Strategic Marketing Management
Planning, implementation and control
Second edition

Richard M. S. Wilson

Professor of Business Administration
The Business School
Loughborough University

Visiting Professor
Sheffield Hallam University

and

Colin Gilligan

Professor of Marketing
Sheffield Business School
Sheffield Hallam University

Butterworth-Heinemann
Linacre House, Jordan Hill, Oxford OX2 8DP
225 Wildwood Avenue, Woburn, MA 01801-2041
A division of Reed Educational and Professional Publishing Ltd

 A member of the Reed Elsevier plc group

OXFORD   AUCKLAND   BOSTON
JOHANNESBURG   MELBOURNE   NEW DELHI

First published 1992
Second edition 1997
Reprinted 1998, 1999

© Richard M. S. Wilson and Colin Gilligan 1992, 1997

British Library Cataloguing in Publication Data
A catalogue record for this book is available from the British Library

ISBN 0 7506 2244 X

Composition by Genesis Typesetting, Rochester, Kent
Printed and bound in Great Britain by The Bath Press, Bath

Contents

Strategic Marketing Management: Planning, implementation and control

The Chartered Institute of Marketing/Butterworth-Heinemann Marketing Series is the most comprehensive, widely used and important collection of books in marketing and sales currently available worldwide.

As the CIM's official publisher, Butterworth-Heinemann develops, produces and publishes the complete series in association with the CIM. We aim to provide definitive marketing books for students and practitioners that promote excellence in marketing education and practice.

The series titles are written by CIM senior examiners and leading marketing educators for professionals, students and those studying the CIM's Certificate, Advanced Certificate and Postgraduate Diploma courses. Now firmly established, these titles provide practical study support to CIM and other marketing students and to practitioners at all levels.

 The Chartered Institute of Marketing

Formed in 1911, The Chartered Institute of Marketing is now the largest professional marketing management body in the world with over 60,000 members located worldwide. Its primary objectives are focused on the development of awareness and understanding of marketing throughout UK industry and commerce and in the raising of standards of professionalism in the education, training and practice of this key business discipline.

Books in the series

Behavioural Aspects of Marketing
Keith C. Williams

Business Law
A. A. Painter and R. Lawson

Economics: an introduction for students of business and marketing
Frank Livesey

Effective Sales Management
John Strafford and Colin Grant

Financial Aspects of Marketing
Keith Ward

The Fundamentals of Advertising
John Wilmshurst

The Fundamentals and Practice of Marketing
John Wilmshurst

International Marketing
S. J. Paliwoda

Marketing Communications
Colin J. Coulson-Thomas

Marketing Financial Services
Edited by Christine Ennew, Trevor Watkins and Mike Wright

The Marketing Primer
Geoff Lancaster and Lester Massingham

Mini Cases in Marketing
Lester Massingham and Geoff Lancaster

The Principles and Practice of Selling
Alan Gillam

Strategic Marketing Management: Planning, implementation and control
Richard M. S. Wilson and Colin Gilligan

Dedication

This book is dedicated to the authors' wives – Gillian and Rosie – and to Ben Gilligan for their support while it was being written.

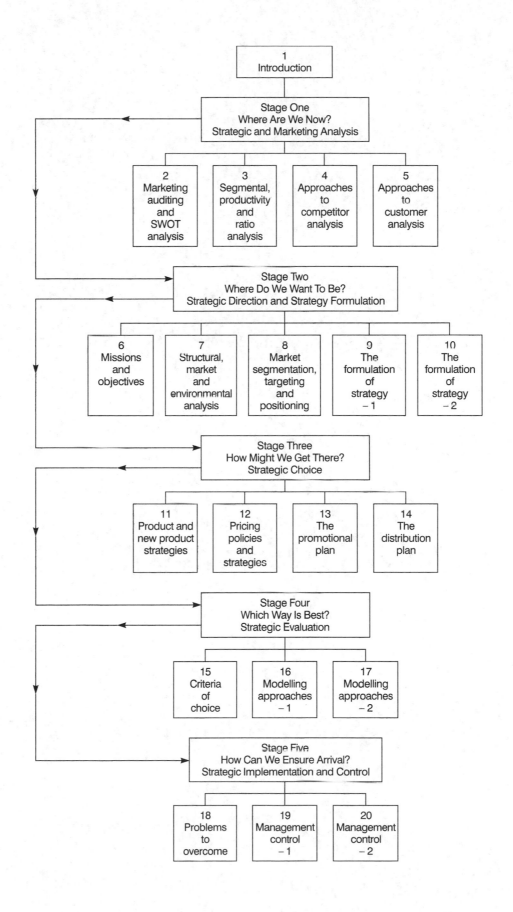

Foreword

As a result of accelerating technological change and the growth of international competition, the discipline of marketing has assumed primary importance in the shaping and implementation of business strategy. Numerous studies confirm that a marketing orientation, with its focus on customer needs and benefits, is critical to the development of effective long-term competitiveness and the creation and maintenance of a sustainable competitive advantage. It follows that sound, clear advice on how to convert a marketing oritentation into successful practice is at a premium.

Irrespective of the level (undergraduate or postgraduate) or degree of specialization (Diploma in Marketing, MSc or MBA) the capstone module is invariably concerned with the subject of this book – *Strategic Marketing Management*. It follows that the creation of a suitable text presents a formidable challenge. Wilson and Gilligan have risen to this magnificently. Having taught this subject for over thirty years, read widely, put it into practice as manager and consultant, and even written about it myself, I can say unequivocally that this book is one of the best structured, comprehensive and, most important, readable texts available today. This second edition is also right up-to-date both in its coverage of the latest thinking from academics and practitioners, as well as in the numerous examples which illustrate and illuminate the issues concerned.

While targeted primarily at students preparing for examination including those of The Chartered Institute of Marketing, the scope and content of this book also makes it a valuable reference source for the practitioner, both as a reminder as well as a guide to current best practice. Whichever category you fit into I recommend this book without reservation.

Michael J Baker
Professor of Marketing
Strathclyde University
President, Academy of Marketing
Dean, CIM Senate

Preface

In writing this book we have been motivated by a concern to help improve the effectiveness of marketing practice – especially in Britain. In focusing on this desired end we have sought to address a number of key questions that logically follow each other in the context of strategic marketing management:

- Where are we now?
- Where do we want to be?
- How might we get there?
- Which way is best
- How can we ensure arrival

The themes of planning, implementing and controlling marketing activities are reflected in the answers to these questions – as offered in the twenty chapters which follow. The structure of the book is designed to take the reader through each of the questions in turn, hence the sequencing of the chapters is significant. We have sought to build the book's argument in a cumulative way such that it will provide guidance in generating effective marketing performance within a strategic framework – once the reader has worked through each chapter in turn.

Against this background we can specify the book's aims as being:

- to make readers aware of the major aspects of the planning and controlling of marketing operations;
- to locate marketing planning and control within a strategic contect;
- to demonstrate how the available range of analytical models and techniques might be applied to marketing planning and control to produce superior marketing performance;
- to give full recognition to the problems of implementation and how these problems might be overcome.

It is not intended that this should be used as an introductory text: we have deliberately assumed that readers will have had some prior exposure to marketing principles if not to marketing practice.

The intended market of the book comprises the following segments;

- students reading for degrees involving marketing (especially MBA candidates and senior undergraduates following business studies programmes);
- students of The Chartered Institute of Marketing who are preparing for the Marketing Planning and Control paper in CIM's Diploma examinations;
- marketing practitioners who will benefit from a comprehensive review of current thinking in the field of strategic marketing planning, implementation and control.

Acknowledgements

In preparing this new edition for publication the authors were very ably helped by Lynne Atkinson at Loughborough and Janice Nunn in Sheffield to whom they would like to offer their thanks. On behalf of the publisher, Stephen Wellings took the risk of accepting a manuscript that was both late and much longer than he had anticipated, for which we are apologetic and appreciative in turn. Alison Boyd looked after the production aspects in a friendly and competent manner.

For granting copyright clearance we are grateful to the following:

- John Wiley & Sons Ltd for Figure 20.32 from R. Amit, et al. 'Thinking One Step Ahead: the Use of Conjectures in Competitor Analysis'. *Strategic Management Journal*, Vol. 9, 1988 © John Wiley & Sons Ltd, 1988.
- Harvard Business School Press for Figure 19.12 from R. N. Anthony, *The Management Control Function*, © 1988 by the President and Fellows of Harvard College; and Figures 17.16–17.19 from T. V. Bonoma and B. H. Clark, *Marketing Performance Assessment*, © 1988 by the President and Fellows of Harvard College.
- MCB University Press Ltd for Figures 20.19 and 20.20 from T. F. Barrett, 'When the Market Says "Beware!"', *Management Decision*, Vol. 24, No. 6, 1986.
- Elsevier Scientific Publishing Co. for Figure 20.28 from J. J. Brock, 'Competitor Analysis: Some Practical Approaches', *Industrial Marketing Management*, Vol. 13, 1984
- The American Marketing Association for Figure 15.14 from G. S. Day and J. R. C. Wensley, 'Assessing Advantage: A Framework for Diagnosing Competitive Superiority', *Journal of Marketing*, Vol. 52, April, 1988; and Figure 20.10, adapted from J. M. Hulbert and N. E. Toy, 'Strategic Framework for Marketing Control', *Journal of Marketing*, Vol. 41, April, 1977.
- The Chartered Institute of Marketing for Figure 20.15 from A. Diamantopoulos and B. P. Mathews, 'A Model for Analysing Product Performance', *Quarterly Review of Marketing*, Vol. 15, No. 3, 1990; Figures 18.11 and 18.13, plus related discussion, from R. M. S. Wilson and N. Fook, 'Improving Marketing Orientation', *Marketing Business*, June, 1990; the Executive Summary in the Preamble to Stage Four from *Manufacturing – the Marketing Solution*; and Illustration 3.2 'Evolution' by Alan Mitchell from *Marketing Business*, February, 1998, p. 18.
- Figure 10.9 reprinted with the permission of The Free Press, a Division of Simon & Schuster from *The PIMS Principles: Linking Strategy to Performance*, by Robert D. Buzzell and Bradley T. Gale, © 1987 by The Free Press.
- Ian Griffith (of Marketing Quality Assurance) for his piece 'Marketing Needs New Sales Pitch', which first appeared in *The Sunday Times*, 7 July, 1991.
- McGraw-Hill, Inc, for Figure 20.16 from J. P. Guiltinan and G. W. Paul, *Marketing Management: Strategies & Programs*, 3rd edition, 1988; and Figure 19.6 from G. Shillinglaw's 'Divisional Performance Review' in C. P. Bonini, R. K. Jaedicke, and H. M. Wagner (eds) *Management Controls: New Directions in Basic Research*, 1964.
- Figures 16.20 and 16.21, plus related discussion from *Marketing* by J. L. Heskett, © 1976. Adapted by permission of Prentice-Hall, Inc., Upper Saddle River, NJ, USA.
- Prentice Hall International (UK) Ltd for Figure 1.10 from G. Johnson and K. Scholes, *Exploring Corporate Strategy*, 2nd edition, 1988; and Figures 14.5, 14.10 and 14.18 from Peter Doyle's *Marketing Management and Strategy*, 1994.
- Cassell plc for Figure 8.4 from P. Feldwick (ed), *Advertising Works – 5*, 1990.
- Butterworth-Heinemann for Figure 1 in the Preamble to Stage Five from P. McNamee, *Management Accounting: Strategic Planning and Marketing*, 1988;

and Figure 14.14 from M. McDonald, *Marketing Plans: How to Prepare Them, How to Use Them*, 1995.

- The Editor of *Accountancy Ireland* for Figure 1.14 from F. Milton and T. Reiss, 'Developing a Competitive Strategy', *Accountancy Ireland*, Vol. 17, No. 5, 1985. (Cartoonist Noel Ford.)
- The cases Bank Corporation of America, Cleveland Clinic, and Eastman Kodak Co., reprinted by permission of *The Wall Street Journal*, © 1989. Dow Jones & Company, Inc. All rights reserved worldwide.
- Professor David W. Cravens and Richard D. Irwin, Inc., for Figures 14.9 and 14.15 from David W. Cravens (1991): *Strategic Marketing*, Homewood, Illinois: Irwin, 3rd edition.
- Frank Pyne (of Problem Resolution) for Figure 15.4 from F. Pyne, 'Better Operating Statements for the Marketing Director', *Accountancy*, Vol. 95, No. 1086, February, 1984.
- The Playboy Enterprises, Inc., case in Chapter 19 reprinted by permission of Professor Subhash C. Jain and South-Western College Publishing from *Marketing Planning & Strategy*, by S. C. Jain, 3rd edition, © 1990, South-Western College Publishing, a division of International Thomson Publishing, Inc., Cincinnati, Ohio 45227, USA.
- Richard Ivey School of Business, The University of Western Ontario, for the Gatorade case in Chapter 16.
- Prentice-Hall, Inc. for Figure 19.17 from D. J. Luck and O. C. Ferrell, *Marketing Strategy and Plans*, 1979; and Figure 2.7 adapted from P. Kotler, *Marketing Management: Analysis, Planning, Implementation and Control*, 6th edition, 1988.
- The Nike, Inc., case in Chapter 15 reprinted with permission of Stanford University, Graduate School of Business, © 1969 and 1977 by the Board of Trustees of the Leland Stanford Junior University.
- The Editor of *Sloan Management Review* for Figure 2.10 adapted from P. Kotler, W. Gregor and W. Rogers, 'The Marketing Audit Comes of Age', *Sloan Management Review*, Vol. 18, No. 1, Winter, 1977.
- *The Independent on Sunday* for Illustration 3.1 'My Biggest Mistake' by David Bruce, 16 December, 1990, p. 20; and Illustration 14.1 'My Biggest Mistake' by Johnnie Boden, 30 January, 1994, p. 24.
- The American Accounting Association for Figure 14.19 from J. K. Shank and V. Govindarajan 'Strategic Cost Management: The Value Chain Perspective', *Journal of Management Accounting Research*, Vol. 4, 1992, p. 181.
- PIMS Associates Ltd for the discussion and exhibits in Chapter 3, Section 3.13, from P. Ceccarelli and Tony Clayton 'How to think about the shape of your business', *The PIMS Letter*, No. 47, 1992; and for the Causaway Plc case in Chapter 3.
- Coopers & Lybrand for the cartoon at the beginning of Chapter 4 which originally appeared in their house journal *Insight*, February, 1994, p. 8.
- Professor David W. Cravens and Richard D. Irwin, Inc., for the cases Bank Corporation of America, Cleveland Clinic, and Eastman Kodak Co., from David W. Cravens (1991): *Strategic Marketing*, Homewood, Illinois: Irwin, 3rd edition, and for Figures 14.9 and 14.15 from the same source.
- Professor Roger A. Kerin and Allyn & Bacon for the cases Masterton Mills, Inc., Solartronics Corporation, and Hanover-Bates Chemical Corporation from R. S. Kerin and R. A. Peterson (1993): *Strategic Marketing Problems*, Boston, Mass.; Allyn & Bacon, 6th edition.
- Professor Subhash C. Jain and South-Western Publishing Co. for the Playboy Enterprises, Inc., case from S. C. Jain (1990): *Marketing Planning & Strategy*, Cincinnati: South-Western, 3rd edition, which is in Chapter 19.
- Professor John R. Kennedy of the University of Western Ontario for the Gatorade case in Chapter 16.
- Dr John Thanopoulos and Dr Joseph W. Leonard for the Engels & Ferrell Industries case in Chapter 20.
- The Board of Trustees of the Leland Stanford Junior University for the Nike, Inc., case in Chapter 15.

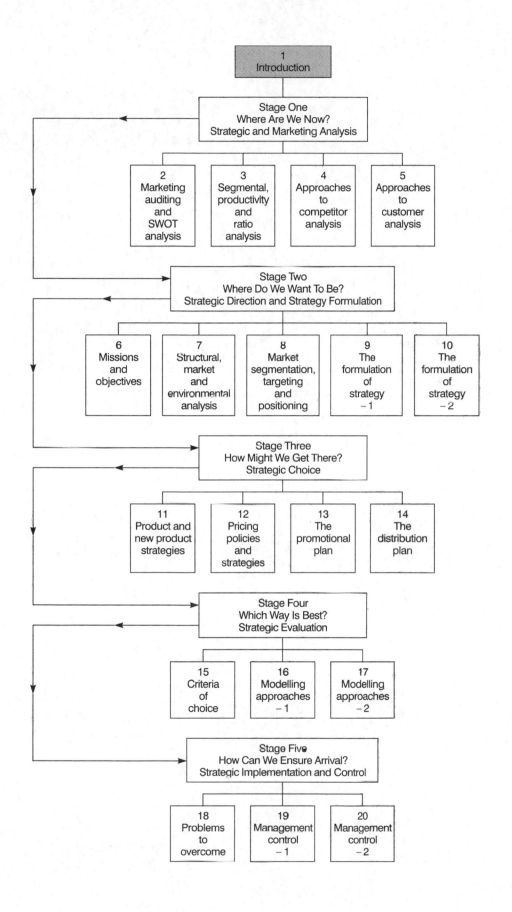

1 | Introduction

1.1 LEARNING OBJECTIVES

When you have read this chapter you should be able to:

(a) define marketing in strategic terms;
(b) understand the basic structure of the book;
(c) appreciate the analytical approach to managerial planning and control that can be achieved through model building;
(d) specify the characteristics of strategy and strategic decisions;
(e) understand the nature of the debate about the future role of marketing and its contribution to management;
(f) appreciate the changing emphases within marketing and the implications for the ways in which marketing strategies are developed.

1.2 THE NATURE OF MARKETING

What is marketing? Many definitions exist with differing emphases on the process of marketing, the functional activities that constitute marketing, and the orientation (or philosophy) of marketing. For example, the Chartered Institute of Marketing defines it as follows:

> Marketing is the management process for identifying, anticipating, and satisfying customer requirements profitably.

A slightly longer but conceptually similar definition of marketing was proposed by the American Marketing Association (AMA) in 1985:

> Marketing is the process of planning and executing the conception, pricing, promotion and distribution of ideas, goods and services to create exchanges that satisfy individual and organizational objectives.

Although this definition, or variations of it, has been used by a variety of writers (see, for example, McCarthy and Perreault, 1990; Kotler, 1991; and Dibb, *et al.*, 1991), Littler and Wilson (1995, p. 1) have pointed to the way in which 'its adequacy is beginning to be questioned in some European textbooks (e.g. Foxall, 1984; Baker (ed), 1997). It could be said that the AMA definition is more of a list than a definition and is therefore clumsy and inconvenient to use; that it cannot ever be comprehensive; and that it fails to provide a demarcation as to what necessarily is or is not *marketing*'.

They go on to suggest that the AMA definition presents marketing as a *functional* process conducted by the organization's marketing department, whereas the general thrust of the more recent literature on marketing theory is that marketing is increasingly being conceptualized as an organizational philosophy or 'an approach to doing business'. This strategic as opposed to a functional approach to marketing is captured both by McDonald:

> Marketing is a management process whereby the resources of the whole organization are utilised to satisfy the needs of selected customer groups in order to achieve the objectives of both parties. Marketing, then, is first and foremost an attitude of mind rather than a series of functional activities. (McDonald, 1989, p. 8)

and by Drucker (1973) who put forward a definition of marketing orientation:

> Marketing is so basic that it cannot be considered a separate function on a par with others such as manufacturing or personnel. It is first a central dimension of the entire business. It is the whole business seen from the point of view of its final result, that is, from the customers' point of view.

A significant shift in emphasis since Drucker wrote this is to be found in the importance that is now attached to *competitive position* in a changing world. Thus the marketing concept is that managerial orientation which recognizes that success primarily depends upon identifying changing customer wants and developing products and services which match these better than those of competitors (Doyle, 1987; see also Wilson & Fook, 1990).

The contrasting emphases on customers and competitors can be highlighted as in Figure 1.1. If an enterprise is managed a little better than customers expect, and if this is done in a slightly better way than competitors can manage, then the enterprise should be successful.

Within Figure 1.1 the customer-oriented and competitor-centred categories speak for themselves. The self-centred category is characterized by an introspective orientation that focuses on year-on-year improvements in key operating ratios, or on improvements in sales volume without making direct comparisons with competitors. Such an orientation is potentially disastrous when viewed in strategic terms. At the opposite extreme is a market-driven approach to marketing which seeks to balance a responsiveness to customers' requirements on the one hand with direct competitor comparisons on the other.

FIGURE 1.1
Customer and competitor orientations

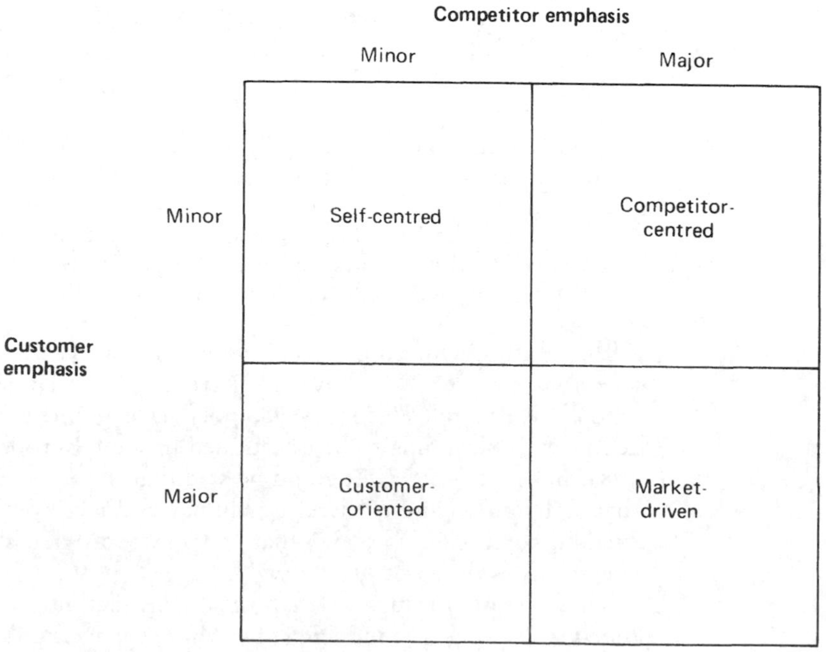

SOURCE: Adapted from Day (1990), p. 126

As pointed out in Wilson (1988, p. 259), the essential requirements of marketing are:

1 the identification of consumers' needs (covering *what* goods and services are bought; *how* they are bought; by *whom* they are bought; and *why* they are bought);
2 the definition of target market segments (by which customers are grouped according to common characteristics – whether demographic, psychological, geographic, etc.);
3 the creation of a *differential advantage* within target segments by which a distinct competitive position relative to other companies can be established, and from which profit flows.

The way in which a differential advantage might be achieved – and sustained – is via the manipulation of the elements of the *marketing mix*. This mix has traditionally been seen to consist of the 'four Ps' of marketing: product, price, promotion and place. Increasingly, however, but particularly in the service sector, it is being recognized that these four Ps are rather too limited in terms of providing a framework both for thinking about marketing and for planning marketing strategy. It is because of this that a far greater emphasis is now being given to the idea of an expanded mix which has three additional elements:

- people;
- physical evidence;
- process management.

The detail of both the traditional 'hard' elements of the mix and of the 'softer' elements appears in Figure 1.2; the individual elements of the mix are discussed in detail in Stage Three of the text.

FIGURE 1.2
The marketing mix

Product management New product development Branding Packaging	Product
Pricing Discount structures Terms of business	Price
Advertising Sales promotion Public relations Personal selling Merchandising	Promotion
Channel management Customer service Physical distribution	Place
Employee selection Employee training Employee motivation	People
Layout Decor Ease of access Forms of presentation	Physical evidence
How customers are handled and managed from the point of very first contact with the organization through to the point of very last contact	Process management

1.3 THE MANAGEMENT PROCESS

Management can be looked at from a variety of viewpoints. It may be seen from one perspective as being largely an *attitude* that reflects a willingness to debate issues and resolve them through the use of appropriate techniques and procedures. Alternatively, management may be viewed in terms of its *responsibility for achieving desired objectives* which requires the selection of means to accomplish prescribed ends as well as the articulation of those ends. This view of management can be analysed further by focusing on its *task orientation* (e.g. in the functional context of marketing) or on its *process orientation* (i.e. the way in which the responsibility is exercised). In either case it has been suggested that decision making and management are the same thing (Simon, 1960, p. 1).

The process of decision making is rendered problematic on account of the existence of risk and uncertainty. In the face of risk or uncertainty some managers postpone making a choice between alternative courses of action for fear of that choice being wrong. What they typically fail to recognize in this situation is that they are actually making another choice – they are deciding *not to decide* (Barnard, 1956, p. 193), which favours the status quo rather than change. This is not a means of eliminating risk or uncertainty since it seeks to ignore them rather than to accommodate them: the imperative to adapt is one that cannot be ignored.

If the central question in the management process concerns the need to make decisions, we need to know *what* decisions should be made and *how* they should be made. This book is intended to deal with both these issues by following a sequence of stages that reflects a problem-solving routine. Each of the five main parts of the book represents one of these stages. Figure 1.3 summarizes these stages.

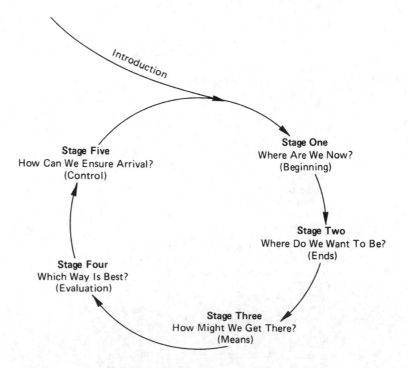

FIGURE 1.3
The framework

Stage 1 raises the question of where the organization is now in terms of its competitive position, product range, market share, financial position and overall effectiveness. In addressing this question we are seeking to establish a base line from which we can move forward. Chapters 2 to 5 address Stage 1.

Stage 2 is concerned with where the organization should go in the future, which requires the specification of ends (or objectives) to be achieved. While top management in the organization will have some discretion over the choice of ends, this is constrained by various vested interests, as we shall see later in this chapter. Chapters 6 to 10 address Stage 2.

Stage 3 deals with the question of how desired ends might be achieved, which begs the question of how alternative means to ends might be identified. This strategy formulation stage requires creative inputs which cannot be reduced to mechanical procedures. Chapters 11 to 14 address Stage 3.

Stage 4 focuses on the evaluation of alternative means by which the most preferred (or 'best') alternative might be selected. The need to choose may be due to alternatives being mutually exclusive (i.e. all attempting to achieve the same end) or a consequence of limited resources (which means that a rationing mechanism must be invoked). Chapters 15, 16 and 17 address Stage 4.

Stage 5 covers the implementation of the chosen means, and the monitoring of its performance in order that any corrective actions might be taken to ensure that the desired results are achieved. Since circumstances both within the organization and in its environment are unlikely to stay constant while a strategy is being pursued it is necessary to adapt to accommodate such changes. Chapters 18, 19 and 20 address Stage 5.

Within these stages are to be found the main managerial activities of:

- planning;
- decision making;
- control.

The entire sequence of Stages 1 to 5 constitutes control, within which the planning activities are to be found in Stages 1 to 4. At every stage it is necessary for decisions to be made, so you will see that these managerial activities are closely intertwined. Moreover, their links are spread across three different time dimensions which are not of equal significance: the past, the present and the future. Let us consider these in turn.

The *past* brought the organization (and its products, competitors, etc.) to their present positions. By gaining an understanding of how the organization arrived in its present position the managers of that organization might develop some insights to help them in deciding how to proceed in the future. However, there is no way in which the past can be influenced, so the best one can do is to attempt to learn from it instead of being constrained by it. If an organization simply continues on unchanging routes its viability is almost certain to be endangered as the environment changes but it does not.

Stage 1 is concerned with establishing the ways in which the past brought the organization to its present position.

The *present* is transient: it is the fleeting moment between the past and the future when one must take one's understanding of the past and link this to the development of one's aspirations for the future. Decisions are made (with both planning and control consequences) in the present, but their impact is intended to be in the future.

The time dimension that is of major relevance in any planning exercise must be the *future* rather than the present or the past. There is nothing about an organization that is more important than its future, and the spirit of this was aptly summarized by C. F. Kettering: 'I am interested in the future because that is where I intend to live.' The past may help us in deciding how to proceed in the future, but there is no way in which we can influence the past, so there is a limit to the amount of effort that should be applied to it as opposed to planning for the future. This is especially relevant when we consider what a constraint to innovation the past might be: in Goethe's terms, we see what we know, and if we are obsessed with carrying on along unchanging routes we must expect our viability to become endangered as the environment changes but we fail to adapt to those changes.

On the other hand, the anticipation of the future should not become too fanciful. In a deliberately extreme mood, de Jouvenal (1967) has stated that:

> ... world population, and also the available labour force in industrial countries, is doubling every 50 years. The GNP is doubling every 20 years, and so are the number of major scientific discoveries. The whole scientific and engineering establishment, including, for example, the numbers of graduates, membership of learned societies, and scientific publications is doubling every 15 years. The money spent on applied research is doubling every 7 years, and so also is the demand for electronics and aviation. If all these processes were to continue unchecked ... within about 100 years every one of us would be a scientist, the entire national output would be absorbed in research, and we should be spending most of our lives airborne at 40,000 feet.

This can be contrasted with a rather more serious comment made by Professor William H. Pickering of Harvard in a speech made during June of 1908 in which his lack of imagination is as extreme as de Jouvenal's excess:

> The popular mind often pictures gigantic flying machines speeding across the Atlantic carrying innumerable passengers in a way analogous to our modern steamship. It seems safe to say that such ideas are wholly visionary, and, even if the machine could get across with one or two passengers, the expense would be prohibitive to any but the capitalist who could use his own yacht.

With this uninspired perspective from a member of the establishment in the early twentieth century, it is not surprising that the vision of writers such as Jules Verne and H. G. Wells were mocked; yet their premonitions have often come to be justified, with surprising speed and accuracy in some instances. We do have Concorde, despite Professor Pickering's pessimism.

It should not be expected that any particular vision of the future will be correct in every detail, nor necessarily very detailed in its conception. Writing in 1959, Drucker made the rather careless statement that '. . . if anyone still suffers from the delusion that the ability to forecast beyond the shortest timespan is given to us, let him look at the headlines in yesterday's paper, and then ask himself which of them he could possibly have predicted ten years ago.' What Drucker does not take into account is the vital *level of resolution*: our interest over a 10-year period may be more in the continued existence of *The Times*, or even of a free press, than in specific headlines, because the level of resolution would have to be relatively low (i.e. broad horizons, broad view, little detail).

A balance must be maintained in dealing with the short-run future on the one hand and the long-run future on the other. Apart from headlines in *The Times* we can note the short-run preoccupation in the UK with financial results and contrast this with the longer-run relevance of market-building strategies; or the risk of being obsessed with tactics to the exclusion of a proper concern for strategy.

1.4 A Modelling Approach

In dealing with managerial processes such as planning, decision making and control it would be inappropriate to presume that *objective rationality* was present. Human beings are unable to act in a wholly objective way as a result of their tendency to use *subjective judgements* in their decision making.

The type of judgement that is intended here is not that which stems purely from 'experience', but rather that which reflects value systems (see Vickers, 1968; 1972). Rationality implies objectivity and thus excludes the subjective reasoning that follows from the values that each decision maker holds. The nature of personal values (such as one's willingness to be involved in marketing cigarettes in full knowledge of the potentially detrimental effect on health by smoking, or the view one has of profit, or of capitalism, or of the use of sexual advertising themes in promoting sexless products) is not well understood, and the choice of personal values is not open to rational economic analysis. Nevertheless, the values of dominant managers will be inherent in the choice of 'organizational' objectives. (Since only individuals can have objectives while collectivities cannot, it follows that organizational objectives must reflect the aspirations of the dominant individuals in the organizational coalition. See March & Simon, 1958, and Cyert & March, 1963.)

The culture of the society in which we live determines the norms for acceptable behaviour and hence for acceptable objectives. Differences among cultures (such as British versus Japanese) will obviously lead to different value systems and different norms of behaviour. (For example, the longer-term focus of Japanese and German financial markets relative to those in the UK and the USA.) However, even within a national culture there are sub-cultures which result in different value systems developing in government, business, the armed forces, and so forth, which can be seen in the very different behaviour patterns of participants in each sub-culture (see Weinshall, 1977).

The recognition that values play such a prominent – and largely unpredictable – role in managerial behaviour may discourage some individuals and cause them to dismiss rational analysis as being inadequate in effective decision making. In the sense that decisions are not made entirely on the basis of economic rationality this may seem reasonable, but if we can apply rational economic analysis to a substantial element in each managerial decision it seems overly pessimistic to assume that this will not be helpful. If alternative courses of action can be analysed and presented in rational, neutral terms to the decision maker, it will help him to make his choice, even though this itself will be biased in accordance with his personal set of values.

The question of personal values to an individual (or perhaps of a cohesive group) can be extended to the question of ethics (or moral values) to a society (see Bartels, 1963; and Kelley in Schwartz, 1965). The consumer movement (see Aaker & Day, 1972 and 1974; Kotler, 1972b, Gaedeke & Etcheson, 1972; and McCarry, 1972) suggests that marketers are not invariably putting other people's interests in an acceptable societal perspective. It is not clear, however, to what extent management is expected to introduce and support gradual social change in so far as this reflects changing its own behaviour towards particular groups (such as consumers, employees, shareholders, and the community at large) and to what extent it should uphold the status quo (see Starr, 1971, pp. 249–58).

Business behaviour will certainly be influenced to some degree by the ethics of the prevailing social system, although defining ethical objectives becomes fraught with difficulties when society is divided in its views. (For example the divergence between the perceived importance in Britain of regenerating economic growth in the private sector, which requires innovative freedom, and the regulation of private enterprise that discourages such regeneration. Similarly, there is conflict between the 'morality' of the environmentalists and the 'morality' of economic growth.) This topic should be kept in mind through the following pages since it constitutes a constraint that may be more restrictive than statutory limitations.

We have seen that the idea of objective economic rationality is not a realistic notion in the context of managerial decision making. Equally, it is unrealistic to proceed purely on the basis of common sense (which might encourage us to think that the world is flat), or arbitrary rules (which might be termed 'conventional wisdom'). What is needed is a theoretical framework for the analysis of managerial problems, and this presupposes a *scientific* orientation.

Science can be defined as a body of knowledge about the phenomena in a particular section of the real world and of the research tools available for obtaining accurate and reliable knowledge about these phenomena. A scientific approach in any field of investigation is the direct antithesis of dogmatism (or conventional wisdom and tradition). In following such an approach the marketing decision maker should learn to rely on evidence from reality instead of hunch. However, whether marketing is, or will ever be, regarded as a science by anyone other than its own adherents is unimportant in relation to the role it has assumed in applying scientific method to the understanding of this important sphere of human activity (see Christopher, et al., 1968, pp. 231–2).

But there is some scope for 'creative intuition' (Fisk, 1967, p. 494), which requires that we view marketing as part *art* (which is usually linked to subjectivity) and part *science* (which is usually linked to a kind of objectivity). At one extreme is a totally objective, scientific approach to decision making, while at the other extreme (of a notional continuum) intuition, experience and subjective knowledge take over the decision. It should be readily appreciated that decision making at higher levels in an organization will require rather more creative intuition than will tend to be the case at lower levels where formal methods can be more widely employed.

In whatever field he is working, a scientist will proceed by attempting to develop theories concerning the behaviour of the phenomena in which he is interested. Rules of thumb and experience are not without some value, but a knowledge of the basic relationships underlying the behaviour of relevant phenomena should allow managers to make decisions even in the absence of traditional guidelines and experience (see Zaltman, et al., 1973).

A good decision maker can be said to be an individual with good theories. This may conflict with the emphasis put on 'practicality' by unenlightened, defensive individuals who are well aware of their own ignorance of the behaviour of marketing phenomena. The aim of marketing theory has been stated, in broad terms, as being '. . . to comprehend what is known and to derive a set of principles or action-guides to enable businessmen to manage their affairs better' (Rodger, 1965, p. 37). It follows therefore that if theory is concerned with knowing, those who dismiss it are recommending a policy of not knowing: the practical individual (operating without a theoretical basis) is the individual who does not really know what he is doing. This is not to say, of course, that practice is not vitally important. It is. But theory and practice are two sides of the same coin, and to emphasize one (or merely neglect the other) is potentially dangerous if one fails to appreciate that sound practice must rest on valid theories, and valid theories must facilitate sound practice.

Scientific theories in marketing enable us to:

1 Explain and understand the behaviour of marketing variables and their interrelationships. The emphais will usually be on causal relations, but one should not expect sets of precise cause-and-effect rules to emerge that are applicable under any potential sets of circumstances. 'In the management field it is never possible to say: "If I do A and B, then C will inevitably happen." The best that [the decision maker] can say is: "If I do A and B, the result is *likely* to be C. And if I neglect to do either A or B, it is *very probable* that the consequences will be unfortunate."' (Dale & Michelon, 1969, p. 11).

2 Predict the future behaviour patterns of marketing variables and their interrelationships. The ability (from (1) above) to explain relationships is a necessary basis for prediction, and it should be apparent that a good explanatory theory can facilitate prediction across a broader range of circumstances than can the practical personal experience of any individual (whose perspective is constrained by the limits of that experience). A theorist can use his knowledge of relevant behaviour patterns in many different situations to indicate the consequences of alternative courses of action among which the decision maker must choose.

3 Produce prescriptions, by which the values of decision makers are aligned with the alternative courses of action available, thereby enabling choices to be made.

4 Achieve control over the outcomes from interactions of marketing variables.

When the marketing analyst has a validated predictive theory of cause-and-effect relationships among phenomena of interest to him, he is able to control the effects by exerting pressure on the causes. Since effects lead to the attainment of objectives this makes the achievements of purpose possible. For example, if it were known how a given amount and type of promotion (cause) affected sales (first-order effect), it would be possible to control the profitability outcome (second-order effect) since profit depends, in part, on the difference between sales revenue and promotional outlays (see Huegy, 1963; Cox, et al., 1964).

Available marketing theories are not yet comprehensive, but appreciating the role of theories and having some awareness of theory construction are essential qualities for the good decision maker. In considering the relationship between sales calls and sales, or that between speed of delivery (or level of service) and sales, a marketing manager might assume that at some stage diminishing returns set in (i.e. no matter how many sales calls are made, or how rapid delivery is, or how many orders can be filled immediately ex-stock, the level of sales will not increase to infinity). It is up to the manager to develop a theory of how, and at what rate, sales vary in response to changes in other variables (see Stasch, 1972, pp. 1–28).

An approach such as this clearly has major implications regarding the provision of data, but it also demands the formal consideration of how particular courses of action lead to particular outcomes, and thus requires an analytical framework for improving decision-making performance. By contrast, the use of practical experience as a basis for decisions is tantamount to uncontrolled experimentation with no formal explanatory foundation, thereby rendering it a faulty guide to the prediction of future events and a totally inadequate basis for control.

We can characterize the main features of theories through a simple systems model (Figure 1.4).

FIGURE 1.4
Theoretical foundations

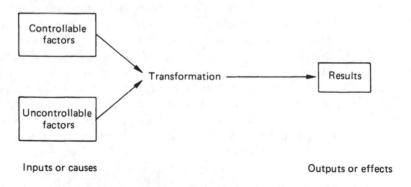

Controllable factors

Uncontrollable factors

Transformation

Results

Inputs or causes   Outputs or effects

Controllable factors in this format are termed 'strategies' and are determined by management. A firm's pricing policy, the range of products it offers, and its forms of promotion are examples of such factors that are entirely within the control (subject to legal constraints) of the firm itself.

The uncontrollable factors are termed 'environments' or 'states of nature', and represent those variables that are independent of the firm's control (such as competitive actions, political events, movements in commodity prices, and so forth).

Together, the uncontrollable and controllable variables in a given situation constitute the inputs, or causal variables, of the theory of that situation. The inputs interact and this produces a transformation that leads to results (which may also be termed pay-offs, effects, or outputs). Since each variable on the input side could assume any one of a vast range of values (such as the controllable expenditure on advertising Product X being anything from, say, £0 to £100,000, and the uncontrollable price of copper, which might be an essential element in Product X, being anything from £750 to £1,050 per ton, and so on), the situation is one of great uncertainty and could therefore lead to any one of a large number of outcomes. Under these circumstances it is necessary for us carefully to limit our concern to states of nature that are likely to occur (given our selected strategies) and that might influence the attainment of our objectives (and hence the desired outputs or effects).

It is worth pointing out that the use of the term 'control' is not unambiguous in managerial parlance. In the phrase 'controllable factors' the sense of the meaning is that the manager can influence, in any way he wishes, the behaviour of each factor. ('Behaviour' means a change in state, or value, over time, and so this covers human behaviour but is by no means restricted to this.) He can, for instance, offer Product X in 25 different colours or only in black. He cannot, however, directly influence the range of colours of competitive products, so this comes under the heading of 'uncontrollable factors' along with other states of nature or environments.

In discussing the role of theories in securing control over the behaviour of phenomena the term 'control' was used in a different sense. If we can anticipate (by predictive means) states of nature, we are in a position to respond to them when they arise, and in this way we are able to survive, adapt, and ultimately reach our objectives. This is the substantive meaning of 'control' in this book.

While the methodology of 'marketing science' is essentially the same as that of the empirical physical sciences (Montgomery & Urban, 1969a, p. 8), with the two central aspects of problem orientation and scientific approach being much in evidence, the facts which are pertinent to marketing science are more inclusive than those which are the subject of investigation in other subject areas. This is demonstrated through the eclectic nature of marketing, which is more in the form of a sub-set of a number of other disciplines rather than being a discipline in itself. As a subject of academic and professional study, marketing is composed of approaches from economics, psychology, sociology, political science, anthropology and history, with assistance from accounting, law, statistics and mathematics. The scientific method is frequently equated with rational rather than emotional deliberation; with objectivity and freedom from personal bias or prejudice; with precision in investigation and measurement; and with honesty in interpreting findings. However, the scientific method is never as easy to apply in the social sciences (which include marketing and management) as it is in the physical sciences (see Schwartz, 1973, pp. 309–10). Directly or indirectly, human behaviour is at the core of marketing problems and this is infinitely more difficult to analyse than is, say, the behaviour of either chemical compounds or white mice under controlled laboratory conditions. (The value of qualitative research, reflecting problems of quantification, is often a controversial topic in marketing; see, for example, Brighton, 1977.) One vehicle that is of great value in helping us cope with studying any form of behaviour is the model, so let us turn our attention to modelling (see Lazer, 1962a).

It is possible to state our knowledge of marketing phenomena in both verbal and quantitative ways, either of which can be equally valid. Analysis is more readily facilitated, however, when information is expressed in quantitative terms. Not only is this likely to be more precise and concise than its verbal counterpart, but it is also amenable to statistical and mathematical manipulation in an effort to explain, predict and control the behaviour of marketing phenomena. Frequently, analysis and manipulation are made possible through the use of models.

We can define a model as a simplified representation of some part of reality. If it were not a simplification of reality it would be both too complex to use and also redundant (since there is little point in a replication of reality). Relevance will determine the features that are to be modelled in relation to a formulated problem situation.

The popularity of models in recent years is due to: an improved competence on the part of decision makers to build and use them (often in conjunction with computing facilities and the availability of spreadsheets); a greater need to incorporate the rapidly increasing uncertainty of problem situations in the decision-making process; and the utility of models in carrying out experiments (e.g. via simulation) which could not be performed in reality. If there were no evidence to suggest that 'scientific' models of marketing processes improved organizational performance the adoption of modelling would not be as popular as it has become. But there is a temptation for models to be developed for their own sake, or to satisfy the curiosity of the analyst, in relation to a matter that is of no real significance to organizational success. Many models suffer from 'rigour without relevance' (Ehrenberg, 1965) in that they are highly refined and elegant in mathematical terms but fail to reflect the key features of marketing processes and problems. It is important to see that marketing models are not ends in themselves but simply a means to an end – the making of better marketing decisions, rather than the 'unlimited postulation of irrelevant truths' (Schwartz, 1965, p. 489). (See Kotler, 1971, for a broad coverage on this theme.)

At a later stage we will look at particular types of models developed specially to tackle particular marketing problems. At this stage, however, it will be helpful to look at one very important type of model (the systems model) and one modelling approach (experimentation), both of which can supply an extremely helpful perspective in considering marketing planning and control.

The *systems model*, in its basic form, is an abstraction that can be related to *any* 'living' system. (A living system is one that is purposive or objective seeking; has interdependent and interacting parts; and exhibits changes of state over time, i.e. it behaves. Such systems are not necessarily live in a biological sense, but exhibit life – as with the economic system – through their changes of state.) (See Beer, 1967; Churchman, 1968; Emery, 1981; Ackoff, 1971; Schoderbek, et al., 1975; Beishon & Peters, 1972.) Every system has inputs, a transformation process in which the various inputs are combined, and outputs that are intended to lead to the attainment of the system's purpose. Figure 1.5 illustrates this in its simplest form.

FIGURE 1.5
A simple systems model

In order that the system might 'learn', and hence adapt its behaviour to ensure it is progressing along an acceptable path towards its objectives, it is necessary to have a link between the outputs and the inputs. This is termed a feedback loop, and it is the essential ingredient that converts a simple systems model into a control model by enabling the system's inputs to be varied in order to ensure that its behaviour (as represented by the system's outputs) is consistent with its objectives (see Figure 1.6).

The example that is usually cited is of a domestic thermostat: whenever the temperature (output) falls below the desired level (which represents the standard of performance, but which is only a surrogate for the objective which will be the welfare of the user of the system), this message passes through the feedback loop

FIGURE 1.6
A simple control system

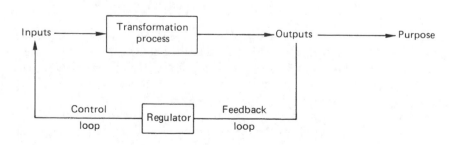

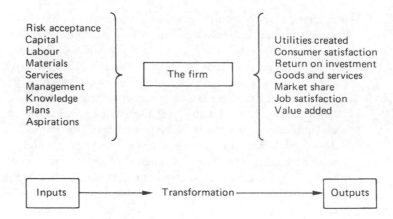

and causes heat to be supplied (through the transformation process) in response to the provision of a signal and fuel (inputs).

To put this simple model into a managerial context we can use the example of Figure 1.7 which shows, in general terms, a range of input factors into a transformation process termed 'the firm', and some of the resulting outputs.

Resources, consisting of managerial skill, materials, funds, labour, etc., constitute a major class of (controllable) inputs, to which must be added such variables as risk and the aspirations or ambitions of individual employees/ managers (over which the firm has little control). In the main, however, input factors are at least identifiable even if some of these represent constraints to the most efficient attainment of objectives. Among the most obvious constraints in marketing systems are the prevailing level of technology, cultural norms, legal restrictions (such as price codes), competition, the pattern and level of demand, and nature (as seen in droughts, floods, climatic variations, etc.), all of which can limit the freedom of action of marketing decision makers.

The outputs from marketing systems indicate how the system is progressing towards its desired purpose. Marketing activities result in the creation of utilities (of time, place and ownership) and in the addition of value to goods passing through the various phases of the marketing process. Consumers derive their satisfaction from the utilities, and business firms derive their profits from the value added.

Output is relative to input, and their relationship gives a measure of efficiency or productivity (see Sevin, 1965; Narver & Savit, 1971, Ch. 15). Efficiency is concerned with the amount of output created from a given mix and amount of inputs and is often encountered in its extreme form when optimizing behaviour is being urged (by which the maximum output from given inputs, or a given output from minimum inputs, is required). Marketing is considered by such authorities as Narver & Savit, 1971, to have low efficiency in comparison with manufacturing or farming, and this gives some indication of the difficulties involved in understanding the complexities of the marketing domain.

But no matter how efficient an activity or process is, we must also have regard to its effectiveness. This refers to a system's ability to achieve its purpose, so we might have effective but inefficient systems, efficient but ineffective ones, or anything in between (see Schoderbek, 1971; Johnson, et al., 1973; Schoderbek, et al., 1975).

The boundary of any system will be drawn by the analyst in accordance with the problem at hand rather than being given in any sense. It is a system's boundary that separates the items over which we have major influence from the environmental variables over which we have little influence but which affect our ability to reach our objectives.

By thinking in terms of purposive systems one gets away from the descriptive view of marketing consisting of a number of separate departments carrying out a range of separable activities. The coherence of its elements distinguishes a system from the jumble of items that might otherwise be perceived, and this simply reflects the real world.

We can represent in systems terms any marketing activity by varying the *level of resolution*. This refers to the spatial (or space) and temporal (or time) dimensions of the problem situation we are examining. For example, if our interest is in media scheduling for a specific advertising campaign we will adopt a high level of resolution which means we will examine the limited number of items in the problem in detail over a short-time horizon. If our interest lay in, say, the adoption of solar heating systems, then we would need to consider many more variables over longer periods of time and consequently we would adopt a lower level of resolution (see Klir and Valach, 1967, Ch. 2; Lowe, 1971, pp. 96–8). The generality of the systems model is such that we can accept its fundamental relevance to the problems of adaptive systems, in general, and then use it to formulate, in precise terms, the characteristics of any particular problem we might come up against.

In summary, then, by using systems models as a means of studying marketing processes and problems we are focusing attention on certain key questions, namely:

1 What purposes are to be served by the system? (In other words, what objective is to be satisfied by the solution to the marketing problem represented by the systems model?)
2 What structure (or organization) should exist among the variables within the system in order that the desired behaviour patterns might emerge?
3 What inputs are required to achieve the system's purpose?
4 What outputs are required, and how should these be measured?
5 What constraints exist to limit the system's ability to behave in the desired manner?
6 With what degree of efficiency and effectiveness is the system operating?

As we have seen, any model is a simplified representation of a larger, more complex slice of reality. In order to make modelling useful in decision making the most general approach has been to enquire about the effects (outcomes) that result from changing the inputs (causes) to the model on a 'What if . . .?' basis. This is one feature of experimentation (in the form of a simulation) which can also be applied by restructuring the model itself.

Sensitivity analysis is one example of *experimentation*. The testing of a model for its sensitivity is aimed at discovering how the output changes in response to variations in input values, or due to variations in model parameters. This should indicate the extent to which outcomes are sensitive (i.e. are subject to change) in response to particular inputs, and which inputs can be varied and have little impact on output. A model's sensitivity should correspond with the sensitivity of the real-world situation, and in this sense there is a link between a model's sensitivity and its validity (see Montgomery & Urban, 1969b, p. 8).

Experimentation in general involves the testing of an item or idea to ascertain its suitability for a particular purpose, or its ability to bring about a desired result. Instances in which an experimental approach might be used abound, and include:

1 determining a product's design;
2 identifying the best method for training sales representative;
3 specifying a package design;
4 ascertaining the most effective advertising copy;
5 selecting a product's price;
6 estimating the demand for a product;
7 choosing the best remuneration scheme for sales representative;

8 evaluating alternative point-of-sale displays;
9 gauging the best shelf arrangements for displaying a product;
10 comparing the efficiency of alternative channels of distribution.

In essence, experiments are observations, but, unlike straightforward observation in which there is no control over either the behaviour of subjects or of the environments in which they are being observed (and hence no real awareness of causal relationships), the experimenting observer deliberately intervenes in the situation. This is done by exercising influence over the variables and conditions within the experimenter's control, and controlled experiments provide the most reliable method of demonstrating causal relationships (see Banks, 1964; Cox & Enis, 1969; Davies, 1970; Venkatesan & Holloway, 1971).

Both 'experimental' and 'control' groups are required representing, say, two matched samples, or two test-market locations, two retail outlets, and so on. Selected stimuli (in the form of controllable inputs) will initially be identical in both the experimental situation and the control situation, but these stimuli will be selectively and systematically varied in the former while being held constant in the latter. Assuming that the uncontrolled extraneous factors (i.e. environmental inputs) vary in the same way between the experimental and control situations, the differences in observed outcomes can be wholly attributed to the changes made in the controllable variables. Let us consider the relationship between sales and advertising for a given product. We could carry out an experiment to determine the nature of this relationship by selecting two matching market situations, one of which would be the control and the other the experimental location. Initially there would be no advertising in either market-place but this would be gradually introduced into the experimental location only. Prior to the introduction of advertising, with all other controllable variables being identical in each location, there would have been sales levels that accorded with existing inputs, so the introduction of a new input should be the main factor in any subsequent variation in the ratio of sales in both locations (subject to the usual tests of statistical significance). In this way it is possible to build up an awareness of the manner in which particular variables (such as sales levels, or profit levels) depend on other variables (such as advertising, or the interaction of cost and revenue functions). Variables of the first type are termed *dependent variables* and those of the second type are termed *independent variables*: the values of independent variables can either be determined by management or emerge from an earlier interaction of variables in which we are not currently interested, and these independent variables then interact to produce the values of the dependent variables in which we are interested.

Diagrammatically, we can portray experimentation in a systems model (see Figure 1.8).

Obvious problems arise in connection with measuring the changes in marketing variables in an acceptably accurate way, especially when the variables of interest are concerned with levels of awareness or degrees of preference on the part of consumers (whether actual or potential). Difficulties also exist in matching groups

FIGURE 1.8
Experimentation

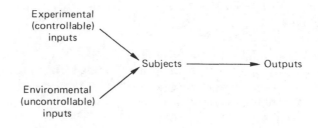

of subjects prior to running an experiment. Following from the matching problem is that of ensuring comparable exposure of the subjects to the same environmental (i.e. non-controllable) stimuli during the experiment, and then ensuring that subjects behave in an authentic manner (which will tend not to be the case when human subjects know that they are participating in an experiment – see Kotler, 1972, pp. 317–18).

If the concept of experimentation brings to mind images of chemical laboratories or white mice, it is as well to remember that the precision of measurements in the physical sciences, and to a lesser extent in the life sciences, is greater than in the social sciences. The controls that are established to ensure the accuracy of experimental results in marketing cannot usually approach the reliability of those employed in scientific laboratories. This can be seen by considering the demographic variations between two towns used in a test marketing experiment, and reflecting on the variations between two samples of a chemical of known formulation. Nevertheless, experimentation is the only means available for verifying causal relationships in marketing, which suggests that it is an important aspect of marketing planning. This in turn suggests that it is essential to know the various components of an experiment. These are shown in Figure 1.9 (after Venkatesan and Holloway, 1971, p. 11), and have an applicability (in this form of abstraction) across a large number of disciplines.

The significance of carefully stating the problem to be solved has already been discussed and might be in the form of evaluating the effectiveness of a specific advertising campaign. Help may be available in the form of existing articles, research reports, etc. (collectively referred to as 'the literature'), and theories to formulate the problem precisely and maybe to provide a solution. Usually, however, it will be necessary to specify one or more hypotheses to be tested. A hypothesis is a conjectural statement about the assumed relationship between two

FIGURE 1.9
Stages of an experiment

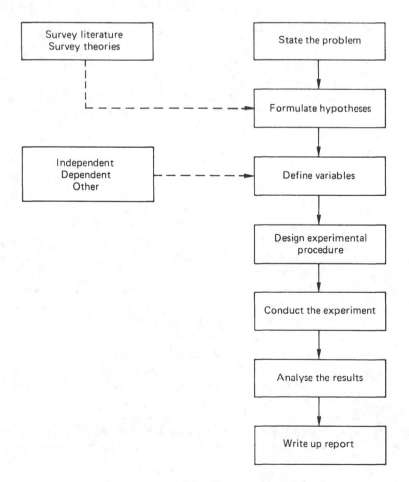

or more variables (see Zaltman, et al., 1973). We might hypothesize, for instance, that the expenditure of £X on advertising in medium A will give more opportunities to see, and have a better effect on sales, than will the expenditure of £Y in medium B. The main relevant variables are advertising expenditure, opportunities to see on the part of members of the target group, and sales response; and their interrelationship is such that sales response depends, *inter alia*, on opportunities to see, which in turn depends on the form of advertising and the medium carrying it. It is advertising that is the independent variable in this case, and an experiment must be designed to determine which type of advertising is most effective (i.e. to test the hypothesis). This raises the problems of measurement, control groups, and so forth, to which reference has already been made. Assuming these problems can be resolved and the experiment carried out the results should then be analysed to see if the hypothesis is supported or refuted.

It will be obvious that well-designed marketing experiments provide a very sound basis for planning and control in marketing, yet they are expensive to carry out, which tends to be a discouraging factor despite the importance of having reliable information in order that the right decisions might be made on the basis of that information. What may be useful is a phasing-in of experimental results over a period covering the preparation of several marketing plans so that the value of this information becomes apparent. Hopefully, this will lead to greater marketing effectiveness, with problems being anticipated so that experiments can be carried out to supply a basis to resolve them before crises emerge (see Adler, 1960; Boyd and Britt, 1965).

1.5 STRATEGIC DECISIONS AND THE NATURE OF STRATEGY

What are the characteristics of strategic decisions?

1 They are concerned with the scope of an organization's activities, and hence with the definition of an organization's boundaries.
2 They relate to the matching of the organization's activities with the opportunities of its substantive environment. Since the environment is continually changing it is necessary for this to be accommodated via adaptive decision making that anticipates outcomes – as in playing a game of chess.
3 They require the matching of an organization's activities with its resources. In order to take advantage of strategic opportunities it will be necessary to have funds, capacity, personnel, etc., available when required.
4 They have major resource implications for organizations – such as acquiring additional capacity, disposing of capacity, or reallocating resources in a fundamental way.
5 They are influenced by the values and expectations of those who determine the organization's strategy. Any repositioning of organizational boundaries will be influenced by managerial preferences and conceptions as much as by environmental possibilities.
6 They will affect the organization's long-term direction.
7 They are complex in nature since they tend to be non-routine and involve a large number of variables. As a result their implications will typically extend throughout the organization.

Decision making (whether strategic or tactical) is but a part of a broader problem-solving process. In essence this consists of three key aspects: analysis, choice and implementation.

1 *Strategic analysis* focuses on understanding the strategic position of the organization, which requires that answers be found to such questions as:

(a) What changes are taking place in the environment?
(b) How will these changes affect the organization and its activities?
(c) What resources does the organization have to deal with these changes?
(d) What do those groups associated with the organization wish to achieve?

2 *Strategic choice* has three aspects:

(a) The generation of strategic options, which should go beyond the most obvious courses of action.
(b) The evaluation of strategic options, which may be based on exploiting an organization's relative strengths or on overcoming its weaknesses.
(c) The selection of a preferred strategy which will enable the organization to seize opportunities within its environment or to counter threats from competitors.

3 *Strategic implementation* is concerned with translating a decision into action, which presupposes that the decision itself (i.e. the strategic choice) was made with some thought being given to feasibility and acceptability. The allocation of resources to new courses of action will need to be undertaken, and there may be a need for adapting the organization's structure to handle new activities as well as training personnel and devising appropriate systems.

The elements of strategic problem-solving are summarized in Figure 1.10 (Johnson and Scholes (1988), p. 16).

FIGURE 1.10
A summary model of the elements of strategic management

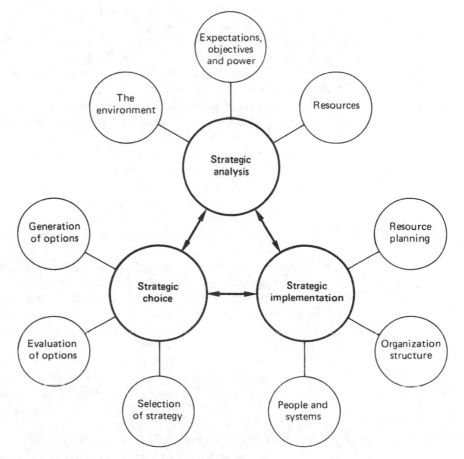

SOURCE: **Johnson and Scholes (1988), p. 16**

We have given some thought to strategic decisions, but what is meant by strategy?

Hofer and Schendel (1978, p. 27) have identified three distinct levels of strategy in a commercial context. These are:

1 corporate strategy, which deals with the allocation of resources among the various businesses or divisions of an enterprise;
2 business strategy, which exists at the level of the individual business or division, dealing primarily with the question of competitive position;
3 functional level strategy, which is limited to the actions of specific functions within specific businesses.

Our main concern is in relation to business strategy (i.e. level (2) above).

Different authorities have defined strategy in lots of different ways; there is no standard definition. However, a range of elements that most writers seem to subscribe to in discussing strategy have been put forward by Simmonds (1980, pp. 7–9), as follows:

- Strategy is applicable to business within defined boundaries. While the boundaries may change, the strategy applies at any one time to actions affecting a delimited area of demand and competition.
- There are specified direct competitors. These are competitors selling essentially the same products or services within the defined demand area. Indirect competitors are those operating outside the defined business and whose products are not direct substitutes. Indirect competition is usually ignored or covered by the concept of price elasticity of demand.
- There is zero-sum competition between the direct competitors for the market demand, subject to competitive action affecting the quantity demanded.
- Demand within the defined market varies over time. This variation in demand is largely independent of supplier strategies and is often referred to as the *product life cycle*. At its simplest it is depicted as a normal curve over time with regularly growing then declining demand.
- Strategy unfolds over a sequence of time periods. Competition evolves through a series of skirmishes and battles across the units of time covered by the product life cycle.
- Single period profit is a function of:
  *the price level ruling for the period;
  *the accumulated volume experience of the enterprise;
  *the enterprise's achieved volume as a proportion of capacity.
- Market share has intrinsic value. Past sales levels influence subsequent customer buying, and costs reduce with single-period volume and accumulated experience.
- Competitors differ in market share, accumulated experience, production capacity and resources. Competitors are unequal, identified and positioned.
- Objectives differ. Enterprises composed of ownership, management and employee factions and operating a range of different businesses have different objectives. Strategic business thinking, however, will usually express these as different time and risk preferences for performance within an individual business, measured in financial terms.
- Within a given situation there will be a core of strategic actions which will be the essential cause of change in competitive position. Non-strategic, or contingent actions, will support strategic actions and should be consistent with them, but will not change competitive position significantly.
- Identification of an optimal core of strategic actions requires reasoning, or diagnosis, is not attained through application of a fixed set of procedures and is situational. In short, thinking is required.

Taken together, these elements present a view of business strategy that sees it as a chosen set of actions by means of which a market position relative to other competing enterprises is sought and maintained. This gives us the notion of competitive position.

It needs to be emphasized that 'strategy' is not synonymous with 'long-term plan' but rather consists of an enterprise's attempts to reach some preferred future state by adapting its competitive position as circumstances change. While a series of strategic moves may be planned, competitors' actions will mean that the actual moves will have to be modified to take account of those actions.

We can contrast this view of strategy with an approach to management that has been common in the UK. In organizations that lack strategic direction there has been a tendency to look inwards in times of stress, and for management to devote their attention to cost cutting and to shedding unprofitable divisions. In other words, the focus has been on *efficiency* (i.e. the relationship between inputs and outputs, usually with a short time horizon) rather than on *effectiveness* (which is concerned with the organization's attainment of goals – including that of desired competitive position). While efficiency is essentially introspective, effectiveness highlights the links between the organization and its environment. The responsibility for efficiency lies with operational managers, with top management having the primary responsibility for the strategic orientation of the organization.

Figure 1.11 summarizes the principal combinations of efficiency and effectiveness (adapted from Christopher, et al., 1987, p. 80).

FIGURE 1.11
Efficiency versus effectiveness

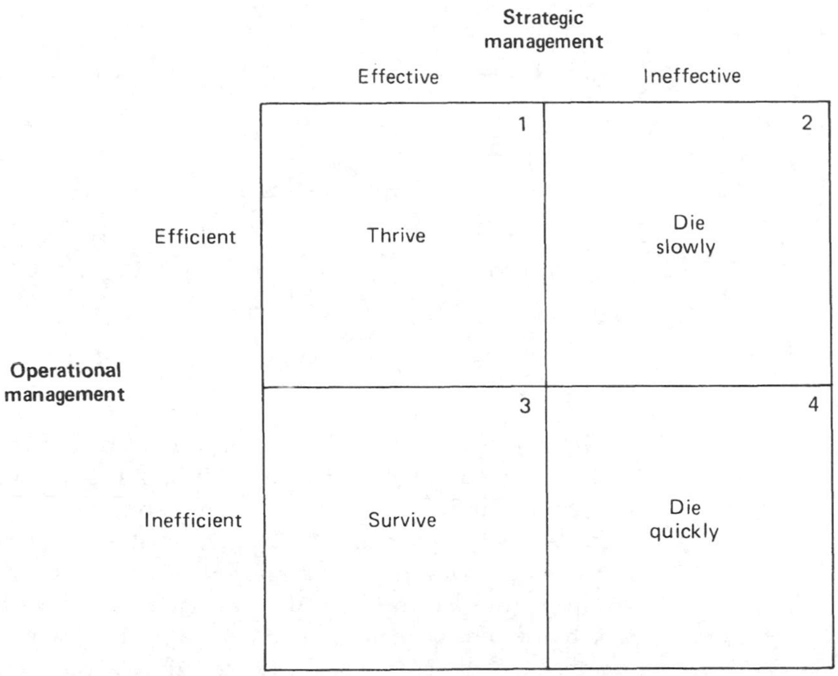

An organization that finds itself in cell 1 is well placed to thrive, since it is achieving what it aspires to achieve with an efficient output/input ratio. In contrast, an organization in cell 4 is doomed, as is an organization in cell 2 unless it can establish some strategic direction. The particular point to note is that cell 2 is a worse place to be than is cell 3 since, in the latter, the strategic direction is present to ensure effectiveness even if rather too much input is being used to generate outputs. To be effective is to survive whereas to be efficient is not in itself either necessary or sufficient for survival.

In crude terms, to be effective is to do the right thing, while to be efficient is to do the (given) thing right. An emphasis on efficiency rather than on effectiveness is clearly wrong. But who determines effectiveness? Any organization can be portrayed as a coalition of diverse interest groups each of which participates in the coalition in order to secure some advantage. This advantage (or inducement) may be in the form of dividends to shareholders, wages to employees, continued business to suppliers of goods and services, satisfaction on the part of consumers, legal compliance from the viewpoint of government, responsible behaviour towards society and the environment from the perspective of pressure groups, and so on. Figure 1.12 illustrates the way in which a range of interest groups come together to sustain (and, indeed, constitute) an organization. In so far as the inducements needed to maintain this coalition are not forthcoming the organization ceases to be effective. Thus, for example, employees may go on strike in furtherance of a pay dispute; shareholders may be unwilling to subscribe further capital if the value of their shares has fallen due to bad management; consumers may have defected in the light of superior market offerings from competitors; and each of these will remove one vital element from the coalition.

FIGURE 1.12
Interest groups

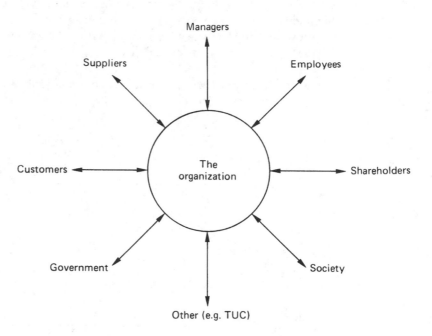

The interest groups within the coalition provide contributions (or resources) without which the organization cannot function: these are the inputs (men, machines, money, etc.) to the systems model we saw earlier in the chapter.

It should be apparent from this view of an organization that management's freedom of movement is constrained by virtue of the expectations of the interest groups within the coalition. We are unable to assume that a clean slate exists on which any strategy might be drawn, since this may be against the interests of members of the coalition. What we can say, therefore, is that any strategy is potentially available in so far as it ensures that the interests of coalition members are protected. If this is not so the organization cannot be effective, and if it is not effective it will not survive.

1.6 THE MARKETING/STRATEGY INTERFACE

On the basis of a literature review Greenley (1986, p. 56) has drawn some distinctions between marketing planning (seen as being an annual exercise) and strategic planning (seen as being of a long-term nature), including the following:

Table 1.1

Strategic planning	Marketing planning
Concerned with overall, long-term organizational direction.	Concerned with day-to-day performance and results.
Provides the long-term framework for the organization.	Represents only one stage in the organization's development.
Overall orientation needed to match the organization to its environment.	Functional and professional orientation tends to predominate.
Goals and strategies are evaluated from an overall perspective.	Goals are subdivided into specific targets.
Relevance of goals and strategies is only evident in the long term.	Relevance of goals and strategies is immediately evident.

These differences indicate that strategic planning logically precedes marketing planning by providing a framework within which marketing plans might be formulated. As Cravens (1986, p. 77) has stated:

> Understanding the strategic situation confronting an organization is an essential starting point in developing a marketing strategy.

This understanding can be derived from an assessment of:

- organizational capabilities;
- threats from environmental forces;
- competitors' strengths and weaknesses;
- customer needs;

and fits into an iterative setting as shown in Figure 1.13.

FIGURE 1.13
The marketing strategy process

The strong interdependence of strategic and marketing planning is clearly seen in this diagram. We can use this interdependence to develop the marketing mix (of Figure 1.2 above) into a set of elements from which a competitive strategy might be developed (as in Figure 1.14). The aim should be to build strength in those elements that are critical to achieving superiority in areas deemed important by customers. In this way the organization should be able to challenge its competitors from a position in which it can use its relative strengths.

The potential benefits of a strategic underpinning to marketing planning are probably apparent, but what about the problem of implementation? If implementation is ineffective the carefully devised strategy will be unable to help in improving the organization's performance. The question becomes, therefore: 'given a specific type of strategy, what marketing structures, policies, procedures, and programs are

FIGURE 1.14
*Elements of a
competitive strategy*

Product
- Functional performance
- Technical developments planned
- Packaging
- Service levels
- Range extensions/deletions

Customer
- Customer targets
- Researching customer needs by segment
- Segmenting the market by customer needs
- Distribution channels
- Export

Distribution
- Identifying appropriate channels
- Accessing successful distributors
- Stock and service levels
- Operating costs

Price
- List prices
- Discount structure

Advertising and promotion
- Target audience
- Communication objective
- Media
- Advertising weight
- Promotion plans and timing
- Point of sale

Sales force
- Customer priorities
- Product priorities
- Incentives and rewards

Manufacturing
- Sustainable quality and volume levels
- Cost reduction programme:
  - raw material usage
  - yields
  - manpower
- Quality enhancement

SOURCE: Milton and Reiss, 1985, p. 23

likely to distinguish high performing business units from those that are relatively less effective, efficient, or adaptable?' (Walker and Ruekert, 1987, p. 15). Part of the answer is undoubtedly the extent to which the organization reflects a customer orientation. We will turn to this question in Part 5.

Left-handed and Right-handed Organizations

The issue of customer orientation has been discussed by Doyle (1994, pp. 7–9) in terms of what he refers to as *left-handed* and *right-handed* organizations. For many senior managers, he argues, the principal business objectives are profitability, growth and shareholder value. There is, however, a danger in these, he suggests, in that they ignore the customer even though:

> satisfied customers are the source of all profits and shareholder value. Customers can choose from whom they buy, and unless the firm satisfies them at least as well as competitors, sales and profits will quickly erode. Customer satisfaction should therefore be a prime objective and measure of the performance of managers (op. cit., p. 7).

This leads Doyle to highlight the differences between the two types of organization. In the case of left-handed or financially-driven organizations, he suggests that the key planning mechanism is the financial plan or budget, with costs, expenses, debt and assets – and the elements of the marketing mix – all being controlled in order to achieve financial goals; this is illustrated in Figure 1.15. The consequence of this is that when sales begin to slip there is a tendency to cut back on areas such as advertising and R & D in order to maintain or boost profits.

By contrast, right-handed or market-driven organizations have as their primary focus the objective of satisfying customers. This involves defining and understanding market segments and then managing the marketing mix in such a way that customers' expectations are fully met or exceeded. The difference between the two approaches, Doyle argues, is that 'Business decisions flow back from an understanding of customers rather than from a financial requirement' (op. cit., p. 9).

He goes on to suggest that the market-led approach, which is based on the idea of achieving market leadership through superiority in meeting customers' needs, has typically been associated with Japanese organizations. By contrast, the

FIGURE 1.15
The left-handed and right-handed organization

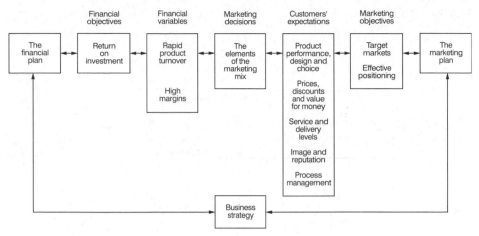

SOURCE: Adapted from Doyle, P. (1994), p. 8

financially-driven approach has all too often been a reflection of British and US organizations. (This is discussed in greater detail in Illustration 4.2.) The idea of a left- versus right-handed orientation leads in turn to the notion of *wrong-side-up* and *right-side-up* organizations. Given the importance to any organization of its customers, it follows that staff must be customer-led. Doyle argues that the *truly* fundamental importance of this has been recognized by relatively few organizations; those which have are the ones that achieve true customer delight.

Among those which have come to recognize the real significance of a customer orientation are McDonald's, Marks & Spencer and, in the 1980s, Scandinavian Airlines. Jan Carlzon, the airline's Chief Executive, recognized at an early stage the importance of what he referred to as 'moments of truth'; these are the occasions when the customer deals with the organization's staff and is exposed to the quality of service and type of personal contact. Carlzon's thinking in turning round and revitalizing what was at the time a poorly performing airline was therefore straightforward. Because the airline's frontline staff, many of whom are in relatively junior positions, are the customer's only really visible point of contact with the airline, managers need to ensure that all staff understand and act out the values that senior management claims are important. This means they need to be the most customer-orientated, best trained and most strongly motivated employees in the business. However, the reality in many cases is that these are the people who least understand the core values and are often only poorly trained. The net effect of this is that the organization fails to deliver to the customer what it promises.

In an attempt to overcome this, organizations have responded in a variety of ways, including downsizing, developing flatter structures and by empowering staff. In this way, a more firmly customer-led business in which frontline employees are more highly trained and motivated to satisfy customer needs should emerge; this is illustrated in Figure 1.16.

Marketing's Mid-life Crisis

We started this chapter by talking about the nature of marketing and its contribution to the overall management process. However, whilst the arguments in favour of marketing, with its emphasis upon the identification of customers' needs and the delivery of customer satisfaction are – or appear to be – strong, there has been an increasing recognition over the past few years that marketing is – or may be – facing what is loosely referred to as a 'mid-life crisis'. The basis for this comment is that, although a whole generation of management writers agree upon the importance of consumer sovereignty, and hence the apparent and pivotal importance of marketing, there is now a widespread and growing concern that 'something is amiss, that the (marketing) concept is deeply, perhaps irredeemably, flawed, that its seemingly solid theoretical foundations are by no means secure and

FIGURE 1.16
*The two types of
organization*

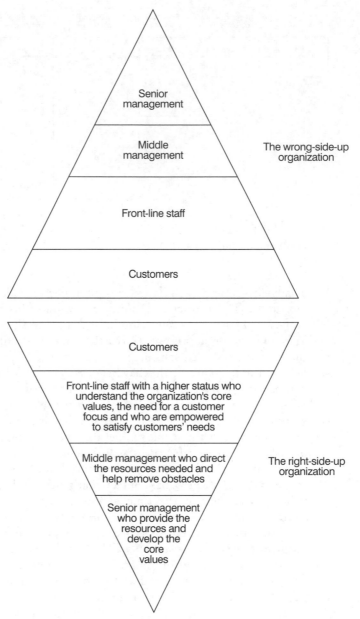

Senior
management

Middle
management

Front-line staff

Customers

The wrong-side-up
organization

Customers

Front-line staff with a higher status who
understand the organization's core
values, the need for a customer
focus and who are empowered
to satisfy customers' needs

Middle management who direct
the resources needed and
help remove obstacles

The right-side-up
organization

Senior management
who provide the
resources and
develop the
core
values

SOURCE: Adapted from Doyle, P. (1994), p. 48

that the specialism is teetering on the brink of serious intellectual crisis'. (Brown, 1995, p. 42).

In developing this argument, Brown makes reference to a variety of commentators:

- Piercy (1991, p. 15), for example, maintains that the traditional marketing concept 'assumes and relies on the existence of a world which is alien and unrecognisable to many of the executives who actually have to manage marketing for real.
- Gummeson (1987, p. 10) states that 'the present marketing concept ... is unrealistic and needs to be replaced'.
- Rapp and Collins (1990, p. 3) suggest that 'the traditional methods ... simply aren't working as well any more'.
- Brownlie and Saren (1992, p. 38) argue that 'it is questionable whether the marketing concept as it has been propagated can provide the basis for successful business at the end of the twentieth century'.
- And Michael Thomas (1993) who has recently made the frank, and frankly astonishing, confession that after thirty years of disseminating the marketing message, he is having serious doubts about its continuing efficacy.

Hooley and Saunders (1993, p. 3), however, have pursued a rather different line of argument, suggesting instead that the marketing concept has come of age in that, whereas even ten years ago many senior managers did not *really* understand marketing, there appears now to be a far deeper and wider appreciation of the concept and of the benefits that it is capable of delivering. To a very large extent this is due to the succession of studies which have highlighted the contribution that effective marketing programmes are capable of making to organizational performance and success; a number of these are summarized in Illustration 1.1. But despite this sort of evidence, there is still a question mark over the direction that marketing should take in the future. Without doubt, one of the triumphs of marketing as a discipline over the past decade has been the way in which it has been accepted in a host of areas by managers who previously had denied its value and scope for contributing to the sector's performance. Included within these are healthcare, not-for-profit organizations, leisure, religious movements, cultural organizations, and the political arena.

Illustration 1.1: But Does Marketing Work?

The question of whether marketing 'works' in the sense that it contributes to or is the principal influence upon higher and more sustained levels of business performance has been the subject of a number of studies. Some of the best known of these were conducted by:

- Hooley and Lynch (1985) who examined 1504 British companies and concluded that the high performing organizations were characterized by a significantly greater market orientation, strategic direction and concern with product quality and design than the 'also rans',
- Narver and Slater (1990) who focused upon the marketing orientation of the senior managers in 140 North American strategic business units (SBUs) and identified not only a very strong relationship between marketing orientation and profitability but also that the *highest* degree of marketing orientation was manifested by managers of the *most profitable* companies.
- Kohli and Jaworski (1990) who conducted a series of semi-structured interviews with marketing practitioners in the US and discovered a high degree of managerial understanding of the three key component parts of the marketing concept (*customer orientation, co-ordination* and *profitability*), and that the perceived benefits of the marketing philosophy included better overall performance, benefits for employees and more positive customer attitudes,
- Wong and Saunders (1993) who, as the result of a study of matched Japanese, American and British companies, demonstrated that organizations classified as 'innovators', 'quality marketeers' and 'mature marketeers' were significantly more successful in terms of profits, sales and market share than those classified as 'price promoters', 'product makers' and 'aggressive pushers'.

Nevertheless, there is still a significant degree of scepticism about the value and future role of marketing. In discussing this, Brown (1995, p. 43) focuses upon four stages of marketing acceptance. The first of these, *realization*, is characterized by a general acceptance that the marketing concept is sound, but that there is often a problem with its implementation; the most common manifestation of this would be that of getting senior management to accept and embrace the concept. The net effect of this in many organizations has been 'a preoccupation with **making**

marketing work through a heightened understanding of organizational politics and inter-functional rivalry . . . (and) a programme of internal marketing' (op. cit., p. 43) designed to ensure that organizational transformation takes place.

The second position is *retrenchment* in which, again, the concept is seen to be sound, but there are certain circumstances in which it is either inappropriate or of little immediate relevance; many managers in the very fastest moving high-tech industries have, for example, argued that this is the case. Other sectors and markets in which its role and contribution is, it is argued, of little real value include commodity markets, public administration and poorly developed markets in which either there is a significant imbalance between demand and supply and/or an almost complete absence of infrastructure.

The third position, *rearrangement*, demands a far more fundamental reappraisal of marketing so that it can more easily and readily come to terms with the very different realities of today's markets. Webster (1988), for example, has argued for a move away from the position in which marketing and strategic management have, for many commentators, become synonymous. Instead of a myopic preoccupation with market share, competitor activity and so on, marketing should, he claims, return to its roots of a true customer focus. A broadly similar line of argument has been pursued by Christopher, et al. (1991) who highlight the fundamental importance of marketing relationships rather than one-off transactions.

The fourth, final and most radical position is that of *reappraisal* which, according to Brown (1995, p. 45), gives acknowledgement to:

> the simple fact that the marketing concept has not succeeded and is unlikely to prove successful in its present form. Despite the latter-day 'triumph' of marketing, the failure rate of new products is as high as it ever was – possibly higher. Consumerism, the so-called 'shame of marketing', is still rampant, especially in its virulent 'green' mutation. Selling has not, contra to the marketing concept, been rendered redundant because few products actually sell themselves. Companies in countries where the marketing message has not been received loud and clear, such as Japan and Germany, continue to outperform their Anglo-American counterparts and, even in the latter milieux, businesses can still succeed without the aid of modern marketing (Piercy (1992) cites The Body Shop, Amstrad, Ratners and Marks and Spencer as prime examples).

Redefining Marketing: Coming to Terms with the Challenges of the Next Millennium

Against the background of our comments so far it is apparent that there is a strong case either for redefining marketing or, at the very least, thinking about the role that it should play in the twenty-first century. For many managers the need for this has been highlighted by the way in which a series of fundamental changes have taken place within many markets which demand a new and possibly radical rethinking of strategies. Prominent among these changes are:

- the decline of the megabrands as the result of attacks from low-branded, low-priced competitors;
- the disappearance within many industrial organizations of staff marketing departments and their replacement by more focused functions with specific line responsibilities;
- the decline in the demand for certain specialist marketing skills, including the collection and analysis of data;
- the emergence of a 'new' type of consumer who demands a far higher value added offer; and
- markets which are characterized by infinitely more aggressive – and desperate – levels of competition.

It was against this background that Kashani (1996, pp. 8–10) conducted an international study of 220 managers with a view to identifying the challenges that marketing managers were facing, how these might best be met and what the implications for marketing might be. The findings suggested that, in order of importance, the principal challenges were seen to be:

- high and rising levels of competition across virtually all markets;
- far higher levels of price competition;
- an increasing emphasis upon and need for customer service;
- a demand for higher levels of product quality;
- higher rates of product innovation;
- changing and less predictable customer needs;
- the emergence of new market segments;
- the growing power of distribution channels;
- growing environmental ('green') concerns;
- increases in government regulations;
- European integration;
- increasing advertising and promotional costs.

The principal implications of these were seen by managers to be the need for constant improvements to product and/or service quality; the development of new products; keeping up with competitors; and adding to or improving customer service.

As part of the study Kashani also asked managers about the sorts of changes that were most likely to affect their markets in the future. The three most significant of these proved to be:

- the consolidation of competition as fewer but larger players emerge;
- changing customers and their demands; and
- the globalization of markets and competition.

In order to cope with these sorts of changes he suggests that marketing needs to respond in several ways. Perhaps the most obvious of these is that it needs to take on a *far more direct line responsibility* within the organization, with an emphasis upon segment or product management, where the focus is upon customer segments or particular products or technologies. The effect of this would be that marketing thinking and action would be better integrated into day-to-day business decisions.

Following on from this, marketing needs to become more strategic and less specialized in its nature so that it becomes part of a more integrated process which might, for example, include upstream product development or downstream distribution management.

The third sort of change which is needed can in many ways be seen to be the underpinning that is needed for the future – that of a marketing or customer orientation becoming far more widespread. This would mean that marketing would no longer be the isolated concern of a few people, but of staff throughout the business. Thus:

> A widespread appreciation of market forces and customer needs and how parts of an organization may contribute to creating a superior customer value is a necessity if the entire organization is to become market responsive. In a fast changing market environment, such an appreciation can make the difference between success and failure (Kashani, 1996, p. 9).

Assuming changes such as these are made, the sorts of skills and competences that managers will need in the future will differ from those which are needed today, with a far greater emphasis being placed upon strategic thinking, communication, and customer sensitivity.

The increasing volatility of markets has also been referred to in a number of recent books, such as *The End of Affluence* (Madrick, 1995) and *The End of Work*

(Rivkin, 1995), both of which argue that the developed western economies are facing a major step change in their fortunes as unemployment levels rise, deficits persist and purchasing power declines. There appear to be two major forces which are contributing to these changes. The first is *globalization* which leads to an opening up of domestic markets and to the threat of low priced foreign entrants. The second contributory factor is that of the seemingly ever faster pace of *technological change*. Together these demand not only that managers have a far more detailed understanding of their current and potential markets and of their organization's ability to capitalize upon the undoubted opportunities that exist, but also of the ways in which these threats might best be minimized; in essence, this is a case for marketers to recognize the fundamental need for their behaviour patterns to be what Ries and Trout (1986) discuss in terms of being faster, more focused and smarter. In the absence of this, an organization's ability to compete is reduced dramatically.

But although the new market environment demands more innovative thinking and more creative ways of tackling the market, there are, in many organizations, significant barriers to this; these are illustrated in Figure 1.17.

FIGURE 1.17
The conflicting environmental and organizational forces

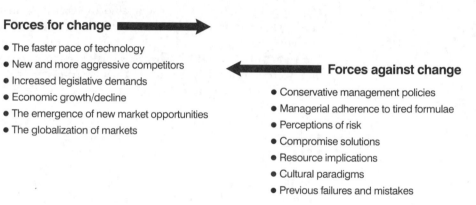

Forces for change

● The faster pace of technology
● New and more aggressive competitors
● Increased legislative demands
● Economic growth/decline
● The emergence of new market opportunities
● The globalization of markets

Forces against change

● Conservative management policies
● Managerial adherence to tired formulae
● Perceptions of risk
● Compromise solutions
● Resource implications
● Cultural paradigms
● Previous failures and mistakes

Given the nature of these opposing forces and of the liklihood of those on the right hand side leading to a failure on the part of the organization to change, the marketing planner needs to focus upon a number of issues including what Hamel and Prahalad (1994, pp. 49–71) refer to in terms of 'learning to forget'. (This is an issue which is developed in detail in Chapter 9.) In arguing for this, they suggest that far too many managers, while acknowledging at an intellectual level the need for change, fail to accept it at an emotional level. In other words, while they are aware of the environmental changes taking place and accept the need to behave more proactively, they are often far too constrained by day-to-day pressures and the organizational culture to make the possibly radical shifts that the environment demands. Because of this, they remain wedded to old patterns of thought, believing that the current ways of doing things will ultimately prove to be adequate.

In order to overcome this myopia, Wind (1996, p. 7) argues that there needs to be a far greater emphasis upon being close to the customer, together with a far more fundamental recognition of the importance of customer satisfaction, the need for customer relationship building, an emphasis upon understanding customer value and the enhanced product offering, and that brand equity stems from a loyal customer base.

The implications of this can be seen to be far-reaching, including the way in which marketing needs to be looked at from a pan-organizational perspective rather than from the far narrower departmental perspective which predominates in many organizations. In turn, this different approach demands a rethinking of an organization's vision, objectives, strategies and structures, as well as of the sorts of skills that its staff need.

In discussing this, Wind (op. cit.) argues that managers need to ask – and answer – twelve questions.

1 Is marketing and its focus on meeting and anticipating customers' needs widely accepted as a business philosophy?
2 Are the business and corporate strategies focused on creating value to all the stakeholders?
3 Do the objectives include customer satisfaction and the creation of value?
4 Is the marketing function integrated with the other functions of the company as part of the key value creating process?
5 Are the key marketing positions market segment (or key account) managers?
6 Are products viewed as part of an integrated product and service offering which delivers the desired benefit positioning for the target segment?
7 Is the marketing strategy global in its scope?
8 Is full use being made of market research and modelling in generating and evaluating marketing and market-driven business strategies?
9 Is there an emphasis upon information technology as an integral part of the organization's marketing strategies?
10 Does a significant part of the marketing effort constitute innovative practices not previously used by the organization and its competitors?
11 Are strategic alliances for co-marketing activities being formed, and are marketing strategies based on the development of long-term relationships with clients?
12 Is there a sufficient focus of attention and resources upon message effectiveness (instead of media power) and value-based pricing (instead of discounting)?

Wind goes on to argue that it is not enough just to answer 'yes' to these twelve questions, but that there is also a need to recognize the interrelationships between many of the questions and that the corporate vision and objectives *must* reflect a marketing orientation. This, in turn, highlights the critical importance of ensuring that the organizational architecture (this embraces the culture, structure, processes, technology, resources, people, performance measures and incentives) is focused upon the implementation of the new marketing paradigm. This paradigm, Wind suggests, can best be summed up in terms of building upon the historical role of marketing as the linkage between the organization and the environment, but which also focuses upon the twelve questions above and which, in turn, has implications for marketing as:

- the leading business philosophy;
- the knowledge and wisdom centre of the company that provides all organizational members with concepts and findings about customers and tools for measuring and forecasting customer behaviour and models and decision-support systems for improving the quality of marketing and business decisions; and
- the growth engine which, through creative marketing strategies that utilise technology and mobilise the other business functions of the company, stimulates the top-line growth of the company.

Given the nature of these comments, it should be apparent that marketing is facing a series of fundamental challenges and that many planners are reappraising how marketing might best contribute to the overall management of an organization. As part of this debate, Figure 1.18 attempts to pull together the kinds of relationships that should or might realistically exist between marketing and other areas of a marketing organization. Within this, there are several areas to which attention needs to be paid, but most obviously the characteristics of corporate management (the long-term perspective, a sense of vision, clear values,

FIGURE 1.18
Marketing and its contribution to effective management

Corporate Management
Lean head office staff
A long-term perspective and a strong sense of vision
An emphasis upon proactivity and the development of long-term relationships with suppliers, distributors and customers
A culture of excellence
Clear (and appropriate) core values
Leadership rather than management
Well-developed internal and external communication patterns
A recognition that creativity is the only remaining competitive edge

Marketing	Design and Engineering	Purchasing	Production	Sales	Customers

Marketing
A proactive competitive stance and an emphasis upon innovation and creativity

An emphasis upon creating and maintaining high levels of customer satisfaction by adding value and 'delighting' the customer

A fundamental recognition of the need to build relationships with customers, suppliers, distributors and the media

Innovative segmentation, targeting and positioning

A search for new markets and opportunities

Detailed competitor and customer analysis with the results being fed into the strategy development process

An emphasis upon adding value and customer 'delight'

Distinctive advertising and promotional appeals

A well-formulated pricing strategy and clear value for money offer

Constant environmental analysis and interpretation

Design and Engineering
Rapid and constant product improvement

Benchmarking inside and outside the industry

Working with customers

Lateral thinking in the search for new ideas

Purchasing
Zero or minimal inventory levels

A policy of not compromising on quality

An emphasis upon developing long-term relationships with a small number of high-quality suppliers

Production
Just in time and lean manufacturing

Zero defects and a culture of right first time, every time

Zero set-up time

A constant search for product, process and quality improvements

Customization offered where possible

Benchmarking inside and outside the industry

An emphasis upon best practice

Sales
The development of long-term relationships with distributors and customers

Aggressive value for money

Low financing changes

Customization offered where possible

A recognition of the need for effective customer process management

Working with customers to identify new leads and opportunities and how they might be met

Customers
Fast and regular customer feedback marketing in order to close the loop

proactive patterns of thought and behaviour, and so on), the process linkages between marketing and the other functions, and the sorts of factors which characterize the effective management of each of the five functions identified.

Changing Emphases Within Marketing

As the part of the organization which interacts most directly and immediately with the environment, there is an obvious need for the marketing planner to investigate, analyse and respond to any environmental changes that are taking place. If this is not done – or if it is done only poorly – not only will opportunities be missed, but potential and emerging threats are more likely to become actual threats, both of which will be reflected in a decline in performance. Because of this, the marketing planner needs to develop a clear vision of the future and of the ways in which the business environment is most likely to develop. In doing this, it is essential that the planner recognizes how patterns of marketing thinking are changing and how the organization might best come to terms with areas of growing importance.

For Doyle (1994, pp. 378–80), the major changes that the marketing planner is faced with include:

- the 'fashionization' of many relatively traditional markets as model changes occur much faster, obsolescence becomes more rapid and markets become more fickle;
- the replacement of mass markets with micro markets;
- rising expectations across virtually all markets and a reduced tolerance to accept poor(er) performance;
- the greater pace of technological change;
- higher levels of competition;
- the globalization of an ever greater number of markets;
- differentiation on the basis of service and the 'soft' rather than the traditional 'hard' elements of the marketing mix;
- the increased commoditization of many markets;
- the erosion of brands; and
- greater government and legislative constraints.

Kotler's (1997, xxxii–xxxiv) views on the changing emphases and priorities within marketing are broadly similar, with a growing emphasis upon:

- quality, value and customer satisfaction;
- relationship building and customer retention;
- managing business processes and integrating business functions;
- global thinking and marketing planning;
- building strategic alliances and networks;
- direct and on-line marketing;
- services marketing;
- ethical marketing behaviour;

In terms of the implications of these changes for marketing strategy, it is apparent that there is a need for companies to adapt – perhaps significantly – or live with the consequences of an erosion of their marketing position. Recognizing this, we can identify a number of marketing priorities for the new millennium:

- As the pace of change increases, the speed of anticipation and response will become ever more important and time-based competition more essential.
- As markets fragment, customization will become more necessary.
- With expectations rising, quality will become one of the *basic* rules of competition (in other words, a 'must have') rather than a basis for differentiation.

- Information and greater market knowledge will provide a powerful basis for a competitive advantage.
- Sustainable competitive advantage will increasingly be based upon an organization's core competences. The consequences of a lack of strategic focus will become more evident and more significant.
- As market boundaries are eroded, the need to think global will become ever more necessary. In this way, the marketing planner will be able to offset temporary or permanent declines in one market against growing opportunities in another. At the same time, of course, the need to recognize the strategic significance of size and scale is increasing. However, in going for size, the marketing planner should not lose sight of the need for tailoring products and services to the specific demands of markets by thinking globally, but acting locally.
- Differentiation will increasingly be based upon service.
- Partnerships with suppliers and distributors will become far more strategically significant.
- Strategic alliances will become more necessary as a means of entering and operating within markets, partly because they offer the advantages of access to greater or shared knowledge, but also because of the sharing of costs and risks.
- A far greater emphasis upon product, service and process innovation.
- A need to recognize the greater number and complexity of stakeholders' expectations.

In turn, these marketing priorities have substantial implications for organizational structures and cultures. Doyle (op cit pp 384–6) identifies the ten most obvious of these as being the need to:

1 Break hierarchies and reorganize around flatter structures.
2 Organize around small(er) business units.
3 Develop self-managing teams.
4 Re-engineer.
5 Focus upon developing networks and alliances.
6 Move towards transactional forms of organization.
7 Become a true learning organization.
8 Emphasize account management in order to integrate specialist expertise across the organization for the benefit of the customer.
9 Recognize the importance of 'expeditionary marketing' so that instead of focusing upon what Hamel and Prahalad refer to as *blockbuster innovation* designed to get it right first time, the organization concentrates upon developing a stream of low cost fast-paced innovative products.
10 Rethink the way in which the board of directors operates so that it focuses to a far greater extent upon strategic direction rather than control and day-to-day management.

1.7 SUMMARY

This chapter seeks to offer some ideas constituting a framework for the rest of the book.

It begins by considering the nature of management and of the management process. The process is often characterized in the following stages:

- planning;
- decision making;
- control.

These are related to a series of questions, around which the book is structured:

1 Where are we now?
2 Where do we want to be?
3 How might we get there?
4 Which way is best?
5 How can we ensure arrival?

Three different time dimensions can be identified:

1 *Past*: which brought us to where we are now and from which we might learn;
2 *Present*: in which we might determine where we wish to go and how we might get there;
3 *Future*: in which our aspirations may – or may not – be realized but which represents the key time dimension.

We can inter-relate managerial processes, key questions, and time dimensions into a multi-faceted framework which can be portrayed as a 'cycle of control'. The next step is to consider the notion of strategy, and then the role of marketing in relation to strategy.

Strategy can be seen as a normative matter concerning what an organization would like to achieve. As such it:

● guides the organization in its relationship with its environment;
● affects the internal structure and processes of the organization;
● centrally affects the organization's performance.

Marketing, via its policies and programmes relating to product, price, service, distribution and communications, can provide the means to facilitate the attainment of a strategy.

The extent to which the strategy is achieved provides a measure of the organization's effectiveness. Any organization's effectiveness depends upon the balance between what is desired and what is achieved on the one hand, and on the other by paying due regard to the requirements of all stakeholders, whether internal or external. It is through the process of organizational control that managers seek to achieve organizational effectiveness, and this gives a reference point for all that follows.

1.8 EXERCISES

1 Referring to Figure 1.1, where would you position the organization that you work for? What factors appear to contribute to this? (*Hint*: think about the nature and demands of the marketing environment and the type of managerial culture that exists.) Assuming that the organization is not market-driven, what would be needed to move the organization towards this position?
2 Turn now to Figure 1.11 and conduct a similar analysis. What are the implications of the organization's position within the matrix?
3 In Figure 1.2, we identify the principal elements of the marketing mix. Looking at your own organization, which of the seven elements of the mix appear to be seen by management to be the most important elements? Do your competitors emphasize the same elements?
4 In Figure 1.16 we illustrate Doyle's idea of the wrong-side-up and the right-side-up organization. Which approach most closely reflects your own organization? Assuming that it is a wrong-side-up organization, (a) what are the

implications for customers and levels of customer service; and (b) what would be needed to change to the right-side-up approach?

5 Figure 1.10 is a summary model of the elements of strategic management. Looking at your own organization, which of the three core elements – strategic analysis, strategic choice and strategic implementation – appears to be (a) the strongest and (b) the weakest? What are the implications of this, and what would be needed in order to achieve a more equal balance?

6 Turning now to Figure 1.17, which of the forces *for* change are proving to be the most significant challenges for your organization? How powerful are the forces *against* change? What is the overall picture that emerges from this, and what appear to be the implications for how the organization will be able to cope with the future?

1.9 CASE STUDY

Penton Ltd

Penton is a medium-sized company which manufactures and markets a range of DIY (Do It Yourself) products under the Easi-Way brand name. Its performance over the past ten years, a period during which the market for DIY products has grown rapidly, has been viewed by those within the industry as steady, but generally unimpressive. In particular, its critics have pointed to performance levels that are below the industry norm, a reliance upon its long-established and now old-fashioned distribution networks, low levels of advertising spend, a failure to exploit the potential strength of the brand name, and a poor profit performance.

Towards the end of 1991, the company was the subject of a takeover bid from a smaller but more aggressive and far more successful competitor. Although Penton's board managed to fight off the bid, the sudden awareness of their vulnerability to further bids has led to a reassessment of their entire manufacturing and marketing strategy.

The problems being faced by the organization were exacerbated by the downturn in retail sales which began to affect the economy at the end of the 1980s. Faced with what was proving to be a static sales curve and a reducing profit margin, the decision was taken to bring in a firm of marketing consultants to conduct a detailed audit of the organization and make recommendations for future strategy. The consultants' initial report highlighted a number of areas of concern which, they suggested, should be the focus of attention:

1 The organization's strong production orientation and a lack of marketing representation at board level.
2 A largely reactive managerial philosophy.
3 Little long-term product or market planning.
4 An over-reliance upon a small number of ageing products.
5 A poorly structured new product planning process.
6 The generally disappointing performance and high failure rate of new product launches over the past few years.
7 A failure to exploit the potential strength of the brand name.
8 Increasing pressure upon margins.

The environmental analysis proved to be more encouraging, with the consultants giving prominence to the size and long-term growth potential of the DIY market, and the major profit opportunities offered by new products. They also pointed to the high level of retail concentration in the market, the need for organizations in this sector to be proactive in their new product development, and for new products to be supported by a strong promotional campaign. In a separate section, the consultants spelled out in detail the implications of the seemingly ever-greater degree of retail concentration, summarizing this with a comment that highlighted the strategic importance of relationship marketing.

The evaluation of the organization's manufacturing capabilities suggested that there was a need for investment in new plant. With regard to the research and development area, the conclusion was that 'whilst the area has potential and the R&D staff are enthusiastic and highly qualified, the activity has suffered from a lack of direction. As a result, the majority of new products have not been related sufficiently directly to market demands.'

Against the background of these findings, the board has attempted to identify the areas of greatest priority and has decided to focus upon the three areas which they believed require the most immediate attention. These are the development of:

- A marketing orientation.
- A far stronger and more effective planning culture.
- A structured and proactive new product development process.

Questions

1 As a member of the team of consultants, you have the responsibility for making recommendations as to how the organization might most effectively achieve the first two of the above points. You are therefore required to prepare a report showing how this might be done. (See pp. 679–85.)
2 What are the implications of your suggestions for approaches to management control?

Required

This is a case study that requires you to be very clear about what is meant by a marketing orientation and how one might be developed within an organization that previously has been product led. Your suggestions must therefore be specific. It is worth remembering that if you can develop the stronger marketing orientation it is likely that the planning and new product development systems will improve as the result of the stronger external focus.

The second question requires you to think about the nature of the control process and how planning and control are two separate but highly interrelated activities. Again, however, your suggestions must be specific.

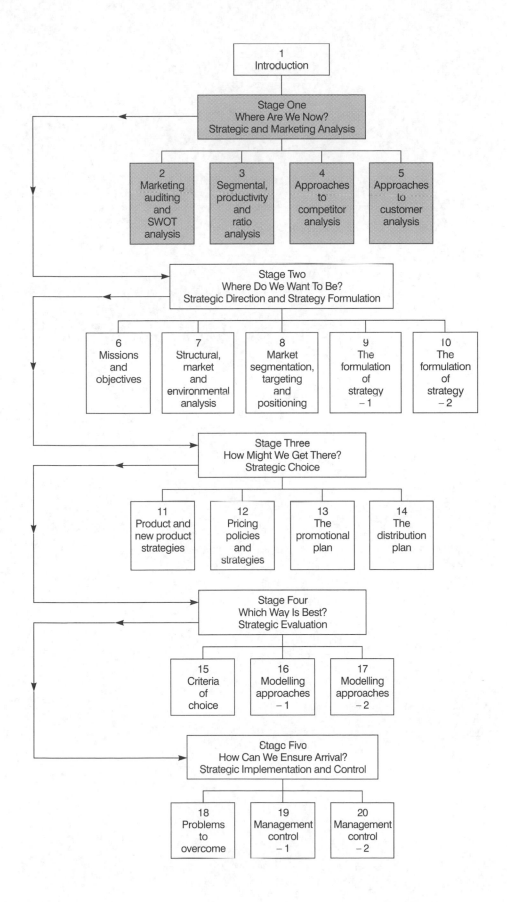

Stage One
Where Are We Now?
Strategic and Marketing Analysis

PREAMBLE

Our primary concern within this stage is with the ways in which organizations can most clearly identify their current position and the extent of their marketing capability. It is against the background of the picture that emerges from this analysis that the strategist should then be in a far better position to begin the process of deciding upon the detail of the organization's future direction and the ways in which strategy is to be formulated.

The starting point in this process of strategic and marketing analysis involves a detailed marketing audit and review of marketing effectiveness. Together, the two techniques are designed to provide the strategist with a clear understanding of:

- the organization's current market position;
- the nature of environmental opportunities and threats;
- the organization's ability to cope with the demands of this environment.

The results of this analysis are then incorporated in a statement of Strengths, Weaknesses, Opportunities and Threats (SWOT).

Although the marketing auditing process is, as we discuss in Chapter 2, a relatively under-utilized activity, a growing number of strategists and writers have over the past few years highlighted the nature of its potential contribution to effective strategy formulation.

Although there is no single format for the audit, it is generally acknowledged that if the process is to be worthwhile, account needs to be taken of six dimensions:

1 the marketing environment;
2 the current marketing strategy;
3 organizational issues;
4 the marketing systems in use;
5 levels of marketing productivity;
6 marketing functions.

Used properly, marketing auditing and a review of marketing effectiveness are recognized as potentially powerful analytical tools that are capable of providing the strategist with a detailed understanding of the organization's marketing capability and the nature of the environment that it is likely to face.

This process of analysis is taken a step further in Chapter 3 in which we discuss the ways in which the strategist can establish patterns of resource allocation and its productivity by relating inputs (resources or costs) to outputs (revenues and profits). By doing this the process of cost-effective planning is capable of being improved significantly.

Against this background we turn in Chapters 4 and 5 to the various ways in which competitors and customers can be analysed.

It has long been recognized that marketing strategy is to a very large extent driven by the strategist's perception of competitors and customers. Because of this the failure to analyse in depth competitors' and customers' potential response profiles is likely to be reflected in strategies which lack an adequate underpinning.

In the case of competitors our understanding of how competitive relationships develop and operate has increased greatly over the past few years, largely as the result of the work of Michael Porter. Porter's work is based on the idea that the nature and intensity of competition within an industry is determined by the interaction of five key forces:

1 the threat of new entrants;
2 the power of buyers;
3 the threat of substitutes;
4 the extent of competitive rivalry;
5 the power of suppliers.

Analysis of these allows, in turn, for the identification of strategic groups and for a far clearer identification of the relative position, strengths and objectives of each competitor. In the light of this the arguments in favour of a competitive intelligence system are compelling. However, as we point out in Chapter 4, the value, and indeed the existence, of such a system is determined to a very large extent by the belief in competitive monitoring on the part of top management. Without this the evidence that emerges from the work of Davidson and others suggests that the organization will be largely introspective, with competitive analysis playing only a minor role in the planning process.

Broadly similar comments can be made about the role and value of customer analysis. As with competitive behaviour, our understanding of how buyers behave has advanced significantly in recent years, largely as the result of the work of researchers such as: Foxall; Turnbull and Cunningham; Webster; Robinson, Faris and Wind; and Hakansson. All too often, however, evidence suggests that firms devote relatively little attention to detailed customer analysis, assuming instead that because they interact with customers on a day-to-day basis they have a sufficient understanding of how and why markets behave as they do. Only rarely is this likely to be the case and, recognizing that customer knowledge is a potentially powerful source of competitive advantage, the rationale for regular and detailed analyses of customers is therefore strong.

2.1 LEARNING OBJECTIVES

When you have read this chapter you should be able to understand:

(a) the nature, structure and purpose of the marketing audit;
(b) the nature of the contribution made by the marketing audit to the overall management audit;
(c) the need for a regular review of marketing effectiveness and how such a review might be conducted;
(d) why a regular review of strengths, weaknesses, opportunities and threats is necessary;
(e) how the marketing effectiveness review, SWOT analysis and the marketing audit contribute to the marketing planning process.

2.2 INTRODUCTION

The process of marketing auditing is for many organizations still a relatively new and under-utilized activity. This is despite a substantial and growing body of evidence which suggests that an organization's performance in the market-place is influenced significantly and directly by the strategist's perception of three factors:

1 the organization's current market position;
2 the nature of environmental opportunities and threats;
3 the organization's ability to cope with environmental demands.

The marketing audit is designed to provide the strategist with a clear understanding of these three dimensions and in this way provide a firm foundation for the development of strategy. This is reflected in a comment by McDonald (1984, p. 14):

> Expressed in its simplest form, if the purpose of a corporate plan is to answer three central questions:
>
> > Where is the company now?
> > Where does the company want to go?
> > How should the company organize its resources to get there?
>
> then the audit is the means by which the first of these questions is answered. An audit is a systematic, critical and unbiased review and appraisal of the environment and of the company's operations. A marketing audit is part of the larger management audit and is concerned (specifically) with the *marketing environment and marketing operations*. [Emphasis added.]

What is a Marketing Audit?

The marketing audit is in a number of ways the true starting point for the strategic marketing planning process, since it is through the audit that the strategist arrives at a measure both of environmental opportunities and threats and of the organization's marketing capability. The thinking that underpins the concept of the marketing audit is straightforward: it is that corporate objectives and strategy can only be developed effectively against the background of a detailed and objective understanding both of corporate capability and environmental opportunity. The audit is, therefore, as McDonald (1984, p. 14) has suggested, 'The means by which a company can identify its own strengths and weaknesses as they relate to external opportunities and threats. It is thus a way of helping management to select a position in that environment based on known factors.'

Definitions of the audit have also been proposed by Shuchman (1950, pp. 16–17) and Kotler (1988, p. 747). Shuchman, for example, has suggested that the audit is:

> ... a systematic, critical, and impartial review and appraisal of the total marketing operation: of the basic objectives and policies and the assumptions which underlie them as well as the methods, procedures, personnel and organization employed to implement the policies and achieve the objectives.

Kotler's view is broadly similar:

> A marketing audit is a *comprehensive, systematic, independent,* and *periodic* examination of a company's – or business unit's – marketing environment, objectives, strategies and activities with a view to determining problem areas and opportunities and recommending a plan of action to improve the company's performance.

Taken together, these definitions highlight the three major elements and potential benefits of the marketing audit:

1 the analysis of the external environment and internal situation;
2 the evaluation of past performance and present activities;
3 the identification of future opportunities and threats.

These three elements can then usefully be viewed against the background of comments made by Ansoff (1968) who has suggested that, 'irrespective of the size of the organization, corporate decisions have to be made within the constraint of a limited total resource'. Recognizing this, the strategist is then faced with the task of producing 'a resource allocation pattern which will offer the best potential for meeting the firm's objectives'. The marketing audit can therefore be seen in terms of providing a sound basis for this process of resource allocation. In this way any strategy that is then developed should be far more consistent both with the demands of the environment and the organization's true capabilities and strengths.

The rationale for the audit is straightforward and in a number of ways can be seen to derive from the more commonly known and widely accepted idea of the financial audit which, together with audits of other functional areas, is part of the overall management audit; the nature of this relationship is illustrated in Figure 2.1.

The Structure and Focus of the Audit

In terms of its structure, the marketing audit consists of three major and detailed diagnostic steps. These involve a review of:

1 the organization's environment (opportunities and threats);
2 its marketing system (strengths and weaknesses);
3 its marketing activities.

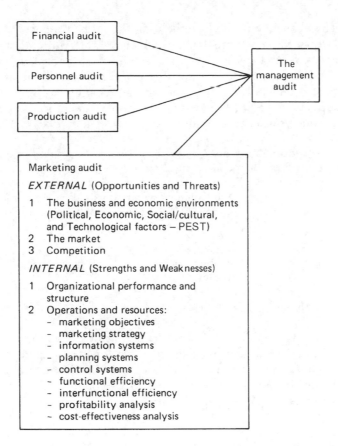

The first of these is designed to establish the various dimensions of the marketing environment, the ways in which it is likely to change and the probable impact of these changes upon the organization. The second stage is concerned with an assessment of the extent to which the organization's marketing systems are capable of dealing with the demands of the environment. The final stage involves a review of the individual components of the marketing mix.

It should be apparent from this that in conducting an audit the strategist is concerned with two types of variable. First, there are the *environmental* or *market variables* over which the strategist has little or no direct control. Second, there are the *operational variables* which can be controlled to a greater or lesser extent. This distinction can also be expressed in terms of the *macroenvironmental forces* (political/legal, economic/demographic, social/cultural, and technological) that affect the business, and *microenvironmental actors* (customers, competitors, distributors and suppliers) who subsequently influence the organization's ability to operate profitably in the market-place. Regardless of which approach to categorization is used, the process and purpose of the audit is the same. It begins with an *external audit* covering the macroenvironmental forces referred to above and the markets and competitors that are of particular interest to the company. The *internal audit* then builds upon this by assessing the extent to which the organization, its structure and resources, relate to the environment and have the capability of operating effectively within the constraints that the environment imposes.

In doing this the auditor should not view the marketing audit and its result in isolation but, as we observed earlier, should instead give full recognition to the way in which it sits within the general framework of the overall management audit and alongside the audits of the other management functions. In this way the strategist should arrive at a true measure not just of environmental opportunity but also of the ability of the organization as a whole to respond effectively.

The Scope and Frequency of Marketing Auditing

The frequency with which the audit should be conducted is influenced by several factors, the most important of which are the nature of the business, the rate of environmental change, and the planning cycle (annual, bi-annual). In so far as it is possible to provide a reasonably definitive guideline it is that the organization should undertake a full audit at the beginning of each major planning cycle, supplemented by less intensive but more frequent reviews of specific or key areas as conditions change. In discussing this, Baker (1985, p. 192) suggests that:

> Detailed inquiry into specific topics, e.g. pricing policy, may well be amenable to some form of rota, so that all areas will be covered within the duration of the planning cycle. For example, if the firm normally operates on an annual cycle then it may be convenient to monitor key indicators such as sales, prices, market share, etc., on a monthly basis, and the 'mix' elements on a bi-monthly rota, e.g.:
>
> Month 2   Pricing
> Month 4   Packaging
> Month 6   Promotion
> Month 8   Distribution
> Month 10 Sales
> Month 12 Market research

A somewhat different view of the frequency of auditing has been put forward by Bureau (1981), who has suggested that 'once every five years is psychologically about the minimum time span between audits. More frequent audits will not only demoralize marketing personnel, but would indicate that the organization's recruitment policies required serious review'.

The Stages of the Audit

In conducting a marketing audit both Grashof (1975) and Cannon (1968, p. 102) advocate a step-wise procedure. In this way, they argue, the approach ensures a degree of consistency that allows for a comparison from one period to another. For Grashof, these steps are:

1 *Pre-audit activities* in which the auditor decides upon the precise breadth and focus of the audit.
2 *The assembly of information* on the areas which affect the organization's marketing performance. These would typically include:

(a) the industry;
(b) the market;
(c) the firm;
(d) the product;
(e) pricing;
(f) promotion;
(g) distribution.

3 *Information analysis*.
4 The formulation of *recommendations*.
5 The development of *an implementation programme*.

Cannon's approach is broadly similar and again consists of five distinct stages as shown in Table 2.1.

Although for many organizations it is the assembly of information which proves to be the most time consuming, it is (in terms of Grashof's suggested framework) Stages 3 and 5 which often prove to be the most problematic. In analysing information the auditor needs to consider three questions:

1 What is the *absolute* value of the information?
2 What is its *comparative* value?
3 What *interpretation* is to be placed upon it?

Table 2.1

	Key elements
Step 1 Define the market	*Develop*: ● Statement of purpose in terms of benefits. ● Product scope. ● Size, growth rate, maturity state, need for primary versus selective strategies. ● Requirements for success. ● Divergent definitions of the above by competitors. ● Definition to be used by the company.
Step 2 Determine performance differentials	● Evaluate industry performance and company differences. ● Determine differences in products, applications, geography and distribution channels. ● Determine differences by customer set.
Step 3 Determine differences in competitive programmes	Identify and evaluate individual companies for their: ● Market development strategies. ● Product development strategies. ● Financing and administrative strategies and support.
Step 4 Profile the strategies of competitors	● Profile each significant competitor and/or distinct type of competitive strategy. ● Compare own and competitive strategies.
Step 5 Determine the strategic planning structure	When size and complexity are adequate: ● Establish planning units or cells and designate prime and subordinate dimensions. ● Make organizational assignments to product managers, industry managers and others.

It is generally acknowledged that if these questions are answered satisfactorily the recommendations will follow reasonably easily and logically. The only remaining problem is then the development of an effective implementation programme; the ways in which this might be done are discussed in detail in Stage Five of the book.

It should be apparent from the discussion so far that a marketing audit, if carried out properly, is a highly specific, detailed and potentially time-consuming activity. Because of this many organizations often do not bother with a full audit, and opt instead for a less detailed, more general and more frequent *review of marketing effectiveness*, coupled with an analysis of strengths, weaknesses, opportunities and threats.

2.3 REVIEWING MARKETING EFFECTIVENESS

Marketing effectiveness is to a very large extent determined by the extent to which the organization reflects the five major attributes of a marketing orientation, namely:

1 a customer-oriented philosophy;
2 an integrated marketing organization;
3 adequate marketing information;
4 a strategic orientation;
5 operational efficiency.

Each of these dimensions can be measured relatively easily, he suggests, by means of a checklist and an overall rating then arrived at for the organization; an example of this appears in Figure 2.2. It needs to be recognized, however, that an organization's marketing effectiveness is not always reflected in current levels of performance. It is quite possible, for example, for an organization to be performing well simply by force of circumstance rather than because of good

FIGURE 2.2
A marketing effectiveness rating instrument

Customer philosophy	Score
1 *To what extent does management recognize the need to organize the company to satisfy specific market demands?*	
The managerial philosophy is to sell existing and new products to whoever will buy them.	☐ 0
Management attempts to serve a wide range of markets and needs with equal effectiveness.	☐ 1
Having identified market needs, management focuses upon specific target markets in order to maximize company growth and potential.	☐ 2
2 *To what extent is the marketing programme tailored to the needs of different market segments?*	
Not at all.	☐ 0
To some extent.	☐ 1
To a very high degree	☐ 2
3 *Does management adopt a systems approach to planning, with recognition being given to the interrelationships between the environment, suppliers, channels, customers and competitors?*	
Not at all; the company focuses solely upon its existing customer base.	☐ 0
To some extent, in that the *majority* of its effort goes into serving its immediate and existing customer base.	☐ 1
Yes. Management recognizes the various dimensions of the marketing environment and attempts to reflect this in its marketing programmes by taking account of the threats and opportunities created by change within the system.	☐ 2

Marketing organization	
4 *To what extent does senior management attempt to control and integrate the major marketing functions?*	
Not at all. No real attempt is made to integrate or control activities, and conflict between areas of marketing exists.	☐ 0
To a limited degree, although the levels of control and coordination are generally unsatisfactory.	☐ 1
To a very high degree with the result that functional areas work together well.	☐ 2
5 *What sort of relationship exists between marketing management and the management of the R & D, finance, production and manufacturing functions?*	
Generally poor, with frequent complaints being made that marketing is unrealistic in its demands.	☐ 0
Generally satisfactory, although the feeling exists that each department is intent on serving its own needs.	☐ 1
Overall very good, with departments working together well in the interests of the company as a whole.	☐ 2
6 *How well organized is the new product development process?*	
Not very well at all.	☐ 0
A formal new product process exists but does not work very well.	☐ 1
It is well structured, professionally managed and achieves good results.	☐ 2

Marketing information	
7 *How frequently does the company conduct market research studies of customers, channels and competitors?*	
Seldom, if ever.	☐ 0
Occasionally.	☐ 1
Regularly and in a highly structured way.	☐ 2

FIGURE 2.2 (contd.)

Customer philosophy	Score

8 *To what extent is management aware of the sales potential and profitability of different market segments, customers, territories, products and order sizes?*

Not at all. □ 0

To some degree. □ 1

Very well. □ 2

9 *What effort is made to measure the cost effectiveness of different levels and types of marketing expenditure?*

None at all. □ 0

Some, but not in a regular or structured way. □ 1

A great deal. □ 2

The strategic perspective

10 *How formalized is the marketing planning process?*

The company does virtually no formal marketing planning. □ 0

An annual marketing plan is developed. □ 1

The company develops a detailed annual marketing plan and a long-range plan that is updated annually. □ 2

11 *What is the quality of the thinking that underlies the current marketing strategy?*

The current strategy is unclear. □ 0

The current strategy is clear and is largely a continuation of earlier strategies. □ 1

The current strategy is clear, well argued and well developed. □ 2

12 *To what extent does management engage in contingency thinking and planning?*

Not at all. □ 0

There is some contingency thinking but this is not incorporated into a formal planning process. □ 1

A serious attempt is made to identify the most important contingencies, and contingency plans are then developed. □ 2

Operational efficiency

13 *How well is senior management thinking on marketing communicated and implemented down the line?*

Very badly. □ 0

Reasonably well. □ 1

Extremely successfully. □ 2

14 *Does marketing management do an effective job with the resources available?*

No. The resource base is inadequate for the objectives that have been set. □ 0

To a limited extent. The resources available are adequate but are only rarely applied in an optimal manner. □ 1

Yes. The resources available are adequate and managed efficiently. □ 2

15 *Does management respond quickly and effectively to unexpected developments in the market-place?*

No. Market information is typically out of date and management responses are slow. □ 0

To a limited extent. Market information is reasonably up to date, although management response times vary. □ 1

Yes. Highly efficient information systems exist and management responds quickly and effectively. □ 2

FIGURE 2.2 (contd.)

The scoring process

Each manager works his way through the 15 questions in order to arrive at a score. The scores are then aggregated and averaged. The overall measure of marketing effectiveness can then be assessed against the following scale:

0–5	= None
6–10	= Poor
11–15	= Fair
16–20	= Good
21–25	= Very good
26–30	= Superior

With a score of *10 or less* major questions can be asked about the organization's ability to survive in anything more than the short term, and any serious competitive challenge is likely to create significant problems. Fundamental changes are needed, both in the management philosophy and the organizational structure. For many organizations in this position, however, these changes are unlikely to be brought about by the existing management, since it is this group which has led to the current situation. The solution may therefore lie in major changes to the senior management.

With a score of *between 11 and 15* there is again a major opportunity to improve the management philosophy and organizational structure.

With a score of *between 16 and 25* scope for improvement exists, although this is likely to be in terms of a series of small changes and modifications rather than anything more fundamental. With a score of *between 26 and 30* care needs to be taken to ensure that the proactive stance is maintained and that complacency does not begin to emerge.

SOURCE: Adapted from Kotler (1977)

management. In other words, good performance may be due to being in the right place at the right time as opposed to anything more fundamental. A change in strategy as the result of an effectiveness review might well have the result of improving performance from good to excellent. Equally, an organization may be performing badly despite seemingly excellent marketing planning. Again, the explanation may well be environmental rather than poor management. Recognizing this, the purpose of going through the process of a marketing effectiveness rating review is to identify those areas in which scope exists for marketing improvement. Action, in the form of revised plans, can then be taken to achieve this.

With regard to the process of arriving at a measure of marketing effectiveness, the procedure is straightforward and involves managers from a number of departments – not just marketing – completing the checklists of Figure 2.2. Scores are then summarized in order to arrive at an overall perception of marketing effectiveness. In practice, and as might be expected, few companies achieve a score in the highest range; among the few to have done this in the US, it is suggested, are McDonald's, Procter & Gamble, IBM, and General Electric. The majority of companies, however, cluster around the fair-to-good range, suggesting that scope exists for improvements in one or more of the five areas.

Having conducted a review of marketing effectiveness, the strategist may decide that the results provide sufficient insight into the organization's strengths and weaknesses. There is, however, a strong argument for viewing the marketing effectiveness rating review as the jumping-off point for the more thorough and detailed marketing audit.

2.4 THE ROLE OF SWOT ANALYSIS

Identifying Opportunities and Threats

Faced with a constantly changing environment, each business unit needs to develop a marketing information system (MIS) to track trends and developments. Each trend or development can then be categorized as an *opportunity* or a *threat*, and an assessment made of the feasibility and action needed if the organization is either to capitalize upon the opportunity or minimize the impact of the threat. However, in examining opportunities and threats the reader needs to recognize a point made by Johnson and Scholes (1988, p. 77) that

> they can never be viewed as 'absolutes'. What might appear at first sight to be an opportunity may not be so when examined against the organization's resources, its culture, the expectations of its stakeholders, the strategies available, or the feasibility of implementing the strategy. At the risk of oversimplification, however, the purpose of strategy formulation is to develop a strategy which will take advantage of the opportunities and overcome or circumvent the threats.

For our purposes an opportunity can be seen as any sector of the market in which the company would enjoy a competitive advantage. These opportunities can then be assessed according to their *attractiveness* and the organization's *probability of success* in this area: this is illustrated in Figure 2.3.

FIGURE 2.3
The opportunity matrix

		Probability of success: High	Probability of success: Low
Attractiveness	High	1	2
	Low	3	4

Cell 1 consists of opportunities offering the greatest scope, and management should focus upon these. Cell 4, by contrast, represents those opportunities which either are too small or which the organization is unlikely to be able to exploit effectively. Cells 2 and 3 offer certain attractions, and management should examine these closely to see whether scope exists either for improving their attractiveness or increasing the probability of success.

The probability of success is influenced by several factors, but most obviously by the extent to which the organization's strengths, and in particular its distinctive competences, match the key success requirements for operating effectively in the target market *and* exceed those of its competitors. Competence by itself is rarely sufficient in anything more than the short term since, given time, competitive forces will erode this competence. Because of this the strategist needs to concentrate upon developing *competitive advantages* which are sustainable over time. The bases of a sustainable competitive advantage are illustrated in Figures 2.4 and 2.5.

The significance of competitive advantage has been highlighted by a wide variety of writers and it is an issue to which we will return on a number of occasions throughout this book. At this stage, however, it is worth quoting from the Boston Consulting Group's Annual Report for 1982:

> In the real world of business competition, each survivor is uniquely superior to all others in some significant way, no matter how subtle the difference. That competitor dominates his unique niche or his life cycle is short.
>
> The nearly infinite possible combinations of customer characteristics, costs, logistics, methodology, etc., make it possible for vast numbers of competitors to co-exist. And each competitor may simultaneously be defending its niche against multiple unique antagonists.

FIGURE 2.4
The bases for developing a competitive advantage

The methods for developing a sustainable competitive advantage can be divided into three main groups:

1 Organizational advantages
- Economies of scope
- Flexibility
- Competitive stance
- Size
- Speed of response
- Past performance
- Financial strengths
- Patterns of ownership
- Reputation

2 Departmental and functional advantages
Marketing
- Customer base
- Customer knowledge
- New product skills
- Pricing
- Communication and advertising
- Distribution
- Sales force
- Service support
- Reputation

Research and development
- Product technology
- Patents

Production
- Technology
- Process efficiency
- Economies of scale
- Experience
- Product quality
- Manufacturing flexibility

Personnel
- Good management–worker relations
- Workforce flexibility

3 Advantages based on relationships with external bodies
- Customer loyalty
- Channel control
- Preferential political and legislative treatment
- Government assistance
- Beneficial tariff and non-tariff trade barriers
- Cartels
- Intra-organizational relationships
- Access to preferential and flexible financial resources

Market share and industry structure are ambiguous terms when such a complex spectrum of individual differences is woven into a web of relationships in which no given competitor has exactly the same competitors as any other.

Strategy development starts with the task of identifying the comparative differentials for each competitor that constitutes a constraint. The next step is to determine the tradeoffs and match-ups that make competitive equilibrium possible. The strategy itself must aim at enlarging either the scope or the depth of the competitive advantage.

Ability to adapt to changing competition determines each competitor's life cycle. The web of customers, suppliers and competitors and the external environment of

FIGURE 2.5
Sources of competitive advantage

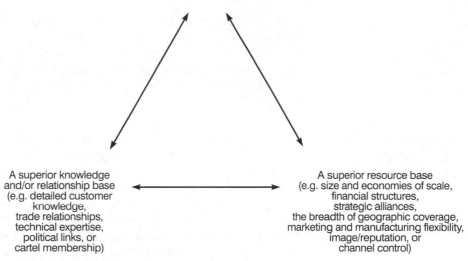

SOURCE: Adapted from McDonald, M. (1990), 'SMEs – twelve factors for success in the 1990s', *Business Growth and Profitability*, Vol. 1, No. 1, pp. 11–19

resources and conditions are constantly shifting. When any competitor adapts to each shift, then the equilibrium between competitors is changed too. Each must adapt. Your competitor is your environment. As a consequence, the whole competitive network is constantly evolving.

Every competitor that survives must be superior to all others with respect to some unique combination of external conditions. Every company dominates its own unique competitive segment. That domination may be by a thin margin, but if a competitor fails to be superior on its own turf, it will inevitably be crowded out.

At the same time as generating opportunities the external environment also presents a series of threats (a threat being a challenge posed by an unfavourable trend or development in the environment that in the absence of a distinct organizational response will lead to the erosion of the company's market position).

Threats can be classified on the basis of their *seriousness* and the *probability of their occurrence*; an example of how this can be done is illustrated in Figure 2.6.

FIGURE 2.6
The threat matrix

Probability of occurrence

	High	Low
High	1	2
Low	3	4

Seriousness

The threats in cell 1 are serious and have a high probability of occurrence. Because of this, the strategist needs to monitor developments closely and have a detailed contingency plan available to cope with any changes that take place. The threats in cells 2 and 3 need to be closely monitored in case they become critical. At this stage, contingency planning is unlikely to be necessary. Threats in cell 4 are very minor and can be largely ignored.

In putting together a picture of the major opportunities and threats facing the business the strategist is attempting to arrive at a measure of *the market's overall attractiveness*. In essence four possibilities exist:

1 an *ideal business* that is characterized by numerous opportunities but few, if any, threats;
2 a *speculative business* that is high both in opportunities and threats;
3 a *mature business* that is low both in opportunities and threats;
4 a *troubled business* that is low in opportunities but high in threats.

Identifying Strengths and Weaknesses

Although in many markets it is often a relatively simple process to identify a whole series of environmental opportunities, few organizations have the ability in terms of competences to capitalize upon more than a small number. Each business needs therefore to evaluate on a regular basis its *strengths* and *weaknesses*. This can be done by means of the sort of checklist illustrated in Figure 2.7.

Each factor is rated by management or an outside consultant according to whether it is a fundamental strength, a marginal strength, a neutral factor, a marginal weakness, or a fundamental weakness. By linking these ratings a general picture of the organization's principal strengths and weaknesses emerges. Of course, not all of these factors are of equal importance either in an absolute sense or when it comes to succeeding with a specific business opportunity. Because of this, each factor should also be given a rating (high, medium or low) either for the business as a whole or for a particular marketing opportunity. Combining performance and importance levels in this way leads to four possibilities emerging; these are illustrated in Figure 2.8 in the form of a performance–importance matrix.

Cell 1 consists of those factors which are important but in which the organization is currently performing badly. Because of this the organization needs to concentrate on strengthening these factors. Cell 2 is made up of factors in which the business is already strong but in which it needs to maintain its strengths. Cell 3 consists of unimportant factors. Improvements here, while often desirable, have low priority. Cell 4 is made up of unimportant factors in which (possibly as the result of over-investment in the past) the business is unnecessarily strong.

On the basis of this analysis it should be apparent that even when a business has a major strength in a particular area this strength does not invariably translate into a competitive advantage. There are several possible explanations for this, the two most prominent of which are that it may not be a competence that is of any real importance to customers, or that it is an area in which competitors are at least equally strong. It follows from this that in order to benefit from the strength it has to be relatively greater than that of the competitor.

Having identified the organization's weaknesses the strategist needs to return to Figure 2.8 and consider again the relative importance of these weaknesses. There is often little to be gained from overcoming all of the organization's weaknesses, since some are unimportant and the amount of effort needed to convert them to a strength would quite simply not be repaid. Equally, some strengths are of little real strategic value and to use them in anything other than a peripheral way is likely to prove of little real value. Recognizing this, the strategist should focus upon those areas of opportunity in which the firm currently has major strengths or where, because of the size of the opportunity and the potential returns, it is likely to prove cost-effective in acquiring or developing new areas of strength. In commenting on this Kotler (1987, p. 54) cites the example of Texas Instruments:

> [The] managers in Texas Instruments (TI) split between those who wanted TI to stick to industrial electronics where it had clear strength and those who urged the company to go into digital watches, personal computers, and other consumer products where it did not have the required marketing strengths. As it turned out, TI

FIGURE 2.7
*Strengths and
weaknesses analysis*

Strengths	Performance					Importance		
	Fundamental strength	Marginal strength	Neutral	Marginal weakness	Fundamental weakness	High	Medium	Low
Marketing factors								
1 Relative market share	___	___	___	___	___	___	___	___
2 Reputation	___	___	___	___	___	___	___	___
3 Previous performance	___	___	___	___	___	___	___	___
4 Competitive stance	___	___	___	___	___	___	___	___
5 Customer base	___	___	___	___	___	___	___	___
6 Customer loyalty	___	___	___	___	___	___	___	___
7 Breadth of product range	___	___	___	___	___	___	___	___
8 Depth of product range	___	___	___	___	___	___	___	___
9 Product quality	___	___	___	___	___	___	___	___
10 Programme of product modification	___	___	___	___	___	___	___	___
11 New product programme	___	___	___	___	___	___	___	___
12 Distribution costs	___	___	___	___	___	___	___	___
13 Dealer network	___	___	___	___	___	___	___	___
14 Dealer loyalty	___	___	___	___	___	___	___	___
15 Geographical coverage	___	___	___	___	___	___	___	___
16 Sales force	___	___	___	___	___	___	___	___
17 After sales service	___	___	___	___	___	___	___	___
18 Manufacturing costs	___	___	___	___	___	___	___	___
19 Manufacturing flexibility	___	___	___	___	___	___	___	___
20 Raw material advantage	___	___	___	___	___	___	___	___
21 Pricing	___	___	___	___	___	___	___	___
22 Advertising	___	___	___	___	___	___	___	___
23 Unique selling propositions	___	___	___	___	___	___	___	___
24 Structure of competition	___	___	___	___	___	___	___	___
Financial factors								
25 Cost of capital	___	___	___	___	___	___	___	___
26 Availability of capital	___	___	___	___	___	___	___	___
27 Profitability	___	___	___	___	___	___	___	___
28 Financial stability	___	___	___	___	___	___	___	___
29 Margins	___	___	___	___	___	___	___	___
Manufacturing factors								
30 Production facilities	___	___	___	___	___	___	___	___
31 Economies of scale	___	___	___	___	___	___	___	___
32 Flexibility	___	___	___	___	___	___	___	___
33 Workforce	___	___	___	___	___	___	___	___
34 Technical skill	___	___	___	___	___	___	___	___
35 Delivery capabilities	___	___	___	___	___	___	___	___
36 Supplier sourcing flexibility	___	___	___	___	___	___	___	___
Organizational factors								
37 Culture	___	___	___	___	___	___	___	___
38 Leadership	___	___	___	___	___	___	___	___
39 Managerial capabilities	___	___	___	___	___	___	___	___
40 Workforce	___	___	___	___	___	___	___	___
41 Flexibility	___	___	___	___	___	___	___	___
42 Adaptability	___	___	___	___	___	___	___	___

SOURCE: Adapted from Kotler (1988), p. 53

FIGURE 2.8
The performance–importance matrix

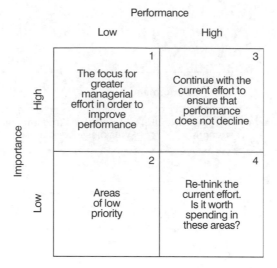

Performance

	Low	High
High	1 The focus for greater managerial effort in order to improve performance	3 Continue with the current effort to ensure that performance does not decline
Low	2 Areas of low priority	4 Re-think the current effort. Is it worth spending in these areas?

Importance

did poorly in these areas, but perhaps its mistake was not in going into these areas, but rather not acquiring the required marketing strengths to do the job right.

On occasions, organizations suffer not because of a lack of individual, departmental or divisional strengths, but quite simply because the various departments or divisions do not work together sufficiently well. As part of the SWOT process the strategist therefore should also pay attention to the quality of interdepartmental and divisional relationships with a view to identifying any dysfunctional areas. One of the ways in which this can be done is by conducting a periodic survey in which each department is asked to identify the strengths and weaknesses both of itself and of each other department. Action can then be taken to overcome areas of conflict, misunderstanding and inefficiency. An example of the results of an attempt to identify interdepartmental strengths and weaknesses appears in Figure 2.9. These are based on a consultancy project conducted by one of the authors at the end of 1989. The northern-based client company operated in the engineering field and was a subsidiary of a far larger multinational organization. The company had a strong financial orientation and was rapidly being overtaken by its competitors; for obvious reasons, the client's name has been omitted.

Making SWOT Analyses More Effective

Although SWOT analysis is a potentially useful input to the strategic marketing planning process, both Piercy (1991, pp. 256–68) and Weihrich (1982, pp. 54–66) have argued that, in practice, its full potential is rarely realized.

In suggesting this, Piercy claims that 'the use of this tool has generally become sloppy and unfocused – a classic example perhaps of familiarity breeding contempt'. There are, he believes, several factors which have contributed to this, the most obvious of which are that:

(a) because the technique is so simple it is readily accessible to all types of manager;
(b) the model can be used without a need for extensive information systems;
(c) it provides planners with a structure that allows for a mixture of the qualitative and quantitative information, of familiar and unfamiliar facts, of known and half-known understandings that characterise strategic marketing planning (op. cit., p. 257).

FIGURE 2.9
Identifying interdepartmental strengths and weaknesses

	Strengths	Weaknesses
Marketing	Market development Advertising Dealer development Competitor analysis	Long-term planning Liaising with sales Liaising with production Profitable new product development Identifying small but potentially profitable gaps in the market Expectations regarding quality and manufacturing capability Pricing Relations with corporate management
Sales	None identified	Expectations regarding delivery times Providing market feedback Often sell what can only be made with difficulty Little apparent awareness of costs Ignores small orders Patchy productivity Levels of training Sales staff turnover
Production	Quality	Slow to change Unwilling to cooperate with marketing and sales Often late in delivering Tend to want to make what they are good at A lack of flexibility caused by a strong trade-union presence Rising costs Lack of strong management Ageing plant Inadequate training in CAD/CAM
Personnel	Junior management and shop-floor training	Representation at board level Long-term senior management development Poor negotiating skills Willingness to give in to trade-union pressure Lack of real personnel management skills
Finance	Tight cost control Credit control Relationship with corporate management Access to significant financial resources	Over-emphasis on short-term returns Lack of vision Unwilling to cooperate with marketing and sales Unwilling to provide finance for major programmes of new product development Unrealistic reporting demands

In order to make better use of the SWOT framework, Piercy proposes five guidelines:

1 *Focus the SWOT* upon a particular issue or element, such as a specific product market, a customer segment, a competitor, or the individual elements of the marketing mix.
2 Use the SWOT analysis as a mechanism for developing a *shared vision* for planning. This can be done by pooling ideas from a number of sources and achieving a team consensus about the future and the important issues.
3 *Develop a customer orientation* by recognizing that strengths and weaknesses are largely irrelevant unless they are recognized and valued by the customer. One of the ways in which this can be done is by applying McDonald's 'so what?' test; in which the planner looks at each of the claimed benefits from the viewpoint of the consumer and by asking 'well so what?' tries to assess its *true* significance. By doing this, the planner is also likely to move away from the trap of making a series of so-called *motherhood statements* (a motherhood statement is warm, reassuring and difficult to argue against). As an example of the most common of motherhood statements to emerge in analyses of strengths is the

suggestion that 'we are committed to the customer'. The reality, Piercy argues, is often far removed from this.

4 In the same way that strengths and weaknesses must always be viewed from the viewpoint of the customer, so the analysis of opportunities and threats must relate to *the environment which is relevant to the organization's point of focus.* Anything else simply leads to a generalized – and largely pointless – set of comments.

5 The final guideline is concerned with what Piercy refers to as *structured strategy generation*. This involves:

- *Matching strategies.* Strengths *must* be matched to opportunities, since a strength without a corresponding opportunity is of little strategic value.
- *Conversion strategies,* which, whilst often difficult, are designed to change weaknesses into strengths and threats into opportunities. As an example of this, competitors may well be growing and proving to be an increasing threat. However, by recognizing that a head-on battle is likely to prove expensive and counter-productive, the emphasis might shift to developing strategic alliances which then provide both organizations with a greater combined strength which, in turn, allows them to capitalize upon growing opportunities.
- *Creative strategies* for developing the business which emerge as the result of a detailed analytical process rather than the vague and unfocused lines of thought to which we referred earlier.
- *Iteration.* As the planner goes through the process of identifying hidden strengths, matching strengths to opportunities, converting weaknesses to strengths, and so on, there is a periodic need to go back to the beginning of the process in order to identify how the situation that is emerging changes the SWOT model and initial assumptions.

SWOT to TOWS

The limitations that Piercy suggests typically characterize SWOT analyses have also been highlighted by Weihrich (op. cit.). His principal criticism of SWOT is that, having conducted the analysis, managers frequently fail to come to terms with the strategic choices that the outcomes demand. In order to overcome this he argues for the TOWS matrix which, while making use of the same inputs (Threats, Opportunities, Weaknesses and Strengths), reorganizes them and integrates them more fully into the strategic planning process. To do this involves the seven steps that are illustrated in Figure 2.10. The TOWS matrix is then illustrated in Figure 2.11.

The matrix outlined in Figure 2.11 does, of course, relate to a particular point in time. There is therefore a need to review the various inputs on a regular or ongoing basis in order to identify how they are changing and the nature of the implications of these changes. It is also often useful if, when planning and having made particular assumptions, the planner then produces TOWS matrices for, say, three and five years ahead with a view to identifying how the strategic options and priorities may change. In this way there is a greater likelihood that the planning team will come to terms with what the future truly demands.

Competitive Advantage and the Value Chain

Having analysed the strengths and resources of the organization, the marketing planner then needs to think about the ways in which these resources can best be used to contribute to the organization's performance. In other words, *how* might these resources best be used as a means of gaining and maintaining a competitive advantage? One of the ways in which this can be done is by means of the *value chain.*

Although value analysis has its origins in accounting and was designed to identify the profit of each stage in a manufacturing process, a considerable amount of work has been done in recent years in developing the concept and applying it

FIGURE 2.10
The TOWS framework

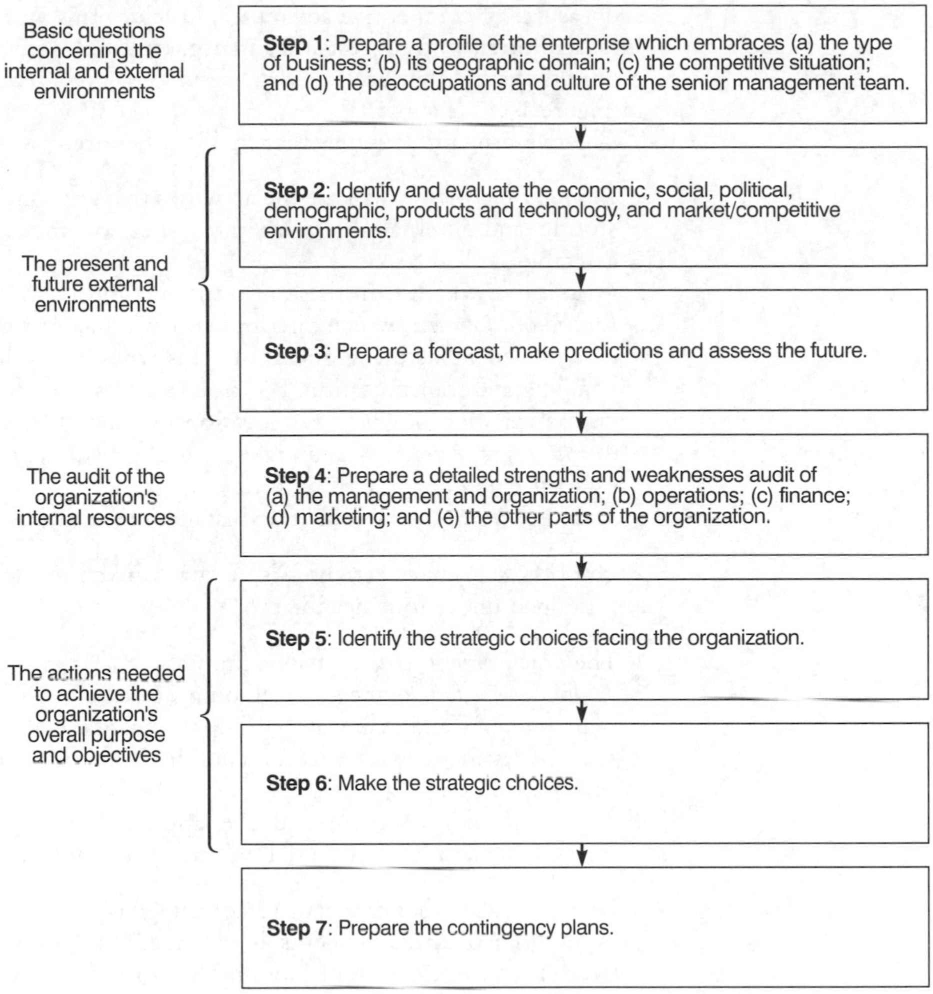

Basic questions concerning the internal and external environments	**Step 1**: Prepare a profile of the enterprise which embraces (a) the type of business; (b) its geographic domain; (c) the competitive situation; and (d) the preoccupations and culture of the senior management team.
The present and future external environments	**Step 2**: Identify and evaluate the economic, social, political, demographic, products and technology, and market/competitive environments.
	Step 3: Prepare a forecast, make predictions and assess the future.
The audit of the organization's internal resources	**Step 4**: Prepare a detailed strengths and weaknesses audit of (a) the management and organization; (b) operations; (c) finance; (d) marketing; and (e) the other parts of the organization.
The actions needed to achieve the organization's overall purpose and objectives	**Step 5**: Identify the strategic choices facing the organization.
	Step 6: Make the strategic choices.
	Step 7: Prepare the contingency plans.

FIGURE 2.11
The TOWS Matrix

External elements \ Internal elements	Organizational strengths	Organizational weaknesses
	Strategic options	
Environmental opportunities (and risks)	**SO**: Strengths can be used to capitalize or build upon existing or emerging opportunities	**WO**: The strategies developed need to overcome organizational weaknesses if existing or emerging opportunities are to be exploited
Environmental threats	**ST**: Strengths in the organization can be used to minimize existing or emerging threats	**WT**: The strategies pursued must minimize or overcome weaknesses and, as far as possible, cope with threats

SOURCE: Adapted from Weihrich, H. (1982), 'The TOWS Matrix: a tool for situational analysis', *Long-Range Planning*, Vol. 15, No. 2, p. 60

to measures of competitive advantage. Much of this work has been conducted by Michael Porter, who suggests that an organization's activities can be categorized in terms of whether they are *primary activities* or *support activities*; this is illustrated in Figure 14.17 (see p. 503).

The five primary activities that he identifies are:

1 *Inbound logistics*, which are the activities that are concerned with the reception, storing and internal distribution of the raw materials or components for assembly.
2 *Operations*, which turn these into the final product.
3 *Outbound logistics*, which distribute the product or service to customers. In the case of a manufacturing operation, this would include warehousing, materials handling and transportation. For a service this would involve the way in which customers are brought to the location in which the service is to be delivered.
4 *Marketing and sales*, which make sure the customers are aware of the product or service and are able to buy it.
5 *Service activities*, which include installation, repair and training.

Each of these primary activities is, in turn, linked to the support activities which are grouped under four headings:

1 The *procurement* of the various inputs.
2 *Technology development*, including research and development, process improvements and raw material improvements.
3 *Human resource management*, including the recruitment, training, development and rewarding of staff.
4 *The firm's infrastructure* and the approach to organization, including the systems, structures, managerial cultures and ways of doing business.

Porter suggests that competitive advantage is determined to a very large extent by how each of these elements is managed and the nature of the interactions between them. In the case of inbound logistics, for example, many organizations have developed just-in-time systems in order to avoid or minimize their stockholding costs. In this way, the value of the activity is increased and the firm's competitive advantage improved. Equally, in the case of operations, manufacturers are paying increasing attention to lean manufacturing processes as a means of improving levels of efficiency. Porter's message is therefore straightforward. Managers, he suggests, need to examine the nature and dimensions of each of the nine activities with a view to identifying how the value added component can best be increased. He then goes on to argue that value chain analysis should not simply stop with the manager's own organization, but in the case of a manufacturer should also include the suppliers and distribution networks, since the value of much of what an organization does will be magnified or constrained by what they do.

Customer Service and Competitive Advantage

We suggest in Chapter 5 that over the past decade customers' expectations have changed in a number of significant and far-reaching ways. The most obvious manifestations of this are that many customers today are far more demanding, much more discriminating, less loyal and much more willing to complain than in the past. In essence, they have become far more brand and supplier promiscuous. Because of this, service has taken on a far more important and obvious role in the search for competitive advantage. In commenting on this, Tschohl (1991, p. 1) cites William Band of the consulting arm of Coopers & Lybrand:

> ... Customer service is not just a competitive edge. In many industries it is *the* competitive edge. Service is the new standard by which customers judge an organisation's performance

However, Zeithaml (1990, p. 135) suggests that far too many organizations have still failed to appreciate the strategic significance of service excellence.

> Service with a smile? Not by a mile. The message of commercials is 'We want you!' The message of the service is 'We want you unless we have to be creative or courteous or better than barely adequate. In that case, get lost'.

Although it might be argued that Zeithaml is being unduly cynical in order to make a point, the reality in numerous cases is that service delivery levels fail to match – or exceed – customers' expectations. The consequences of this are then seen in a number of ways, but most obviously in terms of the organization's failure to exploit the customer base to the extent that might be possible by developing higher levels of loyalty. Because of this, far too many purchases prove to be single transactions with customers who, having been attracted to the product or service, often at considerable cost, are then allowed to walk away without a further commitment. While customer loyalty schemes are designed to overcome this, it needs to be recognized that consistently high levels of service quality stem from a far more fundamental reorientation of the business.

It is the acknowledgement of this, together with an appreciation of the way in which the products and prices of competitors are becoming increasingly similar and difficult to differentiate, which has led to a far greater emphasis upon the 'soft' elements of the marketing mix, but particularly *people* (staff) and *process management* (how customers are managed from the point of very first contact with the organization through to the point of very last contact). In discussing this, Naumann (1995, p. 16) develops a *customer triad*, arguing that competitive advantage stems from the ways in which customers perceive these elements to interact. This is illustrated in Figure 2.12.

FIGURE 2.12
The customer value triad

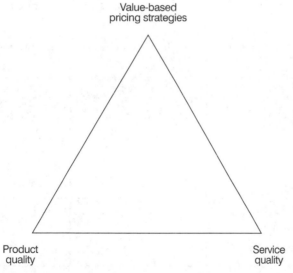

Value-based
pricing strategies

Product
quality

Service
quality

SOURCE: Adapted from Naumann, E. (1995), p. 17

The importance of service and its contribution to competitive advantage was also highlighted by the results of the PIMS research (see pp. 104–7 and 342–7) which suggest that those organizations which achieved high levels of service charged about 9 per cent more for their goods and grew twice as fast, picking up market share at around 6 per cent per annum; the 'also-rans' lost share at 2 per cent per annum. The PIMs research also revealed that the cost of superior service is often little more than for inferior offerings, with Gale (1994, p. 307) arguing that organizations with inferior quality typically have higher relative direct costs than businesses in any other position.

In discussing the attributes of service, Stone and Young (1992, p. 75) suggest that suppliers often see these in terms of technical features which, in practice, may be very different from customers' perceptions. By contrast, the customer's view will typically include factors such as the time taken to deliver the service; the extent to which the customer wants to or perceives the need to be in control; the effort required to receive the service; the relative importance of the service; the efficiency of the supplier; and the level of skill or professional expertise expected of the service staff.

Zeithaml, et al. (1990, p. 20) have developed a similar view based on the results of a series of focus group interviews among representatives from four service sectors – retail banking, credit cards, securities brokerage and product repair and maintenance – from different parts of the United States. From the responses, an underlying pattern emerged which was consistent across all sectors and geographies. These findings were categorized under ten headings or dimensions: tangibles, reliability, responsiveness, competence, courtesy, credibility, security, access, communication and understanding the customer. These ten dimensions were then further grouped into what Zeithaml calls their *SERVQUAL dimensions*:

Tangibles	The appearance of the physical facilities, equipment, personnel and communication materials
Reliability	The ability to perform the promised service dependably and accurately
Responsiveness	The willingness to help customers and provide prompt service
Assurance	The knowledge and courtesy of employees and their ability to convey trust and confidence
Empathy	The caring, individualized attention that the firm provides to its customers

The way in which these come together is illustrated in Figure 2.13

FIGURE 2.13
Correspondence between SERVQUAL dimensions and the original ten dimensions for evaluating service quality

Original ten dimensions	Tangibles	Reliability	Responsiveness	Assurance	Empathy
Tangibles	▓				
Reliability		▓			
Responsiveness			▓		
Competence				▓	
Courtesy				▓	
Credibility				▓	
Security				▓	
Access					▓
Communication					▓
Understanding the customer					▓

SOURCE: Zeithaml, *et al.* (1990), p. 25

The Lessons From Losing Customers

There is clear evidence which suggests that there is a compelling case to adopt a customer service strategy. MacNeill (1994, p. 4), for example, recounts the results of a customer survey carried out in the USA. When customers were asked why they took their business elsewhere, the responses revealed that:

- 3 per cent moved geographically;
- 5 per cent developed other relationships;
- 9 per cent left for competitive reasons;
- 14 per cent were dissatisfied with the product;

but

- 68 per cent left because of an attitude of indifference towards the customer by the owner, manager or some other employee.

Cook (1992, p. 20) supports these results with research conducted by British Airways; these are illustrated in Figure 2.14.

FIGURE 2.14
Factors in passengers' satisfaction and dissatisfaction

	Contribution to satisfaction/ goodwill (%)	Contribution to dissatisfaction/ bad feeling (%)
Staff factors (attitude, how service given)	61	70
Other factors (timing, food, seating, facilities, etc.)	39	30
Total (%)	100	100

SOURCE: *ITC Magazine*, March–April 1987, p. 11

Illustration 2.1: Singapore Airlines and its Pursuit of Service Excellence

Singapore Airlines is one of the world's ten biggest international airlines and, in an industry in which it is notoriously difficult to make money, has consistently proved to be one of the five most profitable.

The history of the airline started in 1947 with the first scheduled flight of Malaysian Airlines from Singapore to Penang. When the two countries became independent in the mid-1960s, the name changed to Malaysia-Singapore Airlines. Singapore Airlines then flew under its own colours for the first time in 1972. Although the company (SIA) was state-owned, the Singapore government's policy was made clear from the outset: there would be no subsidies or preferential treatment. Instead, the government offered foreign carriers the freedom to operate out of Singapore, but only if SIA was given reciprocal rights. It was against this background that the airline developed its strategy and, subsequently, its reputation for service excellence. This strategy has involved focusing upon:

- developing the youngest and most up-to-date fleet of aircraft of all the international carriers; the average age of their aircraft is 4.75 years, compared to an industry average of around 10 years.
- a marketing campaign designed to create an international airline with a strong, distinctive and friendly Asian personality which differentiates SIA from other international carriers.
- innovation: SIA was the first airline to:

  - introduce fully reclining 'snoozer' seats
  - offer free drinks
  - offer free headsets for in-flight movies.

- recognising that the cabin staff are capable of making or breaking any strategy. Because of this, stewardesses are the result of a painstaking recruiting, training and retraining programme and operate with a maximum of three contract terms of five years each. Their pivotal importance to the company is then reflected by their status in the company and their higher than average wages.

- developing trilateral alliances with Swissair and Delta Airlines for customer servicing, interchangeable tour packages, through check-in, joint baggage handling, joint promotions and the sharing of customer lounges.
- investing heavily and consistently in Changi airport with the result that it has consistently been one of the most efficient – if not *the* most efficient – airports in the world.
- investing heavily in technology to speed up the check-in process.
- offering a greater number of meal variations. On most airlines, menus are typically changed four times a year. On SIA's high frequency flights, menus were changed weekly.
- recognising that complaints provide insight to problems and were therefore to be encouraged.
- taking crew members out of the system and giving training when complaints related to a specific in-flight experience.
- ensuring that senior cabin crew members met each Monday for feedback and exchange sessions with service support personnel.
- using research to understand their customers and their expectations *in detail*.

Underpinning everything the airline did was the most fundamental recognition of the need for a customer focused philosophy and a service culture. How its customers were handled at each point of contact was considered to be of paramount importance. With this in mind, the company invested in a $50 million training centre which was used to train employees in how to serve customers. The guiding philosophy involves getting staff to put themselves into the customer's position. As an example of this:

> Key people were sent on special missions to see what other airlines were doing and how customers were handled. Special delay simulation games groomed staff on ways to cope with delay situations, one of the major complaints received from passengers.
>
> One principle remained constant: staff had to be as flexible as possible in their dealings with customers, even if it took more time and effort. Management constantly reiterated that customers could not be told what to do simply because it suited the company. Some passengers wanted to eat as soon as they boarded, others preferred to wait. Customers could not be pigeonholed; they often changed their minds. They might come on board intending to sleep and then decide to watch a movie after all. On long hauls, flexibility was especially important. Most passengers had individual habits that corresponded to their travel agendas, which could include sleeping at the beginning and working later, or vice versa.

In essence, though, the organisation's success can be seen to rest on three pillars:

- modern aircraft
- on-the-ground services
- in-flight services

However, underpinning all of these is something far more fundamental – a managerial culture which stems from the commitment on the part of senior management to service excellence and a painstaking attention to detail.

Source: Singapore Airlines – using technology for service excellence, *IMD case study, 1991*

2.5 THE CHARACTERISTICS OF EFFECTIVE AUDITS

At an earlier stage in this chapter (see p. 44) we made reference to Kotler's definition of the marketing audit. Referring for a moment to this definition, it can be seen that he highlights four dimensions, suggesting that for an audit to be worthwhile it should be *comprehensive, systematic, independent* and *periodic*. The significance of these points is as follows:

1 *Comprehensive.* For the auditing process to be worthwhile it is essential that it covers *all* of the major elements of the organization's marketing activity, including those that seemingly are doing well, rather than just a few apparent trouble spots. In this way a distinction can be drawn between the *marketing audit* and a *functional audit* which would focus far more specifically upon a particular element of marketing activity such as sales or pricing. As an example of this, a functional audit might well suggest that a high sales-force turnover and low morale is due to a combination of inadequate sales training and a poor compensation package. A more fundamental reason, however, might be that the company has a poor or inadequate product range and an inappropriate pricing and advertising strategy. It is the comprehensiveness of the marketing audit which is designed to reveal these sorts of factors and to highlight the *fundamental* causes of the organization's problems.

2 *Systematic.* In carrying out the audit it is essential that a sequential diagnostic process is adopted covering the three areas to which reference was made earlier: the external environment, internal marketing systems, and specific marketing activities. This process of diagnosis is then followed by the development *and implementation* of both short-term and long-term plans designed to correct the weaknesses identified and, in this way, improve upon levels of marketing effectiveness.

3 *Independent.* As with a financial audit, there are several ways in which the marketing audit can be conducted. These include:

(a) a self-audit in which managers use a checklist to assess their own results and methods of operation;
(b) an audit by a manager of the same status but drawn from a different department or division within the organization;
(c) an audit by a more senior manager within the same department or division;
(d) the use of a company auditing office;
(e) a company task force audit group;
(f) an audit conducted by an outside specialist.

Of these it is generally recognized that an audit conducted by an outside specialist is likely to prove the most objective and to exhibit the independence which any internal process will almost inevitably lack. Adopting this approach should also ensure that the audit receives the undivided time and attention that is needed. In practice, however, many large companies make use of their own audit teams (something which 3M, for example, has pioneered).

This question of *who* should conduct the audit has been the subject of a considerable amount of research and discussion in recent years with, as indicated above, the argument revolving around the issue of objectivity (in other words, how objective can a line manager be in conducting an evaluation of activities for which he has direct responsibility?) It is largely because of this that it has been suggested that outside consultants should be used to ensure impartiality. This is likely to prove expensive if done annually, and the answer is increasingly being seen to lie in a compromise whereby an outside consultant is used every third or fourth year, with line managers from different departments or divisions being used in the intervening periods. Alternatively an organization might opt for what is in essence a composite approach, with an external auditor being used initially to validate line managers' self-audits, and subsequently to integrate them to produce an audit result for the marketing function as a whole.

To a large extent, however, it can be argued that the supposed difficulties of achieving impartiality are overstated since a sufficiently well-structured and institutionalized auditing process can overcome many of these difficulties. There is a need, therefore, for managers to be trained in how best to use auditing procedures and, very importantly, for the audit process to be endorsed by senior management; without top management commitment to the audit process and, in turn, to the need to act on the results that emerge, the entire exercise is likely to prove valueless.

4 *Periodic*. If the company is to benefit fully from the auditing process it is essential that it is carried out on a regular basis. All too often in the past companies have been spurred into conducting an audit largely as the result of poor performance. Ironically, this poor performance can often be traced to a myopia on the part of management, stemming from a failure to review activities on a sufficiently regular basis, something which has been pointed to by Shuchman (1950) who has commented that: 'No marketing operation is ever so good that it cannot be improved. Even the best *must* be better, for few if any marketing operations can remain successful over the years by maintaining the status quo.'

Why Bother With a Marketing Audit?

Although we have so far argued the case for marketing auditing to be carried out on a regular basis, many organizations quite simply do not bother to do this until things go wrong. Most typically this would be manifested in terms of declining sales, a loss of market share, under-utilized production capacity, a demoralized sales force, reduced margins, and so on. Faced with these sorts of problems the temptation for management is to firefight and hence fall into the trap of crisis management. In many cases this is characterized by the rapid launching and dropping of products, price cutting, and attempts at drastic cost reduction. While this sort of response will often have an immediate and apparent pay-off, it is unlikely that it will solve any underlying and fundamental problems. The audit is designed to avoid the need for crisis management both by identifying and defining these fundamental problems *before they have any opportunity to affect the organization*. In this way carrying out a regular and thorough marketing audit in a structured manner will go a long way towards giving a company a knowledge of the business, trends in the market, and where value is added by competitors as a basis for setting objectives and strategies. These points have been highlighted in a summary of the 10 most common findings of marketing audits:

1 a lack of knowledge of customers' behaviour and attitudes;
2 a failure to segment markets effectively;
3 the absence of marketing planning procedures;
4 reductions in price rather than increases in volume;
5 the absence of market-based procedures for evaluating products;
6 misunderstanding company marketing strengths;
7 short-term views of the role of promotion;
8 a perception that marketing is limited just to advertising and sales activity;
9 inappropriate organizational structures;
10 insufficient investment in the future, particularly in the area of human resources.

The Auditing Procedure

The auditing process should begin with agreement being reached between the organization's marketing director and the marketing auditor – someone from inside or outside the organization – regarding the specific objectives, the breadth and depth of coverage, the sources of data, the report format and the time period for the audit. Included within this should be a plan of who is to be interviewed and the questions that are to be asked.

With regard to the question of *who* is to be questioned, it needs to be emphasized that the audit should never be restricted to the company's executives; it should also include customers, the dealer network, and other outside groups. In this way, a better and more complete picture of the company's position and its effectiveness can be developed. In the case of customers and dealers, for example, the auditor should aim to develop satisfaction ratings which are capable of highlighting areas in need of attention.

Once the information has been collected, the findings and recommendations need to be presented with emphasis being given to the type of action needed to overcome any problems, the timescale over which remedial action is to be taken, and the names of those who are to be responsible for this.

Components of the Audit

Within the general framework of the external and internal audits, Kotler et al. (1989) suggest there are six specific dimensions that are of direct interest to the auditor. These are:

1 *The marketing environment audit*, which involves an analysis of the major macroeconomic forces and trends within the organization's task environment. This includes markets, customers, competitors, distributors, dealers, and suppliers.
2 *The marketing strategy audit*, which focuses upon a review of the organization's marketing objectives and strategy, with a view to determining how well suited they are to the current and forecasted market environment.
3 *The marketing organization audit*. This aspect of the audit follows on from 2 and is concerned specifically with an evaluation of the structural capability of the organization and its suitability for implementing the strategy needed for the developing environment.
4 *The marketing systems audit*, which covers the quality of the organization's systems for analysis, planning and control.
5 *The marketing productivity audit*, which examines the profitability of different aspects of the marketing programme and the cost effectiveness of various levels of marketing expenditure.
6 *The marketing functions audit* involving a detailed evaluation of each of the elements of the marketing mix.

The audit questions associated with each of these areas appear in Figure 2.15. In answering each of the questions it is essential that the strategist pays particular attention to the implications for the organization and its likely strategic development.

How are the Audit Results Used?

Having conducted the audit the question that then arises is how best to use the results. In some companies a considerable amount of time, effort and expense is given over to the auditing process, but the corrective action that is then needed simply falls by the wayside. To ensure that the results are incorporated most effectively within the strategic planning process which forms the focus of the remainder of this book, the major findings of the audit need to be incorporated within an appropriate framework. This can be done in one of several ways, although undoubtedly the most useful is the SWOT framework discussed earlier. This should focus on the *key* internal strengths and weaknesses in relation to the *principal* external opportunities and threats, and include a summary of the reasons for good or bad performance. It is then against the background of this document that the strategist should begin planning at both the functional and the corporate levels. It is this process which provides the basis for much of the rest of this book.

FIGURE 2.15
The marketing audit

The marketing environment audit

The macro environment

Political/legal/fiscal

1 What legal developments are likely, nationally and internationally, that may affect marketing strategy and tactics?
2 Which governmental bodies (local, national and international) should be monitored?
3 What developments are likely to take place in areas such as product safety, product liability, labelling, packaging, advertising and pricing control, pollution control and employment legislation that might affect marketing planning?
4 What changes are likely in the levels of direct and indirect taxation?
5 Are levels of political risk likely to increase or decrease?
6 How are relations with other countries, regimes and trading blocs likely to develop, and what are their probable implications for marketing?
7 How volatile are trade-union practices likely to be in the short, medium and long term?
8 Are policies regarding nationalization or privatization likely to change?

Economic/demographic

1 What is likely to happen in the short, medium and long term to levels of inflation, unemployment, the availability of credit and savings?
2 What economic growth rates and income levels are forecast both for the organization's existing and potential markets?
3 What changes to the size, structure and regional distribution of population are likely to occur?

Social/cultural

1 What changes to consumer lifestyles and values are taking place?
2 What attitudinal changes towards business and the products/services produced by the organization are occurring?
3 What attitudinal changes are taking place towards such areas as government, the media, and pollution?

Technological

1 What changes are taking place in the areas of product and process technology?
2 What generic substitutes might replace the organization's products?
3 How well placed is the organization to cope with and/or capitalize upon such changes?

Ecological

1 What is likely to happen to the cost and availability of the natural resources and energy required by the organization?
2 What contingency plans exist to cope with shortages or sudden price rises?
3 Have any concerns been expressed about the organization's role in conservation and pollution?

The task environment

Markets

1 What is happening to the size, growth rate and geographical distribution of the organization's markets?
2 Which major market segments exist? How are they likely to grow and which offer the greatest opportunities?
3 Are new market segments emerging?
4 Are new or different market priorities emerging?
5 What scope exists for further market development?
6 What changes in usage patterns can be identified or are likely?
7 Are terms and conditions of sale changing?

Competitors

1 What changes are likely to take place in the structure, bases, and intensity of competition?
2 Who are the major competitors currently and in what ways might they change? Are there any likely new entrants to the market? If so, what capabilities and objectives will they have and what are the probable implications for competition?
3 What are the major strengths and weaknesses of each competitor?
4 What are the objectives, strategies and levels of profitability of each competitor?
5 What trends can be identified in the patterns of future competition and substitutes for the organization's product/service?
6 What patterns of product and market development can be identified among competitors?
7 Are any major changes likely to take place in patterns of market share? Does any competitor appear likely to pursue an aggressive share gaining strategy? If so, how well equipped to do this would they be, what are the implications for the bases of competition, and what is the probability of success?
8 What is the extent of the diversification among each competitor? What international links does each have?

FIGURE 2.15 (contd.)

9 What are the patterns of ownership among competitors and what level of resources can each call upon?
10 What barriers to entry and exit exist currently? In what ways might these change?

Distributors and dealers
1 What changes are taking place in the structure of the distribution network?
2 What are the efficiency levels and growth potentials of each channel?
3 Which channels are currently under-exploited?
4 What is the cost and availability outlook for warehousing and transportation facilities?

Suppliers
1 What changes are taking place in the supplier network and what affect will this have upon balances of power?
2 What new sources of supply are emerging?
3 What are the objectives and strategies of the major suppliers?
4 What changes are taking place in suppliers' patterns of selling?

Advertising and PR agencies
1 How effective are the efforts of the organization's advertising and public relations agencies?
2 What trends in agency practice are emerging?

The marketing strategy audit

The business mission
1 How clearly stated and realistic is the mission statement?
2 To what extent is it consistent and compatible with the corporate and marketing objectives?

Corporate and marketing objectives
1 Do the corporate and marketing objectives provide clear guidelines for marketing planning and control?
2 Are these objectives consistent with the organization's position, capabilities and opportunities?
3 Are the objectives for each business unit clearly stated, realistic and consistent with the overall marketing objectives?

Marketing strategy
1 How clearly stated and appropriate is the marketing strategy?
2 Is the strategy convincing? Has it been properly communicated?
3 Does the strategy take full account of the state of the economy, the stage reached on the product life cycle, and competitors' strategies?
4 Is the basis for market segmentation appropriate?
5 To what extent is there scope for developing and improving upon methods of segmentation?
6 How accurate are the profiles of each segment?
7 How well developed is the positioning strategy for each segment? Does scope exist for repositioning in order to strengthen the competitive stance?
8 Are the available resources sufficient and suitably allocated to the various elements of the marketing mix?
9 Is there scope for reallocating resources to achieve a greater degree of cost-effectiveness?
10 Are there sufficient controls built in to the strategy?

FIGURE 2.15 (contd.)

The marketing organization audit

1 Is the marketing function led by a person with sufficient authority and responsibility over those areas of the organization's activities that affect customer satisfaction?
2 Are the marketing activities optimally structured along functional, product, end-user and geographical lines?
3 What need and scope exists for changing current patterns of authority and responsibility?

Functional efficiency
1 Are the lines of communication and the working relationships between marketing and other areas of the business effective?
2 What scope exists for improving and developing these relationships?
3 What needs exist for training, motivation, supervision, evaluation, and control?

The marketing systems audit

Information systems
1 Is the MIS providing sufficiently accurate and timely information about market developments?
2 Is this information presented in the most appropriate format?
3 Is sufficient market research of the right sort being conducted and are the results being fully and properly utilized?
4 What scope exists for improving upon methods of market and sales forecasting?
5 Is the information generated by the MIS communicated to the appropriate network of staff?

Planning systems
1 How efficient and well conceived are the planning systems?
2 What scope and plans exist for its further development?

Control systems
1 Do the control procedures provide the strategist with a sufficiently clear and accurate picture of absolute and relative performance?
2 Is the performance of individual products, markets, and distribution channels monitored sufficiently regularly?
3 How frequently are marketing costs examined and validated?
4 Is behaviour modified in the light of feedback from the control systems?

New product systems
1 How well organized is the procedure for collecting, generating and evaluating new product ideas?
2 Is sufficient research and analysis conducted before proceeding with new product ideas?
3 Are the levels of product and market testing adequate?
4 Is the rate of new product development and product modification sufficient to achieve marketing objectives?
5 Is the new product success rate satisfactory? Is it better or worse than those of the major competitors?

The marketing productivity audit

Profitability analyses
1 What is the profitability of each of the organization's products, markets, territories and distribution channels?
2 Should the company enter or withdraw from any market segment?
3 Is there a need for expansion or contraction within any market?
4 How do the organization's levels of profitability compare with those of its principal competitors?

Cost-effectiveness analysis
1 Are there any areas of marketing which appear to be incurring unrealistic costs?
2 What scope exists for cost reduction?
3 Are costs monitored sufficiently, regularly and rigorously?
4 What scope exists for modifying approaches to budgeting and control to ensure better resource allocation?
5 Does any one person have direct responsibility for measuring cost effectiveness?

FIGURE 2.15 (contd.)

The marketing functions audit

Products

 1 What are the product line objectives?
 2 How appropriate are these objectives?
 3 How regularly are the objectives reassessed?
 4 Is the current mix of products achieving the objectives?
 5 Which products should be deleted?
 6 What product modifications should be made?
 7 What products should be added to the line?
 8 How well managed is the product line?
 9 What are the product lines' particular strengths and weaknesses?
10 How does the product line compare with those of the organization's competitors?
11 To what extent is the product line differentiated from those of the competitors?

Price

 1 What pricing objectives, strategies and procedures exist?
 2 How appropriate are the pricing objectives?
 3 How consistent is pricing throughout the product range?
 4 Is full advantage taken of the profit opportunities when pricing product options?
 5 Is the pricing stance proactive or reactive?
 6 Is sufficient attention paid to competitive criteria when setting prices?
 7 What knowledge exists of competitors' objectives, costs and price levels?
 8 Are competitors' prices regularly monitored and reviewed?
 9 Are the organization's prices in line with customers' and distributors' perceptions of product value?
10 Is sufficient use made of price promotion?
11 At what level within the organization are pricing decisions made?
12 Are pricing decisions fully integrated with other marketing decisions?
13 How responsive to sudden market changes are prices?

Distribution

 1 What distribution objectives and strategies are pursued?
 2 Are the levels of market coverage appropriate?
 3 What need and scope exists for improvements in service levels?
 4 How effectively are distributors and dealers operating?
 5 What knowledge exists of competitors' distribution structures and costs?
 6 Is there scope or need for changes to be made to the distribution channels being used currently?
 7 Where does the balance of power lie within the channel? In what ways is this changing and what are the implications?
 8 How well motivated is the distribution channel?
 9 How important to the channel are the organization's products?
10 Do distributors have adequate product knowledge? What training needs exist?
11 What scope exists for greater short- and long-term motivation of dealers?
12 What levels of dealer/distributor loyalty exist? Are these adequate? What scope exists for strengthening this loyalty?

Sales force

 1 What are the sales force's short- and long-term objectives?
 2 Is the sales force large enough to achieve the objectives it is set?
 3 Is the organization and structure of the sales force suited to the demands of the market?
 4 Does the sales force give emphasis to volume or to profitability?
 5 Is the sales force made fully aware of the profit associated with different parts of the product line?
 6 Is the sales force kept fully informed of marketing objectives, marketing programmes, and market developments?
 7 Is there sufficient sales force training?
 8 Is the sales force properly motivated? Is full use made of incentives?
 9 Are the sales targets realistic?
10 Is the sales and profit performance measured and the results fed back to sales staff?
11 Is the turnover of sales staff too high? If so, what might be done to reduce it?
12 How does the sales force compare with that of competitors?
13 How is the sales force perceived by customers?
14 Is full use made of the sales force as a means of monitoring market developments?

Advertising and promotion

 1 What are the promotional objectives? Are they appropriate given the overall marketing objectives?
 2 How is the budget set? Is sufficient attention paid to the expenditure levels and patterns of competitors?
 3 What controls over advertising expenditure exist?
 4 How effective is the creative appeal?

FIGURE 2.15 (contd.)

> 5 What advertising research is conducted?
> 6 How well chosen are the media?
> 7 How regularly is the performance of the advertising agency reviewed?
> 8 How important is the account to the agency?
> 9 Are sales promotions used regularly? Are they effective?
> 10 How effective is the publicity programme?
> 11 Is effective use made of sponsorship?
> 12 Who is responsible for publicity?
> 13 What measures of effectiveness are used for advertising, sales promotion and public relations?
> 14 How do the advertising and promotional campaigns compare with those of the competitors?

SOURCE: Adapted from Kotler *et al.* (1977)

2.6 SUMMARY

Within this chapter we have focused upon the role and structure of marketing auditing and SWOT analysis. In doing this we have highlighted the way in which the marketing audit represents an important first step in the marketing planning process and how, as a result, the value of much of what follows within this process is determined by the thoroughness of the audit procedure. It is therefore essential that the audit exhibits a number of characteristics, the four most significant of which are that it is:

1 comprehensive in its coverage of the elements of the organization's marketing activity;
2 systematic;
3 independent;
4 conducted on a regular basis.

The purpose of the audit is to provide the strategist with a clear understanding both of environmental opportunities and threats, and of the organization's marketing capability. In doing this the strategist begins by focusing upon the principal macroenvironmental forces (political/legal, economic/demographic, social/cultural and technological) that affect the business. He then moves on to consider the microenvironmental actors (customers, competitors, distributors and suppliers) who influence the organization's ability to operate effectively in the market-place. The internal audit builds upon this by providing an understanding of the extent to which the organization, its structure and resources relate to the environment and have the capability of operating effectively within the constraints that the environment imposes.

In addition to conducting the marketing audit the strategist needs also to carry out regular reviews of the organization's marketing effectiveness. This can be done most readily by means of a checklist which embraces five principal areas:

1 the nature of the customer philosophy;
2 the marketing organization;
3 marketing information;
4 the strategic perspective;
5 operational efficiency.

Against the background of the picture that emerges from the audit and the review of marketing effectiveness, the strategist should have a clear understanding both of the environment (opportunities and threats) and of the organization's marketing capability (strengths and weaknesses). It is this which then provides the basis for subsequent marketing planning.

Marketing audits are discussed further in Chapter 20, and marketing effectiveness is considered in some detail in Chapter 18.

2.7 EXERCISES

1 Using Figure 2.2, identify your organization's overall level of marketing effectiveness. Which of the five areas (customer philosophy, the marketing organization, the use of marketing information, the strategic perspective and operational efficiency) appears to be the weakest? What would be needed in order to strengthen this?

2 To what extent does your organization (a) have a sustainable competitive advantage and (b) truly exploit this? Referring to Figures 2.4 and 2.5, which of the bases for advantage might your organization best exploit over the next few years?

3 Using Figure 2.7, carry out a performance-importance analysis for your organization and its two principal competitors. Having done this, identify the areas of significant strength and weakness and consider the implications for marketing strategy.

4 Making use of Piercy's guidelines (pp. 57–8), conduct a *detailed* SWOT analysis for one of your organization's products or services. What implications for future strategy emerge from the analysis?

5 Turn to Figure 2.15, select one of the seven principal dimensions of the marketing audit and conduct an audit of one dimension of your organization. What picture emerges from your analysis, and what are its implications?

2.8 CASE STUDIES

New Directions plc

New Directions is a high-street fashion chain which was founded in the late 1950s. After twenty years of slow and generally unspectacular growth, a new Managing Director, Thomas Oakley, was appointed in 1978. Under his very different and aggressively entrepreneurial management style, the company underwent a decade of explosive growth. Many of the old staff left during this period and a far younger team was recruited. The new staff were given considerable operating freedom and high salaries, but were expected to achieve performance levels well above the industry average. By 1988, the company had 400 stores and had become one of the major players in the young (15–25), C1/C2, male and female fashion sectors. Their reputation in the City was that of an ambitious, design-oriented company led by an unconventional, abrasive and maverick figure who inspired considerable loyalty among his employees.

At the beginning of 1987 the company was bought out by a large and cash-rich conglomerate the financial performance of which over the preceding decade had proved to be consistently strong. Despite this, the group's senior management was viewed by the City as being generally staid and unimaginative. The group overall was viewed as having a strong financial orientation with an emphasis upon systems and control. Strategy at the group level was perceived as being risk averse.

New Directions' Managing Director and small senior management team quickly found that operating within a group in which they were accountable to the group's main board constrained their entrepreneurial style and traditional freedom. Not only were they faced with the need to make out a strong written case for anything other than a minor change in strategy but, as they saw it, major restrictions were placed on their ability to capitalize upon short-term opportunities. Profits were remitted to the centre and each division's MD was then required on an annual basis to bid for sums for capital expenditure.

After two years in succession in which his plans for development were rejected by the main board, Oakley resigned. At the heart of the disagreement was his belief that New Directions needed to move up the quality scale and both up and down the age scale. The demographic changes taking place would, he argued, lead to a reduction of at least 20 per cent in the size of the company's traditional target market over the next few years. They should therefore chase the demographic shift by targeting the 30–40 year olds, a sector in which annual growth of 5 per cent was being forecast. At the same time, he suggested, a new chain should be developed that would appeal to the childrens' market. 'Children,' he said, 'are the ultimate fashion accessory. We need to capitalize on this.'

He also pointed to the research evidence which suggested that buyers wanted better quality, something for which New Directions had never had a particularly strong reputation. Instead, they had concentrated on developing a strong fashion element at 'popular' prices. While this strategy had undoubtedly been successful, there was now a need to begin the process of making a series of fundamental changes. Oakley also argued for the need for a rethink in the approach to store design. Competition from other retail chains had become ever more aggressive during the 1980s and evidence existed to suggest that buyers were looking for new and more exciting shopping experiences. An essential element in this was the retail concept, something which had taken a significant step forward in the late 1980s in the repositioning and renaming of one of the company's major competitors. Oakley also pointed to the need to begin looking towards opportunities overseas. 'The British market', he suggested, 'offers only limited scope for growth. We need to get into some of the other European markets and particularly Spain.' He went on to point out that the Spanish market was growing at a faster rate than any other. Indeed, without telling the main board or getting their agreement, he had already gone ahead with plans to begin selling into one of the largest chains of Spanish fashion stores.

Each of these arguments was rejected by the group's main board on the grounds of their cost and the perceived risk.

Following Oakley's resignation, the group appointed as his replacement one of their fast-track corporate finance staff. With little direct retailing experience, he set about reorganizing the company. In doing this, he slashed Oakley's plans for development. Largely because of this, a significant number of the team which had worked with Oakley and who very largely saw themselves as his protegés left. In most cases they were snapped up by competitors who placed considerable value on the training and experience to which they had been exposed.

As the recession of the early 1990s began to bite, turnover dropped. The new MD's almost desperate response was to pursue an aggressive price cutting policy and to reduce overheads as far as possible.

The annual strategic review at the end of 1991 (two years after Oakley's replacement had taken over) painted a dismal picture. Sales were down, market share was slipping, staff were demoralized and, as a market research report highlighted, the image of the chain in the 15–25, 25–30 and 30–40 age groups was confused. In short, New Directions was no longer a leader or even a serious player in the young fashion market.

Questions

1 Prepare a SWOT analysis of the organization both for the period before the takeover and for the period reached at the end of the case study. Having done this, discuss the implications of *one* of your analyses for methods of marketing planning and control.
2 As a consultant to the organization, and in the light of the findings of the strategic review, what course(s) of action would you recommend should be taken?

The Legal Business

The Legal Business is an ambitious and growth-oriented medium-sized firm of lawyers with offices in three major cities. The firm operates with 35 partners supported by 97 other fee earners and 100 support staff. The annual turnover is currently around £10 million. The legal services offered include matrimonial, commercial litigation, corporate law and finance, employment law, insurance litigation, insolvency, debt recovery, licensing, intellectual property, and private client work. The fee-earning potential and the firm's capabilities in each of these areas varies significantly. Each area is the responsibility of one of the senior partners. Until recently, the managing partner has taken responsibility for the marketing effort, but has found the task to be increasingly demanding and difficult.

Because of this the firm hired a marketing consultant to conduct a *brief* and *general* review of the firm's current marketing activities. The results of the review have been summarized for the firm's partners and are as follows:

1 Levels of client satisfaction and client care are far lower than had been expected, with a high proportion of clients suggesting that they were not kept fully or sufficiently informed of the progress of their case.
2 Existing and potential clients appear to have little awareness of the full range of the services that the firm is able to offer. This problem is compounded by the ways in which the individual partners fiercely guard client relationships, with the result that, although there are often opportunities for the cross-selling of services, this seldom happens.
3 There is no real sense of a long-term direction for the firm or of a true competitive stance.
4 There is little planning and no obvious attempt to capitalize upon the firm's strengths.
5 Although there is some advertising, there is no advertising or promotional strategy.
6 Levels of client retention and new client attraction have dropped significantly over the past two years.
7 Market research suggests that the firm is perceived generally to be rather staid.
8 A number of the younger and more promising staff have been attracted away by competitors over the past two years.
9 A number of the competitors, both regionally and nationally, have recently become far more aggressive in their search for new business, with the result that the firm's overall share of the market is dropping.

In discussion with the partners and staff, the marketing consultant discovered that many are unclear about what is meant by marketing or, indeed, how it might contribute to the development of the firm. Instead, there is a culture based on a 'professional approach' characterized by a lack of commerciality and an attitude which prefers to wait for business to come in rather than going out to get it. This was reflected in comments such as:

'Isn't marketing just a different name for selling?'

'Marketing is a cost and so whatever we spend will reduce our profits for the year.'

'If I had wanted to be a salesman, I would have chosen a different career path. I became a lawyer because I want to practise law. It isn't my job to do all of this selling and marketing, is it? Don't expect me to change how I operate.'

Given this, the consultant recommended that a marketing manager be appointed to develop and co-ordinate an external and an internal marketing programme. As the person appointed to do this, you are faced with two tasks:

1(a) *Carrying out a detailed marketing audit of the firm.*
As the first step in this, prepare a briefing paper for the managing partner in which you explain the purpose, focus and components of the audit, how it might be conducted and how the results might be used.

1(b) Against the background of your comments in 1(a), you are required to prepare a report for the managing partner recommending how a strategic marketing orientation might be introduced to the firm. In doing this, you must make *specific* reference to the particular problems that are likely to be encountered within a professional services organization and how these problems might possibly be overcome. (See pp. 679–85.)

3 | Segmental, productivity and ratio analysis

3.1 LEARNING OBJECTIVES

When you have read this chapter you should be able to:

(a) understand how cost analysis can be applied to marketing segments;
(b) appreciate the role of marketing experimentation in improving the allocation of marketing effort;
(c) recognize the value of segmental productivity analysis;
(d) perceive critically how ratio analysis can be used in order to appreciate the current position.
(e) appreciate the relevance of strategic benchmarking.

3.2 INTRODUCTION

In relation to the question 'Where are we now?' it is useful to know how resources have been utilized and with what returns. To this end, it helps to think of the organization as a bundle of projects or activities. This is relevant whether the organization is large or small, commercial or non-commercial, engaged in manufacturing or service rendering. Typical projects might be defined as:

- reformulation and relaunch of product X;
- continued market success with service Y;
- the successful development and launch of project Z.

One might go further and define projects or activities in terms of *missions*: a mission in this context represents the provision of a product or range of products at a particular level of service to a particular customer or customer group in a particular area. Figure 3.1 illustrates this, but see also Chapter 6.

FIGURE 3.1
Multi-dimensional mission characteristics

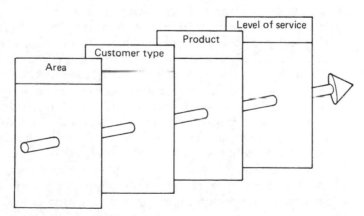

SOURCE: Barrett (1980), p. 143

An organization's mix of projects – or missions – will be constantly changing, and each has resource implications and profit consequences. For example, the scarcity of resources inevitably means that choices must be made in rationing available resources (whether in the form of funds, management time, etc.) among competing activities. It may be that new activities can only be adopted if old ones are deleted, thereby freeing resources. But how might a manager know which activities are worth retaining, which should be added to the portfolio, and which should be deleted? One starting point is to establish the cost of each of the organization's existing activities.

We can think of cost as being equivalent in broad terms to *effort*, so what we are initially seeking to establish is how the available effort has been applied to the various activities in which the organization is engaged. Before we can really get to grips with this, however, we need to clarify our understanding of some important categories of cost.

3.3 THE CLARIFICATION OF COST CATEGORIES

Many of the costs of marketing are not satisfactorily identified since marketing *functions* are not always carried out by the marketing *department*. (It could be argued that any members of an organization who deal with customers, for example, are carrying out a marketing function even though they may not be recognized in any formal sense as members of the marketing staff.) This is one definitional problem, but not the only one.

Another definitional problem concerns the traditional focus that accountants have adopted which puts product costing at the centre of their costing systems. This traditional preoccupation with the manufacturing costs of products and factory processes emphasizes the attributes of whatever is currently being made. Such an orientation fails to deal with patterns of consumer preferences and competitive positioning by market segment. The attributes of market segments – from which profit is derived – are fundamentally different from those attributes that characterize production processes. Any analysis based on product costing will generate insights that are limited by their origins, thereby failing to support marketing orientation.

Whatever cost object (or activity) is selected as the focus of attention, some costs will be *direct* (in the sense of being traceable to the activity – such as direct labour, and direct material inputs into a unit of manufactured output, or a salesperson's salary and expenses in relation to the sales territory), while others will be *indirect*. By definition, indirect costs cannot be traced directly to cost objects, so any procedure whereby these costs are assigned to cost objects will mean that the resulting full (or 'absorbed') cost is inaccurate to an unknown extent. The assigning of a 'fair share' of indirect costs, along with direct costs, to cost objects is at the heart of *absorption costing*.

A particular cost item can only be termed direct or indirect once the cost object has been specified. This could be, for example, a particular product, a product range, a brand, a customer or customer group, a channel, a sales territory, an order, and so on. Thus a salesperson's salary will be indirect in relation to the individual product lines sold (assuming the salesperson carries a range of products), but it will be a direct cost of the territory in which that individual is operating. In the same way the costs of distributing various products to wholesalers may be indirect with regard to the goods themselves but direct if one is interested in costing the channel of distribution of which the wholesalers are part.

The same basic problems arise in attempting to determine the full cost of a cost object in every type of organization, whether a service company, a retailing enterprise, a factory or a non-commercial entity. For example, a garage (as one type of service organization) will treat the servicing of each customer's car as a separate job (or cost object) to which will be assigned the direct cost of the mechanic's time, materials, and parts, plus an allowance (usually applied as an hourly rate and associated with the utilization of mechanics' time) for the use of indirect factors (which will include power, equipment, rent, rates, insurance, salaries of reception, supervisory and stores staff, etc.). A similar approach is applied by firms of solicitors or accountants, by consulting engineers, architects and management consultants. Non-commercial organizations typically provide services (such as health care, defence, education and spiritual guidance) and use resources in carrying out their various activities in much the same way as do commercial undertakings. The logic of absorption costing is equally applicable to non-commercial as to commercial enterprises.

3.4 MARKETING COST ANALYSIS: AIMS AND METHODS

Establishing a base line for marketing planning can be seen to be concerned with the allocation of total marketing effort to cost objects (also known as segments), along with the profit consequences of these allocations. It is generally found, however, that companies do not know the profit performance of segments in marketing terms. Useful computations of marketing costs and profit contributions in the multiproduct company require the adoption of analytical techniques which are not difficult in principle but which are not widely adopted in practice on account of, *inter alia*, the preoccupation with factory cost accounting that exists.

The fact that most companies do not know what proportion of their total marketing outlay is spent on each product, sales territory, or customer group may be due to the absence of a sufficiently refined system of cost analysis, or it may be due to vagueness over the nature of certain costs. For instance, is the cost of packaging a promotional, a production, or a distribution expense? Some important marketing costs are hidden in manufacturing costs or in general and administrative costs, including finished goods inventory costs in the former and order-processing costs in the latter.

Since few companies are aware of costs and profits by segment in relation to sales levels, and since even fewer are able to predict changes in sales volume and profit contribution as a result of changes in marketing effort, the following errors arise:

1 marketing budgets for individual products are too large, with the result that diminishing returns become evident and benefits would accrue from a reduction in expenditure;
2 marketing budgets for individual products are too small and increasing returns would result from an increase in expenditure;
3 the marketing mix is inefficient, with an incorrect balance and incorrect amounts being spent on the constituent elements – such as too much on advertising and insufficient on direct selling activities;
4 marketing efforts are misallocated among missions and changes in these cost allocations (even with a constant level of overall expenditure) could bring improvements.

Similar arguments apply in relation to sales territories or customer groups as well as to products. The need exists, therefore, for planning and control techniques to indicate the level of performance required and achieved as well as the outcome of shifting marketing efforts from one segment to another. As is to be expected, there exists great diversity in the methods by which managers attempt to obtain costs (and profits) for segments of their business, but much of the cost data are inaccurate for such reasons as those listed below.

- Marketing costs may be allocated to individual products, sales territories, customer groups, etc., on the basis of sales value or sales volume, but this involves circular reasoning. Costs should be allocated in relation to causal factors and *it is order-getting marketing expenditures that cause sales to be made* rather than the other way round: managerial decisions determine order-getting marketing costs. A different pattern typically applies to order-fitting (e.g. logistics) costs since sales volume will cause (or **drive**) order-filling costs: order-getting → sales volume → order-filling. Furthermore, despite the fact that success is so often measured in terms of sales value achievements by product line, this basis fails to evaluate the efficiency of the effort needed to produce the realized sales value (or turnover). Even a seemingly high level of turnover for a specific product may really be a case of misallocated sales effort. (An example should make this clear: if a salesman concentrates on selling Product A which contributes £50 per hour of effort instead of selling Product B which would contribute £120 per hour of effort, then it 'costs' the company £70 per hour he spends on selling Product A. This is the *opportunity cost* of doing one thing rather than another and is a measure of the sacrifice involved in selecting only one of several alternative courses of action.)
- General indirect and administrative costs are arbitrarily (and erroneously) allocated to segments on the basis of sales volume.
- Many marketing costs are not allocated at all as marketing costs since they are not identified as such but are classified as manufacturing, general, or administrative costs instead.

Marketing cost analysis has been developed to help overcome these problems and aims to:

1 Analyse the costs incurred in marketing products (embracing order-getting and order-filling aspects) so that when they are combined with product cost data overall profit can be determined.
2 Analyse the costs of marketing individual products to determine profit by product line.
3 Analyse the costs involved in serving different classes of customers, different territories and other segments to determine their relative profit performance.
4 Compute such figures as cost per sales call, cost per order, cost to put a new customer on the books, cost to hold £1's worth of inventory for a year, etc.
5 Evaluate managers according to their actual controllable cost responsibilities.
6 Evaluate alternative strategies or plans with full costs.

These analyses and evaluations provide senior management with the necessary information to enable them to raise questions regarding which classes of customer to cultivate, which products to delete or encourage, which channels may be preferable and so forth. Such analyses also provide a basis from which estimates may be developed of the likely increases in sales volume, value or profit (i.e. outputs) that a specified increase in marketing effort (i.e. input) might create. In the normal course of events it is far more difficult to predict the outcome of decisions that involve changes in marketing outlays in comparison with changes in production expenditure. It is easier, for instance, to estimate the effect of a new machine in the factory than it is to predict the impact of higher advertising outlays. Similarly, the effect on productive output of dropping a production worker is easier to estimate than is the effect on the level of sales caused by a reduction in the sales force.

The basic approach of marketing cost analysis is similar to that of product costing. Two stages are involved:

1 Marketing costs are initially reclassified from their *natural* expense headings (e.g. salaries) into *functional* cost groups (e.g. sales expenses) in such a way that each cost group brings together all the costs associated with a particular marketing activity.

2 These functional cost groups are then apportioned to the cost object/segment of interest (e.g. product lines, customer groups, channels of distribution, etc.) on the basis of measurable criteria that bear as close an approximation as possible to a causal relationship with the total amounts of the functional cost groups.

FIGURE 3.2
*Determining
segmental costs*

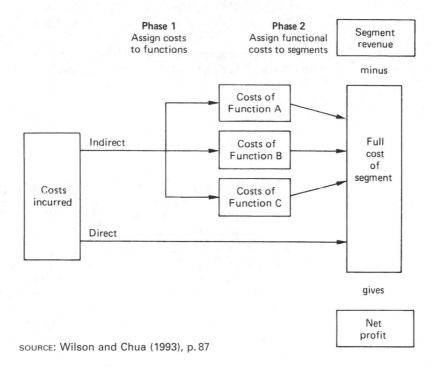

SOURCE: Wilson and Chua (1993), p. 87

These two stages are illustrated in Figure 3.2.

Once the natural indirect expenses have been reclassified on a functional basis they are then charged to the segment in line with the usual benefit criterion (i.e. the segment is only allocated with that portion of each functional cost group that can be related to it on some approximation of a cause and effect basis). The logical basis of allocation may be apparent from an analysis of the underlying data, but it is important to observe that some costs vary with the characteristics of one type of segment only. Thus inventory costs depend on the characteristics of products rather than on those of customers, whereas the cost of credit depends on the financial integrity and number of customers rather than on regional factors. Accordingly, not all functional costs should be allocated to products, customers and territorial segments. Allocation should only be made when an actual or inputed cause and effect relationship between an underlying activity and some resultant cost which is relevant to the segment(s) can be identified.

It must be remembered when using marketing cost analysis that any cost allocation involves a certain degree of arbitrariness which means that an element of approximation is inevitably contained within the allocation. Furthermore, it remains necessary to supplement the analysis of marketing costs with other relevant information and with managerial judgement.

Marketing cost analysis is the joint responsibility of the controller and the marketing manager, with the controller supplying most of the information and the marketing manager supplying most of the judgement. Nevertheless, the marketing manager must be fully aware of the method and limitations of marketing cost analysis. The high cost of establishing and maintaining a marketing costing system is justified by the benefits derived from increasing the efficiency of marketing effort. The risks involved in adopting marketing cost analysis before the benefits have been demonstrated can be reduced by initially confining the analysis to a sample of products, customers, or territories and by making periodic rather than continuous analyses.

Since a fundamental objective of marketing cost analysis lies in increasing the productivity of expenditures and not necessarily in their reduction the manager who wishes to introduce marketing cost analysis must emphasize the desire to make better use of existing resources rather than reducing future budgets. The integration of marketing costing with marketing research can assist in this matter. Confining any costing system to data provided from accounting records risks forcing that system to be historical, but marketing research can provide estimates of future outcomes resulting from variations in marketing effort (with or without experimentation and the building of complex models) which enable the efficiency of alternate expenditure patterns to be pre-determined and evaluated in accordance with corporate aims.

See Illustration 3.1.

Illustration 3.1: My Biggest Mistake; David Bruce

David Bruce, 42, failed his maths 'O' level five times before leaving school to work for a brewery. In 1979, he came off the dole queue to open the Goose and Firkin pub in London after raising a loan against his home. By 1988 he had built a chain of 18 pubs which he sold for £6.6 m, intending to retire with his £2 m share. But he could not resist going back into business and is now trading as Inn Securities and building up a chain of Hedgehog and Hogsheads pubs outside London.

My biggest mistake was not paying proper attention to my accounts in the early days of the Firkin pubs. We had opened the Goose and Firkin in London in 1979 and I was working 18 lousy hours a day, seven days a week, brewing the beer in the cellar and surviving on adrenalin. I had eight staff and a part-time book-keeper.

Everybody said the pub would not work, but people were queuing to get in. It was tremendously exciting and I was on a complete high. The tills were ringing, my break-even point was £2,500 a week but the pub never did less than £4,500.

So why, I thought, if one has created this extraordinary thing, should one scuttle back home to Battersea and spend hours doing boring old paperwork?

The turnover was so good I did not even bother with profit and loss accounts. (And you have to bear in mind that I did not have a natural aptitude for figures.)

In May 1980, I opened the Fox and Firkin in Lewisham. I trained a brewer to look after the Goose, but he promptly broke his leg, leaving me to deal with both pubs. There was even less time to do paperwork.

Then I opened another pub in London, and because the experts doomed us to failure I thought it would be easier if the pubs traded under separate companies. Each one had a different accounting year – it was a good lesson in how not to run a business.

By the time we had opened our fourth pub in 1981, our solicitors, Bishop and Sewell, had watched our progress with great interest and assumed we were incurring a hideous tax bill, so they suggested we met with accountants Touche Ross. My wife Louise and I went along with what little financial information we had, plus a couple of audits which showed we had traded at a loss from day one.

In fact, while the turnover for the first year was £1m, we had made losses of £86,000. One of their corporate finance partners said that if I did not appoint a chartered accountant to the board as financial director immediately we would go bust within a couple of months. So I took on someone from a major brewery who introduced systems such as stock control and weekly profit and loss accounts.

But that did not solve the immediate problems. Touche Ross also said I would have to sell one of the pubs, the Fleece and Firkin in Bristol, because it was costing too much time and money. Reluctantly I put it on the market.

By now it was obvious that I should have appointed a finance director at the beginning. The bank was getting nervous, my borrowings were rising and I was not producing a profit.

If the bank had pulled the rug we would have gone down personally for £500,000. Touche Ross advised me to sell a small percentage of the equity, which of course I did not want to do.

Eventually I struck a satisfactory deal with 3i (Investors in Industry) which bought 10 per cent of the business and gave us a loan. Better cash control enabled us to turn a loss into profit, and the following year, on a turnover of £1.6m we showed a profit of £47,000.

Touche Ross, who charged us under £5,000 to sort the problem out, have done my audits ever since. Paul Adams, our managing director, is the resident chartered accountant. He has kept costs down and introduced budgets which the staff can stick to.

In hindsight the solutions were obvious, but I was a victim of my own success. If the turnover had not been so good I would have realised a lot sooner how close I was to bankruptcy.

Source: As told to journalist Corinne Simcock, The Independent on Sunday: Business, *16 December 1990, p. 20*

3.5 AN ILLUSTRATION OF SEGMENTAL ANALYSIS

As discussed above, a segment is any cost object which is of interest, and is synonymous with the notion of activity, project or mission as appropriate. Thus, for example, marketing segments may be one – or a combination – of the following:

- product line or range;
- channel of distribution;
- sales representative or territory;
- customer or customer/industry group;
- size of order.

It is possible to vary the degree of aggregation of segments as shown in Figure 3.3 (adapted from Ratnatunga, 1983, p. 34).

Initially one must select the segment in which one is interested (e.g. territory, customer, etc.). Then one must select the approach to costing that one prefers. Essentially there are two major alternatives:

1 absorption (or full) costing;
2 variable (or direct or marginal) costing.

Our earlier discussion dealt with the first of these and we saw that this approach involves charging both direct and a portion of indirect costs to the segment in question. When set against the segment's revenue the result is a net profit figure.

FIGURE 3.3
Segmental levels

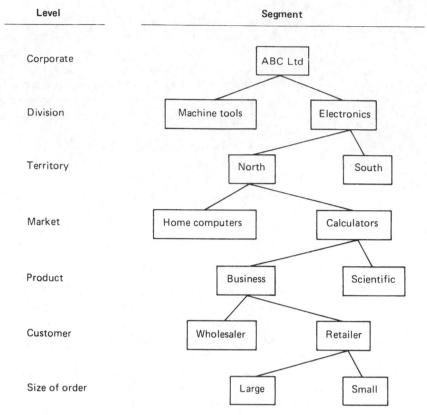

Level	Segment
Corporate	ABC Ltd
Division	Machine tools / Electronics
Territory	North / South
Market	Home computers / Calculators
Product	Business / Scientific
Customer	Wholesaler / Retailer
Size of order	Large / Small

SOURCE: Adapted from Ratnatunga (1983), p. 34

An example is given in Figure 3.4 of the net profit picture in an organization operating through three different channels of distribution.

The net profit figure reflects the result of the allocation of effort as shown by the total of:

cost of goods sold
direct marketing costs
indirect marketing costs

once this allocation has been set against the revenue figure, channel by channel. It is evident that the validity of the net profit figures which emerge depend critically upon the adequacy of the means by which indirect costs are apportioned.

FIGURE 3.4
Profit analysis by channel

£'000s	Channel						Total
	A		B		C		
Revenue	875		950		1,225		3,050
Cost of goods sold	325		285		490		1,100
Gross Profit	550		665		735		1,950
Direct marketing costs	265		245	450		960	
Indirect marketing costs	330		275	250		855	
Total marketing costs	595		520		700		1,815
Net profit	(45)		145		35		135

3.6 AN ALTERNATIVE APPROACH TO SEGMENTAL ANALYSIS

The alternative approach to segmental analysis mentioned above is the variable costing approach in which only direct costs are allocated to arrive at a measure of profit known as *marketing contribution*. Using the data from Figure 3.4 above, this has been reworked in Figure 3.5 to illustrate the variable costing approach.

FIGURE 3.5
A direct costing profit statement

£'000s	Channel			Total
	A	B	C	
Revenue	875	950	1,225	3,050
Variable COGS	225	175	300	700
Manufacturing contribution	650	775	925	2,350
Variable direct marketing costs	115	105	190	410
Variable contribution	535	670	735	1,940
Fixed direct marketing costs	150	140	260	550
Marketing contribution	385	530	475	1,390
Indirect costs				855
Fixed manufacturing costs				400
Net profit				135

It has been assumed that the cost of goods sold figures in Figure 3.4 included £700,000 of variable manufacturing costs and £400,000 of fixed manufacturing costs; that the direct costs are all of a marketing nature and can be split into fixed and variable components as shown in Figure 3.5; and that the indirect costs are all non-allocable to channels. The result is a clear statement that sufficient revenue is being generated via each channel to cover the variable costs and the directly allocable fixed costs. Moreover, there is sufficient total contribution to cover the indirect costs and the fixed manufacturing costs while still making a net profit of £135,000.

3.7 CUSTOMER PROFITABILITY ANALYSIS

An approach to segmental analysis that is of increasing interest is customer profitability analysis (CPA). If marketing effort is to be directed at customers or market segments with the greatest profit potential it is essential that marketing managers have information showing both the existing picture with regard to customer profitability and prospects for the future.

Customer profitability analysis has been defined (Anandarajan & Christopher, 1986, p. 86) as:

... the evaluation, analysis and isolation of:

- all the significant costs associated with servicing a specific customer/group of customers from the point an order is received through manufacture to ultimate delivery;
- the revenues associated with doing business with those specific customers/ customer groups.

The implementation of CPA can be achieved by a series of steps which parallel the steps suggested earlier for other types of segmental analysis. In outline these steps are:

Step 1
Clearly define customer groups and market segments in a way which distinguishes the needs of customers in one group from those of customers in another group.

Step 2
For the customer groups or market segments of interest identify those factors that cause variations in the costs of servicing those customers. This can be done by identifying the key elements of the marketing mix used for each customer group or segment from which some indication of the costs of servicing each group should be drawn.

Step 3
Analyse the ways in which service offerings are differentiated between customer groups. For example, terms of trade may vary between home-based and overseas customers, or between large and small customers, as might the level of service (i.e. speed of delivery) to key accounts.

Step 4
Clearly identify the resources that have been used to support each customer group or segment – including personnel, warehouse facilities, administrative back-up, etc.

Step 5
Determine ways in which the costs of resources (step 4) can be attributed to customer groups.

Step 6
Relate revenues and costs to each customer group, with profit emerging as the difference.

The total of the costs for a given customer group is a measure of the effort that has been allocated to that group, and the profit is a measure of the return from that effort. Until the existing pattern of allocation is known, along with its profitability, it is not possible to devise ways of improving that allocation.

See Illustration 3.2.

Illustration 3.2: Evolution

New technologies are beginning to make mass customisation feasible and information systems are allowing us to identify the profitability of each customer

Tower Records recently started offering its customers the top 40 lines of groceries. It was a publicity stunt, of course. A protest at the way supermarkets have started cherry picking their business by selling records from the Top 40 chart.

Tower's initiative amounts to little more than a puff of hot air, but behind it lies an issue of growing importance. Cherry picking is hardly new, but its extent and nature are changing. Increasingly the most aggressive and successful cherry pickers are coming from 'outside' the industry concerned.

And as such these are invaders with a difference. They're changing the nature of the market itself.

To see what's happening we need to take a step back. Consider, for example, how people acquired their clothes, say, 50 years ago. Basically, they had three ways to do so. First, if they were rich, they could go to their tailor. His was a high quality, high convenience, high service offer, with bespoke fitting at a high price. Second, you could buy mass manufactured garments. They offered standard quality and standard sizes at low prices but with low service and low convenience. Thirdly, you could make them yourself, buying cloth and thread and slaving over a hot sewing machine. This way you got bespoke fitting at a very low price, but the service and convenience elements reduced.

Buying bespoke

Since then, mass manufacturing has swept nearly all before it. Its ongoing technological revolution has forced down prices and improved quality at such a rate that 'Royal' service and DIY have (in most sectors) become tiny niches for the very rich and the very poor respectively. Economies of scale were worth it but came at a price. Everything was standardised and averaged and there was, to varying degrees, cross-subsidisation between customers.

Today, that's changing. New technologies are beginning to make mass customisation feasible and information systems are allowing us to identify the profitability of each customer – marketers are rightly questioning the validity of the mass production trade-off. Inspired by the total quality movement ('you can have better quality and lower prices') they're racing to offer Royal, bespoke products and services at standard prices – an inspiring agenda that will keep them busy for decades.

At the same time, they're realising that their customer base usually falls into three groups. The first group (let's call them the Superprofits) actually generates 150 per cent of their profits, even though it only accounts for, say, 60 per cent of customers and makes a crucial contribution to overheads even if its profitability is marginal. The third group actually costs money to serve.

De-averaging is now the order of the day. The big drive now is to 'fire' or otherwise lose the loss makers while going all out to deepen the relationship with the Superprofits.

So far, so good. This is classic segmentation taken to its next, logical, level. But de-averaging has a sting in the tail. In many a company it threatens to set off a chain reaction that unravels the ties that bound it together into a single entity in the first place. Instead of having one mass production business that dominates the market with its brands, de-averaging implies the return of a three-tiered business structure of Royals, standards and DIY, each with their own distinct brands and marketing strategies.

Cherry picking costs

Without their mass markets and their economies of scale, the advantages that gave mass production its tremendous edge begin to go into reverse. Many of these businesses are, in effect, cross-subsidisation businesses and if cross-subsidisation falls apart, so do they.

Tower Records' beef is that sales of Top 40 records basically subsidise other titles, allowing it to offer a wider range and therefore a better service. If the Top 40 goes, the whole proposition goes. Ditto credit cards. Heavy borrowers who pay extortionate interest rates on high levels of rollover debt are subsidising wily users who pay off their debts each month and get an excellent service for free. But a traditional credit card operator cannot cherry pick its own Superprofits because ending the cross-subsidisation would destroy the rest of its business.

Likewise banks. Current account holders whose balances are so low and transactions so frequent that they cost a fortune to serve are being subsidised by affluent customers with higher balances. Banking is ripe for a redivision into Royal, standard and DIY but it's almost impossible for existing mass players to do so.

Or take insurance. It's all about averaging and cross-subsidisation. Clever marketers have made good money by de-averaging – distinguishing high risk customers from low risk. But the better the match gets between premium and risk, the less incentive there is to bet: high risk people won't be able to afford the premium, and very low risk types will realise they're better off investing their own premiums.

The real challenge comes when an outsider who hasn't got the same sort of cross-subsidising structure targets another industry's Superprofits. Almost by definition, they can make a better offer – like the supermarkets and Tower Records. Or, perhaps, category killers poaching high profit business from mass merchandisers. Or car companies and charities marketing credit cards. In each case, the victim company is no longer doing the segmenting. It is being segmented.

We can expect more of this as technological development reduces the volume a business needs to cover infrastructure costs (thereby lowering barriers to entry); or as specialist operators see big opportunities in creating cherry picking platforms for 'outsider' brands.

It's tempting to label the first type a niche player and the second type a brand extender and to think that's the end of it. But beware: jargon suffocates thought. It may be just the beginning. Behind such brands and marketing strategies there might be much more than meets the eye. A completely new industrial – and brand – landscape may be emerging.

Source: Alan Mitchell (Marketing Business, *February 1997, p. 18*)

An example, ABC Ltd, follows which illustrates in detail how the above approach might be implemented. This approach has been in existence for over 60 years, but renewed interest in it has been generated over the last ten years or so under the banner of activity based costing (ABC).

ABC Ltd: An Exercise on Segmental Analysis

The profit and loss account for last month's operations of ABC Ltd is given in Figure 3.6, showing a net profit of £14,070.

Derek Needham, ABC's chief executive, is interested in knowing the profit from each of the company's three customers. Since this cannot be known from Figure 3.6 as it stands, he asks his management accountant, Philip Randall, to carry out the necessary analysis.

FIGURE 3.6
ABC Ltd profit and loss account

		£
Sales revenue		255,000
Cost of goods sold		178,500
Gross profit		76,500
Expenses		
Salaries	37,500	
Rent	7,500	
Packaging materials	15,180	
Postage and stationery	750	
Hire of office equipment	1,500	
		62,430
Net profit		£14,070

In addition to the five *natural* accounts shown in the profit and loss account Mr Randall has identified four *functional* accounts:

- personal selling;
- packaging and despatch;
- advertising;
- invoicing and collection.

His investigations have revealed that:

1 Salaries are attributable as follows:

- Sales personnel £15,000
- Packaging labour £13,500
- Office staff £9,000

Salesmen seldom visit the office. Office staff time is divided equally between promotional activities on the one hand and invoicing/collecting on the other.
2 The rent charge relates to the whole building, of which 20 per cent is occupied by offices and the remainder by packaging/despatch.
3 All the advertising expenditure related to Product C.
4 ABC Ltd markets three products, as shown in Figure 3.7. These products vary in their manufactured cost (worked out on absorption lines), selling price, and volume sold during the month. Moreover, their relative bulk varies: Product A is much smaller than Product B, which in turn is only half the size of Product C. Details are given in Figure 3.7.

FIGURE 3.7
ABC Ltd basic product data

Product	Manufactured cost per unit	Selling price per unit	Number of units sold last month	Sales revenue	Relative bulk per unit
A	£105	£150	1,000	£150,000	1
B	£525	£750	100	£75,000	3
C	£2,100	£3,000	10	£30,000	6
			1,110	£255,000	

5 ABC's three customers each requires different product combinations, places a different number of orders, and requires a different amount of sales effort. As Figure 3.8 shows, James received more sales calls, Charles placed more orders, and Hugh made up most of the demand for Product C.

FIGURE 3.8
ABC Ltd basic customer data

Customer	Number of sales calls in period	Number of orders placed in period	Number of units of each product ordered in period		
			A	B	C
Charles	30	30	900	30	0
James	40	3	90	30	3
Hugh	30	1	10	40	7
Totals	100	34	1,000	100	10

Using the data that has been presented, and making various assumptions which we feel to be appropriate, we can apply absorption costing principles in order to determine the net profit or loss attributable to each of ABC's customers. On the basis of our analysis we may be able to suggest what course of action be considered next.

Among the given data we are told that office staff divide their time equally between two functional activities:

(i)   advertising (i.e. order-getting);
(ii) invoicing and collections.

It seems reasonable to assume (in the absence of other guidance) that space, postage and stationery, and office equipment are used equally by these two functions. The calculations that follow are based on this assumption, but any other reasonable (and explicit) basis could be acceptable.

Rent is payable on the basis of:

● 20 per cent office space (i.e. £1,500);
● 80 per cent packaging and despatch space (i.e. £6,000).

All packaging materials are chargeable to packaging and despatch (which is a clear-cut example of a direct functional cost). Since packaging costs will vary with the bulk of the products sold rather than with, say, the number of units sold or sales revenue, we need to take note of the causal relationship between the bulk of sales and packaging costs (see Figure 3.9).

FIGURE 3.9
ABC Ltd packaging units

Product	Number of units sold		Relative bulk per unit		Packaging units
A	1,000	×	1	=	1,000
B	100	×	3	=	300
C	10	×	6	=	60
	1,110				1,360

This can be done by computing (as in Figure 3.9) a measure termed 'packaging units' which incorporates both the number of units and their relative bulk. Even though only 10 units of Product C are sold during the month the relative bulk of that product (with a factor of 6) ensures that it is charged with a correspondingly high amount of packaging effort (hence cost) per unit relative to products A and B.

The bases for determining the rates to apply functional costs to segments can be built up in the following way:

(i)   *Assign natural expenses to functional activities.* This is done in Figure 3.10.
(ii) *Select bases for assigning functional costs to segments.*

    ● Sales calls can be used for personal selling expenses (although this assumes all calls took an equal amount of time).

FIGURE 3.10
ABC Ltd assigning natural expenses

Natural expense	Personal selling	Packaging and despatch	Advertising	Invoicing and collection
Salaries	£15,000	£13,500	£4,500	£4,500
Rent	–	£6,000	£750	£750
Packaging materials	–	£15,180	–	–
Postage and stationery	–	–	£375	£375
Hire of equipment	–	–	£750	£750
Total	£15,000	£34,680	£6,375	£6,375

- The packaging costs vary in accordance with the number of packaging units handled, so a rate per product can be established by taking bulk and the number of units handled into account.
- Advertising can be related to the number of units of Product C sold during the period (which assumes that advertising was equally effective for all sales, and that all its benefits were obtained during the period in question).
- The costs of invoicing can be assumed to vary in accordance with the number of orders (hence invoices) processed during the period.

Relevant calculations are given below:

$$\text{Cost per sales call} = \frac{\text{functional costs}}{\text{no. of sales calls}} = \frac{£15,000}{100} = £150.00$$

$$\text{Packaging costs} = \frac{\text{functional costs}}{\text{no. of packaging units}} = \frac{£34,680}{1,360} = £\ 25.50$$

$$\text{Product A} = £25.50 \times 1 \qquad = £\ 25.50$$
$$\text{Product B} = £25.50 \times 3 \qquad = £\ 76.50$$
$$\text{Product C} = £25.50 \times 6 \qquad = £153.00$$

$$\text{Advertising cost} = \frac{\text{functional costs}}{\text{units of C sold}} = \frac{£6,375}{10} = £637.50$$

$$\text{Invoicing cost per order} = \frac{\text{functional costs}}{\text{no. of orders}} = \frac{£6,375}{34} = £187.50$$

(iii) *Assign functional costs to segments.* Before this step can be executed fully it is necessary to calculate the cost of goods sold on a customer-by-customer basis. Data in Figure 3.7 of the question includes the manufactured cost per unit of each product, and from Figure 3.8 in the question we can see how many units of each product are bought by each customer. From this we can calculate the data in Figure 3.11 below.

We can now turn to the assigning of functional costs to segments. If we take the case of Charles we know that he can be attributed with a total of £35,370 (see Figure 3.12).

A similar computation needs to be carried out for James and Hugh, which gives us the data in Figure 3.13.

Finally, the revenue generated from each customer must be calculated as in Figure 3.14.

(iv) *Compile a net profit statement.* All the pieces can now be put together to show the profit or loss of each customer account with ABC Ltd. The resulting figures (Figure 3.15) show that Charles and Hugh are profitable accounts while James is marginally unprofitable.

FIGURE 3.11
ABC Ltd determining cost of goods sold by customer

		Customer					
		Charles		James		Hugh	
Product	**Unit COGS**	Units	COGS	Units	COGS	Units	COGS
A	£105	900	94,500	90	9,450	10	1,050
B	£525	30	15,750	30	15,750	40	21,000
C	£2,100	0	0	3	6,300	7	14,700
			£110,250		£31,500		£36,750

FIGURE 3.12
*ABC Ltd Charles'
costs*

30 sales calls @ £150.00	£4,500
30 orders @ £187.50	£5,625
Packaging costs for:	
Product A 900 × £25.50 £22,950.00	
Product B 30 × £76.50 £2,295.00	
Product C 0	
	£25,245
Advertising	0
Segmental marketing cost	£35,370

FIGURE 3.13
*ABC Ltd costs of
James and Hugh*

James			Hugh		
40 sales calls@	£150.00	£6,000.00	30 sales calls @	£150.00	£4,500.00
3 orders @	£187.50	£562.50	1 order @	£187.50	£187.50
Packaging			Packaging		
A 90 × £25.50	£2,295		A 10 × £25.50	£255	
B 30 × £76.50	£2,295		B 40 × £76.50	£3,060	
C 3 × £153.00	£459		C 7 × £153.00	£1,071	
		£5,049.00			£4,386.00
Advertising 3 × £637.50		£1,912.50	Advertising 7 × £637.00		£4,462.50
Segmental marketing cost		£13,524.00	Segmental marketing cost		£13,536.00

FIGURE 3.14
*ABC Ltd revenue by
customer*

		Customer					
		Charles		James		Hugh	
Product	Unit selling price	Units	Revenue	Units	Revenue	Units	Revenue
A	£150	900	135,000	90	13,400	10	1,500
B	£740	30	22,500	30	22,500	40	30,000
C	£3,000	0	0	3	9,000	7	21,000
			£157,500		£45,000		£52,500

FIGURE 3.15
*ABC Ltd net profit by
customer*

	Customer			
	Charles	James	Hugh	ABC Ltd
Sales revenue	£157,500	£45,000	£52,500	£255,000
COGS	110,250	31,500	36,750	178,500
Gross profit	47,250	13,500	15,750	76,500
Marketing expenses	35,370	13,524	13,536	62,430
Net profit	£11,880	£(24)	£2,214	£14,070

In productivity terms (see pp. 96–8 below) it is evident that there are significant variations from one customer to another. Taking Charles first, we have:

Inputs	£	Outputs	£
COGS	110,250	Sales revenue	157,500
Marketing	35,370		
	£145,620		£157,500

$$\text{Productivity} = \frac{\text{Outputs}}{\text{Inputs}} = \frac{£157,500}{£145,620} = 1.08$$

This productivity index of 1.08 is better than the figure of 1.06 for ABC Ltd as a whole (as shown in Figure 3.16), and considerably in excess of the figures for James and Hugh. It is in excess of unity, which is, *prima facie*, a good thing.

Taking James next, we have:

Inputs	£	Outputs	£
COGS	31,500	Sales revenue	45,000
Marketing	13,524		
	£45,024		£45,000

$$\text{Productivity} = \frac{\text{Outputs}}{\text{Inputs}} = \frac{£45,000}{£45,024} = 0.99$$

Since this index is below unity it follows that a loss is being made, and the loss (£24) is the amount by which the value of the inputs consumed in servicing James exceeds the output generated from his account.

Turning now to Hugh, we have the following picture:

Inputs	£	Outputs	£
COGS	36,750	Sales revenue	52,500
Marketing	13,356		
	£50,286		£52,500

$$\text{Productivity} = \frac{\text{Outputs}}{\text{Inputs}} = \frac{£52,500}{£50,286} = 1.04$$

The index is greater than unity, but not as large as that for Charles, or for that relating to ABC Ltd. as a whole. This overall position is given below:

Inputs	£	Outputs	£
COGS	178,500	Sales revenue	255,000
Marketing	62,430		
	£240,930		£255,000

$$\text{Productivity} = \frac{\text{Outputs}}{\text{Inputs}} = \frac{£255,000}{£240,930} = 1.06$$

A summary is provided in Figure 3.16:

FIGURE 3.16
ABC Ltd: Productivity by segment

	Charles	James	Hugh	ABC Ltd as a whole
Outputs (£)	157,500	45,000	52,500	255,000
Inputs (£)	145,620	45,024	50,286	240.930
Productivity index	1.08	0.99	1.04	1.06

Interpretation of data

A danger in using an absorption-based approach in segmental analysis is that the 'bottom line' might be taken as a criterion for *action*. It should not be; the aim is to determine the net profit as a criterion for *investigation*. (In a sense, of course, this is one type of action, but the type of action that should be avoided is the eliminating of James's account due to the marginal loss revealed in Figure 3.15.)

Charles's account contributed almost 85 per cent of the total net profit, and he bought three times as much from ABC Ltd as did Hugh, and more than three times the purchases of James. However, the number of sales calls to Charles was fewer than to James, although Charles placed a much larger number of orders than both James and Hugh together.

The mix of products purchased clearly affects the profit performance of different customer accounts. While the COGS does not vary from one product to another (being 70 per cent of sales revenue for each product line), the variation in relative bulk of the product lines caused differences in packaging costs. Thus Charles (whose orders were for 900 units of A, 30 of B, and none of C) was charged with relatively less packaging cost than either James or Hugh due to the smaller packaging bulk of Product A. On a similar basis, since Charles bought no units of C his account was not charged with any advertising costs, so the profit performance of Charles's account would clearly be better than either of the others.

One possible way forward could be to consider calling less often on James; encourage Charles to place fewer (but larger) orders; and to rethink the wisdom of the advertising campaign for Product C.

It is vital to recognize that this net profit approach to segmental analysis can only raise questions: it cannot provide answers. (The reason for this, of course, is that the apportionment of indirect costs clouds the distinction between avoidable and unavoidable costs, and even direct costs may not all be avoidable in the short run.)

The application of the above steps to a company's product range may produce the picture portrayed in Figure 3.17.

FIGURE 3.17
Segmental profit statement

Product	% contribution to total profits
Total for all products	100.0
Profitable products:	
A	43.7
B	35.5
C	16.4
D	9.6
E	6.8
F	4.2
Sub-total	116.2
G	−7.5
H	−8.7
Sub-total	−16.2

The segment could equally be sales territory, customer group, etc., and after the basic profit computation has been carried out it can be supplemented (as in Figure 3.18) by linking it to an analysis of the effort required to produce the profit result. (Clearly this is a multi-variate situation in which profit depends upon a variety of input factors – as suggested by Figure 3.1 – but developing valid and reliable multi-variate models is both complex and expensive.) As a step in the direction of more rigorous analysis one can derive benefits from linking profit outcome to individual inputs – such as selling time in the case of Figure 3.18.

FIGURE 3.18
*Segmental
productivity
statement*

Product	% contribution to total profits	% total selling time
Total for all products	100	100
Profitable products:		
A	43.7	16.9
B	35.5	18.3
C	16.4	17.4
D	9.6	5.3
E	6.8	10.2
F	4.2	7.1
Sub-total	116.2	75.2
Unprofitable products:		
G	–7.5	9.5
H	–8.7	15.3
Sub-total	–16.2	24.8

From Figure 3.18 one can see that Product A generates 43.7 per cent of total profits, requiring only 16.9 per cent of available selling time. This is highly productive. By contrast, Product E produces only 6.8 per cent of total profits but required 10.2 per cent of selling effort. Even worse, however, is the 24.8 per cent of selling effort devoted to Products G and H, which are unprofitable.

A number of obvious questions arise from this type of analysis. Can the productivity of marketing activities be increased by:

- increasing net profits proportionately more than the corresponding increase in marketing outlays?
- increasing net profits with no change in marketing outlays?
- increasing net profits with a decrease in marketing costs?
- maintaining net profits at a given level but decreasing marketing costs?
- decreasing net profits but with a proportionately greater decrease in marketing costs?

If these analyses are based purely on historical information they will provide less help than if they relate to plans for the future. One way of overcoming the limitations of historical information is to plan and control the conditions under which information is gathered. This can be achieved through *marketing experimentation*.

3.8 MARKETING EXPERIMENTATION

As we saw in Chapter 1 (see pp. 15–18 above, and see also Chapter 17, pp. 638–40 below), attempts are made in a marketing experiment to identify all the controllable independent factors that effect a particular dependent variable, and some of these factors are then manipulated systematically in order to isolate and measure their effects on the performance of the dependent variable.

It is not possible, of course, to plan or control all the conditions in which an experiment is conducted; for example, the timing, location, and duration of an experiment can be predetermined, but it is necessary to measure such uncontrollable conditions as those caused by the weather and eliminate their effects from the results. Irrespective of these uncontrollable influences, the fact that experiments are concerned with the deliberate manipulation of controllable variables (i.e. such variables as price and advertising effort) means that a good deal more confidence can be placed in conclusions about the effects of such manipulation than if the effects of these changes had been based purely on historical associations.

Studies of marketing costs can provide the ideas for experiments. Questions such as the following can be answered as a result of marketing experimentation.

1 By how much (if any) would the net profit contribution of the most profitable products be increased if there were an increase in specific marketing outlays, and how would such a change affect the strategy of competitors in terms of the stability of, say, market shares?
2 By how much (if any) would the net losses of unprofitable products be reduced if there were some decrease in specific marketing outlays?
3 By how much (if any) would the profit contribution of profitable products be affected by a change in the marketing effort applied to the unprofitable products, and vice versa, and what would be the effect on the total marketing system?
4 By how much (if any) would the total profit contribution be improved if some marketing effort were diverted to profitable territories or customer groups from unprofitable territorial and customer segments?
5 By how much (if any) would the net profit contribution be increased if there were a change in the method of distribution to small unprofitable accounts, or if these accounts were eliminated?

Only by actually carrying out properly designed marketing experiments can management realistically predict with an acceptable degree of certainty the effects of changes in marketing expenditure on the level of sales and profit of each differentiated product, territory, or customer segment in the multiproduct company.

3.9 THE NATURE OF PRODUCTIVITY

Productivity can be considered at either a macro level (i.e. in relation to entire industries or whole economies) or at a micro level (i.e. in relation to particular organizations, or in relation to particular activities within organizations). Our interest is in the latter – productivity at a micro level – although we must avoid being too introspective by focusing exclusively on one organization or function as if it were independent of its context.

At its simplest, productivity can be conceived of as the relationship between outputs and inputs. Thus marketing productivity can be expressed as:

$$\frac{\text{marketing outputs}}{\text{marketing inputs}}$$

Sevin (1965, p. 9) has defined marketing productivity in more specific terms as:

> ... the ratio of sales or net profits (effect produced) to marketing costs (energy expended) for a specific segment of the business.

This equates productivity and profitability, which seems acceptable to some writers (e.g. Thomas, 1984; 1986) but not to others (e.g. Bucklin, 1979). The major objection to Sevin's definition is due to the effects of inflation since sales, net profit, and costs are all financial flows subject to changes in relative prices. For example, any increase in the value of sales from one period to another during inflationary times will be made up of two elements:

1 an increase due to a higher physical volume of sales;
2 an increase due to higher prices.

If the value of the pound sterling were constant this would remove the problem, but since this is not the case it means that any financial data is necessarily suspect. The answer is to make some adjustments to ensure that measurement is made in *real* terms rather than simply in *monetary* terms – and to make these adjustments to both numerator and denominator in a way that allows for differential rates of inflation. Once measurement is made in real terms it is possible to use the ratio that emerges as an index of efficiency. This can be used in relation to two types of question:

1 How much output was achieved for a given input?
2 How much input was required to achieve a given output?

These questions can be asked retrospectively (as above) or prospectively (for example, how much output should be achieved from a given mix and quantity of inputs?). The first relates to the notion of *technical efficiency*, whereby one seeks to maximize the output from a given input, whereas the second relates to the notion of *economic efficiency*, whereby one seeks to minimize the input costs for a given output.

Having specified in operational terms the numerator (output) and the denominator (input), and having eliminated the impacts of inflation, the result represents a measure of resource allocation (i.e. the pattern of inputs) and resource utilization (i.e. the generation of outputs), and these can be depicted via *ratio pyramids* which we will look at later in this chapter. What we need to recognize at this point is that the array of ratios within a ratio pyramid can give us a vivid picture of the manner in which the organization has allocated its resources, and the efficiency with which those resources have been utilized. The next step, of course, is to consider how the allocation and its efficiency might be improved, which will mean changes in inputs and outputs. In turn this requires an understanding of the causal relationships between inputs and outputs.

Let us be a little more specific and consider a particular productivity index from the distribution domain. The relevant output may be expressed in terms of the number of orders shipped during a given period, and the associated input may be the number of labour hours worked in the period. Thus:

$$\text{productivity index} = \frac{\text{number of orders shipped}}{\text{number of labour hours worked}}$$

It will be apparent that this index relates one physical measure to another, hence there is no need to worry about inflationary distortions. However, had the numerator been expressed in terms of the *sales value* of orders shipped, and/or the denominator in terms of the *cost* of labour hours worked, it would have been necessary to adjust the figures to eliminate the effects of inflation – even though the index that results is a true ratio (i.e. it is not stated in terms of specific units).

It should also be apparent that any productivity index that is calculated is meaningless in isolation from some comparative figure. With what should an index be compared? There are a number of alternatives that will be examined later in more detail, but for the present we should be aware of the following:

● *internal comparisons* can be made with either

   1 figures from previous periods, which give a basis for trend analysis;
   2 figures representing efficient or desired performance, which give a basis for budgetary control.

● *external comparisons* can be made with other organizations operating within the same markets.

The importance of external reference points cannot be overemphasized. As Christopher (1977) has stated:

> Business success is achieved where the client is, more than in our plants. External returns from the market are more appropriate measures than internal returns on investment. Success is more in manufacturing satisfied, repeat customers than in manufacturing products.

3.10 THE USE OF RATIOS

Whether one's primary interest is in the productivity of an organization as a whole, or in the productivity of a highly specific activity within an organization, ratios can be computed at a suitable level of aggregation. Their value lies in the relative measures (as opposed to absolute measures) on which they are based.

It is possible to calculate a great range of ratios, but a word of warning is needed to ensure that only useful ratios are calculated. Thus, for example, the ratio of

$$\frac{\text{advertising expenditure}}{\text{miles travelled by salesmen}}$$

within a given period is not likely to be very useful for at least two reasons:

1 it seeks to relate two input factors (rather than one input and one output);
2 the resulting ratio (of advertising expenditure per mile travelled by salesmen) is not meaningful.

On the other hand, the ratio of

$$\frac{\text{incremental sales}}{\text{incremental promotion}}$$

relates one input to a relevant output and is potentially useful as a measure of promotional effectiveness. Discretion, therefore, is most important in choosing which ratios to calculate as a means towards assessing productivity within marketing.

Another warning needs to be given over the way in which ratios tend to average out any patterns in the underlying data. Consider the case of a seasonal business making 90 per cent of its sales in the first six months of every year and the remaining 10 per cent during the other six months. Average monthly sales over the whole year will differ significantly from the average monthly sales in each half year, so one must choose carefully the period over which one gathers data, and the frequency with which one calculates ratios.

At an organizational level the ultimate financial measure of short-term efficiency is the relationship between net profit and capital employed, typically expressed in percentage terms as the rate of return on capital employed or the rate of return on investment (ROI).

$$\frac{\text{Net profit}}{\text{Capital employed}} \times 100 = \text{ROI}$$

This ratio shows the return (i.e. net output) that has been generated by the capital employed (i.e. input) during a given period of time. Problems exist in connection with the definitions, hence measurement, of both numerator and denominator, which highlights another note of caution in using ratios: always be sure to establish the definition of numerators and denominators. For example, is the net profit pre-tax or post-tax? Is the capital employed based on historic cost or replacement cost figures?

Given that profit is the residual once costs have been deducted from sales revenues, it is clear that ROI can be improved by either increasing sales revenues, decreasing costs, or reducing capital employed – or by any combination of these. This gives us the basic idea underlying the ratio pyramid. At the apex is ROI, but this can be decomposed into two secondary ratios:

Primary ratio $\dfrac{\text{net profit}}{\text{capital employed}}$

Secondary ratios $\dfrac{\text{net profit}}{\text{sales revenue}}$ $\dfrac{\text{sales revenue}}{\text{capital employed}}$

Each of the secondary ratios can help explain the ROI. The first is the profit rate on sales and the second is the capital turnover. Their interrelationship is such that:

Profit rate $\times$ capital turnover $=$ ROI

Even the secondary ratios are highly aggregated, so it is necessary to proceed to measure tertiary ratios as one moves down the ratio pyramid using its structure as a diagnostic guide.

The general cause of any deviation in ROI from a target rate may be found by computing the profit ratio and the capital turnover ratio, but this is only a starting point. Before corrective action can be taken a study of specific causes must be made, hence *tertiary ratios* need to be worked out.

Tertiary ratios are those that constitute the secondary ratios. The profit ratio reflects the relationship between the gross profit rate, the level of sales revenue, and operating costs (i.e. net profit + operating costs = gross profit), while the rate of capital turnover is affected by the level of sales revenue and the capital structure mix (of fixed and working capital, etc.). From these details it is a simple step to compute four tertiary ratios as follows (as shown in Figure 3.19):

1    $\dfrac{\text{Gross profit}}{\text{Sales revenue}}$

2    $\dfrac{\text{Sales revenue}}{\text{Operating costs}}$

3    $\dfrac{\text{Sales revenue}}{\text{Fixed assets}}$

4    $\dfrac{\text{Sales revenue}}{\text{Working capital}}$

Figure 3.19 also shows many other levels of the ratio pyramid which can be identified, and the process of decomposing broad ratios into their component parts can be continued further and further until the reasons for overall outcomes are known.

A variation on Figure 3.19 relating specifically to marketing is provided by Figure 3.20.

3.11 ANALYSING RATIOS AND TRENDS

It is possible to indicate trends in a company's performance over time by plotting successive ratios on a graph and thereby showing trends. Some important trends may only become apparent over a number of months (or even years), and ratio

FIGURE 3.19
Ratio pyramid

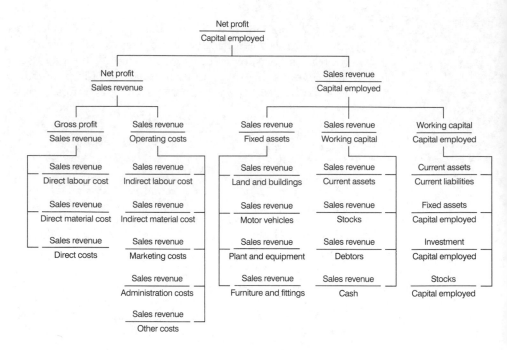

FIGURE 3.20
Marketing ratio pyramid

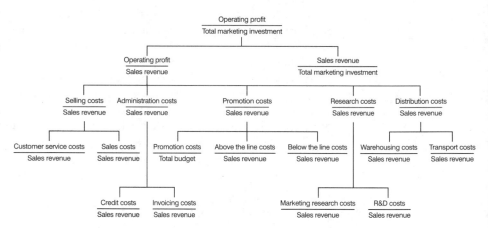

analysis can ensure that such trends do not develop unnoticed. Figure 3.21, for example, shows a continuing decline in a company's profitability. The causes for this trend may be found by breaking it down into its secondary components and so on through the ratio pyramid. These secondary trends – profit rate and capital turnover – are shown in Figure 3.22 and can be seen to be falling and rising respectively. Figure 3.23 then takes the former of these trends (falling profit rate) and decomposes it into a falling gross profit trend and a rising operating cost to sales revenue trend.

It could prove necessary in a specific instance to work right through the ratio pyramid in plotting trends in order to isolate the causes of variations from the desired trend line in higher levels of the ratio hierarchy, and it may also be necessary to apply some imagination and common sense. This last mentioned requirement can be illustrated in two ways. First, the declining ROI noted in Figure 3.21 may be thought, prima facie, to be due to the falling net profit to sales revenue trend shown in Figure 3.22, and so the rising capital turnover trend as in Figure 3.22 may be ignored. But ROI is clearly the combined outcome of a particular level of profit and a particular quantity of capital investment, so any variation in either will inevitably affect the ROI. Furthermore, a rising aggregate trend of capital turnover will almost certainly conceal many more compensating highs and lows in tertiary and subsequent levels of the ratio hierarchy. It follows

FIGURE 3.21
Primary trend

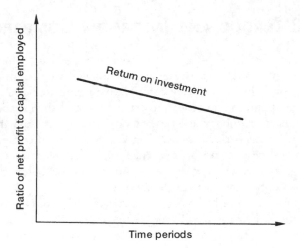

FIGURE 3.22
Secondary trends

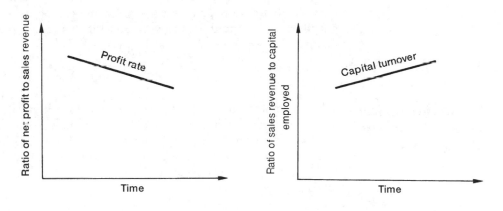

FIGURE 3.23
Tertiary trends

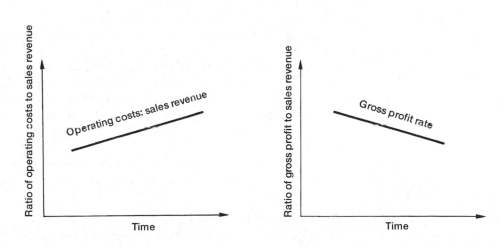

that attention in the light of a falling ROI should not necessarily be focused exclusively on the net profit trend, but some consideration should be given to the rate and trend of capital turnover.

The second common-sense point to note is that a rising operating cost to sales revenue trend, as in Figure 3.23, cannot be controlled until the specific items that cause the trend have been identified and appropriate steps taken to bring them under control. Of course, the extent to which the decline of the profit rate (a secondary trend) is caused by either of its constituent tertiary trends should be carefully established.

3.12 RATIOS AND INTERFIRM COMPARISON

In many industries – and especially in those in which operating methods, technology, product characteristics, and general operating conditions are very similar – it is helpful to have comparative figures for one's own company and for other companies within the industry. From published accounts it is possible to see the primary, secondary, and tertiary ratios (hence trends) of competing companies, but no reasons for divergences between one's own company's results and other companies' results can be discerned from such accounts due to a lack of detail relating to the lower part of the ratio pyramid (i.e. below the tertiary level) and so there is no guidance for future actions.

One major cause of divergence between the results of any two companies can be found in their use of differing accounting techniques and definitions. This will be seen, for example, if two companies purchase a similar asset each at the same point and one company chooses to depreciate the asset over four years while the other company chooses to take a 100 per cent depreciation allowance in the first year. It follows, therefore, that a meaningful comparison must be based on common definitions and usage. This can best be achieved (for comparative purposes) by a central organization and for this reason the Centre for Interfirm Comparison was set up.

Examples of the Use of Interfirm Comparison

While interfirm comparison figures are expressed in relation to quartiles and the median (i.e. if all results are ranked in descending order of size, the median is represented by the figure that comes half-way down, and the third quartile is three-quarters of the way down), the following example (OPQ Ltd) simplifies this by just giving the general approach to interfirm comparisons. The necessary steps in such an exercise are:

1 ensure that the reports, etc., that are to be compared incorporate figures that have been prepared on a comparable basis;
2 compute the required ratios, percentages, and key totals from submitted reports;
3 compare the results of each company with the aggregate results;
4 introduce intangible or qualitative factors that may aid in interpreting the results of each individual company in the light of the whole picture;
5 examine the numerator, denominator, and lower ratios in instances where a ratio differs significantly from the external standard (or average, median, or whatever);
6 determine the adjustment (if any) that is required to bring a given company's divergent ratio into line with the aggregate norm.

OPQ Ltd – Ratio Analysis

The following is a simple example of interfirm comparison. Figure 3.24 shows the ratios of OPQ Ltd, a firm in a light engineering industry, for the two years 1996 and 1997.

This looks like a success story. Profit on assets employed has gone up from 8.25 per cent to 10 per cent due to an increase in the firm's profit on sales (Ratio 2) and the better use it seems to have made of its assets (Ratios 3 and 3a). The higher profit on sales seems to have been achieved through operational improvements which results in a lower ratio of cost of production (Ratio 4). The firm's faster turnover of assets (Ratio 3) is due mainly to a faster turnover of current assets (Ratio 7), and this in turn is due to accelerated turnovers of material stocks (Ratio 9), work in progress (Ratio 10), finished stock (Ratio 11) and debtors (Ratio 12).

FIGURE 3.24
OPQ's own figures

	Ratio	Unit	1996	1997
1	Operating profit / Assets employed	%	8.25	10.0
2	Operating profit / Sales revenue	%	5.5	6.1
3	Sales revenue / Assets employed	times	1.5	1.65
3(a)	Assets employed / Average daily sales revenue	days*	249	222
4	Production cost of sales / Sales revenue	%	71.0	70.4
5	Distribution and marketing costs / Sales revenue	%	17.7	17.7
6	General and administrative costs / Sales revenue	%	5.8	5.8
7	Current assets / Average daily sales revenue	days*	215	188
8	Fixed assets / Average daily sales revenue	days*	34	34
9	Material stocks / Average daily sales revenue	days*	49	45
10	Work-in-progress / Average daily sales revenue	days*	53	46
11	Finished stocks / Average daily sales revenue	days*	52	39
12	Debtors / Average daily sales revenue	days*	61	54

* Days required to turn the asset item over once.

The firm's illusion of success was shattered when it compared its ratios with those of other light engineering firms of its type. Figure 3.25 is an extract from the results – it gives the figures of only five of the 22 participating firms. OPQ Ltd's figures are shown under letter C.

In this year the firm's operating profit on assets employed is well below that of two other firms, and this appears to be due to its profit on sales (Ratio 2) being relatively low. This in turn is mainly due to the firm's high distribution and marketing expenses (Ratio 5). In the actual comparison further ratios were given helping Firm C to establish to what extent its higher Ratio 5 was due to higher costs of distribution and warehousing; higher costs of advertising and sales promotion; or higher costs of other selling activities (e.g. cost of sales personnel).

FIGURE 3.25
*The interfirm
comparison*

Ratio			Firm				
			A	B	C	D	E
1	$\dfrac{\text{Operating profit}}{\text{Assets employed}}$	%	18.0	14.3	10.0	7.9	4.0
2	$\dfrac{\text{Operating profit}}{\text{Sales revenue}}$	%	15.0	13.1	6.1	8.1	2.0
3	$\dfrac{\text{Sales revenue}}{\text{Assets employed}}$	times	1.20	1.09	1.65	0.98	2.0
3(a)	$\dfrac{\text{Assets employed}}{\text{Average daily sales revenue}}$	days*	304	335	222	372	182
4	$\dfrac{\text{Production cost of sales}}{\text{Sales revenue}}$	%	73.0	69.4	70.4	72.5	79.0
5	$\dfrac{\text{Distribution and marketing costs}}{\text{Sales revenue}}$	%	8.0	13.1	17.7	13.7	15.0
6	$\dfrac{\text{General and administrative costs}}{\text{Sales revenue}}$	%	4.0	4.4	5.8	5.7	4.0
7	$\dfrac{\text{Current assets}}{\text{Average daily sales revenue}}$	days*	213	219	188	288	129
8	$\dfrac{\text{Fixed assets}}{\text{Average daily sales revenue}}$	days*	91	116	34	84	53
9	$\dfrac{\text{Material stocks}}{\text{Average daily sales revenue}}$	days*	45	43	45	47	29
10	$\dfrac{\text{Work-in-progress}}{\text{Average daily sales revenue}}$	days*	51	47	46	60	52
11	$\dfrac{\text{Finished stocks}}{\text{Average daily sales revenue}}$	days*	71	63	39	94	22
12	$\dfrac{\text{Debtors}}{\text{Average daily sales revenue}}$	days*	36	84	54	18	26

* Days required to turn the asset item over once.

3.13 A STRATEGIC APPROACH

A strategic-oriented approach to answering the question 'Where are we now?' can be provided from the PIMS database. PIMS stands for *Profit Impact of Market Strategy* and refers to an objective approach to analysing corporate performance using a unique database. Some 3000 strategic business units (SBUs) have contributed over 20 000 years' experience to this database.

PIMS research on what drives business profits has become more widely known over the last 25 years as more evidence has become available. We know that there is, in general, a range of factors which we can quantify and relate to margins or to return on capital employed (ROCE). But does the evidence show that these

FIGURE 3.26
*PIMS can quantify
how strategic factors
drive performance*

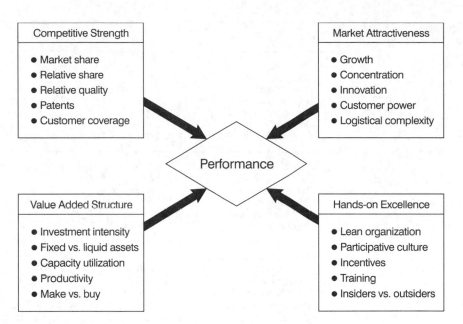

factors work in specific industries – do they actually explain the spread which dwarfs differences between industries?

PIMS results from examining real profits of real businesses suggest that the determinants of business performance can be grouped into four categories:

● Market attractiveness;
● Competitive strength;
● Value added structure;
● People and organization.

These are illustrated in Figure 3.26.

The first category contains factors in the business situation which affect its performance. Customer bargaining power, market complexity, market growth and innovation are obvious examples.

The second group describes how a business differs from its competitors in its market. Share position, customer preference relative to competitors' offerings, market coverage and product range all have an effect.

The third category quantifies the way a business converts inputs into outputs; it includes investment intensity, fixed/working capital split, employee productivity, capacity use and vertical integration.

People and organization, an area in which PIMS has only recently built up comparable data, includes managers' attitudes, skill and training mix, personnel policies and incentives.

Figure 3.27 shows the impact of these factors on business profits tracked across PIMS' 3000 businesses. Some factors are more important than others, but each has an influence which is both measurable and explainable. The positioning of a business on the chart can be described as its 'profile'.

To test whether the profile of a business can explain its profits, irrespective of the industry in which it operates, PIMS looked at the performance of businesses with 'weak' and 'strong' profiles in each of five sectors. Weak and strong profiles were picked in terms of position on each of the fifteen variables in Figure 3.28. Factors related to people and organization were omitted from the exercise because the available sample at the time was not large enough to examine them by sector.

The results are startling! In every industry sector where there were enough observations to test, a business with a weak profit makes a 6 per cent ROS or 10 per cent ROCE over a four year period. In contrast, a strong-profile business

FIGURE 3.27
Impact of strategic factors on performance

Factor	–	Effect on ROCE	+
Market Attractiveness			
Market growth	Low		High
Innovation	Zero, very high		Moderate
R&D spend	Zero, very high		Moderate
Marketing spend	High		Low
Contract size	Large		Small
Customer complexity	Complex		Simple
Competitive strength			
Relative share	Low		High
Relative quality	Worse		Better
Differentiation	Commodity		Differentiated
Customer spread	Narrow		Broader
Product range	Narrow		Broader
Value Added Structure			
Investment/sales	High		Low
Capacity use	Low		High
Vertical integration	Low		High
Employee productivity	Low		High
People and Organization			
Attitudes	Restrictive		Open
Training	Little		Substantial
Incentives	Weak		Strong

SOURCE: PIMS data base

FIGURE 3.28
PIMS Profiles 1

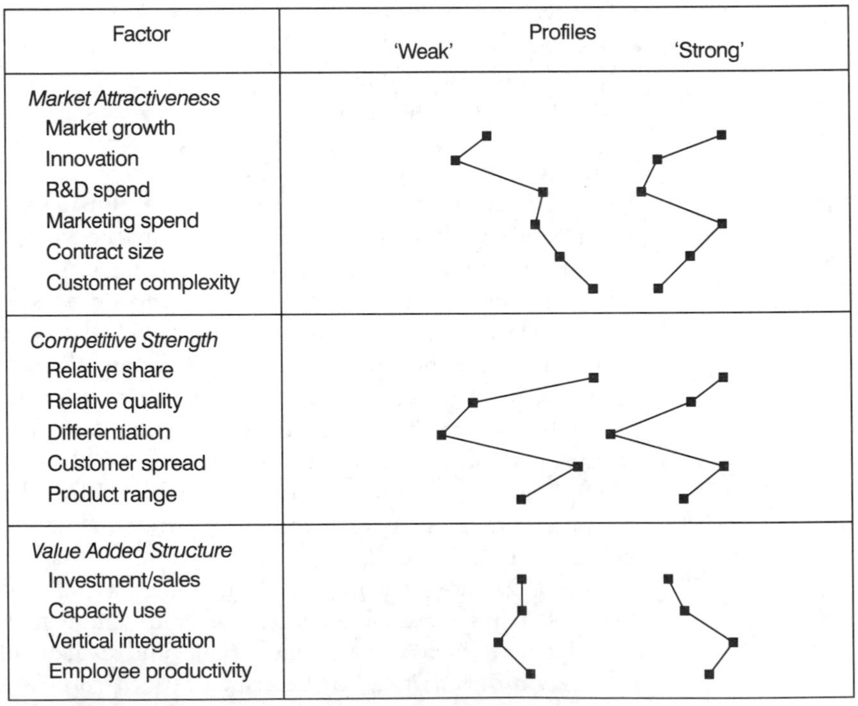

makes 11 per cent ROS or 30 per cent ROCE. The gap in profit performance between strong and weak businesses in each sector is bigger than the standard deviation in each group. So the profile does a better job of explaining differences in performance than the industry each business is in. The profile represents the strategic logic which shapes the real competitive choices facing managers in each business. (See Figure 3.29.)

FIGURE 3.29
PIMS Profiles 2

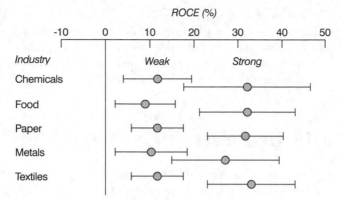

SOURCE: PIMS data base

These new results are critically important. Earlier studies have shown how margins are related to business characteristics, but this is the first time that businesses in different industries with similar profiles have been shown to have more in common when it comes to performance than businesses in the same industry with different profiles.

PIMS also tested the relationships between margins and profile variables in various subsectors in the chemical industry, which is particularly well represented in the PIMS database. In each case the determinants included in the profile have a powerful, and consistent, influence on profits. The effect of each determinant is similar irrespective of the product category. This is true even for what is probably the most subjective of the variables PIMS measure: relative quality.

3.14 SUMMARY

This chapter has been concerned primarily with the pattern of utilization of resources and its efficiency within the enterprise. Both ratio analysis and productivity analysis can help in establishing the pattern of resource utilization and its productivity by relating inputs (resources consumed or costs) to outputs (revenue). From this base, marketing managers will be able to derive greater insights into relationships between inputs and outputs to help them in planning (and controlling) future activities.

If the utilization of 'effort' (i.e. resources) across an organization's various activities can be measured and related to the revenues generated by those activities it is possible to determine their productivity. In essence this is the ratio of outputs/ inputs. While the outputs are fairly easy to establish with precision the same is not true of the inputs, so most of the discussion has focused on the measurement of inputs.

The starting point is the specification of the cost objects of interest, for example, the productivity of operating via different channels, or serving different customer groups. Costs will be *direct* or *indirect*, depending upon the cost objects of interest. Full cost needs to be determined for each cost object (i.e. segment), and the ways in which this can be done were discussed and demonstrated. Once this has been done the productivity of each segment can be measured and from these measurements questions can be raised about the adequacy of each segment's productivity. For example, can effort be reallocated from Segment A to Segment B to improve these segments' productivity?

The key role of ratio analysis and productivity analysis lies in the basis they give for raising questions in the light of the existing state of play. Such techniques cannot generate answers as to what to do next.

A pyramid of marketing ratios was constructed to show the pattern of ratios (reflecting resource utilization and productivity) across relevant activities in a way which highlights interdependencies in an overall context.

Finally, the strategic approach provided by PIMS was outlined, which adds extra dimensions to the analysis of 'Where are we now?'

3.15 EXERCISES

1 While management of RST Company realize that additional marketing/ distribution cost studies are needed, the company lacks the personnel and funds at present to establish accurate cost standards. They do, however, believe that they may be accepting too small an order. As a result, they analyse the order sizes received last year and break their orders down by the simple categories of small (1–20 items), medium (21–100 items) and large (over 100 items).

The actual marketing and distribution costs incurred last year were as follows:

Cost	Amount (£)	Basis for distribution
Marketing personnel salaries	27,000	Number of personnel
Marketing manager's salary	20,000	Time spent
Salespeople's commissions	3,000	Amount of sales
Advertising and direct selling	37,500	Amount of sales
Packaging and shipping	26,250	Weight shipped
Delivery	19,000	Weight shipped
Credit and collection	15,000	Number of orders

An analysis of their records produced the following statistics:

	\multicolumn{3}{c}{Order sizes}	
	Small	Medium	Large	Total
Number of personnel	5	3	1	9
Time spent by marketing manager	60%	10%	30%	100%
Amount of sales (£)	250,000	300,000	200,000	750,000
Weight (kg)	6,090	2,940	1,470	10,500
Number of orders	612	170	68	850

Required:

(a) Prepare a detailed schedule showing the marketing cost per order size and marketing cost as a percentage of sales revenue for each order size.
(b) What recommendations would you make to management regarding the size of order they should accept?

2 Strines & Co. is engaged in marketing three products, X, Y and Z. During May 1997 the sales volume, unit selling price and gross margin of each product was as follows:

	X	Y	Z
Sales (units)	10,000	15,000	25,000
Selling price (£)	50	20	10
Gross margin (%)	45	50	55

Order-getting and order-filling costs for the month were:

	£
Personal selling	180,000
Advertising	70,000
Transportation	90,000
Warehousing and handling	60,000
General	37,500

Certain additional information is available:

	X	Y	Z
Kilos shipped	90,000	50,000	60,000
Sales representative's time	20%	45%	35%
Advertising effort	40%	25%	35%

Required:
Prepare a net profit statement showing the relative profit performance of each product line. Make whatever assumptions you feel to be necessary, but state all the assumptions you have made.

3 The exhibit below shows, for XYZ Ltd, a summary of 1997's operations in the form of a simplified profit and loss account.

XYZ Ltd Basic data for 1997

	£	£
Sales revenue		300,000
Cost of goods sold		195,000
Gross profit		105,000
Operating expenses:		
Salaries	46,500	
Rent	15,000	
Supplies	17,500	
		79,000
Net profit		£26,000

XYZ is a small company engaged in the manufacture and marketing of gardening tools. Its products are sold through three channels of distribution:

- garden centres;
- hardware shops;
- department stores.

The Marketing Director is keen to know the relative net profit performance of each of these channels. In her initial work on this issue she has identified the following marketing functions which are undertaken by XYZ Ltd:

- selling
- advertising
- packaging and delivery
- invoicing and collection

Salaries in 1997 were paid to employees in these functions as shown below, along with use of space and cost of suppliers:

	Selling	Advertising	Packaging and delivery	Invoicing and collection
Salaries	£25,500	£6,000	£7,000	£8,000
Space utilization	–	13.33%	66.66%	20%
Supplies	£2,000	£7,500	£7,000	£1,000

It was easy to identify the sales revenue generated by each channel of distribution (garden centres £150,000; hardware shops £50,000; department stores £100,000) and COGS are believed to be proportional to sales revenue.

Additional information available for 1997 includes:

	Garden centres	Hardware shops	Department stores
Number of orders processed	50	21	9
Number of sales calls	200	65	10
Number of advertisements	50	20	30

Required:

(a) Using the data given, along with any explicit assumptions you consider appropriate, calculate the net profit or loss of each channel using absorption principles.

(b) On the basis of your answer to (a), what scope is there for making improvements?

3.16 DISCUSSION QUESTIONS

1 Why is it useful to know how an organization's 'effort' has been spread across its activities? What problems arise in seeking to measure the 'effort' attributable to marketing activities?

2 What essential characteristic distinguishes a direct cost from an indirect cost? Can a direct cost from one perspective become an indirect cost when viewed from another perspective?

3 How can productivity be defined and measured in the context of marketing operations? What is its value to the marketing manager?

4 In what ways is ratio analysis useful in establishing the adequacy of current marketing operations?

5 How does the PIMS approach to the diagnosis of marketing performance improve upon a more traditional ratio approach?

3.17 CASE STUDIES

The following case study is included in Wilson, R.M.S. (1981), Vol. 1, pp. 240–2.

NUTS

A Tragedy in One Act

The Scene: A small store deep in the jungle of accounting logic.

The Time: Today – and tomorrow, if you are not careful.

The Cast: Joe, owner and operator of a small store-restaurant in the jungle; an accounting efficiency expert.

As the curtain rises we find Joe dusting his counter and casting admiring glances at a shiny new rack holding brightly coloured bags of peanuts. The rack is at the end of the counter. The store itself is like all small store-restaurants in the jungle of accounting logic. As Joe dusts and admires his new peanut rack, he listens almost uncomprehendingly to the earnest speeches of the accounting efficiency expert.

EFF. EX.: Joe, you said you put in these peanuts because some people ask for them, but do you realize what this rack of peanuts is costing you?

JOE: It isn't going to cost anything. Indeed it will make a profit. Sure, I had to pay £20 for a fancy rack to hold the bags, but the peanuts cost only 6 pence a bag and I sell them for 10 pence. I reckon I will sell 50 bags a week at first. It will take 10 weeks to cover the cost of the rack. After that I've got a clear profit of 4 pence a bag. The more I sell, the more I make.

EFF. EX.: That is an anticipated and completely unrealistic approach, Joe. Fortunately, modern accounting procedures permit a more accurate picture which reveals the complexities involved.

JOE: Huh?

EFF. EX.: To be precise, those peanuts must be integrated into your entire operation and be allocated their appropriate share of business over-head. They must share a proportionate part of your expenditures for rent, heat, light, equipment, depreciation, decorating, salaries for waitresses, cook . . .

JOE: The cook? What has he to do with peanuts? He doesn't even know I've got them.

EFF. EX.: Look, Joe, the cook is in the kitchen, the kitchen prepares the food, the food brings people in, and while they're in, they ask to buy peanuts. That is why you must charge a portion of the cook's wages, as well as a part of your own salary to peanut sales. This sheet contains a carefully calculated cost analysis which indicates the peanut operation should pay exactly £1,278 per year towards these general overhead costs.

JOE: The peanuts? £1,278 a year for overhead? That's NUTS!

EFF. EX.: It's really a little more than that. You also spend money each week to have the windows washed, to have the place swept in the mornings, and keep soap in the washroom. That raises the total to £1,313 per year.

JOE: But the peanut salesman said I'd make money. Put them at the end of the counter, he said, and get 4 pence a bag profit.

EFF. EX.: (*With a sniff*) He's not an accountant. Do you actually know what the portion of the counter occupied by the peanut rack is worth to you?

JOE: It is not worth anything. There is no stool there. It is just a dead spot at the end.

EFF. EX.: The modern cost picture permits no dead spots. Your counter contains 60 square feet and your counter business grosses £15,000 a year. Consequently, the square foot of space occupied by the peanut rack is worth £250 per year. Since you have taken that area away from the general counter use, you must charge the value of the space to the occupant.

JOE: You mean I've got to add £250 a year more to the peanuts?

EFF. EX.: Right. That raises their share of the general operating costs to a grand total of £1,563 per year. Now then, if you sell 50 bags of peanuts per week, these allocated costs will amount to 60 pence per bag.

JOE: (*Incredulously*) What?

EFF. EX.: Obviously, to that must be added your purchase price of 6 pence per bag, which brings the total to 66 pence. So you see, by selling peanuts at 10 pence a bag, you are losing 56 pence on every sale.

JOE: Something's crazy!

EFF. EX.: Not at all! Here are the figures. They prove your peanut operation cannot stand on its own feet.

JOE: (*Brightening*) Suppose I sell a lot of peanuts – a thousand bags a week instead of 50?

EFF. EX.: (*Tolerantly*) Joe, you don't understand the problem. If the volume of peanut sales increased, your operating costs will go up – you will have to handle more bags, with more time, more general overhead, more everything. The basic principle of accounting is firm on that subject: 'The bigger the operation the more general overhead costs must be allocated.' No, increasing the volume of sales won't help.

JOE: Okay. You are so smart. You tell me what I have to do.

EFF. EX.: (*Condescendingly*) Well – you could first reduce operating expenses.

JOE: How?

EFF. EX.: Take smaller space in an older building with cheaper rent. Cut salaries. Wash the windows fortnightly. Have the floor swept only on Thursday. Remove the soap from the washroom. This will also help you decrease the square foot value of your counter. For example, if you can cut your expenses by 50%, that will reduce the amount allocated to peanuts from £1,563 down to £781.50 per year, reducing the cost to 36 pence per bag.

JOE: (*Slowly*) That's better?

EFF. EX.: Much, much better. However, even then you would lose 26 pence per bag if you charge only 10 pence. Therefore, you must also raise your selling price. If you want a net profit of 4 pence per bag, you would have to charge 40 pence.

JOE: (*Flabbergasted*) You mean even after I cut operating costs 50% I still have to charge 40 pence for a 10 pence bag of peanuts? Nobody's that nuts about nuts! Who'd buy them?

EFF. EX.: That's a secondary consideration. The point is at 40 pence you'd be selling at a price based upon a true and proper evaluation of your then reduced costs.

JOE: (*Eagerly*) Look! I've got a better idea. Why don't I just throw the nuts out – put them in the ash can?

EFF. EX.: Can you afford it?

JOE: Sure, all I've got is about 50 bags of peanuts. I am going to lose 20 on the rack, but I will be better off out of this nutty business, and no more grief.

EFF. EX.: (*Shaking head*) Joe, it isn't quite that simple. You are IN THE PEANUT BUSINESS. The minute you throw those peanuts out, you are adding £1,563 of annual overhead to the rest of your operation. Joe – be realistic – can you afford to do that?

JOE: (*Completely crushed*) It's unbelievable! Last week I was making money. Now I'm in trouble – just because I thought peanuts on my counter would bring me some extra profit – just because I thought it would be easy to sell 50 bags of peanuts a week.

EFF. EX.: (*With raised eyebrow*) That is the reason for modern cost studies. Joe – to dispel those false illusions.

Required

Discuss this case.

Causaway Plc

Estimating Business Profitability Using Strategic Ratios
Basic Introduction to PIMS Principles and Techniques

Causaway plc is a medium sized engineering company operating from the North of England. In financial year ending March 1996 sales revenue was 200m and operating profits were £14.12m (pre-tax, pre-interest but after depreciation and all other expenses). Capital employed was £118m.

In this (as in recent years) the company's operating return on investment has been considerably short of the 22% (pre-tax, pre-interest) sought by the Board, who were becoming increasingly impatient with the slowness of the management to improve performance within the company. And they were not shy about saying so.

Among the management, opinion was divided about what to do to achieve this hurdle rate. Some members felt that the company was well capable of achieving 22% if only particular divisional managers would pull their weight in implementing the company's plans to improve all round operating efficiency. The divisional managers in question were quick to retort that it was easier for some than others. The company operated in very diverse markets for each of its main product groupings. Trading conditions differed widely and the degree to which the company's name was known and respected also varied.

The problem was compounded by the absence of the right kind of profitability data. While detailed profit contribution analysis was available on each product line no real effort had been made to allocate investment (or overhead costs). Some half-hearted previous efforts had met with scepticism because of what appeared to be arbitrary methods of allocation.

Causaway's new Chief Operating Officer, John Hunt, was not to be put off by such apparent problems. If rate of return was one of the board's major goals, then he felt that he must gain a better insight into where the company's investment was being used and if it was being used to the best effect.

More importantly he wanted to know whether more could be achieved from existing operations as they stood. Was he asking the impossible from some divisional managers – at least in the short term? In addition to accounting studies, he instituted a major examination of the trading conditions under which each of the five major product groupings had to operate. Estimates were also made for the company's market shares of leading competitors in each market area. Also product studies were carried out to test the reputation of the company's products in those markets. Divisional managers were asked for details on recent activities in new product development, technical innovation (R&D) and marketing efforts. Other details concerned production factors and human resources.

By the end of September 1997 Hunt was looking at a summary strategic profile of each of the five discrete operations in the company (see exhibit and notes).

A special management meeting was scheduled for early November to consider the full implications of this strategic analysis. Chief among Hunt's concerns was how to decide what earning power or operating return on investment he could expect from each business operation given the profiles presented to him.

Required

Study the five strategic profiles given in Exhibit 1, and rank the businesses from 1–5 on the basis of the ROI you would expect them to achieve.

Make explicit the logic behind your rankings – including the specification of any assumptions which you felt it necessary to make.

EXHIBIT 1
1996

*Causaway plc Limited
Strategic Data
Business Units*

	A	B	C	D	E
Sales (£m):	30	25	60	45	40
A Competitive position:					
● Market Share (%):	40	15	15	5	50
● Market Share Competitor A (%):	10	30	17	10	18
● Market Share Competitor B (%):	10	15	5	10	5
● Market Share Competitor C (%):	8	5	3	5	5
● Relative Quality (%):	2	18	23	–32	2
● Price Relative to Competition (%):	same	–3	same	–6	+8
B Current Strategic effort:					
● New Product/Sales (%):	30	10	20	5	10
● R & D/Sales (%)	1	1	0	1	4
● Marketing/Sales (%)	15	7	5	8	15
C Capital/production factors:					
● Operating Investments (£m):	15	9	30	36	28
● Plant & Equipment at Cost (£m):	15	6	24	21	37
● Number of Employees:	882	59	1176	816	915
% unionized:	50	30	50	60	70
● Capacity Utilisation (%):	60	70	80	87	90
● Degree of Production Integration (%):	50	60	40	55	70
D Market conditions/factors:					
● Demand (% Volume growth): (1)	2	5	10	2	1
● No. of Immediate Customers accounting for 50% of Sales:	700	3	30	60	60
● % of Demand Controlled by 4 Largest Companies:	68	65	40	30	78
● Typical Order Sizes: (2)	4	5	5	6	4

(1) Average of past three years
(2) See notes for interpretation of index

Notes
1 *Market share (%)*: Sales of the business divided by the total sales of the market which it is actually serving.
2 *Relative quality*: An index reflecting how all customers in the served market appraise our products and services vis-à-vis those available from the main competitors. A relative quality score of zero means that we and our competitors are perceived as being equivalent; below zero means we are inferior; above zero better; well above zero considerably superior.
3 *New products/sales (%)*: This attempts to measure the amount of new product development going on in a business. What percent of current sales is derived from products introduced within the last three years? It is important to remember that usually a new product requires a resource commitment beyond that of a mere product-line extension or a product improvement.
4 *Degree of production integration*: Value added is sales minus total purchases. Purchases include all bought materials, components and

energy. This measures the degree of integration within a business unit and the degree to which the business controls the production and marketing chain. If this percentage is high (above 70%) the business is not very dependent upon vendors and sub-contractors for parts and sub-assemblies. By contrast, if the percentage is low (below 40%), the business adds little value within its plant.

5 *Marketing expenses*: Include expenditures on sales force, operations, advertising and promotion, and other expenses such as market research and staff overheads associated with marketing.

6 *Investment* = operating investment i.e.

Fixed assets at net book value +
working capital (Current Assets – Current Liabilities)

7 *Purchase amount: Immediate customers*: An immediate customer in the case of an industrial company will often be the same as the end user. In the case of a consumer company the immediate customer will usually be the wholesaler or retailer. The index should be interpreted as follows:

Index

1 Less than £1	6 £7,500–£75,000
2 £1–£7.50	7 £75,000–£750,000
3 £7.50–£75	8 £750,000–£7,500,000
4 £75–£750	9 over £7,500,000
5 £750–£7,500	

8 *Employees*: Includes all employees. Includes employee equivalents (e.g. sharing of sales force) 'Overhead' employees have been allocated to each business operation on a plausible and agreed basis.

4 | Approaches to competitor analysis

4.1 LEARNING OBJECTIVES

When you have read this chapter you should be able to understand:

(a) the importance of competitor analysis;
(b) how firms can best identify against whom they are competing;
(c) how to evaluate competitive relationships;
(d) how to identify competitors' likely response profiles;
(e) the components of the competitive information system and how the information generated feeds into the process of formulating strategy.

CARTOONIST: Noel Ford

4.2 INTRODUCTION

We suggest in Chapter 5 that the 1990s have seen the emergence of a new type of consumer who is characterized by a different value system and higher expectations. At the same time, a new type of competitor appears to have emerged along with a different type of competitive environment. This new environment is characterized by:

● generally higher levels and an increasing intensity of competition;
● new and more aggressive competitors who are emerging with ever greater frequency;

- changing bases of competition as organizations search ever harder for a competitive edge;
- the geographic sources of competition are becoming wider;
- niche attacks are becoming more frequent;
- strategic alliances are becoming more frequent (and necessary);
- the pace of innovation is speeding up;
- stronger relationships and alliances with customers and distributors are becoming ever more frequent (and necessary);
- value added strategies are becoming more necessary;
- price competition is becoming ever more aggressive;
- long-term differentiation is becoming more difficult to achieve, with the result that a greater number of enterprises are finding themselves stuck in the marketing wilderness with no obvious competitive advantage;
- 'bad' competitors (i.e. those not adhering to the traditional and unspoken rules of competitive behaviour within their industries) are becoming ever more common and difficult to cope with.

The implications of these changes, both individually and collectively, are significant and demand far more from an enterprise if it is to survive and grow. Most obviously, there is a need for a much more detailed understanding of who it is that the enterprise is competing against and their capabilities. However, in coming to terms with this, the marketing planner needs to focus not just upon the 'hard' factors (e.g. their size, financial resources, manufacturing capability), but also upon the 'softer' elements (such as their managerial cultures, their priorities, their commitment to particular markets and market offerings, the assumptions they hold about themselves and their markets, and their objectives). Without this, it is almost inevitable that the marketing planner will fail to come to terms with any competitive threats.

At the same time, this new competitive environment demands a far more focused approach to marketing based upon a greater understanding of the consumer.

Competitor analysis can be defined as a set of activities which examines the comparative position of competing enterprises within a given strategic sector.

Competitor analysis seeks to:

- provide an understanding of your competitive advantage/disadvantage relative to your competitors' positions;
- help in generating insights into competitors' strategies – past, present and potential;
- give an informed basis for developing future strategies to sustain/establish advantages over your competitors.

Although the vast majority of marketing strategists acknowledge the importance of competitive analysis, it has long been recognized that less effort is typically put into detailed and formal analysis of competitors than, for example, of customers and their buying patterns. In many cases this is seemingly because marketing managers feel that they know enough about their competitors simply as the result of competing against them on a day-by-day basis. In other cases there is almost a sense of resignation, with managers believing that it is rarely possible to understand competitors in detail, and that as long as the company's performance is acceptable there is little reason to spend time collecting information. In yet others, there is only a general understanding of who it is that

FIGURE 4.1
*Attitudinal barriers to
undertaking
competitor analysis*

- Complacency
- It can't happen here
- I don't want to hear it
- We have the information already
- Preconceived assumptions

the company is competing against (see Figure 4.1). The reality, however, is that competitors represent a major determinant of corporate success and any failure to take detailed account of their strengths, weaknesses, strategies and areas of vulnerability is likely to lead not just to a sub-optimal performance, but also to an unnecessarily greater exposure to aggressive and unexpected competitive moves. Other probable consequences of failing to monitor competition include an increased likelihood of the enterprise being taken by surprise, its relegation to being a follower rather than a leader, and to a focus on the short term rather than on more fundamental long-term issues.

Figure 4.2 (opposite) gives four examples of the consequences of failing to adequately monitor the competition. (These examples are drawn from Taylor (1992, pp. 117–18).) It is apparent from these examples and the points made above that competitor analysis is not a luxury but is necessary in order:

- to survive;
- to handle slow growth;
- to cope with change;
- to exploit opportunities;
- to uncover key factors;
- to reinforce intuition;
- to improve the quality of decisions;
- to stay competitive;
- to avoid surprises.

(See Kelly (1987), pp. 10–14.)

It follows from this that competitive analysis should be a central element of the marketing planning process, with detailed attention being paid to each competitor's apparent objectives, resources and competitive stance as well as to their marketing plans and the individual elements of the marketing mix. In this way, areas of competitive strength and weakness can more readily be identified, and the results fed into the process of developing an effective marketing strategy. Better and more precise attacks can then be aimed at competitors and more effective defences erected to fight off competitors' moves. An additional benefit of competitor analysis, in certain circumstances at least, is that it can help in the process of understanding buying behaviour by identifying the particular groups or classes of customer to whom each competitor's strategy is designed to appeal. This can then in turn be used as the basis for determining the most effective probable positioning strategy for the organization.

Recognition of these points faces the strategist with the need to answer five questions:

1 Against whom are we competing?
2 What are their objectives?
3 What strategies are they pursuing and how successful are they?

FIGURE 4.2
Failure to adequately monitor the competition

Example 1

In 1978 Freddie Laker launched low-cost, no-frills transatlantic air travel which was not being provided by any of the other 12 operators. The Laker Skytrain was a huge success and Laker Airlines moved to fifth place among the 13 airlines competing across the Atlantic.

In 1979 Sir Freddie decided to compete against the established transatlantic carriers in the up-market business segment.

But . . . the competitors selectively reduced fares and Laker Airlines went out of business very quickly. Sir Freddie failed to pay sufficient attention to his competitors and their likely reaction to his new strategy.

Example 2

In 1981 Donald Burr launched low-cost, no-frills air travel within the USA which was not being provided by any other airline. The People's Express was an immediate success. In 1985 Burr decided to transform People's Express into a full-service domestic airline to compete directly with major established carriers.

But . . . the competitors selectively reduced fares on Burr's most profitable routes and People's Express quickly went out of business. Burr had paid insufficient attention to his competitors and their likely reactions to his new strategy. (He also ignored the history lesson from Laker Airways' experience.)

Example 3

In 1959 Xerox introduced the world's first plain paper copier. By 1972 Xerox owned the world market for plain paper copiers and its shares were trading at $172.

At this time Ricoh, Canon and Minolta introduced the first smaller, cheaper, plain-paper copiers. Xerox had failed to pay attention to these new competitors and lost a huge chunk of its market as a result.

By 1992 Xerox shares were trading at $25 (in 1972 dollars) and the company had become the subject of continuing speculation regarding its break-up value.

Example 4

In 1983 Reebok developed a strategy to market fashionable athletic footwear to women which generated explosive growth. Reebok relied on products being *image driven* whilst Nike's focus was on *performance-driven* products.

For five years Nike ignored Reebok's success and viewed it as an aberration. As a result, Nike lost significant market share: by 1988 Reebok's market share was 27 per cent as opposed to Nike's 23 per cent.

Nike failed to pay sufficient attention to its competitors, which led to loss of market position, layoffs, and a major management shake-up.

---

4 What strengths and weaknesses do they possess?
5 How are they likely to behave and, in particular, how are they likely to react to offensive moves?

Taken together, the answers to these five questions should provide the marketing strategist with a clear understanding of the competitive environment and, in particular, against *whom* the company is competing, and *how* they compete. An example of this appears in Figure 4.3.

It is then against the background of the picture that emerges from this analysis that the marketing strategist can begin to formulate strategy. In the example cited in Figure 4.3, for example, the central issue for Kodak revolved around the costs, risks, and possible long-term returns from penetrating new markets in instant cameras and office copiers, as opposed to sustaining and defending the company's

FIGURE 4.3
*The competitive
environment for
selected Eastman
Kodak products in the
late 1970s*

Kodak's products	Principal competitor(s)	Kodak's market position	Intensity and bases of competition	Likelihood of new entrants	Kodak's core strategy
Instant cameras and instant film	Polaroid	Challenger to a well-established leader	High and increasing with greater emphasis being placed on innovation	High	Penetration pricing to sell cameras as fast as possible to build a base for the sales of film
Photographic paper	Fuji Photo Film Co	Leader but being threatened by Fuji and other Japanese companies	High – the attack is based on lower prices and statements of quality	Medium	Share maintenance by emphasizing the quality of Kodak paper and making consumers aware that some processors do not use Kodak paper
Office copiers	Xerox, IBM, 3M	Late entrant to a highly competitive market in which Xerox held a 75 per cent share	Very high with ever greater emphasis being given to innovation, cost and service	Very high (particularly from Japanese firms)	The establishment of a separate sales and service network utilizing the firm's image and marketing capabilities in the microfilm equipment area

SOURCE: Adapted from 'The Market Mishandles a Blue Chip', *Business Week*, 20 June 1977.

position as the market leader in the photographic paper market. The principal environmental inputs to the company's strategic planning process at this time were therefore competitive forces and new technology.

Having developed a picture of the market in this way, the analysis can then be taken a step further by a compilation of each competitor's likely response profile; the various inputs needed for this are illustrated in Figure 4.4.

In using this model, the strategist begins by focusing upon the competitor's current strategy and then moves successively through an examination of competitive strengths and weaknesses; the assumptions that the competitor appears to hold about the industry and itself; and then, finally, the competitor's probable future goals and the factors which drive it. It is an understanding of these four dimensions which then allows the marketing strategist to begin compiling the detail of the response profile and to answer four principal questions:

1 Is the competitor satisfied with its current position?
2 What future moves is the competitor likely to make?
3 In which segments or areas of technology is the competitor most vulnerable?
4 What move on our part is likely to provoke the strongest retaliation by the competitor?

Against the background of the answers to those questions, the marketing strategist needs then to consider two further issues: where are we most vulnerable to any move on the part of each competitor, and what can we realistically do in order to reduce this vulnerability?

FIGURE 4.4
Identifying a competitor's response profile

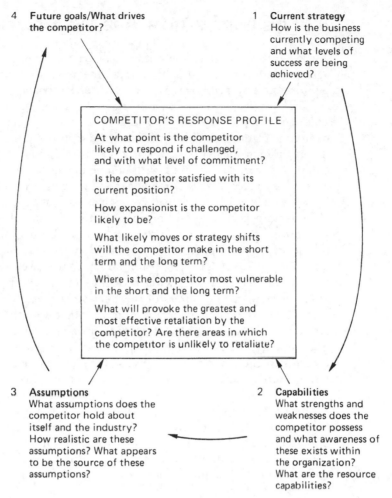

4 **Future goals/What drives the competitor?**

1 **Current strategy**
How is the business currently competing and what levels of success are being achieved?

COMPETITOR'S RESPONSE PROFILE

At what point is the competitor likely to respond if challenged, and with what level of commitment?

Is the competitor satisfied with its current position?

How expansionist is the competitor likely to be?

What likely moves or strategy shifts will the competitor make in the short term and the long term?

Where is the competitor most vulnerable in the short and the long term?

What will provoke the greatest and most effective retaliation by the competitor? Are there areas in which the competitor is unlikely to retaliate?

3 **Assumptions**
What assumptions does the competitor hold about itself and the industry? How realistic are these assumptions? What appears to be the source of these assumptions?

2 **Capabilities**
What strengths and weaknesses does the competitor possess and what awareness of these exists within the organization? What are the resource capabilities?

Porter's Approach to Competitive Structure Analysis

Undoubtedly one of the major contributions in recent years to our understanding of the ways in which the competitive environment influences strategy has been provided by Porter (1980, Ch. 1). Porter's work, which is discussed in detail in Chapter 10, is based on the idea that 'competition in an industry is rooted in its underlying economics, and competitive forces that go well beyond the established combatants in a particular industry' (1979, p. 138). He has also emphasized that the first determinant of a firm's profitability is the attractiveness of the industry in which it operates. The second determinant is competition:

> The second central question in competitive strategy is a firm's relative position within its industry. Positioning determines whether a firm's profitability is above or below the industry average. . . . The fundamental basis of above average performance in the long run is sustainable competitive advantage.

This leads Porter to suggest that the nature and intensity of competition within any industry is determined by the interaction of five key forces:

1 the threat of new entrants;
2 the power of buyers;
3 the threat of substitutes;
4 the extent of competitive rivalry;
5 the power of suppliers.

This work is, as we commented above, examined in Chapter 10 and the reader may therefore find it of value to turn to that chapter before going any further and attempting to answer the five questions referred to on p. 119.

4.3 AGAINST WHOM ARE WE COMPETING?

**Identifying
Present
Competitors
and New
Entrants**

Although the answer to the question of who it is that a company is competing against might appear straightforward, the range of actual and potential competitors faced by a company is often far broader than appears to be the case at first sight. The strategist should therefore avoid competitive myopia both by adopting a broad perspective and recognizing that, in general, companies tend to overestimate the capabilities of large competitors and either underestimate or ignore those of smaller ones. In the 1970s, for example, the large manufacturers of computers were preoccupied with competing against one another and failed for some time to recognize the emergence and growing threat in the PC market posed by what were at the time small companies such as Apple.

In a more general sense, business history is full of examples of companies which have seemingly been taken by surprise by organizations they had failed to identify as competitors, or whose competitive capability they drastically underestimated. In Chapter 9, for example, we discuss the experiences of the Swiss watch industry which was brought to its knees in the late 1960s and early 1970s by new manufacturers of inexpensive watches which incorporated digital technology, a technology that, ironically, the Swiss themselves had developed. Equally, in the reprographic market, companies such as Gestetner suddenly and unexpectedly found themselves in the 1970s having to fight aggressive new entrants to the market such as Xerox. Xerox entered this market with a new, faster, cleaner, and infinitely more convenient product to which Gestetner, together with a number of other companies in the market at the time, experienced difficulties in responding. Similarly, the British and US television and motorcycle manufacturers either failed to recognize the Japanese threat or underestimated their expansionist objectives. The result today is that neither country has a domestic manufacturing industry of any size in either of these sectors. Less drastic but in many ways equally fundamental problems have been experienced in the car industry.

It is because of examples such as these that astute strategists have long acknowledged the difficulties of defining the boundaries of an industry and have recognized that companies are more likely to be taken by surprise and hit hard by *latent* competitors than by *current* competitors whose patterns of marketing behaviour are largely predictable. It is therefore possible to see competition operating at four levels:

1 *Competition consists only of those companies offering a similar product or service to the target market, utilizing a similar technology, and exhibiting similar degrees of vertical integration.* Thus, Nestlé sees General Foods with its Maxwell House brand as a similar competitor in the instant coffee market, while Penguin sees its direct competitors in the chocolate snack bar market to be Kit-Kat's six pack, Twix and Club.

2 *Competition consists of all companies operating in the same product or service category.* Penguin's indirect competitors, for example, consist of crisps and ice-creams.

3 *Competition consists of all companies manufacturing or supplying products which deliver the same service.* Thus, long-distance coach operators compete not just against each other, but also against railways, cars, planes and motorcycles.

4 *Competition consists of all companies competing for the same spending power.* An example of this is the American motorcycle manufacturer, Harley Davidson, which does not necessarily see itself as competing directly with other motorcycle manufacturers. Instead, for many buyers it is a choice between a Harley Davidson motorcycle and a major consumer durable such as a conservatory or a boat; this is discussed in greater detail in Illustration 4.1.

Illustration 4.1: Harley Davidson and Its Perception of Competition

Harley Davidson, the last remaining American motorcycle, is seen by many as one of the icons of the design world. As a symbol of freedom and adventure, the socio-economic profile of Harley Davidson owners differs significantly from that of virtually all other motorcycle riders. The late Malcolm Forbes, the owner of *Forbes* magazine, for example, rode Harleys with his 'gang' called the Capitalist Tools and did much to promote the bike among clean-cut executives known as Rich Urban Bikers – RUBs. This image has been reinforced by the bike's appearance in numerous commercials, including a Levis' advertisement in which a monstrous Harley is ridden on to a Wall Street dealing-room floor.

Although it is acknowledged that the bikes are technically antiquated, few current or aspiring owners see this as a drawback. Most Harley owners do not actually ride them a great deal. They are, as one commentator has observed, social statements rather than forms of transport. One consequence of this is that Harley Davidson, at least in the UK, competes only very indirectly with other motorcycle manufacturers. Instead, as Steve Dennis of Harley Street, a dealership specializing in used and customized bikes, puts it: 'We're competing against conservatories and swimming pools, not other bikes.'

Source: Sunday Times, 23 September 1990

It should be apparent from this that the marketing strategist needs not only to identify those competitors who reflect the same general approach to the market, but also to consider those who 'intersect' the company in each market, who possibly approach it from a different perspective, and who ultimately might pose either a direct or an indirect threat. As part of this, he needs also to identify potential new entrants to the market and, where it appears necessary, develop contingency plans to neutralize their competitive effect. Newcomers to a market can, as Abell and Hammond (1979, p. 52) have pointed out, enter from any one of several starting points:

- They already sell to your customers, but expand their participation to include new customer functions which you currently satisfy (e.g. they initially sell a component of a computer system and expand into other system components which you supply).
- They already satisfy customer functions which you satisfy but expand their participation into your customer market from activities in other customer markets (e.g. they initially sell pumps for oil exploration only and then expand into the marine pump business where you are active).
- They already operate in an 'upstream' or 'downstream' business (e.g. Texas Instruments entered calculators from its position as a semi-conductor manufacturer, while some calculator manufacturers have integrated backwards into the manufacture of semi-conductors).
- They enter as a result of 'unrelated' diversification.

Taken together, these comments lead to two distinct viewpoints of competition: the industry point of view and the market point of view.

The Industry Perspective of Competition

The industry perception of competition is implicit in the majority of discussions of marketing strategy. Here, an industry is seen to consist of firms offering a product or class of products or services that are close substitutes for one another; a close substitute in these circumstances is seen to be a product for which there is a high cross-elasticity of demand. An example of this would be a dairy product such as butter, where if the price rises a proportion of consumers will switch to margarine. A logical starting point for competitor analysis therefore involves understanding the industry's competitive pattern, since it is this which determines the underlying competitive dynamics. A model of this process appears in Figure 4.5.

FIGURE 4.5
The competitive dynamics of an industry

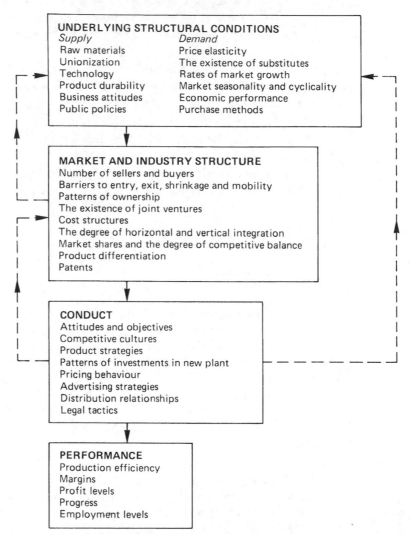

SOURCE: Adapted from Scherer (1980), p. 4

From this it can be seen that competitive dynamics are influenced initially by conditions of supply and demand. These in turn determine the *industry structure* which then influences *industry conduct* and, subsequently, *industry performance*.

Arguably the most significant single element in this model is the structure of the industry itself, and in particular the number of sellers, their relative market shares, and the degree of differentiation which exists between the competing companies and products; this is illustrated in Figure 4.6.

FIGURE 4.6
*Five industry
structure types*

		Differentiated product	Undifferentiated Product
	One	1 Pure monopoly	
Number of sellers	Few	2 Differentiated oligopoly	3 Pure oligopoly
	Many	4 Monopolistic competition	5 Pure competition

Characteristics and marketing implications

1 *Pure monopoly*: prices tend to be high, there is little advertising, service levels tend to be low, and barriers to entry often exist.
2 *Differentiated oligopoly*: differentiation is achieved by pursuing a strategy of quality, adding features or styling. The extent to which leadership or premium pricing can be achieved is a measure of the success of the strategy.
3 *Pure oligopoly*: differentiation is difficult to achieve and prices are set at the going rate. The only way in which to achieve a sustainable competitive advantage is by means of cost reductions.
4 *Monopolistic competition*: companies typically focus on particular market segments where scope exists either for minimizing the degree of direct competition or in which scope for premium pricing exists.
5 *Pure competition*: at its most extreme, there is no scope for differentiation and prices are at the same level. Advertising is only worthwhile if it can create a degree of psychological differentiation (where this is feasible, the market should be more correctly labelled as monopolistically competitive). Relative profit levels are directly determined by each company's ability to manage costs.

The interrelated issue of the number of sellers and their relative market shares has long been the focus of analysis by economists who have typically categorized an industry in terms of five types:

1 an absolute monopoly in which because of patents, licences, scale economics, or some other factor, only one firm provides the product or service;
2 a differentiated oligopoly where a few firms produce products that are partially differentiated;
3 a pure oligopoly in which a few firms produce broadly the same commodity;
4 monopolistic competition in which the industry has many firms offering a differentiated product or service;
5 pure competition in which numerous firms offer broadly the same product or service.

Although industries can at any given time be categorized in these terms, competitive structures do of course change. British Rail, for example, faced significant competition from National Express coaches after deregulation within the industry in 1980 and was forced into making a series of changes to its marketing strategy which have continued following the privatized break-up of BR. Equally, patterns of competition in many other industries such as cars, consumer electronics, and white goods, have changed dramatically in a relatively short period as the result of the growth of import penetration. In the case of white goods such as refrigerators, washing machines, tumble driers and freezers, for example, the domestically-based manufacturers such as Hoover and Hotpoint found themselves in the 1970s facing new, aggressive and often price-based competition from, among others, Zanussi, Indesit, Electrolux and Candy. The issue that then needs to be faced is how best the challenged company can respond.

Although a substantial increase in levels of import penetration are in many ways the most conspicuous causes of a change in competitive structures, a series of other factors exist which can have equally dramatic implications for the nature and bases of competition. These include:

- changes within the distribution channels – the emergence of large national DIY retailers such as Homebase, B & Q and Do-It-All, for example, has led to a shift in the balance of power between manufacturers and retailers, with the retailers adopting an ever more proactive stance regarding product acceptance, new product development, price points, and advertising support;
- changes in the supplier base;
- legislation;
- the emergence of new technology.

The Market Perspective of Competition

As an alternative to the industry perspective of competition, which takes as its starting point companies making the same product or offering the same service, we can focus on companies which try to satisfy the same customer needs or which serve the same customer groups. Theodore Levitt has long been a strong advocate of this perspective and it was this which was at the heart of his classic article 'Marketing Myopia'. In this article, Levitt (1960, pp. 45–56), pointed to a series of examples of organizations which had failed to recognize how actual and potential customers viewed the product or service being offered. Thus in the case of railways, the railway companies concentrated on competing with one another and in doing this failed to recognize that, because customers were looking for transport, they compared the railways with planes, buses and cars. The essence of the market perspective of competition therefore involves giving full recognition to the broader range of products or services which are capable of satisfying customer needs. This should, in turn, lead to the marketing strategist identifying a broader set of actual and potential competitors and adopting a more effective approach to long-run market planning. See Illustration 4.2.

4.4 EVALUATING COMPETITIVE RELATIONSHIPS AND ANALYSING HOW ORGANIZATIONS COMPETE

Any analysis of *how* firms compete falls into four parts:

1 What is each competitor's current strategy?
2 How are competitors performing?
3 What are their strengths and weaknesses?
4 What can we expect from each competitor in the future?

However, before moving on to the detail of these four areas, the strategist should spend time identifying what is already known about each competitor. There are numerous examples of companies which have collected information on competitors only to find out at a later stage that this knowledge already existed within the organization but that, for one reason or another, it had not been analysed or disseminated. In commenting on this Davidson (1987, p. 133) has suggested that:

> Recorded data tends not to be analysed over time, and often fails to cross functional barriers. Observable data is typically recorded on a haphazard basis, with little evaluation. Opportunistic data is not always actively sought or disseminated.

Illustration 4.2: Substitutes for Aluminium

The need to have a clear understanding of who exactly your competitors are and the nature of their strengths and weaknesses is illustrated in the table below. In this we list some of the alternatives to aluminium. Although not all of the materials listed in the left-hand column are alternatives in each and every situation in which aluminium is used, the table goes some way towards illustrating how an overly narrow competitive perspective could well lead to an organization's being taken by surprise as customers switch to the alternatives.

Material	*Advantages*	*Drawbacks*
Mild steel	Very cheap Widely available	Weight Rusts easily
Low-chrome ferritic stainless steel	Similar price Widely available	Weight Rusts in sea water
Titanium	Strength (especially at temperature) Corrosion resistance	Cost Processing (not easily extrudable)
Magnesium	Very lightweight	Vulnerable to fire
Polystyrene unplasticated PVC	Lightweight Reasonably cheap	Low strength No temperature/fire resistance
ABS, nylon engineering plastics	Lightweight Strong	Cost
Wood	Cheap Widely available	Variable quality Rots
Composites		
Aluminium MMCs	Stiffer Stronger Harder	Extra cost Processing difficulties
Fibre reinforced plastics	Lighter for quality Stiffness/strength	Can lack toughness Extra cost

This failure to collect, disseminate or make full use of competitive information is, for the majority of organizations, a perennial problem and often leads to the same information being collected more than once. It is, however, an issue that we discuss in greater detail at a later stage, and at this point we will therefore do no more than draw attention to it.

In attempting to arrive at a detailed understanding of competitive relationships, it is essential that each competitor is analysed separately, since any general analysis provides the strategist with only a partial understanding of competitors, and tells little either about potential threats which might emerge, or opportunities which can be exploited. It is worth remembering, however, that what competitors have done in the past can often provide a strong indication of what they will do in the future. This is particularly the case when previous strategies have been conspicuously successful. Companies such as Mars, for example, have traditionally pursued an objective of market leadership, while the Japanese are often willing to accept long pay-back periods. Recognition of points such as these should then be used to guide the ways in which strategy is developed.

Other factors that need to be borne in mind include:

- patterns of investment in plant;
- links with other competitors;
- patterns of advertising expenditure;
- relative cost positions;
- major changes in the senior management structure and in particular the appointment of a new chief executive who might act as an agent for change.

Identifying Strategic Groups

In the majority of industries competitors can be categorized, at least initially, on the basis of the similarities and differences that exist in the strategies being pursued. The strategist can then begin to construct a picture of the market showing the strategic groups that exist; for our purposes here, a strategic group can be seen to consist of those firms within the market which are following a broadly similar strategy. An example of how strategic groupings can be identified is illustrated in Figure 4.7.

FIGURE 4.7
Strategic groups in the construction industry

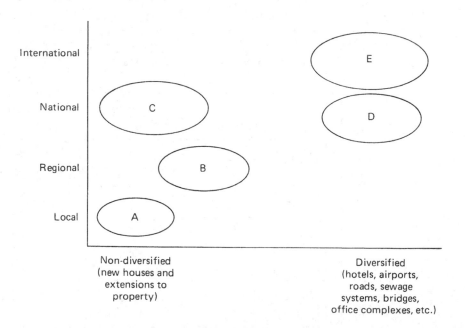

Having identified strategic groups in this way, the strategist then needs to identify the relative position and strength of each competitor. This can be done in one of several ways, including the categorizing of firms on the basis of whether their position within the market overall and within the strategic group is dominant, strong, favourable, tenable, weak or non-viable. Having done this, the strategist needs to consider the bases of any competitive advantages that exist; this is illustrated in Figure 4.8.

The experiences of many companies suggest that the easiest starting point from which to improve an organization's competitive position is Level 3, since this can often be achieved by good management. One example of a company which did this with considerable success was Beecham with its Lucozade brand.

FIGURE 4.8
The five types of competitive status and the implications for competitive advantage

Level	Competitive status	Examples
1	One or more sizeable advantages	Honda, Sony, Seiko & Coca Cola
2	A series of small advantages which combine to form one large advantage	McDonald's
3	Advantages exist but these are either not recognized or not exploited fully	
4	No obvious or sustainable competitive advantages	Petrol retailers, estate agents and high street banks
5	Competitive disadvantages because of the organization's limited size, inflexibility, inefficient manufacturing practices, distribution networks, cost structures, culture, lack of skills, or poor image	Eastern European car manufacturers

SOURCE: Adapted from Davidson (1987), p. 160

There are several points that emerge from identifying strategic groups in this way. The first is that the height of the barriers to entry and exit can vary significantly from one group to another. The second is that the choice of a strategic group determines which companies are to be the firm's principal competitors. Recognizing this, a new entrant would then have to develop a series of competitive advantages to overcome, or at least to neutralize, the competitive advantages of others in the group.

There is, of course, competition not just *within* strategic groups but also *between* them, since not only will target markets develop or contract over time and hence prove to be either more or less attractive to other firms, but customers might not fully recognize major differences in the offers of each group. One consequence of this is that there is likely to be a degree of comparison buying across groups, something which again argues the case for the marketing strategist to adopt a market, rather than an industry, perspective of competition.

Although in Figure 4.7 we have made use of just two dimensions in plotting strategic groupings, a variety of other factors can typically be expected to be used to differentiate between companies and to help in the process of identifying group membership. A summary of these characteristics appears in Figure 4.9.

The particular relevance to any given industry of these characteristics is in practice influenced by several factors, the most significant of which are the history and development of the industry, the types of environmental forces at work, the

FIGURE 4.9
Some characteristics for identifying strategic groups

- *Size* and relative share
- The extent of *product* or *service diversity*
- The degree of *geographic coverage*
- The number and type of *market segments served*
- The type of *distribution channels* used
- The *branding* philosophy
- Product or service *quality*
- *Market position* (leader or follower)
- *Technological position* (leader or follower)
- *R & D capability*
- *Performance*
- *Cost structure* and behaviour
- Patterns of *ownership*
- Organizational *culture*
- The degree of *vertical integration*
- *Reputation*

SOURCE: Adapted from Johnson and Scholes (1988), p. 75

nature of the competitive activities of the various firms, and so on. It should be evident from this that each company does therefore have a different strategic make-up which needs to be profiled separately. Often, however, a strategy proves difficult to describe since it encompasses so many different dimensions, but Abell and Hammond (1979, p. 53) have outlined a useful framework for thinking about the strategic decision process:

- How does the competitor define the business in terms of customer groups, customer functions, and technologies, and how vertically integrated is he? And at a lower level of aggregation, how is he segmenting the market and which segments are being pursued?
- What mission does this business have in his overall portfolio of businesses? Is it being managed for sales growth? market share? net profit? ROI? cash? What goals does he appear to have for each major segment of the business?
- What is his marketing mix, manufacturing policy, R & D policy, purchasing policy, physical distribution policy, etc.?
- What size are his budgets and how are they allocated?

In so far as it is possible to generalize, it is the third of these areas in which marketing managers find it most easy to collect information. This should not, however, be seen as a reason for ignoring the other three areas, since it is here that insights into what really drives the competition can best be gained.

This leads us to a position in which we are able to begin to construct a detailed list of the areas in which we need to collect competitive information. In the case of each competitor's current performance, this list includes sales, growth rates and patterns, market share, profit, profitability (return on investment), margins, net income, investment patterns and cash flow. Other areas to which attention needs to be paid include the identification of the importance of each market sector in which the competitor is operating, since this allows the marketing strategist to probe the areas of weakness or least concern at the minimum of risk.

The Character of Competition

The final area that we need to consider when examining how firms compete is what can loosely be termed 'the character of competition'. Because competition within a market is influenced to a very high degree by the nature of customer behaviour, the character of competition not only takes many forms but is also likely to change over time. One fairly common way of examining the character of competition is therefore by means of an analysis of the changes taking place in the

FIGURE 4.10
A comparison of the value added components across the product life cycle

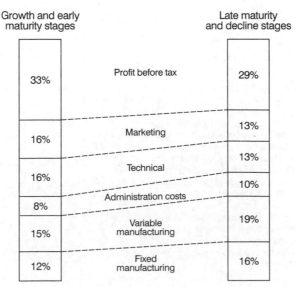

SOURCE: Adapted from Abell and Hammond (1979), p. 59

composition of *value added* by different firms. (The term 'value added' is used to describe the amount by which selling prices are greater than the cost of providing the bought out goods or services embodied in market offerings.) An analysis of changes in the value added component can therefore give the strategist an understanding of the relative importance of such factors as product and process development, selling, after-sales service, price, and so on, as the product moves through the life cycle. See Figure 4.10 for an example of this for a hypothetical product.

The marketing strategist can also arrive at a measure of the character of competition by considering the extent to which each competitor develops new total industry demand (primary demand) or quite simply competes with others for a share of existing demand (selective demand). When a competitor's objective is the stimulation of primary demand, it is likely that efforts will focus upon identifying and developing new market segments. Conversely, when a competitor concentrates upon stimulating selective demand, the focus shifts to an attempt to satisfy existing customers more effectively than other companies. The obvious consequence of this is that the intensity of competition on a day-to-day basis is likely to increase significantly.

4.5 IDENTIFYING COMPETITORS' OBJECTIVES

Having identified the organization's principal competitors and their strategies, we need then to focus upon each competitor's objectives. In other words, what drives each competitor's behaviour? A starting point in arriving at an answer to this is to assume that each competitor will aim for profit maximization either in the short term or the long term. In practice, of course, maximization is an unrealistic objective which for a wide variety of reasons many companies are willing to sacrifice. A further assumption can be made – that each competitor has a variety of objectives, each of which has a different weight. These objectives might typically include cash flow, technological leadership, market share growth, service leadership, or overall market leadership. Gaining an insight into this mix of objectives allows the strategist to arrive at tentative conclusions regarding how a competitor will respond to a competitive thrust. A firm pursuing market share growth is likely to react far more quickly and aggressively to a price cut or to a substantial increase in advertising than a firm which is aiming for, say, technological leadership.

The differences that exist between the objectives of companies has been referred to by a variety of writers, including Doyle, Saunders and Wong (1986) who have contrasted the objectives typically pursued by Japanese and British firms. See Illustration 4.3 for a discussion of their work.

In a general sense, however, company objectives (as is pointed out in Chapter 6) are influenced by a wide variety of factors, but particularly the organization's size, history, culture, and the breadth of the operating base. Where, for example, a company is part of a larger organization, a competitive thrust always runs the risk of leading to retaliation by the parent company on what might appear to be a disproportionate scale. Conversely, the parent company may see an attack on one of its divisions as being a nuisance, but little more, and not bother to respond in anything other than a cursory fashion. This has been discussed in some detail by Rothschild (1989, Ch. 5) who argues that the potentially most dangerous competitive move involves attacking a global company for which this is the only business.

It follows that the marketing strategist should give explicit consideration to the relative importance of each market to a competitor in order to understand the probable level of commitment that exists. By doing this, it is possible to estimate the level of effort that each competitor would then logically make in order to

Illustration 4.3: The Difference Between Japanese and British Company Objectives

In 1986, Doyle, Saunders and Wong published the results of a study in which they compared the objectives and strategies of 15 leading Japanese companies operating within the United Kingdom with those of their British counterparts. Their findings proved to be illuminating, and highlighted some of the principal causes of Japanese success. In commenting subsequently on their research, Saunders (1987, pp. 24–26) has given emphasis to several points:

> There was a striking contrast between these two national groups in the clarity of their strategic thinking, and in their determination to achieve the objectives that they set themselves. Indeed, only one-third of the British (compared with two-thirds of the Japanese) even believed themselves to be good at sales and marketing. When entering a new market, the British usually arrived late, and few had a strong commitment to it. Two-thirds of UK companies gave defensive reasons for entry: 'We had to in order to survive'. Several admitted that they 'had never really thought it out'. In contrast, the Japanese were much more professional: over 70 per cent said that their moves were 'part of a planned global expansion', or related to the 'potential of the UK market'. Once in the market, the British lack of commitment to beating the competition was again striking. Some 87 per cent of the Japanese gave 'aggressive growth' or 'market domination' as their goal, but only 20 per cent of the British thought these targets applied to them. Maintenance of the status quo or the prevention of decline were the most typical British objectives. Short term profit was also much more important to the UK companies (93 per cent) than to the Japanese (40 per cent). The British were willing to allow their market position to be eroded in order to bolster short term profitability.

He went on to emphasize the difference that exists between the strategic focus, customer targets, competitor targets, differential advantages, management of the marketing mix, and approaches to organization and implementation.

In the case of strategic focus, for example, the Japanese concentrated on stimulating primary demand, entering newly emerging market segments and building market share by weaning customers away from their competitors. By contrast, the British tended to focus on cost cutting, range reduction and rationalization as ways of preventing margin erosion.

In the area of customer targets, equally significant differences emerged with the Japanese concentrating on high-potential segments while the British either made little attempt to focus their efforts or positioned themselves at the lower and cheaper end of the market.

It was perhaps because of this that only 20 per cent of Japanese companies in the study saw European firms as their major rivals; the remainder saw their main competition in the UK coming from other Japanese groups. This was in turn reflected in the recognition by many British companies of their lack of skill at differentiating themselves from the competition. By contrast, 87 per cent of the Japanese pointed to superior quality, reliability and customer service as their bases of differentiation and competitive advantage.

Source: Saunders, J., 'Marketing and Competitive Success' in The Marketing Book, *edited by Baker, M. (1987), Heinemann. See also: Doyle, P., Saunders, J. and Wong, V. (1986), 'A Comparative Study of Japanese Marketing Strategies in the British Market',* Journal of International Business Studies, *17(1), Spring.*

defend its position. Several factors are likely to influence this level of commitment, the five most important of which are likely to be:

1 the proportion of company profits which this market sector generates;
2 the managerial perceptions of the market's growth opportunities;
3 the levels of profitability that exist currently and which are expected to exist in the future;
4 any interrelationships between this and any other product or market sector in which the organization operates;
5 managerial cultures – in some companies, for example, any threat will be responded to aggressively almost irrespective of whether it is cost effective.

As a general rule of thumb, therefore, competitive retaliation will be strong whenever the company feels its core business is being attacked. Recognizing this, the marketing strategist should concentrate on avoiding areas which are likely to lead to this sort of response, unless of course the target has a strong strategic rationale. This sort of issue is discussed in detail in Chapter 10.

4.6 IDENTIFYING AND EVALUATING COMPETITORS' STRENGTHS AND WEAKNESSES

By this stage it should be apparent that the identification and evaluation of competitors' strengths and weaknesses is at the very heart of a well-developed competitive strategy. The marketing strategist should as a first step therefore concentrate upon collecting information under a number of headings as a prelude to a full comparative assessment. These include:

- sales;
- market share;
- cost and profit levels and how they appear to be changing over time (discussed in some detail in Chapter 12);
- cash flows;
- return on investment;
- investment patterns;
- production processes;
- levels of capacity utilization;
- organizational culture;
- products and the product portfolio;
- product quality;
- the size and pattern of the customer base;
- the levels of brand loyalty;
- dealers and distribution channels;
- marketing and selling capabilities;
- operations and physical distribution;
- financial capabilities;
- management capabilities and attitudes to risk;
- human resources, their capability and flexibility;
- previous patterns of response;
- ownership patterns and, in the case of divisionalized organizations, the expectations of corporate management.

The signs of competitive strength in a company's position are likely to be:

- Important core competences;
- Strong market share (or a leading market share);

- A pace-setting or distinctive strategy;
- Growing customer base and customer loyalty;
- Above-average market visibility;
- In a favourably situated strategic group;
- Concentrating on fastest-growing market segments;
- Strongly differentiated products;
- Cost advantages;
- Above-average profit margins;
- Above-average technological and innovational capability;
- A creative, entrepreneurially alert management;
- In a position to capitalize on opportunities.

Obtaining this sort of information typically proves to be more difficult in some instances than in others. Industrial markets, for example, rarely have the same wealth of published data that is commonly available in consumer markets. This should not, however, be used as an excuse for not collecting the information, but rather emphasizes the need for a clearly developed competitive information system which channels information under a wide variety of headings to a central point. This information needs to be analysed and disseminated as a prelude to being fed into the strategy process.

The sources of this information will obviously vary from industry to industry, but will include most frequently the sales force, trade shows, industry experts, the trade press, distributors, suppliers and, perhaps most importantly, customers. Customer information can be gained in several ways, although periodically a firm may find it of value to conduct primary research among customers, suppliers and distributors to arrive at a profile of competitors within the market. An example of this appears in Figure 4.11 where current and potential buyers have been asked to rate the organization and its four major competitors on a series of attributes. A similar exercise can then be conducted among suppliers and distributors in order to build up a more detailed picture.

FIGURE 4.11
The comparative assessment of competitors

Significant buying factors	Our company	Competitors		
		1	2	3
Products				
Product design	Good	Exc	Fair	Good
Product quality	Good	Exc	Fair	Exc
Product performance	Good	Good	Fair	Good
Breadth of product line	Fair	Fair	Poor	Good
Depth of product line	Fair	Fair	Poor	Good
Reliability	Good	Exc	Fair	Exc
Running costs	Fair	Good	Equal	Good
Promotion and pricing				
Advertising/sales promotion	Fair	Exc	Fair	Good
Image and reputation	Fair	Exc	Fr/Pr	Exc
Product literature	Poor	Exc	Poor	Good
Price	Equal	Fair	Good	Equal
Selling and distribution				
Sales force calibre	Fair	Good	Poor	Good
Sales force experience/knowledge	Fair	Good	Fair	Exc
Geographical coverage	Good	Good	Poor	Good
Sales force/customer relations	Fair	Exc	Poor	Exc
Service				
Customer service levels	Fair	Exc	Poor	Exc
Performance against promise	Fair	Exc	Poor	Exc

The classification of factors from excellent (Exc) to poor should be determined by marketing intelligence, including studies of the perceptions of current and potential buyers, as well as those of suppliers and distributors.

A variation on this approach is shown in Figures 4.12 and 4.13. In the first of these, a list of characteristics which can be associated with success in the sector in question has been identified and each main competitor (including ourselves – ABC Co) has been evaluated on each of the characteristics. From the total scores it appears that Rival 2 is the strongest competitor, with Rival 1 being only marginally weaker than ABC Co. However, while the relative strengths of each competing enterprise are clearly visible in Figure 4.12, there is no indication of the relative importance of each of the key success factors. For example, it may be that relative cost position and ability to compete on price are the most important factors for competitive success within this sector, with technological skills, advertising effectiveness and distribution being relatively unimportant. These priorities can be indicated by weights, as in Figure 4.13. From this it is now evident that Rival 1 is the market leader, followed by Rival 2 which is ahead of ABC Co. These profiles indicate quite clearly the relative importance of key success factors and the relative strength of each competitor on each of those factors.

FIGURE 4.12
Unweighted competitive strength assessment

Rating scale: 1 = Very weak; 10 = Very strong

Key success factor/strength measure	ABC Co	Rival 1	Rival 2	Rival 3	Rival 4
Quality/product performance	8	5	10	1	6
Reputation/image	8	7	10	1	6
Raw material access/cost	2	10	4	5	1
Technological skills	10	1	7	3	8
Advertising effectiveness	9	4	10	5	1
Distribution	9	4	10	5	1
Financial strength	5	10	7	3	1
Relative cost position	5	10	3	1	4
Ability to compete on price	5	7	10	1	4
Unweighted overall strength rating	61	58	71	25	32

FIGURE 4.13
Weighted competitive strength assessment

Rating scale: 1 = Very weak; 10 = Very strong

Key success factor/strength measure	Weight	ABC Co	Rival 1	Rival 2	Rival 3	Rival 4
Quality/product performance	0.10	8/0.80	5/0.50	10/1.00	1/0.10	6/0.60
Reputation/image	0.10	8/0.80	7/0.70	10/1.00	1/0.10	6/0.60
Raw material access/cost	0.10	2/0.20	10/1.00	4/0.40	5/0.50	1/0.10
Technological skills	0.05	10/0.50	1/0.05	7/0.35	3/0.15	8/0.40
Advertising effectiveness	0.05	9/0.45	4/0.20	10/0.50	5/0.25	1/0.05
Distribution	0.05	9/0.45	4/0.20	10/0.50	5/0.25	1/0.05
Financial strength	0.10	5/0.50	10/1.00	7/0.70	3/0.30	1/0.10
Relative cost position	0.30	5/1.50	10/3.00	3/0.90	1/0.30	4/1.20
Ability to compete on price	0.15	5/0.75	7/1.05	10/1.50	1/0.15	4/0.60
Sum of weights	1.00					
Weighted overall strength rating		5.95	7.70	6.85	2.10	3.70

Competitive Product Portfolios

In many cases, one of the most useful methods of gaining an insight into a competitor's strengths, weaknesses and general level of capability is by means of portfolio analysis. The techniques of portfolios analysis, which include the Boston Consulting Group matrix, are by now well developed and are discussed in detail in Chapter 9. The reader might therefore find it of value at this stage to turn to pages 311–20 in order to understand more fully the comments below.

Having plotted each major competitor's portfolio, the marketing strategist needs to consider a series of questions:

1 What degree of internal balance exists within each portfolio? Which competitors, for example, appear to have few, if any, 'cash cows' but a surfeit of 'question marks' or 'dogs'? Which of the competitors appears to have one or more promising 'stars' which might in the future pose a threat?
2 What are the likely cash flow implications for each competitor's portfolio? Does it appear likely, for example, that he will be vulnerable in the near future because of the cash demands of a disproportionate number of 'question marks' and 'stars'?
3 What trends are apparent in each portfolio? A tentative answer to this question can be arrived at by plotting the equivalent growth-share display for a period three to five years earlier, and superimposing on this the current chart. A third display that reflects the likely development of the portfolio over the next few years, assuming present policies are maintained, can in turn be superimposed on this to show the direction and rate of travel of each product or strategic business unit (SBU).
4 Which competitors' products look suited for growth and which for harvesting? What are the implications for us and in what ways might we possibly pre-empt any competitive actions?
5 Which competitor appears to be the most vulnerable to an attack? Which competitor looks likely to pose the greatest threat in the future?

In plotting a competitor's portfolio the marketing strategist is quite obviously searching for areas of weakness which subsequently can be exploited. In commenting on this, Davidson (1987, pp. 139–40) identifies 17 major sources of vulnerability. A summary of his ideas appears in Illustration 4.4.

Illustration 4.4: What Makes a Competitor Vulnerable?

A knowledge of a competitor's weaknesses can often be used to great effect by an astute marketing strategist. According to Davidson (1987, pp. 139–40), the sorts of factor that make a competitor vulnerable include:

- a lack of cash;
- low margins;
- poor growth;
- high cost operations or distribution;
- overdependence on one market;
- overdependence on one account;
- strength in falling sectors;
- short-term orientation;
- people problems;
- taking their eyes off the ball;
- predictability;
- product or service obsolescence/weakness;
- high market share;
- low market share;
- premium price positioning;
- slow moving/bureaucratic structures;
- fiscal year fixation.

Source: J. H. Davidson, 1987, Offensive Marketing, *Penguin*

At this point it is perhaps worth uttering a word of caution. The marketing strategist should not of course limit competitive analysis just to a series of marketing factors, but should also focus upon other areas, including financial and production measures. In this way it is possible to identify far more clearly which competitors within the industry are relatively weak and might therefore be vulnerable to a price attack or a takeover. Equally, it can identify which competitors within the industry should, by virtue of their financial strength or production flexibility, be avoided.

4.7 IDENTIFYING COMPETITORS' LIKELY RESPONSE PROFILES

Although a knowledge of a competitor's size, objectives and capability (strengths and weaknesses) can provide the strategist with a reasonable understanding of possible responses to company moves such as price cuts, the launch of new products, and so on, other factors need to be examined. One of the most important of these is the organization's culture, since it is this which ultimately determines how the firm will do business and hence how it will act in the future.

The issue of how a competitor is likely to behave in the future has two components. First, how is a competitor likely to respond to the general changes taking place in the external environment and, in particular, in the market-place? Second, how is that competitor likely to respond to specific competitive moves that we, or indeed any other company, might make? For some companies at least there is also a third question which needs to be considered: how likely is it that the competitor will initiate an aggressive move, and what form might this move be most likely to take? In posing questions such as these we are trying to determine where each competitive company is the most vulnerable, where it is the strongest, where the most appropriate battleground is likely to be, and how, if at all, it will respond.

Kotler (1988, p. 247) identifies four common reaction profiles among competitors:

1 *The laid-back competitor.* Some competitors do not react quickly or strongly to a given competitor move. They may feel that their customers are loyal; they may be harvesting the business; they may be slow in noticing the initiative; they may lack the funds to react. The firm must try to assess the reasons for the competitor's laid-back behavior.

2 *The selective competitor.* A competitor might react to certain types of assault and not to others. It might, for example, always respond to price cuts in order to signal that these are futile. But it might not respond to advertising expenditure increases, believing these to be less threatening. Knowing what a key competitor reacts to gives a clue as to the most feasible types of attack.

3 *The tiger competitor.* This company reacts swiftly and strongly to any assault on its terrain. Thus P & G does not let a new detergent come easily into the market. A tiger competitor is signalling that another firm had better avoid any attack because the defender is going to fight to the finish if attacked. It is always better to attack a sheep than a tiger.

4 *The stochastic competitor.* Some competitors do not exhibit a predictable reaction pattern. Such a competitor might or might not retaliate on any particular occasion, and there is no way to foresee what it will do based on its economics, history, or anything else.

This general theme has, in turn, been developed by Bruce Henderson (1982) of the Boston Consulting Group who, in discussing competition, argues that much depends on the competitive equilibrium. Henderson's comments on this have been summarized by Kotler (1988, p. 247) in the following way:

1 *If competitors are nearly identical and make their living in the same way, then their competitive equilibrium is unstable.*
There is likely to be perpetual conflict in industries where competitive ability is at parity. This would describe 'commodity industries' where sellers have not found any major way to differentiate their costs or their offers. In such cases, the competitive equilibrium would be upset if any firm lowers its price. This is a strong temptation, especially for a competitor with over-capacity. This explains why price wars frequently break out in these industries.

2 *If a single major factor is the critical factor, then competitive equilibrium is unstable.*
This would describe industries where cost differentiation opportunities exist through economies of scale, advanced technology, experiences curve learning, etc. In such industries, any company that achieves a cost breakthrough can cut its price and win market share at the expense of other firms which could only defend their market shares at great cost. Price wars frequently break out in these industries as a function of cost breakthroughs.

3 *If multiple factors may be critical factors, then it is possible for each competitor to have some advantage and be differentially attractive to some customers. The more the multiple factors that may provide an advantage, the more the number of competitors who can coexist. Each competitor has his competitive segment defined by the preference for the factor trade-offs that he offers.*
This would describe industries where many opportunities exist for differentiating quality, service, convenience, and so on. If customers also place different values on these factors, then many firms can coexist through niching.

4 *The fewer the number of competitive variables that are critical, the fewer the number of competitors.*
If only one factor is critical, then no more than two or three competitors are likely to coexist. Conversely, the larger the number of competitive variables, the larger the number of competitors, but each is likely to be smaller in its absolute size.

5 *A ratio of 2 to 1 in market share between any two competitors seems to be the equilibrium point at which it is neither practical nor advantageous for either competitor to increase or decrease share.*

The Significance of Costs

In attempting to come to terms with the structure of competition, the marketing strategist should also take account of *cost structures* and *cost behaviour*. Cost structure is usually defined as the ratio of variable to fixed costs and is typically capable of exerting a significant influence upon competitive behaviour. In businesses where, for example, the fixed costs are high, profits are sensitive to volume. Companies are therefore forced to behave in such a way that plants operate as near to full capacity as possible. Where demand is price sensitive, the industry is likely to be characterized by periodic bouts of aggressive price wars. Where, however, it is the case that variable costs are high, profits are influenced far more directly by changes in margins. Recognizing this, the marketing strategist needs to focus upon differentiating the product in such a way that prices and hence margins can be increased.

The second cost dimension is that of its behaviour over time and in particular how the organization can make use of learning and experience effects, as well as scale effects; these are discussed in detail in Chapter 12.

The Influence of the Product Life Cycle

Competitive behaviour is typically affected in several ways by the stage reached on the product life cycle (PLC). Although the product life cycle (see Chapter 9) is seen principally as a model of product and market evolution, it can also be used as a framework for examining probable competitive behaviour. Used in this way, it can help the strategist to anticipate changes in the character of competition. In the early stages of the life cycle, for example, advertising and promotion is generally high, and prices and margins are able to support this. The natural growth of the market allows firms to avoid competing in an overtly direct way. As maturity approaches and the rate of growth slows, firms are forced into more direct forms of competition, a situation which is in turn exacerbated by the often generally greater number of companies operating within the market. This greater intensity of competition manifests itself in several ways, but most commonly in a series of price reductions. The role of advertising changes as greater emphasis is placed upon the search for differentiation. In the final stages, some firms opt to leave the market, while others engage in perhaps even greater price competition as they fight for a share of a declining sales curve. It follows from this that the PLC is yet one more of the myriad of factors that the marketing strategist needs to consider in coming to terms with competitors.

4.8 THE COMPETITIVE INFORMATION SYSTEM (CIS)

It should be apparent from the discussion so far that the need for an effective competitive intelligence system (CIS) is paramount. In establishing such a system, there are five principal steps:

1 setting up the system and deciding what information is needed;
2 collecting the data;
3 analysing and evaluating the data;
4 disseminating the conclusions;
5 incorporating these conclusions into the subsequent strategy and feeding back the results so that the information system can be developed further.

A framework for developing a CIS is given in Figure 4.14.

FIGURE 4.14
Approaches to competitor analysis

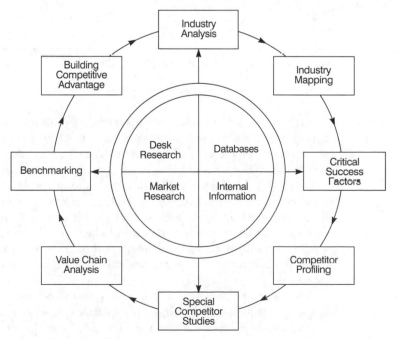

SOURCE: Harbridge House

The mechanics of an effective CIS are straightforward, as Davidson (1987, p. 134) has pointed out:

- Select key competitors to evaluate. Focus on three or four per market at most.
- Select and brief data collectors in each department. This should include people in sales, purchasing, engineering, marketing, R & D and finance.
- Apply the right resource levels to the task. It is usually worthwhile having at least a part-time competitive analyst, to chase, coordinate and evaluate competitive data.
- Insist on regular returns from data collectors.
- Publish regular tactical and strategic reports on competition. The tactical ones could be fortnightly and widely circulated. The strategic ones would be less frequent, perhaps quarterly, and go to senior management only.

The sources of data are, as we observed at an earlier stage, likely to vary significantly from one industry to another. However, a useful framework for data collection involves categorizing information on the basis of whether it is recorded, observed or opportunistic. The major sources of data under each of these headings are shown in Figure 4.15.

FIGURE 4.15
The major sources of competitive data

Recorded data	Observable data	Opportunistic data
Market research	Competitors' pricing	Raw material suppliers
Secondary data sources, e.g. Mintel	Promotions	Equipment suppliers
Business press	Patent applications	Trade shows
Trade press	Competitive advertising	Customers
Technical journals	Planning applications	Packaging suppliers
BRAD (British Rate & Data)	Sales force feedback	Distributors
Government sector reports, e.g. Monopolies Commission	Buying competitors' products and taking them apart to determine costs of production and manufacturing methods	Sub-contractors
Stockbrokers' reports		Internal newsletters
Credit reports		Disgruntled employees
Annual reports		Poaching competitors' employees
Public documents		Conferences
		Placing advertisements and holding interviews for jobs that do not exist in order to entice competitors' employees to spill the beans
		Private investigators

SOURCE: Adapted from Davidson (1987), p. 134

With regard to the question of precisely what information is needed, this will of course vary from one industry to another and from one company to another. It is, nevertheless, possible to identify with relative ease the sorts of headings under which information should be gathered: these are identified in Figure 4.16.

Given this information, the strategist should be able to determine far more precisely which competitors are operating in the same strategic group. From here, he can then go on to decide far more readily which competitors to attack and when and the basis on which this should be done. Equally, he is also able to decide which competitors are to be avoided. Although these issues are discussed in some detail in Chapter 10, there are several points that can usefully be made at this stage.

Assuming that the company is to go on the offensive, the strategist needs to begin by deciding *which competitors* to attack. In essence, this represents a choice between strong and weak competitors, close and distant competitors, and good and bad competitors.

FIGURE 4.16
What companies need to know about their competitors

Although it is not possible to develop an exhaustive list of headings under which competitive information should be collected, these are nine principal areas to which the strategist should pay attention on a regular basis:

1 **Sales**
Number of units sold
Sales by product line
Sales trends
Market shares
Share trends

2 **Customers**
Customer profiles
Buying motives
Patterns of usage
New accounts/buyers
Lost accounts/buyers
Proportion of repeat business/degree of brand loyalty
Depth of brand loyalty
Identity and image among buyers
Satisfaction levels with the product's design, performance, quality and reliability
The existence of special relationships

3 **Products**
Breadth and depth of the product range
Comparative product performance levels
New product policies
Investment in R & D
New product introduction and modifications
Size assortments
New packaging

4 **Advertising and promotion**
Expenditure levels and patterns
Effectiveness
Product literature
Sales promotions
Customers' brand preferences
Image and levels of recognition

5 **Distribution and sales force**
Types of distribution network used
Relationships and the balance of power
Cost structures
Flexibility
Special terms and the existence of agreements
Dealer objectives
Distributors' performance levels

Size, calibre and experience of the sales force
Sales force customer coverage
Levels of technical assistance available
Dealer support levels and capabilities
Stock levels
Shelf facings
After-sales service capabilities
Customer service philosophy
Location of warehouses
Degree of customer satisfaction

6 **Price**
Cost levels
Cost structure
List prices and discounts by product and customer type
Special terms

7 **Finance**
Performance levels
Margins
Depth of financial resources
Patterns of ownership and financial flexibility

8 **Management**
Objectives (short and long term)
Philosophy and culture
Expectations
Attitudes to risk
Identity of key executives
Skills and special expertise
Competitive strategies
'Ownership' of strategies and the commitment to them
Organizational structures
Investment plans
Key success factors

9 **Other**
Sales per employee
Plant capacity utilization
Type of equipment used
Labour rates and relationships
Raw material purchasing methods
Principal suppliers
Degree of vertical and horizontal integration
Commitment to market sectors.

Although *weak competitors* are by their very nature the most vulnerable, the potential pay-off needs to be examined carefully. It may be the case, for example, that the share gained, while useful, is of little long-term strategic value since it takes the company into segments of the market offering little scope for growth. Equally, these segments may require substantial long-term investment. By contrast, competing against *strong competitors* requires the firm to be far leaner, fitter and more aggressive, a point that has been argued in some considerable detail for almost two decades by Porter, and which was developed further in his book *The Competitive Advantage of Nations* (1990).

The second decision involves deciding between *close* and *distant competitors*. We have already commented that the majority of companies compete against those within the strategic group they most resemble. Thus, as we observed earlier, Nestlé's Nescafé is in direct competition with General Foods' Maxwell House. The strategist needs, in certain circumstances at least, to beware of destroying these close competitors, since the whole competitive base may then change. In commenting on this, Porter (1985, pp. 226–7) cites several examples:

> Bausch & Lomb in the late 1970s moved aggressively against other soft lens manufacturers with great success. However, this led one after another competitor to sell out to larger firms such as Revlon, Johnson & Johnson, and Schering-Plough, with the result that Bausch & Lomb now faced much larger competitors ...

> A speciality rubber manufacturer attacked another speciality rubber manufacturer as its mortal enemy and took away market share. The damage to the other company allowed the speciality divisions of the large tyre companies to move quickly into speciality rubber markets, using them as a dumping ground for excess capacity.

Porter expands upon this line of argument by distinguishing between 'good' and 'bad' competitors. A good competitor, he suggests, is one which adheres to the rules, avoids aggressive price moves, favours a healthy industry, makes realistic assumptions about the industry growth prospects, and accepts the general status quo. Bad competitors, by contrast, violate the unspoken and unwritten rules. They engage in unnecessarily aggressive and often foolhardy moves, expand capacity in large steps, slash margins and take significant risks.

The implications of this is that good competitors should work hard to develop an industry which consists only of good companies. They can do this, Kotler (1988, p. 252) suggests, by coalitions, selective retaliation and careful licensing. The pay-off will then be that:

1 competitors will not seek to destroy each other by behaving irrationally;
2 they will follow the rules of the industry;
3 each player will be differentiated in some way;
4 companies will try to earn share increases rather than buying them.

He goes on from this to develop the larger point:

> that a company really needs and benefits from competitors. The existence of competitors confers such strategic benefits as the following: (1) They lower the antitrust (monopolies) risk, (2) they may increase total demand, (3) they lead to more differentiation, (4) they provide a cost umbrella for the less efficient producers, (5) they share the cost of market development and legitimise a new technology, (6) they improve bargaining power versus labour or regulators, and (7) they may serve less-attractive segments.

4.9 SUMMARY

Within this chapter we have emphasized the need for constant competitor analysis and for the information generated to be fed into the strategic marketing planning process.

Although the need for competitor analysis has long been acknowledged, a substantial number of organizations still seemingly fail to allocate to the process the resources that are needed, relying instead upon a far less detailed understanding of competitive capabilities and priorities. It does therefore need to be recognized that if an effective system of competitive monitoring is to be developed, and the results used in the way intended, it is essential that top management commitment to the process exists.

In developing a structured approach to competitive analysis the strategist needs to give explicit consideration to five questions:

1 Against whom are we competing?
2 What are their objectives?

3 What strategies are they pursuing and how successful are they?

4 What strengths and weaknesses do they possess?

5 How are they likely to behave and, in particular, how are they likely to react to offensive moves?

Taken together, the answers to these five questions can be used to develop a detailed response profile for each competitive organization, and the probable implications for competitive behaviour fed into the planning process.

Several methods of categorizing competitors were discussed, including Porter's notion of strategic groups. We then examined the ways in which these ideas can be taken a step further by focusing upon the character of competition and how this is likely to change over the course of the product life cycle.

Particular emphasis was given to the need for the strategist to take account of each competitor's probable objectives, its competitive stance, and the relative importance of each market sector. Again, a variety of frameworks which can help in this process of understanding were discussed, including portfolio analysis.

Against this background we discussed the ways in which an effective competitive intelligence system (CIS) might be developed and the nature of the inputs that are required. Much of the information needed for such a system is often readily available, and emphasis therefore needs to be placed upon developing a framework which will ensure that this information is channelled, analysed and disseminated in the strategically most useful way. This theme is further developed in Chapter 20.

4.10 FURTHER READING

The following sources are recommended:

Cvitkovic (1993); de Chernatony, Daniels and Johnson (1993); Fuld (1995); Howell (1994); Kahaner (1996); Kelly (1987); McGonagale and Vella (1993); and Taylor (1992).

4.11 EXERCISES

1 Identify your organization's three principal competitors. How much detailed information exists on each of these? Identify what other information would be of value and how you might go about collecting it.

2 Using Figure 4.11, prepare a comparative assessment of your organization's performance against its three principal competitors.

3 Looking at Figure 4.8 and making reference to your own industry, identify examples for each of the five levels of competitive status. Where within this would you put your own organization?

4 Using Figure 4.4, develop a response profile for one of your principal competitors. What picture emerges from this, and what are the implications for the way in which the competitor might be 'managed'?

5 Look at your own organization and consider the following questions:

   • Which competitive perspective – the industry perspective or the market perspective – predominates?

   • What sorts of competitive changes are occurring in each of your major markets?

   • Are these changes being led by your own organization or by another firm?

   • To what extent does it appear that the full and long term significance of these changes has been recognized?

- How well equipped to cope with the major competitive changes does your organization appear to be?
- Can you find any examples of the organization having been taken by surprise by competitors in the past? If so, what were the causes of this, and what lessons appear to have been learned?

6 How would you go about establishing an effective competitive monitoring system (CMS) within an organization? What sort of monitoring system does your own organization have, and how effectively does it appear to work? What suggestions would you make to improve its effectiveness? How well do you think each of your competitors understands your organization?

7 How would you categorize each of the organizations against which you are competing? How would you categorize your own organization? What are the implications of each type of competitor for how you might best handle them?

4.12 DISCUSSION QUESTIONS

1 What factors should be taken into account in conducting a detailed analysis of your competitors? How might the information then be used in developing your organization's marketing strategy?

2 Your company's markets are becoming increasingly competitive. Explain how you would develop an effective competitive monitoring system, the nature of the inputs that the system would require and how the outputs from the system might be used to improve the strategic marketing planning process.

3 Your company is coming under increasing attack from a number of competitors. Identify the information that you would need in order to develop competitive response profiles and how this information might subsequently be used in the development of strategy.

4 It has been suggested that the sales force is a potentially valuable but under-utilized source of competitive information. Given this, explain how a sales force might be used as a structured source of information. What types of information might the sales force be expected to generate, and how might this information be used?

5 What factors should be taken into account when conducting a detailed competitor analysis? What models or frameworks might be useful in this exercise?

6 What information might a marketing manager need in order to understand a competitor? Where might this information come from? What problems might be encountered in collecting and analysing the information?

4.13 CASE STUDIES

BankAmerica Corporation

'I want my people to destroy our competitors. I want them to kill and crush them,' barks Thomas Peterson, a BankAmerica Corp. executive vice president and chief of its far-flung branch network.

Standing in a 43rd-floor conference area in BankAmerica's down-town tower, the former Army sergeant adds, 'This is the war room.' Charts bearing zigzagging red and blue lines compare BankAmerica's performance with those of its main California rivals, Wells Fargo & Co., Security Pacific Corp. and First Interstate Bancorp. On one wall hangs a cartoonlike painting of BankAmerica executives riding in a tank and waving a banner reading 'Annihilate the competition.'

These days, a retail-banking war is rumbling with the big talk and loud hype more traditional on a used-car lot. Recent months have seen the rise of late-night banking, Saturday banking, Sunday banking, 24-hour-a-day loan-by-phone dial-a-banker banking and African-safari sweep-stakes banking. BankAmerica has been leading the pack, handing out free checking accounts and pushing credit lines with no up-front charges. Its Seattle-based Seafirst Corp. unit is offering five bucks to any customer who has to wait in line more than five minutes (it's paid out about $2,000 so far).

This 'combat banking,' as some at BankAmerica call it, has played a key role in the biggest turnaround in U.S. banking history. A little more than two years' ago, BankAmerica's survival was in doubt: now, largely on the strength of retail profits and remarkably low domestic loan losses, its net income is up 114% for the 1989 first half, to $579 million, or $2.88 a share. After losing $1.8 billion from 1985 through 1987, BankAmerica is expected this year to post record net income of more than $1 billion.

Of course, lifting its loan-loss reserves for Third World debt, as several other money-center banks have done in recent days, could wipe out much of that anticipated profit. BankAmerica's reserves now stand at about 37% of its $7.4 billion of nontrade foreign debt. By comparison, Chase Manhattan Corp. has increased its reserves on nontrade debt to 46%, and J. P. Morgan & Co. has gone up to about 100%. BankAmerica won't comment on its plans. But despite its Third World problems, its stock has jumped nearly fivefold, from a 1987 low of $6.875 to Friday's close of $35.875 on the New York Stock Exchange. Last week it traded as high as $36.125, an all-time peak.

Much of the credit for the company's turnaround is going to Richard M. Rosenberg. He joined the bank in April 1987 and now heads its California banking group, which includes the booming retail business. Mr. Rosenberg is the frontrunner to succeed the 66-year-old chairman and chief executive, A. W. 'Tom' Clausen, who was brought out of retirement by BankAmerica's board in the dark days of late 1986 and is expected to retire again in a year or two.

An acknowledged retail-banking whiz, Mr. Rosenberg, 59, is the foremost member of a cadre of former Wells Fargo executives (Mr. Peterson is another) brought to BankAmerica when it was at low ebb. Even with an 850-branch network that is the envy of its rivals, BankAmerica's retail operations had been stagnant for years. Mr. Rosenberg's plan for revitalizing the bank through retail operations, a former executive recalls, boiled down to 'sell and sell and cut and cut.'

In an interview in his office, Mr. Rosenberg puts it more diplomatically. 'We had to win back the confidence of the market and of our own people,' he says. He is truly a marketing man: Hanging on the wall behind his desk is a framed, poster-sized reproduction of a BankAmerica ad. 'Morale was bad. Expenses were bad.' he adds. 'We needed something to show the world out there that we had a lot to offer.'

What Mr. Rosenberg offered is a mix of product doodads, marketing hype and cost cutting. He came up with Alpha, a package linking checking and savings accounts with a credit line that kicks in when customers' accounts are overdrawn – and carries a 16.8% charge. Alpha has helped reverse a disconcerting slide in deposits.

Mr. Rosenberg offered home-equity loans with no up-front charges; that helped increase customer loans outstanding to $16.2 billion, up 29% from year-earlier levels. Mortgage loans, aggressively priced by BankAmerica for the first time in years, have mushroomed 28%.

Meanwhile, costs as a percentage of revenues have been slashed 21% since 1986, transforming an expense structure that had been obese into one that's merely plump.

BankAmerica's efforts mirror a national trend, behind which lies a fundamental truth: 'Wholesale banking stinks,' says John Lyons, a New

York banking consultant. Deregulation and global economic developments have made lending to big companies and countries a low-profit or no-profit proposition.

That leaves the retail market – credit cards, auto loans and other loans and services for individuals – as the chief source of loan growth, cheap deposits and bank profits. Since 1985, U.S. banks' consumer loans have swollen 50% to $677.9 billion, almost double the rate of growth for commercial and industrial loans. Last year, for the first time in memory, U.S. banks had more loans outstanding to consumers than to businesses. Commercial and industrial loans currently total about $622.5 billion.

For consumers, this isn't entirely a blessing. While competition is driving down rates on some loans, banks are often accused of gouging consumers on credit cards, deposit fees and wherever else the banks think consumer apathy lets them raise their charges without driving customers away.

And despite the high margins, banks themselves face numerous pitfalls: Consumer bankruptcy filings have doubled in the past four years and would undoubtedly explode in a recession. Furthermore, so many banks are racing so furiously after the same customers that they inevitably crash into each other, resulting in pricing pressure and losses.

Still, so far so good for BankAmerica. Alpha was one of its major opening salvos in the marketing war. Mr. Rosenberg pushed the credit-line link and the bank in general with a multimillion-dollar marketing blitz – billboards, television spots, direct mail pitches. He met with Bank-America's longtime advertising firm. Grey Advertising, bluntly criticized BankAmerica's ads and laid out the objective for future marketing campaigns: 'Show people that it's not stupid to bank here and that it is stupid not to.' Alpha was pitched as the 'first step in simplified banking' – one-stop shopping for bank customers.

Alpha and other products got a big boost last May 6, BankAmerica's annual 'Founder's Day' honoring A. P. Giannini, the bank's immigrant founder. BankAmerica combined the celebration with offers of checking accounts that are free for the first three years. BankAmerica opened 40,000 accounts that day, a Saturday.

'I'm forced to admit that it was a very clever marketing double-whammy,' says one marketing executive at a sizable competitor. 'They hyped product and they hyped Saturday banking.'

Since introducing Alpha accounts in mid-1988, BankAmerica has opened more than 500,000 of them. Its share of the California deposit pie, which had plummeted to an estimated 35% in 1987 from 44% two years earlier, edged up to 36% by mid-1988 and is believed to be higher now.

People at the bank now rhapsodize about the flowering 'sales culture' – a buzzword for an atmosphere in which bankers are sent out to hawk products. Such a transformation, if true, would be amazing: Even some of BankAmerica's own executives have compared its traditional culture to a listless, bloated Third World ministry. By contrast, Wells Fargo is known for some of the most aggressive efficiency in the business.

At BankAmerica barbecues throughout the state, ex-Wells Fargo executives Rosenberg and Peterson have pounded home the notion that the main job of BankAmerica employees is to sell. Lending officers are ordered to call clients with long lists of questions designed to ferret out their other credit relationships. The idea is to 'cross sell' existing customers services that they never dreamed they needed.

Competitive fires are stoked by publicly listing each branch's results – and ranking each employee as well. 'If you're in the cellar, you'll work your tail off to get out,' Mr. Peterson explains. At newly instituted weekly sales meetings, managers and employees swap stories and hand out awards for 'sales of the week.'

Isn't some of this silly? 'Of course, a lot of this stuff is hokey,' concedes Martha Monroe, assistant manager of BankAmerica's branch in Novato, as she stands beneath lavender and turquoise banners promoting Alpha accounts. But, she says, 'Hokey works.'

The hokey often seems balanced by judicious use of terror. After a quick tour of one branch, a disgusted Mr. Peterson began lecturing the manager on the shabby condition of the place. At one point, he grabbed a handful of BankAmerica brochures and used them to swab down a grimy automated teller machine as the manager looked on with a stricken expression. 'The place looked like a dump,' Mr. Peterson recalls.

Asked about the key to transforming work-a-day bankers into sales dynamos. Frank Schultz, a senior vice president who heads Bank-America's residential-real-estate operations, responds: 'Greed.' He elaborates: 'You tell them they'll make a lot of money if they perform and they'll have serious problems if they don't.'

One of the first things the new regime did was to freeze salaries of branch managers and many other employees and set up incentive-pay programs that compensate managers largely on the basis of production – new accounts opened, consumer loans generated, transactions processed. Production targets are set for each branch, and branch managers who don't measure up don't last. A former branch manager recalls a friend, also a branch manager, who was busted down to a simple loan-officer status for failing to achieve quotas. 'He had some bad quarters and, whammo, they dunked him,' the former manager recounts.

Though such cutthroat practices appall some people, they clearly produce results. One example: Mr Schultz's real-estate operation. Bank-America got burned by making fixed-rate mortgage loans in the 1970s and had largely avoided home loans of any kind for a long while. At the end of 1987, it ranked 21st in California in real-estate loan originations. Shortly thereafter, Mr. Schultz hired a battalion of more than 100 sales people – some had sold cars and computers – put them on commission and unleashed them on California's torrid housing market.

Now, BankAmerica ranks third in California, having blown by all its bank rivals and trailing only two giant thrift holding companies, H. F. Ahmanson & Co. and Great Western Financial Corp. Lately, BankAmerica has been making over $1.5 billion in mortgage loans a month; it has $11.5 billion in residential-real-estate loans outstanding. Much of the lending is in adjustable-rate mortgages that limit the bank's exposure to interest-rate swings. Despite the explosive growth, Mr. Schultz says, BankAmerica's delinquency rate is only 1.2%, less than half the California average and even further below the 4.6% nationwide rate.

BankAmerica also has begun charging for more and more services it used to give away. Its automated-teller-machine transactions, once free, now cost customers 30 cents a pop. Subpoenas for customer records, formerly handled in the branches, now are processed by a central office – for a fee that depends on how quickly they are needed.

But selling is only half the battle in retail banking; driving down expenses is also crucial. Retail operations are inherently expensive because servicing accounts costs a lot, but BankAmerica's expenses had ballooned by the mid-1980s. That partly reflected a paternalistic attitude fostered by Mr. Giannini; the founder had coddled his employees and basically gave them jobs for life. As recently as three years ago, BankAmerica bragged that it rarely fired anyone.

That attitude is gone. Since 1984, BankAmerica has trimmed about 33,000 workers off its payroll, reducing employment to about 54,700 world-wide. Most of that cutback has come on the international and wholesale sides of the bank through divestitures, but some 5,000 people have been cut from its retail division just since 1987.

The branch network's costly structure has been overhauled. Its 62 'area management groups,' clusters of branches, were cut to 31. The four regional managers, each of whom formerly had staffs of about 40 people, now have 10 apiece.

Cost cutters identified 90 functions performed by each branch, everything from making loans to returning hot checks. 'We discovered that we had 850 branches doing the same things 850 different ways,' says Larry McNabb, executive vice president for operations in the California banking group. Of those 90 functions, 80 are now handled by factory-like processing centers.

The cutbacks have been rough on employees. Mr. Rosenberg, Mr. Peterson and other executives have given soothing speeches, and internal surveys find that morale has improved. But many employees still grumble. 'B of A is making money now, but the pressure to cut and cut and cut is still horribly demoralizing,' says one former branch manager who recently quit.

And the ascendency of the Wells Fargo expatriates continues to gall some employees, especially old-timers. 'We've viewed Wells as the evil empire forever,' one says, adding that Wells Fargo's approach to banking – its ferocious cost control – 'is sort of heartless.' Many BankAmerica employees now ruefully call their bank 'Wells of America.'

Nonetheless, the cutting and whipcracking have been vital to turning BankAmerica around. Its spending to earn one dollar of revenue has been slashed to about 64 cents – still high compared to Wells Fargo, where the

EXHIBIT 1
Fashioning a Turnaround at BankAmerica

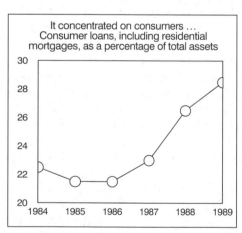

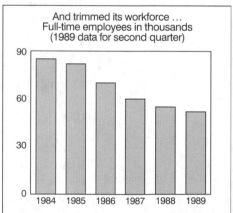

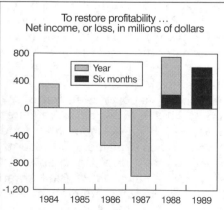

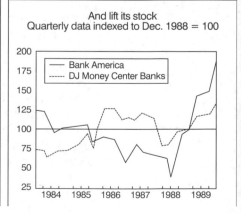

ratio is 52 cents to the dollar – but a big improvement from the roughly 80 cents that BankAmerica was spending in 1985. Its return on assets climbed to a robust 1.26% at June 30 from a mediocre 0.69% a year earlier. Its net interest margin – the difference between its cost of funds and what it receives on loans – has risen to 4.74% from 3.79% a year ago, largely because of the high-yielding consumer loans.

However, not everything has gone well on the retail side. BankAmerica's credit card loans of roughly $4.4 billion have been pretty much stagnant over the past several years; credit cards are one of retail banking's most lucrative areas, and competitors such as Citicorp have vastly expanded their card operations. One BankAmerica credit card promotion, under which consumers piled up points that later could be swapped for catalog gifts, got out of hand. BankAmerica drastically underestimated how many gifts it would have to give away, a mistake that cost the bank $11 million, according to former executives.

Moreover, many observers believe that BankAmerica's forced retreat from wholesale and international operations – and the overhang of dubious foreign loans – will permanently hobble its ability to compete with global financial powers such as Japan's giant banks and even U.S. internationals.

That possibility is known to trouble Mr. Clausen. Before retiring the first time, he served as the bank's chief executive from 1970 to 1981 and oversaw the vast expansion of its international operations and other activities that badly damaged it after he left. Yet he clearly feels vindicated by the bank's turnaround.

'When I came back, people said, "My God, they've brought that fool Clausen back, he caused all these problems in the first place. ... The board must be crazy,"' he muses in an interview. 'Well, we've come a fur piece. Maybe I'm not as dumb as people thought.'

But friends say Mr. Clausen still sees BankAmerica as a global bank and worries that the emphasis on retail banking may jeopardize that. They add that he is occasionally peeved at the seeming glee that some retail executives take in slashing costs. A former executive tells of a meeting at which Mr. Peterson's enthusiastic description of how he was saving money by making tellers part-timers and stripping them of some benefits prompted Mr. Clausen to snap: 'Let me remind you that I started as a teller.' (Mr. Peterson, who also worked once as a teller, says Mr. Clausen meant it as a joke.)

These issues weigh on Mr. Clausen as he considers whom to anoint as his successor. Mr. Rosenberg is the clear leader because he has engineered the most visible aspect of the turnaround. But he has scant international experience. Furthermore, a clause in his contract pays him roughly $800,000 if he quits before 1990 or if he is fired for any reason other than being fired for gross misconduct.

'Dick is 59 himself, and if Clausen dithers, he may just take the money and go run something else,' a former executive says.

In any event, Mr. Clausen doesn't seem in any hurry to go. 'The job isn't done yet,' he says. He won't speculate on how much longer he will stay. As for Mr. Rosenberg, he still has plenty of work to do in his present job. He notes that, considering bank documents and customer forms, certain BankAmerica real estate loans require 98 different pieces of paper.

'We intend to cut that by 65%,' he says, waving a stack of pie charts and graphs. 'Thirty-four [forms] ain't great, either, but it's progress.'

Source: Charles McCoy, 'Combat Banking: BankAmerica's Rebound Stems from No-Holds-Barred Attack on the Retail Trade,' *The Wall Street Journal*, October 2, 1989, pp. A1, A8.

Discussion questions

1 Define and describe the generic, product type, and brand product markets for BankAmerica's customer loans in California.
2 Do you agree with top management's combat strategy against other regional and national banks? Discuss.
3 Discuss the competitive situation and identify key competitors on different levels.
4 Suggest important marketing strategy guidelines for marketing BankAmerica's services in the future.

The Cleveland Clinic

For years, Ohio's Cleveland Clinic has ranked with the top world-class providers of medical care. It pioneered coronary bypass surgery and developed the first kidney dialysis machine. King Hussein of Jordan uses the clinic, so too the royal family of Saudi Arabia.

But to Diran M. Seropian, chief of the medical staff of the largest hospital in Broward County, Fla., the clinic is the Carl Icahn of medicine – 'a hostile corporation with a hostile corporation mentality.' Its unforgivable mistake, in Dr. Seropian's view: It opened an outpatient facility here 18 months ago as part of a plan to expand into this market. Local politicians and businesses cheered the idea. But many local physicians were outraged, and an extraordinary campaign to keep the clinic out was begun.

The battle between the Cleveland Clinic and the South Florida physicians is part of a larger war sweeping the health care industry and can ultimately be boiled down to one issue: competition. Big-name health-care institutions are after new markets for their state-of-the-art medicine, and are posing a new threat to local physicians. The expansions are also disrupting traditional relationships between physicians and their patients, physicians and their hospitals and physicians and their fellow physicians.

In the Cleveland Clinic's case, Carl C. Gill, the chief executive of the Clinic's Florida enterprise, and a surgeon who has done 4,000 openheart operations, was denied local hospital privileges. The credentials committee of Broward General Medical Center said he lacked enough experience in the emergency room, among other things. In fact, for 15 months, the

EXHIBIT 1 Projected Population Growth 1990–2000 in the Cleveland Clinic's Markets

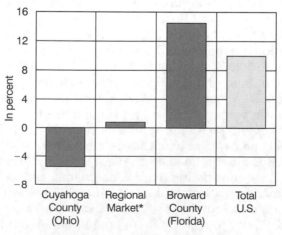

*Includes portions of Ohio, Indiana, Kentucky, Michigan, New York, Pennsylvania and West Virginia

SOURCE: Cleveland Clinic Foundation, Broward Economic Development Board based on U.S. Bureau of the Census data.

clinic was blocked from conducting heart surgery in Florida. When one hospital finally opened its doors, some local physicians, apparently in protest, began snubbing the facility and referring their patients elsewhere. And when some patients told their local physicians that they wanted to consult physicians at the clinic, they were handed their medical charts and told not to come back.

In a recent full-page advertisement in the Miami Herald, Dr. Seropian, who has led the charge, pulled out the stops. He likened the clinic to Dingoes – wild Australian dogs – 'which roam the bush eating every kind of prey.'

In May, the clinic filed suit in federal district court in Fort Lauderdale, charging, among other things, that some physicians had conspired to 'hamper' its entry into Broward County. In a countersuit, Amjad Munim, a pulmonologist and one of two individual defendants named in the complaint, maintained the clinic had tried to recruit him to spy on his fellow physicians so it could build a legal case against them. Meanwhile, the Federal Trade Commission is investigating whether the battle has involved violations of antitrust laws.

The Cleveland Clinic, which had revenue of $672 million in 1988, isn't alone in its desire to expand. The Mayo Clinic, based in Rochester, Minn., has recently set up satellite operations in Jacksonville, Fla., and Scottsdale, Ariz. The M. D. Anderson Cancer Center in Houston is negotiating to open a branch in Orlando, Fla. Several other, smaller institutions and academic centers have also established regional branches, intended to feed patients to their main facilities.

In part, these institutions are victims of their own success. Many once-exotic procedures that they invented are now routinely available across the country, reducing the need for patients to travel to the medical meccas. For instance, the Cleveland Clinic might once have had a hold on coronary bypass surgery, but no more: Last year more than 250,000 patients had the operation at hospitals throughout the U.S.

'These clinics used to be the court of last resort for complex medical cases,' says Jeff Goldsmith, national health-care adviser to Ernst & Whinney, the accounting firm. 'Now, the flooding of the country with medical specialties and high-technology equipment has forced them to adopt a different strategy.'

Their expertise and reputation spell formidable competition for the local medical community. On one level, says Jay Wolfson, a health-policy expert at the University of South Florida in Tampa, 'it's like bringing in a McDonald's. If you're a mom-and-pop sandwich shop on the corner, you could get wiped out.'

In Fort Lauderdale, physicians insist they aren't threatened by the Cleveland Clinic. Instead, they say they resent what they see as special favors the institution was given to invade their turf. They also maintain the clinic will lure fully insured patients from local hospitals, leaving behind the burden for indigent care. And they bristle at the suggestion that the clinic dispenses a better brand of medicine. 'They've implied the doctors here are dummies, that they're bringing enlightened medicine to the hinterlands,' Dr. Seropian says.

Since its founding in 1921, the not-for-profit Cleveland Clinic has built its business taking on complex, high-risk cases, and leaving more routine primary care to family physicians. In addition to treating patients, its salaried physicians do research and train new physicians, tasks the clinic says set it apart from everyday medical practice. 'Basic fee-for-service practice doesn't advance medicine,' says Dr. Gill.

Clinic physicians claim they aren't interested in stealing patients. But they make no apology for provoking a battle with their fee-for-service brethren that is both cultural and economic. Says Dr. Gill: 'Let's let the marketplace sort out what the best way to deliver health care is.'

The conflict began early in 1986 over modest ambitions: a proposed joint venture between the clinic and the North Broward Hospital District, a tax-supported agency that operates Broward General and three other county hospitals. Under the plan, the clinic would build an out-patient facility adjacent to Broward General Medical Center. The medical center would provide surgical and other major services.

But word of the idea leaked prematurely and a hastily-arranged meeting to explain it to the district's physicians erupted into a verbal pummeling of William Kiser, chairman of the Cleveland Clinic Foundation board of governors. Soon after, hospital officials halted the negotiations.

'The [physicians] really had a problem with a bunch of carpetbaggers from the North.' Dr. Kiser said.

The clinic, however, moved ahead with its expansion plans. Like any business, it keeps close tabs on its core market, and the outlook wasn't all that bright. Seven states provide 90% of the clinic's business and population growth in that region is expected to be flat through the year 2000. But not so southeastern Florida, where the population is still growing and, in many areas, is highly affluent.

On the surface, the region – Dade, Broward, and Palm Beach Counties – is a dream market. Yachts lining the canals of the Intracoastal Waterway and a ubiquitous building boom reflect wealth and growth so palpable that clinic officials have come to call it 'immaculate consumption.' Moreover, about 20% of the 3.7 million residents in Dade, Broward and Palm Beach Counties are over 65 years old. By the year 2000, about 50% of the population will be over 45 – a potential motherlode of patients.

'We felt there was room for us,' Dr. Kiser said. 'We decided to go on our own rather than wait to be invited.'

Others have been drawn by the same flame. Throughout the 1970s, for-profit hospital chains rushed here to cash in on the growing elderly population, whose medical tab was paid in full by Medicare. But in 1983, when the U.S. instituted new Medicare payment guidelines called DRGs, or diagnosis related groups, to control surging medical costs, hospital occupancy rates began to plummet. Now, the region is glutted with health care: There are 240 physicians for every 100,000 residents in southeastern Florida – the national average is 189 – and a surplus of 3,500 hospital beds.

Glut or not, the clinic drew up big plans: a $200 million complex, anchored by a state-of-the-art, 400-bed hospital. Health planners blanched, but the business community was enthralled.

'We looked at this as a world-class health facility that we would use to build business around,' said James Garver, president of the Broward Economic Development Board.

In May 1987, with help from a politically connected law firm and after some of its physicians had made about $2,000 in campaign contributions to local legislators, the clinic won passage of crucial legislation: a law granting it tax-exempt status and waiving the state medical exam for 25 senior physicians who would move from Cleveland to launch the new facility.

Local physicians were enraged. 'Twenty-five thousand physicians have taken that exam to practice in this state,' fumes Dr. Seropian. The Cleveland physicians shouldn't have been exempted, he says.

The clinic says it received the same consideration previously afforded the Mayo Clinic and academic institutions hiring out-of-state faculty. (Ultimately, 13 of its physicians accepted exemptions before the waiver expired.)

With the bill's passage, the clinic pressed forward to build its out-patient facility, which opened in February 1988. But more battles loomed. For one, to build its proposed hospital, which it hoped to open in the early 1990s, the clinic had to get a 'certificate of need' from the state, proving that the community actually needed the services. The local hospital association and health planners allied with local physicians to oppose it.

The clinic's physicians meanwhile had no place to operate, and started hunting for a hospital that would open its doors. The clinic found two allies, one of which was North Beach Hospital, a 153-bed facility that was filling only 28 of its beds. There was just one problem: North Beach lacked a certificate of need for cardiac service.

Enter Richard Stull, the chief executive of the North Broward Hospital District. Mr. Stull had played a key role in the early joint-venture discussions between the clinic and the District, and he held steadfast to his hope of an affiliation with the clinic.

'In this county there are 20 acute-care hospitals that are known for nothing,' Mr. Stull says. 'All I was looking for was adding something so that we'd stand out.' He was also worried about offsetting competition from a new source: Some of his own physicians were setting up clinics that siphoned off outpatient business from the hospital.

When a cardiac team left Broward General at the beginning of 1988, Mr. Stull thought the clinic's heart specialists could fill the void. But once again, the hospital's medical staff was opposed.

In the resulting battle:

– The hospital's credentials committee denied practice privileges to the clinic's five-person cardiac team, including Dr. Gill, because the clinic is 'an acknowledged potential competitor' of the hospital, the committee said.
– The district's board, in the face of political pressure, overruled the committee and last January signed a five-year contract with the clinic to provide cardiac services at Broward General. In protest, some physicians apparently diverted their patients to other hospitals, helping to depress February revenues at Broward General $3.5 million below projections.
– When the clinic asked for privileges for its other specialists to consult on cardiac cases, the local credentials committee refused to act. Mr. Stull had to fly in a panel of physicians from outside the area to approve their qualifications.

On May 15, more than 14 months after the clinic's outpatient facility opened, Dr. Gill performed the first open heart operation at Broward General for the Cleveland Clinic, Florida.

But that victory was tempered by a serious setback. In January, state health officials denied the clinic a certificate of need for its hospital. They said there were already too many surplus hospital beds in the area, and rejected the clinic's claim that it offered unique services.

For now, the clinic's hospital plans are on hold. But, in the meantime, it says its Florida practice is thriving. More than 12,000 patients have sought treatment since it opened; some wait as long as three months for an appointment with one of its 48 physicians.

Specialty-care and exotic procedures remain its stock-in-trade. In one recent operation, three clinic surgeons replaced a Fort Lauderdale resident's cancerous throat with a piece of his small intestine. In another, a physician used two ribs to make a new forehead for a man whose own had been removed to relieve pressure in his brain. Then there is Beth Acker. Told by a local neurosurgeon that she had an inoperable spinal cord tumor and four months to live, the 29-year-old mother went to the clinic where she had successful surgery. 'They handled it like an everyday thing,' she said.

Gradually, local physicians are sending patients its way, the clinic says, but the vast majority come in on their own. That is prompting the clinic to expand its services, and add a general medical practice to its group of specialists.

Source: Ron Winslow, 'Medical Clash: Big Hospitals Move into New Territories. Draw Local Staffs' Ire,' *The Wall Street Journal*, August 18, 1989, pp. A1.4

Discussion questions

1 Define and describe the competitive arena(s) in which the Cleveland Clinic competes.
2 Discuss the legal and ethical issues concerning the competition between the Cleveland Clinic and its key competitors.
3 Evaluate the competitive threats that the clinic poses to Broward County medical services organizations.
4 Compare and contrast the Cleveland Clinic's competitive advantage(s) with those of its key competitors.
5 Identify and evaluate the marketing strategies that may be adopted by the Cleveland Clinic's key competitors in Florida.

5 | Approaches to customer analysis

5.1 LEARNING OBJECTIVES

When you have read this chapter you should be able to understand:

(a) the factors that influence consumer behaviour;
(b) the structure of the consumer buying decision process;
(c) the nature of organizational buying;
(d) how an understanding of buying processes can be used in the development of marketing strategy;
(e) why relationship marketing is becoming an increasingly important strategic marketing tool and how a relationship marketing programme can be developed.

5.2 INTRODUCTION

It has long been recognized that marketing planning is ultimately driven by the marketing strategist's perception of how and why customers behave as they do, and how they are likely to respond to the various elements of the marketing mix. See Illustration 5.1.

In the majority of markets, however, buyers differ enormously in terms of their buying dynamics. The task faced by the marketing strategist in coming to terms with these differences is consequently complex. In consumer markets, for example, not only do buyers typically differ in terms of their age, income, educational levels and geographical location, but more fundamentally in terms of their personality, their lifestyles and their expectations. In the case of organizational and industrial markets, differences are often exhibited in the goals being pursued, the criteria employed by those involved in the buying process, the formality of purchasing policies, and the constraints that exist in the form of delivery dates and expected performance levels.

Despite these complexities, it is imperative that the marketing strategist understands in detail the dynamics of the buying process, since the costs and competitive implications of failing to do so are likely to be significant. In the case of new product development, for example, it is generally recognized that some 80 per cent of all new products launched fail, a statistic that owes much to a lack of understanding of customers' expectations. It is for these sorts of reasons that a considerable amount of research has been conducted in the post-war period in order to provide us with a greater understanding of buying patterns, and to enable us to predict more readily *how* buyers will behave in any given situation. Within this chapter we therefore focus upon some of the factors which influence behaviour and how subsequently they influence marketing strategy. It does need to be emphasized, however, that a series of interrelationships exist between this material and the areas covered in Chapter 8 in which we examine approaches to segmentation, targeting and positioning. The reader might therefore find it useful at this stage to turn briefly to Chapter 8 to identify the nature of these interrelationships before reading the present chapter in detail.

Illustration 5.1: The Advantages of Understanding Customer Needs

Although the arguments for constant and detailed customer analysis have been well rehearsed, numerous organizations fall into the trap of believing that because they deal with their customers on a day-to-day basis, they have a clear understanding of their needs and motivations. The reality is, however, often very different, as is shown for example by the ways in which companies are seemingly taken by surprise by the decline of major market sectors, the loss of long-standing accounts, and by the way in which some 80 per cent of all new products launched fail. There is therefore an overwhelming argument for regular assessments (and reassessments) of what customers really want, their current levels of satisfaction, and the scope that exists for developing new products and services that existing customers might buy. Among those to have done this are:

- Accounting firms which having been heavily committed to a mature product – the annual company audit – used this as the entry point for developing a wide range of consultancy services. They are now firmly positioned in the rapidly-expanding management consultancy market, having retained their stable core auditing business.
- One of the great success stories of the 1980s was the Sony Walkman. Its development was brought about as the result of Sony's Chairman, Akio Morita, observing that the quality of stereo on planes was poor. The Sony Walkman technology was therefore developed initially for global travellers. Once the technology was available, Sony recognized the product's potential for a younger and far larger market.
- Dulux Solid Emulsion Paint which overcame the perennial problem faced by the DIY decorator, that of paint spattering over the floor. The advantages of the product were capitalized upon in an intensive advertising campaign and confirmed Dulux's position as the market leader.

Source: Davidson, J. H. (1987) Offensive Marketing, *Penguin p. 60*

5.3 A Simple Model of Buyer Behaviour

Irrespective of whether the marketing strategist is operating in a consumer, industrial or organizational market, there are seven questions which underpin any understanding of buyer behaviour:

1 Who is in the market and what is the extent of their power with regard to the organization?
2 What do they buy?
3 Why do they buy?
4 Who is involved in the buying?
5 How do they buy?
6 When do they buy?
7 Where do they buy?

It is the answers to these questions which should provide the marketing strategist with an understanding of the ways in which buyers are most likely to respond to marketing stimuli. It then follows from this that the organization which makes the best use of the information should be in a position to gain a competitive advantage. For this reason, a considerable amount of time, effort and money has been spent over the past few decades in attempting to provide the marketing strategist with a series of answers.

The starting point for much of this work has been a straightforward stimulus-response model of the sort illustrated in Figure 5.1.

FIGURE 5.1
A stimulus-response model of buyer behaviour

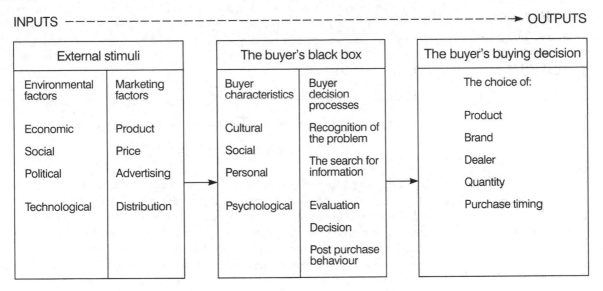

INPUTS — → OUTPUTS

External stimuli		The buyer's black box		The buyer's buying decision
Environmental factors	Marketing factors	Buyer characteristics	Buyer decision processes	The choice of:
Economic	Product	Cultural	Recognition of the problem	Product
Social	Price	Social	The search for information	Brand
Political	Advertising	Personal		Dealer
			Evaluation	Quantity
Technological	Distribution	Psychological	Decision	Purchase timing
			Post purchase behaviour	

Here, stimuli in the form both of the external environment and the elements of the marketing mix enter the buyer's 'black box' and interact with the buyer's characteristics and decision processes to produce a series of outputs in the form of purchase decisions. Included within these is the question of whether to buy and, if so, which product and brand, which dealer, when, and in what quantities. The task faced by the marketing strategist therefore involves understanding how the black box operates. To do this, we need to consider the two principal components of the box: firstly, the factors which the individual brings to the buying situation, and secondly, the decision processes that are used. We will therefore begin by focusing upon these background factors – cultural, social, personal and psychological – as a prelude to examining the detail of the decision process itself. However, as a general background to this discussion, the reader should first read Michael Porter's analysis of competitive structures which we examine in detail on page 121. In essence, Porter argues that five forces of competition can be at work in any market. It is then that interplay between these elements that determines the attractiveness and intensity of competition within any given market sector. Included within these five forces are the issues of buyer and supplier power. *Buyer power*, he suggests, is likely to be at its highest when:

● there is a concentration of buyers;
● there are alternative sources of supply;
● buyers have access to useful information and tend to shop around;
● there is a threat of backward integration if the buyer does not obtain satisfactory supplies and prices.

By contrast, *supplier power* is likely to be high if:

● there is a concentration of suppliers;
● the costs of switching from one supplier to another are high;
● suppliers are likely to integrate forward if they do not obtain the price/profits they seek;
● the organization has little countervailing power.

The nature of buyer-seller relationships is therefore of potentially considerable significance and needs to be taken into account when examining any market sector. In the majority of consumer markets, for example, buyer power is typically low, while supplier power is high. In many industrial markets, however, the situation is reversed and it is the buyer who is often in the position of greatest power. The implications of these different relationships are reflected most obviously in terms of how marketing strategy is developed and the relative degree of freedom that the market structure gives to the strategist. An important element therefore of any customer analysis is the insight that it provides to our understanding of buyer–supplier relationships, and hence to the market's competitive structure.

Illustration 5.2: The Emergence of the New Consumer

In many ways, the most significant and far-reaching legacies for marketing of the economic and social changes and turbulence of the late 1980s and early 1990s are reflected in what we might loosely refer to as the emergence of the 'new' consumer and the 'new' competitor (the dimensions of the new competitor were discussed in Chapter 4). Although neither is necessarily new in any absolute sense, they differ in a series of ways from traditional consumers and competitors in that their expectations, values and patterns of behaviour are all very different from that with which marketing planners traditionally had to come to terms. The consequences of this are manifested in several ways but, in the case of the new consumer, by the way in which the degree of understanding of customers' motivations must be far greater and the marketing effort tailored more firmly and clearly to the patterns of specific need. We can therefore see the new consumer as being characterized by:

- the development of new value systems;
- a greater emphasis upon value for money;
- higher levels of price awareness and price sensitivity;
- an increased demand for and a willingness to accept more and exciting new products;
- less technophobia;
- lower levels of brand and supplier loyalty;
- a greater willingness to experiment with new products, ideas and delivery systems;
- a greater cynicism;
- higher levels of environmental awareness (the way in which Volkswagen responded to this is discussed in Illustration 5.4);
- a greater scepticism about politicians, big business and the traditional institutions;
- the changed and changing roles of men and women;

Taking just one of these eleven characteristics – the changed and changing roles of men and women – its significance can perhaps be appreciated by the fact that 35 per cent of new cars that are bought privately are now bought by women; this compares with less than 6% in 1970. From the viewpoint of the car manufacturers the implications have been enormous and have had to be reflected not just in terms of the design of cars, but also the nature of the market research that is conducted, the advertising and promotion that is carried out, and the approach to selling.

5.4 FACTORS INFLUENCING CONSUMER BEHAVIOUR

From the viewpoint of the marketing strategist, the mix of cultural, social, personal and psychological factors which influence behaviour and which are illustrated in Figure 5.2 are largely non-controllable. Because of the influence they exert upon patterns of buying, it is essential that as much effort as possible is put into understanding *how they interact* and, ultimately, *how they influence* purchase behaviour. In doing this, the reader should not lose sight of the differences that exist between customers and consumers, and the implications of these differences for strategy. The term 'consumer' is typically taken to mean the final user, who is not necessarily the customer. In the case of foodstuffs such as breakfast cereals, for example, the buyer (generally still the housewife) acts on behalf of her family. For the marketing mix to be effective, it is quite obviously essential that the strategist therefore understands not just what the *customer* wants (e.g. value for money) but also what the *consumer* wants (e.g. taste, free gifts, image).

FIGURE 5.2
Factors influencing consumer behaviour

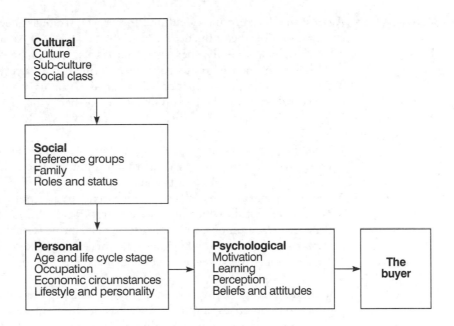

The Significance of Culture

The most fundamental of the four influencing forces, and hence the logical starting point for any analysis of behaviour, is the buyer's set of *cultural* factors. These include culture, subculture and social class. Of these, it is the culture of the society itself which typically proves to be the most fundamental and enduring influence on behaviour. Human behaviour is, as Kotler (1988, p. 175) has observed, 'largely the result of a learning process and as such individuals grow up learning a set of values, perceptions, preferences and behavior patterns as the result of socialization both within the family and a series of other key institutions'. From this we develop a set of values which, in the western world at least, Schiffman and Kanuk (1983, pp. 404–20) suggest include achievement, success, efficiency, progress, material comfort, practicality, individualism, freedom, humanitarianism, youthfulness and practicality. It is these which to a very large extent determine and drive our patterns of behaviour.

This broad set of values is then influenced in turn by the subcultures in which we develop. These include nationality groups, religious groups, racial groups and geographical areas, all of which exhibit degrees of difference in ethnic taste, cultural preferences, taboos, attitudes and lifestyle.

The influence of subcultures is subsequently affected by a third set of variables, that of *social stratification* and, in particular, *social class*. The significance of social class as a determinant of behaviour is discussed in some detail in Chapter 8. At this stage we will simply highlight its key characteristics which, traditionally at least, it has been suggested are as follows:

1 people within a particular social class are more similar than those from different social classes;
2 social class is determined by a *series* of variables such as occupation, income, education and values rather than by a single variable;
3 individuals can move from one social class to another.

Although research in recent years has led to a modification of these ideas, the most important single implication of social class is the still valid assumption that it exerts a significant degree of influence in areas such as clothing, cars, leisure pursuits and media preferences.

Social Factors

Against this background of cultural forces, the strategist needs then to turn to an examination of the influence exerted by a series of social factors, including reference groups, family, social role and status.

Although influence groups have been defined in a variety of ways, one of the most useful definitions is that of 'all the groups that have a direct (face-to-face) or indirect influence on the person's attitudes or behavior' (Kotler, 1988, p. 177).

Reference groups can be divided into four types.

1 *Primary membership groups*, which are generally informal and to which individuals belong and within which they interact. These include family, neighbours, colleagues and friends.
2 *Secondary membership groups*, which tend to be more formal than primary groups and within which less interaction typically takes place. Included within these are trade unions, religious groups and professional societies.
3 *Aspirational groups* to which an individual would like to belong.
4 *Dissociative groups* whose values and behaviour the individual rejects.

The influence exerted by reference groups tends to vary considerably from one product and brand to another, as well as at different stages of the product life cycle. Among the products and brands that Hendon (1979, pp. 752–61) found were influenced most directly by reference group behaviour were cars, beer, clothing, restaurants and cigarettes. He went on to highlight the ways in which this behaviour changes over the course of the product life cycle. In the introductory stage, for example, the question of *whether* to buy is heavily influenced by others, although the influence upon the choice of brand is not particularly significant. In the growth stage, the group influences both product and brand choice, while in maturity it is the brand but not the product which is subject to this influence. The influence of reference groups in the decline stage is almost invariably weak in terms of both the product and brand choice.

The implications of these findings are significant and provide the marketing strategist with a series of guidelines, the most important of which centres around the need to identify the *opinion leaders* for each reference group. Our understanding of opinion leadership has developed considerably over the past few years, and whereas at one time it was believed that opinion leadership was limited primarily to prominent figures within society this is now no longer seen to be the case. Rather, it is recognized that an individual may well be an opinion leader in certain circumstances, but an opinion follower in others. Quite obviously, this makes the task of identifying opinion leaders more difficult and gives emphasis to the need to understand not just the demographic, but particularly the psychographic characteristics of the group which the strategist is attempting to influence.

For many products, however, it is the family which exerts the greatest single influence on behaviour. This includes both the *family of orientation* (parents, brothers and sisters) and the *family of procreation* (spouse and children). The significance of the family as a determinant of buying behaviour has long been recognized and for this reason it has been the subject of a considerable amount of research in order to identify the roles and relative influence exerted by different family members. Although it is not our intention to examine this area in detail, there are several general conclusions that have emerged from this research and that at this stage merit emphasis:

1 Husband and wife involvement in purchase decisions varies greatly from one product category to another, with women still playing the principal role in the purchasing of food and clothing. Although this has changed somewhat over the past few years as the proportion of working women has increased and divorce rates have escalated, the Institute of Grocery Distribution has estimated that women still account for some 78 per cent of food purchases.
2 Joint husband and wife decision making tends to be a characteristic of more expensive product choices where the opportunity cost of a 'wrong' decision is greater.

At a more general level, however, research in the United States (see, for example, Davis, 1970) has identified three patterns of decision making within the family and the sorts of product category with which each is typically associated. These are:

- husband dominant: life insurance, cars, and televisions.
- wife-dominant: washing machines, carpets, kitchenware and non-living-room furniture.
- equal: living-room furniture, holidays, housing, furnishings and entertainment.

Although this research is useful in that it distinguishes between the different decision-making patterns, the results need to be treated with a degree of caution, if only because of the ways in which roles within the family have, and indeed still are, changing significantly.

The final social factor that typically influences purchase behaviour consists of the individual's actual and perceived *roles* and *statuses* both within society in general and within groups in particular. The significance of status symbols and the messages they communicate has long been recognized and is discussed in some detail in Chapter 13. The obvious implication, however, for the marketing strategist is to position products and brands in such a way that they reinforce the messages suited to particular individuals and groups.

Personal Influences on Behaviour

The third major category of influences upon behaviour is made up of the buyer's set of *personal characteristics*, including age and life-cycle stage, occupation, economic circumstances, lifestyle, and personality (see Illustration 5.4). The majority of these factors have been used extensively by marketing strategists in segmenting markets, and the reader should therefore turn to pages 283–95 in which we discuss this.

Psychological Influences

The fourth and final set of influences upon behaviour consists of the four principal *psychological factors* - motivation, perception, learning, and beliefs and attitudes. The first of these, motivation, is in many ways both the most important to understand and the most complex to analyse. The starting point involves

Illustration 5.3: Understanding the Muddled, Anxious, Happy Shopper

Over the last 20 years, the entire retail sector has undergone a major transformation, with the rapid growth of out-of-town superstores, a corresponding decline in high street outlets, a dramatic increase in own label brands, the development of relationship marketing in the form of loyalty schemes, and the emergence of home shopping.

The fiercer rivalry that has emerged from these changes has, in turn, led to a demand for a far greater degree of understanding of shoppers, the roles they play, their needs, attitudes, frustrations; the decision processes involved in choosing between stores; and their product choices both prior to the shopping trip as well as within the store.

In discussing this, Lunn and Blamires (1996) suggest that

> Housewives typically experience a number of frustrations in supermarket shopping, including: the perception of shopping as a chore; irritations provoked by the in-store environment such as narrow aisles; confusion and depersonalisation in very large superstores; the often traumatic experience of shopping with very young children.
>
> However, supermarket shopping is far from a totally negative experience. It can provide a number of important satisfactions, including: a pretext for getting out of the house; social motivations; a key manifestation of their basic role of housewife, mother and provider; and pleasure can be derived from the very act of replenishing store cupboards and fridges.
>
> A bonding relationship can be developed over time with a single favourite store or repertoire of stores. The combination of familiarity with ambiance, layout and stock can reinforce the woman's confidence in the total shopping activity.

Against this background, Lunn and Blamires have identified a number of basic attitudinal differences which have a marked bearing on supermarket shopping needs and behaviour. For example, shoppers differ significantly in the extent to which they are or are not organized and methodical about shopping; confident in their approach to shopping; involved in shopping; experimental (like trying out new and different products, shopping at different stores); bargain seeking; sociable/extrovert. These basic attitudes have, in turn, been used to develop shopper typologies, with six basic types having emerged:

* the conservative shopper;
* the inefficient, extravagant shopper;
* the reluctantly well-organized shopper;
* The happy, impulsive shopper;
* the efficient, model-housewife shopper;
* the anxious, muddled shopper.

Taking just two of these, Lunn et al. suggest that the reluctantly well-organized shopper does not really enjoy shopping, yet is confident about the products and brands she chooses, and organizes her shopping carefully.

In contrast, the happy, impulsive shopper, who thoroughly enjoys trying out new products, uses several stores to make sure she is not missing any opportunities. She likes looking out for bargains.

Equally, life cycle or life stage segmentation (see pp. 291–5) provides a basis for segmenting shoppers. For example, with young childless couples there is a major change from their single state. Now they have partners to consider, not just themselves. Shopping is often perceived as an encroachment upon leisure time and is consequently especially likely to arouse feelings of frustration.

Families with older children present a total contrast. They have become highly experienced at shopping, know how long they are prepared to spend during a main shop, and in this time they know they can purchase what they need. They know they have provided for the family, and so experience considerable feelings of satisfaction and self-esteem.

Source: Lunn, A. Blamires, C. and Browne, P. 'The revitalisation of Mothercare', proceedings of the Market Research Society Annual Conference, 1996

Illustration 5.4: The Influences of Personality on Product Choice

A large number of writers and researchers over the past 30 years have argued that an individual's personality influences his or her choice of product and brand. Assuming that this is indeed the case, the scope that should then exist for using personality to guide marketing strategy by, for example, segmenting markets, repositioning brands, developing new products, and modifying advertising messages, would be considerable. In practice, however, consumer researchers have, as Foxall (1987, p. 132) has pointed out,

> ... failed to find more than a handful of significant relationships between measures of personality and aspects of consumer choice despite a great many empirical investigations. Particularly disappointing was the fact that personality measures often turned out to be less accurate predictors of consumer behaviour than more traditional segmentation variables such as social class, age and previous patterns of choice.

Foxall's comment is based very largely on the inconclusive results which have emerged from a series of studies, the best known of which was conducted by Evans (1959). This study was stimulated by the way in which in the United States Fords and Chevrolets were promoted as having different personalities. Ford buyers, for example, were identified as 'independent, impulsive, masculine, alert to change and self-confident', while Chevrolet owners were 'conservative, thrifty, prestige conscious, less masculine, and seeking to avoid extremes'. Evans investigated the validity of these descriptions by applying the Edwards Personal Preference Test which measures needs for achievement, dominance, change, aggression, and so on, to Ford and Chevrolet owners. The scores achieved by the two groups of owners proved not to be significantly different and Evans concluded that 'the distribution of scores for all needs overlap to such an extent that (personality) discrimination is virtually impossible'.

recognizing the differences between *biogenic* needs which are physiological (hunger, thirst and discomfort) and *psychogenic* needs which are essentially psychological states of tension (these include the need for esteem and the desire for recognition or belonging). It is these needs which, when they become sufficiently intense, create a motivation to act in such a way that the tension of the need is reduced. The search to understand the detail of this process has led to a considerable amount of research over the past 100 years and, in turn, to a variety of theories of human motivation. The best known of these are the theories of Marshall, Freud, Veblen, Herzberg and Maslow.

The first of these, the Marshallian model, is in many ways the most straightforward and is based on the idea that a person's behaviour is inherently rational and motivated by economic factors. The economic individual therefore attempts to maximize total satisfaction by buying goods and services from which the marginal utility is, in theory at least, equivalent to the marginal utility of the alternatives. Although such an overtly rational view of behaviour has long been criticized as being too partial and inadequate an explanation, Kotler (1972) has highlighted several ways in which the Marshallian model contributes to our understanding of buyer behaviour:

1 It is axiomatic that every buyer acts in the light of his own best interest. The question is whether an economist would describe these actions as 'rational' or not.
2 The model is normative in the sense that it provides a logical basis for purchase decisions, i.e. how one should decide rather than being descriptive, i.e. how one actually decides.
3 The model suggests a number of useful behavioral hypotheses, e.g. the lower the price, the greater the sales; the lower the price of substitute products, the lower the sales of this product; the lower the price of complementary products, the higher the sales of this product; the higher the real income, the higher the sales of this product, provided that it is not an 'inferior' good; the higher the promotional expenditure, the higher the sales.

Freud's work, by contrast, suggests that the psychological factors which influence behaviour are for the most part unconscious, and that as a consequence we can only rarely understand our true motivations. Equally, in the process of growing up and conforming to the rules of society, we repress a series of urges. The obvious implication of this for marketing is that a consumer's *stated* motive for buying a particular brand or product may well be very different from the more fundamental *underlying* motive. Thus, in the case of a fast car, the stated motive might be the ability to get from A to B quickly. The underlying motive, however, might well be the desire for status and to be noticed. Similarly, with an expensive watch the stated motive might be the product's reliability, while the real – and unconscious – motive might again be status and the desire to impress others.

The best known exponent of Freudian theory in marketing is Ernest Dichter who in the 1950s developed a series of techniques, under the general heading of *motivational research*, designed to uncover consumers' deepest motives. Motivation research was subjected to a considerable amount of criticism on the grounds that buyers were subsequently being manipulated and persuaded to act against their own interests. Two of the most vociferous opponents of motivation research proved to be Galbraith and Packard. Galbraith (1958), for example, levelled a series of criticisms against the development of the consumer society, arguing that consumers were being persuaded to act against their true interests. Packard's criticisms, in his book *The Hidden Persuaders* (1957), were aimed even more specifically at techniques of motivation research and raised the spectre of the wholesale manipulation of society by marketing people for their own ends. Largely because of the subsequent publicity, motivation research became a less acceptable research technique and this, coupled with a whole series of problems experienced in its use, led to its gradual decline.

The Freudian view that a consumer's stated motives may well be very different from the true motives is echoed in Veblen's social-psychological interpretations of behaviour (1899). Many purchases, he argued, are motivated not by need but by a desire for prestige and social standing. Although Veblen's views, and in particular his emphasis upon conspicuous consumption, have subsequently been modified by research findings, his contribution to our understanding of buyer behaviour is significant, not least because it stresses the importance of social relationships as an influence upon choice.

The fourth major theory of motivation and one which has received considerable attention from marketing analysts over the past 15 years, was developed by Herzberg. Labelled the 'Two Factor Theory' of motivation, it distinguishes between *satisfiers* (factors that create satisfaction) and *dissatisfiers* (factors that create dissatisfaction). In the case of a car, for example, the absence of a warranty would be a dissatisfier. The existence of a warranty, however, is not a satisfier since it is not one of the principal reasons for buying the product. These are more likely to be the car's looks, its performance and the status that the buyer feels the product confers upon the driver.

There are several implications of this theory for marketing, the two most significant of which are, first, that the seller needs to be fully aware of the dissatisfiers which, while they will not by themselves sell the product, can easily 'unsell' it. The second implication, which follows logically from this, is that the strategist needs to understand in detail the various satisfiers and then concentrate not just upon supplying them, but also giving them full emphasis in the marketing programme.

The fifth and final principal theory of motivation was put forward by Maslow who suggested that behaviour can be explained in terms of a hierarchy of needs; this is illustrated in Figure 5.3.

The model suggests that a person begins by concentrating upon satisfying the most important and most basic physiological needs before moving on to the higher levels of need. Thus, as each level is satisfied, the next level is likely to become the focus of attention.

Although from the viewpoint of the marketing strategist Maslow's theory is arguably of less direct value than that of, say, Herzberg, it is of value in that it provides yet another insight into the ways in which products fit into the goals and lives of consumers.

FIGURE 5.3
Maslow's hierarchy of needs

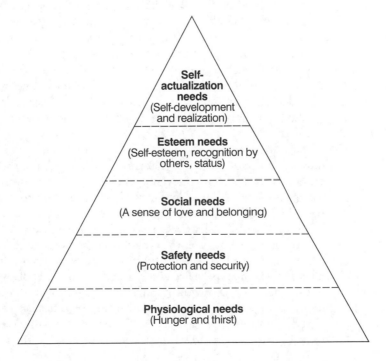

Issues of Perception

Against the background of an understanding of the factors influencing motivation, the marketing strategist needs then to consider the influence of *perception*, since it is the way in which motivated individuals perceive a given situation that determines precisely how they will behave. It has long been understood that because of the three elements of the perceptual process – selective attention, selective distortion and selective retention – individuals can perceive the same object in very different ways. It is the failure to recognize and take account of this that often leads to a confusion of, for example, advertising messages. Research in this area has provided a series of insights into the perceptual process, and subsequently to a series of guidelines for marketers. In the case of *selection attention*, for example, simply because of the enormous number of stimuli that we are exposed to each day (more than 1000 advertisements alone), a substantial number are either ignored or given only cursory attention. If a marketing message is to succeed it therefore has to fight against this screening process. This can be done in one of several ways, including:

1 the use of black and white advertisements when others are in colour, or vice versa;
2 the use of shock messages – in 1990, for example, the RSPCA drew attention to the number of stray dogs being destroyed each year by showing a mountain of bodies;
3 the sheer size of the advertisement;
4 substantial money-off offers;
5 the unexpected – a glue manufacturer used his product to stick a car to a hoarding in London some 15 feet above the pavement.

Even when a message does reach the consumer, there is no guarantee that it will be interpreted in the way that was intended. Each person modifies information in such a way that it fits neatly into the existing mind set. This process of *selective distortion* means that messages that confirm preconceived notions are far more likely to be accepted than those that challenge these notions. Although a mind set can be changed, this is typically both costly and time consuming. However, one example of where this has been done with considerable success is with Japanese products. The image reputation of the majority of Japanese products in the 1960s was undoubtedly poor, and a factor which had implications for, among other areas, distribution and pricing. Throughout the 1970s and 1980s, however, the Japanese concentrated on quality and product innovation to the point at which even the most die-hard and conservative European or American has been forced to admit that in many markets it is now the Japanese who set the lead.

A similar example is likely to be provided in the 1990s by the Czechoslovakian car manufacturer, Skoda. Long seen as rugged, cheap and utilitarian, their take-over by Volkswagen in the early part of the decade and the strategic changes which will inevitably be made will force changes in the ways in which the product is perceived.

The third element of perception is that of *selective retention*. Quite simply, individuals forget much of what they learn. To ensure therefore that a message is retained, it needs to be relevant, generally straightforward, one which reinforces existing positive attitudes, and in the case of certain products, catchy. Many people for example still remember simple advertising slogans such as 'Beanz Meanz Heinz', 'Drinka Pinta Milk A Day', 'Go to work on an egg', and 'Guinness is good for you', even though in some cases the message has not been used for well over a decade.

Once individuals have responded to an advertisement, they go through a process of learning. If the experience with the product is generally positive, the likelihood of repeat purchase is obviously increased. If, however, the experience is largely negative, not only is the likelihood of repeat purchase reduced, but the negative attitude that develops is likely to be extended to other products from the same manufacturer and possibly the country of origin. It is the set of *beliefs* and *attitudes*

Illustration 5.5: Volkswagen's Environmental Car : Marketing to New Age Customers

Founded in 1938, Volkswagen is the world's fourth largest car manufacturer with an annual output of 3.5 million cars. Although General Motors, Ford and Toyota are all bigger than VW, the company is Europe's largest car producer with the greatest share of market – 18 per cent or so compared with the 12–13 per cent of its largest rival, GM-Opel.

With 80 per cent of Volkswagen's sales being made within Europe, the state of the European market is at the heart of the company's success. The economic downturn of the late 1980s and early 1990s therefore hit the organization particularly hard, with net earnings in 1992 having dropped by 70 per cent. However, despite the downturn in the market and a series of budgetary cuts, VW had pushed ahead with its plans for the launch of an environmentally safer car. The new model, which was launched to the media at the 1993 Frankfurt Auto Show, was felt by the management team to be exactly the sort of car that the regulatory bodies and European consumers had long been asking for, and had led to VW investing millions of DM in the project on the assumption that they would sell 20 000 vehicles.

Environmental concerns and the manufacturers' responses
The car has long been seen by governments and the public alike to be one of the – or the – key causes of environmental pollution. The car manufacturers have responded to this in a variety of ways, including the development of recyclable materials and the recycling of parts and components, more economical engines, lighter-weight vehicles, and through research into alternative fuels such as natural gas, solar power and hydrogen. Against this background and the market research which:

> seemed to confirm that consumers everywhere – especially in Germany, Switzerland, Austria, the USA and Sweden – were environmentally aware and concerned, and that they wanted to do something about the perceived crisis. In other countries – such as Italy, France and the UK – the awareness was not yet as intense but was expected to become so in the very near future. Instinctively sensing this new 'feeling' out in the market place, VW's top management decided that the company had to take the lead and design a car specifically to solve rather than create environmental problems.

The response to this proved to be surprisingly easy, as Karlheinz Keller, Head of Speciality Cars, commented:

> We had an *immediate* solution to top management's request – and it had been sitting in the bottom drawer for the past seven years! We'd already made such a car in 1982 and had offered it to the market. So, why not try again to do what we had intended to do seven years earlier? Why not use the technological capabilities we already had to reduce gas consumption?

The car that he was referring to had been launched in 1982 and, although a technological success, had proved to be a marketing failure. The vehicle's key feature had been a unique engine brake which did not slow the car down when the driver took his foot off the accelerator. The effect of this was to improve fuel consumption by 10–30 per cent.

In rejuvenating these ideas, the company's senior management recognized that the profit potential of the new car would almost inevitably be low:

If this project had been judged solely as other profit-making opportunities, it would never have gone further than the Board. It was, of course, expected to make a profit, but we also believed that our technology should be used as part of our responsibility to keeping the earth clean. The real point was to show our customers that we were reliable, to make them aware that VW is a company which has always been dedicated to environmental responsibility.

The target market

In identifying those parts of the market which appeared to offer the greatest potential, VW's manager categorized the public in terms of their environmental attitudes:

1 *The deep green ecologists*, who were typically regarded as being 'on the fringe', advocated public transport and bicycles in place of cars, and who were frequently associated with Greenpeace and other movements (a relatively small group).
2 *The environmentally concerned consumers*, who actually changed their behaviour and were also prepared to pay extra for environmentally sound offerings (a relatively small group that was growing).
3 *The environmentally aware consumers*, who were willing to change their behaviour, e.g. separate their refuse or return recyclable items, but were not generally willing to pay extra (a relatively large group that was growing).
4 *The environmentally interested*, who voiced some concern about the environment, but whose behaviour did not change (a reasonably sized group of people 'waiting to see').
5 *The environmentally unconcerned*, who felt that the focus on environmental issues was totally foolish and unwarranted (still the largest group, amounting to around 30 per cent of the population).

For Volkswagen, it was groups 2 and 3 which were seen to be essential to success. But although group 2 was seen to be a relatively easy target, it was group 3 that ultimately would determine whether the project would achieve the momentum and critical mass that would stop competitors getting into the market.

In the event, the market proved to be far less enthusiastic than had been expected and this, coupled with the development within the group of far more efficient, powerful, less polluting diesel engines, led to the model being dropped.

that emerge both from our own experiences and from those of individuals in our reference groups that build up a set of product and brand images. These, in turn, lead us to behave in relatively consistent ways. An obvious problem that can therefore be faced by a manufacturer stems from the difficulties of changing attitudes and images once they have been established.

5.5 THE BUYING DECISION PROCESS

Having identified the various factors which influence behaviour, the marketing strategist is then in a position to examine the buying process itself. This involves focusing on three distinct elements:

1 the buying roles within the decision-making unit;
2 the type of buying behaviour;
3 the decision process.

The Five Buying Roles

In the majority of cases and for the majority of products, identifying the buyer is a relatively straightforward exercise. In some instances, however, the decision of what to buy involves several people, and here we can identify five distinct roles:

1 the *initiator* who first suggests buying the product or service;
2 the *influencer* whose comments affect the decision made;
3 the *decider* who ultimately makes all or part of the buying decision;
4 the *buyer* who physically makes the purchase;
5 the *user(s)* who consumes the product or service.

Identifying who plays each of these roles, and indeed *how* they play them, is important since it is this information which should be used to determine a wide variety of marketing decisions. In the case of advertising, for example, the question of who plays each of the buying roles should be used to decide on who the advertising is to be aimed at, the sort of appeal, the timing of the message, and the placing of the message.

The Types of Buying Behaviour

So far in our discussion, we have referred simply to 'buying behaviour'. In practice, of course, it is possible to identify several types of buying decision and hence several types of buying behaviour. The most obvious distinction to make is based on the expense, complexity, risk and opportunity cost of the purchase decision – the process a consumer goes through in deciding on a new car or major holiday, for example, will be radically different from the process in deciding whether to buy a chocolate bar. Recognition of this has led Assael (1987, Chapter 4) to distinguish between four types of buying behaviour, depending on the degree of buyer involvement in the purchase and the extent to which brands differ. This is illustrated in Figure 5.4.

FIGURE 5.4
The four types of buying behaviour

		Low	High
Significant differences between brands	Few	1 Habitual buying behaviour (e.g. baked beans)	3 Dissonance reducing behaviour (e.g. furniture)
	Many	2 Variety seeking behaviour (e.g. chocolate bars and breakfast cereals)	4 Complex buying behaviour (e.g. computers)

SOURCE: Adapted from Assael (1987), p. 87

Understanding the Buying Decision Process

The third and final stage that we are concerned with here is the structure of the buying decision process that consumers go through. In other words, precisely how do consumers buy particular products? Do they, for example, search for information and make detailed comparisons, or do they rely largely upon the advice of a store assistant? Are they influenced significantly by price or by advertising? Questions such as these have led to a considerable amount of research into the buying process (see Illustration 5.6) and subsequently to consumers being categorized either as deliberate buyers or compulsive buyers.

To help in coming to terms with this, a series of models have been proposed which focus not simply upon the purchase *decision*, but upon the *process* leading

Illustration 5.6: Using Research to Get into the Consumer's Mind

Customer analysis is designed to provide the strategist with a clear understanding of *how* and *why* people behave as they do. To help with this, two sets of techniques have been developed.

1 *Consumer research* which deals with attitudes and opinions towards existing products and possible new ones. The techniques used include simple structured interviews of large samples of consumers and lengthy discussions with small groups.
2 *Market research* which observes what happens in the market-place. The findings are then projected into estimates of total market size, trends, brand shares, and so on.

Although both sets of research techniques have developed significantly over the past 20 years, Davidson (1987, pp. 48–9) has argued that:

> Despite much clever talk in the marketing world about complicated and novel research techniques, it is apparent that most of the really successful new consumer products introduced in the past decade have fulfilled relatively obvious needs which the simplest form of investigation would have revealed. The critical reason for their success was not shrewd investigation, but skilful design and selling. Most of the outstanding new products of the 1980s succeeded for these reasons.

Source: Davidson, J. H. (1987), Offensive Marketing, *Penguin*

up to this decision, the decision itself, and then subsequently post-purchase behaviour. An example of this sort of model is illustrated in Figure 5.5.

This process begins with the consumer's *recognition of a problem*, or perhaps more commonly, a want. This may emerge as the result of an internal stimulus (hunger or thirst) or an external stimulus in the form of an advertisement or a colleague's comment. This leads to the *search for information*, which might be at the level simply of a heightened awareness or attention to advertising, or at the deeper level of extensive information searching. In either case, the search process is likely to involve one or more of four distinct sources:

FIGURE 5.5
A sequential model of the buying process

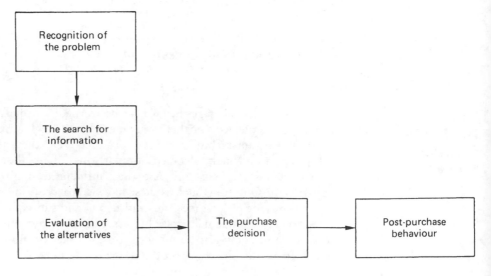

1 *personal sources* such as family, friends, colleagues and neighbours;
2 *public sources* such as the mass media and consumer organizations – a typical example would be the Consumers' Association *Which?* magazine;
3 *commercial sources* such as advertising, sales staff and brochures;
4 *experimental sources* such as handling or trying the product.

The relative importance of each of these varies greatly from person to person and product to product, a point that has been emphasized by Kotler (1988, p. 196):

> Generally speaking, the consumer receives the most information exposure about a product from commercial sources, that is, marketer-dominated sources. On the other hand, the most effective exposure come from personal sources. Each type of source may perform a somewhat different function in influencing the buying decision. Commercial information normally performs an informing function and personal sources perform a legitimizing and/or evaluation function.

To illustrate this, Kotler goes on to cite an example of doctors learning about the existence of new pharmaceuticals from commercial sources, but who then typically rely upon other doctors for evaluative information.

By gathering information in this way consumers develop an awareness, knowledge and understanding of the various brands in the market. An obvious task then faced by marketing strategists is how best to ensure that their brand stands out from the others available and is subsequently purchased. In essence this involves moving the product or brand from the *total set* available, through to the consumer's *awareness set* and *consideration set* to the *choice set* from which the consumer ultimately makes the buying decision; this is illustrated diagrammatically in Figure 5.6.

However, for this to be done effectively, the strategist needs to have a clear understanding of the evaluative criteria used by consumers in comparing products. Much of the research in this area has focused primarily upon the cognitive element, suggesting that consumers make product judgements on a rational basis (see Illustration 5.7). Whether this is the case in practice is debatable.

FIGURE 5.6
The move from the consumer's total set to the choice set

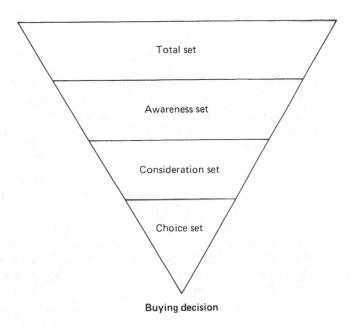

Total set

Awareness set

Consideration set

Choice set

Buying decision

Illustration 5.7: Customers Buy Benefits, Not Products

Recognition of the idea that customers do not buy products but are instead interested in the benefits gained from using the product has long been at the heart of successful marketing. This has been commented on by, among others, Malcolm McDonald (1984, p. 56):

> The difference between benefits and products is not just a question of semantics. It is crucial to the company seeking success. Every product has its features: size, shape, performance, weight, the material from which it is made, and so on. Many companies fall into the trap of talking to customers about these features rather than what those features mean to the customer. This is not surprising. For example, if, when asked a question about the product, the salesman could not provide an accurate answer, the customer might lose confidence and, doubting the salesman, will soon doubt his product. Most salesmen are therefore very knowledgeable about the technical features of the products they sell. They have to have these details at their fingertips when they talk to buyers, designers and technical experts.
>
> However, being expert in technical detail is not enough. The customer may not be able to work out the benefits which particular features bring and it is therefore up to the salesman to explain the benefits which accrue from every feature he mentions.
>
> A simple formula to ensure that this customer-oriented approach is adopted is always to use the phrase 'which means that' to link a feature to the benefit ir brings:
>
> 'Maintenance time has been reduced from 4 to 3 hours which means that most costs are reduced by . . .'
>
> 'The engine casing is made of aluminium which means that six more units can be carried on a standard truck load, which means that transport costs are reduced by . . .'

McDonald goes on to argue that companies should undertake detailed analyses to identify the full range of benefits *they are able to offer* the customer as a prelude to identifying the range of benefits that *customers actually want* or will respond to. Benefits typically fall into four categories:

1 *standard benefits* which arise from the company and its products;
2 *double benefits* which bring a benefit to the customer and subsequently, through an improvement in the customer's product, to the end user;
3 *company benefits* which emerge as the result of a relationship that develops by virtue of having bought a particular product – a typical example would be worldwide service back-up;
4 *differential benefits* which distinguish the product from those offered by competitors.

Among others to have discussed the significance of benefits is Theodore Levitt who takes as an example drill bits. The customer, he suggests, does not buy a quarter-inch drill for its own sake, but for the quarter-inch holes it gives. The implication for the manufacturer is that he needs to define his business in terms of the means of making holes in materials. By limiting the definition to the manufacture of drills he is likely to fail to recognize the opportunity offered by, for example, industrial lasers which are capable of making holes more rapidly and accurately.

Nevertheless, there are several influencing factors which have emerged from this research which merit consideration. These include:

1 the *product's attributes* such as its price, performance, quality and styling;
2 their *relative importance* to the consumer;
3 the consumer's perception of each *brand's image*;
4 the consumer's *utility function* for each of the attributes.

By understanding consumers' perceptions in this way, the strategist can then begin modifying the product offer. This can be done in one of six ways:

1 changing the physical product by, for example, adding features (real repositioning);
2 changing beliefs about the product by giving greater emphasis to particular attributes (psychological repositioning);
3 changing beliefs about competitors' products by comparative advertising and 'knocking copy' (competitive depositioning);
4 changing the relative importance of particular attributes – as a product moves through the product life cycle, for example, and consumers become more familiar with the concept and the technology, the emphasis in the advertising can be shifted from, say, reassuring consumers about reliability and service back-up, to a range of additional uses;
5 emphasizing particular product features which previously have been largely ignored;
6 changing buyers' expectations.

Against the background of these comments, the strategist should then be in a position to consider the act of purchase itself, and in particular *where* the purchase will be made, the *quantities* in which it will be made, the *timing*, and the *method* of payment.

An Overview of Models of Consumer Behaviour

Throughout the 1960s attempts were made to integrate a variety of theories, research findings and concepts from the behavioural sciences into a general framework which could be used to explain and predict consumer behaviour. In doing this, the principal writers, such as Nicosia (1966), Engel, Kollat and Blackwell (1968), and Sheth (1969), moved away from the general perspective that had previously been adopted by economists and which in a number of ways is typified by Marshall's work and the Marshallian model of 'economic man'. Instead of viewing consumer behaviour simply as a single act made up of the purchase itself and the post-purchase reaction, a far greater recognition was given to the consumer's psychological state before, during and after the purchase. This process has been summarized by Howard (1983) who suggested that buyer behaviour is 'largely determined by how the customer thinks and processes information'.

This idea of an information – attitude – intention – purchase sequence has also been commented on by Foxall (1987, p. 126):

All of the models . . . are founded upon such a rational decision sequence. They credit consumers with considerable capacities for receiving and handling quantities of information and undertaking extensive prepurchase searches and evaluations. They rely heavily upon the idea of cognitive decision making in which information is received and classified by the individual and, via mental processing, transformed into the attitudes and intentions which determine brand choice and related aspects of purchase and consumption. Consumer information processing has sometimes been described as analogous with that of computers; the consumer has been depicted in terms of a 'central control unit' and the cognate elements of information technology. Whatever the details of explanation, however, hypothesized decision makers use evaluation criteria to predict the outcomes of each available option in terms of their objectives; employ decision rules or other methods of comparative evaluation in order to decide upon a course of action; receive and process information, storing it in and retrieving it from memory – all in the course of making a decision or solving a problem before purchasing a brand.

The three best known of these so-called comprehensive models were developed in the United States by Nicosia, Engel et al., and Sheth. A brief summary of their structure and key features appears in Illustration 5.8.

Although these models have been of value in extending our understanding of the decision process, their value has been questioned in recent years. The principal criticisms that have been made by Foxall (1987, p. 128) are as follows:

1 the models assume an unrealistic degree of consumer rationality;
2 observed behaviour often differs significantly from what is described;
3 the implied decision process is too simplistic and sequential;
4 insufficient recognition is given to the relative importance of different types of decisions – each decision is treated by comprehensive models as significant and of high involvement, but the reality is very different and by far the vast majority of decisions made by consumers are relatively insignificant and of low involvement;
5 the models assume consumers have a seemingly infinite capacity for receiving and ordering information – in practice, consumers ignore, forget, distort, misunderstand or make far less use than this of the information with which they are presented;
6 attitudes towards low involvement products are often very weak and only emerge after the purchase and not before as comprehensive models suggest;
7 many purchases seem not to be preceded by a decision process;
8 strong brand attitudes often fail to emerge even when products have been bought on a number of occasions;
9 consumers often drastically limit their search for information, even for consumer durables;
10 when brands are similar in terms of their basic attributes, consumers seemingly do not discriminate between them but instead select from a repertoire of brands.

In the light of these criticisms, it is perhaps not surprising that the results that have emerged from attempts to test the models have proved disappointing.

5.6 ORGANIZATIONAL BUYING BEHAVIOUR

Although there are certain factors common to both consumer and organizational buying behaviour, there are also numerous points of difference. Perhaps the most obvious feature of commonality in approaching the two areas is the fundamental need to understand how and why buyers behave as they do. There are, however, certain features of organizational buying which are not found in consumer markets. Kotler (1988, p. 208) identified these as being:

- Organizations buy goods and services to satisfy a variety of goals: making profits, reducing costs, meeting employee needs, and meeting social and legal obligations.
- More persons typically participate in organizational buying decisions than in consumer buying decisions, especially in procuring major items. The decision participants usually have different organizational responsibilities and apply different criteria to the purchase decision.
- The buyers must heed formal purchasing policies, constraints, and requirements established by their organizations.
- The buying instruments, such as requests for quotations, proposals, and purchase contracts, add another dimension not typically found in consumer buying.

Illustration 5.8: Comprehensive Models of Consumer Behaviour

The Nicosia Model

The Nicosia model consists of a flow diagram designed to illustrate how a potential consumer responds to news of a new brand. The model's three-stage sequence begins with the consumer being made aware of the brand's existence and then traces the decision process through from purchase to post-purchase evaluation and feedback. This sequence is assumed to begin with advertising which makes the consumer aware of the brand's existence and an unfilled want. Perception of the message is influenced by attributes of both the company and the consumer, and may lead to the development of an attitude towards the brand. The consumer is then assumed to search for alternative brands which are evaluated by means of other consumers, advertising messages, previous experiences with each company, and so on. This search process leads the consumer either to dismiss or to purchase the product. The experience of purchase and consumption then has the effect of modifying the consumer's psychological state and acts as a feedback loop leading either to a decision to repeat the purchase or not to buy it again.

The Engel, Kollat and Blackwell Model

The starting point for the EKB model is the consumer's perception of a want which must be satisfied. This stimulates a search for information internally (memory), externally (neighbours, colleagues, and friends), and from market sources (advertisements, trade literature, magazine reports). This search process identifies the various ways in which the want can be satisfied and leads to the consumer setting the criteria by which the alternatives can be compared and evaluated. This leads in turn to the emergence of a set of attitudes and beliefs which ultimately determine choice. The outcome of this choice then feeds back to influence future behaviour.

The Howard and Sheth Model

Howard and Sheth's approach is broadly similar to those of Nicosia and Engel, et al., in that it again attempts to pull together a disparate set of variables. These are grouped under four main headings:

1 *inputs* which stimulate the buying process. These include product related factors (price, quality and distinctiveness), symbolic factors (images that stem from the mass media and sales people), and social factors (family, reference groups and social class influences);
2 *perceptual constructs* which explain the consumer's cognitive activity in terms of information processing;
3 *learning constructs* which represent the results of information processing;
4 *outputs* which include not just the purchase itself but also the implications for perception and learning.

As with the two previous models, the output acts as a feedback loop to influence attitudes and future behaviour.

These points are in turn reflected in Webster and Wind's (1972, p. 2) definition of organizational buying as 'the decision making process by which formal organizations establish the need for purchased products and services, and identify, evaluate, and choose among alternative brands and suppliers'.

The significance of organizational buying practices has been pointed to by a variety of writers, including Turnbull (1987, p. 147) who has highlighted the impact of professional procurement on profitability in the telecommunications equipment market:

> Some telecommunications equipment manufacturers now buy in items accounting for up to 80 per cent of total cost. Thus even a 2 per cent procurement saving can have a marked effect on profitability or give the company a significant price advantage in the marketplace. Additionally, professional purchasing also helps secure long term and improved sources of supply.

The strategic significance of consistently good buying has long been recognized within the Dixons retail chain and has been a major contributor to their performance in recent years. Their experiences are discussed in Illustration 5.9.

Although quite obviously, as with consumers in consumer markets, no two companies behave in the same way, both research and experience have demonstrated that patterns of similarity do exist in the ways in which organizational buyers approach the task of buying, and that they are sufficiently uniform to simplify the task of strategic marketing planning.

In analysing patterns of organizational buying, the starting point is in many ways similar to that for consumer markets, with the strategist posing a series of questions:

- *Who* makes up the market?
- What *buying decisions* do they make?
- Who are the *key participants* in the buying process?
- What are the *principal influences* upon the buyer and what organizational rules and policies are important?
- What *procedures* are followed in selecting and evaluating competitive offerings and how do buyers arrive at their decisions?

Who Makes Up the Industrial Market?

The term 'industrial market' is used to refer to individuals who and organizations which buy goods and services that are then used in the production of other goods and services subsequently supplied to others. As a group, it therefore includes agriculture, manufacturing, construction, transportation, communications, banking, financial services, insurance, mining, and so on. These markets typically possess a set of characteristics which are not shared with consumer markets and which have a series of implications for the way in which the marketing strategist needs to approach the marketing task. The most significant of these characteristics are:

1 the existence of a smaller number of buyers each of whom typically buys in larger quantities than is the case in consumer markets;
2 a (high) degree of buyer concentration, with a limited number of buyers often accounting for the bulk of purchasing within the industry;
3 geographical concentration;
4 close relationships between suppliers and customers, with products often being modified to fit the specific needs of the customer;
5 inelastic demand, particularly in the short term;
6 demand is generally derived, with the result that the strategist needs to examine the secondary markets which influence the demand for the primary product;
7 professional purchasing which is performed by buyers who often work as part of a buying team and who in attempting to satisfy particular performance or

---

Illustration 5.9: The Dixon's Success Story: a Lesson in Buying

'Retailing is about buying rather than selling,' according to Stanley Kalms, the founder of Dixons. 'It is based on products and is about "competitive edge" and unique propositions.' Certainly the success of Dixon's, the high street electrical and camera retailer, owes much to its professional purchasing operations.

Buyers at Dixon's are seasoned veterans who know their industry inside out. Buying activities break down into three categories. Firstly there are the deals with leading manufacturers of brown goods (e.g. TVs; videos; computers) and white goods (e.g. washers; cookers, fridges and freezers). Dixon's has a successful record of working with leading manufacturers to develop new products, too. Secondly, and of growing importance are Dixon's own label products (labelled with Japanese type names such as Saisho). These are made for Dixon's by foreign manufacturers and provide the organisation with the opportunity to beat famous brand prices and still make bigger margins. Finally, and most excitingly (according to some Dixon's buyers), are the 'one off' bargain deals Dixon's are able to strike with manufacturers. Such deals are forged with manufacturers who need to move stocks. Often the success of such transactions is down to Dixon's better understanding of what will sell and how to sell in the market place. The financial capability of Dixon's enables it to take massive stocks (the entrepreneurial spirit within the organisation makes acceptable the risk involved). This capability often means very low purchasing prices per unit. In the summer of 1985, for example, Dixon's doubled its order of computer stock from the troubled Sinclair organisation. Ten thousand units represented an order of such magnitude that it might well have been beyond the scope of Dixon's prior to their takeover of the family firm, Curry's the year earlier. As it turned out an aggressively marketed package of a Spectrum computer together with software, disc drive and joystick, all at a lower price, made reordering possible.

The marketing operation is the mirror image of purchasing. Purchasing managers work closely with their marketing counterparts – even share the same office. They are jointly responsible for the selection of product ranges and for their margins. While according to the firm, 'good purchasing personnel ripen with age', marketing people are constantly moved to new product areas to maintain a continuous injection of new ideas.

The constant search is to find ways of making customers feel 'it is worth their while coming into Dixon's, always worthwhile passing by someone else'. Exclusive merchandise, own label products, 'how to' books, better credit, better ranges, longer guarantees and an exciting, 'sexy' shop atmosphere have been hallmarks of the Dixon marketing approach.

Source: Richardson and Richardson (1989), Business Planning: an approach to strategic management, *Pitman.*

---

quality criteria employ a greater degree of overtly rational thinking than is generally the case in consumer markets;

8 reciprocal trading patterns often exist, making it difficult for new suppliers to break into the market.

The Three Types of Buying Decision

Much of the research conducted over the past 25 years into the nature of the industrial buying process has made either explicit or implicit use of a categorization first proposed in 1967 by Robinson, Faris and Wind. There are, they suggested, three distinct buying situations or buy classes, each of which requires a different pattern of behaviour from the supplier. They are the *straight rebuy*, the *modified rebuy*, and the *new task*.

Of these, the straight rebuy is the most straightforward and describes a buying situation where products are reordered on a largely routine basis, often by someone at a fairly junior level in the organization. Among the products ordered in this way is office stationery. Here, the person responsible for the ordering simply reorders when stocks fall below a pre-determined level and will typically use the same supplier from one year to another until either something goes wrong or a potential new supplier offers a sufficiently attractive incentive for the initial decision to be reconsidered. The implications of this sort of buying situation are for the most part straightforward and require the supplier to maintain both product and service quality. Perhaps the biggest single problem in these circumstances stems from the need on the part of the supplier to avoid complacency setting in and allowing others to make an approach which causes the customer to reassess the supplier base.

The second type of buying situation – the modified rebuy – often represents an extension of the straight rebuy and occurs when the buyer wants to modify the specification, price or delivery terms. Although the current supplier is often in a relatively strong position to protect the account, the buyer will frequently give at least cursory consideration to other possible sources of supply.

The third type of buying situation – the new task – is the most radical of the three and provides the marketing strategist with a series of opportunities and challenges. The buyer typically approaches the new task with a set of criteria which have to be satisfied, and in order to do this will frequently consider a number of possible suppliers each of whom is then faced with the task of convincing the buyer that his product or service will outperform or be more cost-effective than the others. The buyer's search for information is often considerable and designed to reduce risk. Where the costs are high there will typically be several people involved in the decision, and the strategist's task is therefore complicated by the need not just to identify the buying participants, but also their particular concerns and spheres of influence. In doing this, the strategist should never lose sight of the significance of attitudes to risk and the ways in which individuals may work to reduce their exposure to it. Chisnall (1989, p. 72), for example, has commented that: 'A buyer's professional activities may be tempered by the fundamental instinct he has for survival and for enhancing his career.' This point has also been made by McClelland (1961): 'A great part of the efforts of business executives is directed towards minimising uncertainties.'

This general theme has been examined in detail by Cyert and March (1963) who in their behavioural theory of the firm identify four types of buying determinants: individual, social, organizational, and environmental. Within this framework they then distinguish between 'task' and 'non-task' factors. Task factors are for the most part rational and include price, delivery, quality, performance levels, and so on. The non-task factors include personal values, and political, cultural and social elements, as well as the personality traits of the decision maker. Although identifying and analysing the impact and relative importance of these 'soft' elements is difficult, their effects should be neither underestimated nor ignored.

Who is Involved in the Buying Process?

A major characteristic of organizational buying is that it is a group activity, and only rarely does a single individual within the organization have sole responsibility for making all the decisions involved in the purchasing process. Instead, a number of people from different areas and often with different statuses are involved either directly or indirectly. Webster and Wind (1972, p. 6) have referred to this group both as the decision-making unit (DMU) of an organization and as the buying centre, and define it as 'all those individuals and groups who participate in the purchasing decision-making process, who share some common goals and the risks arising from the decisions'. There are, they suggest, six roles involved in this process, although on occasions all six may be performed by the same person:

1 *users* of the product or service who in many cases initiate the buying process and help in defining the purchase specifications;
2 *influencers* who again help to define the specification, but who also provide an input to the process of evaluating the alternatives available;
3 *deciders* who have the responsibility for deciding on product requirements and suppliers;
4 *approvers* who give the authorization for the proposals of deciders and buyers;
5 *buyers* who have the formal authority for selecting suppliers and negotiating purchase terms (a summary of the different types of buyer that have been identified appears in Illustration 5.10).
6 *gatekeepers* who are able to stop sellers from reaching individuals in the buying centre. These can range from purchasing agents through to receptionists and telephone switchboard operators.

Illustration 5.10: The Seven Different Types of Buyer

The issue of the buyer's style and its implications for marketing strategy has been the subject of research in the United States by Dickinson (1967, pp. 14–17) who identified seven types of buyer:

1 *loyal* buyers who remain loyal to a source for considerable periods;
2 *opportunistic* buyers who choose between sellers on the basis of who will best further his long-term interests;
3 *best deal* buyers who concentrate on the best deal available at the time;
4 *creative* buyers who tell the seller precisely what they want in terms of the product, service and price;
5 *advertising* buyers who demand advertising support as part of the deal;
6 *chisellers* who constantly demand extra discounts;
7 *nuts and bolts* buyers who select products on the basis of the quality of their construction.

Although Webster and Wind's categorization of buying centre roles is the best known and the most widely used, a variety of other analytical approaches have been developed. Hill (1972), for example, has argued the case for analysing the buying centre not on the basis of the participants' roles, but on the basis of functional units. There are, he suggests, five such units:

1 *control units* which are responsible for the policy making which influences buying and which imposes certain constraints – these might include buying where possible only from British suppliers or from local small firms;
2 *information units* which provide information relating to the purchase;
3 *the buying unit* which consists of those with formal responsibility for negotiating the terms of the contract;
4 *user units* consisting of anyone in the organization who will be involved in using the product or service;
5 *the decision-making unit* which consists of those in the DMU who will make the decision.

Of these, it is only the control, information and decision-making units that he believes are of any real importance in influencing buying decisions. Regardless of which of these two frameworks the strategist uses in trying to understand the organizational buying process, a considerable amount of research has been

Illustration 5.11: Research Findings on Roles within the Buying Centre

Each of the roles in the organizational decision-making unit has been subjected to a substantial amount of research. Among the findings to have emerged from this, Turnbull (1987, p.149) has highlighted 12 of the most significant:

- The buyer or purchasing agent in many circumstances is little more than a clerical officer whose input to the buying decision is limited to filling out the order forms (Weigand, 1968).
- The buyer's role and influence is determined to a very large extent by senior management's purchasing philosophy. Where this is seen to be significant, the role and influence of the buyer will be far greater than is otherwise the case (Feldman and Cardozo, 1968).
- Buyers' perceptions of their role and status can be major determinants of the influence they exert. Where the buyer is ambitious, they work to enhance their role by feeding information on new technical developments to management and by trying to become involved in as many aspects of the buying process as possible (James, 1966).
- Where buyers have little authority, they often attempt to simplify the purchasing process (Kettlewood, 1973).
- Users with specialist knowledge may exert sufficient influence to override traditional commercial considerations such as delivery times and price (Weigand, 1966).
- Purchasing staff and technologies in certain European countries such as Germany and Sweden have been shown to be more highly qualified and demanding than their British counterparts. This apparent lack of technical competence on the part of British companies has led in turn to exporters facing unexpected barriers to entry (Turnbull and Cunningham, 1981).
- The composition of the buying centre is heavily dependent upon the company's orientation. Where, for example, it is technology orientated, engineers dominate the buying process and decisions (Sheth, 1973).
- The larger the company, the greater the number of buying influences (Sheth, 1973).
- Large organizations typically exhibit a far greater degree of purchasing expertise and formality than smaller firms (Various).
- The composition of the buying centre tends to vary depending upon the characteristics of the product being purchased and, in particular, the degree of perceived risk (Cyert and March, 1963).
- The composition of the buying centre is influenced by the organization's previous experience with the seller (Robinson, Faris and Wind, 1967).
- Buyers often only examine a limited range of suppliers, largely because of the costs of collecting information (Buckner, 1967). This finding has subsequently been taken a step further by White (1969) whose research suggested that a major reason for limiting the search process is in fact to avoid or simplify work.

conducted that provides a series of interesting insights to each of these elements; a brief summary of a selection of these findings appears in Illustration 5.11.

Although the size, structure and formality of the buying centre will quite obviously vary depending both upon the size of the organization and the product decision involved, the strategist needs always to consider five questions:

1 Who are the principal participants in the buying process?
2 In what areas do they exercise the greatest influence?
3 What is their level of influence?
4 What evaluative criteria do each of the participants make use of and how professional is the buying process?
5 To what extent in large organizations is buying centralized?

In considering these questions, there are several pieces of research which are worth examining because of the insights they provide to the ways in which buying centres behave. The findings of two of the most useful studies are illustrated in Figures 5.7 and 5.8.

FIGURE 5.7
Buying influences and company size

Number of employees	Average number of:	
	(I) Buying influences	(II) Contacts by members of the sales force
0–200	3.42	1.72
201–400	4.85	1.75
401–1000	5.81	1.90
More than 1000	6.50	1.65

SOURCE: Adapted from McGraw-Hill (1963)

FIGURE 5.8
Sources of information

	Small firms (%)	Large firms (%)
Trade and technical press	27	60
Calls by the sales force	46	19
Direct mail	19	9
Exhibitions	8	12

SOURCE: McLean Hunter

The Principal Influences on Industrial Buyers

Much of the early research into industrial buying processes was based on the assumption that industrial buyers, unlike consumers, are wholly rational. More recently it has been recognized that while economic factors play a significant role, a variety of other elements also needs to be taken into account. Chisnall (1989, p. 71), for example, in recognizing this, says that:

> Organisational buyers do not live like hermits; they are influenced by the personal behaviour of their colleagues, by the trading practices of other enterprises, and by the standards of the society to which they belong.
>
> It is unrealistic, therefore, to approach the study of buying behaviour – personal or organisational – without an appreciation of the multiplexity of buying motivations. A balanced view is necessary; explanations of buying behaviour should not go from the one extreme of regarding 'rational' economic factors as solely responsible to the equally extreme view that emotional or 'irrational' influences entirely account for the purchase of products and services.

A similar view has been expressed by Harding (1966, p. 76) who has suggested that:

> Corporate decision-makers remain human after they enter the office. They respond to 'image'; they buy from companies to which they feel 'close'; they favour suppliers who show them respect and personal consideration, and who do extra things 'for

them'; they 'over-react' to real or imagined slights, tending to reject companies which fail to respond or delay in submitting requested bids.

This point has in turn been developed by Kotler (1988, p. 214) and reflected subsequently in a model of the influences on industrial buying behaviour proposed by Webster and Wind (1972, pp. 32–7). Kotler, for example, has said:

Industrial buyers actually respond to both economic and personal factors. Where there is substantial similarity in supplier offers, industrial buyers have little basis for rational choice. Since they can satisfy the purchasing requirements with any supplier, these buyers can place more weight on the personal treatment they receive. On the other hand, where competing products differ substantially, industrial buyers are more accountable for their choice and pay more attention to economic factors.

Webster and Wind's model classifies the influences on industrial buyers under four headings: environmental, organizational, interpersonal, and individual influences. These are illustrated in Figure 5.9.

FIGURE 5.9
Factors influencing industrial buying behaviour

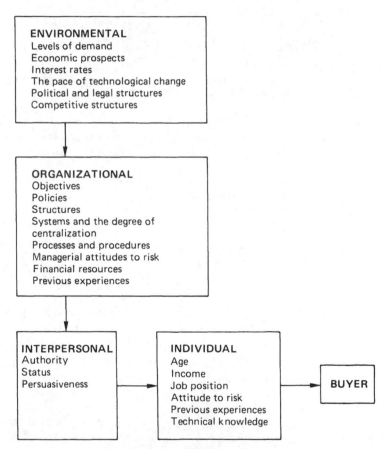

SOURCE: Adapted from Webster and Wind (1972), pp. 33–7

The question of what influences buyers and how various sources of information are perceived has also been examined by Webster (1970). He was particularly interested in the relative importance of formal and informal information sources and how they differ from consumer markets. His findings suggest that informal sources tend to be used far less frequently in industrial markets than in consumer markets and that sales people are often regarded as highly reliable and useful sources of information. By contrast, opinion leadership, which often plays a significant role in consumer markets, was found to be largely ineffective; a possible explanation of this is the perception that no two companies experience the same problem and that there is therefore little to be gained. Perhaps the most significant single finding to emerge from Webster's research was the significance of the role that the industrial sales person is capable of playing *throughout* the buying process; this is illustrated by the summary of Webster's work which appears in Figure 5.10.

The relative importance of sources of information has also been examined by Martilla (1971) and Abratt (1986). Martilla's work led to a series of conclusions that are broadly similar to those of Webster, although in addition he highlighted the importance of word of mouth communication within firms, particularly in the later stages of the adoption process. Abratt's research, which focused on high technology laboratory instrumentation, adds a further dimension to our understanding of the buying process, suggesting that in markets such as these buying personnel often have 'only a token administrative function'. Instead, the question of what to buy is the responsibility of groups of two to three people, with the most significant purchasing criteria proving to be product reliability and technical and sales service back-up, while price was relatively unimportant.

FIGURE 5.10
Percentage of respondents considering information sources to be important at each stage of the buying process

	Awareness	Interest	Evaluation	Trial	Adoption
Manufacturer's sales staff	84	90	64	70	56
Trade journals and the technical press	90	38	22	16	8
Buying staff in other companies	18	22	28	16	8
Engineering staff in other companies	26	34	44	20	18
Trade associations	42	24	14	4	8
Trade shows and exhibitions	76	38	16	12	4

SOURCE: Adapted from Webster (1970)

Perhaps the most underestimated and, in research terms, ignored elements of the buying process is that of the *gatekeeper*. Although the identity of the gatekeeper is often difficult to determine, it is the gatekeeper who in many organizations either blocks or facilitates access and who can therefore play a pivotal role in determining which products are considered. This has been recognized by Pettigrew (1975) who, in a study of the way in which a computer system was purchased, demonstrated how the gatekeeper is capable of filtering the information flow to suit his own objectives.

Although as Chisnall (1989, p. 78) has observed, 'Generalisations about buying behaviour – industrial or consumer – appear to be unwise,' it is generally acknowledged that the role and status of buyers is typically lower in high technology organizations than elsewhere. There are several explanations for this, the most obvious being the need for specialist inputs from technical staff. The ways in which this erodes the authority of the professional buyer and how they typically respond has been examined by Strauss (1962). He identified a series of techniques ranging from the rigid enforcement of highly routinized techniques through to extremes of persuasion and cooperation. This led him in turn to propose a five-part framework:

1 rule-orientated tactics;
2 rule-evading tactics;
3 personal–political tactics;
4 persuasion–educational tactics;
5 organizational–interactional tactics.

The success of the buyer's behaviour was, he suggested, ultimately due to whether the strategy pursued was broadly expansionist or contractionist. Those who tried to expand their role and sphere of influence and who subsequently succeeded did so, he concluded, where: managerial relationships were still developing (perhaps because of new management); the technology of the industry was complex; and there was a need for learning.

How do Buyers Arrive at Their Decisions?

One of the major differences between consumer and industrial buying decisions is the buying motive. Whereas the majority of consumer purchases are made for the individual's personal consumption or utility, industrial purchases are typically designed to reduce operating costs, satisfy legal obligations, provide an input to the manufacturing process, and ultimately to make money. In order to provide a greater understanding of this process, Robinson, Faris and Wind (1967) of the Marketing Science Institute have identified eight stages or buy-phases of the industrial buying process. They then related these to the three types of buying situation that we discussed earlier to form what they referred to as the *buy-grid framework*. This is illustrated in Figure 5.11.

FIGURE 5.11
The Buygrid model

		Buy classes		
		Straight rebuy	Modified rebuy	New task
Buy phases	1 Problem recognition	No	Possibly	Yes
	2 Determination of the general need	No	Possibly	Yes
	3 Specific description of the required product	Yes	Yes	Yes
	4 Search for potential suppliers	No	Possibly	Yes
	5 Evaluation of suppliers	No	Possibly	Yes
	6 Selection of a supplier	No	Possibly	Yes
	7 Order-routine established	No	Possibly	Yes
	8 Review of performance and feedback	Yes	Yes	Yes

SOURCE: Adapted from Robinson, et al. (1967)

This buying process, which begins with the recognition of a problem, can be sparked off by either internal or external stimuli. Internal stimuli typically include: the decision to develop a new product, and the recognition that this will require new equipment or materials; machine breakdowns; the belief on the part of the purchasing manager that better prices or quality can be obtained from an alternative supplier; curiosity; and organizational policy decisions. External stimuli include: the launch of a new product by a competitor; advertisements; sales representatives; and ideas that emerge as the result of trade shows.

This recognition of a problem is then followed by a *general need description* in which the buyer identifies the characteristics and quantity of the products required to overcome the problem. This leads to the development of *product specifications* and subsequently to a *search for suppliers*.

The question of precisely *how* buyers select suppliers has been the subject of a considerable amount of research with some of the most significant findings emerging from the work of Dempsey (1978), Cunningham and Roberts (1974), Lehmann and O'Shaughnessy (1974), and Green, Faris and Wind (1968). Dempsey, for example, in a survey of purchasing managers found the 20 most important selection criteria to be:

1 delivery capability;
2 quality;
3 price;
4 repair and after sales services;

  5 technical capability;
  6 performance history;
  7 production facilities;
  8 help and advice;
  9 control systems;
10 reputation;
11 financial position;
12 attitude towards the buyer;
13 compliance with bidding procedures;
14 training support;
15 communications on the progress of the order;
16 management and organization;
17 packaging;
18 moral/legal issues;
19 location;
20 labour relations.

Cunningham and Roberts' research, which covered the British valve and pump industry, highlighted a series of similar factors: delivery reliability; technical advice; test facilities; replacement guarantee; speed of quotations; ease of contact; and a willingness/ability to supply a wide range.

Lehmann and O'Shaughnessy's findings were again broadly similar, although they introduced an additional element in the form of the *type of buying situation*. This led them to suggest that:

1 for routine order products delivery, reliability, price and reputation are extremely important;
2 in the case of procedural-problem products (e.g. computers and other types of office machinery) the important criteria are technical service, supplier flexibility, and product reliability;
3 for political-problem products which are capable of creating organizational rivalries, the most important attributes are price, the reputation of the supplier, product reliability, service reliability, and supplier flexibility.

These general patterns were in turn reflected in the research findings of Green, Faris and Wind (1968), which are illustrated in Figure 5.12.

FIGURE 5.12
The relative importance of product selection criteria in industrial markets

Performance characteristics	Scaling value
Price/quality ratio	3.61
Reliability of delivery	2.94
Technical knowledge and abilities	1.95
Information services	1.86
Reputation and image	1.65
Location geographically	1.63
Technical and related issues	1.61
Degree of previous contact	1.44
Significance of client-supplier reciprocal relations	0.61

SOURCE: Adapted from Green, et al. (1968)

In so far as it is possible to identify a common theme in this process of deciding between suppliers, it is the reduction, containment and management of risk. In commenting on this, Chisnall (1989, p. 83) has suggested that:

The element of risk in buying decisions could be considered along a continuum ranging from routine (low risk purchases) at one extreme to novel (high risk) purchases at the other end of the scale. In the centre would fall many industrial transactions where the hazards could reasonably be calculated sufficiently to allow decisions of tolerable risk to be made.

FIGURE 5.13
The buying risk
continuum

Reasonable risk

Low risk ◄ — — — — — — — — — — — — — — — — — — — ► High risk
(Routine purchases)   (Occasional purchases   (New purchases
                          for which hazards can be   involving high
                          calculated to allow for   absolute or
                          reasonable risk   opportunity
                          minimization or   costs)
                          avoidance)

SOURCE: Adapted from Chisnall, P. M. (1989), *Strategic Industrial Marketing* (second edition),
Prentice Hall, p. 83

This is illustrated in Figure 5.13.

Buyers typically cope with these risks in several ways, including:

1 exchanging technical and other information with their customers and prospects;
2 dealing only with those suppliers with which the company has previously had favourable experiences;
3 applying strict (risk reducing) decision rules;
4 dealing only with suppliers who have a long-established and favourable reputation;
5 the introduction of penalty clauses for, for example, late delivery;
6 multiple sourcing to reduce the degree of dependence upon a single supplier.

Although for many buyers the pursuit of a risk-reducing strategy has a series of attractions, it needs to be recognized that such a strategy can also possess drawbacks. The most obvious of these stems from the way in which it is likely to lead to the company becoming and remaining a follower rather than becoming a leader. Developments both in product and process technology on the part of a supplier often provide significant opportunities for the development of a competitive edge, and unless this is recognized by the company it runs the risk of adopting new ideas only when they have been well tried by others. In commenting on this, Chisnall (1989, p. 84) has said:

> The industrial buyer is, to some extent, in a dilemma regarding innovating products. He will not wish to retard the development of his own organisation but, at the same time, he will be reluctant to accept unduly heavy risk. Yet he will be conscious of his status within the management hierarchy and of the opportunities which he should use to enhance his career. It has been seen that progressive buyers . . . deliberately involved technical managers in discussions and decisions regarding supplies, and were skilled in using formal and informal approaches. In this way the corporate or organisation man aims to steer a careful course between satisfying his personal need for status and security and the development of his company as a progressive organisation . . . Suppliers should obviously (therefore) try to reduce the element of risk as perceived by buyers, through imaginative marketing strategies, particularly where new products are being introduced.

Perhaps the final aspect of risk that needs to be considered here stems from the significance of post-purchase dissonance. Undoubtedly the best known writer on dissonance is Festinger (1957), who has referred to it as a state of psychological discomfort. This discomfort is, in essence, the result of the individual questioning whether the decision made is correct. According to Festinger, a buyer will try to reduce this discomfort by seeking reassurance for the decision. This can be done by, for example, seeking the support of others, avoiding conflicting messages such as competitive advertising, and searching for editorials and advertisements which state how good the product just purchased is. The more expensive and significant the purchase, the greater the dissonance is likely to be. The implications for a supplier in these circumstnaces should be obvious: buyers need reassurance and this can best be provided by continuing to 'sell' the product and providing supporting evidence of the wisdom of the decision even after the sale itself has been made. Other ways in which dissonance can be reduced include giving emphasis to the quality of the after-sales service, maintaining regular contact with customers, and giving prominence in advertising to the market leaders who have also bought the product. One example of an organization that recognizes the need for managing dissonance is IBM, whose experiences are discussed in Illustration 5.12.

Illustration 5.12: IBM and its Development of the Total Sales Programme

IBM says that it sells solutions, not products. In doing this, the company concentrates upon gaining – and retaining – the customer's confidence from the moment of contact through until well after the sale has been made. One result of this is that long-term relationships are established, repeat purchases are guaranteed, and the likelihood of post-purchase dissonance reduced so that it is to all intents meaningless. Some of the ways in which this is done are listed below:

- Inviting the customer contact and other members of the company to conferences and seminars that may be useful to them. Often these seminars feature major international figures.
- Inviting the contact to visit prestigious customers who have successful IBM installations.
- Inviting the contact and others in the company to visit IBM's factories to look at projects that may be of interest.
- Sending out articles, newsletters and house magazines.
- Ensuring that IBM's service engineers and systems specialists channel back information gained when working at the customer's plant so that as full a picture as possible is built up of the client's needs.
- The development of 'account planning sessions' in which IBM, together with the customer, draws up an action plan for the next few years covering the systems and products that the customer may need.
- Ensuring a regular and worry-free relationship is developed and maintained.

Adapted from Duro, R. (1989) Winning the Marketing War, *John Wiley & Son*

Having decided upon the choice of supplier, the buyer moves on to the *order-routine specification* by identifying such features as the technical specification, the order quantities, delivery schedules, maintenance requirements and payment terms.

The final stage involves a *review of suppliers' performance* and is designed, in one sense at least, to close the loop by feeding back information that will be used when purchasing in the future.

An Assessment of the Buygrid Framework

Although the buygrid framework is undoubtedly useful and provides a series of insights into the various phases of buying, the reader should recognize that it fails to give full recognition of the complexity of the behavioural factors which are likely to influence those involved in making specific purchase decisions. Because of this, other models of organizational buying have been proposed, four of which are discussed in Illustration 5.13.

Illustration 5.13: An Overview of Models of Organizational Buying Behaviour

During the past 25 years a wide variety of models of industrial buying behaviour have been developed. These fall into four main categories:

1 task related models;
2 non-task related models;
3 complex and multidisciplinary models;
4 interactive models.

The first of these – *task related models* - is by far the most straightforward and is the organizational equivalent of the Marshallian model of economic man that we discussed at an earlier stage. These models, which have to a large extent been invalidated by subsequent research, emphasize rationality and constrained choice:

By contrast, *non-task models* recognize the personal interests of the decision maker. In discussing this, Turnbull (1987, pp. 155–6) identifies the key concepts as being:

- Individual desire for ego enhancement or personal gain.
- Desire to avoid risk in decision making.
- Gratification of buyer and seller through a dyadic relationship.
- Lateral relationships between buyer and colleagues.
- Relationships with significant other persons from within the company and their effect on transmission and interpretation of information.

The third category consists of *complex* and multidisciplinary models which incorporate a larger number of variables. Included within this are Robinson, Faris and Wind's buygrid model, and Sheth's multidisciplinary model, both of which are discussed in the text. A key feature of complex models is that explicit recognition is given to social, cultural, psychological and economic variables.

The final category – the *interaction approach* - places far greater emphasis upon the nature of the process and relationships which develop both within and between buying and selling organizations. Thus:

- buyers and sellers are both active participants and buyers often attempt to influence what they are offered;
- relationships are often long term and based on mutual trust rather than any formal commitment;
- patterns of interaction are frequently complex and extend within the organizations as well as between them;
- emphasis is given to supporting these relationships as well as to the process of buying and selling;
- links between buyers and sellers often become institutionalized.

The best known of the multidisciplinary models was developed by Sheth (1973). Within this model he attempts both to identify and show the interrelationship of the multiplicity of factors involved in industrial buying. These factors, he suggests, can be examined under three headings:

1 the psychological world of the individuals involved in organizational buying;
2 the conditions which precipitate joint decisions among these individuals;
3 the process of joint decision making with the inevitable conflict among the decision makers and its resolution by resorting to a variety of tactics.

In putting forward this model, Sheth does not argue that it is definitive. Rather it is a framework which illustrates the complexity of the process and attempts to present the various inputs to this process systematically.

This approach to modelling industrial buying has in turn provided one of the foundations for the work of Hakansson and the IMP (International Marketing and Purchasing of Industrial Goods) group. Their research focused upon industrial buying and selling behaviour in five European countries – West Germany, the United Kingdom, France, Italy and Sweden – and led to the development of a model which views this behaviour as a process in which both sides play active roles within a given environment. They suggest that four elements influence the patterns of buyer–seller interaction. These elements, which are illustrated in Figure 5.14, are:

1 the interaction process;
2 the participants in this process;
3 the interaction environment;
4 the atmosphere created by this interaction.

FIGURE 5.14
The interaction model of industrial marketing and purchasing

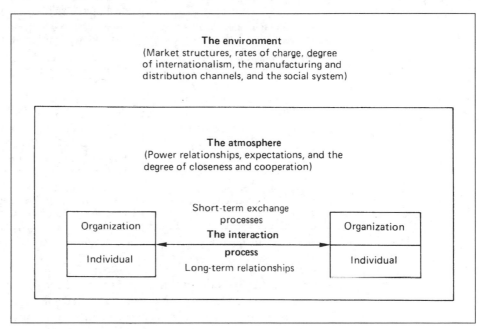

SOURCE: Adapted from Hakansson (1983)

The real value of this model, which makes use both of inter-organizational theory and new institutional economic thinking, is that it gives far greater emphasis than earlier work to the idea that industrial buying and selling is concerned with the management of relationships. In commenting on this, Chisnall (1989, p. 93) has said:

> That business negotiation is essentially a dynamic process will hardly surprise experienced executives who, although they may not be able to articulate the theory, know full well the complexities involved in successful business deals. The interdependence of buyers and sellers in industrial product and service markets is well recognised in practice, although even long-established relationships and loyalties may be vulnerable to new levels of competition from, for instance, the newly industrialised countries.

Hakansson's theory is helpful in drawing attention to the need for executives – in both purchasing and marketing – to develop negotiating skills appropriate to specific products and market conditions. Both formal and informal contacts contribute to the establishment of relationships that can result in mutually satisfactory business transactions. Since the research enquiries covered several countries, it is perhaps not surprising that attitudes towards participation and authority were found to be 'quite different' in France and Germany compared with Sweden, although it was considered that more extensive research would be needed before this cultural phenomenon could definitely be established.

The Growth of Relationship Marketing

It has long been recognized that the costs of gaining a new customer, particularly in mature and slowly declining markets, are often high. Given this, it is argued, the marketing planner needs to ensure that the existing customer base is managed as effectively as possible. One way of doing this is to move away from the traditional and now largely outmoded idea of marketing and selling as a series of activities concerned with transactions, and to think instead of their being concerned with the management of long(er)-term relationships. This is illustrated in Figure 5.15.

FIGURE 5.15
Transaction versus relationship marketing

Transaction marketing	Relationship marketing
A focus on single sales	A focus on customer retention and building customer loyalty
An emphasis upon product features	An emphasis upon product benefits that are meaningful to the customer
Short timescales	Long timescales, recognizing that short-term costs may be higher, but so will long-term profits
Little emphasis on customer retention	An emphasis upon high levels of service which are possibly tailored to the individual customer
Limited customer commitment	High customer commitment
Moderate customer contact	High customer contact, with each contact being used to gain information and build the relationship
Quality is essentially the concern of production and no-one else	Quality is the concern of all, and it is the failure to recognize this that creates minor mistakes which lead to major problems

SOURCE: Adapted from Christopher, Payne and Ballantyne (1994), *Relationship Marketing*, p. 9.

The potential benefits of this are considerable and can be seen not just in terms of the higher returns from repeat sales, but also in terms of the opportunities for cross-selling, strategic partnerships and alliances. (Clutterbuck (1993) cites a study by Bain and Co. who suggest that, depending upon the type of business, a 5 per cent increase in customer retention can result in a profitability boost of anywhere from 25 per cent to 125 per cent. The advantages are, of course, then increased further when the potential lifetime value of the customer is taken into account.) In developing a relationship marketing programme, there are several important steps:

● Identify the key customers, since it is with these, particularly in the early stages, that the most profitable long-term relationships can be developed.
● Examine in detail the expectations of both sides.
● Identify how the two organizations can work together more closely.
● Think about how operating processes on both sides might need to be changed so that co-operation might be made easier.
● Appoint a relationship manager in each of the two organizations so that there is a natural focal point.
● Go for a series of small wins in the first instance and then gradually strengthen the relationship.
● Recognize from the outset that different customers have very different expectations and that these need to be reflected in the way in which the relationship is developed.

FIGURE 5.16
Relationship marketing and the customer loyalty chain

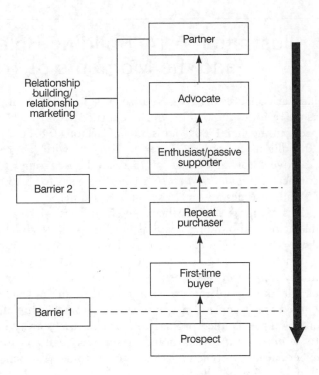

The position of relationship marketing within the customer loyalty chain is illustrated in Figure 5.16. The ways in which it was used strategically by SAS is discussed in Illustration 5.14.

Although it might be argued that the movements of a buyer through the various stages from prospect to partner should be straightforward and seamless, the reality in many instances is that organizations unwittingly erect a series of barriers which slow down or stop this movement. The first can be seen to be that of the way in which, in many cases, organizations make it difficult to do business with them. While this might seem to be something of a paradox, these barriers often exist in terms of inappropriate opening hours, unhelpful sales staff, uncompetitive prices, poor product configurations, slow delivery, and so on. The second barrier occurs at a later stage, when the customer deals with the organization on a regular basis, but no real effort is made to get close to the customer by building a relationship. Instead, each sale takes the form of a one-off transaction, an approach which goes at least part of the way towards explaining why long-standing customers 'suddenly' move to another supplier.

Given this, the arrow on the right-hand side of Figure 5.16 shows how customers can – and almost inevitably will – move back down the loyalty chain if the relationship is not managed proactively.

5.7 THE INFLUENCE OF THE PRODUCT ON MARKETING STRATEGY

Although a variety of frameworks for classifying products have at one time or another been proposed, one of the most useful was put forward by Aspinall (1962). There are, he suggests, five product characteristics that should provide the basis for identifying the product's potentially most effective marketing strategy. These are:

1 the rate at which the product is purchased, consumed and replaced (*the replacement rate*);
2 the *gross margin*;

Illustration 5.14: Building Relationships and the Moments of Truth

Jan Carlzon, president of Scandinavian Airlines System (SAS), achieved fame as the result of the way in which he turned SAS from heavy losses to healthy profit in the mid-1980s. In his book, Carlzon (1987, p. 3) says that each of his 10 million customers came in contact with approximately five SAS employees for an average of 15 seconds each time. He referred to these contacts as *moments of truth*, suggesting that, for SAS, these were 'created' 50 million times a year, 15 seconds at a time.

It is statistics such as these which indicate the scale of opportunity for managing and building relationships, or, as Clutterbuck, et al. (1993, p. 101) define these critical encounters, OTSUs – Opportunities to Screw Up.

When things do go wrong – and almost inevitably they will sooner or later in any long-term relationship – the question is how well the organizations handle the complaint. In examining this, the TARP organization in the United States concluded that when a customer complains and feels that the complaint is handled properly, he or she comes away satisfied and is likely to be *more loyal* to that brand or supplier than a customer who has never experienced a problem. Related to customer segment brand loyalty, the findings were as follows:

- experienced no problem   87%
- satisfied complainant   91%
- dissatisfied complainant   41%
- non-complainant   59%

Two key issues emerge here: firstly, dissatisfied customers should be encouraged and assisted to complain, but secondly, the complaint must be resolved to the customer's complete satisfaction.

Where customers remain dissatisfied, the implications are significant because not only will they fail to buy again, they tend not to keep quiet about their experiences. Statistics surrounding this issue are quoted ubiquitously, but all tend to tell the same story. Gerson (1992, p. 18), for example, states that a dissatisfied customer will tell ten people about his experiences; approximately 13 per cent of dissatisfied customers will tell up to twenty people. Customers who are satisfied or have had their complaints satisfactorily resolved will tell between three and five people about their positive experience.

The stark reality of these statistics is that three to four customers have to be satisfied for every one who remains dissatisfied – a 4:1 ratio against.

3 the *amount of adjustment* that needs to be made to the product so that it matches the precise needs of the customer;
4 the *time of consumption* over which the product delivers the utilities demanded by the consumer;
5 the amount of *searching time* that the consumer is willing to give to the product. This is typically a measure of the average time and distance from the retail outlet.

Aspinall argues that this framework can then be used as the basis for a scoring system and the subsequent classification of products into broad categories. He then goes on to identify three categories of products, each of which is assigned a colour. Thus:

- *Red goods* which have a high replacement rate, a low gross margin, require little adjustment, and have a limited consumption and searching time;
- *orange goods* which have a medium score across all five dimensions;
- *yellow goods* which have a low rate of replacement, a high gross margin, require substantial adjustment, and have a significant consumption and searching time.

5.8 SUMMARY

Within this chapter we have focused on the detail of consumer and industrial buying structures and processes and on the ways in which an understanding of these contributes to effective marketing planning.

A variety of factors influence consumer behaviour, the most significant of which are a network of cultural, social, personal, and psychological forces. Each of these was discussed in some detail and the nature of their interrelationships explored. Against this background we then considered the structure of buying decision processes, and in particular:

- the buying roles within the decision-making unit;
- the different types of buying behaviour;
- the process through which a consumer goes in making a decision.

A variety of attempts have been made over the past 25 years to model the complexities of the buying process, the best known of which are those proposed by Nicosia; Engel, Kollat and Blackwell; and Sheth. These models have been the subject of a certain amount of criticism, one consequence of which has been that the strategist's ability to predict with any real degree of accuracy the probable response of consumers to marketing behaviour is still relatively limited.

Research into organizational buying behaviour has pursued broadly similar objectives to that in the consumer field, with attention being paid to the questions of:

- Who makes up the market?
- What buying decisions do they make?
- Who are the key participants in the buying process?
- What influences the buyer?
- How do buyers arrive at their decisions?

Each of these areas was examined in some detail and the best known of the models of organizational buying behaviour were reviewed. As with models of consumer behaviour, the majority of these have been heavily criticized, largely because of their poor analytical or predictive ability. There are, however, exceptions to this, as we discussed, including Robinson, Faris and Wind's buygrid model, and Hakansson's interaction approach in which use is made of inter-organizational theory and new institutional economic thinking. It is in these areas that future developments in our understanding of organizational buying processes are most likely to be made.

5.9 EXERCISES

1 How might the model illustrated in Figure 5.2 be used to increase our understanding of consumer buying patterns for

- foodstuffs?
- cigarettes?
- fashion clothing?
- cars?

Which are the seemingly most important influences upon consumer choice in each case? What are the implications for the marketing planner?

2 Using Figure 5.4, identify examples of the four types of buying behaviour and consider the implications for marketing planning.

3 Turn to Illustration 5.10 and, using the categorization of the seven types of buyer, identify the style that appears to predominate within your own organization. Given the environment in which your organization operates, do you feel that it is the most appropriate?

4 Take two different types of purchase that you make (e.g. a low-cost and frequent purchase and a more expensive and less frequent purchase) and attempt to build a model which not only explains the thinking process that you go through in making a decision, but which would also enable someone else to predict how you are likely to behave in the future.

5 Look at the purchasing process within your organization and think about the following questions:

- How is the purchasing process organized?
- How influential within the organization is the person who has overall responsibility for purchasing?
- How often are suppliers reviewed?
- What sort of criteria are used for this?
- What evidence is there that purchasing is viewed *strategically* and as a potential source of competitive advantage?

6 Identify examples within your organization of each of the three types of buying situation referred to by Robinson, et al. (p. 184). What sort of criteria are employed in each case when buying decisions are taken? Who is involved at each stage?

7 Select two very different types of product bought by your organization and, using the framework of the six buying roles (p. 179) identify those who play each of the roles.

8 Which approach to marketing appears to predominate in your organization – a transactional approach or a relationship approach?

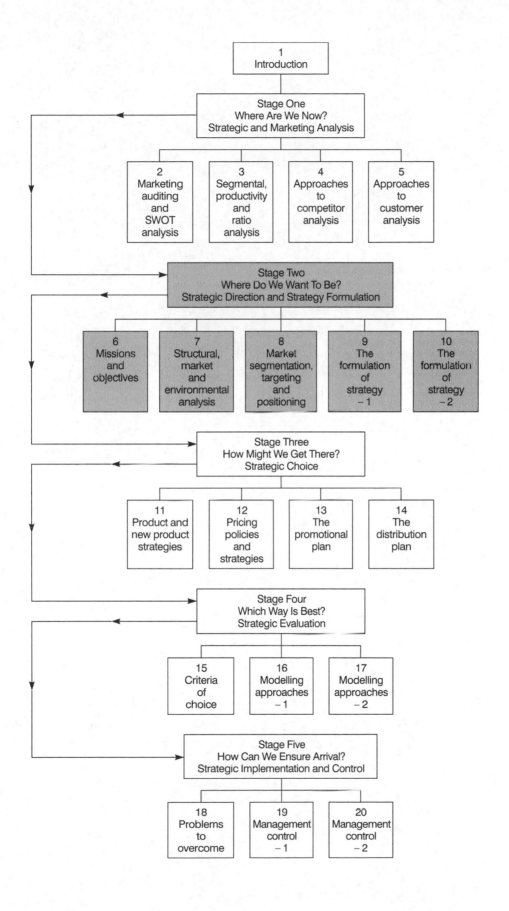

Stage Two
Where Do We Want To Be?
Strategic Direction and Strategy Formulation

PREAMBLE

Within this stage we focus on where the organization wants to go. In doing this we take as our foundation the material of Stage One in which we examined where the organization is currently, and the nature of its marketing capability.

We begin by considering the organizational mission and the nature of marketing objectives (Chapter 6). We then turn to an examination of the changing structure of the marketing environment (Chapter 7) and to the ways in which this structure needs to be reflected in the approach adopted when segmenting the market (Chapter 8). In the following chapter we examine a number of the models that have been developed to help in the process of strategy formulation, as a prelude – in Chapter 10 – to a discussion of the factors that influence the nature of the strategy pursued.

Mission statements have been the subject of considerable discussion in recent years, with the majority of commentators pointing to their potential for providing employees with a clear understanding of core corporate values. Although many organizations still lack a mission statement, while others have statements which reflect a degree of wishful thinking rather than reality, the guidelines for developing a meaningful corporate mission are now well developed. The significance of the mission statement can be further highlighted by recognizing that it is against the background of the mission statement that the strategist should set objectives at both the corporate and the functional level (in the case of marketing, these objectives revolve around two major dimensions: products and markets). It follows from this that a poorly developed mission statement is likely to have consequences for the nature and appropriateness of any subsequent objectives.

As well as being influenced by the corporate mission, organizational objectives are typically influenced by a wide variety of other factors, including the nature and demands of the environment. The marketing strategist typically analyses the environment within the PEST (Political, Economic, Social and Technological) framework, the individual elements of which are in the majority of markets undergoing a series of significant and often unprecedented changes, each of which needs to be taken into account both when setting objectives and formulating strategies.

The changing environment also has consequences for methods of segmentation. Effective segmentation is at the heart of a well-developed marketing strategy, and has implications for virtually everything else that follows in the strategy process. It is therefore a source of concern that work by Saunders has highlighted the fact that senior managers in many British organizations seemingly fail to recognize this, and pay little or no attention either to the need for segmentation or to the ways in which it can be carried out most effectively.

The strategic significance of segmentation is reinforced by the way in which decisions on how the organization's markets are to be segmented subsequently has implications for targeting and market positioning. The failure to segment effectively is therefore likely to weaken much of the marketing process.

In Chapters 9 and 10 we focus upon approaches to the formulation of marketing strategy. In the first of these chapters we consider some of the developments that have taken place over the past 20 years in techniques of portfolio analysis. The portfolio approach to management emerged largely as a result of the turbulence of the early 1970s and is based on the idea that an organization's businesses should be viewed and managed in a similar way to an investment portfolio, with a strategic perspective being adopted in the management of each major element.

Although a wide variety of portfolio techniques have been developed and have contributed to a greater understanding on the part of management of what is meant by strategy, research findings are beginning to emerge which suggest that usage levels of even the best-known methods are low. Several explanations for this have been proposed, including unrealistic expectations on the part of managers, difficulties with the data inputs, and an over-zealous adherence to the strategic guidelines that typically accompany the models. Nevertheless, models of portfolio analysis need to be seen as one of the major developments in strategic thinking over the past 20 years and, if used wisely, are capable of contributing greatly to a structured approach to marketing management. (See Morrison and Wensley (1991).)

The type of marketing strategy pursued by an organization is often the result of the interaction of a series of factors, including past performance, managerial expectations and culture, competitive behaviour, the stage reached on the product life cycle, and the firm's relative market position. Porter has attempted to provide a structure for examining the strategic alternatives open to an organization and suggests that in order to compete successfully the strategist needs to select a generic strategy and pursue it consistently. The three generic strategies that he identifies are:

- cost leadership;
- differentiation;
- focus.

Dangers arise, Porter suggests, when the firm fails to pursue one of these and instead is forced or drifts into a 'middle-of-the-road' position where the message to the market is confused and the likelihood of a successful competitive attack is increased.

A considerable amount of work has been done in recent years in drawing parallels between military warfare and marketing strategy with a view to identifying any lessons that the marketing strategist might learn. A number of general lessons have emerged from this, and guidelines on how best either to defend a market position or attack other organizations are now well developed. Within this chapter we have attempted to draw upon the experiences of successful organizations and to highlight particular dangers. Included within these is the danger of adhering to a particular strategy for too long a period, labelled 'strategic wear out'. There is an obvious attraction in sticking to a well-proven strategy, although evidence exists to suggest that even the best formulated strategy has a limited life. The marketing strategist should therefore closely monitor the effectiveness of any given strategy and be willing to change it in order to reflect the environment, different managerial expectations, and the progression through the product and market life cycles.

6 | Missions and objectives

6.1 LEARNING OBJECTIVES

When you have read this chapter you should be able to understand:

(a) the purpose of planning;
(b) the nature of the corporate mission and how a mission statement can best be developed;
(c) the factors influencing objectives and strategy;
(d) the nature of corporate objectives;
(e) the nature of marketing objectives.

6.2 INTRODUCTION

To be effective, a strategic planning system must be goal driven. The setting of objectives is therefore a key step in the marketing planning process, since unless it is carried out effectively, everything that follows will lack focus and cohesion. In terms of its position within the overall planning process that forms the basis of this book, objectives setting can be seen to follow on from the initial stage of analysis and, in particular, the marketing audit which provided the focus of Chapter 2 (see Figure 6.1).

FIGURE 6.1
The strategic planning process

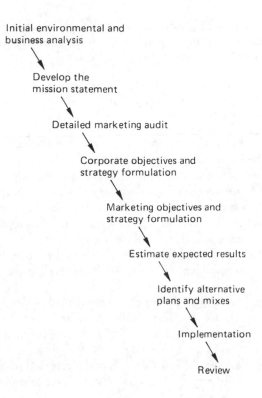

Initial environmental and business analysis

Develop the mission statement

Detailed marketing audit

Corporate objectives and strategy formulation

Marketing objectives and strategy formulation

Estimate expected results

Identify alternative plans and mixes

Implementation

Review

By setting objectives, the planner is attempting to provide the organization with a sense of direction. In addition, however, objectives provide a basis for motivation as well as a bench-mark against which performance and effectiveness can subsequently be measured. The setting of objectives is thus at the very heart of the planning process and is the prelude to the development of strategies and detailed plans. (For a discussion of the interrelationships between objectives, strategies and plans, refer to Illustration 6.1). Perhaps surprisingly therefore in view of its fundamental importance, the literature on *how* to set marketing objectives is surprisingly thin, something that is reflected in a comment by McDonald (1984, p. 82):

> The literature [on marketing planning] is not very explicit, which is surprising when it is considered how vital the setting of marketing objectives is. An objective will ensure that a company knows what its strategies are expected to accomplish and when a particular strategy has accomplished its purpose. In other words, without objectives, strategy decisions and all that follow will take place in a vacuum.

A possible explanation of this is that, in principle at least, the process of setting objectives is relatively straightforward and as such merits little discussion. In practice, however, the process is infinitely more difficult, particularly in divisionalized organizations, or where the company has an extensive product range being sold across a variety of markets. Regardless of whether we are talking about principles or practice, the sequence should be the same, beginning with an identification of the organization's current position and capabilities, a statement of assumptions about environmental factors affecting the business, and then agreement among stakeholders as to the objectives themselves.

In moving through this process, the majority of commentators recommend that the planner moves from the general to the specific and from the long term to the short term. This frequently translates into statements on three aspects of the business:

1 the nature of the current business (what business *are* we in?);
2 where it should go (what business *should* we be in?);
3 how it should get there.

Identifying where the company is currently is often far more difficult than it might appear, something which is reflected in a comment by the ex-Chairman of ICI, Sir John Harvey-Jones (1988):

> There is no point in deciding where your business is going until you have actually decided with great clarity where you are now. Like practically everything in business this is easier said than done.

Recognizing the validity of this point should encourage the strategist to focus not just upon the business's current position, but also *how* and *why* it has achieved its current levels of success or failure. Having done this, he is then in a far better position to begin specifying the *primary* or *most important* corporate objectives, as well as a series of statements regarding the key results areas such as sales growth, market penetration, and new product development in which success is essential to the organization. Following on from this, the strategist should then begin developing the *secondary* or *sub-objectives* such as geographical expansion and line extension which will need to be achieved if the primary objectives are to be attained.

This process of moving from the general to the specific should lead to a set of objectives which are not just attainable within any budgetary constraints that exist, but which are also compatible with environmental conditions as well as organizational strengths and weaknesses. It follows from this that the process of setting objectives should form what is often referred to as an internally consistent and mutually reinforcing hierarchy. As an illustration of this, if we assume that corporate management is concerned first and foremost with, say, long-term profits and growth, it is these objectives which provide the framework within which the more detailed subset of operational objectives, including market expansion and product specific increases in sales and share, are developed. Taken together, these then contribute to the achievement of the overall corporate objectives.

It is these operational objectives which are the principal concern of those in the level below corporate management. Below this, managers are concerned with objectives that are defined even more specifically such as creating awareness of a new product, increasing levels of distribution, and so on. This hierarchy points in turn to the interrelationship, and in some cases the confusion, that exists between corporate objectives and marketing objectives. The distinction between the two is an important one and is discussed at a later stage in this chapter. However, as a prelude to this, and indeed to the process of objectives setting, there is a need for the strategist to decide upon the business mission. We therefore begin this chapter with a discussion of the role and purpose of planning as the background against which we can more realistically examine approaches to the development of the mission statement and, subsequently, corporate and marketing objectives. See Illustration 6.1.

Illustration 6.1: Objectives, Strategies and Plans

The interrelationships between objectives, strategies and plans have been spelled out by Davidson (1987, p. 122) who, in discussing BMW's recovery efforts in Germany in the 1960s, comments:

> In 1960 BMW was on the verge of bankruptcy. It was producing motor cycles for a dwindling market, and making a poor return on its bubble cars and six-cylinder saloons. A takeover bid by Daimler-Benz, the makers of Mercedes, was narrowly avoided, and the group was rescued by a Bavarian investment group.
>
> Paul G. Hahnemann, Opel's top wholesale distributor, was appointed Chief Executive. His first objective was obviously to get BMW back on an even keel, where it was sufficiently profitable to survive in the long-term. Having got there, he would then move to a more ambitious objective of challenging Mercedes for leadership of the market for high-quality executive cars.
>
> He was convinced that there was an unexploited market for a sporty saloon car, which Mercedes was not tapping. As he pointed out, 'If you were a sporty driver and German, there was no car for you. The Mercedes is big, black and ponderous. It's for parking, not driving.'
>
> Consequently, he evolved a strategy for producing a range of high-quality cars with better performance and a more sporty image than any other saloon. This strategy has remained broadly unchanged since. But the plans for executing it have evolved and been refined.

Source: Davidson, H. (1987), Offensive Marketing, Penguin

6.3 THE PURPOSE OF PLANNING

In discussing the nature and role of the planning process, Jackson (1975) comments that:

> Planning attempts to control the factors which affect the outcome of decisions; actions are guided so that success is more likely to be achieved. To plan is to decide what to do before doing it. Like methods, plans can be specially made to fit

circumstances or they can be ready made for regular use in recurrent and familiar situations. In other words, a methodical approach can be custom built or ready made according to the nature of the problems involved.

The purpose of planning can therefore be seen as an attempt to impose a degree of structure upon behaviour by allocating resources in order to achieve organizational objectives. This is in turn reflected in a somewhat cumbersome but nevertheless useful comment by Drucker (1959) who suggests that:

> business planning is a continuous process of making present entrepreneurial decisions systematically and with best possible knowledge of their futurity, organizing systematically the effort needed to carry out these decisions against expectations through organized feedback.

While not particularly succinct, this definition has a certain value in that it highlights the three major elements of planning:

1 the need for systematic decision making;
2 the development of programmes for their implementation;
3 the measurement of performance against objectives, as a prelude to modifications to the strategy itself.

It follows from this that if the planning process is to be effective, then the planner needs to give full recognition to the changing nature and demands of the environment, and to incorporate a degree of flexibility into both the objectives and the plan itself. Any failure to do this is likely to lead to a plan that quickly becomes out of date. Simmons (1972) has pointed to the dangers of this both in the planning carried out by the Eastern bloc countries and by American business. In the case of the Eastern bloc countries in the 1940s, 50s and 60s, for example, he suggests that:

> They tried to impose a fixed five year plan on changing conditions. Unfortunately, some American businesses are still making this mistake ... frequently a well constructed plan only six months old will be found to be very much out-of-date.

If planning is to prove effective, there is an obvious need for a regular review process, something which is particularly important when the environment in which the organization is operating is changing rapidly. As an example of this, Chisnall (1989, pp. 133–34) has pointed to the Post Office and the increasingly competitive environment it faced following the Post Office Act of 1969, which:

> ... transformed the Post Office from a Department of State into a State Corporation that had to achieve a predetermined level of profits. The establishment of a marketing department in 1972 added to the keen commercial awareness and new professional skills which were needed to tackle, for instance, the fast-growing and aggressive competition in parcels traffic from several new market suppliers.

The principal purpose and indeed benefit of planning can therefore be seen in terms of the way in which it imposes a degree of order upon potential chaos and allocates the organization's resources in the most effective way. Among the other benefits are the ways in which the planning process brings people together and, potentially at least, leads to 'a shared sense of opportunity, direction, significance and achievement'. The planning process can therefore be seen to consist of four distinct stages:

1 evaluation (where are we now, where do we want to go, and what level of resource capability do we have?);
2 strategy formulation (how are we going to get there?);
3 detailed planning;
4 implementation and review.

For many organizations, it is the implementation stage which proves to be the most difficult but which paradoxically receives the least attention. There are several possible explanations for this. Peters & Waterman (1982, pp. 9–12), for example, suggest that all too often emphasis is placed upon what they refer to as the 'hard-ball' elements of strategy, structure and systems, with too little recognition being given to the significance of the 'soft-ball' elements of style, skills, staff and subordinate systems. (This is discussed in greater detail on page 681.)

The Problems with Marketing Planning

Although marketing planning has an inherent logic and appeal, McDonald (1995, p. 64) suggests that the vast majority of organizations experience significant problems in developing truly effective planning systems and cultures. There are, he believes, ten factors that contribute to this:

1 Too little support from the chief executive and top management. As a result, the resources that are needed are not made available and the results are not used in a meaningful way.
2 A lack of a plan for planning. As a consequence, too few managers understand how the plan will be built up, how the results will be used, the contribution that they are expected to make and the timescales that are involved.
3 A lack of support from line managers.
4 A confusion over planning terms: remember that not everyone is familiar with Ansoff and the Directional Policy matrix.
5 Numbers are used instead of written objectives and strategies.
6 An emphasis upon too much detail, too far ahead.
7 Planning becomes a once-a-year ritual instead of an integral part of the day to day management process.
8 Too little thought or attention is given to the differences between operational or short term planning and strategic planning.
9 There is a failure to integrate marketing planning into the overall corporate planning system.
10 The task of planning is left to a planner who fails to involve those who are actually managing the business.

McDonald goes on to suggest that far too many plans fail to take sufficient account of the issues associated with the plan's implementation. The consequences of this, which have also been discussed by Bonoma, are illustrated in Figure 6.2.

FIGURE 6.2
The planning and implementation matrix

	Bad (inappropriate)	Good (appropriate)
Marketing Implementation — Bad (ineffective)	**1 Failure** The marketing programme fails to exploit environmental opportunities and build upon the resource base	**2 Trouble** The answer lies in focusing upon issues of implementation
Marketing Implementation — Good (effective)	**3 Trouble** The plan is flawed and any attempt at implementation is therefore of little value	**4 Success** The marketing programme achieves its objectives

SOURCE: Adapted from Bonoma, T. (1985), *The Marketing Edge: Making Strategies Work*

6.4 ESTABLISHING THE CORPORATE MISSION

Referring back to Figure 6.1 (see page 199), it can be seen that following an initial environmental and business analysis, the development of a mission statement is the starting point both for corporate and marketing planning since it represents a vision of what the organization is or should attempt to become. This is typically expressed in terms of the two questions to which we have already referred: 'What business are we in?' and 'What business should we be in?' It is the answer to this second question in particular which sets the parameters within which objectives are subsequently established, strategies developed, and action programmes implemented. The mission statement should therefore be capable of performing a powerful integrating function, since it is in many ways a statement of core corporate values and is the framework within which individual business units prepare their business plans, something which has led to the corporate mission being referred to as an 'invisible hand' which guides geographically scattered employees to work independently and yet collectively towards the organization's goal. A similar sentiment has been expressed by Ouchi (1983, p. 74) who suggests that the deliberate generality of the mission statement performs an integrating function of various stakeholders over a long period of time. This is illustrated in the case of the earth-moving equipment manufacturer J. C. Bamford which has a clearly stated policy of quality and product improvement, something of which everyone in the organization is fully aware and which acts as a consistent guideline in determining behaviour at all levels, but particularly within the planning process.

For a mission statement to be worthwhile, it should be capable of providing personnel throughout the company with a shared sense of opportunity, direction, significance and achievement, factors which are particularly important for large organizations with divisions which are geographically scattered.

The potential benefits of a strong binding statement of fundamental corporate values and good communication have been highlighted by a variety of writers, including Pilditch (1987, p. 34) who has pointed to research in the United States which 'found that companies that do better had excellent communications. Everyone knew the corporate goals and was encouraged to help to achieve them'. Equally a study of European managers by Management Centre Europe found that what gave highly successful companies an edge over their competitors was the importance they attached to basic corporate values. In commenting on these findings, Chisnall (1989, pp. 138–39) has said:

> As with comparable studies in the United States, there often seemed to be a rather curious inverse relationship between those companies which emphasised profitability as a primary corporate value and the actual profitability achieved. On the other hand, companies generally ranking customer satisfaction as the most important corporate value were highly profitable. It is important to note, however, that professed commitment to high corporate values needs to be translated into practice: strong declarations themselves may sound impressive, but implementation has to be effected by management at every level of organisation and expressed in many ways, such as high standards of customer service, good teamwork between executives in different departments as well as in the same section, keeping promised delivery dates, etc. Clearly, these duties should always be undertaken by those responsible for them but, too often, such everyday tasks are just not well done.

In many ways, therefore, the mission statement, the position of which within the overall planning process is illustrated by the acronym MOST (Mission, Objectives, Strategy, Tactics), represents a visionary view of the overall strategic posture of an organization and, as Johnson & Scholes (1988, p. 8) comment 'is likely to be a persistent and resistant influence on strategic decisions'. Richards (1983, p. 104) has referred to the mission in much the same way, calling it 'the 'master strategy' and suggesting that it is a visionary projection of the central and overriding concepts on which the organization is based. He goes on to suggest that 'it should not focus on what the firm is doing in terms of products and markets currently served, but rather upon the services and utility within the firm'.

It follows from this that any failure to agree the mission statement is likely to lead to fundamental problems in determining the strategic direction of the firm. Recognizing this, Debenhams, Sainsbury, and Marks & Spencer have all concentrated upon developing *and communicating to their staff* their mission statements. The rationale in each case is straightforward and is a reflection of the fact that a mission statement is of little value unless it is understood by everyone in the organization and *acted upon*.

In the case of Debenhams, for example, the mission statement is printed on a card which employees are expected to carry with them:

We will be the leading countrywide speciality store, the first choice for fashion and home furnishings for middle and upper income customers, characterised by our:

- Visual excitement and easy to shop environment
- Fashion authority
- Dominance in the most wanted merchandise categories
- Above average quality and value for money
- Merchandise organised by end use, activity or emerging trend
- Customer dedication

We will produce above average profits for Department Stores to meet Group financial objectives.

We will develop an organisational environment which will attract, retain, develop and motivate high calibre staff, dedicated to the implementing of our mission.

Similarly, Sainsbury has stated its mission as being:

To discharge the responsibility as leaders in our trade by acting with complete integrity, by carrying out our work to the highest standards, and by contributing to the public good and to the quality of life in the community.

To provide unrivalled value to our customers in the quality of the goods we sell, in the competitiveness of our prices and in the range of choice we offer.

In our stores, to achieve the highest standards of cleanliness and hygiene, efficiency of operation, convenience and customer service, and thereby create as attractive and friendly a shopping environment as possible.

To offer our staff outstanding opportunities in terms of personal career development and in remuneration relative to other companies in the same market, practising always a concern for the welfare of every individual.

To generate sufficient profit to finance continual improvement and growth of the business whilst providing our shareholders with an excellent return on their investment.

Marks & Spencer's mission is broadly similar:

. . . a commitment to putting the customer first at all times. To this end we are determined to sell only merchandise of the highest quality at outstanding values. We are determined to offer the highest standard of customer care in an attractive shopping environment and aim to improve standards continually throughout our operations using the latest technology. We establish mutually rewarding, long-term partnerships with our suppliers, developing overseas sources to serve our expanding international business, at the same time maintaining support for our British supply base. We aim to minimise the environmental impact of our activities. We nurture good human relations with staff, customers and the community, and ensure staff and shareholders share in our success.

In all three cases the mission statement represents a reflection of basic corporate values and in doing this provides an overall purpose and sense of direction, something which is illustrated by BT which expresses its central purpose as being:

- to provide world class telecommunications and information   products and services, and
- to develop and exploit our networks at home and overseas

... so that we can

- meet the requirements of our customers,
- sustain growth in the earnings of the group on behalf of our shareholders, and
- make a fitting contribution to the community in which we conduct our business.

This, in turn, is underpinned by a statement of the organization's core values:

- We put our customers first
- we are professional
- we respect each other
- we work as one team
- we are committed to continuous improvement.

The Characteristics of Good Mission Statements

Good mission statements can be seen to exhibit certain characteristics, the most notable being that they are, as Wensley has commented, 'short on numbers and long on rhetoric while (still) remaining succint' (1987, p. 31). Having said this, Toyota's mission statement, expressed in 1985, did contain a useful and significant number. Sometimes called the Global 10 mission, it expressed Toyota's intention to have 10 per cent of the world car market by the 1990s. In many cases, however, the mission statement emerges as little more than a public relations exercise. In making this comment we have in mind the temptation that exists for over-ambition which is typically reflected in the too frequent use of phrases such as 'first in the field', 'excellent', and so on. For a mission statement to be worthwhile, it is essential that it is realistic and specifies the business domain in which the company will operate. According to Abell (1980, Ch. 3) this domain is best defined in terms of three dimensions;

1 the *customer groups* that will be served;
2 the *customer needs* that will be met;
3 the *technology* that will satisfy these needs.

Modifying the Mission Statement Over Time

Having developed a mission statement, it should not be seen as a once-and-for-all expression of the organization's purpose, but rather as something which changes over time in response to changing internal conditions and external environmental opportunities, and threats. A mission statement developed in the 1970s, for example, is unlikely to be appropriate in the 1990s when issues such as environmentalism and the green consumer are of considerably greater importance. Equally, the mission statement needs to reflect changing emphases as the organization grows, adds new products and moves into new markets. Over the past decade, for example, Uniroyal has gradually moved out of the tyre business and in doing this has redefined its mission statement on several occasions.

Influences on the Mission Statement

In developing the mission statement for a company there are likely to be five major factors which need to be taken into account:

1 *The company's history and in particular its performance and patterns of ownership.* In commenting on this, Kotler (1988, p. 37) has pointed out that 'every organization has a history of aims, policies and accomplishments. In reaching for a new purpose, the organization must honour the salient characteristics of its past history.'
2 *The preferences, values and expectations of managers, owners and those who have power within the organization.* In commenting on this in the context of the nature of strategic decisions, Johnson & Scholes (1988, p. 7) suggest that 'strategy can be thought of as a reflection of the attitudes and beliefs of those who have the most influence in the organization. Whether an organization is expansionist or more concerned with consolidation, or where the boundaries are drawn for a company's activities, may say much about the values and attitudes of those who most strongly influence strategy'.
3 *Environmental factors,* and in particular the major opportunities and threats that exist and are likely to emerge in the future.
4 *The resources available*, since these make certain missions possible and others not.
5 *Distinctive competences.* While opportunities may exist in a particular market, it would not necessarily make sense for an organization to enter the market if it would not be making the fullest use of its areas of distinctive competence.

For the majority of organizations, the development of a mission statement often proves to be a difficult process, involving a series of decisions on strategic trade-offs between different groups of stakeholders both inside and outside the organization. These stakeholders can conveniently be grouped under three main headings (see Figure 1.12, p. 22):

1 *internal stakeholders* including owners, decision makers, unions and employees;
2 *external stakeholders* such as the government, the financial community, trade associations, pressure groups and society;
3 *market-place stakeholders* including customers, competitors, suppliers and creditors.

Of these three groups it is the *internal stakeholders* who undoubtedly exert the greatest and most immediate effect upon the mission and subsequently the objectives pursued, since it is their expectations and patterns of behaviour which influence the organization most directly on a day-to-day basis.

The impact of *external stakeholders* is by contrast less direct although still felt in a variety of ways. The implications of legislation, for example, in the form of, say, compulsory seat belts in the rear of cars has an effect both upon the manufacturers of cars and seat belts. Equally, the financial community represents a significant influence in that the availability and cost of finance, as well as financial expectations in terms of returns, will all force the planner to behave in particular ways. In the case of pressure groups, the most obvious factor in recent years has been the emergence of environmental issues with the 'greening' of business policies having subsequently been felt across a wide spectrum of products, including petrol, foodstuffs, and white goods such as refrigerators.

The third category of stakeholders is made up of those in the *market-place*. Of the four major types of market-place stakeholders, it is customers and competitors who have the most obvious and direct impact upon planning, since in order to succeed the company needs to understand in some detail their expectations and likely patterns of behaviour. It follows from this that both the organizational mission and the objectives pursued must of necessity be a direct reflection of both elements. By contrast, the influence of suppliers is generally seen to be less direct. There is, however, an obvious need for planning to take account of issues of supply availability, consistency and quality, since without this problems of shortfall or irregular supply are likely to be experienced.

Before attempting to write a mission statement the strategist needs to spend time preparing a meaningful statement about the purpose of the firm. In doing this he needs to recognize the organization's capabilities, the constraints upon it both internally and externally, and the opportunities that exist currently and that might feasibly develop.

For a mission statement to be useful therefore it needs to exhibit certain characteristics. It should, for example, focus upon *distinctive values* rather than upon every opportunity that is likely to exist. A statement that includes comments on producing the highest-quality product, offering the most service, achieving the widest distribution network, and selling at the lowest price is both unrealistic and too ambitious. More importantly, it fails to provide the sorts of guidelines needed when trade-offs are necessary. Equally, the mission statement must define what we can refer to as the *competitive domain* within which the organization will operate. This competitive domain can be classified by a series of statements on scope:

1 *Industry scope*: this is the range of industries that are of interest to the organization. Some organizations, for example, will operate in just one industry sector, while others are willing to operate in a series. Equally some organizations will only operate in an industrial or consumer goods market while others are willing to operate in both.
2 *Geographical scope*: the geographical breadth of operations in terms of regions, countries or county groupings is again part of the mission statement, and varies from a single city right through to multinationals which operate in virtually every country of the world.
3 *Market segment scope*: which covers the type of market or customer that the company is willing to serve. For a long time, for example, Johnson & Johnson sold its range of products only to the baby market. Largely because of demographic shifts, the company redefined its market segments and, with considerable success, moved into the young adult market.
4 *Vertical scope*: which refers to the degree of integration within the company. Thus Ford, as part of its car manufacturing operations, also owns rubber plantations, glass manufacturing plants and several steel foundries. Others, by contrast, buy in everything and simply act as middlemen.

It should be apparent therefore that in developing the mission statement a variety of considerations need to be borne in mind. The end purpose, however, should be that of *motivation* by ensuring that stakeholders recognize the significance of their work in a far broader sense than simply that of making profits.

The third aspect of the mission statement is that it should only give emphasis to the *major policies* that the organization wishes to pursue. These policies are designed to narrow the range of individual discretion, with the result that the organization should operate in a more consistent manner.

The Need for Communication

Once a mission has been developed it is of course imperative that it is communicated to employees so that everyone in the organization is aware of it, since as we suggested earlier, the statement is designed to provide a sense of vision and direction for the organization over the next 10 to 20 years. A mission statement is of little value therefore if employees are either not made aware of it or misunderstand it, or if it is revised every few years in response to minor environmental changes. There is, however, a need for it to be redefined either when it has lost its appropriateness or when it no longer defines the optimal course for the organization.

But although mission statements have an undoubted value in that they are capable of highlighting an organization's core values, many mission statements have been criticized in recent years on the grounds that they are far too general ('to be the best'), too ambitious ('to be the world leader') and too similar. If therefore a mission statement is to be meaningful, it is essential that it is firmly rooted in the organizational realities, capabilities and competences. Without this, it is quite simply empty rhetoric.

It is partly in recognition of this that a greater emphasis is now being given to the idea of *visioning*. The thinking behind visioning is straightforward and designed to encourage management teams at the corporate level, the business unit or the brand level to think in detail about what they are trying to create. In doing this, there is an obvious need for a clear understanding both of the ways in which the environment might develop (or be encouraged to develop) and of the organization's competences. Against this background, an initially broad but increasingly detailed vision of the organization or brand in, say, three, five and ten years' time can be developed. An example of this in the case of Swatch appears in Illustration 6.2. This vision would typically embrace several dimensions, including the organization or brand's size, its market position, the corporate or brand values, the segments served, the geographic coverage, the competitive stance, the links with other organizations, and so on.

Having created the vision, the management team can then begin to focus upon the development of the specific objectives and the detail of the strategy. However,

---

Illustration 6.2: The Swatch Vision

One of the major successes of the 1980s and 1990s has been the Swiss Corporation for Microelectronics and Watchmaking (SMH). The company was formed in 1983 by the merger of two of Switzerland's biggest watchmakers, both of which were insolvent. The new company, under the leadership of Nicholas Hayek, developed the Swatch watch (a detailed discussion of this appears in Illustration 7.1) which, Hayek openly admits, was the result not of detailed financial analysis but of a burning desire to rebuild the Swiss watch industry and a vision of how this might be done.

Hayek recognized, that in order to beat his Asian competitors, he would have to produce something distinctive. In the event, this was a watch with a European sense of style which, despite being built in a high labour cost environment, was able to compete against – and beat – watches from SMH's Japanese competitors such as Seiko.

In commenting on this, Hayek said

> Everywhere children believe in dreams. And they ask the same question: Why? Why does something work a certain way? Why do we behave in certain ways? We ask ourselves those questions every day.
>
> People may laugh – the CEO of a huge Swiss company talking about fantasy. But that's the real secret of what we've done.
>
> Ten years ago, the people on the original Swatch team asked a crazy question: Why can't we design a striking, low-cost, high-quality watch and build it in Switzerland? The bankers were sceptical. A few suppliers refused to sell us parts. They said we would ruin the industry with this crazy product. But this was our vision and we won!

Others who have taken a similar and seemingly impossible approach include the management team of Toyota, who pursued a vision of creating a car that would allow them to undercut the prices of German luxury cars while at the same time beating them on quality. The result was the Lexus.

it is not enough for this strategy to be appropriate in that it builds upon organizational capabilities and environmental demands, it must also be implementable. Although implementation is discussed in greater detail later in the text, the reader needs to recognize at this stage that there are numerous barriers to the effective implementation of any strategy and that good leadership and well developed patterns of communication are a fundamental part of overcoming these barriers. Without these, it is almost inevitable that the staff will have little real understanding of the core values or what is expected of them.

It is because of this that considerable emphasis in recent years has been given to the idea of *internal marketing*. The term 'internal marketing', which is used to describe the work that is done within the organization in terms of training, motivating and communicating with the employees, was developed largely within the service sector. Increasingly, however, it is becoming recognized that it is a fundamental part of the marketing equation for any organization, since in its absence the ways in which employees interact with customers will lack true focus; this is illustrated in Figure 6.3.

FIGURE 6.3
The three dimensions of marketing

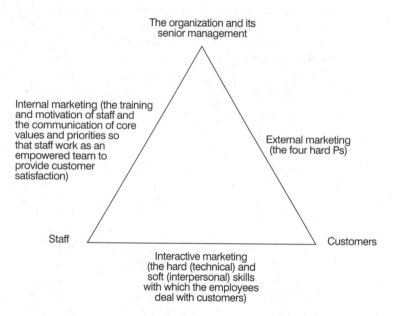

6.5 INFLUENCES ON OBJECTIVES AND STRATEGY

Having developed the mission statement, the strategist is then in a position to turn to the objectives and strategy. It has long been recognized that any organization represents a complex mix of cultural and political influences, all of which come to bear in some way on the objectives that are pursued. It follows from this that objectives and strategy are not simply set in a vacuum or just by reference to environmental factors, but rather that they emerge as the product of a complex interaction at various levels of the organization. This is reflected in Figure 6.4 which illustrates the various layers of cultural and political influences on objectives (and subsequently strategy), ranging from the values of society to the far more specific influences such as organizational objectives, individuals' expectations, and indeed the power structures that exist within and around the organization.

It follows from this that if we are to understand fully the process of setting objectives, we need to recognize the complexities of these interrelationships.

FIGURE 6.4
Influences on organizational objectives (and strategy)

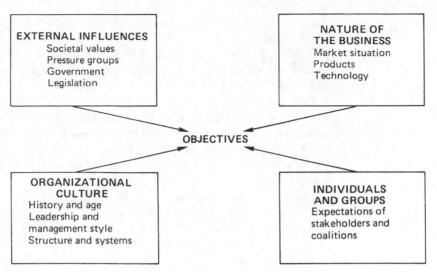

SOURCE: Adapted from Johnson and Scholes (1988), p. 114

These have been commented on by Johnson & Scholes (1988, pp. 113–15), and it is worth quoting them at some length:

- There are a number of cultural factors in an organization's *environment* which will influence the internal situation. In particular the values of society at large and the influence of organized groups need to be understood.
- The *nature of the business*, such as the market situation and the types of product and technology are important influences not only in a direct sense but in the way they affect the expectations of individuals and groups.
- Most pervasive of all these general influences is the organizational *culture* itself.
- At a more specific level, individuals will normally have shared expectations with one or more groups of people within the organization. These shared expectations may be concerned with undertaking the company's tasks and reflect the formal structure of the organization, e.g. departmental expectations. However, *coalitions* also arise as a result of specific events, and can transcend the formal structure.
- Internal groups and individuals are also influenced by their contacts with *external stakeholders* - groups who have an interest in the operation of the company such as customers, shareholders, suppliers or unions. For example, sales staff may be pressurized by customers to represent their interests within the company.
- Individuals or groups, whether internal or external, cannot influence an organization's strategies unless they have an influencing mechanism. This mechanism is called *power*, which can be derived in a variety of ways.
- Organizational *objectives* traditionally have been afforded a central/dominant role in influencing strategy, i.e. strategy is seen as the means of achieving preordained and unchangeable objectives. That is not our view. Whereas organizations do have objectives, which are often valuable in strategy formulation, they should not be regarded as an unchangeable set of expectations. They should be viewed as an important part of the strategic equation, and open to amendment and change as strategies develop.
- Objectives tend to emerge as the wishes of the most dominant coalition, usually the management of the organization although there are notable exceptions. However, in pursuing these objectives the dominant group is very strongly influenced by their reading of the political situation, i.e. their perception of the power struggle. For example, they are likely to set aside some of their expectations in order to improve the chance of achieving others.

External Influences on Objectives

By referring to Figure 6.4 above it can be seen that the most general of the influences upon individuals and groups, and hence on organizational objectives and strategy, are external factors, the nature of the business, and the organizational culture. Taking the first of these, arguably the two most important external factors are the *values of the society* in which the organization is operating and the *behaviour of organized groups* both inside and outside the organization. The influence of social values is likely to be felt in a variety of ways, but most significantly in terms of what society will and will not tolerate in terms of business behaviour. As an example of this, it is worth considering how attitudes to environmental pollution have changed dramatically over the past 20 years. An obvious consequence of this has been to force changes on business behaviour and to increase the pressures for safer and more environmentally friendly products. In the case of petrol, for example, a growing awareness of the dangers of airborne lead pollution and an increasing unwillingness on the part of society to accept this prompted the oil companies to develop unleaded petrols. Equally, it was an awareness of a growing opposition to the testing of products on animals that led Anita Roddick's Body Shop to offer a range of cosmetics that has been developed without the need for testing on animals.

Objectives and strategy are also affected by the behaviour of organized groups within the organization. The most obvious of these are trade unions and trade associations which attempt to influence members both formally and informally through codes of conduct and norms of behaviour. In the case of the travel industry, for example, ABTA (the Association of British Travel Agents) has over the past few years worked hard to monitor and improve the standards within the industry so that clients receive better and more professional standards of service.

The Nature of the Business

The second general influence on objectives and strategy is the *nature of the business itself*, and in particular the market situation faced by the organization, the life-cycle stages of its products, and the types of technology being used. The influence of market situation can perhaps best be understood by referring back to the mid-1980s when much of British industry was undergoing fundamental restructuring in order to survive. The markets in which the industries were operating had changed dramatically over a 20-year period with an upsurge in the market of often low priced foreign competition which made operating profitably difficult. Faced with this, organizations such as British Steel and the National Coal Board (subsequently renamed British Coal) were forced into the position of massive restructuring, changed working practices and radically different product/ market strategies in order to survive. This, in turn, was reflected in the type of technology that could be used, attitudes within the industry, and subsequently in the ways in which employees viewed policy.

Organizational Culture

The third general influence on objectives and strategy is *organizational culture*. Culture has been defined in a variety of ways over the past few years but for our purposes here it can be seen as the commonly held core beliefs of the organization. As such, it determines how people within the organization behave and respond. In examining and trying to understand organizational culture, Johnson & Scholes (1988, pp. 39–43) argue the case for what is referred to as the 'cultural web'. This web, they suggest, is made up of four major dimensions:

1 stories and myths;
2 rituals and symbols;
3 leadership and management style;
4 structure and systems.

Together, these four factors determine the type and profile of the organization and hence how it is likely to behave in the market-place. Factors such as these led Miles and Snow to identify three types of organization: defenders, prospectors

FIGURE 6.5
Different types of organizational culture and their influences on policy making

Organization type and dominant objectives	Characteristics of policy making (preferred strategy)	Nature of the planning and control systems
1 *Defenders* Desire for stability	Specialization with cost efficient production; a marketing emphasis on price and service to defend current business A tendency for vertical integration	Generally, centralized with detailed control and an emphasis on cost-efficiency Extensive use of formal planning procedures
2 *Prospectors* Search for and exploitation of new product and market opportunities	Growth through product and market development Constant monitoring of environmental change Multiple technologies	Emphasis on flexibility and decentralization with use of ad-hoc measurements
3 *Analysers* Desire to match new ventures to present shape of business	Steady growth through market penetration Exploitation of applied research Followers in the market	Often extremely complicated Coordinating roles between functions Intensive planning

SOURCE: Adapted from Miles and Snow (1978)

and analysers. The implications of each type for objectives, strategies, and planning and control systems appear in Figure 6.5.

Individual and Group Expectations

The fourth and final influence on objectives and strategy is that of the *expectations of individuals, stakeholders and coalitions*. In most cases it is the expectations of coalitions that exert the greatest influence on the organization, in that while individuals may well have a variety of personal aspirations, they often share expectations with a number of others. This, together with the relative inability of any single individual to exert a major influence upon the organization, leads to the emergence of groups within departments, regions and levels of the hierarchy, all of which attempt in one way or another to influence the direction of the organization. In practice, however, and particularly in the case of a multinational or large divisionalized organization, the ability of any one group to exert any significant degree of influence may well be limited. Almost inevitably, of course, conflicts between the expectations of different groups are likely to exist and this, in turn, leads to a series of trade-offs. This was referred to in a slightly different context at an earlier stage in this chapter when talking specifically about marketing objectives. More generally, the sorts of conflicts that are likely to emerge are between growth and profitability; growth and control/independence; cost efficiency and jobs; and volume/mass provision versus quality/specialization.

6.6 GUIDELINES FOR ESTABLISHING OBJECTIVES AND SETTING GOALS AND TARGETS

Few businesses pursue a single objective; instead they have a mixture, which typically includes profitability, sales growth, market share improvement, risk containment, innovativeness, usage, and so on. Each business unit should therefore set objectives under a variety of headings and then *manage by objectives*. In other words, it is the pursuit of these objectives which should provide the framework both for the planning and control processes. However, for this to work, several guidelines must be adhered to, with objectives being:

1 *hierarchical*: going from the most important to the least important;
2 *quantitative*: in order to avoid ambiguity – the objective 'to increase market share' is not as satisfactory a guideline as 'to increase market share by 5 per cent' or indeed 'to increase market share by 5 per cent within 18 months';
3 *realistic*: it is only too easy for objectives to reflect a degree of wishful thinking – instead they should be developed as the result of a detailed analysis of opportunities, corporate capability, competitive strengths and competitive strategy;
4 *consistent*: it is quite obviously unrealistic to pursue incompatible objectives. As an example of this, to aim for substantial gains in both sales and profits simultaneously is rarely possible.

Primary and Secondary Objectives

Although for a long time economists argued that firms aimed to maximize profits, it is now generally recognized that the modern large corporation, managed by professionals, pursues a far broader and infinitely more diverse set of objectives. As a consequence, traditional views of profit maximization as the principal objective have been challenged by the reality of the behaviour of corporate management. With this in mind, two types of objective can be identified: *primary* and *secondary*.

Traditionally the primary objective was, as we observed above, profit maximization. Other objectives are, however, often seen by managers to be of more immediate relevance and, as Chisnall (1989, p. 137) points out, may affect the organization's profit-earning ability:

These secondary objectives which are not in any way inferior to the primary objective, are necessary if a company is to plan effectively for its future progress. In the short term, for instance, a profit maximisation policy may be affected by changes in economic conditions which demand some restructuring of corporate resources to meet new levels of competition. Survival or market share defences may, in fact, become primary objectives.

This issue of the multiplicity of objectives has also been discussed by Drucker (1955) who isolated eight areas in which organizational objectives might be developed and maintained:

1 market standing;
2 innovation;
3 productivity;
4 financial and physical resources;
5 manager performance and development;
6 worker performance and attitude;
7 profitability;
8 public responsibility.

See also the discussion in Chapter 15 on the GE approach to multiple objectives.

Objectives and Time Horizons

It should be apparent by this stage that in setting objectives the marketing planner needs to take account of a wide variety of factors. Perhaps the final influence that we need to examine here before focusing upon the detail of corporate and marketing objectives is that of the time horizons involved. In the case of those industries which are highly capital intensive, for example, the planning horizons tend to be considerably longer than is the case in faster-moving consumer goods markets. We can therefore usefully distinguish between the short, medium and long term.

From the planner's point of view, the short term is concerned essentially with issues of tactics, while the long term is concerned with the major issues of strategy and the allocation and reallocation of resources. The medium term then sits neatly between these in that it provides the focus for determining how effectively resources are being used. Although there is a perhaps understandable temptation to tie each of these phases to specific periods of time (e.g. up to one year in the case of the short term, one to five years for the medium term and over five years for the long term), such an exercise is generally only useful when carried out in relation to a specific industry or company.

At a more general level, the significance of planning time horizons relates rather more to the degree of environmental change being experienced and the ability of the organization to respond by reallocating resources. The significance of this from the point of view of establishing objectives can therefore be seen in terms of the need to identify objectives both for the short term and the long term. The long-term objectives will then be concerned with the direction in which the organization is heading, while the short-term objectives will be allied far more closely with the stages through which the organization will have to move in order to achieve this position.

The Nature of Corporate Objectives

In the light of our discussion here and in Chapter 1 (see page 21) it should be apparent that corporate management, having established the corporate mission, then has to take the mission a stage further by developing a series of specific objectives for each level of management. Most typically these objectives are expressed in terms of sales growth, profitability, market share growth and risk diversification. Because the majority of organizations generally pursue a number of objectives, it is, as we have seen, important that they are stated in a hierarchical manner going from the most important to the least important, with this hierarchy being both internally consistent and mutually reinforcing. By doing this, the strategist is clarifying priorities so that if at a later stage a conflict of objectives emerges, a decision can then be made on which particular objective is to dominate. At the same time it is essential that the objectives established are realistic both in terms of their magnitude and the time scale over which they are to be achieved. Almost invariably, however, organizations experience difficulties and conflicts in establishing objectives, problems which are in turn compounded by the need to establish multiple objectives. It is seldom, if ever, possible for example for an organization to satisfy concurrently objectives of rapid growth *and* risk aversion, or to maximize both sales *and* profits. Recognizing this, Weinberg (1969) has identified eight basic strategic trade-offs facing firms. These are, he suggests:

1 short-term profits versus long-term growth;
2 profit margins versus competitive position;
3 direct sales effort versus market development effort;
4 penetration of existing markets versus the development of new markets;
5 related versus non-related new opportunities as a source of long-term growth;
6 profit versus non-profit goals;
7 growth versus stability;
8 a 'riskless' environment versus a high-risk environment.

It follows from this that the strategist has to decide upon the relative emphasis that is to be given to each of these dimensions. Any failure to do this is ultimately likely to lead to conflict and reduce the extent to which the objectives provide useful strategic guidelines.

However, while the need for clear objectives may well be self-evident, it is rare, as Baker (1985, p. 41) has pointed out, 'to find any explicit reference as to just *how* one should set about formulating these objectives in the first place'. One of the few who has attempted to provide guidelines for formulating objectives is McKay (1972), who suggests that it is possible to identify two categories of issues that should be considered: the general issues which apply to all organizations, and the more specific which force a more detailed examination. These general issues are:

(i)   *business scope*: what business should we be in?
(ii) *business orientation*: what approach is most appropriate for our business scope and to our purposes of survival, growth and profit?
(iii) *business organization*: to what extent is our organizational style, structure and staff policy suited to the orientation chosen?
(iv) *public responsibility*: is there a match between our selection of opportunities and the existing and future social and economic needs of the public?
(v)   *performance evaluation*: is there a match between our appraisal and planning systems?

The *specific* areas that then follow from this he suggests relate to each strategic business unit (SBU) and include:

- customer classes;
- competitors;
- markets and distribution;
- technology and products;
- production capability;
- finance;
- environment.

Taking Account of Competitors' Objectives

Objectives should never be set in a vacuum. Instead they should be set against the background of a detailed understanding of environmental demands and opportunities. In doing this particular attention needs to be paid to the objectives that are likely to be pursued by competitors, since these will often have a direct impact upon subsequent levels of performance.

A competitor's objectives are likely to be influenced by many factors, but particularly by its size, history, managerial culture, and performance. They are also affected by whether the company is part of a larger organization. If this is the case, the strategist needs to know whether it is being pressured to achieved growth or whether it is viewed by the parent as a 'cash cow' and is being milked. Equally, we need to know just how important it is to the parent; if it is central to the parent company's long-term plans, this will have a direct influence upon how much money will be spent in fighting off an attack. Rothschild (1984, Ch. 5), for example, argues that the worst competitor to attack is the competitor for whom this is the sole or principal business, and who has a global operation.

There is therefore, as we discussed in Chapter 4, a strong argument for the strategist to develop a detailed competitive map in which issues of competitive capability and priority figure prominently. In doing this, a useful assumption, at least initially, is that competitors will aim for profit targets and choose their strategies accordingly. Even here, however, organizations differ in the emphasis they put on short-term as opposed to long-term profits. In reality, of course, few organizations aim for profit maximization, be it in the short or long term, but instead opt for a degree of satisficing. They have target profit figures and are satisfied to achieve them, even if greater profits could have been achieved by other strategies with perhaps a greater degree of risk. In discussing this, Kotler (1988, p. 242) suggests that:

> An alternative assumption is that each competitor has a mix of objectives with different weights. We want to know the relative weights that a competitor places on current profitability, market share growth, cash flow, technological leadership, service leadership, and so on. Knowing a competitor's weighted mix of objectives allows us to know whether the competitor is satisfied with its current financial results, how it might react to different types of competitive attack, and so on. For example, a competitor that pursues low cost leadership will react much more strongly to a manufacturing process breakthrough by another competitor than to an advertising step-up by the same competitor.

The argument for looking in detail at your competitors as a prelude to developing your own objectives has also been pursued by Davidson (1987, p. 136):

> You know what your competitors have done in the past, and buried in there are many clues as to what they are likely to do in the future . . . The attitudes and philosophies of your competitors (therefore) deserve close study. With successful competitors, their attitudes tend to be deeply ingrained and change little, if at all. Any competitor of General Electric or Mars will know that their objective in any market is likely to be brand leadership, with little interest in being number two or number three for long. Many Japanese competitors are prepared to wait five or ten years before receiving a return on their investments when entering new markets.

Competitive attitudes, objectives and strategies do, of course, change over time, even when a particular strategy is proving to be successful. History has shown that the probability of change is far greater when a particular strategy is not working, or when there is a change in management at the top of the organization. There are therefore several specific factors that should be taken into account as well as the rather more general issue of competitive posture referred to above. These include:

1 *Each competitor's previous successes and failures*. It is quite normal to continue with a successful formula and to change one that is not working.
2 *The volume and direction of investment in advertising and plant*. A rational competitor will concentrate his advertising effort on the products and markets which appear to offer the greatest scope. Monitoring patterns of competitive advertising spend can therefore provide the strategist with a good indication of the directions in which to concentrate. Equally, a knowledge of competitors' investment in plant, which can often be picked up from equipment suppliers, planning applications and the trade press, provides an invaluable guide to profitable future plans.
3 *Each competitor's relative cost position*. The starting point for this is to arrive at an assessment of each competitor's relative cost position in each major market sector. Working on the assumption that each competitor will have conducted a similar exercise, it is reasonable to suppose that they will give priority to cost-reduction strategies in those markets in which they are currently high-cost operators.

By focusing upon areas such as these, the strategist should be in a far better position to answer four fundamental questions:

1 What is each competitor seeking?
2 What is it that drives each competitor?
3 What is each competitor's true competitive capability?
4 In what ways might this capability be translated into objectives and strategy?

It is against this background that the strategist can then define and perhaps redefine his own organization's objectives.

Developing Offensive Corporate Objectives

Firms can be broadly classified as *proactive* or *reactive*. The former are characterized by an entrepreneurial and highly positive attitude to their markets, with a constant searching and pursuit of new business opportunities; in essence they try to shape the environment to fit the organization's resources and objectives. By contrast, reactive firms adopt a far more passive and less entrepreneurial posture, responding to rather than initiating environmental change. These contrasting styles have an obvious effect upon the sorts of objectives pursued and indeed, in most cases, upon subsequent levels of trading performance.

The implications of this for marketing have been spelled out by Davidson (1987, p. 149) who suggests that:

> Objective setting is a good measure of a company's success in offensive marketing. Unless ambitious objectives are established, there is little incentive for executives to apply the offensive marketing approach.

With regard to the specific objectives that an offensive or proactive organization might pursue, these will depend to a large degree upon the organization's market position. If, for example, it is intent on increasing its market share, the starting point involves deciding upon which competitor(s) to attack. The options open to it are essentially:

1 *to attack the market leader*: this is typically a high risk but potentially high return strategy and one which makes sense if the leader is generally complacent or not serving the market as well as he might – Xerox, for example, chose to attack 3M by developing a cleaner, faster and more convenient copying process (dry copying rather than wet);
2 *it can attack firms of its own size*: firms that are either underfinanced or undermanaged;
3 *it can attack local and regional firms*: again, firms that again are underfinanced or undermanaged – this strategy was pursued with considerable success in the 1960s and 70s by a small number of large brewers who gobbled up the small, regional brewers.

This question of *who* to attack is at the very heart of an effective offensive strategy, since to make the wrong choice is likely to prove immensely costly. Thus while in the razor market BIC might well try to increase its market share, it carefully avoids attempting to topple Gillette.

The differences between reactive and proactive organizations have also been the subject of a considerable amount of analysis at the national level over the past few years. In part this has been due to the relatively poor economic performance of British companies in world markets. Japanese organizations, by contrast, have achieved far greater levels of success; it is the reasons for this and the apparent differences between British and Japanese marketing approaches that has provided the focus for a considerable body of research. In essence, the results of this research have highlighted a largely proactive approach on the part of Japanese firms, but an essentially reactive approach on the part of British firms. One example of this research is summarized in Illustration 6.3.

Establishing the Marketing Objectives

Against the background of the comments made so far, we can identify a firm's competitive situation and hence its marketing decisions as being concerned with just two major elements: products and markets. This has been discussed by a variety of writers but most obviously by McKay (1972), Guiltinan and Paul (1988)

Illustration 6.3: The Differences Between Japanese and Western Business Objectives

That major differences exist betwen the objectives of Japanese companies and their European and North American counterparts has long been recognized. Kotler (1988, p. 242), for example, has stated that:

> US firms operate largely on a short-run profit maximization model, largely because their current performance is judged by stockholders who might lose confidence, sell their stock, and cause the company's cost of capital to rise. Japanese firms operate largely on a market share maximization model. They need to provide employment for more than 100 million people in a resource-poor country. Japanese firms have lower profit requirements because most of the capital comes from banks that seeks regular interest payments rather than high returns at somewhat higher risks. As a result, Japanese firms can charge lower prices and show more patience in building and penetrating markets. Thus competitors who are satisfied with lower profits have an advantage over their opponents.

A similar line of argument has been pursued by Doyle, et al., (1986) who, in a comparative investigation of Japanese marketing strategies in the British market, highlighted a variety of differences between Japanese and British companies. Prominent among these were:

1 market share versus short-term profitability – the marketing of western companies, they suggest, is oriented to profitability, that of the Japanese to market share;
2 an emphasis upon fast market adaption rather than innovation;
3 more aggressive marketing tactics on the part of the Japanese;
4 a greater orientation by Japanese firms towards environmental opportunities.

Underpinning these four points were fundamental differences in the strategic objectives being pursued:

> The marketing objectives of a company express its ambition and commitment. There was a striking contrast between the two groups in these strategic objectives. In entering a new market the British usually arrived late and few had a strong commitment to it. Two-thirds of British companies gave defensive reasons for entry: 'we had to in order to survive' and several admitted they 'had never really thought it out'. In contrast, the Japanese were much clearer and professional: over 70% noted the motives were 'part of a planned global expansion' or 'potential of the UK market'. Once in the market, the British lack of commitment to beating competition was again striking. Whereas 87% of the Japanese gave 'aggressive growth' or 'market domination' as the goal, only 1 in 5 British companies thought these statements applied to them. 'Maintenance' or the 'prevention of decline' were the most the typical British competitor sought. As hypothesized, short-term profit was much more important to the British than the Japanese (93% vs 40%), and they were willing to cut costs and allow their market position to erode if necessary to bolster short-term profitability. If these attitudes are typical, the poor record of much of British manufacturing industry in defending its home market becomes more comprehensible.

The authors went on to suggest that a company can improve profitability by a strategic focus based either upon raising volume or improving productivity. Organizations with ambitious strategic objectives would be expected to focus on the former, a defensive one on the latter. The Japanese firms in their sample almost invariably chose volume. By contrast, the British, rather than pushing aggressively into new, high-growth markets or competing for market share, tended to focus on cost cutting, range reduction and rationalization as the basis for preventing margins being eroded. The differences between these British and Japanese firms can perhaps best be illustrated by the two tables below:

What was your market share/sales strategy?

	British (%)	Japanese (%)
Prevent decline	20	0
Defensive	20	0
Maintain position	40	0
Steady growth	0	13
Aggressive growth	13	60
Dominate market	7	27

How well does 'good short-term profits are the objective' describe your company?

British (%)	Japanese (%)
93	40

The differences between western and eastern managerial orientations and preoccupations have also been discussed by the management consultants Arthur Andersen. These are discussed in Illustration 6.4.

and Ansoff (1968). McKay, for example, identifies just three fundamental marketing objectives:

1 to enlarge the market;
2 to increase market share;
3 to improve profitability.

McKay's ideas of three principal marketing objectives have been taken several steps further by Guiltinan and Paul, who argue that there are six objectives which should be given explicit consideration:

1 market share growth;
2 market share maintenance;
3 cash flow maximization;
4 sustaining profitability;
5 harvesting;
6 establishing an initial market position.

In many ways, however, the thinking underpinning both approaches can be seen to come together in Ansoff's ideas of a product/market matrix. This is illustrated in Figure 6.6.

FIGURE 6.6
*Ansoff's growth
vector matrix*

		Product		
		Current	New	
Market	Current	Market penetration 1	Product development 3	
	New	Market extension 2	Diversification 4	

SOURCE: Ansoff (1957)

This matrix, which focuses upon the product (what is sold) and to whom it is sold (the market), highlights four distinct strategic alternatives open to the strategist:

1 selling existing products to existing markets;
2 extending existing products to new markets;
3 developing new products for existing markets;
4 developing new products for new markets.

Although in practice of course there are *relative* degrees of newness both in terms of products and markets, and hence the number of strategies open to the organization is infinite, Ansoff's matrix is useful in that it provides a convenient and easily understood framework within which marketing objectives and strategies can be readily developed.

It follows from this that setting objectives and strategies *in relation to products and markets* is a fundamental element of the marketing planning process. These marketing objectives then represent performance commitments for the future and are typically stated in terms of market share, sales volume, levels of sterling distribution, and profitability. For these to be worthwhile, however, they need to be stated both quantitatively and unambiguously. In this way they are capable of measurement, something which is not possible if they are stated only in broad directional terms. In commenting on this McDonald (1984, p. 88) suggests that:

> Vague objectives, however emotionally appealing, are counter-productive to sensible planning, and are usually the result of the human propensity for wishful thinking which often smacks more of cheerleading than serious marketing leadership. What this really means is that while it is arguable whether directional terms such as 'decrease', 'optimize', 'minimize' should be used as objectives, it seems logical that unless there is some measure, or yardstick, against which to measure a sense of locomotion towards achieving them, then they do not serve any useful purpose.

The argument for explicit and quantitatively expressed objectives is therefore overpowering, since any failure to do this simply offers scope for confusion and ambiguity at a later stage, not just in terms of the sort of action required but also in terms of the performance measurement standards that are to be used. In stating objectives they also need to be related to the fundamental philosophies and policies of a particular organization, something which again argues the case for a clear and well-communicated mission statement. The *process* of setting objectives is therefore central to its effectiveness, a comment reflected by McDonald (1984, p. 30) who, in discussing the findings of a research programme carried out at the Cranfield School of Management, has suggested that:

> ... it is inadequacies in the objective-setting process which lie at the heart of many of the problems of British companies. Since companies are based on the existence of markets, and since a company's sole means of making profit is to find and maintain profitable markets, then clearly setting objectives in respect of these markets is a key

business function. If the process by which this key function is performed is inadequate in relation to the differing organizational settings in which it takes place, it follows that operational efficiency will be adversely affected.

Some kind of appropriate system has to be used to enable meaningful and realistic marketing objectives to be set. A frequent complaint is the pre-occupation with short-term thinking and an almost total lack of what has been referred to as 'strategic thinking'. Another complaint is that plans consist largely of numbers, which are difficult to evaluate in any meaningful way, since they do not highlight and quantify opportunities, emphasize key issues, show the company's position clearly in its markets, or delineate the means of achieving the sales forecasts. Indeed, very often the actual numbers that are written down bear little relationship to any of these things. Sales targets for the sales force are often inflated in order to motivate them to higher achievement, while the actual budgets themselves are deflated in order to provide a safety net against shortfall. Both act as demotivators and both lead to the frequent use of expressions such as 'ritual', 'the numbers game', 'meaningless horsetrading', and so on.

Ansoff's Matrix Revisited

Against the background of the comments so far it should be apparent that marketing objectives relate to the four categories of Ansoff's product/market matrix, with decisions being needed on:

1 existing products in existing markets;
2 new products in existing markets;
3 existing products in new markets;
4 new products in new markets.

The general nature and direction of these decisions is influenced both by the product life cycle and the current shape of the company's product portfolio. This in turn leads to a series of choices for each product/market condition, choices which can be expressed in terms of five types of strategy:

1 *Maintenance* of the current competitive position.
2 *Improvement* of the current competitive position.
3 *Harvesting* which involves reducing or relinquishing the current competitive position in order to capitalize upon short-term profit and improve cash flow.
4 *Exiting*. This typically occurs when the company is suffering from a weak competitive position or recognizes that the cost of staying in the market and/or improving upon the position is too high. As an example of this, ICI sold its loss-making European fertilizer business to Europe's second largest fertilizer producer, the Finnish company Kemira Oy. The decision to withdraw from this market sector was made after ICI had experienced losses for four years, despite having made major attempts to improve the business including vigorous cost reductions and investment in new technology.
5 *Entry* to a new sector.

However, while considering either the need or the feasibility of each of these strategies, the marketing manager needs to recognize the danger of adhering slavishly to any particular set of rules relating to the five categories and to be fully aware of the major constraints within which he is operating. Among the most commonly used and useful frameworks for identifying these is the concept of the limiting factor (see Illustration 6.4) and techniques of gap analysis which are designed to highlight any gaps that exist between long-term forecasts of performance and the sales or financial objectives that have been set (see Figure 6.7).

In the case of Figure 6.7(a), the lowest curve represents a projection of expected sales from the organization's current portfolio of businesses. The highest curve traces the sales targets for the next 10 years which, as can be seen, are more

Illustration 6.4: BOC and the Limiting Factor

A few years ago, the British Oxygen Company recognized that its limiting factor was the nature of demand for its products: this was essentially reactive and dependent on industrial activity. In addition, BOC products could not economically be transported more than 150–200 miles from the point of production.

The invasion of the British market by Air Products faced BOC with an entirely new competitive situation; for years they had enjoyed a virtual monopoly situation in the British gas market. BOC, in the words of the chairman of their industrial and medical cases group, were forced to start marketing gases: a task for which they were ill prepared. The defensive posture adopted against Air Products' aggressive marketing in the late 1960s was abandoned and BOC sought to regain ground by positive marketing not only of gases but of the technological expertise and advice which they could offer to customers.

Another outcome of the changed market environment was that BOC vigorously pursued a policy of diversification, so that its activities now range across welding products, vacuum engineering, medical equipment, refrigeration equipment, frozen food retailing and specialized food distribution.

Source: Chisnall, P. M. (1989), Strategic Industrial Marketing, Prentice Hall International, p. 143.

FIGURE 6.7
The strategic planning gap

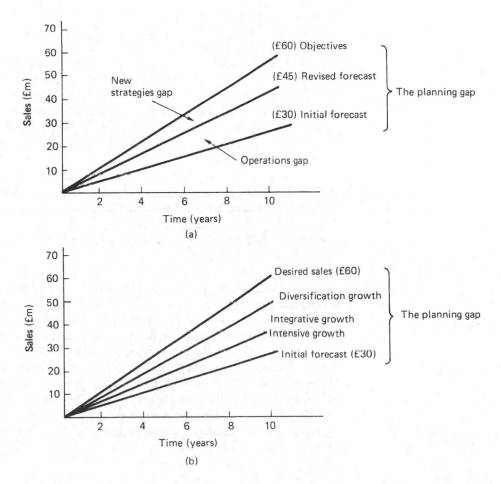

ambitious than the current portfolio will permit. The question that then quite obviously follows is how best to fill this strategic planning gap. The courses of action open to the strategist can then be examined in several ways. The first involves subdividing the gap into the *operations gap* and the *new strategies gap*. In the case of the *operations gap*, the approaches to reducing or eliminating it totally include:

1 greater productivity by means of reduced costs;
2 improvements to the sales mix or higher prices;
3 higher levels of market penetration.

In the case of the *new strategies gap*, the courses of action include:

1 a reduction in objectives;
2 market extension in the form of new market segments, new user groups or expansion geographically;
3 product development;
4 diversification by selling new products to new markets.

An alternative way of looking at the strategic planning gap is illustrated in Figure 6.7(b). Here, the solutions to the shortfall have been categorized as:

1 identifying further opportunities to achieve growth within the company's current business (intensive growth);
2 identifying opportunities to build or acquire businesses related to the current sphere of operations (integrative growth);
3 adding businesses that are unrelated to current operations (diversification).

In weighing up which of these alternatives to pursue, the planner needs to give consideration to a variety of issues. For many companies the most attractive option proves to be greater market penetration since this is concerned with existing products and markets and typically therefore involves less cost and risk than would be incurred by moving outside existing areas of knowledge. Equally, it generally pays an organization to search for growth within existing and related markets rather than moving into new markets, since by doing this it is more readily able to build upon its reputation. If, however, the company decides to move into new and possibly unrelated areas, there is then a need not only to establish itself against a new set of competitors but also to build new distribution networks and come to terms with a different technology. This should not in itself be seen as an argument against moving into new markets with new products, but rather an argument for the planner to develop objectives and strategies against the background of a firm understanding of the organization's strengths and weaknesses and overall corporate capability, all of which should emerge clearly from the marketing audit.

The levels of risk associated with each of the strategic alternatives identified in the Ansoff matrix can perhaps be better understood by considering an extension to the basic model. While undoubtedly useful as a framework, Ansoff's four-cell matrix is not able to reflect different *degrees* of technological or market newness, or indeed of the risk associated with the four alternatives. By returning for a moment to Figure 6.6, it should be apparent that, all other things being equal, the lowest level of risk is associated with the market penetration strategy of Cell 1. This then increases through Cells 2 and 3, peaking in Cell 4 with a strategy of diversification. The diagrams that appear in Figures 6.8 and 6.9 are both designed to add a further dimension to Ansoff's original model.

Figure 6.8, for example, gives recognition to the fact that strategies involving new products (hence technology) generally entail a greater degree of risk than those limited just to new markets.

FIGURE 6.8
Levels of risk associated with various product/ market combinations – 1

Product

	Existing	New
Market Existing	1	4
New	2	16

FIGURE 6.9
Levels of risk associated with various product/ market combinations – 2

Newness of product

Newness of market	Same product	Extended model	Modified or improved design	New product
Same market	1	2	4	8
Better market coverage	2	4	8	16
New coverage but in related areas	4	8	16	32
Totally new market	8	16	32	64

SOURCE: Adapted from Ward (1968)

Figure 6.9 takes this model somewhat further by distinguishing between the different types and degrees of market and product development, and in doing this illustrates the relative degrees of risk more precisely. It can be seen from this how risk levels escalate as the organization moves away from its existing product and market base. It then follows that the issue of corporate capability, and in particular the ability of the organization to cope with risk, needs to be understood in some detail by the marketing planner. Without this understanding there is a very real danger that the organization will move too far and too fast into areas in which it will find difficulties in operating effectively. Again, however, this should not be seen simply as an argument for the company to stay where it is currently, since the product life cycle alone necessitates changes both to products and markets if sales and profits are to be maintained or increased. Rather it is an argument for strategic development to reflect objectives, opportunities and capabilities, together with an understanding of the entry and exit barriers to possible market areas. The implications of entry and exit barriers for a market's attractiveness are illustrated in Figure 6.10.

The most attractive segment from the viewpoint of profit is one in which entry barriers are high and exit barriers are low. Few new firms are able to enter, and the

FIGURE 6.10
Barriers and profitability

Exit barriers

	Low	High
Entry barriers Low	Low, stable returns	Low, risky returns
High	High, stable returns	High, risky returns

poor performers can exit easily. When both entry and exit barriers are high the profit potential is high, although this is generally accompanied by greater levels of risk as the poorer performers, finding it difficult to leave, are forced to fight for share. When both entry and exit barriers are low, firms find it easy both to enter and leave, and returns tend to be stable and low. The worst case scenario is when barriers to entry are low but exit barriers are high: here firms enter when the market is buoyant, but then find it difficult to leave when there is a downturn. The result is overcapacity which affects all the players.

6.7 THE DEVELOPMENT OF STRATEGIES

In the light of what has been discussed so far it should be apparent that a marketing objective is what the organization wants to achieve in terms of sales volume, market share, and so on. How the organization then sets out to achieve these objectives is the *strategy*. An effective strategy statement should therefore make reference not just to the allocation of resources but also to timescales; inevitably it is broad in scope. Following on from this, the planner then moves to develop the *tactics* and *programme for implementation*. From the viewpoint of the marketing planner, the major aspects of strategy with which he is involved are the individual elements of the marketing mix, each of which is covered in greater detail at a later stage in the book. Before moving on, however, it is worth focusing on one of the other major influences upon strategic success. Although decisions are typically taken against a background of resource constraint, their effects can often be minimized by the strategist giving full recognition to the importance of the *leverage* that can be gained by the development of one or more *distinctive competences* to gain a comparative marketing advantage. Although the importance of distinctive competences has long been recognized, their strategic significance was highlighted by the results of a study carried out by the American management consultants, McKinsey & Co. Prominent among their findings was that:

> the distinguishing characteristic shared by (successful companies) was that they did one particular thing well. They had developed significant strength in one feature of their business which gave them a comparative advantage over their competitors.

This theme has, in turn, been developed by Chisnall (1989, p. 143) who has made the observation that while the concept of a distinctive competence is well known and understood, one of the main problems of applying it is that of changing the basis of competitive advantage in line with changes in the environment. Among the companies which have failed to come to terms with this are Bowman in the hand-held calculator market, Sinclair in home computers, and Texas Instruments in digital watches.

It follows from this that in developing strategies the planner needs to identify these distinctive competences, and to build on them. As an example of how this can be done, the Dominos Pizza chain in the United States developed as its USP (unique selling proposition) rapid delivery times with a refund to the customer if delivery of the pizza took longer than it should.

The Changing Focus of Strategic Planning

Although portfolio analysis has been subjected to a number of criticisms, its contribution to strategic planning has undoubtedly been significant. However, at the beginning of the 1990s, a number of writers, including Mintzberg (1994) and Stacey (1991), began questioning the traditional and well-established lines of thinking about strategic planning. With its origins in the late 1960s and early 1970s, strategic planning had been held up by many as the most logical and effective way of devising and implementing the strategies which would improve the competitiveness of a business unit. However, Mintzberg argues that the

Illustration 6.5: East meets West
(or does it?)

In a major study conducted jointly with the Batey Research and Information Centre in Singapore, and with support from *Fortune* magazine, consultants from Arthur Andersen interviewed some 400 senior executives across Asia, the US and Europe. The aim of the study was to test the proposition that east–west management styles and business practices are converging to produce a 'new international manager'. The conclusion that the researchers arrived at was that sharp differences do, in fact, still exist and need to be recognised and understood by those working across market boundaries.

The principal differences which were identified were that almost all respondents characterised western styles as open, direct and confrontational, while the predominant Asian style was seen as placing value on seniority, relationships and family ties. Both eastern and western managers were in broad agreement on the qualities of the ideal manager, focusing on the ability to anticipate future trends and the efficient use of resources; a summary of the results under four headings appears below:

(i) Differences in management style

Western managers: ...	Eastern managers: ...
1 are more open, direct and confrontational;	put greater value on seniority, relationships and family ties;
2 emphasise flexibility and creativity;	are more likely to be paternalistic;
3 encourage the empowerment of line workers;	support life-time employment and oppose hire-and-fire;
4 favour databases and statistics and resist intuition;	place more emphasis on corporate loyalty;
5 are more productivity-oriented than people-oriented;	are more resistant to women assuming senior positions; and
6 are characterised more by individual initiative than by group consensus; and	are more likely to stress quality rather than quantity.
7 put greater importance on short term profits.	

(ii) The importance of connections

	Local westerners	Expatriate westerners	Local Asians
	%	%	%
Business connections	93	96	90
Government connections	50	81	80
Personal friendships	72	78	73
Family	25	60	65
Gifts or favours	13	48	32
Alumni contacts	25	44	32
Bribes	4	23	24

(iii)   Measures of success

Western	Asian
Respected by the business community	Respected by the business community
Good salary	Good salary
Respected by subordinates	Rapid promotions
Rapid promotions	Important job title
–	Respected by subordinates

(iv) Perceptions of the characteristics of the ideal manager

Western	Asian
Offer full support/motivation for staff;	Have a well-developed ability to anticipate future trends/changes;
Have a well-developed ability to anticipate future trends/changes;	Act as a role model for co-managers and subordinates;
Are able to identify and recruit talented people;	Offer full support/motivation for staff;
Are willing to give subordinates wider responsibilities;	Make efficient use of resources to meet sales/profit targets;
Make efficient use of resources to meet sales/profit targets.	Are able to identify and recruit talented people.

Adapted from Differences and Similarities Between Western and Eastern Managers, *published by Arthur Andersen, 1997*

creation in many large organizations of specialist departments staffed by strategic planners who were involved in the thinking but not the doing or the implementation has created a series of difficulties and tensions. The net effect of this, he suggests, is that 'strategic planning has long since fallen from its pedestal' (1994, p. 107). He goes on to say that:

> But even now, few people really understand the reason: *strategic planning* is not *strategic thinking*. Indeed, strategic planning often spoils strategic thinking, causing managers to confuse real vision with the manipulation of numbers. And this confusion lies at the heart of the issue: the most successful strategies are visions, not plans.

In making this comment, Mintzberg highlights the way in which the traditional approach to strategic planning is, in essence, *strategic programming*, an activity which involves articulating strategies or visions which already exist. What is needed, he believes, is that managers should understand the differences between planning and strategic thinking so that they can then focus upon what the strategy development process should really be. This process, he suggests, involves capturing what the manager learns from all sources (both the soft insights from his or her personal experiences and the experiences of others throughout the organisation and the hard data from market research and the like) and then synthesizing that learning into a vision of the direction that the business should pursue

Recognition of this means that the role of the planner changes significantly and, for Mintzberg, highlights the way in which the planner's contribution should be *around* rather than *inside* the strategy-making process. In other words, they should provide the analyses and data inputs that strategic thinkers need and not the one supposedly correct answer to the strategic challenge being faced.

This redefinition of roles illustrates, in turn, the distinction that needs to be made between the analytical dimension of planning and the synthesis, intuition and creativity that characterize true strategic thinking. It also goes some way towards highlighting the way in which the formal and traditional approach to planning:

> ... rests on the preservation and rearrangement of established categories, the existing levels or strategy [corporate, business, functional], the established types of products (defined as "strategic business units"), and overlaid on the current units of structure [divisions, departments, etc].
>
> But real strategic change requires not merely rearranging the established categories, but inventing new ones. Search all those strategic planning diagrams, all those interconnected boxes that supposedly give you strategies, and nowhere will you find a single one that explains the creative act of synthesizing experiences into a novel strategy. Strategy making needs to function beyond the boxes, to encourage the informal learning that produces new perspectives and new combinations. As the saying goes, life is larger than our categories. Planning's failure to transcend the categories explains why it has discouraged serious organisational change. This failure is why formal planning has promoted strategies that are extrapolated from the past or copied from others. Strategic planning has not only amounted to strategic thinking but has often impeded it. Once managers understand this they can avoid other costly misadventures caused by applying formal technique, without judgement and intuition, to problem solving (1994, p. 109).

These criticisms of the traditional logical and sequential approach to planning have, in turn, been developed by Stacey who, in his book, *Managing Chaos*, argues for a managerial emphasis upon adaptability, intuition, paradox and entrepreneurial creativity in order to cope with an unpredictable and, indeed, inherently unknowable future.

In many ways, Stacey's ideas are a reflection of chaos and complexity theories ('chaos' in these terms refers not to muddle and confusion, but to the behaviour of a system which is governed by simple physical laws but is so unpredictable as to appear random) in which the complexity of interaction between events is so great that the links between cause and effect either disappear or are so difficult to identify as to be meaningless. The implication of this for strategic planning is potentially far-reaching and, according to Stacey, highlights the importance of intuition and the need for managers to deal with problems in a truly holistic fashion. He goes on to suggest that managers 'must learn to reason through induction rather than deduction; and to argue by analogy, to think in metaphor and to accept paradox' (1994, p. 64).

Like Mintzberg, Stacey argues for a greater creativity within organizations and refers to the scientific concept of the 'edge of chaos' as a metaphor for more independence of managerial thought:

> Tucked away between stability and instability, at the frontier, non-linear feedback systems generate forms of behaviour that are neither stable nor unstable. They are continuously new and creative. This property applies to non-linear feedback

systems no matter where they are found. All human organisations, including businesses, are precisely such non-linear feedback systems; and while it is not necessary or indeed desirable for all organisations to be chaotically creative all the time those that do should not think in terms of stability and adapting to their environment but in terms of using amplifying feedback loops or self-reinforcing mechanisms to shape customer needs (1994, p.65)

With regard to the detail of planning and strategy, Stacey's views rest upon the idea that, because of the nature and complexity of the business system, anything useful about the future is essentially unknowable, something which negates the value of the conventional planning wisdom that success depends upon developing a vision of where the company wants to be in five, ten or twenty years' time, the strategy that will achieve this, and a shared culture. Instead, he believes that:

> ... managers should recognise that these strategic planning meetings every Monday morning serve a ritual rather than a functional purpose rather like the ceremonial laying of the foundation stone on a building. They should recognise too that those elaborate computer-modelled forecasts presented to the board to convince them of the wisdom of a proposed business venture are a fiction, and that their purpose is to allay anxiety rather than perform any genuinely predictive purpose. Real strategy is not derived from this sort of planning. No, real strategy emerges from group dynamics, from the politicking and informal lobbying in the corridors, from the complicated patterns of relationships and interplay of personalities, from the pressure groups that spring up after the formal meeting is over and real success lies not in total stability and 'sticking to your knitting', but in the tension between stability (in the day-to-day running of the business) and instability (in challenging the status quo). Instability is not just due to ignorance or incompetence, it is a fundamental property of successful business terms (Stacey quoted in *Management Today*, November 1994, p.65).

Given this, he suggests that creative organizations deliberately set out to encourage counter-cultures and subversion. Among the examples that he cites of organizations which have done this with a high degree of success is Honda which, during the past decade, has hired large numbers of managers in mid-career from other organizations as a means of introducing a series of pressures, challenges and contention into the organization. The effect of this has been to encourage a culture of creative destruction, greater learning and an increase in flexibility.

6.8 Summary

In this chapter we have focused on three main areas:

- the nature and purpose of planning;
- the significance of the corporate mission;
- the nature and purpose of corporate and marketing objectives.

The starting point in the planning process involves the strategist in identifying where the organization is currently (where are we now?) and the short- and long-term direction for the organization (where should we go?). In addressing this second question a variety of issues need to be considered, including:

- environmental opportunities and threats (see Chapter 2);
- the organization's strategic capability (again, see Chapter 2); and
- stakeholders' expectations.

Having done this it then becomes possible to give far more explicit and realistic consideration to the question of how the organization should go about achieving its objectives.

As a background to the planning process there needs to be agreement on the corporate mission, the mission statement being a vision of what the organization is or should attempt to become. The significance of the mission statement has been highlighted by a wide variety of writers, most of whom have given emphasis to its integrating role and to the way in which it provides a strong binding statement of fundamental corporate values.

In developing a mission statement the strategist needs to take account of a variety of factors, including:

- the organization's history, performance and patterns of ownership;
- managerial values and expectations;
- the environment;
- resource availability;
- the existence of any distinctive competences.

Having developed a mission statement the strategist is in a far stronger position to begin the process of establishing corporate and marketing objectives. Objectives are typically influenced by several issues, including:

- the nature of the business (products, markets and technology);
- external factors (societal values, pressure groups, government and legislation);
- organizational culture;
- individuals and groups within the organization.

Having identified the organization's corporate and marketing objectives the strategist needs to ensure that they satisfy certain criteria, the four most significant of which are that they are arranged hierarchically, that they are expressed quantitatively, that they are realistic and that there is internal consistency. It is at this stage also that the strategist is in a position to identify the nature and size of any gaps that are likely to emerge between where the organization wants to go and where in practice it is capable of going. Once this has been done it then becomes possible to begin the process of developing the strategies that are to be used to achieve the agreed objectives.

6.9 EXERCISES

1 Which approach to planning appears to predominate in your organization?
2 Take your organization's mission statement and apply the test of the characteristics of good mission statements which appears on page 206. What are the implications of your findings?
3 Are mission statements of any real value?
4 Looking at Figure 6.2, how would you categorize your organization?
5 What evidence do you see of vision in your organization at the corporate, divisional, business unit and brand level? How well communicated is this vision?
6 What appear to be the principal influences on your organization's objectives and strategies?
7 On page 215, we identify eight basic strategic trade-offs facing firms. To what extent can you find examples of these within your organization?
8 What objectives do your principal competitors appear to be pursuing? How do these compare with those pursued by your organization?

9 How offensive are (a) your organization's objectives; and (b) those pursued by your principal competitors?

10 Using the Ansoff matrix, identify the various ways in which your organization might develop. Which approach has predominated so far?

11 Is there a planning gap in your organization? (refer to pages 222–4). What evidence is there of one or more limiting factors? (see Illustration 6.4).

6.10 CASE STUDY

Anderson Marine Construction Ltd

Anderson Marine Construction (AMC) is a well-established and financially successful builder of medium-sized, high-performance yachts and power boats. Based on the south coast of England, the company's products have developed a strong reputation for quality and performance, and an intensely loyal and knowledgeable customer base.

The company has traditionally adopted a largely reactive approach to selling, justifying this partly on the grounds that for the past twenty years they have been able to sell everything they have been able to make, and partly because the firm's founder and Managing Director, Tom Anderson, saw the firm facing little direct competition in its principal target markets. At the end of the 1980s, however, sales began to drop as demand for expensive luxury goods declined. As a response to this, AMC cut its prices by 6 per cent in real terms for the 1991 season and then by a further 4 per cent for 1992. Despite this, sales remained sluggish.

Faced with this and with no sight of an upturn in demand, Tom Anderson called in a marketing consultant to advise on what AMC should do next. The consultant argued that further price cuts were likely to achieve little and that in the long term they would probably be detrimental to the image developed by AMC. Instead, he suggested, AMC should capitalize upon its reputation and the very strong brand values associated with its name by moving down the size and price scale by developing a new range of smaller and lower priced boats. Although this sector of the market had a greater number of direct competitors, the consultant suggested that patterns of demand would be more consistent and less susceptible to fluctuations in the economy.

Although the idea had an initial appeal. Anderson recognized that the firm's approach to marketing and selling would have to change. Previously, the firm's sales effort had been limited to very occasional advertisements in the boating press and a small stand every other year at a regional boat show. This, together with the strength of the firm's reputation and word of mouth recommendation, had, he felt, been adequate. Boats were made to order with a delivery time of 9–15 months and prices, which were negotiated individually with clients, reflected the specification demanded. Once completed, they were either delivered by AMC or the customer collected the boat himself.

The consultant emphasized that the new range would need to be targeted at buyers for whom the sailing skills and buying motives and processes would be very different from those of AMC's traditional customers. The implications of this were spelled out in a report:

1 Buyers within the proposed target group are less knowledgeable about boats and sailing and would expect a greater degree of what he referred to as 'active selling' of the product's benefits.

2 There would be a need for a structured distribution network with at least ten distributors throughout the country.

3 Buyers would not be prepared to wait for delivery but would expect boats to be available from stock.

4 A communications programme would be required.

5 A formal pricing and distributor discount structure would be needed.

6 Because the new range would bring AMC into more direct competition with other boat builders, a competitive monitoring system should be developed.

7 A marketing budget should be set as a matter of priority and the responsibility for the marketing effort clearly allocated.

Recognizing that these recommendations called for a far more proactive approach to marketing than had previously been adopted, Anderson decided to appoint a marketing manager. As the person appointed to this post, you have the immediate responsibility for developing the marketing plan to support the new range which is scheduled for launch for the 1994 sailing season.

Questions

1 Prepare an outline of the marketing plan for the launch and subsequent market development of the new range. In doing this, you should make specific reference to the nature of any additional information that you might require.

2 In the light of AMC's previous approaches to selling, what, if any, organizational problems might you expect to encounter in implementing the marketing plan? In what ways might these problems be overcome or minimized?

7 | Structural, market and environmental analysis

7.1 LEARNING OBJECTIVES

When you have read this chapter you should be able to understand:

(a) why a regular and detailed analysis of the organization's environment is important;
(b) the key elements of the environment;
(c) how firms go about analysing the environment;
(d) how environmental factors are changing;
(e) the dimensions of environmental scanning systems.

7.2 INTRODUCTION

The Changing Business Environment (or the New Marketing Reality)

If there is a single issue or theme which now links all types and sizes of organization, it is that of the far faster pace of environmental change and the consequently greater degree of environmental uncertainty than was typically the case even a few years ago. This change and uncertainty has been manifested in a wide variety of ways and has led to a series of environmental pressures and challenges with which managers need to come to terms; a number of these are illustrated in Figure 7.1. Although the fourteen points identified in Figure 7.1 are not intended either as a complete or a definitive list of the sorts of challenges that managers now face, they go some way towards illustrating the nature of the ways in which organizational environments are changing and how the pressures upon managers are increasing. They also illustrate the point made in the introduction to this book that strategic marketing is an essentially iterative process. It is iterative for a number of reasons, the most significant of which is that as the company's external environment changes, so opportunities and threats emerge and disappear only to re-emerge perhaps in a modified form at a later stage. Because of this, the marketing strategist needs to recognize the fundamental necessity both for an environmental monitoring process that is capable of identifying in advance any

FIGURE 7.1
Environmental pressures and the strategic challenges of the new millennium

1	The stagnation of many markets
2	Market fragmentation
3	Product proliferation
4	Growing product parity
5	Shorter product life cycles
6	Increasingly frequent niche attacks by competitors
7	Greater customer sophistication and increased customer demands
8	Downward price pressures
9	Rising promotional costs and lower promotional returns
10	Increasing sales force costs
11	Changing patterns of distribution and shifts in the balance of power as intermediaries become more dominant
12	The erosion of many of the traditional bases of competitive advantage
13	An increased emphasis upon environmental and 'green' issues
14	The increasingly global nature of many markets

possible opportunities and threats, and for a planning system and organizational structure that is capable of quite possibly radical change to reflect the environment so that the effects of threats are minimized and that opportunities are seized.

In essence, therefore, the formulation of marketing strategy is concerned with matching the *capabilities of the organization* with the *demands of the environment*. In doing this, the strategist is faced with a difficult problem, since what we typically refer to as the environment encapsulates a wide variety of influences. The difficulty lies therefore in coming to terms with this diversity in such a way that it contributes to effective decision making, since it is this that has a direct influence upon performance. This difficulty in coping with the environment can be viewed under two headings:

1 understanding the *extent* to which the environment affects strategy;
2 understanding the ways in which environmental pressures can be *related* to the capabilities of the organization.

A possible danger that has been highlighted by several commentators is that of adopting a 'balance sheet' approach to environmental analysis and simply listing all possible environmental influences and then categorizing each as either an opportunity or a threat. If environmental analysis is limited to this alone, the strategist is left with far too broad and unsophisticated a picture of what really affects the organization. In addition, such an approach is likely to lead to the organization responding in a fragmented way rather than in a more integrated and strategic fashion.

Within this chapter we therefore focus on the various elements of the marketing environment with a view to illustrating the nature of their interaction and, subsequently, their effect on the organization. Against this background, we then move on to consider the ways in which an effective environmental monitoring process can best be developed and then, subsequently, how environmental forces are capable of determining the nature of the strategy pursued. We begin, however, by examining an approach to analysing the environment.

7.3 ANALYSING THE ENVIRONMENT

In analysing the environment, Johnson and Scholes (1988, p. 54) argue for a step-wise approach. This involves an initial audit of general environmental influences, followed by a series of increasingly tightly focused stages that are designed to provide the strategist with an understanding of the *key opportunities and threats* as a prelude to identifying the organization's *strategic position*. This process, which is illustrated in Figure 7.2, consists of five stages:

1 The starting point in this process is the *general audit of environmental influences*. The purpose of this is to identify the types of environmental factors that have influenced the organization's development and previous performance, and to arrive at an initial conclusion of the likely important influences in the future.
2 From here the strategist moves to an *assessment of the nature of the environment* and the degree of uncertainty and change that is likely to exist. If from this the strategist concludes that the environment is relatively static then historical analysis is likely to prove useful. If, by contrast, the environment shows signs of instability, then a stronger emphasis upon the future is needed.
3 The third phase then involves focusing upon *specific environmental factors* such as the nature and structure of the market.
4 This in turn leads to an analysis of the firm's *competitive position*. A detailed discussion of how this can be done appears in Chapter 4. In essence, however,

FIGURE 7.2
*The five stages of
environmental
analysis*

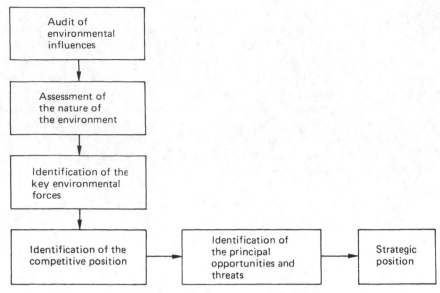

SOURCE: Adapted from Johnson and Scholes (1988), p. 54

this involves a combination of *strategic group analysis* in which competitors are mapped in terms of their similarities, dissimilarities, their capabilities and the strategies they follow, and *market share analysis* to highlight their relative degrees of market power.

5 This information is then used as the basis for identifying *in detail* how environmental forces are likely to affect the organization and, in particular, the *opportunities and threats* that are likely to exist. This in turn provides the basis for a detailed understanding of the organization's strategic position and the degree to which there is match between strategy, structure and environment.

At this point we will examine the first three stages of this step-wise approach; the fourth stage is discussed at the end of this chapter, while the fifth stage was covered in some detail in Chapter 2.

Referring back to Figure 7.2, it can be seen that the first step in the process involves the *general audit of environmental influences*. The starting point for this involves the strategist in developing a list of those factors which are likely to have an impact on the organization and which will therefore need further analysis. In doing this, the purpose is to develop a detailed understanding of what environmental factors have influenced the organization in the past, and the degree to which any changes that are taking place are likely to increase or reduce in impact. Although quite obviously such a list has to be company specific, it is possible to identify a broad framework to help with this audit. This framework, which is typically referred to as PEST (Political, Economic, Social and Technological) analysis, is illustrated in Figure 7.3.

Against this background, the strategist can then move to an assessment of the *nature of the environment*. In essence, this is concerned with answering three questions:

1 How uncertain is the environment?
2 What are the sources of this uncertainty?
3 How should this uncertainty be dealt with?

Levels of uncertainty are directly attributable to the extent to which environmental conditions are dynamic or complex. *Dynamism* is due largely to the rates and frequency of change, while *complexity* is the result either of the diversity of

FIGURE 7.3
The PEST framework for environmental auditing

POLITICAL/LEGAL FACTORS
Legislative structures
Monopoly restrictions
Political and government stability
Political orientations
Taxation policies
Employment legislation
Foreign trade regulations
Environmental protection legislation
Pressure groups
Trades union power

ECONOMIC FACTORS
Business cycles
Money supply
Inflation rates
Investment levels
Unemployment
Energy costs
GNP trends
Patterns of ownership

SOCIO-CULTURAL FACTORS
Demographics
Lifestyles
Social mobility
Educational levels
Attitudes
Consumerism

TECHNOLOGICAL FACTORS
Levels and focuses of government
and industrial R & D expenditure
Speed of technology transfer
Product life cycles
Joint ventures

environmental influences, the amount of knowledge required to cope with them, or the extent to which environmental factors are interconnected. The implications for environmental analysis of these different types of environmental condition are illustrated in Figure 7.4.

FIGURE 7.4
Handling different environmental conditions

	Conditions		
	Simple/static	**Dynamic**	**Complex**
Aims	To achieve thorough (historical) understanding of the environment	To understand the future rather than simply relying on past experiences	The reduction of complexity Greater structural understanding
Methods	Analysis of past influences and their effect on organizational performance Identification of key forces Analysis of existing relationships	Managers' sensitivity to change Scenario planning Contingency planning Sensitivity planning	Specialist attention to elements of complexity Model building
Dangers	The sudden emergence of unpredicted change Mechanistic organizational structures Lack of skills Focus on existing relationships Lack of willingness to accept that conditions are changing Stereotyped responses	Management myopia Mechanistic organizational structures Lack of skills Inappropriate forecasting Failure to recognize significant new players	Unsuitable organizational structure or control systems Inappropriate reactions Inappropriate focuses Over-reaction

SOURCE: Adapted from Johnson and Scholes (1988)

Environment Types

The question of *how* to categorize environments has been discussed in some detail by Miles (1980, Ch. 8) who developed a framework for a comprehensive and systematic analysis of environment types. The model calls for a 'measurement' response by those performing the analysis and is based upon the answers to six questions:

1 How complex is the environment? (Complexity is a measurement of the number of different environmental forces which have an impact, or potential impact, upon the organization.)
2 How routine and standardized are organizational interactions with elements of the environment?
3 How interconnected and how remote, initially, are the significant environmental variables?
4 How dynamic and how unpredictable are the changes taking place around the organization?
5 How receptive is management to the ways in which environmental pressures adversely affect the input and output processes of the organization?
6 How high is flexibility of choice and to what extent is the organization constrained from moving into new areas?

Using this checklist of questions, the strategist should then be able to establish the organization's environmental position on a number of continuums:

Simple ↔ Complex
Routine ↔ Non-routine
Unconnected ↔ Interconnected
Proximate ↔ Remote
Static ↔ Dynamic
Predictable ↔ Unpredictable
High input receptivity ↔ Low input receptivity
High output receptivity ↔ Low output receptivity
High domain choice flexibility ↔ Low domain choice flexibility

The Implications of Environmental Change

Undoubtedly one of the major problems faced by managers comes when the organization, having operated for some time in a largely predictable environment, is faced with having to come to terms with a far more complex, uncertain and possibly malevolent environment. Among those who have had to do this in recent years are solicitors, estate agents and opticians, all of whom have been affected by the Conservative government's moves to reduce barriers to competition. Solicitors, for example, have had to come to terms with a new form of competition in the form of licensed conveyancers. Similarly, the structure of estate agency changed dramatically in the mid to late 1980s as a series of financial institutions moved into the business by buying individual agencies and regional chains, and then offered clients packages of financial services in addition to the normal estate agency service. Prominent among those doing this were Lloyds Bank, Prudential Insurance, and the large building societies such as the Halifax and Abbey National. Those estate agents which were still independent found themselves having to cope with a radically different and generally more sophisticated form of competition than that to which most were accustomed.

The significance of changes such as these needs to be seen in terms of *how* the organization monitors the environment and, subsequently, *how* it *responds*. Quite obviously, what is appropriate to a static environment is not suited to either a dynamic or a complex environment.

Static, Dynamic and Complex Environments

With regard to the question of how the organization monitors the environment, evidence suggests that in *broadly static conditions* straightforward environmental scanning is likely to be a useful and generally adequate process. In a *dynamic environment*, however, the organization is typically faced with major change in the areas of technology and markets with the result that decisions can no longer be based upon the assumption that what broadly has happened in the past will continue in the future. As a consequence of this, the focus needs to be upon the future with a far greater degree of inspirational interpretation. Among the techniques that have been used to do this is Delphic forecasting. The results are then used as the basis for building alternative scenarios.

This idea of alternative futures can then be used to identify the likely impact upon consumers, suppliers, competitors, government, the financial institutions, their probable responses, and subsequently their impact upon the organization.

For organizations faced with a *complex* environment, many of the issues and problems to which reference has been made are exacerbated. In discussing how to cope with this, Johnson and Scholes (1988, p.61) suggest that there are organizational and information processing approaches:

> Complexity as a result of diversity might be dealt with by ensuring that different parts of the organisation responsible for different aspects of diversity are separate and given the resources and authority to handle their own part of the environment. Where high knowledge requirements are important it may also be that those with specialist knowledge in the organisation become very powerful because they are relied upon, not only to make operational decisions, but are trusted to present information in such a way that a sensible strategic decision can be made: or indeed they themselves become responsible for the strategic decisions. As an information processing approach there may be an attempt to model the complexity. This may be done through a financial model, for example, which seeks to simulate the effects on an organisation of different environmental conditions. In its extreme form there may be an attempt to model the environment itself. The Treasury Office draws on a model of the UK economy for example. However, for most organisations facing complexity, organisational responses are probably more common than extensive model building.

Regardless, however, of the degree of complexity in the environment, there appear to be certain common strands in the ways in which managers cope with their environments. The most significant of these is that managers develop over time what can loosely be referred to as the accepted wisdom of the industry and the workable solutions to the various situations that are likely to emerge. One consequence of this is that the major competitive threats to organizations often come from companies *outside* the industry which, on entering the market, adopt a strategy which falls outside this area of standardized expectation which allows for the conventional wisdom of response to change to be adopted.

7.4 THE NATURE OF THE MARKETING ENVIRONMENT

The marketing environment has been defined in a variety of ways. Churchman (1968), for example, has referred to it in terms of factors which are outside the system's control but which determine, in part at least, how the system performs.

For our purposes, however, the most useful working definition is that proposed by Kotler (1988, p.135):

> The company's marketing environment is made up of the sectors and forces outside the firm's marketing function which infringe upon the ability of marketing management to develop and maintain a successful relationship with the firm's target group.

Within the environment there are two distinct components: the *micro-environment* and the *macroenvironment*. These are illustrated in Figure 7.5.

FIGURE 7.5
The organization's marketing environment

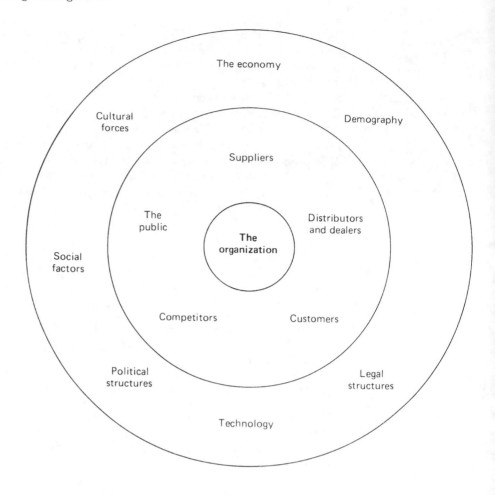

The *microenvironment* is made up of those elements which are closest to the company and which exert the greatest and most direct influence over its ability to deal with its markets. This includes the organization itself, its suppliers, its distribution network, customers, competitors, and the public at large. The *macroenvironment* consists of the rather broader set of forces that have a bearing upon the company, including economic, demographic, technological, political, legal, social and cultural factors. Together, these elements of the environment combine to form what we can loosely refer to as the non-controllable elements of marketing which, in many ways, act as a series of constraints on the parameters within which the marketing planner is required to operate.

In labelling these elements as non-controllable, the reader should recognize that, in some cases at least, the marketing planner may well adopt a highly proactive stance in an attempt to alter the nature and impact of the environment upon the organization. He might, for example, attempt a merger or take-over in order to minimize a competitive threat. Equally, a large organization may well lobby the government in order to have legislation developed or changed so that the company benefits in some way. The car, foodstuffs, cigarettes, and brewing industries, for example, all have powerful lobby groups that attempt to exert a degree of influence over government to ensure that any legislation is beneficial or at least not harmful to their interests. In other cases, however, the organization may adopt a rather more reactive stance and simply view the environment as something that has to be lived with and responded to.

Regardless of which approach an organization adopts, it needs to be recognized that the environment is a significant determinant both of strategy and organizational performance, something which has been reflected in the work of a considerable number of writers including Baker (1985, p. 85) who has described it as 'the ultimate constraint upon the firm's strategy', Drucker (1969) who referred to the environment of the 60s and 70s as the 'age of discontinuity', and Toffler (1970, p. 28) who, in looking ahead, referred to it as a time of 'future shock'. In making these comments, each author was giving recognition to the volatility, and indeed the potential malevolence, of environmental factors. As an example of this, the early 1970s witnessed the oil crisis, which in turn precipitated an economic upheaval throughout the world which was reflected for some considerable time in higher levels of unemployment, interest rates, the development of new economic thinking, and perhaps most importantly, levels of business confidence. However, although the oil crisis was without doubt a significant environmental upset, its impact was obviously felt far more directly by some organizations than others. It needs therefore to be remembered that what is a key environmental issue for one organization is not necessarily a key environmental issue for another. For a multinational corporation, for example, the major areas of concern are likely to be government relations, spheres of influence and the various political complexions throughout the world. For a retailer, the more *directly* important environmental influences are likely to be customer tastes and behaviour, and interest rates, while for a manufacturer in the high technology fields it is issues of technical development and speeds of obsolescence that are important.

The question of the extent to which environmental change, particularly of something as significant as the oil crisis, can be anticipated by business organizations has been the subject of considerable discussion, and in the case of the oil crisis, has led to both a 'yes' and a 'no' answer. 'Yes' in the sense that the techniques of environmental analysis undoubtedly existed at the time, but 'no' in that few people were willing, or indeed able, to recognize that one economic era was in the process of coming to an end, that another was about to start and that balances of power throughout the world were beginning to change in a number of significant ways.

Although a number of commentators have suggested that environmental change of this magnitude is so rare as to be seen almost as a one-off, other writers' views differ and suggest that it is simply the *scale* of the oil crisis that separates it from the more commonly experienced and less dramatic forms of environmental change. The lesson to be learned in either case is straightforward, in that it points to the need for companies to engage in careful, continuous and fundamental monitoring of the environment with a view to identifying *potential* threats before they become *actual* threats, and opportunities before they are missed. In the absence of this, the organization runs the risk of falling victim to what Handy (1995, pp. 7–8) refers to as the boiled frog syndrome; this is discussed in Illustration 7.1. This has in turn led to the idea of 'strategic windows', a concept which has been discussed by Abell and Hammond (1979, p. 63):

> The term strategic window is used to describe the fact that there are often only limited periods when the 'fit' between the 'key requirements' of a market and the particular competences of a firm competing in that market are at an optimum. Investment in a product line or market area has to be timed to coincide with periods in which a strategic window is open, i.e. where a close fit exists. Disinvestment should be considered if, during the course of the market's evolution, changes in market requirements outstrip the firm's capability to adapt itself to the new circumstances.
>
> The strategic window concept can be useful to incumbent competitors as well as to would-be entrants into a market. For the former it provides a way of relating future strategic moves to market evolution and of assessing how resources should be allocated to existing activities. For the latter it provides a framework for diversification and new entry.

The consequences of failing to identify strategic windows can, of course, be significant and is typically manifested in terms of a loss of opportunity, market share or competitive advantage. This was illustrated by the Swiss watch industry in the 1970s and 1980s when it failed to recognize the significance of new, low price market segments, new quartz technology, and a new, low cost and aggressive form of

Illustration 7.1: The Parable of the Boiled Frog

All organizations are faced with a series of environmental changes and challenges. The principal difference between the effective and the ineffective organization is how well it responds, something that was encapsulated several years ago in one of the most popular of management fables, the parable of the boiled frog. What is now referred to as 'the boiled frog syndrome' is based on the idea that if you drop a frog into a pan of hot water, it leaps out. If, however, you put a frog into a pan of lukewarm water and turn the heat up very slowly, it sits there quite happily not noticing the change in the water's temperature. The frog, of course, eventually dies.

The parallels with the management and development of any organization are – or should be – obvious. Faced with sudden and dramatic environmental change, the need for a response is obvious. Faced with a much slower pace of change, the pressures to respond are far less (this is the 'we are doing reasonably well and can think about doing something else at some time in the future' phenomenon), with the result that the organization becomes increasingly distant from the *real* demands of its customers and other stakeholders. Given this, think seriously about whether you are one of the frogs that is sitting quite happily in a pan of increasingly hot water. If so, why, what are the possible consequences and what, if anything, are you going to do about it?

competition from Japan and, subsequently, Hong Kong. The net effect of this was that the Swiss saw their share of the world watch industry drop from 80 per cent in 1948 to just 13 per cent in 1985; this is discussed in detail in Illustration 7.2.

That they have subsequently fought back with the Swatch watch is, in one sense at least, incidental. Perhaps the more important lesson to be learned from their experience is that a different approach to environmental monitoring might well have led to the industry avoiding the traumas that it undoubtedly faced.

The New Marketing Environment

We suggested at the beginning of Chapters 4 and 5 that among the legacies of the economic and social turbulence of the late 1980s and early 1990s has been the emergence of a new type of consumer and the development of a new type of competitive environment. Taken together, these changes have led to what is for

FIGURE 7.6
Patterns of environmental change

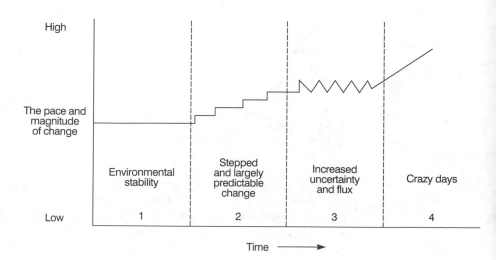

Illustration 7.2: The Swiss Watch Industry and the Consequences of New (and Unexpected) Competition

In 1948 the Swiss watch industry accounted for 80 per cent of all watches sold in the world. By 1985 its share of the market had dropped to just 13 per cent with the Japanese, a relatively new entrant to the market, having taken over as market leader (see Figure 7.7).

FIGURE 7.7 *Estimated breakdown of world watch production*

	World production*	Switzerland	Japan	Hong Kong	USA	Rest of world
1948	31	80	–	–	–	20
1970	174	43	14	–	11	32
1975	218	34	14	2	12	38
1980	300	29	22	20	4	25
1985	440	13	39	22	0.4	25

* million watches and movements

SOURCE: Federation of the Swiss Watch Industry

This surprising and remarkably rapid change in the market's structure was attributable to several factors, the most important of which can be identifed as:

1 A failure on the part of the Swiss to come to terms with the explosive growth in the less expensive sector of the market.
2 The speed of the switch away from mechanical (i.e. spring-powered) watches to the far more accurate quartz-powered watches. Whereas 98 per cent of all watches and movements produced in 1974 were mechanical and only 2 per cent were quartz, in 1984 the breakdown was 24 per cent mechanical and 76 per cent quartz. Ironically, in the light of the source and the technological base of the attack upon the Swiss watch industry, the quartz electronic watch was invented in Switzerland in 1968, but first marketed in the United States.
3 A failure to come to terms with the increasing Asian penetration of the large and lucrative American market. While Switzerland's estimated contribution to American import volume decreased from 99 per cent in 1950 to 4 per cent in 1984, the percentage of import volume from Asia increased from 10 per cent in 1970 to 92 per cent in 1984.

The Japanese, and subsequently the Hong Kong manufacturers, owed their success to a combination of aggressive marketing, a high degree of production concentration, and perhaps most importantly, a relatively complacent competitor who was taken by surprise by the sudden inroads made by the Japanese and who subsequently found it difficult to retaliate. With regard to the first two points, the nature of the challenge has been summed up in the following way.

The Japanese industry was highly concentrated with the two major firms, Hattori Seiko and Citizen, stressing the development of automated production lines and maximum vertical integration of operations. Compared with the multitude of Swiss watch brands, the combined product lines of these two plus Casio, the third major Japanese watchmaker, did not exceed a dozen brands. In contrast, the industry in Hong Kong was highly fragmented, with several manufacturers producing 10 – 20 million watches per year, and hundreds of small firms producing less than 1 million annually. These firms could not afford to invest in quartz analog technology but with virtually no barriers to entry for watch assembly, they produced complete analog watches from imported movements and modules, often Swiss or Japanese. Design costs were also minimized by copying Swiss or Japanese products. The competitive advantages of the Hong Kong firms were low-cost labour, tiny margins and the flexibility to adapt to changes in the market.

The spectacular rise of Japan and Hong Kong, particularly in the middle and low-price categories, was primarily due to their rapid adoption of quartz technology, a drive to achieve a competitive cost position through accumulation of experience, and economies of scale. Whereas in 1972 the digital watch module cost around $200, the same module cost only $50 in 1984. The Asian watchmaking industry had been ensuring a chronic state of world oversupply, mainly in the inexpensive quartz digital range. This had been the cause of a number of bankruptcies and had incited watch manufacturers to turn to the quartz analog market where added value was higher. Since in contrast to quartz digital technology, quartz analog technology was available only within the watch industry, the hundreds of watch assemblers scattered throughout the world were increasingly dependent on the three major movement manufacturers, Seiko, ETA and Citizen.

The fightback by the Swiss began at the beginning of the 1980s and was spearheaded by Dr Ernest Thomke. Thomke concluded that '... the future was in innovative finished products, aggressive marketing, volume sales and vertical integration of the industry'. Quartz analog technology was more complex than digital, but as ETA was known for the technology it possessed for the production of high-priced, ultra-thin 'Delirium' movement, Thomke decided to develop a 'low-price prestige' quartz analog wristwatch that could be mass produced in Switzerland at greatly reduced cost. Two ETA micromechanical engineers specializing in plastic injection moulding technology, Jacques Muller and Elmar Mock, were given the challenge of designing a product based on Thomke's concept. This required inventing entirely new production technology using robots and computers for manufacture and assembly. By 1981 a semi-automated process had been designed to meet Thomke's goal of a 15 SF ex-factory price, and seven patents were registered. The watch's movement, consisting of only 51 instead of the 90 – 150 parts in other watches, was injected directly into the one-piece plastic case. The casing was sealed by ultrasonic welding instead of screws, precluding servicing. The watch would be simply replaced and not repaired if it stopped. The finished product, guaranteed for one year, was shock resistant, water resistant to 100 feet (30 metres) and contained a three-year replaceable battery.

Launched as the Swatch, the success of the marketing campaign is now legendary. However, the question that must be faced is to what extent might the problems faced by the Swiss watch industry have been avoided by a far more careful monitoring of the environment and the identification of a major competitive and technological threat?

Source: I've Got a Swatch *case study, INSEAD, 1987*

many organizations a radically different and far more demanding marketing environment than has been the case in the past; this is illustrated in Figure 7.6 with organizations facing a general shift towards stages 3 and 4. The consequences of this shift have been felt in a variety of ways, but most obviously in terms of the need for a different approach to management; this would typically be discussed in terms of the need for managers to be more creative, innovative, flexible, dynamic, forward looking and willing to take risks. However, in making this comment and identifying the characteristics of a new approach, we run the risk of making a series of largely self-evident points, but then failing to develop the sort of culture in which these elements prosper.

Returning for a moment to Figure 7.6, it is stages 3 and 4 which are of the greatest importance to us here. Environmental uncertainty and its implications have been discussed by numerous commentators over the past few years, including Charles Handy (1994) in *The Empty Raincoat* and Tom Peters (1992) who, in *Liberation Management*, referred to the extreme changes that some organizations now face as 'crazy days'. Crazy days, he argued, are increasingly being faced by managers, and call for responses which often fall outside the traditional, well-understood and well-rehearsed patterns of managerial behaviour. Often, he suggests, it is the case that if an organization is to survive, let alone prosper, managers need to pursue much more radical and truly innovative strategies than ever before. He refers to these new patterns of behaviour as 'crazy ways'. Thus, he argues, crazy days demand crazy ways.

Although others have suggested that Peters perhaps goes too far in his ideas of how to respond, it can be argued that they provide a useful starting point or underpinning of thinking about how best to manage the marketing process. In essence, what Peters is arguing for is a move away from the traditional to the more radical. This post-modern approach has, in turn, been developed by a wide variety of other commentators (see, for example, Brown, 1995, and Nilson, 1995), all of whom have argued in one way or another for more innovative responses and patterns of managerial thinking and behaviour.

This theme has also been developed by Hamel and Prahaled who, in *Competing for the Future* (1994), encapsulate many of these ideas in terms of what they label 'the quest for competitiveness'. This quest, they suggest, typically involves one or more of three possible approaches: *restructuring*, *re-engineering*, and *reinventing the industry and/or strategies*; these are discussed in Chapter 10. In many cases, however, they claim that, although many managers over the past few years have placed emphasis upon the first two of these, they have failed to recognize the real significance – and, indeed, the strategic necessity – of the third.

The implications of this are significant, and highlight one of the two key themes of this book: firstly, that in common with many other parts of a business, the marketing process needs to be managed in a truly strategic fashion and, secondly, that there is an ever greater need for innovation. These changes also highlight the need for organizations to be far closer to their markets than has typically been the case in the past and to have a far more detailed understanding of market dynamics. Without this, it is almost inevitable that any marketing programme will lack focus.

7.5 THE EVOLUTION OF ENVIRONMENTAL ANALYSIS

Recognition of the potential significance of environmental change highlights the need for a certain type of organizational structure and culture which is then reflected both in a balanced portfolio of products and in an adaptive management style supported by a well-developed intelligence and information monitoring system. Without this, the likelihood of the firm being taken unawares by environmental changes of one sort or another increases dramatically. Against the background of these comments, the need for environmental analysis would appear self-evident. All too often, however, firms appear to pay only lip service to such a need. In commenting on this, Diffenbach (1983, pp. 107–16) has identified three distinct stages in the evolution of corporate environmental analysis. These are, he suggests:

1 An *appreciation stage* typically resulting from the emergence of books and articles which argue the case for looking beyond the short term and for considering the wider implications of the economic, technological, social and political factors which make up the business environment.
2 An *analysis stage* which involves 'finding reliable sources of environmental data, compiling and examining the data to discuss trends, developments and key relationships. It also includes monitoring developments and anticipating the future'. It was the emergence of this thinking which led to the appearance in the 1960s and 1970s of numerous books on environmental scanning, Delphic analysis and environmental forecasting.
3 The *application stage* in which very real attempts are made to monitor the environment, assess the implications for change and incorporate staff evaluations into strategy and plans.

Assuming therefore that a firm intends to develop an effective system for environmental analysis, there is a need first to identify those dimensions which are likely to have the greatest impact upon the organization, and second to establish a mechanism whereby each of these elements is monitored on a regular basis. For most companies these elements are contained within the PEST analytical framework referred to earlier. Although in practice other factors can be added to this list, we will for convenience use this framework as a prelude to illustrating how environmental factors influence, and occasionally dictate, strategy. However, before examining these various dimensions, it is worth making reference to the way in which environmental analysis has developed, and to the areas upon which managers typically focus. In doing this, the most obvious starting point is Aguilar's (1967) work.

In what is now seen as a classic study, Aguilar interviewed 137 managers drawn from 41 chemical firms in Europe and the United States. His work highlighted the lack of a systematic approach to environmental monitoring, something which has been reinforced more recently by the work of, among others, Thomas (1980, pp. 20–8) and Fahey, et al. (1981, pp. 32–9).

In carrying out his research, Aguilar identified that managers typically collected 16 types of environmental information. These he subsequently classified under five headings:

1 market tidings;
2 acquisition leads;
3 technical tidings;
4 broad issues (e.g. general conditions and government actions);
5 other tidings (e.g. suppliers and resources).

These information needs are developed in Figure 7.8.

Of these, market tidings proved to be the most commonly collected pieces of environmental information, with 52 per cent of participants placing emphasis upon them. This was followed by technical tidings (17 per cent) and broad issues (12 per cent). The research also revealed four approaches to market monitoring:

1 undirected viewing;
2 conditioned viewing;
3 informal search;
4 formal search.

FIGURE 7.8
*The types of
environmental
information required
by managers*

Market tidings

Market potential
Structural change
Competitors and industry
Pricing
Sales negotiations
Customers

Acquisition leads

Leads for mergers, joint ventures or acquisitions

Technical tidings

New products, processes and technology
Product problems
Costs
Licensing and patents

Broad issues

General conditions
Government actions and policies

Other tidings

Suppliers and raw materials
Resources available
Miscellaneous

SOURCE: Adapted from Aguilar (1967)

Aguilar concluded from this work that for a process of environmental monitoring to work effectively and make a worthwhile contribution to a company's operations, it must be carried out systematically and not in the fragmented and frequently purposeless fashion (i.e. largely undirected viewing) revealed by his study. In suggesting how best to overcome these problems, Aguilar gave prominence both to the necessity for *top management commitment* to environmental monitoring and to the *incorporation* within the decision-making process of the information generated. This should, he argued, lead to a far greater degree of top management involvement in the specification of the information to be collected, and hence to a sense of 'ownership'. Without this, the benefits of the system are likely to be limited.

Subsequent work in this area has continued to reveal a general picture of the partial and largely unstructured development of environmental monitoring processes, although Fahey, et al. (1981, pp. 32–9) identified a more positive picture in a sample of 12 large American firms. This work led them to suggest a typology of models of scanning characterized by an increasing degree of structure, systemization, sophistication and resource intensity. These are:

1 *Irregular systems* which predominate in companies with a poorly developed planning culture and in which the focus is upon *responding* to environmentally generated crises. The net effect of this is that emphasis is simply placed upon finding solutions to short-term problems with little real attention being paid to identifying and assessing the likely impact of future environmental changes.
2 *Periodic models* which represent a general development of the irregular system and which are more systematic, resource intensive and sophisticated. The environment is reviewed regularly and a longer-term perspective is developed.
3 The *continuous model* which is yet a further development and involves focusing upon the business environment generally and upon the long term as opposed to short term and specific issues.

Fahey, et al., went on to suggest that although there is a general shift within American companies towards more sophisticated systems, this movement is slow and compared with its apparent impact, has still to justify the level of resources required.

Nevertheless, the argument for continuous environmental monitoring in order to identify strategic issues and market signals in advance of their impact upon the company is a strong one and has led Brownlie (1987, pp. 100–5) to identify the three basic premises upon which continuous environmental analysis is based. These are, he suggests, that:

1 the determinants of success are dictated by the business environment;
2 the firm's response to environmental change therefore represents a fundamental strategic choice;
3 a knowledge of the business environment must precede the acquisition of any degree of control over it.

Acknowledging the validity of these three assumptions leads to a recognition that effective management cannot take place in an information vacuum, or indeed in circumstances in which information is at best partial and poorly structured. There is, therefore, an obvious need for the organization to develop an effective information system which *collects, analyses* and then *disseminates* information both from within and outside the company.

There are, however, problems that are commonly associated with the first of these, that of information collection and the development of a worthwhile database. Brownlie identifies these as being that all too often the information is:

• poorly structured;
• available only on an irregular basis;
• often provided by unofficial sources;
• qualitative in nature;
• ambiguous in its definitions;
• opinion based;
• poorly quantified;
• based on an insecure methodology;
• likely to change.

Because of problems such as these, the need to collect and analyse environmental information in a well-structured and useable fashion is essential, and it is this that frameworks such as PEST are designed to achieve. It must be emphasized, however, that the organization should avoid focusing just upon the immediate task environment, since all too frequently history has demonstrated that the most significant threats faced by companies often come from firms outside the task environment. We have already pointed to the example of the Swiss watch industry which was significantly damaged by the introduction of microchips and digital technology on the part of firms that the Swiss did not see as competitors. Equally, companies in markets as prosaic as carbon paper were decimated by photocopying technology, while in the same period the British motorcycle manufacturers of the 1960s, seeing their competitors as being one another, were taken by surprise by the Japanese. In making these comments we are therefore arguing for a *breadth* of perspective within the general structure of PEST analysis.

However, although the environment exerts a significant and obvious influence upon the organization, it should not necessarily be seen as the most direct determinant of strategy. Porter (1980, Ch. 1), for example, has argued that industry structure is a more important factor than environmental conditions:

Industry structure has a strong influence in determining the competitive rules of the game as well as the strategies potentially available to the firm. Forces outside the industry are significant primarily in a relative sense; since outside forces usually affect all firms in the industry, the key is found in the differing ability of the firms to deal with them.

Before going on to consider some of the ways in which industry structure influences strategy, we need to examine the various dimensions of the political, economic, social and technological environments. It is this that provides the basis of the next section.

7.6 THE POLITICAL, ECONOMIC, SOCIAL AND TECHNOLOGICAL ENVIRONMENTS

At the beginning of this chapter we suggested that effective marketing planning is based on two important analytical ingredients. First, market opportunity must be analysed, and second, the company's ability to take advantage of these opportunities and cope with threats must be assessed.

Under the first heading, there are four basic building blocks:

1 customers must be analysed to determine how the market can be segmented and what the requirements of each segment are;
2 competitors must be identified and their individual strategies understood;
3 environmental trends (social, economic, political, technological) affecting the market must be isolated and forecasted;
4 market characteristics in terms of the evolution of supply and demand and their interaction must be understood.

It is point 3 to which we now turn our attention.

The Political (and Legal) Environment

Marketing decisions are typically affected in a variety of ways by developments in the political and legal environments. This part of the environment is composed of laws, pressure groups and government agencies, all of which exert some sort of influence and constraint on organizations and individuals in society.

With regard to the legislative framework, the starting point involves recognizing that the amount of legislation affecting business has increased steadily over the past two decades. This legislation has been designed to achieve a number of purposes, including:

1 protecting companies from each other by means of laws such as the Restrictive Trade Practices Acts (1956 and 1976) and the Fair Trading Act (1973), all of which are designed to prevent unfair competition;
2 Protecting consumers from unfair business practice – legislation such as this, which includes the Trade Descriptions Act (1968), the Consumer Credit Act (1974), the Sale of Goods Act (1979), and the Unfair Contract Terms Act (1977), is intended to ensure that certain safety standards are met, that advertising is honest, and that generally companies are not able to take advantage of the possible ignorance, naivety and gullibility of consumers;
3 protecting society at large from irresponsible business behaviour.

It is important therefore that the marketing planner is aware not only of the current legislative framework, but also of the ways in which it is likely to develop and how, by means of industry pressure groups and lobbying of parliament, the direction of legislation might possibly be influenced so that it benefits the company. At a broader level the strategist should also be familiar with the way in which legislation in other countries differs, and how this too might provide opportunities and constraints. The Scandinavian countries, for example, have developed a legislative framework to protect consumers that is far more restrictive than is generally the case elsewhere in Europe. Norway, for example, has banned many forms of sales promotion such as trading stamps, contests and premiums as being inappropriate and unfair methods for sellers to use in the promotion of their products. Elsewhere, food companies in India require government approval to launch a new brand if it will simply duplicate what is already on offer in the market, while in the Philippines food manufacturers are obliged to offer low price variations of their brands so that low income groups are not disadvantaged.

Although legislation such as this tends to be country-specific, examples such as these are potentially useful in that they highlight the need for marketing managers to be aware not just of the situation in their immediate markets, but also of how legislation might develop in order to restrict marketing practice. In a broader sense, marketing planners also need to monitor how public interest groups are likely to develop and, subsequently, influence marketing practice. In commenting on this in the context of American pressure groups, Salancik and Upah (1978) have said:

> There is some evidence that the consumer may not be King, nor even Queen. The consumer is but a voice, one among many. Consider how General Motors makes its cars today. Vital features of the motor are designed by the United States government; the exhaust system is redesigned by certain state governments; the production materials used are dictated by suppliers who control scarce material resources. For other products, other groups and organizations may get involved. Thus, insurance companies directly or indirectly affect the design of smoke detectors; scientific groups affect the design of spray products by condemning aerosols; minority activist groups affect the design of dolls by requesting representative figures. Legal departments also can be expected to increase their importance in firms, affecting not only product design and promotion but also marketing strategies. At a minimum, marketing managers will spend less time with their research departments asking 'What does the consumer want?' and more and more time with their production and legal people asking 'What can the consumer have?'

In the light of comments such as these, the need for careful and continual monitoring of the political and legal environment should be obvious, since at the heart of all such analysis is the simple recognition of the idea of political risk.

The Economic and Physical Environments

Within the majority of small and medium sized firms, the economic environment is typically seen as a constraint, since the ability of a company to exert any sort of influence on this element of the environment is to all intents and purposes negligible. As a consequence, it is argued, firms are typically put into the position of responding to the state of the economy. Having said this, larger companies, and particularly the multinationals (MNCs), are perhaps able to view the economic environment in a rather different way, since they are often able to shift investment and marketing patterns from one market to another and from one part of the world to another in order to capitalize most fully on the opportunities that exist. For a purely domestic operator, however, the ability to do this is generally non-existent. For both types of company there is still a need to understand *how* the economic environment is likely to affect performance, a need which received a significant boost in the 1970s in the wake of the oil crisis when parallels were being drawn between that period and the Great Depression of the 1930s. More specifically, however, the sorts of change that are currently taking place in the economic environment can be identified as:

1 an increase in real income growth;
2 continuing inflationary pressures;
3 changings in the savings/debt ratio;
4 concern over levels of Third World debt;
5 different consumer expenditure patterns.

The significance of changes such as these should not be looked at in isolation, but should be viewed instead against the background of changes in the *political/ economic balances of power* (e.g. the rise of Japan over the past 20 years, the opportunities today in Central and Eastern Europe, and the possible economic development of China), and major changes in the *physical environment*.

Concern with the physical environment has increased dramatically over the past few years, with the origins being traceable to the publication in the 1960s of Rachael Carson's book *Silent Spring* (1963). In this Carson drew attention to the possibly irrevocable damage being done to the planet and the possibility that we would exhaust the world's resources. This concern was echoed in the coining of the phrase 'eco-catastrophe' and reflected subsequently in the formation of powerful lobby groups such as Friends of the Earth who have had an impact upon business practice. The four major areas of concern expressed by pressure groups such as these are:

1 an impending shortage of raw materials;
2 the increasing costs of energy;
3 increasing levels and consequences of pollution;
4 an increasing need for governments to become involved in the *management* of natural resources.

It should be apparent from this that a broad perspective needs to be adopted in looking at the economic environment. From the viewpoint of the marketing planner, analysis of short-term and long-term economic *patterns* is of vital importance. Although it is not possible to develop an all-embracing list of economic issues to which attention needs to be paid, the strategist almost invariably needs to take account of the following areas:

1 patterns of real income distribution;
2 patterns of saving and debt;
3 expenditure patterns;
4 inflationary and deflationary pressures.

The Social, Cultural and Demographic Environments

In analysing this aspect of the environment, arguably the most useful and indeed logical starting point is that of demography, since not only is demographic change readily identifiable, but it is the size, structure and trends of a population that ultimately exert the greatest influence on demand. There are several reasons for this, the two most significant of which are, first, that there is a strong relationship between population and economic growth, and second, that it is the absolute size of the population that acts as the boundary condition determining potential or primary demand. A detailed understanding of the size, structure, composition and trends of the population is therefore of fundamental importance to the marketing planner. It is consequently fortunate that in the majority of developed countries information of this sort is generally readily available and provides a firm foundation for forecasting; a number of these are referred to in Illustration 7.3.

At the same time, a variety of other equally important and far reaching changes are currently taking place including the following.

1 *A growth in the number of one-person households*. The size of this SSWD group (single, separated, widowed, divorced) has grown dramatically over the past few years, partly as the result of more young adults leaving home early and partly by a rise in the divorce rate. The significance of this has been highlighted by a government forecast that the number of one-person households will have increased by more than 34 per cent in the period 1976–2000. At the same time, the number of pensioner one-person households is expected to have increased from 2.9 million in 1979 to almost 4.5 million by the turn of the century. The

Illustration 7.3: The Changing Consumer: the Growth of the 'Grey' Pound

In 1996, the findings of the TGI Gold survey of the 50–plus market conducted by the British Market Research Bureau International gave an insight to the size of the 'grey' market and the value of the 'grey' pound.

- In Britain, 17.5 million people are currently aged 50 or over. By the year 2000, this will have risen to 19.7 million, one third of the population.
- The over-50 market currently accounts for 38% of the adult population and is expected to grow by 12% by 2001.
- Families in which the head of household is over 50 have a total income of £245 billion. By contrast, those headed by someone under 50 spend only £135 billion annually.

These spending figures are even more impressive when it is recognised that many of these households are usually small, with the children having left home (the empty nester market) and major debts such as mortgages have been paid off. Combined with this, as the 1996 edition of *Social Trends* notes, recently retired pensioner units (either a single person over 65 or a couple where the husband is over state pension age) had a gross income of £225.50 a week in 1993 against £170.20 for all pensioners. Incomes are therefore gradually improving because of the rise in occupational pensions, and will continue to do so.

But despite the enormous spending power of the 'grey' market, not only do relatively few organisations specifically target 'grey' consumers (Saga is, of course, one of the most obvious and notable exceptions), but in many instances actively discriminate against it. However, given the changing demographic structure not just of Britain, but of virtually all developed markets, the question is how long will this remain so?

Source: Bush, J. Power of the 'grey' pound. The Times, 6 August 1996, p. 7.

net effect of changes such as these, together with a rather more general move towards smaller families, will lead to a drop in the average household size from 2.7 in 1979 to 2.2 in 2000.

The implications for marketing of changes such as these have already proved significant in a variety of ways and have been reflected in an increase in demand for more starter homes, smaller appliances, food that can be purchased in smaller portions, and a greater emphasis on convenience products.

2 *A rise in the number of two-person cohabitant households.* It has been suggested by several sociologists that cohabitation is becoming increasingly like the first stage of marriage, with more people of the opposite sex sharing a house. At the same time, the number of households with two or more people of the same sex sharing has also increased.

3 An increase in *group households* with three or more people of the same or opposite sex sharing expenses by living together, particularly in the larger cities. This figure looks set to increase yet further.

The needs of these non-family households differ in a variety of ways from those of the more conventional family household which in the past has typically provided the focus for marketing attention. By virtue of their increasing importance, non-family households are likely to require ever more different strategies over the next few years if full advantage of the opportunities they offer is to be realized.

At the same time a variety of other significant demographic shifts are taking place throughout the world, all of which need to be reflected in the planning process.

1 *An explosion in the world's population.* With an annual and exponential growth rate of 1.8 per cent, the world population will have grown from 4.4 billion in 1980 to 6.2 billion by the year 2000. Much of this growth will be concentrated in those nations which, by virtue of currently low standards of living and economic development, can least afford it. Nevertheless, significant opportunities will be generated as a result of this growth both domestically and internationally.

2 *A slowdown in birth rates* in many of the developed nations. Many families today, for example, are opting for just one child and this has had significant implications for a variety of companies. Johnson & Johnson, for example, responded to the declining birth rate by very successfully repositioning its baby oil, baby powder and baby shampoo in such a way that the products also appealed to young female adults. Similarly, cosmetics companies have placed a far greater emphasis on products for the over-fifties.

3 *An ageing population* as advances in medical care allow people to live longer. One result of this trend, which has in turn been exacerbated by the slowdown in birth rate, has been an increase in the number of empty nesters (see the section on the family life cycle on pp. 284–5) who have substantial sums of discretionary income and high expectations.

4 *Changing family structures* as a result of:

- later marriage
- fewer children
- increased divorce rates
- more working wives
- an increase in the number of career women.

5 *Higher levels of education* and an increasing number of families in what has traditionally been seen as the middle class.

6 *Geographical shifts* in population and, in Britain at least, the emergence of a north-south divide characterized by radically different levels of economic activity and employment.

7 *A growth in the number of people willing to commute long distances to work*, and an upsurge in the opportunities for telecommuting whereby people work from home and interact with colleagues via computer terminals.

The net effect of changes such as these has been significant, and is continuing to prove so, with the marketing strategies of nearly all companies being affected in one way or another. At their most fundamental, these changes have led to a shift from a small number of mass markets to an infinitely larger number of micromarkets differentiated by age, sex, lifestyle, education and so on. Each of these groups differs in terms of its preferences and characteristics, and as a consequence requires different, more flexible and more precise approaches to marketing which no longer take for granted the long established assumptions and conventions of marketing practice. The implications of these trends are therefore of considerable significance and from the viewpoint of the strategist have the advantage of being both reliable and largely predictable, at least in the short and medium term. There is thus no excuse either for being taken unawares by them or for ignoring them.

Against the background of fundamental demographic and social shifts such as these a wide variety of other changes can be seen to be taking place, particularly in the area of social and cultural factors. Albrecht (1979), for example, has identified five major lifestyle changes that are currently taking place. There are, he suggests, shifts:

- from rural living to urban living;
- from stationary to mobile;
- from self-sufficient to interconnected;
- from isolated to interconnected;
- from physically active to sedentary.

The full impact of these changes is in many cases still to be felt, although Albrecht highlights their physiological and psychological effects, which have increased levels of stress and in turn influenced lifestyle. At the same time, however, the social and cultural environment is being influenced by a seemingly ever greater concern with the environment. At one level this has seen the development of consumerism and concern for equal opportunities while at another level, however, it is reflected in a far deeper and more fundamental concern for the physical environment and the way in which certain products such as the fluorocarbons contained in some aerosols have harmed the ozone layer. Equally, attitudes with regard to such things as acid rain, pollution of the seas, and the danger of nuclear power have all changed over the past decade and, directly or indirectly, seem likely to influence marketing behaviour, with an ever greater emphasis being given to environmentally friendly products. In part this can be seen as a result of: the possible shift in emphasis from a 'me society' to a 'we society' that is characterized by less self-interest and a greater concern with longer lasting relationships; an increase in the number of people concerned with a healthy lifestyle; a decline in the work ethic and institutional loyalty; and a greater concern with the physical environment. Others have argued that the shift in social and cultural values is in fact the other way.

Regardless of the direction in which attitudes are shifting, the relationship between people and society can be expressed in terms of the Stanford Research Institute's *life ways concept* which suggests that people fall into one of six groups. The key elements of each of these groups have been summarized by Kotler (1988, p. 162) as being:

- *Makers*. Makers are those who make the system work. They are the leaders and the up-and-comers. They are involved in worldly affairs, generally prosperous and ambitious. They are found in the professions and include the managers and proprietors of business.
- *Preservers*. Preservers are people who are at ease with the familiar and are proud of tradition. They are a powerful force in promoting stability in a changing world.
- *Takers*. Takers take what they can from the system. They live only marginally in the work world, finding their pleasures outside. They are attracted to bureaucracies and tenured posts.
- *Changers*. Changers tend to be answer-havers; they commonly wish to change things to conform with their views. They are the critics, protestors, radicals, advocates, and complainers – and a significant segment of the doers. Their focus is chiefly outward.
- *Seekers*. Seekers are the ones who search for a better grasp, a deeper understanding, a richer experience, a universal view. The pathways of their seeking and the rewards sought tend to be internal. They often originate and promulgate new ideas.
- *Escapers*. Escapers have a drive to escape, to get away from it all. Escape takes many forms from dropping out, to addiction, to mental illness, to mysticism.

These life groups differ in a variety of significant ways and need to be seen as market segments with specific material and symbolic needs. The makers, for example, are high achievers for whom success symbols such as cars, houses and brand names are important forms of expression, while changers, represent a far more austere lifestyle, characterized by smaller cars and less emphasis in their clothing on fashion. This shift in cultural values has also led to the following trends:

Other centredness → self-fulfilment
Postponed gratification → immediate gratification
Hard work → the easy life
Formal relationships → informal open relationships
Religious orientation → secular orientation

Taken together, the changes that we have pointed to in this section can be seen as fundamental, and have been described by Albrecht (1979) in the following ways:

> The period from 1900 until the present stands apart from every other period in human history as a time of incredible change. Mankind, at least in the so-called 'developed' countries, has lost its innocence entirely. The great defining characteristics of this period – the first three-quarters of the twentieth century – have been change, impermanence, disruption, newness and obsolescence, and a sense of acceleration in almost every perceptible aspect of American society.
>
> Philosophers, historians, scientists, and economists have given various names to this period. Management consultant Peter F. Drucker (1968) has called it the Age of Discontinuity. Economist John Kenneth Galbraith (1977) has called it the Age of Uncertainty. Media theorist Marshall MacLuhan (1964, 1968) called it the Age of the Global Village. Writer and philosopher Alvin Toffler (1970, 1975) called it the Age of Future Shock. Virtually all thoughtful observers of America, Americans, and American society have remarked with some alarm about the accelerating pace with which our life processes and our surrounds are changing within the span of a single generation. And this phenomenon is spreading all over the industrialized world. I call this the Age of Anxiety.

The Technological Environment

The fourth and final strand of the environment is that of technology. Seen by many people as the single most dramatic force shaping our lives, technological advance needs to be seen as a force for 'creative destruction' in that the development of new products or concepts has an often fatal knock-out effect on an existing product. The creation of the Xerography photocopying process, for example, destroyed the market for carbon paper, while the development of cars damaged the demand for railways. The implications for the existing industry are often straightforward: change or die. The significance of technological change does, however, need to be seen not just at the corporate or industry level but also at the national level, since an economy's growth rate is directly influenced by the level of technological advance (see Wills, et al., 1972).

Technology does, therefore, provide both opportunities and threats, some of which are direct while others are far less direct in their impact. As an example of this, the development of the contraceptive pill led to smaller families, an increase in the number of working wives, higher levels of discretionary income and then subsequently to a greater emphasis on holidays, consumer durables, and so on. Recognizing then that the impact of technology is to all interests inevitable, the areas to which Kotler (1988, pp. 154–6) suggests the marketing planner should pay attention include:

1 *The accelerating pace of technological change.* In his book *Future Shock*, Toffler (1970) makes reference to the accelerative thrust in the invention, exploitation, diffusion and acceptance of new technologies. An ever greater number of ideas are being developed, and the time period between their development and

implementation is shortening. This theme was developed further by Toffler in *The Third Wave* (1980) in which he forecast the rapid emergence and acceptance of telecommuting (the electronic cottage) with direct implications for such things as family relationships, home entertainment and, less directly, levels of car exhaust pollution.

2 *Unlimited innovational opportunities* with major advances being made in the areas of solid state electronics, robotics, material sciences and biotechnology.

3 *Higher research and development budgets*, particularly in countries such as Japan. One implication of this is that organizations are likely to be forced into the position of spending ever greater amounts on R & D simply to stay still.

4 *A concentration of effort in some industries on minor product improvements* that are essentially defensive, rather than on the riskier and more offensive major product advances.

5 *A greater emphasis upon the regulation of technological change* in order to minimize the undesirable effects of some new products upon society. Safety and health regulations are most evident in their application in the pharmaceutical, foodstuffs and car industries, although across the entire spectrum of industry far more emphasis today is being given to the idea of technological assessment as a prelude to products being launched commercially.

From the viewpoint of marketing, the implications of each of these areas is of potential significance, and argues the case for careful technological monitoring in order to ensure that emerging opportunities are not ignored or missed. This, in turn, should lead to more market-oriented, rather than product-oriented, research and to a generally greater awareness of the negative aspects of any innovation.

Underlying all of these points is, of course, a recognition of the product life cycle (PLC) concept. The pros and cons of the PLC are detailed elsewhere in this book, and at this stage we are therefore concerned with the way in which simple recognition of the concept argues the case for the development of a formal technological forecasting system which then acts as an input to the process of developing marketing strategy.

Coming to Terms with Industry Breakpoints

A fundamental element of any competitive marketing strategy should be the anticipation – or precipitation – of major structural change. Sometimes referred to as *industry breakpoints*, the consequences of major change are seen in a variety of ways, but most obviously in terms of how a previously successful strategy is made obsolete. An understanding of how breakpoints work and how they might best be managed is therefore an essential part of strategic marketing.

In discussing industry breakpoints, Strebel (1996, p. 13) defines them as:

> . . . a new offering to the market that is so superior in terms of customer value and delivered cost that it disrupts the rules of the competitive game : a new business system is required to deliver it. The new offering typically causes a sharp shift in the industry's growth rate while the competitive response to the new business system results in a dramatic realignment of market shares.

There are numerous examples of industries in which the phenomenon has been experienced (see, for example, our discussion of the Swiss watch industry in Illustration 7.2 and the launch of Häagen Dazs in Illustration 10.12), although in many instances it appears that managers have learned little from the lessons of other markets in which traumatic change has already taken place. However, given the seemingly ever greater pace of competition, shorter product, market and brand life cycles, and the consequently more intensive search for competitive advantage, it is almost inevitable that at some stage a majority of managers will be faced with the problems that breakpoints create. The experiences of the personal computer industry are discussed in Illustration 7.4.

Illustration 7.4: Industry Breakpoints and the Personal Computer Industry

When Apple launched its first PC, it provided the market with a low-cost product that was infinitely more convenient than traditional centralised computing systems. However, few, if any, of the established players appear to have seen Apple as any sort of threat. By contrast, numerous small firms recognised the opportunities that Apple's simplicity offered, with the result that competition in the PC market escalated as firms tried to define the form and content of a PC.

With IBM's entry to this part of the market, an industry standard began to emerge, production volumes grew, prices dropped and the pace of technological change escalated. Many of the smaller players were unable to match the shifts that took place and were shaken out of the market. Indeed, even Apple was hit hard by the changes that were taking place and eventually responded by ousting its founders in favour of a consumer marketing expert.

Levels of competition continued to increase dramatically as firms focused upon expanding the market and capturing market share by offering the product at even lower prices. The intensity of this price competition created major difficulties as more and more firms tried to find a way out of the downward spiral.

However, it was not until Apple launched the Macintosh with its much higher levels of user-friendliness that things really began to change. Amongst the numerous competitors, it was only those who recognised that customers' values had changed in that they were ready for hard disks, better graphics, faster operating speeds and new software who managed to cope with this new breakpoint. Others, however, were quickly forced out. It was therefore something of an irony that Apple appear not to have recognised the real

FIGURE 7.9
Breakpoints within the PC industry

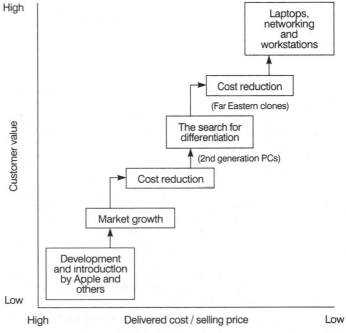

SOURCE: Adapted from Strebel, P. (1966), Breakpoint: how to stay in the game, *Financial Times, Mastering Management*, Vol. 17, p. 14

value of the shift they had generated and, as a consequence, failed to capitalise upon it to the extent that they might have done. By contrast, Bill Gates of Microsoft saw the opportunities of graphics software and began creating the equivalent for the IBM standard.

The next breakpoint was created by the recession of the late 1980s. Given the size of the market, it was inevitable that it would be affected by the downturn in spending and so, as sales dropped, each company's cost base became crucial. Those who were best placed to benefit from this were the firms in the Far East and companies such as Compaq.

As the recession eased, the industry was affected by yet another breakpoint as more powerful chips and software emerged, and the market shifted towards laptops, integrated networks and workstations; these are all illustrated in Figure 7.9. At the same time, there was a major shift in the supplier base with Intel having emerged as the dominant supplier of chips, and Microsoft of software. Meanwhile, the fortunes of IBM, Apple and many of the Far Eastern manufacturers had all declined dramatically.

Source: Strebel, P. (1996) Breakpoint: how to stay in the game, Financial Times, Mastering Management, Vol. 17, p. 13

According to Strebel (1996, p.13), there are two basic types of breakpoint:

1 *Divergent breakpoints*, which are associated with sharply increasing variety in the competitive offerings and consequently higher value for the customer; and
2 *Convergent breakpoints*, which are the result of improvements in the systems and processes used to deliver the offerings, with these then being reflected in lower delivered costs.

These are illustrated in Figure 7.10.

FIGURE 7.10
The evolutionary cycle of competitive behaviour

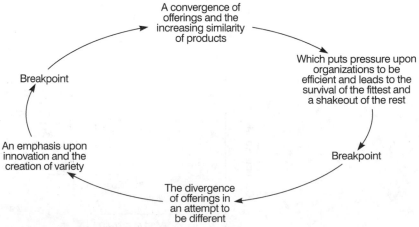

SOURCE: Adapted from Strebel (1996)

With regard to the specific causes of breakpoints, it appears that they can be created by a variety of factors, including:

● technological breakthroughs which provide the innovative organization with a major competitive advantage but which, in turn, put competitors at a disadvantage;

- the economic cycle which, in a downturn, forces a radical rethink of the product and how it is to be marketed;
- a new source of supply which offers scope for major reductions in cost;
- changes in government policy;
- shifts in customer values and/or expectations;
- the identification by one company of new business opportunities, with the result that there is a divergence in competitors' responses and behaviour as they try to work out how best to exploit these opportunities;
- shifts within the distribution network which lead to changes in the balance of power between manufacturers and retailers and very different sets of expectations;
- new entrants to the market who bring with them different sets of skills and expectations, as well as a different perspective;
- declining returns which force a radical rethink of how the company is operating and how it should develop in the future.

Given the significance of breakpoints, it is obviously essential that, wherever possible, the marketing planner identifies when breakpoints are most likely to occur and the form they will take. In the absence of this the organization will be forced into a responsive mode. However, it can be argued that a majority of managers are particularly badly equipped to identify breakpoints, especially in organizations with a closed culture, since their experience is largely irrelevant in new markets and new business systems. As an example of this, the established players in the computer industry focused much of their effort upon their existing products, markets and technologies, and had little cause or incentive to look at a redefinition of the product and market in the way that Apple did. Equally, difficulties arise when an upstream or downstream company begins to adopt a radically different approach; this is touched upon in Illustration 7.4, with the moves made by Intel and Microsoft.

Nevertheless, planners need to come to terms with the dynamics of their industry and, in particular, the sorts of pressures which we referred to earlier and which, sooner or later, lead to breakpoints occurring. Insofar as a framework for this can be identified, it stems from the way in which there is a tendency for the competitive cycle to fluctuate between *divergence* (variety creation) and *convergence* (the survival of the fittest).

7.7 APPROACHES TO ENVIRONMENTAL ANALYSIS AND SCANNING

Against the background of our discussion so far it should be clear that environmental analysis and forecasting are capable of making a major contribution to the formulation of strategy. Indeed it has been argued by a number of strategists that environmental analysis and forecasting is the true starting point of any effective planning system, since strategy is based not only on a detailed understanding of the firm's capacity but also on a full knowledge and appreciation of environmental forces and changes that are likely to have an impact on the firm. At its most extreme, the failure to do this is highlighted by Theodore Levitt's ideas of 'Marketing Myopia' which he discussed in his now classic *Harvard Business Review* article (1960, pp. 45–56).

In this article Levitt argued that declining or defunct industries generally reached this position because of a product rather than a marketing orientation. In other words, they focused too firmly on products rather than the environment in which they operated. As a consequence, these companies were often taken by surprise by environmental change, found it difficult to respond, and in many cases, either lost significant market shares or were forced into liquidation.

A system of environmental analysis and forecasting consists of two elements: the first of these is concerned with the *generation* of an up-to-date data base of information, while the second involves the *dissemination* of this information to decision makers and influencers. The effectiveness of such a system, and in particular of this second part, is in practice likely to be influenced by a variety of factors, including:

1 the technical skills of those involved in the process of analysis and forecasting;
2 the nature of the managerial environment that exists within the company.

The significance of this second point is in many companies all too often ignored, but highlights the importance of a planning culture which is both endorsed and promoted by top management. In addition, the managerial environment affects the process in the sense that in large companies at least, those who are involved in the mechanics of analysis and forecasting are rarely the decision makers themselves. Instead, they are generally in an advisory role. This role can lead to the emergence of an important political process within the system whereby the analyst presents information in such a way that the decision maker's perception of the environment and, in turn the options open to the company, is distorted in a particular way. By the same token, the decision maker will often place a particular interpretation on the information presented by the analyst, depending on his perception of the analyst's track record. In commenting on this political process, Brownlie (1987, p. 99) suggests that:

> students of history will recognise that many a bloody political intrigue was spawned by the jealously guarded, and often misused privilege of proximity to the seat of power which was conferred on privy counsellors and advisors. Thus in addition to the technical skills demanded of environmental analysts and forecasters, astute political skills could be said to be the hallmark of an effective operator.

It should therefore be recognized that the effectiveness of a planning system is not determined solely by its methodology, but that it is also affected by several other factors, including the willingness and ability of a management to recognize and subsequently respond to the indicators of coming environmental change.

Taken together, these comments argue the case for what we can refer to as *formal environmental scanning*, a process which covers the full spectrum of activities firms use in order to understand environmental changes and their implications. The essential element of formal environmental scanning is that it should be seen as an activity that becomes an *integral* part of the ongoing process by which companies develop, implement, control and review strategies and plans at both the corporate and the business unit level.

The Benefits of Environmental Scanning

In practice, the precise role of an environmental scanning process is influenced by a variety of factors, the most significant of which is typically that of management expectations. This, in turn, is often a function of the size of the organization and managerial perceptions of the complexity of its environment. Thus in the case of many small firms the focus is likely to be on the general trends that are likely to influence short- and medium-term levels of performance. In large firms, however, and in particular the multinationals, the focus tends to be far broader with a greater emphasis being placed upon longer-term and more fundamental issues, including possible changes in the political, economic, social and technological variables which provided the focus for the first part of this chapter.

With regard to the specific benefits of environmental scanning Diffenbach (1983, pp. 107–16), in a study of 90 American corporations, has suggested that there are seven principal pay-offs:

1 an increased general awareness by management of environmental changes;
2 better planning and strategic decision making;
3 greater effectiveness in government matters;
4 better industry and market analysis;
5 better results in foreign business;
6 improvements in diversification and resource allocations;
7 better energy planning.

It should be noted that from this study Diffenbach found that although environmental scanning is widely practised and generally considered to be important by the majority of those firms that do it (73 per cent), a sizeable number of companies (27 per cent) simply did not bother with scanning, or did it but found it to be of only limited value (28 per cent).

These benefits of environmental scanning have also been expanded upon by Jain (1985, p. 250) who has listed the major attractions to be that the process:

1 helps firms to identify and capitalize upon opportunities rather than losing out to competitors;
2 provides a base of objective qualitative information;
3 makes the firm more sensitive to the changing needs and wishes of customers;
4 provides a base of 'objective qualitative information' about the business environment that can subsequently be of value to the strategist;
5 provides a level of intellectual stimulation for strategists;
6 improves the image of the firm with the public by illustrating that it is sensitive to its environment;
7 provides a continuing broad based education for executives in general, and the strategist in particular.

Having said this, the complexity of the scanning process varies greatly from one company to another. In commenting on this, Ansoff (1984) has suggested that it is determined by two factors:

1 perceptions within the company of the degree of environmental uncertainty (most typically this is a function of the rate of environmental change);
2 perceptions of the degree of environmental complexity (this is generally influenced by the range of activities and markets in which the firm is currently and prospectively involved).

The significance of this second factor needs to be seen in terms of the implications for the structure of the scanning process which the firm then develops. Recognizing the dangers of overload within a system, there is a need for those involved in scanning to organize the process in such a way that the environment can be reduced to something manageable, while at the same time ensuring that extraneous factors are not ignored. What this means in practice is that a process of filtration generally operates in which the full breadth of environmental stimuli is reduced to something more manageable.

The question of who should decide on these elements has been referred to by Ansoff (1984) who has argued that it is the *user* of the information who should exert the major influence; in practice, however, it is often the scanner who determines the choice of approach.

Returning for a moment to the filtration process through which a structure is imposed upon the full breadth and complexity of the environment, Brownlie (1987, pp. 110–12) identifies three levels:

1 *The surveillance filter* which provides a broad and generally unstructured picture of the business environment. However, although this picture is broad it

will, by virtue of the perceptions of those involved, 'be selective and partial' (Brownlie, 1987, p. 110).

2 *The mentality filter* which emerges as the result of past successes and failures and which in turn leads to the idea of bounded rationality allowing those involved to cope with the volume and complexity of the information being generated. However, while this mentality filter is undoubtedly useful in helping to provide a structure, bounded rationality can create problems in that environmental signals which are extreme in nature and outside the manager's historical experience are likely to be perceived to be of little significance and subsequently screened out. There is a need therefore to balance the benefits of the mentality filter with a willingness to assess and possibly incorporate novel and perhaps extreme signals.

3 *The power filter* which is in essence an attitude of mind on the part of top management and which reflects a willingness to incorporate material in the strategic decision-making process that falls outside the bounds of previous practice and preconceived notions. Recognition by the scanner of the existence of an attitude such as this is then likely to be reflected in the scanner's own willingness to build into the process a breadth of perspective rather than a straightforward identification and assessment of largely predictable environmental changes.

Against the background of comments such as these, it is possible to identify the features which are most likely to lead to an effective environmental scanning system. These include:

1 top management involvement and commitment;
2 a detailed understanding of the dimensions and parameters of the scanning model that it is intended should operate;
3 an established strategic planning culture.

In addition, attention needs to be paid to the *boundaries of the firm's environment* and hence to those areas which are deemed to be either relevant or irrelevant, and to the *time horizon* which is felt to be meaningful. In the case of the chemicals and pharmaceuticals industries, for example, the planning time horizon – and hence the scanning period – may easily be in excess of 30 years, while in the clothing industry it may be a year or less.

The Responsibility for Scanning

Brownlie's work (1983, 1987) suggests that environmental scanning is typically the responsibility of one of three levels of management.

1 *Line management* with one or more line managers being given the task of scanning in addition to their normal responsibilities. In practice, however, such an approach typically suffers from limitations, the most obvious of which is that it is an additional responsibility and may not therefore get the attention it deserves. On top of this, the perspective is likely to be at best medium term, since the manager is unlikely to have the full range of specialist skills needed for the task to be performed effectively.

2 *Strategic planning* in which environmental scanning is made part of the overall process of strategic analysis. While this is arguably more likely to succeed than is the case if responsibility is passed to line management, other problems are likely to emerge largely because corporate staff may not necessarily understand the detail of the firm's business on a day-to-day basis. Because of this, it is argued, they are unlikely to be able to define and interpret the relevant parameters of the environment any more effectively than a line manager.

3 *A specialist organizational unit* with specific responsibilities for environmental monitoring.

Of these, the third approach may be seen as an ideal that few firms have yet to embrace. As a result, it is a mixture of the first two that predominates in business today. Most typically the mixture operates on a largely unstructured basis, with corporate planners focusing upon the general environment, while line managers focus upon the product market. The two perspectives, together with the general forecasts that can be bought from consultants and organizations such as the Henley Centre, are then assessed before the overall picture is developed.

Recognizing these sorts of organizational problems has led Diffenbach (1983) to identify the specific difficulties of environmental analysis that act as deterrents to the development and implementation of an effective scanning system:

1 the interpretation of results and the assessment of their specific impact upon the organization is rarely clear-cut;
2 the output of environmental analysis may be too inaccurate, general or uncertain to be taken seriously;
3 a preoccupation with the short term pre-empts attention being paid to longer-term environmental issues;
4 long-term environmental analyses are often treated sceptically;
5 in diversified businesses the amount of analysis needed is likely to be both considerable and complex, particularly when interrelationships are considered;
6 perceptions and interpretations of scenarios identified may differ significantly between one manager and another.

Market Understanding and Competitive Advantage: the Importance of Market Learning

For many marketing managers, one of the biggest and most enduring problems is that of understanding their markets. Without this understanding, they lose touch with the market, are taken by surprise by shifts in customer expectations, are slow to react to competitors, and fail to make full use of their distribution channels. The net effect of this is that they then fail to anticipate the nature and direction of changes within the market, constantly miss opportunities and, when they do respond, typically behave slowly and counter-productively. By contrast, managers within the truly market-driven organization are notable for the way in which they sense how their markets are likely to change, the nature of the opportunities that this is likely to create and how these opportunities can then best be exploited.

In discussing the difference between the two types of organization and what determines whether an organization is market-driven, Day (1996, p. 12) highlights the importance of market learning:

> Market learning involves much more than simply taking in information. The learning process must give managers the ability to ask the right questions at the right time, absorb the answers into their mental model of how the market behaves, share the new understanding with others in the management team and act decisively. Effective learning about markets is a continuous process that pervades all decisions. It cannot be spasmodic.

This effective learning process, which is illustrated in Figure 7.11, consists of several distinct stages:

- *Open-minded enquiry* based on the belief that decisions need to be based on a detailed and broad understanding of the market and that conventional wisdoms and preconceived notions and beliefs are dangerous;
- *Widespread information distribution* to ensure that managers across the organization develop a greater market understanding;
- *Mutually informed mental models* which are used in the interpretation of information and ensure that issues that are deemed to be strategically important are examined;

FIGURE 7.11
*The organizational
learning process*

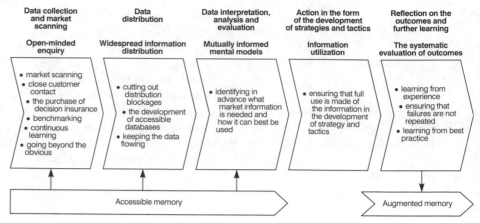

SOURCE: Adapted from Day, G. (1996), How to Learn about Markets, *Financial Times,
Mastering Management*, Vol. 12, p. 12

- *An accessible organizational memory* to ensure that the organization keeps track of what has been learned and so the information and knowledge can continue to be used.

The process is then reinforced by a deliberate reflection on the outcomes of the strategies and tactics that have been developed and, by means of integrated databases, the augmentation of the organizational memory.

7.8 SUMMARY

Marketing strategy is concerned with matching the capabilities of the organization with the demands of the environment. There is therefore a need for the strategist to monitor the environment on an ongoing basis so that opportunities and threats facing the organization are identified and subsequently reflected in strategy.

In analysing the environment a step-wise approach is needed. This begins with an initial audit of general environmental influences followed by a series of increasingly tightly focused stages designed to provide the strategist with a clear understanding of the organization's strategic position.

Although a variety of approaches can be used for analysing the environment, arguably the most useful is the PEST framework. This involves the strategist focusing in turn upon the Political/legal, Economic, Social/cultural, and Techno-logical elements of the environment. Each of these elements was discussed in detail.

The environmental conditions faced by an organization are capable of varying greatly in their complexity and need to be reflected both in the ways in which environmental analysis is conducted and in the ways in which strategy is subsequently developed. The consequences of failing to take account of a changing environment have, as we discussed, been illustrated by a wide variety of organizational experiences, including those of the Swiss watch industry in the 1970s.

It is widely recognized that the pace of environmental change is increasing and that the need for organizations to develop a structured approach to environmental analysis with the results then being fed into the strategic marketing planning process is greater than ever. Despite this the evidence suggests that in many organizations environmental scanning systems are only poorly developed. If this is to change, top management commitment both to the development of a scanning system and to the incorporation of the results into the planning process is essential.

7.9 EXERCISES

1 Identify two examples of organizations which appear either to have failed to monitor their environment, or have misread it, and as a consequence have been taken by surprise by changing market structures (which might include the emergence of new competitors, a different marketing approach by the firm's current competitors, and so on).

2 Identify examples of each of the three environmental types referred to in Figure 7.4. What are the marketing implications of each type for how an organization might operate?

3 Look at the environment in which your organization operates and compare it with the sort of environment that existed, say, five and ten years ago. What problems have been experienced by the management team in coming to terms with this new environment? In what ways does it appear that the environment will change over the next few years? To what extent does it appear that the organization's existing strategies, structures, systems and people will be able to cope with this?

4 How well developed is the environmental monitoring system within your organization? Who has the *explicit* responsibility for environmental scanning?

5 Conduct a detailed PEST analysis for your organization. Which of the PEST elements appears to be the most influential when the marketing strategy is being formulated?

7.10 CASE STUDY

Watergate Pumps Ltd

Watergate Pumps Ltd manufactures and markets a range of water pumps and control systems for domestic and industrial central heating systems. For the past three years total industry sales of domestic pumps have been stable at an average of 1.3 million units per annum (£40 million at manufacturers' average selling prices). Sales are forecast to grow only slowly over the next few years and are expected to reach a peak of 1.55 million units p.a. in 1998.

Within the domestic sector, there are four principal markets for the product: local authorities; the privatized utilities such as British Gas; regional/national building companies; and small firms of builders/plumbers and individuals repairing their own heating systems.

The company, which is a subsidiary of a far larger organization which has interests throughout the building supplies industry, has three competitors. Selected market data collected from various sources appear in Tables 1, 2 and 3.

Watergate has been taken by surprise by a variety of developments in the marketplace over the past few years, including:

- The entry into the market in 1991 by Pump Suppliers, a Dutch-owned company which set up a factory in southern England.
- The launch by B G Industrial (BGI) and Northern Pumps of several modified and new products.
- A general competitive repositioning (see Figure 1).
- An extension by all three competitors of the guarantees offered on their products from one to three years.
- The three-year stagnation of the market.
- A significant shift in customers' buying motives, with quality and ease of fitting having become increasingly important (see Figure 2).

- A series of improvements by all three competitors in their control systems.
- The move by BGI and Northern Pumps into a number of profitable overseas markets.

Because of this, there is now recognition that the company's understanding of the market is poor and that some form of structured external environment monitoring is needed.

Table 1 Watergate Pumps – selected market data

	Market shares within the domestic pumps sector (1990–93)				Total manufacturing capacity (000 units)	Total output in 1993 (000 units)	UK overseas split of sales in 1993
	1990 (%)	1991 (%)	1992 (%)	1993 (%)			
Watergate Pumps	35	29	27	24	475	320	100/0
BG International	50	50	48	48	850	830	75/25
Northern Pumps	15	13	15	16	300	280	74/26
Pump Suppliers	0	8	10	12	300	300	52/48

Table 2

	Sales in 1993 by type of buyer (000 units)	Expected percentage increase/ (decrease) by 1998	Market position of each company by type of buyer (1993)			
			No 1	No 2	No 3	No 4
Local authorities	400	(25)	WGP	NP	PS	BGI
Privatized utilities	300	66	BGI	PS	WGP	NP
Regional/national builders	400	25	BGI	PS	NP	WGP
Local builders/plumbers and private individuals	200	25	BGI	NP	PS	WGP

Key: WGP – Watergate Pumps
　　BGI – BG International
　　NP – Northern Pumps
　　PS – Pump Suppliers

Source: Trade Data

Table 3 Rank order of the principal buying motives of different customer groups

	Local authorities	Privatized utilities	Regional/ national builders	Local builders/ plumbers and private individuals
Price	1	3	3 =	3
Availability off the shelf	N/A	N/A	3 =	1 =
Reliability	3	1	1	4
Ease of fitting	2	2	2	1 =

N/A: Not applicable, since supplies are delivered in bulk to regional warehouses

Source: Compiled from trade data

FIGURE 1
Competitive positioning (1990 and 1993)

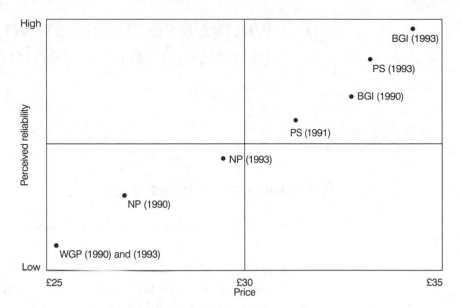

FIGURE 2
Principal buying motives

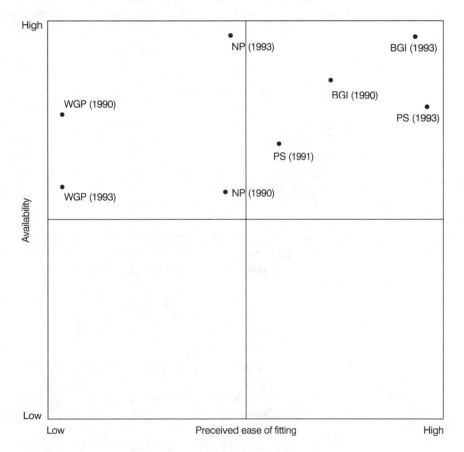

Questions

1 As the company's newly appointed market analyst, you are required to prepare a detailed report for the marketing director recommending how an effective external environment monitoring system for the company might best be developed and implemented. Included within the report should be your suggestions on the structure of the system, the expected inputs and outputs, the probable organizational and resource implications, and the nature of any benefits that should emerge.

2 In the light of the information contained in the mini case, what recommendations for future marketing action would you make?

<table>
<tr><td>8</td><td>Market segmentation, targeting and positioning</td></tr>
</table>

8.1 LEARNING OBJECTIVES

When you have read this chapter you should be able to understand:

(a) the nature and purpose of market segmentation;
(b) the contribution of segmentation to effective marketing planning;
(c) how markets can be segmented, and the criteria that need to be applied if segmentation is to prove cost effective;
(d) how product positioning follows from the segmentation process and the bases by which products and brands can be positioned effectively.

8.2 INTRODUCTION

In the previous chapter we focused on approaches to environmental analysis and the frameworks within which strategic marketing planning can best take place. Against this background we now turn to the question of market segmentation and to the ways in which companies need to position themselves in order to maximize their competitive advantage and serve their target markets in the most effective manner. It does need to be recognized, however, that for many organizations the strategic issues of segmentation and positioning often take on only a minimal role. Saunders (1987, p. 25), for example, points to research which suggested that a substantial proportion of British companies still fail to segment their market. He quotes the marketing director of one consumer durables company as saying:

> We have not broken the customers down. We have always held the opinion that the market is wide . . . and the product has wide appeal, therefore why break the market down at all?

A similar comment emerged from a sales director who stated:

> We do not see the market as being made up of specific segments. Our market is made up of the whole industry.

There are several possible reasons for views such as these, although in the case of companies with a broadly reactive culture, it is often due largely to a degree of organizational inertia, which leads to the firm being content to stay in the same sector of the market for some considerable time. It is only when the effects of a changing environment become overwhelmingly evident that serious consideration is given to the need for repositioning in order to appeal to new sectors of the market. For other organizations, however, a well thought out policy of segmentation plays a pivotal role in the determination of success. It is the recognition of this that has led to the suggestion in recent years that the essence of strategic marketing can be summed up by the initials STP – segmentation, targeting and positioning. This is illustrated in Figure 8.1.

FIGURE 8.1
The eight stages of the segmentation, targeting and positioning process

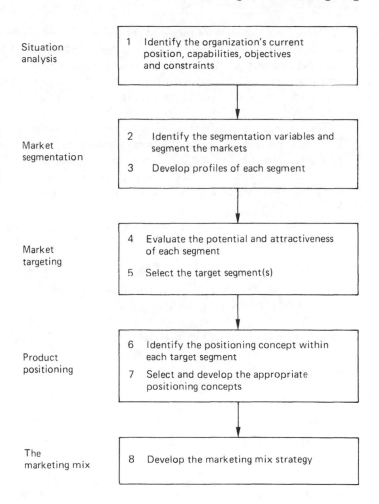

Situation analysis

1 Identify the organization's current position, capabilities, objectives and constraints

Market segmentation

2 Identify the segmentation variables and segment the markets

3 Develop profiles of each segment

Market targeting

4 Evaluate the potential and attractiveness of each segment

5 Select the target segment(s)

Product positioning

6 Identify the positioning concept within each target segment

7 Select and develop the appropriate positioning concepts

The marketing mix

8 Develop the marketing mix strategy

Not all writers are in favour of segmentation and before we examine the methods used to segment markets, it is worth looking briefly at their views. Bliss (1980), for example, has suggested that while many marketing managers acknowledge the rationale of segmentation, many are dissatisfied with it as a concept, partly because it is inapplicable or difficult to apply in many markets, but also because emphasis is too often given to the techniques of segmentation at the expense of the market itself and the competitive situation that exists. Equally, Resnik, Turney and Mason (1979, pp. 100–6) have suggested that changing values, new lifestyles and the rising costs of products and services argue the case for what they call 'countersegmentation'; in other words, an aggregation of various parts of the market rather than their subdivision. The majority of writers, however, acknowledge the very real strategic importance of segmentation and, in particular, the ways in which it enables the organization to use its resources more effectively and with less wastage.

8.3 THE NATURE AND PURPOSE OF SEGMENTATION

During the past 20 years market segmentation has developed and been defined in a variety of ways. In essence it is the process of dividing a varied and differing group of buyers or potential buyers into smaller groups within which broadly similar patterns of buyers' needs exist. By doing this, the marketing planner is attempting to break the market into more strategically manageable parts which can then be targeted and satisfied far more precisely by making a series of perhaps small changes to the marketing mix. The rationale is straightforward and can be expressed most readily in terms of the fact that only rarely does a single product or marketing approach appeal to the needs and wants of all buyers. Because of this, the marketing strategist needs to categorize buyers on the basis both of their characteristics and their specific product needs with a view then to adapting either the product or the marketing programme or both to satisfy these different tastes and demands.

The potential benefits of a well-developed segmentation strategy can therefore be considerable since an organization should be able to establish and strengthen its position in the market and in this way operate more effectively. Not only does it then become far more difficult for a competitor to attack, but it also allows the organization to build a greater degree of market sector knowledge and customer loyalty.

Although the arguments for segmentation appear strong, it is only one of three quite distinct approaches to marketing strategy which exist. These are:

1 undifferentiated or mass marketing;
2 product-variety or differentiated marketing;
3 target or concentrated marketing.

These are illustrated in Figure 8.2.

FIGURE 8.2
Undifferentiated, differentiated and concentrated marketing

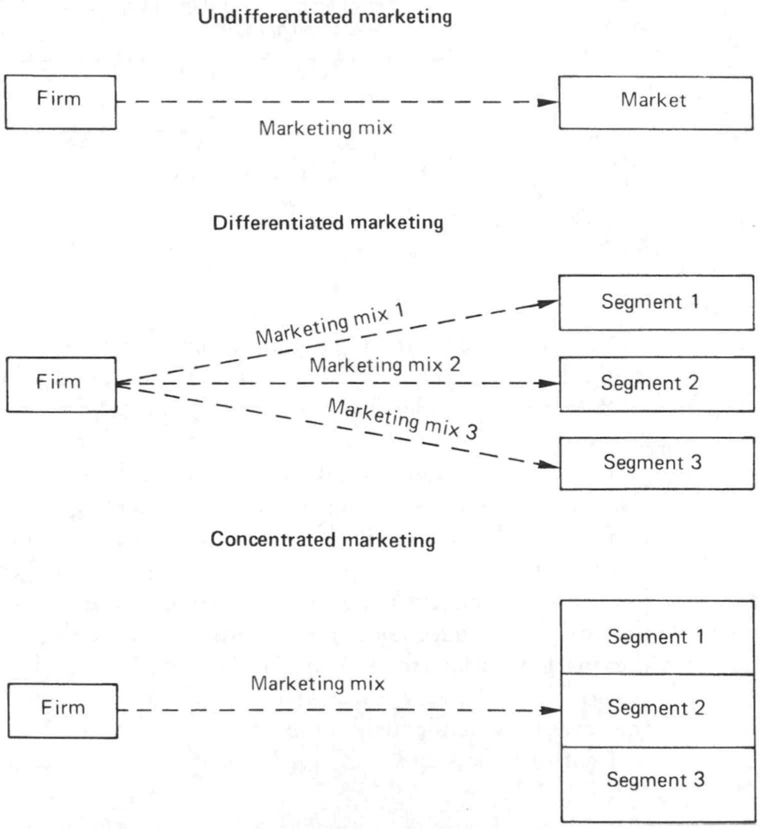

Undifferentiated, Differentiated and Concentrated Marketing

A policy of *undifferentiated or mass marketing* emerges when the firm deliberately ignores any differences that exist within its markets and decides instead to focus upon a feature that appears to be common or acceptable to a wide variety of buyers. Perhaps the best known and most frequently quoted example of this is Henry Ford's strategy with the Model T that buyers could have 'in any colour as long as it is black'. A more recent example of undifferentiated marketing is provided by Black & Decker which in the late 1970s was faced with a drop in its worldwide market share of the power tool market from 20 per cent to 15 per cent as Japanese firms began marketing their brands in a far more aggressive manner. In an attempt to counter this, Black & Decker moved away from a policy of customizing products for each market and concentrated instead on making a smaller number of products that could be sold everywhere with the same basic marketing approach. The success of this undifferentiated global marketing strategy was subsequently reflected in the fact that by the mid 1980s Black & Decker had more than regained its 20 per cent share of the market.

The obvious advantage of an undifferentiated strategy such as this is that it offers scope for enormous cost economies in production, promotion and distribution, since the organization is dealing with a standardized product. At the same time it needs to be recognized that undifferentiated marketing is becoming increasingly rare, largely because of ever greater degrees of competition and the increasingly sophisticated and fragmented nature of the majority of developed markets. In these circumstances, the scope that exists for marketing a product aimed at a broad sector of the market is reduced significantly.

This de-massification of markets has led many organizations towards strategies of *product-variety marketing* and, ultimately, target marketing. As an example of this, Coca-Cola for many years produced only one type of drink for the entire market in the expectation that it would have a mass market appeal. The success of the strategy is now part of marketing folklore. The company's strategy was changed, however, partly to cope with an increasingly aggressive competitive environment and partly to develop and capitalize on different patterns of consumer demand. As a result, the company's marketing effort today now reflects buyers' needs for a far wider variety of tastes and demands which are packaged in a number of different sizes and types of container. It should be emphasized that the move on the part of many organizations in recent years towards product differentiated or product-variety marketing has often had as its primary purpose the need to offer existing buyers greater variety, rather than to new and different market segments. In many ways, therefore, product variety marketing can be seen as an interim step in the move towards *target marketing* in which the strategist identifies the major market segments, targets one or more of these segments, and then develops marketing programmes tailored to the specific demands of each segment.

For some organizations target marketing leads to a concentration of effort on a single target market with a single marketing mix. Referred to as *concentrated segmentation*, it is a strategy that has been pursued with great success by the piano makers Steinway. The company defines its market as the concert and professional pianist and while, quite obviously, others may buy the product, they are not part of the strategic target market. The obvious advantage of an approach such as this is that having identified a particular market, the firm can then control costs by advertising and distributing *only* to the market it views as its primary target.

In so far as disadvantages exist with a strategy of concentration, they stem from the possibility of missed opportunities; it may be the case, for example, that significant opportunities exist elsewhere but that the firm's single-minded approach to just one part of the market fails to recognize this. Equally, the organization can prove vulnerable either to a direct and sustained attack by a competitor or to a downturn in demand within the target market. Because of this, many marketing strategists pursue a policy of *multiple segmentation* in which the firm focuses upon a variety of different segments and then develops a different marketing mix for each. This is often described as a 'rifle' rather than a 'shotgun' approach in that the company can focus on buyers they have the greatest chance of satisfying rather than scattering the marketing effort. An example of its use is that of the Burton Group which during the 1980s has developed and refined a highly segmented strategy. In doing this specific attention was paid to a variety of distinct customer groups by means of different types of retail outlet, each with its own distinct target market, image and customer appeal.

The ways in which a segment's characteristics influence the allocation of marketing effort has been illustrated in the case of the retail banking sector by Channon (1987) who identified four distinct customer groups:

1 *the very rich*: a small but strategically significant group with substantial assets in excess of £1 million – customers within this category are typically over 50 years of age and expect a high level of personal service;
2 *the rich*: a far larger group with assets of around £100,000;
3 *high net worth individuals (HNWIs)*: a semi-mass market with assets available for investment of £15,000 to £100,000.
4 *medium net worth individuals (MNWIs)*: the bulk of the market both for the high street banks and building societies.

Each of these groups has very different sets of expectations which need to be reflected in the organization's marketing strategy.

The rationale for target marketing and multiple segmentation can be seen to be straightforward and stems from an expectation on the part of the organization that it will be able to generate a higher total level of sales by making specific appeals to a variety of different target groups. At the same time, however, a strategy of multiple segmentation almost invariably leads to cost increases in several areas, including production, promotion, distribution, inventory and administration. The choice between undifferentiated marketing, product-variety marketing, and target marketing does therefore involve a series of trade-offs, the most obvious of which is an increase in cost against an expectation of higher total returns. As a prelude to deciding which of these three approaches to adopt, the strategist needs to identify clearly the organization's capability, the opportunities that exist and the level of market coverage that is possible or realistic.

Perhaps the most extreme example of a trade-off is to be seen in *customized marketing* where the product or service is modified to match the specific demands of each buyer. This is discussed in Illustration 8.1.

Where there are no apparent natural segments, a more formal procedure needs to be adopted. Several approaches exist, the most popular of which consists of three steps and has been spelled out by Kotler (1988, p. 284):

1 *Survey stage*. The researcher conducts informal interviews and focus groups with consumers to gain insight into their motivations, attitudes and behaviour. Based on these findings, the researcher prepares a formal questionnaire that is administered to a sample of consumers to collect data on:

- Attributes and their importance ratings.
- Brand awareness and brand ratings.
- Product usage patterns.
- Attitudes toward the product category.
- Demographics, psychographics, and mediagraphics of the respondents.

The sample should be large in order to gather enough data to profile each segment accurately. If the researcher guesses that there are, say, four segments, and generally two hundred interviews are desired per segment, then the questionnaire might be administered to eight hundred consumers.

2 *Analysis stage*. The researcher applies factor analysis to the data to remove highly correlated variables. Then the researcher applies cluster analysis to create a specified number of maximally different segments. Each cluster is internally homogenous and externally very different from every other cluster.

3 *Profiling stage*. Each cluster is now profiled in terms of its distinguishing attitudes, behaviour, demographics, psychographics, and media consumption habits. Each segment can be given a name based on a dominant distinguishing characteristic. Thus in study of the leisure market, Andreasen and Belk (1980, pp. 112–20) found six market segments:

- The passive homebody.
- The active sports enthusiast.
- The inner-directed self-sufficient.
- The culture patron.
- The active homebody.
- The socially active.

They found, for example, that the culture patron is the best target for both theatre and symphony subscriptions. The socially active can also be drawn to symphonies (though not theatres) in order to satisfy social needs.

Illustration 8.1: Levi's and its Use of One-to-one Marketing

The idea of one-to-one marketing in the high street clothing market reached a peak in the 1950s and 1960s when Burton's the Tailors developed a large and loyal customer base who often saved weekly through clothing accounts to buy several suits during the year, each of which was made to order. The customer went into the local Burton's for a fitting and the size, style and details of the chosen cloth were sent off to the company's factory. Several weeks later the suit arrived. The measurements were then stored so that they could be used the next time the customer wanted a suit.

Although bespoke tailoring still exists at the top end of the market, a combination of rising costs and more varied customer demands for off-the-peg led Burton's in the 1970s to begin pursuing a very different mass-market strategy. However, the thinking behind one-to-one marketing is potentially attractive and led to its trial in 1994 by the jeans manufacturer Levi's:

> Levi's 'Personal Pair' trial was tested in four sites across America: New York, Cincinnati, Columbus, Ohio and Peabody, Massachusetts. It used customised clothing softwear developed by a specialist American company to fit a pair of tapered-leg jeans precisely to the body. Customers are measured for their jeans by a trained sales assistant who feeds details into the computer. The PC then generates the code number of a pair of trial jeans with the correct measurements, which the customer tries on. From this point, small changes, as little as half an inch, can be made to perfect the fit.

Levi says that on average it takes two to three prototypes before a customer is totally satisfied. When the buyer is happy, the co-ordinates of the final prototype are sent by modem over ordinary phone lines to the Levi jeans factory in Mountain City, Tennessee, where a dedicated team of sewing operators makes the final pair, delivering them within three weeks. Sewn into the waist-band of the jeans is a barcode with an individual customer number kept on computer by the company. The owner of the jeans can call Levi at any time and order a new pair, in a range of colours and finishes, using the barcode.

Source: The Sunday Times, *11 June 1995, p. 6*

The Development of Segments Over Time

Having identified segments within a market, the strategist needs to recognize that this is not a once-and-for-all exercise, but rather that it is one which needs monitoring and updating if it is to maintain its usefulness. This is illustrated by the ways in which attitudes to a given product's country of origin can change, possibly dramatically, over time. Twenty years ago, for example, attitudes in Britain to Japanese products were generally negative, largely because of perceptions of poor quality and inadequate levels of after-sales support. These attitudes began changing in the 1970s and today Japanese products are generally perceived very differently. The implications of this for preference patterns is significant and does, of course, need to be reflected in methods of segmentation.

8.4 APPROACHES TO SEGMENTING MARKETS

The majority of markets can be segmented in a variety of ways. For the marketing strategist, the process of identifying the potentially most effective way begins with an initial examination of the market with a view to identifying whether 'natural segments' already exist.

In the United States in the 1960s, for example, both Volkswagen and Toyota identified the growth potential of a market sector that was concerned with car size and fuel economy, a segment that the three major domestic manufacturers had either failed to identify or had chosen to ignore. Following the Arab–Israeli conflict of the early 1970s and the subsequent oil crisis, consumers became far more energy conscious and this part of the market grew dramatically. It was several years before domestic manufacturers were able to capitalize on these opportunities.

There are several lessons to be learned from this sort of example, including the ways in which new segments can be identified by examining the sequence of variables that consumers consider when choosing a product. One way of doing this involves categorizing current consumer segments on the basis of a hierarchy of attributes. There are those, for example, whose major preoccupation is price (price-dominant), while others are more concerned with the brand (brand-dominant), quality (quality-dominant), or country of origin (nation-dominant).

In the case of hi-fi and audio equipment, for example, a buyer might only be willing to consider products from a Japanese manufacturer; this would be the first-level preference. The second-level preference may then be for, say, Sony. After this, issues of the price range and choice of outlet begin to emerge.

Recognition of hierarchies of attitudes such as these has led to the emergence of market-partitioning theory, with segments being determined on the basis of particular combinations such as quality/service/brand, price/type/brand, and so on. Underlying this is the belief that each combination will then reflect distinct demographic and psychographic differences.

The question of *how* to segment the market provides the basis for much of the remainder of this chapter. In essence, however, this involves deciding between *a priori* and *post hoc* methods. An *a priori* approach is based on the notion that the planner decides in advance of any research which basis for segmentation he intends using. Thus typically he will categorize buyers on the basis of their usage patterns (heavy, medium, light, and non-users); demographic characteristics (age, sex, and income); or psychographic profiles (lifestyle and personality). Having decided this, he then goes on to conduct a programme of research in order to identify the size, location and potential of each segment as a prelude to deciding on which of the segments the marketing effort is to be concentrated.

Post hoc segmentation, by contrast, involves segmenting the market on the basis of research findings. Thus, research might highlight particular attitudes, attributes or benefits with which particular groups of customers are concerned. This information can then be used as the basis for deciding how best to divide the market. As an example of this, Haley's research into the toothpaste market in the early 1960s highlighted levels of concern among mothers about tooth decay in their children (1963, pp. 30–5). Although a number of brands claiming decay prevention existed at the time, the size and potential for the growth of this segment had not previously been recognized. One result of Haley's work was to increase the number of companies that recognized the value of targeting this segment.

In making these comments, it must be emphasized that both approaches to segmentation have their place and that their real value to the strategist depends largely on how much knowledge of the market the strategist has. If, for example, previous research or experience has enabled the planner to identify key segmentation dimensions within the market, then an *a priori* approach is likely to be adequate. When, however, the market is new, changing or unrelated to the planner's experience, a *post hoc* approach to determine the key segmentation variables is likely to prove more valuable. See Illustration 8.2.

8.5 FACTORS AFFECTING THE FEASIBILITY OF SEGMENTATION

For a market segment to justify attention, six conditions typically need to be satisfied. The segment must be:

1 *Measurable*. Although in many consumer markets measurement is generally a relatively straightforward exercise, it is often a more difficult process with industrial or technical goods. This is due largely to the relative lack of specific published data.
2 *Accessible*. In some cases it may be possible to identify a sizeable and potentially profitable segment, but then either because of a lack of finance or in-house expertise this potential may be difficult to exploit.
3 *Substantial*. If the strategist is to justify the development of a segment the exercise must be cost effective. The size and value of the segment is therefore an important determinant of this decision. Size should, of course, be seen in relative rather than absolute terms, since what may be too small to be considered by one organization may be appropriate to another, smaller, company. Morgan, for example, has concentrated on a very small and specialized part of the car market which is of no interest to the larger firms such as Ford, Toyota and Volkswagen.
4 *Unique* in its response, so that it can be distinguished from other market segments.
5 *Appropriate* to the organization's objectives and resources.
6 *Stable*, so that its behaviour in the future can be predicted with a sufficient degree of confidence.

8.6 APPROACHES TO SEGMENTATION

Although a wide variety of methods of segmentation have been developed over the past 30 years, their real value to the strategist in any given situation depends to a very large extent on the nature and characteristics of the product and the market in which the company is operating. The task that the strategist is faced with involves deciding upon the most appropriate single method or combination of methods for dividing up the market. In the case of consumer goods, for example, the most commonly used methods have typically been geographic, demographic and benefit measures, while in the industrial sector they have typically been usage rate, source loyalty and location. Most of these measures, however, are at best partial, and the past few years have witnessed a growing willingness on the part of many companies, particularly in the consumer sector, to make greater use of more complex methods of segmentation in order to build up more detailed and useful pictures of their target markets. One result of this has been an upsurge of the interest expressed in behavioural and psychographic techniques as a means of gaining a greater insight into the question of *why* people behave in particular ways.

Illustration 8.2: The Changing Nature of Segmentation

Thinking on segmentation is changing in a variety of ways. In discussing this, Fifield and Gilligan (1996, p. 97) highlight a number of issues, arguing that far too many organizations base their approaches to segmentation on the sort of thinking that is reflected in the left-hand column rather than in the right.

Past	→	Future
Correlation	→	Causality
Description	→	Motivations

Past and future   When asked how they segment what they are doing in the area, almost invariably managers will start to describe their past experiences with customers; how people reacted; what they did; and even an analysis of where the last three years' sales have come from. As we all know, the future is unlikely to be a straight-line extrapolation from the past, much as we would like it to be so.

As marketers trying to put together a marketing strategy which will deliver what the business needs, our concerns must be for the future. Our attention must centre on where we should invest our marketing spend and our energy for both short and long-term returns from the marketplace. The past has gone. There is some value to be gained from understanding the lessons of the past, but only if they can improve our future activity.

Correlation and causality   The second problem is that when your managers are pressed to explain the rationale behind their segments you are often presented with a whole series of correlations. What we need to uncover is some degree of causality. There may be some relationships which an in-depth study of our existing customers could expose; however, it is dangerous to build a strategy on relationships which lack an identifiable cause. In other words, is there an underlying motivational reason why people act in a certain way that we can understand from their circumstances?

Description and motivation   Finally, there is a general misunderstanding between description and motivation. An in-depth description of our existing customer base and our existing 'segments' in terms of age profiles, sex, income, occupation, education, family life stage or even socio-economic grouping is only really valid if we believe that these characteristics are motivational. Descriptors tend to come from the past. 'This is how last year's customers looked'. Only very rarely will a customer group described in these terms surprise us by acting in a way unique from the rest of the market.

The only thing we know for sure about the future is that our ideas and predictions will be wrong; but it is still worthwhile working to reduce the margin of error. It is our job to ensure that we make the best possible return on the funds which the organisation invests in its markets. Returns are based upon informed judgement of how a segment will respond to our offer and what will motivate it to buy (op. cit., p. 97).

The thread that runs through all of these approaches is the need to understand in detail the structure of the market. This is most typically done by focusing on three areas:

1 developing a spatial map of consumers' perceptions of brands within a given market sector;
2 identifying consumers' ideal points on this map so that demand for a particular product might then be estimated by examining its position in relation to the ideal;
3 developing a model which will provide a basis for predicting consumers' responses to new and modified products.

An example of a perceptual map that was developed for the launch of Paul Masson California Carafes at the beginning of the 1980s appears in Figure 8.3.

FIGURE 8.3
A perceptual map of the wine market

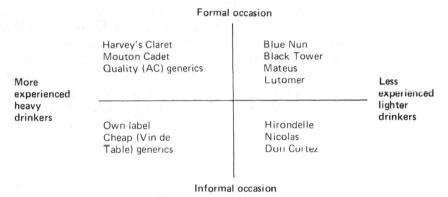

Formal occasion

Harvey's Claret
Mouton Cadet
Quality (AC) generics

Blue Nun
Black Tower
Mateus
Lutomer

More experienced heavy drinkers

Less experienced lighter drinkers

Own-label
Cheap (Vin de Table) generics

Hirondelle
Nicolas
Don Cortez

Informal occasion

SOURCE: TGI (1982)

Here, the wine market is mapped on two key dimensions: heavy versus light drinkers, and above and below average usage according to the most often usage occasion.

By mapping the market in this way, the company's advertising agency, Abbott Mead Vickers, was able to examine the duplication or repertoires of brand usage among wine drinkers and establish the degrees of overlap between the different brands. By doing this, clusters of brands emerged according to usage and provided the agency/strategist with an understanding of the market's structure, the existence of any gaps, the nature and intensity of competition, and the type of marketing mix needed to establish or support a brand.

This sort of picture of the market can then be taken a step further by superimposing a second map illustrating in greater detail consumer profiles. This might typically include sex (male versus female), age (young, middle-aged, old), income group (high earners versus low earners), and marital status (married versus single).

The importance and role of brand mapping is also illustrated by the way in which Brooke Bond's Red Mountain brand of coffee was positioned and then subsequently repositioned in the instant coffee market. This is discussed in Illustration 8.3.

8.7 BASES FOR SEGMENTATION

In 1978, Wind (1978, p. 317) commented that 'over the years almost all variables have been used as bases for market segmentation'. There are several possible explanations for this, the most significant of which is the difficulty that is typically

Illustration 8.3: Brand Mapping of the Coffee Market

The British Coffee market has long been dominated by two major companies, Nestlé (Nescafé) and General Foods (Maxwell House). The decision by Brooke Bond to enter the market with its Red Mountain brand was therefore one which had significant competitive and financial implications. The brand, a quality freeze-dried instant coffee, was launched on a platform of 'Move Up to the Bigger Taste' with advertising that attempted to capture the spirit of adventurous outdoor people who liked their coffee strong. This imagery with its use of, among others, cowboys backfired with consumers perceiving it as a cheap coffee but finding at the point of purchase that it was more expensive than the market leader, Nescafé. In an attempt to overcome this, the company tried to build on the launch strategy by appealing to those with a sense of adventure. This was then followed by a relaunch to highlight a new, improved blend, together with a reduction in price to below Nescafé levels.

Dissatisfaction by Brooke Bond with the drift in positioning of the brand led to the appointment of a new advertising agency, Still Price Court Twivy D'Souza. The brief given to the agency centred around the need for repositioning and in particular to provide reassurance about the taste and to associate the brand with quality and aspirational images.

The respositioning exercise began with a market research programme which concentrated initially on developing a brand map. The results are illustrated in Figure 8.4.

FIGURE 8.4 *Initial perceptions of instant coffee brands*

Expensive ←————————————————————————————————→ Cheap			
Gold Blend Blend 37	Nescafé Maxwell House	Red Mountain	Own label

● The best instants
● Special
● Expensive
● When one has
  people round
● Christmas
	● Popular
	● Everyday
	● Reliable
	● 'The Standard'
	● Frequent use
	● Old favourites
	● Ordinary
		● Cheaper
		● Not as classy
		● Middle of
		  the road
		● Cheap and
		  cheerful
			● Cheap and nasty
			● Weak
			● Bitter
			● Lack flavour

SOURCE: Feldwick (1990) p. 210

These perceptions of Red Mountain were in turn confirmed by qualitative research which had elicited the image and personality as being:

Outdoor, rugged, American, working class, eccentric, ordinary, scruffy, lumberjack, macho, farmer, normal, dull, boring, rough and ready, strange, untidy, basic.

Against the background of these findings, the decision was made not to compete directly with Gold Blend but at the half of the market accounted for by Nescafé and Maxwell House. The brand proposition eventually decided on was 'Ground coffee taste without the grind'.

The first commercial was the highly successful 'Dinner party' in which the hostess goes in the kitchen, pushes the filter coffee maker to one side, turns on the kettle, spoons Red Mountain into the jug of the coffee maker and then mimics the clacking noise that coffee makers make as they finish brewing.

This was followed over the next few months by several other commercials such as 'Apartment' and 'Restaurant' in which one of those involved goes through the same routine.

The campaign proved to be a significant success with levels of spontaneous awareness, attitude ratings, sales and brand share all increasing dramatically. Equally significantly, rival brands were forced to retaliate with higher levels of advertising spend and/or new advertising. Gold Blend, for example, started a 'soap opera' campaign.

Source: Advertising Works 5, *Holt, Rinehart Winston, 1990*

encountered in putting into practice the normative theory of segmentation. In other words, while the marketing planner might well recognize that customer characteristics should determine strategy, all too often this is reversed with managers focusing on the probable response of different segments to a previously determined strategy. Although quite obviously in the majority of circumstances feedback will ensure that changes are subsequently made to the strategy to take account of the response received, it is often the case, as Baker (1985, p. 142) has pointed out, that 'the managerial approach is more closely akin to product differentiation than a normative approach to market segmentation'.

Although, as we observed earlier, a wide variety of variables have been used to segment markets, the majority of these can be grouped into four categories:

1 geographic and geo-demographic;
2 demographic;
3 behavioural;
4 psychographic.

Only rarely, however, can just one of these dimensions be used to segment a market effectively, something which is reflected both in Illustration 8.4 and in a comment by Wind (1978, p. 318).

> In contrast to the theory of segmentation that implies that there is a single best way of segmenting a market, the range and variety of marketing decisions suggest that any attempt to use a single basis for segmentation (such as psychographic, brand preference, or product usage) for all marketing decisions may result in incorrect marketing decisions as well as a waste of resources.

FIGURE 8.5
The major bases for segmenting consumer markets

Geographic and geodemographic

Geographic: region, climate, population density.
Geodemographic: ACORN, MOSAIC, PiNPOINT, SUPERPROFILES, DEFINE, PiN, FiNPiN

Demographic

Age, sex, education, occupation, religion, race, nationality, family size, family life cycle, SAGACITY

Behavioural

Attitudes, knowledge, benefits, user status, usage rate, loyalty status, readiness to buy, occasions

Psychographic

Personality, lifestyle, VALS, AIO, 4Cs, Monitor

Illustration 8.4: Recommendations for the Bases of Segmentation

Some of the most interesting work on market segmentation has been carried out in the United States by Yoram Wind (1978). One of the undoubted attractions of his work is its strong element of pragmatism and the recognition that he gives to the problems typically experienced by marketing managers in trying to develop and implement an effective segmentation strategy. This has led him to a series of recommendations for the bases of segmentation which Baker (1985, pp. 142–3) has neatly summarized:

For general understanding of a market:
- benefits sought (in industrial markets, the criterion used is purchase decision);
- product purchase and usage patterns;
- needs;
- brand loyalty and switching pattern;
- a hybrid of the variables above.

For positioning studies:
- product usage;
- product preference;
- benefits sought;
- a hybrid of the variables above.

For new product concepts (and new product introduction):
- reaction to new concepts (intention to buy, preference over current brand, etc.);
- benefits sought.

For pricing decisions:
- price sensitivity;
- deal proneness;
- price sensitivity by purchase/usage patterns.

For advertising decisions:
- benefits sought;
- media usage;
- psychographic/lifestyle;
- a hybrid of the variables above and/or purchase/usage patterns.

For distribution decisions:
- store loyalty and patronage;
- benefits sought in store selection.

8.8 GEOGRAPHIC AND GEODEMOGRAPHIC TECHNIQUES

Geographic Techniques

Geographic segmentation – one of the earliest and still most commonly used methods of segmentation both within the consumer and the industrial sectors – involves dividing markets into different geographical units such as countries, regions, counties and cities. The strategist then chooses to operate either in just a few or in all of these. Typically, however, if a company pursues this second approach, minor modifications are often made to the marketing mix used for different geographical areas in order to take account of different regional tastes and preferences. In the case of the car industry, for example, manufacturers such as Ford and General Motors, while selling a particular model throughout Europe, will typically make a series of minor changes to the design and to the way in which the product is promoted and sold in order to reflect local differences, preferences and legislative demands. Similarly, the manufacturers of potato crisps modify the taste of the product to cater for regional taste differences, with a greater emphasis being placed upon strong flavours in the north of England and Scotland. In the United States, General Foods with its Maxwell House brand of coffee varies the flavour regionally to reflect preferences for stronger or weaker coffees. With other products such as consumer electronics, geographical differences also need to be reflected in strategy. Makers of stereophonic equipment, for example, offer products that vary by region. Europeans tend to want small, unobtrusive, high-performance equipment, while many Americans prefer large speakers that, as one anonymous commentator said, 'rise from the floor of living rooms like the columns of an ancient temple'.

Among the undoubted attractions of geographic segmentation to the strategist is its flexibility and its apparent simplicity. It is the combination of these, together with its broad applicability, that has led to its widespread use. At the same time, however, it is a relatively unsophisticated approach to categorization and one that at best gives only a partial view of buying motives.

Geodemo-graphic Techniques

Largely because of the limitations of geography, a considerable amount of work has been done in Britain over the past few years in an attempt to improve on the traditional methods of geographic segmentation. One outcome of this has been the development of a variety of geodemographic systems such as ACORN (A Classification Of Residential Neighbourhoods) which classify people by where they live. Based on the idea that 'birds of a feather flock together', it gives recognition to the fact that people with broadly similar economic, social and lifestyle characteristics tend to congregate in particular neighbourhoods and exhibit similar patterns of purchasing behaviour and outlook, something which is reflected in a comment by Rothman (1989, p. 1) who in discussing the central theme of geodemographics suggests that:

> ... two people who live in the same neighbourhood, such as a Census Enumeration District, are more likely to have similar characteristics than are two people chosen at random. . . . neighbourhoods can be categorized in terms of the characteristics of the population which they contain, and ... two neighbourhoods can be placed in the same category, i.e. can contain similar types of people, even though they are widely separated.

The essential purpose of geodemographics is therefore to provide the base for targeting customers in particular areas who exhibit similar behaviour patterns.

The first attempt to formalize this and demonstrate its potential to the strategist was carried out in Liverpool in 1973 by Richard Webber. Working subsequently with the Census Office at a national level, Webber applied techniques of cluster analysis to identify 38 separate neighbourhood types, each of which was different in terms of its population, housing and socio-economic characteristics. The potential value of this to the market research industry was subsequently recognized by Kenneth Baker (1982) of the British Market Research Bureau, who identified the scope that the system offered for controlling the fieldwork of the bureau's Target Group Index (TGI). The 2400 respondents in the TGI survey were categorized on the basis of Webber's neighbourhood groups, and illustrated graphically 'that respondents in different neighbourhood groups displayed significantly different propensities to buy specific products and services'.

FIGURE 8.6
The 1981 ACORN profile of Great Britain

ACORN groups		1981	
		Population	**%**
A	Agricultural areas	1811485	3.4
B	Modern family housing, higher incomes	8667137	16.2
C	Older housing of intermediate status	9420477	17.6
D	Poor quality older terraced housing	2320846	4.3
E	Better-off council estates	6976570	13.0
F	Less well-off council estates	5032657	9.4
G	Poorest council estates	4048658	7.6
H	Multi-racial areas	2086026	3.9
I	High status non-family areas	2248207	4.2
J	Affluent surburban housing	8514878	15.9
K	Better-off retirement areas	2041338	3.8
U	Unclassified	388632	0.7

Following this, Webber subsequently joined Consolidated Analysis Centres Inc. (CACI) and concentrated on developing the technique further in order to achieve higher levels of discrimination. The result was the 11-group classification (see Figure 8.6) which today is used as a major method of market location. Specific applications of the technique include:

1 the identification of new retail sites;
2 the selection of sales territories;
3 the allocation of marketing resources;
4 media selection;
5 leaflet distribution;
6 decisions on which products and services to promote in particular retail outlets.

Using this profile, specific areas of high and low consumption can be identified from the ACORN 'buying power' indices. As an example of this, ACORN type J35, which consists of 'villages with wealthy older commuters, have 2.4 times the national average proportion of households with two cars, and 2.7 times the proportion of those living in seven or more rooms'. Using information such as this, market targeting becomes both easier and far more accurate.

This work on the ACORN system of classification has led subsequently to a major reassessment of the ways in which geographic techniques might be used in the most effective way. One result of this has been the development of a variety of other geodemographic forms of classification, including CCNs MOSAIC, CDMSs SUPERPROFILES, Infolink's DEFINE, and PiNPOINT Analysis's PiN and FiNPIN.

The common element in all geodemographic systems is their use of census enumeration district (ED) data. ACORN, for example, uses 40 regularly updated census variables which take account of the demographic, housing, and social aspects of EDs. Their clustering techniques then enable customers to be matched to an ACORN type and, by the postcode, to the relevant ED.

Other geodemographic systems are broadly similar to this, although each uses a variety of other variables. MOSAIC, for example, includes financial data at postcode level and then relies on aggregated individual addresses within a postcode to reduce the errors encountered in matching postcodes to EDs. Other systems such as PiNPOINT base their clustering techniques on a larger sample and improvements to the grid referencing of EDs so that they more accurately match postcodes. Such developments represent a very real attempt to overcome some of the inevitable problems and inaccuracies of geodemographic analysis. In commenting on this, Joseph and Yorke (1989, p. 12) have said:

> It must be recognized that despite claims from commercial companies, there are inaccuracies within all the geodemographic systems. Many of the errors are bound up firstly with the difficulty of matching EDs to postcodes and secondly trying to reflect as far as possible the changes in housing since the last census.

These sorts of problem have also been referred to by Openshaw (1989, p. 121) who, in discussing how geodemographics should develop, has said that:

> ... users with a large customer data base spending big sums of money on segmentation based direct mail ... banks, building societies, insurance companies, home shopping organisations, telemarketers, etc., should be seriously considering using a system which has been explicitly tailored to meet their own unique purposes in preference to any of the standard geo-demographic products.

Although on the face of it, comments such as these might appear to suggest that geodemographic techniques are, at least in part, questionable, the reality is that they represent an enormous step forward in accurate targeting. Recognizing this, a considerable amount of work in recent years has been devoted to developing industry and market specific systems. One example is PiNPOINT's FiNPIN, a 40-variable classification system that uses data from Financial Research Services to define geographical areas in terms of financially active/inactive customers.

8.9 DEMOGRAPHIC SEGMENTATION

The second major method of segmentation, and probably the one most frequently used, rests on the assumption that markets can be subdivided into groups on the basis of one or more demographic variables such as age, sex, income, education, occupation, religion, race, nationality, family size and stage reached in the family life cycle. Here, we will concentrate on just three of these variables: age and the family life cycle, income and occupation, and sex.

An undoubted attraction of demographic segmentation is the wide availability and easy interpretation of the data, and it is this, together with the fact that not only can most consumer markets generally be divided relatively easily along these lines but also that purchase behaviour often correlates highly with demographic segmentation, that have combined to make it such a convenient, easily understood and frequently used approach. In recent years, considerable attention has been paid to the ways in which specific demographic variables can be used more effectively, with the result that variables such as age and life cycle, income, and sex have all been greatly refined. As an example of this, firms such as Fisher Price give full recognition to the differences that exist between children of various ages, with the result that toys are now designed to fall into highly specific age categories. In this way not only is the development potential of the child maximized, but the task of choosing toys by parents, friends and relatives is made infinitely easier. A similar if perhaps rather more esoteric recognition of the importance of age and life cycle is reflected in the marketing strategies of various petfood manufacturers who over the past few years have developed different dog foods for puppies and adult dogs. In the United States, this has been taken several steps further by General Foods which has also targeted owners of older dogs and overweight dogs. More frequently, however, the significance of life cycle is reflected in the notion of a *family life cycle* (FLC), the details of which are illustrated in Figure 8.7.

FIGURE 8.7
The family life cycle and its implications for buying behaviour

Stages in the family life cycle	Buying patterns
1 Bachelor stage: young, single people living at home	Few financial commitments. Recreation and fashion orientated. Buy: cars, entertainment items, holidays
2 Newly married couples: young, no children	Better off financially than they are likely to be in the near future. High purchase rate of consumer desirables. Buy: cars, white goods, furniture
3 Full nest 1: youngest child under six	House buying is at a peak. Liquid assets are low. Dissatisfied with level of savings and financial position generally. Buy: medicines, toys, baby food, white goods
4 Full nest 2: youngest child six or over	Financial position is improving. A higher proportion of wives are working. Buy: wider variety of foods, bicycles, pianos
5 Full nest 3: older married couples with dependent children	Financial position is improving yet further. A greater proportion of wives work and some children get jobs. Increasing purchase of desirables. Buy: better furniture, unnecessary appliances and more luxury goods
6 Empty nest 1: older married couples, no children at home, head of household still in the workforce	Home ownership is at a peak. The financial situation has improved and savings have increased. Interested in travel, recreation and self-education. Not interested in new products. Buy: holidays, luxuries and home improvements
7 Empty nest 2: Older married, no children living at home, head of household retired	Substantial reduction in income. Buy: medical products and appliances that aid health, sleep and digestion
8 Solitary survivor in the workforce	Income still high but may sell home
9 Solitary survivor, retired	Same medical and product needs as group 7. Substantial cut in income. Need for attention and security.

SOURCE: Adapted from Wells and Gubar (1966)

The Family Life Cycle

The idea of a family life cycle can be traced back to Rowntree's work at the beginning of the century and while changes have occurred since then to the pattern through which the family passes, the concept is still the same. Today, the nine-stage FLC proposed by Wells and Gubar (1966, pp. 355–63) is the one to which reference is made most frequently. The potential strategic value of the FLC stems from the way in which it highlights the different and changing financial situation and priorities of the family as it moves through the nine stages. By recognizing and taking account of these differences, the strategist should be more easily able to develop a marketing programme that satisfies the *specific* rather than the general demands of target groups.

Despite its apparent attractions, the FLC has been subjected to a series of criticisms in recent years. For the most part, these stem from the significance and implications of changes taking place within society which are at best reflected only marginally in the basic FLC model. Implicit in FLC thinking, for example, is a particular view of the role of women which is some way removed from today's reality where the proportion of women working even during the early stages of their children's lives is high. Equally, the model fails to reflect high divorce rates and the large numbers of single-parent families. Because of criticisms such as these, fundamental questions have been raised about the model's validity and usefulness. Defenders of the model, however, have argued that it is a summary demographic variable that combines the effects of age, marital status, career status (income), and the presence or absence of children. This can then be used *together* with other variables to reflect reality. This view is supported by a number of writers, including Dominguez and Page (1984) whose research in the United States for a mid-Western bank found that the FLC is a major determinant of consumer banking interest and behaviour. Similarly, Reading (1988, p. 9) has pointed out that:

> There is a distinctive life time pattern to saving and spending when we are in our twenties and thirties – getting married, buying houses, having children – we borrow and spend. When we are old and retired, we 'dissave' and spend. In middle age, therefore, we have to save like blazes to repay debts and build up capital for our old age.

A slightly different version of the family life cycle has in recent years been proposed by Research Services in the form of SAGACITY. The basic thesis of the SAGACITY grouping is that people have different aspirations and behaviour patterns as they go through their life cycle. Four main stages of the life cycle are defined which are subdivided by income and occupation groups. This is illustrated in Figure 8.8.

FIGURE 8.8
The SAGACITY life-cycle model

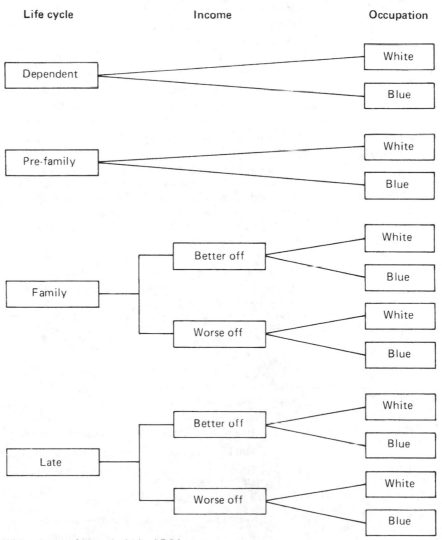

White: head of household in ABC1 groups
Blue: head of household in C2DE groups

The Psychological Life Cycle

As an extension both to the traditional thinking and the family life cycle and to the more current ideas of SAGACITY, work recently has focused upon the idea of a *psychological life cycle* in which chronological age by itself is not necessarily the factor of greatest significance in determining consumption patterns. Rather it is the transformation of attitudes and expectations that becomes a more important factor; something which is reflected in the Neugartens' research in the United States:

> Age has become a poor predictor of the timing of life events, as well as a poor predictor of a person's health, work status, family status, and therefore, also of a person's interests, pre-occupations, and needs. We have multiple images of persons of the same age: there is the 70-year-old in a wheelchair and the 70-year-old on the tennis court. Likewise, there are 35-year-olds sending children off to college and 35-year-olds furnishing the nursery for newborns, producing in turn, first-time grandparenthood for persons who range in age from 35 to 75.

Income and Occupation

The second major category of demographic variable focuses upon *income* and *occupation*, the combination of which is reflected in the JICNARS approach to social classification; this is illustrated in Figure 8.9.

Developed in the immediate post-war period, the JICNARS classification of social class has proved to be a popular, enduring and easily understood method of classification. It is, however, an imprecise method of segmenting a market since social class today is a far less accurate predictor of income and spending patterns than was once the case. It has also been argued that social class is unable to give any real insight into a household's level of disposable income, particularly where there are several wage earners. Largely because of this, a considerable amount of work has been done in recent years in an attempt to develop it further and to identify better alternative methods of discrimination.

The problems of social class as a basis for segmentation have been highlighted by O'Brien and Ford (1988, pp. 289–331) who have commented,

> The trends today are towards a more disparate family group, less inclined to share their meals and leisure time as a household unit, but following their own interests and tastes with like minded peers. Whether peer groups share the same 'social' background is less important than their shared pursuit. Equally, Social Class does not act as an accurate guage of disposable income. A C2 or D may not intellectually be performing the same role in the job market as a B or C1, but may well have more cash with which to acquire the trappings of our society. The financial chains of private education are likely to constrain the AB as much as the black economy and overtime can enhance the apparently lower wage of the C2 and D. From a different standpoint, social class categories are difficult to apply consistently. The variety and complexity of people's jobs make many social classifications inherently subjective rather than objective.

FIGURE 8.9
The JICNARS social classification

Grade	
A	Upper middle class: higher managerial administrative or professional
B	Middle class: middle to senior management, up and coming professionals
C1	Lower middle class: Junior management, supervisory, secretarial, and clerical grades
C2	Skilled working class: manual trades
D	Working class: semi and unskilled workers
E	Pensioners and widows and those on the breadline, using social security and state benefits

It is because of problems such as these that Coleman (1961, pp. 171–84) has drawn a distinction between the 'underprivileged' and the 'overprivileged' segments of each social class. 'The most economical cars are not bought by the really poor', he argues, but rather 'by those who think of themselves as poor relative to their status aspirations and to their needs for a certain level of clothing, furniture, and housing which they could not afford if they bought a more expensive car'. He goes on to point out that medium-priced and expensive cars tend to be purchased by the overprivileged segments of each social class.

Recognition of the problems of defining social class and of the limitations of traditional methods of social classification led the Market Research Society in 1990 to publish an up-to-date guide to socio-economic status. The guide, which defines the pecking order of 1500 jobs, is based not on earnings, but on qualifications and responsibility. A summary of this appears in Figure 8.10.

FIGURE 8.10
The Market Research Society's occupation groupings

A: admiral, advocate, air marshal, ambassador, archbishop, attorney, bank manager, bishop, brigadier, chemist shop manager (more than 25 staff); chief constable, chief engineer, chief fire officer, chief rabbi, chiropodist (more than five staff); national orchestra conductor, coroner, university dean, dental surgeon with own practice, chartered estate agent, self-employed farmer (more than 10 staff), financier, general practitioner (own practice/partner), school head-teacher (more than 750 pupils), homoeopath, insurance underwriter, magistrate, hospital matron, judge, MP, professor and town clerk.

B: advertising account director, archdeacon, area sales manager, ballistics expert, qualified brewer, bursar, church canon, chef (more than 25 staff), police chief inspector, computer programmer, stock exchange dealer, deputy power station manager, drawing office manager, fund manager, master mariner, orchestra leader, parish priest, parson, prison governor, probation officer, rabbi, senior buyer, senior engineer, qualified social worker, secondary-school teacher, television newscaster, lecturer and nursing sister.

C1: advertising account executive, accounts clerk, announcer (television, radio or station platform), art buyer, articled clerk, athlete, band master, bank cashier, boxer, bus inspector, calligrapher, campanologist, telephone canvasser, cardiographer, cartographer, chef (five to 24 staff), chemist dispenser, chorister, chorus girl, clown, sports coach, coastguard, computer operator, skilled cook, police constable, advertising copywriter, travel courier, curate, cricketer, dancer, dental hygienist, private detective, dietician, driving examiner/instructor, estate agent (not chartered), fashion model, film projectionist, golfer, hospital houseman, book illustrator, disc jockey, juggler, domestic loss adjuster, magician, maitre d'hotel, masseur/masseuse, midwife, monk, nun, staff nurse, non-manual office worker, pawn-broker, plant breeder, RSPCA inspector, receptionist, secretary, telephone operator, sports umpire, youth worker.

C2: AA patrolman, self-employed antique dealer, boat builder, bus driver, shoe-maker, bricklayer, carpenter, chimney sweep, bespoke tailoring cutter, deep-sea diver, dog handler, hair-dresser, skilled electrician, fireman, thatcher, train driver, Rolls-Royce trained chauffeur, skilled miner.

D: au pair, bingo caller, dustman, bodyguard, bus conductor, chauffeur, croupier, dog breeder, lumberjack, unskilled miner, nursemaid and ratcatcher.

E: anyone brave enough to admit it.

SOURCE: MRS (1990)

Sex

The third demographic category is that of sex. While this variable has obvious applications to such products as clothes, cosmetics, magazines and so on, ever greater attention has been paid in recent years to the ways in which it can be used as a key element in the strategies to market a far wider range of products. In part, this has been brought about by a series of fundamental changes that are taking place within society, including a greater number of working women and the generally higher levels of female independence. One result of this has been an increase in the number of marketing campaigns targeted specifically at women; examples include cigarettes, cars and hotels.

8.10 BEHAVIOURAL SEGMENTATION

The third major approach to segmentation is based on a series of behavioural measures including attitudes, knowledge, benefits sought by the buyer, a willingness to innovate, loyalty status, usage rates, and response to a product. Of these, *benefit segmentation* is probably the best known and most widely used and is based on the assumption that it is the benefits people are seeking from a product that provide the most appropriate bases for dividing up a market.

In applying this approach the marketing planner begins by attempting to measure consumers' value systems and their perceptions of various brands within a given product class. The information generated is then used as the basis for the marketing strategy. One example of this is the work conducted on the watch market by Yankelovich (1964, pp. 83–90). His findings that 'approximately 23 per cent of the buyers bought for lowest price, another 46 per cent bought for durability and general product quality, and 31 per cent bought watches as symbols of some important occasion' were subsequently used by the US Time Company which created its Timex brand to capitalize on the first two of these segments. The majority of other companies at this stage focused either largely or exclusively on the third segment and Timex therefore faced little direct competition in the early years.

Benefit segmentation begins therefore by determining the principal benefits customers are seeking in the product class, the kinds of people who look for each benefit, and the benefits delivered by each brand. Amstrad, for example, a late entrant into the microcomputer market, gained market share largely as the result of concentrating on two distinct benefit segments: initially, those who were non-computer literate and who wanted a basic machine they could simply plug in and use, and then, subsequently, those who wanted a cheap and easy-to-use word processor.

One of the first pieces of benefit research, and probably the best known, was conducted by Russell Haley (1963, pp. 30–5). On the basis of his work in the toothpaste market, Haley identified four distinct segments which, he argued, were sufficiently different to provide a platform for selecting advertising copy, media, commercial length, packaging and new product design; the four segments he identified were: seeking economy, decay prevention, cosmetic, and taste benefits respectively.

Haley demonstrated that each group exhibited specific demographic, behavioural and psychographic characteristics. Those concerned primarily with decay prevention, for example, typically had large families, were heavy toothpaste users and were generally conservative in their outlook. By contrast, the group which was more concerned with bright teeth (the cosmetic segment) tended to be younger, were more active socially and, in many cases, were smokers. Each of these groups, he then demonstrated, exhibited preferences for particular brands: Crest in the case of those concerned with decay prevention, and Macleans and Ultra-Brite for those preoccupied with bright teeth.

In a similar type of study, Doyle and Newbould (1974) examined the building society market and identified three distinct categories of customer and the benefits each is seeking:

1 a building society's investors currently;
2 investors who also have accounts in other building societies;
3 those without any building society investments.

Having identified these three primary segments, they went on to identify a secondary stage:

- bankers: those who use the society in a similar way to a bank – they typically have an account with few funds and have a high withdrawals to deposit rate;
- savers: who use their account primarily as a means of saving for special purchases – balances tend to be high and withdrawals infrequent;

● investors: who have relatively large accounts, and who switch funds to maximize interest payments.

The information generated by studies such as these can, as we observed earlier, be used in a variety of ways. Most obviously they prove useful in classifying the specific benefits being sought by particular customer groups, the segment's behavioural, demographic and psychographic characteristics, and the major competitive brands. An additional by-product of this sort of research can also be that it highlights a benefit that customers are seeking, but which currently is not being satisfied. As an example of this, General Foods identified a sizeable and predominantly female segment which found the majority of instant coffees to be too strong and bitter. Using this as the starting point, the company went on to develop and launch Mellow Birds instant coffee which took as its major appeal a far less bitter taste. More recently, benefit segmentation research has also highlighted the size of the potential market for caffeine-free coffees. The result has been a substantial upsurge in the number of coffees targeted at this segment which was served previously only by Café Hag.

In many markets benefit segmentation results in the company focusing upon satisfying just one benefit group, with the benefit offered being the unique selling proposition (USP). This is, however, just one of four choices that exist:

1 single benefit positioning;
2 primary and secondary benefit positioning;
3 double benefit positioning;
4 triple benefit positioning.

These will be discussed in greater detail at a later stage in the chapter (see pp. 302–4).

User Status

As an alternative to benefit segmentation, markets can be subdivided on the basis of what is referred to as *user status*. Thus a number of segments can typically be identified including non-users, ex-users, potential users, first-time users and regular users. These final two categories can then be subdivided further on the basis of *usage rate* (this is sometimes referred to as *volume segmentation*).

For many firms the marketing task is seen in terms of moving buyers and potential buyers along the buying continuum; thus non-users and potential users all need to be persuaded to try the product, while first-time users need to be persuaded to become medium users, and medium users to become heavy users. The essence of this approach is reflected in the strategies of a variety of organizations, including those of a number of cigarette companies which, having been affected by changing smoking habits over the past two decades, have targeted particular user status groups. In the United States, for example, young females in particular have been identified as a potentially valuable segment and a variety of brands developed to appeal specifically to this part of the market.

The attraction of different user status groups tends to vary from one type of organization to another. High market share companies, for example, typically focus on converting potential users into actual users, while smaller and lower share firms will often concentrate upon users of competitive brands with a view to persuading them to switch brands.

Loyalty Status and Brand Enthusiasm

The third technique encompassed by behavioural segmentation is that of *loyalty status* in which buyers are categorized on the basis of the extent and depth of their loyalty to particular brands or stores. Most typically this leads to the emergence of four categories: hard core loyals, soft core loyals, shifting loyals, and switchers.

- *Hard core loyals* consist of consumers who consistently buy the same brand or use the same store. Their buying pattern over time can therefore be represented as XXXXXX.
- *Soft core loyals* are those willing to choose from a limited brand set. Their buying pattern of XXYXYY reflects their divided loyalty between brands X and Y.
- *Shifting loyals* who shift their loyalty from one brand to another. Their buying pattern is therefore likely to be XXXYYYZZZ.
- *Switchers* who show no loyalty to any single brand. Their buying pattern is typically determined either by the special offers available ('offer prone'), or by their search for variety (variety prone). This is then reflected in a buying pattern of XYXZYX.

The implications of loyalty are of course significant, since in the case of those markets in which high patterns of loyalty exist, the ability to persuade buyers to shift from one brand to another is likely to be limited, even in the face of high levels of marketing expenditure. Thus, in these circumstances, a share gaining or market entry strategy may well prove to be at best only marginally cost effective. However, the process of categorization referred to above is not by itself sufficient for the strategist. Rather it is the starting point from which the specific characteristics of each category then need to be examined. It may be the case, for example, that those buyers with the highest degrees of loyalty exhibit certain common characteristics in terms of age, socio-economic profile, and so on, while those with lower degrees of loyalty exhibit a very different but common set of characteristics. Research designed to identify these differences may well then provide the planner with a far greater understanding and insight to the ways in which patterns of loyalty may prove vulnerable to attack. Equally, analysis of this sort can provide an insight into the ways in which a competitor's products are vulnerable to attack. In the case of soft core loyals, for example, the strategist needs to identify the brands which compete either directly or indirectly with its own. By doing this, it can then strengthen its position, possibly by means of knocking copy or direct comparison advertising.

Analysis of the final group – the switchers – is also of potential strategic value since this can provide the basis for understanding in greater detail the brand's weaknesses and the basis for attack.

As an alternative or addition to loyalty status, consumers can often be categorized on the basis of their *enthusiasm* for the product, the five categories that are used most frequently being *enthusiastic*, *positive*, *indifferent*, *negative* and *hostile*. Its major value as a technique is principally as a screening step, in that having identified the category within which the consumer falls the organization can then focus its energies on the most likely prospects. This process can then be taken a step further by focusing on the *occasions* on which consumers develop a need, purchase or use a product.

Greeting cards companies, for example, have concentrated on increasing the number of occasions on which cards are given in relation to what was the case, say, 20 years ago. A glance at the shelves of any newsagent will reveal the enormous variety of cards that now exist, ranging from Father's Day and Mother's Day through to Get Well and Congratulations on Your Examination Success/New Baby/Moving House/New Job/Passing Your Driving Test, and so on. Ice-cream manufacturers have pursued a broadly similar strategy in order to move away from a pattern of sales that was overly dependent on hot, sunny weather. The result in this case has been the development of a whole series of ice-cream based desserts such as Vienetta, and ice-cream cakes that can be used throughout the year.

Critical Events   As a further development of occasion-related segmentation, the past few years have seen the emergence of what is usually referred to as *critical event segmentation* (CES). This is based on the idea that major or critical events in an individual's life generate needs that can then be satisfied by the provision of a collection of products and/or services. Typical examples of these critical events are marriage, the death of someone in the family, unemployment, illness, retirement and moving house. Among those who have recognized the potential of CES are estate agents, who during the past decade have moved away from simply selling houses to providing the whole range of legal and financial services surrounding house sale and purchase.

8.11 PSYCHOGRAPHIC AND LIFESTYLE SEGMENTATION

The fourth and increasingly popular basis of consumer segmentation stems from work in the early 1950s by Riesman, et al. (1950) which led to the identification of three distinct types of social characterization and behaviour:

1 *tradition directed behaviour* which changes little over time and which as a result is easy to predict and use as a basis for segmentation;
2 *other directedness* in which the individual attempts to fit in and adapt to the behaviour of the peer group;
3 *inner directedness* where the individual is seemingly indifferent to the behaviour of others.

Although this relatively simplistic approach to categorization has subsequently been subjected to a degree of criticism, it has provided the basis for a considerable amount of further work, all of which has been designed to provide the strategist with a far more detailed understanding of personality and lifestyle.

The attempts to use personality to segment markets began in earnest in the United States in the late 1950s when both Ford and Chevrolet gave emphasis to the brand personalities of their products in order to appeal to distinct consumer personalities (see Illustration 5.2, p. 158). Buyers of Fords, for example, were identified as 'independent, impulsive, masculine, alert to change, and self confident, while Chevrolet owers were conservative, thrifty, prestige-conscious, less masculine, and seeking to avoid extremes'. The validity of these descriptions was subsequently questioned by Evans (1959, pp. 340–69) who, by using a series of psychometric tests, argued that Ford and Chevrolet owners did not in fact differ to nearly the extent that had been suggested. More recent research has with just one or two possible exceptions been equally inconclusive. Among these exceptions is the work of Westfall (1962, pp. 34–40) and Young (1972, pp. 61–82). Westfall, for example, has reported finding evidence of personality differences between the buyers of convertible and non-convertible cars, with the former seemingly being 'more active, impulsive and sociable', while Young has pointed to the successful development of personality trait based segmentation strategies in the cosmetics, drinks and cigarettes markets.

Largely because of the difficulties encountered in using personality as an easy, consistent and reliable basis for segmentation, attention in recent years has switched to *lifestyle* and to the ways in which it influences patterns of consumer demand. Lifestyle has been defined in a variety of ways, but is in essence, as Kotler (1988) states:

> the person's pattern of living in the world as expressed in (their) activities, interests and opinions ... [it] portrays the 'whole person' interacting with his or her environment. Lifestyle reflects something beyond the person's social class, on the one hand, or personality, on the other ... [it] attempts to profile a person's way of being and acting in the world.

Illustration 8.5: Russian Lifestyles and Purchasing Patterns

In a study of the Russian market in 1992, the advertising agency D'Arcy, Masius, Benton & Bowles identified five types of consumer:

- Kuptsi (merchants);
- Cossacks;
- Students;
- Business Executives;
- Russian Souls.

The Cossacks proved to be ambitious, high spending, extrovert, independent, oriented to the west, searching for status and preoccupied by brand names. By contrast, the Russian Souls, although hopeful, were passive, less socially active, cautious, and fearful of choice. These differences were then reflected in the types of product the two groups bought, with the Cossacks driving BMWs, smoking Dunhill cigarettes and drinking Scotch, while the Russian Souls drove Ladas, smoked Marlboros (or a local brand) and drank vodka.

Because of the apparent insights offered by lifestyle analysis, an example of which appears in Illustration 8.5, a variety of models for categorizing consumers have emerged over the past few years, prominent among these being the VALS and AIO frameworks, Young and Rubicam's 4Cs, and Taylor Nelson's Monitor.

The VALS Framework

Developed in the United States by Arnold Mitchell of the Stanford Research Institute, the VALS framework used the answers of 2713 respondents to 800 questions to classify the American public into nine value lifestyle groups. These nine groups, together with estimates of the percentages of the US population within each group, are:

1 *survivors* who are generally disadvantaged and who tend to be depressed, withdrawn, and despairing (4%);
2 *sustainers* who are again disadvantaged but who are fighting hard to escape poverty (7%);
3 *belongers* who tend to be conventional, nostalgic, conservative and generally reluctant to experiment with new products or ideas (33%);
4 *emulators* who are status conscious, ambitious and upwardly mobile (10%);
5 *achievers* who make things happen, and enjoy life (23%);
6 *'I-am-me'* who are self-engrossed, respond to whims and generally young (5%);
7 *experientials* who want to experience a wide variety of what life can offer (7%);
8 *societally conscious* people with a marked sense of social responsibility and who want to improve the conditions of society (9%);
9 *integrateds* who are psychologically fully mature and who combine the best elements of inner and outer directedness (2%).

The thinking that underpins the VALS framework is that individuals pass through a series of developmental stages, each of which influences attitudes, behaviour and psychological needs. Thus people typically move from a stage which is largely need driven (survivors and sustainers) towards either an outer-directed hierarchy of stages (belongers, emulators and achievers) or an inner-directed hierarchy (I-am-me, experientials, societally conscious); relatively few reach the nirvana of the integrated stage.

From the marketing point of view, the need-driven segments have little apparent appeal since it is this part of society which lacks any real purchasing power. Outer-directed consumers, by contrast, represent a far more attractive part of the market and in general buy products with what has been described as 'an awareness of what other people will attribute to their consumption of that product'. Typically, therefore, brand names such as Rolex, Gucci, Benetton, Chanel and Cartier will prove to be important. Inner directed consumers by contrast are those people who in their lives place far greater emphasis on their individual needs as opposed to external values. Although in terms of overall numbers this group represents only a small part of the total market, it is often seen to be an important sector in terms of its ability to set trends. It is this group also which currently is showing the fastest growth rate within society, while the number of need-driven consumers declines and outer-directed remains about the same.

The AIO Framework

The AIO framework is broadly similar in concept to VALS in that again it attempts to classify distinctive lifestyle groups. This is done by means of a questionnaire designed to measure Activities, Interests and Opinions (AIO). Using this, the advertising agency Needham, Harper and Steers has identified the five major male and five major female lifestyle types:

Male Lifestyle Types
1 the self-made businessman (17 per cent);
2 the devoted family man (17 per cent);
3 the frustrated factory worker (19 per cent);
4 the successful professional (21 per cent);
5 the retiring homebody (26 per cent).

Female Lifestyle Types
1 the socialite (17 per cent);
2 the contented housewife (18 per cent);
3 the militant mother (20 per cent);
4 the suburbanite (20 per cent);
5 the traditionalist (25 per cent).

Against the background of this sort of classification, the strategist needs then to decide the group(s) at which the product is targeted, and an advertising message that should appeal specifically to the AIO characteristics of that lifestyle group.

This sort of thinking was used by Levi Strauss at the beginning of the 1980s in their development of a new range of clothes as the company diversified away from their core business of denim jeans. Although the new line eventually proved disappointing, their research identified five basic lifestyle segments, each of which exhibited specific characteristics. These are:

● Q1: *mainstream traditionalist* – over 45, he is a department-store shopper, conservative, and the main target for Levi action slacks and action suits (semi-smart casual wear). He shops with wife and values her opinion.

Proportion of population 19 per cent

● Q2: *classic independent* – aged between 20 and 60, a specialist store shopper, he dresses traditionally, but not unfashionably. Looking right is important. Shops alone and spends more on clothes than any other group.

Proportion of population 20 per cent

- Q3: *utilitarian jeans buyer* – all ages, a department store shopper who doesn't care much about clothes, he wears jeans for work and play; a Levi loyalist.

  Proportion of population 26 per cent

- Q4: *trendy casual* – aged 16–45, he shops in department and specialist stores, likes to be noticed, may wear jeans for work, certainly wears them for play sometimes.

  Proportion of population 19 per cent

- Q5: *price shopper* – all ages, department and discount store shopper who looks for bargains. Appearance is only important within certain parameters.

  Proportion of population 15 per cent

Young and Rubicam's 4Cs and Taylor Nelson's Monitor

Developed by the advertising agency, Young & Rubicam, 4Cs (A Cross-Cultural Consumer Characterization) divides people into three main groups, each of which is further subdivided along the following lines:

(a) *the constrained*
    (i) the resigned poor;
    (ii) the struggling poor.
(b) *the middle majority*
    (i) mainstreamers;
    (ii) aspirers;
    (iii) succeeders.
(c) *the innovators*
    (i) transitionals;
    (ii) reformers.

The largest single sub-group in the United Kingdom is the mainstreamers, said to account for between 30 and 35 per cent of the population.

The principal benefit of 4Cs is that it defines in a fairly precise manner individual or group motivational needs. It does this by acknowledging the multidimensional nature of people and groups by taking the key motivational factors (e.g. success in the case of a succeeder) and overlaying this with other important motivational values to develop a motivational matrix. The technique has been used by Young and Rubicam over a number of years to develop strategic frameworks for marketing and advertising campaigns both domestically and internationally. In the case of the domestic market, for example, both the British Gas 'Tell Sid' shares campaign and Legal and General's 'Umbrella Campaign' were based on 4Cs analysis.

In the case of Legal and General, the objectives of the campaign were to make L & G sound new, interesting and at the forefront of innovating policies (without weakening its solid, safe, secure, mainstream image), as they wished to introduce new and larger investors without alienating their mainstream investors. Here, the 4Cs was used to identify the main motivational factors that would influence succeeders and aspirers to invest with them, while at the same time not alienating mainstreamers.

A similar framework, labelled Monitor, has been developed by the market research agency, Taylor Nelson. The Monitor typology again divides people into three main groups which are then subdivided:

1 *Sustenance-driven.* Motivated by material security, they are sub-divided into:
    (a) aimless, who include young unemployed and elderly drifters and comprise 5 per cent of the UK population;
    (b) survivors, traditionally-minded working class people (16% of the population);
    (c) belongers. These conservative family-oriented people form 18 per cent of the population, but only half of them are sustenance driven.

2 *Outer-directed.* Those who are mainly motivated by the desire for status. They are subdivided into:
   (a) belongers;
   (b) conspicuous consumers (19 per cent).
3 *Inner-directed.* Subdivided into:
   (a) social resisters, who are caring and often doctrinaire (11 per cent);
   (b) experimentalists, who are hedonistic and individualistic (14 per cent);
   (c) self explorers, who are less doctrinaire than social resisters and less materialistic than experimentalists.

The development of approaches such as these has also led to the emergence of a wide variety of acronyms and labels; an example of this in the grocery retailing market appears in Illustration 8.6. Prominent among these are Yuppies (Young Upwardly Mobile Professional), Bumps (Borrowed-to-the-hilt, Upwardly Mobile Professional Show-offs), Jollies (Jet-setting Oldies with Lots of Loot), Woopies (Well Off Older Persons), and Glams (Greying Leisured Affluent Middle Aged). Although a number of these labels are now rather passeé – Yuppies, for example, proved to be a phenomenon of the 1980s and the Big Bang – they have proved to be useful in that they characterize in an easily understood fashion a particular style of life.

Illustration 8.6: Consumer Profiling and Shopping Habits

In an attempt to reflect the diversity of society – and to determine our response to certain stimuli – the market research company AC Nielsen has separated shoppers into six categories:

- The habit-bound diehard: These tend to be older people for whom routine and loyalty are important. They have limited funds; they are cautious with an eye for a bargain.
- The self indulgent shopper: They are younger professionals, with no money worries or commitments and a fondness for the exotic and unusual. They are confident, self-assured and eager to experiment with a multiplicity of foods.
- Struggling idealists: Not much respected or desired by supermarkets, they are pedantic and particular, favouring organic and 'natural' ingredients. They never spend much.
- Comfortable and contented: Loosely called Middle Englanders, they are the most sought-after shopper, encompassing young comfortable mothers and housewives to middle-aged couples with disposable income. They tend to be admirers of Delia Smith and luxuriate in abundance in surplus.
- The frenzied coper: Professional without much time, or mothers juggling a career and family, they spend freely but move quickly. They return to the same supermarkets, especially if they offer crèche facilities and consistent layouts.
- Mercenaries. They are fickle, transient, often impoverished. They favour own-brand goods, promotions, discounts and damaged goods – anything cheap.

Source: The Times, *1 February 1997, p.17*

8.12 APPROACHES TO SEGMENTING INDUSTRIAL MARKETS

Although much of the work that has been done on segmentation analysis over the past 20 years has focused on consumer markets, many of the variables such as benefits sought, geography, and usage rates can be applied with equal validity to industrial markets. Recognizing this, a number of writers, including Cardozo (1983, pp. 264–76), and Bonoma and Shapiro (1983) have concentrated on demonstrating, developing and refining their applicability. Cardozo, for example, has identified four dimensions which can be used either separately or collectively to classify organizational buying situations.

1 familiarity with the buying task and in particular whether it is a new task, modified rebuy or straight rebuy;
2 the type of product and the degree of standardization;
3 the significance of the purchase to the buying organization;
4 the level of uncertainty in the purchase situation.

Baker (1985, p. 159) has argued that these last two factors are of particular significance in that they reflect the fact that buyers too try to segment potential suppliers by developing assessment criteria and establishing formal vendor rating systems. This general line of thinking has been developed by Johnson and Flodhammer (1980, pp. 201–5) who, in arguing that the need to understand buyers' needs is as important in industrial markets as in consumer markets, have

FIGURE 8.11

The major industrial market segmentation variables

Demographic

Industry: on which industries that use this product should we concentrate?

Company: on what size of company should we concentrate?

Location: in which geographical areas should we concentrate our efforts?

Operating variables

Technology: which customers technologies are of the greatest interest to us?

User status: on which types of user (heavy, medium, light, non-user) should we concentrate?

Customer capabilities: should we concentrate on customers with a broad or a narrow range of needs?

Purchasing approaches

Buying criteria: should we concentrate on customers seeking quality, service, or price?

Buying policies: should we concentrate on companies that prefer leasing, systems purchases, or sealed bids?

Current relationships: should we concentrate on existing or new customers?

Situational factors

Urgency: should we concentrate on customers with sudden delivery needs?

Size of order: should we concentrate on large or small orders?

Applications: should we concentrate on general or specific applications of our product?

Personal characteristics

Loyalty: should we concentrate on customers who exhibit high or low levels of loyalty?

Attitudes to risk: should we concentrate on risk taking or risk avoiding customers?

SOURCE: Adapted from Bonoma and Shapiro (1983)

suggested that 'Unless there is knowledge of the industrial users' needs the manufactured product usually has the lowest common denominator – price. Quality and service are unknown qualities.'

A slightly different line of argument has been pursued by Bonoma and Shapiro (1983) who have concentrated on developing a classification of industrial segmentation variables and listing the questions that industrial marketers should pose in deciding which customers they want to serve. A summary of these questions in declining order of importance appears in Figure 8.11.

From this it can be seen that the starting point is the question of which industry to serve, followed by a series of decisions on customer size and purchase criteria.

This method has been employed to great effect by, among others, IBM. IBM's starting point for segmentation has always been the idea that the company sells solutions rather than products. They therefore segment the market by commercial type: banking, transportation, insurance, processing industry, and so on, so as to be able to tailor solutions to specific problem areas. Each segment is then divided in a series of subsegments. Transportation, for example, can be divided into road, air, sea and rail.

8.13 MARKET TARGETING

Having decided how best to segment the market, the strategist is then faced with a series of decisions on how many and which segments to approach. Three factors need to be considered.

1 the size and growth potential of each segment;
2 their structural attractiveness;
3 the organization's objectives and resources.

The starting point for this involves examining each segment's size and potential for growth. Obviously, the question of what is the 'right size' of a segment will vary greatly from one organization to another. Morgan, for example, as mentioned earlier, has chosen to concentrate on a very small and specialized segment of the car market. Its customers are seeking the nostalgia of a pre-war sports car and the company has tailored its marketing mix accordingly. In commenting on this and giving the product a four-star rating, *What Car?* (1985) said:

> The ride's as hard as a rock, comfort and space minimal, noise levels deafeningly high, and overall the sports car has about as much refinement as a tractor. Wonderful!

This is neither a specification nor a segment that has any appeal for, say, General Motors or Ford, but Morgan operates within it with a degree of success.

In so far as it is possible to develop broad guidelines, we can say that large companies concentrate on segments with large existing or potential sales volumes and quite deliberately overlook or ignore small segments simply because they are rarely worth bothering with. Small firms, by contrast, often avoid large segments partly because of the level of resource needed to operate effectively, and partly because of the problems of having to cope with a far larger competitor.

With regard to the question of each segment's *structural attractiveness*, the strategist's primary concern is profitability. It may be the case that a segment is both large and growing but that, because of the intensity of competition, the scope for profit is low. Several models for measuring segment attractiveness exist, although arguably the most useful is Michael Porter's five-force model. This model, which is discussed at the beginning of Chapter 10, suggests that segment profitability is affected by five principal factors:

1 *industry competitors* and the threat of segment rivalry;
2 *potential entrants* to the market, and the threat of mobility;
3 the threat of *substitute products*;
4 *buyers* and their relative power;
5 *suppliers* and their relative power.

Having measured the size, growth rate and structural attractiveness of each segment, the strategist needs then to examine each one in turn against the background of the organization's objectives and resources. In doing this, the strategist is looking for the degree of compatibility between the segment and the organization's long-term goals. It is often the case, for example, that a seemingly attractive segment can be dismissed either because it would not move the organization significantly forward towards its goals, or because it would divert organizational energy. Even where there does appear to be a match, consideration needs to be given to whether the organization has the necessary skills competences, resources and commitment needed to operate effectively. Without these, entry is likely to be of little strategic value.

There are therefore two questions which need to be posed:

1 *Is the segment growing or declining*? Here we are interested in two broad aspects of growth and decline. What is the projected future of the segment in terms of volume sales and profit? Despite much argument to the contrary there need not be a link between volume sales and profit. Declining volumes in certain market segments can still be extremely profitable for the organizations which service them. It is therefore often more a question of how the segment is managed rather than what the segment is doing.
2 *Is the segment changing*? There are three aspects to this question of change. First, we need to understand how the structure and make-up of the segment is likely to change over time. Is the segment starting to attract new and slightly different members to its centre? What effect will this have on the segment's needs? The second aspect of change relates to the nature of the products and services which we would expect this segment to be demanding in the future. In other words, do we see any significant change in the way in which the members of the segment are likely to translate their needs into buying behaviour? Will they want different products or services in three years' time? The third area of segment change must consider the movements of the segments over time. Do we, for example, see the overall array of segments changing? There are two ways in which this structural change can occur. Segments may merge and combine to create larger, more 'shallow' segments. Alternatively, larger segments may fragment over time into smaller, more precise market targets for the organization to approach, something which led to Cafédirect's decision to target a particular type of consumer. (This is discussed in Illustration 8.7.)

8.14 DECIDING ON THE BREADTH OF MARKET COVERAGE

The final segmentation decision faced by the strategist, is concerned with which and how many segments to enter. In essence, five patterns of market coverage exist:

1 *Single segment concentration* in which the organization focuses on just one segment. Although a potentially high risk strategy in that the firm is vulnerable

---

Illustration 8.7: Charity Coffee Aims for a Richer Blend

In 1995, Cafédirect launched its first major advertising campaign under the heading 'Richer, mellower and distinctly less bitter'. With this, the company was not talking just about the taste of its coffee, but also its Latin American and African growers.

The company, which is backed by four charities, Oxfam, Traidcraft, Twin Trading, and Equal Exchange Trading, started life in 1991 when it began selling coffee through the charities' mail order catalogues. Its selling proposition is 'that it guarantees to pay farm cooperatives a minimum of 10 per cent above the world coffee price for their produce and to ship the product directly to the UK where it is marketed. The farmers use the money they receive to benefit their communities and provide health care and education. The long-term basis of Cafédirect's relationship means farmers can make plans for the future rather than survive from one harvest to the next.'

With the strong Central and South American heritage of the coffee, the traditional customer base for the product proved to be consumers who had above average levels of political awareness, and church groups which sold the product to the members. However, in 1995 the company faced a classic marketing dilemma – how to move the brand on and attract new customers without alienating its core market.

The solution was seen to lie in the targeting of 'semi-ethical' women; these are defined in terms of those who have a reasonable interest in green and world issues and feel that they want to do the right thing, but only if it is not too difficult or too painful.

In order to capture this market, the advertising focused primarily on the quality of the product, something which had been made possible by the advice on growing and quality control techniques that had been given to the farmers, and only in a secondary way upon the background to the product.

Source: The Financial Times, *12 November 1995, p. 8*

to sudden changes in taste or the entry of a larger competitor, concentrated marketing along these lines has often proved to be attractive to small companies with limited funds. Left to itself, an organization which opts to concentrate upon a single segment can develop a strong market position, a specialist reputation, and above average returns for the industry as a whole.

2 *Selective specialization*. As an alternative to concentrating upon just one segment, the strategist may decide to spread the risk by covering several. These segments need not necessarily be related, although each should be compatible with the organization's objectives and resources. One organization to have done this with a high degree of success is Land Rover. Launched at the end of the 1940s as a rugged, utilitarian and easily maintained off-road vehicle, the Land Rover was targeted at a wide variety of geographically dispersed agricultural and military markets. Having dominated these markets for a considerable time the company subsequently developed the far more luxurious (and expensive) Range Rover which proved to have an immediate appeal to a very different type of market altogether. Their strategy was then developed further in 1990 by the launch of the Land Rover Discovery (see Gabb, 1991).

3 *Product specialization* in which the organization concentrates on marketing a particular product type to a variety of target markets. As an example of this, the

Burton Group has concentrated upon selling fashion clothing to a predominantly young market.

4 *Market specialization.* Here the organization concentrates on satisfying the range of needs of a particular target group. An example of this would be an agro-chemicals manufacturer whose principal target market is farmers.

5 *Full market coverage.* By far the most costly of the five patterns of market coverage, a strategy of full market coverage involves serving all customer groups with the full range of products needed.

In deciding which of these five approaches to adopt, the marketing planner needs to take account of two interrelated issues:

● *The nature of the current strategy.* In discussing this, Fifield and Gilligan (1996, p. 98) suggest that 'market segments ought to be selected according to the broader strategic decisions taken by the company'. For example, the organization aiming for a 'differentiated' position in the market place will need to retain a certain degree of flexibility which will allow it to operate in a number of related market segments while still retaining its differentiated market position. The 'focused' organization, on the other hand, will necessarily have to get much, much closer to its fewer market segments, and will have to predict fragmentation and merging long before this phenomenon arises. It must be prepared and be able to continue to service changing segment needs as they arise. Failure to do this by the focused organization will leave it very vulnerable to competitive attack in its core markets.

● *Organization resources and capability* so that the customers' needs within the segments that are chosen are capable of being properly served.

Against the background of the answers to these two questions, the planner can then begin the process of ordering the segments so that a measure of their relative attractiveness across a series of dimensions can be arrived at: a framework for this appears in Figure 8.12.

FIGURE 8.12
Identifying segment attractiveness

Criteria	Weight	Segments				
		1	2	3	4	5
1 Long-term volume growth 2 Long-term profit growth 3 Short-term volume growth 4 Short-term profit growth 5 Organizational image 6 Offensive strategic reasons 7 Defensive strategic reasons 8 Internal resource/capability 9 Relative competitive strength 10 Competitive vulnerability 11 Legislative constraints 12 Technological change 13 New product demands 14 Levels of price competition 15 Advertising levels 16 Distributor power 17 Life cycles						
Total						
Priority						
(Ratings 1–10, 10 = highly attractive)						

SOURCE: Adapted from Fifield, P. and Gilligan, C. T. (1996), *Strategic Marketing Management: planning and control and analysis and decision – a workbook*, p. 99

Market Niching and Focusing

For small companies in particular, market niching offers a degree of security that is often denied to them if they try to compete in segments which, by virtue of their size, appeal to larger and better funded organizations.

An undoubted attraction of many niche markets is the scope they offer for premium pricing and above-average profit margins. In addition, an effective niche strategy has for many firms provided a convenient jumping off point for entry into a larger market. Both Volkswagen and Toyota, for example, niched when they first entered the North American car market. Their strategies, together with the subsequent growth of the small car market, combined to change what had previously been a niche into a sizeable segment which the American big three (Ford, General Motors, and Chrysler) found difficult to attack because of the entrenched positions of VW and Toyota. Elsewhere, the Japanese have often used a niche as the entry point to a larger market. In the case of motorcycles, for example, 50cc 'toys' proved to be the niche which gave Honda in particular the basis for expansion. Similarly, Volvo developed what was previously a niche that wanted a safe, functional and long-lasting car into a mass market.

There is, however, a hidden danger in looking at what appear to be niche markets. Many strategists with small brands often deceive themselves by believing they have a niche product. The reality may in fact be very different with the product being a vulnerable number four or number five brand in a mass market. To clarify whether a brand is a true market nicher, Davidson (1987, p. 168) therefore suggests posing three questions:

1 Is the niche or segment recognized by consumers and distributors, or is it just a figment of marketing imagination?
2 Is your niche product distinctive, and does it appeal strongly to a particular group of consumers?
3 Is your product premium-priced, with above average profit margin?

Unless the answer to all three of the questions is 'yes', he argues, it is unlikely that the brand is a true nicher, but is instead a poor performer in a far larger market segment. He goes on to say:

> Anyone can find a niche ... The secret is to ensure that it is the right size – large enough to be profitable, but not sufficiently large to attract the supertankers, at least not in the early days when you are establishing a position. Some niche marketers are small companies. Others are large but have developed the knack of operating with small-volume products. Two of the most skilful exponents of niche marketing – American Home Products and Reckitt & Colman – are major companies.

In the light of comments such as these, the characteristics of the ideal niche are:

1 it is of sufficient size to be potentially profitable;
2 it offers scope for an organization to exercise its distinctive competences;
3 it has the potential for growth.

Other characteristics that favour niching would be patents, a degree of channel control, and the existence of customer goodwill.

Niching should not, however, be seen as a strategy limited just to small organizations. Among the large firms to have recognized the benefits of niching is 3M, which has long pursued a highly effective niching strategy by finding sectors of the market that have either been missed or ignored by others.

8.15 PRODUCT POSITIONING

The third strand of what we referred to at the beginning of this chapter as STP marketing involves deciding on the position within the market that the product is to occupy. In doing this, the strategist is stating to customers what the product means and how it differs from current and potential competing products. Porsche, for example, is positioned in the prestige segment of the car market with a differential advantage based on performance, while Mothercare is positioned to appeal to mothers of young children. Its differential advantage is based on the breadth of merchandise for that target group.

Positioning is therefore the process of designing an image and value so that customers within the target segment understand what the company or brand stands for in relation to its competitors. This can perhaps best be understood by considering an example such as grocery retailing where the major UK retailers have set out to establish distinct market positions. Marks & Spencer, for example, occupies a service and quality position. Kwik Save, Aldi and Netto, by contrast, have pursued the low price/no frills position, while Sainsbury and Tesco occupy the quality, breadth of range, and convenience position. In doing this, the organization is sending a message to consumers and trying to establish a competitive advantage that it hopes will appeal to customers within a subsegment of the target segment. In the case of M & S, therefore, the company hopes that its quality/service position will appeal to the customer to whom these two dimensions are far more important than low prices.

It should be apparent from this that positioning is a fundamental element of the marketing planning process, since any decision on positioning has direct and immediate implications for the whole of the marketing mix. In essence, therefore, the marketing mix can be seen as the tactical details of the organization's positioning strategy. Where, for example, the organization is pursuing a high quality position, this needs to be reflected not just in the quality of the product that is to be sold, but in every element of the mix including price, the pattern of distribution, the style of advertising, and the after-sales service. Without this consistency, the believability of the positioning strategy reduces dramatically.

For some organizations the choice of a positioning strategy proves to be straightforward. Where, for example, a particular positioning strategy and image has already been established in a related market, there are likely to be synergistic benefits by adopting the same approach in a new market or with a new product. For other organizations, however, the choice of position proves to be more difficult or less clear and the firm ends up by pursuing the same position as several others in the market. Where this happens the degree and costs of competition increase dramatically. There is a strong case therefore for the strategist to decide in detail on the basis of differentiation; in other words, the organization must identify and build a collection of competitive advantages that will appeal to the target market and then communicate these effectively.

In the light of these comments, it should be apparent that the process of positioning involves three steps:

1 identifying the organization's or brand's possible competitive advantages;
2 deciding on those that are to be emphasized;
3 implementing the positioning concept.

Points 1 and 2 are discussed in detail in Chapter 10 and here we will therefore consider only point 3.

Capitalizing on the Competitive Advantage

Having identified the competitive advantage (see Chapter 10) that appears to offer the greatest potential for development, the final step in the process involves communicating this to the market. Ries and Trout (1982), who in the eyes of many are the founding fathers of positioning theory, argue that positioning is first and foremost a communication strategy and that any failure to recognize this will undermine the whole of the marketing mix. All too often, however, and despite having identified potentially valuable competitive advantages, organizations fail to signal these advantages sufficiently strongly. This then leads to one of three errors:

1 confused positioning where buyers are unsure of what the organization stands for;
2 over-positioning where consumers perceive the organization's products as being expensive and fail to recognize the full breadth of the range;
3 under-positioning where the message is simply too vague and consumers have little real idea of what the organization stands for.

Recognition of these dangers has led to the development of six major positioning strategies:

1 positioning by attribute;
2 positioning by price/quality;
3 positioning by competitor;
4 positioning by application;
5 positioning by product user;
6 positioning by product class.

In order to select the most effective market position, the strategist needs to begin by identifying the structure of the market and the positions currently held by competitors. This can be done in a variety of ways, including by means of the sort of brand map to which we referred to earlier in Figure 8.3. With maps such as these the planner sets out firstly to plot where the product lies in relation to competitive products, and secondly, to identify those areas in which marketing opportunities might exist either for a new brand or for the existing brand if it was to be repositioned. In taking this second step the strategist is setting out to position the product in such a way that its marketing potential is fully realized. As an example of this, the West German car manufacturer Audi set out in the 1980s to reposition its range of products in order to move further up-market. In doing this, the company recognized that the organizations against which it would be competing would change and that in this particular case it would bring itself into more direct competition with both BMW and Mercedes-Benz. In electing for a repositioning strategy, the strategist therefore needs to feel confident that, first, he will be able to reach the new market position he is aiming for, and second, that he will be able to operate and compete effectively and profitably in this new position. It was with this in mind that the Rover Group began its repositioning exercise in the mid-1990s.For many organizations, however, repositioning proves to be a less than successful exercise. Among those that have succeeded are Lucozade and Babycham.

Against the background of these comments, it should be recognized that very different positioning strategies need to be followed depending upon whether the firm is a market leader, follower or challenger, and that as a general rule market followers should try to avoid positioning themselves too closely or directly against the market leader. The reasoning behind this is straightforward, since a smaller firm is most likely to succeed if it can establish its own position within the market and develop its own customer base. To compete head-on against the market leader is to invite retaliation and a costly marketing war. See Illustration 8.8.

Illustration 8.8: The repositioning of the Rover Group

When BMW took over the Rover Group in the mid-1990s, the management team recognized the need for a series of fundamental changes. Though partially transformed from the unwieldy mess of British Leyland, the company was faced with the problem of how to become a globally competitive car manufacturer. In many ways, the problem stemmed from the size of the organization : it was too small to operate effectively in the high-volume mass market, but its products were not sufficiently focused for it to be an upmarket niche operator.

Faced with this, the Rover Group's management team, led by a German, began to focus upon the ways in which Rover might be repositioned and turned into an upmarket global brand. The solution, it was felt, lay in creating cars which recaptured an image of Britishness that would appeal to the rest of the world in much the same way that Burberry does with clothes and Crabtree & Evelyn does with soaps. In terms of how this was to be achieved, the planning team set about a major new product development policy designed to produce cars which fitted a series of niches and which complemented BMW's own range.

8.16 SUMMARY

Within this chapter we have focused upon the ways in which a well-developed strategy of market segmentation, targeting and positioning contributes to effective marketing planning.

The rationale for segmentation is straightforward and based on the idea that only rarely can a single product or marketing approach appeal to the needs and wants of a disparate group of potential customers. Because of this there is a need for the marketing strategist to categorize buyers on the basis both of their characteristics and their specific product needs with a view then to adapting either or both of the product and the marketing programme to satisfy more specifically these different tastes and demands. An effective policy of segmentation is therefore a key contributory factor to the development of a competitive advantage.

A wide variety of approaches to segmentation have been developed and these were discussed in some detail in the text. Many of the early approaches to segmentation are uni-dimensional and are incapable of providing the marketing planner with a sufficiently detailed picture of buyers' motives to be of real value. A considerable amount of work has therefore been conducted over the past decade to improve segmentation techniques, with the greatest emphasis being placed upon geodemographics and psychographics.

Work within the industrial products sector has for the most part tended to lag behind that in the consumer goods field, although the work of Cardozo, and Bonoma and Shapiro has gone some way towards rectifying this.

Having segmented the market the strategist should then be in a position to identify those segments which, from the organization's point of view, represent the most attractive targets. In deciding where to focus the marketing effort the strategist needs to give consideration to three elements:

1 the size and growth potential of each segment;
2 the structural attractiveness of different segments;
3 the organization's objectives and resources.

Once a decision has been made on the breadth of market coverage the strategist needs then to consider how best to position the organization, the product range, and brand within each target segment. A number of guidelines for market positioning were discussed and emphasis was placed upon the need to avoid making any one of the three most common positioning errors:

1 confused positioning;
2 over-positioning;
3 under-positioning.

We concluded by returning to the significance of competitive advantage and to the ways in which a well-conceived and properly implemented strategy of segmentation, targeting and positioning can contribute to a truly effective marketing programme.

8.17 EXERCISES

1 On page 268, we suggest that a conscious approach to segmentation, targeting and positioning (STP) is at the heart of effective strategic marketing. Can you identify a company which has followed this process? How has segmentation led to targeting and then led to positioning? How do the final marketing mixes differ for the eventual product-market matches?

2 Looking at your organization:

- How does it appear to segment its markets?
- Can you count more than one approach?
- How well does the organization use its segmentation approach to improve customer satisfaction?
- How do your competitors segment the market?
- Is segmentation used as a strategic tool?

3 Applying the tests of segmentation to your own organization (page 275), how robust is your segmentation approach? What changes (if any) would you recommend?

4 Look at your organization and apply the analysis of market/segment attractiveness tests to the segments that are targeted. What does this imply for the way that you organize your marketing for the various segments?

5 Looking at your organization and its markets, can you identify any emerging segments – the segments where tomorrow's profits will be made?

6 From a review of TV or trade press, can you find examples of what appears to be good and bad practice in:

- Targeting?
- Positioning?

What are the consequences of bad decisions in these two areas?

8.18 CASE STUDY

MAS Marketing: an exercise in repositioning

MAS Marketing is a medium-sized marketing consultancy which was established fifteen years ago. The company has a well-established local, regional and national client base, to which it offers a range of largely tactical services including advice on strategic planning, competitor analysis, market research, international marketing, distribution and logistics, and pricing.

Although for the past few years growth has been fairly consistent, the company's management recognizes that there are numerous market opportunities which it has been ignoring. At the same time, levels of competition for its traditional business have increased significantly, with the result that margins have been dropping. Because of this, the decision has been taken to reposition the firm and offer an additional range of client services. These include advice on direct marketing, new product development, sales force and customer incentive schemes, and conference organization. The company also intends to focus far more specifically on *strategic* issues. However, while it *appears* that these areas offer potential, little real research has yet been done to identify the detail of this or how the firm will need to operate if it is to succeed in these areas. It is recognized, though, that the firm will be faced with a number of new and possibly well-established competitors.

A client satisfaction survey has recently been conducted and, while the results were generally positive, a number of the clients suggested that the firm's current skills are 'adequate' rather than 'very good'.

At the same time, a study of staff satisfaction was also carried out, the results of which suggested that morale was 'reasonable' rather than 'high'. There appear to be several reasons for this, the most significant of which is that a number of the staff claim to be overworked and underpaid.

The firm's senior managers believe that although some of the new services will appeal to the existing client base, there will be a need to attract a substantial number of new clients. Exactly how this will be done has not yet been decided. The current approach to attracting new clients is generally unstructured, with the responsibility for this being only loosely allocated. Equally, little has yet been agreed about how the new work will be managed and handled internally. However, what is obvious is that a number of highly specialized new staff will need to be recruited and that, particularly in the area of new product development and strategic planning, salary levels will be higher than those paid to most staff working for the firm currently.

Areas for discussion:
1 What issues need to be taken into account in the repositioning exercise? How would you suggest the firm should go about this?
2 What problems, if any, would you expect to face?

9	The formulation of strategy 1: analysing the product portfolio

9.1 LEARNING OBJECTIVES

When you have read this chapter you should be able to understand:

(a) how strategic perspectives have developed over the past 20 years;
(b) how the responsibilities for planning vary throughout the organization;
(c) how portfolio analysis has developed and how it can be used in the development of strategy;
(d) the limitations and current status of portfolio analysis.

9.2 INTRODUCTION

Against the background of the material covered so far we are now in a position to turn our attention to the ways in which organizations approach the development of a marketing strategy. In this, the first of two chapters on strategy, we begin by examining how strategic perspectives have developed over the past 20 years. We then turn our attention to a variety of models of portfolio analysis. In Chapter 10 we concentrate upon the issues surrounding growth, the approaches that are most typically used to achieve it, methods of developing a sustainable competitive advantage, and the ways in which market position influences strategy.

9.3 THE DEVELOPMENT OF STRATEGIC PERSPECTIVES

Although a considerable amount has been written on strategic planning, it should be recognized that as a discipline strategic planning and the associated concepts and techniques did not emerge fully until the early 1970s. There are several reasons for this, perhaps the most significant of which is that, as Kotler (1988, pp. 33–4) has pointed out, largely because of the growing and continuously buoyant markets of the 1950s and 1960s, many companies prospered on the back of largely short-term operational planning. The turbulence of the early 1970s that followed a series of crises, including oil supply restrictions, energy and material shortages, high inflation, economic stagnation, labour unrest, increased unemployment and then recession, caused many managers to search for a radically different approach to the running of their businesses. At the same time an influx of low-price but relatively high-quality products from countries such as Japan began to flood Western markets, changing drastically the economics of manufacturing. The revised approach to management planning that emerged was designed to provide organizations with a far stronger and more resilient framework that would enable managers both to recognize opportunities more readily and overcome threats more easily. This new planning process was based on three central premises:

1 The company's business should be viewed and managed in a similar way to an investment portfolio with each aspect of the business being closely monitored and decisions subsequently made on which products or specific parts of the business should be developed, maintained, phased out, or deleted.

2 Emphasis should be placed upon identifying in detail the future profit potential of each aspect of the business.

3 A strategic perspective to the management of each major element of the business should be adopted. This notion of what has sometimes been referred to as a 'game plan' for achieving long-term objectives, required the strategist to plan on the basis of industry position, objectives, opportunities and resources.

It needs to be recognized, however, that for the strategist to be able to adopt this approach to management, there is a need to understand in detail the complexities of the interrelationships that exist between different parts of the organizational structure. In the majority of businesses, three different organizational levels can be identified: the corporate level, the business unit level, and the product level.

At the corporate level, the decisions made are concerned principally with the corporate strategic plan and how best to develop the long-term profile of the business. This, in turn, involves a series of decisions on the levels of resource allocation to individual business units, be it a division or subsidiary, and on which new potential business should be supported. Following on from this, each business unit should, within the resources allocated by corporate headquarters, then develop its own strategic plan. Finally, marketing plans need to be developed at the product level. Plans at all three levels need then to be implemented, the results monitored and evaluated and, where necessary, corrective action taken; this cycle of planning, implementation and control, which underpins the structure of this book, is illustrated in Figure 9.1.

FIGURE 9.1
The strategic planning, implementation and control cycle

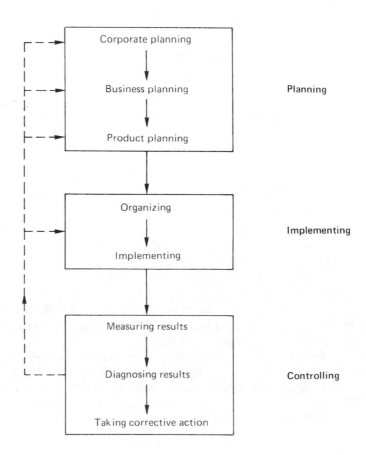

Strategic Planning and Issues of Responsibility

It should be apparent from what has been said so far that the ultimate responsibility for the planning process rests firmly with corporate management. This process, which involves statements of mission, policy and strategy, establishes the broad framework within which plans at the business unit level are then developed. In practice, of course, organizations differ greatly both in how they go about this and in the degree of freedom given to the managers of individual business units. Some organizations, for example, allow business units considerable scope in developing their own objectives and strategies, requiring only that the promised levels of performance are then obtained; this is typically referred to as *bottom-up planning*. Others, by contrast, adopt an approach which is diametrically opposed to this in that they not only establish the objectives, but also subsequently insist on being involved in the development and implementation of strategy (*top-down planning*). Still others are content to establish the goals and then leave the business unit to develop the strategies for their achievement (*goals down/plans up*). Irrespective of which approach is adopted, however, corporate management has the ultimate responsibility for the four major dimensions of planning:

1 the definition of the business mission;
2 establishing the company's strategic business units (SBUs);
3 evaluating the existing business portfolio;
4 identifying new areas for the business to enter.

The first of these – the definition of the business mission – provided the focus for Chapter 6 and, as we emphasized at that stage, is designed to provide the organization with an overall sense of purpose. Once this has been done, the strategist is then in a position to move on and identify the organization's *strategic business units* (SBUs).

The idea of SBUs as the basis for planning first emerged in the 1960s and gave recognition to the fact that the majority of companies operate a number of businesses, not all of which will necessarily be immediately apparent or identifiable. It does not follow, for example, that a company with four operating divisions will have four businesses and hence four SBUs, since one division may in practice contain several quite separate businesses. This typically comes about when the division produces different products for very different customer groups. Equally, two or three divisions may overlap or be interrelated in such a way that in effect they form a single business. It is therefore important that the planner understands in detail the nature and extent of these interrelationships so that the organization's strategy can be developed in the most logical way.

In commenting on this, Levitt (1960, pp. 45–56), along with a number of other writers, has warned against the dangers of simply defining businesses in terms of the products being made. Doing this, he argues, is myopic since the demand for a particular product is likely to be transient. By contrast, basic needs and customer groups are far more likely to endure. In arguing this, Levitt is reminding us that businesses need to be seen as a *customer satisfying process* rather than as a *goods-producing process*. Numerous examples exist of industries that have failed to recognize this, including the American railway companies in the 1950s, the British motorcycle industry in the 1960s, and the Swiss watch industry in the 1970s. (For a more detailed discussion of the problems experienced by the Swiss watch industry, refer to Illustration 7.2). The net effect of this has been either that opportunities have been missed, or the business – and on some occasions the entire industry – has gone into decline. It was in an attempt to force managers to recognize the transient nature of demand that Drucker (1973, Ch. 7) recommended that periodically they should pose the questions 'What business are we in?' and 'What business should we be in?'

This general theme has also been pursued by Abell (1980, Ch. 3) who suggests that businesses should be defined in terms of three elements:

1 the customer groups that will be served;
2 the customer needs that will be satisfied;
3 the technology that will be used to meet these needs.

Having done this, the planner can then move on to consider how best to manage each business strategically. A variety of frameworks to help with this have emerged over the past 20 years, although at the heart of virtually all of them is the concept of the *strategic business unit* or *strategy centre*. The term 'strategy centre' was first used by the American management consultants Arthur D. Little (1974) who defined it as:

> A business area with an external market place for goods or services, for which management can determine objectives and execute strategies independently of other business areas. It is a business that could probably stand alone if divested. Strategic Business Units are the 'natural' or homogeneous business of a corporation.

It follows from this definition that SBUs exhibit a number of characteristics, the three most important of which are that an SBU:

1 is a single business or a collection of related businesses which offer scope for independent planning and which might feasibly stand alone from the rest of the organization;
2 has its own set of competitors;
3 has a manager who has responsibility for strategic planning and profit performance, and who has control of profit-influencing factors.

Planning with SBUs

The ideal of planning based on SBUs developed throughout the 1970s and has proved to be useful, not least because for many managers it has to a very large extent clarified what is meant by strategic marketing planning. The identification of SBUs is therefore a convenient starting point for planning since once the company's strategic business units have been identified, the *responsibilities* for strategic planning can be more clearly assigned. In practice, the majority of companies work on the basis that strategic planning at SBU level has to be agreed by corporate management. Thus plans are typically submitted on an annual basis with corporate management then either agreeing them or sending them back for revision.

In going through this process of review, corporate management attempts to identify future potential and hence where investment can most profitably be made. This has in turn led to the development of a variety of frameworks in which products are categorized on the basis of their potential. One of the best known of these was put forward by Drucker (1963) who labelled products as:

1 tomorrow's breadwinners;
2 today's breadwinners;
3 products that are capable of making a contribution assuming drastic remedial action is taken;
4 yesterday's breadwinners;
5 the also-rans;
6 the failures.

By categorizing products or SBUs in this way, corporate management is moving towards a position where decisions regarding patterns of investment in the overall portfolio can be made with a far higher degree of objectivity than is typically the case when each SBU is viewed in partial or total isolation. To help with this and in order to ensure that the process is analytical rather than impressionistic, a number of models of portfolio evaluation have been developed. Among the best known of these are the Boston Consulting Group's Growth-Share and Growth-Gain matrices.

9.4 MODELS OF PORTFOLIO ANALYSIS

The Boston Consulting Group's Growth-Share and Growth-Gain Matrices

Undoubtedly the best-known approach to portfolio analysis, the Boston Consulting Group's (BCG) growth-share model, involves SBUs being plotted on a matrix according to the *rate of market growth* and their *market share relative to that of the largest competitor.* This is illustrated in Figure 9.2.

In using these dimensions as the basis for evaluating the product portfolio, the Boston Consulting Group forces management to give explicit consideration both to the *future potential of the market* (i.e. the annual growth rate) and to the *SBU's competitive position.* (At this stage it might be worth referring back to Chapter 4 and our discussion of Michael Porter's work concerned with the forces governing competition in an industry.) Within the model, competitive position is measured on a logarithmic scale against the share of the firm's largest competitor; thus a relative market share of 0.3 in Figure 9.2 signifies that the SBU's sales volume is 30 per cent of the leader's sales volume, while 4.0 would mean that the company's SBU is the market leader and has four times the market share of the next largest company in the market. A ratio of 1.0 signifies joint leadership. The vertical axis is then used to illustrate the largely uncontrollable annual rate of market growth in which the business operates. In Figure 9.2 this ranges from 0 to 20 per cent, with a growth rate in excess of 10 per cent being seen as high.

FIGURE 9.2
The Boston Consulting Group's growth share matrix

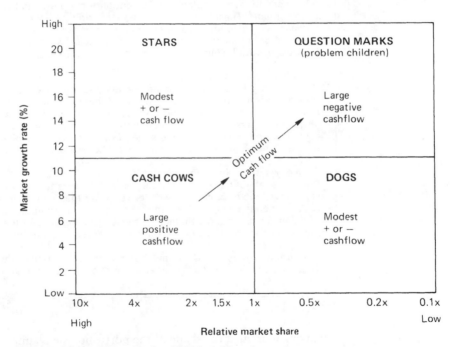

SOURCE: Adapted from Hedley (1977), p. 12

The 2 × 2 matrix that emerges from this is based on four assumptions:

1 margins and the funds generated increase with market share largely as the result of experience and scale effects;
2 sales growth demands cash to finance working capital and increases in capacity;
3 increases in market share generally need cash to support share gaining tactics;
4 growth slows as the product reaches life-cycle maturity and at this stage a surplus of cash can often be generated without the organization experiencing any loss of market share; this can then be used to support products still in the growth stages of their life cycles.

The matrix itself is divided into four cells, each of which indicates a different type of business with different cash using and cash generating characteristics; the characteristics of each of these cells are discussed in Figure 9.3.

Having plotted the position of the organization's SBUs, the balance and health of the portfolio can be seen fairly readily. A balanced portfolio typically exhibits certain characteristics, including a mixture of cash cows and stars. By contrast, an unbalanced and potentially dangerous portfolio would have too many dogs or question marks and too few stars and cash cows; the likely consequence of this is that insufficient cash will be generated on a day-to-day basis to fund or support the development of other SBUs.

FIGURE 9.3
The Boston Consulting Group's SBU classification

Dogs (low share, low growth)
Dogs are those businesses that have a weak market share in a low-growth market. Typically they generate either a low profit or return a loss. The decision faced by the company is whether to hold on to the dog for strategic reasons (e.g. in the expectation that the market will grow, or because the product provides an obstacle, albeit a minor one, to a competitor). Dog businesses frequently take up more management time than they justify and there is often a case for phasing out (shooting) the product.

Question marks (low share, high growth)
Question marks are businesses operating in high-growth markets but with a low relative market share. They generally require considerable sums of cash since the firm needs to invest in plant, equipment and manpower to keep up with market developments. These cash requirements are, in turn, increased significantly if the company wants to improve its competitive position. The title of *question mark* comes about because management has to decide whether to continue investing in the SBU or withdrawing from the market.

Stars (high share, high growth)
Stars are those products which have moved to the position of leadership in a high growth market. Their cash needs are often high with the cash being spent in order to maintain market growth and keep competitors at bay. As stars also generate large amounts of cash, on balance there is unlikely to be any positive or negative cash flow until such time as the state of market growth declines. At this stage, provided the share has been maintained, the product should become a cash cow.

Cash cows (high share, low growth)
When the rate of market growth begins to fall, stars typically become the company's cash cows. The term *cash cow* is derived from the fact that it is these products which generate considerable sums of cash for the organization but which, because of the lower rate of growth, use relatively little. Because of the SBU's position in the market, economies of scale are often considerable and profit margins high.

Two further groups of SBU's have been identified by Barksdale and Harris (1982). These are *war horses* (high market share and negative growth) and *dodos* (low share, negative growth).

Having identified the shape of the portfolio, the planner needs then to consider the objectives, strategy and budget for each SBU. In essence, four major strategies can be pursued:

1 *Build*. In following a building strategy, the primary objective is to increase the SBU's market share in order to strengthen its position. In doing this, short-term earnings and profits are quite deliberately forsaken in the expectation that long-term returns will be far greater. It is a strategy which is best suited to question marks so that they become stars.
2 *Hold*. The primary objective in this case is to maintain the current share. It is the strategy which typically is used for cash cows to ensure they continue to generate the maximum amounts of cash.
3 *Harvest*. By following a harvesting strategy management tries to increase short-term cashflows as far as possible, even at the expense of the SBUs's longer term future. It is a strategy best suited to cash cows that are weak or which are in a

market with seemingly only a limited future life. It is also used on occasions when the organization is in need of cash and is willing to mortgage the future of the product in the interests of short-term needs. Harvesting is also used for question marks when there appear to be few real opportunities to turn them into stars, and for dogs.

4 *Divest*. The essential objective here is to rid the organization of SBUs that act as a drain on profits or to realize resources that can be used to greater effect elsewhere in the business. It is a strategy which, again, is often used for question marks and dogs.

Having decided which of these four broad approaches to follow, the strategist needs then to give consideration to the way in which each SBU is likely to change its position within the matrix over time. SBUs typically have a life cycle which begins with their appearance as question marks and their progression through the stages of star, cash cow and, finally dog. It is essential therefore that the BCG matrix is used not simply to obtain a snapshot of the portfolio as it stands currently, but rather that it is used to see how SBUs have developed so far and how they are likely to develop in the future. In doing this, it is possible to gain an impression of the probable shape and health of the portfolio in several years' time, any gaps that are likely to exist, and hence the sort of strategic action that is needed in the form of decisions on new products, marketing support, and indeed product deletion. This process can then be taken a step further if similar charts are developed for each major competitor, since by doing this the strategist gains an insight to each competitor's portfolio strengths, weaknesses, and potential gaps. The implications can then be fed back into the organization's own strategy.

The Pitfalls of Portfolio Analysis

Although portfolio analysis is capable of providing a picture of the organization's current position, the strategists need to adopt a degree of care in their interpretation and when developing a future policy. A common mistake in portfolio analysis is to require each SBU to achieve an unrealistic growth rate or level of return; the essence of portfolio analysis involves recognizing that each SBU offers a different potential and as such requires individual management. Other typical mistakes include:

1 Investing too heavily in dogs hoping that their position will improve, but failing.
2 Maintaining too many question marks and investing too little in each one with the result that their position either fails to change or deteriorates. Question marks should either be dropped or receive the level of support needed to improve their segment position dramatically.
3 Draining the cash cows of funds and weakening them prematurely and unnecessarily. Alternatively, investing too much in cash cows with the result that the money available for question marks, stars and dogs is insufficient.

It should be apparent from the discussion so far that cash cows are essential to the health and long-term profitability of the organization since they provide the funds needed if it is to develop and realize its full potential. The reality in many companies, however, is that cash cows are often in short supply and may already have been too vigorously milked. Booz, Allen & Hamilton (1988), for example, have estimated that, in traditional portfolio analysis terms, 72 per cent of business units in the United States are dogs, 15 per cent are cash cows, 10 per cent question marks, and only 3 per cent stars. There is little evidence to suggest that the proportions in the UK are radically different. Recognizing this, the strategist needs to focus upon the long term and consider how best to manage the portfolio and ensure that the organization benefits from a succession of cash cows. Any failure to do this is likely to lead to suboptimal management and the sorts of disaster sequences that are illustrated in Figure 9.4.

FIGURE 9.4
*Success and disaster
sequences in the
product portfolio*

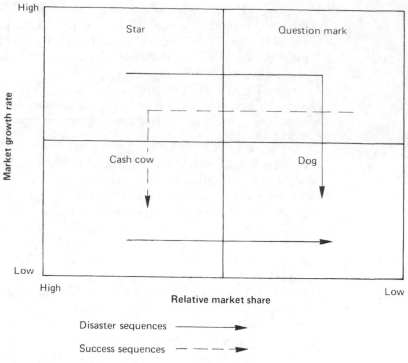

SOURCE: The Boston Consulting Group (1970)

A second model developed by the Boston Consulting Group – the growth-gain matrix – can go some way towards helping the strategist avoid problems such as those shown in Figure 9.4. The alternative matrix, which is often used in conjunction with growth-share analysis, illustrates the extent to which the growth of each product or SBU is keeping pace with market growth. The matrix, which is illustrated in Figure 9.5(a), features the growth rate of the product (or of its capacity) on the horizontal axis, and the growth rate of the market on the vertical axis. Products with a growth rate just equal to the market growth rate are located on the diagonal. Share losers therefore appear above the diagonal, while share gainers are below.

Figure 9.5(b) shows the ideal location of products within a portfolio. Here, the dogs are clustered along or near the market growth axis, a position which reflects zero capacity growth. Cash cows are concentrated along the diagonal showing that market share is being maintained. Stars should appear in the high-growth sector since they should be gaining, or at the very least holding, market share. Question marks then appear in two clusters with one group receiving little support, while the other is receiving the considerable support needed to maximize its chances of producing stars.

In discussing how best to use and interpret the growth-gain matrix, Alan Zakon (1971) of the Boston Consulting Group highlights the significance of the firm's *maximum sustainable growth*; this is plotted as a solid vertical line on the matrix. 'The weighted average growth rate of the products within the portfolio cannot', he emphasizes, 'exceed this maximum sustainable rate.' Where, however, the 'centre of gravity' (i.e. the weighted average growth rate) is to the left of this line, scope exists for further growth. This would typically be achieved by a series of strategy changes to reposition products. As an example of this, extra funds might be shifted to one of the stars in order to achieve even higher rates of growth.

Used in this way, the growth-gain matrix provides a basis for moving the portfolio closer to the 'ideal' position of maximum sustainable growth. Equally, by plotting growth-gain matrices for each major competitor, the strategist can, as with growth-share analysis, gain an insight into the areas of competitive emphasis and react accordingly.

FIGURE 9.5
The product portfolio and maximum sustainable growth

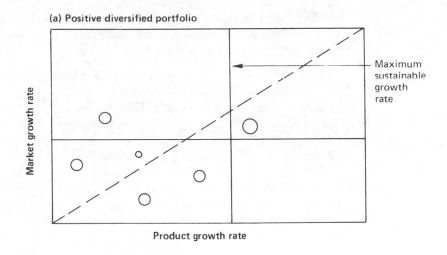

(a) Positive diversified portfolio

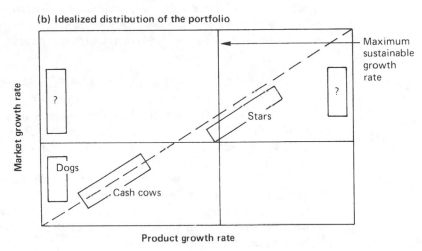

(b) Idealized distribution of the portfolio

SOURCE: The Boston Consulting Group (1971)

Portfolio Analysis: An Initial Assessment

Although the BCG matrices have a number of obvious attractions, a word of caution needs to be uttered, since they do not represent the ultimate management panacea that many of their advocates in the early days argued. It should be recognized that the practical value of portfolio analysis is influenced significantly both by the quality of the basic data inputs, many of which are difficult to define and measure, and the broader political and social environments within which decisions are made. It was therefore in an attempt to give greater specific recognition to a broader spectrum of factors that other approaches to portfolio analysis, including the General Electric multifactor matrix, the Shell directional policy matrix, the Arthur D. Little strategic condition matrix, and Abell and Hammond's 3 × 3 relative investment opportunity chart have been developed. It is to these models, which are concerned with market attractiveness and business position, that we now turn our attention.

9.5 MARKET ATTRACTIVENESS AND BUSINESS POSITION ASSESSMENT

The two BCG matrices we have discussed so far are capable of providing the strategist with an understanding of several important strategic relationships, including internal cashflows, and market share and growth trajectories. It is generally acknowledged, however, that while the insights provided by these models is undoubtedly of significant value, they are in the majority of cases insufficient if truly worthwhile investment decisions affecting the future of the business are to be made. More specifically, critics such as Abell and Hammond (1979, pp. 211–12) have highlighted the three major shortcomings of relying simply on growth-share analysis:

1 Often, factors other than relative market share and industry growth play a significant role in influencing cashflow.
2 Cashflow may well be viewed as being of less significance than ROI as a means of comparing the attractiveness of investing in one business rather than another.
3 Portfolio charts provide little real insight into how one business unit compares with another in terms of investment opportunity. Is it the case, for example, that a star is always a better target for investment than a cash cow? Equally, problems are often encountered in comparing question marks when trying to decide which should receive funds to make it a star, and which should be allowed to decline.

Recognition of these sorts of problems has led to the development of an approach which is labelled '*market attractiveness – business position assessment*', the best known of which is the General Electric model.

The General Electric Multifactor Portfolio Model

The thinking behind General Electric's multifactor model is straightforward and based on the argument that it is not always possible or appropriate to develop objectives or to make investment decisions for an SBU solely on the basis of its position in the growth-share matrix. The General Electric model therefore takes the general approach a step further by introducing a greater number of variables against which the position of SBUs might be plotted. This model, which appears in Figure 9.6, involves SBUs being rated against two principal dimensions: *industry attractiveness* and *competitive position*.

The circles then represent not the size of the SBU, but rather the size of the market in question, with the shaded part of the circle representing the SBU's market share.

The thinking behind the choice of the two axes is based on the notion that the success of a company is determined, first, by the extent to which it operates in attractive markets, and second by the extent to which it possesses the sorts of competitive business strengths needed to succeed in each of these markets. The failure on the part of the company to recognize this is likely to lead to long-term problems, since, as Kotler (1988, p. 43) suggests, 'neither a strong company operating in an unattractive market nor a weak company operating in an attractive market will do very well'.

FIGURE 9.6
The General Electric multifactor portfolio model

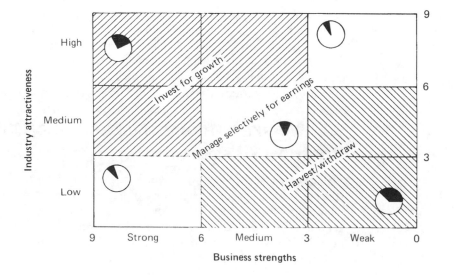

Recognizing this requires the planner to measure each of the two dimensions. In order to do this, the factors underlying each dimension must be identified, measured and then combined to form an index. Although within each dimension the list of factors that combine to form a measure of attractiveness will be specific to each company, it is possible to identify the sorts of factor that will in nearly every instance be of relevance. Industry attractiveness, for example, is determined to a very large extent by the market's size, its rate of growth, the degree of competition, the pace of technological change, the extent to which it is constrained by government or legislative regulations, the sorts of profit margins that historically have been achieved, and so on. Equally, business strength is influenced by such factors as market share, product quality, the brand's reputation, the distribution network, production capacity and production effectiveness. (See Chapter 16 for a fuller discussion.)

It can be seen from Figure 9.6 that the nine cells of the General Electric matrix fall into three distinct areas, each of which requires a different approach to management and investment. The three cells at the top left of the matrix are the most attractive in which to operate and require a policy of investment for growth. The three cells that run diagonally from the top right to the bottom left have a medium attractiveness rating; the management of the SBUs within this category should therefore be rather more cautious with a greater emphasis being placed upon selective investment and earnings retention. The three cells at the bottom right of the matrix are the least attractive in which to operate and management should therefore pursue a policy of harvesting and/or divestment.

As with the BCG matrix, it needs to be recognized that the General Electric approach to portfolio analysis also needs to take account of the probable future of each SBU. The planner should therefore attempt to look ahead by considering life cycles, new forms of technology and their probable impact, likely competitive strategies, and so on. This can then be reflected in the matrix by adding a series of arrows showing how each SBU is likely to move over the next few years.

Other Portfolio Models

Although the BCG and GE models are undoubtedly the best-known approaches to portfolio analysis, a variety of other models have appeared over the years, including the Shell directional policy matrix (DPM) (1975), Abell and Hammond's 3 × 3 matrix (1979), and the Arthur D. Little strategic condition model (1974).

Shell's directional policy matrix which is illustrated in Figure 9.7 again has two key dimensions, the company's *competitive capabilities* and the *prospects for sector profitability*. As with the General Electric matrix, each dimension is then

FIGURE 9.7
The Shell directional policy matrix

Prospects for sector profitability

		Unattractive	Average	Attractive
Enterprise's competitive capabilities	Weak	Disinvest	Phased withdrawal	Double or quit
	Average	Phased withdrawal	Custodial Growth	Try harder
	Strong	Cash generation	Growth Leader	Leader

SOURCE: Shell Chemical Co. (1975)

FIGURE 9.8
*Abell and Hammond's
3 × 3 investment
opportunity matrix*

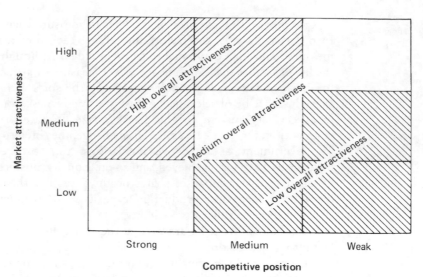

SOURCE: Adapted from Abell and Hammond (1979), p. 213

subdivided into three categories. SBUs are located within the matrix and the strategic options open to the company then identified. The directional policy matrix has, in turn, provided the basis for Abell and Hammond's 3 × 3 chart (see Figure 9.8), which is designed to depict relative investment opportunities.

Although the terminology used by Abell and Hammond differs slightly from that of Shell's DPM – company competitive capability, for example, is referred to as business position, while prospects for sector profitability is termed market attractiveness – the thinking behind the model is similar and indeed can be seen to link back to the General Electric approach.

The Arthur D. Little model (ADL) (Wright, 1974) which is illustrated in Figure 9.9 is again similar in concept, although here the two dimensions used are the

FIGURE 9.9
*The Arthur D. Little
strategic condition
matrix*

Competitive position	**Stage of industry maturity**			
	Embryonic	Growth	Mature	Ageing
Dominant	Grow fast. Build barriers. Act offensively.	Grow fast. Aim for cost leadership. Defend position. Act offensively.	Defend position. Increase the importance of cost. Act offensively.	Defend position. Focus. Consider withdrawal.
Strong	Grow fast. Differentiate.	Lower cost. Differentiate. Attack small firms.	Lower cost. Differentiate. Focus.	Harvest.
Favourable	Grow fast. Differentiate.	Focus. Differentiate. Defend.	Focus. Differentiate. Hit smaller firms.	Harvest.
Tenable	Grow with the industry. Focus.	Hold-on or withdraw. Niche. Aim for Growth.	Hold-on or withdraw. Niche.	Withdraw.
Weak	Search for a niche. Attempt to catch others.	Niche or withdraw.	Withdraw.	Withdraw.

SOURCE: Adapted from ADL

firm's *competitive position* and the *stage of industry maturity*. Competitive position, they suggest, is influenced by the geographical scope of the industry and the specific product – market sectors in which the SBU operates. It is not therefore simply market share that influences competitive position but also competitive economics and a series of other factors, including technology. This led ADL to the recognition of five main categories of competitive position:

1 *Dominant*. This is a comparatively rare position and in many cases is attributable either to a monopoly or a strong and protected technological leadership. The implications are that the firm is able to exert considerable influence over the behaviour of others in the industry and has a wide variety of strategic options open to it.
2 *Strong*. By virtue of this position, the firm has a considerable degree of freedom over its choice of strategy and is often able to act without its market position being unduly threatened by competitors.
3 *Favourable*. This position, which generally comes about when the industry is fragmented and no one competitor stands out clearly, results in the market leaders having a reasonable degree of freedom. Companies with a favourable market position often have strengths that can be exploited by particular strategies and hence a greater than average opportunity to increase market share.
4 *Tenable*. Although firms within this category are able to perform satisfactorily and can justify staying in the industry, they are generally vulnerable in the face of increased competition from stronger and more proactive companies in the market. The opportunities for an organization to strengthen its position tend to be lower than average. The profitability of the tenable firm is best achieved and sustained through a degree of specialization.
5 *Weak*. The performance of firms in this category is generally unsatisfactory although opportunities for improvement do exist. Often, however, the firm is either too big and inefficient to compete with any real degree of effectiveness, or it is too small to cope with competitive pressures. Unless the firm changes, it is ultimately likely to be forced out of the market or exit of its own accord.

A sixth position, that of *non-viability*, can be added to this list and applies when the firm's performance is unsatisfactory and there are few, if any, opportunities for improvement. In these circumstances it is essentially a case of the strategist recognizing the reality of the situation and withdrawing from the market in the least costly way.

The second dimension of the model – the *stage of industry maturity* ranging from embryonic to ageing – has, ADL argue, significant implications for the strategies open to the organization. Thus once a basic strategy has been identified, there are certain things the strategist must do, might do, and should not do if consistency is to be maintained.

This combination of competitive position and industry maturity provides the basis for determining the SBU's strategic condition and subsequently the identification and evaluation of the strategic options open to the company; this typically is a choice between investing in order to strengthen or maintain position, spending in order to maintain the status quo, harvesting, or exiting from the industry. In commenting on this, ADL state that 'there is a finite set of available strategies for each Business Unit' and that these can be seen in terms of six generic strategic groups:

● market strategies (domestic and international);
● product strategies;
● technology strategies;
● operations strategies;
● management and systems strategies;
● retrenchment strategies.

In choosing among these, ADL identify several guiding principles, the most important of which is that 'strategy selection (should) be driven by the condition of the business, not the condition of its managers'. In making this comment, ADL are arguing for realism in strategic planning and that it is this that should prevail if the organization is not to overreach itself.

9.6 CRITICISMS OF PORTFOLIO ANALYSIS

Despite the rapid growth, adoption and indeed the apparent attractions of the underlying logic of portfolio analysis, it has been subject to a considerable and growing volume of criticism over the past 10 years. Although it is acknowledged by its critics that the sort of models referred to here have encouraged managers to think strategically, consider the economics of their businesses in greater detail, examine the nature of interrelationships, and adopt a more proactive approach to management, many writers have argued that the models are generally too simplistic in their structure. In commenting on this, Kotler (1988, p. 46) suggests that:

> Portfolio analysis models must be used cautiously. They may lead the company to place too much emphasis on market-share growth and entry into high growth businesses, to the neglect of managing the current businesses well. The results are sensitive to the ratings and weights and can be manipulated to produce a desired location in the matrix. Furthermore, since an averaging process is occurring, two or more businesses may end up in the same cell position but differ greatly in the underlying ratings and weights. A lot of businesses will end up in the middle of the matrix due to compromises in ratings, and this makes it hard to know what the appropriate strategy should be. Finally, the models fail to accommodate the synergies between two or more businesses, and this means that making decisions for one business at a time may be risky.

These sorts of criticisms have been echoed by others, including Baker (1985, p. 75) who has pointed to the way in which many firms managed to cope with the recession of the 1970s and early 1980s not because of a portfolio of products or even a high market share, but rather as the result of a strategy of concentrating upon a single product and market. Equally, many other firms, and especially those in mature markets, he suggests, have not only survived but have also prospered despite having products which in portfolio analysis terms would be universally classified as dogs. Brownlie (1983) also discusses these criticisms in some detail, and is worth quoting at length. He suggests that:

> Additional criticism of the BP [business portfolio] approach tends to focus on its over-simplified, and somewhat misleading, representation of possible strategy positions; and its use of the dimensions growth rate and market share, which are themselves considered to be inadequate measures of, respectively, industry attractiveness, and competitive position. As Wensley concludes, this approach to strategy development 'encourages the use of general rather than specific criteria as well as implying assumptions about mechanisms of corporate financing and market behaviour which are rather unnecessary or false'. Indeed, it has been observed that market leadership does not always offer the benefits of lower costs, more positive cash flow and higher profits. On the contrary: the number of highly viable companies occupying market 'niches' is legion, and growing by the day. Recent trends that have favoured the development of greater specialisation in some markets include the growth of private label consumer products and the emergence of differential preferences in some industrial markets, for example computers, as customers become familiar with product, or develop relevant in-house expertise.
> The BP also tends to overlook other important and strategic factors which are more a function of the external competitive environment, for example, technological change; barriers to entry; social, legal, political and environmental pressures; union and related human factors; elasticity of demand; and cyclicality of sales. The

application of the BP to strategic decision-taking is in the manner of a diagnostic rather than a prescriptive aid in instances where observed cash flow patterns do not conform with those on which the four product-market categories are based. This commonly occurs where changes in product-market strategies have short-term transient effects on cash flow.

The limitations and problems of portfolio analysis have also been highlighted by McDonald (1990, p. 2), albeit from a rather different viewpoint from that of most writers. McDonald suggests that the gap between theory and practice is greater in the case of marketing than any other discipline. One consequence of this according to McDonald is that little evidence exists to show that some of the more substantive techniques such as the Ansoff Matrix, the Boston Matrix, and the Directional Policy Matrix are used in practice. This is supported by research findings not just in the UK but also in Australia and Hong Kong. Reid and Hinckley (1989, p. 9), for example, concluded:

> Respondents were asked which techniques they were familiar with. The results were skewed towards ignorance of all the techniques to which they were exposed. The majority were not familiar with any by name.

Similarly, from a study of Australian management practice, McColl-Kennedy, et al. (1989, p. 28) stated that 'The awareness and usage of planning tools is low.' McDonald suggests that there are three possible explanations for this:

1 companies have never heard of them;
2 companies have heard of them, but do not understand them;
3 companies have heard of them, have tried them and found that they are largely irrelevant.

More fundamentally, however, he argues that the gap between theory and practice is due to the failure of most writers' attempts to explain the strategic methodologies underpinning such techniques. He illustrates this by discussing the directional policy matrix which, he suggests, is a well-known but under-utilized and misunderstood planning tool. This misunderstanding is in one form or another common to virtually all approaches to portfolio analysis. However, in the case of the DPM, the problems stem from the complexity of the analytical process that is needed if the model is to be used effectively. Thus:

> The criteria for the vertical axis (market attractiveness) can only be determined once the population of 'markets' has been specified. Once determined, those criteria cannot be changed during the exercise. Another common mistake is to misunderstand that unless the exercise is carried out twice – once for t0 and once for t+3 – the circles cannot move vertically. Also, the criteria have to change for *every* 'market' assessed on the horizontal axis each time a company's strength in that market is assessed. Some way has also to be found of quantifying the horizontal axis to prevent every market appearing in the left hand box of the matrix. If we add to this just some of the further complexities involved, such as the need to take the square root of the volume or value to determine circle diameter, the need to understand that the term 'attractiveness' has more to do with future *potential* than with any externally derived criteria, and so on, we begin to understand why practising managers rarely use the device.

Despite criticisms such as these, portfolio analysis has many defenders, including Day (1983) who suggests that

> current criticisms (of portfolio analysis) are unwarranted because they reflect a serious misunderstanding of the proper role of these analytical methods ... what must be realised is that these methods can facilitate the strategic planning process and serve as a rich source of ideas about possible strategic options. But on their own,

these methods cannot present the appropriate strategy or predict the consequences of a specific change in strategy.

In many ways, Day's comments help to put the true role and value of portfolio analysis into perspective. It is not as some managers appeared to believe in the early days a set of techniques that guarantees greater success. Rather it is an approach to the formulation of strategy which, if used in the way intended, should force a deeper analysis and give far greater recognition to the interrelationships and implications of these interrelationships to the portfolio of brands or businesses being managed by the company. This, in turn, should lead to a far firmer base for effective decision making.

This final point in particular was highlighted in 1979 by the results of a *Harvard Business Review* sponsored study of strategic portfolio planning practices in *Fortune*'s 1000 companies. The study by Haspeslagh (1982) found that portfolio planning helped managers to strengthen their planning processes, particularly in divisionalized and diversified organizations. The secret to success, however, was found to lie not just in the techniques themselves, but also in the challenge of incorporating the theory of the techniques into managerial practice. The findings of the study did highlight several problems of portfolio planning including:

1 if done properly, the process is time consuming and firms often experience difficulties of implementation;
2 if the techniques are seen simply as analytical tools, the company sees only limited benefits;
3 all too often, the strategist focuses upon factors that are in a sense inappropriate e.g. levels of cost efficiency rather than organizational responsiveness;
4 the techniques are of only limited value in addressing the issue of new business generation.

Despite problems such as these, the techniques were found to be popular for a number of reasons:

1 they were felt to lead to improvements in strategies;
2 the allocation of resources was improved;
3 they provided an improved base for adapting planning to the needs of individual businesses;
4 levels of control improved.

9.7 SUMMARY

In this, the first of two chapters on strategy, we took as our primary focus the nature and development of portfolio analysis. As a prelude to this we examined the development of strategic perspectives over the past 20 years, highlighting the way in which the environmental turbulence that characterized the early 1970s led to many managers rethinking their approaches to running their businesses. The new planning perspective that emerged was, we suggested, based on three central premises:

1 a need to view and manage the company's businesses in a similar way to an investment portfolio;
2 an emphasis upon each business's future profit potential;
3 the adoption of a *strategic* perspective to the management of each business.

The starting point for portfolio analysis involves identifying the organization's *strategic business units*, an SBU being an element of the business as a whole which:

- offers scope for independent planning;
- has its own set of competitors;
- has a manager with direct profit responsibility who also has control over the profit-influencing factors.

A variety of approaches to portfolio analysis and planning have been developed, the best known of which are:

- the Boston Consulting Group's growth-share matrix;
- the General Electric multifactor matrix;
- the Shell directional policy matrix;
- the Arthur D. Little strategic condition matrix;
- Abell and Hammond's 3 × 3 investment opportunity chart.

The conceptual underpinnings in each case are broadly similar, with consideration being given in one form or another to the SBU's *competitive position* and *market attractiveness/potential*. Each of the portfolio models also encompasses a series of strategic guidelines and these were examined.

Against this background we focused upon the limitations of portfolio analysis. Although it is acknowledged that these models have encouraged managers to think strategically, to consider the economics of their businesses in greater detail, and to adopt a generally more proactive approach to management, critics have argued that the models are overly simplistic in their structure, and often require data inputs which are complex and difficult to obtain. Because of this, it is suggested, usage levels are generally low.

9.8 EXERCISES

1 What do you think are the major advantages and disadvantages of each of the three main approaches to planning? Which approach predominates in your own organization?

2 Using Drucker's framework (p. 310), conduct an initial analysis of your organization's SBUs. What picture emerges? Is it one with which senior management can be happy?

3 Using the BCG growth-share matrix, plot the position of your organization's SBUs. What sort of picture regarding the balance and health of the portfolio emerges? To what extent can you identify *explicit* strategies for each of the SBUs? In what ways do they correspond with the four strategies identified above? (*Authors' tip*: in plotting the position of the SBUs, always start with the market growth rate. In the case of Figure 9.2, this goes from 1–20 per cent, although you may have to change this to reflect the specifics of your market; the key issue is that you distinguish between low and high growth. Turn then to the horizontal axis which focuses upon relative competitive position. This is measured logarithmically against the market share of the firm's largest competitor. If you have half the share of this firm, your relative position is 0.5x. If you are joint leader, you have 1.0x. If you have the biggest SBU and your next biggest competitor has half the share that you have, you would position yourself at 2.0x.)

4 What characterizes:

- a balanced portfolio?
- an unbalanced portfolio?

5 What sorts of factors do you feel contribute to:

- industry attractiveness?
- business strength?

6 Applying the Shell Directional Policy matrix (pp. 317–18) to your organization, what strategic guidelines emerge?

9.9 CASE STUDY

RTJ Engineering Ltd

Established in 1952, RTJ Engineering is a fabricator of highly specialized engineering components. Selected sales and financial data appear in Figure 2. The company's operations are divided between five strategic business units: Nuclear, Aerospace, Defence, Marine and General Engineering (see Figure 3).

The firm has an international reputation for engineering excellence and prides itself on the very high quality of its work and its ability to tackle projects of extreme technical complexity. However, the sales department within the organization has traditionally operated with a highly reactive approach to selling, relying heavily upon word-of-mouth and repeat business from its established customer base.

In 1992 and 1993, total sales declined partly as the result of a downturn in its core markets, but also because of the loss of three medium-sized and long-standing customers to competitors. Because of this, the managing director hired a marketing consultant who, as part of a programme of activities, conducted a study designed to reveal current and potential customers' perceptions of the firm's three principal SBUs (see Figures 1(a) and 1(b) for a selection of the results). The consultant's report gave full recognition to the depth and breadth of the firm's technical expertise, but

Figure 1(a)
Customers' perceptions of RTJ Engineering and its principal competitors

	Nuclear		Aerospace		Defence	
	RTJ	Others	RTJ	Others	RTJ	Others
Design skills	8	6	8	7	6	7
Sales expertise	2	4	3	5	3	5
Customer management	3	5	3	6	4	5
Quality of literature	1	4	2	4	2	4
Production flexibility	7	7	7	7	7	7
Ability to cope with complex specifications	9	7	9	8	8	7
Adherence to promised delivery schedules	4	7	4	6	3	6
Price competitiveness	4	6	3	6	4	7
Quality of work	9	6	9	7	9	6
Unprompted technical support	4	6	3	6	3	5
Helpfulness of sales staff/ sales support	3	5	3	6	2	5

(1 = Low, 9 = High)

Figure 1(b)
Selected quotations that emerged from the customer research

'They work at their speed rather than ours.'
'Technically, they're the best in the industry but they haven't got the first idea about marketing or selling.'
'Do they ever deliver on time?'
'They are the most frustrating company that I've ever dealt with, but nobody can match their quality.'
'Have their sales staff ever had any training in anything other than being rude to customers?'
'Have you seen their sales literature? It's a joke.'
'I'd never go anywhere else when I've got a complex job that needs doing.'
'Superb quality, but very expensive.'

Figure 2
*Selected sales and
financial information*

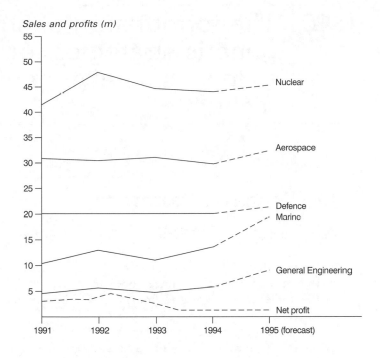

Figure 3

	RTJ's sales 1994 (£m)	Number of direct competitors	Sales of the three largest firms in the sector (£m)	Forecast annual growth rate (%)
Nuclear	13	5	13*, 13, 8	3
Aerospace	12	8	12*, 9, 6	4
Defence	9	12	15, 12, 11	(6)
Marine	6	7	18, 12, 6*	15
General engineering	4	16	15, 14, 10	8
	44 (forecast)			

Note: Figures asterisked represent RTJ's sales within the sector

was highly critical of the approaches to marketing and selling. In particular, he pointed to the results of the customer study, arguing that unless a series of changes were made, the company would almost inevitably lose sales and market share to its ever more numerous and aggressive competitors. Against this background, it has been agreed that a far more proactive approach to customer care will be introduced.

Questions

1 Using a model of your choice, comment upon the apparent state of the firm's portfolio. In doing this, you should specify any assumptions that you make, the limitations of the model and any other information that you would require before recommending how the firm's portfolio should be developed. You should also identify briefly any other approach to portfolio analysis that might be used to evaluate the portfolio.

2 In the light of the research findings, prepare a report for the managing director identifying the key dimensions of a customer-care programme and how such a programme might be introduced into the organization. In doing this, you should pay particular attention to issues of implementation.

10 | The formulation of strategy 2: generic strategies for leaders, followers, challengers and nichers

10.1 LEARNING OBJECTIVES

When you have read this chapter you should be able to understand:

(a) the need for a clear statement of marketing strategy;
(b) the types of marketing strategy open to an organization;
(c) the forces which govern competition within an industry and how they interact;
(d) the sources of competitive advantage;
(e) the influence of market position on strategy;
(f) how organizations might attack others and defend themselves;
(g) how the product life cycle influences strategy.

10.2 INTRODUCTION

Having used the techniques discussed in the previous chapter to identify the strengths and weaknesses of the product portfolio, the strategist should be in a far stronger position to focus upon the ways in which the organization is best capable of developing. Against this background, we now turn our attention to an examination of some of the principal factors that influence marketing strategy. We begin by examining Michael Porter's work in which emphasis is given to the need for a clear statement of a generic strategy and for this to be based upon a detailed understanding of corporate capability and competitive advantage. This is then used as the basis for a discussion of the ways in which the organization's position in the market, ranging from market leader through to market nicher, influences strategy. Finally, we turn our attention to the ways in which market and product life cycles need to be taken into account.

10.3 TYPES OF STRATEGY

Throughout this book we have tried to give full emphasis to the need for objectives and strategy to be realistic, obtainable, and based firmly on corporate capability. In practice, of course, this translates into an almost infinite number of strategies that are open to an organization. Porter (1980) has, however, pulled them together and identified three generic types of strategy – *overall cost leadership, differentiation*, and *focus* - that provide a meaningful basis for strategic thinking (see Figure 10.1). In doing this, he gives emphasis to the need for the strategist to identify a clear and meaningful selling proposition for the organization. In other words, what is our competitive stance, and what do we stand for in the eyes of our customers? Any failure on the part of the strategist to identify and communicate the selling proposition and strategy is, he suggests, likely to lead to a dilution of the offer and to the company ending up as stuck in the middle or, as it appears in Figure 10.1, a middle-of-the-roader.

FIGURE 10.1
Porter's three generic strategies

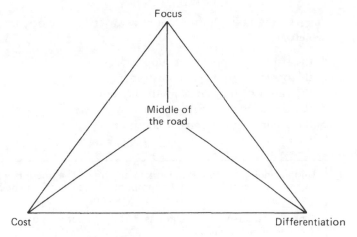

SOURCE: Adapted from Porter (1980)

Porter's thesis is therefore straightforward: to compete successfully the strategist needs to select a generic strategy and pursue it consistently; the ways in which this might be done and the benefits and the problems that might possibly be encountered are referred to in Figure 10.2. Obviously, there is no single 'best' strategy even within a given industry, and the task faced by the strategist involves selecting the strategic approach which will best allow it to maximize its strengths vis-à-vis its competitors. This needs to be done, Porter (1979, pp. 137–45)

FIGURE 10.2
Porter's three generic strategies

Type of strategy	Ways to achieve the strategy	Benefits	Possible problems

Cost leadership	Size and economies of scale
	Globalization
	Relocating to low-cost parts of the world
	Modification/simplification of designs
	Greater labour effectiveness
	Greater operating effectiveness
	Strategic alliances
	New sources of supply
		The ability to:
		  outperform rivals
		  erect barriers to entry
		  resist the five forces
			Vulnerability to even lower cost operators
			Possible price wars
			The difficulty of sustaining it in the long term

Focus	Concentration upon one or a small number of segments The creation of a strong and specialist reputation	A more detailed understanding of particular segments The creation of barriers to entry A reputation for specialization The ability to concentrate efforts	Limited opportunities for sector growth The possibility of outgrowing the market The decline of the sector A reputation for specialization which ultimately inhibits growth and development into other sectors
Differentiation	The creation of strong brand identities The consistent pursuit of those factors which customers perceive to be important High performance in one or more of a spectrum of activities	A distancing from others in the market The creation of a major competitive advantage Flexibility	The difficulties of sustaining the bases for differentiation Possibly higher costs The difficulty of achieving true and meaningful differentiation

suggests, by taking into account a variety of factors, the five most significant of which are:

1 the bargaining power of suppliers;
2 the bargaining power of customers;
3 the threat of new entrants to the industry;
4 the threat of substitute products or services;
5 the rivalry among current competitors.

FIGURE 10.3
Porter's approach to competitive structure analysis

Understanding the forces at work in any market segment is a necessary prerequisite to deducing whether – and if appropriate, how – the firm should use that segment as a strategic business area. The five forces are:

1 new entrants, potential entrants and the threat of entry;
2 substitute products/services;
3 buyers and buyer power;
4 suppliers and supplier power;
5 competitors and the nature of inter-firm rivalry.

The greater the intensity of any of these sources of competition, the harder it will be for an organization to earn profits and the greater will be the need for strategic sophistication. In the UK the intensity of competition in markets is growing. A checklist of questions can assist strategists in thinking through the strategic implications of the competitive structures of an industry:

1 What is the threat of entry into the industry and from where does it arise?
2 Where are present and potential substitute products/services located and what is their impact or likely impact on the organization and the industry?
3 Who are the buyers and what is the extent of their power with regard to the organization?
4 Who are our suppliers and what is their power with regard to the organization?
5 Who are our present and potential competitors and how intense is (or will be) present and potential competitive rivalry?

Each of these key areas can in turn be analysed to determine the intensity of competition:

1 *Potential entrants.* Threat of entry depends on the extent of barriers to entry, so:
  ● Is the potential customer base sufficient to support new operations?
  ● How heavy is the capital investment requirement in the industry? Is finance available?
  ● Is there a strong brand image to overcome?
  ● How costly will be access to distribution channels?
  ● What operating cost advantages might existing competitors hold (e.g. experienced staff, patent protection, etc.)?
  ● Is there governmental/legislative protection afforded to existing organizations?
  ● How vigorously will existing operators react against new entry attempts?
2 *Substitute products/services* will be more prevalent if:
  ● customers perceive other offers to perform the same function as ours;
  ● substitute products offer higher value for money;
  ● substitute products earn higher profits.
3 *Buyer power* is likely to be high if:
  ● there is a concentration of buyers;
  ● there are alternative sources of supply;
  ● buyers have access to useful information and tend to shop around;
  ● there is a threat of backward integration if the buyer does not obtain satisfactory supplies and prices.
4 *Supplier power* is likely to be high if:
  ● there is a concentration of suppliers;
  ● the costs of switching from one supplier to another are high;
  ● suppliers are likely to integrate forward if they do not obtain the price/profits they seek;
  ● the organization has little countervailing power.
5 *Intensity of rivalry* will be greater if:
  ● competitors are of equal size and are seeking dominance;
  ● the market is mature and subject to 'shake out' activities;
  ● high fixed costs provoke price wars to maintain capacity;
  ● product homogeneity necessitates activity to maintain share;
  ● new influxes of capacity have created excess capacity;
  ● high 'exit' barriers (legal constraints; high cost non-transferable plant and equipment; emotional commitment) exist.

SOURCE: Richardson and Richardson (1989), pp. 52–3

Taken together, these factors represent the forces governing the nature and intensity of competition within an industry, and they are the background against which the choice of a generic strategy should be made. The key features of these five forces are shown in Figure 10.3.

In identifying these three generic strategies, Porter suggests that the firms that pursue a particular strategy aimed at the same market or market segment make up a *strategic group*. It is the firm that then manages to pursue the strategy most effectively that will generate the greatest profits. Thus in the case of firms pursuing a low-cost strategy, it is the firm that ultimately achieves the lowest cost that will do best.

10.4 PORTER'S THREE GENERIC COMPETITIVE STRATEGIES

Overall Cost Leadership

By pursuing a strategy of cost leadership, the organization concentrates upon achieving the lowest costs of production and distribution so that it has the *capability* of setting its prices at a lower level than its competitors. Whether it then chooses to do this depends on its objectives and its perception of the market. Saunders (1987, p. 12) for example, points to IBM and Boeing, both of which are cost leaders who have chosen to use their lower costs not to reduce prices but rather to generate higher returns which have subsequently been invested in marketing, R & D and manufacturing as a means of maintaining or strengthening their position. More commonly, however, firms that set out to be cost leaders then use this lower cost base to reduce prices and in this way build market share – Amstrad in the 1980s was a case in point.

Although cost reduction has always been an important element of competitive strategy, Porter has commented that it became increasingly popular in the 1970s, largely because of a greater awareness of the experience curve concept. For it to succeed, he suggests that:

> Cost leadership requires aggressive construction of efficient-scale facilities, vigorous pursuit of cost reductions from experience, tight cost and overhead control, avoidance of marginal customer accounts, and cost minimisation in areas like R & D, service, sales force, advertising, and so on (1980, p. 35).

In tackling costs the strategist therefore needs to recognize in advance the potential complexity of the task, since the evidence suggests that true cost leaders generally achieve this by very tight and consistent control across *all* areas of the business, including engineering, purchasing, manufacturing, distribution and marketing. An important additional element of course is the scale of operations and the scope that exists for economies of scale. However, scale alone does not necessarily lead to lower costs; rather it provides management with an *opportunity* to learn how the triad of technology, management and labour can be used more effectively (see Chapter 12). Whether these opportunities are then seized depends on the management stance and determination to take advantage of the *potential* that exists for cost cutting. Research has shown, for example, that the Japanese are most adept at gaining experience, doing so at a faster rate than the Americans, who in turn are faster than the Europeans.

While the experience curve (see pp. 450–2) can provide the basis for cost reductions, manufacturers can also turn to a variety of other areas including:

1 *the globalization of operations*, including brands, in order to benefit from the economies that are not possible by operating purely on a regional basis;
2 *concentrating the manufacturing effort* in one or two very large plants in countries such as South Korea, Taiwan, and the Philippines which, currently at least, offer a low-cost base;

3 *modifying designs* to simplify the manufacturing process and make use of new materials;

4 *achieving greater labour effectiveness* by investing in new plant and processes.

The potential benefits of being a low-cost producer are quite obviously significant, since the organization is then in a far stronger position to resist all five competitive forces, out-perform its rivals, and erect barriers to entry that will help protect the organization's long-term position. In practice, however, many organizations find the long-term pursuit and maintenance of a cost-leadership strategy to be difficult. The Japanese, for example, based much of their success in the 1960s on aggressive cost management but then found that because of a combination of rising domestic costs and the emergence of new and even lower-cost competitors such as Taiwan, the position was not necessarily tenable in the long term. Although this realization coincided in many cases with a desire on the part of firms to move further up market where the scope for premium pricing is greater, the Japanese experience helps to illustrate the potential danger of an overreliance upon cost leadership. It is largely because of this that many organizations opt sooner or later for an alternative policy such as that of differentiation.

The difficulties of maintaining a cost-leadership position were also illustrated in the late 1980s and early 1990s in the UK grocery retailing sector where the low cost position had been occupied with some considerable success for a number of years by Kwik Save. The organization came under attack from an aggressive new German entrant to the market, Aldi, and from the Danish company, Netto. Faced with this, Kwik Save was forced into deciding whether to place greater emphasis on differentiation.

The effect of Aldi's entrance was not felt just by Kwik Save. Others, such as Sainsbury and Tesco, both of which had for a number of years pursued with considerable success a strategy of differentiation, were also forced to respond, albeit in a less direct way. In part, this need to respond can be seen as virtually inevitable in any mature market where the opportunities for substantial growth are limited and a new entrant is therefore able to gain sales only at the expense of firms already in the market. (This is sometimes referred to as a zero-sum game in that one organization's gain is necessarily another organization's loss.)

It is largely because of the difficulties of maintaining the lowest cost position over time and the vulnerability to a price-led attack that many organizations view cost leadership with a degree of caution and opt instead for one or other of Porter's generic strategies. Most frequently this proves to be differentiation.

Differentiation

By pursuing a strategy of differentiation, the organization gives emphasis to a particular element of the marketing mix that is seen by customers to be important and that as a result provides a meaningful basis for competitive advantage. The firm might therefore attempt to be the quality leader (Mercedes Benz with cars, Bang and Olufsen with hi-fi, and Marks and Spencer with food), service leader (McDonald's), marketing leader (the Japanese with cars), or the technological leader (Makita with rechargeable power tools in the early 1980s, and Dolby with noise suppression circuits for tape decks).

Differentiation can also be achieved by means of the brand image and packaging, a ploy that is particularly suited to mature markets in which the products are for the most part physically indistinguishable. This might arguably include cigarettes and beer where blind tests have shown that even highly brand loyal customers experience difficulties in identifying their favourite brand. The significance of labels and brand images, and hence their potential for differentiation, is also shown in the fashion clothing industry where brand names and logos such as Benetton, Nike and Lacoste are often prominently displayed and, by virtue of the images associated with them, used as the basis for premium pricing.

In discussing how a strategy of differentiation can be developed most effectively, Saunders (1987, p. 13) discusses the airlines industry:

> Perhaps one of the most difficult differentiation tasks is faced by the airlines who, because of bilateral agreements, are all forced to fly the same aeroplanes, to the same destinations, and charge the same prices. But as any international traveller will know, there is wide divergence in the services offered by the airlines. Singapore Airlines, Thai Airlines and Japanese Airlines have all gained their high reputation on the basis of the inflight services they provide. Some of these are on the basis of better food with more choice, free movies, many accessories freely available to passengers, and slightly more modern aircraft, but it all depends upon the attentiveness and professionalism of their cabin crews.

Differentiation can, however, prove costly if the basis for differentiation that is chosen subsequently proves to be inappropriate. Sony, for example, developed the Betamax format for its video recorders, but ultimately found that the market preferred JVC's VHS system. Despite this, differentiation is potentially a very powerful basis for strategic development, as companies such as Marks and Spencer and Sainsbury have demonstrated. Its potential is also illustrated by a McGraw-Hill study of industrial buying which estimated that most buyers would require incentives that equated to a price reduction of between 8 and 10 per cent before considering a switch to a new supplier. In commenting on this, Baker (1985, p. 110) suggests that:

> Assuming this applies to the average product with a minimum of objective differentiation, it is clear that sellers of highly differentiated products can require an even larger premium. Given higher margins the firm following a differentiated strategy is able to plough back more into maintaining the perception of differentiation through a policy of new product development, promotional activity, customer service, etc., and thereby strengthen the barriers to entry for would-be competitors.

It should be apparent from this that if a strategy of differentiation is to succeed there is a need for a very different set of skills and attitudes than is suited to cost leadership. Instead of a highly developed set of cost control skills, the strategist needs to be far more innovative and flexible so that me-too companies are kept at a distance.

Focus

The third of the generic strategies identified by Porter involves the organization in concentrating its efforts upon one or more narrow market segments, rather than pursuing a broader based strategy. By doing this the firm is able to build a greater in-depth knowledge of each of the segments, as well as creating barriers to entry by virtue of its specialist reputation. Having established itself, the firm will typically then, depending upon the specific demands of the market, develop either a cost-based or differentiated strategy. Among those that have used this approach successfully, at least in the short term, are both Laura Ashley and Land Rover. Other firms that have used a focused strategy are Morgan with cars, Steinway with pianos, and in its early days, Amstrad with microcomputers which were designed for those with a low level of computer literacy and those who wanted low-price, easy-to-use word processing equipment.

One of the biggest problems faced by companies adopting this approach stems paradoxically from its potential for success, since as the organization increases in size, there is a tendency both to outgrow the market and to lose the immediacy of contact that is often needed. As a general rule, therefore, a focused strategy is often best suited to smaller firms since it is typically these which have the flexibility to respond quickly to the specialized needs of small segments.

Specializing in this way also enables the organization to achieve at least some of the benefits of the other two strategies since, although in absolute terms the scale of operations may be limited, the organization may well have the largest economies of scale *within* the chosen segment. Equally, the greater the degree of concentration upon a target market, the more specialized is the firm's reputation and hence the greater the degree of perceived product differentiation.

Although Porter presents competitive strategies in this way, many companies succeed not by a blind adherence to any one approach, but rather by a combination of ideas. In commenting on this, Saunders (1987, p. 14) has suggested that:

> It is apparent ... that some leading companies have not succeeded by being exclusively cost leaders, differentiators or focused. Many top companies are both cost leaders and differentiators. The buying power and expertise of Marks and Spencer make it a low cost company but it trades on quality, service and its brand name; IBM is a cost leader which also trades on customer service and Boeing has lower costs than any other aeroplane manufacturer but the 747, its most profitable product, is unique. Many of the successful low volume manufacturers complement differentiation with a clear focus. For example, Jaguar, Land Rover and Morgan in the automobile industry, and J. C. Bamford in earthmoving. Lastly, Amstrad's success needs explaining in terms of both cost leadership and focus. Its success in the hi-fi market has been based on integrated systems at the bottom of the market which the major Japanese manufacturers were neglecting. Equally, although Amstrad were cost leaders, it was its identification of segment needs which enabled it to become a major supplier with the audacity to challenge IBM.

It follows from this that the identification, development and maintenance of a competitive advantage, and hence a strong selling proposition, is at the very heart of an effective marketing strategy. In practice though, many organizations find this to be a difficult exercise. Without an advantage, however, the stark reality is that the organization runs the risk of drifting into the strategic twilight zone of being a middle of the roader or, in Porter's terms, 'stuck in the middle'.

10.5 IDENTIFYING POTENTIAL COMPETITIVE ADVANTAGES

Making Use of the Value Chain

In discussing competitive advantage, Porter (1985, Ch. 2) suggests that it:

> grows out of the value a firm is able to create for its buyers that exceeds the firm's cost of creating it. Value is what the buyer is willing to pay, and superior stems from offering lower prices than competitors for equivalent benefits or providing unique benefits that more than offset a higher price. There are two basic types of competitive advantage: cost leadership and differentiation.

He goes on to suggest that a convenient tool for identifying and understanding the potential competitive advantages possessed by a firm is by means of value chain analysis. In making this comment, Porter gives recognition to the way in which a firm is a collection of activities that are performed to design, produce, market, deliver and support its product.

The value chain disaggregates a firm into nine strategically significant activities so that the strategist is more easily able to understand the source and behaviour of costs in the specific business and industry, and the existing and potential sources of differentiation; these nine value activities consist of five primary activities and four support activities. (The value chain is also discussed on pp. 502–4.)

The five *primary* activities that Porter refers to are concerned with the process of bringing raw materials into the organization and then modifying them in some way as a prelude to distribution, marketing and servicing them. The *support* activities, which take place at the same time, are then concerned with procurement, technology development, human resource management, and the firm's infra-structure (i.e. its management, planning, finance, accounting, and legal affairs). The strategist's job therefore involves focusing upon the levels of cost and performance in each of the nine value areas in order to identify any opportunities for improvement. The extent to which this is achieved is a measure of competitive advantage.

In searching for competitive advantage through the value chain, Porter also gives emphasis to the need to look outside the organization and to consider the value chains of supplier, distributors and customers, since improvements to each of these will also help in the search for an advantage. As an example of this, a supplier or distributor might be helped to reduce costs, with all or part of the savings then being passed to the company and used as another means of gaining cost leadership. Equally, an organization might work closely with its suppliers to ensure that particular levels of quality or service are achieved. Marks and Spencer, for example, has traditionally worked very closely with its suppliers to ensure that quality levels are maintained. Similarly, the major food retailers work with their suppliers in areas such as product development and cost control. In each case, the rationale is the same – that of achieving a competitive advantage.

Although the value chain is generally recognized to be a useful framework for searching systematically for greater competitive advantage, its usefulness in practice has been shown to vary from one industry to another. Recognition of this has led the Boston Consulting Group to develop a matrix in which they distinguish between four types of industry (see Figure 10.4).

FIGURE 10.4
The Boston Consulting Group's strategic environment matrix

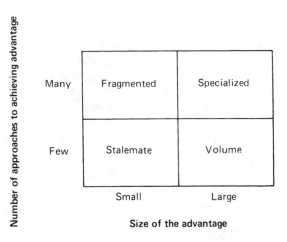

The two dimensions they identify in doing this are concerned with the *size of the competitive advantage* and the *number of approaches to gaining advantage*. The characteristics of the four types of industry are outlined in Figure 10.5.

It can be seen from this that the scope for benefiting from cost or performance opportunities can vary considerably from one type of industry to another. In some industries, for example, it will be the case that the only opportunities for advantage are small and easily copied. Faced with this, an organization needs to institutionalize the process for searching for new ideas so that although it is unlikely ever to gain a significant or long-term advantage, it benefits from a whole series of small and constantly updated advantages.

FIGURE 10.5
Industry type and the scope for competitive advantage

Volume industry. A volume industry is one in which organizations can typically gain only a few, but generally large, advantages. In the construction equipment industry, for example, firms can pursue either the low-cost position or the highly differentiated position, and succeed in either case. Profitability is therefore a function both of size and market share.

Stalemated industry. Here there are few potential competitive advantages and those that do exist are generally small. An example of this is the steel industry where scope for differentiation is limited, as indeed are the opportunities for significant cost reduction. In these circumstances, size is unrelated to profitability.

Fragmented industry. A fragmented industry is one in which companies have numerous opportunities for differentiation, although each is of limited value. The hairdressing industry typically exhibits this characteristic where hairdressers can be differentiated in a wide variety of ways but increases in market share tend to be small. Profitability is rarely related to size and both small and large operations can be equally profitable or unprofitable.

Specialized industry. In a specialized industry the opportunities for differentiation are numerous and the payoffs from each can be significant. An example would be the specialist machine tool industry where machinery is made for specific customers and market segments. Here profitability and size are rarely related.

Developing a Sustainable Advantage

This need to understand the bases of competition and the way in which competitive advantage is achieved has also been referred to by Bruce Henderson (1981, p. 8), the founder of the Boston Consulting Group:

> A market can be viewed in many different ways and a product can be used in many different ways. Each time the product-market pairing is varied, the relative competitive strength is varied too. Many businessmen do not recognise that a key element in strategy is choosing the competitor whom you wish to challenge, as well as choosing the market segment and product characteristics with which you will compete.

The problem faced by many companies, therefore, is not how to *gain* a competitive advantage, but how to *sustain* it for any length of time. Most marketers are, for example, fully aware of the profit potential associated with a strategy based on, say, premium quality or technological leadership. The difficulty that is all too often faced in practice, however, is how to guard against predators and capitalize on these benefits *over the long term*. Business history is full of examples of companies that having invested in a particular strategy, then fall victim to a larger organization. The question faced by many marketing strategists at one time or another is therefore how best to sustain a competitive advantage. In discussing this, Wensley (1987, p. 34) has suggested that there are three possible approaches:

1 advantages residing in the organization;
2 advantages stemming from specific functional areas;
3 advantages based on relationships with external entities.

These points were discussed in some detail in Figure 2.4.

The issue of how to develop and sustain a competitive advantage has also been discussed in detail by Davidson (1987, p. 153) 'Competitive advantage', he suggests,

> is achieved whenever you do something better than competitors. If that something is important to consumers, or if a number of small advantages can be combined, you have an *exploitable* competitive advantage. One or more competitive advantages are usually necessary in order to develop a winning strategy, and this in turn should enable a company to achieve above-average growth and profits.

For Davidson, the eight most significant potential competitive advantages are:

1 *a superior product benefit* such as the application by the Japanese of solid state technology in televisions in the 1970s,
2 *a perceived advantage*: Marlboro, with its aggressively masculine image featuring cowboys, holds a 22 per cent share of the US cigarette market; the brand is well marketed but there is no reason to believe the cigarettes are objectively superior in consumer acceptance;
3 *low-cost operations* as the result of a combination of high productivity, low overheads, low labour costs, better purchasing skills, a limited product range, or low cost distribution;
4 *legal advantage* in the form of patents, copyright, sole distributorships, or a protected position;
5 *superior contacts*;
6 *superior knowledge* as the result of more effective market research, a better understanding of costs, or superior information systems;
7 *scale advantages*;
8 *offensive attitudes* or, as Procter & Gamble label it, an attitude of competitive toughness and a determination to win.

A fundamental understanding of the significance of competitive advantage has long been at the heart of Marks and Spencer's strategies. Their performance has consistently outstripped the vast majority of retailers and has led not just to the company maintaining its position as the market leader in the clothing market, but also to its enormously successful development of food retailing. The company has concentrated on developing a series of competitive advantages which, taken together, represent a strong selling proposition, provide consumers with a powerful reason to buy, and put competitors at a disadvantage. These advantages are summarized in Illustration 10.1.

Creating Barriers to Entry

Although the development and exploitation of competitive advantage is at the heart of any worthwhile marketing strategy, relatively few organizations prove to be successful at doing this over the long term. Innovators are almost invariably followed by imitators and, because of this, few manage to maintain a truly dominant market position. Tagamet, for example, one of the best-selling and most revolutionary drugs of all time, was quickly eclipsed by an imitator, Zantac. Equally, Thorn-EMI with its body scanner and Xerox with a series of innovations which helped develop and define the personal computer are just two companies which, having innovated, failed to capitalize upon their ideas.

The issue that emerges from these and a host of other examples is straightforward: all too often, the resources devoted to *creating* a significant competitive advantage are of little value unless that advantage is subsequently aggressively exploited and sustained. In order to do this and benefit fully from the innovation, Geroski (1996, p. 11) argues that planners need to focus upon understanding two areas:

- the market's *barriers to entry* – these are the structural features of a market which protect the established companies within a market and which allow them to raise prices above costs without attracting new entrants; and
- *mobility barriers*, which protect companies in one part of a market from other companies which are operating in different parts of the same market.

The bases of entry and mobility barriers fall into one of three principal categories:

Illustration 10.1: Marks and Spencer and its Use of Competitive Advantage to Create Distinctive Competences

Marks and Spencer have consistently been one of the most successful organizations in the UK retail sector. This success has been due to a combination of factors, but in particular to a well-developed marketing strategy that builds on a series of competitive advantages that have been used to create several distinctive competences.

Sources of competitive advantage	Competition most affected	Distinctive competence
Multiple operation	Independents	
Systems retailer	Independents	
Simplified business	Department stores	
Emphasis on quality 100 per cent own label	Most other retailers	Control
Involvement in product technology	Multiples	
Emphasis on economic rather than market planning	Many multiples and coops	Management of change
Family influence	Some 'corporate' multiples	
Increase in income and mobility of customers	Independents	
Theory Z company	Most employers	
Attitude to staff	Many other retailers	Human relations
Community involvement	Some retailers	
Returns policy	Many other retailers	
Public image	Most retailers	

Source: Davies, G. (1988) Marks & Spencer UK Case Study, Manchester Metropolitan University

---

1 *product differentiation advantages*, which lead to high switching costs and which stem from:

- superior quality;
- superior levels of service;
- strong brand names;
- high levels of brand loyalty;
- distribution strengths;
- product interrelationships which would mean that a change from one product to another would have consequences for other product choices.

2 *absolute cost advantages*, which allow prices to be set below the levels of competitors. The bases of this include:

- a consistently high investment in R & D;
- high levels of process technology and production efficiency;
- patents;
- privileged access to scarce resources;
- vertical integration;
- tariff barriers;
- distribution access and efficiency;
- cartels.

3 *scale-related advantages*, which emerge as the result of high production and sales levels.

Because entry and mobility barriers rarely emerge in any natural way, the marketing planner needs to think strategically about the ways in which they can best be created and exploited. In doing this, there are three main types of strategy that can be used: sunk costs, the squeezing of new entrants, and raising competitors' costs.

The first of these, the use of *sunk costs*, involves the firm locking itself into a market in such a way that any competitor then finds it difficult to force the firm out. This is done most frequently by a heavy investment in plant and equipment, since this also provides the basis for economies of scale and hence absolute cost advantages. In discussing this, Geroski (op cit., p. 12) cites the example of cross-Channel travel:

> Eurotunnel has an enormous potential competitive advantage over the ferry companies it competes against, since once built the tunnel can never be redeployed on another route. Whatever else they may do, it is certain that the ferry companies cannot launch a price war with a reasonable hope of driving the tunnel out of the market.

The second and third strategies are to a large extent interrelated, and involve *squeezing competitors* and *raising their costs* so that it becomes more difficult for them to achieve a positive return. Among the most obvious of the ways in which this can be done is by raising advertising levels, increasing R & D expenditures, developing fighting brands, and limiting their access to distribution channels.

Taken together, these strategies are capable of providing an organization with a far stronger long term market position than would otherwise be the case. However, it needs to be remembered that some of the steps that an existing player might take might appear at first sight to be irrational in that they have the effect of raising the firm's costs without necessarily generating additional revenue. However, when they do succeed, they can be justified by the way in which the existing revenue stream is protected; it is this which to a large extent provides the rationale for investment in entry and mobility barriers.

10.6 THE INFLUENCE OF MARKET POSITION ON STRATEGY

In discussing how best to formulate marketing strategy, we have focused so far on the sorts of model and approach to planning that can help to formalize the analytical process. In making use of models such as these the strategist needs to pay explicit attention to a series of factors, including the organization's objectives and resources, managerial attitudes to risk, the structure of the market, competitors' strategies and, very importantly, the organization's position within the market. The significance of market position and its often very direct influence upon strategy has been discussed in detail by a wide variety of writers, most of whom suggest classifying competitive position along a spectrum from market leader to market nichers:

- *Market leader.* In the majority of industries there is one firm which is generally recognized to be the leader. It typically has the largest market share, and by virtue of its pricing, advertising intensity, distribution coverage, technological advance, and rate of new product introductions, it determines the nature, pace and bases of competition. It is this dominance which typically provides the benchmark for other companies in the industry.
- *Market challengers and followers.* Firms with a slightly smaller market share can adopt one of two stances. They may choose to adopt an aggressive stance and attack other firms, including the market leader, in an attempt to gain share and perhaps dominance (*market challengers*), or they may adopt a less aggressive stance in order to maintain the status quo (*market followers*).
- *Market nichers.* Virtually every industry has a series of small firms which survive, and indeed often prosper, by choosing to specialize in parts of the market which are too limited in size and potential to be of real interest to larger firms; a case in point would be Morgan specializing in traditional sports cars. By concentrating their efforts in this way, market nichers are able to build up specialist market knowledge and avoid expensive head-on fights with larger companies.

This approach to classification has in turn led to a considerable discussion of the strategic alternatives for leaders, challengers and nichers, with numerous analogies being drawn between business strategy and military strategy. The idea has been to show how the ideas of military strategists, and in particular Von Clausewitz, Sun-Tzu and Liddell-Hart, might be applied to the alternatives open to a company intent on gaining or retaining a competitive advantage. Within this section we will therefore examine some of these ideas and show how market leaders might defend their current position, how challengers might attempt to seize share, and how followers and nichers are affected by this; an overview of how this might be done appears in Figure 10.6.

FIGURE 10.6
Leaders, followers, challengers and market nichers

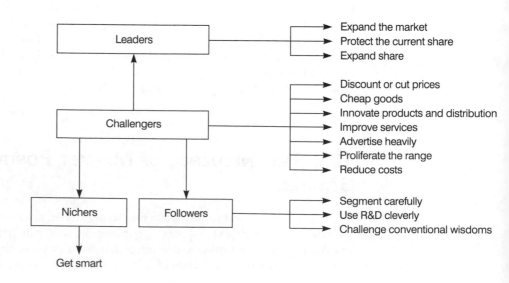

10.7 STRATEGIES FOR MARKET LEADERS

Although a position of market leadership has undoubted attractions both in terms of the scope that often exists to influence others and a possibly higher return on investment, leaders have all too often in the past proved to be vulnerable in the face of an attack from a challenger or when faced with the need for a major technological change. If therefore a market leader is to remain as the dominant company, it needs to defend its position constantly. In doing this, there are three major areas to which the marketing strategist needs to pay attention:

1 how best to expand the total market;
2 how to protect the organization's current share of the market;
3 how to increase market share.

A summary of the ways in which leaders might do this appears in Figure 10.7.

FIGURE 10.7
Strategies for market leaders

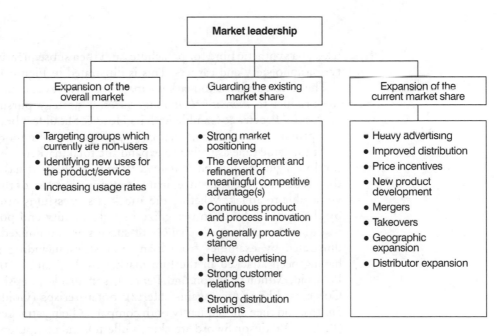

Of these, it is an *expansion of the overall market* from which the market leader typically stands to gain the most. It follows from this that the strategist needs to search for new users, new uses and greater usage levels of his or her firm's products. This can be done in a variety of ways. In the 1960s and 1970s, for example, Honda increased its sales by targeting groups that traditionally had not bought motorcycles. These groups, which included commuters and women, were seen to offer enormous untapped potential. The company unlocked this by developing a range of small, economic and lightweight machines which they then backed with a series of advertising campaigns giving emphasis to their convenience and style. Moving into the 1980s, the strategy began to change yet again as the company recognized the potential for selling motorcycles almost as an adjunct to fashion. Styling therefore became far more important. This repositioning was then taken several steps further in the late 1980s as Honda, along with other manufacturers, began targeting the middle-aged executive market with a series of larger motorcycles that were supported by advertising campaigns giving emphasis to the re-creation of youthful values.

As a second stage the strategist might search for *new uses* for the product. Perhaps the most successful example of this is Du Pont's Nylon which was first

FIGURE 10.8
Nylon's product life cycle

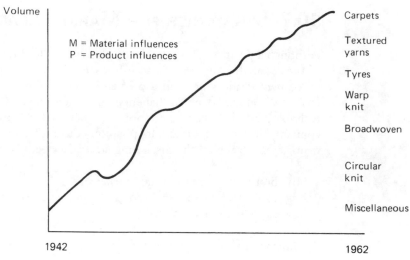

SOURCE: Adapted from Yale (1964), p. 33

used as a synthetic fibre for parachutes and then subsequently for stockings, shirts, tyres, upholstery and carpets. This is illustrated in Figure 10.8.

The third approach to market expansion involves encouraging *existing users* of the product to *increase their usage rates*, a strategy pursued with considerable success by Procter & Gamble with its Head & Shoulders brand of shampoo which was promoted on the basis that two applications were more effective than one.

At the same time as trying to expand the total market, the market leader should not lose sight of the need to *defend its market share*. It has long been recognized that leaders represent a convenient target since, because of their size, they are often vulnerable to attack. Whether the attack is successful is often determined largely by the leader's ability to recognize its vulnerability and position itself in such a way that the challenger's chances of success are minimized. The need for this is illustrated by examples from many industries including photography (Kodak having been attacked in the film market by Fuji and in the camera market by Polaroid, Minolta, Nikon and Pentax); soft drinks (Pepsi Cola attacking Coca Cola); care hire (Avis against Hertz), potato crisps (Golden Wonder attacking Smiths, and then subsequently both companies being attacked by Walker's), razors (Bic and Wilkinson Sword attacking Gillette), and computers (IBM being attacked by, among others, Apple and Amstrad).

Although there are obvious dangers in generalizing, the most successful strategy for a leader intent on fighting off attacks such as these lies in the area of continuous innovation. This, Kotler (1988, p. 321) argues, involves the leader refusing

> to be content with the way things are and leading the industry in new-product ideas, customer services, distribution effectiveness, and cost cutting. It keeps increasing its competitive effectiveness and value to customer. The leader applies the 'military principle of the offensive': the commander exercises initiative, sets the pace, and exploits enemy weaknesses. The best defence is a good offence. The dominant firm, even when it does not launch offensives, must at least guard all of its fronts and not leave any exposed flanks. It must keep its costs down, and its prices must be consonant with the value customers see in the brand. The leader must 'plug holes' so that attackers do not jump in.

Among the ways in which this can be done in the consumer goods sector at least is by producing a product in several forms (e.g. liquid soap as well as bars of soap) and in various sizes (small, medium, large and economy) to tie up as much shelf space as possible.

Although the cost of 'plugging holes' in this way is often high, the cost of failing to do so and being forced out of a product or market segment can often be infinitely higher. As an example of this, Kotler cites the camera market and the way in which Kodak withdrew from the 35 mm sector because its product was losing money. The Japanese subsequently found a way of making 35 mm cameras profitably at a low price and took share away from Kodak's cheaper cameras.

Similarly, in the United States, the major car manufacturers paid too little attention in the 1960s and early 1970s to the small car sector because of the difficulties of making them at a profit. Both the Japanese (Toyota, Mazda and Honda) and the Germans (Volkswagen) took advantage of this lack of domestic competition and developed the small car sector very profitably. The long-term consequence of this has been that the domestic manufacturers, having initially conceded this market sector, have subsequently entered into a series of joint ventures with the Japanese (e.g. Ford with Mazda, General Motors with Toyota, Isuzo, and Suzuki, and Chrysler with Mitsubishi).

The third course of action open to market leaders intent on remaining leaders involves *expanding market share*. This can typically be done in a variety of ways including by means of heavier advertising, improved distribution, price incentives, new products and, as the brewers demonstrated in the 1970s, by mergers and take-overs.

It should be apparent from what has been said so far that leadership involves the development and pursuit of a consistently proactive strategy, something which Pascale has touched upon; this is discussed in Illustration 10.2.

Illustration 10.2: Change, Transformation and a Market Focus: Reasserting Market Leadership

Three of the best known and most successful organizational change programmes over the past decade have taken place at British Airways ('from Bloody Awful to Bloody Awesome'), Grand Met and SmithKline Beecham. In each case, a slow-moving and increasingly unsuccessful organization has been refocused and transformed into a marketing leader. However, the problems of achieving transformation *and maintaining* a successful profile are highlighted by the way in which only five years after the publication of Peters and Waterman's 1982 bestseller *In Search of Excellence*, all but 14 of its 43 'excellent' companies had either grown weaker or were declining rapidly.

In commenting on this, Richard Pascale (1990) argues that too few managers really understand what is involved in transforming an organization. To him, transformation involves not only a discontinuous shift in an organization's capability, but also the much more difficult task of sustaining that shift. Faced with the need for change, he suggests, companies come to a fork in the road. About 80 per cent take the easy route, stripping themselves 'back to basics', searching for the latest tools and techniques and going on to risk stagnation or decline. Only a fifth of companies take the much tougher, alternative route. This involves three big steps: the first he refers to as 'inquiring into their underlying paradigm' (that is, questioning the way they do everything, including how managers think); attacking the problems systematically on all fronts, notably strategy, operations, organization and culture; and 'reinventing' themselves in such a way that the transformation becomes self-sustaining. It is only in this way that truly intellectual learning is matched by the emotional learning that is needed and transformation truly becomes embedded in the organization.

The PIMS Study and the Pursuit of Market Share

The significance of market share, and in particular its influence upon return on investment, has long been recognized, and has been pointed to by a variety of studies over the past 25 years, the best known of which is the PIMS (Profit Impact of Market Strategy) research. (Aspects of the PIMS research are also discussed on pp. 104–7.)

The aim of the PIMS programme, which now has a database of more than 2800 businesses, has been to identify the most significant determinants of profitability. The factors that have shown themselves to be persistently the most influential are:

1 *competitive position* (including market share and relative product quality);
2 *production structure* (including investment intensity and the productivity of operations;
3 the *attractiveness of the served market* (as shown by its growth rate and customers' characteristics.

Taken together, these factors explain 65–70 per cent of the variability in profitability among the firms in the PIMS data base. By examining the determinants of profitability it is possible to address a series of strategic questions such as:

● What rate of profit and cash flow is normal for this type of business?
● What profit and cashflow outcomes can be expected if the business continues with its present strategy?
● How will future performance be affected by a change in strategy?

One of the key notions underlying strategic marketing management is, as we have already emphasized, that of the relative position of a firm among its competitors, particularly with regard to unit costs, profitability and market share. This is reflected in the PIMS approach which is illustrated in Figures 10.9 and 10.10.

The respective contribution of each of the variables in Figure 10.10 to overall profitability is estimated by means of a multiple regression model. This allows the impact of weak variables to be offset by strong variables; a low market share might,

FIGURE 10.9
Some PIMS linkages

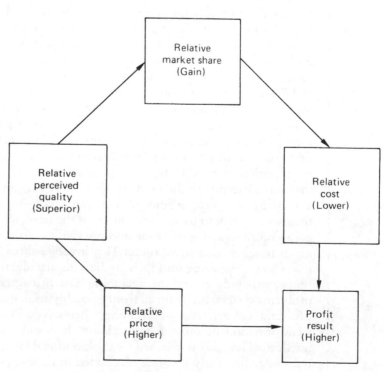

SOURCE: Buzzell and Gale (1987), p. 81

for example, be offset by high product quality. Once the model has been applied to a given company, it can then be used to assess the relative strengths and weaknesses of competitors in order to identify the best source of competitive advantage. From the viewpoint of the marketing strategist, this has most typically been seen in terms of the organization's relative market share, a factor which has been given considerable emphasis by successive PIMS reports: 'The average ROI for businesses with under 10 per cent market share was about 9 per cent . . . On the average, a difference of 10 percentage points in market share is accompanied by a difference of about 5 points in pretax ROI.' The study has also shown that businesses with a market share of more than 40 per cent achieve ROIs of 30 per cent, or three times that of firms with shares under 10 per cent.

In the light of these findings, it is not at all surprising that many organizations have pursued a goal of share increases, since it should lead not just to greater profits but also to greater profitability (that is, return on investment). Williams Holdings, for example, has consistently – and successfully – pursued an acquisition and marketing strategy that reflects this by focusing upon current or potential market leaders (see Illustration 10.3).

Illustration 10.3: Williams Holdings and Its Pursuit of Market Leadership

In just eight years, Williams Holdings PLC, under the chairmanship of Nigel Rudd, grew from an annual turnover of £6 million to more than £1000 million. This was achieved by aggressive management of the firm's portfolio and a series of carefully targeted acquisitions.

The company, which now operates throughout Europe and the United States, has relentlessly pursued an objective of growth by focusing much of its efforts on 'businesses which are pre-eminent in their sphere of operations' (Annual Report for 1989, p. 13). The company's publicly stated policies include:

- owning businesses which have significant shares in their relevant markets;
- generating above average margins and cashflow to enable the companies to market their products and services aggressively;
- to invest capital consistently to create the position of lowest cost producer.

Source: Williams Holdings PLC Annual Report, 1989, pp. 13–14

Although the findings and conclusions of the PIMS study have an initial and pragmatic appeal, the general approach has been subjected to an increasing amount of critical comment in recent years. In particular, critics have highlighted:

- measurement errors;
- apparent deficiencies in the model;
- the interpretations of the findings.

Perhaps the main concern, however, is over the practice of deriving prescriptions about strategy from unsupported causal inferences. It is therefore important in using PIMS data to understand the limitations of the approach. When used in this way the PIMS programme can, its defenders argue, provide valuable insights to effective marketing and corporate strategy. In particular, they point to some of the broad conclusions from the programme which can be summarized as:

1 In the long-run, the single most important factor affecting performance is the quality of an enterprise's products/services relative to those of its competitors.
2 Market share and profitability are strongly related:

- ROI increases steadily as market share increases;
- enterprises having relatively large market shares tend to have above-average rates of investment turnover;
- the ratio of marketing expenses to sales revenue tends to be lower for enterprises having high market shares.

The PIMS programme has demonstrated the linkages among superior relative quality, higher relative prices, gains in market share, lower relative costs and higher profitability. These linkages are portrayed in Figures 10.9 and 10.10 which indicate the causal role that relative quality plays in influencing business performance.

3 High investment intensity acts as a powerful drag on profitability:

- the higher the ratio of investment to sales, the lower the ROI;
- enterprises having high investment intensity tend to be unable to achieve profit margins sufficient to sustain growth.

4 Many dog and wildcat activities generate cash, while many cash cows do not.
5 Vertical integration is a profitable strategy for some kinds of enterprise but not for others.
6 Most of the strategic factors that boost ROI also contribute to long-term value.

FIGURE 10.10
The determinants of profitability

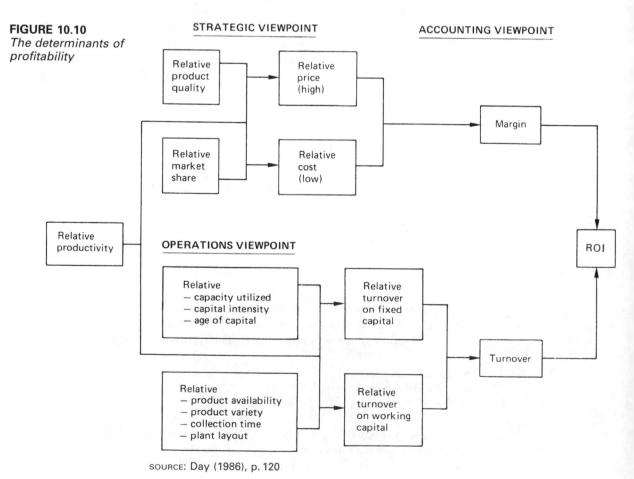

SOURCE: Day (1986), p. 120

Despite these comments, however, the reader should bear in mind the very real reservations that have been expressed about the study. Baker (1985, p. 110), for example, has said that 'one should be cautious about accepting too readily the relationship between profit and market share claimed as the result of the PIMS study which is more the result of flexible definitions than reality'. Similarly, Porter (1980, p. 44) suggests:

> There is *no single relationship* between profitability and market share, unless one conveniently defines the market so that focused or differentiated firms are assigned high market shares in some narrowly defined industries and the industry definitions of cost leadership firms are allowed to stay broad (they must because cost leaders often do not have the largest share in every sub-market). Even shifting industry cannot explain the high returns of firms who have achieved differentiation industry wide and held market shares below that of the industry leader.

A number of other writers have also argued that the study's findings are generally spurious. Hamermesh, et al. (1987) for example, have pointed to numerous successful low-share businesses. Similarly Woo and Cooper (1982) identified 40 low-share businesses with pretax ROIs of 20 per cent or more.

Findings such as these suggest the existence not of a linear relationship between market share and profitability but, in some industries at least, of a V-shaped relationship. This is illustrated in Figure 10.11.

In such an industry there will be one or two highly profitable market leaders, several profitable low-share firms, and a number of medium-share, poorly focused

FIGURE 10.11
The relationship between market share and profitability

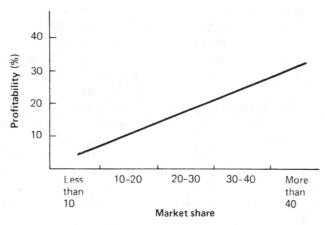

(a) Linear relationship between market share and profitability as indicated by the PIMS findings

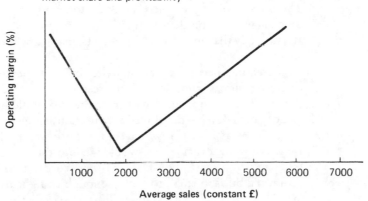

(b) V-shaped relationship between market share and profitability

and far less profitable organizations. This has been commented on by Roach (1981, p. 21):

> The large firms on the V-curve tend to address the entire market, achieving cost advantages and high market share by realising economies of scale. The small competitors reap high profits by focusing on some narrower segments of the business and by developing specialised approaches to production, marketing, and distribution for that segment. Ironically the medium sized competitors at the trough of the V-curve are unable to realise any competitive advantage and often show the poorest profit performance. Trapped in a strategic 'No-Man's Land', they are too large to reap the benefits of more focused competition, yet too small to benefit from the economies of scale that their larger competitors enjoy.

Perhaps the most important point to come from this sort of observation is that the marketing strategist should not blindly pursue market share in the expectation that it will automatically improve profitability. Rather it is the case that the return will depend upon the *type* of strategy pursued. In some cases, for example, the cost of achieving a share gain may far exceed the returns that are possible. There are therefore twelve factors which need to be taken into account in deciding whether to pursue a share gaining strategy:

1 The cost of gaining share and whether this will be higher than the returns that will follow. This is likely to occur in various situations, but most obviously when the market is in or near maturity, since in these circumstances sales (and hence share) can only be gained on the basis of what would typically be a zero sum game (this would in effect lead to a pyrrhic victory in which the benefits of victory are outweighed by the costs of achieving that victory). In other words, the only way in which a company can gain sales is at the expense of someone else in the market. By contrast, when the market is in the growth stage, sales can be gained without the need to pursue a confrontational strategy.

2 When the implication of gaining extra share has a knock-on effect to another part of the organization. This might happen when a firm is already operating at full capacity and any increase would involve a heavy investment in new capacity and the likelihood of achieving a positive ROI is then small.

3 There is already a high degree of loyalty to competitors' products among the customer base and this loyalty can only be broken down at a disproportionately high cost.

4 The company intent on gaining share has few obvious or sustainable competitive advantages and hence a weak selling proposition.

5 The future life cycle of the product or market is likely to be short.

6 An increase in share is likely to lead to the firm running foul of anti-monopoly legislation.

7 The increase in share can only be gained by moving into less appealing and less profitable segments.

8 The pursuit of higher share is likely to spark off a major – and potentially unmanageable – competitive fight.

9 It is unlikely that any gain in share can be maintained for anything other than the short term.

10 By increasing share, a larger competitor begins to perceive the organization as an emerging threat and decides to respond in a way which, assuming the organization had not decided to grow, the two would have co-existed peacefully.

11 The organization has developed a reputation as a specialist or niche operator and any move away from this would compromise brand values and the brand equity.

12 By growing, the organization would fall into a strategic 'no-man's land' in which the firm is too big to be small (in other words, it would no longer be a niche operator), but too small to be big enough to fight off the large players in the market on an equal footing; this is illustrated in Figure 10.11.

In addition, of course, share gaining strategies can also be argued against when the management team has neither the ability nor the *fundamental* willingness to develop and sustain an appropriate and offensive strategy.

These sorts of points have also been referred to by Jacobson and Aaker (1985) who in an article entitled 'Is Market Share All That It's Cracked Up To Be?' raised a series of fundamental questions about the value of chasing share gains. It is, however, possible to identify the two conditions under which higher share generally does lead to higher profits. These are, first, when the company offers a superior quality product which is then sold at a premium price which more than offsets the extra costs of achieving higher quality, and second, when unit costs fall significantly as sales and share increase.

These two points have been developed by Buzzell and Wiersema (1981) who, by using PIMS data, concluded that companies which successfully achieved gains in market share generally out-performed their competitors in three areas: *new product activity, relative product quality*, and *levels of marketing expenditure*. Thus:

1 the successful share gainers developed and added a greater number of new products to their range than their competitors;
2 companies that increased their relative product quality achieved greater share gains than those whose quality stayed constant or declined;
3 those companies which increased their marketing expenditures more rapidly than the rate of market growth gained share;
4 companies that cut their prices more rapidly than competitors rarely – and perhaps surprisingly – did not achieve significant share gains.

10.8 MARKETING STRATEGY AND MILITARY ANALOGIES: LESSONS FOR MARKET LEADERS

The greater intensity of competition that has taken place throughout the world in recent years has led to many managers developing an interest in models of military warfare with a view to identifying any lessons that might be learned and applied to business. From the viewpoint of a market leader intent on defending his position, there are six military defence strategies that can be used: position defence, mobile defence, flanking defence, contraction defence, pre-emptive defence, and counter-offensive defence. However, if military history is to teach the marketing or business strategist anything at all, it has to be that some of these strategies are likely to be far less successful than others.

Position Defence   Arguably one of the consistently least successful methods of defence, the position defence or fortress, relies on the apparent impregnability of a fixed position. Militarily, parallels are often drawn between this and the wartime French Maginot and German Siegfried lines, neither of which achieved their purpose. To overcome a position defence an attacker therefore typically adopts an indirect approach rather than the head-on attack that the defender expects. Among the companies that have adopted a position defence only to see it fail is Land Rover which was attacked by Toyota, Suzuki and Subaru. The company, which had developed a strong international reputation for well-made and very rugged four-wheel drive vehicles, did relatively little in the 1960s and 1970s either in terms of product or market development, and subsequently fell victim to an attack based on a lower price and 'fun' appeal. Rather than responding in an aggressive way to this, Land Rover continued with only small modifications to its strategy of selling primarily to farmers and the military, and was then faced with a second wave attack from Mitsubishi.

There are therefore several lessons to be learned from examples such as this, as Saunders (1987, p. 15) has highlighted:

> A company attempting a fortress defence will find itself retreating from line after line of fortification into shrinking product markets. The stationary company will end up with outdated products and lost markets, undermined by competitors who find superiority in new products in the market place. Even a dominant leader cannot afford to maintain a static defence. It must continually engage in product improvement, line extensions and product proliferations. For instance, giants like Unilever spread their front into related household products; and Coca-Cola, despite having over 50 per cent of the world soft drinks market, has moved aggressively into marketing wines and has diversified into desalination equipment and plastics. These companies defend their territory by breaking it down into units and entrenching in each.

Mobile Defence

The second approach, a mobile defence, is based in part on the ideas discussed by Theodore Levitt in 'Marketing Myopia' (1960), in that rather than becoming preoccupied with the defence of current products and markets through the proliferation of brands, the strategist concentrates upon market broadening and diversification. The rationale for this is to cover new territories that might in the future serve as focal points both for offence and defence. In doing this the intention is to achieve a degree of strategic depth which will enable the firm not just to fight off an attacker, but to retaliate effectively. At the heart of a mobile defence therefore is the need for management to define carefully, and perhaps redefine, the business it is in. Several years ago, for example, the bicycle manufacturer Raleigh redefined its business by recognizing that its future was that of leisure and health rather than that of cheap and generally functional transport. Similarly, Coloroll in the mid 1980s recognized that its future was the home fashion market, including textiles and ceramics, rather than simply the wallpapers that it was making at the time.

However, in pursuing a strategy of market broadening, the marketing stategist should never lose sight of two major principles – the *principle of the objective* (pursue a clearly defined and realistic objective) and the *principle of mass* (focus your efforts upon the enemy's point of weakness). The implications of these are perhaps best understood by considering for a moment the oil industry. Faced with the likelihood of oil reserves being exhausted in the twenty-first century, the oil companies have been encouraged to redefine their business from that of petrol and oil to that of 'energy'. This has led several companies to experiment with, and in some cases invest in, nuclear energy, coal, hydroelectric power, solar energy and wind power. In the majority of cases, however, success has at best been limited and in some instances has diluted the company's mass in the markets it is operating in currently. A strategy of market broadening should therefore be realistic and reflect not just the two principles referred to above but also, and very importantly, company capability.

The second dimension of a mobile defence involves *diversification* into unrelated industries. Among those who have done this, in some cases with considerable success, are the tobacco manufacturers who, faced with a declining market, have moved into industries such as food and financial services, both of which offer greater long-term stability and profits. The net effect of this has been that their vulnerability to predators has been reduced significantly.

Flanking Defence

It has long been recognized that the flank of an organization, be it an army or a company, is often less well protected than other parts. This vulnerability has several implications for the marketing strategist, the most significant of which is that secondary markets should not be ignored. This lesson was learned the hard way in the 1960s by Smith's Crisps, which at the time dominated the potato crisp market. This market consisted primarily of adults, with distribution being achieved mainly through pubs. The children's market was seen by the company to be of secondary importance and it was therefore this flank that Imperial Tobacco's Golden Wonder attacked with a strategy aimed at children. Distribution to this market then took place through newsagents, sweet shops and the grocery trade. The net effect of this was that within just a few years Golden Wonder had taken over as market leader.

This need to monitor closely the organization's flanks is shown also by Birds Eye's experiences in the frozen foods market. Although the company was subjected initially to a head-on attack from Findus, this achieved little. By contrast, a series of flanking moves at a later stage had the effect of changing the market structure in a variety of dramatic ways. These are discussed in Illustration 10.4.

Illustration 10.4: The Frozen Foods Battleground

One of the consistently most aggressive business battlegrounds of the past 30 years has been the market for frozen foods. Pioneered in the UK by Birds Eye, the company in the 1960s held a 60 per cent market share. The remaining 40 per cent was split between Findus with 20 per cent, a number of smaller brands and a few private labels.

The first move in the market was a series of generally half-hearted head-on attacks by Findus which copied Birds Eye's strategy of superior quality – premium price. This was fought off with relative ease. A few years later in the 1970s, however, two rather more successful flanking moves took place, the first by Ross Foods and the second by stores seeking to build their private label portfolios. The private label move concentrated initially upon sectors of the market which were of little real interest to Birds Eye – the low price, moderate quality almost commodity sectors such as peas, fish fingers and burgers. Although these moves were successful, Birds Eye continued to dominate the high-quality end of the market.

Having established themselves in the commodity sector, the private label operators such as Tesco and Sainsbury shifted from a flanking strategy to a head-on attack as they concentrated on moving up-market, strengthening their reputation for frozen foods, and developing new products. At the same time, Ross Foods, which previously had been a very small player with just 2–3 per cent share of the market made use of flanking to displace Findus as the number two brand. It achieved this initially by developing a wide range of reasonable quality products in large economy packs, and then aggressively concentrating upon the private label market. Neither of these sectors was of interest either to Birds Eye or Findus. By the mid 1980s, however, the success of this strategy encouraged Ross to shift from flanking to a series of head-on attacks against Birds Eye. At the same time as this was taking place, a number of other companies were, in Michael Porter's words, jockeying for position. One of the most successful was McCain. Its strategy in the 1970s was straightforward and designed to create a niche. By the early 1980s this had changed to a flanking attack on Birds Eye, Findus and Ross. Towards the end of the 1980s this had changed yet again and began exhibiting all the characteristics of an emerging head-on attack.

The effects of these moves upon market share were significant. Although in 1985 Birds Eye was still the market leader, this was with a reduced share. Ross held 9 per cent of the market, while Findus was firmly in third place. Most dramatically, store private labels held 34 per cent.

Source: Davidson, J. H. (1987) Offensive Marketing, *Penguin, pp. 163–4*

Contraction Defence

There are occasions when, faced with an actual or potential attack, a company will recognize that it has little hope of defending itself fully. It therefore opts for a withdrawal from those segments and geographical areas in which it is most vulnerable or in which it feels there is the least potential. It then concentrates its resources in those areas in which, perhaps by virtue of its mass, it considers itself to be less vulnerable. Militarily, it is a strategy which was used by Russia to great effect in defending itself against Napoleon and, subsequently, Hitler. It was, however, a strategy that was used far less effectively by the British motorcycle industry in the 1960s and 1970s, as Saunders (1987, p. 17) illustrates:

> The British motorcycle industry provides an example of a contracting defence that failed. When the Japanese attacked the moped market, and particularly the markets in South-East Asia, the British retreated and convinced themselves that the Japanese development of the sector would, in the long term, stimulate demand for larger British bikes. The retreat continued through 125 cc bikes, to 250 cc and 350 cc bikes, until eventually the only British manufacturers remaining were the super-bike manufacturers – Norton and Triumph. By the time Honda launched its own super-bikes these two, now small, British manufacturers were in no position to defend against the now much larger Honda.

Pre-emptive Defence

Recognizing the possible limitations both of a position defence and a contraction defence, many strategists, particularly in recent years, have begun to recognize the potential value of pre-emptive strikes. This involves gathering information on potential attacks and then, capitalizing upon competitive advantages, striking first. This strike can take one of two broad forms: either the company behaves aggressively by, for example, hitting one competitor after another, or it uses psychological warfare by letting it be known how it will behave if a competitor acts in a particular way, a strategy which has been labelled FUD marketing – that is spreading 'fear uncertainty and despair'.

Among the companies that have successfully used pre-emptive defences are Procter & Gamble, and Seiko. In the case of P & G, pre-emptive behaviour has been a fundamental element of their strategy for the past few decades and takes the form of consistent and broad ranging product development, heavy advertising, aggressive pricing and a general philosophy of what is sometimes referred to as 'competitive toughness'. A similar philosophy has been pursued by Seiko which, with more than 2000 different models of watch worldwide, has made it difficult for competitors to get a foothold. The general lesson to be learned from these two companies, and indeed other market leaders, is that the company should never rest even after it has achieved domination, but should instead offer a broad range of products which are replaced frequently and supported aggressively. Any competitor is then faced with a target that is infinitely more difficult to penetrate.

Counter-Offensive Defence

The final form of defence tends to come into play once an attack has taken place. Faced with a competitor's significant price cut, major new product, or increase in advertising, a market leader needs to respond in order to minimize the threat. This response can take one of three forms:

1 meet the attack head-on;
2 attack the attacker's flank;
3 develop a pincer movement in an attempt to cut off the attacker's operational base.

Of these, it is the first which arguably is the most straightforward and was seen in the way in which airlines responded in the 1970s to Freddie Laker's attack on prices on the North Atlantic routes. Faced with Laker's price cutting, other airlines flying these routes also cut their prices. Laker's company was eventually forced into liquidation though an inability to service its debts.

As an alternative to this sort of response, market leaders can try searching for a gap in the attacker's armour, a strategy that was used in the United States by Cadillac when faced with a stronger marketing push by Mercedes. Cadillac responded by designing a new model, the Seville, which, it claimed, had a smoother ride and more features than the Mercedes.

The final counter-offensive move involves fighting back by hitting at the attacker's base. In the United States, for example, Northwest Airlines was faced with a price cutting attack on one of its biggest and most profitable routes by a far smaller airline. Northwest responded by cutting its fares on the attacker's most important route. Faced with a significant drop in revenue, the attacker withdrew and prices were restored to their original levels.

Market Leadership and a Customer Focus

It should be apparent from what has been said so far that for an organization to become a market leader and – perhaps more importantly – retain its leadership position over anything other than the short term, the marketing planner needs to develop a clear view of what the future will or can be. As part of this, it is typically argued that there needs to be a strong focus upon the customer and that the organization must, of necessity, be customer-led; indeed, this is a fundamental element of the marketing concept. However, it needs to be recognized that a strong argument can be developed *against* being wholly customer-led in that customers only rarely have a detailed or useful vision of what they will want in the future. (The reader needs to recognize that, in arguing against being customer-led, we are not arguing against customer satisfaction.) As an example of this, if Sony had relied upon the results of customer research when developing the Walkman they would have dropped the product at an early stage since few customers appeared to value the concept. Equally, 3M persevered with its Post-it notes despite initially negative customer research findings.

The lesson that many market leaders have learned from these and, indeed, numerous other examples of products which have succeeded in the face of customer myopia, was summed up by Akio Morita, the chairman of Sony:

> Our plan is to lead the public with new products rather than ask them what kind of products they want. The public does not know what is possible, but we do. So instead of doing a lot of market research, we refine our thinking on a product and its use and try to create a market for it by educating and communicating with the public.

This sentiment, which has been echoed by many other consistently innovative companies such as Toshiba with its Lifestyle Research Institute, highlights the need for the marketing planner to ask – and answer – two questions:

● What benefits will customers see to be of value in tomorrow's products?
● How, through innovation, can we deliver these benefits and in this way pre-empt our competitors?

In posing the first of these two questions, the marketing planner must, of course, take a very broad view of who the customer is, in that if tomorrow's customers are defined in the same way as those of today it is almost inevitable that the firm will be eclipsed by others in the market. Recognition of this leads to us being able to identify three types of organization:

1 companies which insist on trying to take customers in a direction in which they do not really want to go;

FIGURE 10.12
*The step beyond
'customer-led'*

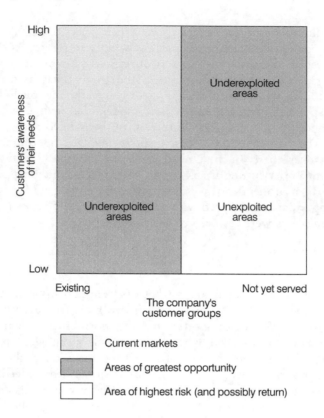

2 companies which listen to their customers and then respond by producing products and services which customers are aware they want, but which others in the market are either producing currently or will produce shortly;
3 companies which take their customers where they want to go, even though they may not yet be aware that this is a direction in which they want to go and that the product will deliver value to them.

It is this third type of organization which can be seen to have moved beyond being customer-led and which, as a result, is creating its own future. In doing this, the matrix which is illustrated in Figure 10.12 is of value in helping managers to focus their thinking. See also Illustration 10.5.

10.9 STRATEGIES FOR MARKET CHALLENGERS

Companies that are not market leaders are faced with a straightforward strategic choice: either they attack other firms – including perhaps the market leader – in an attempt to build market share and achieve leadership themselves (*market challengers*), or they pursue a far less aggressive strategy and in doing so accept the status quo (*market followers*). In deciding between the two, several factors need to be taken into account, the most significant of which are the costs of attacking other firms, the likelihood of success, the eventual probable returns, and the willingness of management to engage in what in most cases will prove to be a costly fight. In commenting on the issue of returns, Fruhan (1972, p. 100) has highlighted the dangers of spending unwisely, arguing that, particularly in mature markets, management can all too easily fall into the trap of chasing market share which proves not to be cost effective.

This theme has, in turn, been picked up by Dolan (1981) who has suggested that competitive rivalry is typically most intense in industries faced with stagnant demand, high fixed costs and high inventory costs. The implications for a firm in this situation are potentially significant, since, while there may well be a need to gain share in order to benefit from greater economies of scale, not only are the

Illustration 10.5: Marketing Dangerously – and Succeeding

In 1994, the Marketing Society took as its conference theme 'Who Dares Wins – Success through Intelligent Risk'. Intelligent risk taking, it was argued, is at the heart of successful innovation, but in many organisations had been one of the first victims of the economic recession. However, amongst the exceptions to this the case histories of which were featured at the conference were Tizer, Carling Black Label, Peperami, and the Nissan Micra.

In the case of Tizer, sales of the soft drink had dropped dramatically over a ten-year period, and with the retail trade threatening to delist it the product's death seemed inevitable. The first step in reversing this was a programme of research which highlighted the way in which the core target market of under-24s saw it to be old-fashioned, 'giggly' and 'pathetic'. The company responded by targeting a tightly defined group of opinion leaders and a series of 'in-yer-face', heavy-on-the-attitude advertisements. The result was that distribution was maintained as sales leapt by 500,000 litres and unit profits increased as the result of a shift from two litre bottles to 330ml cans.

Carling Black Label was forced to make equally radical shifts in its marketing strategy when, in 1992, and with sales of £900m (this amounts to over 20 pints a second) increasing competition led to the threat of it becoming a commodity product. The response involved completely regenerating the advertising campaign and focusing upon the product's strength and integrity so that drinkers would be proud of having chosen the brand. The result was that between October 1992 and April 1994, Carling's volume sales increased by 10 per cent at a time when the market dropped by 8 per cent.

A radical step was also taken by Unilever with its Peparami sausage which was portrayed in its advertising as a maniacal, meat-munching beast which 'could easily have scared the living daylights out of one-third of its target audience : mothers with young children, at a time when caring, sharing "right-on-ness" was at its peak'. The result of the 'It's a bit of an animal' campaign was 95 tonnes of incremental business, the second highest ever score on Millward Brown's awareness index and tracking studies, and distribution acceptance in a variety of new types of outlet including pubs and garages.

Caricaturing the product was also the basis for Nissan's launch at the beginning of the 1990s of its revised Micra. Its portrayal as a funny little blob of a car gave it a personality which led to customers buying the car on its own merits rather than just a price and helped the company to raise the price by 20 per cent at a time when the market average dropped by 3 per cent.

The strength and success of these campaigns (Nicholas suggests), lies not merely in their creativity – although many are undoubtedly 'creative', results such as these cannot be achieved by grafting on great ads as a bolt-on-goody, no matter how big the idea. They are expressions of genuinely daring marketing: behind each is the ability and a willingness to be bold, based on thorough research, sound, if wacky-sounding, strategic thinking and an understanding of bravery's commercial worth.

Source: Nicholas, R., The value of marketing dangerously, Marketing, 8 September 1994, pp.22–3

costs of doing this high, but the likelihood of the sort of pyrrhic victory referred to above also increases dramatically. Recognition of this should then lead the strategist to a clearer perception of the course of action that is likely to be the most cost effective. In practice, this means choosing between:

1 attacking the market leader;
2 attacking firms of similar size to itself but which are either under-financed or re-active;
3 attacking smaller regional firms.

In making this choice a variety of factors need to be considered, but particularly the competitive consequences. Picking off a series of small regional players is, for example, often far more profitable than attacking the market leader. This point has been highlighted by Porter (1985, p. 91) who suggests that:

> trying to take business away from the competitor that holds the largest share of a market, or makes the most money from that market, may be the most dangerous move a company can make ... the leader, by virtue of its preeminent position, can afford to cut prices, rain down new products on rivals, or bury their offerings under an advertising blitz – in short the big guy can make the business miserable for everyone else.

If, however, a company does take on the market leader and succeeds, the rewards both in terms of the power and financial returns that are possible can be considerable. It is largely because of this that many challengers opt for the high risk–high return route. For those who do pursue this route there are several guidelines that emerge from the experience of others. These involve the challenger meeting three basic conditions:

1 He must have a *sustainable* competitive advantage either in terms of cost or differentiation.
2 He must be able to partly or wholly neutralize the leader's advantages, typically by doing almost as well as the leader that which the leader does best.
3 There must be some impediment to the leader retaliating. Most commonly this might be because the leader will run foul of anti-monopolies legislation or has an enormous and inflexible commitment to a particular technology that the challenger can side-step. (For a discussion of how this was used by Michelin, see Illustration 10.6.)

Although ideally the challenger will meet all three of these conditions, fulfilling just one or two can often offset a degree of weakness in meeting the others. In the United States, for example, the no-frills airline People Express began with the benefits of a lower cost base than its competitors – pilots' salaries were lower than the norm, staffing levels were low, and there was little job demarcation – which were passed on to customers in the form of lower prices. Their product, a cramped seat, was sufficiently similar to the cramped seats of other operations for the market leaders to be unable to persuade customers there was a difference. The condition that People Express was unable to meet was the lasting impediment to retaliation, and eventually others in the industry fought back by matching the People Express prices. Having exhausted the growth potential offered on routes that the majors had largely neglected, People Express was forced to look to the more competitive routes if it was to continue growing, and this sparked off a further round of price cutting and retaliation (see Richardson (1988) pp. 17–19, 38).

A successful attack by a challenger is therefore typically based on a degree of reconfiguration of the activities that make up the business, be it in the form of design, manufacture or delivery. If the challenger is unable to do this, the safest

Illustration 10.6: Michelin and Its Use of Technological Flanking

Michelin, the French tyre manufacturer, used a strategy of technological flanking to enormous effect in the United States when it moved from an exporting base to local manufacture in 1975. The market at the time was dominated by four US manufacturers – Goodyear, Firestone, Uniroyal and Goodrich – who had for years concentrated on supplying the original equipment market (OEM) with cross-ply tyres. Although the profit margins were very low (according to one analyst, they were only pennies per tyre), the strategy guaranteed long production runs, kept brand names in front of consumers, ensured a lucrative replacement market 12–15000 miles later and, because the technology was well established, meant only a minimal sum needed to be spent on research and development. Michelin, by contrast concentrated its efforts on supplying the specialist replacement market with high quality radial tyres.

In the mid to late 1970s, the market for tyres began to change in a number of fundamental ways. The catalyst for this was the Arab–Israeli war at the beginning of the 1970s and the consequent rise in fuel prices. Motorists responded by driving fewer miles, with the result that the lucrative replacement market slowed down. The major car manufacturers responded to the call for greater fuel efficiency by switching to radial tyres as original equipment; radial tyres can reduce fuel consumption by 5–7 per cent. Michelin capitalized on this by aggressively forcing its way into the OEM market and by careful use of its reputation for quality and innovation, captured 25 per cent of the $4 billion market.

Faced with this, the US manufacturers' response was disorganized. More significantly, they were hampered by a lack of manufacturing know-how. Firestone's response, for example, involved counter-attacking with its '500' series, but this failed because of problems of quality. Other, and broader, problems also began to emerge as the industry slowly came to terms with the consequences for the replacement market of the new technology. Radial tyres typically last twice as long as cross-plys and, given the average car, reduced the replacement market opportunities substantially. Faced with a rapidly shrinking market, fixed capacity and substantial inventories, the US manufacturers were forced into an agressive and unprofitable cut-throat price war.

Source: James, B. G. (1985) Business Wargames, *Penguin, p. 54*

option is often to ignore the leader and to pursue instead others in the industry who are of equal size or who are smaller and potentially more vulnerable. In this way, any competitive response is likely to be more manageable.

The choice of *who* to challenge is thus fundamental and is a major determinant not just of the likelihood of success, but also of the costs and risks involved. However, once this has been done, the strategist is then in a position to consider the detail of the strategy that is to be pursued. Returning to the sorts of military analogies discussed earlier, this translates into a choice between five strategies: a frontal attack, a flanking attack, an encirclement attack, a bypass attack, and a guerilla attack. But before choosing among these we need to return for a moment to the more fundamental issue referred to above of *who* to attack and *when*. In deciding this, the options, as we have suggested, can be seen in terms of an assault on the market leader (a high-risk but potentially high-return strategy); an attack upon companies of similar size; or an attack upon the generally larger number of

FIGURE 10.13
Attack strategies for market challengers

It has long been recognized that market challengers only rarely succeed by relying on just one element of strategy. Instead, success depends on designing a strategy made up of several strands which, by virtue of their cumulative effect, give the challenger a competitive advantage. The 10 most commonly used and successful strategic strands used by challengers are:

1 *Price discounting*. Fuji attacked Kodak by offering photographic film and paper which they claimed was of the same quality as the market leader, but 10 per cent cheaper. A similar strategy was pursued by Amstrad in the personal computer market.
2 *Cheaper goods*. Aldi's attack in the grocery retailing market was based on providing a different quality–price combination than that of the other players in the market. Similarly, the coach travel company National Express has based its attack upon British Rail on a strategy of lower prices.
3 *Product innovation*. By offering a constant stream of new and updated products, a challenger gives buyers a powerful reason for changing their purchasing patterns. Among those to have done this successfully are Polaroid with cameras and, in the 1970s, Apple with microcomputers.
4 *Improved services*. Avis challenged Hertz, the market leader in the car hire market, with a strategy that promised a faster and higher level of service. Its advertising slogan, 'Avis, we're number two, we try harder', is now part of advertising mythology.
5 *Distribution innovation*. Timex watches achieved considerable sales success as the result of a strategy which pioneered a new approach to watch distribution. Rather than selling the product through specialist jewellery stores, the company opted for a far broader approach by distributing through chain stores and supermarkets.
6 *Intensive advertising*.
7 *Market development*. Walker's Crisps achieved considerable success in the 1960s by focusing on the previously ignored market sector of children. The market leader, Smiths, had traditionally concentrated on adults and had distributed through pubs. The attack on such a different front took Smiths by surprise.
8 *Prestige image*. Much of the success achieved in the car market by Mercedes and BMW has been based on the development of an image of quality, reliability and consumer aspiration.
9 *Product proliferation*. The success of Seiko's attack on other watch manufacturers owes much to its strategy of developing some 2400 models designed to satisfy fashion, features, user preferences and virtually anything else that might motivate consumers.
10 *Cost reduction*. Many Japanese companies entered the European and North American markets in the 1960s and 1970s on the back of a cost-reduction, price-led strategy designed to put pressure on domestic manufacturers. Subsequently, a large number of these Japanese companies have modified their approach and repositioned by, for example, emphasizing quality, reliability and prestige. Their place has now been taken by a second wave of companies, this time from Korea, Taiwan and the Philippines which are emphasizing cost reduction and lower prices.

smaller and possibly more vulnerable firms in the industry. In choosing among these various targets, the strategist is likely to be influenced by a variety of factors, including perception of the leader's likely response, the availability of the resources needed to launch an effective attack, and the possible pay-offs. In addition, however, the strategist should also perhaps be influenced by the findings of the military historian, Liddell-Hart. In an analysis of the 30 most important conflicts of the world from the Greek wars up to World War One (this included 280 campaigns), Liddell-Hart concluded that a direct head-on assault succeeded on only six occasions. By contrast, indirect approaches proved not only to be far more successful, but also more economic. This thinking, when applied to business, has led to a series of guidelines for challengers which are summarized in Figure 10.13.

Frontal Attacks

The conventional military wisdom is that for a frontal or head-on attack to succeed against a well-entrenched opponent, the attacker must have at least a 3 :1 advantage in firepower; history suggests that broadly similar lessons apply to business.

In launching a frontal attack, a market challenger can opt for either the *pure frontal atack* by matching the leader product for product, price for price, and so on, or a rather more *limited frontal attack* by attracting away selected customers. Although the record of success with a pure frontal attack is, as we commented above, generally limited, examples of companies that have adopted this approach and succeeded do exist. Included among these is Xerox who in the copying market attacked companies such as Gestetner and 3M and who by virtue of a better product captured the market. (Subsequently, Xerox has itself been attacked by a large number of companies including Sharp, Canon, Panasonic, Toshiba and Mita.)

A similar frontal attack was used to great effect by the Japanese producers of magnetic recording tape. Having pioneered the market in the 1960s, 3M fell victim to a series of aggressive pricing moves in the 1970s led by TDK. The effect on 3M was significant and by 1982 it had been forced into the position of a minor player.

More frequently, however, it is the case that, as Saunders (1987, p. 18) has pointed out, a pure frontal attack proves to be an expensive failure as was shown by Laker's attack on larger airlines such as British Airways, Pan Am and TWA, and in the main frame computer market in the early 1970s by the attacks by RCA, Xerox and General Electric upon IBM.

Returning for a moment to 3M, the company seemingly learned a great deal from its experience with magnetic tape and acted to ensure that the same thing did not happen with videotapes. As the market leader and with a strong reputation for quality, 3M launched a second brand, EXG, to ensure dominance in the premium-quality, premium-priced sector. It then capitalized on its distribution strengths by opting for intensive distribution covering office suppliers to chain stores. With regard to price, it matched the Japanese blow for blow to ensure that it maintained its leadership position.

Flank Attack

As an alternative to a costly and generally risky frontal attack many strategists have learned the lesson from military history that an indirect approach is both more economical and more effective. In business terms, a flanking attack translates into an attack on those areas where the leader is geographically weak and in market segments or areas of technology which have been neglected. It was the geographical approach that was used in the late 1960s and early 1970s by Honeywell in competing in the United States against IBM. Quite deliberately, the company concentrated its efforts on the small- and medium-sized cities in which IBM's representation, while still high, was not as intense as in the major cities. A similar geographical approach was adopted by the Japanese motorcycle industry which concentrated its efforts progressively on Asia, the United States and then Europe.

As an alternative, many companies have opted for *technological flanking* or leap-frogging. Among those to have done this with considerable success are the Japanese in the car industry who rewrote the rules of how to mass produce cars to such an extent that not only did they manage to undercut the traditional market leaders, but also reversed the flow of technology transfer in the industry.

Others to have used technological flanking include Michelin, whose experiences were discussed in Illustration 10.6, and the state-owned French helicopter manufacturer, Aerospatiale. Aerospatiale's competitors – Bell Helicopter, Sikorsky and Boeing – worked to full capacity for several years to satisfy the enormous military demand for helicopters in the Vietnam war and had little time for major technological developments. Aerospatiale took advantage of this and in 1980 simultaneously introduced three new generation fast twin-turbine models designed to cover all conceivable military and civilian needs. These models all featured Aerospatiale developed fail-safe rotor blades manufactured not from conventional metal but from composite materials.

Segmental flanking has been used to equal effect by numerous companies, including Hewlett-Packard with mini computers, Apple with micros, and Toyota and Volkswagen in the United States with small, economical cars. The lesson in each case is straightforward: identify the areas of market need not being covered by the market leader and then concentrate resources on building both size and share. In doing this, it is, however, essential that the attacker moves quickly, since the challenge becomes clearer over time and can lead to a sudden competitive response in which the company being attacked regains the initiative. In the majority of cases, however, the company being attacked either fails to recognize the significance of the challenge or is unsure of how best to retaliate and as a result responds only slowly. Bic, for example, flanked Gillette in razors by developing the low-priced sector, while Knorr and Batchelor flanked Heinz with the introduction of low-priced soups shortly after Heinz had fought off a head-on attack by Campbells. In both cases, the defender was slow to respond, possibly because of a fear that a stronger reaction would speed up the growth of the low-price sector. See Illustration 10.7.

Illustration 10.7: How Okidata Lost Its Leadership Position to Hewlett-Packard

In the 1970s, Okidata launched a dot-matrix printer which took a substantial share of the North American printer market. Hewlett-Packard quickly responded by importing from the Far East a technically superior inkjet model. They then followed this up with their range of laserjets which, based on a technological breakthrough, proved not only to be far faster, quieter and more reliable than anything else on the market, but also offered a better print quality and a substantial resale value.

Surprisingly, Okidata failed to respond and, with its market share dropping, carried on offering customers 'the best damned (dot matrix) printers on the market'. By continuing to offer a product which was no longer of real value to its customers, Okidata rapidly lost its leadership position to Hewlett-Packard which, through a series of product launches and distribution initiatives, it then quickly consolidated.

Encirclement attack

Whereas flanking in its purest form involves an attack on just one front, encirclement has parallels with a blitzkrieg in that it involves launching an attack on as many fronts as possible in order to overwhelm the competitor's defences. In this way, the defender's ability to retaliate effectively is reduced dramatically. Although quite obviously an expensive strategy to pursue and one which is almost guaranteed to lead to significant short-term losses, its record of success in the hands of certain types of company is impressive. Seiko, for example, has made use of a strategy of encirclement not just with the sheer number of models which are changed constantly, but also by acquiring distribution in every watch outlet possible and by heavy advertising which gives emphasis to fashion, features, user preferences, and everything else that might motivate the consumer. Equally, the Japanese motorcycle, audio and hi-fi manufacturers, having started with flanking strategies, quickly developed these into encirclement strategies with an emphasis on rapid product life cycles, frequent and radical new product launches, wide product ranges, aggressive pricing, strong dealer support and, in the case of the motorcycle companies, a successful racing programme. Other companies that have made use of encirclement, admittedly with varying degrees of success, include Yamaha against Honda (see Illustration 10.8), and the Japanese construction machinery manufacturer Komatsu in its attack on the market leader, Caterpillar.

Illustration 10.8: Yamaha and Its Attack Upon Honda

By the early 1960s, Honda had established itself in the United States as the undisputed market leader in the motorcycle market. Its aggressive sales, distribution, and product development strategy had had a significant effect on the size and profitability of the market, and led Yamaha to enter the market against Honda. It began by identifying Honda's weaknesses and areas of potential vulnerability. These included a number of successful but complacent dealers, a series of management changes, and the discouragement of some new and more aggressive franchise seeking dealers.

Yamaha offered its own franchises to the best of these dealers and recruited an ambitious sales force to train and motivate them. It then invested heavily in the design of its motorcycles so that it could justifiably claim and demonstrate their mechanical superiority. The company capitalized on this with an extensive and costly advertising programme designed to increase buyer awareness and dealer motivation. When motorcycle safety became a significant issue, Yamaha invested in safety features and promoted them extensively.

The combined effect of these strategies led to Yamaha achieving the clear number two position in the market. Yamaha's president, Hisao Koike, then launched a major attack on Honda in order to achieve leadership. With an advertising slogan 'Yamaha take the lead', new models were launched in an attempt to encircle Honda. The plan failed and Yamaha found itself with high inventory levels. This forced the company to reduce its workforce by 2000 employees. Koike resigned, and what was subsequently labelled 'Yamaha's Kamikaze attack' was withdrawn.

In the case of Komatsu and Caterpillar, Komatsu's attack on the market leader was based on the slogan used internally, 'Encircle Caterpillar'. This translated into a series of attacks on market niches, improvements in product quality, extensions to its product range, and pricing at levels 10–15 per cent lower than those of Caterpillar.

Bypass Attack

The fourth approach, a bypass attack, is in the short term at least the most indirect of assaults, in that it avoids any aggressive move against the defender's existing products or markets. Instead, the strategist typically concentrates on developing the organization by focusing on *unrelated products* (the Japanese consumer electronics firms developing video recorders and compact discs rather than traditional audio-visual products); *new geographical markets* for existing products and, in the case of the hi-tech industries, by *technological leap-frogging*. Among those to have used a bypass attack successfully are Sturm Ruger and YKK.

Sturm Ruger, a small US gun manufacturer, recognized in the early 1950s that it did not have the resources to develop a product range that would enable it to compete effectively against Colt, Remington and Browning. It therefore concentrated on a bypass strategy by producing a limited range of high quality and competitively produced guns that earned a reputation for being the best in their class. In this way, Sturm Ruger managed over a 30-year period to capture almost 20 per cent of the US domestic sporting guns market.

A broadly similar strategy was pursued in the zip fasteners market by YKK. The North American market had long been dominated by Talon. YKK therefore concentrated on avoiding a head-on confrontation with the market leader and, by selling direct to fashion houses, managed both to bypass Talon and turn their zip fasteners into a high-fashion item which commanded a premium price. By doing this, YKK captured 30 per cent of the US market. The same strategy was subsequently used in Europe to achieve broadly similar results.

Guerilla Attack

The fifth option open to a challenger is in many ways best suited to smaller companies with a relatively limited resource base. Whereas frontal attacks, flanking, encirclement and even bypass attacks are generally broad based and costly to pursue, a guerilla attack is made up of a series of hit-and-run moves designed to demoralize the opponent as a prelude to destabilizing and keeping the competitor off-balance. In practice, this typically involves drastic short-term price cuts (see Illustration 10.9), sudden and intensive bursts of advertising, product comparisons, damaging public relations activity, poaching a competitor's key staff, legislative moves, and geographically concentrated campaigns. The success of such a strategy has been shown to depend in part upon the competitor's response. In some cases, for example, the competitor chooses to ignore the attack, as has been seen with the way in which the major airlines have deliberately not responded to Virgin's lower prices on the North Atlantic routes. In others, however, the competitor fights back quickly and aggressively in order to minimize any long-term threat. All too often, dealing with guerilla attacks proves to be difficult. In the cream-cracker biscuits market, for example, Nabisco's Jacob's brand has long been the market leader. United Biscuits, which has only a small share of the market with its Crawford's brand, has made use of the brand to harass Jacob's with a series of guerilla attacks, normally in the form of low-priced activity.

The value of guerilla attacks is also shown by the way in which Lever Bros responded to a new formulation of Daz by Procter & Gamble. The new formulation, which involved adding more bleach and a fluorescer to the product, gave P & G the opportunity to claim a superior whiteness, something which is, of course, a major selling proposition in the washing powder market. The product's selling price was not increased, even though the costs of development and

---

Illustration 10.9: Boots and Its Guerilla Pricing Strategy in the United States

The success of an unconventional and aggressive approach to competition was graphically illustrated by Boots' launch of its Rufen brand of ibuprofen, an anti-arthritic drug, into the US in the late 1980s. The company had previously licensed ibuprofen to Upjohn who had marketed the drug as Motrin.

On entering the market with Rufen, Boots pursued an unexpectedly radical penetration pricing strategy to gain market share. The drug was sold at a 20 per cent discount under Motrin's price, plus a $1.50 rebate to patients every time they bought a 100-tablet bottle, an approach which had never previously been used in the industry.

Because the government's Medicare and Medicaid programmes reimbursed pharmacists only for the lowest cost drug suited to the treatment, Boots rapidly gained a substantial part of the 20 per cent of Motrin's sales to the two programmes. In addition, because a substantial proportion of arthritis sufferers are elderly, Boots' strategy proved to be particularly appealing to a large number of price-sensitive consumers who paid for treatment themselves.

Source: James, B. G. (1985) Business Wargames, Penguin, p. 64

advertising were high; P & G's assumption seemingly was that the major competitor, Omo, would be deterred from following because of this cost. In the event, Lever Bros responded not with Omo, but instead with its smaller fighting brand, Surf. In this way, Lever managed to invalidate the Daz claim at a relatively low cost.

10.10 STRATEGIES FOR MARKET FOLLOWERS

As an alternative to challenging for leadership, many companies are content to adopt a far less proactive posture simply by following what others do. The attractions of this have been pointed to by a variety of writers, including Levitt (1966, p. 63) and Kotler (1988, p. 339). Levitt, for example, suggested that a strategy of product imitation can often be as profitable as a strategy of innovation. Similarly, Kotler has pointed to the way in which

> the innovator bears the huge expense of developing the new product, getting it into distribution, and informing and educating the market. The reward for all this work and risk is normally market leadership. However, another firm can come along, copy or improve the new product, and launch it. Although this firm probably will not overtake the leader, the follower can achieve high profits, simply because it did not bear any of the innovation expense.

For many firms, therefore, the attractions of being and indeed remaining a market follower can be considerable. This is particularly so when the true costs and risks of challenging an entrenched leader are recognized. If a company is to challenge a market leader successfully, it is essential that the basis for challenging is truly worthwhile and meaningful; in practice, this would generally mean a major breakthrough in terms of innovation, price or distribution, something which in relatively long-established and stable industries is often difficult to achieve. Without a major breakthrough such as this, any attack is almost certain to fail since most market leaders will not only have the benefit of better financing, but will also be more firmly entrenched.

Recognizing this leads the majority of market followers to accept the status quo, and to pursue a course of action that avoids the risk of confrontation and retaliation. In strategic terms this often translates into copying the market leaders by offering broadly similar products, prices and levels of service; this is sometimes referred to as a *me-too strategy*. The net effect is that direct competition is avoided and market shares tend to remain relatively stable over a considerable period.

These comments should not, however, be taken to mean that market followers do not have their own distinct strategies. Indeed, as Saunders (1987, p. 21) has pointed out, the strategies of successful low-share followers tend to exhibit a number of common characteristics, including:

1 Careful market segmentation, competing only in areas where their particular strengths were highly valued.
2 Efficient use of limited R & D budgets – they seldom won R & D battles but channelled their R & D spending into areas that were most likely to generate the greatest financial payoff, in terms of return on R & D expenditure. Where R & D capabilities were available, they concentrated on truly innovative products.
3 They thought small and stayed small. They tended to emphasise profitability rather than sales growth and market share, concentrating on specialisation rather than diversification, high value added rather than mass products, quality rather than quantity.
4 The companies were willing to challenge conventional wisdom – their leaders were often strong willed, committed and involved in almost all aspects of their companies' operations.

It follows from this that the need for a follower to develop a clear and well-formulated strategy is just as great as it is for an infinitely more proactive market leader or challenger. In practice, however, many market followers fail to recognize this and pursue a 'strategy' that is largely implicit and derivative. At the very least a follower needs to recognize the importance of positioning itself so that its customer base is not eroded, that sales increase in line with rates of market growth, and that it is not overly vulnerable to more aggressive and predatory market challengers. This is particularly important when it is remembered that challengers can gain share in three ways, including by taking sales from smaller or equal sized competitors (see page 338). A market follower in these circumstances can often prove to be an attractive and vulnerable target.

Followers do therefore need to decide how they intend operating and, in particular, how closely they intend following the market leader. In doing this it is essential that the firm reduces its vulnerability as much as possible by a combination of tight cost control, an early recognition of developing opportunities, and a clear product and service strategy. This final point is particularly significant since there is a danger of seeing market followers quite simply as imitators of the market leader. Where this does happen the dangers of confusion among customers increases and the reasons for buying from the follower decrease markedly.

It is possible to identify three quite distinct postures for market followers, depending on just how closely they emulate the leader:

1 *following closely* with as similar a marketing mix and market segmentation combination as possible;
2 *following at a distance* so that although there are obvious similarities, there are also areas of differentiation between the two;
3 *following selectively* both in product and market terms so that the likelihood of direct competition is minimized.

10.11 STRATEGIES FOR MARKET NICHERS

The fourth and final strategic position for a firm is that of a market nicher. Although niching is typically associated with small companies, it is in practice a strategy that is also adopted by divisions of larger companies in industries in which competition is intense and the costs of achieving a prominent position are disproportionately high. The advantages of niching can therefore be considerable, since if properly done it is not only profitable, but also avoids confrontation and competition.

The attractiveness of a market niche is typically influenced by several factors, the most significant of which Kotler (1988, p. 342) identifies as follows:

1 [It] is of sufficient size and purchasing power to be profitable;
2 the niche has growth potential;
3 the niche is of negligible interest to major competitors;
4 the firm has the required skills and resources to serve the niche effectively;
5 the firm can defend itself against an attacking major competitor through the customer goodwill it has built up.

It is specialization that is at the heart of effective niching, something which was recognized by retailers such as Sock Shop, Tie Rack and Knickerbox in the 1980s, and, as discussed in Illustration 10.10, by Avon in the tyre market.

Specialization can, however, prove dangerous if the market changes in a fundamental way either as the result of greater competition or an economic down

Illustration 10.10: Avon and the Development of a Niche Market

As one of the world's smallest tyre producers, Avon is dwarfed by multinationals like Goodyear, Michelin, Pirelli and Continental. Despite this, the organization proved to be remarkably successful during a period in which the industry was plagued with problems of chronic overcapacity, inefficient production processes, and a series of changes in buying patterns as radial tyres took over from cross-plys and the sales of remoulds and secondhand tyres increased.

Faced with changes such as these, Avon's initial response in the early 1980s was to cut its manufacturing capacity by a third and make 800 people redundant. Recognition, however, that this was at best a short-term solution led to a slow but fundamental change in the entire business and in particular to the search for market niches. The two that were identified as offering the greatest scope were high-performance motorcycle tyres and high-performance car tyres.

Although the motorcycle market is small in comparison with the car market – 50 000 tyres against some 20 million – it has the advantage not just of being far easier to target, but more discerning, selective and potentially far more brand loyal.

Although the company also still makes conventional car tyres, the strategy has concentrated upon developing an image of high quality to avoid being sucked into the bottom end of the market. In doing this, Avon invested in developing a car racing division and, by avoiding Formula One racing where tyres are supplied free of charge to the racing teams, makes a profit.

The third part of the organization's strategy involved developing tyres for the high-performance sector of the car market. This sector accounts for around 25 per cent of the UK car market and within this Avon has built its reputation on its involvement with racing and on the fact that it has long been an original equipment supplier to Rolls Royce, Bentley and Aston Martin.

Source: Crainer, S. (1990) A Niche for High Performance, Marketing Business, 13 October, pp. 14–15

turn and the nicher is left exposed. For this reason, there is often a strong argument for multiple niching rather than single-sector niching.

The potential profitability of niching has been pointed to by a variety of consultants and authors over the past few years, including McKinsey, and Biggadike. Two of McKinsey's consultants, Clifford and Cavanagh (1985) for example, found from a study of successful mid-size companies that their success was directly attributable to the way in which they niched within a large market rather than trying to go after the whole market. Equally, Biggadike (1977) in a study of 40 firms that entered established markets found that the majority chose to concentrate upon narrower product lines and narrower market segments than the rather better established incumbents.

In terms of how market nichers operate, there are several guidelines that can be identified. These include:

1 specializing geographically;
2 specializing by the type of end user;
3 specializing by product or product line;
4 specializing on a quality/price spectrum;
5 specializing by service;
6 specializing by size of customer;
7 specializing by product feature.

Competitive Strategy as a Game

It has long been recognized that competition between organizations can be seen in much the same way as a game, in that the outcome in terms of an organization's performance is determined not just by its own actions but also by the actions and reactions of the other players, such as competitors, customers, governments and other stakeholders. However, as the pace of environmental change increases and the nature, sources and bases of competition alter, markets become more complex and the competitive game consequently becomes more difficult to win, something which has been illustrated by a spectrum of markets including colas, films and cameras, airlines, detergents, disposable nappies, tyres, computer hardware and software, and newspapers. In markets such as these, the ever present danger is of one company taking a step such as a price cut which then proves to be mutually destructive as everyone else responds in a desperate attempt to avoid losing customers, volume and share. From the customers' point of view, of course, moves such as these are often attractive, particularly as they can lead to a different set of expectations which any individual firm then finds difficult to reverse.

It follows from this that the need to manage competition and the competitive process, while often difficult, is essential. Although there are no hard and fast rules, it is possible to identify a number of very broad guidelines which companies might follow. These include:

- *Never ignore new competitors*, particularly those who enter at the bottom end of the market since, almost inevitably, once a firm gains a foothold it will start targeting other segments of the market. Examples of this include the early manufacturers of calculators who ignored Casio; IBM, which ignored a series of initially small players such as Apple, Dell and Compaq; the UK motorcycle manufacturers who underestimated the Japanese such as Honda, Yamaha, Kawasaki and Suzuki; and Xerox, which was hit hard by Canon.
- *Always exploit competitive advantages* and never allow them to disappear unless they are being replaced by an advantage which, from the customer's point of view, is more powerful and meaningful.
- *Never launch a new product or take a new initiative without working out how the competition will respond* and how you will be affected by this.

Although these three guidelines are in many ways self-evident, the reality is that numerous organizations develop and implement strategies which reflect little real understanding or awareness of the competition. Others, however, do manage to develop competitive strategies in the truest sense. According to Day (1996, p. 2), there appear to be several factors which set these companies apart, including:

- an intense focus upon competitors *throughout* the organization;
- the desire and determination to learn as much as possible about each competitor, its strategies, intentions, capabilities and limitations;
- a commitment to using this information and the insights it provides in order to anticipate how they are most likely to behave.

The outcome of this sort of approach is, as Day (op cit., p. 3) comments:

> They formulate strategies by devising creative alternatives that minimise or preclude or encourage cooperative competitive responses. They adroitly use many weapons other than price, including advertising, litigation, and product innovation. They play the competitive game as though it were chess, by envisioning the long term consequences of their moves. Their goal is long term success, rather than settling for short run gains, or avoiding immediate losses.

However, in developing a competitive strategy, many managers appear to make the mistake of focusing upon what competitors have done in the past rather than what they are most likely to do in the future. Although, quite obviously, behaviour in the future is often influenced by what has been done previously, even small changes on the part of a competitor can invalidate the assumptions being made.

At the same time, much thinking about competitors and the interpretation of competitive intelligence is based on mental models which reflect a simplification of reality. Although this simplification is understandable – and may well prove to be adequate in relatively static markets – it is unlikely to be suited to markets in which there is any real degree of competitive intensity. Because of this, competitively successful organizations appear to put a great deal of effort into learning, not just about competitors, but also into developing a detailed understanding of distributors' perceptions and expectations and the extent to which these are being met. They appear also to devote significant resources to learning from their own experiences so that future strategies can then be built upon this understanding.

Marketing Strategy and the Search for Future Competitiveness

We suggested earlier that, if an enterprise is managed a little better than customers expect, and if this is done in a slightly better way than competitors can manage, then the enterprise should be successful (refer to page 4). Although the need for a competitively superior approach has long been at the heart of marketing strategy, the search for greater competitive capability has increased dramatically over the past few years. There are several factors which have contributed to this, a number of which are referred to in our discussion of the strategic challenges facing organizations (see page 234) and the dimensions of the new customer and the new forms of competition (pages 158 and 116–17 respectively). Together, these have put pressures on managers to develop strategies which not only are far more clearly focused upon the market, but which are also infinitely more proactive, flexible and innovative. However, for many managers, the problem is not necessarily that of identifying or gaining an advantage initially, but of *sustaining* it over any length of time. In highly competitive and largely mature markets, for example, an ever greater number of organizations are having to compete directly against competitors who offer almost identical products across 70–80 per cent of the range. Because of this, the focus of competitive advantage is increasingly shifting away from major product and technological breakthroughs to an emphasis upon a series of process improvements, these are illustrated in Figure 10.14.

FIGURE 10.14
The contribution of process improvements to greater competitiveness

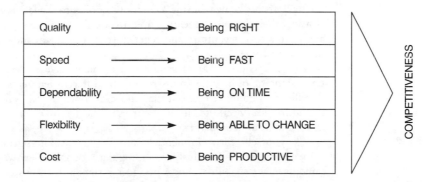

However, in order to achieve this, it is essential that the interrelationships which exist both internally between marketing and other functional areas of the business and externally between the organization and its suppliers and distributors are refined – and perhaps rethought – so that the five dimensions of quality, speed dependability, flexibility and cost referred to in Figure 10.14 are operating as optimally as is possible.

As part of this, the marketing planner also needs to develop a far more detailed understanding of what customers see to be of importance and how the organization's product range compares with those of its competitors. A framework for this is illustrated in Figure 10.15.

FIGURE 10.15
*Performance against
competition*

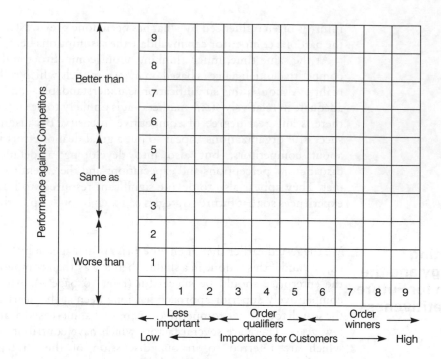

This search for competitiveness has been pursued by numerous writers over the years, including Hamel and Prahalad (1994) who, in *Competing for the Future*, one of the most influential management books of the 1990s, argue that in competing for the future managers need to rethink their strategies in a series of fundamental ways. However, in many organizations they argue that all or most managers have still failed to come to terms with this and are wedded to old patterns of thinking and old formulae. As a test of this, they suggest posing a series of questions:

> Look around your company. Look at the high profile initiatives that have been launched recently. Look at the issues that are preoccupying senior management. Look at the criteria and benchmarks by which progress is being measured. Look at the track record of new business creation. Look into the faces of your colleagues and consider their dreams and fears. Look toward the future and ponder your company's ability to shape that future and regenerate success again and again in the years and decades to come.
>
> Now ask yourself: Does senior management have a clear and broadly shared understanding of how the industry may be different ten years in the future? Are its 'headlights' shining further out than those of competitors? Is its point of view about the future clearly reflected in the company's short-term priorities? Is its point of view about the future competitively unique?
>
> Ask yourself: How influential is my company in setting the new rules of competition within its industry? Is it regularly defining new ways of doing business, building new capabilities, and setting new standards of customer satisfaction? Is it more a rule-maker than a rule-taker within its industry? Is it more intent on challenging the industry status quo than protecting it?
>
> Ask yourself: Is senior management fully alert to the dangers posed by new, unconventional rivals? Are potential threats to the current business model widely understood? Do senior executives possess a keen sense of urgency about the need to reinvent the current business model? Is the task of regenerating core strategies receiving as much top management attention as the task of re-engineering core processes?
>
> Ask yourself: Is my company pursuing growth and new business development with as much passion as it is pursuing operational efficiency and downsizing? Do we have as clear a point of view about where the next $100 million, or $1 billion of revenue growth will come from as we do about where the next $10 million, $100 million, or $1 billion of cost savings will come from? (op. cit., pp. 1–2).

The answer to these and a number of other questions, they suggest, is that far too often, far too little really detailed thinking about how best to compete in the future is going on.

As a first step in overcoming this, they suggest that managers focus upon the factors which contribute to greater competitiveness. These are illustrated in Figure 10.16.

FIGURE 10.16
The search for greater competitiveness

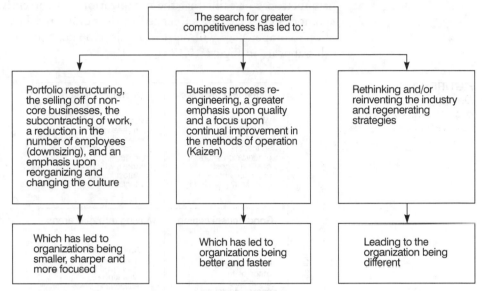

SOURCE: Adapted from Hamel, G. and Prahalad, C. K. (1994), p. 15

However, they go on to argue that although many managers have focused upon the first two dimensions (which, it needs to be emphasized, are inward-looking), relatively few have managed to come to terms with the third, even though it is this area which offers the greatest opportunity for an organization to make a major competitive advance. At the same time, of course, it is this area which offers the scope for the greatest competitive disadvantage if a competitor reinvents the industry or strategy first.

Among the organizations which have successfully reinvented the industry and/or regenerated strategy are Xerox, which in the 1970s redefined the document copying market; Pentax and Canon, which developed highly reliable and low-cost 35mm cameras; Canon, which, in the 1980s, developed small, low-cost photocopiers and, in so doing, opened up vast new markets which, despite its initial innovatory zeal, Xerox had largely ignored; Compaq, which developed the low-cost PC market; Swatch, with fashion watches; The Body Shop, which pioneered the environmentally friendly health and beauty market; Sony, with, among other products, the Walkman; Direct Line, which developed the direct selling of insurance; and Häagen Dazs, the experiences of which were discussed in Illustration 10.12 (see pp. 377–8).

At the heart of Hamel and Prahalad's thinking on strategy is the idea that, in order to cope with the demands of the future, managers need to make a series of fundamental changes. The starting point in this process, they suggest, involves getting off the treadmill of day-to-day activities and moving away from existing patterns of thought. A fundamental part of this involves managers in 'learning to forget'. In other words, managers need to recognize that, by adhering to the old but possibly successful formulae and to the existing cultural paradigms, failure is almost certain. There needs therefore to be an emphasis upon a series of steps, including:

- *Competing for industry foresight* by identifying how the market will or can be encouraged to develop. 'The trick', Hamel and Prahalad suggest, 'is to see the future before it arrives' (op cit., p. 73);

- Having developed a picture of the future, the emphasis then shifts to *crafting the strategic architecture* or blueprint for developing the skills and structures that will be needed in order to compete in the new environment
- In turn, this leads to the *stretching and leveraging of strategy* so that the organization's resources are focused, developed and exploited to the full.

Underpinning all of this is the need for a clear understanding of the core competences or skills that the organization has currently, the nature of the core competences that will be needed in the future and how therefore the organization's competences will need to be developed. A framework for thinking about this appears in Figure 10.17.

FIGURE 10.17
Developing the organization's core competences

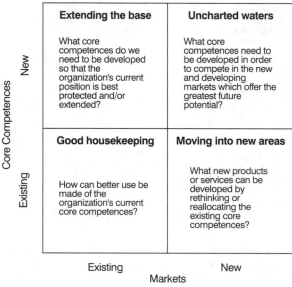

SOURCE: Adapted from Hamel, G. and Prahalad, C. K. (1994), p. 227

10.12 THE DANGERS OF STRATEGIC WEAR-OUT

Regardless of whether the company is a leader, follower, challenger or nicher, the marketing strategist needs to recognize that even the most successful of strategies will, sooner or later, begin to wear out and lose its impact. It is therefore essential that strategies are modified both to anticipate and meet changing competitive challenges and consumer needs. Among the companies that have failed to do this are Polaroid and the large mail order companies. In the case of Polaroid, its winning strategies of the 1960s and 1970s failed to change sufficiently to come to terms with the radically different markets of the 1980s as non-instant competitors improved product performance and the high street witnessed an explosion in the number and reliability of shops offering one-hour and 24-hour photographic development services.

Similarly, the mass market mail-order companies failed in the 1970s to come to terms with the changing role of women, their greater spending power, the smaller numbers staying at home during the day, the greater attractions of the high street, and the greater availability of instant credit. The result was a rapid decline in their share of consumer spending, an increasingly tired looking sales formula, and perhaps more fundamentally, an apparent absence of any real understanding of how to fight back.

Quite obviously, the vulnerability of a company to a predator in these circumstances increases enormously and highlights the need for regular reviews of strategy. In many cases, however, and particularly when a company has been successful, management often proves reluctant to change what is seen to be a winning strategy. The need for change often becomes apparent only at a later stage when the gap between what the company is doing and what it should be doing increases to a point at which performance and prospects begin to suffer in an obvious way. It is by this stage that an observant and astute competitor will have taken advantage of the company's increased vulnerability. The argument in favour of regular environmental and strategic reviews is therefore unassailable and reinforces the discussion of Chapter 2. Specifically, the sorts of factor which contribute to strategic wear-out and strategic drift include:

- changes in market structure as competitors enter or exit;
- changes in competitors' stances;
- competitive innovations;
- changes in consumers' expectations;
- economic changes;
- legislative changes;
- technological changes; these include in some instances the emergence of a new technology which at first sight is unrelated or only indirectly related to the company's existing sphere of operations;
- distribution changes;
- supplier changes;
- a lack of internal investment;
- poor control of company costs;
- a tired and uncertain managerial philosophy.

We commented at an earlier stage in this book that for many companies strategic development often proves to be a painful and unnatural process. Recognizing this, it is perhaps understandable that having developed a seemingly successful strategy, many management teams are content either to stick with the strategy or change it only marginally over time.

10.13 THE ATTRACTIONS OF BEING A MARKET PIONEER

A variety of studies over the past decade covering a broad range of mature consumer and individual goods businesses have shown that market pioneers – the companies that did most to develop particular market sectors in their early days – typically have a substantially higher market share than late entrants to the market. The attractions of market leadership have already been highlighted within this chapter and it follows from this that a pioneering approach can therefore have considerable benefits. Among those who have pointed to this are the PIMS researchers, and Robinson and Fornell.

Within the PIMS research a business is classified as:

1 one of the *pioneers* responsible for developing products or services within the market;
2 an *early follower* of the pioneer in a still growing and dynamic market;
3 a *later entrant* to a longer established market sector.

Using this framework, Robinson and Fornell (1985 and 1986) examined average market shares for each of these categories. The results are shown in Table 10.1.

Recognizing the potential attractions in this way should lead a market pioneer to consider carefully the strategic options open to the firm. In doing this, the strategist needs to take account of a variety of factors, but especially the anticipated life of the market. If, for example, it seems likely that the market will have only a short life, the strategy should be designed to maximize short-term returns. If, however the market offers longer-term scope, the pioneer should identify first which particular product markets it should focus on, and then second

Table 10.1 Average market share

	Consumer goods	Industrial goods
Pioneer	29%	29%
Early follower	17%	21%
Late entrant	13%	15%

who best to sustain its competitive advantage. Returning for a moment to the work of Robinson and Fornell, there appear to be several guidelines for success which can be summarized as 'pioneers tend to have higher product quality and broader product lines than late entrants ... [and] they gain a brand name advantage because being first is an effective way to secure a position in the consumer's mind. This is especially important in markets where consumers buy out of habit'. Perhaps surprisingly they did not find that pioneers benefited from significant direct cost savings:

> while cost savings are roughly 1 to 2 per cent, the associated market share impact is less than one share point. In these mature markets, patents and trade secrets do not benefit pioneers ... sustainable competitive advantages are typically developed in the market place and not in the patent office.

For a firm to remain as a market pioneer requires therefore a degree of forethought, with attention being paid both to the short- and long-term profit opportunities of each segment and to the likely entry points and strategies of competitors. In commenting on this, Frey (1982) discusses the shape and implications of the competitive life cycle that pioneers are likely to encounter. This begins with the pioneers being in the position of the sole supplier with 100 per cent of the market's production capacity and sales. There follows a stage of competitive penetration in which the pioneer's share of production capacity and sales begins to fall. As others enter the market the degree of price competition tends to increase, with the result that the scope for premium pricing on the part of the pioneer declines. As the market develops yet further and more firms enter the market the perceived value of the product tends to decline, with the result that there is a gradual shift towards what Frey describes as 'commodity competition'. At this stage profit margins throughout the industry tend to be low and one or more firms may decide to withdraw. The pioneer, who is likely still to dominate the market, may take this opportunity either to increase his share further or instead withdraw from the market altogether. This cycle is illustrated in Figure 10.18.

FIGURE 10.18
The competitive life cycle

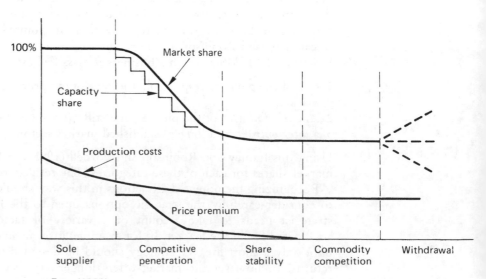

SOURCE: Frey (1982)

10.14 THE INFLUENCE OF PRODUCT EVOLUTION AND THE PRODUCT LIFE CYCLE ON STRATEGY

The product life cycle is arguably one of the best-known but least understood concepts in marketing. In making this comment, we have in mind the idea that although the concept has an inherent appeal and logic, there is little hard evidence that marketing managers use it in a particularly effective manner when developing strategy. There are several reasons for this, the most obvious being the difficulty in identifying the precise shape of the life-cycle curve and the position of the company on the curve at any particular time. Nevertheless, the idea of the product life cycle has undoubtedly influenced the thinking of many marketing strategists, albeit at a general rather than a specific level.

The rationale of the life cycle is straightforward and reflects the way in which, as Kotler (1988, p. 347) points out,

> not only are economic conditions changing and competitors launching new assaults, but in addition, the product is passing through new stages in the role that it plays in its market. Consequently, the company needs to plan for a succession of strategies appropriate to each stage in the product's life cycle. The company must think about how to extend the product's life and profitability in the face of knowing that it will not last forever.

The strategic implications of the life cycle are thus potentially significant and can be summarized as follows:

1 products have a finite life;
2 during this life, they pass through a series of different stages, each of which poses different challenges to the seller;
3 virtually all elements of the organization's strategy need to change as the product moves from one stage to another;
4 the profit potential of products varies considerably from one stage to another;
5 the demands upon management and the appropriateness of managerial styles also varies from stage to stage.

In terms of operating practice, the most obvious and immediate implication of a model of product and market evolution such as this can be seen as the need for

FIGURE 10.19
Sales and product life cycles

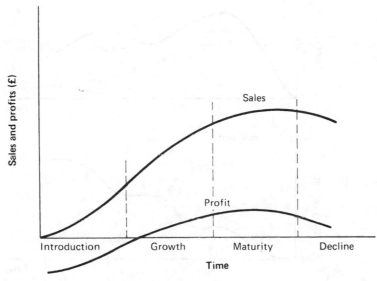

strategy to change over time and to reflect the particular demands of the different stages. These stages, which are illustrated in Figure 10.19, are typically designated as introduction, growth, maturity and decline, and follow an S-shaped curve.

However, despite the simplicity and apparent logic of the life cycle concept, a series of problems are typically experienced in its use. The most common of these stems from the difficulty of identifying where on the life cycle a product is and where each stage begins and ends. In most cases, the decision is arbitrary, although several commentators have proposed rather more objective criteria. Probably the best known of these is an approach devised by Polli and Cook (1969) which is based on a normal distribution of percentage changes in real sales from year to year. Others such as Cox (1967) advocate an historically based approach whereby the strategist examines the sales histories of similar products in his industry. If this reveals that in the past the average length of the introductory, growth and maturity periods has been five, 14 and 48 months respectively, these time-scales are, all other factors being equal, are assumed to apply to the product in question. The problem of course is that other factors almost invariably do intrude with the result that historical analysis is at best only a vague guide to strategy and at worst misleading. This is particularly so when levels of competitive intensity increase. Equally, the strategist should not lose sight of the way in which life cycles generally are shortening. Other problems with historical analysis stem from the very different life-cycle curves that products exhibit; one particular piece of research, for example, has identified 17 different life-cycle patterns (see Swan and Rink, 1982), the three most common of which are illustrated in Figure 10.20. The combined effect of these few points raises a significant question mark over historical analysis and argues the case for a rather more cautious and individual approach than is normally suggested.

FIGURE 10.20
Three common product life-cycle curves

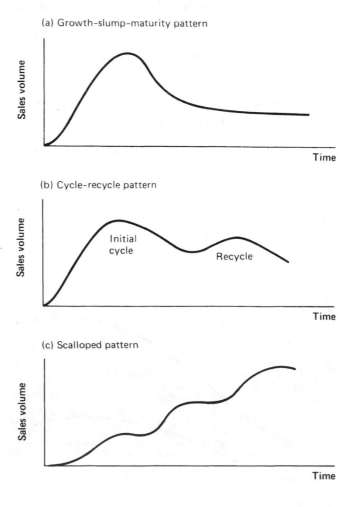

(a) Growth–slump–maturity pattern

(b) Cycle–recycle pattern

(c) Scalloped pattern

FIGURE 10.21
The characteristics of the PLC and the implications for strategy

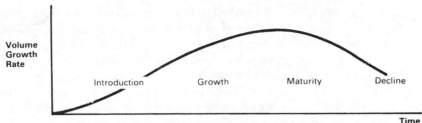

Market characteristics

	Introduction	Growth	Maturity	Decline
Sales	Low	Increasing rapidly	Peaking	Declining
Costs per customer	High	Average	Low	Low
Profits	Negative	Increasing	High	Declining/negative
Customer type	Innovators	Early adopters	Middle and late majority	Laggards
Competitors	Few	Increasing. Some emulators	High but beginning to decline	Declining with rapid shake-out
Competitors' strategies	Unfocused and indirect	Attempting to achieve trial. Undifferentiated products, services. Emphasis on fighting for share.	Price cutting to achieve volume. Fighting for market share but difficulties experienced in doing this. Emphasis on efficiency and low cost. Shake-out of weakest players.	Exit of some competitors
Managerial style	Entrepeneurial/nursemaid	Sophisticated manager/tank driver	Critical administrator/housewife	Opportunistic milker/lemon squeezer
Marketing objectives	Create awareness and trial	Rapid share increases/Maximize share	Defend share and capitalize upon profit opportunities	Reduce spending, milk the brand and prepare for withdrawal

Marketing mix strategies

	Introduction	Growth	Maturity	Decline
Product	Basic product	Develop product extensions and service levels	Modify and differentiate. Develop next generation.	Phase out weak brands
Price	Low price strategy	Penetration strategy	Price to meet or beat competitors	Reduce
Distribution	Selective	Intensive. Limited trade discounts.	Intensive. Heavy trade discounts.	Selective. Phase out weak outlets.
Advertising	Heavy spending to build awareness and encourage trial among early adopters and distributors	Moderate to build awareness and interest in the mass market. Greater word of mouth.	Emphasize brand differentiation and special offers	Reduce to a level that maintains hard core loyalty. Emphasize low prices to reduce stock.
Sales promotion	Extensive to encourage trial	Reduce to a moderate level	Increase to encourage brand switching	Reduce
Planning time frame	Short to medium	Long range	Medium range	Short
Communication system	Informal/expedient	Formal/tailor made	Formal/uniform	Little or none
Structure	Task force	Product division	Business division together with task force for new product development	Reduced
Compensation	High variable/low fixed. Linked to performance.	Balanced variable & fixed	Low variable/high fixed	Fixed

Nevertheless, despite these criticisms, the PLC does offer some scope as a broad planning, control and forecasting tool. As a planning tool its value should be seen in terms of the way in which it highlights the need for marketing strategy to change over time and indeed identifies the types of strategy that are best suited to each of the four stages. As a control tool it can be used as a basis for a comparison of a product's performance against broadly similar products in the past, while as a means of forecasting it provides a broad indication of how a product might develop. These are brought together in Figure 10.21 which summarizes the characteristics of the life cycle, and the objectives and strategies best suited to each of the four major stages.

The Influence of Market Evolution on Strategy

The product life cycle is, as we commented earlier, a model of both product and market evolution. In practice, emphasis tends to be placed on the *product's* life cycle rather than that of the *market*, with the result that many strategists work to a product-oriented picture rather than to a market-oriented picture. There is, however, a strong argument for the strategist to take a step sideways and to focus periodically upon the market overall in an attempt to identify how it is likely to evolve and how it will be affected by changing needs, new technology, developments in the channels of distribution, and so on. This, in turn, points to the need for the strategist to recognize the nature of the interrelationships between the demand life-cycle curve and the technology life-cycle curve, and how in turn these should be reflected in the management of particular brands.

In doing this, the starting point involves focusing upon the demand life cycle, since it is the demand life cycle which is concerned with the underlying need. The technology life cycle, by contrast, is concerned with the particular ways in which this need is satisfied. One of the most commonly used examples to illustrate this point is that of the need for calculating power. The demand life cycle for this is still growing rapidly and looks as if it will continue to do so for the foreseeable future. The technology life cycle is concerned with the detail of how this need is met. This was done initially with fingers and then subsequently with abacuses, slide rules, adding machines, handheld calculators and then, most recently, with computers. Each of these has a technology life cycle which exists within the overall framework of the demand life cycle. The strategic implications of this need to be seen in terms of what and who the firm is competing against, something which takes us back to Peter Drucker's questions of 'what business *are* we in?' and 'what business *should* we be in?' In practical terms, this can be seen by a manufacturer of slide rules in the 1960s continuing to see its competitors as other manufacturers of slide rules rather than the new and emerging forms of technology such as adding machines and low-priced calculators which subsequently forced slide rules into decline. For a computer manufacturer today the issues are broadly similar.

The need for a company to identify clearly what type of demand technology to invest in and when to shift emphasis to a new technology has been discussed in some detail by Ansoff (1984) who refers to a demand technology as a *strategic business area* (SBA), 'a distinctive segment of the environment in which the firm does or may want to do business'. The problem faced by many firms, however, is that, confronted by a variety of different markets and technologies, all of which are changing, there is little scope for mastering them all. The strategist is faced with the need to decide where the firm's emphasis is to be placed. In essence this involves a choice between investing heavily in one area of technology or less heavily in several. This latter strategy, while offering less risk, has the disadvantage of making it less likely that the firm will either become or retain market leadership. Rather it is the pioneering firm that invests heavily in the new technology that is likely to emerge and remain as the leader.

FIGURE 10.22
Competitive strategies for leaders, followers and challengers

	Stage of industry development		
	Growth	**Maturity**	**Decline**
Strategic position of the firm Leader	Keep ahead of the field Discourage other possible entrants Raise entry barriers Develop a strong selling proposition and competitive advantage 'Lock in' distributors Build loyalty Advertise extensively	Hit back at challengers Manage costs aggressively Raise entry barriers further Increase differentiation Encourage greater usage Search for new uses Harass competitors Develop new markets Develop new products and product variations Tighten control over distributors	Redefine scope Divest peripherals Encourage departures Squeeze distributors Manage costs aggressively Increase profit margins
Challenger	Enter early Price aggressively Develop a strong alternative selling proposition Search for the leader's weaknesses Constantly challenge the leader Identify possible new segments Advertise aggressively Harass the leader and followers	Exploit the weaknesses of leaders and followers Challenge the leader Leapfrog technologically Maintain high levels of advertising Price aggressively Use short-term promotions Develop alternative distributors Take over smaller companies	If the challenging strategy has not been successful, manage the withdrawal in the least costly way to you but in the most costly way to others
Follower	Imitate at lower cost if possible Search for joint ventures Maintain vigilance and guard against competitive attacks Look for unexploited opportunities	Search for possible competitive advantages in the form of focus or differentiation Manage costs aggressively Look for unexploited opportunities Monitor product and market developments	Search for opportunities created by the withdrawal of others Manage costs aggressively Prepare to withdraw

This line of thought can be taken a step further by relating the development stage of an industry – growth, maturity, or decline – to the organization's strategic position – leader, challenger, or follower. The strategic implications of the interplay between these two dimensions is illustrated in Figure 10.22. See also Illustration 10.11.

Life Cycles and Managerial Style

Although a considerable amount has been written on product and market life cycles and how strategies need to reflect life cycle stages, relatively little has been said about the appropriateness of managerial style. There is, however, a strong argument for the style of management to be tailored to the particular demands of different stages. In the introductory stage, for example, there is a need for an *entrepreneurial* style of management in which emphasis is placed upon the rapid identification and seizing of opportunities, flexible structures and a risk-taking culture. In the growth stage this needs to be modified slightly with greater attention being paid to long-term planning and control. In maturity this needs to change again in order to capitalize on the profit opportunities that exist, something which argues the case for what Arthur D. Little refers to as a *critical administrator* and which is particularly important bearing in mind that the

---

Illustration 10.11: Zero Sum Games and Negative Sum Games

In mature markets breakthroughs which lead to a major change in competitive positions and to the growth of the market are rare. Because of this, competition becomes a zero sum game in which one organization can only win at the expense of others. However, where the degree of competition is particularly intense, a zero sum game can quickly become a negative sum game, in that everyone in the market is faced with additional costs. As an example of this, when one of the major high street banks in Britain tried to gain a competitive advantage by opening on Saturday mornings, it attracted a number of new customers who found the traditional Monday–Friday bank opening hours to be a constraint. However, faced with a loss of customers, the competition responded by opening on Saturday as well. The net effect of this was that, although customers benefited, the banks lost out as their costs increased but the total number of customers stayed the same.

In essence, this proved to be a negative sum game.

---

majority of products spend most of their lives in the mature stage. In the final stage of the life cycle the managerial needs change yet again with the focus tending to shorten, costs being reduced and the need for an increased emphasis upon *opportunities milking* styles. These ideas have been expressed in a slightly different, albeit more colourful, way by Clarke and Pratt (1985) who argue for four styles of management: nursemaid, tank driver, housewife and lemon squeezer. See also Illustration 10.12.

10.15 ACHIEVING ABOVE AVERAGE PERFORMANCE AND EXCELLENCE

Throughout this book we have tried to emphasize the importance of internal and external analysis, and for strategy to be based not just on corporate objectives, but also on a fundamental understanding of corporate capability. This theme is a reflection of the paradigm which can be traced back to the work of Mason in the late 1950s and Chandler (1962) in the early 1960s which 'relates the constructs of strategy, structure, environment and performance in a formulation which verbally states that a firm's performance is a function of its environment, its strategy and its structure'. These ideas have been reflected in a series of empirical studies in recent years by, among others, Peters and Waterman (1982), Goldsmith and Clutterbuck (1985), and Hooley et al. (1983). Of these, it is undoubtedly the work of Peters and Waterman that has had the greatest impact. Their research, which has subsequently provided the basis for a variety of other studies, was designed to identify the organizing characteristics of successful American companies. The characteristics which they suggested led to above average performance and excellence in ambiguous environments were:

1 *A bias for action.* Successful organizations showed an ability and desire to try things – to respond to situations rather than to sit back and hope for environments to change in favour of the organization.
2 *Closeness to the customer.* Success for these firms was founded on understanding customers and in serving them well.

Illustration 10.12: The Regeneration of a Market: the Launch of Häagen-Dazs Ice Cream

In 1989, as part of their objective of building the biggest ice cream brand in the world, Grand Met took the decision to launch Häagen-Dazs into Europe. At the time of the launch, the European market was dominated by three large multinationals: Unilever, which had a worldwide market share of 40%, Mars, and Nestlé. However, despite the size, strength and undoubted marketing expertise of their competitors, Grand Met believed that it had identified a number of areas in which the three companies were vulnerable to an attack by a new entrant. The most significant of these was that no real attempt had been made to develop either a global or a Eurobrand.

FIGURE 10.23 *Annual per capita consumption of ice cream (1990)*

	Litres
Sweden	13.6
Norway	11.9
Finland	11.0
UK	7.8
France	6.5
Germany	5.5

There were several apparent reasons for this, including the way in which patterns of ice cream consumption varied significantly from one country to another (see Figure 10.23); taste differences (85% of ice cream in the UK was non-dairy, whilst almost everywhere else in Europe, except for Portugal and Ireland, it was **dairy** ice cream); and buying and eating patterns (in France, the impulse sector accounted for 28% of sales and the take home sector for 72%. By contrast, the impulse sector in Italy accounted for 41% of sales, whilst in the UK and Germany it was 43% and 62% respectively). These differences were then compounded by the product's highly seasonal nature and by the way in which the European ice cream market had stagnated since 1985. Because of this, the sector was seen generally to be an unexciting market which offered few real opportunities for growth. The majority of consumers were children, the average life expectancy of a brand was around three years, new brands needed heavy advertising support in order to gain national distribution, and the new product failure rate was high.

Despite this, Häagen-Dazs was launched in 1989 and, with only a modest marketing budget, achieved sales in 1990 of $10 million. By September 1991, this had tripled to $30 million and, by 1992, had reached $100 million, making it the European market leader in the premium sector.

So what led to the brand's success?
In a number of ways, Häagen-Dazs illustrates Hamel and Prahalad's thinking on the need for managers to focus upon reinventing their industry and/or regenerating the strategy, (refer to p. 367). At a time when the quality of ice cream was generally poor (as one commentator remarked, ice cream had deteriorated to the point at which it was just cheap, cold and sweet) and marketed very largely on the basis of a pull strategy with heavy television spending supported by trade and consumer promotions, Häagen-Dazs chose to pursue a very different three-pronged marketing push strategy

designed to increase the awareness of the brand, achieve a high trial rate, and generate substantial word-of-mouth. One consequence of this was that 'it radically changed the rules of the game in the European ice cream market (Joachimsthaler, 1994, p. 4).

The principal dimensions of this strategy involved:

1 the opening of a series of ice cream parlours in large European cities;
2 targeting food service accounts in expensive hotels and restaurants; and
3 targeting major retail accounts including supermarket chains, delicatessens, cinemas and convenience stores. In doing this, Häagen-Dazs opted for extensive sampling and retailer support packages which included upright freezer display cabinets.

However, underpinning this were four further factors which, for many observers, are the real keys to success:

● the product's demonstrably superior quality and taste which stems from the very high dairy (butter) fat content, the use of 100% natural ingredients and the absence of stabilisers;
● a superb product delivery service;
● premium pricing (in the UK its prices were 30–40% higher than its immediate competitors, whilst in Germany it was twice as expensive as the local premium product); and
● a highly distinctive and provocative advertising campaign which featured black and white photography inspired by the movie *Nine and a Half Weeks*, a theme of 'The Ultimate Experience in Personal Pleasure', and the ending on every piece of advertising copy, 'Häagen-Dazs – dedicated to pleasure'.

The effect of the Häagen-Dazs strategy upon the market proved to be significant. By taking their competitors by surprise and redefining both the product and the market, the competition was forced to respond. In the event, nearly all did this by launching their own premium quality and premium priced products in an almost desperate attempt to capitalise upon the new market. By the end of 1993, however, it was clear that Häagen-Dazs was the winner of what was labelled the ice cream wars. Not only had it managed to increase its market share yet further, it had maintained a significant price premium.

Source: Joachimsthaler, E. A. (1994), Häagen-Dazs Ice Cream: the making of a global brand *(case study), International Graduate School of Management*

3 *Autonomy and entrepreneurship.* In order to avoid some of the problems of 'bigness', many successful firms pushed responsibility and authority (autonomy) 'down the line' to product managers and venture teams. In addition they encouraged staff to be entrepreneurial.
4 *Productivity through people.* The 'excellent' companies treated their workers as mature people who would respond better to high expectations and peer-group assessment rather than to heavy handed 'boss' control.
5 *Hands-on value-driven.* This characteristic refers to the way that leaders, through personal example and involvement, have indoctrinated their organizations to accept and adhere to those core values that are essential to the organization's identity and success.
6 *Sticking to the knitting.* According to Peters and Waterman, organizations that do branch out into new operating areas which are related enough to benefit

from existing 'excellent' skills perform more successfully than the 'out and out' conglomerates.

7 *Simple form, lean staff*. The successful companies had avoided two dangers that expansion creates – complex organization structures and large numbers of staff personnel. Excellent companies seem to have few people working at corporate level – most are out 'in the field' getting things done. Despite the hugeness of many of these winning organizations, staff knew their job and their place in the structure – even though jobs and structures might be in a constant state of flux.

8 *Simultaneous loose–tight properties*. While the excellent firms encouraged autonomy and entrepreneurship, employees knew that discretionary decision making operated within the constraints of adherence to the organization's core values. Excellence in these areas was often achieved through attention to, and control of, the finest detail.

Although Peters and Waterman's work has had a significant influence on management thinking, a number of critics have pointed out that by the time their book was published in 1982 several of its 'excellent' firms, including Hewlett Packard and Caterpillar, had begun to experience difficulties. In the case of Caterpillar, for example, it was, as we observed earlier (see p. 359), coming under increasing attack from the Japanese firm Komatsu, and finding it difficult to respond effectively. Their response to this was that this did not in any way invalidate their research, but rather it was an illustration of the difficulties of adhering to the characteristics of excellence. This has in turn been reflected in a comment by Brownlie (1987, p. 101) who has suggested that, 'Despite the lessons of Peters and Waterman, the history of many firms reveals that success and excellence remain temporary and elusive phenomena.' Recognition of this highlights the need for constant monitoring of the businesses environment and for the results to be reflected in an updating of the assumptions underpinning the firm's strategic thinking.

This theme has in turn been discussed in detail by Hugh Davidson in his book *Offensive Marketing* (1987). Davidson argues that offensive marketing is a practice which combines the age-old virtues of risk taking with a modern approach to marketing. It is practised, he suggests, by only a handful of successful companies and differs enormously from the sluggish and specialized concept that passes for marketing in most companies. For Davidson (1987(b), pp. 24–9), offensive marketing is summed up by the acronym POISE – Profitable, Offensive, Integrated, Strategic, and Effectively Executed. These elements work as follows:

Profitable: marketing is not just to increase market share or provide good value for consumers, but to increase profit. Offensive marketers will encounter conflicts between giving the consumer what he or she wants, and running the firm efficiently. One of their skills is to reach the right balance between these sometimes opposing elements.
Offensive: an offensive approach calls for an attitude which decides independently what is best for a company, rather than waiting for competition to make the first move.
Integrated: where marketing is integrated it permeates the whole company. It challenges all employees to relate their work to the needs of the marketplace and to balance it against the firm's profit needs.
Strategic: winning strategies are rarely developed without intensive analysis and careful consideration of alternatives. A business operated on a day-to-day basis, with no long-term marketing purpose, is more likely to be a follower than a leader.
Effectively executed: an intelligent approach is no use without effective execution, which is vitally dependent on the relationship between marketing and other departments, and on the existence of common strategies.

Offensive marketing is, Davidson suggests, 'less a matter of intelligence and ability – since most companies have plenty of both – than of attitudes, structure and strategy. It is also a set of attitudes and approaches leading to winning strategies executed with flair, and a serious approach to providing excellent value to the consumer and strong profit growth' (1987(b), p. 29).

In the period since the publication of *In Search of Excellence* (1982), Peters has continued to pursue the interrelated themes of excellence and high performing organizations in a series of books, including *Thriving on Chaos* (1987). In this, as with much of what he has written, he adopts a highly prescriptive and evangelical tone, arguing that for managers to succeed in ever more demanding environments they need to follow certain rules. These involve:

1 redefining the mundane;
2 listening to and measuring customer satisfaction in order to become a customer responsive organization;
3 cherishing and empowering front-line people;
4 responding quickly to customers' needs and pursuing strategies of fast-paced innovation;
5 focusing on quality and service;
6 learning to love change.

This general theme has, in turn, been developed by Treacy and Wiersema (1995) who, in the introduction to their book *The Discipline of Market Leaders*, suggest that

> The challenge facing corporate leaders today is nothing less than the reinvention of their companies. Something is happening to the nature of competition, something fundamental and inevitable. The signs are all around us. Market leadership is increasingly hard to win – and even harder to keep. Customers are more demanding and less loyal than ever before, yet many markets are so saturated that the customer finds it impossible to distinguish between one "me-too" product and another. In this landscape, the maps and compasses of traditional business strategy will not serve. The navigation charts need to be redrawn.

Because of this, they argue that marketing planners need to ask a number of fundamental questions:

> Is your company willing to cannibalize its hottest product with a risky, untested new one? Offer a service at a loss hoping to establish a long-term relationship? Link up with an adversary to drive its costs even lower?
>
> If not – or if you believe the answer isn't of paramount importance – get used to mediocre market performance and to playing competitive catchup continuously. Your company will never be a market leader. Not until it learns discipline.

In a number of ways, these ideas can be seen to be an extension of the sort of thinking that Hammer and Champy (1993) proposed in *Re-engineering the Corporation*. In essence, they suggest, *Re-engineering the Corporation*, which introduced many managers to the ideas of business process re-engineering, was about how to run a competitive race. *The Discipline of Market Leaders* builds upon this in that it is 'about choosing the race to run' (op cit., p. xiii). Success, they argue, is increasingly based on a recognition that no company can succeed by trying to be all things to all people. Instead, it must identify the unique value which it alone can deliver to its chosen markets. In doing this, managers need to come to terms with three essential concepts:

> The first is the value proposition, which is the implicit promise a company makes to customers to deliver a particular combination of values – price, quality, performance, selection, convenience, and so on. The second concept, the value-driven operating model, is that combination of operating processes, management systems, business structure, and culture that gives a company the capacity to deliver on its value

proposition. It's the systems, machinery, and environment for delivering value. If the value proposition is the end, the value-driven operating model is the means. And the third concept, which we call value disciplines, refers to the three desirable ways in which companies can combine operating models and value propositions to be the best in their markets (op. cit., p. xiv)

The three value disciplines which Treacy and Wiersema consider to be so important are operational excellence, product leadership and customer intimacy:

1 *Operational excellence.* Companies which pursue this value and discipline are not product or service innovators, and nor are they concerned with developing deep and long-lasting relationships with their customers. Rather, they offer middle market products at the best price with the least inconvenience; it is this no-frills approach which characterizes many of the low price grocery retailers such as Netto, Lidl, Kwik Save, Lo-Cost and Aldi.
2 By contrast, *product leadership* involves focusing upon developing and offering products which consistently push at the boundaries of innovation; both Intel and Nike are examples of this.
3 The third value discipline is *customer intimacy* and is based on the idea that the organization concentrates upon building relationships and, in many cases, satisfying specialized or unique needs.

A summary of the bases of each of the three value disciplines appears in Figure 10.24.

FIGURE 10.24
The discipline of market leaders

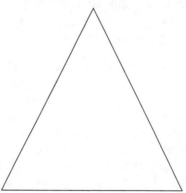

Operational excellence
- develop teams, run them together
- optimize systems
- integrate internal and external activities
- use IT
- aim for the highest levels of customer service

Product leadership
- direct the portfolio of activities
- create flexibile structures and robust structures
- nurture talent

Customer intimacy
- assemble, integrate and retain talented people
- coordinate expertise
- create deep relationships

It is important to recognize that the choice of which value discipline to pursue cannot be chosen in an arbitrary way. Instead, it involves a detailed understanding both of the company and its markets. Equally, Treacy and Wiersema argue, it cannot simply be grafted onto an organization but is instead 'a central act that shapes every subsequent plan and decision a company makes, coloring the organisation from its competencies to its culture. The choice of value discipline, in effect, defines what a company does and therefore what it is' (op cit., p. xv).

10.16 SUMMARY

Within this chapter we have focused on the need for a clear statement of marketing strategy and for this strategy to be based on a detailed understanding of corporate capability and competitive advantage. In doing this we took as our initial framework the work of Michael Porter. Porter's thesis is straightforward and suggests that in order to compete successfully the strategist needs to select a generic strategy and pursue it consistently. In deciding on this strategy consideration needs to be given to a variety of factors, the most significant of which Porter suggests are:

- the bargaining power of suppliers;
- the bargaining power of customers;
- the threat of new entrants to the industry;
- the threat of substitute products or services;
- the intensity of competitive rivalry.

The generic strategies that he identifies as being open to an organization are:

- cost leadership;
- differentiation;
- focus.

The failure to pursue one of these positions is likely to lead to a confused strategic message both internally and externally and to the organization being 'stuck in the middle'.

Any strategy needs to be based on a firm understanding of corporate capability and, in particular, any competitive advantages possessed by the organization. Several approaches to identifying and developing competitive advantage exist, including Porter's approach to value-chain analysis which is designed to help the strategist understand more readily the source and behaviour of costs within the industry, and the existing and potential sources of differentiation.

Against the background of an understanding of the organization's competitive advantages the strategist needs then to begin developing the detail of the strategy. In doing this explicit consideration needs to be given both to the organization's objectives and to its position within the marketplace. In part this position is determined by the competitive stance that has been adopted in the past. Thus organizations have a choice between a *market leader* strategy, a *market challenger* strategy, a *market follower* strategy, and a *market nicher* strategy. Each of these requires distinct courses of action and these were explored in some detail with parallels being drawn between marketing strategy and military strategy.

An important marketing objective for many private sector organizations is the pursuit of market share. The attractions of market share were explored and the findings of the PIMS research examined. Included within these is that:

- market share and profitability are strongly related;
- in the long run the single factor most affecting performance is the organization's relative product/service quality;
- most of the strategic factors which boost ROI also contribute to long-term value.

Marketing strategy needs also to take account of the stage of market evolution and the position reached on the *product life cycle* (PLC) by the product or brand. Although the PLC has been the subject of considerable criticism over the years, work recently has improved our understanding of the ways in which the concept can be used and these were incorporated into a model highlighting the implications of the PLC for strategy.

We concluded by making reference to the work done over the past decade in identifying the characteristics of high performing organizations. In doing this we made particular reference to the work of Peters and Waterman, who suggested that excellence comes from:

- a bias for action;
- autonomy and entrepreneurship;
- a closeness to the customer;
- productivity through people;
- 'sticking to the knitting';
- hands-on, value-driven;
- simple form, lean staff;
- simultaneous loose–tight properties.

10.17 EXERCISES

1 In Porter's terms, which of the three generic strategies is being pursued by each of your organization's SBUs? Is there any evidence of a middle-of-the-road or a stuck-in-the-middle strategy?

2 Making reference to examples, suggest how Porter's ideas of generic competitive strategies can be used by the marketing planner.

3 Which of Davidson's eight possible bases of competitive advantage (see p. 335) does your organization appear to have? To what extent are these (a) recognized and (b) exploited? Which competitive advantage(s) does each of your principal competitors have?

4 Select a market sector and identify the position (market leader, challenger, follower or nicher) that each firm *appears* to occupy. To what extent can you find evidence of a challenger's strategy? How successful does it appear to be?

5 Identify an organization which is very firmly a market leader and identify which of the three approaches to the defence of its position that are illustrated in Figures 10.6 and 10.7 it appears to be using. How successful does the strategy appear to be?

6 Identify examples of market challengers for each of the ten bases of attack that are identified in Figure 10.13. How successful does each one appear to have been?

7 In what circumstances would you recommend that an organization should pursue a market follower strategy?

8 On p. 363, we identify the seven guidelines for market niching. Identify an example for each of these.

9 What evidence do you see in your organization of strategic drift and strategic wear-out?

10 Where on the life cycle does each of your organization's major products or services appear to be? What are the implications of the overall picture that emerges from your analysis?

11 We refer on pp. 375–6 to Clarke and Pratt's ideas of management styles across the life cycle. Which style appears to predominate within your organization?

12 How would you categorize your organization? Is it a market leader, challenger, follower or nicher?

10.18 CASE STUDY

The MJS Catering Supplies Company

The MJS Catering Supplies Company is a specialist supplier of ready-prepared meals which are then reheated before serving. The company operates with four principal strategic business units serving the airlines, restaurants, hotels and educational markets. Selected sales and market data appear in Figure 1.

FIGURE 1
Selected sales and market data

	Sales (1996–97) £ million	Annual forecast market growth rate 1997–2000 (%)
Airlines	190	12
Hotels	163	10
Restaurants	120	8.5
Educational institutions	105	6.2
	578	

The company has grown rapidly over the past few years and has seen little need for detailed environmental analysis. Equally, little thought has been given by the management team to the development of an explicit marketing strategy. Instead, they have operated with a strong sales orientation and what they believe is an instinctive and unerring feel for the market which has led to the company identifying and exploiting a series of market opportunities.

The company's selling propositions centre around the quality of its products, its innovative recipes, strong service back-up and a high value for money offer. Although MJS is not a market leader in any of the sectors in which it operates, the company is seen by industry analysts to be a major player in all four of its markets.

Over the past two years, a number of changes have occurred in the catering supplies market, the three most significant of which have been the entry to the market of several new competitors; the takeover of two medium-sized firms by cash-rich and growth-oriented firms; and the merger of three of the smaller players. The net effect of this has been that the structure of the market has begun to change fairly dramatically, as have the nature and bases of competition.

Although MJS has not previously viewed its competitors as a real threat and has relied instead upon its strong market position and established reputation, there is now a recognition that patterns of competition in the future will be very different. The company has recently lost two of its most profitable airline and hotel customers to medium-sized and increasingly aggressive organizations, and has been unsuccessful in five of the last six contracts for which it has submitted tenders. The majority of these tenders appear to have been lost to relatively small companies which have been market niching within the airlines and hotels markets.

Because of this, an element of panic has hit the company and there is now a recognition of the need for a far more offensive approach to its markets. In commenting on this, the managing director said, 'As a company, we're fat, lazy and complacent. If we carry on like this, we simply won't survive.'

As the firm's marketing manager, you have the responsibility for advising on the development and implementation of a new and more offensive marketing approach.

Areas for Discussion

1 Prepare a briefing paper for the main board outlining the dimensions of an offensive marketing strategy and, in particular, how the company might fight off the emerging market challengers and nichers. You should also include within the paper comments on the organizational and cultural implications of adopting a more offensive competitive stance.

2 In response to the findings of a market research exercise (see Figure 2), prepare a report for the managing director outlining the principal dimensions of a relationship marketing programme and how such a programme might most effectively be implemented.

FIGURE 2
A summary of market research findings

MJS's customers' perceptions of MJS		
	1994	**1996**
Product quality	4.3	3.1
Product innovation	4.6	3.3
Customer support	4.0	2.9
Value for money	4.2	3.7
Breadth of the product range	4.1	3.6

Note: Ratings are based on a five-point scale:
1 = very poor, 5 = very good)

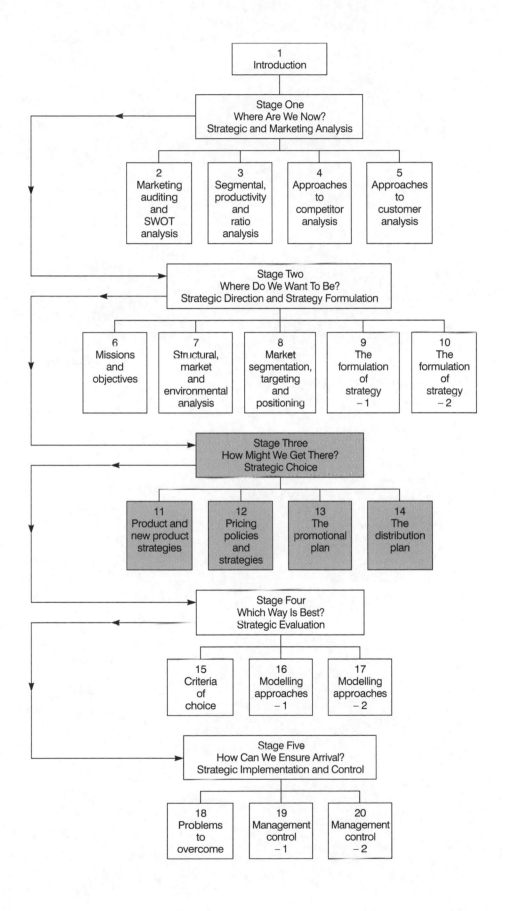

Stage Three
How Might We Get There?
Strategic Choice

PREAMBLE

The principal contribution made by marketing to the achievement of objectives is via the marketing mix. In essence, this entails developing products and services to meet the needs of the target segment(s) (established by marketing research), communicating their benefits to target audiences and ensuring that they are available in the right place, at the right price and at the right time.

In writing here on the marketing mix, we have recognized that most readers will already be familiar with the basics; also that several books are available which are devoted to the individual elements of the marketing mix, such as selling, advertising, pricing and distribution, for those readers looking for a more detailed treatment.

As we said in Chapter 1, at its simplest, the marketing mix can be seen to consist of four major elements which were referred to by McCarthy (1974) as the four Ps, namely:

P1: Product (or service)
P2: Price
P3: Promotion (communications)
P4: Place (distribution)

However, in recent years a number of writers have argued that the traditional mix is too limited, particularly when talking about the marketing of services, and that there is therefore a strong case for its expansion. It is this which has led to the idea of the 7Ps, to which brief reference was made in Chapter 1. This expanded mix gives emphasis to the so-called 'soft' elements of marketing – people, physical evidence and process management. Here, however, we focus upon the traditional four 'hard' Ps of marketing.

11 | Product and new product strategies

11.1 LEARNING OBJECTIVES

When you have read this chapter you should be able to understand:

(a) the nature and importance of product strategy;
(b) the role of the product within the overall marketing mix;
(c) the dimensions of brand strategy;
(d) the strategic importance of new product development;
(e) how the new product development process should operate.

These objectives are contained within Figure 11.1.

FIGURE 11.1
The product plan and its likely submix

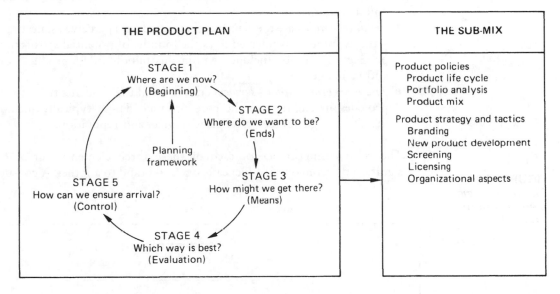

11.2 INTRODUCTION

In this chapter, the first of four dealing with the elements of the marketing mix, we focus on what is commonly acknowledged to be the most important single element of the marketing mix, the product. Product policy is or should be the principal preoccupation of marketing managers since it is as Thomas (1987, p. 238) has pointed out 'the product or service offering of a company or organisation [which] ultimately determines the nature of the business and the marketplace perception of the business. In this sense it is the core of the marketing management function'. In making this comment Thomas gives implicit recognition to the idea that, although in an ideal world marketing management starts with the identification and selection of opportunities, in practice resources have generally already been committed. The principal concern of most organizations is therefore *product* policy and management rather than *market* policy and management. Given this, the task faced by the strategist in developing an effective product policy can be seen to consist of two distinct but interrelated elements: first, the management of the organization's existing range of products or services, and second, the development of new or modified products or services. It is to these two areas that we now turn our attention.

11.3 WHAT IS A PRODUCT?

The term 'product' is used throughout this chapter to refer both to physical goods and to intangibles: Hoover, for example, sells vacuum cleaners which are *goods*; Prudential sells insurance and pension schemes which are *services*; and Weight Watchers sells an *idea* - that of losing weight through changed eating habits and greater self-control. An organization's 'product' may therefore fall into any one of these three categories.

In discussing the nature of the product, Kotler (1988, p. 446) suggests that three distinct elements need to be considered: the product's attributes, its benefits, and the nature of the support services. These are illustrated in Figure 11.2.

- *Product attributes* are associated with the core product and include such elements as features, styling, quality, brand name, packaging, and size and colour variants.
- *Product benefits* are the elements that consumers perceive as meeting their needs – this is sometimes referred to as the 'bundle of potential satisfactions' that the product represents. Included within this bundle is the product's performance and its image.
- *The marketing support services* consist of all the elements that the organization provides in addition to the core product. These typically include delivery, installation, guarantees, after-sales service, and reputation.

The relative importance of each of these three elements can of course vary significantly from one product category and brand to another. A consumer buying

FIGURE 11.2
The three basic elements of the product

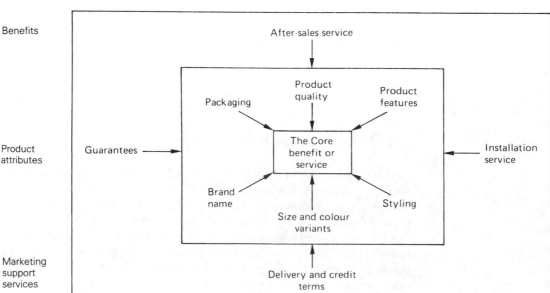

SOURCE: Adapted from Kotler (1988), p. 446

a car such as a Porsche, for example, is likely to be more concerned with the intangible attributes such as image, brand and quality than with the economic benefits of the car. The significance of this from the viewpoint of the manufacturer and the dealer needs to be seen in terms of how the product is presented through advertising and supported by the dealer network.

Recognition of this leads in turn to two distinct views of the product:

1 that the product is simply a physical entity which has a precise specification;
2 that it is a far broader concept which consists of anything, be it favourable or unfavourable, that a buyer receives in the exchange process.

From the viewpoint of the marketing strategist, it is the second of these two views which is the most meaningful and which is encapsulated in the idea of the product as a 'bundle of potential satisfactions'. This has been elaborated upon by Abbott (1955, p. 9) who has emphasized that 'What people really desire are not the products but satisfying experiences.' This view has in turn been expanded upon by Levitt (1976) who argues that products need to be seen in terms of the benefits they provide rather than the functions they perform. Thus, he suggests, 'One million quarter-inch drills were sold not because people wanted quarter-inch drills, but because they wanted quarter-inch holes.'

Views such as this provide strong support for the suggestion that in developing product policy the strategist needs to give explicit recognition both to the objective and the subjective elements of the product. The objective elements in the form of, for example, the physical specification and price are often easily copied by a competitor. The subjective element, however, which consists of among other things the image and reputation is generally more difficult to copy and in many markets provides the most effective basis for differentiation. In practice, of course, the objective and subjective dimensions are interrelated: a strong image and positive reputation, for example, develop largely as the result of high quality and reliability. It is therefore the recognition of this sort of interrelationship that is at the heart of effective product policy, since it is the combination of the two which delivers 'value' to the customer. This point has been elaborated on in the context of the American car industry by Bennett and Cooper (1982, pp. 52–69). The success of the Japanese and the Europeans in the 1970s in taking share away from domestic manufacturers was due, they suggest, not simply to lower prices and better fuel economy. Rather, it was the case that 'The European and Japanese car makers have simply been better competitors; they anticipated market needs; they built a better product – one that is more reliable, has better workmanship, and is better engineered; and they did it effectively. In short, these manufacturers delivered better value to the American consumer.'

11.4 THE DIMENSIONS OF PRODUCT POLICY

Effective product management is to a very large extent based on an understanding and application of two major concepts, the product life cycle and portfolio analysis, both of which were discussed in some detail in Chapters 9 and 10. The reader should therefore return briefly to the discussion on pp. 311–20 and 371–5 for a detailed discussion of these two concepts, since here we will concentrate simply on some of the key points.

The Product Life Cycle: Its Contribution to Product Policy

In our earlier discussion we referred to the product life cycle (PLC) as one of the best-known but least understood concepts in marketing. The ideas that underpin the concept are, as we pointed out, straightforward, suggesting that sales following a product's launch are initially slow but then increase as awareness grows. Maturity is reached when the rate of sales growth levels off and repeat purchasers account for the majority of sales. Ultimately, sales begin to decline as new products and new technologies enter the market, leading eventually to the product being withdrawn.

Although a considerable amount has been written about the product life cycle and how it might or should be used, surprisingly few empirical studies of the concept's real scope for application within an organization's product policy have been conducted. It is perhaps because of this that the literature on the life cycle still tends to lean towards one extreme or the other, with some arguing that life-cycle analysis offers a strong foundation for effective product management, while others dismiss the idea as being conceptually attractive but pragmatically worthless. Prominent among those within this second category are Dhalla and Yuspeh (1976, pp. 102–112) who, in an article entitled 'Forget the Product Life Cycle', argued that the PLC is conceptually and operationally flawed. The bases of their argument were that:

- The biological metaphors used to suggest that products are living entities is misleading.
- Attempts to match empirical sales data to life-cycle curves have proved difficult and the results are largely meaningless.
- The life cycle of a product and hence the shape of the curve is determined by how the product is managed over time. It is not an independent variable as is suggested by traditional PLC theory.
- The PLC is not equally valid for product class, product form and for brands as is often argued.
- The stages of the life cycle are difficult to define.
- Identifying where on the life cycle a product is at any particular time is difficult to determine.
- The scope for using the concept as a planning tool is limited.
- Evidence exists to suggest that where organizations have tried to use the PLC as a planning tool, opportunities have been missed and costly mistakes made.

In the light of these comments, what then is the status of the PLC and what contribution might it be expected to make to product policy? Quite obviously, it is not a model with universal applicability, but rather an ideal type from which insights into the general behaviour of most product forms can be deduced, but which in its application requires a possibly high degree of caution. This is reflected in a comment by Thomas (1987, p. 242) who suggests that:

> as a means to an end – that end being more sensitive management of the product over time, no sensible product manager should ignore the intellectual inheritance represented by the product life cycle literature. Using the product cycle concept is a means to creating an optimal life cycle, rather than being controlled by it. Sales history is a fundamental tool of the product manager, but sales history is not the only variable controlling the future of the product.

This general line of argument has also been pursued by Michael Porter (1980) who has highlighted the significance of the context in which the PLC is applied. Porter argues that the nature of the industry and its evolution from embryonic to declining is at least of equal importance as the stage of the product's life cycle. (For a more detailed discussion of this, refer to pp. 329–32.)

The Role of Portfolio Analysis in Product Policy

The second key contributor to effective product policy is portfolio analysis and management. The techniques of portfolio analysis are discussed in detail in Chapter 9 and so here we will limit ourselves to identifying some of the principal elements of its contribution to product policy. The starting point involves recognizing that portfolio analysis provides a firm foundation both for developing and evaluating marketing plans. The data required, for example, for the growth-share and market-attractiveness/business-position type matrices help not only in the process of allocating resources, but also in deciding upon the current and future mix and balance of the organization's portfolio. This in turn provides the basis for identifying the contribution that each strategic business unit (SBU) is capable of making to short-term and long-term strategy and, where this contribution is perceived to be inadequate, for adjustments to be made.

For Haspeslagh (1982), the principal role of portfolio analysis within product policy is that of resource allocation and, subsequently, a series of decisions regarding each product or SBU. These decisions revolve around the issue of how to manage each product and, in particular, whether to adopt a custodial, harvesting, penetration, phased withdrawal, divestment, acquisition, or new product development stance.

In many ways, this view of portfolio analysis represents a neat summary of its potential role and contribution. Portfolio displays are not intended as strategic answers to the resource allocation problem, but are instead designed to help in the process of communication and decision making at brand management and strategic management levels.

The Product Mix and the Product Line: The Issue of Definition

The group of products sold by a company is referred to as the firm's *product mix*. Thus all of the products sold by Heinz, including soups, baby foods, and baked beans, make up its product mix. Although the number of products within a firm's mix can vary enormously, the majority of firms begin with a single product. Ford, for example, began in this way and satisfied consumers' needs for a low-cost car. Over time, however, companies typically recognize that their single product does not satisfy the needs of all consumers and that other opportunities exist. At this stage it begins to develop a *product line*. Thus, in the case of Ford, it began developing other types of car. A product line can therefore be seen as a group of broadly similar products targeted at a broadly similar group of consumers who will use them in a broadly similar fashion. In many cases, of course, companies develop multiple product lines either to capitalize on other opportunities or to reduce a potential competitive threat. Volvo, for example, has developed a series of product lines including cars, trucks, buses and marine engines. Equally, Procter & Gamble which began life as a soap manufacturer has developed or acquired product lines in, among other areas, foods, coffee, paper products and baby products.

The advantages of multiple product lines can be considerable and not only help a company to grow more rapidly than would be the case with a single product line, but also help to reduce the risk associated with being overly dependent on one product and market sector.

The Product as a Strategic Variable

Because the product is at the very heart of marketing strategy, the need to manage it strategically is of paramount importance, since how well this is done is the key both to the organization's overall financial performance and to the gaining and retaining of market share. The question of *how* to manage the product strategically is not necessarily answered easily, however, and for many firms involves a careful balancing of costs, risks and returns. In doing this, explicit consideration needs to be given to competitors and in particular to the probable implications of any moves that they are likely to make.

In many cases, time is a critical dimension of product strategy and exerts a significant influence on any marketing manager's freedom of movement. In the long term, say five to 10 years, products can be changed radically in almost all industries and can therefore make a major contribution to corporate objectives. In the short term, however, the product is often much more inflexible. In the car industry, for example, a period of four years or so is often needed to develop and introduce a totally new model. In the shorter term, the strategist's flexibility is consequently more limited and restricted to a series of minor and often cosmetic changes. For this reason, innovation tends not to be a major element of short-term marketing strategy. Instead, the strategist is limited to a series of package and label changes, new varieties, accessories, options, and combinations of products that inject a degree of newness into the market.

In developing an effective product strategy, a variety of factors need to be considered. The first, and in many ways the most important, is the question of the *type* of product strategy that is to be pursued. Is it, for example, to be broadly offensive or broadly defensive? If it is to be offensive the strategist needs to consider not just how this is to be translated into action, but also its feasibility and the costs and risks that are associated with it. We can identify four types of product strategy:

1 a market leader product strategy;
2 a leadership challenging product strategy, which might translate, initially at least, into 'the strategy of the fast second' whereby the firm allows the existing leader to incur the costs and risks of developing a new product and then moves in rapidly after the launch with a copy or an improved version of the product;
3 a product following strategy;
4 a me-too product strategy.

The issue of how firms pursue a strategy of leading, challenging or following was examined in detail in Chapter 10 and the reader may find it useful to turn back to pp. 337–63 for a discussion of the key points. Where, however, an organization is intent either on leading or challenging, the implications for product strategy are considerable and are likely to make heavy demands upon resources. The majority of leaders retain their leadership position by means of a series of small and large innovations, supported by a heavy investment in advertising and distribution. For a challenger to succeed, the implications are straightforward and in many industries require an even greater level of investment.

The question of which strategy to pursue cannot be made in isolation, but requires a detailed understanding both of the organization's current position and capabilities, and of each competitor's stance and likely response pattern when challenged. The starting point should therefore be an assessment of the organization's current portfolio. Such an assessment can be carried out in one of several ways, including using the product life cycle and techniques of portfolio analysis, both of which were reviewed briefly at an earlier stage in this chapter. Based on this sort of analysis, Drucker (1963) recommends classifying products in one of six ways:

1 tomorrow's breadwinners;
2 today's breadwinners;
3 products that are capable of making a contribution assuming that drastic action is taken;
4 yesterday's breadwinners;
5 the also-rans;
6 the failures.

This approach to classification then provides the basis for posing three questions:

● Should we continue to market the product?
● If so, should the strategy and level of resource allocation be changed in a minor way?
● Should there be a major rethink of the product's strategy (e.g. a relaunch, a repositioning, or a major styling change)?

In answering these questions, the strategist needs to consider a variety of factors, but most importantly how the product is perceived by consumers and distributors; its probable future sales pattern; the scope that exists for repositioning or extending the life of the product; the availability of resources; the returns that are being generated currently; the ways in which returns are likely to increase or decrease in the future; possible competitive moves that will affect consumers' perceptions of the product; and the nature of any competing demands for the resources currently being absorbed by the product. In addition, consideration needs to be given to the relative rates of product and market growth, and whether the product is growing at a faster or slower rate than the overall market. Regardless of whether the growth rate is faster or slower, the strategist needs to consider first why this is the case and second the strategic implications (see Figure 11.3).

FIGURE 11.3
Product and market growth rates

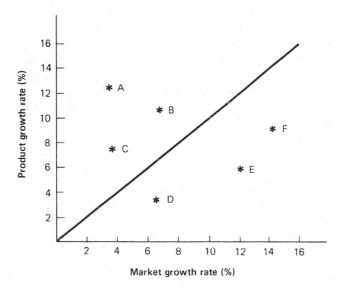

Products A, B and C are all growing at a faster rate than the rate of market growth. Products D, E and F are growing more slowly than the market. In both cases, the strategist needs to consider why this is so.

Much of the information needed for this should be generated on a regular basis by the organization's marketing information system, although in some instances specific studies of buyers, distributors, and competitors will be needed. By studying the product on a regular basis and, in particular, by focusing upon changing consumer needs and competitors' moves, the strategist should be able to identify more readily any inadequacies that exist and the scope or need for product development. As an example of this, the chewing gum manufacturers Wrigley identified that denture wearers would not buy gum because its stickiness loosened their dentures. The solution the company came up with was Freedent gum.

11.5 BRAND STRATEGIES

An important element of any product strategy is the role played by brand names. Brands are designed to enable customers to identify products or services which promise specific benefits. As such, they are a form of shorthand in that they create a set of expectations in the minds of customers about purpose, performance, quality and price. This, in turn, allows the strategist to build added-value into products and to differentiate them from competitors. Because of this, well-known brand names such as Rolex, Cartier, Chanel and Lacoste are of enormous strategic and financial value and are in many cases the result of years of investment in advertising. The significance of this in the case of IBM has been highlighted by the suggestion that the company's brand name is worth more than the gross national product of many nations. It also helps to explain why pirating of brand names has developed with enormous rapidity over the past decade.

In developing a brand strategy, an organization can pursue one of four approaches:

1 corporate umbrella branding;
2 family umbrella branding;
3 range branding;
4 individual branding.

The first of these – *corporate umbrella branding* - can be used in one of two ways: either as a lead name such as Heinz, Kellogg's or Cadbury's, or as a supporting brand name such as Allied-Lyons. In the case of Cadbury's, for example, the umbrella is used to cover a wide variety of chocolates and sweets including Cream Eggs, Flake, Dairy Milk, Milk Tray, Bournville, Roses, Fry's Chocolate Cream, and Turkish Delight.

Family umbrella names, by contrast, are used to cover a range of products in a variety of markets. A case in point is Marks and Spencer with its St Michael brand which is used for food, clothing and household textiles. The common link exists in terms of the quality, style and packaging. A broadly similar approach is used by C & A with its Canda label.

Range brand names are used for a range of products which have clearly identifiable links in a particular market. An example of this is the Lean Cuisine ranges of low calorie foodstuffs.

The fourth approach – *individual brand names* - is typically used to cover one type of product in one type of market, possibly with different combinations of size, flavour and service options or packaging formats. Examples of this include Lucozade, Marmite and Penguin.

Approaches to Brand Development

To be truly effective, a brand strategy has to develop over time and reflect environmental conditions. There is therefore a need for brand development, the seven principles of which have been identified by Davidson (1987, pp. 299–303):

1 understand your brands;
2 determine how all your brand names fit;
3 decide which brand names can be stretched and how far;
4 know when to develop new brand names;
5 consider licensing your brand name;
6 cover your tracks;
7 have a five-year brand development plan.

The starting point for this involves analysing the brand in order to understand in detail what it means to customers. In doing this, the strategist needs to identify the core values, the scope that exists for extending the brand name into other product or market sectors, and the areas which must at all costs be avoided. The core values relate to the essential meaning of the brand and can be subdivided into the *inner core values* or intrinsic qualities which if altered would seriously damage the brand's integrity, and the *outer core values* which have a greater degree of flexibility.

From here, the strategist needs to move on to consider the interrelationships between the brand names used. In the case of the Volkswagen Golf GTi, for example, Volkswagen is the umbrella name, Golf the model, and GTi the designation for performance. The issue here therefore is the extent to which names can be used, how they might be extended and how they might be used in combination with other models in the range.

The third stage involves deciding how far brand names can be stretched and still be meaningful. A company that has done this with considerable success in the 1990s is Mars which, having developed a very strong brand name and image with Mars Bars, then stretched the name into a Mars drink and Mars ice cream. Similarly, Johnson & Johnson, best known for its babycare products, stretched its brand name to cover a range of toiletry products for men, while Marks & Spencer stretched its name for clothes into foods and home furnishings.

In attempting to stretch a brand, the strategist needs to tread carefully. The obvious danger, of course, is that of moving into an area in which the brand name has little relevance or which detracts from the value of the brand in its core market. The aim should therefore be to operate only in the three cells in the bottom right-hand corner of Figure 11.4.

FIGURE 11.4
Brand stretching and market attractiveness

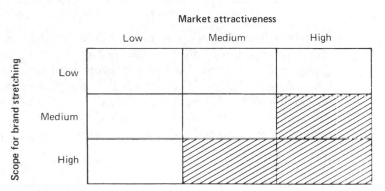

SOURCE: Adapted from Davidson (1987)

As an alternative to brand stretching, or indeed in addition to brand stretching, the strategist can opt for the development of new brand names. There are, of course, significant costs associated with this, particularly when put against the background of the traditionally high failure rate of new products. Estimates of the costs of successfully developing a new brand name vary considerably, but as a broad rule of thumb in the food or confectionery market it is unlikely to be much less than £3 million. Again, therefore, the strategist needs to tread carefully and consider developing a new brand name only when certain criteria can be satisfied. These include:

1 the product has a series of distinctive values;
2 the consumer benefits are both strong and obvious;
3 acceptance of the new product is highly likely;
4 when using an existing brand name would be inappropriate because there is little apparent linkage between the existing and new products;
5 when using an existing name would weaken the novelty impact of the new product.

For those organizations with very strong brand names there is often scope for generating additional profits by means of licensing. Among those to have done this with considerable success are Disney and Christian Dior.

The sixth stage of offensive brand development involves 'covering your tracks', a step which is designed to safeguard the brand name from the often illegal moves of others, particularly in the form of pirating.

The final stage of offensive brand development stems from the need for an explicit brand development plan. There is little real evidence to suggest, despite the growing recognition of the need for planning, that this extends into the area of brand name development. Because of this, and because of the significance of the brand name, the strategist should concentrate upon developing a brand development plan showing how each brand name is to be used over the next five years. In doing this, Davidson (1987, p. 303) suggests that five areas be considered:

1 What is the meaning of the brand today and what do we want it to mean in five years' time?
2 What line extensions and new products do we wish to develop under this brand name?
3 What changes in market needs and consumer demographics do we forsee that will require us to modify or change the brand meaning?
4 What are the detailed plans by year for achieving these changes in the next five years? What are the sales, spending and profit implications?
5 Bearing in mind the new markets we wish to enter, which ones can be covered with existing brand names and which need new brand names?

A final issue that needs to be considered at this stage stems partly from the developments taking place in the media with the emergence of larger media footprints, and partly from the growing internationalism of companies. The combination of these factors has led several manufacturers to reconsider their branding policies. Whereas previously different brand names have been used for the same product in different countries, there is now a move towards a greater commonality. Among those to have done this is Mars which changed its Marathon bar to Snickers.

Developing a Brand Strategy

For many organizations, branding is a fundamental element of the product strategy and provides the basis for a consumer franchise which, if managed effectively, allows for greater marketing flexibility and a higher degree of consumer loyalty. However, it needs to be recognized that branding involves a great deal more than simply putting a name on a package. Instead, it is about creating, maintaining and proactively developing perceived consumer value. It is only in this way that the organization is able to promise and continue delivery to the consumer a superior value to that offered by competitors.

It follows from this that any brand strategy is, of necessity, a long-term process which involves an investment in and commitment to the development of the brand over time. This long-term perspective involves the dovetailing of a number of issues, but in essence can be seen to be concerned with two principal issues:

1 where the brand is currently and how it is perceived;
2 how the brand is to be perceived in three, five and ten years' time and how this might best be achieved.

With regard to the first of these, the starting point for any brand strategy involves identifying:

1 the brand's current market positioning;
2 competitors' positioning strategies and resource bases;
3 the ways in which the market is likely to develop and the implications of product, brand and market life cycles;
4 customers' perceptions of the portfolio of brands in the market;
5 customers' expectations and the extent to which these are being met both by the brand and its competitors;
6 levels of customer loyalty across the market;

7 distributors' expectations and how they are being met by the various players in the market;

8 the financial, managerial and operational resources that can be called upon in managing the brand;

9 the bases of competition;

10 the relative importance of the brand to the organization; and

11 managerial expectations of the brand.

It is only against this background that the strategist is able to develop a vision for the brand. Having done this, attention needs then to turn to the planner who needs to focus upon issues of detail including:

- the sales, market share and profit objectives that will be pursued;
- the geographic markets in which the brand will be sold. Is there, for example, an objective of operating purely in the domestic markets or moving into a series of overseas markets? If the latter, how many markets will be involved; what will be their relative importance; and what timing will be involved?
- the competitive stance which is to be adopted;
- the segments which are to be targeted and their relative importance to the brand;
- the positioning and, in the long term, the repositioning strategy within each of these segments;
- the brand values that are to be developed;
- whether the brand is to be developed as an individual name (e.g. the Procter & Gamble policy); under a blanket family name (e.g. the Heinz policy); under a separate family name (e.g. Marks & Spencer with its St Michael brand); or under the banner of a company trade name combined with individual brand names (e.g. Kellogg's with Rice Crispies);
- the strategy towards brand extensions (e.g. Mars extending its name from chocolate bars to drinks and ice creams);
- the pricing points that the company is aiming for both in the short and the long term;
- the brand development policy. Is it the intention, for example, to concentrate upon developing a regular series of (small) modifications to the brand or to make a smaller number of larger modifications on a less frequent basis?
- whether there is scope for licensing the product for sale in other markets and, if so, how, where and over what time period;
- the policy towards generics.

Finally, in developing the brand strategy, the planner needs to give consideration to a series of financial issues, including the margins and contribution that the brand is required to generate in both the short and the long term, and the levels of investment that the brand needs if it is to achieve the objectives set.

How Much is a Brand Worth?

Towards the end of the 1980s a number of companies, some threatened by takeovers, argued that a substantial part of their net worth was the ownership of well-known and strategically valuable brand names. As such, they should be treated as assets and should appear in the balance sheet. Among those to have done this were Guinness who in their 1988 accounts recognized acquired brands to a value of £1695 millions, and Ranks-Hovis-McDougall (RHM) whose inclusion of more than 50 brands added £678 millions to their 1988 balance sheet.

Although the inclusion on the balance sheet of an intangible fixed asset is allowed under the 1985 Companies Act, valuing brands was seen to be potentially problematic. The starting point for valuation that has subsequently emerged attempts to simplify this by distinguishing between brands that have been acquired, perhaps as the result of a take-over, and brands which have been created and developed internally. In the case of Guinness, the figure of £1695 millions referred to above was arrived at by considering a series of criteria including:

1 title to the brand had to be clear and separately disposable from the rest of the business;
2 its value had to be substantial and long term, based on separately identifiable earnings that had to be in excess of those achieved by unbranded products.

RHM's approach was somewhat more elaborate and was developed by the Interbrand Group. Here the method was based on an elaborate scoring system against seven criteria:

1 The brand's market position. A market leader clearly counts for more than those in lower positions.
2 The age of the brand and its stability.
3 The nature of the market. Food and drink brands score more highly than those in, say, fashion or computers where names are less well known and often have a shorter life cycle.
4 Geographic spread. Is the brand known overseas and how much has been spent overseas on its promotion?
5 The market trend. Is it growing or declining?
6 The existence of trade marks or any other form of protection.
7 The levels and consistency of advertising and promotion.

Once a score had been arrived at against these criteria, account was taken of the brand's earning power. This was done by taking a weighted average of the profits over the preceding three years, minus any depreciation, tax and costs. The two factors were then put together to produce an earnings multiple.

The strategic value of a brand name was dramatically highlighted in 1990 when it was announced that minute traces of benzene, a carcinogenic substance, had been found in bottles of Perrier water in the United States. The company's subsequent action to reassure the public and minimize the damage to the brand are now seen to be a model for others as the company fought desperately not to retain short-term sales, but rather to safeguard the meaning and value of the brand. The company's experiences are discussed in Illustration 11.1.

A still more detailed approach to the measurement of brand equity has been put forward by Ambler (1996, p. 40–41), who advocates that consistent monitoring of 22 dimensions:

● prompted and unprompted brand awareness;
● market share, either by volume or value;
● relative price, market share by value and share by volume;
● levels of aided and unaided awareness;
● consumers' perceptions of the product's quality;
● economic profit or other bottom line indicators;
● market size and its total value;
● AMP (advertising, merchandising and promotion) expenditure;
● advertising as a percentage of AMP;
● share of voice (i.e. brand advertising as a proportion of total category advertising);
● penetration (i.e. the percentage of consumers buying in the last year);
● levels of loyalty;
● the number of product lines;

Illustration 11.1: And If One Green Bottle Should Accidentally Fall

Although the strategic importance and commercial value of strong brand names has long been recognized, their potential vulnerability was dramatically illustrated on a number of occasions in the 1980s and early 1990s. In the United States, for example, Procter & Gamble had to contend with rumours, based on the company's corporate logo, of satanic influences within the company. Equally, Heinz and Johnson & Johnson were both hit by cases of product tampering and contamination. In each case it was shown that the company's ability to defend the brand depended on the nature and speed of the response.

The need for a fast and decisive response was also illustrated in 1990 when minute traces of benzene, a carcinogenic substance, were found in bottles of Perrier water in the United States. The company responded immediately and very publicly by withdrawing 160 million bottles of Perrier from shelves throughout the world. The cause of the problem, a faulty filter at the company's Vergeze plant in south-west France, was replaced, the public was given unequivocal reassurances of the product's safety, and quality control measures were stepped up.

This need for a fast response can be seen both in terms of a company's social responsibility and because of the necessity of defending the market value of the brand. In the case of Perrier, the company's success owes much to the public's perceptions of the product's purity, and any erosion of this has dramatic and obvious implications for the brand itself, particularly when the brand has a high profile.

The growth of the bottled water market throughout the 1980s had been dramatic, with total annual sales for 1989 of £1.2 billion in the United States, £851 million in France, £1.4 billion in West Germany, £791 million in Italy, and £150 million in the UK. As the market leader in many of these markets (60 per cent in the UK, for example), the stakes were therefore high. Having withdrawn its bottles from the shelves and having seen many of its competitors gaining sales and share, Perrier then went on the offensive. This began with a series of advertising campaigns, and continued with an aggressive policy of selling into the distribution network new stock with a green flash on the pack saying 'New Production'. In doing this, Perrier was acutely aware of the costs of failure. Having spent enormous sums of money achieving market leadership and with more than half its FFr 1 billion profits derived from mineral water, the value of the brand was immeasurable.

- the percentage of sales generated by products launched in last *n* years (*n* can be three or five, for example);
- some measure of distribution strength;
- the strength of retailer relationships;
- pipeline inventory (i.e. stock sold into channels but not yet bought by consumers);
- leadership in terms of the product's influence upon the market;
- the percentage of sales spent on promotional activity;
- levels of price elasticity;
- absolute and relative quality;
- other image measures such as fashionability and modernity.

The Future of the Brand: the Challenge of the New Market-Place

Brand strategies involve focusing upon three key dimensions:

1 creating, building, maintaining and delivering consumer values that cannot be matched by others;
2 giving emphasis to strong positioning, consistent brand building and differentiation in order to avoid the brand's values being eroded and the product being seen as a commodity; and
3 developing a superior product or service through continuous innovation.

At the beginning of the 1990s, the marketing and financial performance of numerous major brands across a spectrum of market sectors began to decline. There were several reasons for this, the most significant of which were that consumers had become more sceptical and less willing to pay the price premium that many major brands demanded; competition in the form of higher quality 'me too' products from less well-known companies had begun to emerge; and retailers had begun developing own-label products which, for the first time, were able to match branded products at a lower price.

Among the most prominent of those to have been affected by these sorts of changes were:

- IBM which lost its position as the world's largest maker of personal computers to Compaq which, until then, had been a relatively poorly known manufacturer of PC clones
- Procter & Gamble, which was forced to rethink its premium pricing policy in order to cope with a flood of private-label products and the erosion of its market share; and
- Marlboro, which in order to fight back against intense competition in the cigarettes market slashed its prices by 19 per cent on what became known as 'Marlboro Friday'.

FIGURE 11.5
The changing fortunes of brands

The changing brand environment	Compounded by poor brand management	The fight back
The different types of consumer • Better educated • Better informed • More sceptical • More willing to experiment • Less brand-loyal • Much more media-aware • Higher expectations of service and the total package	**Low investment** • Inadequate product development • Poor consumer communication • An emphasis upon quick paybacks rather than true long-term brand building • Too little innovation and an emphasis upon small modifications	**Get lean** • Avoid the temptation to live off past successes • Cut costs to improve cost structures • Provide a basis for aggressive pricing • Prune weak brands and reallocate resources
Different types of competition • Generally higher quality levels • More aggressive • The more rapid launch of 'me too' products • Higher quality 'me toos'	**Lazy pricing** • Insufficient attention to value creation • Pricing arrogance • Insufficient product differentiation • Poor value for money • High cost bases	**Invest** • Innovate in the product and services • Create more consumer value **Listen to the market** • Get closer to customers
Different/better retailers • Better point of sale technology • A greater awareness of the performance of brands • More price competition • Greater financial pressures • The launch of private labels	**Management complacency** • A comfortable status quo • Short-termism • Risk aversion • Bureaucracy • Little long-term vision • Little innovative thinking • The decline of the killer instinct • Insufficient interaction with customers and distributors	**Be bold** • Think creatively • Set new paths • Retain existing customers • Set new market and performance standards • Take risks **Think globally** • Launch sequentially and rapidly across markets • Go for world brands

At the same time, own-label products were managing to capture an unprecedented share of many markets. In the UK in 1995, for example, private label accounted for 30 per cent of sales, in Germany and Switzerland it was 23 per cent, in France and Sweden it had reached 20 per cent, and in Portugal, Norway, Italy and Spain it was 10 per cent.

To a large extent, it can be argued that many of the problems brand marketers now face are at least partially self-inflicted. In Figure 11.5 we identify the changing environment within which many brands operate and, in particular, the different types of consumer, competition and retailer. However, rather than responding proactively to these, too many brand and marketing managers have responded by failing to invest enough in the brand, have pursued lazy pricing strategies and are generally guilty of at least a degree of management complacency. The net effect of this is that many brands have become far more vulnerable to attack than has been the case in the past.

But although brands have declined, this is not to say that there is no future for them. However, if brands are to fight back, there is a need for a series of proactive strategies; it is these which are outlined in column 3 of Figure 11.5. The starting point for this is a move away from the complacency that has characterized many brand strategies over the past few years and the need for a greater degree of innovation and for far higher levels of investment in the product and in innovation. At the same time, there is also a need for rather bolder strategies which open up new market sectors and set higher performance standards. Without a series of steps such as this, the gap between brands and private labels can only get smaller. See also Illustration 11.2.

Illustration 11.2: Handling Brand Crises and Brand Rage

At the beginning of the 1990s, a number of marketing managers were faced with problems which threatened to undermine their brands and destroy the brand equity that had been developed over the years. Labelled 'brand rage', the phenomenon highlighted the way in which gaps can open up between a product's real risks and how consumers perceive them. Amongst those to be hit by this were Intel's Pentium chip and Lever's Persil Power.

In the case of the Pentium chip, it was found that although it was the most thoroughly tested microprocessor ever, it had a small flaw which, Intel calculated, a commercial user would hit every 2700 years. Nevertheless, Intel was forced into a product recall costing $400 million. Equally, Persil Power was hit hard when its major competitor, Procter & Gamble, claimed that Persil's new ingredient caused damage to certain fabrics and dyes if washed at higher than usual temperatures. The damage, which seemingly could not be seen by the naked eye, was exploited by a series of Procter & Gamble advertisements and led to an embarrassing and expensive retreat by Persil.

The lessons from these and a series of other examples reinforce the Perrier experience (referred to in Illustration 11.1); if there is a problem with the brand, face up to it and act quickly. In this way, although short-term earnings will be affected, the long term will probably see the brand getting back to normal. Recognising this, Heineken responded immediately with a recall of 17 million bottles in 152 markets when a bottling fault led to slivers of glass in the bottles. By behaving so proactively, the possible or threatened crisis quite simply failed to develop.

Source: Management Today, *August 1996, pp. 76–77*

11.6 THE DEVELOPMENT OF NEW PRODUCTS

The development and introduction of new products has traditionally been seen to be a costly and risky activity. For an organization intent on either maintaining or improving its position in the market-place there are, however, few alternatives to new product activity of one sort or another. The issues faced by many marketing strategists thus revolve around the issue of the type of new product activity that is to be pursued and how best to manage and, hopefully, reduce risk levels.

In the majority of industries, there are two principal ways in which new products can be added to the product range: first, acquisition and second, internal new product development. Of the two, acquisition is often the faster and involves one of three approaches:

1 the organization can buy other firms;
2 the organization can buy a licence or franchise;
3 the organization can buy patents.

New product development (NPD) can in turn involve two approaches with products either being developed internally by an in-house R & D team, or by means of outside agencies used to develop products that satisfy internally generated criteria.

In the majority of firms, of course, both routes are pursued with a greater or lesser emphasis being placed on one or other activity as environmental conditions and pressures change.

What is a New Product?

Definitions of what constitutes a new product have over the years varied greatly. For our purposes, however, the term is used to refer to products that are *totally new to the world*, *product improvements*, *product modifications* and *new brands*. This issue of definition has been discussed in detail by the American management consultants Booz, Allen and Hamilton (BAH) (1982). There are, they suggest, two principal dimensions that need to be considered: how new is the product to the company, and how new is it to the market-place? This led them to propose a six-stage classification, as shown below. The figures in brackets represent the percentage of products appearing in each of these categories in the United States at the beginning of the 1980s and which are felt by BAH still to be broadly valid:

1 New to the world products that create an entirely new market. An example would be the launch of the Sony Walkman (10 per cent).
2 New product lines that are designed to enable a company to enter for the first time an existing product sector (20 per cent).
3 Additions to existing product lines (26 per cent).
4 Improvements and revisions to existing products (26 per cent).
5 Repositionings where existing products are retargeted in order to appeal to new market segments (7 per cent).
6 Cost reductions where products are modified to provide similar performance but at a lower cost (11 per cent).

An alternative approach to classification has been proposed by Robertson (1967) who placed innovations in three groups:

1 Continuous innovations which simply involve the modification of existing products and lead to few if any changes in consumer behaviour.
2 Dynamically continuous innovations which, while more disruptive than the previous category, do not change behaviour patterns in any fundamental way.

3 Discontinuous innovations which are dramatically new and which lead to significant changes in patterns of behaviour and usage. Included within this are the jet engine, television, stainless steel, antibiotics, and so on.

The Increasing Risks of New Product Development

We commented earlier that new product development has traditionally been seen as a high-risk activity. There are several sources of this risk, the most significant of which represent a mixture of financial, social, psychological and physical elements. For a variety of reasons these risks have increased over the 1980s and seem likely to continue increasing throughout the 1990s. There are several explanations for this, the most obvious of which are that buyers are becoming increasingly demanding and discriminating; markets are becoming more fragmented; product life cycles are shortening, with the result that pay-back periods are reducing; the expectations of distributors and dealers are increasing; the pace of technology is becoming ever faster; and competition generally is increasing. Recognition of this has led to what can be referred to as 'the new product development dilemma' in which, while there is widespread agreement that new products are needed if the firm is to grow, the likelihood of success appears to be getting ever smaller.

The causes of the high failure rate of new products have been examined within a variety of organizations and have led to a series of conclusions, the most prominent of which are:

- the size of the market is frequently overestimated;
- the product fails to perform at the levels demanded or expected by users;
- competitors prove to be too firmly entrenched;
- the product is poorly positioned, inadequately advertised, or priced at too high a level;
- distributors lack commitment to the launch and fail to provide the support needed;
- the new product is pushed through the development by a senior executive, despite market research findings which point to the product's likely failure.

These points are elaborated on at a later stage in this chapter.

If anything, however, failure rates seem likely to increase over the next decade as the new product development process becomes more complex. For Kotler (1988, p. 407) this greater complexity is due to seven pressures:

1 the growing shortage of new product ideas in certain areas;
2 increasingly fragmented markets which means smaller market segments, more precise needs and reduced sales and profit potentials;
3 increased societal and governmental constraints;
4 the costliness of the NPD process;
5 shortages of capital;
6 shorter time spans between the emergence of the idea and the physical launch of the product;
7 shorter life spans as competitors either copy the product idea or develop improved technologies.

In the light of these factors, it seems likely that the pressures on the marketing strategist will increase, possibly dramatically, over the next decade. Insofar as it is possible to identify how this might be dealt with most effectively, it is clear that attention needs to be paid first to the new product development process, and second to the organizational arrangements for dealing with new products.

The Role of New Product Development

Although organizations have in the past demonstrated that they develop new and modified products for a wide variety of reasons, the underlying strategic purpose should always be either to help create and maintain a competitive advantage or to reduce the advantages of a competitor. Recognizing this, the specific role of new product development can be stated in terms of:

1 ensuring that the product mix matches changing environmental conditions and that product obsolescence is avoided;
2 enabling the organization to compete in new and developing segments of the market;
3 reducing the organization's dependence upon particular elements of the product range or vulnerable market segments;
4 matching competitive moves – where, for example, a competitor moves into a new and potentially valuable segment there is often a strong argument for following so that the competitor's advantage is kept to a minimum;
5 filling excess capacity;
6 achieving greater long-term growth and profit.

The relative importance of these factors is influenced both by the nature and culture of the organization and by the nature of the market. Where, for example, the organization is either poorly resourced or has a risk averse culture, the perceived role and importance of new products is likely to be fairly minimal. Where, however, there is a greater availability of resources and the competitive stance is more proactive, new product development is likely to take on a far more important role. At the same time, the nature of the market often exerts a series of pressures which are capable of dictating levels of new product activity. Where, for example, competition is intense, the need both for differentiation and a regular flow of new and modified products increases dramatically. The strategist should nevertheless avoid falling into the trap of seeing the solution purely in terms of new products.

Recognizing that products consist of two interrelated dimensions, an *objective* or *physical* element and a *subjective* or *perceived* element, changes in the product's advertising and packaging can often be achieved with *relatively* low levels of investment in cost and time, but lead to strategically significant different sets of perceptions. These then provide the strategist with a foundation for moving into new sectors of the market both at a lower cost and with a smaller degree of risk.

It should be apparent from this that the parameters for new product development must be set by corporate management. These parameters need to cover the product categories and market sectors in which the organization intends operating in the future, and should be set against the background of the general stance of leader or follower that the organization intends adopting. What the strategist should never lose sight of is that NPD is often a slow process and one which cannot simply be turned on or off as economic conditions dictate. The most successful companies in the field of NPD have tended to be those that recognize its *strategic* role and that allocate resources consistently. Recognizing this, Drucker (1955) has emphasized that not only is innovation a slow process, but that many market leaders owe their position to the NPD activity of earlier generations. The real consequences of cutting back on innovation and new product development are therefore likely to be felt by the next generation of management who will be faced with a significant reduction in competitive capability.

This question of the strategic role of new product development has been examined in detail by Booz, Allen and Hamilton. Their research highlighted six principal roles. The figures in percentages below show the proportion of new products in each category:

1 maintain the organization's position as a product innovator (46 per cent);
2 defend a market share position (44 per cent);
3 establish a foothold in a new market sector (37 per cent);

4 preempt a market segment (33 per cent);
5 exploit technology in a new way (27 per cent);
6 capitalize on distribution strengths (24 per cent).

Perceptions of the role of NPD have also been examined by Ansoff (1968) who subsequently classified firms as reactors, planners or entrepreneurs. 'Reactors', he suggested, wait for problems to occur (e.g. the decline of an existing product) before trying to solve them; 'planners' try to anticipate problems; while 'entrepreneurs' deliberately focus upon and attempt to anticipate both problems and opportunities. The implications for the ways in which new product development is then handled are significant, with reactors typically assigning it a low status. In entrepreneurial firms, by contrast, NPD is seen to be of central strategic importance and allocated resources accordingly.

This general theme has in turn been reflected in Myers and Marquis's (1969) idea that NPD is broadly either *offensive* or *defensive*. Offensive NPD is designed to open up new markets or enlarge existing ones by a conscious effort to introduce new products. Defensive NPD is, by contrast, often stimulated by competitive forces or other changes in the market-place and is typically designed to maintain market share or current rates of growth.

These ideas can be taken a step further by categorizing firms as *pioneers* or *imitators*. Firms that are broadly imitative can then be further subdivided into those content to follow at a distance, and those that adopt a deliberate policy of monitoring the leaders (the pioneers) and move in as soon as the market begins to grow or a new product shows signs of success (a wait and see approach). By behaving in this way it is often possible to capitalize at a relatively low cost on the mistakes made by the pioneer. The attractions of this approach were highlighted by Freeman (1965) in a study of the electronic capital goods market.

> The performance of the first laboratory prototypes and early commercial deliveries almost always leaves a great deal to be desired, so that the scope for improvement is very great. For this reason, some entrepreneurs have followed a deliberate policy of being *second* with a new product development rather than first. Success in such a policy often requires a greater capacity for moving fast with new developments once the time is considered ripe.

The attractions of imitation have also been pointed to by Majaro (1972), who suggested that 'imitation is not only more abundant than innovation, but actually a much more prevalent road to business growth and profits. IBM got into computers as an imitator. Texas Instruments into transistors . . . Holiday Inns into motels'.

Proactive and Reactive New Product Strategies

Although for many organizations the idea of a proactive new product strategy has a certain appeal, the reality is that proactive strategies are typically associated with a significant degree of risk and a need for heavy and sustained investment in money, skill and time, not only in the development and launch stages, but also throughout the product's life. If, therefore, an organization is intent on adopting a proactive stance, certain criteria need to be met. Included within these are:

- a fundamental and sustained commitment to new product development and a willingness to accept the associated costs and risks;
- an ability to protect the new product, possibly by patents, but certainly by a sustained and aggressive investment in marketing;
- an ability to target high-volume or high-margin markets, and subsequently to capitalize on them;
- the availability of the financial, staff, and time resources needed, as well as a willingness to commit them;

- a degree of flexibility so that the strategy can be modified to reflect changing environmental conditions;
- top management commitment;
- a previously successful NPD track record (the new product chicken and egg syndrome).

Where these criteria cannot be met, the organization is likely to do far better by opting for a less proactive stance. This typically translates into one of four postures:

1 rapidly responsive;
2 second but better;
3 imitative (me-too);
4 defensive.

Overall, therefore, reactive strategies are best suited to an organization when:

- its strengths lie in managing existing products;
- it is faced with a competitor who has an aggressive and successful new product strategy and who has the capability and willingness to increase the pace of innovation within the industry;
- there is a lack of specialist NPD skills within the organization;
- organizational resources are relatively limited;
- only limited protection of an innovation exists;
- markets are too small to guarantee the recovery of development costs.

In making these comments, a point that needs emphasizing is that neither a proactive nor a reactive stance is inherently better than the other. Rather it is the case that their suitability is a function of the organization's capability and as such needs to be reflected in the NPD strategy pursued.

New Product Development: the Lessons from Japan

The Walkman is one of several highly successful products developed in the laboratory at Sony, the Japanese consumer-electronics giant.

Sony's managers believe a large part of the group's achievement stems from getting products to market quickly. Exciting new gadgets fetch premium prices, and rival manufacturers are left struggling to catch up.

This philosophy pervades Japanese industry. The success of the motor industry, for example, lies in the skill of the Japanese at getting new models into production faster than their western rivals. It accelerates the payback time on investment and also strengthens their competitive position.

The Different Types of Innovation

The question of what drives new product development has been the subject of considerable research. There are, in essence, two extremes: technology push and demand pull. Technology push is based on the idea that a discovery is made for which an application then needs to be found. Demand pull, by contrast, represents a customer need that must be satisfied. In discussing this, Langrish, et al. (1972) have identified two subdivisions within each approach:

1 *Discovery push*

- science discovers, technology applies;
- technological discovery, e.g. Pilkington's float glass process.

2 *Need pull*

- customer needs which emerge as the result of customer requests or from marketing research;
- management by objectives where, for example, by recognizing the need to lower costs, research into new processes achieves positive results.

The relative importance of technology push or demand pull varies greatly from one industry to another. In the packaged goods industry, for example, the majority of new products are driven by demand pull. This typically begins with a programme of market research designed to identify unsatisfied needs, segments or niches. The attributes of the ideal product can be determined by means of techniques such as attribute listing. The R & D team is then asked to develop a product that matches this specification. Following this, preference and taste testing can be used to refine the product, which is then launched with a specific positioning strategy.

Illustration 11.3: Canon and Honda and their Approaches to Technology Push

Canon, the Japanese camera and office equipment manufacturer, has a straightforward approach to new product development: 'You create good technology and then you try to make a business out of it. Some products succeed and some don't; the process is painful.' In making this comment, Canon's senior managing director and head of research, Dr Hajime Mitarai, summarized an approach used by many large Japanese corporations with a reputation for innovation.

Canon's view of the process begins with a belief in the need to master the key areas of technology. Useful products, it is believed, will then to a large degree flow automatically. Despite the demonstrable success of this approach, the majority of Western companies have been reluctant to pursue such an explicitly technologically-driven philosophy, the normal argument being that R & D staff would tend to lose sight of the market. The Japanese technology-driven businesses overcome this problem with a highly system-ized communication process designed to keep their researchers in constant touch with sales and production staff. In this way, it is argued, the R & D teams become more aware of market trends and manufacturing techniques with the result that the number of blind alleys pursued is reduced dramatically. Nevertheless, Canon acknowledges that a significant proportion of the projects started each year by the company's 4000 R & D staff fail to move into the production cycle.

A similar philosophy is pursued at Honda, a company which, despite its marketing successes, does not have a marketing department. Instead, the majority of the marketing functions, such as identifying customers' future needs, are carried out by the company's research staff who work in a separate company, Honda R & D. This company operates with a budget fixed at 6 per cent of the total sales of the group, and a general absence of parent company formal guidelines.

Again, as with Canon, Honda recognizes that a substantial proportion of the research conducted does not lead anywhere, at least in the short term, and accepts this as one of the by-products of such a heavy focus upon innovation.

The emphasis that both Honda and Canon place on formal liaison betwen research staff and commercial people is a characteristic of many Japanese firms which, critics argue, inhibits scientists from moving into radically new areas of research and taking risks. Others argue that the approach leads to a far greater degree of continuity and that the discontinuity that characterizes many Western companies is avoided. One result is that over the medium and long term, researchers in Japan are likely to come up with more good ideas than their industry can realistically commercialize.

By contrast, in the consumer durables and industrial sectors there is typically a far greater emphasis on technological push. There is a danger, however, that technologial push can lead to innovations emerging with no obvious or sizeable market. There is thus a strong need for R & D and marketing to work closely together, something to which both Canon and Honda have paid considerable attention. Their experiences are discussed in Illustration 11.3.

11.7 THE NEW PRODUCT DEVELOPMENT PROCESS

Some of the most pragmatic and operationally useful research on the new product development process has been carried out by Booz, Allen and Hamilton. Success, they suggest, is most likely to occur when organizations adopt a conscious step-by-step approach that begins with a search for possible new product ideas and then moves progressively through a series of evaluative stages culminating in the launch of the new product. All too often, they argue, organizations for one reason or another rush through the NPD process paying too little attention to the need for detailed evaluation and are then surprised by the product's subsequent poor performance.

The step-by-step approach that Booz, Allen and Hamilton advocate consists of eight stages: idea generation; initial screening; concept development and testing; the development of marketing strategy; business analysis; product development; market testing; and commercialization. These are illustrated in Figure 11.6, which begins with a statement of the new product development strategy.

This process is designed to act as a series of filters with a large number of ideas being poured in at the beginning in the hope and expectation that one or more commercially sound products will emerge at the end. From their initial research in the 1970s, Booz, Allen and Hamilton found that an average of 58 initial ideas were needed in order to generate one worthwhile product. In their latest research, however, this has been reduced to just seven. There are, they suggest, several explanations for this, the most encouraging of which is that many organizations appear to have come to terms with the structure and complexity of new product development and are now far less likely to waste resources by using the shotgun approach that dominated during the 1970s.

Idea Generation

The first stage in the new product development process is a search for ideas. Although these ideas can come from a variety of sources (see Illustration 11.4), the search process typically benefits by being structured and by being set against the background of a tight statement of the product and market sectors that are seen by senior management to be of strategic importance.

In addition, the objectives of new product development need to be clearly stated. Are they, for example, related to market share increases or to short-term cash flow? Are they designed to achieve technological leadership or to reduce risk? How much effort should be devoted to developing totally new products and how much to copying competitors and to modifying existing products?

Idea Screening

Having generated a series of ideas, the strategist needs then to move on to the first and broadest stage of the evaluative process. In doing this, the purpose is to begin eliminating those ideas which are either weak in absolute terms or which, while possibly attractive to other firms, are of little immediate interest to the organization. In screening ideas, two types of error can be made: drop errors which occur when an idea with potential is dismissed, and go errors when a product that subsequently proves to be of little value is allowed to move on to the next stage and thereby incur extra costs.

FIGURE 11.6
*The new product
development process*

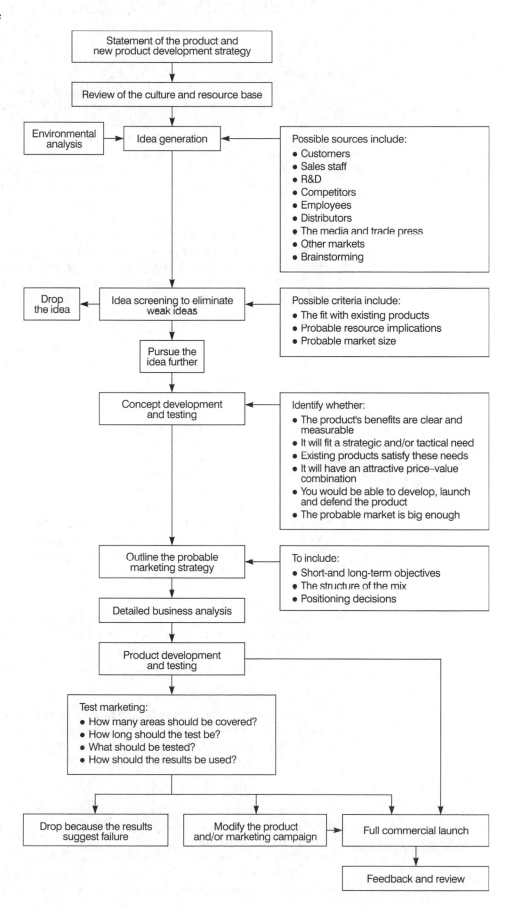

Illustration 11.4: Sources of Ideas

Ideas for new products can come from a wide variety of sources. The task faced by the strategist is to ensure that these ideas are collected in a systematic fashion, channelled to those who are best able to assess their initial feasibility, and then either discarded, shelved, sold on to another organization, or passed into the next stage of the NPD process. The first step therefore involves setting up a system for collecting ideas. In doing this, attention needs to be paid to customers, competitors, distributors, sales staff, R & D staff, employees in general, the media, and research organizations.

The starting point involves studying *customers' needs and wants*. The richness of this source has been pointed to by a number of writers with the techniques including surveys, group discussions, suggestions, customer complaints and projective techniques.

The second major source consists of the firm's direct and indirect competitors. This can include imitating or improving competitors' products, with particular attention being paid to competitive weaknesses.

Distributors are often a valuable source of ideas, since in many markets it is the distributors or dealers who have the closest and most frequent contact with customers.

The company's *sales staff* are again often close to customers and this contact, together with the insights they have to the distribution network and competitors' products, should provide a breadth and depth of perspective. All too often, however, the views of sales staff are either not canvassed sufficiently regularly or are dismissed as being unimportant.

R & D staff are particularly valuable in the high-technology industries and here their ideas should be examined within the more general framework of ideas emerging from other scientists, research bodies, inventors, patent lawyers, university and polytechnic laboratories, consultants, advertising agencies and market researchers.

Employees, even if they are not in R & D, sales or marketing, should be encouraged, either by the general culture of the organization or by a system of rewards, to search for ideas and put them forward for consideration. Although the number of ideas that have emerged from employees has not been shown to be high and the ideas have generally been biased towards processes rather than products (i.e. improving the organization's manufacturing process in some way), this represents a low-cost source which on occasions proves useful.

The *media* including not only the specialist and technical press, but also newspapers since they can provide general insights to market opportunities and competitors' moves, should be watched closely.

A variety of criteria can be used to screen products at this stage and in order to ensure that the process is both consistent and systematic, the majority of organizations make use of standardized forms. An example of this sort of form appears in Figure 11.7. See also Illustration 11.5.

Concept Development and Testing

Once the idea has passed through the initial screening process it moves into concept development and testing. Until this point, ideas are, for the most part, only broadly formed. Here, however, the idea is refined into a distinct concept which can be expressed in terms that buyers will understand and which also allows the strategist to begin developing a product and brand positioning map so that the nature of the probable competition can be clearly identified.

FIGURE 11.7
A new product development checklist

PART A

NEW PRODUCT JUSTIFICATION REPORT NO...

PRODUCT

I. Discounted cash flow rate... % Payback...years

	Stage Reached				
Business Analysis	Development	Testing	Commercial-ization	Follow-up

Year 1	Year 2	Year 3	Year 4	Year 5

II. Product Contribution
    Sales   A
    Contribution to overheads   B
    Return on sales (B/A × 100)   C

%	%	%	%	%

III. Return on investment (cumulative)
     Total investment in new product
         Fixed
         Working capital
         Introduction expenses

                              Total   D

Return on investment (B/D × 100)
    (before tax)
Basic Data
    Volume
    Selling price per unit
    Contribution per unit

%	%	%	%	%

PART B

NEW PRODUCT JUSTIFICATION
(Supplementary Schedule)

PRODUCT

REPORT NO.

II. Product Contribution

Year 1	Year 2	Year 3	Year 4	Year 5

    Unit: volume per annum   A
    Selling price per unit   B
    Sales (A × B)   C
    Variable cost per unit
        Raw materials
        Labour
        Overheads
        Distribution
                              Total   D
    Variable Cost (A × D)   E
    Contribution to product fixed expenses
        (C − E)   F
    Product fixed expenses (1)
        Depreciation
        Factory Overheads
        Selling
        Advertising (2)
        Market Research (2)
        R. & D. (2)
                              Total   G
    Loss of contribution by other products (3)   H
    Contribution to overheads and profits
        (F − G − H)   I

Notes: 1. Additional fixed costs arising solely due to introduction of new product. No allocation of existing fixed costs.
        2. Excluding special introduction expenses treated as part of initial investment.
        3. Calculated identically to the contribution by this product.

PART C

NEW PRODUCT JUSTIFICATION
(Supplementary Schedule)

PRODUCT

REPORT NO.

Total Investment
    Fixed Assets
    Land and buildings
    Plant and machinery
    Patents, etc.
    Future obligations (5th year)
    Less recovery of existing plant no longer
    required   Total

Year 1	Year 2	Year 3	Year 4	Year 5

Working Capital
    Stocks
    Debtors
    Less creditors
    Less working capital released on any
        product discontinued or reduced   Total

Introduction Expenses
    Development expenditure
    Special launching expenses (advertising)
    Marketing research prior to commencement
    Losses in early years
    Other (specified)   Total

Total Investment in New Product

SOURCE: Wilson, R. M. S. (1979), *Management Controls and Marketing Planning*, Heinemann: London, pp. 184–6

Illustration 11.5: How to Stop the Flow of Creative Thinking in Your Company

Although creativity and innovation are widely recognized to be fundamental contributors to organizational development and success, traditional structures and mindsets act as powerful inhibitors upon the creative process. Recognizing this, The Chartered Institute of Marketing, perhaps slightly tongue in cheek, has identified the comments that are most frequently used within organizations to stifle innovative or creative thinking and preserve the status quo:

We've never done it that way before . . .
It won't work . . .
We've not got the manpower . . .
It's not in the budget . . .
We're not ready for it yet . . .
It's all right in theory but you can't really put it into practice . . .
You don't understand our problem . . .
We're too small for that . . .
It's been the same for 20 years so it must be good . . .
Let's form a committee . . .
Let's think it over for a while and watch developments . . .
It's not our problem . . .
It won't work in my territory . . .
You'll never sell that to management . . .
Don't move too fast . . .
The Unions will scream . . .
We can't do it under the regulations . . .
It will mean more work . . .
It's not in the manual . . .
It's not our responsibility . . .
Yes, but . . .
It will increase overheads . . .
It's too early . . .
It's too late . . .
It will offend . . .
It won't pay off . . .
Our people won't accept it . . .
You don't understand the problem . . .

The process itself involves testing the concept either physically or symbolically with a group of target buyers. Kotler (1988, p. 420) recommends at this point a series of questions about the concept:

1 *Are the benefits clear to you and believable?*
   This measures the concept's communicability and believability. If the scores are low, the concept must be refined or revised.
2 *Do you see this product as solving a problem or filling a need for you?*
   This measures the need level. The stronger the need, the higher the expected consumer interest.
3 *Do other products currently meet this need and satisfy you?*
   This measures the gap level between the new product and existing products. The greater the gap, the higher the expected consumer interest. The need level can be multiplied by the gap level to produce a need-gap score. The higher the need-gap

score, the higher the expected interest. A high need-gap score means that the consumer sees the product as filling a strong need and is not satisfied with available alternatives.

4 *Is the price reasonable in relation to the value?*
This measures perceived value. The higher the perceived value, the higher the expected consumer interest.

5 *Would you (definitely, probably, probably not, definitely not) buy the product?*
This measures purchase intent. We would expect it to be high for consumers who answered the previous three questions positively.

6 *Who would use this product and how often would it be used?*
This provides a measure of user targets and purchase frequency.

In the light of the results that emerge from this, the strategist should then be able to gauge the degree of buyer appeal, the nature and intensity of the probable competition, the broad price bands that are appropriate, and so on.

The Development of Marketing Strategy

Having formalized the product concept and gained an understanding of probable buyer reactions, the strategist should be able to begin drafting the preliminary statement of marketing strategy covering, first, the short- and long-term sales, profit and market share objectives, and second, the structure of the marketing mix.

Business Analysis

Having developed both the product concept and an initial marketing strategy, the strategist is in a far firmer position to determine the product's attractiveness, and in particular whether sales, costs and profit projections are satisfactory. The problem most commonly encountered is that of predicting the likely level and pattern of sales with any real degree of accuracy. Where the product represents only a small change to what has been offered before, these problems are of course reduced. Where, however, there is any degree of product novelty or when the company is entering a new market segment, the problems of forecasting sales and market share increase significantly. In these circumstances the strategist can take one of several approaches, including comparing the product with similarly radical new products that the organization has launched in the past. There is no easy solution to the task, particularly when it is recognized that sales will depend not just on the product and its qualities, but also on the nature of the marketing mix used to support it, and any competitive action the product's launch might stimulate. However, in order to provide some sort of structure to the forecasting process, the strategist needs to focus on three dimensions:

1 the level and speed of first-time sales;
2 the level of replacement sales;
3 the likelihood and possible level of repeat sales.

Each of these dimensions needs to be calculated for each market segment in which the organization intends to operate, and the results then combined. In this way, the speed of market adoption (see Illustration 11.6), and the probable shape of the product life cycle can be determined.

By contrast, forecasting cost levels is often a relatively straightforward process and the net contribution is calculated with relative ease. This can then be compared with target ROCEs and a decision made on whether the product should move to the next stage or be dropped or shelved.

Illustration 11.6: The Diffusion of Innovation

Within any given market, potential buyers differ greatly in their speed and willingness to accept new ideas. Recognition of this has led many organizations to move away from mass-market launches of new products to those that are targeted far more precisely on *heavy users* and *early adopters*. Although numerous theories of product adoption have been proposed, the conclusions are all broadly the same:

- adopters of new products move successively through the stages of awareness, interest, evaluation, trial and adoption;
- individuals differ greatly in their willingness to try new products;
- personal influence exerts a significant influence on whether individuals are willing to adopt a new product and, if so, the speed of adoption;
- the nature of the innovation and in particular its novelty and its perceived relative advantages affect the speed of adoption.

These ideas have to a large extent been brought together by Rogers (1962) (see Figure 11.8) who suggested that the five adopter groups that can be identified differ greatly in their value orientations and demographic characteristics. Thus:

- *Innovators* are adventurous and willing to accept risk. They tend to be young, and have higher than average incomes and expectations.
- *Early adopters* are often opinion leaders and, whilst willing to accept a degree of risk, often behave with a degree of caution. Again, they tend to be young, come from higher social groups, and have a high discretionary income. Their sources of information tend to be more numerous, impersonal and cosmopolitan than later adopters. They also typically exhibit a high degree of psychological independence.
- *The early majority* are only rarely leaders and are willing to experiment with new ideas when the risk factor appears not to be unduly high.
- *The late majority* tend to be sceptical and willing to accept new ideas only after their reliability has been thoroughly demonstrated. They tend to place emphasis upon word of mouth and often seek the security conferred by large institutions such as the major retailers.
- *Laggards* are traditionalists, suspicious of change and only accept an idea once it has been available for a considerable period and when in one sense it has become part of a tradition. In demographic terms they tend to be older and from lower social groupings.

FIGURE 11.8
A categorization of adopters based on the speed of innovation

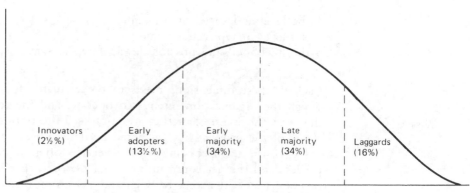

SOURCE: Adapted from Rogers (1962), p. 162

Product Development

For those product ideas that satisfy the business analysis criteria the next stage involves the physical development of the product in the form of a prototype and, in most cases, a substantial increase in commitment and investment. Once this has been done, the product can then again be tested, although here the tests take on a physical nature. They can, for example, be tested for their functionality to make sure that they perform safely and effectively, and that they achieve the performance levels expected. In the case of foodstuffs, they can be tested for taste and for shelf life. Pharmaceuticals can be tested both for their clinical effectiveness and for any side effects.

Market Testing

The final stage of the evaluative process is designed to provide a far more formal and realistic setting for the product. The most commonly used technique is that of test marketing where the product is launched into one or more relatively small geographical areas that are seen to be representative of the market as a whole. In doing this, the primary objectives are, first, to arrive at a more reliable forecast of sales, and second to pretest marketing plans. Where, for example, more than one geographical area is being used, it is often possible to compare the sales and profit implications of different marketing mix combinations such as high price/heavy advertising as opposed to low-price/redeemable coupons.

Other possible benefits of test marketing are that weaknesses in the product that have not previously been identified may come to light, insights may be gained into distribution problems, and the behaviour of customers can be seen in greater detail. There are, however, many critics of test marketing who argue that, at best, the results are of only marginal value. In particular, they point to:

- the difficulties of finding areas that are representative of a market as a whole;
- the dangers of competitors either becoming aware of the organization's plans and responding by copying, or of them altering their current sales strategies in order to invalidate the results;
- the difficulties of translating national media plans into local equivalents.

Where, however, a firm does opt for a test market, it has to make a series of decisions:

1 How many test areas should be used?
2 Which test areas should be used?
3 How long should the test last in order to gain a sufficiently valid insight into purchase and repeat purchase patterns?
4 What information should be collected?
5 How should the information collected be used?

Largely because of the difficulties and costs of test marketing, a number of alternatives have been proposed over the past few years. These include *store tests* in which, in return for a fee, a small number of stores carry the product, and *simulated store techniques*.

In the case of a store test, a variety of factors can be tested including shelf location, facings, price levels, and point-of-sale promotions. In a simulated store technique, groups of consumers are invited to view a number of television commercials both for existing and new products, including the one under test. They are then given a sum of money and taken into a store where they can either keep the money or spend it on any item. Researchers then take note of how many opt to buy the product being tested and how many opt for a competitive brand. The group is then asked for its reasons for purchase or non-purchase. Those who did buy are subsequently followed up by telephone to determine usage patterns and satisfaction levels. The results are then put into a mathematical model designed to forecast national sales.

Few of the techniques described so far can be used in industrial markets and here a different approach altogether is often needed. These include: *product-use tests*, where a selection of customers use the product for a short period and report both on their experiences and their likelihood of purchase; *trade shows* where potential buyers can see the product and express interest; and *dealers' display rooms* where the product stands next to existing and possibly competitive products.

Regardless of which approach to testing is used, be it in a consumer or an industrial market, the results from market testing need to be treated with a degree of caution. It is unrealistic to expect to be able to take the results and simply gross them up in order to arrive at a precise measure of sales when the product's full launch takes place. Instead, the strategist should see market testing as an opportunity to gain a greater insight into buyers' reaction patterns and to identify possible faults and problems.

Commercialization

Because of the sorts of problem that are typically experienced in market testing, many organizations go straight from product development into a full-scale product launch. Regardless of the approach used, the issues in commercialization are the same:

1 *When* should the product be launched? Should it, for example, be launched so that the company is first into the market, or should the launch be delayed until after a competitor has spent money developing the market? Doing this also allows the strategist to learn from the competitor's experiences.
2 *Where* should it be launched? Should the product be launched regionally, nationally or internationally in one go, or should there be a more gradual roll-out in order to learn from localized experiences and reduce the initial expenditure?
3 *Which groups* should be targeted? Should the organization, for example, concentrate on existing customers or new sectors of the market? The answer to this will in practice depend upon both the nature of the product and perceptions of the target market and how it is likely to respond.
4 *How* should it be launched?

A New Product Development Checklist

Against the background of our discussion so far it is possible to identify a series of questions that need periodically to be posed within the NPD process:

- Does the development strategy reflect the best long-term interests of the organization?
- Are sufficient resources being allocated to the up-front phases?
- Are we targeting the right market sectors?
- Are R & D and marketing working together *effectively*?
- Are we fully utilizing the organization's creative skills?
- Does the product have a core benefit proposition?
- Does the product fulfil the core benefit proposition?
- When we test market, do we make full and effective use of the information generated?
- Do we have a control system to follow the launch?
- Are we maximizing the potential of our mature products?
- Do we have the best people working on and managing our new product development process?

Taken together, these questions lead to a further but very fundamental question:

- *Do we really have a well-formulated new product strategy or do we approach new product development in a haphazard fashion that lacks any real strategic rationale and structure?*

The Role of Licensing and Technology Transfer

As an alternative to developing new products in-house, an ever greater number of organizations have over the past decade opted for licensing. The thinking behind this move is straightforward and based on the idea that rather than re-inventing the wheel, substantial savings in time and money, as well as a significant reduction in risk, can be made by making use of the technology developed by others. As an example of this, although there are no properly researched figures available, general agreement exists among those who have made use of technology transfer that time savings of between 50 and 80 per cent can be achieved. These sorts of saving are particularly important given the general trend towards shorter product life cycles and the consequently greater pressures on organizations to achieve a return on investment at the earliest opportunity.

The potential benefits of technology transfer can be considerable, and can be summarized in terms of:

- *Lower costs* with savings that can go as high as 90–95 per cent of going it alone.
- *Reductions in risks.* Commercializing a technology that has already been proven elsewhere is less likely to result in failure.
- *Shorter time-scales and faster reaction periods* are possible as the initial stages of the traditional R & D phases can be short-circuited; an example of how this was done by ICI's Plant Protection Division in the 1970s is cited by Chisnall (1989, p. 240):

(The company) searched for a suitable post-emergence herbicide to control grass weeds as part of their consistent research programme during which about 10,000 different chemical compounds active against major crop pests are screened each year. Work was stopped on a compound of its own when ICI's toxicological studies revealed that it might not meet the safety standards in crop protection. After 2½ years of complex negotiations, an agreement was reached with a Japanese chemical company for rights to a suitable compound which had been synthesised by them. This enabled ICI to produce Fusilade, which was first marketed in 1981 in Central America and Romania. Later, clearance was obtained virtually worldwide, and so within seven years of first hearing about a potential active ingredient ICI had been able to launch a major new crop protection product. Success was achieved through the efficient co-operation of many innovative scientists and technologists.

Despite the apparent attractions of technology transfer, there are a number of arguments that have been put forward against its wholesale use. It is suggested, for example, that:

- Technology transfer takes the focus away from internal R & D.
- It can make the firm overly reliant upon external sources which can in certain circumstances put the organization at a disadvantage.
- It can reduce the organization's capacity to innovate.
- Transferring technology to another firm can in the long term lead to the creation of another competitor. Michael Porter (1985) is among those who have highlighted the potentially detrimental long-term effects: 'Firms often hurt rather than help their competitive position by awarding licences . . . Firms often fail to perceive who their potential competitors are, and thus award licences that come back to haunt them.'

The validity of these criticisms has been questioned by a number of writers, many of whom have pointed to the ways in which the Japanese have over the past 45 years made very real strategic use of technology transfer. The key issue appears therefore to be that of management attitudes to new technology. When used as an adjunct to R & D, technology transfer becomes an additional weapon in the NPD armoury, speeding up in-company development processes.

Among those to have used technology transfer successfully are Mazda, Dolby, and Pilkington. In the case of Mazda, the company licensed the technology for the Wankel rotary engine from NSU Wankel. NSU had experienced several problems with the technology, particularly with engine seals. Mazda took the technology, refined it, solved the technical problems and subsequently achieved considerable success.

Both Dolby and Pilkington are examples of companies that have developed a technology which they have then licensed out. In the case of Dolby, the company recognized that they were too small to take on the hi-fi companies, and therefore licensed out their technology to the principal manufacturers partly as a pre-emptive move and partly to generate royalties that have subsequently been used to develop the system further. A similar strategy was used by Pilkington who, having developed the revolutionary 'float glass' process, licensed the process technology first to plate glass manufacturers and later to sheet glass manufacturers.

From the viewpoint of the organization that develops the technology there are six main reasons for engaging in licensing negotiations with others:

1 an inability on the part of the firm to exploit the technology in-house (e.g. Sinclair, who licensed the ZX81 to Timex in the USA);
2 the opening up of markets which other firms are more capable of exploiting;
3 the achievement of a faster standardization of technology;
4 a fragmented industry structure;
5 the creation of 'good' competitors (the issue of good and bad competitors is discussed on p. 142);
6 the development of relationships with firms which can then be capitalized on in other areas.

The significance of buying in ideas has also been highlighted by Langrish, et al. (1972) who in a study of 25 important product and process innovations in DuPont, a company with a strong reputation for its success, found that only 10 came from DuPont's own staff.

11.8 Reasons for New Product Failure

It is often suggested that the majority of new products fail, with perhaps the most frequently quoted figure for failure being 80 per cent. There is a problem in identifying with any degree of precision what is meant by failure, and for this reason it is best to see it in terms of products that fail to meet the expectations of their developers. Recognizing the lack of precision and that the term 'failure' can include total and partial failures, Crawford (1979) published a summary of every new product success or failure study covered in the new product's management literature. A summary of his results appears in Figure 11.9.

Regardless of just how accurate these figures are, it is generally acknowledged that failure rates are (too) high, that they seem not to change to any great degree over time, and that many firms see failure as one of the prices to be paid for success.

FIGURE 11.9
Studies of new product failure

Study	Percentage of failure
Booz, Allen and Hamilton	37 (Consumer)
	38 (Industrial)
Buzzell	27 (Food)
Cochran	30 (Various)
Gallagher	41 (Various)
Graf/Nielsen	42 (Food)
Hopkins and Bailey	40 (Consumer)
	20 (Industrial)
Mansfield and Wagner	27 (Industrial)

SOURCE: Barclay and Benson (1990)

The costs of new product failure can be examined under three headings:

1 *the financial costs* associated with the development and launch processes;
2 *the marketing costs*, which include any damage to the organization's relations with its distributors and customers, lost opportunities, and any publicity given to the product's failure;
3 *the organizational costs*, including any loss of confidence on the part of those involved with the development and launch of the product, and a reduction of top management commitment to future NPD activity.

Although it is typically the first of these three areas that receives the greatest attention, the marketing and organizational consequences of failure should never be either underestimated or ignored. Where failures do occur there is an understandable tendency on the part of those associated with it to distance themselves from the project as far as possible. Often the causes of failure are identified only in broad terms with the result that organizations do not learn as much from the experiences as they otherwise might. The argument for examining failures in considerable detail are therefore strong with the results then being fed back into future new product approaches and strategies.

The research that has been conducted into the causes of failure has tended to pursue one of two themes, with attention being paid either to the reasons for the failure of a specific product (e.g. the Ford Edsel in the 1950s), or to the more general causes of failure across a spectrum of product or market sectors. The first of these has led to the emergence of case histories which, while interesting, have tended to be of relatively limited general applicability. By contrast, the work of, among others, Davidson (1987) and Cooper (1979), has provided a series of guidelines that are of potential value to the strategist.

Davidson, for example, in a study of the groceries market, found that successful products almost invariably exhibited one or more of three characteristics:

1 a significant price or performance advantage;
2 a significant difference from existing products;
3 they were the first into the market.

Although Davidson recognizes that exceptions to these rules exist, they are, he emphasizes, the exception.

Cooper's work among Canadian firms provides an equally useful insight into the causes of failure. His research led him to conclude that the principal sources of failure among industrial firms tended to be market related rather than technical. Thus:

- competitors proved to be too firmly entrenched with the result that the necessary levels of sales proved difficult to achieve (43 per cent of cases);
- overestimations were made of the numbers of potential users (36 per cent);
- prices were set at too high a level (35 per cent);
- the marketing effort was misdirected (28 per cent).

In only one-third of the companies he examined were technical difficulties experienced.

This pattern of results led Cooper to examine the root causes of failure and to conclude that the areas with the biggest deficiency ratings were:

1 detailed studies of the market (a 74 per cent deficiency rating);
2 test marketing (a 58 per cent deficiency);
3 product launch activities (a 53 per cent deficiency).

A broadly similar pattern of results emerged from work in the United States by Hlavacek, with the causes being identified as:

- inadequate market size;
- distribution problems;
- internal conflicts;
- impatience and resistance on the part of marketing staff;
- poor marketing research.

These sorts of results have led researchers to develop a series of guidelines. The market researchers A. C. Neilsen, for example, have suggested that:

1 the product should be of demonstrably higher quality than those that it will be competing against;
2 it must compare favourably with the competition in terms of:
    - the new product idea,
    - packaging excellence,
    - price/value for money,
    - advertising support,
    - sales support,
    - benefits for the distribution network;
3 it should be capable of bidding for a strong position in the market if levels of brand loyalty are low;
4 care should be taken to guard against distribution hiccups, particularly in the early stages of the product's life;
5 it should not be too far ahead of its time.

Although the bulk of these findings and comments are straightforward and the guidelines for success that emerge largely self-evident, far too many organizations still appear to lack the objectivity that is needed for new products to succeed. In commenting on this, Davidson (1987, pp. 340–2) suggests that there are six possible explanations:

1 *New product development time schedules are often unrealistic*, particularly when the organization is faced with a competitive move. Crash action timetables are brought into play and a lead time of, for example, 18 months is reduced to four. The product that then emerges from this process is likely to be a copycat and lack the strategic thinking and differentiation needed for success.

2 *New product targets are frequently too ambitious* with those responsible for NPD being expected to develop, say, two new products each year. While this can be done, it can often only be achieved by sacrificing quality and strategic thinking in at least one of the two products.

3 *A lack of courage* in stopping a product idea once it has gone beyond the initial stages of the development process.

4 *Vested interests* on the part of those who develop the idea initially and who subsequently fight against the idea being dropped even in the face of evidence which suggests that success is unlikely.

5 *A degree of arrogance* which stems from the size of the company or the strength of its brands and which leads its staff to believe that all new products are guaranteed to succeed.

6 *An over-absorption in the process* which prevents those involved viewing the product objectively (not being able to see the wood for the trees).

Broadly similar patterns of results have emerged from a variety of other studies, including Project Sappho which focused upon the factors influencing successful industrial innovations. The research findings suggested that two marketing factors directly influenced the likelihood of success, first, a detailed understanding of user needs, and second, the attention paid to marketing. In the relative absence of these, failure rates increased dramatically.

11.9 LESSONS FROM NEW PRODUCT SUCCESS

The first major study of the factors which contribute to success was conducted in the UK by Carter and Williams (1956). Although the study was somewhat general, their findings highlighted the importance of management talent and the need for communication, both of which have emerged with a high degree of consistency in a variety of subsequent studies. Langrish (1972), for example, published a list of factors associated with success in the area of technological innovation which again gave emphasis to managerial factors. There is, he sugggested, a need for:

- a top person – the presence of an outstanding person in a position of authority;
- other person – some other type of outstanding individual (the 'mechanical genius');
- a clear identification of market needs;
- a realization of the discovery's potential usefulness;
- high levels of cooperation within the organization;
- the availability of resources;
- help from government sources.

The combination of these first two factors has been found to exist in the vast majority of successful companies, particularly the larger ones.

Rothwell (1972, 1974, 1977) and Project Sappho highlighted broadly similar elements:

- successful companies had a higher than average understanding of user needs;
- greater attention was paid to marketing;
- development work was performed effectively, but not always quickly;
- use was made of outside technology and advice;
- the individuals involved in NPD held senior positions and had significant authority.

For Carson and Rickards (1979), the key elements proved to be:

- the establishment of new product teams;
- the creation of an entrepreneurial spirit and approach;
- the development and use of structures designed for systematic opportunity searches;
- a staged progression from idea generation through to commercialization.

The significance of a systematic approach was again reinforced by Project Industriele Innovatie (1980) – as cited in Barday and Benson (1990) – in the Netherlands:

- a step-by-step approach;
- a strong emphasis on teams;
- a strong external focus;
- extensive use of creativity techniques;
- a process-oriented consulting role.

The majority of these factors were brought together by Peters and Waterman (1982) in *In Search of Excellence* (see pp. 376 and 378–9). Their findings on consistently innovative companies led them to suggest that success is the result of blending four dimensions:

1 *People*: Emphasize autonomy and entrepreneurship; encourage innovators and leaders; respect the individual; achieve productivity through people; and encourage a bias for action.
2 *Attitude*: Emphasize hands-on, value-driven management, and give leadership and managerial support.
3 *Organization*: Strive for a simple form and lean staff; encourage simultaneous loose/tight properties.
4 *Market*: Get close to the customer and stay close to the business you know (stick to the knitting).

A detailed review of research into new product success led Barclay and Benson (1990, p. 10) to identify five key attributes associated with success:

1 an open-minded, supportive and professional management;
2 a good market knowledge and strategy;
3 a unique and superior product that clearly meets customers wants and needs;
4 good communications and coordination;
5 proficiency in technological activities.

Together, these five attributes form a complex and interrelated set of variables which, perhaps most significantly, are all within the company's control. Success is not, therefore, something which is either entirely or even largely determined by uncontrollable external factors. (See Illustration 11.7.)

11.10 ORGANIZING FOR NEW PRODUCT DEVELOPMENT

We suggested at an earlier stage that two principal factors contribute to new product success: first, the structure and effectiveness of the NPD process, and second, the nature of the organizational structure and culture. The significance of this second dimension was for a long time underestimated, although over the

Illustration 11.7: The Twelve Lessons of Innovation Success

Although it is both dangerous and naive to suggest that there are six, ten or twelve elements which will guarantee successful innovation, it is possible to identify the sorts of factors which inhibit innovation. By recognizing these and working to overcome them, the marketing planner should be in a position to begin moving towards being able to create the structures, processes and, most importantly, the culture in which innovation has a greater opportunity in which to flourish.

These twelve 'lessons' can be seen to include:

1 Persevere and do not be disheartened by initial failures.
2 Avoid bureaucratic structures and hierarchies.
3 Empower staff and avoid imposing central thinking and diktats.
4 Appoint champions and recognize that these can come from anywhere in the organization.
5 Truly understand the customer.
6 Don't rush to advertise breakthroughs.
7 Develop open communication patterns and share ideas.
8 Break the established rules.
9 Revisit old ideas with new eyes.
10 Work to overcome the 'not invented here' success.
11 Shout about success.
12 'Celebrate' failure by being willing to accept it and learn from it. Above all, don't punish failure.

And one more:

13 Look internationally and across product sectors with a view to collecting ideas and learning from others.

---

past decade a dramatically increased recognition has emerged. At the heart of this has been the acknowledgement that new product development is a process which, if it is to be effective, needs to be handled in a very different way from the vast bulk of day-to-day activities. The implication is that if the organization simply sees NPD as something that can run alongside normal ongoing activities, failure rates are likely to be high. Recognizing this, Booz, Allen and Hamilton (1982) have suggested that the consistently most successful innovators exhibit three characteristics:

1 a significant and sustained commitment of resources to new product development;
2 a new product strategy that is closely linked to the strategic planning process;
3 formal and sophisticated organizational arrangements.

A variety of approaches to organizing for NPD have been suggested, ranging from the responsibility resting with brand managers through to new product venture teams. The pros and cons of each of these approaches are listed in Figure 11.10.

In so far as it is possible to identify the key determinant of success, it is the development and maintenance of an entrepreneurial climate. Where the organi-

FIGURE 11.10
Approaches to organizing for new product development

	Advantages	Disadvantages
Brand managers	Close to the market	The more immediate need to focus upon existing brands and products A short-term and narrow perspective A lack of specialist NPD skills
New product managers	Provides a strong focus for NPD Adds professionalism	Often lack real authority A tendency to focus upon 'quick-fixes' in the form of a series of small modifications
New product committees	Adds weight to the process because members are often drawn from senior positions	Tend to ignore the small, routine changes needed Bureaucratic Often slow and cumbersome Political conflicts frequently emerge Often ad hoc and focus on specific proposals
New product departments	Strong focus Adds weight to the process Suited to large organizations with large portfolios	Need strong strategic guidelines Often suffer from communication problems
Venture teams (see below)	Encourages entrepreneurial behaviour Can lead to major developments	Expensive if the results are not significant Staff often experience problems re-entering the main body of the organization

A *venture team* consists of staff brought together from different departments and given the specific responsibility for developing a new product or business. Members are taken away from their normal duties and often moved into a separate physical location. Emphasis is placed upon informal relations and getting the job done, including launching it on to the market. Among those to have used venture teams with some success are Olivetti, 3M, and Dow.

zation has a poor track record of NPD, the causes can often be traced back to this, as well as to a lack of teamwork. In commenting on this, Kotler (1988, p. 411) suggests that:

> The traditional model of innovation calls for the R & D department to get a bright idea and research it, then have an engineering team design it and the design turned over to the manufacturing department to produce, and then over to sales to sell. But this 'serial' model of innovation led to many problems. The manufacturing people would often send the design back to the engineers saying they could not produce it at the targeted cost; the engineers would then spend time redesigning the product. When the sales force later showed the product to customers, they would realise that it could not be sold at the targeted price, since consumer needs and wants were not met. The sales people would be mad at the engineers, the R & D people would call the sales force a bunch of incompetents who could not sell, and mutual blaming would be rife.
>
> The solution is clear. Effective product development requires closer teamwork among design, manufacturing, and marketing from the beginning. The product idea must be researched from a marketing point of view, and a marketing person must follow and advise on the idea through its development. Design engineers and manufacturing people must jointly work on the design so that the prototype passes smoothly into manufacture. Studies of Japanese companies show that their new-product success is due in large part to building in much more teamwork in product development from the beginning.

Although effective teamwork undoubtedly makes an important contribution to new product success, the strategist needs also to recognize the potential significance of the *product champion* who, believing strongly in the product, pushes the product forward, argues for resources, and ensures that it receives serious consideration. The importance of the champion was graphically illustrated by a study within Texas Instruments of 50 or so new product introductions which found that failures were *always* associated with the lack of a *volunteer* champion. This work has in turn led to the identification of three types of champion:

- *the product champion* who believes in the project and who is likely to be egotistical and a loner;
- *the executive champion* who is almost invariably an ex-product champion and who has therefore been through the process of fighting for resources;
- *the godfather* who is likely to be older, a leader, and who provides a model for championing.

11.11 THE R & D AND MARKETING INTERFACE

The amounts of money spent on research and development (R & D) vary greatly from one industry to another. In some of the high technology industries, for example, it is often around 10 per cent of sales, while in the food area it rarely reaches 1 per cent. The key to success is not expenditure for its own sake, but rather the way in which the money is spent and how it relates to customer needs. Gluck (1985), for example, in discussing 'big-bang' research for companies such as Apple has suggested:

> The raw materials for the big bang are detailed understanding of customers, competitors, markets, and technologies, and the implications of how they are changing.

A similar line of argument applies to virtually every other market.

The need to integrate R & D and marketing is therefore paramount. There are difficulties in doing this, however, largely because of the often very different outlooks of the two departments. In commenting on this, Davidson (1987, p. 189) suggests that whereas marketers give emphasis to risk/reward ratios, speed and timing, a desire for certainty, the short/medium term, facts, and profit-related issues, R & D staff focus on technical issues, detailed insight even at the expense of time, are willing to accept greater uncertainty, the medium/long term, creativity, and the 'validity' of the project.

In an attempt to overcome the potential for conflict that emerges from this, it is possible to identify a series of guidelines:

1 Give priority to priority setting. Recognizing that only a very small minority of ideas ever become commercially viable propositions, R & D efforts need to be focused and priorities allocated. This can be done by considering three questions:

- What is the idea's marketplace profit potential?
- What is the likelihood of technical success?
- What R & D costs and time are likely to be involved in taking the idea through to completion?

2 Turn uncertainty into measures of risk which can then be assessed and a decision made concerning whether to go further.
3 Recognize the need for continuous product improvement.
4 Concentrate on developing superior product benefits.
5 Recognize that small differences can be of strategic significance.
6 Concentrate on *profit* improvements.

11.12 SUMMARY

In this chapter we have focused on the nature and importance of product strategy, its role within the marketing mix, and the strategic significance of new product development.

In developing a product strategy recognition needs to be given to the three interrelated elements of the product:

1 the product's physical attributes including its performance, style, and quality;
2 the benefits or 'bundle of satisfactions' that it delivers to the buyer;
3 the marketing support services such as delivery, installation and after-sales service.

The relative importance of these elements can vary considerably from one product to another with buyers in some instances being concerned almost exclusively with the product's physical or objective elements while in other cases their concern is predominantly with the product's image and subjective elements.

An effective product policy is based on an understanding of two main concepts:

1 the product life cycle;
2 portfolio analysis.

Although both the product life cycle and techniques of portfolio analysis have been subjected to a considerable amount of criticism in recent years, both are capable of providing strategic guidelines for the marketing planner.

In developing a product strategy consideration needs to be given to a variety of elements, including environmental factors, past performance, organizational objectives, resource availability and corporate capability. Taken together these elements provide the framework within which the strategist needs to decide among policies based on:

● market leadership;
● market challenging;
● product following;
● me-too.

Within the general framework of the product strategy consideration also needs to be given to the nature of the brand strategy that is to be pursued. Four principal alternatives are open to the organization:

1 corporate umbrella branding;
2 family umbrella branding;
3 range branding;
4 individual branding.

Regardless of which approach is adopted attention needs also to be paid to the various ways in which the brand can be developed. Included within this is the scope that exists for brand stretching.

Against this background we discussed the role of new product development (NPD) and the various ways in which new product development can be carried out cost effectively. We highlighted the differences between proactive and reactive strategies and the implications of each for the NPD process.

Considerable work has been done in recent years in an attempt to extend our knowledge of the determinants of new product success. The findings of this research have pointed to the significance of procedural and structural issues. The principal implications of this are that there is a need for a sequential evaluative approach, adequate resourcing, and a commitment on the part of top management which creates a positive new product development culture. Without this it is likely that the new product development process will lack true direction and the organization's product mix will rapidly become obsolete.

11.13 EXERCISES

1 Using Drucker's framework, classify the products or services offered by your organization. What picture emerges from this?
2 What evidence is there of a true brand strategy in your organization? What would be needed to strengthen it?
3 Is there an understanding within the organization of the value of the brand portfolio? What would be needed to increase its value?
4 How would you categorize the new product strategy pursued by your organization? Is it more or less proactive than that of your competitors?
5 How effective does the new product strategy pursued by your organization appear to have been? What are its strong and weak points? How might it be improved?
6 To what extent does your firm make use of licensing and technology transfer?
7 How well developed are the links between marketing and other functional areas within your organization? Where the links are only poorly developed, what are the implications?
8 To what extent does the management team appear to be aware of the causes of new product success and failure?

11.14 CASE STUDY

Kanko Ltd

Kanko Ltd is a wholly owned subsidiary of a highly diversified listed public company which has traditionally allowed its subsidiaries to operate with a high degree of autonomy.

Kanko markets a wide range of plumbing accessories, heating systems and small air-conditioning units both for domestic and industrial use. Its products are sold through iron-mongers, specialist builders' merchants and, increasingly, very large do-it-yourself (DIY) outlets (see Table 1 below). The company's sales force of forty is split fairly evenly into three geographical regions, each of which is headed by a Regional Sales Manager who has the sales but not the profit responsibility for that

Table 1 Kanko's sales turnover by type of outlet (1991–97)

	1991 %	1992 %	1993 %	1994 %	1995 %	1996 %	1997* %
Ironmongers	28	27	25	22	19	20	20
Builders' merchants	64	63	62	61	63	63	63
Do-it-yourself	8	10	13	17	18	17	17
* Estimate							

region. This profit responsibility rests with the Sales and Marketing Director. Each member of the sales team handles the entire range of products and is expected to cover all types of sales outlet in his/her territory.

Following the publication of the interim results in mid-1997 (see Table 2 below), the Managing Director, Finance Director and the Sales and Marketing Director were asked by the parent company to resign. A new senior management team was appointed and far higher levels of accountability than had been the case previously were introduced.

Table 2 Selected sales and profit data (1993–97)

	1991 %	1992 %	1993 %	1994 %	1995 %	1996 %	1997* %	1997** %
Sales turnover (£m)	57	63	62	63	55	56	28	53
Profit (loss) net of tax and parent company management charges (£m)	3.4	3.2	3.0	2.6	0.7	0.5	(1.3)	(3.1)
Net profit as a percentage of turnover	6	5.1	4.8	4.1	1.3	0.9	(4.6)	(5.8)

* First six months
** Projection for the full year

Under the new team, an initial review of the entire sales and marketing function was conducted. Although the clarity of the findings was clouded somewhat by the poor costing and control systems that existed, it appeared that the company had previously been run in a highly haphazard fashion. This haphazard approach was manifested in a variety of ways, including:

1 An unstructured and seemingly indiscriminate new product development programme which had led to numerous products being launched with seemingly little real attention having been paid to their sales or profit potential.
2 Poor day-to-day management of the product range with the result that some 30 per cent of the product range appeared to be unprofitable.
3 Rising costs of distribution and an apparent willingness to appoint distribution intermediaries regardless of their sales potential or ability to provide after sales support.
4 A failure to address the rising levels of complaints about variable product quality and inadequate levels of service support.
5 The generally poor sales and profits performance of the sales team, with little attention paid to market development.
6 Uninspiring and tired sales literature and advertising.

Because of this latter point, the decision to fire the existing advertising agency has already been taken.

In 1996, the nature and intensity of competition throughout the industry increased significantly as Kanko's two principal competitors, both of which have a similar product range to Kanko, used aggressive price competition to gain market share.

In the same period, overall market demand remained stagnant as domestic buyers, affected by economic uncertainties, demonstrated a high degree of price consciousness, whilst sales to industrial buyers were constrained by the downturn in housebuilding and factory construction. In parallel with this, the structure of the distribution networks continued to change, with an ever greater proportion of sales being channelled through the major DIY outlets (see Table 3 below). Because of the strength of the latters' buying power, the terms that their centralized buying teams were able to demand from their suppliers, as well as the far higher levels of marketing support they required, meant that margins on the sales made by Kanko to these outlets were, at best, slim. Kanko's penetration of the major DIY outlets is currently lower than that of each of its two principal competitors.

Table 3 Industry Sales by Type of Outlet (1991–98)

	1991 %	1992 %	1993 %	1994 %	1995 %	1996 %	1997 * %	1998 ** %
Ironmongers	25	25	23	20	18	15	10	8
Builders' merchants	65	57	52	52	50	50	47	47
Do-it-yourself	10	18	25	28	32	35	43	45

* Estimated
** Forecast

It is against this background that the detailed review of every aspect of the company's sales and marketing operations is taking place.

Questions

1 As a member of the new management team, you have been given the responsibility for recommending how the product and distribution strategies should develop. You are required to prepare a report detailing the criteria by which the current product range and sales and distribution networks should be evaluated and possibly rationalized.

2 You are also required to make recommendations on the appointment of the new advertising agency. You should prepare a short briefing paper identifying the criteria by which agencies pitching for the account should be shortlisted.

WGP Industries Ltd

To: The Group Managing Director
From: The Group Marketing Director
Date: 1 June 1997

Review of WGP Industries Ltd

As you know, in the three months since my appointment as Group Marketing Director I have been reviewing the marketing activities of each of our subsidiary companies. The company that concerns me most is WGP Industries Ltd (referred to hereafter as WGPI).

The firm is currently manufacturing industrial and domestic cleaning machines that are sold in Great Britain, France and parts of northern Germany. The market, particularly in the volume sector, is dominated by a small number of major international players and so WGPI has traditionally pursued what might loosely be described as a market niching strategy, with an emphasis upon very high quality, high performance, high prices, exclusive distribution, limited advertising, a series of significant product innovations, and strong after-sales support. By contrast, the major players have pursued strategies of price competition, the frequent introduction of small and often cosmetic changes to their products, heavy advertising, frequent trade and consumer sales promotion campaigns, and regular – and often fairly pointless – confrontations with each other.

It is obvious that both the industrial and consumer markets are in long-term maturity and that there is a growing problem of over-capacity. This, coupled with the entry to the European market of a large and aggressive Far Eastern manufacturer, has led to the market becoming highly price-competitive. We know that nearly everyone in the industry is now searching for underexploited market sectors and that WGPI's traditional markets are likely to come under increasing attack over the next few years as other firms develop new products for the lower volume but higher quality/higher price/higher margin sectors of the market. The management team first identified this as a possible threat three years ago and a strategy that was designed to safeguard the firm's long-term position was put in place. This strategy has been based upon a four-pronged approach:

1 the early identification and exploitation of market sectors with areas of specialist needs which appear to offer scope for growth (e.g. domestic consumers who suffer from air-borne allergies and who need a particularly clean environment);
2 the application of their existing technologies to new markets (e.g. high-performance air filtration systems for use in industrial environments where dust pollution must be kept below very tightly defined levels);
3 the entry to a greater number of overseas markets; and
4 a programme of product innovation in order to retain and possibly develop further the technological and performance leads that the company's products possess.

Although I am generally happy with the strategy, I feel that we have major problems with how it is being implemented. The company's performance in the areas of new product and new market development has been consistently disappointing, with the firm having found itself beaten to the market by one or more of its competitors on four occasions over the past two years. It appears that there are two major causes of these problems:

(a) the very traditional and sequential approach to new product development that is being used and the consequent length of time between idea formulation and the commercialization of the product; and
(b) an insufficiently detailed understanding of the characteristics of the new target markets.

Because of this, I am about to conduct a detailed review of the firm's new product and new market development activities; I will keep you informed of my progress.

Questions

As the marketing analyst working with the Marketing Director on this review, you have been given two tasks:

1 The preparation of a report suggesting how the current sequential approach to new product development might possibly be improved. In doing this you should make reference to any lessons that emerge from the experiences of other organizations and to the research work that has been carried out into the typical causes of new product success and failure.
2 The development of a brief for a market research agency explaining what information you require in order to develop a detailed picture of any new markets that the company might be interested in entering.

Required

The first of the two questions asks you to make a series of recommendations on how the company's new product development (NPD) processes might be improved. Although the problems are most obviously those of it taking too long to get new products to market and that much of the new product development activity is poorly focused, it can be argued that the solution involves tackling a far more fundamental issue, that of the organizational culture. In the event, however, many candidates simply talked about the Booz, Allen and Hamilton framework for NPD and ignored the issues of structure and culture. The question also asked candidates to make reference to any lessons that might emerge from other organizations and to the research that has been carried out into the causes of new product success and failure. Far too many failed to do this with the result that marks were often lower than might have been expected.

The second question asked candidates to prepare a brief for a market research agency. In doing this, they had to identify the nature of the information that would be needed in order to develop a clear picture of new markets that the company was thinking of entering. Answers to this question were generally reasonable, although few candidates made use of models such as that proposed by Harrell and Keifer (the model is included in the specimen answer).

12 | Pricing policies and strategies

12.1 LEARNING OBJECTIVES

When you have read this chapter you should be able to understand:

(a) the strategic role and significance of price;
(b) the ways in which price can be used tactically;
(c) the factors which need to be taken into account when setting a price;
(d) the nature of pricing objectives;
(e) methods of pricing.

12.2 INTRODUCTION

For many organizations price is potentially the most controllable and flexible element of the marketing mix. It is also in many cases one of the most important elements and, together with the product, a key component of an organization's marketing strategy. In this chapter we therefore focus on the strategic and the tactical roles that price is capable of playing and how pricing decisions influence and interrelate with the other elements of the marketing mix.

12.3 THE ROLE AND SIGNIFICANCE OF PRICE

It is generally acknowledged that pricing decisions are among the potentially most difficult that marketing managers are required to make. There are several reasons for this, the most significant of which is the nature and complexity of the interaction that commonly exists between three groups – consumers, the trade, and competitors – and the need that exists to take this interaction into account when either setting or changing a price. An added complexity is that pricing decisions often have to be made quickly and without testing, but almost invariably have a direct effect upon profit. Largely because of this, many marketing managers work to reduce the relative importance of price by, for example, giving far greater emphasis to the product's distinctive values and to its image. In other cases, the pricing decision is taken out of the hands of the marketing strategist by a combination of market-related factors. Prominent among these is the presence of a large and aggressive competitor who in effect determines prices for the industry as a whole and who, with the exception of just one or two small niche players, all other organizations are obliged to follow. The issue faced then by the strategist revolves not around the question of what price to set, but rather how to ensure that costs are contained in such a way that profits can still be made.

Price is undoubtedly a significant strategic variable and in many markets, despite a growth in the importance of non-price factors, it is still the principal determinant of consumer choice. Its significance is further emphasized by the fact that price is the only element of the mix that generates revenue – the others

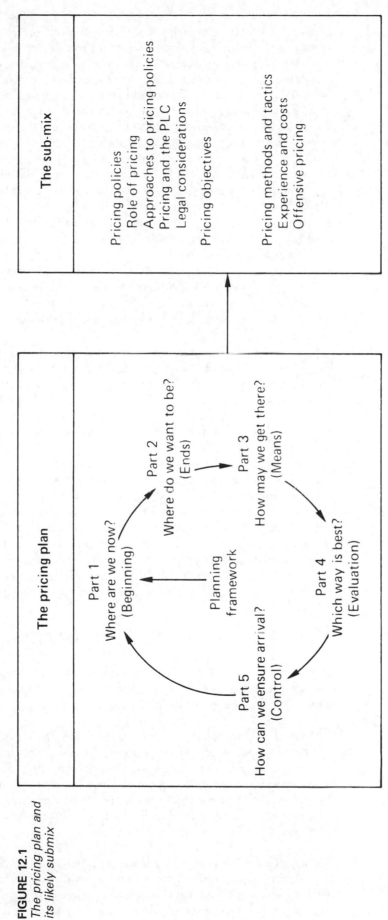

FIGURE 12.1
The pricing plan and its likely submix

The pricing plan

Part 1
Where are we now?
(Beginning)

Part 2
Where do we want to be?
(Ends)

Part 3
How may we get there?
(Means)

Part 4
Which way is best?
(Evaluation)

Part 5
How can we ensure arrival?
(Control)

Planning framework

The sub-mix

Pricing policies
Role of pricing
Approaches to pricing policies
Pricing and the PLC
Legal considerations

Pricing objectives

Pricing methods and tactics
Experience and costs
Offensive pricing

produce costs. It is perhaps understandable therefore that many marketing strategists treat pricing decisions with an extra degree of caution, which helps to explain why studies on both sides of the Atlantic have suggested that setting prices and dealing effectively with price competition is one of the biggest problems faced by marketing managers. The combination of these factors also goes some way towards explaining why it has often been suggested that relatively few organizations handle pricing well, and why a series of mistakes are commonly made. The most common of these are that:

1 pricing decisions are often too heavily biased towards cost structures and fail to take sufficient account of either competitors' or customers' probable response patterns;
2 prices are often set independently of other mix elements and without sufficiently explicit account being taken of, for example, advertising strategies and market positioning;
3 too little account is taken of the opportunities to capitalize on differentiation;
4 prices often do not vary sufficiently greatly between different segments of the market;
5 prices often reflect a defensive rather than an offensive posture.

Taken together, these points suggest that pricing decisions run the risk of emerging largely as the result either of historical factors or of expediency, rather than of detailed strategic thinking. The likelihood of this risk is further increased by the often haphazard way in which the focus of responsibility for pricing is allocated. In many small firms, for example, pricing decisions are often made not by sales and marketing staff, but by senior management. In larger organizations, although the responsibility for price setting is often devolved downwards, senior management typically retains an overseeing brief.

Perhaps the biggest single source of the problems that are typically associated with pricing stems from the question of whether pricing should be the responsibility of marketing or finance. Although writers on marketing have long argued that price is a marketing variable, a substantial body of evidence exists to suggest that in many organizations price is still seen to be the responsibility of the finance department, and that finance staff guard their possession of this with a degree of jealousy that makes it difficult for marketing to do little more than exert a minimal influence. This is of course a stance to which we do not subscribe.

12.4 APPROACHES TO PRICE SETTING

Our earlier comment that in some industries at least organizations have little choice other than to follow the prices set by the market leader, leads to the hypothesis that there are two types of firm:

1 *Price takers* which, by virtue of their size and market position, lack of product differentiation, or passive organizational culture, are either unable or unwilling to adopt a proactive pricing stance. As a result, they follow the lead set by one or more larger and more aggressive organizations within the industry.
2 *Price makers* which, largely as the result of their size and power within the market, are able to determine the levels and patterns of price which others then follow.

It is the price makers with which we are principally concerned here.

In setting a price either for a new or modified product, or for an existing product which is being introduced into a new sector of the market, the strategist needs to give explicit consideration to a variety of factors. These are summarized in Figure 12.2.

FIGURE 12.2
A summary of the influences on pricing strategy

The firm's corporate and marketing objectives
The firm's product range
The existence or scope for unique selling propositions
The degree of product differentiation
Costs (own and competitors)
Resources
The firm's market position
Previous strategies
The nature of the market
The nature and structure of competition
Opportunities for market growth
Demand elasticities
Consumers' perceptions and expectations
The need for credit
Government influences and constraints upon price
Inflation rates
The costs of raw materials and, when these are brought in from overseas, the effects
of currency fluctuations
Interrelationships within the product line

SOURCE: Gilligan and Hird (1986)

Of these, the most significant are:

1 the organization's corporate objectives;
2 the nature and structure of competition;
3 the product life cycle;
4 legal considerations;
5 consumers and their response patterns;
6 costs.

Taken together, these factors allow the strategist to develop the market's price profile (see Figure 12.3) and, subsequently, to gain a greater insight into the market's pricing dynamics.

FIGURE 12.3
The dimensions of a market's price profile

Competition
- Who are our direct and indirect competitors?
- What pricing strategies does each pursue?
- Is price competition an important element of their marketing mix?
- How are they likely to behave when faced with price competition?
- What financial resources do they have available to cope with a price war?
- Are competitors' prices related to particular market segments?

Legal
- Are there any constraints upon pricing and re-pricing decisions?
- Are there legal constraints upon margins within the distribution network?
- Is there freedom to engage in price promotions?
- Do prices have to be printed on the product and/or package?
- Does retail price maintenance exist?

Customers
- How do consumers perceive these types of product?
- How important is the product's country of origin?
- How is our organization perceived?
- Do any social or cultural factors exist that might influence the prices that consumers are willing to pay?

Distribution
- What are the implications of the patterns of distribution for costs and subsequent prices?
- What margins typically exist throughout the channel?
- How are price promotions and special offers likely to be received?

Other
- Are there any trade associations that might usefully be consulted before setting prices?
- Is there a consumer group (e.g. The Consumers' Association) which publishes comparative analyses of products which might influence consumers' perceptions of prices?
- Will our price strategy be affected by the behaviour of others in the market in the past?
- How is the market as a whole likely to respond to price changes?

SOURCE: Gilligan and Hird (1986)

Corporate Objectives

By starting with a statement of the firm's overall objectives and of what it is trying to achieve within each sector of the market, it is possible to identify the broad dimensions of the pricing strategy and the role that price is expected to play. In commenting on this, Majaro (1978, pp. 111–12) suggests that:

> A firm may achieve a volume of profit by catering for a small number of consumers with a high quality product and at a high price. A competitor may opt for a different approach: he may wish to attain a substantial penetration of the market with a lower quality product at a lower price and yet achieve virtually the same amount of profit. The net result of these two extremes may be the same in terms of profit but totally different in terms of turnover, production load, productivity and so on. The underlying considerations in each situation will be different, and it is essential for a person responsible for determining the price of a product to understand these considerations and the goals of the firm that result therefrom. It is the role of the strategic level of the firm to communicate such a fundamental 'input' to the marketing personnel wherever they may be located.

The Nature and Structure of Competition

Having identified the firm's overall objectives, the focus of attention switches to the nature of competition and to the ways in which the competitive environment is likely to influence the implementation of a pricing strategy. If, for example, the market is dominated by a large and aggressive competitor the firm is likely to be forced into the position of having to follow the market leader with little or no real control over the price charged. This, in turn, may have consequences for prices in other markets either because a policy of price standardization is being pursued, or because it is seen to be necessary to increase prices elsewhere to compensate for these pressures. In other circumstances the firm may find itself in a market in which it has a degree of technological leadership or in which its manufacturing or marketing expertise provides it with a significant competitive advantage and hence a greater degree of pricing flexibility.

The significance of competitive factors in influencing pricing decisions was highlighted by the results of a study conducted by Farris and Reibstein (1979) in which they examined the relationship between relative price, relative quality, and relative advertising. The study, which covered 227 businesses, found that:

1 brands, and particularly those in mature markets, which had an average relative quality but a high relative advertising budget were able to charge higher prices than was possible for less well-known brands;
2 brands with a high relative quality and high relative levels of advertising spend achieved the highest prices;
3 brands with low relative quality and levels of advertising were unable to move away from the lowest prices;
4 the relationship between high prices and high advertising was strongest in the later stages of the product life cycle (PLC).

The Product Life Cycle

The role of the product life cycle (see pp. 371–6) in marketing strategy was discussed in some detail at an earlier stage in the text and at this point we will do little more than remind the reader that as the firm's products move through their life cycle, so the role of each element of the marketing mix changes. In determining the pricing policy, consideration should therefore be given to three main factors:

1 the probable length of the product's life cycle;
2 the scope that exists for a competitor to introduce a new product or new

technology – possibly from another market – thereby artificially shortening the length of the life cycle;

3 the firm's profit expectations.

The specific implications of the PLC for pricing are spelled out in Figure 12.4.

FIGURE 12.4
The implications of the PLC for pricing decisions

Product life-cycle stage	The nature of price decisions
1 Pre-launch	Establish price objectives. Analyse the various influences upon price (e.g. forecast levels of demand, costs, competitors, product characteristics, supply factors, legal and other environmental issues).
2 Introduction	Penetration or skimming prices depending on objectives and market characteristics. Determine trade discount structure. Develop special offers to encourage trial.
3 Growth	Use price to combat competition. Make use of economies of scale. Strengthen dealer ties, improve price/value perceptions.
4 Maturity	Price to protect position. Identify incremental opportunities via product differentiation. Increase options. Introduce a low-price fighting brand. Identify alternative distribution channels offering scope for higher prices.
5 Decline	Price to maximize profits, even at the expense of market share. Use price reductions in short-life segments.

Legal Considerations

In many markets the pricing policies of large companies and particularly the multinationals are a potentially controversial issue, with some governments, particularly those in the Third World, viewing their strategies as unduly manipulative and against the consumer interest. Because of this a number of countries, including those in the developed world, have at various times experimented with price legislation in one form or another. The nature and significance of this legislation has varied enormously, but most frequently has taken the form of anti-monopoly rules in an attempt to protect small companies, domestic manufacturers and consumers from abuses by large firms.

A second area of concern for governments which has also led to the emergence of legislation is that of *price dumping* whereby an international firm uses its revenues from one market to subsidize abnormally low prices in another. The consequences of dumping have often proved to be disastrous for indigenous manufacturers and at one time or another have affected the steel industry, textile manufacturers, electronics companies, and agricultural machinery manufacturers throughout the world.

At a rather broader level, the influence of the government regulations upon prices has been discussed by Henley (1976, p. 10):

> Perhaps the most obvious difference can be found in the realm of legal and philosophical approaches toward competition. Europe, Japan, and the U.S., for example, have far different approaches toward competition policy. In the U.S., antitrust has a long history. Structure and conduct are the principal bases upon which public policy toward competitive activity is formulated. In Europe, antitrust has a history of less than 15 years. Performance is far more important than structure and conduct which would be unheard of in the U.S., provided that performance in terms of public benefits (price, products, service, stable employment, etc.) is acceptable. The Japanese, if the literature is to be believed, coordinate industry, financial institutions, unions, and governments in a manner impossible to duplicate in the other advanced countries. In the developing countries, antitrust is virtually unknown and competition may even be seen as wasteful of fixed plant and equipment.

The final legal issue which needs to be considered here relates to price collusion. In some circumstances, companies may attempt to reduce price competition and establish a greater degree of control over the market by some form of collusion since, by doing this, price is to all intents taken out of the competitive equation. Collusion, however, is seen in many developed countries to be anti-competitive and as such is typically subject to legal sanctions.

Consumers' Response Patterns and Costs

The last two of the six principal factors which need to be taken into account when setting prices are consumers' response patterns and costs; both elements are discussed in detail at later stages of the chapter.

12.5 DECIDING ON THE PRICING OBJECTIVES

Having developed the framework within which pricing decisions are to be made, the marketer needs then to decide upon the specific pricing objectives that are to be pursued. Although the nature of these objectives and their implications for the eventual price charged can vary greatly, the most commonly pursued are described below.

Survival

Survival is arguably the most fundamental pricing objective and comes into play when the conditions facing the organization are proving to be extremely difficult. Thus prices are reduced often to levels far below cost simply to maintain a sufficient flow of cash for working capital.

Return on Investment

Prices are set partly to satisfy the needs of consumers, but more importantly to achieve a predetermined level of return on the capital investment involved.

Market Stabilization

Having identified the leader in each market, the firm determines its prices in such a way that the likelihood of the leader retaliating is minimized. In this way, the status quo is maintained and market stability ensured.

The Maintenance and Improvement of Market Position

Recognizing that price is often an effective way of improving market share, the firm uses price partly as a means of defending its current position, and partly as a basis for gradually increasing its share in those parts of the market where gains are most likely to be made and least likely to result in competitive action. Toys 'Я' Us is just one example of a company that has used price in this way with considerable success.

Chevalier and Carty (1974), however, have highlighted the dangers of using price to pursue market share. Among the disadvantages to which they give emphasis are:

1 gaining market share, particularly in mature markets, is often prohibitively expensive and only rarely cost effective;
2 share gaining price strategies tend to be blunt weapons which do not reflect differences between buyers;
3 at particular stages of the life cycle, market share is an inappropriate goal and can lead to the organization ignoring strategically more important areas such as distribution.

Meeting or Following Competition

Having entered a market in which competitors are firmly entrenched, the firm may decide quite simply to take its lead in pricing from others until it has built up sufficient experience and established a firm reputation on which it can subsequently build.

Pricing to Reflect Product Differentiation

For a firm with a broad product range, differences between the products can often be made most apparent by means of price variations related to each market segment. The differences in price are not necessarily linked to the costs of product, but are instead designed to create different perceptions of their products' value, and indirectly to increase profits. Among those who do this with a high degree of success and skill are the volume car manufacturers who offer a variety of derivatives from a basic model.

Market Skimming

With a skimming objective the marketer enters the market with a high price and only gradually lowers it as he seeks a greater number of market segments. In this way, profits are likely to be relatively high and, by minimizing the degree of commitment at any one time, the levels of risk are minimized. However, for this to be a realistic objective, certain conditions must exist, the most important of which is that the firm has a degree of security in the form of patents, a strong selling proposition (i.e. a high degree of differentiation exists), unique new technology or a new product which discourages or prevents others from undercutting the price and upsetting the strategy. Among the products for which this has been used successfully are compact disc players. Development costs were high and manufacturers wanted to recover these as quickly as possible. At the same time, consumers' perceptions of the product's value were high, allowing a premium pricing strategy to be used. Where barriers to entry are low, however, and there are few if any forms of protection, price skimming is almost invariably doomed to failure since it provides a price 'umbrella' allowing competitors to enter with unnecessary ease.

Market Penetration

As an alternative to the gradual entry strategy of market skimming, the firm may adopt a far more aggressive approach in which prices are set at a deliberately low level to ensure a high level of sales and to keep competitors at a distance. Among those to have done this consistently and successfully, particularly when entering new markets, are the Japanese.

Early Cash Recovery

Faced with problems of liquidity or a belief that the life of the product or market is likely to be short, the firm may opt for a policy designed to generate a high cashflow and lead to an early recovery of cash. This can be achieved in a variety of ways, including a rigorous credit control policy, and by a series of special offers and discounts designed to increase immediate sales and achieve prompt payment.

Preventing New Entry

Because of the potentially powerful role that price can play, a low price may have the effect of preventing others from entering the market as they recognize the low returns available and the dangers of becoming involved in a price war. In this way, the firm may be able to minimize the amount of competition, while recognizing that the returns may be relatively unattractive.

Pricing Objectives and the Time Dimension

In deciding on the objective(s) to be pursued, the strategist needs to give consideration not just to the organization's general competitive stance, but also to the issue of time. It is of course always possible for short-term objectives to conflict with long-term objectives; perhaps the most obvious example of this is the scope for conflict that exists between high short-term and long-term profits. Only rarely can the strategist pursue the two simultaneously. Because of this and because of the uncertainty regarding the future, many organizations pursue pricing methods which reflect an essentially short- to medium-term orientation, rather than the long term. This has been commented on by Fisher (1966) who has identified what he suggests are the eight most commonly pursued specific short-term pricing objectives:

1 to penetrate the market and preempt competitors by offering a low price;
2 to skim the market and aim for early profits by opting for a high price;
3 to phase out an old product by raising the price and making it unattractive;
4 to discourage competitors from entering the market;
5 to develop the company's image;
6 to be regarded as 'fair' by customers;
7 to encourage market growth by a low price/high volume policy;
8 to avoid unnecessary provocative action.

Pricing Problems

Although in an ideal world the strategist would simply determine the pricing objective(s) and then move on to develop the detail of the pricing structure, there are in practice several problems that are commonly encountered and that conspire to prevent the objectives being achieved unless an allowance is made for them. In commenting on these, Oxenfeldt (1973, p. 50) suggests that they include:

1 prices may be too high when compared with those of competitors and lead either to a reassessment of objectives or an acceptance of an erosion of market share;
2 a given price, while acceptable in one sector of the market, may be too high or low elsewhere;
3 the price may be viewed by sections of the market as exploitative and the company consequently seen as untrustworthy;
4 price differentials across the product line may be illogical;
5 the price may destabilize a previously stable market;
6 the price may lead to a degree of confusion in the market;
7 the price may damage or inhibit brand loyalty;
8 the strategy may well lead to an increase in buyers' price sensitivity.

12.6 METHODS OF PRICING

Against the background of our discussion so far it should be apparent that there are four principal factors which influence the pricing decision:

1 the company's marketing objectives;
2 the company's pricing objectives;
3 the determinants of demand including costs, competitors and consumers;
4 the product itself and the extent to which it has any distinguishing features.

The relative importance of these varies considerably from one product and market sector to another. All four, however, need to be taken into account in the choice of the pricing method. This is illustrated diagrammatically in Figure 12.5.

In deciding *how* to price, the strategist has a choice between a range of techniques which, for our purposes here, can be seen to be broadly either *cost oriented* or *market oriented*.

FIGURE 12.5
*A framework for
systematic pricing
decisions*

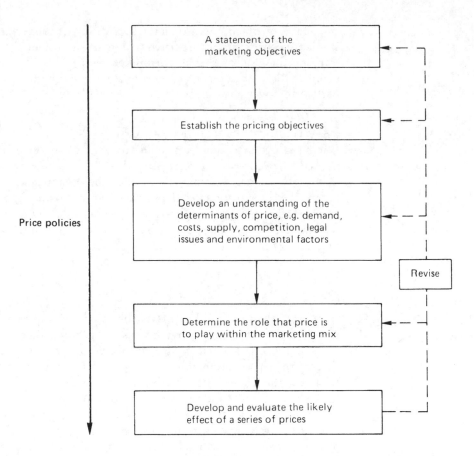

Cost-Oriented Techniques

The three most commonly used cost oriented pricing techniques are mark-up pricing, target return on investment pricing, and early cash-recovery pricing.

Mark-up Pricing

In many ways the most straightforward technique available, mark-up or cost-plus pricing simply involves adding a standard mark-up to the total fixed and variable costs of the product. In so far as operational difficulties are encountered with the technique, they stem largely from the problems of identifying and allocating the product's full costs.

Although a commonly used method of pricing, the technique has little to commend it other than its simplicity, since it links prices to the known variable of costs rather than to the uncertainties and realities of demand. It therefore lacks any real logic, and, because it fails to take account either of competitors or the nature of demand, is unlikely to lead to an optimal price. A further limitation of the technique is that when costs rise, prices follow almost irrespective of the implications for demand.

Target Return on Investment Pricing

The second cost-oriented technique is based on the idea that the organization sets prices in order to achieve a particular level of return on investment. Among those to have used this in the past have been the privatized utilities and, in the United States, General Electric and General Motors. The calculation is straightforward:

Price to achieve the target ROI =

$$\text{Unit cost} + \frac{\text{Target percentage return} \times \text{Capital invested}}{\text{Unit sales}}$$

In so far as problems exist with the application of the technique, they are broadly similar to those that are associated with mark-up pricing: the method is essentially introspective and market opportunities are likely to be missed. There is also a problem if the price that emerges proves to be too high to achieve the level of sales needed to cover costs and the target return.

Early Cash-Recovery Pricing (ECR)

Pricing in order to achieve a rapid recovery of the investment involved is often needed when forecasts suggest either that the life of the market is likely to be short (e.g. a fashion-related product), or when the organization anticipates that a larger company will shortly enter the market and, by lowering prices, force others out. In these circumstances emphasis needs to be placed upon pricing at a level which will, as far as possible, maximize short-term revenues and reduce the firm's medium-term risk.

Market-Oriented Techniques

Because of the shortcomings of cost-oriented techniques, many organizations opt instead for methods of pricing that take a far greater and more explicit account of market and market-related factors. Prices in these circumstances are to be determined by a combination of competitive forces and consumers' perceptions of relative value. In using this general approach, the justification for a price increase has to be that it will add to profit or help gain or increase a competitive advantage. The central focus therefore is the question of what will happen in the short, medium and long term to the sales revenue trend. The most common manifestations of a demand-oriented approach are perceived value pricing, and going rate pricing.

Perceived Value Pricing

This is based on the idea that in setting a price, costs should be of secondary rather than primary importance. The more important factor is the question of how *customers* perceive the value of the product. This perception can be influenced by several factors, the majority of which are under the control of marketing managers. They include the positioning strategy that is used, the image, the level of support services, and how the lifetime operating costs of the product compare with those of a competitor.

Going Rate Pricing

As with perceived value pricing, going rate pricing is based on the notion that costs are of only limited direct value when setting a price that customers will respond to most meaningfully. Instead, the benchmark is the price set by a major competitor. The firm then sets its price at the same level or, depending upon the existence or absence of any additional distinguishing features, either just above (premium pricing) or just below (discount pricing) this level.

As a method of pricing, going rate pricing has proved popular not just because of its apparent simplicity and that it appears to reflect what is sometimes referred to as the collective wisdom of the industry, but also because it tends to reduce the likelihood of price wars emerging.

Although going rate pricing involves focusing specifically on competitors, the strategist should, when using this and indeed when using any of the other techniques, take account of the probable impact of the price on others in the market-place. This includes the *distribution network* (how will they view the price?), the *sales force* (will they be able to sell the product at this price?), *suppliers* (will they see an opportunity for increasing their prices of raw materials?), and the *government* (will they perhaps see the price as evidence of a monopoly?).

Consumers and their Response Patterns

In setting a price the strategist quite obviously needs to understand in as much detail as possible what effect it will have on levels and patterns of demand. To do this involves taking account of competitors and their probable patterns of behaviour, and of consumers' sensitivity to price. The issue of competition is discussed in the section that follows and here we will focus only on how best to take account of price sensitivity.

Although a number of approaches to measuring price sensitivity have been developed, one of the most useful has been proposed by Nagle (1987, Ch. 3) who suggests that there are nine principal influencing factors:

1 the *unique value effect*: the more distinctive a product is, the less price sensitive buyers become;
2 the *substitute awareness effect*: the more aware consumers become of substitutes, the greater their price sensitivity;
3 the *difficult comparison effect*: the more difficult it is to make direct comparisons between products, the less price sensitive they are likely to be;
4 the *total expenditure effect*: the lower the expenditure is as a proportion of their total income, the lower the degree of price sensitivity;
5 the *end benefit effect*: as perceived benefit increases, so price sensitivity reduces;
6 the *sunk investment effect*: when the product is used in association with products bought previously, price sensitivity is reduced;
7 the *shared cost effect*: price sensitivity is reduced when the costs are shared with one or more other parties;
8 the *price-quality effect*: the greater the degree of perceived quality or exclusiveness, the lower the price sensitivity;
9 the *inventory effect*: when the product cannot be stored and consumption takes place immediately, price sensitivity again reduces.

Taking Account of Competitors

One of the recurring themes of this book has been the need for competitive analysis and for the information that is generated through this to be taken into account when developing strategy. In the case of pricing decisions the need to understand competitors' cost levels and their likely patterns of price behaviour is particularly important, since in many industries a competitive attack can be launched most readily and effectively through the price mechanism. Recognizing this, the strategist should monitor particularly closely each competitor's prices and price movements for any evidence of a possible price offensive. By doing this it is possible to build a price profile for each competitor which includes a statement of the firm's likelihood and ability to engage in a price war. This involves taking account of nine factors:

1 each firm's general competitive posture – is it, for example, offensive or defensive and, in Porter's terms (see Chapter 4), a 'good' or a 'bad' competitor?
2 their cost levels and hence the scope that exists for price cutting;
3 the level of resources that would be available in the event of a price war breaking out (see Illustration 12.1);
4 their relative dependence upon each product and market sector;
5 the potential returns from cutting prices;
6 the relative importance of each market sector to competitors and hence their probable depth of commitment;
7 their past price history (offensive or defensive);
8 the distinctiveness of each competitor's major products and the apparent degree of brand loyalty that exists;
9 the probable response of distributors and any others in the distribution channel.

Illustration 12.1: Price Competition and the Brand Leaders

On 2 April, 1993, Philip Morris USA launched an elaborate integration programme of consumer and retail promotions which effectively slashed the retail price of its flagship brand, Marlboro, by 20 per cent in the US market. This programme represented a major shift in strategy designed by Philip Morris to reverse the alarming declines in Marlboro's market share which had occurred in the face of severe price competition from discount brands. Given Marlboro's status as one of the world's premier brands and the changing environment of consumer marketing, the date these actions were announced was immediately labelled 'Marlboro Friday' and heralded as a milestone in marketing history.

The Marlboro experience threw into stark relief the vulnerability of even the very strongest of brands to sustained price competition and, in the minds of many brand strategists, raised the question of whether any brand is safe.

Although the information needed under most of these headings is often difficult to obtain with any degree of precision (this is particularly so in the case of costs), the strategic and tactical need for this information should never be under-estimated. The strategist should therefore begin by focusing on the two or three most significant competitors and build the price profile for each firm. The framework can then gradually be developed for the next and less direct level of competition.

12.7 USING PRICE AS A TACTICAL WEAPON

The bulk of our discussion so far has centred around the strategic role played by price. In many cases, however, price is used very largely as a tactical weapon, a role to which, because of its flexibility, it is well suited. There are several ways in which this tactical role can be performed, including:

- varying prices to reflect geographic differences;
- offering discounts for early payment, off-season buying, and to encourage high volume purchases;
- trade-in allowances to boost sales when the economy generally is sluggish;
- discriminatory pricing in order to capitalize upon the ability or willingness of particular market segments to pay a higher price;
- optional feature pricing which allows the price of the basic product such as a car to be kept low, but for substantial profits then to be made by adding accessories such as a sunroof;
- hitting at competitors who appear particularly vulnerable.

Perhaps the most obvious and most important tactical role that can be played by price stems from the periodic need or opportunity to raise or lower prices in order to gain or retain a competitive advantage.

Price cutting, for example, can be used to put pressure on competitors and reverse a falling market share. Equally, it can be used to solve the problem of short-term excess capacity. Raising prices can often be a means of overcoming the problems of excess demand and generating an increase in profits.

However, before making any changes to prices, the strategist needs to consider the impact on the triumvirate to which we referred at the beginning of the chapter – consumers, the trade, and competitors – and hence their likely reaction. Faced with a price increase, buyers and distributors may, for example, both respond negatively: buyers by turning to another product and distributors by focusing their attention on competitive products. A price increase might also provide competitors with an opportunity which they then become determined to exploit as far as possible.

Price cutting can, in certain circumstances at least, also create difficulties. Buyers may respond by perceiving the quality to have been lowered, while distributors may feel their margin has been eroded. Even where sales increase, this may simply be as the result of the lower price and does not necessarily lead to any degree of brand loyalty. The implication of this is that when either the price rises at a later stage or when a competitor lowers his price, sales drop. However, perhaps the biggest problem with price cutting is the danger of sparking off a price war.

Faced with a price change that is initiated by a competitor, the strategist has a number of choices:

- follow by increasing prices by the same amount;
- keep prices the same in the hope that those who have previously bought from the competitor will be encouraged to shift supplier;
- cut prices to increase the price differential.

There are of course no hard and fast rules that can be applied. Rather it is the case that the strategist should give full consideration both to the short- and to the long-term implications of any move that is made.

The Price/ Quality Relationship

The price of a product is capable of communicating a great deal to consumers and can play a powerful role both in attracting attention and gaining sales. It is also, together with the product's performance, the main determinant of a brand's value. The question of where to position a product on quality and price is therefore at the heart of marketing strategy. There are in essence nine possible combinations of price and quality, and it is the decision on these that subsequently effects how the other elements of the marketing mix are used; these nine combinations are illustrated in Figure 12.6.

FIGURE 12.6
The nine price/quality strategies

		Price		
		Low	Medium	High
Product quality	Low	1 Cheap-value strategy	2 Out-of-step strategy	3 Exploitative strategy
	Medium	4 Above average value strategy	5 Middle-of-the-road strategy	6 Overcharging strategy
	High	7 Superb value strategy	8 High-value strategy	9 Premium strategy

The three most offensive price/quality positioning strategies are 4, 7 and 8; it is these which provide the strongest basis for an attack since each one offers the buyer above average value for money. By contrast, strategies 2, 3 and 6 all involve setting the price above its real value and, particularly in the medium and long-term, are unlikely to succeed. (For a further discussion of how price and quality interrelate to influence patterns of product success and failure, the reader should turn back to p. 423 in which we refer to Davidson's work and consider the lessons which emerge from Illustration 12.2.)

> # Illustration 12.2: Price Cuts and Zero Sum Games
>
> At the beginning of 1996, Procter & Gamble launched its 'Every Day Low Pricing Strategy', which saw the prices of many of its brands cut by up to 17%. The strategy, which was led by Pampers and Lenor, had a dramatic effect upon the market, forcing competitors such as Kimberly-Clark and Lever Brothers to match P & G's lower prices. However, twelve months later, faced with static market share figures and squeezed profit margins, P & G made a dramatic U-turn and began raising prices. Within days, its competitors followed suit.
>
> In commenting on the price war in just one of P & G's markets, the disposable nappy sector, a trade buyer commented: 'You cannot grow volumes in the nappy market. The cuts did not help anyone'.

Source: Marketing, *13 February 1997, p. 1*

Pricing Decisions and Portfolio Analysis

In our discussion of portfolio analysis in Chapter 9 we commented that cashflow and profitability are both closely related to sales volume. Recognizing therefore that products typically follow a well-trodden path through the matrix, portfolio analysis is capable of providing a series of general pricing guidelines. *Question marks*, for example, offer scope either for skimming in order to quickly regain investment (this would be appropriate if the strategist sees the market as having only a limited life), or rapid penetration by means of low prices in order to build share and keep competitors at bay.

In the *star* stage, high prices are appropriate when buyer loyalty is high and/or if a high level of development costs still needs to be recovered. In other markets, a low price may be needed in order to retain share. In the *cash cow* stage, prices are likely to drift down partly because of a general increase in competition as late entrants to the market appear, and partly because the significance of differentiation is often reduced.

For a *dog*, the pricing choice is straightforward. Either price aggressively in order to build share, or where this is felt either not to be possible or worthwhile, raise prices in order to maximize very short-term profits as far as possible and then withdraw.

12.8 THE BEHAVIOUR OF COSTS OVER TIME

It has long been recognized that size and market share are primary determinants of profitability. The principal reason for this is that large firms usually have a lower unit cost base. These lower costs are due partly to *economies of scale* in manufacturing, distribution, purchasing and administration, and partly to the *experience effect* whereby the costs of most products decline by a fixed percentage each time an organization's experience of producing and selling them doubles.

Of the two, the nature and sources of economies of scale are by far the best known and it is therefore not our intention to do anything more than to draw the reader's attention to its significance and to emphasize that these economies can provide a significant input to the pricing decision.

The less well-known *experience effect*, however, is of equal, and in some instances of even greater, strategic significance. The concept is based on the discovery that costs decline with cumulative production and that this decline is measurable and predictable. The origins of the effect can be traced to the idea of the *learning curve* which recognizes that the time needed to perform a task decreases as workers become more familiar with it. In the 1960s, however, evidence emerged to suggest that phenomenon was limited not just to labour costs, but applied also to all total value-added costs, including administration, sales, marketing, distribution, and so on. A series of studies by the Boston Consulting Group then found evidence of what was subsequently labelled the *experience effect* in a wide variety of industries covering high technology to low technology products, service to manufacturing, consumer to industrial products, new to mature products, and process to assembly plants. The key feature in each case was, as Abell and Hammond (1979, p. 107) have pointed out:

> That each time cumulative volume of a product doubled, total value-added costs . . . fell by a constant and predictable percentage. In addition, the costs of purchased items usually fell as suppliers reduced prices as their costs fell, due also to the experience effect. The relationship between costs and experience was called the experience curve.

Sources of the Experience Effect

The experience effect has a variety of sources, the seven most significant of which have been identified as:

1 greater labour efficiency;
2 work specialization and methods improvement;
3 new production processes;
4 obtaining better performance from existing equipment;
5 changes to the resource mix;
6 greater product standardization;
7 product redesigns.

While these are the principal sources of experience, they do not emerge naturally but are instead, as Abell and Hammond (1979, p. 113) point out:

> the results of substantial, concerted effort and pressure to lower costs. In fact, if left unmanaged, costs rise. Thus experience does not *cause* reductions but rather provides an opportunity that alert managements can exploit. Consequently strategies resulting from market planning should explicitly address how cost reductions are to be achieved.

The strategic implications of the experience curve are potentially significant, since by pursuing a strategy to gain experience faster than competitors (this would normally mean high market share), an organization lowers it cost base and has a greater scope for adopting an aggressive and offensive pricing strategy. This is illustrated in Figure 12.7 in which three organizations are competing.

FIGURE 12.7
The implications of experience for pricing and profitability

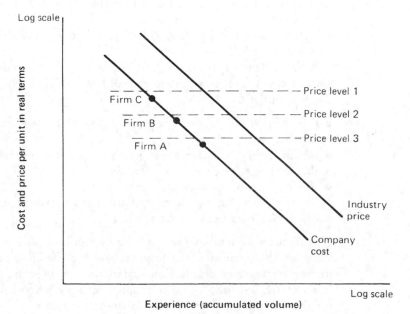

In this example Firm A has the greatest experience, Firm C has the least. Firm A therefore has a choice of strategies open to it. By setting the price at level 1, all three firms make a profit. However, by forcing the price down initially to level 2 and subsequently to level 3, Firm A puts ever greater pressure on its two competitors and forces firstly Firm C and then Firm B into making a loss. Faced with this, the two firms either make a loss which has to be absorbed or they withdraw from the market.

Although the industry prices are shown in Figure 12.7 to fall steadily, in practice they tend to follow a somewhat different pattern. This is illustrated in Figure 12.8.

FIGURE 12.8
The development of costs over time

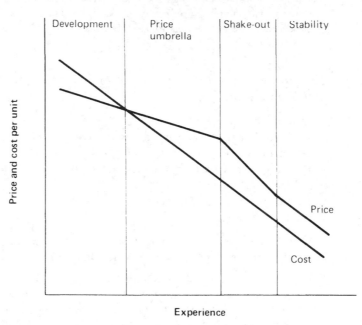

SOURCE: Adapted from Boston Consulting Group (1972), p. 21

In the development phase, prices are below costs.

In the umbrella phase, prices remain relatively stable and profits are readily obtainable. The shake-out occurs either as the result of one company deliberately slashing prices to gain share (this was done with enormous success both in the hand-held calculator market in the early 1970s and in the personal computer market in the 1980s), or as a defensive move to preempt a competitor's move. At this stage, some companies are likely to withdraw, and the industry then returns to a degree of stability.

Although the experience effect has, as we commented earlier, been found to exist in a wide variety of markets, problems are typically encountered in its use. These include:

● the mistake of plotting cost data against time rather than cumulative experience;
● the difficulties of analysing experience on different cost components;
● the need to take account of inflation;
● the implications of shared experience;
● identifying the correct starting point when measuring experience;
● cost differences between competitors.

Despite these difficulties, the experience effect is of potentially enormous strategic value and has considerable implications for the development of a long-term pricing strategy. A detailed understanding of the experience effect and, more importantly, how it can be used has, for example, provided a strong underpinning for the strategies pursued by the Japanese car industry.

12.9 THE PRINCIPLES OF OFFENSIVE PRICING

We commented at an earlier stage that pricing decisions are among the potentially most difficult that marketing managers are required to make. Recognizing this, a number of writers have developed models that are designed to provide the basis for a more highly structured approach to price setting. Among those to have done this is Davidson (1987, Ch. 10) who identifies what he refers to as 'The Eight Principles of Offensive Pricing'. These principles are listed below.

1 Know Your Price Dynamics
Pricing decisions must be based on a detailed understanding of the nature and degree of price sensitivity that exists. In some markets, for example, *overall demand* may be generally inelastic whilst the demand for *individual brands* may be highly price responsive. The strategist should therefore consider:

- the frequency of purchase – as a general rule of thumb, levels of price sensitivity increase with the frequency of purchase;
- the degree of necessity – the greater the need, the lower the sensitivity;
- unit price – high prices lead to greater price consciousness;
- the degree of comparability – when this is easy, price awareness increases;
- the degree of fashion or status – as this increases, the direct importance of price reduces.

2 Strengthen Your Pricing Muscles
By giving a greater emphasis to non-price features such as higher quality, packaging, advertising and after-sales service, the nature of the selling proposition can be changed in the organization's favour. An example of a company to have done this with considerable success is Marks & Spencer 'which succeeded in widening its price premium by steadily strengthening the appeal of its products over time. Its food products earn a premium because customers perceive them as fresher, of higher quality and more exciting. They also generate (higher) profits' (Davidson, p. 234). Learning from this, other food retailers such as Sainsbury and Tesco have both made significant changes to their product mixes over the past few years.

3 Choose Your Price Segments
In choosing segments of the market in which the company is to operate, consideration needs to be given to the implications for pricing and to the organization's ability to operate effectively. In certain market sectors, for example, the prerequisite is not simply that the organization has a low cost base currently, but that it is capable of maintaining this cost base over time. The issues which must therefore be considered include:

- the relative profitability of each segment;
- the degree of organization – segment fit;
- competitors' intentions and capabilities.

4 Consider the Alternatives
In what ways might price be integrated most effectively with other elements of the marketing mix and hence the direct significance of price be reduced? (See Illustration 12.3.)

5 Manage the Ripples
In most competitive industrial or distributor markets, different buyers pay different prices depending upon their purchase volumes, delivery methods,

---

Illustration 12.3: The Rise of 'Confusion Marketing'

Faced with increasing competitive markets and more demanding customers, retailers in the United States in the mid 1990s developed an approach to marketing which was subsequently labelled 'confusion marketing'. Its purpose is to frustrate consumers' increasing emphasis on price by offering them a bewildering range of deals, discounts and bonuses. In the past, the approach has been made possible by the development of technology which allows the marketing planner to introduce and change special offers on a weekly or daily basis without ever losing sight of the effect upon profitability.

From the viewpoint of the best known brands, confusion marketing has a particular attraction in that it makes shopping around on the basis of price far more difficult, with the result that consumers are more likely to make a choice on the basis of name recognition. By contrast, where prices are transparent, price comparisons are easy, with the result that shopping around – the enemy of brand loyalty - begins to dominate.

---

servicing demands and negotiating skills. Because of the potential sensitivity of this, the strategist needs to give emphasis to:

- a clearly communicated trading strategy;
- understanding the profit implications of altering each of the variables referred to above;
- building long-term relationships so that the implications of problems at a particular level in the organization can be reduced.

6 Beware of Profit Cannibalization

This applies where a marketing initiative with one product significantly reduces the profit on another.

7 If You Make a Pricing Mistake, Admit it and Remedy it Fast

8 Beware of Markets with Falling Prices

This is the case unless you are confident that your organization has a competitive edge which can be maintained and be used to keep competitors on the defence.

12.10 How Does British Industry Price?

The question of how industrial firms approach the pricing task was the subject of a major study, *How British Industry Prices*, published in 1975 but which still provides a clear insight to current practices. The study highlighted a series of points including:

- in most industrial companies, cost-oriented methods predominanted;
- prices were seemingly influenced by marketing policy to only a limited extent;
- little variation in pricing behaviour was found to exist between the three markets covered by the study (capital goods, components and materials);
- the majority of organizations stated that prices were set either by the cost-plus technique or by the target return on investment method;

- less than one-fifth of companies said that prices were primarily affected by factors other than costs;
- the pricing stance was almost invariably defensive;
- prices tended to follow or reflect the patterns set by competitors;
- discounts were only rarely used within the overall framework of marketing objectives, and were instead mechanistically linked to individual or aggregate order size;
- giving discounts appeared to be largely routinized;
- only some 30 per cent of companies conducted any research to determine price acceptability before setting or modifying a price;
- the results of pricing decisions were seldom monitored;
- in general, pricing tended to be handled in an ad hoc rather than a systematic fashion.

12.11 SUMMARY

It is generally acknowledged that pricing decisions are among the potentially most difficult decisions that marketing managers are required to make. Within this chapter we explored the complexities of the pricing decision and discussed how the marketing strategist can use price both tactically and strategically.

Organizations can be broadly characterized as being either *price takers* or *price makers*. Our concern within this chapter was with the price makers (those firms which are able to operate with at least a degree of pricing freedom).

Prices are influenced by a series of factors, the most significant of which are:

- corporate objectives;
- the competitive stance;
- the nature and structure of competition;
- the product life cycle;
- legal considerations;
- consumers and their response patterns;
- cost structures.

A detailed understanding of each of these elements *and their interrelationships* is needed whenever setting or modifying a price.

A variety of pricing objectives exist, the most common of which are:

- survival;
- return on investment;
- market stabilization;
- the maintenance or improvement of market position;
- meeting or following competitive moves.

Methods of pricing can be broadly categorized as:

- cost oriented (mark up, target ROI, and early cash recovery);
- market oriented (perceived value and going rate pricing).

Because of its flexibility price can be used in a variety of ways as a tactical weapon, including boosting short-term sales, and reflecting geographical or segmentation differences.

Strategically, price can be a powerful marketing tool although if its full potential is to be used the strategist needs a detailed understanding of competitive objectives and relative cost structures. This was discussed in the context of the experience curve.

We concluded by examining the eight principles of offensive pricing and the various ways in which British industry goes about pricing. The starting point for an offensive approach involves understanding the organization's pricing dynamics and choosing price segments with care, two points which according to the research tend to be understood only by a minority of British organizations.

12.12 EXERCISES

1 Looking at your own organization, identify whether a price-taking or price-making approach is adopted. To what extent is there evidence of a *strategic* approach to pricing?
2 Looking again at your own organization, what other factors appear to influence the prices charged? What about, for example, the following?:

  - distributor's expectations;
  - managerial fears about sparking off a price war;
  - the cost and marketing interrelationships between different parts of the product mix;
  - price dumping by an overseas competitor;
  - collusion between firms in the form of cartels (while often illegal, implicit cartels exist in many markets);
  - prices that have been set in the past and a lack of willingness on the part of management to sit down with a clean sheet of paper and pose a series of fundamental questions about precisely what the price strategy is designed to achieve.

3 Speak to one or more financial managers in the organization and identify how detailed an understanding exists of cost structures for:

  - each product;
  - each market sector in which you operate in.

4 What evidence do you see within your organization of pricing being related to the stages of the life cycle?
5 What pricing objectives and approaches to pricing appear to predominate within your organization?
6 To what extent does the experience effect appear to influence your organization's approach to pricing?
7 How might you apply the principles of offensive pricing?
8 What competitive information would you need when setting prices?

12.13 CASE STUDY

The Midas case

Midas plc is in the business of high-security printing. Between them, Midas plc and their main competitor Alpha plc, have consistently held an 80 per cent share of the market for years (see Figure 1) and the rest of the market is held by smaller firms.

In preparation for a Midas plc Board meeting in December, 1997, figures have been prepared which show Midas' market share and average price per item for the last eight years, all inflation-adjusted. Alpha's figures are included for comparison. Figures for revenue and operating profit for both companies are also available (see Figure 1).

There are two schools of thought among the directors. One is that prices should be increased, as they often have been in the past. This would put up the average price to something like 39 pence at current prices. 'After all, we project the total market in 1998 to be something like 600 million items – why don't we just keep on doing what we have been doing, successfully!'

Figure 1
Basic information – Midas and Alpha

Year	Total market volume (million items)	Market share Midas	Alpha	Average price (£) Midas	Alpha	Revenue (£m) Midas	Alpha	Profit (£m) Midas	Alpha
1990	340	50%	30%	0.21	0.21	35.7	21.4	3.6	(13.3)
1991	380	47%	33%	0.23	0.22	41.2	27.6	4.1	(11.2)
1992	420	49%	31%	0.23	0.23	47.4	29.9	5.2	(3.9)
1993	395	42%	38%	0.30	0.23	49.8	34.5	6.4	(1.5)
1994	430	36%	44%	0.34	0.26	52.7	49.2	7.5	11.4
1995	440	38%	42%	0.28	0.28	46.8	51.7	6.5	12.8
1996	485	34%	46%	0.35	0.33	57.8	73.6	8.7	29.0
1997	525	36%	44%	0.35	0.35	66.2	80.9	19.0	37.0

The other is that the price should be held for another year. 'We've got room to move, and Alpha haven't, if we maintain price parity. It would give us the chance to expand as fast as we're investing in new technology.'

The problem, then, is to calculate the probable effect of the two pricing strategies on the 1998 profits of Midas plc and Alpha plc, on the basis of the data provided above, in order that an appropriate decision might be made.

One way in which this problem might be addressed can be developed from the following analysis of the given data.

We can start by producing an analysis of the relative market share, as shown in Figure 2.

The next step is to generate relative price indices, followed by average cost per unit for each company plus relative cost indices, and then profit summaries, as in Figures 2 and 3.

From Figure 2 it is evident that there has been a change in relative position over the period 1990–1997. In the earlier years Midas had a larger share of the market

Figure 2
Summary analysis of market share, price and cost

Year	Relative market share	Relative price	Cost (£) Midas	Alpha	Average cost (£) Midas	Alpha	Relative cost
1990	0.60	1.00	32.1	34.7	0.19	0.34	1.79
1991	0.70	0.96	37.1	38.8	0.21	0.31	1.48
1992	0.63	1.00	42.2	33.8	0.20	0.26	1.30
1993	0.90	0.77	43.4	36.0	0.26	0.24	0.92
1994	1.22	0.76	45.2	37.8	0.29	0.20	0.69
1995	1.11	1.00	40.3	38.9	0.24	0.21	0.88
1996	1.35	0.94	49.1	44.6	0.30	0.20	0.67
1997	1.22	1.00	47.2	43.9	0.25	0.19	0.76

Figure 3
Profit

Year	Midas Revenue (£m)	Cost (£m)	Profit (£m)	Average profit (£)	Alpha Revenue (£m)	Cost (£m)	Profit (£m)	Average profit (£)	Relative profit
1990	35.7	32.1	3.6	0.02	21.4	34.7	(13.3)	(0.13)	–
1991	41.2	37.1	4.1	0.02	27.6	38.8	(11.2)	(0.09)	–
1992	47.4	42.2	5.2	0.03	29.9	33.8	(3.9)	(0.03)	–
1993	49.8	43.4	6.4	0.04	34.5	36.0	(1.5)	(0.01)	–
1994	52.7	45.2	7.5	0.05	49.2	37.8	11.4	0.06	1.20
1995	46.8	40.3	6.5	0.04	51.7	38.9	12.8	0.07	1.75
1996	57.8	49.1	8.7	0.05	73.6	44.6	29.0	0.13	2.60
1997	66.2	47.2	19.0	0.10	80.9	43.9	37.0	0.16	1.60

than Alpha – as revealed by the relative market share index: when this is less than unity it means that Midas has a larger share than Alpha, but when it exceeds unity it means the opposite. The index is calculated as:

$$\frac{\text{Alpha's market share}}{\text{Midas' market share}}$$

Relative market share is a primary indicator of competitive position. In a growing market, with an increase of 54 per cent (from 340m items in 1990 to 525m items in 1997), it is apparent that Midas has failed to achieve the same growth rate (170m to 189m represents an increase of only 11 per cent). In contrast, Alpha's growth rate has been much higher (102m to 231m represents an increase of 126 per cent). Midas has achieved a smaller share of a growing market and has clearly been losing competitive position relative to Alpha.

From Figure 2 we can also see the relative price index which is calculated as:

$$\frac{\text{Alpha's average price}}{\text{Midas' average price}}$$

When this is less than unity it means that Alpha has a price advantage (i.e. is charging a lower price), and when it exceeds unity it means that Midas has a price advantage. In no year did this index exceed unity, suggesting that Alpha always had a price advantage – and this was especially evident in 1993 and 1994. It was during these two years (see Figure 2) that Alpha's relative market share overtook that of Midas.

Over the span of eight years the increase in price of both companies was 67 per cent (from £0.21 to £0.35), but at no time was Alpha's price greater than that of Midas. In fact, by increasing its price by large amounts in the middle years Midas lost out in terms of its competitive position.

Turning from revenue to costs, we can see from Figure 2 that the relative cost position of the two competitors changes significantly over the years in question. This index is measured by:

$$\frac{\text{Alpha's average cost}}{\text{Midas' average cost}}$$

The *total* cost figure is computed by deducting profits from revenue (or adding losses to revenue) year by year. An average figure is arrived at by dividing costs by the number of items.

In relative cost terms Midas had a clear advantage in the period 1990–1992 when the index was greater than unity. However, Alpha established an advantage from 1993 when the index dropped below unity. This coincided with the marked improvements in Alpha's relative price and relative market share position. Over the entire span of eight years Alpha's average unit cost has fallen by 44 per cent (from £0.34 to £0.19) whereas Midas' average unit cost has increased by 32 per cent (from £0.19 to £0.25).

The profit picture is portrayed in Figure 3. It can be seen that Midas had an advantage in the period 1990–93, but that Alpha secured the advantage in the years from 1994 onwards. The relative profit figure is given by:

$$\frac{\text{Alpha's average profit}}{\text{Midas' average profit}}$$

When this exceeds unity it means that Alpha has the advantage.

Midas improved its average profit per unit from £0.02 in 1990 to £0.10 in 1997 – an increase of 500 per cent. But Alpha's improvement was from a loss of £0.13 to a profit of £0.16 – an improvement of £0.29 per unit.

In terms of relative price, relative cost, relative profit, and relative market share we can conclude that, prior to the decision that needs to be made, Midas has been losing out to Alpha in its competitive position. The graph that follows shows the patterns in a slightly different format for costs (see Figure 4).

Figure 4
Cost–volume relationships: Midas and Alpha

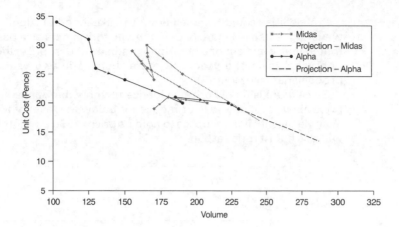

What we need to do is establish some relationship between volume and costs that can be projected into the future, and some relationship between market share and price that can also be projected into the future. (All cost and revenue flows are deemed to be inflation free.)

Taking cost–volume relationships first, as Figure 4 shows, the higher the volume the lower is the unit cost. This is much clearer in the case of Alpha, but it is still broadly the case for Midas. We would expect this to be applicable in the future too, so we might use Figure 4 as a basis for projecting cost data in the light of anticipated volumes.

In 1990 Midas was the market leader (50 per cent share), whereas Alpha had become the leader by 1997 (44 per cent share). When price parity prevails Midas tends to gain share at Alpha's expense, but when there is no price parity (i.e. Alpha's prices are lower than those of Midas) Alpha gains share at Midas' expense. See Figure 5.

Figure 5
Brand switching patterns

Year	Change in Midas' market share (% points)	Price difference (pence)	Change in Alpha's market share (% points)
1990	–	0	–
1991	–3	1	+3
1992	+2	0	–2
1993	–7	7	+7
1994	–6	8	+6
1995	+2	0	–2
1996	–4	2	+4
1997	+2	0	–2

In quantitative terms we can say that Midas gains 2 per cent p.a. in market share when price parity exists, and that Alpha gains (on average) 1 per cent p.a. in market share for each 1p difference in price.

If Midas increases its price (Option 1) from 35p to 39p it is likely that one of the following outcomes will occur (see Figure 6).

Taking the total volume for 1998 as 600m items (as given in the case) the figures in Figure 6 can readily be turned into physical quantities (relating to market share) and revenue possibilities.

Figure 6
1998 price and share projections

Price		Market share	
Midas	Alpha	Midas	Alpha
39p	35p	–4%	+4%
39p	36p	–3%	+3%
39p	37p	–2%	+2%
39p	38p	–1%	+1%
39p	39p	+2%	–2%

Probabilities could be attached to the likelihood of Alpha reacting in any of the ways suggested in Figure 6. Using the historical data as a basis for this we can see that in four years out of eight Alpha matches Midas' price; the difference was 1p in one year; 2p in one year; and more than 2p in two years. Let us adopt these probabilities (see Figure 7).

Since there is no historical evidence to show that Alpha has either increased its price above that of Midas or reduced it below the level of Midas, it seems safe to assume that, if Midas chooses to hold its price at 35p through 1998 (Option 2), Alpha will also hold its price at 35p.

Figure 7
Probabilities

Price		Probability
Midas	Alpha	
39p	35p	0.125
39p	36p	0.125
39p	37p	0.125
39p	38p	0.125
39p	39p	0.500
		1.000

We can now compute the probable effects on the profits of Midas and Alpha of the two pricing options. This is shown in Figure 8 and reveals that Midas will be better off if Option 1 is adopted since this gives it a higher expected value for profit than Option 2.

Figure 8
Overall analysis: 1998 projections

	Midas price (p)	Alpha reaction (p)	Brand switch M (%)	A (%)	Market share M (%)	A (%)	Volume M (m)	A (m)	Revenue M (£m)	A (£m)	Unit cost M (p)	A (p)	Costs M (£m)	A (£m)	Profit M (£m)	A (£m)	Prob-ability	Expected value M (£m)	A (£m)
Option 1	39	35	−4	+4	32	48	192	288	74.9	100.8	24.5	13.5	47.0	38.9	27.9	61.9	0.125	4.0	7.7
	39	36	−3	+3	33	47	198	282	77.2	101.5	23.5	14.0	46.5	39.5	30.7	62.0	0.125	3.8	7.8
	39	37	−2	+2	34	46	204	276	79.6	102.1	22.5	14.5	45.9	40.0	33.7	62.1	0.125	4.2	7.8
	39	38	−1	+1	35	45	210	270	81.9	102.6	22.0	15.0	46.2	40.5	35.7	62.1	0.125	4.5	7.8
	39	39	+2	−2	38	42	228	252	88.9	98.3	21.0	17.0	47.9	42.8	41.0	55.5	0.5	20.5	27.8
																		37.0	58.9
Option 2	35	35	+2	−2	38	42	228	252	79.8	88.2	21.0	17.0	47.9	42.8	31.9	45.4	1.0	31.9	45.4

On the other hand, under Option 1 the expected value of the market shares are: Midas 35.75 per cent, Alpha 44.25 per cent, which is a weaker situation for Midas than is the market share picture under Option 2. Moreover, under Option 1 it is clear that the expected profit outcome for Alpha is much better than it would be under Option 2. In other words, given that market share is the main source of profit and that the greater the relative profit performance of competitors the greater is their scope for investing in improving their competitive position, there could be some logic in Midas selecting Option 2. Midas' relative cost position is expected to be much better under Option 2 than it is likely to be under Option 1. This would give a basis – coupled with the larger market share under Option 2 – for fighting back against Alpha's superior position.

After all this analysis it is still a matter of judgement – preferably *informed* judgement – that should underpin Midas' choice between the two options. The analysis is relevant if not wholly precise. For example, using the cost curves in Figure 4 instead of experience curves is a rather crude proxy, and the anticipated level of sales in 1998 (600m items) is taken at face value as a reliable point estimate. Nevertheless, the analysis generates insights into the competitive position of Midas relative to Alpha and these insights should lead to better decisions, hence enhanced organizational effectiveness.

13 | The promotional plan

13.1 LEARNING OBJECTIVES

When you have read this chapter you should:

(a) have achieved an understanding of the role of promotion in the marketing mix;
(b) understand that promotion is composed of a sub-mix of elements which need to be integrated to increase their total impact;
(c) be familiar with the promotional planning process and the major decision areas within this element of the marketing mix;
(d) be able to interrelate promotional planning with other aspects of the overall marketing plan.

13.2 INTRODUCTION

For many organizations marketing communications represent the most visible face of the organization. The question of how the communications programme is to be managed is therefore a fundamental part of the strategic marketing task. In deciding how best to do this the planner needs to come to terms with a variety of issues, including the question of how the communications programme can be integrated with the other elements of the marketing mix in order to achieve the greatest degree of synergy. The relationships which exist between the communications or promotions mix and the other elements of the marketing mix are illustrated in Figure 13.1.

Although eight elements of the promotions mix are identified in Figure 13.1, it needs to be recognized that this is not an exhaustive list of the communications tools that the marketing planner has available. The area of communications is perhaps the fastest moving element of the marketing mix and, because of this, new ways of communicating with the market are constantly emerging. As an example of this, *product placement*, which involves the deliberate featuring of a product or brand in a film or television programme, was in its infancy even five years ago. Today, however, it represents a useful – if still marginal – element of the communications programme for many consumer goods organizations. By the same token, *advertorials*, which are print advertisements that have an editorial style and format similar to newspaper or magazine articles, are a small but growing part of the communications mix.

Within this chapter it is not our intention to focus in detail upon the individual elements of the communications mix, but rather to highlight the sorts of issues to which the marketing planner needs to pay attention when developing the guidelines for the communications programme.

FIGURE 13.1
*The promotions mix
and its contribution to
marketing strategy*

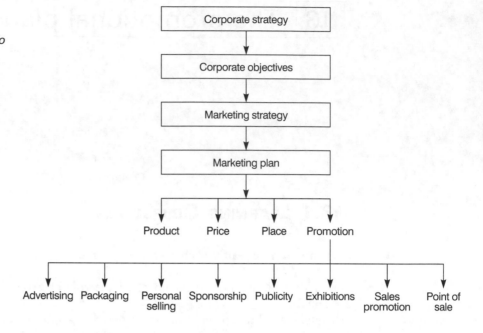

Planning the Communications Programme

In developing the communications programme, the marketing planner needs to take account of eight areas:

1 the nature of the target audience(s);
2 the short- and long-term communications objective(s);
3 the messages that are to be used;
4 the communication channels that will carry the message;
5 the budget;
6 the promotions mix;
7 the ways in which the elements of the promotions mix are to be integrated and how, in turn, the promotions mix is to be integrated with the marketing mix;
8 how the results of the campaign are to be measured.

Although these eight areas are laid out sequentially, it needs to be recognized that, almost inevitably, a degree of iteration will be involved in arriving at a firm decision in at least some of these areas. This is perhaps most obvious in terms of the constraints which might be imposed by the budget. It could well be the case, for example, that having identified the target audience, the communications objectives, the messages and the channels, the costs of implementing the campaign are simply too high for the organization. Given this, the planner is likely to be faced with having to go back and revise the objectives and/or timescales.

Stage 1   Deciding Upon the Target Audience

The starting point in the planning of any communications programme involves a detailed statement of the target audience. Without this, it is likely that anything that follows will lack any real focus. The planner therefore needs to think initially about the ways in which the market might possibly be categorized and then how the messages might be or need to be tailored to fit the needs of each of the target groups. Although an audience might be broken up in a variety of ways, the most obvious of these involves a categorization on the basis of whether the target market consists of current or potential users, their needs, their role in the buying process (users, influencers, deciders), their levels of knowledge, their levels of loyalty, and their perceptions of the various products and brands in the market. It is only against this background that decisions can then be taken about what to say, how to say it, when to say it, where to say it, and to whom to say it. (For a more detailed discussion of the ways in which buyers might be categorized and markets segmented, the reader should refer to Chapters 5 and 8.)

Stage 2   Setting the Communications Objectives

Having identified the target audience, the planner's focus needs then to shift to the question of the communications objectives. In essence, these objectives relate to the cognitive, affective or behavioural responses which the campaign is designed to achieve. In other words, the planner might be aiming to put something into the consumer's mind, change the consumer's attitude or encourage the consumer to behave in a particular way. Labelled *response–hierarchy models*, a summary of the four best known of these appears in Figure 13.2.

FIGURE 13.2
Response–hierarchy models and the communications process

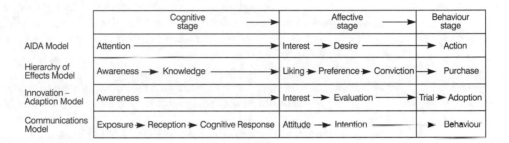

The four models illustrated are based on the idea of a 'learn–feel–do' process, in which the buyer discovers something in general terms about the product, moves on to a more detailed understanding and then – and only then – takes action in the form of trying the product and possibly becoming a regular user. However, it needs to be recognized that this sequence, although logical, is not necessarily the one that will always be followed. In the case of products in sectors in which there

FIGURE 13.3

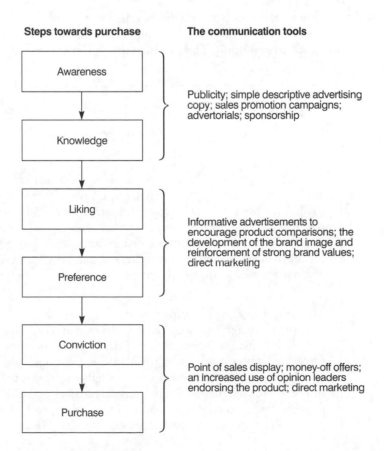

is little real or obvious differentiation and with which the buyer has little real involvement, the sequence may be that of 'learn–do–feel'. In these circumstances, the buyer buys the product and only after having used it develops a more detailed understanding of it and possibly a degree of brand loyalty. Examples of this would be kitchen rolls and aluminium cooking foil.

From the point of view of the marketing planner, an understanding both of the sequence of stages that buyers go through and of the stage reached by each of the target groups is important in that it determines the type of message that needs to be used (e.g. how much detailed information is needed and the type of appeal), its frequency and the communication vehicles. This is illustrated in Figure 13.3.

Stage 3 Developing the Message

Having developed an understanding of the sort of response that the communications campaign needs to achieve, the planner can then begin to focus upon the design of the message, a task which involves deciding upon four issues:

1 What to say (the content);
2 How to say it logically (the structure);
3 How to say it emotionally or symbolically (the format);
4 Who should say it (the source).

In deciding upon the first of these – what to say – the planner is faced with a number of choices, including whether to use a highly *rational appeal* (by buying this product you will gain this distinct and tangible benefit), or an *emotional appeal*. Emotional appeals can, in turn, be either positive or negative. In the case of a positive emotional appeal, the planner sets out to associate the product with an especially favourable image; an obvious example would be the ways in which cars, perfumes and expensive watches are advertised. *Negative* emotional appeals include fear, shame and guilt; an example of this would be how the advertisers of toothpastes typically play upon these sorts of emotions by emphasizing bad breath or the fear of tooth decay.

However, irrespective of whether the appeal is positive or negative, the planner needs to identify the theme or unique selling proposition that the campaign is designed to rest upon. This is discussed in Illustration 13.1.

Illustration 13.1: Selecting the Creative Approach

Having analysed the characteristics of both the market and the product, the advertiser is in a position to decide upon the creative approach that is to be used. Very broadly, there are two main schools of thought concerning the development of creative appeals: there are those who suggest that the potentially most successful advertisements are based on the creation of a distinct *brand image*, whilst others argue that success is more likely if emphasis is placed on developing a *unique selling proposition* (USP).

The brand image philosophy

The brand image philosophy was developed very largely by one of the founding fathers of advertising, primarily from the approach to advertising of David Ogilvy, and refers to all those emotional and aesthetic qualities which people associate with a brand. Ogilvy calls this the 'complex symbol' of the brand and suggests that many advertisers make the mistake of trying to be all things to all people and end up with a product that has little or no personality with which consumers can identify. He argues that an infinitely more worthwhile strategy involves creating a personality for the product in order to conjure up strong images in the public mind.

The development of a distinct brand image therefore begins with finding out what the brand means to the consumer and then emphasizing the product as a means of self-fulfilment. The idea of a self-concept or self-image and its value as a means of determining the advertising appeal has been investigated by a number of people in recent years, including Walters and Paul (1970). They point out that there are, in fact, five different concepts of self-image: the real self, the ideal self, the self-image, the apparent self, and the reference group image. The *real self* is made up of the individual's physical and emotional characteristics and is 'the total person as an objective entity'. The *ideal self* represents what the person would like to be. The individual's *self-image* is how he sees himself and combines the real and ideal self. The *apparent self* refers to the way in which others see him and therefore has an effect on his social interactions. The *reference group image* is the way in which the individual perceives significant others seeing him.

Walters and Paul suggest that much of our behaviour is the result of an attempt to enhance or maintain some concept of the self and that this is reflected in five main patterns of behaviour:

1 People buy products which are consistent with their self-image.
2 They avoid products which conflict with the self-image.
3 They buy products which reflect an improved self-image.
4 They avoid products which represent a departure from group norms.
5 They buy products which relate favourably to reference group norms or behaviour.

The obvious implication of these ideas is that people are likely to buy a product if they feel that its image is compatible with their own image. By recognizing this and developing a strong and potentially favourable brand image through advertising, the advertiser is likely to enhance the performance of his product in the marketplace.

Unique selling proposition

The development of the almost diametrically opposed approach of the unique selling proposition (USP) philosophy is generally attributed to Rosser Reeves, who believed that all really successful advertising campaigns are based on a product's unique selling proposition. For Reeves, the theory of USP is based on three rules:

1 Each advertisement must make a definite proposition to the consumer: 'buy this product and you will get this specific benefit'.
2 The proposition must be unique: it must be one which competitors either do not or cannot offer.
3 The proposition must be sufficiently strong and attractive to persuade people to switch from the competing products they are presently using to your product.

The credibility and memorability of this theme can, in turn, be influenced either positively or negatively by the source of the message. It is for this reason that many campaigns feature celebrities who are selected for their credibility, trustworthiness or general likeability. At the same time, however, the planner needs to understand how messages are received, since this too has an impact upon message design. The three principal influences upon this are:

1 *Selective exposure*. Most people find it uncomfortable to be exposed to messages that are not reasonably compatible with their existing attitudes. Because of this they will, as far as possible, avoid messages which they find incompatible, boring or irritating.

2 *Selective perception*. If the intended meaning of a message differs from the attitudes held by a recipient it is likely that, to ensure congruity, the perception of the message will be distorted.

3 *Selective retention*. If the meaning of a message is substantially different from the attitudes held by a person it is more likely to be forgotten than one which reinforces or confirms an existing attitude.

Stage 4 Selecting the Communication Channels

For the message to reach the target market, the planner needs to select the channels through which contact and communication can be made in the most effective way. These channels fall into one of two categories: *personal influence channels* and *non-personal influence channels*. In turn, personal influence channels can be sub-divided into (a) *advocate channels*, consisting primarily of the sales force and others who are employed by the company; (b) *expert channels*, which consist of those whose views are seen to be independent and respected (these include independent authorities and advisers such as consumer groups, research institutes, *Which?* magazine and other bodies not employed by the company but which comment on the value of a product); and (c) *social channels* made up of neighbours, friends, business associates and reference groups. (For a discussion of reference groups, refer to pages 160–1.)

Non-personal influence channels include the mass media, such as newspapers, television, magazines, the cinema and posters, which have the advantage, not generally enjoyed by personal influence channels, of reaching large numbers of people. However, in doing this, they lack any personal element, with the result that the message is more easily ignored and misinterpreted.

The relative value to a prospective consumer, and therefore the planner, of either of these two categories of channel is influenced by several factors, but particularly by the importance of the purchase to be made and the opportunity cost of buying the 'wrong' product. With many low-price, frequently bought consumer non-durables, for example, the opportunity cost of buying the wrong product is small and non-personal influence channels are therefore likely to be able to satisfy the individual's requirements for information. However, when the purchase is expensive, bought infrequently and is likely to be owned for a considerable time (e.g. most consumer durables), then the opportunity cost of buying the wrong product is high. In these circumstances, the prospective purchaser is likely to search for as much information as possible; it is then that personal influence channels, and expert and social channels in particular, are likely to take on a more important role.

Stage 5 Setting the Budget

Although there are various ways in which the communications budget might be set, the most common of these are the *affordable approach, competitive parity*, a *percentage of sales*, and the *objective and task technique*. These are discussed in greater detail at a later stage in the chapter.

Stages 6 and 7 Deciding Upon and Integrating the Elements of the Promotions Mix

In deciding upon which promotional tools should be used, the marketing planner needs to take account of eight elements:

1 the degree of control that is needed in terms of how the message is delivered;
2 the financial resources that are available;

3 the credibility of each of the tools in the eyes of the buyer;
4 the size of the target markets and their geographic spread;
5 the nature of the product and market and, in particular, whether it is an industrial or a consumer product (see Figure 13.4);

FIGURE 13.4
The consumer and industrial communications mixes

	% of the marketing budget	
	Industrial markets	Consumer markets
Advertising	3	25
Sales promotions	7	33
Sales force	70	32
Other	20	10

SOURCE: PIMsLetter (1992), No. 50

6 whether a push or a pull strategy is being used. (A *push* strategy, involving a heavy use of the sales force and trade promotions, is best suited to situations where there is a low level of brand loyalty, the choice is generally made at the point of purchase and the benefits are well understood by the buyer. A *pull* strategy, by contrast, is more appropriate when brand loyalty is high, differences between brands are easily perceived and there is a higher degree of involvement in the purchase);
7 the stage reached by the product in its life cycle (this is illustrated in Figure 13.5 and referred to in Figure 10.21);

FIGURE 13.5
The cost-effectiveness of different promotional tools throughout the life cycle

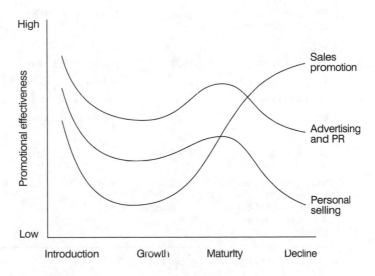

8 the buyer's readiness stage. Advertising and publicity are generally the most effective tools for raising levels of buyer awareness in the early stages and are more cost effective than either personal selling or sales promotion. However, as levels of awareness and readiness increase, so personal selling takes on a more direct and valuable role. Closing the sale is also achieved most effectively by personal selling and sales promotion, while advertising then begins to increase in importance again at the re-ordering stage. This is illustrated in Figure 13.6.

FIGURE 13.6
The buyer decision process

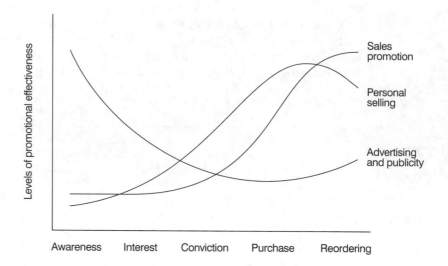

FIGURE 13.7
The principal characteristics of marketing communications tools

The characteristics of the principal elements of the mix in relation to the most significant of these eight criteria are illustrated in Figure 13.7.

	Advertising	Sales promotion	Public relations	Personal selling	Direct-response media
Communications					
Ability to deliver personal messages	Low	Low	Low	High	High
Scope for reaching large audiences	High	Medium	Medium	Low	Medium
Degree of interaction	Low	Low	Low	High	High
Perceived credibility by target audiences	Low	Medium	High	Medium	Medium
Costs					
Absolute costs	High	Medium	Low	High	Medium
Cost per contact	Low	Medium	Low	High	High
Wastage levels	High	Medium	High	Low	Low
Level of investment	High	Medium	Low	High	Medium
Control					
Scope for targeting specific audiences	Medium	High	Low	Medium	High
Management's ability to adjust the deployment of the tool as circumstances change	Medium	High	Low	Medium	High

SOURCE: Adapted from Fill, C. (1995), p. 12

Against this background the planner needs then to focus upon the ways in which the various communication tools might possibly be brought together in the form of an integrated marketing communications programme. The thinking behind this is that, by achieving a high(er) level of integration between the individual elements of the communications mix, the planner should achieve a greater degree of clarity and consistency, with the result that there will then be a seamless integration of messages and a correspondingly greater impact in the marketplace. But although there is an obvious logic to the idea of integrating the elements of the communications mix, the reality is that in many organizations too little effort is placed upon achieving this. There are several reasons for this, the most obvious of which is that large organizations in particular often make use of different communications specialists to deal with each of the individual elements of the communications programme. As a result, the focus for integration is the brand or marketing manager, many of whom have little direct experience either of the detail of the individual tools or of the ways in which integration might best be achieved. However, the consequences of *not* achieving a high level of integration are potentially significant since the messages to the market are then likely to lack the degree of unity and consistency that is needed in an ever more competitive arena.

Stage 8   Measuring the Results

An important part of any marketing activity is the measurement of the results that have been achieved. In the case of communications, this can be done using two dimensions: *qualitative measures* and *quantitative measures*. In the case of qualitative issues, the planner is concerned largely with attitudinal changes; quantitative measures relate to changes in sales levels, levels of satisfaction, and trial levels. The extent to which a campaign is successful is, however, influenced by a whole series of factors, many of which are outside the control of the marketing planner. A number of these are illustrated in Figure 13.8.

FIGURE 13.8
The marketing mix and the countervailing forces affecting buyer progression

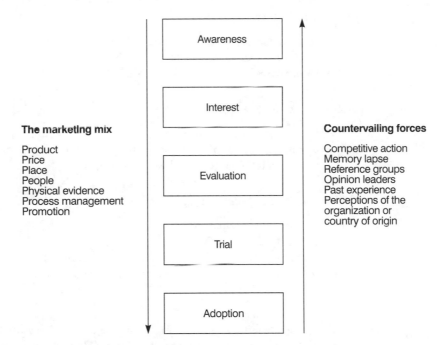

The marketing mix

Product
Price
Place
People
Physical evidence
Process management
Promotion

Awareness

Interest

Evaluation

Trial

Adoption

Countervailing forces

Competitive action
Memory lapse
Reference groups
Opinion leaders
Past experience
Perceptions of the organization or country of origin

13.3 THE ADVERTISING PLAN

In discussing the role of advertising and the nature of advertising objectives, Gilligan and Crowther (1976, p. 27) suggest that:

> Those who contend that the task of advertising should be to achieve a communication goal argue that sales cannot serve as a realistic objective primarily because they are the result not only of advertising but of advertising in conjunction with the other marketing variables. There is the consequent difficulty, therefore, of determining the extent to which advertising has contributed to the achievement of any particular level of sales experienced. By way of contrast, the degree of communication achieved can be measured relatively easily and accurately by the use of research techniques.

Advocates of this latter view – known as DAGMAR (Defining Advertising Goals, Measuring Advertising Results) – therefore suggest that the task of advertising is best stated in terms of communication effects.

However, although the adoption of communications objectives overcomes the disadvantages inherent in the use of a sales goal, a significant drawback still exists. With few exceptions, the ultimate purpose of advertising is to create sales and, unless there is clear cut evidence regarding the relationship between communication and subsequent sales, it is not necessarily realistic to assume that a high degree of brand awareness or the existence of a favourable attitude towards a product will lead to an increase in the company's sales performance. The attainment of a communication goal may therefore be misleading in so far as it is not always reflected in the company's performance in the market place.

With these considerations in mind the reader should appreciate that it is not feasible to generalise about the type of objectives which should be pursued by advertising or to state that a sales objective is either any better or any worse than a communication objective. Instead, the choice should be seen to be dependent upon the particular circumstances in which the company is operating. For example, if it is possible to determine that there is a direct functional relationship between communication and subsequent sales, it is safe to use communication objectives. If there are not these obvious relationships then the task of advertising should be expressed in terms of both sales and communication objectives.

With this in mind, advertising objectives can be categorized on the basis of:

Broad objectives:

1 to enhance organizational effectiveness;
2 to generate greater profits;
3 to improve our competitive position.

Specific objectives (quantitative):

4 to increase sales from X to Y;
5 to raise the level of awareness of a given product from P to Q;
6 to generate N enquiries/coupon responses.

Sub-objectives (qualitative):

7 to convey information;
8 to create desire;
9 to improve the image of product X or brand Y;
10 to mitigate the effect of a premium price (e.g. Heinz Beans).

Advertising Strategies

When deciding how best to attain the objectives described above, the advertiser needs a clear idea of the target audience. This audience may be existing and/or potential buyers, deciders or influencers, individuals or groups, particular publics or the general public.

The target audience will, to a large extent, influence advertising decisions on what we want to say, how best to say it, where and when it is to be said.

Generally speaking, the bigger the investment in advertising, the greater the number of people that can be made aware of the advertiser's products or services. However, the law of diminishing returns will eventually operate, in that, in general, the extra cost of the extra people reached will outweigh the extra sales potential.

However, no matter how many people are made aware of a company's products through advertising, the potential sales effectiveness is to a large extent governed by the nature of the advertisements themselves. If these are not believed and/or remembered then it is unlikely that people will be persuaded to buy.

Deciding the Advertising Spend

Kotler (1988, pp. 604–6) and other authors offer evidence to show that there are four or five generally used methods of deciding on the advertising spend, namely:

1 what the organization can currently afford;
2 matching competitors' spends or the norm for the industry;
3 a fixed percentage of past sales;
4 a fixed percentage of past profit;
5 the objective and task approach.

We can evaluate these methods as shown below.

1 Affordable Approach

In the affordable approach, the advertising budget is set simply on the basis of an assessment of what the company can afford to spend in the forthcoming financial year. It is therefore an extremely arbitrary method which, although it has the advantage of being simple to operate and of ensuring that the company does not over-extend itself, suffers from several severe limitations.

The two fundamental weaknesses of the affordable approach are, first, that it does not encourage the development of long-term planning of advertising expenditure (the amount the company can afford to spend may vary greatly from year to year and these variations cannot easily be predicted), and second, that short-term advertising opportunities are likely to be overlooked. Despite these weaknesses many companies use the affordable approach, seemingly without encountering problems. Difficulties are likely to arise, however, if the company's sales revenue begins to decline. Faced with this situation the instinctive reaction is to spend less on 'luxuries' such as advertising. But any decrease in the amount of advertising may well lead to a further decrease in sales. The effects of using the affordable approach in such a situation are therefore likely to be cumulative.

A slight variation of the basic affordable approach has been suggested by Joel Dean (1951, pp. 363–75) who pointed out that the utility to management of any funds left over after allowing for an acceptable return on capital is low compared with the possible return to the organization of diverting all of these excess funds into advertising.

However, the value of Dean's idea notwithstanding, the affordable approach to setting the appropriation has little to commend it and offers little promise to the advertiser who wishes to determine the appropriation in a logical manner by attempting to relate advertising costs and advertising effects.

2 Competitive Parity

When applying the principle of competitive parity, the advertiser sets the budget at a level to match the advertising outlay of a competitor. This can be done in one of two ways: either by setting the budget to match exactly, or nearly exactly, the expenditure of a competitor, or by setting it on the basis of a ratio of share of market to share of advertising. To apply this second method it is necessary to collect data on total sales and total advertising by all the firms in the market. If, having collected this information, a correlation appears to exist between advertising expenditure and subsequent sales performance it is possible to compute approximately how much money needs to be spent on advertising to achieve any given market share. To illustrate this, assume that the information in Table 13.1 has been collected.

On the basis of the figures in Table 13.1 the marketer can conclude that for every 1 per cent share of the market gained by a specific brand, an expenditure of 2 per cent of total industry advertising was required. Therefore, if the manufacturer of Brand B wishes to maintain his 15 per cent share of the market, he must ensure that his advertising appropriation is at least 30 per cent (15 times 2) of the industry's advertising expenditure. Knowledge of the existence of any

Table 13.1

	Percentage of industry sales	*Percentage of industry advertising*
Brand A	30	60
Brand B	15	30
Brand C	3	6
Others (including private brands)	52	4
	100%	100%

such relationship is obviously of value although in practice it is likely to occur only in a very stable market in which there is no aggressive action on the part of any one company.

Two justifications are normally advanced for the competitive parity approach. The first is that in some mystical way competitors' expenditure represents what is known as 'the collective wisdom of the industry'. The second is that by maintaining a competitive parity, aggressive action is minimized and advertising wars avoided.

In practice both arguments lack validity. The only true justification for basing the appropriation upon that of a competitor is if both companies are facing exactly the same market conditions, have exactly the same opportunities, are pursuing the same goals, have the same reputations, are intending to allocate advertising funds in the same way to the same media, and are operating the company in the same manner. However, even if we assume that these conditions are satisfied (which in itself is most unlikely), then there still exists the distinct possibility that the competitor from whom the company takes its lead is allocating money unwisely. In addition, there are two practical difficulties in implementing this approach. Companies traditionally handle their financial affairs with some attempt at secrecy and there are likely to be problems encountered in discovering the amount a competitor intends to spend in the forthcoming period. Finally, even assuming that this information is obtained, the imitator may be unable to afford to spend the money necessary to achieve parity.

With regard to the second justification of the approach, little or no evidence exists to suggest that maintaining parity does stabilize industry expenditures.

Thus, although an awareness of a competitor's advertising appropriation is undoubtedly useful, the competitive parity approach is unlikely to lead to an optimal solution to the problem. A worthwhile guideline in this respect was laid down by Burton and Miller (1970, p. 99): 'Watch what your competitor does. Profit from what he does; but set your own course.'

3 & 4 Percentage of Sales or Profit

Of the numerous approaches to determining the budget, the concept of percentage of sales is the most popular. In its simplest form percentage of sales involves applying a predetermined percentage figure to the value of sales achieved in the previous financial period. This percentage figure remains constant for a number of years. Thus, if the advertiser had sales last year of £1 million and the percentage figure used in the past is 5 per cent, the appropriation for the forthcoming year is £50,000 (5 per cent of £1 million). A slight variation which has gained ground in recent years involves the percentage being applied not to the previous year's sales, but to a forecast of sales for the period covered by the appropriation.

The obvious attraction of a percentage of sales or profit is its simplicity. In addition, the amount of funds allocated to advertising will tend to vary with what the company can afford, and, assuming that competing firms tacitly agree to let advertising expenditures follow a percentage of sales, some degree of competitive stability will result.

However, despite these advantages, the method represents a very mechanistic approach to decision making, and is hard to support analytically. The weaknesses of the method are, first, that circular reasoning is employed as sales act to determine advertising, rather than the other way round. Second, because the funds made available will vary as sales or profits fluctuate, there is likely to be only limited scope for engaging in long-term planning of advertising programmes. Third, because funds will vary with what the company can afford, there is no facility for engaging in counter-cyclical advertising. Fourth, there is no apparent logical figure which should be employed. In the example given earlier the percentage could equally be 4 per cent or 6 per cent. In addition, implicit in the approach is the fact that once the percentage figure has been chosen it is adhered to rigidly. This inflexibility is obviously undesirable in the face of changing goals and market conditions and is likely to lead to short-term opportunities being overlooked. Finally, having used percentage of sales to determine the appropriation, there is a tendency to allocate the budget in the same way rather than in a more constructive fashion such as on the basis of opportunities.

Thus, despite its popularity, the percentage of sales or profit approach has no apparent logical foundation and, like the affordable and competitive parity methods, is unlikely to lead the advertiser to the profit maximizing outlay.

5 Objective and Task

In the objective and task method, the approach used in the previous four methods is reversed. Instead of determining the size of the appropriation and then allocating it by product and sales area, objective and task requires the advertiser to set the appropriation on the basis of the cost of achieving the advertising objectives.

The approach can be illustrated by the following five steps:

(i) establish the advertising objectives;
(ii) select the media and determine the number of insertions needed to achieve these objectives;
(iii) calculate the cost of the media programme and add to it the production costs;
(iv) examine the relationship between costs and objectives to determine whether the cost of achieving the objectives is justified and whether the company can 'afford' the costs;
(v) if necessary, revise the goals and methods to a level the company can afford.

Although objective and task is accepted as being logically the most superior of all those in common use, many advertisers avoid using it because of the amount of analysis required initially to operate it properly. In addition, an interesting observation has been made by Frey and Halterman (1970, p. 372) who point out that advertisers:

who state that they use the method often have trouble in explaining just how they arrived at the amount of advertising necessary to reach the established objectives. They may even find it difficult to explain how they arrived at the objectives. The objectives themselves may be established with too little regard for their implications.

Selecting an Advertising Agency

In selecting an agency, a variety of factors need to be taken into account, including:

● the *type* of agency that is required and the breadth of service needed. The alternatives range from a full-service agency, which is capable of handling all aspects of any promotional campaign, through to creative hot-shops, which concentrate upon the development of the creative appeal leaving the client to organize, either directly or indirectly, other elements of the promotional task, such as media buying;

- the agency's size and the relative importance of the account;
- their current and past client portfolio, since this gives an understanding not just of the breadth of their client range, but also of the types of promotional work that they have undertaken;
- their understanding of the marketing problems which the company faces and their views of the ways in which a new promotional campaign might possibly contribute to their resolution;
- their apparent levels of creativity. These can be assessed, in part at least, by reference to previous campaigns;
- their reputation;
- the nature of their pitch and the extent to which it appears to reflect an understanding of the organization and its market;
- the costs that are likely to be incurred;
- their areas of specialist expertise;
- their financial stability.

An additional and possibly very important factor which should be taken into account is *the degree of empathy* which exists between the agency and the client since it is essential that a fruitful and profitable relationship is developed. However, in doing this, the client needs to be very clear about the role that advertising and promotion are expected to play, the marketing and promotional objectives that will be pursued, and the levels of promotional spend.

When selecting an advertising agency the question of terms will almost certainly arise. There are a number of different ways in which an agency may be paid for its services but these fall mostly into three basic systems: a flat fee, a retainer or by commission received from the media.

Evaluation and Control of the Advertising Plan

Much has been written about the difficulties of evaluating advertising and the small amount spent on research to this end when compared with total advertising expenditure.

There are, however, marketing research agencies which specialize in the pre-tracking and post-tracking of advertising campaigns. For campaigns aimed at establishing a new or improved corporate image, pre-tracking would establish the bench-marks and post-tracking the extent to which favourable change had occurred.

Continuous tracking, i.e. studies taking place during the campaign, can be helpful in that changes can be made before it is too late to avoid damage.

Post-tracking on the government's campaign against the spreading of AIDS showed that while attitudinal and behavioural changes had been wrought in the population at large, the minority of people most responsible for the spread of AIDS had scarcely been affected. It was alleged therefore that insufficiently accurate targeting had occurred, but the real problem was that of specifically identifying the people most at risk.

Advertisements can be pre-tested using a variety of research techniques. Such techniques would normally be pre-tested for attributes of:

- communications effectiveness (copy-testing);
- sales effectiveness.

Communications effectiveness research would focus upon testing a proposed advertisement for the quality of impact and retention. For example, in the case of a magazine advertisement a dummy magazine can be passed among the readers who are asked to say which advertisements they can remember having seen and what the advertisements said.

Sales effectiveness research would test a proposed advertisement for its qualities of liking, conviction and propensity to buy. Taken a stage further, test-marketing could establish the actual number of trials achieved and the proportion of repeat purchases, but it should be noted that these would be affected by other elements in the marketing mix as well as advertising.

13.4 SALES PROMOTION

Americans use the term 'sales promotion' in the same way that some British authors use the term 'promotion', i.e. to describe all forms of communication including advertising and personal selling. McDonald (1984, p. 110) in bemoaning the state of confusion caused by the various definitions states that, in practice, 'sales promotion is a specific activity, which can be defined as the making of a featured offer to defined customers with a specific time limit'.

The Institute of Sales Promotion defines sales promotion as 'a range of tactical marketing techniques designed within a strategic marketing framework to add value to a product or service in order to achieve specific sales and marketing objectives'.

For the purposes of this discussion, sales promotion can be best defined as any marketing communications other than personal selling, advertising and PR.

The increase in expenditure on sales promotion relative to advertising which has taken place over the past decade can be accounted for partially by its efficacy. Certain forms of sales promotion such as incentive schemes and exhibitions lend themselves to cost-benefit analysis to a greater extent than advertising. For example, the sales effect of a precise markdown and the number of redemptions of prize incentives (i.e. people claiming prizes) can be calculated with a high degree of accuracy, as can the amount of orders taken at a particular exhibition.

Most larger companies in consumer goods and service have sales promotion managers and departments whose activities need to be audited in the same way as other elements of the promotional mix.

The sales promotion audit should cover at least the following items:

1 the effectiveness of sales promotion activites in total;
2 a review of the extent to which various types of sales promotions are used relative to competitors;
3 costs of the various types of sales promotions employed, together with trends;
4 results of individual sales promotions against objectives set;

The benefits of sales promotion can therefore be seen in terms of the way in which it helps to maintain a high level of awareness of the supplier and of the brand in several ways:

- through packaging impact at the point of sale;
- through other point-of-sale display materials;
- by obtaining prime positions in retail outlets;
- through the use of in-store merchandising activities such as free sampling;
- by special offers and other incentives, e.g. competitions;
- through exhibitions;
- by the use of sponsorship;
- by the use of sales literature and other selling aids (videos, samples, etc.).

Not only do sales promotions win and help to maintain the patronage of customers but they also build the goodwill of dealers and distributors who enjoy increases in store traffic and rates of stockturn. They also encourage the trial and repeat purchases of services.

While sales incentives such as price markdowns are used to boost sales of a product line it should be remembered that the majority of the boost can only be temporary. Buyers may switch loyalties only for the period of the promotional offer and then revert to their normal brand purchase. The real benefit of a good promotion is to convert some of the brand switchers to loyal repeat purchasers of your brand. In this way market share can be increased by a *series* of promotions as illustrated in Figure 13.9.

FIGURE 13.9
Sales promotion series as a means of building market share

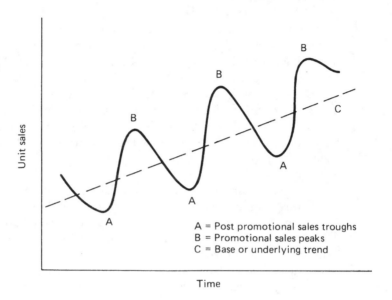

The positions marked A are the pre- and post-promotion sales troughs, while those marked B represent the promotional peaks. It can be seen that position A settles progressively at a higher sales point due to the retention of a proportion of the previous promotional increase. The dotted line C indicates steadily rising sales stimulated by the series of product-line promotions.

Sales Promotion Strategies

We referred to the idea of push and pull promotional strategies in the introduction to this chapter. When we examine the role of sales promotion in relation to these two notions in more detail we can observe that its various techniques can be used in both contexts; see Figure 13.10.

When deciding whether or not to stock a new product a distributor can often be swayed by the amount and quality of consumer sales promotion support. This is because the distributor's main fear is that of the product not selling, and consumer incentives will help to ensure that products stocked are sold. In this way consumer incentives can help a sales force to sell in to the distribution channel.

FIGURE 13.10
Sales promotion as a push and pull strategy

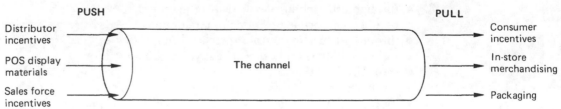

However, many manufacturers will also offer distributors some special incentives to stock and display a new product or to feature an existing product, such as case bonuses, special trial offers, special display fittings, etc.

In the above ways sales promotion can be seen as an important contributor to the selling in process as well as to that of selling out. More detail on particular techniques follows in the next section.

Sales Promotion Tactics

A variety of techniques can be employed in a short-term or tactical way to increase sales without committing the promoter to longer-term changes. For example, a consumer markdown may be used to clear out stocks of winter fashions at the end of a season. This does not constitute a permanent reduction in prices.

The wide variety of sales promotion techniques can be categorized as shown below.

Consumer Incentives

Some of these can be retailer originated as well as supplier originated, and take a wide variety of forms which seem to increase each year as more ideas are created. Some of the more well known of these are:

- *Price markdowns*: which can be on-pack or off-pack, on showcards or in the form of coupons featured in newspapers/magazines or distributed door to door, which customers then offer for redemption.
- *Premium offers*: these can be extra quantities of the same product at the regular price or small free gifts either in the pack or attached to it, e.g. plastic toys or more specifically the inclusion of sachets of Ovaltine in Shredded Wheat packs.
- *Self-liquidating premium offers*: these are where, for example, a cake slicer at a specially reduced price is offered by a cake supplier in return for proof of purchase of N cake cartons. The offer is usually made on-pack. The cake supplier will usually have negotiated a bulk purchase of cake slicers from the slicer manufacturer at a big discount allowing the cake supplier to offer the cake purchaser a slicer at say half its normal price. The cake purchaser thus obtains a premium. The cost of the offer is self-liquidating to the cake supplier on account of the discount negotiated with the slicer manufactuer and the extra cake sales made. That is to say the cost of the promotion is compensated by the profit on the extra sales made and an increment on the price paid for the slicer.
- *Banded packs*: these are usually related items such as a toothbrush banded to toothpaste at a reduced price for the two combined.
- *Stamp collecting schemes*: stamps are given to purchasers in proportion to the spend usually by retail outlets such as the Co-op and petrol stations as a patronage incentive. Other forms include free prize game or 'scratch' cards and coupons which can be collected and exchanged for promotional offers.
- *Free sample or tasting offers*: the giving away, often in-store, of samples, usually by a merchandising person supplied by the promoter. Popular for food and drink items such as cheeses and wines.
- *Prize competitions*: usually on-pack and with questions related to knowledge of the supplier's goods.
- *Personality promotions*: are used to attract greater in-store traffic as well as promote sales of particular items. Thus a well-known footballer may be seen at a bookshop giving autographs or personally signing books on football.
- *In-store demonstrations*: of new gadgets or machines again help to build store traffic and sales.
- *Special displays*: help to attract attention and build sales. These can be assisted by the provision of materials and/or staff by the suppliers – see merchandising/ POS.

Dealer Incentives

- *Cash bonuses*: may be in the form of one extra case for every 10 ordered, cash discounts or straight cash hand-outs to encourage volume sales, period stock-building, display or in support of a cut-price to consumers.
- *Credit terms*: may be extended to support promotions aimed at bulk retail buyers.
- *Staff incentives*: may be payments or prizes provided by suppliers for the attainment of particular promotional targets. Staff training by suppliers could also be considered as falling under this heading.

Sales Force Incentives

These usually take the form of cash payments or prizes for the achievement of specific promotional objectives. Holmes and Smith (1987, pp. 35–40) give typical objectives for sales force incentives as:

1 to increase sales volume (total);
2 to increase sales of specific products;
3 to increase sales of a high profit product;
4 to reduce high inventory;
5 to introduce new products;
6 to balance seasonal sales variations;
7 to gain new accounts;
8 to reactivate 'old' customers;
9 to decrease credit exposure.

The ultimate objectives, however, may be to increase market share and/or profit.

A higher motivational effect may be gained from a sales force if a competitive incentive element is introduced (e.g. an exotic holiday for two is offered for the best performance within a group) in addition to individual rewards. Incentives can be applied on a team rather than on an individual basis where appropriate.

Non-financial incentives involving an appeal to pride or status can also prove extremely effective, such as 'best sales person' awards, the use of a special car or the temporary use of the best sales person's special car-parking spot.

For companies that continuously offer sales force incentives, special services have been developed by a number of promotional entrepreneurs. One of these is a system whereby prize points are continuously available and can be exchanged for goods and services featured in a catalogue. The service company will normally handle all the administration of such a scheme on behalf of its clients.

Exhibitions

Exhibitions are widely used in industrial, commercial and consumer goods and services markets as a means of promoting sales (see pp. 480–2 for their role in PR).

At some exhibitions such as the Boat Show, the Ideal Home Exhibition and the Motor Show, orders may be actually taken on the exhibition stand, thereby enabling their cost effectiveness to be established.

Companies need therefore to take decisions as to:

- aims to be achieved;
- which exhibitions if any they need to show at;
- the size of stand to hire;
- the location of the stand;
- the layout of the stand and its facilities;
- staffing of the stand.

Choice criteria would include:

- the nature of the exhibition and the types of people likely to attend;
- the numbers of people likely to attend and their geographical locations (e.g. whether groups from overseas countries will be attending);
- costs;
- competitors showing or likely to book stands;
- timing: whether exhibitions might coincide with the launch of a new product;
- assessments of impact on customer relations;
- opportunities for publicity and enhancement of corporate image.

Packaging

Davidson (1972, p. 214) claims that 'packaging is one of the lowest cost and highest leverage areas of marketing activity. Changes in design are relatively expensive but can bring quite large business gains ... Packaging unlike advertising, can close a sale once it operates at the point of purchase'.

The word 'leverage' here is taken to mean positional advantage and return on cost. Davidson also provides a checklist for packaging development based upon the following four aspects:

- protection of contents;
- consumer convenience;
- trade appeal;
- consumer sales appeal.

The importance of the aspect of trade appeal is echoed by Cox and Brittain (1988, p. 173) in their comment on pack design:

> Because so many products are prepacked and because there is such a fight for shelf space, pack design is important to the retailer who may decide to accept or reject a pack just on the basis of its design rather than its contents, e.g. because of its dimensions or its 'stackability'.

Packaging is therefore the 'silent salesman' in a self-service world, and without packaging noticeability, the product will be unlikely to be selected from the supermarket shelves.

Opportunities exist through the package design for uniqueness and to add value. The shape and attractiveness of a bottle can greatly influence the sale of a liqueur or perfume, while secondary uses (e.g. empty coffee jars for storage) add value to the product.

Other ways in which the packaging can add value have been described above under the heading of consumer incentives and branded packs.

A great deal of thought is put into packaging impact across the range of products being offered by major companies. When Boots last redesigned their packaging for the entire range of own-label medicines great care was taken to ensure *total* harmony and impact in-store. Sales improved dramatically as a result and Boots regained share against competitive proprietary medicines.

Character Merchandising

The use of characters such as 'Mr Men' can greatly enhance sales of items like mugs and T-shirts to children. Manufacturers pay a royalty and/or a fee for the privilege to the owners of the copyright of the character.

Some companies invest in building up their own characters as promotional devices, such as the famous Spillers flour graders or the Tetley Tea Bag characters.

Coulson-Thomas (1983, pp. 283–4) refers to the practice of associating sportswear and goods with particular sporting personalities under this heading. He also cites the application of the technique to the Pope's visit to Ireland when the Catholic Church entered into a joint venture arrangement with a professional merchandising company in order to profit from the product of an extensive range of 'official' souvenirs.

Sponsorship

The practice of sponsorship has increased greatly in recent years, and databanks exist which record the companies active in this form of promotion and the types of sponsorship in which they are involved. The association of Cornhill with test cricket is a good example.

Some reference to the PR elements of sponsorship has already been made earlier in this chapter – Jefkins (1990, p. 200) points out that, while sponsorship may be genuinely altruistic, it more usually fulfils a PR, advertising or marketing communications objective of some kind and that many sports sponsorships aim quite blatantly to gain TV coverage.

TI Raleigh, the bicycle manufacturers, sponsored a Tour de France team for several years at a reputed cost of over £500,000 per annum before the team finally succeeded. However, the company found that the benefits simply in terms of the cost of the TV coverage obtained more than compensated for the costs of sponsorship. TI Raleigh's share of the European cycle market increased considerably as a result of their win.

Jefkins (1990, p. 201) cites a list of 16 potential objectives of sponsorship, some of which are concerned with PR, advertising, corporate identity and product positioning rather than sales promotion *per se*. However, some ways in which sponsorship can be seen to contribute to sales promotion objectives are:

- inspiring the sales force, making them proud and providing extra talking points in building better customer relations;
- giving a boost to the trade which is seen to be selling products associated with major events and constantly in the news (e.g. Jaguar dealers following motor-racing success);
- providing a means of offering greater hospitality to very important customers as when sponsoring horse racing and show jumping.

13.5 PUBLIC RELATIONS

Public relations (PR) is at its simplest the way in which an organization manages its relations with its publics. In some companies there appears to be relatively little management or even recognition of this important function.

Marketing is concerned with satisfying the needs of customers. In endeavouring to satisfy customer needs, marketing also has to manage relations with those people who are responsible for producing and distributing goods and services. Thus marketing and PR are very much interlinked and there is a public relations element in every aspect of marketing communications. However, PR extends beyond marketing in that it is concerned with the total communications of the organization, embracing the community as a whole, funding bodies and shareholders, political and legal interfaces, the media, the organization's employees and their trade unions; these are illustrated in Figure 13.11.

A PR strategy needs therefore to be based upon dicisions in three areas:

1 the extent and frequency of the communications with that public;
2 the degree of importance attached to the communications in terms of their ability to harm or help the organization;
3 the effectivenes of these communications in achieving objectives.

FIGURE 13.11
Eight basic publics for PR

> 1 **The community at large** – people living near the site and/or affected by it
>
> 2 **Employees** – categorized by type, e.g. factory workers, office staff, management and their trade unions
>
> 3 **Customers** – past, present and future
>
> 4 **Suppliers of materials and services** (other than financial)
>
> 5 **The money market** – shareholders, banks, insurance companies, potential investors
>
> 6 **Distributors** – agents, wholesalers, retailers, etc.
>
> 7 **Potential employees**
>
> 8 **Opinion leaders** – all those whose opinions may help or harm the organization, including media editors

It can be seen that some aspects are quantifiable (e.g. frequency of communications), while other aspects are qualitative or judgemental (e.g. degrees of importance). The extent to which the PR audit needs to be conducted by a specialist agency is perhaps conditioned by these considerations. Some parts (for example, that of customer relationships) might be better conducted by an outside agency on the grounds of objectivity, while other parts (e.g. the number and seriousness of complaints received), are better handled by the organization itself. The extent to which complaints are monitored and acted upon has a direct relationship with the level of customer service.

The amount of publicity gained in the media can be assessed quantitatively (in terms of space) but the extent to which this publicity is favourable or unfavourable requires the exercise of judgement.

PR Evaluation and Control

Since PR is about effecting change for the better, a basic evaluation procedure involves taking stock of the current situation prior to conducting a PR campaign and then establishing the new situation following the campaign. This procedure is similar to the pre-advertising and post-advertising tracking studies referred to in a previous section.

In this way checks can be made on the improvement of the corporate image, assuming this to be one of the PR objectives. An organization might find that its image scored high rankings on some attributes such as reliability, but a low ranking on modernity (i.e. was considered old fashioned by a majority of potential customers). A campaign to improve the modernity ranking might include the development of articles highlighting R & D activities targeted at particular media with copies direct mailed to particular buyers. This could be coupled with a series of in-company visits to computerized/robotized production plants again targeted at particular buyers. Such a campaign would of course need to be scheduled over a period of time and would incur costs which would need to be budgeted and approved. The extent to which buyers' attitudes had then changed could be established by a post-campaign survey and increases in orders measured against set targets.

A simpler way of evaluating PR activity as a whole is to measure the amount of media coverage in terms of the amount of space gained in newspapers/magazines and/or the amount of viewing/listening time gained on television and radio. Assessing its value would be more problematical but subjective judgements could be made by a panel of company executives.

More specific measures can be made against specific objectives. For example, a PR objective of establishing a better reputation as an employer in the local community might evaluate results by comparing labour turnover rates prior to and following the activities carried out and/or the amount of new recruits from the area involved.

Internal marketing PR could be assessed by means of staff surveys or group discussions. These could focus on particular aspects such as the rating of an in-house journal or the knowledge of and understanding of the company's mission statement.

In summary, therefore PR (which is thought by many to be the most ephemeral element of the marketing mix) can and indeed should be subject to the planning, evaluation and control process which govern other elements of the promotional mix, whether conducted in-house or through PR consultants. In the latter case, clear briefs covering objectives, budgets, reporting and evaluation procedures will be required in much the same way as when briefing advertising agents.

13.6 PLANNING PERSONAL SELLING

In a sense, the sales plan is of focal importance in that the income generated by it provides most of the means for expenditure not only on marketing research, promotion and distribution but also on the production of goods or the supply of services in the majority of companies. There are of course exceptions! For example, when a company markets its products and/or services by mail-order gaining sales by receiving direct orders against offers advertised in newspapers and magazines and where no personal selling is involved. However, even in this extreme example, receivers of goods may have complaints or queries and contact the company by telephone, asking for the sales department and being put through to a person who could be categorized as dealing with customers and therefore in telephone sales.

In a number of ways it could be argued that the sales function is the most extensively and continuously monitored aspect of the marketing mix, in that sales volumes and values are totalled at least weekly in most organizations and compared against targets or budgets. This recording and checking is usually carried out at the individual sales person's level, as well as at area, regional and national levels.

However, we perhaps need to go beyond these basic measures when auditing the sales function and endeavour to identify the sales force's effectiveness in carrying out sales strategies and as an element of the promotional mix. This may involve, for example, determining the numbers of new customers gained or the proportion of sales achieved for new products. Certainly we also need to measure the selling costs involved in each of these activities in order to determine sales force effectiveness.

The sales audit might therefore seek to establish customer/non-customer attitudes toward the sales force and sales force attitudes towards the company. It would also normally involve comparisons of the sales force with competitors on aspects such as those listed below in an effort to determine its relative effectiveness and form a basis for improvement:

- relative size of the sales force;
- reward systems and levels of earnings;
- rate of sales force turnover;
- sales per sales person;
- sales force support systems;
- relative level of training;
- recruitment system;
- control systems;
- relative images of sales forces.

Sales objectives are perhaps the most quantified and time-scaled of any objectives within the marketing mix, probably because revenue is so important to the

FIGURE 13.12
Major quantified sales objectives

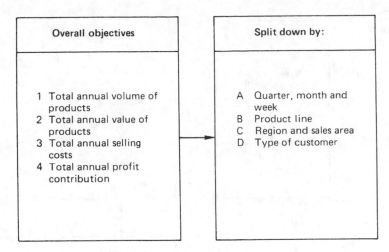

Overall objectives	Split down by:
1 Total annual volume of products 2 Total annual value of products 3 Total annual selling costs 4 Total annual profit contribution	A Quarter, month and week B Product line C Region and sales area D Type of customer

company's ability to pay bills, and hence to its survival. They are also the most easily measured and monitored. Quantified objectives would, for example, normally be set covering at least items 1, 2 and 3 in Figure 13.12.

As pointed out in Chapter 6, marketing mix objectives are means to ends (strategies) at corporate planning level, and this is known as the cascade effect or hierarchy of objectives as described in McDonald (1984, p. 98). Overall marketing objectives have to be broken down into sub-objectives which, when taken all together, will achieve the overall objectives.

Sales Strategies

In a very real sense the sub-objectives and the splits of overall quantified sales objectives contained in the above figures represent some of the sales strategies to be employed.

For example, overall sales revenue objectives might be reached by concentrating on particular areas or on particular types of customers with particular product lines.

The establishment of POS display material and/or the training of customers' sales forces are means of obtaining sales.

Lancaster and Jobber (1985, pp 50–3) in their discussion of sales strategies confine this to the marketing mix rather than addressing sales strategy *per se* - an approach shared by most authors on selling and sales management. This might be because until recently personal selling has been seen as a rather more tactical element in the marketing mix. However, it is increasingly being recognized that personal interfaces with customers and potential customers present an important opportunity for which a clearly defined strategy is required.

West (1987, p. 215) observes that:

> Surprisingly, there is little discussion of the implications of the interaction between a firm's salesforce and its marketing strategy and tactics . . .
>
> The substantial growth in the service sector has led certain authors to identify further factors; people (the nature of the people employed in the organisation), process (the way in which the service is carried out), and physical (the environment in which the service is performed). The salesforce will have important influences in almost all these areas . . .

Sales strategies – like any other element in the marketing mix – are linked to overall marketing objectives so that a marketing objective of increased market share could be translated into a market penetration strategy, which would then become a sales objective of selling more of Product X to existing customers, as illustrated in Figure 13.13.

FIGURE 13.13
The relationship of sales strategies to marketing and corporate plans

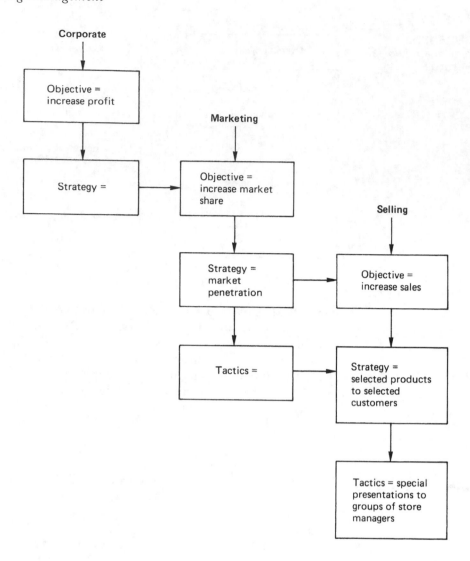

How to sell more of Product X to existing customers entails the selection of a sales strategy which might be that of initiating a series of presentations emphasizing the benefits of Product X to groups of store managers in convenient hotels using incentives of refreshments and post-presentation entertainment.

At an individual sales person's level an objective of increased sales from existing customers with existing products will demand an individual strategy or way of getting there. He/she may decide to give more attention to a particular geographic area or select particular customers who are known to possess the most potential for increased business.

There are other ways of viewing sales strategy. For example, we can take an *organizational approach* to selling as a means achieving sales objectives. Some companies organize their sales forces on levels which reflect those of their major customers. In the case of a manufacturer marketing through multiple grocers, van salesmen may call on individual store managers, area sales managers on group store managers (i.e. those over-managers of a small group of stores), regional sales managers on regional store managers, and so on.

Similarly in industrial marketing the sales organization can be tailored to better represent its market segment customers. Thus for the same product – such as industrial cooling equipment – a company can have a sales engineer calling on mechanical engineering companies, a chemical engineer on companies in the chemical industry, etc. This strategy enables the company to offer specialist advice on different applications for the same types of equipment. It improves communications over the alternative of using sales personnel to cover a wide variety of complex technologies and can lead to increased sales and greater organizational effectiveness.

A further approach to the formulation of sales strategy lies in the choice of broad selling methods and the type of relationship that is desired with the prospective customer. Companies can choose between a hard sell approach and a soft sell approach. Hersey (1989) distinguishes between these two approaches in a manner similar to that shown in Figure 13.14.

FIGURE 13.14
Hard sell versus soft sell strategies

Hard sell	Soft sell
● Concern for self	● Concern for customer
● Canned presentation	● Questions for discussion
● Talking	● Listening
● Pushing product	● Providing buying opportunity
● Presenting features	● Presenting benefits
● Advocating without acknowledging	● Acknowledging needs

Sales Force Remuneration

There are five basic ways of remunerating the sales force. These are shown in Figure 13.15.

A bonus can be defined as a specific and discretionary payment for a specific purpose or task, as opposed to a commission on sales which is ongoing and previously agreed. Thus a bonus can be used to compensate a salesperson for losses of commission due to staffing exhibitions or training new sales personnel. It can also be used to reward a team of salespeople where no one particular person could be said to have been solely responsible for the gaining of a national contract. Bonuses in the form of a share in profits or the issue of free shares are used by some managements as sales force incentives but are of course conditional on a profit being achieved during the trading period in question.

FIGURE 13.15
Sales force remuneration options

1 Salary only
2 Commission only
3 Salary plus commission
4 Salary plus bonus
5 Salary plus commission plus bonus

The choice of remuneration method is to some extent conditioned by custom and practice in the sales setting concerned. Companies can, however, evaluate the options by considering the advantages and disadvantages of each from the respective viewpoints of the company and the salesperson.

Some of the advantages and disadvantages are general. For example, an advantage of commission-only schemes may be that payment is related to results for both the company and the representative. A common disadvantage of commission-only schemes may be the uncertainty involved, which may be more meaningful to representatives worried about paying the mortgage than to the company which may be more concerned with the difficulty of administering the scheme.

However, since all five payment systems are in use (sometimes within a given sales setting), it is clear that different companies see particular advantages in the various methods. This may well be due to considerations of image and product positioning and whether a hard sell or a soft sell approach is being adopted. Hence a long-established company positioning its product well up-market, using exclusive distribution and sustaining a campaign of prestige advertising/PR, may prefer to reward its sales force with a high salary only system so as to discourage hard selling techniques and engender a greater degree of stability in terms of staff turnover.

Direction and Motivation

Training can of course be used as a means of direction and motivation. It can be the prime reason why the person applied for a selling job with the company in the first place. Equally, poor training can de-motivate. In this context Allen (1989), in writing on the psychological bases of training, points to the individual's reasons for becoming a salesperson, which may be:

● to make more money;
● as a means of self-development;
● out of a liking for travel and meeting people;
● numerous other reasons.

When examining incentives as a means of motivation it can be useful to distinguish between financial incentives (such as salary, commission, bonuses, prizes, car, travelling and out-of-pocket expenses) and non-financial incentives (such as training, level of management support, prestige of company, longevity, opportunities for promotion, etc.).

A mix of financial and non-financial incentives would seem to comprise the best motivation for a sales force in that it is more likely to generate the right degree of enthusiasm combined with a sense of team spirit and pride. Such a working environment can be dynamic without suffering from the high rates of staff turnover experienced by companies relying on financial incentives alone.

In directing the sales force, sales managers need to appreciate the relatively high degree of independence and initiative in the typical sales person's character. Over-direction can cause resentment and be counter-productive, while under-direction can lead to chaos. Certainly the sales manager needs to be a leader and to maintain discipline. Equally, leadership studies suggest that the sales manager will gain the most commitment from a team of salespeople if he or she can be seen to work with them, to listen to them and to champion their causes when appropriate.

West (1987) also points to the interaction which can take place between the firm's sales force and its marketing strategy and tactics. Thus the sales force can influence the setting of prices, the development of products and the nature of sales promotions.

Good communications play a vital role in the directing of a sales force. Two-way verbal communications are the most flexible and effective form, which is why a heavy emphasis tends to be placed on meetings and conferences in the selling function.

The degree of direction the sales manager needs to give is to a large extent governed by the product-market situation. In fmcg, where young sales forces tend to be the mode, the number of visits to be made, their sequence, the amount of time to be given to each call and even the journey plan can be strictly laid down by sales management.

This would contrast with a technical sales engineer who would tend to be older, technically qualified, more experienced and who might be left to his own devices to a much greater extent.

Evaluation and Control

In evaluating sales force performance comparisons should be made with competitors with regard to what has been achieved both quantitatively in terms of market share and qualitatively in terms of image in the market-place. This will typically entail the use of competitor intelligence and market research.

Some companies use a field sales trainer who will accompany sales representatives intermittently to appraise selling skills and give practical advice.

At the individual sales person's level it is not necessarily the person with the highest sales who should receive the most praise. There could be territorial advantages applying. High sales might have been achieved by high-pressure tactics leading to customer alienation. Such a high performer might be forced into obtaining a high proportion of businesses from new customers at the expense of losing existing customers. Similarly, a high total sales performance might not be achieved with the right degree of balance throughout the product range or throughout the year.

Other factors to be taken into account are the amount of competitor intelligence obtained, the quality of reporting, contribution to team events and the level of selling expenses incurred.

Where possible the contribution towards profits generated by a given salesperson's territory should be evaluated, particularly when that person has responsibility for price or discount negotiation. High sales do not necessarily mean high contributions. Quite apart from low prices, too many small orders can decrease the profit contribution considerably.

What we should be most concerned with are productivity and effectiveness (issues which have been discussed earlier in Chapters 1 and 3) and how best to evaluate overall performance, a problem which is addressed more fully in Chapters 15, 16 and 18.

13.7 SUMMARY

We began this chapter by suggesting that, for many organizations, marketing communications represent the most visible face of the organization and that, because of this, the question of how the communications programme is to be managed is a fundamental strategic issue.

In developing the communications plan, the marketing planner needs to begin by recognizing that the various tools of communication such as advertising, public relations, sales promotion and so on cannot be looked at and managed in isolation. Instead, they need to be seen as the component parts of a promotions or communications mix which, in turn, is just one part of the organization's overall marketing mix. Because of this, it is essential that the planner develops a clear understanding of the nature of the interrelationships that exist between the individual elements of the communications mix and how these then influence and are in turn influenced by the elements of the marketing mix. However, it is often still the case that either these interrelationships are not fully understood or, because of a series of organizational constraints, the elements of the communications programme are managed largely independently.

The consequences of this are typically seen in a number of ways, but most obviously in terms of the organization's failure to deliver a consistent and seamless message to the marketplace. In order to overcome these sorts of problems the planner needs to begin the process of planning the communications programme with a clear understanding of the nature of the corporate and marketing objectives. Without this, anything that follows will lack a true strategic focus and fail to make the contribution to the overall marketing programme that is needed and, indeed, that might be possible. It is then, and only then, that the detailed planning of the communications programme is possible.

However, at the same time as managing the integration of the various parts of the communications mix, the planner also needs to manage each of the individual elements in as optimal a way as possible. Although a strong case can be made out for doing this against the background of an initially unconstrained budget so that the promotions budget can then be built up to reflect the objective and task approach that is outlined in the text, the reality in most cases is that the budget is given and the planner is then faced with having to manage within this in as optimal a fashion as possible.

Having developed and implemented the communications programme, the planner then needs to measure its effectiveness. Although this is typically a difficult task in that only rarely can *precise* measures of a campaign's effects be determined, there is a need to develop a detailed feedback loop so that the lessons for the future might be learned.

13.8 EXERCISES

1 Look at your own organization and identify the extent to which there is a conscious attempt to integrate the elements of the communications mix. What else would be needed to improve the degree of integration?

2 Identify three examples of good communications practice. What factors appear to contribute to this, and what lessons might other organizations learn?

3 Select an industry sector and compare the approaches to communication used by the organization which is recognized to be the market leader with one of the market followers and, assuming that one exists, the market challenger. What differences exist in terms of the communication tools that are being used, how they are being used and their apparent effectiveness?

4 In the case of your own organization, what scope do you feel exists for a radically different approach to communicating with the market? What changes would be needed?

5 Do you think that internal marketing will become more or less important over the next few years? What barriers do you think will need to be overcome for it to become a widely accepted and conventional part of the communications programme in most organizations?

6 To what extent is internal marketing used – and used effectively – within your own organization? What would be needed to develop a more effective internal marketing programme?

14 | The distribution plan

14.1 LEARNING OBJECTIVES

When you have read this chapter you should be able to:

(a) understand the range of decisions to be taken with regard to the distribution plan;
(b) identify alternative channel structures and relevant criteria of choice;
(c) recognize the distinctive characteristics of logistics management (including its role within the value chain);
(d) appreciate the contribution that distribution makes to overall marketing strategy.

14.2 INTRODUCTION

Having discussed in Chapter 13 the process by which orders are obtained (i.e. the promotional mix), we now need to turn our attention towards the problem of fulfilling these orders.

A significant and increasing part of many organizations' expenditure is that incurred in keeping their products on the move through the channels of distribution to the final consumer. The distribution plan focuses on the set of decisions relating to the processes which are concerned with the flow of supplies, components, products and services between sources of supply, the producer, intermediaries, and end-users.

The success of order-getting activities will determine the volume and hence the scale of order-filling activities. This influences distribution planning (and control) in a significant way. Similarly, the level of customer satisfaction engendered by order-filling activities will affect the placing of repeat orders, which again illustrates the interdependency of the elements of the marketing mix.

There are two major areas to consider under the broader heading of order-filling. One relates to channel management decisions, given that few organizations distribute their outputs directly to the final user. The other relates to the management of physical distribution activities, such as transportation, inventory management, warehousing and order-processing (collectively known as *logistics*). (See Figure 14.1.)

We will deal with each of these aspects of the distribution plan in turn.

FIGURE 14.1
Two major aspects of order filling

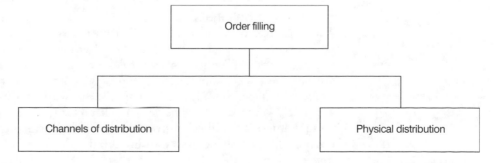

14.3 CHANNEL MANAGEMENT

Channel management embraces the analysis, planning, organizing and controlling of an enterprise's channel of distribution. This is an increasingly demanding element of the marketing domain due, in part, to pressures from global competition. In addition, the following are among the major trends which impact upon channel management:

- *An increasing emphasis on the development of channel strategy.* There is a relatively recent recognition that channel strategy can be an important means for achieving competitive advantage.
- *The emergence of new retailing concepts.* The novelty characterized by Argos (i.e. the combination of retail outlets selling products from catalogues) is being repeated in a variety of other retail settings. For example, buying clubs and cash and carry outlets are emerging.
- *The increasing importance of channel power.* Channel-driven strategies are being employed by an increasing number of companies which seek to develop or acquire products which can be marketed through their existing channels. For example, Gillette acquired Oral-B Laboratories due to the scope for increasing the usage of existing channels (i.e. razors and razor blades are sold through the same intermediaries as toothbrushes and other dental hygiene products).
- *Growth of partnerships and strategic alliances.* Every year sees the establishment of close working relationships between producers and key intermediaries with a view to generating competitive advantages. (This is an example of *supply chain management*, which will be dealt with later in this chapter.)
- *The development of direct marketing.* The emergence of database marketing in recent years has resulted in a huge increase in the use of direct mail and the telephone as distribution channels. A significant proportion of insurance business is now conducted by telephone.
- *Enhanced distribution productivity.* There has been a considerable increase in the use of information technology (IT) within distribution, along with re-engineering to develop more streamlined organizational arrangements which have resulted in both cost reduction and better management in distribution channels.

While it is possible to consider channel management from the point of view of, say, the retailer (or other final reseller) by looking 'up the channel' towards the producer, it is much more usual for the perspective to be that of the producer looking 'down the channel' towards the market. This latter perspective will be adopted here.

Key Decision in Channel Management

Rosenbloom (1995) has identified six major decision areas in channel management. These are illustrated in Figure 14.2.

The remainder of this section will deal with those decisions which are of greatest significance to the development of a distribution plan.

Formulating Channel Strategy

The objectives to be served by a distribution strategy will typically cover how, when and where the enterprise's market offerings should be made available to the targeted markets. The strategy provides a means to these ends. Perhaps the most crucial aspect is the choice of a *level of service* by which an enterprise might seek to secure competitive advantage. This is dealt with later in the chapter.

It is also necessary to consider the characteristics of orders: large orders will require different distribution strategies from those which are appropriate for small orders. The analysis necessary to underpin a decision on minimum order size is illustrated in Figures 14.3 and 14.4.

FIGURE 14.2
Major decision areas in channel management

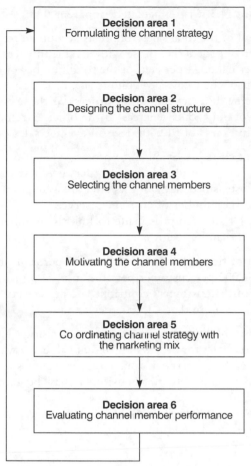

SOURCE: Rosenbloom (1995), p. 443

FIGURE 14.3
Analysis – Order size v. sales volume

Size of order	No. of orders	% of total orders	Sales value	% of total sales	Average sales value/order $
(1)	(2)	(3)	(4)	(5)	(6) [(4) ÷ (2)]
Under $10	477	17.2	$ 2,599	0.3	$ 5.45
$10 to $25	462	16.8	8,607	1.0	18.63
$26 to $50	558	20.3	21,059	2.4	37.74
$51 to $100	388	14.1	29,798	3.4	76.80
$101 to $200	151	5.5	23,450	2.7	155.30
$201 to $500	156	5.7	50,039	5.7	320.76
$501 to $1,000	209	7.6	163,559	18.7	782.58
Over $1,000	352	12.8	576,588	65.8	1,638.03
	2,753	100.0	$875,699	100.0	$ 318.09

SOURCE: Blecke (1957)

FIGURE 14.4
Sales analysis – Number of customers v. sales volume

Sales volume category	No. of customers	Sales volume $	Average sales per customer $	% customers to total	% volume to total
(1)	(2)	(3)	(4) [(3) ÷ (2)]	(5)	(6)
Under $4,000	310	$ 353,324	$ 1,140	79.7	24.8
$4,000 to $5,000	16	69,392	4,337	4.1	4.8
$5,001 to $7,500	24	149,431	6,226	6.2	10.4
$7,501 to $10,000	11	98,898	8,991	2.8	6.9
$10,001 to $15,000	13	156,036	12,003	3.3	10.9
$15,001 to $25,000	9	177,036	19,671	2.3	12.4
$25,001 to $50,000	5	194,028	38,806	1.3	13.5
Over $50,000	1	232,799	232,779	0.3	16.3
	389	$1,430,924	$ 3,678	100.0	100.0

SOURCE: Blecke (1957)

From Figure 14.3 it is immediately apparent that:

- 84.5 per cent of the total sales volume is accounted for by only 20.4 per cent of the number of orders (i.e. those with a value in excess of $500);
- on the other hand, 34 per cent of the total number of orders only accounts for 1.3 per cent of the total sales volume (i.e. orders up to a value of $25);
- at one extreme, 17.2 per cent of the orders (i.e. those below $10) have an average sales value of only $5.45 whereas, at the other extreme, 12.8 per cent of orders (i.e. those in excess of $1,000) have an average sales value of $1,638.03.

In general, it costs just as much to process a small order as it does to process a large order, with the result that small orders give rise to disproportionately high distribution costs, since many of the latter are a function of the number of orders processed and the number of customers served.

In Figure 14.4 an attempt is made to link the number of customers to annual sales revenue. It can be seen that:

- 20 per cent of the customers contribute 75 per cent of the sales volume (i.e. in excess of $4,000 per customer per annum);
- 4 per cent of the customers contribute 42 per cent of the total sales value (i.e. those ordering more than $15,000 per annum).

On the basis of this type of analysis a decision should be made regarding distribution strategies for orders of different value in a way which is cost-effective. For example, cash and carry may be appropriate for small orders, whereas direct delivery from producer to final customer may be more appropriate for large orders.

As Rosenbloom (1995, p. 554) has pointed out, the importance of channel strategy is likely to depend upon the existence of one or more of the following conditions:

- target markets (or customers) demand a strong emphasis on distribution;
- competitive parity exists in other marketing mix variables, with the need for channel strategy to provide some differential advantage (as in the case of McDonald's);
- competitive vulnerability exists because of distribution neglect;
- opportunities for synergy exist through channel strategy (e.g. via partnerships and strategic alliances).

Designing the Channel Structure

Doyle (1994) has suggested that there are three generic channel options: *direct marketing, via a sales force,* or *via intermediaries.* These are illustrated in Figure 14.5.

FIGURE 14.5
Three generic marketing channels

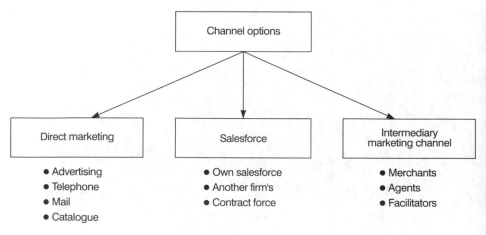

SOURCE: Doyle (1994), p. 318

To some extent, the choice between these generic options will depend on answers to the following questions:

- Can we effect distribution better than intermediaries at an equivalent cost?
- Can we effect distribution as well as intermediaries at a lower cost?

If the answer to either of these questions is yes, then the enterprise should consider direct distribution. However, a barrier to direct marketing might exist in the form of *entrenched buying behaviour*. That is to say, people get used to buying certain products through particular intermediaries and have an in-built inertia to change.

Figures 14.6 and 14.7 illustrate potential savings through the use of intermediaries (or middlemen). It can be seen that the total number of transactions has been reduced from 20 in Figure 14.6 to 12 in Figure 14.7. The customer now has to deal with only one supplier instead of two. Each producer deals with just one middleman instead of ten customers. As a result, substantial savings are possible in the ordering system and in transportation costs. Lead times will be potentially reduced by the middleman holding stocks. The mark-up he charges will cover the cost of this aspect of customer service.

Within the UK context it is possible to expand on the generic channel options given in Figure 14.5; these are shown in Figure 14.8.

From this array of alternatives we can see that voluntary retail groups (i.e. independent retailers trading under a common group symbol such as Spar which acts as a group for purchasing purposes) will buy from wholesalers outside the group as well as from within the group. Co-operative Society retailers will act in a similar way when expedient.

FIGURE 14.6
Direct marketing to 10 customers by two manufacturers

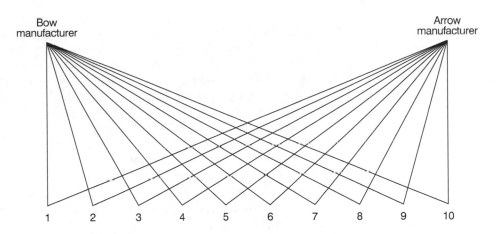

FIGURE 14.7
Marketing to 10 customers by two manufacturers through one middleman

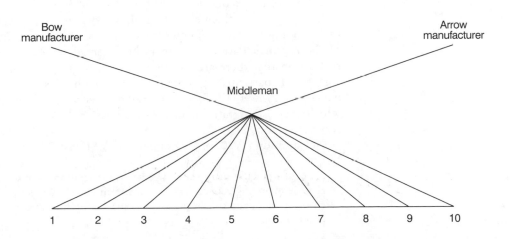

FIGURE 14.8
*Principal UK channels
of distribution*

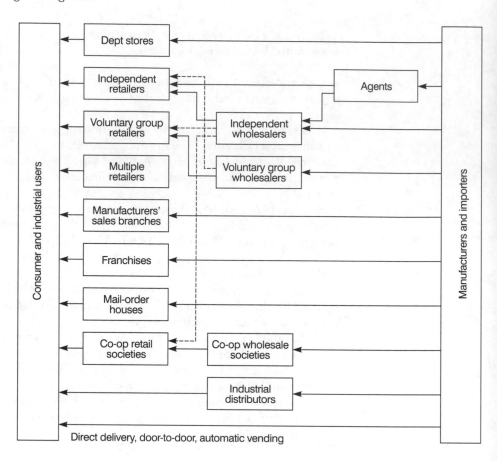

Co-operative Society wholesalers will buy from other manufacturers as well as from their own manufacturing units in the same way that Boots the Chemists do in order to offer their customers a more attractive choice of products. Producers can, of course, use more than one channel of distribution, and this is fairly common in the clothing industry, for example, where a manufacturer might sell direct to the public ex-factory while supplying garments to mail order companies, multiple retailers, agents and even market traders.

Not all retailers will want to stock all manufacturers' products. Assuming a manufacturer of matches was able to offer small independent retailers an equivalent product at a lower price than competitors, with the scope for the retailer to add a higher mark-up, it may not be worth the latter's while to deal with that manufacturer for a single item – especially when the weekly sales value of matches might be very small. The small independent retailer is likely to deal with a local cash and carry wholesaler for a full range of items on the grounds of convenience and economy of effort.

A conventional channel of distribution consists of independent intermediaries each looking after its own interests with little concern for the overall performance of the channel. Part of the emerging interest in *supply chain management* is a realization that there are advantages in managing the channel as a co-ordinated system of participating organizations. Such a system is termed a *vertical marketing system* (VMS) and the retailing sector is dominated by such systems, which are also significant in the business to business, industrial products and services sectors.

McCammon (1970, p. 43) has defined VMS as:

> . . . professionally managed and centrally programmed networks pre-engineered to achieve operating economies and maximum market impact . . . through integration, co-ordination, and synchronization of marketing flows from point of production to points of ultimate use.

There is a need within VMS for one of the participating organizations to act as channel manager in order to co-ordinate the whole channel. The links through which co-ordination might be facilitated might include prescribed rules, operating guidelines, contractual arrangements, services provided by the channel manager, and so on. Procter & Gamble acts as channel manager in connection with its own brands. Similarly, where franchising arrangements exist (e.g. fast foods, print shops, hotels) the franchiser will typically act as channel manager. Within the channels used by most motor manufacturers there will typically be a contractual VMS agreement between manufacturers and dealers.

In deciding on the most appropriate configuration of distribution channels it must be decided whether to aim to sell products through all available outlets, through a selection of the available outlets in a particular area, or to limit distribution to one outlet in each area. These three alternative strategies are known as:

- *intensive distribution*, which is often sought by manufacturers of high-volume, low-value products in mass demand for which the typical pattern of buying behaviour is that of habit and convenience. An obvious example is soft drinks which are distributed intensively in outlets ranging from vending machines to theatre foyers and fish and chip shops;
- *selective distribution*, which is used by manufacturers of consumer durables for which the typical pattern of buying behaviour is that of 'shopping around'. Most consumers will make an effort to compare the offerings available in different outlets. For this reason, the manufacturer need not distribute his products through all the available outlets. For example, a dishwashing machine might be distributed via electricity company showrooms and department stores in town centres rather than via all available outlets. Selective distribution involves less communication effort than does intensive distribution and also offers opportunities to develop closer relationships within the channel from which adequate market coverage might be achieved with lower cost and greater control than is possible with intensive distribution;
- *exclusive distribution*, which arises when the producer limits the number of intermediaries more strictly to one per geographical area. The dealer will receive exclusive rights to distribute the producer's offerings in that geographical area in return for agreeing not to carry competing products. The producer will consequently receive a greater commitment from the outlet and more control over image and price. Rolls Royce cars are a good example of this type of distribution strategy.

Figure 14.9 illustrates distribution intensity.

FIGURE 14.9
Distribution intensity

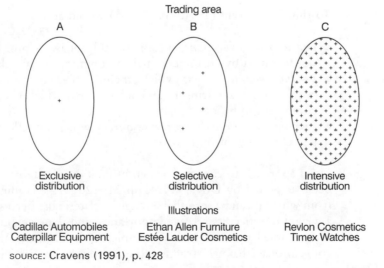

SOURCE: Cravens (1991), p. 428

The choice among the alternatives will depend to a large extent on the nature of the market offering, the target market segment and the product positioning. Lancaster and Massingham (1988) suggest that some of the factors which might persuade a company to prefer a more exclusive form of distribution include:

- where the customer needs or expects specialist advice, facilities or service;
- where the manufacturer and/or distributor would gain from the enhanced image associated with selective/exclusive distribution;
- where potential sales volume would not warrant more intensive distribution;
- where the manufacturer wishes to exercise more control over channel members' marketing activities;
- where more intensive distribution might result in conflicts between channel members.

Channels of distribution, once selected and established, involve the enterprise in relatively long-term commitments to other organizations (such as wholesalers and retailers) as well as affecting in a very significant manner every other major marketing decision. It is important therefore to ensure that the implications of each alternative choice are carefully evaluated. We now turn to this question.

The importance of correct channel structure is vividly illustrated in Johnnie Boden's *Biggest Mistake* (see Illustration 14.1) and in Daewoo's entry into the U.K. car market (see Illustration 14.2).

Selecting the Channel Members

In developing this part of the distribution plan consideration needs to be given to (see Wilson (1983, p. 572)):

- *economic criteria*, which will reflect the pattern and levels of costs, sales revenue and profit. As each alternative channel configuration is likely to produce different levels of sales revenue and costs, the best alternative is not necessarily that producing the most or the least respectively, but the one which produces the best relationship between the two – i.e. profit;
- *control criteria*, which relate to the degree of influence, motivation and conflict among channel members. For example, an agent who handles many different manufacturers' lines will probably not be seen favourably by manufacturer A because the agent will put his own interests ahead of A's in endeavouring to sell *any* line – not just A's – and this can lead to friction;
- *adaptive criteria*, by which the manufacturer is able to preserve some flexibility in responding to changing conditions. Long-term franchise agreements are antithetical to adaptive behaviour within distribution channels.

To this list Cravens (1991, pp. 429–31) would add:

- *end-user considerations*, since it would not be helpful to select intermediaries not favoured by customers further down the supply chain;
- *product characteristics*, which include the complexity, special application requirements, servicing needs and so forth which channel members must be competent to handle;
- *manufacturer's capability and resources*, which are reflected in bargaining power and channel control.

An approach to carrying out an evaluation of alternative channel options has been suggested by Doyle (1994, pp. 319–20). This is illustrated in Figure 14.10, from which it can be seen that a range of criteria has been specified, each accorded a weight to reflect its relative importance, and then weighted scores produced for each channel option. In this example, VMS produces the highest score and a conventional channel structure (i.e. involving intermediaries but without any

Illustration 14.1: 'My Biggest Mistake', Johnnie Boden

The 32-year-old former banker and stockbroker set up Boden, the mail-order clothing company, two-and-a-half years ago. Based in north London, it now has 30,000 customers, a turnover of £1.5m – and just 10 employees

I have made so many mistakes that I often consider it a miracle that we've survived. However, as someone once put it, if 51 per cent of your decisions are correct, you're laughing.

In setting up a business after several years of corporate life, one is beset with indecision. I spent days agonising over problems to which I was convinced there was a 'right' answer.

The head ruled the heart: so-called professionals were consulted (at no inconsiderable cost) to make decisions which, in truth, they had no business making. These decisions were mine to make. I was merely being weak. If I were to pass on one piece of information to any budding entrepreneur, it would be this: don't be frightened of making mistakes.

For each problem, there tend to be only two possible solutions (or variations of the same). Make a decision trusting your guts. If you don't and the decision is the wrong one, you'll kick yourself; if it's the right one, you won't have learnt anything. So within reason, follow your guts. If you are right, you will feel great. If you're wrong, you'll have learnt a lot. Most importantly, you won't regret it.

My greatest mistake emanated from a head-based decision that almost crippled the business. On the advice of an expensive firm of consultants, I decided to entrust the 'fulfilment' arm of the business to a third party. 'Fulfilment' is mail-order jargon for the taking, processing and despatching of customer orders. We paid an outside company to deal with our existing and potential customers.

Fortunately, the orders rolled in. According to the daily information I received, orders were taken, goods were sent out, cheques were cashed and everyone was happy. All I did was monitor the operation from afar and count my blessings, rather pompously, that I was spared the nitty-gritty and could thus devote my energies to the 'major issues' – or so I thought.

Cracks soon started to appear. Tales of inefficient service and slow delivery filtered back to me, normally indirectly, or at great parties which were thereby ruined.

Not only did such tales catch me completely unawares, but I was utterly powerless. The frustration of such impotence in an ultimate service industry was indescribable. This fulfilment company held our stock, its telephone numbers were printed in our catalogue and it had all our data.

On reflection (as my guts, wife and mother had told me all along), how could I expect someone else, all nine-to-fivers, to care as passionately as I did about customer service? These were *our* customers, *our* livelihood. I would have stayed up all hours to satisfy them. What were they to the fulfilment company but a very indirect means to an end?

We eventually parted company. But as a result of our experience, many of our valued and ill-treated customers will never return, thereby wasting considerable amounts of money spent on attracting them in the first place.

Now we speak to the customers direct. I no longer delegate important aspects of the business to people over whom I have little control. Of course, we continue to make massive mistakes. But at least we've only got ourselves to blame.

Source: As told to journalist Corinne Simcock, The Independent on Sunday: Business, *30 January 1994*, p. 24

Illustration 14.2: Daewoo and Its Approach to Distribution Innovation

In 1995, Daewoo, the Korean car manufacturer, made a spectacular UK debut. With sales in its first month of operations of 1500 cars, the company based its strategy upon a radically different approach to selling and distributing its cars.

The majority of car companies use a well-developed and long-established dealer system which acts as a buffer between them and their customers. Daewoo, however, opted for a rather different approach with an advertising campaign which placed customer care as high as the mechanical quality of its cars and establishing a network of its own direct sales centres, together with a partnership with Halfords, the retail parts and service group. In doing this, they overcame one of the major problems which small car companies and new entrants to the market typically face, that of starting a sales and distribution network from scratch and ensuring that the network then achieves – and maintains – the standards of customer care they are aiming for.

The principal benefits of the two-strand strategy were that it gave Daewoo an immediate nationwide sales and service network and enabled Halfords' 30 million annual customers to see the cars every time they visited one of the 136 participating Halfords stores, each of which has a Daewoo-trained mechanic and a computer terminal with access to Daewoo's parts warehouse.

The partnership between the two companies emerged as the result of a major customer survey. In interviews with 100,000 potential customers, Daewoo uncovered the depth of dissatisfaction with the traditional approach to selling cars. The findings of the survey were used to develop the final Daewoo product that was based upon the notion of 'customer delight' and selling a complete motoring package and not simply a car. Halfords was then recruited as a partner after the research suggested that it had a more positive image than any other potential third party partner.

Prominent amongst the survey findings was that customers find haggling over price to be highly stressful. Daewoo responded to this by basing its sales approach around 'sales advisors' who are not paid on a commission basis and who are therefore not under pressure to clinch the sale at almost any cost. In addition, the sales advisors very deliberately do not approach customers but instead wait until the customer approaches them.

Once the car has been sold, it comes with a 30-day money-back guarantee, provided that it has been driven no more than 1000 miles. Other innovations which were introduced largely as the result of the research findings included the installation of childrens's play areas; because the surveys revealed that car buying is a family activity, it follows that something should be done specifically for the children.

The link with Halfords allowed the company to include within the price a significant service element. Thus, each car is sold on a fixed non-negotiable price that includes three years' free servicing at Halfords. Included with this is all servicing, labour and consumables, except tyres. In taking this approach, Daewoo was aiming for a totally trouble-free servicing operation. Customers are 'phoned before the service in order to identify the work that needs doing. Cars are then collected and returned to any location, with a free courtesy car being provided if needed. Within 72 hours of the service, a Daewoo representative 'phones the customer to check that everything has been done satisfactorily.

The results – and success – of the Daewoo approach were seen in several ways, but most obviously by the much higher level of product demand than had been anticipated and by a series of very high customer satisfaction scores.

Source: The Sunday Times, *11 June 1995, p. 3*

FIGURE 14.10
Evaluating alternative channel options

Criteria	Importance Weight	Channel options			
		Direct	Franchise	Conventional	Vertical
Channel objectives					
1 Goals	0.1	5	2	3	4
2 Resources	0.1	1	2	5	3
3 Positioning	0.1	1	4	2	5
Channel strategy					
4 Target market	0.15	3	3	4	4
5 Differential advantage	0.2	4	4	1	5
Channel reliability					
6 Motivation	0.15	5	4	2	4
7 Control	0.1	5	3	1	4
8 Risk	0.1	2	2	2	3
Weighted scores	**1.0**	**39**	**35**	**26**	**45**

SOURCE: Doyle (1994), p. 320

attempt at managing the channel as a whole) produces the lowest score. However, the numbers themselves are not the most important feature of this approach. The main aim is to encourage managers to identify the attributes which they consider to be necessary if a channel is to operate effectively. In this way the strengths and weaknesses of alternative channel options can be highlighted.

While accepting that a variety of criteria are relevant in choosing a channel of distribution, there are several approaches available which deal specifically with the economic criteria. For example, Figure 14.11 illustrates the choice between using a sales agent and establishing a branch sales office.

The level of fixed costs of the agent (in the form of a retainer) will probably be lower than the fixed costs of setting up a branch sales office (which involves rent, salaries, etc.) but the variable cost of the agent (i.e. commission) will almost certainly be greater per unit sold than would be the case with the branch office's variable costs. If the level of sales is expected to be below point S on the horizontal scale of Figure 14.11 then a sales agency arrangement is preferable financially, but otherwise a branch office is to be preferred. Taking another example, if a company has, say, four channels of distribution in operation, the cost pattern of each can be identified as shown in Figure 14.12.

For each channel the variable costs applicable to that channel and the specific (i.e. separable) fixed costs appertaining to each channel can be charged directly to

FIGURE 14.11
Break-even chart for channel decisions

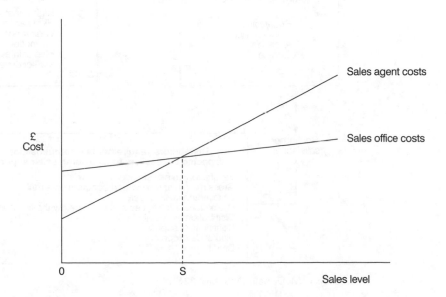

FIGURE 14.12
Channel profitability –
1

		Channels			
	Total	A	B	C	D
Sales revenue	37 000	6 000	7 000	5 000	19 000
Variable costs	15 000	1 000	3 000	4 000	7 000
Separable fixed costs	14 000	3 000	4 000	2 000	5 000
Contribution	8 000	2 000	0	– 1 000	7 000
Non-separable costs	5 000				
Net profit	£ 3 000				

FIGURE 14.13
Channel profitability –
2

		Channels		
	Total	A	B	D
Sales revenue	32 000	6 000	7 000	19 000
Variable costs	11 000	1 000	3 000	7 000
Separable fixed costs	12 000	3 000	4 000	5 000
Contribution	9 000	2 000	0	7 000
Non-separable costs	5 000			
Net profit	£ 4 000			

FIGURE 14.14
Distribution
objectives and
consumer satisfaction

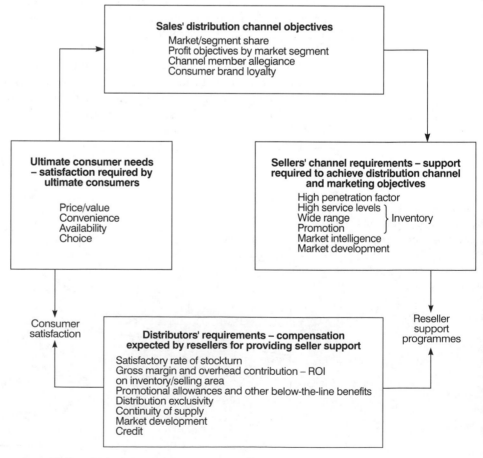

SOURCE: McDonald (1995), p. 324

the channels which, when deducted from the sales revenue generated through each channel, gives a contribution (by channel) to the common (i.e. non-separable) fixed costs of the company as a whole.

Figure 14.12 illustrates that channel C is distinctly unprofitable and that channel B is neither profitable nor unprofitable (i.e. is in a break-even situation). By eliminating channel C the variable and separable fixed costs incurred in connection with this channel will be eliminated – as will the sales revenue – and the net profit will improve by £1,000 (as shown in Figure 14.13).

Eliminating channel B would bring no benefit, and if some new initiatives can be taken within channel B it may be possible to make it profitable (e.g. by improving efficiency and thereby reducing costs and improving its contribution).

McDonald (1995) makes useful distinctions between sellers' distribution objectives, sellers' requirements of middlemen and distributors' requirements of sellers: see Figure 14.14.

It can be seen from Figure 14.14 that manufacturers and middlemen need to co-operate fully in their common objective of satisfying consumer needs profitably. However, conflict can occur when a manufacturer or a middleman seeks domination and/or becomes dissatisfied with the relationship. Such conflict can be resolved to some extent by *backwards or forwards integration* within the supply chain (as when a retailer takes over a manufacturer or a manufacturer sets up its own retail outlets). Conflict also occurs, of course, between competing retailers within a channel, and can even occur between branches of the same retail chain when, for example, a regional promotion involves some branches but excludes others.

By way of summary of the channel issues which we have considered, Figure 14.15 shows their interrelationships.

FIGURE 14.15
Channel choice decisions

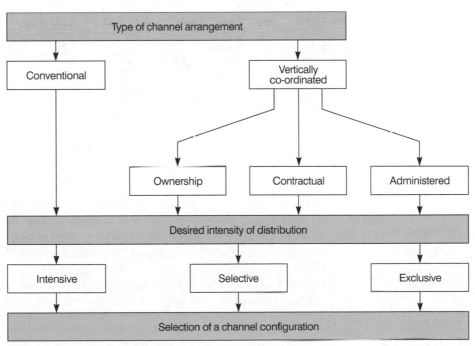

SOURCE: Cravens (1991), p. 433

14.4 LOGISTICS

Logistics, or *physical distribution management* (PDM), consists of a number of activities which are essential to linking marketing, manufacturing and administration but which have received little co-ordinated study until recent years. A major reason for this is that attention has been directed from time to time to elemental parts of PDM (such as inventory control) without viewing the parts in the context of the whole process. In a similar way, it is an oversimplification to extract, say, advertising from its order-getting setting of marketing.

The activities encompassed by PDM include:

- order processing;
- inventory management;
- warehousing;
- materials handling;
- traffic management;
- transport facilities;
- packaging;
- customer services (e.g. credit control);
- depot/warehouse location.

The costs of these activities constitute a major part of total marketing outlays. It has been suggested (Bowersox and Closs (1995, p. 586)) that, on average, logistics consumes about 11 per cent of the gross domestic product and employs approximately 20 per cent of a nation's workforce. In more specific terms, Figure 14.16 gives an indication of logistics costs by industry sector across Europe.

FIGURE 14.16
Logistics costs by sector as percentage of sales

Sector		Storage	Inventory	Transport	Admin	Packaging	Total
Food, Drink & Tobacco	Manuf	1.05	1.23	2.36	2.13	0.58	7.35
	W'sale	0.74	0.79	2.80	0.46	0.21	5.01
	Retail	1.42	0.46	0.94	0.59	0.18	3.59
Consumer Goods	Manuf	0.96	1.04	1.76	1.76	0.25	5.77
	W'sale	1.05	1.23	2.36	2.13	0.58	7.35
	Retail	1.57	0.65	1.26	1.22	0.32	5.03
Industrial Manufacturing		0.94	1.00	1.49	1.64	0.43	5.50

SOURCE: "Euorpean Logistics Comparative Costs & Practice Survey 1995", Institute of Logistics

Previous studies have shown that small companies in general operate at a cost disadvantage compared with their larger competitors. This situation is particularly noticeable among industrial companies and through nearly all the manufacturing sectors. The situation is less critical for retailers and wholesalers, since factors such as the product range and the type of outlets will have a significant impact on the results. However, these results are entirely consistent with previous surveys and indicate significant economies of scale for many larger operators.

The Value Chain

Porter (1985) introduced the *value chain* as a way of breaking down an enterprise's strategically relevant activities in order to understand the behaviour of costs and the sources of differentiation as alternative approaches to securing competitive advantage. (See discussion in Chapter 2 above – pp. 58–60.)

The value chain of an enterprise consists of nine categories of interrelated activities, as shown in Figure 14.17.

These activities are, in part, primary activities and, in part, support activities: the latter exist to facilitate the former, with the particular arrangement reflecting any

FIGURE 14.17
The value chain

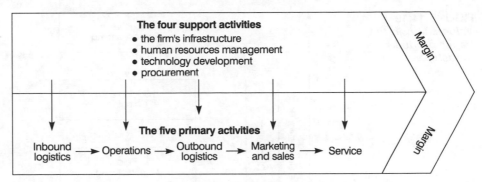

SOURCE: Adapted from Porter, M. E. (1985), *Competitive Advantage*

given enterprise's history, strategy and the underlying economics of its situation. The value aspect is to be found in the price that customers are willing to pay; hence, the margin depends on the cost-effectiveness of the primary and support activities on the one hand and the market's perception of the enterprise's offering on the other.

Each activity in the value chain has operating costs associated with it, and any given enterprise's cost position (relative to its competitors) is derived from the cost behaviour patterns associated with the activities constituting its value chain. Doyle (1994) has modified the generic value chain to highlight the outbound logistics aspects and their linkage to other marketing channel activities: see Figure 14.18.

This way of viewing the activities of an enterprise emphasizes the crucial interrelationships of the different value generating activities. However, while it does encourage managers to think of the cost-effectiveness of each primary and support activity relative to competing firms in a *horizontal* sense, it does run the risk of ignoring the *vertical* linkages. Figure 14.19 illustrates the value chain in the context of the paper product industry. In this vertical illustration it can be seen that Competitor A operates at all levels within the industry whereas Competitor

FIGURE 14.18
Value chain and the marketing channel

		Firm infrastructure		
Human resource management	Information systems development	Recruitment Training	Recruitment Training	
Technology management	Computer services	Market research Sales literature	Service manuals Procedures	Margin
Procurement	Transport	Advertising agency Travel	Spare parts Subsistence	
	Support activities			

| Inbound logistics | Operations | *Outbound logistics* • order processing • warehousing • inventory | *Marketing and sales* • packaging • pricing • promotion • salesforce | *Service* • delivery • installation • repair • servicing | Margin |

Primary activities · Marketing channel activities

SOURCE: Doyle (1994), p. 312

FIGURE 14.19
Value chain in the paper products industry

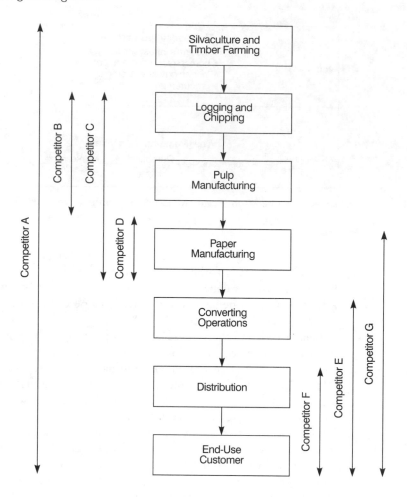

D is only active at one stage (paper manufacturing), with other competitors spanning two or more links of the value chain. In this format we can see that the value chain is that linked set of value creating activities which range from basic raw material sources to the ultimate consumer. The scope which Competitor D has for operating profitably is dependent to some extent on both *inbound logistics* (from pulp manufacturing) and *outbound logistics* (to converting operations).

Supply Chain Management (SCM)

This perspective has been gaining ground in recent years. If an enterprise has PDM objectives such as:

- reducing unit transportation costs from £5 per case to £4.50;
- reducing delivery times from seven days to five days;
- reducing the incidence of stock-outs from 10 per cent to 5 per cent,

then it is more likely to be able to achieve these costs if a supply chain perspective is adopted as opposed to a perspective which fails to recognize a series of customer-supply relationships which can be managed to mutual advantage. See Illustration 14.3.

The Level of Service

The level of service which an enterprise provides might be the key distinguishing factor in its marketing mix. Christopher, et al. (1979) define customer service as:

> . . . a system organised to provide a continuing link between the time that the order is placed and the goods are received with the object of satisfying customer needs on a long-term basis.

Illustration 14.3: Supply Chain Management at BOC

Look at the appointments section of any newspaper these days and you will see advertisements calling for supply-chain managers. But until now only a handful of vanguard companies have been aware of the significant cost savings and improved service that supply-chain management can bring. BOC is one company that does. In 1994 it began a global initiative which focused on bought-in goods and services.

BOC is a corporate giant. It operates in about 60 countries and has four main businesses: industrial gases, health care, vacuum products and distribution services. And, for various reasons, all seemed conducive to a review of their purchasing processes. Each had examples of best practice. The distribution services company, for example, had a 25-year relationship with Marks and Spencer in the UK.

The benefits of supply chain management can be seen in all the group's businesses but a good example is in the vacuum business. The headquarters of that part of BOC is in the UK. It manufactures in the UK, Korea and Japan. Unusually for UK manufacturing, 90 per cent of products manufactured there are exported. This part of BOC has seen exceptional business over the last few years due in part to the new processes of supply-chain management. Now, instead of the 25–week delivery time, vacuum pumps can be delivered in three weeks. This has resulted in a dramatic reduction in the level of stocks held and consequently in costs.

Source: Management Accounting, *Vol. 74, No. 6, June 1996, p. 64*

This definition omits pre-sales services. A broader perspective is offered by Blenel and Blender (1980) who suggest three distribution missions:

1 The first mission of service is to protect the company's customer base;
2 The second mission is to enhance the product's saleability;
3 The third mission, from a marketing perspective, is to generate profit.

La Londe and Zinszer (1976) and other writers have suggested a number of common elements of customer service from a logistics viewpoint:

- speed of response (time taken to deliver from receipt of order);
- consistency and reliability of delivery;
- stock availability;
- order size constraints;
- convenience of ordering system (customer friendliness);
- flexibility of delivery times;
- invoicing procedures and reliability;
- claims and complaints procedures;
- order status information system;
- condition of goods on delivery;
- service and support.

The problem of determining an appropriate level of service is a complex one involving the reconciliation of two conflicting issues. On the one hand, managers are keen to keep distribution costs low while, on the other hand, the level of service offered by PDM is a major source of competitive advantage. The higher the

FIGURE 14.20
Level of service

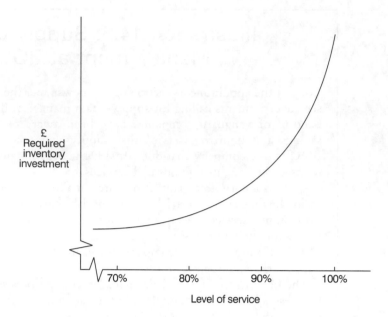

level of customer service the higher will be the level of PDM costs, hence a trade-off is needed in achieving a suitable balance.

If we define the level of service as being the percentage of orders which can be filled from existing stocks, we can plot the required inventory investment needed to achieve different levels of service, as in Figure 14.20. This shows an exponential increase in the inventory investment as the level of service increases.

If the perspective is broadened to include the costs of quicker transportation and faster order processing as well as inventory-carrying costs, these will be seen to increase as the level of customer service increases. However, the loss of profit due to lost sales (whether due to stock-outs, slow transportation, inefficient order processing, etc.) reduces as the level of customer service increases. The pattern is shown in Figure 14.21 and a total cost curve can be derived to identify the optimal level of customer service to offer (i.e. at the lowest point of the total cost curve).

This approach is helpful to a point, but it risks being introspective in linking service level purely to costs rather than to customers' requirements. A better

FIGURE 14.21
Relationship between service levels and costs

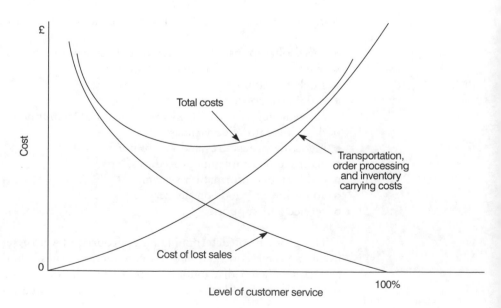

approach to distribution planning is given by Doyle (1994, p. 330) involving the following sequence of steps:

1 Identify the dimensions of service which customers value.
2 Weight the service dimensions by their relative importance.
3 Obtain customers' evaluations of the enterprise and its competitors along the dimensions specified in 2.
4 Estimate the effect on revenue of changes in the level of service.
5 Estimate the costs of providing different service levels.

If one pursues this approach it is possible to compile the graph shown in Figure 14.22. This shows, for example, that it is more profitable to offer a level of service (defined in terms of ordered items being in stock) of 93 per cent rather than 99 per cent which is currently being offered. However, in planning the level of service it is important to recognize that different market segments may warrant different levels of service. Some customers may be willing to pay high prices in order to receive premium service, while others will accord a high priority to low prices and be willing to accept lower levels of service as a consequence.

FIGURE 14.22
Setting customer service levels

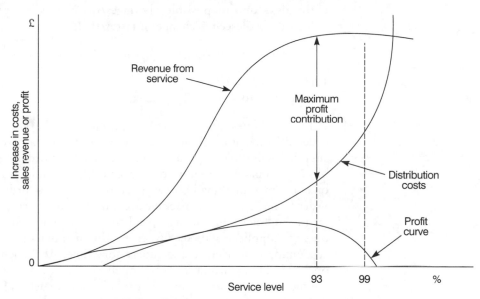

SOURCE: Adapted from Ballou, Ronald H. (1985), *Business Logistics Management: Planning and control*, 2nd edn, p. 66

Inventory management

For inventories there is an optimum level of investment below which opportunities are lost through having too little and above which more opportunities are lost through idleness of excess stock. Idle assets or non-existent assets (as exemplified by inventories which are too high or too low) cannot earn a return and this results in the cost of lost opportunities. Inventory management should aim to facilitate the manufacturing–distribution–marketing cycle at minimum cost for a given level of service.

The costs that can be associated with inventories which are too large are:

● loss of return on the capital tied up in excess stocks;
● risks from obsolescence;
● storage costs;
● handling costs;
● clerical costs;
● insurance premiums.

On the other hand, if inventories are too low, production may be disrupted by short runs for urgently required items, and sales may be lost due to the lack of availability of goods when they are required. The costs that stem from low inventories include:

- the profit element in foregone sales;
- foregone purchase discounts;
- loss of customer goodwill;
- increased unit costs of purchasing and transportation;
- extra costs of uneconomic production runs.

In formulating an inventory policy for finished goods, management must take into account at least the following points:

- the perishability of the goods;
- the demand pattern (i.e. sales requirements);
- the length of the product/order cycle;
- storage facilities (including capacity);
- carrying costs;
- capital requirements;
- the risks due to possible shortages/price increases/price reductions/techno-logical obsolescence/change in tastes/theft.

Following this, two major questions must be answered:

1 How much to order.
2 When to order.

The first question will now be discussed. The amount of inventory to be ordered (either as a call on productive output or via a purchase order to an outside supplier) will directly influence the frequency of ordering (i.e. an annual demand of 20 000 units may require one order of 20 000 units for stock, 20 000 orders of one unit, or something in between). Since placing an order involves costs (stamps, order forms, envelopes, machine accounting time, clerical and supervisory time in raising and checking the order, and so on, when an order is to be placed with an outside supplier, and set-up costs for manufacture, order forms, machine accounting time, clerical and supervisory time, etc., when the order is an internal one) and holding inventories also involves costs (the larger the inventory the larger are the costs of storage capacity, capital charges such as interest, rates, insurance, depreciation, etc.), the decision as to how much to order must come from a balancing of two opposing effects.

Figure 14.23 shows the inventory carrying cost curve rising with the amount of inventory (i.e. size of order) and it also shows the cost of ordering falling the larger the order size (i.e. the fewer the number of orders per period).

If the two costs are summated into a total inventory cost curve, the optimum order size is given by this curve's lowest point: the answer to the question how much to order is given by point X (as shown in Figure 14.23).

In addition to this graphical analysis, a simple formula can be employed to compute the *economic order quantity* (EOQ) given by point X. The formula is:

$$X = \sqrt{\frac{2QP}{S}}$$

where

X = economic order quantity (in units)
Q = annual usage (in units)
P = cost of placing an order
S = annual storage cost per unit

FIGURE 14.23
Inventory cost curves

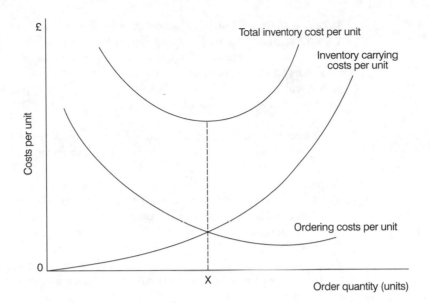

The number of orders required per period is given by $Q \div X$. Clearly, from this equation, X will increase as either Q or P grows larger, or as S decreases, and vice versa. Furthermore, the true re-order quantity (X) is determined by means of this formula regardless of discrete periods of time. This can be illustrated by Figure 14.24 which shows a hypothetical re-order situation.

The best frequency of ordering appears to be four orders per annum, giving a total inventory cost of £1,700. However, it may be the case that the optimum situation is not given in Figure 14.24 because it falls outside the specified frequencies or order size (e.g. it may be 3½ months' supply) and the formula method will precisely identify the solution.

FIGURE 14.24
Annual inventory costs

Number of months' supply per order	1	2	3	4	6	12
Orders per annum	12	6	4	3	2	1
Average inventory costs	£1,500	£3,000	£4,500	£6,000	£9,000	£12,000
Annual order costs @ £200	£2,400	£1,200	£800	£600	£400	£200
Annual carrying costs @ 20%	£300	£600	£900	£1,200	£1,800	£3,600
Total costs	£2,700	£1,800	£1,700	£1,800	£2,200	£3,800

The second question – when to order – requires a study of the rate of usage of the item under consideration. In the formula above, Q represents the annual usage, but variations in the rate of usage during the year, along with variations in lead time (i.e. the time between placing an order and receiving delivery of the items ordered), can cause severe problems. If usage is steady at, say, 50 units per month, and delivery is reliable at twice a month, then an order for 25 units could be placed every half-month in anticipation of the goods being delivered before the inventory ran out; this would mean that the last units of inventory were used on the day the new delivery arrived, and the re-order point would be an inventory level of 25 units (in other words, a new order for 25 units would be placed when the last order was delivered, and the usage between orders would be exactly equal to the quantity of each delivery). This is the basis of *just-in-time* (JIT) and is somewhat ambitious; variations will be unavoidable in delivery schedules and the rate of usage, with the result that stock-outs will arise from time to time as well as situations involving overstocking. To counter the disruptive danger of stock-outs, it is common practice to have a safety stock. An order will therefore be placed when the level of inventory has fallen to the safety stock level, and the size of the order will be given by the EOQ. The relationship between usage rate and lead time is given by the formula:

Re-order point (in units) = rate of usage (units per day) × lead time (days)
+ safety stock (in units)

Figure 14.25 illustrates the re-order point in the usual conditions of uncertainty in which a safety stock is needed. An order will be placed at point X and delivery will be expected at point Y (both on a time scale). Between ordering and receiving goods the level of inventory will have fallen (in conditions of normal usage) from the re-order level to the safety stock level. If, however, the rate of usage is greater than normal, then the stock level will be below the safety level, so the safety stock must be set by balancing the probability of a high rate of usage against the costs of holding extra stocks.

FIGURE 14.25
Re-order points

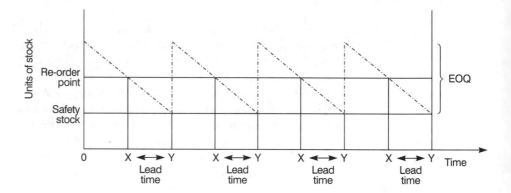

Over the last ten years or so there has been a major development in *just-in-time* (JIT) approaches to inventory management. The object of JIT is for incoming supplies to arrive at the factory, warehouse or retail outlet at the point when they are needed. The underlying principle is that, if delivery is dependable, inventory levels can be reduced substantially with enormous savings in cost. Problems arise, of course, when delivery dates are not met. Figure 14.26 illustrates a straightfor-

FIGURE 14.26
Delivery control statistics

Delivery pattern	Number of orders	Percentage of total
As promised	186	37.2
Late: 1 day	71	14.2
2 days	49	9.8
3 days	35	7.0
4 days	38	7.6
5 days	28	5.6
6 days	14	2.8
7 days	13	2.6
8 days	10	2.0
9 days	8	1.6
10 days–2 weeks	17	3.4
2 weeks–3 weeks	15	3.0
3 weeks–4 weeks	10	2.0
4 weeks–5 weeks	6	1.2
Total	500	100.0

ward analysis of deliveries in relation to agreed dates. It is not possible in a supply chain context to plan for JIT if more than 60 per cent of deliveries are later than the agreed date.

JIT is one example of time-based logistics strategies which shift co-ordination activities among members of a supply chain in order to increase inventory velocity and to reduce performance cycle lengths. While JIT is manufacturing focused the other time-based strategies are market-focused, hence must react to changes and uncertainties in market demands. The following are some of the leading-edge strategies currently emerging:

1 *Quick response* (QR) is a co-operative effort to provide merchandise supply closely matched to consumer buying patterns. It requires that retail sales of specific products be regularly monitored and this information shared across the value chain to ensure that the right product assortment will be available when and where required.
2 *Continuous replenishment* (CR) is an extension of QR which eliminates the need for replenishment orders. The aim is to create a supply chain arrangement which is so flexible and efficient that inventories in retail outlets are continuously replenished by means of daily transmissions of either retail sales information or details of warehouse shipments, with the manufacturer assuming responsibility for replenishing retail inventories as necessary.
3 *Profile replenishment* (PR) is a strategy which extends QR and CR by giving manufacturers the right to anticipate future requirements based on their overall knowledge of what is important to a merchandise category (see Bowersox and Closs (1995, p. 585)). The 'profile' reflects the combination of colours, sizes, etc., that typically sell in a particular merchandise category, which enables the manufacturer to eliminate retailers' efforts in tracking sales and inventory levels for fast-moving lines.

One thing which these time-based strategies all have in common is the co-ordination of logistics throughout the supply chain in order that the channel partner which can perform appropriate responsibilities most efficiently is in a position to do so.

Other Aspects of Logistics

Having decided on the configuration of the distribution channels and dealt with the choice of service levels, inventory management and supply chain management, there are some additional issues which also need to be considered.

Order Processing
PDM planners need to specify, *inter alia*:

- the minimum size of order (as discussed above);
- conditions of sale and purchase;
- the system to be used to process orders;
- the time taken to process orders.

To some extent these are interdependent, since the time taken to process an order will depend on the order processing system in use, which then determines the costs of order processing, which in turn, dictates the minimum size of order which can be economically handled.

Mention might be made here of *electronic point-of-sales systems* (EPOS), which link sales ordering systems with automatic stock control and stock re-ordering systems. A further development is *electronic funds transfer at the point of sale* (EFTPOS), which simultaneously debits the buyer's bank account. Cox and

Brittain (1988, p. 267) give the major benefits of EPOS to retailers in both 'hard' and 'soft' varieties as follows:

- *hard benefits*
  - up to 15 per cent increase in checkout productivity;
  - labour savings in not having to price individual items;
  - reduced 'miss-rings' at the checkout;
  - easier price changing;
- *soft benefits*
  - more management information on customer flows, line sales over time periods, merchandising/promotional effectiveness;
  - better stock control.

Warehousing

Attention needs to be paid to achieving cost-effective results through the efficient utilization of labour and equipment in this area. In particular:

- *Space utilization.* Since warehouse space and its related costs (such as rent, lighting, heating) are expensive, a high rate of utilization, hence low unit cost, should be sought.
- *Labour utilization.* Work study should be applied to goods received, stacking, materials handling, order assembly, outward loading, and stock control activities.
- *Equipment utilization.* The high costs of materials handling equipment should be justified by fairly intensive usage.

Delivery

The overall aim should be a high level of utilization of both vehicles and drivers. Three issues warrant particular attention:

- *Terminal time.* To avoid reducing the driver's time on the road, his vehicle should be loaded in his absence by the warehouse staff (e.g. in the evenings or during the night).
- *Running time.* In multiple delivery work, attempts should be made to ensure that as high a proportion of running time as possible is spent in delivery goods.
- *Delivery time.* This is a critical element of PDM, and careful traffic planning should ensure that as little delay as possible is incurred between deliveries by determining the best routes to be taken. It has often been argued that it is at those points in the distribution flow where goods stop moving that they accumulate costs.

14.5 SUMMARY

In this chapter we have dealt with aspects of planning the order-filling activities of channel management and logistics. These complement the order-getting activities dealt with in the earlier chapters of Stage Three.

Channel management is concerned with developing a channel strategy, designing its structure and selecting channel members. In dealing with these issues it is necessary to decide on distribution intensity (whether intensive, selective or exclusive) and to choose between conventional and vertical marketing systems. (The latter is the dominant choice for consumer products, and it is of increasing importance for business and industrial products.)

Logistics planning includes consideration of service levels in terms which reflect the revealed preferences of customers. There is no substitute for research-based decisions. In developing a logistics system its specification will consist of a unique physical distribution network reflecting decisions on transport, warehousing, inventory management, order processing and the level of service to be provided. The total cost of such a system is given by the simple equation:

D = T + FW + VW + S

where

D = total distribution cost
T = total transportation costs
FW = fixed warehousing costs
VW = variable warehousing costs (including inventory costs)
S = cost of lost sales due to stock-outs or delivery delays.

Each alternative system should be evaluated using this equation before the best one (on economic grounds) can be selected.

Both channel management and physical distribution management involve strategic decisions of a crucial nature, since they can make or break long-term customer relationships through the level of customer service which they afford.

In developing the distribution plan there are clear opportunities for gaining distinctive advantages over competitors. While one enterprise may offer good products at competitive prices, communicated effectively to the right people, all these factors can be let down if the products are not available in the right quantities, of the right quality, in the right place, at the right time, in the right form, and with the right packaging. Distribution can be seen to either take away from or add value to other elements in the marketing mix.

14.6 EXERCISES

1 Assume the role of Distribution Manager for a new company which has been established to develop and market computer games. What would be a suitable distribution strategy for your company?
2 What criteria do you think Daewoo used in selecting its approach to distribution when entering the UK car market?
3 Portray the value chain (in both its *horizontal* and *vertical* forms) for an enterprise with which you are familiar. Indicate the aspects which are of particular significance to the distribution function (reflecting channel management on the one hand and logistics on the other).
4 If the annual demand for a component is 5 000 units, the cost of placing an order is £5, the cost of the component is £4, and the annual storage cost is £0.50 per unit, what is the distributor's economic order quantity?
5 XYZ Ltd has a national distribution system via six warehouses selling to wholesale customers. Ninety-five per cent of orders are delivered within 24 hours of receipt. Some figures from the last financial year are:

Sales	£5 m
Net profit (after tax)	£250,000
Finished goods inventory at factory*	£750,000
Finished goods inventory at warehouse*	£1 m

(*average)

There is only one factory, and this works on a system of minimum-maximum levels of finished goods inventory to maintain the 95 per cent level of service. Each warehouse orders weekly from the factory, with special interim orders for urgent requirements. Warehouse inventory levels are based on lead times of 2–12 days from the factory.

The firm's marketing director asks what the effect on costs would be if the warehouses were eliminated and direct delivery was made to customers by outside carriers. The estimated effects for the next year are given below:

		Shipments to warehouses	Shipments to customers
Transport	To warehouses	150,000	
	Local	37,500	
	Direct		330,000
Warehousing	Rent	52,500	2,500
	Salaries	65,000	20,000
	Insurance	17,500	10,000
	Rates	7,500	5,000
	Other	15,000	5,000
	Communications	22,000	30,000
Total distribution costs		£365,500	£402,500

Required
Advise the marketing director.

14.7 Discussion Questions

1 Identify the advantages and disadvantages facing a producer using multiple channels of distribution.
2 What factors are likely to increase the trend towards the use of vertical marketing systems?
3 Can you identify any environmental changes which might prompt an enterprise to revise its distribution strategy?
4 Explain the differences between channel decisions and physical distribution management decisions and show how these functional areas are linked.
5 How might the level of customer service be improved in ways which are cost-effective?

14.8 Case Studies

Masterton Mills, Inc.

In January 1998, Suzanne Goldman was scheduled to meet with Robert Meadows, President of Masterson Mills, Inc. Goldman knew that the meeting would relate to the recent board of directors meeting. In her position as Special Assistant to the President, or 'troubleshooter,' as she called herself, Goldman had noticed that such meetings often led to a project of some type. Her expectations were met, as Meadows began to describe what had happened at the board meeting:

The directors are not pleased with the present state of affairs. The cyclical nature of carpet sales is again proving itself, as disposable personal income and new house construction have plateaued and actually declined in many areas of the country. Our wholesalers are complaining about slow payments from retailers. In many cases, their receivables are taking 60 days to collect, and we are extending our receivables to satisfy them at a 15-percent annual carrying cost. Wholesalers are cutting back on inventory as costs of carrying inventory approach 15 percent annually. Our inventories have increased, and our delivery costs have risen as we attempt to service our wholesalers. Costs of servicing wholesalers are running about 4 percent of sales. I could go on, but you get the picture. The possibility of establishing our own warehouses or wholesale operation was raised, but I was unprepared to discuss it. Needless to say, I was somewhat embarrassed. Would you examine such a program for me and prepare a position paper for the May board meeting? Focus only on the retail sales business, since we handle contract sales on a direct basis, and assume the same sales level as in 1997. Remember that our policy is to finance programs from internal funds. I'd like to see you do the same comprehensive job that you did on the advertising and sales program last November.

The Industry
The carpet and rug industry reported sales of $10 billion at manufacturers' prices in 1997. Sales in 1998 would reach $10.5 billion, according to Meadows. Industry sales are evenly divided between 'contract,' or commercial, sales and retail sales for household use.

The industry is moderately concentrated. In 1997, 15 companies out of over 250 carpet and rug manufacturers accounted for approximately two-thirds of total industry carpet and rug volume. Burlington Industries is the industry leader.

Three major types of retail outlets account for the vast majority of carpet and rug volume in the retail segment. The latest statistics available indicate that floor covering specialty stores account for 58 percent of industry volume; department stores, 21 percent; and furniture stores, 19 percent. Although no statistics exist, industry observers believe that discount stores are increasing their share of carpet and rug sales volume.

Industry trends suggest that significant cost pressures arising from raw material prices will accelerate in the next five years. This trend is likely to compress profit margins, since upwards of 80 percent of the typical producer's cost of goods sold is for materials. A second trend is the increasing emphasis on nylon in carpet and rug manufacturing. Nylon is used in 75 percent of all carpet face yarn consumed. Nylon's popularity will continue because of its excellent bulk, flexible styling, easy printing and dyeing capabilities, and usefulness as a flame retardant. A third trend is the relatively strong market for higher-quality carpets and rugs despite sluggishness in the industry as a whole. Higher-quality products should experience better sales results than popular-priced lines over the next few years.

Carpet purchase for household use is important and often time-consuming for the buyer. The purchase process is similar to that observed in furniture buying: (1) multiple store shopping, (2) joint decision making between a husband and wife, and (3) considerable ego involvement. Questionnaires completed by *Better Homes and Gardens* Consumer Panel members revealed the following:

1 Almost one-half of panel members purchasing carpet in the past two years bought it to replace another carpet or rug. (*Note*: Industry estimates indicate a carpet replacement cycle of eight years.)
2 About three in five panel members said that the brand name of carpet was a very important or somewhat important consideration in determining quality.

3 Surface appearance, color, durability, and soil resistance/cleanability were designated as very important factors in choosing a carpet/rug by over one-half of panel members responding.[1]

The Company

Masterton Mills, Inc. is a manufacturer of a full line of medium- to high-priced carpets for household use. Contract sales to apartment and office builders are also made but account for only 10 percent of total company sales. Total company sales in 1997 were $60 million, with a net profit before tax of $2.4 million. Exhibit 1 shows abbreviated financial statements.

EXHIBIT 1
Masterton Mills, Inc. – Abbreviated Financial Statements, 1997

Income Statement	
Net sales	$60,000,000
Less cost of goods sold	45,000,000
Gross margin	$15,000,000
Distribution expenses	$ 1,800,000
Selling and administrative expenses	9,000,000
Other expenses	1,800,000
Net profit before tax	$2,400,000
Balance Sheet	
Current assets	$21,550,000
Fixed assets	19,200,000
Total assets	$40,750,000
Current liabilities	$ 8,250,000
Long-term debt and net worth	32,500,000
Total liabilities and net worth	$40,750,000

The company currently distributes its line through seven wholesalers located throughout the country. These wholesalers, in turn, supply 4000 retail accounts, including department stores, furniture stores, and floor-covering specialty stores. Inspection of distribution records revealed that 80 percent of total company sales are made through 50 percent of its retail accounts. This relationship exists within all market areas served by Masterton Mills. Meadows commented that these sales-per-account percentages indicate that at the retail level the company is gaining adequate coverage, if not over-coverage.

Advertising by Masterton Mills is primarily in magazines and newspapers. The emphasis in advertisements is on fiber type, colors, durability, and soil resistance. A cooperative advertising program with retailers had been expanded on the basis of Goldman's recommendation. According to Goldman, 'The coop program is being well received and has brought us into closer contact with retail accounts.' The company employs two regional sales coordinators, who act as a liaison with wholesalers, assist in managing the cooperative advertising program, and make periodic visits to large retail accounts. In addition, they are responsible for handling contract sales.

Independent wholesalers play a major role in the company's marketing strategy. Wholesalers maintain extensive sales organizations, with the average wholesaler employing ten salespeople. Carpet manufacturers expect that retail accounts receive at least one call per month. Goldman's earlier evaluation of the sales program revealed that wholesaler sales representatives perform a variety of tasks, including checking inventory

[1] *INQUIRY: A Study on Home Furnishings from the Better Homes and Gardens Consumer Panel.* Copyright Meredith Corporation.

and carpet samples, arranging point-of-purchase displays, handling retailer complaints, and taking orders. About 25 percent of an average sales-person's time is spent on nonselling activities (preparing call reports, acting as a liaison with manufacturers, traveling, and so forth). About 40 percent of each one-hour sales call is devoted to selling Masterton Mills carpeting; 60 percent is devoted to selling noncompeting products, such as furniture accessories and draperies. This finding disturbed company management, who felt that a full hour was necessary to represent them. In addition to making sales, wholesalers also carry carpet inventory. Masterton Mills's wholesalers typically carry sufficient inventory to keep the number of turnovers at five per year. Masterton Mills's executives felt that inventory levels sufficient for four turns per year were necessary to service retailers properly. Finally, wholesalers extend credit to retail accounts. In return for these services, wholesalers receive a 22 percent margin on sales billed, at the price to retailers.

Direct Distribution Experience of Competitors

In February and March 1998 Goldman sought out information on competitors' experience with direct distribution. Despite conflicting infor-mation from trade publications and knowledgeable industry observers, she was able to arrive at several important conclusions. First, competitors with their own warehousing operations located them in seven metropolitan areas: Atlanta, Chicago, Cleveland, Dallas-Fort Worth, Los Angeles, New York, and Philadelphia. Masterton Mills had wholesalers already operating in these metropolitan areas, except for Dallas-Fort Worth and Atlanta. The company serviced these two areas from wholesalers located in Houston, Texas, and Richmond, Virginia, respectively. Second, approximately $5 million in sales was necessary to operate a warehouse operation economically. The average warehouse operation could be operated at an annual fixed cost (including rent, personnel, operations) of $700,000. Goldman was informed that suitable warehouse space was available in the metropolitan areas under consideration; therefore, the company would not have to embark on a building program. Third, salaries, expenses, and fringe benefits of highly qualified sales representatives would be about $60,000 each annually. One field sales manager would be needed to manage eight sales representatives. Salary, expenses, and fringe benefits would be approximately $70,000 per field sales manager per year. Finally, sales administration costs were typically 40 percent of the total sales force and management costs per year. Though these figures represented rough approximations, in Goldman's opinion and in the opinion of others with whom she conferred they were the best estimates available.

In March 1998 Goldman received a disturbing telephone call from a long-time successful wholesaler of the company's products. The whole-saler told her that he and others were aware of her inquiries about direct distribution possibilities. Through innuendo, the wholesaler threatened a mass exodus from Masteron Mills once the first company warehouse was opened. He implied that plans were already under-way to establish a trade agreement with a competitor. This conversation would have significant impact on her recommendation if direct distribu-tion was deemed feasible. In short, a roll-out by market area looked less likely. A rapid transition would be necessary, which would require sizable cash outlays.

Source: This case was prepared by Professor Roger A. Kerin, Edwin L. Cox School of Business, Southern Methodist University, as a basis for class discussion and is not designed to illustrate effective or ineffective handling of an administrative situation. Certain names and data have been disguised.

Required

What course of action should Suzanne Goldman recommend to Robert Meadows? Would it be in the interests of Masterton Mills to pursue a strategy of direct distribution? Support your recommendations with appropriate analyses.

Solartronics Corporation

It was early November, 1997. The corporate planning process for Solartronics Corporation had just concluded, and Richard Hawly, Vice-President of Marketing, was reviewing the corporate goals for 1998. Even though Hawly had participated in the deliberations and the drafting of the final document, he was impressed with the ambitious goals. For example, the corporate plan established a sales goal of $37 million for 1998, when sales volume for 1997 was estimated to be $27 million.

During the planning process, a number of fellow executives had voiced concern over whether the distribution approach used by Solartronics was appropriate for the expanded sales goals. Hawly felt that their concerns had merit and should be given careful consideration. Though he had considerable latitude in devising the distribution strategy, the final choice would have to be consistent with the overall marketing program for the company in 1998. A recommendation and supporting documentation had to be prepared in a relatively short time to permit an integrated marketing program introduction in January 1998.

The Company

Solartronics Corporation was formed in 1961 by Mark Speerson, who had a Ph.D. in electrical engineering. The company introduced a stereo radio unit in 1964 and a line of television sets in 1966. By the early 1980s, the company had expanded its product line to include a full line of home entertainment equipment.

Solartronics is an assembler rather than a manufacturer of home entertainment equipment. As an assembler, the company purchases components under contract from large (usually foreign) manufacturers. These components are then identified as Solartronics Corporation products and placed in consoles or other packages for sale.

Solartronics distributes its products directly to 425 independent specialty home entertainment dealers and 50 exclusive dealers which are of standard industry size in terms of selling space. Combined, these 475 dealers service 150 markets in eleven western and Rocky Mountain states. The exclusive dealers, however, are the sole company representatives in 50 markets. According to Hawly, this disparity in market coverage occurred as a result of the company's early difficulty in gaining adequate distribution.[1]

The independent dealers typically carry ten or more brands of home entertainment equipment products, whereas the exclusive dealerships carry only Solartronics products and noncompetitive complementary products. Dealerships are located in market areas with populations of approximately 100,000 or less. In contrast, major competitors tend to be national in scope. Partially as a result of that – and partially because of economies of scale in advertising and distribution – these firms had been

---

[1]Exclusive dealerships had chosen to operate in this manner. This was not the policy of Solartronics Corporation. However, Solartronics did not pursue additional dealers in these markets for the purpose of carrying company products.

selling an increasing proportion of their products through mass merchandisers such as chain and discount stores. The overwhelming majority of these stores were located in retail trading areas with 1 million or more inhabitants.

The company employs ten sales representatives, each responsible for a territory that is generally delineated by state borders. These representatives deal primarily with the independent dealers and call on them twice a month on average.

The Home Entertainment Industry

The home entertainment industry grew considerably in the 1980s with the rise in consumer disposable income, changes in lifestyles, and product innovation. Estimates of the actual dollar volume of the industry are extremely vague, partly because of the rapidly changing product mix encompassed by the general term *home entertainment* and constant product innovation.

Despite the difficulty in estimating market size, it is generally accepted that Thomson (GE and RCA brands), Zenith, Matsushita (Panasonic and Quasar brands), Sony, and North American Philips (Magnavox, Sylvania, and Philco brands) account for the bulk of total dollar volume. Private brands, produced by several of these firms and many others, are also important in the industry. The total market was estimated to be growing at a rate of 6 percent annually.

Though it is difficult to define specifically the product mix in the industry at any one time, eight general product categories exist: television, compact disc players, video cassette recorders, radios, phonographs, tape recorders, tape decks, and high-fidelity stereo system components. Product categories vary dramatically in terms of saturation. For example, 99 percent of the households in the United States have a television set, 65 percent have a video cassette recorder, and 48 percent have a portable radio or tape player. By comparison, 14 percent of households in the United States have a compact disc player and only 6 percent have a portable compact disc player. Exhibit 1 shows the incidence of first purchase and replacement purchases for selected home entertainment products.

EXHIBIT 1
First Purchase and Replacement Purchases for Selected Home Entertainment Products

	Percentage of Households Buying			
	For First Time	As Replacement	In Addition to One Now Owned	Total Market
Color console TV	37	49	14	100
Color portable TV	41	30	29	100
Color table-model TV	44	31	25	100
Stereo receiver/amplifier	58	23	19	100
Stereo speakers	55	21	24	100
Tape deck	71	14	15	100
Tape recorder	61	15	24	100
Video cassette recorder	85	10	5	100

SOURCE: Company records.

In 1987 the company commissioned a study on the socioeconomic characteristics and purchase behavior of buyers of home entertainment products. Exhibit 2 shows selected demographic characteristics of buyers of selected home entertainment products. The study reported that these purchasers had median household incomes above the median household income of the U.S. population as a whole. The research also revealed the following:

1 In-store demonstration, friend or relative recommendation, dealer or sales-person presentation, and advertising are dominant influences when buyers decide what brand of home entertainment products to purchase.
2 The median number of shopping trips made before purchasing home entertainment products was 2.4.
3 The most frequently shopped outlets for home entertainment products were radio/TV stores.

EXHIBIT 2
Demographic Characteristics of Heads of Households Buying Selected Types of Home Entertainment Products

	For First Time	As Replacement	In Addition to One Now Owned
Color console TV			
Median age	38	50	42
Median number of household members	3.3	3.3	4.3
College graduate	21.3%	15.4%	30.6%
Color table-model TV			
Median age	36	45	46
Median number of household members	3.4	3.2	4.3
College graduate	44.0%	22.5%	30.8%
Color portable TV			
Median age	41	43	43
Median number of household members	3.1	2.9	3.8
College graduate	24.2%	32.2%	33.9%
Stereo receiver/amplifier			
Median age	39	40	46
Median number of household members	3.6	3.3	4.3
College graduate	32.1%	43.8%	46.8%
Stereo speakers			
Median age	37	34	41
Median number of household members	3.5	3.0	4.1
College graduate	34.7%	38.8%	38.7%
Video cassette recorder			
Median age	39	39	NA
Median number of household members	3.2	3.4	NA
College graduate	42.1%	20.1%	NA
Tape recorder			
Median age	43	44	43
Median number of household members	3.7	4.2	3.9
College graduate	28.1%	39.4%	39.1%
Tape deck			
Median age	40	34	49
Median number of household members	3.9	3.5	4.2
College graduate	27.5%	20.5%	29.6%

SOURCE: Company records.

The vast majority of home entertainment products are distributed through five types of retail outlets: (1) home furnishings/furniture stores, (2) housewares/hardware stores, (3) auto supply stores, (4) department stores/mass merchandisers (such as Circuit City), and (5) radio/TV stores. The volume of home entertainment merchandise sold by these outlets is unknown because of the variety of merchandise offered. However, selected data on the radio/TV store group with a more homogeneous product mix are available (see Exhibit 3). These types of dealers represent all of Solartronics's accounts and operate with a gross margin of 27.5 percent.

EXHIBIT 3
Number and Retail Sales of Radio/TV Stores in the Western and Rocky Mountain States

State	Number	Sales (thousands of dollars)
Arizona	289	$ 164,870
California	2,375	1,581,046
Colorado	331	180,119
Idaho	86	30,029
Montana	81	38,408
Nevada	88	55,397
New Mexico	113	42,749
Oregon	286	132,726
Utah	124	57,204
Washington	457	182,993
Wyoming	59	20,252
Eleven-state total	4,289	$2,485,793

SOURCE: *Census of Retail Trade* and Solartronics Corporation estimate

Solartronics Corporate Policy for 1998
The following is an excerpted version of the company's statement of policy.

General Corporate Objective
Our customer is the discriminating purchaser of home entertainment products who makes the purchase decision in a deliberate manner. To this customer we will provide, under the Solartronics brand, quality home entertainment products in the higher-priced brackets that require specialty selling. These products will be retailed through reputable electronics specialists who provide good service.

Marketing Objectives and Strategy
The company's marketing objective is to serve the discriminating purchaser of home entertainment products who approaches a purchase in a deliberate manner with heavy consideration of long-term benefits. We will emphasize home entertainment products with superior performance, style, reliability, and value that require representative display, professional selling, trained service, and brand acceptance – retailed through reputable electronics specialists to those consumers whom the company can most effectively service. This will be accomplished by:

1 A focused marketing effort to serve the customer who approaches the purchase of a home entertainment product as an investment
2 Concentration on our areas of differential advantage: high-technology television, audio, and related home entertainment products with innovative features, superior reliability, and high performance levels – products that generally sell for more than $600 at retail
3 Emphasis on products requiring display, demonstration, and product education, which must be delivered to and serviced in the home, to be sold through reputable merchants who specialize in home entertainment products and provide good service
4 Concentration on distribution in existing markets, and general exclusion of large core cities with populations of 1 million or more
5 Developing brand acceptance by obtaining in every market served a market position of at least $6.50 sales per capita, which our research indicates is possible

Solartronics's 1998 policy statement and marketing strategy represented a significant departure from the company's previous marketing posture. For many years the company had manufactured and marketed good-quality, medium- and promotionally priced home entertainment products. In the last few years, however, the company had begun to emphasize more expensive and more luxurious home entertainment equipment.

Although this was not stated in the overall marketing strategy, the company had also become more aggressive in its advertising. The advertising budget for 1998 included television advertising, which the company had previously eschewed in favor of local newspaper advertising on a cooperative basis with dealers. In 1998, television advertising would be allotted $3 million and would be directed at the 100 highest-potential markets, 50 markets served by exclusive dealers and 50 other current markets that had the next highest potential.

The overall direction of the marketing program had been reaffirmed in the recent corporate planning sessions. The sales target of $37 million was viewed as both ambitious and necessary. Solartronics's senior managers were of the firm belief that the company had to attain a larger, critical mass of sales volume to preserve its buying position with component suppliers, particularly with respect to component prices and discounts.

Even though there was agreement on the marketing effort and the need to expand sales volume, different viewpoints were raised concerning the capacity of present dealers to deliver $37 million in sales. This matter had consumed much of Hawly's time recently.

The Distribution Strategy Issue

Hawly was well aware of the value that Solartronics placed on its dealers and the importance of developing a close linkage between the company and the dealers. The company had long emphasized that dealers are an asset and must be consistently supported.

Hawly saw his charge as determining the characteristics, the number, and the locations of the dealers Solartronics would need to meet its sales goal of $37 million in 1998. Initially this would involve identifying the types of dealers who would satisfy the needs of the kind of customer the company sought and who would work closely with the company in meeting corporate objectives.

A number of different viewpoints had been voiced by Hawly's fellow executives. One viewpoint favored increasing the number of dealers in the markets currently served by the company. The reasoning behind this position was that it would be difficult for existing dealers to attain the $37 million sales goal specified in the corporate plan. Executives expressing this view noted that even with a 6 percent increase in sales following the industry trend, it would be necessary to add at least another 100 dealers. They said these dealers would be likely to be independent (nonexclusive) dealers located in the 100 markets not served by exclusive dealerships. Hawly believed that adding another 100 dealers over the next year would not be easy and would require increasing the sales force that serviced nonexclusive dealers. Executives acknowledged that this plan had more merit in the long run of, say, three to four years. However, their idea had merit as a long-term distribution policy, they thought. The incremental direct cost of adding a sales representative was $50,000 per year.

A second viewpoint favored the development of an exclusive franchise program, since 27 nonexclusive dealers had posed such a possibility in the last year. Each of these dealers represented a different market and each of these markets was considered to have high potential and be a candidate for the new advertising program. These dealers were prepared to sell off competing lines. They would sell Solartronics home entertainment products exclusively in their market for a specified franchise fee. In exchange for the dealer's contractual obligation to promote, merchandise, and service Solartronics products in a specified manner consistent with corporate objectives, Solartronics would drop present dealers in their markets and not add new dealers. Further, these dealers noted, the company's current contractual arrangements with its independent dealers allowed for cancellation by either party, without cause, with 90 days advance notification. Thus, the program could be implemented during the traditionally slow first quarter of the upcoming year. If adopted, Solartronics executives believed the franchise program in these 27 markets could be served by the television advertising program. The other 50 markets served by exclusive dealers would be unaffected, since this advertising program was already being applied. The remaining 73 markets would also be unaffected, except for increased advertising in 23 high-potential markets.

A third viewpoint called for a general reduction in the number of dealerships without granting any exclusive franchises. Executives supporting this approach cited a number of factors favoring it. First, analysis of dealers' sales indicated that 10.5 percent of Solartronics dealers (all exclusive dealers) produced 80 percent of company sales. Second, an improvement in sales force effort and possibly increased sales might result if more time were given to fewer dealers. Third, committing Solartronics to an exclusive franchise program would limit its flexibility in the future. Although a number had not been set, some consideration had been given to the idea of reducing the number of dealers in the 150 markets served by the company from 475 to 250. This would mean that the 50 exclusive dealers would be retained and 200 nonexclusive dealers would operate in the remaining 100 markets, of which the top 50 would benefit from the television advertising program.

A fourth viewpoint voiced by several executives was not to change either the distribution strategy or the dealers. Rather, they believed that the company should do a better job with the current distribution system. It was their opinion that additional sales personnel and the expanded television advertising budget should be sufficient. Moreover, they argued that because of a recessionary environment, the early 1990s was not the time for major changes in distribution policy and practices.

Source: This case was prepared by Professor Roger A. Kerin, Edwin L. Cox School of Business, Southern Methodist University, as a basis for class discussion and is not designed to illustrate effective or ineffective handling of an administrative situation. Certain names and data have been disguised.

Required
Evaluate the four alternative approaches to distribution for Solartronics and produce a recommendation (with supporting documentation) to help Richard Hawly reach a decision.

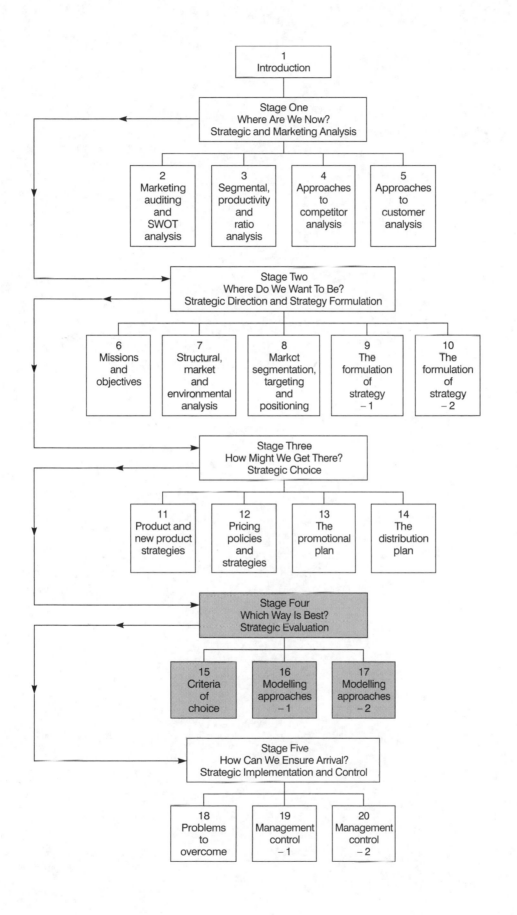

Stage Four
Which Way Is Best?
Strategic Evaluation

PREAMBLE

The overall concern within this stage is with the choice among alternative marketing strategies that were suggested in Stages Two and Three. This concern reduces to two principal questions:

1 What criteria of choice should be employed? This is dealt with in Chapter 15.
2 How might alternative marketing programmes be evaluated given the criteria articulated in 1? This is addressed in Chapter 16 and 17.

Prior to moving on to Chapters 15–17 it may be useful to consider some of the evidence that is available on the effectiveness of marketing activities within the UK. This will provide useful background material as we move through Stages Four and Five of the book.

In their study on the effectiveness of British marketing (Lynch, et al., 1988), the Bradford-based research team followed up an earlier study they had undertaken (Hooley, et al., 1984). Their main interest was in identifying the characteristics of the more successful organizations across a sample that was broadly representative of British companies in terms of size, sector and business type.

No magic formula was found that might guarantee the success of marketing activities. However, the better performers showed a firmer grasp of the key marketing concepts and a greater consistency in applying those concepts across their range of operations. There was, in fact, a stronger commitment to marketing principles resulting in a consistent marketing-oriented culture within the more successful enterprises. In summary, the prevalent attitudes among the better performers were found to be:

- a greater emphasis on identifying and meeting customers' needs;
- the chief executive sees marketing as a guiding philosophy for the whole organization;
- more aggressive, expansionist objectives;
- more likely to pursue longer-term marketing goals rather than short-term financial objectives;
- great importance is attached to marketing training.

With regard to marketing practices, the better performing companies exhibited the following characteristics:

- a greater input was made by marketing to overall strategic planning;
- there was more evidence of formal, long-term marketing planning;
- marketing objectives were more aggressively specified;
- prepared to attack the whole market and take on any competition;
- more prepared to take calculated risks;
- adopted superior quality, high-price positioning strategies;

- competitive advantages are built through reputation and quality;
- more active in new product development in order to achieve market leadership.

In overall terms the more successful enterprises showed impressive consistency in implementation derived from a combination of their clearer marketing grasp and their more focused marketing structures and systems.

Other studies that have examined the success of marketing activities include those by Verhage and Waarts (1988) who looked at Dutch and British companies on a comparative basis, and those by Doyle, Saunders and Wright (1988) and Wong, Saunders and Doyle (1988) who looked at the comparative quality of marketing activities in British, Japanese and US companies. Results from the last two studies highlighted significant weaknesses in the marketing effectiveness of British companies which were exacerbated by an excessive emphasis on short-run financial gains. Given that the focus was on comparative performance within UK markets it was found that US firms were less committed to the UK market than were their Japanese rivals. While the Japanese were working to close the technological gap between themselves and their US competitors, the latter were demonstrating a short-term profit focus. This makes it likely that US market positions will deteriorate since the Japanese showed themselves to be unmistakably aggressive, single-minded in their pursuit of market share, and undeniably more market-oriented than their US or British counterparts.

In 1994 a report prepared by the Cranfield School of Management for the Chartered Institute of Marketing revealed scepticism about the contribution of marketing to business success. (See Simms (1995, p. 12).) The Chartered Institute of Marketing subsequently commissioned a further study (see Parkinson (1995)) to measure marketing's contribution to the competitive performance of British manufacturing industry. The aim was 'to develop and validate a framework which companies could use to assess and improve their competitive performance through effective and efficient marketing'. The Executive Summary of the report *Manufacturing – the Marketing Solution* is reproduced below (with permission of the CIM).

Executive Summary

Objectives

UK manufacturing industry has experienced considerable problems over the last 25 years. From a position of market dominance in the mid 1960's, British companies have steadily lost international market share. Turnover and employment in manufacturing have steadily declined, and overseas competitors have increased their share of world markets.

This report has two objectives.

- To measure marketing's contribution to the competitive performance of British manufacturing industry
- To develop and validate a framework which companies in British manufacturing industry can use to assess and improve their competitive performance through effective and efficient marketing

The Excellence Framework

Marketing, particularly in a business to business setting, involves a much wider range of activities than those typically taking place in the sales or marketing department. These functional areas make an important contribution, frequently providing specialist services such as market research, competitive analysis and business planning services. However in an effective company the whole of the organisation is market focused. All of its capabilities are focused on the market.

These capabilities include internal processes such as research and development, operations management and manufacturing. They also include external processes such as supply chain management, customer development, and the management of strategic alliances with suppliers, distributors and other competitors. Effective companies manage this alignment more effectively and more efficiently than their competitors. Such companies are also capable of modifying and developing new ways of meeting market needs to maintain superior market positions.

Improving competitive performance involves managing key marketing processes more effectively. This involves four stages, namely:

- defining the processes which influence business performance
- measuring performance against these processes and then
- comparing the company's performance with those companies which achieve superior performance
- investing in (or redesigning) those processes which are most likely to give competitive advantage

An increasing number of case histories are now appearing in management literature on how to use business process engineering to improve competitive performance. However, little attempt has been made to date to review the processes which really contribute to competitive success, and there are few practical diagnostic frameworks available to help in the analysis.

Such a framework was developed for this project, and has been used to assess critical marketing processes in over 40 companies operating in British manufacturing industry.

The following key processes were seen to be critical.

- marketing strategy development
- quality strategy development
- product and process innovation
- customer development and management
- brand management
- supply chain management
- integration of marketing and operations

To succeed organisations should have a clearly defined strategic marketing planning process, in which customer and competitor analysis are major elements. This process should be driven by a determination to allocate resources in a systematic way to reflect different levels of market opportunity and competitive strengths and weaknesses. Equally importantly, the process should be firmly led, with a clear sense of vision and purpose, and explicit communication of the company's objectives to employees and other stakeholders.

FIGURE 1
Marketing excellence framework

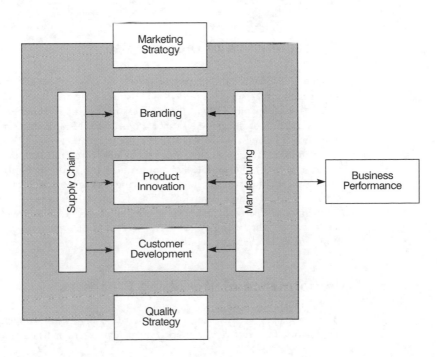

However, having a strategic direction alone is not sufficient. A well worked out strategic marketing plan will founder if there is no system to ensure that such a plan is effectively implemented. In the framework the company's quality strategy is the second key enabling factor. If strategic marketing planning is about vision and direction, then quality strategy relates to making things happen in a direct and accountable way.

Five sub-processes have been identified which link together within the broad overall framework of strategic marketing planning and quality strategy. These are product and process innovation, manufacturing and operational support, supply chain management, branding, and customer development. Together these seven processes make up the Marketing Excellence Framework. See Figure 1.

Method

To develop the marketing excellence framework each of the seven processes was disaggregated into individual components. These components enabled the project team to conduct a detailed analysis of each of the seven elements of the model. They also provided a basis for a company to score itself in terms of competitive marketing performance. A section of the full report discusses how readers can use this approach in their own organisations. These components were derived from the marketing literature, combined with the research team's own experience. In addition the original framework was piloted to ensure that the main elements made practical sense to UK manufacturing industry.

The study approach required considerable co-operation from participating companies. Interviews were required with the members of the senior management team responsible for each of the processes in the marketing excellence framework. To implement the research required the participation of up to six managers in each company. At an early stage in the research a decision was taken to build the sample in an incremental way. Considerable negotiation was required with each company to agree participation in the project.

Although the study was focused on individual operating companies, many of these companies had several different divisions. Within each of these divisions there were also potentially many different products and markets. The chief executive of each company was asked to designate the business area within the company where the analysis should be based.

The sample is well distributed, both in terms of industrial sectors and size of companies. In addition data has been collected at the business unit level, where day to day decisions are made about the future of the organisation. Perhaps most importantly the project team interviewed almost 200 managers responsible for different functional areas within each company. Jointly these managers defined and developed the companies' competitive strategies.

Characteristics of the Sample

Of the companies in the sample 66% (29) described their major business area as a major cash generator. 27% (12) regarded the business as an area to invest in for the future. In only 7% of the companies (3) was the business regarded as declining. This was consistent with the description of the growth rate of the markets. 55% of the companies (24) believed that their major business was operating in a mature market place. Approximately one third (17 companies) characterised their markets as new or established and growing.

Over 50% of the sample (25 companies) felt that competition for their core (most important) market was intense and growing. For 16 companies (36%) it was still moderate and stable. Only three companies (7%) felt that there was little effective competition. 13 companies (29%) faced markets where the competition was well established and stable. However in the majority of cases competition was either gradually changing (19 companies), or changing rapidly (12).

Performance of Marketing Processes

The companies in this sample do not score highly on any element of the excellence framework (see Figure 2). In particular scores are markedly lower for branding as a business process, reflecting a lack of concern with branding as a strategic process and a potential source of competitive advantage. For most companies, significant changes would need to be made to achieve 'best in class' performance.

Companies were classified into one of four main groupings. Those scoring up to 13 on the excellence framework were termed the '**stragglers**'. Stragglers have been left behind in terms of the use of best-practice techniques. There are 12 such companies in this sample. The second major grouping is the '**copers**'. These companies have adopted some best-practice techniques and are coping with their environment, albeit in an imprecise way. Copers manage some processes effectively but there is still considerable room for improvement. Copers have been defined as those companies scoring between 13 and 19 on the framework. There are 14 copers in the sample.

The third grouping includes companies which score heavily on some elements of the framework but not necessarily well everywhere. These companies have been defined as those scoring over 19 and up to 25 on the framework. They are frequently in transition to excellence. Such companies have been termed the '**travellers**'. There are 12 travellers in the sample. The final group is those companies which have already developed 'best in class' practice, defined by scores over 25 on the framework. These companies have been labelled the '**professionals**'. Professionals manage all of the processes in the framework effectively. Many processes are managed excellently. There are six professionals in the sample.

FIGURE 2
Scores on each business process

Business Process	1	2	3	4	5	Total No. (%)	Average
Marketing Strategy	4 (9)	13 (30)	14 (32)	10 (23)	3 (7)	44 (100)	2.9
Quality Strategy	8 (18)	7 (16)	9 (20)	10 (23)	10 (23)	44 (100)	3.1
Branding	29 (66)	7 (16)	6 (14)	2 (4)	–	44 (100)	1.5
Innovation	6 (14)	9 (20)	13 (29)	9 (20)	7 (16)	44 (100)	3.0
Customer Development	4 (9)	11 (25)	10 (23)	14 (32)	5 (11)	44 (100)	3.1
Supply Chain Management	6 (14)	9 (20)	13 (29)	8 (18)	8 (18)	44 (100)	3.0
Manufacturing	4 (9)	9 (20)	11 (25)	10 (23)	10 (23)	44 (100)	3.3

Stragglers are predominantly smaller companies. Copers, travellers and professionals are increasingly larger organisations, although there is still a significant number of relatively small travellers. The adoption of best-practice techniques increases with size, perhaps reflecting the greater range of skills available. Increasing complexity of tasks and greater resources are available to devote to 'planning rather than doing'. Stragglers are to be found predominantly in the mechanical engineering industry. Automotive supply, aerospace and chemicals have a greater proportion of more sophisticated companies.

A company's customers can have a major impact on the way it manages itself. Companies which are suppliers to the automotive industry have had to respond to increasingly demanding international customers in the last few years. This is reflected in higher overall scores on the excellence framework. Professionals are concerned about the impact of technical change on their business. Moving through to stragglers, each successive category is less concerned about the impact of changing supply market technologies, new products, and changes in manufacturing technology.

Marketing Ability and Business Performance

There is a positive relationship for a significant number of companies between the total score on the marketing excellence framework and return on sales (profit before interest and tax to sales turnover). This is encouraging since better performance on critical business processes is related to better financial performance. For these companies, getting key processes right makes a difference to financial performance.

Companies which are better at strategic marketing planning, product innovation, customer development, branding, and supply chain management make better return on sales. Funds and time invested in these processes will yield tangible business returns.

Some companies are relatively good at managing business processes, but still show relatively poor return on sales (high scorers–low performers). Better management of critical processes does lead to improved profitability in most circumstances, but not necessarily all.

High scorers–high performers are significantly more likely to operate in markets where there is a high rate of technical change in supply markets. Eight companies out of 22 (36%) high performers were in this situation. High scorers–high performers were also experiencing rapid technical changes in their products. 11 of the 22 (50%) high performing companies operated in markets with high rates of product change. By contrast only one of the nine high scoring–low performing companies (11%) operated in markets with high rates of product change.

Individual case studies show considerable variations in marketing practice across a range of different settings. Analysis of the scores of individual components reveals wide variety in the levels of sophistication with which marketing processes such as strategic planning, quality, product innovation, branding, and customer development are managed.

Application of the Findings

There are several ways to use the findings of this survey. These are as follows:

- to provide an indication of how well the company is managing each element of the excellence framework and enable the company to benchmark itself against the companies in this sample
- to provide an agenda for action aimed at improving performance on critical processes which can be monitored and evaluated over time
- to create a debate about critical business processes which is based on a structured approach

Reviewing the processes requires a degree of objectivity in analysis. The project team defined evidence for each performance dimension which was used in the scoring. Two members of the team scored each company. Readers may not have the time or resources to analyse their own organisation to the same level of detail. However, more evidence will lead to greater objectivity in the resultant scores, and greater management consensus about the final result.

Conclusions

One of the most satisfying conclusions from this research is the simple one that the application of marketing processes actually makes a quantifiable difference in U.K. manufacturing industry. Companies which scored higher on the excellence framework showed higher levels of return on sales. The study is encouraging to those involved with improving the quality of marketing practice. The depth of analysis and the focus on tightly defined business units in this study gives the project team confidence in the findings.

Considerable effort is required to implement a benchmarking study thoroughly. Critical problems include the definition of the framework including main processes, components and individual performance dimensions. The project team is confident in the framework. Statistical tests of the relationship show that the model was a good fit and explained over 65% of the variance in return on sales.

In a few of the best performing companies the project team found evidence of a genuine attempt to organise the business on a process basis rather than around conventional business functions. In one such company one job title seemed to the research team to summarise the philosophy of the whole project, namely Director of Customer Satisfaction.

Where companies had begun to focus on key processes there was greater evidence of awareness of the importance of measurement of market-led performance indicators, such as customer or supplier satisfaction. The positive evidence between process improvement and performance presented in this study should provide encouragement to companies to push ahead with this approach.

The final conclusion from this study is that excellent performance on the framework may be a necessary but not sufficient condition for business success. In some sectors companies were excellent when compared with their peers but still showed lower profit return on sales. This was due to the intensely competitive markets in which such companies were operating. The simple message for these companies is that it is not sufficient to be excellent in a comparative way with the rest of manufacturing industry. Such companies must continue to set even more demanding targets for process improvement, if they are to stay in business and achieve competitive parity or leadership.

15.1 LEARNING OBJECTIVES

When you have read this chapter you should be able to:

(a) understand the role of criteria of choice in the decision-making process;
(b) distinguish between financial and non-financial criteria;
(c) recognize the limitations of using single criteria for making strategic choices;
(d) appreciate the relevance of multiple criteria approaches to strategic choice.

In 1993 a group of chairmen, chief executives and other senior executives from 25 of Britain's top businesses came together to form the Royal Society of Arts (RSA) Inquiry *Tomorrow's Company*. This inquiry was prompted by the recognition that Britain has a long tail of underperforming companies and that the prime responsibility for correcting this situation lay with the business community. The inquiry team has now reported, and a summary of its Inclusive Approach is shown in Illustration 15.1. This contrasts *Tomorrow's Company* with *Yesterday's Companies*. One of the key means of moving forward successfully is to improve the way in which strategic decisions are made.

Tomorrow's Companies (or New Products, New Markets, New Competitors and New Ways of Thinking)

In his book *Thriving on Chaos*, Peters (1987) argues that at least ten major forces are at work which are influencing how managers think and how they need to behave. By themselves, each of these forces represents a powerful agent for change. Together, he suggests, they are overturning virtually every well-known precept of corporate management. The ten forces that he highlights are:

1 *Unprecedented uncertainty.* Despite the attention that has seemingly been paid to environmental flux over the past ten years, the majority of the managerial tools – basic accounting practice, patterns of organisation, and approaches to the formulation of strategy – are, he suggests, still predicated on stability.
2 Increasingly, *time* will be the main weapon of competition, with speed, flexibility, adaptiveness and information technologies providing enormous scope for the exploitation of opportunities.
3 *The fragmentation of markets* and the consequent need to customize products, services and the marketing effort negates the old ideas of niche markets. Niche marketing is, Peters argues, no longer meaningful, since there are no non-niche markets any more.
4 *Quality, design and service* are the fundamental expectations of customers in virtually all markets. Yet in far too few companies are these areas obsessions.
5 *Giant firms can no longer behave as they used to.* In *Time, Chance and Organisation*, Herbert Kaufman argues that 'the survival of some organisations for great lengths of time is largely a matter of luck'. Skill plays a minor role and attempts to induce flexibility are often in vain: the ravages of time that

Illustration 15.1: RSA Inquiry
Tomorrow's Company

The Inclusive Approach

Some of the Inquiry's comparisons between TOMORROW'S COMPANY and yesterday's companies are:

Purpose and Values

- TOMORROW'S COMPANY clearly defines its purpose and values, and communicates them in a consistent manner to all those important to the company's success.
- *Yesterday's companies do not see the need to have a distinctive purpose or values, and often confuse purpose with measures of success (for example, upper quartile earnings per share) or are content to leave the definition of their purpose to habit or to others. Yesterday's companies have different messages for different audiences (for example to providers of capital, employees are costs to be cut, while to the employees 'you are our greatest asset').*

Measuring Success

- TOMORROW'S COMPANY uses its stated purpose and values, and its understanding of the importance of each relationship, to develop its own success model from which it can generate a meaningful framework for performance measurement.
- *Yesterday's companies take it for granted that 'everyone knows' what success is and allow existing systems of measurements to define it for them. They are content to measure returns. Because they have no measures of the value embedded in their relationships, when hard decisions have to be made they are taken in the dark. They risk destroying value rather than creating it. Yesterday's companies measure what they have always measured in the past.*

Relationships

- TOMORROW'S COMPANY values reciprocal relationships and works actively to build them with customers, suppliers and other key stakeholders through a partnership approach and, by focusing on and learning from all those who contribute to the business, will be best able to improve returns to shareholders.
- *Yesterday's companies are locked in adversarial relationships. They think in terms of zero-sum, imagining that if they were to make customers, employees, suppliers or the community more important, the shareholders would be the losers.*

beset large organizations are generally irreversible. The only hope is to create brand-new autonomous units with very different cultures from the parent.

6 *New organizational configurations* based on local networks inside the firm and electronic data interchange outside it becoming the keys to success. The flattening of hierarchical pyramids is simply a belt-tightening exercise and only a partial – and temporary – solution.

7 *Old ideas about economies of scale are no longer meaningful.* Scale, Peters suggests, needs to be redefined. Although size may well continue to be effective, it is more likely in the future to be based on the ideas of the collections of smaller firms in new organizational combinations rather than the monolithic ideas of the past.

8 *The growth of competitive networks.* Traditionally, organizations have operated at arm's length with their suppliers and forced one to bid against another in order to keep prices as low as possible. Such an approach is, however, incompatible with ideas of competing on time, constant innovation and improvement, and even simple efficiency. To overcome this, organizations need to develop partnership relationships with a smaller number of suppliers, with each side aiming to make the other profitable. These value added partnerships (VAPs) are based on the idea that each player in the value added chain has a stake in each other's success and it is therefore the entire VAP – not just one part of it – which is the competitive unit.

9 *Internationalization for all.* Although tailoring products or services to local needs is vital, almost any national market today offers an opportunity for the enterprising firm of any size, irrespective of where it is located.

10 *The line worker committed to constant improvement and retraining* must become the chief agent for adding value and achieving continuous innovation.

15.2 INTRODUCTION

In choosing between alternative courses of action or strategies it is, of course, desirable to choose the best; but how is the 'best' to be recognized? The best from the viewpoint of one stakeholder may not be the best from another stakeholder's viewpoint. Similarly, what is best in the short term may not be best in the long term. Specifying the criteria by which choices are to be made among competing alternatives is a crucial step in working towards improved marketing performance.

It has traditionally been the case that financial criteria have dominated choice processes irrespective of the initial emphasis that may have been given to non-financial criteria. Recent changes in strategic thinking (as reported, for example, by Munro and Cooper (1989)) have suggested that the dominance of financial measure may no longer be appropriate. For instance, the emphasis placed by McDonald's on quality, service, cleanliness and value shows that a financial criterion is insufficient, although there will invariably be one or more financial measures within any enterprise's set of *critical success factors* (see pp. 552–60 below).

A selection of the most important financial and non-financial criteria is given in Figure 15.1, many of which will be discussed in this chapter.

Within the marketing literature there is surprisingly little coverage of effectiveness (i.e. doing the right things) as opposed to efficiency (i.e. doing things

FIGURE 15.1
Financial and non-financial criteria

Financial	Non-financial
Liquidity	Sales volume
Cash generation	Market share
Value-added	Growth rate
Earnings per share	Competitive position
Shareholders' value	Consumer franchise
Share price	Risk exposure
Profit	Reliance on new products
Profitability	Customer satisfaction
Cost leadership	Sustainable competitive advantage

right). However, it is implicit in the extensive coverage of efficiency that the results of marketing activities are effective: it is not suggested that effectiveness should be traded off for greater efficiency. Nevertheless, the preoccupation that has existed with inputs rather than outputs tends to mean that outputs such as increased sales revenue, greater market share, or higher profits are taken as being self-evident measures of effectiveness.

The various inputs and outputs cited in the literature on marketing efficiency include those shown in Figure 15.2.

FIGURE 15.2
Marketing efficiency
criteria

Inputs		Outputs
Marketing expense Investment Number and quality of employees Quality of decisions Technology Administrative support	**Marketing activities**	Profit Sales value Sales volume Market share Cash flow Value added Consumer franchise

If we consider market share to be an appropriate output measure we can relate this back to the discussions of the BCG growth-share matrix and the PIMS approach (see Chapter 9, pp. 311–15 and Chapter 10, pp. 342–7 below).

The growth-share matrix was developed for use in portfolio planning (i.e. to generate a balanced portfolio of business activities with reference to cash generation and cash use). Relative market share serves as a proxy for cash generation, with market growth acting as a proxy for cash use.

Market share as an output measure also features prominently in the PIMS approach (see Abell and Hammond (1979), Buzzell and Gale (1987), Day (1990)). ROI is the dependent variable in the PIMS approach (see pp. 342–7 above) with market share playing a key role in the following sequence:

1 superior relative quality is established by a business for its products;
2 this superiority facilitates the building of market share;
3 greater share brings with it cost advantages due to higher volume and experience curve effects;
4 superior quality allows premium prices to be charged which, in association with lower costs, ensures higher profits.

Whatever measures of input and output are used in an attempt to assess efficiency – and Figure 15.2 offers only a limited number of each – the overriding emphasis is typically on readily quantifiable factors. This gives a means of both asking and answering the question as to whether the enterprise is getting as much output per unit of input as it should, or whether the efficiency of marketing activities might be improved. As we have seen, however, this concern with 'doing things right' begs the question of whether the right things are being done, which requires a fuller consideration of marketing effectiveness. This is provided in Chapter 16 when we deal with such approaches as the marketing audit (which was also covered in Chapter 2) and Bonoma's approach to assessing marketing programmes.

We will proceed through this chapter by examining a range of individual criteria from both the financial and non-financial categories, and then look at more broadly-based, multiple-criteria approaches to evaluating alternatives.

15.3 FINANCIAL CRITERIA

**Cash
Generation**

Poor liquidity is a greater threat to the survival prospects of an enterprise than poor profitability, hence it is vitally important in choosing a marketing strategy to consider carefully the cashflow implications of available alternatives. This can be vividly illustrated via the BCG growth-share matrix (as discussed in Chapter 9) which classifies products into four categories (see Figures 9.2 and 9.3 on pp. 311–12):

- stars;
- question marks (or wildcats);
- dogs;
- cash cows.

Use of the product portfolio as a frame of reference should ensure that all products, business units, or profit centres are not treated alike and that investment decisions are not seen as being independent of continuing business activities. Nevertheless, a strategic success sequence is likely to emerge through following these steps:

1 The cash generated by cash cows (high market share, low market growth) should be invested in building the market share of question marks. If this is done well sustainable advantage will be provided by which question marks will become stars and then cash cows, and will thereby become capable of financing subsequent strategies.
2 To be avoided is the sequence by which question marks are not supported so that they become dogs when the market matures: low relative share in a low growth market is not the place to find oneself.
3 Also to be avoided is the sequence by which stars lose position and become question marks as market growth slows, with the risk of their becoming dogs.

It should be mentioned that, in focusing on the balancing of operating cashflows, the BCG matrix ignores the existence of capital markets which also have a role to play in balancing cashflows. Moreover, the BCG matrix fails to allow for differential risk.

Cost Leadership

A particular strategy may be more desirable than others if it is likely to secure cost leadership (which is one of Porter's key generic strategies). This notion can be illustrated through the *experience curve* which was introduced in Chapter 12 (see pp. 450–2).

The essence of the experience curve is that the real costs of generating products and services decline by 20–30 per cent whenever cumulative experience doubles.

Several causes of cost reduction act together within the experience curve, such as:

- the learning experience;
- the effect of labour specialization;
- scale effects due to increased volume.

The experience curve is derived not from accounting costs but by dividing the cumulative cash inputs by the cumulative output of end products, and the cost decline is shown by the rate of change in this ratio over time. From this rate of change managers can see how – and why – their competitive costs are shifting. If estimates can be made of competitors' experience curve effects this should reveal which are the low-cost competitors and which are not, hence which are at risk and from whom.

The main strategic message from the experience curve is that if costs per unit in real terms decrease predictably with cumulative output, then the market leader has the potential to achieve the lowest costs and the highest profits. This is illustrated in Figure 12.7 (see p. 451).

Given the empirical existence of the experience curve it is apparent that the use of cash will be less than directly proportional to a product's rate of growth. Similarly, the generation of cash will be a function of the product's market share, which links back to the BCG product portfolio matrix.

Profitability Analysis

Profitability can be defined as the rate at which profit is generated. This may be expressed as profit (i.e. an output measure) per unit of input (e.g. investment, or some measure of effort such as sales calls). Apart from limiting our focus to one output measure (profit) to represent effectiveness, this approach also overlooks such issues as the quality of services rendered, hence its partiality needs to be kept in mind.

As a criterion for strategic decision making, profitability has been criticized by Robinson, et al. (1978), as being insufficient in:

- failing to provide a systematic explanation as to why one business sector has more favourable prospects than another and why one enterprise's position in a particular sector is strong or weak;
- not providing enough insight into the underlying dynamics and balance of an enterprise's individual business units and the balance among them.

Other writers (including Chakravarthy (1986) and Day (1990)) have also criticized profitability as a performance criterion due to its remoteness from the actions that actually create value: it represents an outcome rather than a determinant of performance and cannot be managed directly, hence employees are likely to attach limited importance to it on the grounds that their day-to-day actions would appear to have little impact on profitability.

Feder (1965) has defined good marketing performance as existing when investment in each market segment is made to the point where the expenditure of an additional $1 or £1 would produce greater immediate profits if spent elsewhere. This approach reflects the *marginal responsiveness* that is characteristic of marketing experimentation (i.e. where can the greatest response in terms of improved profit be achieved for a marginal increase in effort?). To take an example, if investment of £1 million in advertising within a given market produces sales of £20 million and a gross margin of £10 million, then the *average* response of profit to advertising is 10:1. If an increase in advertising expenditure of £100,000 produced additional sales of £3 million and a gross margin of £1.5 million, then the *marginal* response would be 15:1.

In assessing marketing performance using this approach it would be logical to determine the average response for the existing allocation of marketing effort, segment by segment, which would highlight those areas in which the company has underspent or overspent relative to their profit potential. Improvements can be made by allocating additional effort in accordance with the anticipated marginal response: the greater the anticipated marginal response the more efficient will be the allocation of effort. In considering whether additional effort might be exerted through direct selling, advertising, or improved terms for intermediaries within distribution channels, for example, the need exists to consider the timing factor since different actions bring results over different time scales.

A less dynamic approach emphasizing profit (rather than profitability) has been suggested by a number of writers. Goodman (1970) and Pyne (1984) both offer

FIGURE 15.3
*Marketing-oriented
income statement*

	£	£
Proceeds from sales		100.0
Variable cost of goods sold:		
Raw materials	10.0	
Packing	10.0	
Direct labour	5.0	
Variable gross profits (manufacturing contribution margin)		75.0
Other variable expenses:		
Freight	3.0	
Warehousing	2.0	
Spoilage	1.0	
Commissions	5.0	
Discounts	3.0	
Variable profit (distribution contribution margin)		61.0
Direct product costs:		
Advertising	9.0	
Promotion	3.0	
Direct product profits		49.0
Direct division costs:		
Sales management	12.0	
Product management	3.0	
Sales force	2.8	
Sales incentives	1.0	
Market research	0.2	
Division profit contribution (net contribution margin)		30.0
Allocated fixed expense:		
Factory indirect costs	21.0	
Supervision	4.0	
Other indirect costs	19.0	
Corporate administration	5.0	
Net division profit before taxes		(19.0)

SOURCE: Adapted from Goodman (1970), p. 38

modified versions of financial operating statements as bases for assessing marketing performance. These are illustrated in Figures 15.3 and 15.4.

In Figure 15.3 Goodman distinguishes carefully between direct and apportioned costs which is a more relevant distinction than, say, that between fixed and variable costs if one is concerned to identify the performance of a marketing segment: relevance is given priority over the question of cost behaviour. In principle it makes sense to separate the profit attributable to manufacturing, distribution, and so forth, on a direct cost basis. The operational difficulty in doing this stems from the problems associated with identifying the direct costs of Product 123 within a product range of 10,000 items.

Apart from the quantity of profits as a measure of performance we might also consider the quality of profits. This depends upon the position of a particular product within its life cycle. It is evident that the profits from products in the growth phase of the cycle are likely to be more valuable than those in the decline phase since the former have a more promising future.

Pyne's approach is similar in some respects to that of Goodman. For instance, both authors emphasize the need for conventional operating statements (i.e. those having a legalistic format) to be modified to reflect marketing's circumstances and, in so doing, to highlight direct costs.

In Figure 15.4 we can see that Pyne's approach differs in some significant ways from that of Goodman:

- revenue is analysed more fully;
- marketing costs are analysed more fully with headings that help in distinguishing operating from policy-related costs;

FIGURE 15.4
Marketing-oriented profit statement

Full revenue sales (at full sale price to end user)	£
Lost revenue Distributors' mark-ups and margins Mark-downs, offers, deals and allowances Third-party costs of delivery to end user paid by the purchaser	_____
Sales proceeds Sales taxes and customs duties	£ _____
Net sales proceeds	£

Direct marketing expense
Direct selling – field sales expenses
Sales promotion – merchandising and display
                 – samples, point of sales aids
                 – cooperative allowances to distributors
Product packaging and branding expense
Product service – installation, warranty and returns
Warehousing – storage, receiving and marking, shipping
Transportation outward – truck, rail, air; cost, insurance,
                                freight and delivery
	_____

Direct marketing contribution	£
Managed marketing expense Order processing Sales and distribution management Brand and product management Marketing direction and administration	_____
Marketing policy costs Advertising and publicity Market research and customer relations Product planning, design and development Marketing team training and development	£ _____
Committed marketing costs Inventory carrying – expense and financing Cost of credit – collection and financing Marketing equipment – maintenance, insurance, financing	£ _____
Net marketing contribution	£ _____

Note: where appropriate, lost revenue may be broken down by the marketing channels in use, e.g. wholesalers, stockists, retail chains, stores, direct vending outlets, etc.

SOURCE: Pyne (1984), p. 90

- the orientation is more radical than that of Goodman in giving a basis for assessing marketing performance in strategic terms.

The amount of profit an enterprise earns is a measure of its effectiveness if that enterprise has a profit objective. (In this sense we can define effectiveness in terms of achieving that which one sought to achieve.) Since profit = revenue (output) – cost (input), it can be seen to be a measure of efficiency also in that it relates outputs to inputs. Thus an organization having revenues of £100 million and costs of £60 million is more efficient than one in the same industry having revenues of £100 million and costs of £70 million since the former uses less input to produce a given output.

Despite its ability to act as a measure both of effectiveness and efficiency, profit is a less than perfect measure because:

1 it is a monetary measure, and monetary measures do not measure all aspects of either input or output;
2 the standards against which profits are judged may themselves be less than perfect;
3 at best, profits are a measure of what has happened in the short run, whereas we must also be interested in the long-run consequences of management actions.

Nevertheless, profit measures can still play a distinctly valuable role in the control effort. For example:

1 A profit measure can provide a simple criterion for evaluating alternatives. (Although it will be necessary to take into account many factors other than profit in making a choice among alternative courses of action, on the face of it option A is more attractive than option B if A will produce more profit than B.)
2 A profit measure will permit a quantitative analysis of alternatives to be made in which benefits can be directly compared with costs. (Assuming a market exists for an enterprise's output, these benefits will be measured by the revenue flow from its sale.)
3 A profit measure can provide a single, broad measure of performance in that it is arrived at after all financial costs and revenues have been taken into account, and it thus subsumes many other aspects of performance.
4 Profit measures permit the comparison of performance to be made over time for one organization, or comparisons at a point in time to be made for a group of organizational units (e.g. divisions or competing enterprises within an industry), even if they are performing dissimilar functions. This is not possible with other measures, although it may be necessary to standardize accounting practices in measuring profits for this purpose and to ensure that the valuations of assets are made on the same bases.

This all sounds very promising, but we need to bear in mind the limitations of the profit measure. Among these are:

1 Organizations have multiple objectives and will often forgo profit opportunities in order to avoid conflict over some other objective (or constraint) such as the desired image for the company or some ethical standard.
2 Social costs and benefits are excluded from corporate profit figures. At best profit is a measure of an enterprise's success as an economic entity, but this does not measure that enterprise's net contribution (or cost) to society such as the training programmes it might offer, or the pollution it might cause.
3 As already mentioned, profit measures typically focus on current rather than long-run performance: actions can be taken to improve the former at the expense of the latter (e.g. by cutting advertising, R & D, training and maintenance budgets).
4 Profit is an inadequate basis for comparing organizations' relative performance or for monitoring one organization's performance over time. The real test is actual versus target profit, but we are really unable to specify this latter figure in any sensible way because it should be based on *profit potential* and a company's profit opportunities are not all identified. It follows that an apparently high profit figure, even when this corresponds with the target figure, may in reality be poor when related to missed opportunities.
5 Accounting rules are also inadequate since they often do not permit the recording of economic reality. (Costs should reflect the use of resources, but accounting practice does not allow this to be measured when it values assets on the basis of historical cost rather than their opportunity cost, i.e. current value in an alternative use, which has an impact on the depreciation charge, etc.)
6 Profit measures are not applicable in certain segments of a business, notably those that incur costs but do not generate revenue (unless a transfer pricing system is introduced to impute revenue flows). Examples of these types of segment are R & D, the legal department, the personnel department and the accounting department.

Creating Shareholder Value

Perhaps the majority of evaluative criteria advocated in the literature and used in practice focus on the maximization of profit, profitability, or sales rather than on the return to shareholders (see, for example, McGuire et al. (1986); Chakravarthy (1986)). The key idea behind *creating shareholder value* (e.g. Rappaport (1986); Wenner and LeBer (1989); Reimann (1989)) is that investors only willingly invest in an enterprise when they think that the managers of that enterprise will be able to secure a better return on their funds than they could on their own without additional risk. In contrast to ROI and other short-term measures the creation of shareholder value emphasizes the market's assessment of the long-term health and wealth of the enterprise. Evidence exists to indicate that movements in an enterprise's share price are due (at least in part) to the impact of management's decisions on the long-term value of the enterprise. This is covered by the *efficient markets hypothesis* which suggests that financial markets are adept at capturing information and reflecting the significance of that information in changes in share prices. It follows that decision makers in enterprises having listed shares (which only applies to some 2200 of more than one million companies incorporated in the UK) should pay due attention to the impacts of their decisions on share prices.

Day and Fahey (1988) have sought to demonstrate how a value-based approach can be applied to the evaluation of marketing strategies. The starting point is the recognition that value is only created when the financial benefits of a strategic activity exceed its costs. Since strategic activities are carried out over time – often involving several years – it is necessary to apply discounting methods to the relevant cash inflows and outflows. This is equivalent to the long-established practice of applying discounting techniques to new investments in plant and equipment: the extension of the practice to marketing strategies involves dealing with more intangible elements and embracing a series of issues rather than simply the investment in a single item of plant. We will return to this approach in Chapter 16.

15.4 NON-FINANCIAL CRITERIA

Growth

The importance of growth as a criterion of choice stems from the following:

1 Its relationship to gaining market share. Consider, for example, the sad case of the motorcycle industry in Britain. During the 1960s the level of output of British motorcycles was fairly constant (at 80 000 units per annum) whereas the exports from Japan increased from 60 000 in 1960 to 2.5 million in 1973, with their production volumes tripling over this period. The British manufacturers failed to recognize the strategic importance of market share *on a worldwide basis* for long-term profitability related to the experience curve effect. While UK production during the 1960s ensured that manufacturing facilities were being adequately employed the significant strategic issue was that Japanese manufacturers' costs were falling whereas those of British manufacturers were not, hence the collapse of the UK motorcycle industry in the early 1970s.

2 The opportunities it provides for investment: as funds are generated they can be reinvested to produce a compound return.

Growth has a significant relevance to an enterprise's relative competitive position. This is most readily measured by relative market share which is defined as the enterprise's market share divided by that of its largest competitor. Since the stronger the relative competitive position the higher the margins should be (due to the effect of the experience curve) this measure has a strategic importance.

The need for growth is shown in Figure 15.5 in which a gap can be discerned between the enterprise's present position and its preferred future position. (Figure 15.5 is a variation on Figure 6.7.) By continuing with current activities on the same scale the level of profits will decline (e.g. due to increasing competition, product

FIGURE 15.5
Gap analysis

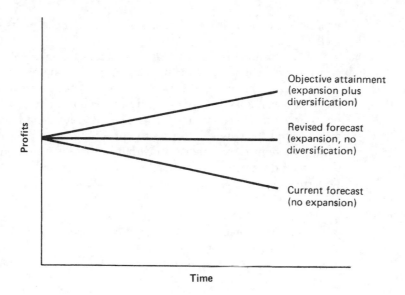

obsolescence, etc.). By expanding in either existing markets (i.e. larger market share) or by entering new markets with existing products, or by improving existing products, it may be possible to maintain the level of profits into the future. (Note: these alternatives employ known technology and, in two out of three cases, known markets.)

By expanding the scale of activity within existing markets, improving existing products *and* diversifying into new markets with new products, a much higher level of profit may result, thereby meeting the desired profit target. The choice of strategy, therefore, will be that by which the gaps in Figure 15.5 might be closed.

Growth will usually involve a move outside the enterprise's existing range of activities. Alternative paths for expansion are shown in Figure 6.6 (see p. 221).

- *Market penetration* entails an increasing share of existing markets with existing products – this would involve more aggressive promotion and distribution;
- *market extension* results from taking existing products into new markets;
- *product development* requires that new products be created to replace existing products in present markets;
- *diversification* involves the development (or acquisition) of new products for new markets.

The risk levels associated with these strategies tend to increase in the sequence in which they are listed above, so a change in product technology is likely to be riskier than a change in target markets, and a change in markets and products will be riskier than a change in only one of these (see Figures 6.8 and 6.9, p. 225).

Sustainable Competitive Advantage

(See also Chapter 10, pp. 332–7)

Wensley (1981), Day and Wensley (1988) and Cravens (1988) argue that the most meaningful guidance for strategic decision makers is to be found in returning to basics and focusing on the search for *sustainable competitive advantage*. This focus implies that strategic alternatives should be evaluated in terms of the organization's strengths and weaknesses. Sustainable competitive advantage will be found when opportunities are taken to build on an enterprise's unique capabilities. These capabilities reflect the adequacy of the match between the current core activities of an enterprise and the strategic alternatives under consideration. Thus, for example, if we consider Ansoff's growth matrix (see Figure 6.6) an enterprise's greatest competitive advantage is likely to be found in product-market situations that are similar to those of its core activities (i.e. in Cell 1).

A clear example is that of Gillette. Razors for men were followed by shaving cream for men and razors for women. Razors – whether for men or women – can be manufactured using the same facilities and the marketing has similarities whether it is razors or shaving cream one is considering. A common brand name helps develop a consumer franchise. The distribution system in use for razors can also be used for shaving cream – the products are bought in the same outlets.

At first sight it may appear odd that Gillette ventured into disposable lighters since they do not fit synergistically with the marketing of razors, etc. However, Gillette's special capabilities include:

- mass production of low cost products;
- utilization of precision plastic moulded parts;
- use of mass distribution;
- marketing of low cost, disposable consumer products under the Gillette brand name.

The manufacturing and marketing capabilities ensured Gillette secured competitive advantage in disposable lighters even if the brand name itself was not particularly useful.

Competitive Position

In considering financial criteria it is usually found that a rather introspective approach is adopted (i.e. *this* enterprise's profit, or *this* enterprise's cashflow). There is a need to adopt a more strategic perspective in dealing with an enterprise's competitive position.

The strategic dimension emerges when the performance of the business in question is compared with that of its competitors. Viewing the business within its competitive context is possible within the framework suggested by Figure 15.6.

FIGURE 15.6
Strategic comparisons

	Economic performance of competitive units				
	Market leader	Dominant challenger	Own business unit	Closest competitor	
				A	B
Revenues **Resource costs**					

SOURCE: Adapted from Pyne (1984), p. 90

The details from Figure 15.4 would be entered in the rows of Figure 15.6 under the given headings.

A variation on this theme, focusing on the notion of competitive position, has been developed by Simmonds (1986). This is covered in some detail in the following discussion.

The key notion here is that of an enterprise's position *relative to* competitors' positions. In so far as strategy is concerned with competitive position it has been largely ignored by management accountants, but in a number of papers Simmonds (1981, 1982, 1985, 1986) has proposed how this failing might be overcome.

A basic plank in his argument is the preoccupation that accountants have with the recording, analysing and presentation of cost data relating to existing activities. This 'data orientation' begs some fundamental questions, such as why the data is being collected in the first place. An alternative and preferable approach is one of 'information orientation' which starts with the diagnosis of problems, leading to the structuring of decisions, and thence to the specification of information that will help in making appropriate decisions. The focus shifts from the analysis of costs *per se* to the value of information.

The manager wishing to make decisions that will safeguard his organization's strategic position must know by whom, by how much, and why he is gaining or being beaten. In other words, strategic indicators of performance are required. Conventional measures, such as profit, will not suffice.

Let us take comparative costs as a starting point. It is intuitively the case that organizations having a cost advantage (i.e. lower unit cost for a product of comparable specification) are strong and those having a cost disadvantage are weak. If we relate this to the idea of the experience curve (which was introduced on p. 450–2 above) it will be appreciated that, if costs can be made to decline predictably with cumulative output, then the enterprise that has produced most should have the lowest unit cost and therefore the highest profits.

Apart from cost, an enterprise may seek to gain strategic advantage via its pricing policy. In this setting the management accountant can attempt to assess each major competitor's cost structure and relate this to their prices, taking care to eliminate the effects of inflation from the figures being used. Applying cost–volume–profit analysis to one's competitors is likely to be more fruitful than simply applying it internally. As Simmonds (1982, p. 207) states:

> Clearly, competitor reactions can substantially influence the outcome of a price move. Moreover, likely reactions may not be self-evident when each competitor faces a different cost-volume-profit situation. Competitors may not follow a price lead nor even march in perfect step as they each act to defend or build their own positions. For an adequate assessment of the likelihood of competitor price reactions, then, some calculation is needed of the impact of possible price moves on the performance of individual competitors. Such an assessment in turn requires an accounting approach that can depict both competitor cost-volume-profit situations and their financial resources.

After dealing with costs and prices the next important (and related) variable to consider is volume – especially market share. By monitoring movements in market share an enterprise can see whether it is gaining or losing position, and an examination of relative market shares will indicate the strength of different competitors.

Reporting market share details along with financial details can help in making managerial accounting reports more strategically relevant.

The significance of competitive position has been highlighted by Simmonds (1986) as being the basic determinant of future profits and of the business' value. Moreover, since competitive position can change over time, so can profits and value, but it should not be assumed that an improvement in competitive position will be associated with an improvement in short-run profits. In fact, the opposite is likely to be the case due to the need to incur costs in building up a competitive position which has the effect of depressing current profits in favour of future profits. This raises the question as to whether competitive position can be measured in accounting terms – not just for a given business, but also for its main competitors; and not just at a point in time, but also over time. Simmonds has attempted to do this by applying strategic management accounting. He makes it clear, however, that it is not possible to express competitive position as a single figure. Instead it is possible to offer an array of indicators relating to the competitive situation. From these indicators managers can gain insights into the competitive position of a business which will help them in judging whether or not things are moving in their favour.

Simmonds recommends that competitive data be built up for the market leader, close competitors, and laggards rather than for all competitors. The following data* might most usefully be developed:

1 Sales and Market Share

Sales revenue of each firm relative to the total market is a cornerstone, and changes in market share should be closely monitored. A decrease in market share suggests a loss of competitive position, with unfortunate implications for future profits. Conversely, an increase in market share suggests an improved competitive position with the prospect of improved future profits. By adding market share details to management accounting reports managers are able to make much more sense of what is happening.

FIGURE 15.7
Sales and market share data, Product X

	Firm A	Total market
Sales (£'000)		
Last year	1,000	5,200
This year	1,200	7,500
% change	+20	+44
Market share (%)		
Last year	19	100
This year	16	100

Figure 15.7 gives sales and market share data for Firm A and the total market for Product X.

We can see from Figure 15.7 that, despite an increase in sales revenue of 20 per cent for Firm A, the market share has slipped from 19 per cent to 16 per cent. This is explained by the growth in the total market of 44 per cent. It seems probable that the firm's failure to keep pace with the overall market growth will be reflected in a poorer competitive position: not only might competitors have gained market share at the firm's expense, but this is likely to be accompanied by cost advantages – hence improved profits. Some details are given in Figure 15.8.

Relative market share is calculated by dividing each competitor's market share by that of one's own firm, and it indicates any gains or losses. As Figure 15.8 makes clear, Firm A has slipped relative to both the market leader and its closest competitor. The leader's market share has increased to three times that of Firm A, and it will almost certainly have lowered its unit costs.

FIGURE 15.8
Relative market shares

	Sales (£'000s)	Market share (%)	Relative market share
Total market:			
Last year	5,200		
This year	7,500		
Firm A:			
Last year	1,000	19	
This year	1,200	16	
Leading competitor:			
Last year	2,200	42	2.20
This year	3,600	48	3.00
Close competitor:			
Last year	1,200	23	1.20
This year	2,200	27	1.67

*The example that follows is derived from that given in Simmonds (1986) and is used with permission.

FIGURE 15.9
Sales, market shares, and profits for all suppliers of Product X

	Sales (£'000s)	Market share (%)	Relative market share	Profit (£'000s)	(%)
Firm A:					
Year 1	700	17.5		90	12.8
Year 2	1,000	19.2		130	13.0
Year 3	1,200	16.0		170	14.2
Leading competitor:					
Year 1	1,400	35.0	2.0	200	14.3
Year 2	2,200	42.3	2.2	400	18.2
Year 3	3,600	48.0	3.0	800	22.2
Close competitor:					
Year 1	1,000	25.0	1.4	120	12.0
Year 2	1,200	23.1	1.2	170	14.2
Year 3	2,000	26.6	1.7	260	13.0
Laggard 1:					
Year 1	500	12.5	0.71	55	11.0
Year 2	500	9.6	0.50	60	12.0
Year 3	500	6.7	0.42	50	10.0
Laggard 2:					
Year 1	400	10.0	0.57	40	10.0
Year 2	300	5.8	0.30	20	6.7
Year 3	200	2.7	0.17	5	2.5
Total market:					
Year 1	4,000	100.0		505	12.6
Year 2	5,200	100.0		780	15.0
Year 3	7,500	100.0		1,285	17.1

2 Profits and Return on Sales

If a competitor has a high return on sales than Firm A it may well reduce price, or improve quality, or increase its marketing efforts in order to improve its competitive position further.

The data in Figure 15.9 shows sales, market share, relative market share and profit (before tax but after interest) over the last three years for all firms supplying Product X. Over that period the market leader's profit has quadrupled, the closest competitor's has more than doubled, and Firm A's has not quite doubled. In absolute terms the market leader's profit in Year 3 is almost five times that of Firm A, giving a huge source of funds for expansion, R & D, etc., while in relative terms the leader's return on sales of 22.2 per cent in Year 3 is well ahead of any other competitor.

Firm A's task seems to be to reinforce its competitive position relative to both laggard firms on the one hand, and to develop a defence against the strong competitors on the other.

3 Volume and Unit Cost

Details of volume and costs are given in Figure 15.10. Changes in unit costs reveal each firm's relative efficiency: the further a competitor's relative cost falls below unity the more of a threat this becomes, and vice versa. (Costs are calculated by subtracting profit from sales revenue, and unit costs are obtained by dividing the costs by volume, year by year.)

The market leader has a cost advantage in Year 3 of 69p per unit relative to Firm A, whereas Laggard 2 has a cost disadvantage relative to Firm A of 73p per unit. Perhaps more significant than these figures are those that compare volume and cost changes. Thus, for example, Firm A's two main competitors both increased volume between Years 2 and 3 by more than 70 per cent, yet the close competitor's cost per unit only fell by 3 per cent or so while the market leader's cost per unit fell by more than 9 per cent. Is the explanation to be found in the close competitor's investment in competitive position – such as in R & D, marketing programmes, or new plant?

FIGURE 15.10
Volume, costs and unit costs

	Volume in units (000s)	Increase (%)	Cost (£'000s)	Cost per unit (£)	Relative cost per unit
Firm A:					
Year 1	100		610	6.10	
Year 2	156	56	870	5.58	
Year 3	192	23	1,030	5.36	
Leading competitor:					
Year 1	200		1,200	6.00	0.98
Year 2	350	75	1,800	5.14	0.92
Year 3	600	71	2,800	4.67	0.87
Close competitor:					
Year 1	140		880	6.29	1.03
Year 2	190	36	1,030	5.42	0.97
Year 3	330	74	1,740	5.27	0.98
Laggard 1:					
Year 1	70		445	6.36	1.04
Year 2	75	7	440	5.86	1.05
Year 3	80	7	450	5.62	1.05
Laggard 2:					
Year 1	56		360	6.42	1.05
Year 2	45	(20)	280	6.22	1.16
Year 3	32	(29)	195	6.09	1.14
Total:					
Year 1	566				
Year 2	816	44			
Year 3	1,234	51			

4 Unit Prices

In Figure 15.11 are shown the unit prices charged for Product X by each competitor over the last three years, along with costs and the profits and market shares that have resulted. (Unit prices are simply calculated by dividing sales revenue by units sold.)

The pattern of price changes reflects the use of price as a competitive variable, and this can be related to cost and market share data to see how competitive positions are changing. For example, the market leader has reduced the price by

FIGURE 15.11
Unit prices, profits and market shares

	Average price per unit (£)	Average cost per unit (£)	Profit per unit (£)	Market share (%)
Firm A:				
Year 1	7.00	6.10	0.90	17.5
Year 2	6.41	5.58	0.83	19.2
Year 3	6.25	5.36	0.89	16.0
Leading competitor:				
Year 1	7.00	6.00	1.00	35.0
Year 2	6.29	5.14	1.15	42.3
Year 3	6.00	4.67	1.33	48.0
Close competitor:				
Year 1	7.14	6.29	0.85	25.0
Year 2	6.31	5.42	0.89	23.1
Year 3	6.06	5.27	0.79	26.6
Laggard 1:				
Year 1	7.14	6.36	0.78	12.5
Year 2	6.66	5.86	0.80	9.6
Year 3	6.25	5.62	0.63	6.7
Laggard 2:				
Year 1	7.14	6.42	0.72	10.0
Year 2	6.66	6.22	0.44	5.8
Year 3	6.25	6.09	0.16	2.7

more than any other firm, but its price reductions have not been as great as its cost reductions, hence profit per unit has increased each year – as has the number of units. This places that firm in a very strong competitive position.

Patterns of price, cost, profit and volume change for Firm A and its closest competitor are less clear, but for the laggards the picture of a downward spiral is clear enough.

5 Cashflow, Liquidity and Resource Availability

Competitive gains and losses will arise over longer periods than the financial year, and the capacity of a competitor to continue in the fray is a function of more than simply profit or market share at a particular point in time. A firm's ability to continue to compete will also depend on its liquidity position and the availability of other resources over time. For example, a firm with poor cashflow, a high level of debt, and out-of-date production facilities is not likely to be able to compete for long.

6 The Future

Having analysed the relative positions of each firm supplying Product X over the past three years the real challenge comes in attempting to make the next move.

The management of Firm A will be able to see that the market leader is controlling the competitive situation with the highest volume and profits, plus the lowest unit costs and price. If that firm reduced its price by, say, 10 per cent, it would force the laggards out of the market and limit the close competitor's profit (assuming it followed suit and reduced its own price). Firm A needs to reduce its costs and strengthen its position against its two main competitors while there is scope for growth in the overall market for Product X.

Using Figures 15.8 to 15.11 as a basis, various possibilities can be projected for the future, each building on explicit assumptions regarding:

- future market demand;
- likely competitive actions;
- likely competitive reactions;
- competitors' liquidity and solvency.

This takes us a long way from conventional single entity, single-period management accounting, yet the adaptations that need to be made are not so difficult to comprehend – but the benefits from gaining a clearer picture of one's competitive position and how this is changing should be enormous. Strategic management accounting can help realize these benefits.

After seeing the appeal of the approaches suggested by Pyne and Simmonds one might wonder how the necessary competitive information might be gathered. Brock (1984), Pyne (1985), Beerel (1986), Jones (1988), Robert (1990) and others offer a variety of ways forward. We will return to this theme in Chapter 20.

Consumer Franchise

It has been argued by Mehotra (1984) that market share and profit measures are unsatisfactory for gauging efficiency since they ignore the purpose of marketing which he sees as being the identification of, and meeting, the needs and wants of end users. His proposed measure is *consumer franchise* which he has developed from an approach within General Electric. The basis of this approach is to be found in a continuum with consumers being arrayed along it in accordance with the probability of their buying a particular brand. An enterprise's core consumer franchise for its brand is represented by consumers having a consistently high probability of buying that brand. Those consumers with a low probability of buying that brand are likely to be either committed to another brand or uncommitted to any brand. It is apparent, therefore, that a brand's sales can be represented by the following equation:

$$\text{Sales} = (P_1 \times N_1) + (P_2 \times N_2)$$

Where: P_1 is probability of buying if committed
      N_1 is number of committed buyers
      P_2 is probability of buying if uncommitted
      N_2 is number of uncommitted buyers

The level of sales can be increased by increasing the probability of purchasing by a given consumer or by increasing the proportion of high probability buyers, i.e. the consumer franchise. To achieve the former it is likely that sales promotion methods will be used, whereas advertising and product improvements are more likely for the latter. It can be argued that the use of sales promotions (as inputs) is likely to influence market share but this may only be temporary. On the other hand improvements in the consumer franchise are more likely to be lasting, hence a more desirable output. There is always a risk that some approaches to increasing market share (or sales or profit) may only achieve this in the short term and thereafter actually erode the consumer franchise – this would be reflected in a temporary improvement in efficiency but a reduction in effectiveness. In contrast a brand's consumer franchise might be enhanced by a more substantive and coordinated improvement in the market offering.

15.5 MULTIPLE CRITERIA

Let us broaden our perspective and consider criteria that go beyond the single criterion approach we have been focusing on so far in this chapter. The use of a single criterion is inadequate because:

1 organizations behave ineffectively from some points of view if a single criterion is used;
2 organizations fulfil multiple functions and have multiple goals, some of which may be in conflict. It would be inappropriate to assess strategies purely on the basis of any one criterion.

The difficulty, as will be apparent, lies in identifying those multiple criteria that are necessary and sufficient to ensure corporate well-being and survival. One way is via the application of *Pareto's Law*.

Pareto's Law (or the 80/20 rule) is widely thought to apply to a range of situations in which most of the behaviour or value of one factor is deemed to depend on only a little of another factor. For example, it is often asserted that 80 per cent of inventory movements within an organization are attributable to 20 per cent of items stocked, 80 per cent of sales volume comes from 20 per cent of customers, or 80 per cent of profits are derived from 20 per cent of product lines. The main point here, of course, is that one can effectively control an inventory if one can focus attention on the critical 20 per cent of active items, or one can control the level of sales if the key customers are properly serviced. This can be greatly beneficial both in terms of cost savings (through eliminating unnecessary control effort on the 'insignificant' 80 per cent of items that only make up 20 per cent of stock issues) and in terms of improved organizational effectiveness (due to better control of the key elements).

The application of Pareto's Law is known by a number of different names. Perhaps the most frequently encountered are: key variables, critical success factors (CSF), and key result areas.

FIGURE 15.12
A general example of key variables

Sphere of activity	Critical factors
Environment	Economic – interest rates inflation rates concentration Political stability
Marketing	Sales volume Market share Gross margins
Production	Capacity utilization Quality standards
Logistics	Capacity utilization Level of service
Asset management	Return on investment Accounts receivable balance

FIGURE 15.13
Specific industry examples of key variables

Food processing:
- new product development
- good distribution
- effective advertising

Motor vehicles:
- styling
- efficient dealer networks
- tight control over manufacturing costs

Life assurance:
- development of agency managerial personnel
- effective control of clerical staff
- innovation in creating new types of policies

Oil:
- decentralization
- liquidity
- government business relationships
- societal image
- new ventures (to broaden its base)

SOURCE: Adapted from Rockart (1979)

To illustrate the idea further we can consider a generalized example, and then a number of specific industry examples (see Rockart (1979)). Figure 15.12 identifies for each main sphere of activity the factors that are likely to be of some major significance to corporate performance. Each factor has financial implications, and if they can be controlled it is probable that the overall company can be controlled.

Within specific industries there is likely to be considerable variation in key variables, as Figure 15.13 illustrates. Johnson (1967), for example, looks in more detail at this key question.

The variables that are critical are those that are causally related to desired outcomes. In seeking to measure the values of variables great care must be taken to avoid the trap of giving attention to variables that are amenable to measurement and overlooking more important variables that are not amenable to measurement (e.g. quantities are more readily measured than qualities, but it does not follow that the latter are less important than the former). Similarly, variables that reflect a short-run focus, such as reported profit or EPS (earnings per share), should not be allowed to dominate the measurement process when variables with a longer-run focus, such as competitive position, are being ignored in that process.

In a study of more than 250 US organizations Steiner (1969) sought to determine the factors most likely to influence future success. He did this by asking the senior managers in the chosen companies to rank 85 factors. The top 10 are shown below:

1 attract and maintain high quality top management;
2 develop future managers for domestic operations;
3 motivate sufficient managerial drive for profits;
4 assure better judgement, creativity, and imagination in decision making at top management levels;
5 perceive new needs and opportunities for products;
6 develop a better long-range planning programme;
7 improve service to customers;
8 provide a competitive return to shareholders;
9 maximize the value of shareholders' investment;
10 develop a better willingness to take risks with commensurate returns in what appear to be excellent new business opportunities in order to achieve growth objectives.

A variety of alternative approaches have been put forward for identifying key variables or critical success factors (see, for example, Leidecker and Bruno (1984); Jenster (1987); Freund (1988); Dace (1990); De Vasconcellos and Hambrick (1989); Hitt and Ireland (1985)). Such approaches usually rely on the views of managers and other experts within the particular industries. It is inherent in these approaches that their validity is questionable and that they do not constitute a clear basis for action. Is it helpful in the food processing industry, from the viewpoint of formulating action plans, to know that NPD, good distribution, and effective advertising are the prescribed critical success factors (as in Figure 15.13)? However plausible the CSFs might be it is difficult to know how they will impact on an enterprise's competitive position.

An alternative approach that Day and Wensley (1988) argue gives more defensible insights is one that relates current *sources* of advantage to the achievement of advantageous competitive *positions* hence superior *performance*. By relating causes (i.e. sources) to effects (i.e. performance) this approach emphasizes linkages in a more explicit way. It is illustrated in Figure 15.14.

An example of operational linkages between CSFs and actions (in the form of specified strategies) is given by Freund (1988) for a life insurance company. These emerged from a process in which:

1 top management identified what it considered were the company's CSFs;
2 departmental managers then identified financial strategies that would allow the CSFs to be achieved.

While CSFs can serve as criteria for choosing among competing strategies they are not equivalent to performance indicators. Figure 15.15 shows CSFs, a selection of strategies, and some performance indicators. The performance indicators are designed to show when – and by how much – strategies are not being achieved once they have been implemented.

In a study of US companies D'Aveni and MacMillan (1990) found that, under normal circumstances, managers in successful enterprises pay equal attention to their internal and external environments but pay more attention to their output environment than to their input environment. When crises relating to demand decline arise they focus their attention on the critical aspects of their external environments.

In contrast, the managers of enterprises that subsequently fail tend to ignore output factors during crises and to pay more attention to their input and internal environments.

FIGURE 15.14
*Comparing
competitors*

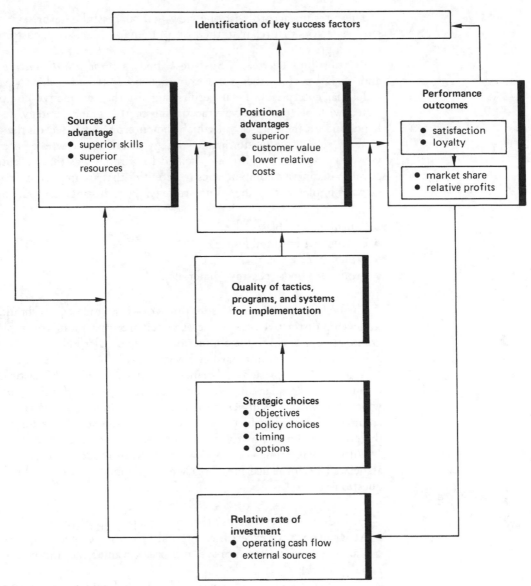

Identification of key success factors

**Sources of
advantage**
- superior skills
- superior
  resources

**Positional
advantages**
- superior
  customer value
- lower relative
  costs

**Performance
outcomes**
- satisfaction
- loyalty
- market share
- relative profits

**Quality of tactics,
programs, and systems
for implementation**

Strategic choices
- objectives
- policy choices
- timing
- options

**Relative rate of
investment**
- operating cash flow
- external sources

SOURCE: Day and Wensley (1988), p. 13

FIGURE 15.15
*Critical success
factors in action*

Critical success factor	Strategies	Performance indicators
Ability to achieve critical mass volumes through existing brokers and agents	- Develop closer ties with agents - Telemarket to brokers - Realign agents' compensation	- Policies in force - New business written - Percent of business with existing brokers
Be able to introduce new products within six months of industry leaders	- Underwrite strategic joint ventures - Copy leader's products - Improve underwriting skills	- Elapsed time to introduce - Percent of products introduced within six months - Percent underwriters having additional certification
Be able to manage product and product line profitability	- Segment investment portfolio - Improve cost accounting - Closely manage loss ratio	- Return on portfolio segments - Actual product cost/revenue versus plan - Loss ratio relative to competitors

SOURCE: Adapted from Freund (1988), pp. 22–3

These results accord with the view that successful enterprises attend to critical success factors that relate to their output environments (e.g. customers' needs and demand growth).

Relationships between CSFs (described as *corporate distinctive competencies*) and overall performance were examined by Hitt and Ireland (1985) in 185 US industrial enterprises. Their results suggest that distinctive competencies associated with performance vary according to the 'grand strategy' used on the one hand, and on the industry in which the enterprise is based on the other. A grand strategy refers to a predominant strategy covering the whole enterprise, and the view put forward by Hitt and Ireland for testing was that an enterprise should develop distinctive competencies in activities that are important from the point of view of implementing the grand strategy. They distinguish four industry types:

- consumer durables;
- consumer non-durables;
- capital goods;
- producer goods (e.g. raw materials).

The message that emerges from this work is that managers should be concerned to develop distinctive competencies which are appropriate for implementing their grand strategies within the context of their particular industries. It is important to match these matters in a balanced way.

A particular approach to balance which has been enthusiastically received in recent years is Kaplan and Norton's *Balanced Scorecard Framework* (1992, 1993) which 'provides executives with a comprehensive framework that translates a company's strategic objectives into a coherent set of performance measures, thereby providing a powerful tool for decision making'.

Within their framework Kaplan and Norton specify four sets of goals and associated performance measures which focus attention on the following basic questions:

- How do customers see us? (i.e. customer perspective);
- At what must we excel? (i.e. internal business perspective);
- Can we continue to improve and create value? (i.e. innovation and learning perspective);
- How do we look to our shareholders? (i.e. financial perspective).

These elements of the scorecard are illustrated in Figure 15.16, from which it will be apparent that this approach has the potential to overcome two of the most pervasive problems associated with, on the one hand, univariate performance measures and, on the other, linking goals and measures of performance.

To implement the balanced scorecard approach it is necessary that senior managers address four further questions regarding:

- their vision of the future;
- the ways in which they will be seen to differ in shareholders' perceptions, customers' perceptions, internal management activities and their ability to innovate and grow if their vision succeeds;
- the specification of CSFs from financial, customer, internal and innovating perspectives;
- the critical measurements which should be used for each of the four goal and performance areas shown in Figure 15.16.

As Murray and O'Driscoll (1996, p. 386) point out, the balanced scorecard framework improves on traditional approaches in some significant ways. For example:

FIGURE 15.16
The balanced scorecard

	Goals	Measures
How do we look to our shareholders? *Financial perspective*	• survive • succeed • prosper	• cash flow • sales growth and operating income at division level • ROE, share of market
How do customers see us? *Customer perspective*	• new products • responsiveness • preference • partnership	• new products as % sales • OTIF delivery • % key account purchases • no. of joint projects
What must we excel at? *Internal business perspective*	• technology ability • operations excellence • R&D productivity • NPD activity	• application turnaround • yield % • fastest output • introduction schedule vs plan
Can we continue to improve and create value? *Innovation and learning perspective*	• technology leadership • process improvement • time to market	• first with next generation • downtime % • cycle time vs industry norm

SOURCE: Adapted from R. S. Kaplan and D. P. Norton (1992). 'The balanced scorecard – measures that drive performance', *Harvard Business Review*, Jan–Feb, p. 76

(i) It is based on the company's strategic objectives and competitive demands; by demanding that managers select a small number of critical indicators it promotes greater focus on strategic vision.

(ii) By including financial and non-financial measures it provides a basis for managing both current and future success.

(iii) It balances external and internal goals and measures and reveals trade-offs that managers should or should not make.

(iv) It facilitates coherence among various strategic initiatives and special projects (such as re-engineering, total quality and empowerment initiatives) by providing a goal-related context and an approach to integrated measurement.

It will be apparent that the choice of critical variables is neither neutral nor objective: in choosing what to measure the manager is indicating his/her personal view regarding factors that are considered important in the control process. This can be illustrated via the well-documented (e.g. Lewis (1955), Greenwood (1979)) case of the American company, General Electric (GE).

GE set up a major measurement project which had three principal component parts dealing with:

1 measures designed to assess the overall performance of a department or division as an economic entity;

2 measures designed to assess the performance of the functional activities within the organization (such as engineering, production, marketing, finance, employee relations, and community relations);

3 measures designed to assess the performance of departmental or divisional managers.

The overall measurement project was based on the following principles:

• measures should be designed to provide factual inputs to support judgements in appraising the performance of departments or divisions;

• measures should be designed so as to provide performance indicators relating both to short-run and long-run goals;

● a minimum number of measures should be used at each level within an organization.

In order to determine whether or not a variable qualified as a key success factor (which would require it to be measured) the following question was asked: 'Will continued failure in this area prevent the attainment of management's responsibility for advancing General Electric as a leader in a strong, competitive economy, even though results in all other key result areas are good?'

A range of eight key success factors emerged from this project – see Figure 15.17.

FIGURE 15.17
General Electric's key results areas

1 Profitability
2 Market position
3 Productivity
4 Product leadership
5 Personnel development
6 Employee attitudes
7 Public responsibility
8 Balance between short-run and long-run goals.

While these eight factors might seem to be generally applicable, it is their precise definition within the context of a particular company's activities that determines how critical they are. This highlights a fundamental aspect of designing any control system: it must be highly 'situational' if it is to be effective. In other words, it must be tailored to the specific characteristics of the situation, which means *this* company's objectives, *this* company's operations, *this* company's managers, and *this* company's environment.

The General Electric approach seeks to balance two conflicting tendencies: on the one hand, the diffusion of effort over multiple goals and the failure to perform as well as might be expected in any one area; and on the other hand, the tendency to emphasize one particular goal with the result that other goals are not attained.

The most common tendency in commercial enterprises is to focus on the short-run maximization of net profit (or sales) without considering the damage that this might do to the long-run position (e.g. by postponing repairs or maintenance work; by cutting back on advertising or on research, training or quality control expenditure; by deferring capital investment outlays; or through exhortations to employees to increase productivity). Short-term 'gains' achieved in this way tend to be illusory because the subsequent need to make up lost ground (e.g. via heavier advertising or training in later periods) more than outweighs short-term gains.

Saunders (1987) has observed that an enterprise only has two basic ways of increasing wealth: it can do this by innovating to increase its volume or by seeking to improve its productivity via production of the same output but at lower cost. It is much simpler to look inwards and seek to cut costs rather than to look outwards and seek to innovate, compete more effectively or increase margins through better marketing planning. Cost cutting is referred to by many Europeans as 'a British solution', since it is easy to do in the short term but with unfortunate long-term consequences (as suggested in the previous paragraph). Figure 15.18 summarises the alternative approaches to improving long run returns.

As is apparent from Figure 15.19, a preoccupation with short-term profit reflects an introspective concern with aspects of productivity. A longer-term perspective requires a shift of focus from internal productivity improvement to external factors – such as beating the competition and innovating (by developing new markets, new products or both).

FIGURE 15.18
Strategic alternatives

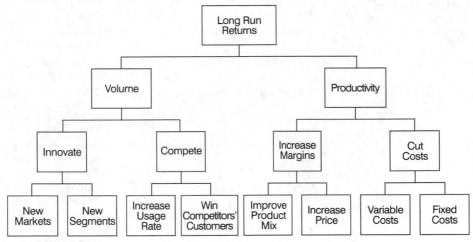

SOURCE: Saunders (1987), p. 174

FIGURE 15.19
Routes to success

Success ⟶

OBJECTIVES	Short-Term Profit	Medium-Term Profit	Innovation
FOCUS	Productivity	Beat Competition	New Product (Market)
TARGET MARKET	Own Customers	Competitors' Customers	New Customers
TARGET COMPETITION	Own Staff	Competition	The Unknown
DIFFERENTIAL ADVANTAGE	Cost Control	Segmentation	Differentiation
MIX	Price	Promotion/Place	Product
ORGANIZATION	Financial	Marketing	Entrepreneurial

SOURCE: Saunders (1987), p. 176

To the extent that effectiveness is a multi-faceted criterion we must avoid the trap of focusing too sharply on one contributing factor. It would be a mistake to assume that effectiveness would be assured simply through selecting and training the right people. Given our definition of effectiveness in Chapter 1, effectiveness may be assessed in terms of a system's capacity:

1 to survive, adapt, maintain itself, and grow – regardless of the functions it fulfils;
2 to achieve 1 through its bargaining position with its environment in relation to the acquisition of resources.

Against this background of criteria for effectiveness at an enterprise level it can be argued that any attempt to deal with the effectiveness of individual elements of marketing, such as advertising or personal selling, is problematic for two major reasons:

1 It is not possible to separate the impact of, say, advertising on the attainment of goals from the impacts of other elements of the marketing mix. The interdependence of the elements of the mix ensures that the selling task is influenced by advertising and by the nature of the product, the price and the channel decisions, all on a *mutatis mutandis* basis. It would not be sensible,

FIGURE 15.20
Criteria for functional activities

Activity	Criteria
● New product programmes	Trial rate Repurchase rate
● Product programmes	Contribution margin Controllable margin as percentage of sales
● Sales programmes	Contribution by region, salesman Controllable margin as percentage of sales Number of new accounts Travel costs
● Advertising programmes	Awareness levels Attribute ratings Cost levels
● Promotion programmes	Redemption rates Displacement rates Stock-up rates
● Pricing programmes	Price relative to industry average Price elasticity of demand
● Distribution programmes	Number of distributors carrying the product

therefore, to attempt to consider marketing effectiveness at any level below that of the marketing programme (i.e. the integrated set of marketing activities embracing the entire mix formulated to pursue a given strategy directed at a particular segment).

2 Most criterion measures relating to individual elements of marketing are measures of efficiency rather than effectiveness, focusing on the maximization of output for a given input or the minimization of input to achieve a given level of output. One exception to this is the use of sales quotas which represent output measures and performance is assessed by reviewing how close each sales person came to achieving his/her quota. We can see that this is a measure of effectiveness, albeit on a small scale relative to the overall scheme of things.

With these caveats in mind it is possible to identify criteria that are regularly applied in choosing among alternative plans for specific elements of the mix (see, for example, McNamee (1988), pp. 131 and 143; Guiltinan and Paul (1988), pp. 396–8). Examples are given in Figure 15.20.

15.6 SUMMARY

In this chapter we have looked at a range of possible criteria for assessing marketing strategies as a basis for making choices. Distinctions have been made among:

- short-term versus long-term criteria;
- financial versus non-financial criteria;
- single versus multiple criteria;
- criteria focusing on overall strategies versus criteria focusing on specific activities;
- criteria focusing on efficiency versus criteria focusing on effectiveness.

Apart from the variety of input and output measures that have been discussed there are additional approaches that deal with factors ranging from the degree of realism in the assumptions underlying the strategy to the capacity of the enterprise to implement successfully the chosen strategy. To take specific examples, Tilles

(1963) and Day (1990) both outline sets of criteria that might be applied in assessing strategies. These include:

1 Is there an effective matching of the enterprise's competences with the threats and opportunities from the environment? (If not then there is unlikely to be a basis for achieving sustainable competitive advantage.)

2 Will the strategy place the enterprise in a position to counter known threats, exploit opportunities, enhance current advantages, or provide new sources of advantage?

3 Is the strategy robust enough to adapt to a broad range of anticipated environmental events or is it only likely to work under very specific conditions?

4 Will it be difficult for competitors to deal with the expected advantages to be gained from the strategy?

5 Are the assumptions underlying the formulation of competing strategies realistic? (Such assumptions might relate to price levels, relative market share, market growth, cost levels, timing aspects, competitive reactions, and so on.)

6 What are the potential risks to which the strategy (hence the enterprise) may be vulnerable? (These may be internal – in the form of resource availability or implementation factors – as well as external.)

7 Is the strategy feasible from the viewpoint of the enterprise having the necessary skills and resources? (These would include access to technology, markets, and servicing facilities as well as adequate managerial capabilities.)

8 Is the strategy capable of being effectively communicated so that those who will be responsible for its implementation can understand what is required of them?

9 Will the strategy challenge and motivate key personnel? (This implies that strategies must be accepted by those who are charged with their implementation.)

10 Are the elements within the strategy internally consistent so that it hangs together in a coherent way?

11 Will the expected results from the strategy be acceptable relative to the anticipated risks? (This will require evidence of a clear competitive advantage from which enhanced value to shareholders and other stakeholders' gains will flow.)

12 Does the strategy have an appropriate time frame? (Strategies cannot be achieved overnight, so sufficient time must be allowed for their effective implementation.)

15.7 EXERCISES

1 Select a recent major marketing programme (such as the launch of a new product or a new promotional campaign for an existing product. At the time of writing this, for example, McDonald's in Manhattan have just announced the '99 cents burger' as a competitive move against Burger King.).

   What criteria do you think were employed by the company's marketing team in choosing the programme you have selected?

2 Identify the critical success factors which you consider to be appropriate for enterprises in two distinct sectors.

   Justify your answer.

3 In collaboration with colleagues from the accounting sphere within your organization, attempt to generate marketing-oriented profit statements (such as those illustrated in Figures 15.3 and 15.4).

4 Devise a 'balanced scorecard' for:

   (a) a financing company;

   (b) a business-to-business enterprise;

   (c) a service organization in the not-for-profit sector.

5 Carry out a comparative evaluation of the General Electric approach to key results areas and Kaplan and Norton's balanced scorecard approach.

15.8 Discussion Questions

1 From a marketing perspective, are financial criteria more important than non-financial criteria?
2 In what ways are single criterion approaches to decision making in marketing unsatisfactory?
3 What problems arise in developing and implementing multiple criteria in marketing approaches to strategic choice?
4 Is it the case that choice criteria employed in marketing decision making emphasize efficiency at the expense of effectiveness?
5 Why is it problematic seeking to capture a measure of *competitive position*?
6 Is growth necessarily a good thing?

15.9 Case Studies

Nike, Inc.

During the fall of 1982, the Nike Company was recognized generally as one of the phenomenal success stories of the recent decade. From its small base in 1972, by 1981 the firm had blossomed into a $450,000,000 giant and expected sales to reach $650,000,000 in 1982. It had passed Adidas in the United States and held an estimated 30 percent of the American market. Most Nike executives were confident that a $1 billion sales year was imminent. Although the company owed much of its success to a vibrant management team, it was also very much the brainchild of a remarkable entrepreneur, Phil Knight, who still served as president, CEO, and major stockholder.

The company's incredible growth rate was not without its problems. As Phil Knight reflected:

> There has been a severe overload on marketing compounded by our need to organize for new opportunities as our old products and markets mature. We are geared to handle existing lines where we have 30% or 40% of the market. But how about new areas which must be developed, like leisure products, international, the children's line, clothing and cleated shoes? I question whether our existing approaches can successfully pioneer these many opportunity areas, particularly given the increase in competition and changes in consumer habits.

The Industry

Nike competed in two industries: sports and athletic shoes; and also sportswear. Each of these categories was estimated to exceed $10 billion in 1982 sales. Starting from its running heritage, Nike had branched out rapidly into an assortment of other sports (tennis, soccer, basketball, etc.) as well as leisure ('look-like') markets. Running, still the company's wellhead, was essentially an American phenomenon, though it had been copied in varying degrees elsewhere. By 1980, however, the running boom showed signs of leveling off. In the words of Phil Knight: 'We see only a couple more years of strong growth in running shoes in the United States, though we are sure fitness is here to stay.'

Because of the industry's evolution, there was a wide range of competitors and strategies. In running, for example, there were Adidas (the largest firm in total, worldwide sales), Puma, Converse Rubber, Pony International, Asics (Tiger brand), New Balance, and Brooks (acquired by Wolverine in 1982), to mention the most obvious. Reliable data about these competitors was sketchy because many were either privately owned or divisions of larger companies. Moreover, market share estimates were based primarily on one commercial service that regularly surveyed 200 specialty retailers for competitive comparisons. Omitted from their sample were discounters, mass merchandisers, and most large department stores.

The market segments were diverse. In addition to the serious runners, the interested student might distinguish the faddist, the casual exerciser, the trend follower, the price buyer, the leisure-time devotee, the amateur sportsman, the high-fashion, status-conscious user, and any other number of variants. In recent months some observers felt that color coordination (between shoes and clothing) was a coming consumer preference. Indeed, one competitor (New Balance) had succeeded in drawing favorable comments about its grey, light brown, burgundy, and navy colors early in 1982. This same firm had recently increased its margins to the trade (to 55% compared to Nike's 48%–50%), upped its innovation rate, and put heavy emphasis on the specialty retailers. These actions appeared to have increased that firm's penetration of the innovator segment.

The clothing business was even more fragmented, consisting of thousands of designers, cutters, finishers, stylists, knitters, weavers, and so forth. Raw materials ranged from cotton and wool to a great variety of synthetics and blends. In the relevant world of Nike, the key actors were such competitors as Levi Strauss, Head, Adidas, and hundreds of prestige designers (e.g., Pierre Cardin, Bill Blass). There were, in addition, many retailer brands such as Brooks Brothers, Saks and I. Magnin.

During the '60s and '70s, Levi Strauss grew spectacularly on the basis of its 'Western-cowboy' look and, thanks partly to the well publicized acceptance by James Dean and Marlon Brando, jeans became the uniform for every self-respecting teenager or young adult. By 1980, however, there was some speculation that 'the look' was about to shift to a new life-style – the fit, the jock, the athlete-winner. If this shift materialized, the implications were great for the trade.

It was also reasonably obvious that traditional manufacturer labels in fashion merchandise were under siege by the aforementioned designer labels. Large numbers of department stores and mass merchandisers were trying to gain distinction handling such 'prestige' labels and the use of the 'boutique look' within their stores. It almost seemed that there were two fundamental strategies at work – the price-oriented mass market appeal and the high-income, status appeal. The distinction between these two was somewhat clouded by the adoption of prestige labels by the more aggressive mass merchandisers. Even Sears Roebuck had relaxed its policy of carrying only house labels.

Adidas, Head, and Nike represented firms that had expanded into clothing from 'hardware lines' (that is, shoes), whereas Levi Strauss experimented, not too successfully, with shoes. All of these firms, of course, vied for the same basic distribution system. At the retail level, the outlets could be classified as mass merchandisers (Sears), discounters (Marshalls and Mervyn's), department and specialty stores (R.H. Macy and I. Magnin), and a wide variety of small independents (sporting goods, shoe stores, running stores). These outlets could be reached through company sales personnel, manufacturers' representatives, distributors, or even direct mail. Adidas, for example, covered the United States with four independent distributors; Levi Strauss used company sales representatives; Nike employed manufacturers' representatives; and Sears Roebuck sold direct through mail order and/or retail stores.

Nike's niche in the industry was substantial. The firm appealed to the market on the basis of quality, technical innovation, and high performance, all of which attracted the serious runner. This acceptance by the experts was the lever to open up the mass markets. The product diffused into the channels starting with the high performance specialists and spreading into the mass outlets on the basis of this 'expert' endorsement. Nike had also been aggressive in product line extensions (such as leisure shoes and clothing). Whether or not to introduce a second label was a topic being discussed by senior management.

Nike Organization

One of the distinguishing characteristics of the company was its informal organization. From its beginning, Nike had been run as a small operation by a close-knit group of top managers. Most of them were sports enthusiasts and athletes and thus understood and appreciated the Nike line. A surprisingly large percentage also had legal or accounting backgrounds. But, as Phil Knight explained, 'We mostly want people who are company experts, not functional experts.' Problem solving, not specific technical knowledge, was the valued skill.

The organization chart, which is reproduced below, is therefore deceptive. It portrays the formal pieces of the organization, but not the way it works:

Because apparel was a relatively new product line, it was still associated with footwear marketing (the same sales reps, for example, were involved), though sourcing and product development were separately handled.

Management assignments across functions were normal. One senior manager had moved from legal to R&D, to lobbying, to marketing, and there were other equally dramatic assignment changes. Territorial imperatives were held to a minimum and such words as budgeting, planning, and control were dirty ones – even though the company did have working systems. The emphasis was upon informality, willingness to change, experimentation, and mutual decision making. The Friday Club was the chief management tool of the company. This group of 11 top managers[1] was called together regularly, as Phil Knight laughingly described, 'to shout at each other.' The meetings were open and informal and everyone contributed with enthusiasm his ideas and solutions. Phil Knight played the catalyst role in eliciting ideas and in meshing the various personalities. There were no functional restrictions. The informality of these sessions was evident on one occasion when a visitor commented that Nike management

---

[1] These included in 1982: Chairman, Executive Vice President, Vice Presidents of Apparel, Finance, Production, Chief Counsel, Manager MIS, Vice President International, Director of Marketing, Treasurer, and Manager Far East Operation.

'was a shambles.' The next day at a follow-up meeting, each executive wore a T-shirt that said, 'It's a shambles.'

Even though the Friday Club was a key decision-making group, it wasn't as omnipotent as it might appear. In the first place, it was in practice a floating group with varying degrees of autonomy. There were five so-called old-timers who were really 'the chairman's office' and who were considered the ultimate decision-making unit. The Friday Club itself could expand or shrink in size depending on the issue. There had been some meetings, to illustrate, at which over 30 managers participated. Perhaps more important was the fact that reporting to these senior executives was a 'conventional' organizational hierarchy. Marketing, to select one example, included research and advertising components while manufacturing had plant and quality assurance managers. The unique aspects of the Nike organization were the degree of mobility, the generalist perspective of the senior group, and the participative decision-making style.

History

Knight's enthusiasm for sports started early, and by his senior year in high school he was already an accomplished runner who had caught the eye of Bill Bowerman, the track and field coach at the University of Oregon. Knight attended that university and then received his MBA from Stanford in 1962. For one of his term papers, the budding entrepreneur developed an idea for a new business. He knew that running shoes were dominated by two German firms, Adidas and Puma, and he wondered why the Japanese couldn't do in shoes what they had already done in TV and cameras. After graduation from Stanford, Knight joined a CPA firm in Portland, Oregon, but as a sideline decided to import and sell Japanese running shoes. He traveled to Japan and contracted with Onitsuka to supply him with their Tiger line, as their exclusive agent for the 13 western states. He also persuaded his former track coach to join in the venture. Between them they invested $1,000 in inventory for shoes that cost $3.50 a pair but which they sold for $9.95. By 1966 the fledgling company had branched out to the East Coast, and by 1971 sales had reached just over $1,000,000. At this point Knight broadened his product line to include soccer, basketball, and tennis shoes.

In 1972 Onitsuka sought more control of its marketing and Knight decided to strike out on his own. Furthermore, even though his growth had been rapid – virtually doubling every year – it was still a small company and Knight was hardpressed to obtain adequate financing. For each purchase, he had to put up a letter of credit that would tie up his credit for approximately 90 days. As luck would have it, he read a *Fortune* magazine article suggesting that Japanese trading companies could, among other things, extend credit on flexible terms, though at a slight premium. A few inquiries unearthed Nissho-Iwai, the sixth-largest trading company in Japan, and Knight and Nissho-Iwai soon agreed to a deal. Through Nissho-Iwai, Knight also acquired some manufacturing contacts who agreed to produce shoes to Nike's specifications.

The Nissho-Iwai deal gave Nike an important financial and business ally which made subsequent rapid growth possible. By putting up the necessary letters of credit every month, Nissho-Iwai freed Nike to concentrate on operating matters. In fact, the trading company went well beyond the strict limits of the agreement and gave Nike much needed flexibility. Nissho-Iwai served, furthermore, as the financial and administrative intermediary between Nike and the contract manufacturers. During these same early days, Phil established a strong Accounts Receivable group, which managed to keep receivables in line despite the explosive growth in sales.

The development of these contract manufacturers was an early preoccupation of top management. A traditional problem in the leisure shoe industry had been the lack of dependable supply and delivery, particularly for the retailers. Knight saw this as an opportunity. He first tied up a considerable percentage of the available shoe capacity in Japan and later in Taiwan and Korea. These vendors were delighted to supply such a fast-growing and profitable customer. By 1982 the company's production was centered in 28 plants, and over 80% of this production was in Taiwan and Korea. There were three plants in the United States. Knight also introduced a futures program for retailers, whereby the company guaranteed the price and delivery terms for any retailer who ordered six months in advance. The system worked as follows:

Illustrative Data	Event	Elapsed Time
March 30	Retailer places order with Nike (order is non cancellable by the retailer & guaranteed by Nike)	0
April 15	Nike places order with NIAC (Nisso-Iwai American Corp.)	15 days
April 25	NIAC orders from the plant	25 days
July 30	Plant completes manufacturing and ships order	120 days
September 1	Shoes come to warehouse in Seattle, Boston, or Memphis	150 days
September 15	Shoes shipped to retailer	165 days

Since 65% of the orders followed this sequence, the futures program in effect served as a planning device by giving Nike reasonably accurate sales forecasts and shipment schedules. By 1982 monthly shipments were averaging 4.5 million pair. The other 35% of the orders were placed by the dealers on a 'when needed' basis. Delivery, in this second case, was not guaranteed.

Production costs were low and flexible but quality was high because all output was made to Nike specifications and the firm maintained its own quality control staff at each plant. In fact, the first expatriate employee was assigned to Taiwan in 1976. The table below summarizes the cost buildup from a hypothetical $1 manufacturing base:

Cost Buildup

Cost to Manufacturer (for a Korean plant)	$1.00
Price from Nissho-Iwai Corp. (Japan)	1.04
Price from Nissho-Iwai, U.S. (this is Nike cost)	1.08 + interest (near prime)
Price to the retail store	1.60
Price to the consumer	2.80–3.00

As one of the early employees of the firm said: 'Product control is our forte.' Indeed, the plants had considerable product flexibility and could easily handle volume swings of 25%–35%. The three U.S. plants were useful as a backup to the overseas contractors.

Innovation

Another early focus of Nike management was product innovation. Bowerman, for example, was a particularly creative individual who contributed the famous 'waffle sole' (though at the expense of his wife's waffle iron). In fact, when Nike originally split from the Onitsuka group, the founders took with them two important product innovations which they had developed on their own time. Management's interest in innovation was so high that in 1974, while still small, the firm bought a factory in Exeter, New Hampshire, and dedicated it to R&D. This group subsequently developed a number of major innovations, including the airsole, the nylon top, and the full-cushioned mid-sole.

Innovation, in practice, was a constant give-and-take between marketing, production, and Exeter. For example, as marketing identified new product needs, it asked Exeter to conduct extensive research and testing in design and biomechanics.

Phil Knight was an important innovator in an even broader sense – not only in product but also in several aspects of the operations. He was described by one colleague as 'farsighted and alert to new opportunities.' To be specific, Knight foresaw the desirability of expanding production out of Japan, the opportunity in a guaranteed retailer delivery system, the potential of manufacturing in China, and the advantages of working with a trading company instead of a bank. Moreover, be anticipated a number of market changes and moved his company into other sports shoes (basketball, court, cleated, etc.), a children's line, nonathletic leisure and work shoes, and clothing. The firm's early concentration on running represented superb timing (either by luck or brilliant deduction) and positioned Nike in the consumer's mind as 'a running company.'

Marketing

The marketing program was developed over several years. To start, the company hired sales representatives who, of necessity, were new, enthusiastic, hardworking shoe amateurs. They were supervised by East Coast and West Coast field managers. The number of representatives was gradually increased and their territories decreased, until in 1982 there were 28 representative organizations employing 180 salespeople. Some carried other lines; some did not. But all had thrived under Nike and depended upon the firm for their well-being. Sales were so large that representative commissions averaged 2½% instead of the more traditional 6%.

The representatives sold to 8,000 retailers who operated 13,000 outlets. Almost 2,500 of these outlets were classified as mass merchandisers, 2,500 specialty (i.e., running) stores, 1,500 sporting goods, and the rest shoe stores and miscellaneous. The premier mass merchandiser for Nike was J.C. Penney, which was added in 1977 before Nike was particularly well-known. (Adidas elected to go through J.C. Penney in 1981.) Quite obviously, the distribution system was effective and covered a wide range of clientele – from low-end to high-end specialty. Furthermore, the Nike line, priced between $19.95 and $70, was broad enough to accommodate each segment. These relatively few dealers who sold primarily the top of the line to the serious, innovative runners were handled through a 'Torch program' and received special attention. For all dealers, Nike offered a number of special inducements: a generous 46% margin, guaranteed prices and delivery, and a coordinated program of promotions, advertising, training, and sponsorships. As between footwear and apparel, the retail stores employed by Nike split out as follows: Shoes only 25%; Apparel only 25%; Both 50%.

Nike also owned and operated seven retail stores. Their volume of $4 million was minor, but they were regarded as valuable training centers. There were no expansion plans.

The distribution story was different overseas where Nike was just beginning to expand. In Europe the jogging boom had not yet taken off, though Nike expected that it would. Adidas and Puma dominated the European distribution system and concentrated on the huge soccer market. These German competitors would not be easy to replace, particularly since their loss of market in the United States. As one industry executive stated: 'Adidas and Puma will let the other American companies do whatever they want in Europe because they're not much of a threat. But after what Nike did to them in the U.S., they simply will not let themselves be embarrassed in their own backyards.' It would not be easy for Nike to gain dealers whose livelihood depended on Adidas and Puma.

Japan was an easier target. Not only did the Japanese perceive American products as high quality, but also Nike had had years of contact with that market. England was another attractive market. Nike acquired its distributorships and also opened a manufacturing plant there to permit in-expensive access to the European markets.

Nike's promotion and advertising strategy was another ingredient of its success. The company, to start, employed a pull, not a push, approach built around its distinctive 'swoosh' trademark. Its recent $18 million budget was spent as follows:

25% Product advertising in such vertical publications as *Running* and *The Runner* – stressing general concepts like cushioning and shoe weight.

Point-of-sale devices such as a retailer poster program, the use of technical tags and brochures, and dealer clinics.

25% Dealer co-op advertising where Nike would match the dealers' advertising outlays up to a specified limit.

50% Promotions that included free goods and/or cash payment to about 2,500 athletes as well as the sponsorship of selected athletic events (including a women's pro-tennis circuit).

The critical part of Nike's selling approach was the endorsement by these athletic 'heroes.' From the firm's first endorsers – Steve Prefontaine and Geoff Petrie – the list grew to include 40% of the players in the National Basketball Association, a large percentage of the top runners, and such individual stars as John McEnroe, Sebastian Coe and Dan Fouts. As one of the Nike managers said: 'These athletes are our promotional team.'

The effectiveness of Nike's strategies was reflected in their financial statements. (See Exhibits 1 and 2.)

Current Concerns

Obviously, Nike had been a tremendous success. Nonetheless, size created its own problems and caused Phil Knight to review, more specifically, some of the important marketing issues.

The channels, as a case in point, represented one such area of concern. To quote from a company document:

Given the present management's obsession with increased 'numbers,' it is not surprising that we are witnessing an increased emphasis on self-service in branded footwear retail sales. You need only look as far as the local G.I. Joe's, J.C. Penney, Meir & Frank, or Athletic Shoe Factory Outlet to see why

Exhibit 1
Nike, Inc.

Profit and Loss Summaries

	1981	1980	1979
Revenues	457,742	269,775	149,830
Cost of Sales	328,133	196,683	103,466
Selling and Administrative	60,953	39,810	22,815
Interest	17,859	9,144	4,569
Other	92	107	(443)
Income Before Taxes	50,705	24,031	19,423
Taxes	24,750	11,526	9,700
Net Income	25,955	12,505	9,723
Earnings per Share	1.52	.77	.58

Breakdown of Sales

	1981	1980	1979
Domestic Footwear	398,852	245,100	143,400
Domestic Apparel	33,108	8,100	2,200
Foreign Sales	25,782	16,575	4,230
Total	457,742	269,775	149,830

Exhibit 2
Nike, Inc.

Balance Sheet

	May 31, 1981	May 31, 1980
Cash	1,792	1,827
Accounts Receivable	87,236	63,861
Inventories	120,229	55,941
Deferred Taxes	1,300	135
Prepaid Expenses	2,487	2,151
Current Assets	213,044	123,915
Property, Plant, Equipment	23,845	14,193
Accumulated Depreciation	(7,673)	(4,027)
Other Assets	1,073	534
Total Assets	230,289	134,615
Liabilities		
Current Portion of Debt	6,620	3,867
Notes Payable	61,190	36,500
Accounts Payable	42,492	36,932
Accrued Liabilities	15,401	10,299
Income Taxes Payable	12,654	6,693
Current Liabilities	138,357	94,291
Long Term Debt	8,611	11,268
Common Stock	28,600*	71
Retained Earnings	54,721	28,985
Total Liabilities	230,289	134,615

* In 1981 Nike went public with the sale of 1,360,000 shares of common stock, with Knight retaining 51% of the outstanding shares.

the technical portion of our line is so badly misunderstood. In self-service retail outlets, you are hard pressed to find any sales help, let alone well-informed assistance from users of athletic footwear. Perhaps it is a function of our stagnant economy, but every retailer is talking about how to reduce his 'selling costs' by employing mass merchant mentality, i.e., read *Proportionally Fewer Customer Service-Oriented Retail Outlets* to intelligently sell our technical line.

With a significantly smaller and diminishing percentage of our products being sold in specialty or Torch accounts, it is no wonder that our reputation is being redefined in the consumer's mind with descriptive phrases such as, 'Low-End, Non-Technical, Pricepoint and Promotional.' The bulk of our sales volume is now attributable to dealers who are providing less and less point-of-purchase information about how our shoes perform to customers as retailers strive for more volume and fine tune their selling efficiency. The result of this shift in selling technique and brand identity puts increased pressure on Nike to pre-sell our products while making the shoes easily visible and recognizable as high-quality, innovative products.

In the midst of the recent frenzied growth of mass consumption of branded athletic footwear, there has developed a reaction among both the more technically aware and prestige-seeking affluent consumers to distinguish themselves from the pack. With increased discretionary buying power, these consumers are demanding high-tech products and are willing to 'pay a little more to get just what I wanted.' This is the segment of the market we have ignored and, as a result, have been losing to New Balance, Tiger, and Saucony. If Nike is going to continue to have mass volume sales and retain a strong share of the high-end sales, it is obvious we need to segment the product line and distinguish the product in this market so that it appeals to the high-tech, affluent consumers.

The High-Tech segment of the branded market is becoming substantially more crowded with new products and new brands. This is particularly true of running flats. Avia, for example, is gearing its entire entrance into the technical branded segments of the athletic footwear market with advertising and packaging that connotes high technology and new design innovations. Advanced technologies (materials, construction techniques) are creating a more confusing product environment for consumers to make buying decisions in. The expanded array of products and advertised product features, each (Puma, New Balance, Tiger) claiming to perform breakthroughs in sports research, is making our brand prey to slick (well-segmented) marketing strategies.

Of particular note was the recent incursion by some mass merchandisers into the high end of the shoe market. Mervyn's, to be specific, in early 1982 sold 300 pairs of Nike's newest technical product at very low prices. Nike received the income, to be sure, but was unable to capitalize in the consumer's mind on the technical advantage of the new product. To the consumer, it was only a price deal.

Another matter of worry had to do with individual responsibilities as opposed to company-wide responsibilities. Size had increased the breadth and depth of the various lines. For example, there were over 200 shoe types alone. But, as no one was responsible for any one line, this led to a lack of focus and attention to details in several lines. Moreover, as implied earlier, there were few formal lines of communication and very little hierarchy between managers and locations. And finally, in Phil's opinion, the company was relying on too few key people who were close friends and saw the company as fun more than as a business.

It was within this special environment that Phil was considering his possible moves. It was not easy to trade off more control and formality against the current organizational culture. And yet he was very much aware that the market's and his own company's evolution required a new look at how to organize for growth.

Although he had thought about the implications and was well aware that there were other choices, Knight thought he might ask the Friday Club to consider the implications of eight alternatives:

1. Do Nothing

Knight was sensitive to the real possibility that any kind of significant move might 'spoil' the existing ambiance. After all, the organization had worked and had evolved a number of valuable attributes – informality, dynamism, and flexibility. Moreover, there was a minimum of territorial imperative within Nike: managers were not expected to build walls around their piece of the operation. On the contrary, open teamwork was expected. Over time, it was not surprising that the culture of the firm was well understood. The nuances of day by day interaction were as well developed as small talk between husband and wife.

Knight also considered it valuable that the footwear and apparel operations had been closely associated. Even though production for each was individually supervised, the marketing and sales were interdependent. The sales reps, to be specific, carried both lines.

It should be recognized, finally, that the organization with its functional orientation (namely marketing and manufacturing) focused upon these broad skills rather than separate products and markets. Presumably the functions would receive greater focus and hence deliver a higher level of generic expertise.

2. Divisionalize (and Decentralize) by Product Category

But size and rapid growth still bothered Knight: could the old informality continue?

One alternative format might be:

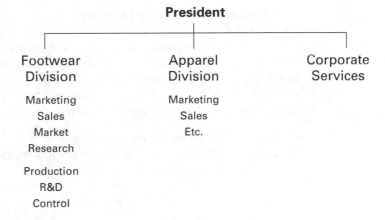

Each division would be a profit center and control a number of key activities. If this option were accepted, there remained a number of knotty questions:

a) Which activities would you assign to the divisions and which to corporate?
b) Would you totally separate footwear and apparel and, if so, how would you handle the salesforce?
c) Would the corporate services respond to divisional requests or initiate the requests?

3. Organize by Channel

Since there were two levels of buyers, customers (or the retailers) and consumers, why not two levels of organization? The advertising and promotional efforts would be directed at consumer segments while the in-store selling and other channel efforts would be directed at retail segments.

Thus, one might consider:

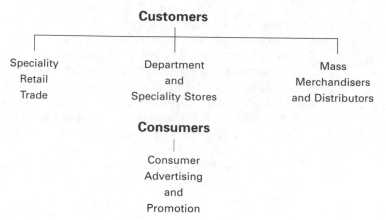

Customers

Speciality	Department	Mass
Retail	and	Merchandisers
Trade	Speciality Stores	and Distributors

Consumers

Consumer
Advertising
and
Promotion

Such an orientation would recognize the power of the trade and the need to comprehend the needs and strategies of each major retail type.

There would be, of course, some tough problems such as duplicate product managers since the channels are not mutually exclusive in their choice of products. This organizational variation would marry footwear and apparel, which would facilitate the use of a single salesforce. Unfortunately the distribution of retail outlets between shoes and apparel might cause complications.

Maybe the biggest problem would be that of finding executives sufficiently skilled in retail operations to make everything work.

4. Organize by Markets or Segments

This variation would be a further recognition that consumer segmentation is primary. Perhaps there should be geographic 'operations' such as Nike East, West, South, and North. This orientation already existed to the extent that there was an International and Domestic operation.

There were, needless to say, other segmentation alternatives such as demography, income, or application (runners vs. spectators).

5. Fragment the Marketing Function

This approach would permit the various marketing activities (research, sales, advertising, etc.) to specialize and develop as 'service centers' for the operations. The other extreme would be to pool all of these pieces into a centrally directed marketing department.

6. Product Management System

An illustration of this orientation might include:

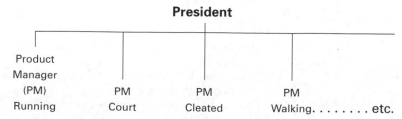

President

Product			
Manager			
(PM)	PM	PM	PM
Running	Court	Cleated	Walking. . . . . etc.

Each PM would be similar to a division manager but would probably have fewer responsibilities and be responsible primarily for the marketing mix.

In traditional product management systems, the manager has no direct authority over the separate business activities, rather the PM serves as a strategist, coordinator, and persuader who gets the job done through the efforts of others. One of the problems associated with this form of organization is to identify and develop young managers able to assume considerable responsibility without much authority.

7. *Split the Marketing Group into 'Established Businesses' and 'New Opportunities'*

Knight recognized that this organizational variation was a bit unorthodox, but he was intrigued with its recognition of two fundamental skills: old and new businesses. Whether such a split should include all the activities of the business or just selected ones, such as sales, R&D, and advertising, was an open question.

8. *Establish 'Task Forces' to Handle Critical Problem Areas as They Arise*

The comforting aspect of this alternative was that it was reasonably similar to the present policy of 'throwing' people at problems. The concept of a series of task forces, however, was a bit more formal but had the potential danger of developing a 'keep-your-hands-off' attitude among the teams.

Task forces, nevertheless, did reinforce the company's flexible approach to management and would permit the firm to concentrate on critical issues. The question might be raised, however, that task forces might be difficult to coordinate: the results might be a series of discrete, although separately effective, decisions.

Source: This case was written by Robert T. Davis, Professor of Marketing. Reprinted with permission of Stanford University Graduate School of Business. Copyright 1982 by the Board of Trustees of the Leland Stanford Junior University. Revised in 1986. All rights reserved.

Required

What criteria are applicable to the evaluation of the eight alternatives identified by Phil Knight?

Lazy Days Holidays

Lazy Days Holidays is a London-based company offering packaged holidays (flights, accommodation and some meals). Its two primary destinations are North Africa, in which it offers beach holidays in the summer and golfing holidays in the winter, and Eastern Europe, in which it offers low-cost skiing holidays from December to April.

Although for the past three years the company has been relatively successful (see Figure 1), the management team believes that its current destinations offer little real scope for growth.

Figure 1
Selected sales and financial data

	1992	1993	1994	1995*
Number of holiday makers ('000)	69	82	87	95
Turnover (£m)	15	18	20	22
Gross margin (%)	16	15	13	11
Gross profit (£m)	2.4	2.7	2.6	2.42
Net profit (£000)	450	530	420	390

* Estimated

The company sells its holidays primarily through travel agents. However, because of the growth of the major tour operators and their increased share of the overall market, Lazy Days is now finding it increasingly difficult to achieve shelf space for its brochures in travel agents' showrooms. It is also finding the growing levels of price competition throughout the industry difficult to manage.

Faced with these problems, the company has recently used a marketing consultant to conduct a review of the business. The consultant's final report highlighted several issues, including:

(a) The firm currently has little detailed information on its customers. What information is available suggests that customers are drawn predominantly from social groups C1 and C2, are between 38 and 60 years old, and see the price of the holiday as being a very important or the most important buying consideration.

(b) There appears to be little customer loyalty and no real evidence of much repeat business.

(c) In the absence of a sizeable marketing campaign, the summer destination appears to offer relatively little scope for growth. However, if a campaign was to be developed, it is felt that it might well have the effect of attracting some of the larger players in the industry, who currently view the area as being of only marginal interest.

(d) Winter golfing holidays are felt to offer significant growth prospects.

(e) The skiing market is likely to continue growing for at least the next five years, but will become subject to increasing price competition (see (g) below).

(f) The company currently has a policy of pricing at 5–8 per cent below the average of the industry leaders, and gives emphasis in its promotional material to this.

(g) With the substantial growth in the capacity of the Austrian, French and Italian ski resorts over the past few years, price competition in these markets has increased significantly. One result of this has been that the price advantage from which the Eastern European market benefited previously has very largely been eroded.

(h) The firm's sales brochures are uninspiring, and reflect the lack of any real basis for differentiation.

(i) The company has high fixed costs.

Against this background, the consultant has emphasized the general importance of moving up-market in order to increase the value added element of the holidays and allow for a greater degree of premium pricing. The specific recommendations that have been made are that:

- The company should continue to promote its current destinations, but over the next three years should attempt to reposition these in order to attract clients from higher socio-economic groups.
- It should gradually withdraw from the Eastern European ski resorts and concentrate instead upon higher-margin skiing holidays in the United States.
- A new range of holidays in Africa which would feature ballooning and safaris and targeted firmly at young high-spending customers in social groups A and B should be launched. These should be sold direct to clients and not via travel agents.

Questions

As Lazy Days' newly appointed marketing analyst, you have been given two tasks:

(a) Prepare a report for the managing director, identifying the criteria by which the three recommendations might best be evaluated.

(b) Prepare an outline marketing plan for the launch of a new holiday destination. In doing this, you should make detailed reference to the sort of financial and non-financial information that would be needed to underpin the plan.

Pentagon Balloons Ltd

Established by three flying enthusiasts in 1980, Pentagon Balloons Ltd started life as manufacturers of hot air balloons capable of carrying up to six passengers. These were sold primarily to a middle-aged and relatively wealthy market of ballooning enthusiasts, and positioned as 'the gift that you always promised yourself'.

In 1984 the company recognized the potential of hot air balloons as a promotional vehicle and began designing and manufacturing hot air balloons for clients in a wide variety of shapes, including various types of clothes, bottles and cans, running shoes, a car, and so on. Although the approach to marketing was largely reactive, this proved to be a highly successful venture and the company developed a reputation both for its high quality and its ingenious, if expensive, designs. Although the recession of the late 1980s had little impact upon sales, the decision was taken in 1990 to sell a 51 per cent stake in the company in order to inject a large sum of cash into the business to fund future growth. This stake was bought by a mini-conglomerate which, until recently, has allowed Pentagon to operate without interference.

In 1991, Pentagon's management recognized that the promotional hot air balloon market had reached what appeared to be a long-term maturity which offered relatively few opportunities for real or sustained profitable growth. Faced with this, the company began looking for new market opportunities. Amongst those identified was the market for microlight aircraft. These aircraft, which weight about 150 kg, are made of a tubular framework and the man-made textile, Dacron. Powered by a 500 cc engine, they require a 30-metre runway for take-off and 130 metres for landing. Like a hang-glider, the wing can be folded down to fit into a tube and, with the cockpit loaded onto a small trailer, the machine can be taken and stored almost anywhere. Prices range from £6,000–£10,000.

After an initial and admittedly superficial assessment of market opportunities, the company enthusiastically entered the market by coming to a loose and largely informal arrangement with an American designer and manufacturer of very high-quality microlights. Encouraged by their first six months' sales results, they then entered into a more formal 10-year marketing licence in late 1992. Under the terms of the licence they import the aircraft and have the marketing rights for Great Britain, Scandinavia, and the Benelux countries, with an option for the French and German markets. The licence requires Pentagon to achieve sales targets which are agreed every five years. Failure to achieve these targets leads to substantial financial penalties.

Although sales of the microlights proved initially to be healthy and profitable, the company has for the past 18 months failed to hit the sales target, and the penalty clause has been invoked. The company therefore employed a marketing consultant three months ago to conduct a detailed marketing audit. The consultant's subsequent report proved to be scathing, and highlighted a series of issues (see Figure 1).

With regard to marketing and sales (see Figure 2), the consultant concluded that 'a significant and underexploited sales potential exists throughout the territories for which you have the marketing rights . . . levels of competition are still relatively low . . . [and] the product's undoubted quality and performance give you a significant marketing edge. However, given the current approach, this potential will not be realized ... My biggest single recommendation must therefore be that the organization adopts a far stronger and more proactive approach to marketing.'

Figure 1
Selected extracts from the consultant's report

1 Despite the firm's initial success in this market, the impression gained is that the company is being run almost as a hobby by a group of flying enthusiasts.
2 Little or no real attention has been paid to structured market development.
3 There has been no sales effort in any of the markets outside Great Britain, even though the company's marketing licence covers several for which there is now hard evidence that a considerable sales potential exists.
4 There is an absence of formal market and marketing planning.
5 The sales effort has been largely reactive and has relied too heavily upon word-of-mouth and the general interest generated by the occasional newspaper feature or television programme.
6 No real segmentation or positioning policy exists.
7 There is little understanding of buyers' motives or where the marketing effort should be focused.

Figure 2
Market sectors for microlight aircraft

- Police forces, for low-cost traffic monitoring.
- Local authorities, for land surveys.
- Flying enthusiasts, who either cannot afford a 'proper' aircraft or who are attracted by the way in which microlights re-create the early days of flying.
- The military, for a variety of uses.

Of these, it is the third and fourth sectors which offer the greatest potential.

Questions

1 Working with the consultant, you have been given the responsibility for preparing a report recommending how a stronger marketing orientation might be introduced to the organization. Within the report you should make reference to, amongst other areas, the organizational and managerial implications of your recommendations, as well as the implications for marketing practice.
2 Identify the marketing and financial criteria that should be employed to assess the markets identified in Figure 2 by the consultant.

Required

The first of the two questions asks you to recommend how the organization might be refocused so that it has a far stronger external (marketing) orientation and less of an inward-looking approach. As many organizations have discovered, this is not necessarily an easy task, since it requires a major change in the management culture and ways of thinking. The solution is therefore far more complex than simply appointing a marketing director. You should therefore discuss how a change in culture might be brought about, and the sorts of problems that are likely to be experienced. Following on from this, you need to discuss the organizational (structural) implications of your recommendations, the ways in which management practice would need to change, and the consequences for marketing practice.

The second question is relatively straightforward, and asks you to identify the variety of financial and marketing criteria that marketing planners should take into account in assessing the alternatives open to them.

16 | Modelling approaches – 1

16.1 LEARNING OBJECTIVES

When you have read this chapter you should be able to:

(a) understand more fully the role of modelling approaches;
(b) apply financial models to the short-run and long-run evaluation of marketing plans;
(c) appreciate the contribution which cost–volume–profit analysis can make;
(d) carry out appraisals of marketing programmes using discounting methods.

16.2 INTRODUCTION

In broad terms a model is anything that is used to represent something else, and models may be classified as descriptive – those that aim to describe real-world processes; predictive – describing both objectives and events as well as attempting to predict future events; and control models – describing current events, predicting future events, and providing a basis for choice among alternative courses of action.

Management science models are typically mathematical in nature, being sets of equations or other expressions that specify the significant variables in a particular situation and indicate the relationship among them. A variable can be defined as any factor that can take on different values under different circumstances, such as:

$$y = a + bx$$

Where: y represents sales turnover (the effect);
   x represents consumer income (the cause);
   a and b are constants (or parameters), one of which may, for instance, be a time lag.

This shows that management science models are symbolic and are based on the axioms of mathematics. The axioms of probability theory, for example, as one branch of mathematics, will be briefly stated (see pp. 617–18 below). Furthermore, most mathematical models are based on a small number of highly aggregated factors that are of overriding importance in explaining the way a system works and determining the outcome of different actions.

Models are useful in that they facilitate conceptions of reality that allow the effects of alternative courses of action to be more readily anticipated and measured. Such conceptions, however, are necessarily simplifications of the real situation because this is usually so complex that it could not possibly be explained by a model. The danger is always present that models may be *over*-simplifications of reality, and this renders them useless. Over-simplification is often a trait of corporate model-building.

The balance sheet is a form of simplified corporate model governed by the principles of financial accounting, but the annual budget is a better operational example of a corporate model. Such models can be used to examine how the workings of a system affect the flow of inputs and outputs and are being used with increasing frequency.

Budgeting, as a means of modelling, is limited in its traditional application by:

1 the inclusion of too few alternative possibilities from which the most satisfactory is to be selected;
2 the difficulty of adjusting traditional operating budgets to rapidly changing conditions – they are at best 'flexible' with respect to changing sales or production levels (see Chapter 8).

It follows that a model permitting the calculation of a larger number of alternatives (based on a larger range of flexible variables and changing parameters) should yield a closer approximation to the ideal solution.

This can be achieved via simulation models, the idea of which is to handle relationships that are too complex to be reduced to simple conclusions by means of mathematical or statistical analysis. These models can then be used to generate predictions about the future course of events.

Two types of simulation are readily identifiable:

1 analogue simulation which tends to be a physical representation – such as the use of a model aircraft to predict the behaviour of a full-scale version;
2 symbolic simulation via mathematical modelling, in which the manipulation of the variables within the model simulates the interaction process and is thereby able to predict the outcomes of particular courses of action.

Sensitivity analyses (see pp. 623–4 below) can be performed in the symbolic simulation model by varying the inputs to the system (e.g. time, quantities, funds, etc.) and observing the outputs from each alternative combination of inputs. In this way a pattern of responses can be built up to permit predictions to be made of likely future outcomes.

Probability theory is important in any form of simulation since, for instance, the application of probabilities allows the manipulator to estimate the risk of predictions proving to be wrong. This and related techniques show that the value of simulation to management is in its providing the equivalent of a laboratory in which past or proposed strategies can be examined and experimental evidence produced concerning the probable future outcomes of present decisions.

The building of any model should be carried out by following a *systematic method* such as the following:

1 specify the objectives to be achieved;
2 formulate the problem to be solved;
3 determine the relationships and major variables in the problem situation, including constraints;
4 construct a model to represent the system under review in such a way that it expresses the effectiveness of the system as a function of the variables isolated in step 3, with at least one of these variables being subject to direct manipulation;
5 derive a solution from the model;
6 test both the solution and the model to ensure that the effect of changes in the system are accurately predicted in the system's overall effectiveness;
7 establish controls over the solution to allow for variations in the relationships among the variables, otherwise the solution may become invalid;

8 implement the tested solution by translating it into a set of operating procedures capable of being understood and applied by the personnel who will be responsible for this use;
9 appraise the results.

Within marketing many models have been developed that have general application in such areas as brand share and loyalty determination, media selection, measurement of message effectiveness, competitive strategies, transportation and warehouse location, pricing and the determination of competitive bids. However, these models are usually more complex and less precise than those developed for production and administration purposes. This is due to two major factors:

1 The ease of model construction will generally depend on the number of variables involved and the accuracy with which the costs associated with these variables can be measured. The general absence of well-developed costing systems for marketing means that marketing models must handle less precise data than is desirable.
2 The sheer number of variables in the typical marketing decision is huge, many of which are beyond the decision-maker's influence. This results in complex models as well as the need to make a large number of simplifying assumptions.

In many marketing decisions it is behavioural relationships that are of the essence rather than more easily measured physical or economic factors, and, along with other environmental variables, behaviour is difficult to measure in order to accommodate it into a mathematical model. The nature of a behavioural model is shown in Figure 16.1 for predicting sales in the convenience food industry.

FIGURE 16.1
Buyer behaviour model

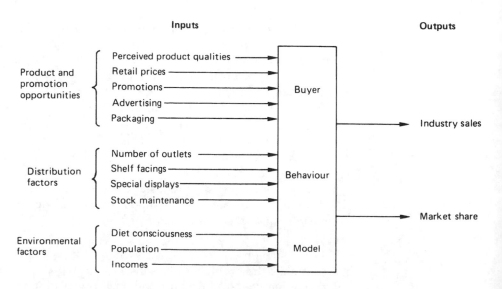

This is a *black-box* model that aims to show which given inputs result in a particular output rather than attempting to explain exactly how this occurs.

Decision models (as illustrated in Figure 16.2) permit a higher degree of explanation than is possible with *black-box* models because the variables contained within them are more readily quantified, and the interrelationships contained within these models are less tenuous than in behavioural models.

Analytical decision models (based on the programming techniques discussed later in Chapter 17) can result in the selection of the best marketing mix to adopt for both the trade and the consumer. Simulation models, on the other hand, can

FIGURE 16.2
Decision model

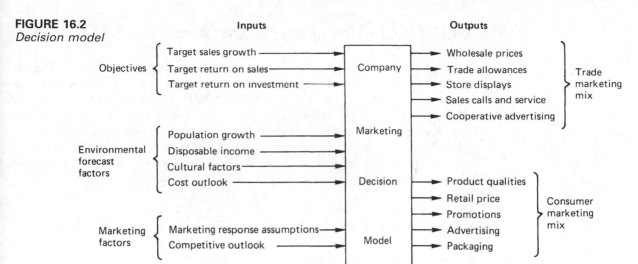

FIGURE 16.3
Company sales and profit model

> *Company profit equation:*
> $Z = (P - c) Q - F - A - D$
>
> *Company sales equation:*
> $Q = sQi$
>
> *Industry sales equation:*
> $Qi = mKN$
>
> *Market share equation:*
> $s = R(aA + dD)/\Sigma [R(aA + dD)]$
>
> Where: Z = Company profit in Year T
> $\quad\quad\quad\ P$ = Average price of the company's product in Year T
> $\quad\quad\quad\ c$ = Average variable manufacturing cost of the company's product in Year T
> $\quad\quad\quad\ Q$ = Number of units of product sold by the company in Year T
> $\quad\quad\quad\ F$ = Fixed manufacturing costs of company in Year T
> $\quad\quad\quad\ A$ = Advertising and promotion costs of the company in Year T
> $\quad\quad\quad\ D$ = Distribution and sales force costs of the company in year T
> $\quad\quad\quad\ s$ = Average market share of company in Year T
> $\quad\quad\ Qi$ = Industry sales in Year T
> $\quad\quad\ m$ = Convenience food share of total food market
> $\quad\quad\ K$ = Consumption of food per head in Year T
> $\quad\quad\ N$ = Population of market in Year T
> $\quad\quad\ R$ = Preference rating for company's product in Year T
> $\quad\quad\ a$ = Advertising effectiveness index
> $\quad\quad\ d$ = Distribution effectiveness index

start from a different point and attempt to evaluate the effect of alternative marketing mix combinations on the company's sales and profits as shown in Figure 16.3.

There can be little doubt that models can assist considerably in marketing planning and control, but this will only happen if models are developed and used properly.

Models must be designed on a systematic basis to ensure that they are geared to the decision maker's objectives and requirements. In addition, models must function as part of the management process, which means that they should not be developed in isolation of an appreciation of the changes in the balance of power that they can produce: political implications are a significant feature of management science applications.

Once developed, the risk exists that models will be incorrectly used. This does not mean that the decision maker must become a specialist in the development of models, but he should understand the essential features of model building and how to apply a model that has been built.

16.3 COST–VOLUME–PROFIT ANALYSIS

In deciding on future courses of action management pays a great deal of attention to the alternatives that are available. However, in the case of alternatives that involve changes in the level of business activity with no changes in scale itself it is generally found that profit does not vary in direct proportion to changes in the level of activity. This is due to the interactions of costs, volume, and profits.

For short-run decision-making purposes, costs can be classified as fixed, variable, and mixed. In a marketing context the costs which are typically fixed in relation to the level of activity (within a specified time-span) are:

- salaries;
- sales administration costs;
- advertising appropriations;
- market research allocations;
- establishment costs of premises.

Many costs depend very much on the level of activity (e.g. volume of business) and are often computed on a per unit basis. Such variable costs include:

- commissions which may vary with sales revenue;
- delivery costs which may vary with weight shipped;
- after-sales service costs which may vary with units sold;
- cost of credit which may vary with debtors' balances;
- order processing/invoicing costs which may vary with number of orders received.

Mixed costs are those that are neither constant over a period nor directly variable on a per unit basis. An example could be the cost of additional sales staff: a particular level of business may require 30 sales staff to service the relevant outlets, but a rise in business of, say, 10 per cent that involves new outlets will probably require additional sales staff.

The patterns that emerge are shown in Figure 16.4.

FIGURE 16.4
Cost behaviour patterns

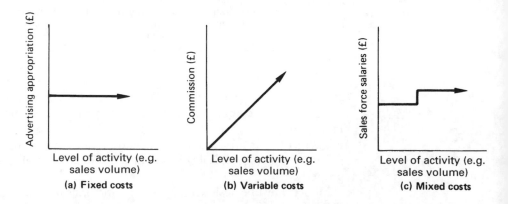

(a) Fixed costs   (b) Variable costs   (c) Mixed costs

Sales revenue is an increasing function of the level of activity and therefore has the behavioural characteristics of the variable cost curve (see Figure 16.4(b)). Profit is a residual that depends on the interaction of sales volume, selling prices and costs. The non-uniform response of certain costs to changes in the level of activity can have a serious impact on profit in companies having a high proportion of fixed costs with the result that a seemingly insignificant decline in sales volume from the expected level may be accompanied by a major drop in expected profit.

(This is particularly prevalent in capital-intensive companies producing expensive but specialized industrial equipment.)

On account of the difficulties involved in many industries in accurately predicting the volume of business that may be expected during a forthcoming planning period it is a wise policy to consider the cost–volume–profit picture for each likely level of activity. This can be done by means of a profitgraph (or break-even chart) that illustrates the profit emerging from different cost/revenue combinations.

FIGURE 16.5
Profitgraph

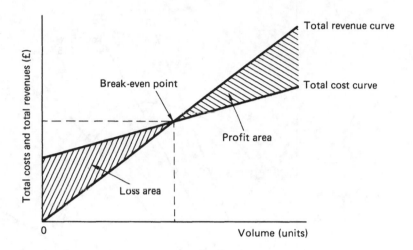

The simple profitgraph in Figure 16.5 is compiled by combining the cost and revenue curves. The total revenue curve is simply the expected unit sales multiplied by price for each level of activity, whereas the total cost curve is made up by splitting mixed costs into their fixed and variable costs elements, and superimposing the total fixed cost curve on to the variable cost curve as shown in Figure 16.6.

It is characteristic of this modelling technique that significant simplifying assumptions underlie its application. For example:

1 it is assumed that fixed costs are constant and that variable costs vary at a constant rate;
2 it is assumed that all costs can be broken into either fixed or variable categories;
3 it is assumed that only one selling price applies.

FIGURE 16.6
Total cost curve

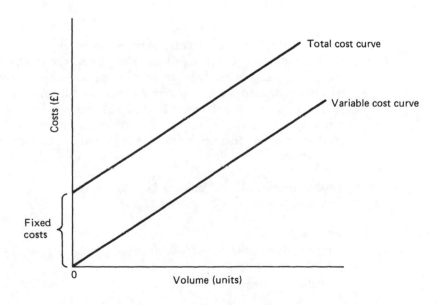

FIGURE 16.7
CVP analysis with a market demand schedule

Unit price (£)	Market demand (units)	Total revenue (£)	Total costs (£)	Break-even point (units)	Profit (£)
5	65 000	325 000 (a^1)	362 500	80 000 (a)	(37 500)
10	55 000	550 000 (b^1)	337 500	26 667 (b)	212 500
15	45 000	675 000 (c^1)	312 500	16 000 (c)	362 500
20	30 000	600 000 (d^1)	275 000	11 429 (d)	325 000

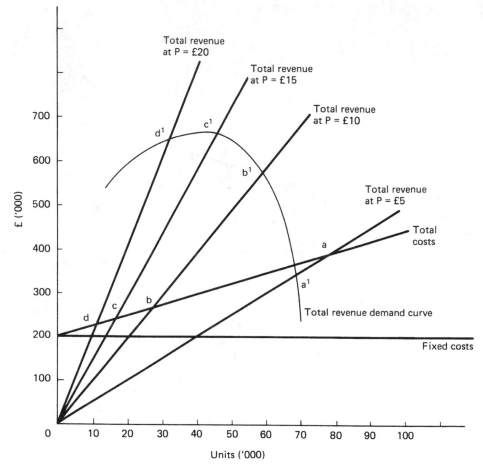

SOURCE: Adapted from Cravens and Lamb (1986)

Any of these (and other) assumptions underlying cost–volume–profit analysis can be modified in order to produce a more realistic model that is better suited to specific circumstances. This can be demonstrated by reference to Figure 16.7 in which assumption 3 above is relaxed (modified from Cravens and Lamb (1986), p. 31). Fixed costs are given at £200,000, the unit variable cost is £2.50, and demand forecasts are shown for a number of different prices: £5, £10, £15 and £20. The greatest profit is generated by the £15 price and can be confirmed by the following calculation:

Sales revenue (45 000 units at £15.00)	£675,000
Variable costs (45 000 units at £2.50)	£112,500
Contribution	£562,500
Fixed costs	£200,000
Profit	£362,500

The break-even volume is derived from the formula:

$$\frac{\text{Fixed costs}}{\text{Unit contribution (i.e. SR/unit–VC/unit)}}$$

$$= \frac{£200,000}{£15.00 - £2.50} = 16,000 \text{ units}$$

At £15.00 per unit the break-even point (i.e. the point at which TR = TC, hence P = 0) expressed in terms of revenue is:

16,000 × £15 = £240,000

This gives a margin of safety of

$$\frac{£675,000 - £240,000}{£675,000} \times 100 = 64\%$$

In other words, sales could fall by 64 per cent before a loss would be incurred.

In Figure 16.7 the line connecting the points a^1, b^1, c^1 and d^1 constitutes the market demand curve for the product in question.

An alternative form of presentation to the profitgraph is the profit–volume chart. This shows the same relationships but simplifies the picture by netting costs and revenues to show the profit for each level of activity. Figure 16.8 shows such a chart.

FIGURE 16.8
Profit-volume chart

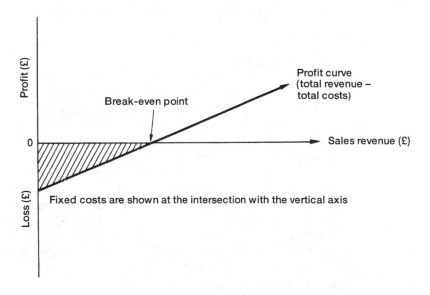

The reason why the total cost curve of Figures 16.5 and 16.6 does not pass through the origin is the same as the reason why the profit curve of Figure 16.8 cuts the vertical axis below the point of zero profit: even when there are no sales the fixed costs must still be paid, and consequently the area below the break-even sales volume represents one of loss, being at its greatest at zero sales.

When constructed, the profitgraph represents in essence a wide range of profit statements for various levels of activity. As such, it can be used as a bench-mark for judging the adequacy of actual performance, or it can be used in the planning phase to portray alternative courses of action. The graphical analysis described above is a simple means of illustrating cost–volume–profit interrelationships, but the managerial applications can also be facilitated by algebraic analysis.

The basic equation is simple once mixed costs have been split into their fixed and variable elements and shown as such:

Sales revenue = variable costs + fixed costs + profit.

The break-even (BE) equation is even simpler since at the break-even point there is no profit:

BE sales revenue = variable costs + fixed costs.

In physical volume terms the break-even point can be calculated as follows:

$$\text{BE volume} = \frac{\text{Fixed costs}}{(\text{Sales revenue} - \text{variable costs})/(\text{units sold})}$$

Thus if a firm has fixed costs of £10,000, variable costs of £15,000, and sells 5000 units for £30,000, the break-even volume is:

$$\frac{10\,000}{(30\,000 - 15\,000)/5000} = 3333 \text{ units}$$

In monetary terms the break-even volume can be derived by applying the formula:

$$\frac{\text{Fixed costs}}{1 - (\text{Variable costs/sales revenue})} = \frac{\text{Fixed costs}}{\text{Contribution margin ratio}}$$

Using the data referred to above the break-even volume is equal to:

$$\frac{10\,000}{1 - (15\,000/30\,000)} = \frac{10\,000}{0.5} = £20,000$$

The proof is simple: unit price is £6.00 (i.e. £30,000/5000) and the unit variable cost is £3.00 (i.e. £15,000/5000). The unit contribution towards fixed costs and profit is therefore £6.00–£3.00 = £3.00 and sufficient units must be sold to cover the fixed costs of £10,000. The solution is thus 3333 units, and at a unit price of £6.00 the break-even revenue is £20,000.

Reference was made in the above example to the contribution margin ratio. This is an important concept that expresses the percentage of a volume change that is composed of variable costs. In the example the revenue from an additional sale is £6.00 and the additional variable cost is £3.00. The contribution margin ratio is therefore $1 - \frac{3}{6} = 0.5$ or 50 per cent. In other words, half the revenue from a change in volume is sufficient to cover the variable costs and the other half contributes to

FIGURE 16.9
Profit-volume variations

	Original volume	Increase in volume	Decrease in volume
	(£)	(£)	(£)
Sales	30,000	+10,000	−10,000
Variable costs	15,000	+5,000	−5,000
Fixed costs	10,000	Unchanged	Unchanged
Total costs	25,000	+5,000	−5,000
Profits	5,000	+5,000	−5,000

fixed costs and profits. (The slope of the curve in Figure 16.8 is given by the contribution margin ratio.)

The application of this ratio is based on the assumption that other factors remain constant and it should be evident that this is a somewhat unrealistic assumption. Nevertheless, to continue the above example, if a change in sales of £10,000 takes place the change in profits will be as shown in Figure 16.9.

Figure 16.9 shows that with a contribution margin (or profit–volume) ratio of 50 per cent the profit variation for an upward move is the same as that for a downward move, with the former being positive and the latter negative, and with both being equal to one half of the change in sales revenue.

A further equation can be devised to measure the excess of actual (or budgeted) sales over the break-even volume. This is known as the *margin of safety* and is given by the equation:

(Actual sales – sales at break-even point)/actual sales

Again taking data from the earlier example, in monetary terms the margin of safety is:

(£30,000 – £20,000)/£30,000 = ⅓ or 33⅓%

In physical terms it is:

(5,000 – 3,333)/5,000 = ⅓ or 33⅓%

This ratio means that sales can fall by one-third before operations cease being profitable – assuming that the other relationships are accurately measured and remain constant.

The combination of cost–volume–profit analysis with budgeting enables alternative budget figures to serve as the basis for profitgraphs. If a particular budget is shown to be unsatisfactory then the parameters can be recast until a more suitable budget results. It is not surprising that cost–volume–profit analysis has been compared to flexible budgeting in being able to show what the cost and profit picture should be at different levels of sales, but flexible budgets are essentially concerned with cost control whereas cost–volume–profit analysis is more concerned with the predictions of profit.

As with other techniques, cost–volume–profit analysis has its strengths and weaknesses. In its favour is its value as a background information device for important decisions – such as selecting distribution channels, make or buy, and pricing decisions. In this role it offers an overall view of costs and sales in relation to profit requirements.

If simplicity is a virtue, then cost–volume–profit analysis has this virtue since it is easily understood. However, this very simplicity points the way to the weaknesses and limitations of cost–volume–profit analysis. As suggested earlier in this section, the major weakness is in the underlying assumptions: profit varies not only in relation to changes in volume, but also with changes in production methods, marketing techniques, and other factors. cost–volume–profit analysis is unable to allow for these possibilities, and at best indicates the profit that may be expected under a single set of assumed conditions regarding external factors as well as managerial policies. Thus it is a static representation of the situation it purports to illustrate: a different set of circumstances would obviously result in a different series of cost–volume–profit relationships.

Furthermore, cost–volume–profit analysis can only accommodate objectives that relate to profits, costs and sales levels/revenues, and it tends to treat costs, volume, and profit as if they were independent of each other.

These limitations do not outweigh the value of cost–volume–profit analysis provided that the user is aware of the assumptions and limitations. It is necessary, of course, to supplement the assistance given by any technique with managerial judgement, and cost–volume–profit analysis is no exception to this principle.

The roles of budgeting and cost–volume–profit analysis are illustrated below in another example.

Examples

1 ABC Ltd

This is a single-product company with a profit objective that is expressed as 10 per cent of net sales revenue.

For the next planning period the total market potential is estimated to be 500 units. Figure 16.10 indicates the cost and profit outlook at each level of sales that ABC Ltd can expect to achieve.

FIGURE 16.10
Manufacturing costs and revenues

Forecast percentage share of market	10%	12%	14%	16%
Unit sales	50	60	70	80
Average net price per unit	£1,500	£1,500	£1,450	£1,400
Forecast net sales revenue	£75,000	£90,000	£101,500	£112,000
Variable manufacturing costs at £300 per unit	£15,000	£18,000	£21,000	£24,000
Contribution	£60,000	£72,000	£80,500	£88,000
Fixed manufacturing costs	£20,000	£20,000	£20,000	£20,000
Gross profit	£40,000	£52,000	£60,500	£68,000

The behaviour of marketing costs is shown in Figures 16.11 and 16.12 for fixed and variable costs respectively.

The unit costs from Figure 16.12 can be extended to show the variable marketing costs of each anticipated sales level:

Market share	10%	12%	14%	16%
Variable marketing cost	£5,000	£6,000	£7,000	£8,000

The combination of Figures 16.10, 16.11 and 16.12 gives the total cost–volume–profit situation shown in Figure 16.13.

FIGURE 16.11
Fixed costs

Fixed costs	10%	12%	14%	16%
Sales force (excluding commission)	£6,000	£6,000	£9,000	£9,000
Sales administration	£10,000	£10,000	£12,000	£12,000
Advertising appropriation	£5,000	£5,500	£8,000	£12,000
Establishment costs	£10,000	£10,000	£12,000	£12,000
Marketing research costs	£2,000	£2,000	£2,000	£2,000
Office services	£3,000	£3,100	£3,200	£3,300
Totals	£36,000	£36,600	£46,200	£50,300

FIGURE 16.12
Variable cost per unit

Delivery	£10
Order processing/invoicing	£2
Commission	£10
Average cost of credit	£30
After-sales service	£48
	£100

FIGURE 16.13
Net profits

Net profit statement	10%	12%	14%	16%
Gross margin (Figure 16.10)	£40,000	£52,000	£60,500	£68,000
Marketing costs (Figures 16.11 and 16.12)	£41,000	£42,600	£53,200	£58,300
Net profit (loss)	£(1,000)	£9,400	£7,300	£9,700
Net profit as percentage sales revenue	−1.33%	10.44%	7.19%	8.66%

The profit objective of 10 per cent of net sales revenue is only achieved if ABC Ltd secures a 12 per cent market share, but control effort must be rigorously applied because the margin for error is very small.

This gives the basic budget for the forthcoming period, and this can be illustrated in a profitgraph as in Figure 16.14.

For the selected course of action (i.e. that aiming for a 12 per cent market share) the total cost make-up is:

Variable manufacturing costs	£18,000	
Variable marketing costs	£ 6,000	
		£24,000
Fixed manufacturing costs	£20,000	
Fixed marketing costs	£36,600	
		£56,600
Total costs		£80,600

The break-even point is computed by applying the formula given earlier in this section:

$$\frac{£56,000}{(£90,000 - £24,000)/60} = 51 \text{ units}$$

FIGURE 16.14
Cost–volume–profit relationships

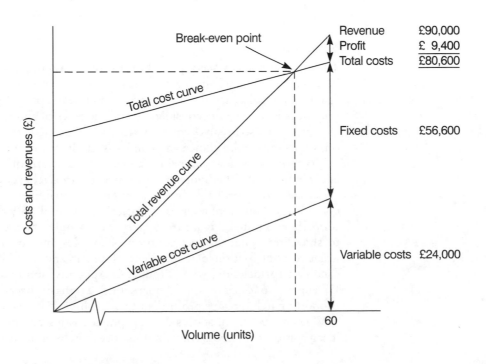

This gives a margin of safety of only 15 per cent calculated thus:

$(60 - 51)/60 = 15\%$

A clear and concise summary is given in this way of one particular course of action that provides a standard for management purposes. Separate charts and analyses can easily be drawn up for other alternative courses of action prior to making a choice.

Cost–volume–profit analysis can be used to aid the decision maker faced with such choices as:

1 leasing or buying premises;
2 leasing or owning vehicles;
3 using agents or setting up branch offices.

In the case of warehousing Figure 16.15 summarizes the situation, showing the storage space at which ownership costs are identical with leasing charges (B). At greater volume requirements ownership is cheaper, and at lesser volumes leasing is to be preferred.

FIGURE 16.15
Break-even chart for warehousing

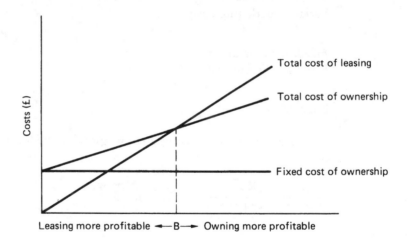

2 Product Line

The product mix is a major part of the overall marketing plan, and the relationship between the mix and the level of profit can be seen to be one of the basic areas against which alternatives can be reviewed in developing the marketing plan. Not only does it involve the consideration of the roles of single products and product groups but it also involves considerations of the related effects of decisions bearing on, for example, the choice and emphasis of alternative sales areas.

However, very few companies appear to be aware of the actual gross profit contributions of either individual products or product groups. Furthermore, large variations would probably be found in gross contributions in most cases, and this could suggest different courses of marketing action if only the gross margins were properly computed. Figure 16.16 gives the example of a six-product mix analysed to show how each product contributes to sales and to profit. Product F has a negative contribution of 5 per cent of profit and would thus appear to be a candidate for deletion, while Product C especially, and to a lesser extent Product D, appear to deserve special marketing emphasis because they both have a proportionately greater profit than their relative volume.

When management adopts direct product costing and distribution cost analysis it can compute the gross contribution of each item in the product range so that the

FIGURE 16.16
Product mix analysis

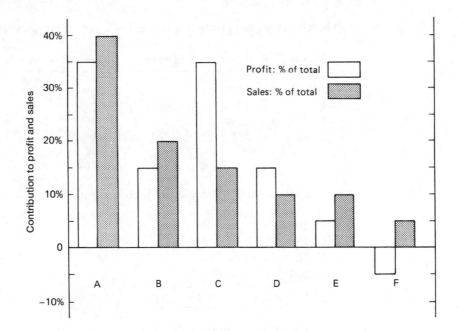

tactical significance of the mix in relation to profit objectives becomes apparent. This can reveal cases of under-recovery of direct costs (as in Product F in Figure 16.16) that could possibly be corrected by modifications in price or cost reduction if it is decided that the product should be retained to fill out the product line.

Direct costing requires the separation of fixed and variable costs, with the latter being treated as 'period costs' (i.e. they are charged to the profit and loss account on a periodic basis rather than being apportioned to units of output). An example should make the picture clear. LMN Ltd markets four products, the most recent financial data for which are shown in Figure 16.17. For each £1 of sales of the

FIGURE 16.17
Product costs and contributions

Product	Selling price (SP)	Variable cost (VC)	% contribution (SP-VC)/SP × 100	% of total sales	Contribution as % of total sales
A	£5	£4	20%	10%	2.0%
B	£6	£5	16.6%	20%	3.3%
C	£8	£6	25%	30%	7.5%
D	£10	£7	30%	40%	12.0%
				100%	24.8%

existing product mix, therefore, 24.8p is profit contribution. If the fixed costs of LMN Ltd amount to £50,000 and total sales are £250,000, then profit (P) is equal to:

(Sales × 24.8/100) – fixed costs
∴ P = £62,000–£50,000 = £12,000

If it is decided to vary this mix it will be necessary to forecast the costs and sales for the modified mix. For instance, Product E may be launched to replace Product B, having the following characteristics:

Selling price per unit	£7
Variable cost per unit	£5.6
Percentage contribution	20%
Increase in fixed costs	£1,000

The effects on the product mix are, for a new total sales level of £275,000:

Product	Former % of sales	Forecast % of sales
A	10%	25%
C	30%	30%
D	40%	30%
E	–	15%
		100%

The total contribution picture then becomes:

A: $20 \times 25/100 = 5\%$
C: $25 \times 30/100 = 7.5\%$
D: $30 \times 30/100 = 9\%$
E: $20 \times 15/100 = 3\%$

$$24.5\%$$

$$\therefore \ P = (275,000 \times 24.5/100) - (50,000 + 1,000)$$
$$P = £67,375 - £51,000 = £16,375$$

The profit improvement is thus £4,357 (i.e. £16,375 – £12,000) on additional sales of £25,000 and this gives ROS of 17.6 per cent.

This example emphasizes the fact that product decisions should be made on the basis of their contribution to fixed costs and profit, and on the basis of their percentage share of total sales, rather than being considered in isolation.

Future planning and control are both aided by studying the progress of each product over its life cycle since no product can hold its market position indefinitely in the face of changing conditions. The typical curves of Figure 16.18 show the lagged profit curve and the sales revenue curve for a product over the phases of its life. (See also the discussion in Chapter 10 above.) Rates of technological change, market acceptance, and ease of competitive entry will collectively determine the lifespan of the product. However, it may be possible to extend the lifespan by either modifying the product, changing its image to appeal to new market segments, or finding new uses for it. Generally it will be necessary to adapt the marketing effort in each phase, and the ideal situation is one in which new products are introduced at such a rate that optimum profits can be maintained

FIGURE 16.18
The product life cycle

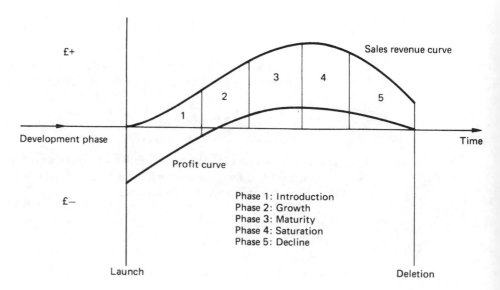

Phase 1: Introduction
Phase 2: Growth
Phase 3: Maturity
Phase 4: Saturation
Phase 5: Decline

by some products reaching maturity at the time when others are beginning to decline, and so on.

In Figure 16.18 the product in question is deleted at the time when it ceases to be profitable, even though it is still generating sales revenue. But any deletion decision should be preceded by serious consideration of the areas in which it may be possible to improve the product's performance. In particular, areas to consider are selling methods, channels, the advertising message, promotions, the brand image, the pack, the quality and design of the product, and the adequacy of the service offered.

Under no circumstances should a declining product be allowed to continue in decline without evaluation because it may be consuming resources that could more fruitfully be employed elsewhere. A declining product will tend to take up a disproportionate amount of management time; may require frequent price adjustments; will involve short – hence expensive – production runs; and may damage the company's image. Pareto's law will often apply in that 80 per cent of sales will come from 20 per cent of products and the weakest 20 per cent of products may absorb 80 per cent of management's attention.

Reviewing the product line should not be a rare action but should rather be undertaken in a regular and planned manner. For example, all products could be reviewed every three months and any that are less profitable than, say, the average for the range should be the subject of revised plans to improve their performance.

3 SRD Example

Heskett (1976, pp. 410–18) gives the example of a marketing proposal from the Safety Razor Division of the Gillette Company for a line of blank audio cassettes. The market penetration of the SRD's razors and blades was such that no further increase was likely, thus growth would have to come via diversification. Estimates of the size and rate of growth of the market for blank audio cassettes made it particularly attractive.

In the USA the most popular tape was the 60-minute one, available as follows:

Type	Price
Budget quality	$1.00
Standard quality	$1.75–$2.00
Professional quality	$2.98

Competition was fierce and price-oriented: some 50 per cent (by value) of tape sales were of budget quality, typically unbranded, with well-known companies supplying standard and professional quality tapes under such brand names as Sony, 3M, Memorex.

If SRD used 10 per cent of its existing sales force's effort to sell cassettes via existing outlets with the 50 per cent discount off retail price that was customary for cassettes, and if an advertising budget for Year 1 was set at $2 million (and $1.2 million per annum thereafter), and if unit costs were as follows:

Cassette case (bought out)	$0.159
Standard quality tape (60 minutes)	$0.214
Professional quality tape (60 minutes)	$0.322
Assembly labour	$0.200

and if the fixed annual costs of an assembly plant with capacity to handle 1 million cassettes per month were $500,000, there is the basis for an economic appraisal of alternative marketing programmes.

Figure 16.19 shows an outline programme offering standard quality cassettes at a price that is a little higher than that applicable to budget cassettes. The break-

FIGURE 16.19
Economic appraisal of marketing strategy-standard quality at budget prices

Item		Computation
Price to final consumer		$1.30 per tape
Price to retailer or wholesaler (50 per cent of list price)		$0.650
Variable costs per tape:		
cassette case	$0.159	
standard quality tape	$0.214	
assembly labour	$0.200	
Total		$0.573
Contribution		$0.077
Fixed costs per annum:		
assembly plant	$500,000	
sales force costs (10%)	$550,000	
advertising	$2,000,000	
Total		$3,050,000

Break-even sales volume: $\dfrac{\$3,050,000}{\$0.077}$

$$= 39,600,000 \text{ tapes}$$

$$39,600,000 \times \$1.30 = \$51.5 \text{ million retail value}$$

SOURCE: Adapted from Heskett (1976)

even volume is almost 40 million units per annum, which is greatly in excess of the capacity of the assembly plant. It also represents 85 per cent of the total retail market of budget-priced cassettes (totalling $65 million). On grounds of feasibility this does not appear to be a viable proposition.

Alternative marketing programmes to allow SRD to enter the cassette market might entail:

- raising list price (with or without an increase in quality);
- reducing trade margins;
- using a small sales team and only selling via wholesalers;
- reducing the proposed advertising budget;
- investing in manufacturing facilities (rather than just assembly).

These alternatives might be considered individually (on a *ceteris paribus* basis) or interactively (on a *mutatis mutandis* basis) and there would be knock-on effects for other elements of the marketing mix also.

Significant effort would need to be applied (via market research) to define the market, its segments, growth rates, etc., in order to determine the viability of alternative marketing programmes. Relevant factors would include:

- the quality of forecasts;
- the rate at which market conditions favourable to entry might change;
- alternatives to blank cassette tapes as vehicles for SRD's growth;
- assumed buyer behaviour patterns within the cassette market;
- assumptions about other elements of the marketing mix.

Three alternative marketing programmes have been developed by SRD. The steps through which they were developed are shown in Figure 16.20 and the evaluated alternatives are shown in Figure 16.21. These alternatives are the marketing of budget cassettes, the marketing of standard cassettes at a low price, and the marketing of professional cassettes. Only the last two would use the Gillette brand name, although all three would have to generate an equivalent profit to Gillette's overall level (at 20 per cent of sales revenue). It is clear from Figure 16.21 that alternative 3 is non-viable and that alternative 1, while viable, is more challenging than alternative 2.

FIGURE 16.20
A conceptual scheme for the economic appraisal of a marketing programme

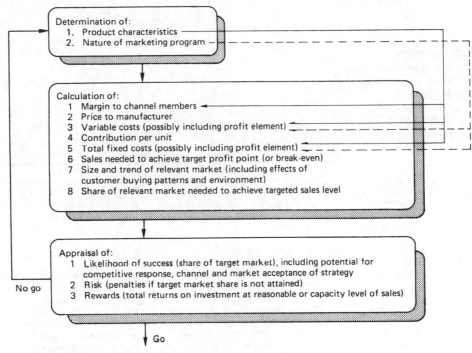

Determination of:
1. Product characteristics
2. Nature of marketing program

Calculation of:
1 Margin to channel members
2 Price to manufacturer
3 Variable costs (possibly including profit element)
4 Contribution per unit
5 Total fixed costs (possibly including profit element)
6 Sales needed to achieve target profit point (or break-even)
7 Size and trend of relevant market (including effects of
customer buying patterns and environment)
8 Share of relevant market needed to achieve targeted sales level

Appraisal of:
1 Likelihood of success (share of target market), including potential for
competitive response, channel and market acceptance of strategy
2 Risk (penalties if target market share is not attained)
3 Rewards (total returns on investment at reasonable or capacity level of sales)

No go

Go

SOURCE: Heskett (1976), p. 415

16.4 INVESTMENT APPRAISAL

Any investment involves the outlay of resources at one point in time in anticipation of receiving a larger return at some time in the future. This return must repay the original outlay as well as providing a minimum annual rate of return (or interest) on that outlay. If an individual invests £100 in a building society he will expect to receive that £100 back at some future time along with compound interest. This is a typical investment situation.

The aim will usually be to secure the maximum net cash flow (after tax) from the investment, and this will be achieved only from investments having the highest rate of return of those available.

Characteristically, an investment decision involves a largely irreversible commitment of resources and is generally subject to a significant degree of risk. Such decisions have far-reaching effects on an enterprise's profitability and flexibility over the long term, thus requiring that they be part of a carefully developed strategy that is based on reliable forecasting procedures.

Typical examples of investment projects are:

1 expansion projects;
2 replacement projects;
3 buy or lease decisions.

Projects for analysis and appraisal do not just appear – a continuing stream of good investment opportunities results from hard thinking, careful planning, and often from large outlays on R & D. Replacement decisions are ordinarily the simplest to make as the enterprise will have a very good idea of the cost savings to be obtained by replacing an old asset along with the consequences of non-replacement. (A central problem is that of accurately predicting the revenues and costs associated with particular projects for many years into the future.)

FIGURE 16.21
*An economic analysis
of three alternative
strategies for
designing and
marketing SRD
cassettes*

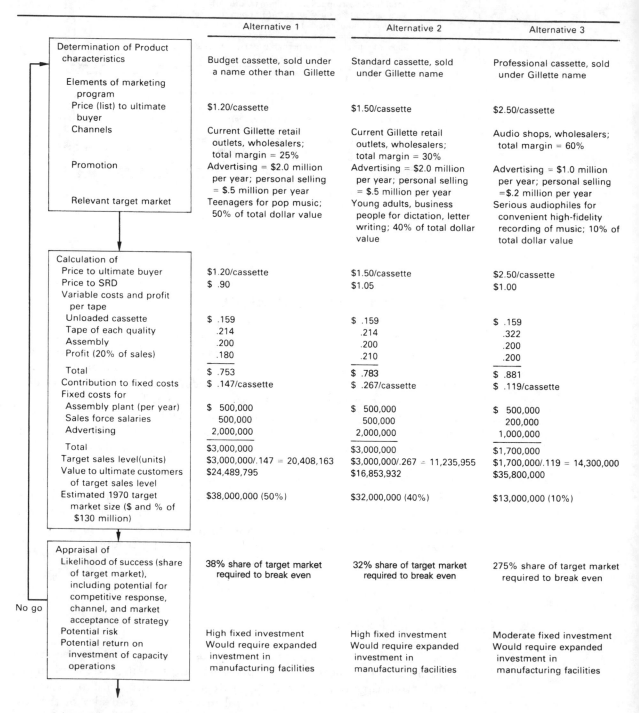

	Alternative 1	Alternative 2	Alternative 3
Determination of Product characteristics	Budget cassette, sold under a name other than Gillette	Standard cassette, sold under Gillette name	Professional cassette, sold under Gillette name
Elements of marketing program			
Price (list) to ultimate buyer	$1.20/cassette	$1.50/cassette	$2.50/cassette
Channels	Current Gillette retail outlets, wholesalers; total margin = 25%	Current Gillette retail outlets, wholesalers; total margin = 30%	Audio shops, wholesalers; total margin = 60%
Promotion	Advertising = $2.0 million per year; personal selling = $.5 million per year	Advertising = $2.0 million per year; personal selling = $.5 million per year	Advertising = $1.0 million per year; personal selling = $.2 million per year
Relevant target market	Teenagers for pop music; 50% of total dollar value	Young adults, business people for dictation, letter writing; 40% of total dollar value	Serious audiophiles for convenient high-fidelity recording of music; 10% of total dollar value
Calculation of			
Price to ultimate buyer	$1.20/cassette	$1.50/cassette	$2.50/cassette
Price to SRD	$ .90	$1.05	$1.00
Variable costs and profit per tape			
Unloaded cassette	$ .159	$ .159	$ .159
Tape of each quality	.214	.214	.322
Assembly	.200	.200	.200
Profit (20% of sales)	.180	.210	.200
Total	$ .753	$ .783	$ .881
Contribution to fixed costs	$ .147/cassette	$ .267/cassette	$ .119/cassette
Fixed costs for			
Assembly plant (per year)	$ 500,000	$ 500,000	$ 500,000
Sales force salaries	500,000	500,000	200,000
Advertising	2,000,000	2,000,000	1,000,000
Total	$3,000,000	$3,000,000	$1,700,000
Target sales level(units)	$3,000,000/.147 = 20,408,163	$3,000,000/.267 = 11,235,955	$1,700,000/.119 = 14,300,000
Value to ultimate customers of target sales level	$24,489,795	$16,853,932	$35,800,000
Estimated 1970 target market size ($ and % of $130 million)	$38,000,000 (50%)	$32,000,000 (40%)	$13,000,000 (10%)
Appraisal of			
Likelihood of success (share of target market), including potential for competitive response, channel, and market acceptance of strategy	38% share of target market required to break even	32% share of target market required to break even	275% share of target market required to break even
Potential risk	High fixed investment	High fixed investment	Moderate fixed investment
Potential return on investment of capacity operations	Would require expanded investment in manufacturing facilities	Would require expanded investment in manufacturing facilities	Would require expanded investment in manufacturing facilities

No go

SOURCE: Adapted from Heskett (1976), pp. 416–17

Over-investment in capital projects will result in heavy fixed costs, whereas under-investment may mean:

1 an enterprise's activities are not sufficiently modern to enable it to operate competitively; or
2 it has inadequate capacity to maintain its share of a growing market.

Investment is one of the main sources of economic growth. The application of reliable means of appraising investment proposals brings out more systematically and reliably the advantages of investing where it will improve performance and thus help to secure faster growth.

Various criticisms have been put forward in relation to the methods of appraisal that many companies employ. Among the most important are:

1 although most companies only make investment decisions after careful consideration of the likely costs and benefits as they see them, these decisions are often reached in ways that are unlikely to produce the pattern or level of investment that is most favourable to economic growth – or even most profitable to the company;
2 many companies apply criteria for assessing investment projects that have little relevance to the measurement of the expected *rate of return on investment* (ROI) by which subsequent performance will be gauged;
3 even when a calculation of the anticipated ROI of each project is made, the methods used vary widely and are sometimes so arbitrary as to give almost meaningless results – for instance, a failure to assess returns *after* tax is a frequent weakness of many widely used methods since alternative opportunities can only be effectively compared and appraised on an after-tax basis.

This faulty use of (or use of faulty) means of investment appraisal may result in over-cautious investment decisions in which too high a rate of return is demanded before a proposal is accepted. This will cause delay in economic growth. Alternatively, faulty methods may mean that investment decisions are made that result in the selection of projects that yield an unduly low return. This causes a waste of scarce capital resources which is also unfavourable to economic growth.

From an information flow point of view the use of inadequate means of investment appraisal results in a damaging restriction in the flow of information to top management since these methods are incapable of fully exploiting relevant data. Because a company's future is inextricably linked to its investments, poor appraisal methods that give poor information that leads to poor decisions are likely to result in many mistakes.

Realistic investment appraisal requires the financial evaluation of many factors, such as the choice of size, type, location, and timing of investments, giving due consideration to the effects of taxation and alternative forms of financing the outlays. This shows that project decisions are difficult on account of their complexity and their strategic significance.

No matter which technique is adopted for investment appraisal the same steps will need to be followed. These steps are:

1 determine the profitability of each proposal;
2 rank the proposals in accordance with their profitability;
3 determine the cut-off rate (e.g. minimum acceptable rate of return);
4 determine which projects are acceptable and which unacceptable in relation to the cut-off rate; and
5 select the most profitable proposals in accordance with the constraints of the company's available funds.

Cashflows

In considering investment decisions it does not matter whether outlays are termed 'capital' or 'operating', nor whether inflows are termed 'revenue', 'tax allowance', or whatever. All outlays and inflows must be taken into account in cash flow terms.

Cash flow in this context is not the same as the cash flow through a bank account nor is it identical to accounting profit since changes in the latter can occur without any change taking place in the cash flow.

For purposes of investment appraisal the cash flow is the incremental cash receipts less the incremental cash expenditures solely attributable to the investment in question.

The future costs and revenues associated with each investment alternative are:

1 *Capital costs.* These cover the long-term capital outlays necessary to finance a project, and working capital. (Since residual working capital is recoverable at the termination of a project's life, this leads to the investment having a terminal value that should be taken into account.) Typically, additional working capital will be required to cover a higher inventory, or a larger number of debtors, and to be worthwhile the project must earn a return on this capital as well as on the long-term capital.
2 *Operating costs.*
3 *Revenue.*
4 *Depreciation.* In the case of the discounting methods of appraisal (discussed below) the recovery of capital (i.e. depreciation) is automatically allowed for from the net cash flow so depreciation need not be included as an accounting provision. This has the important advantage that the discounted profitability assessment is not affected by the pattern of accounting depreciation chosen.
5 *Residual value.* As with working capital, the residual assets of the project may have a value (as either scrap or in an alternative use or location). This residual value (net of handling costs and tax allowances or charges) should be included within the net cash flow.

An investment decision implies the choice of an objective, a technique of appraisal, and a length of service – the project's life. The objective and technique must be related to a definite period of time. In a static world that period would quite naturally be taken as being equal to the commercial life of the plan that is the purpose of the investment, which may be known with a good deal of certainty on the basis of past experience. However, in a dynamic world the life of the project may be determined by:

1 technological obsolescence; or
2 physical deterioration; or
3 a decline in demand for the output of the project – such as a change in taste away from the market offering.

No matter how good a company's maintenance policy, its technological forecasting ability, or its demand forecasting ability, uncertainty will always be present because of the difficulty of predicting the length of a project's life.

Time Value of Money

To permit realistic appraisal the value of a cash payment or receipt must be related to the time when the transfer takes place. In particular it must be recognized that £1 received today is worth more than £1 receivable at some future date because £1 received today could be earning interest in the intervening period. This is the concept of the *time value of money*.

To illustrate this, if £100 was invested today at 5 per cent per annum compound interest it would accumulate to £105 at the end of one year (i.e. £100 × 1.05), to £110.25 at the end of two years (i.e. £100 × 1.05 × 1.05, or £105 × 1.05), and so on. In other words, £110.25 receivable in two years' time is only worth £100 today if 5 per cent per annum can be earned in the meantime (i.e. £110.25/(1.05 × 1.05) = £100).

The process of converting future sums into their present equivalents is known as *discounting*, which is simply the opposite of *compounding* (see Figure 16.22). Compounding is used to determine the *future value of present* cash flows.

FIGURE 16.22
Discounting and compounding

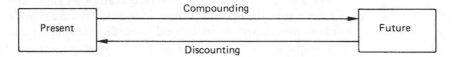

Another example will clarify this further. An investor who can normally obtain 8 per cent on his investments is considering whether or not to invest in a project that gives rise to £388 at the end of each of the next three years. The present value of these sums is:

$$\frac{£388}{1.08} + \frac{£388}{1.08 \times 1.08} + \frac{£388}{1.08 \times 1.08 \times 1.08} = £1,000$$

If the investment's capital cost is less than the present value of its returns (say £800) then it should be accepted since the present value of the return on this outlay is a larger amount (i.e. £1,000 – £800 = £200 gain from the investment). The gain is the *net present value* of the investment.

The interest rate does not always relate to an outlay of borrowed cash as the concept of interest applies equally to the use of internal funds. The reason why interest must be considered on *all* funds in use, regardless of their source, is that the selection of one alternative necessarily commits funds that could otherwise be invested in some other alternative. The measure of interest in such cases is the return foregone by rejecting the alternative use (i.e. the opportunity cost).

Financial Evaluation

The techniques of financial evaluation fall into two categories, as shown below.

Traditional Methods of Evaluation

The payback period is the most widely used technique and can be defined as the number of years required to recover the initial investment. By definition, the payback period ignores income beyond this period and it can thus be seen to be more a measure of liquidity than of profitability. In addition, it fails to take account of the time value of money, and these limitations make it seriously defective in the aim of reflecting the relative financial attractiveness of projects.

Projects with long payback periods are characteristically those involved in strategic planning and which determine an enterprise's future. However, they may not yield their highest returns for a number of years and the result is that the payback method is biased against the very investments that are likely to be most important to long-term success.

The accounting rate of return is defined as the average profit from the project (after allowing for accounting depreciation but before tax) as a percentage of the average required investment.

This method is superior to the payback period but is fundamentally unsound. While it does take account of the earnings over the entire economic life of a project, it fails to take account of the time value of money. This weakness is made worse by the failure to specify adequately the relative attractiveness of alternative proposals. It is biased against short-term projects in the same way that payback is biased against longer-term ones.

These traditional methods of investment appraisal are misleading to a dangerous extent. A means of measuring *cash* against *cash* that allows for the importance of time is needed. This is provided by the discounting methods of appraisal, of which there are basically two, both of which meet the objections to the payback period and accounting rate of return methods.

Discounting Methods of Evaluation

Both discounting methods relate the estimates of the initial cash outlays on the investment to the annual net after-tax cash flows generated by the investment. As a general rule, the net after-tax cash flows will be composed of profit less taxes (when paid), plus depreciation. Since discounting techniques automatically allow for the recoupment of the capital outlay (i.e. depreciation) in computing time-adjusted rates of return it follows that depreciation implicitly forms part of the discounting computation and so must be added back to profit in specifying cash flow.

The *internal rate of return* (IRR) (or discounted cash flow) method consists of finding that rate of discount that reduces the cash flows (both inflows and outflows) attributable to an investment project to zero – this being, in principle, the true rate of return. (In other words, this 'true' rate is that which exactly equalizes the discounted net cash proceeds over a project's life with the initial investment outlay.)

If the IRR exceeds the minimum required rate (or *cost of capital*) then the project is *prima facie* acceptable.

Instead of being computed on the basis of the average investment the IRR is based on the funds in use from period to period.

The actual calculation of the rate is a hit-and-miss exercise because the rate is unknown at the outset, but tables of present values are available to aid the analyst. These tables show the present value of future sums at various rates of discount, and are prepared for both single sums and recurring annual payments (i.e. annuities).

The *net present value* (NPV) method discounts the net cash flows from the investment by the minimum required rate of return, and deducts the initial investment to give the yield from the funds invested. If this yield is positive then the project is *prima facie* worthwhile, but if it is negative the project is unable to pay for itself and is thus unacceptable. An index can be developed for comparative purposes by relating the yield to the investment to give the yield per £1 invested. This is the *present value index* and facilitates the ranking of competing proposals in order of acceptability. (It is not important in their evaluation in terms of profitability that competing proposals require widely different outlays since the index reduces alternatives to a common base.)

Comparison of Discounting Methods

In ordinary circumstances the two discounting approaches will result in identical investment decisions. However, there are differences between them that can result in conflicting answers in terms of ranking projects according to their profitability.

In formal accept/reject decisions both methods lead to the same decision since all projects having a yield in excess of the minimum required rate will also have a positive net present value. Figure 16.23 shows that this is so.

FIGURE 16.23
Ranking comparisons, 1

Internal rate of return:	A = 15%	
	B = 12%	
Net present value	A = (1,150 × 0.926) − 1,000 = £65	
	B = (1,405 × 0.794) − 1,000 = £115	

Note: 0.926 is the factor that reduces a sum receivable one year hence, at a discount rate of 8 per cent, to its present value; and 0.794 is the discount factor that reduces a sum due three years hence to its present value. These discount factors are derived easily from published tables.

Example: Projects A and B both require an outlay of £1,000 now to obtain a return of £1,150 at the end of Year 1 in the case of A, and £1,405 at the end of Year 3 in the case of B. The minimum required rate of return is 8 per cent.

Both projects have rates of return in excess of 8 per cent *and* positive net present values; but on the basis of the IRR method Project A is superior, while on the basis of the NPV method Project B is superior.

Confusion arises because the projects have different lengths of life and if only one of the projects is to be undertaken (i.e. they are mutually exclusive) the IRR can be seen to be unable to discriminate satisfactorily between them. As with any rate of return there is no indication of either the *amount* of capital involved or the *duration* of the investment. The choice must be made either on the basis of net present values or on the return on the *incremental investment* between projects. (In the above example, of course, the same amount of investment is required for each, thus Project B is to be preferred on the strength of its higher net present value.)

The two methods make different implicit assumptions about the reinvesting of funds received from projects – particularly during the 'gaps' between the end of one and the end of another.

Considering the example further, if it is explicitly assumed that the funds received from Project A can be reinvested at 10 per cent per annum between the end of Years 1 and 3, the situation will be as shown in Figure 16.24.

FIGURE 16.24
Ranking comparisons, 2

IRR	A =	$(15 + 10 + 10) \div 3$	= 11.667%
	B	(as Fig. 16.24)	= 12%
NPV	A =	$[(150 \times 0.926) + (115 \times 0.857) + (1126 \times 0.794)] - 1,000$	= £32
	B	(as Fig. 16.24)	= £115
Terminal value:	A =	$(1,150 \times 110\% \times 110\%)$	= £1,391
	B	(as given)	= £1,405

All three formulations clearly show Project B to be superior, illustrating the importance of project characteristics when only one can be undertaken.

The NPV approach assumes that cash receipts can be reinvested at the company's minimum acceptable rate of return, thereby giving a bias in favour of long-lived projects.

In contrast, the IRR approach assumes that cash receipts are reinvested at the same rate (i.e. a constant renewal of the project), giving a bias in favour of short-lived projects.

It follows that the comparison of alternatives by either method must be made over a common time-period with explicit assumptions being made about what happens to funds between their receipt and the common terminal date.

Aspects of Application

Alternative Proposals
The selection of a particular proposal should follow a careful appraisal of both alternative uses for funds and alternative means of performing a particular project. For instance, a company may wish to double the capacity of its production line and determine three means of accomplishing this, namely:

- introduce double-shift working;
- install a second production line;
- scrap the existing production line and build a new line with double the initial capacity.

The choice of a particular alternative will depend on how it accords with the enterprise's established investment objectives, and the choice of projects will depend on both corporate objectives and the availability of funds. But the fact remains that if the most advantageous alternative has been overlooked no amount of technical evaluation and appraisal can overcome this basic omission.

Capital Rationing

In terms of financing investment projects three essential questions must be asked:

- What funds are needed for capital expenditure in the forthcoming planning period?
- What funds are available for investment?
- How are funds to be assigned when the acceptable proposals require more than are currently available?

The first and third questions are resolved by reference to the discounted return on the various proposals since it will be known which are acceptable and in which order of preference.

The second question is answered by a reference to the *capital budget*. The level of this budget will tend to depend on the quality of the investment proposals submitted to top management. In addition, it will also tend to depend on:

- top management's philosophy towards capital spending (e.g. is it growth-minded or cautious?);
- the outlook for future investment opportunities that may be unavailable if extensive current commitments are undertaken;
- the funds provided by current operations;
- the feasibility of acquiring additional capital through borrowing or share issues.

It is not always necessary, of course, to limit the spending on projects to internally-generated funds. Theoretically, projects should be undertaken to the point where the return is just equal to the cost of financing these projects.

If safety and the maintaining of, say, family control are considered to be more important than additional profits, there may be a marked unwillingness to engage in external financing, and hence a limit will be placed on the amounts available for investment.

Even though the enterprise may wish to raise external finance for its investment programme there are many reasons why it may be unable to do this, for example:

- the enterprise's past record and its present capital structure may make it impossible, or extremely costly, to raise additional debt capital;
- its record may make it impossible to raise new equity capital because of low yields – or even no yield;
- covenants in existing loan agreements may restrict future borrowing.

Furthermore, in the typical company, one would expect capital rationing to be largely self-imposed.

Post-audit

Each major project should be followed up to ensure that it conforms to the conditions on which it was accepted, as well as being subject to cost control procedures.

FIGURE 16.25
Cash flow projections

Proposal	Add a new line of toys.
Cash investment (£'000s)	
Production equipment	1,000
Recruiting and training salesmen	100
Promotional material	10
Inventory and debtors	190
	1,300
Projected sales volume (£'000s)	
Year 1	600
Year 2	1,000
Year 3	1,200
Year 4	1,000
Year 5 (final year)	800
Cost of sales	30% of sales value
Direct operating costs	£100,000 per annum
Depreciation of equipment	£200,000 per annum. No salvage value.

SOURCE: Adapted from Winer (1966)

An Example

The following example illustrates the importance of accurate forecasts of cash flows (representing sales value, cost of sales, operating costs, and initial investment). Taxation is deliberately ignored. (The example is adapted from Winer (1966).)

A proposal has been put forward in the form of a marketing plan to launch a new line of toys. Cash flow forecasts are shown in Figure 16.25. Note that depreciation is not, in fact, a cash cost. It is shown here simply as a footnote to indicate that there will be no cash inflow at the end of Year 5 from the sale of the equipment since that equipment is not expected to have any residual value at that point in time.

The evaluation of the plan is shown in Figure 16.26 which is largely self-explanatory. Cost of capital is shown as being 18 per cent. This can be taken to be the minimum required rate of return from the plan (thus reflecting equivalent returns from alternative plans of comparable risk). The plan's net present value is £447,000 which results when the discounted inflows and outflows are summed and the initial investment deducted from the total:

Total discounted value of inflows and outflows from Year 1 to Year 5	£1,747,000
Initial investment	£1,300,000
Net present value	£ 447,000

FIGURE 16.26
Cash flow analysis and evaluation

(£'000s)	Year 0	Year 1	Year 2	Year 3	Year 4	Year 5
1 Cash investment	(1,300)					
2 Sales revenue		600	1,000	1,200	1,000	800
3 Cost of sales		(180)	(300)	(360)	(300)	(240)
4 Operating costs		(100)	(100)	(100)	(100)	(100)
5 Recovery of investment in inventory and debtors						190
6 Cash flows	(1,300)	320	600	740	600	650
7 Discount factor at 18%	1.00	0.847	0.718	0.609	0.516	0.437
8 Discounted cash flow	(1,300)	271	431	451	310	284
9 NPV	447					

SOURCE: Adapted from Winer (1966)

From these figures it is also possible to calculate the PV index:

$$\frac{£1,747,000}{£1,300,000} = 1.34$$

In other words, the plan promises to generate £1.34 for every £1.00 invested in it, expressed in terms of current £s. Since the PV index exceeds unity, hence the NPV is positive, the plan appears to be economically viable. However, various additional questions need to be raised, such as:

- Is there sufficient funding available to meet the initial investment requirements of £1,300,000?
- Can the plan be modified to earn even more than £1.34 per £1.00 of investment?
- Are there alternatives available that may be more attractive?
- How sensitive is the plan's NPV to changes in flow estimates, including their timing?

From the data given in Figure 16.26 it is possible to calculate the payback period of the plan and the accounting rate of return, as follows:

Payback period is the length of time it takes to recover the initial investment.

		£'000s
	Year 1	320
	Year 2	600
380/740	Year 3	380
		1,300

It will be 2 years and 187 days (assuming an even pattern of inflows). The investment is exposed, therefore, over half of the anticipated life of the plan.

The accounting rate of return is an accounting (rather than cash flow) measure of the average profitability of the plan.

- Average profits will be (in £'000s):

$$\frac{£(320 + 600 + 740 + 600 + 460)}{5} - £200$$

$$\frac{£2,720}{5} - £200 = £344$$

It is necessary to deduct depreciation as an expense in calculating the average accounting profit.

- Average investment will be (in £'000s)

$$\frac{£1,300 - £190}{2} = £555$$

- The ARR will be:

$$\frac{£344}{£555} \times 100 = 62\%$$

Valuing Market Strategies

Mention was made in Chapter 15 of the criterion of enhanced shareholder value. This has been adopted by Day & Fahey (1988) in their approach to strategy evaluation. Since the basic premise of this approach is that shareholders' interests should be maximized it will be apparent that it is a partial approach that ignores other stakeholders' interests. Moreover, since maximizing the current market value of shareholders' interests presumes that the shares themselves are listed, this restricts Day & Fahey's approach to a little over 2200 of the total of more than one million limited companies incorporated within the UK.

Value is created whenever the financial gains from a strategy exceed its costs. The use of discounting methods allows for both the timing of cash flows and the inherent riskiness of marketing strategies in measuring the value of the latter. A potential shareholder will only invest in an enterprise if it is his expectation that the management of that enterprise will generate a better return than he could obtain himself, at a given level of risk. The minimum expected return is the cost of capital (i.e that rate used in discounting), hence shareholder value is only created when activities are undertaken that generate a return in excess of the cost of capital.

The usual approach adopted in assessing the shareholder value of an enterprise is to discount the anticipated cash flows by the risk-adjusted cost of capital. If a new strategy is in prospect then the shareholder value will be the sum of the value to be derived from the new strategy plus the 'baseline' value reflecting the value that is expected to result from continuing the existing strategy. This gives a basis for comparing strategic alternatives in a way that highlights their respective contributions to value. Thus:

$$
\begin{array}{l}
\text{Estimated shareholder} \\
\text{value if strategy X} \quad = \quad
\begin{array}{l}
\text{Estimated value} \\
\text{contributed} \\
\text{by strategy X}
\end{array}
\quad + \quad
\begin{array}{l}
\text{Baseline} \\
\text{shareholder} \\
\text{value}
\end{array} \\
\text{is selected}
\end{array}
$$

$$
\therefore
\begin{array}{l}
\text{Estimated value} \\
\quad \text{of strategy X}
\end{array}
\quad = \quad
\begin{array}{l}
\text{Estimated} \\
\text{shareholder value} \\
\text{if strategy X} \\
\text{is selected}
\end{array}
\quad - \quad
\begin{array}{l}
\text{Baseline} \\
\text{shareholder} \\
\text{value}
\end{array}
$$

When several competing strategies are being evaluated in a situation where there are insufficient resources to undertake all available strategies that meet the specified economic criterion (e.g. offer a positive net present value when discounted at the risk-adjusted cost of capital), the recommended basis for ranking acceptable strategies is by use of the PV index. This shows how much value is created per £1 of investment.

$$
\text{PV index} = \frac{\text{Present value of strategy}}{\text{Investment required}}
$$

In using this approach to evaluating strategies there needs to be available:

1 cash inflow and outflow forecasts relating to each alternative strategy;
2 cash flow forecasts relating to the baseline strategy;
3 a suitable discount factor (i.e. the risk-adjusted cost of capital);
4 alternative scenarios to allow the sensitivity of the outcomes to changes in the inputs to be tested.

Even if all these information requirements can be met there is inevitably a large element of subjectivity involved: in part this will be included within the estimates of cash flows, etc., and in part it will reflect both the specification of the strategy and the interpretation of results from the analysis. It is suggested that all assumptions involving judgments be specified explicitly in order that their appropriateness can be gauged by others.

The steps to follow in carrying out a strategic evaluation to enhance shareholder value are:

1 derive cash flow forecasts from the managerial judgments relating to competitive and market responses to each strategic alternative;
2 adjust the forecasts from 1 for risk and timing prior to calculating the NPV of each strategy and relating these NPVs to baseline expectations in order to gauge the increase in shareholder value from each alternative;
3 select the strategy that offers the greatest increase in shareholder value and implement it.

It is implicit in this sequence of steps that:

- the value creation potential of each strategic alternative relative to the baseline strategy can be accurately predicted;
- the shareholder value criterion is applicable to all strategic alternatives having cash flow implications;
- the stock market will recognize and reward strategies that enhance shareholder value.

Each of these matters raises fundamental questions. For example, our ability to predict accurately is limited for reasons of uncertainty as well as personal bias, and the stock market is not a perfect market (and so does not have perfect information on which to base its reactions). Nevertheless, by focusing on cash flows rather than accounting data, and by taking a long-term perspective rather than a short-term one, the approach advocated by Day & Fahey has distinct benefits as well as limitations.

Support for variations on this 'economic value' approach has come from a range of sources. Buzzell and Chussil (1985), for example, have argued that it is rare for managers to evaluate strategies in terms of their effects on future value. This suggests that many enterprises are failing to achieve their full potential by using inappropriate methods for strategic evaluation, and by emphasizing short-run financial results at the expense of long-term competitive strength.

16.5 SUMMARY

Given the specification of marketing programmes in Chapters 11 to 14, and the specification of choice criteria in Chapter 15, this chapter has sought to show some of the ways in which marketing programmes might be evaluated by using financial modelling approaches embodying the appropriate criteria.

The principles of modelling were reviewed and developed via a consideration of short-run financial modelling (using cost–volume–profit analysis) and long-run financial modelling (using investment appraisal methods).

A model is, in essence, a simplified representation of a situation or process which needs to be analysed, evaluated or controlled. The representation can be symbolic, mathematical or physical. In using financial models such as those dealt with in this chapter it is necessary to bear in mind the limitations of such models. In particular, financial systems measure those things which can be measured by financial systems, and in a marketing context there are typically many additional issues which cannot be adequately reflected in financial models.

16.6 EXERCISES

1 Assume the following:

Present sales: £400,000
Variable cost: £0.75 per £ of sales
Fixed cost: £80,000

(a) Find the effect on profit of:

    (i) a decrease of 20 per cent in sales;
    (ii) an increase of 20 per cent in sales.

(b) Same as (a) above, except the variable costs equal £0.60 per £ of sales.

(c) Assuming the same data as in (a), what is the effect on profit at present unit volume of:

    (i) an increase in sales price of 10 per cent, other factors remaining the same?

    (ii) a decrease in sales price of 10 per cent, other factors remaining the same?

(d) Assuming the same data as in (a), what is the effect on profit at present unit volume of:

    (i) an increase of 6 per cent in the variable cost?
    (ii) a decrease of 6 per cent in the variable cost?

(e) Assuming the same data as in (a), what is the effect on profit at present unit volume of:

    (i) an increase of 10 per cent in the fixed cost?
    (ii) a decrease of 10 per cent in the fixed cost?

2 Produce a profitgraph (as in Figure 16.5) for a marketing project with which you are involved.

3 Specify the cash flows of a marketing project with which you are involved. Show the actual and anticipated inflows and outflows over the expected life of the project.

4 Evaluate the project you have specified in Exercise 3 above via:

(a) payback;
(b) net present value.

(assume the appropriate discount rate is 10 per cent).
Discount tables are provided in Appendix A.

5 What questions are prompted by your evaluation in Exercise 4 above?

16.7 DISCUSSION QUESTIONS

1 What do you understand a *model* to be, and what roles can a model play in the context of strategic marketing management?

2 What are the limitations of cost–volume–profit analysis?

3 Explain the essence of *investment* and why investment decisions are typically complex.

4 Define the *time value of money*. Why is this of relevance in evaluating competing marketing proposals?

5 Outline the advantages and disadvantages of using a *shareholder value* approach to evaluating marketing proposals.

16.8 Case Studies

Gatorade

'If we decide to introduce Gatorade to Canada,' said Yves Lafortune in September 1985, 'it will be our first beverage product. Although we have information on our U.S. experience, there are some differences in the market here. That makes planning for a Gatorade introduction an exciting challenge.' Lafortune was the New Business Development Manager for the grocery products division of The Quaker Oats Company of Canada Limited. The previous month he had been invited to give a presentation to senior management on the Gatorade potential in Canada. The outcome of that meeting was that Lafortune had been asked to prepare a detailed proposal for the possible introduction of Gatorade into Canada in 1986.

Gatorade

Gatorade was developed at the University of Florida in 1965 by a team of scientists led by Dr. Robert Cade. Their goal was to develop the ultimate rehydration beverage by producing a drink with a good taste that would encourage athletes to use it. The beverage they developed was tested on the Gators, the football team at the University of Florida. The Gators loved the product and soon began to outscore opponents in the second half of the game. Players reported that they felt fresher and not as energy-depleted when they drank the beverage during a game. The Gators went on to win the Orange Bowl, after which losing Georgia Tech coach Bobby Dodd told the press that his team did not have the mysterious and effective beverage he called 'Gatorade.' The name stuck, and it remains the name of the beverage today.

Dr. Cade formulated Gatorade to contain water, carbohydrates, and electrolytes. As a result of this formulation, Gatorade can be absorbed quickly and easily into the body thereby allowing rapid fluid replacement and enhancing athletic performance.

The product was not protected by patent, but had trade mark protection.

The Quaker Oats Company of Canada

Quaker Oats of Canada Limited has two divisions; the grocery products division and the Fisher-Price toys division. The company reported combined sales of $240 million and profits of $12 million for the year ending June 30, 1985.

Since it started in Peterborough, Ontario in 1901, the company has grown to employ 900 people, and it has assets valued at $110 million. The Canadian company is the wholly-owned subsidiary of an American parent, which reported after-tax income of $138 million on 1984 sales of $3.3 billion.

Gatorade in the United States

In 1967, two years after Gatorade was developed, Stokely Van-Camp in the United States bought the rights from Dr. Cade. Initial efforts were focused on sports teams. The product developed a 'cult' status, and its user group broadened to include serious athletes in all sports activities. Finally, in the southern United States, Gatorade became widely accepted as the ultimate thirst quencher, appealing to individuals with serious thirst.

Under Stokely's direction, marketing and sales efforts were concentrated in the United States Sun Belt region, with limited consumer promotion support and a professional sponsorship program confined primarily to the NFL. In the decade prior to 1983, sales grew sixfold to $80 million. Eighty percent of yearly sales were made between April and October.

The original Gatorade was a liquid with a lemon-lime flavor. An orange flavor was added in 1971, and a fruit-punch flavor in the summer of 1983. Instant Gatorade was added to the line in 1979.

Quaker USA purchased Stokely Van-Camp in 1983, thereby acquiring the rights to Gatorade. Upon acquiring Gatorade, Quaker USA established the objective of achieving dramatic volume growth for the brand while maintaining profitability. In order to achieve this objective, a strategy was implemented of aggressively promoting Gatorade on a national basis to physically active males 18–34. This move meant that much more emphasis was placed on market development in the northern United States.

Although it was estimated that Gatorade had a 97-percent share of the sports beverage market, in fact it competed with many beverages, including water, tea, iced tea, soft drinks, and beer. The uniqueness of the product made it difficult to categorize for purposes of retail store location and beverage comparison. It was determined that in the United States the most effective grocery store location for both the liquid and crystal forms was the ready-to-serve juice drink section, which attracted adult buyers/users. It was estimated that Gatorade had a 10 to 11 percent share of this category in 1983.

Convenience stores had become an important part of Gatorade's distribution. In 1984, it was estimated that 20 percent of Gatorade sales were made in these stores. Smaller-sized containers stored in the cooler produced the highest sales, with buyers in very large part being the target audience of males 18–34, who purchased for immediate consumption. This led Quaker personnel to talk about obtaining distribution 'at point of sweat.' It was estimated that 50 percent of Gatorade consumption took place outside the home. Furthermore, it was estimated that 60 percent of purchases were made by women and that 40 percent of users were women.

The year 1984 was a highly successful year for Gatorade. Sales increased to $120 million. Exhibit 1 shows that shipments and market share increased sharply, particularly in the non-Sun Belt area. The volume gain data in Exhibit 2 show that the Gatorade franchise was expanded and solidified in 1984.

Exhibit 1

1984 Grocery Distribution[a]			
	Shipments	**Share**	**Change**
Sun Belt	+13%	22.7%	+2.6%
Non-Sun Belt	+63%	7.9%	+3.4%
Total U.S.	+27%	13.5%	+2.9%

[a] Does not include convenience stores.

The Canadian Opportunity

The 1984 success of Gatorade in the northern United States attracted the interest of Quaker management in Canada. After some preliminary discussions, Lafortune was asked to prepare a presentation that would provide senior management with a full picture of the U.S. Gatorade experience, identification of the key success factors, and an assessment of Gatorade's potential in Canada.

Exhibit 2

Source of 1984 Volume Gain		
	Trial Customers	Repeat Customers
Sun Belt	23%	77%
Non-Sun Belt	53%	47%

As part of that presentation, Lafortune provided information on the U.S. product mix and pricing (see Exhibits 3 and 4). He noted that although Quaker had earlier research showing that the 32-ounce size was considered a one-serving size by a large majority of target-audience males in the Sun Belt, recent research had determined that this pack size was considered to be more than a one-serving size by a majority of target-audience males in the non-Sun Belt region. He also provided information on the growth of non-Sun Belt sales from 28 percent in April-October 1983, to 36 percent in April-October 1984, and up to 42 percent in April-June 1985, which strongly suggested that the Gatorade concept was viable in Canada. Lafortune's assessment of the factors contributing to the 1984 U.S. success is given in Exhibit 5. Exhibit 6 contains information developed by Lafortune that supported the idea that general market trends favored a Gatorade introduction in Canada.

It was at this meeting that Lafortune was asked to develop a detailed proposal for the possible Canadian introduction of Gatorade in 1986.

Exhibit 3

1985 U.S. Gatorade Produce Mix	
Size[a]	Share of Line
32 oz glass	68.9%
46 oz glass	20.8
6 pack (12-oz cans)	7.9
1 gal. glass	.9
2 qt. instant	.3
8 qt. instant	1.2
	100.0%
Flavor	Share of Line
Lemon-lime	52.7
Orange	30.1
Fruit punch	17.2
	100.0%

[a] The gallon size is available in the lemon-lime flavor only. All other sizes are available in lemon-lime, orange, and fruit punch.

Exhibit 4

1985 U.S. Gatorade Pricing[a]		
Pack/Size	Average Retail Price	Average Retail Margin
10/32 oz. glass	$0.93	20.4%
6/46 oz. glass	1.28	22.6
4/1 gal. glass	3.44	19.4
4/6 12 oz. cans	2.81	20.9
24/2 qt. instant	1.03	23.3
12/8 qt. instant	3.91	21.4

[a]Retail prices represented about a 20-percent premium over soft drinks and a 10-percent premium over fruit drinks. In 1985, $1.00 U.S. equaled $1.38 Canadian.

Exhibit 5

Factors Contributing to 1984 U.S. Success

Advertising
- Clearly communicated benefit and uniqueness
- Broadened target to weekend warrior
- Increased usage rate through continuity plan

Promotion
- Maximized trial in the North
- Spurred multiple purchases in the Sun Belt
- Capitalized on merchandiseable events

Sales Force
- Dramatically increased non-Sun Belt distribution
- Provided excellent display support

Production/Distribution
- Dramatically increased efficiency to improve margins
- Improved product availability

Exhibit 6

General Market Trends Favorable to Gatorade

In Canada, changing lifestyle patterns and a more serious attitude toward health, fitness, weight control, and nutrition all indicate increasing potential for 'good for you'-type beverages. A general shift in beverage consumption patterns, stimulated to some degree by concern over alcohol abuse, coupled with the growing acceptance of non-alcoholic drinks, suggests that an opportunity exists for a unique 'thirst quencher' alternative like Gatorade.

It should be noted that the population 'bubble' consisting of post-war baby boomers has and will continue to greatly influence consumer beverage trends. This group (34 percent of the population) is the most fitness-oriented generation in recent history, and it is probable that their health orientation will continue into the twenty-first century.

Usage information in the United States indicates that Gatorade is consumed almost exclusively (over 90 percent in the Frank Sun Belt study) in conjunction with a strenuous physical activity. More specifically, 63 percent of Gatorade consumers say that they usually use the product in conjunction with a sports activity. *The 1983 Canadian Fitness Survey* reports that 53 percent of Canadians exercise at least three hours weekly, while the *Lite Sports Study* indicates that 44 percent of the U.S. population makes a similar claim. It is evident that a significant group of Canadian consumers exhibits one of the key behavioral traits associated with heavy Gatorade usage.

Another favorable indicator for Gatorade in the Canadian market is the level of consumption of 'good for you' beverages as represented by the juice market. Per capita, Canadians consume approximately 24.5 liters of juice per annum – the highest level in the world.

Senior management placed just one constraint on the development of a marketing strategy – the product formulation, aside from flavors, must remain identical to that in the United States.

The development of the proposal

Early Decisions

Early work on the proposal focused on the development of market and packaging data. 'Ontario represents 40 percent of the Canadian market,' said Lafortune, 'and we decided early that we would confine ourselves to that province for the first few years of operation. We estimate that each 1 percent of the Ontario grocery ready-to-serve juice drink market represents about $500,000 in revenue to the company. Category growth, excluding Gatorade, is increasing at 2 percent per year, and we estimate an inflation rate of 7 percent for the next few years.

'We also looked at packaging options for both liquid and instant. For liquid, we disqualified Tetra Pak for strategic reasons, and plastic as well as aluminum for technological and cost reasons.[1] That left glass as the best option. Based on U.S. experience and a review of the Canadian market, we concluded that the best alternatives for instant Gatorade were canisters and/or foil pouches.' Subsequently, the decision was made to use co-packers, which meant that no production investment would be required.

Target Audience(s)

It seemed clear to Lafortune that the primary target audience for Gatorade was physically active males 18–34, who accounted for 50 percent of the current U.S. sales and potential. The remaining 50 percent of U.S. sales and potential came from physically active females 18–34, physically active teens 13–17, and physically active males 35–44. Lafortune was undecided as to whether one or more of these three groups should be identified specifically as a secondary target audience, or whether he should focus his attention on the primary target audience and depend on a rub-off effect from this group to influence the other groups.

Distribution

Although Lafortune knew that the primary distribution thrust of a Gatorade introduction would be grocery stores, he was considering whether he should put emphasis on two other kinds of distribution, neither of which the Quaker organization was well equipped to service. One of these, of course, was convenience stores. Convenience chains are similar to grocery chains in that they both require selling at the head office to get 'listed' and selling effort at the individual store level to get stocking against that listing. Although the sales force currently did not service convenience stores, it might be possible to schedule two or three 'blitz' days during which the sales force could cover 70 percent of the 2,900 Ontario chain and major independent convenience stores once.

Alternatively, a summer student sales force could be created specifically to sell to convenience stores. Lafortune estimated that a student salesperson could make 25 calls per day and be put on the road for approximately $1,500 per month in salary and expenses for the four summer months, from May through August.

Lafortune was also interested in obtaining Gatorade distribution in sports stores, because he believed it would have a highly positive effect on the image of Gatorade for all of the possible target audiences. He saw the instant product form as the one appropriate to this type of distribution. He thought that if he were to develop this option, then he would probably have to negotiate an arrangement with a sporting goods distributor, which worked on a margin of 30 percent on cost. One of the things that concerned Lafortune about this option was that the distributor margin, combined with

---

[1] Tetra Pak was a patented package that provided long shelf life to the package contents. These packs were being used increasingly to package juices in 250-milliliter and 1-liter rectangular 'bricks.'

the 40–50 percent retail margin in sports outlets, was much higher than the 29 percent expected by grocery and convenience stores. This difference meant that it would be difficult to have the same product item in all three types of distribution.

Flavors, Product Formats, Pack Sizes, and Prices

Decisions had to be made also on flavors, product formats, pack sizes, and prices. Although Lafortune wanted to introduce all three Gatorade flavors because it would give the product much more shelf visibility, he was aware that this course of action could create some problems for the future. If sales for a particular flavor were low, then there was a high probability that the flavor would be delisted. Lafortune knew that if this occurred, it would be very difficult to get that flavor relisted at any future date.

A similar kind of situation held for product formats and pack sizes. Lafortune had decided tentatively that for grocery and convenience stores he should have no more than two or three liquid pack sizes, and no more than one instant pack size. He thought that he should consider no more than two sizes of instant Gatorade for sports outlets, should he decide to include them in his plan. Grocery and convenience store pack sizes, in particular, posed a problem. First, these outlets in Canada expected 29-percent margins on juice drink products, substantially higher than the 20 percent that was normal in the United States. Further, Gatorade would be subject to a 12-percent manufacturer's tax in Canada, a tax that was not levied in the United States.[2]

This suggested that, unless Quaker was willing to accept less than its traditional contribution rate of 45 percent on the selling price (including freight but before manufacturer's tax), Canadian retail prices would be substantially higher than those for equivalent product sizes in the U.S. However, product concept testing in Canada for a pack size comparable to the U.S. 32-ounce size produced intent-to-purchase figures for a $1.65 retail price that were comparable to northern U.S. data for the lower U.S. price. The $1.65 price represented a 40-percent premium over soft drinks and a 10-percent premium over fruit drinks.[3] The available cost date for various Gatorade packages are given in Exhibit 7. Although Lafortune did not believe that he had to select pack sizes identical to those of other products in the supermarket fruit-drink section, he did not think that he could ignore them either. He discovered that the most common glass pack sizes were 28 ounces, 1 liter (35.28 ounces), 40 ounces, and 48 ounces.[4] The predominant can pack size was 48 ounces, with the next most common size being 19 ounces. He was already aware that the most common pack sizes for soft drinks were 250 milliliter cans and 1 liter bottles.

Advertising and Merchandising Support

Annual Ontario advertising expenditures on the total juice drinks (including frozen) and nectars category was estimated at $3.9 million.

---

[2] The tax was not applicable to all components of the selling price. The effective rate was about 9 percent of the selling price.

[3] This comparison was based on shelf prices. In 1985, soft drinks and Gatorade were subject to a 7-percent Ontario sales tax.

[4] Canadian packaging regulations required that metric measurement appear on packaging. However, many manufacturers continued to put the ounce equivalent on the package as well. One fluid ounce is equal to 28.34 milliliters.

Exhibit 7

Variable Cost Data for Various Gatorade Packages[a]				
Type	Size[b]	Material, Direct Manufacturing, and Packaging Costs per 100 ml	Freight Costs per 100 ml	Probable Units per Case
Glass	1500 ml	$0.0485[c]	$0.0056	8
	1000 ml	0.0543	0.0056	12
	500 ml	0.0701	0.0056	24
	250 ml	0.0781	0.0056	24
Canister	520 g (7500 ml mixed)	0.0144	0.0003	12
	140 g (2000 ml mixed)	0.0193	0.0003	48
Foil	240 g (3400 ml mixed)	0.0163	0.0004	96
	60 g (850 ml mixed)	0.0372	0.0004	144

[a] Some costs have been changed to protect confidentiality.
[b] 907 ml = 32 oz = 1 qt (U.S. measure).
[c] Costs are approximately linear for sizes between those shown.

Within this broad category, juice drink expenditures were estimated to be $1.1 million. Lafortune thought that it would require an expenditure of 50 to 75 percent of this figure to get a share of voice sufficient to establish Gatorade in the market. He was not sure what proportion he should commit to TV relative to print. Further, he believed that this level of expenditure would be required for at least two years before it could be cut back to 25 to 35 percent of category expenditures.

He estimated that it would cost approximately $200,000 in the first year to get 70 to 75 percent distribution in grocery and convenience stores. A further $150,000 would be required in trade deals during the first year, together with $75,000–$100,000 in co-op advertising. Distribution, trade deal, and co-op advertising costs were expected to be close to 10 percent of company sales in future years. Consumer promotions to get trial were estimated to cost 10 percent of company sales for the first two years and fall to 5 percent in following years.

Lafortune believed that substantial effort should be put into public relations and sports marketing activities to create exposure for and awareness of Gatorade. He perceived a key objective to be the achievement of the same high visibility for Gatorade during NHL games as existed for NFL football. He did not have sufficient background to estimate closely what the costs of such a program might be. However, his preliminary estimate was in the range of $200,000 to $400,000 on a continuing basis. He estimated that one-time development costs for such activities as research, licenses, package development, and sales aids would total close to $300,000, and annual costs of a product manager would be about $50,000. Finally, his estimate for working capital was 11 percent of sales.

The Days Ahead

'We've done preliminary analysis on a lot of areas,' said Lafortune, 'and some decisions have been made that start to put some focus on the proposal. However, a great deal of work must still be done before we have a proposal which I will have confidence in taking to top management. At the same time, I'm encouraged by some very recent research we've done, which shows that 69 percent of physically active English

Canadians have already heard of Gatorade and are familiar with the basic product proposition.'

Source: This case was prepared by Paul Bandiera under the direction of Professor John R. Kennedy, The University of Western Ontario, as a basis for class discussion and is not designed to illustrate effective or ineffective handling of an administrative situation. The University of Western Ontario acknowledges the financial support of the Government of Canada through the Canadian Studies Directorate of the Department of Secretary of State. Although some data have been disguised, the relationships among them have been maintained. Copyright © The University of Western Ontario, 1987. Used with permission.

Required
Attempt to model the proposal given in the case.

17 | Modelling approaches – 2

17.1 Learning Objectives

When you have read this chapter you should be able to:

(a) understand more fully the role of modelling approaches;
(b) recognize and handle the problems of allowing for risk and uncertainty in carrying out evaluations;
(c) appreciate the contribution that non-financial modelling approaches – such as matrix models and Bonoma's MPA model – can make to evaluating marketing plans;
(d) see the applicability of programming approaches to the evaluation of marketing plans.

17.2 Introduction

In Chapter 16 we looked at the nature of models and modelling with particular reference to short-run financial modelling (via cost–volume–profit analysis) and long-run financial modelling (using investment appraisal methods). In general, little attention was paid to the problems of risk and uncertainty. These will be dealt with in this chapter.

In addition, matrix models of a non-financial type will be covered as an extension of the discussion in Chapter 9 above. For example, the directional policy matrix, multi-factor portfolio matrix, product positioning matrix and Bonoma's Marketing Performance Assessment (MPA) model will be discussed and illustrated.

We will also extend the discussion (see Chapter 1 above) on marketing experimentation and introduce aspects of programming and network analysis which can be used to evaluate marketing programmes.

17.3 Allowing for Risk and Uncertainty

In dealing with risk and uncertainty we will draw heavily from management science. Management science is a method or approach to management problem solving rather than a discipline within its own right. The various techniques of management science offer managers an analytical, objective, and (usually) quantitative basis for making better decisions.

The basic requirement in decision making is information and a major branch of management science is concerned with the provision of information under conditions of risk and uncertainty. This is the role of *decision theory*.

Information should preferably be in quantitative form, and this presupposes some means of measurement. Furthermore, the information presented should relate to the objective of the decision – it is easier to make the correct decision when one keeps in mind what one is trying to achieve. If there exists more than one objective the decision maker must balance one against the other by making a *trade-off*. For example, the decision maker may trade speed for quality in deciding on a particular means of distribution if this appears to reflect accurately the relative importance of multiple objectives.

Decisions are made in relation to objectives and they are well made if the objectives are achieved. However, doubts about the future mean that a choice can be wrong, and it also means that a single choice can have several possible outcomes. The sales of a new product, for instance, may be at any one of several levels estimated at the time of its launch. The systematic approach of decision theory allows good decisions to be made even in the presence of severe doubts about what the future may hold in store.

Views of the future are of four types:

1 *ignorance* - where the future is seen as a blank;
2 *assumed certainty* - which is a pretence, for all practical purposes, that the future is known exactly and estimates become deterministic;
3 *risk* - where it is not known exactly what will happen in the future but the various possibilities are weighed by their assumed probability of occurrence;
4 *uncertainty* - where a variety of outcomes is possible but probabilities cannot be assigned.

There is little that can be done in cases of ignorance, other than following a systematic approach and attempting to delay making the decision until further information has been gathered. In cases of certainty, of course, there is no such need for delay. This covers situations in which the decision maker has full knowledge.

In relation to decision making under conditions of risk and uncertainty the purpose of expressing an opinion about the likelihood of an event occurring is to facilitate the development of decision-making procedures that are explicit and consistent with the decision maker's beliefs. (See Illustration 17.1.)

Illustration 17.1

Lou Gerstner, the chief executive of IBM, when asked about his vision of the company said, 'The last thing IBM needs now is a vision for the future. What is required is to take control of the immediate problems before we can even consider what lies ahead'.

Allowing for Risk

Risk describes a situation in which there are a number of actions or strategies that may be taken, a number of conditions or events that may be experienced (known as *states of nature* because they are beyond the decision maker's control), and consequently a number of possible outcomes each of which will depend on a particular combination of strategy and state of nature.

In the risk situation *probability theory* is central in rational decision making. The probability of a particular outcome of an event is simply the proportion of times this outcome would occur if the event were repeated a great number of times. Thus the probability of the outcome 'heads' in tossing a coin is 0.5 since a large number of tosses would result in 50 per cent heads and 50 per cent tails.

By convention, probabilities follow certain rules, such as:

- the probability assigned to each possible future event must be a positive number between zero and unity, where zero represents an impossible event and unity represents a certain one;

- if a set of events is mutually exclusive (i.e. only one will come about) and exhaustive (i.e. covers all possible outcomes), then the total of the probabilities of the events must add to one.

The probability of an outcome is a measure of the certainty of that outcome. If, for instance, a sales manager is fairly confident that his division will be able to sell 10 000 units in the forthcoming period, he may accord a probability of 0.8 to this outcome (i.e. he is 80 per cent certain that 10 000 units will be sold). By simple deduction, there is a 20 per cent probability that the outcome will be something other than 10 000 units (i.e. 100 − 80 = 20 per cent).

A development of this approach gives rise to the concept of *expected value*. This results from the multiplying of each possible outcome of an event by the probability of that outcome occurring, and this gives a measure of the *pay-off* of each alternative. An example should make this clear: Company XYZ has two new marketable products but only sufficient resources to manufacture and market one of these. The relevant estimates of sales, costs, and profits are shown in Figure 17.1 for the various anticipated levels of sales activity.

FIGURE 17.1
Decision information

	Sales £	Costs £	Profit £	Probability	Expected value £
Product A	1,000	500	500	0.1	50
	1,250	600	650	0.4	260
	1,500	700	800	0.3	240
	1,750	800	950	0.2	190
				1.0	£740
Product B	2,000	800	1,200	0.2	240
	2,300	950	1,350	0.4	540
	2,500	1,050	1,450	0.2	290
	2,700	1,150	1,550	0.1	155
	3,000	1,300	1,700	0.1	170
				1.0	£1,395

The calculations are very simple. If sales of product A amount to £1,000, the associated costs – as shown above – are £500, and thus the profit is also £500. But there is only a probability of 0.1 that this outcome will eventuate, giving an *expected value* of £50 (i.e. £500 × 0.1).

This procedure is followed for the other possible outcomes of Product A sales, costs, and profits, and the expected values of each outcome summated to give an expected pay-off of £740. (This is nothing more than a weighted arithmetic average of the data given in Figure 17.1.)

In contrast, Product B has an expected pay-off of £1,395 and this choice is, therefore, the better one of the two, provided that profit is the desired objective, as measured by the pay-off computation.

Apart from the externally given economic and physical conditions surrounding a decision (i.e. the 'states of nature'), the decision maker's own attitudes towards the alternatives must also be taken into account. His scale of values will determine the *desirability* of each possible course of action, whereas the conventional prediction systems merely assign probabilities. Desirability has connotations of 'best' that are unrelated to profit and may be measured in terms of utility, thus:

Expected utility = (Probability of success × value of success) −
(Probability of failure × value of failure)

As a result of his sense of values the decision maker will have a general attitude towards risk that may cause him to act as either a *risk acceptor* or a *risk averter*. In the latter case the decision maker will tend to request more and more information before he attempts to make a decision, and this will often mean that decisions are made too late to be optimal, whereas the risk acceptor makes rapid decisions that may not be the correct ones.

Risk attitudes are one of four essential elements to be ascertained in any decision, these being:

1 What are the available courses of action?
2 What are the relevant states of nature?
3 What are the possible outcomes?
4 What is important to the decision maker?

Applying Risk Analysis

The application of simple risk analysis is best illustrated by means of an example. Let it be assumed that RST Ltd has two new products, A and B, but only has the resources to launch one of these. The relevant states of nature relate to competitive activity: no matter which product is launched, it may be assumed that the competition will:

1 do nothing; or
2 introduce a comparable product; or
3 introduce a superior product.

On the basis of past experience and current knowledge the management of RST Ltd attach probabilities of 0.25, 0.5 and 0.25 respectively to these states of nature. In the light of these alternative conditions the profit of each strategy can be shown in a *pay-off matrix* (Figure 17.2).

FIGURE 17.2
Pay-off matrix

Strategy	State of nature		
	Do nothing	Introduce comparable product	Introduce superior product
Launch A	£40,000	£30,000	£20,000
Launch B	£70,000	£20,000	£0

This matrix shows that if Product B is launched and a comparable competitive product is introduced a profit of £20,000 will be made, and so forth for the other five possible outcomes. The best decision would *appear* to be to introduce Product B and *hope* that competitive action does not change. But is this so?

By using the concept of expected value it is possible to calculate the expected profit (or pay-off) from each strategy by multiplying the probability of each outcome by the profit from that outcome. Thus, for strategy A (the introduction of Product A), the expected pay-off is given by:

$$(40,000 \times 0.25) + (30,000 \times 0.5) + (20,000 \times 0.25)$$

and is equal to £30,000.

Similarly, for strategy B the expected pay-off is:

$$(70,000 \times 0.25) + (20,000 \times 0.5) + (0 \times 0.25)$$

which equals £27,500.

This analysis clearly shows that strategy A is to be preferred as it has a larger expected profit or pay-off. It is vital, however, that the distinction between the *expected* pay-off and the *most probable* pay-off is understood and attention focused on the former rather than the latter. The most probable pay-off for strategy A is that with the competitive introduction of a comparable product, which has a probability of 0.5 and a profit estimated at £30,000. The most probable pay-off for strategy B has the same state of nature, and a profit estimate of £20,000. But the most probable outcome cannot be used as the basis for decision making because it ignores the other possible outcomes. It is thought to be 50 per cent certain that a comparable competitive product will be launched which means that it is also 50 per cent *uncertain* that this will occur and allowance for this eventuality should accordingly be made. The use of expected pay-off allows for this.

From the information contained in the above example a *decision tree* can be constructed as in Figure 17.3.

FIGURE 17.3
Decision tree

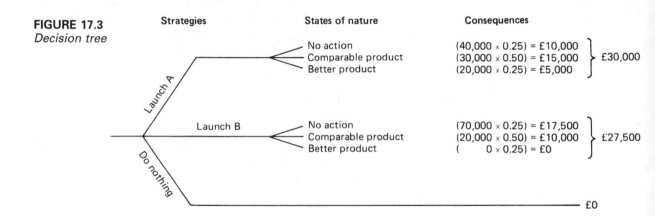

Strategies	States of nature	Consequences	
Launch A	No action	(40,000 × 0.25) = £10,000	
	Comparable product	(30,000 × 0.50) = £15,000	£30,000
	Better product	(20,000 × 0.25) = £5,000	
Launch B	No action	(70,000 × 0.25) = £17,500	
	Comparable product	(20,000 × 0.50) = £10,000	£27,500
	Better product	(0 × 0.25) = £0	
Do nothing			£0

Strategies and states of nature are represented by the branches of the decision tree, and at each fork there are as many branches as there are identified possibilities. Only if all of the possible courses of action have been observed and included will the tree be complete. For each alternative combination of strategy and state of nature the outcome can be computed, and the expected pay-off for each strategy derived.

A decision tree is a diagrammatic representation of the relationships between decisions, states of nature, and pay-offs (or outcomes) that helps in structuring problems in a way that allows risk to be assessed at each stage. Further examples will show how a decision tree can be used. Imagine a research project that is in progress with a view to developing a new product for commercial launch. There are several aspects to this issue.

1 the project may be aborted or it may be allowed to continue;
2 if it is continued it may or may not result in a potentially marketable new product;
3 if it does result in a marketable product the organization may choose to launch it immediately or to postpone the launch;
4 competitors may or may not be able to match the organization's endeavours.

Figure 17.4 spells out these aspects and specifies the two major decisions that need to be made. (The squares represent points at which decisions need to be made, while the circles represent subsequent events.) It can be seen that each decision, combined with the states of nature that are assumed to prevail, produces distinct outcomes.

FIGURE 17.4
A basic decision tree

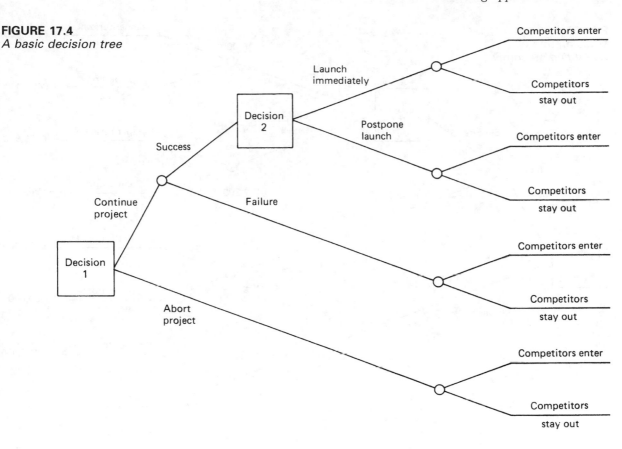

The next step is to introduce quantitative data, so let us assume the following:

1 it will cost an estimated £50,000 to continue the project (which is itself probabilistic);
2 if the company decides to postpone the launch of the product (assuming the project is successful) and competitors enter the market there will be a loss of current business amounting to £125,000;
3 if the project is successful and an immediate launch is undertaken, the company will generate incremental cash flows of £450,000 if competitors stay out of the market but only £250,000 if competitors enter the market.

These figures are shown at the end of each branch of the decision tree in Figure 17.5. We now need to incorporate the probabilities of the events leading to the various possible outcomes, and these are also shown in Figure 17.5. By working back from the right-hand side of the decision tree it is a simple matter to compute expected values. Taking the branch dealing with the immediate launch of a successful project as an example, the expected value is derived as follows:

£250,000 × 0.7 = £175,000
£450,000 × 0.3 = £135,000

Expected value   £310,000

The figures show that an immediate launch is the better alternative if the project is successful than is postponing it (which has an expected value of − £112,500). But this only gives part of the picture, so the expected values need to be worked through to the next event in the tree (moving across from right to left). The logic in doing this is straightforward: if the project is successful and the launch is

FIGURE 17.5
*Decision tree with
quantified outcomes*

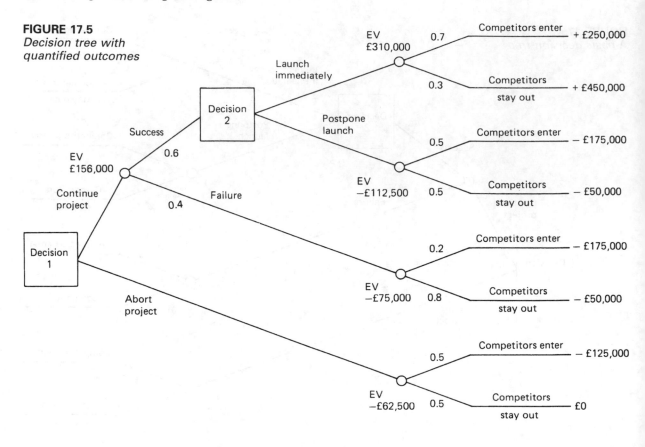

immediate there will be a larger pay-off than if the launch is postponed, so the latter branch can now be ignored. This gives an expected value for continuing the project of £156,000 calculated thus:

$$£310,000 \times 0.6 = £186,000$$
$$-£75,000 \times 0.4 = -£30,000$$

Expected value   £156,000

A comparison of this pay-off with the expected value of aborting the project (-£62,500) shows the desirability of continuing with the project.

Risk analysis is applicable to most pricing decisions, such as the situation in which a company can adopt one of three pricing policies for a new product:

1 skimming pricing – P_1;
2 intermediate pricing – P_2;
3 penetration pricing – P_3;

and in which three estimates of demand are available:

1 optimistic forecast – Q_1;
2 most probable demand – Q_2;
3 pessimistic forecast – Q_3;

and in which two sizes of plant are available:
1 small plant – F_1;
2 large plant – F_2.

FIGURE 17.6
Pricing decision tree

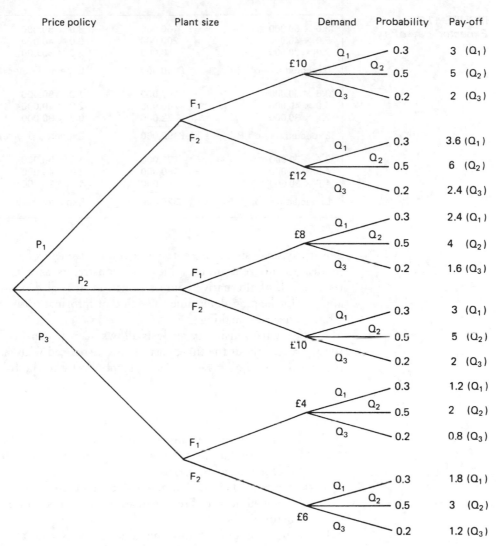

The various interrelationships of price, demand and capacity are illustrated in a decision tree format in Figure 17.6.

The pay-off is computed by taking the probability of each level of demand and multiplying it by the forecast level of demand, and then multiplying this by the price. Thus for a penetration pricing policy (P_3) with a small factory (F_1) and a pessimistic sales forecast (Q_3), the pay-off is given by multiplying the P_3F_1 price of £4 by 0.2, which is the probability of Q_3 occurring, and expressing this in terms of Q_3. If values of 50 000, 40 000 and 30 000 are ascribed to Q_1, Q_2, and Q_3, the pay-off column in Figure 17.6 becomes Figure 17.7.

Clearly strategy P_1F_2 has the highest expected pay-off because it has the highest price, but each expected pay-off must be related to objectives in order to select the most appropriate in a given situation.

There are several alternatives to the basic decision tree approach to allowing for risk which can be employed. It is not possible within the limits of this volume to cover them, but there is space to refer to *sensitivity analysis*. In its applied organizational setting this has been broadly defined by Rappaport (1967, p. 441) as:

> ... a study to determine the responsiveness of the conclusions of an analysis to changes or errors in parameter values used in the analysis.

FIGURE 17.7
Expected pay-offs

3.0 × 50,000	=	150,000	3.0 × 50,000	=	150,000
5.0 × 40,000	=	200,000	5.0 × 40,000	=	200,000
2.0 × 30,000	=	60,000	2.0 × 30,000	=	60,000
Expected pay-off P_1F_1		£410,000	Expected pay-off P_2F_2		£410,000
3.6 × 50,000	=	180,000	1.2 × 50,000	=	60,000
6.0 × 40,000	=	240,000	2.0 × 40,000	=	80,000
2.4 × 30,000	=	72,000	0.8 × 30,000	=	24,000
Expected pay-off P_1F_2		£492,000	Expected pay-off P_3F_1		£164,000
2.4 × 50,000	=	120,000	1.8 × 50,000	=	90,000
4.0 × 40,000	=	160,000	3.0 × 40,000	=	120,000
1.6 × 30,000	=	48,000	1.2 × 30,000	=	36,000
Expected pay-off P_2F_1		£328,000	Expected pay-off P_3F_2		£246,000

Sensitivity analysis seeks to test the responsiveness of outcomes from decision models to different input values and constraints as a basis for appraising the relative risk of alternative courses of action. It is also possible to use sensitivity analysis for helping determine the value of information in addition to its role in strategic decision making.

In effect what sensitivity analysis allows management to do is to experiment in the abstract without the time, cost or risk associated with experimenting with the organization itself. This can be seen symbolically in the following expression:

$$V = f(X,Y)$$

where:

V = a measure of the value of the decision that is to be made;

X = the set of variables that can be directly regulated by the decision-maker (i.e. the decision variables);

Y = the set of factors (variable or constant) that affects outcomes but which is not subject to direct regulation by the decision maker (i.e. the states of nature);

f = the functional relationship amongst V, X and Y.

One can manipulate any element within X or Y and see the consequent impact on V.

Reference has been made in earlier chapters of this book to balancing the cost and value of information. The broad picture is given in Figure 17.8 from which it will be seen that the optimum amount of information in a given situation (OM) is to be found when the difference between the value and cost curves is greatest. For a number of reasons (including overload) the value of information starts to decline as more is made available whereas the cost of providing information increases at an accelerating rate as more is made available (due to increasing accuracy, faster transmission, etc.).

In operational terms how can we assess the value of information? We can readily grasp the principle that by evaluating the consequences of a particular decision based on a given amount of information on the one hand, and then evaluating the consequences of the same decision made with additional information on the other, the difference (in consequences) reflects the value of the extra information. This value gives the maximum sum that should be spent on generating the extra information. To apply this principle requires that we:

1 enumerate the possible outcomes of future information collection efforts;
2 compute the probabilities of these outcomes;
3 indicate how the information will change the decision maker's view of this choice.

These are demanding requirements!

FIGURE 17.8
Cost and value of information

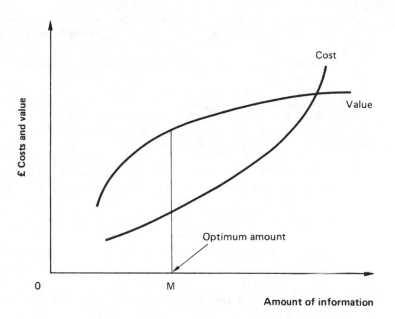

Allowing for Uncertainty

Uncertainty arises from a lack of previous experience and knowledge. This results in the decision maker's inability to assign probabilities to the elements within alternative strategies.

Inevitably decision making under conditions of uncertainty is more complicated than is the case under risk conditions. In fact, there is no single *best* criterion (such as expected pay-off) that should be used in selecting a strategy. Of the various available techniques company policy or the decision maker's attitude will determine that which is selected. Four possible criteria are given below.

1 Maximin – Criterion of Pessimism

The assumption underlying this technique is that the worst outcome will always come about and the decision maker should therefore select the largest minimum pay-off. Referring back to Figure 17.2, this would mean that strategy A should be adopted; the worst outcome for A is £20,000 and the worst for strategy B is £0 which means that strategy A maximizes the minimum – hence maximin. The philosophy is that the actual outcome can only be an improvement in the majority of instances – the probabilities accorded to strategy A suggest that there is a 75 per cent chance that a better result than £20,000 will be obtained and a 25 per cent chance of its being £20,000.

2 Maximax – Criterion of Optimism

This is the opposite of maximin and is based on the assumption that the best pay-off will result from the selected strategy. Referring again to Figure 17.2, the highest pay-offs are £40,000 and £70,000 for A and B respectively. Strategy B has the highest maximum pay-off and will be selected under the maximax criterion.

3 Criterion of Regret

This criterion is based on the fact that, having selected a strategy that does not turn out to be the best one, the decision maker will regret not having chosen another strategy when he had the opportunity.

Thus, if strategy B had been adopted (see Figure 17.9) on the maximax assumption that competitors would do nothing, and competitors actually did nothing, there would be no regret; but if strategy A had been selected the company would have lost £70,000 – £40,000 = £30,000. This measures the *regret* and the aim of the regret criterion is to minimize the maximum possible regret. A regret matrix (Figure 17.9) can be constructed on the above basis.

FIGURE 17.9
Regret matrix

Strategy	State of nature		
	Do nothing	Introduce comparable product	Introduce superior product
Launch A	£30,000	£0	£0
Launch B	£0	£10,000	£20,000

The maximum regret is, for strategy A, £30,000, and for strategy B £20,000. The choice is therefore B if the maximum regret is to be minimized.

4 Criterion of Rationality – Laplace Criterion

The assumption behind this criterion is that, since the probabilities of the various states of nature are not known, each state of nature is equally likely. The expected pay-off from each strategy is then calculated and the one with the largest expected pay-off selected.

For strategy A the expected pay-off under this criterion is:

$$(40,000 \times 0.33) + (30,000 \times 0.33) + (20,000 \times 0.33)$$

which equals £30,000; and for strategy B it is:

$$(70,000 \times 0.33) + (20,000 \times 0.33) + (0 \times 0.33)$$

which is also equal to £30,000.

By chance neither strategy in this example is preferable under this criterion, with the result that the choice must be made on another basis (e.g. in terms of desirability) or under another criterion (e.g. minimax).

Under conditions of risk or uncertainty the decision may appear to be to select one of the available courses of action or to accept none of them. However, another alternative is to postpone the decision and gather more information to aid in the selection process.

Perfect information is rarely available, so the decision maker must be satisfied with imperfect data which will reduce even if it does not eliminate his uncertainty. But there comes a point when it is unnecessary or pointless collecting further information, and at this point a decision must be made. An increasingly popular approach to determining this point is given by the Bayesian approach to statistical decision theory.

The theory of Bayesian inference is one that provides the basic rules whereby one set of probabilities can be mathematically (i.e. logically) determined from another. For example, the probability of heads in tossing a coin is 0.5, and Bayesian inference puts the probability of there being 10 heads in a row as 0.5^{10} (about 0.001). Bayesian inference is not restricted to accepting the input of observed data only: it will also accept the decision maker's subjective probabilities.

The most common form of Bayesian inference is prior-posterior analysis which involves the derivation of probabilities posterior to evidence by reweighing prior probabilities according to likelihoods indicated by this evidence. This procedure is an important one. However, since it is beyond the scope of this book to present a detailed exposition of Bayes' theorem the interested reader is referred to Day (1964).

In general the benefits of decision theory are that it requires the decision-making manager to make his uncertainties and other judgments explicit in such a way that they can be incorporated into a formal analysis that will lead to the best decisions being made. This process need not be time consuming, but it does prevent the hurried selection of the most obvious course of action and encourages creative thinking in seeking new solutions to problems.

This is the best way to determine the value of information prior to carrying out research. It differs from traditional statistical techniques by allowing the assignment of numerical probabilities to *unique* rather than to repetitive events, with probabilities being subjectively determined by the decision maker. For example, in relation to a new product launch, Bayesian analysis argues that the manager has some idea of how well it will do based on his experience with other products, and that these expectations can be translated into quantitative terms by assigning probabilities to the various sales levels that may be achieved. The key concept is the 'opportunity loss' which represents either:

1 the actual financial loss due to the new product failing to reach its break-even sales volume; or
2 the potential loss of profit from failing to introduce the product when sales would have been profitable.

In Figure 17.10 the probabilities of the expected sales levels are shown in columns (1) and (2), and the profit/loss consequences are shown in column (3) with the break-even point being 1 400 000. At a sales level of 1 800 000 a profit of £450,000 is expected, and the opportunity *loss of not* introducing the product (if this level of sales could be achieved) is £450,000 (i.e. the profit of launching the product is foregone by not launching it). The *expected* opportunity loss is given by the product of the estimated probability and the opportunity loss. For a sales level of 1 800 000 the expected loss is (0.10 × £450,000) = £45,000. The same analysis can be applied to all the other possible sales levels as shown in columns (4) to (7). The sums of columns (6) and (7) show the overall expected opportunity loss of each course of action – introduce the product on the one hand, or do not introduce it on the other. Since the 'introduce' choice has the lowest expected opportunity loss it should be the chosen course of action, and £67,500 is the maximum value of research expenditure.

FIGURE 17.10
Bayesian analysis for product launch

Unit sales (1)	Estimated probability (2)	Profit/ loss (3)	Opportunity loss Introduced (4)	Opportunity loss Not introduced (5)	Expected opportunity loss Introduced (6)	Expected opportunity loss Not introduced (7)
1,800,000	0.10	450,000	0	450,000	0	45,000
1,600,000	0.25	200,000	0	200,000	0	50,000
1,400,000	0.35	0	0	0	0	0
1,200,000	0.15	−150,000	150,000	0	22,500	0
1,000,000	0.10	−250,000	250,000	0	25,000	0
800,000	0.05	−400,000	400,000	0	20,000	0
Totals	1.00				£67,500	£95,000

Although analytical methods can be applied to the evaluation of risk and uncertainty, management may prefer to take other courses of action to reduce risk and uncertainty. Perhaps the best method is to increase the information available to the decision maker prior to his making a decision. For instance, marketing research can supply further information prior to new product launches via product testing or test marketing.

Alternatively, the scale of operations may be increased, or product diversification pursued. Figure 17.11 illustrates the case of two products, with Product A having a seasonal demand pattern that is the opposite of the pattern of Product B.

FIGURE 17.11
Diversified products

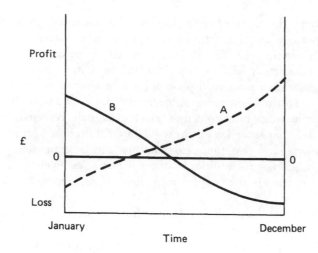

FIGURE 17.12
*Combined
profitability*

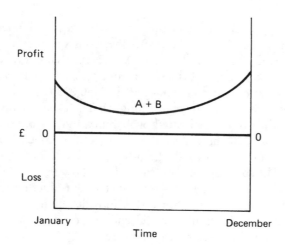

But in combination Figure 17.12 shows that the overall result is one of continuous profitability, whereas either product in isolation would result in a loss during part of its demand cycle.

17.4 MATRIX MODELS

A number of analytical matrix models were discussed in Chapters 9 and 10 above. In this section we will focus on three available models: the directional policy matrix, the multifactor portfolio matrix, and the product positioning matrix.

**Directional
Policy Matrix**

This was developed to help in identifying:

1 the principal criteria by which a business unit's prospects may be assessed:
2 the criteria by which an enterprise's position in a particular market may be evaluated.

The criteria that emerge are useful in defining *business sector prospects* on the one hand, and the *enterprise's competitive capabilities* on the other. These can be used to label the axes of the matrix itself, as shown in Figure 9.7 (see p. 317).

There are nine cells in this matrix. On the x axis business sector prospects increase in attractiveness as one moves from left to right. The strength of the enterprise's competitive capabilities increases as one moves down the scale on the y axis. Locating an enterprise in any cell of the matrix implies different strategic actions, although the boundaries between cells are less precise than this might suggest: it is more helpful to consider zones rather than cells – even though the zones may be of irregular shapes. Strategies appropriate to the zones shown in Figure 9.7 are (after Cohen (1988), pp. 36–7):

- leader – allocate major resources to the product group;
- try harder – acceptable in the short run but may be vulnerable over the longer run;
- double or quit – major future sources of competitive advantage and profitability should be developed from this zone;
- growth – sufficient resources should be allocated to match market growth;
- custodial – maximize cash generation without any further commitment of resources;
- cash generator – a cash generator with little further need for finance or expansion;
- phased withdrawal – resources can be reallocated to better uses by withdrawing gradually;
- divest – withdraw immediately and redeploy resources elsewhere.

Among the criteria by which business sector prospects might be assessed are:

- market growth rate
  - market growth is needed if profits are to grow;
- market quality, reflected in such factors as
  - whether profitability is high and stable,
  - whether or not margins can be maintained when demand falls below the level of normal capacity,
  - whether the market is supplied by a few or by many enterprises,
  - whether a small group of powerful consumers dominates the market,
  - whether the market offering is free from risks of substitution;
- environmental aspects (e.g. regulations applying to distribution, marketing, or manufacturing).

The criteria for assessing an enterprise's competitive capabilities include:

- its market position (usually specified in terms of market share);
- production capability (including location, number of plants, capacity, access to supplies, technological state of facilities);
- product R & D (as a complete technological package to cover product range, quality, developments in applications, competence of technical service).

It is probably most beneficial if the enterprise in question reviews its competitive capabilities relative to those of significant competitors. Ratings are best determined by a team of relevant personnel attempting to reach a consensus. Alternatively, a more complex set of weights (see multifactor portfolio matrix below) may need to be devised when some criteria (or critical success factors) are deemed to be more important than others.

Multifactor Portfolio Matrix

This was developed jointly by General Electric and the consulting firm of McKinsey & Co in order to overcome the limitations of the BCG's growth-share matrix. Like the directional policy matrix it has nine cells with the axes relating to similar notions: industry attractiveness (rather than business sector prospects) and business strengths (rather than the enterprise's competitive capabilities). Figure 9.6 (see p. 316) illustrates the multifactor portfolio matrix. There are three zones dealing with strategies relating to:

- invest;
- manage selectively for earnings;
- harvest or divest;

and these are more clearly defined than are the zones within the directional policy matrix.

Criteria that might be used in establishing industry attractiveness include:

- market size;
- size of key segments;
- market growth rate;
- diversity of market;
- demand seasonality;
- demand cyclicity;
- sensitivity of market to price;
- opportunities;
- competitive structure;
- entry and exit barriers;
- extent of integration;
- degree of concentration;
- bargaining power of suppliers;
- bargaining power of distributors;
- capital intensity;
- capacity utilization;
- raw material availability;
- inflation vulnerability;
- environmental aspects;
- profitability;
- value added.

Measures that reflect business strength include:

- market share;
- enterprise (or SBU) growth rate;
- breadth of product line;
- distributive effectiveness;
- sales effectiveness;
- price competitiveness;
- promotional effectiveness;
- facilities (location, age, capacity, etc.);
- experience curve effects;
- investment utilization;
- raw material cost;
- relative product quality;
- R & D capabilities;
- personnel skills;
- relative market position;
- relative profitability;
- value added.

An enterprise can select whichever measures of industry attractiveness or business strength best suit its circumstances when evaluating plans. The relative importance weightings of the selected measures will need to be determined in order to locate a plan within the matrix. This can be carried out in the following way (after Cohen (1988), pp. 32–5).

1 Identify the major measures of industry attractiveness that are applicable. Let us suppose these are:

- size of market;
- growth of market;
- ease of entry;
- favourable position in PLC.

2 Weights must be assigned to the chosen measures to indicate their relative importance. If the weightings are 0.30, 0.30 ,0.25 and 0.15 respectively for the criteria shown in 1 above we can see the overall picture in Figure 17.13.

FIGURE 17.13
Weighted score for industry attractiveness

Industry attractiveness criteria	Relative importance weightings	Point ratings	Weighted scores
Size of market	0.30	9	2.70
Growth of market	0.30	4.5	1.35
Ease of entry	0.25	9	2.25
Favourable PLC position	0.15	0	0
Total weighted score			6.30

3 Figure 17.13 also shows the points that might be awarded to any given marketing plan in relation to the extent to which the selected criteria are seen to be met by that plan. Points might be awarded on the following basis:

- very attractive   9
- attractive   7
- fair   4.5
- unattractive   3
- very unattractive   0

4 A weighted score relating to industry attractiveness can be calculated for each alternative marketing plan: this is equal to 6.30 for the plan covered by Figure 17.13.

5 Steps 1–4 need to be repeated for business strength in relation to each marketing plan. Let us assume that the applicable criteria are image, productivity, product synergy, and price competitiveness, with weights of 0.40, 0.30, 0.15 and 0.15 respectively. The assessment of points to indicate the extent to which any given plan meets the applicable criteria would be carried out as outlined in 3 above, with the results being shown in Figure 17.14.

6 Having calculated weighted scores of 6.30 for industry attractiveness and 6.825 for business strength it is now possible to locate these scores within the matrix.

FIGURE 17.14
Weighted score for business strength

Business strength criteria	Relative importance weightings	Point ratings	Weighted scores
Image	0.40	9	3.60
Productivity	0.30	7	2.10
Product synergy	0.15	3	0.45
Price competitiveness	0.15	4.5	0.675
Total weighted score			6.825

Using the scales shown in Figure 9.6 it is apparent that the coordinates interesect in the top left-hand cell within the *invest* zone of the matrix.

7 Similar plots can be made for alternative marketing plans and an appropriate choice made in accordance with strategic priorities.

It will be evident that the weightings and scoring within this procedure involves considerable subjective judgement. This makes it important that all underlying assumptions should be made explicit to facilitate peer review.

Product Positioning Matrix

Among the many other available matrix approaches that can be used for evaluating marketing programmes is that of Wind and Claycamp (1976). This focuses on product line strategy and is comprehensive in that it deals with all the major measures (sales, market share, profitability) that are essential in positioning products by segment.

The first step involves defining:

1 the product (including its subcategories at both the enterprise and industry levels);
2 the strategic market for the product and the key segments within it;
3 the appropriate forms of measurement (e.g. sales in value or volume terms, sales per capita, quarterly time periods).

Following the establishing of suitable definitions the analysis can be undertaken. This will involve the generation of:

• Sales position for the given product within the strategic market, showing enterprise and industry sales along with an indication of when the product is expected to reach each stage within the product life cycle. For this purpose the PLC can be characterized as having three stages:
  – growth (when sales are expected to increase by more than 10 per cent year on year);
  – maturity (where sales are expected to increase in the range of 0–10 per cent year on year);
  – decline (when sales growth is expected to be negative).
• Market share position which can also be characterized by means of a set of decision rules such as:
  – marginal (if market share is likely to be less than 10 per cent).
  – average (if market share is likely to be within the range 10–24 per cent).
  – leading (if market share is expected to be over 25 per cent).
• Profit position, which can be characterized by distinguishing among:
  – above par (where profit from a given segment is expected to be greater than from the rest of the enterprise's business when expressed as a rate of return);
  – par (where the profitability expected from the segment is comparable to that from other segments);
  – below par (where the profitability of the segment is expected to fall below that of other segments).

The expectations relating to product sales, industry sales, market share, and profitability can then be plotted on to the comprehensive product evaluation matrix as shown in Figure 17.15.

It is possible to plot the anticipated positions of the product in question under different assumptions regarding sales, market share and profitability. A time dimension can be built in as suggested in Figure 17.15.

FIGURE 17.15
Product positioning matrix

Industry sales	Profitability / Market share	Decline Below par	Decline Par	Decline Above par	Maturity Below par	Maturity Par	Maturity Above par	Growth Below par	Growth Par	Growth Above par
Growth	Leading									
Growth	Average									
Growth	Marginal									
Maturity	Leading							B_{19X2}		
Maturity	Average						B^1_{19X2}	B_{19X1}	B^2_{19X2}	
Maturity	Marginal									
Decline	Leading									
Decline	Average	A_{19X1}			A^1_{19X2}					
Decline	Marginal	A_{19X2}		A^2_{19X2}						

SOURCE: Adapted from Wind and Claycamp (1976)

This figure shows for two products – A and B – the current position (i.e. A as at 19X1 and B as at 19X1) along with projections into the future. Such projections are built up from estimates of each constituent element (sales, market share, profit outcome) for each alternative marketing programme. We can see, for example, that Product A is a poor performer as at 19X1: it is in a declining industry with declining sales, has only an average market share and is achieving a profit performance that is below par. If no change occurs it is anticipated that Product A's position will get worse. In an attempt to improve the position of Product A two alternative marketing plans are proposed: plan A^1 is predicted to reposition Product A in an improved situation in 19X2 by moving it from its 19X1 position to a position offering stable sales and profits at par, although it is not expected that the decline in industry sales can be changed.

An alternative to plan A^1 is given by plan A^2 which anticipates an improvement in the profit performance but a continuing decline in sales and also in market share between 19X1 and 19X2.

Product B is in a much stronger position in 19X1. It is increasing its sales level within a mature market, thereby increasing its market share but showing poor profit performance. If no changes occur in the marketing plan for B the expectation is that, by 19X2, it will have achieved a leading market position with profit performance continuing to be below par. Two alternative marketing plans are proposed for Product B. The first, B^1, will lead to a stable level of sales and an improvement in profit performance from below par to above par. Plan B^2 is expected to produce continuing growth and a better profit position.

For Product A management must consider the trade-off between a modest improvement in profit with an increase in sales, and a large improvement in profit with a decrease in sales. In the case of Product B the choice is between taking profits in the near future (plan B^2) or investing for the longer term in increased market share.

17.5 THE MARKETING PERFORMANCE ASSESSMENT MODEL

Bonoma and Clark (1988) set out to develop a means of assessing the performance of marketing programmes in a way that avoids the limitations of measures that focus narrowly on either economic issues or efficiency. They do this by relating programme results to management's expectations, thereby focusing on effectiveness via a measure of satisfaction. Efficiency is assessed by means of the effort that needs to be expended to achieve a given level of satisfaction. The effort comprises the skills that must be exercised by a marketing programme's managers and the support structures that are provided for the programme.

Finally, Bonoma and Clark allow for those factors that are beyond the enterprise's control but that affect the performance of the marketing programme – such as competitors' actions, changes within distribution channels or in legal, economic, or demographic variables. It is possible to determine programmes that succeed (or fail) on the basis of luck rather than effort by utilizing these factors.

In summary, they seek to offer an approach to marketing performance assessment that measures:

1 the degree to which a marketing programme satisfies strategic requirements;
2 the effort that is necessary to produce the satisfaction in 1, above;
3 the effect of uncontrollable variables on the programme.

The approach is operationalized via a testable model of *marketing performance assessment* (MPA) which is defined as the adjudged quality of marketing programmes, directed by strategy, as these programmes are executed in the market-place. The model seeks to combine elements of efficiency and effectiveness in assessing marketing performance. In addition it incorporates managers' judgements in an explicit way.

The motivation behind this work was a concern to identify whether a set of principles exists that explains 'quality marketing practice' (i.e. the *doing* of marketing in an effective and efficient way rather than just the *planning* of marketing). In part this motivation stemmed from the following dissatisfactions that Bonoma felt with the literature on marketing practice:

1 there is a widespread tendency to ignore the role of managers, hence their values, etc., which implies that all managers act in similar ways – something we know is not the case;
2 it is implicit in the advice offered to guide marketing practice that the causal link is strategy – causes – practice whereas there is good reason to believe that the reverse causal link exists (i.e. practice – causes – strategy) in some circumstances, which is akin to ex post-rationalization.

Bonoma conceives of marketing practice as an attempt by managers with particular skills (relating to organizing, allocating, interacting and monitoring), values and expectations to achieve specified results. The managers in question operate within an organizational context characterized by particular ways of doing things – whether through particular programmes, systems or policies – which collectively represent a structure for guiding marketing actions. In turn the organization is located within its environment, with its array of threats, opportunities and constraints, and the link between the organization and its environment is found via the marketing strategy of the organization.

These relationships are portrayed in Figure 17.16 which represents a rudimentary model of marketing implementation.

FIGURE 17.16
*A rudimentary model
of marketing
implementation*

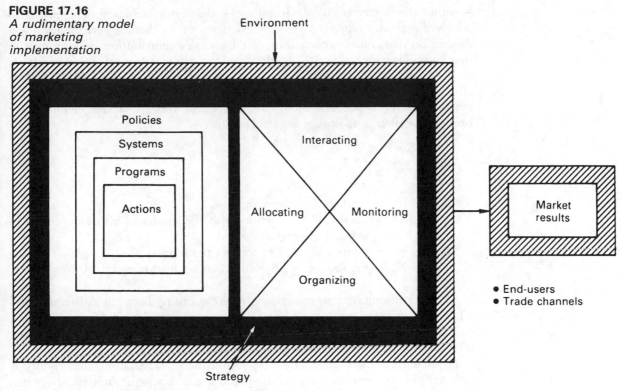

Quality practice = f (Marketplace results) = f (Environment, Strategy, Structure, and Skills)

SOURCE: **Bonoma and Clark (1988), p. 59**

Implementation

Notes to Figure 17.16

Structural variables	**Skills**
Actions relate to low-level execution issues (e.g. selling, NPD, distributor management, etc.).	*Interaction skills* focus on how managers deal with each other and with staff, customers, etc., in order to influence events.
Programs deal with integrated sets of actions (e.g. a specific marketing mix tailored to a particular segment).	*Allocation skills* relate to an ability to assign resources to tasks in an effective and efficient way.
Systems focus on formal controls and decision aids (e.g. decision-support systems, order processing systems, etc.).	*Monitoring skills* concern the design and use of feedback mechanisms to measure and control marketing activities.
Policies are broad rules of conduct promulgated by top management to guide marketing operations (e.g. segments to develop, technology to use in NPD).	*Organizing skills* deal with 'networking' behaviour by which a manager copes when the formal organization is not relevant.

Adapted from Bonoma and Crittenden (1988)

It is suggested by Figure 17.16 that:

Quality marketing practice = f (market results)
and
Market results = f (environment, strategy, structure, skills).

The combination of structure (in the form of programmes, systems and policies) and skills on the part of individual managers allows strategies to be implemented

– within the organization's environment – and results achieved. The extent to which the results represent an effective level of marketing performance will depend on managerial expectations, but Bonoma's contribution is significant in that he builds into his model the idea of effort expended in achieving results as well as the level of satisfaction that managers derive from the results of their efforts plus an explicit recognition that results are influenced by events outside the enterprise over which managers have no direct control. These elements are brought together in the following expression:

$$MP = \frac{SAT}{EFF} \times EXT$$

Where MP = marketing performance
SAT = managers' satisfaction with the results of effort expended in marketing programmes
EFF = effort expended to achieve the results
EXT = the impact of external events on marketing effort.

A variety of implications concerning the relationship between satisfaction and effort stem from the discussion above. These are summarized in Figure 17.17 and indicate how the MPA model predicts optimal marketing performance when a low level of effort is associated with a high level of satisfaction.

The determinants of satisfaction are seen as being expectations and results: if expectations are not met the consequences can be high satisfaction (when expectations are exceeded) or high dissatisfaction (when expectations are not realized). Figure 17.18 shows how the lowest level of satisfaction occurs when

FIGURE 17.17
Marketing performance: satisfaction and effort

		Management's perceived effort is	
		Low	High
Management's perceived satisfaction with results is		Maximum performance	Adequate performance
	High	Achieving the most results with the least effort, in complete contravention of the Protestant ethic. By definition, low effort is more easily achieved through, systematized or routinized procedures than through 'exception management'.	High satisfaction is the 'due consequence' of high effort. Effort, however, is costly, resulting in only adequate performance because much was expended to produce the results. Usually, effort is high when routinized systems and procedures cannot be delegated to do the job 'automatically'.
		Adequate performance	Low performance
	Low	There is little to be satisfied with, but little effort was expended in achieving the low performance. The lack of effort is seen as justifying or explaining the lack of performance.	Much effort was expended to little avail in terms of results. This is the worst possible state.

SOURCE: Bonoma and Clark (1988), p. 65

FIGURE 17.18
The determinants of satisfaction: results and expectations

| | Results from marketing efforts are | |
	Poor	**Good**
Management's expectations for results are	High dissatisfaction	Moderate satisfaction
High	Results achieved do not live up to expectations. Management is unhappy with performance given prior expectations and promise.	Results match goals – which, after all, is only what should have happened. There are no surprises, either pleasant or unpleasant.
	Moderate dissatisfaction	High satisfaction
Low	Poor results match the low expectations held for the program. The poor results are only moderately unsettling because of the low expectations.	Good results far exceed what was hoped or planned. Top management loves these kinds of surprises, despite its suspicion about being sandbagged.

SOURCE: Bonoma and Clark (1988), p. 66

FIGURE 17.19
The determinants of effort: management skills and marketing structures

| | Marketing structures are | |
	Flexible	**Rigid**
Management's marketing skills are	Maximum effort	Moderate effort
Strong	Weak structures cannot help routinize repetitive decisions; all problems receive 'custom' solutions from strongly skilled managers. While all get solved, the fixes are expensive and people-dependent.	Strong structures help routinize decisions, but strongly skilled managers come into conflict with structural constraints. Decisions with which the system cannot cope are handled on an exception basis by management. This is expensive but highly effective as long as systems and managers do not conflict destructively.
	Low effort	Minimal effort
Weak	Weak structures do not routinize well. Poorly skilled management does not or cannot exert itself to bridge the shortcomings between structural shortfalls and marketing requirements.	Strong structures routinize marketing decisions. Weakly skilled managers let the structure do the job, and are not compelled to intervene in its operation. This works superbly efficiently, and is effective as long as the environment remains stable.

SOURCE: Bonoma and Clark (1988), p. 70

poor results and high expectations interact, and the highest level of satisfaction arises when low expectations interact with good results.

Within any organization the quality of marketing skills will depend on the availability of suitably trained and motivated staff. The application of marketing skills through the organization's marketing structure (i.e. programmes, systems, policies) will determine the effort that is to be expended in order to achieve results. Skills might be strong or weak, and structures might be flexible or rigid. As shown in Figure 17.19, there are various combinations of skills and structure that determine the effort available, and the way in which that effort might be applied.

17.6 SOME OTHER APPROACHES TO MODELLING

In this section we will reinforce earlier coverage of marketing experimentation as a modelling approach by which marketing plans might be assessed. In addition we will look at programming and networking as further approaches to modelling by which alternative plans can be evaluated.

Marketing Experimentation

In an experiment attempts are made to identify all the factors that affect a particular independent variable, and these factors are then manipulated systematically (in so far as it is within the firm's power to do so) in order to isolate and measure their effects on the performance of the dependent variable (see pp. 15–18 above).

It is not possible to plan or control all the conditions in which an experiment is conducted; for example, the timing, location, and duration of an experiment can be predetermined, but it is necessary to measure such conditions as the weather and eliminate their effects from the results.

The independent variable that is the subject of marketing experimentation may be the demand for one of the company's various products, or one of the environmental factors it faces, and the dependent variable may be one of the company's objectives. Profit is a dependent variable of both the particular marketing strategy adopted and of the external conditions prevailing at the time that strategy is executed.

Because experiments are concerned with the deliberate manipulation of controllable variables (i.e. such variables as prices and advertising effort), a good deal more confidence can be placed in conclusions about the effects of such manipulation than if the effects of these changes are based purely on historical associations or vague projections rather than on the basis of experimentation.

Ideas for experiments can result from marketing cost studies. The following questions are fairly representative of those that can be answered as a result of experimentation (as we saw in Chapter 3):

1 By how much (if any) would the net profit contribution of the most profitable products be increased if there were an increase in specific marketing outlays, and how would such a change affect the strategy of competitors in terms of the stability of, say, market shares?
2 By how much (if any) would the net losses of unprofitable products be reduced if there were some decrease in specific marketing outlays?
3 By how much (if any) would the profit contribution of profitable products be affected by a change in the marketing effort applied to the unprofitable products, and vice versa, and what would be the effect on the total marketing system?
4 By how much (if any) would the total profit contribution be improved if some marketing effort were diverted to profitable territories or customer groups from unprofitable territorial and customer segments?

5 By how much (if any) would the net profit contribution be increased if there were a change in the method of distribution to small unprofitable accounts or if these accounts were eliminated?

Only by actually carrying out properly designed marketing experiments can management realistically predict with an acceptable degree of certainty the effects of changes in marketing expenditure on the level of sales and profit of each differentiated product, territory or customer segment in the multi-product company.

Experiments must be conducted under conditions that resemble the real-life conditions of the market-place insofar as this is possible. It is pointless, for example, carrying out an experiment to prove that the sale of £1's worth of Product X in Southampton through medium-sized retailers contributes more to profit than does the sale of £1's worth of Product Y through small retailers in Leeds, if the market for Product X is saturated and no reallocation of marketing resources can change the situation. This points to the danger of confusing what is happening now with what may happen in the future – ascertaining that Product X is more profitable than Product Y may be the right answer to the wrong question.

The style of question should be 'What will happen to the dependent variable in the future if the independent variables are manipulated now?' If the concern is with the allocation of sales effort, the aim of an experiment may be to show how changes in the total costs of each sales team can be related to changes in the level of sales. In such a simple case where only one type of marketing effort is being considered this effort should be reallocated to those sales segments where an additional unit of effort will yield the highest contribution to profits.

The experiment can be designed to show which sales segment produces the highest value when the following equation is applied to each:

(Additional sales – additional variable costs)/additional expenditure

If an additional budget allocation of £1,000 to the London sales force results in extra sales of £5,000 with additional variable costs amounting to £2,000, then the index of performance is $(5,000 - 2,000)/1,000 = 3$. It may happen that the same index computed for the Midlands sales force has a value of 4, in which case selling effort should be reallocated to the Midlands *provided* due consideration has been given to the expected level of future demand.

As a result of the high costs involved, experiments must usually be conducted with small samples of the relevant elements. This is generally valid so long as the samples are properly determined and representative. However, it is believed by some that marketing experimentation is not a feasible means by which information can be obtained as a basis for making important decisions.

There are certainly a lot of difficulties to be overcome in planning and executing experiments, and the need to keep special records and make repeated measurements is both expensive and time consuming. The risk is always present that the results of an experiment will not be of any value because they may not be statistically significant. A further risk is that even temporary and limited experimental variations in the marketing mix may damage sales and customer relationships both during and after the experiment.

Other problems that are involved in marketing experimentation include:

1 the measuring of short-term response when long-term response may be of greater relevance;
2 accurate measurements are difficult to obtain – apart from the high expense involved;
3 it is almost impossible to prevent some contamination of control units by test units since it is difficult to direct variations in the marketing mix solely to individual segments;

4 making experiments sufficiently realistic to be useful is hindered by such difficulties as the national media being less flexible than may be desired, and the fact that competitors may not react to local experimental action in the same way as they would to a national change in policy.

These problems and difficulties, while discouraging, are insufficient to discount completely the use of experimentation as a valuable means of obtaining information to increase the efficiency of marketing operations. Indeed, it is likely that the use of experimental techniques will become increasingly widespread, as has been the case with test marketing which is the best known form of experimentation in marketing.

Programming

Programming is a form of analytical modelling that is useful in allocation problems. The most widely-used technique is *linear programming* which aims to determine the optimum allocation of effort in a situation involving many interacting variables: in other words, it produces that solution which maximizes or minimizes a particular outcome in accordance with given constraints (e.g. how should sales effort be allocated among regions to maximize the level of sales subject to a maximum availability of 10 000 units of product per period, or what product mix should be sold – subject to demand – in order to give the maximum profit?). Other forms of programming include integer programming which is concerned with optimizing subject to the constraint that the solution must be in the form of whole numbers, and dynamic programming which is applicable to problems involving a series of interdependent decisions.

In all cases the marketing manager will be interested in making the best use of his limited resources and the constraints that exist will set the upper limit to the level of performance that is possible. The company cannot spend more on advertisng each product than it has in its advertising appropriation, thus:

$$a_1(W) + a_2(X) + a_3(Y) + a_4(Z) \leq A$$

Where: $\leq$ means 'equal to or less than'
        A is the total advertising appropriation
        $a_1(W)$ is the amount spent on advertising Product W
        $a_2(X)$ is the amount spent on advertising Product X
        $a_3(Y)$ is the amount spent on advertising Product Y
        $a_4(Z)$ is the amount spent on advertising Product Z

Similarly, a constraint exists in relation to every fixed budget or limited resource such as sales force time and warehouse space:

$$b_1(W) + b_2(X) + b_3(Y) + b_4(Z) \leq B$$

Where: B is the total available sales force time
        $b_1(W)$ is the time devoted to selling Product W, etc.

And:

$$c_1(W) + c_2(X) + c_3(Y) + c_4(Z) \leq C$$

Where: C equals the available warehouse space
        $c_1(W)$ is the space occupied by the inventory of Product W, etc.

The basis on which resources are allocated is the *marginal response*. If the expenditure on advertising of £100,000 produces sales amounting to £500,000 then the *average response* is 5/1; and if an increase in advertising expenditure of £1,000 produces additional sales totalling £10,000 this gives the measure of marginal response, which is equal to 10/1. Marginal response can thus be seen to be a measure of the value of opportunities presented.

If a company's advertising budget is set at £100,000 for a period, the optimal allocation to each of the company's products (A, B, and C) is given by equating the marginal responses because this gives the situation where it will not be beneficial to reallocate funds from one product to another. The requirement is to find the best solution to the equation:

$$a_1(A) + a_2(B) + a_3(C) = £100,000$$

where $a_1(A)$ is the advertising budget for product A, $a_2(B)$ for product B, and $a_2(C)$ for product C. This is given when:

$$d\ YA/d\ XA = d\ YB/d\ XB = d\ YC/d\ XC$$

where $d\ YA/d\ XA$ is the marginal response for product A measured as change in sales/change in advertising outlay, and so on for products B and C.

Linear programming must be applied in the absence of uncertainty, which means that uncertainty must be eliminated before variables are incorporated into a linear programme. Moreover, all the relationships of problems put into a linear programming format are assumed to be linear, and this may not apply under all possible conditions. For example, costs rarely rise in direct proportion to increases in sales. But even with this discrepancy linear programming is able to indicate the best direction for allocating resources to segments. This technique can be used to determine the best (i.e. optimal) solution to allocation decisions in the following circumstances:

1 where there is a clear, stated objective;
2 where feasible alternative courses of action are available;
3 where some inputs are limited (i.e. where constraints exist);
4 where 1 and 2 can be expressed as a series of linear equations or inequalities.

Let us consider the application of linear programming to a short-run product selection problem in which the decision maker's objective is to maximize profits. (This illustration is adapted from Dev (1980).) The products in question both offer positive contributions, and market demand is buoyant and likely to be sustained, but there are insufficient resources in prospect to allow for unlimited output. The problem is, therefore, to choose that allocation of available resources which leads to maximized profits.

Boam Brothers produce two products, M and S, and the following data reflects estimated prices, variable manufacturing costs, and contributions for each product for the following financial year:

		Product M			*Product S*
Selling price per unit		£22.20			£14.00
Less avoidable costs:					
Material A @ £1.00 per kilo					
12 kilos	12.00		4 kilos	4.00	
Labour @ £3.00 per hour					
1 hour	3.00		2 hours	6.00	
		15.00			10.00
Contribution per unit		£7.20			£4.00

It is assumed that the material and labour input requirements per unit and the contribution per unit are constant no matter what the level of output. This emphasizes the 'linear' aspect of linear programming.

Available inputs for next year are expected to be subject to possible constraints as suggested below:

Material A   1,200,000 kilos
Labour   400,000 hours

Fixed costs have been budgeted at £560,000. Assume that there are no opening or closing inventories of M, S or A, and that the selling price will stay constant irrespective of the level of sales.

Three possible situations can be envisaged:

1 *No resource constraints*, in which case Boam Brothers would produce as much of M and S as they are able (since both make a positive contribution).
2 *One resource constraint*, which we might take as material A being limited to 1,200,000 kilos. The solution is derived via the limiting factor: priority will be given to the product generating the highest contribution per unit of the limiting factor. We can see that this is product S from the following computation:

	Product M	Product S
Contribution per unit	£7.20	£4.00
Kilos of A per unit	12	4
Contribution per kilo of A	£0.60	£1.00

With the available amount of A the maximum output would be:

$$\frac{1,200,000}{12} = 100,000 \text{ units M; } \frac{1,200,000}{4} = 300,000 \text{ units S,}$$

and the maximum contribution would be:

M: 100,000 × £7.20 = £720,000 S: 300,000 × £4.00 = £1,200,000

(or 1,200,000 × £0.60 = £720,000 for M, and 1,200,000 × £1.00 = £1,200,000 for S).

The optimal choice is to produce 300,000 units of S and to give up producing M.

If, on the other hand, the scarce resource was labour hours the analysis would show the following:

	Product M	Product S
Contribution per unit	£7.20	£4.00
Labour hours per unit	1	2
Contribution per labour hour	£7.20	£2.00

The maximum output with 400,000 labour hours available would be:

$$\frac{400,000}{1} = 400,000 \text{ units M; } \frac{400,000}{2} = 200,000 \text{ units S}$$

and their respective contributions would be:

M: 400,000 × £7.20 = £2,880,000 S: 200,000 × £4.00 = £800,000.

The optimal output is to produce 400,000 units of M and no units of S.

3 *Two resource constraints*. This is a more difficult situation than 2 above since the material constraint favours production of S and the labour constraint favours the production of M. Four logical alternatives present themselves:

- produce M but no S;
- produce S but no M;
- produce some combination of M and S;
- produce neither M nor S.

The last alternative can be discarded because the contributions of both products are positive. A choice from the remaining alternatives can be made by formulating the problem as follows:

Maximize C = 7.20 Q_m + 4.00 Q_s

Subject to 12Q_m + 4 Q_s ≤ 1,200,000
Q_m + 2 Q_s ≤ 400,000
Q_m ≥ 0; Q_s ≥ 0
Where: C   = total contribution
Q_m = units of product M to be produced
Q_s = units or product S to be produced

The resource constraints are expressed as inequalities (i.e. 'less than or equal to') because it may not be necessary to use all 1,200,000 kilos of A or all 400,000 labour hours. In addition, a non-negativity constraint is included in the problem formulation to show that negative quantities of either M or S are not desired.

A solution can be derived either by algebraic or graphic methods (and can easily be handled by standard computer programs). Figure 17.20 shows a graphic approach to the solution. Units of M and S are shown on the x and y axes respectively, with line AB showing the maximum output of each under the labour constraint and line CD showing the maximum output of each under the material constraint. AB connects all the possible combinations of M and S within the labour constraint while CD connects all the combinations that are feasible within the material constraint. However, when we take both constraints into account the combinations of M and S within the triangles ACE and DBE are not feasible because they require more labour and material respectively than is available. This leaves OAED as a *feasible region* within which all the combinations of M and S can be achieved. But which is the best combination (in terms of maximizing profit)?

To determine the answer we need to move from quantities to relative contributions. Let us take a contribution figure of, say, £1,800,000. This can be generated by

$$\frac{1,800,000}{7.20} = 250,000 \text{ units M} \quad \text{or} \quad \frac{1,800,000}{4.00} = 450,000 \text{ units S.}$$

A curve showing these limits is superimposed on the graph in Figure 17.20 but none of the possibilities suggested by this line is within the feasible region. By moving back towards the origin with parallel contribution lines we arrive at point E which is within the feasible region, and this gives us the optimal combination of M and S. (The lines will be parallel because the contribution per unit of M and S will be the same regardless of the level of output.) It should be apparent that the closer the contribution line is to the origin the lower will be the total contribution (since the smaller will be the output), so the best point is at a tangent to the feasible region: point E.

The output levels at this point (from the graph) are 40 000 units of M and 180 000 units of S, with the following financial outcome:

FIGURE 17.20
*Graphical
presentation of
solution*

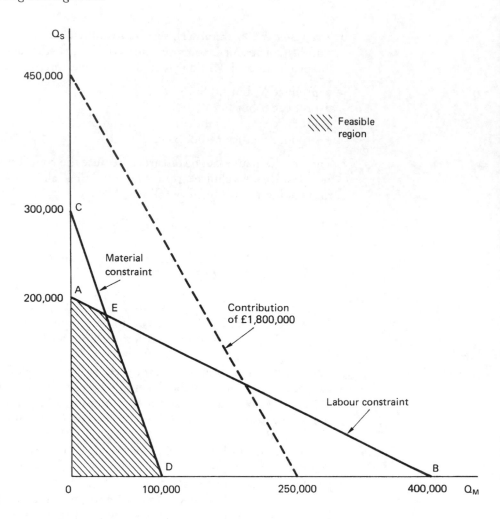

Contribution:

M	40,000 × £7.20	288,000
S	180,000 × £4.00	720,000
Total contribution		1,008,000
Fixed costs		560,000
Net profit		£448,000

You may care to manipulate the combination of M and S represented in this solution to see if any marginal change could improve the profit outcome. (For example, if five units less M were produced this would free 60 kilos of A and five hours of labour which could be used to produce two more units of S – with one hour of labour and 52 kilos of A left over. However, the contribution gained from S would only be £8.00, whereas the contribution lost by M would be £36.00, so it would be a suboptimal change.)

Networks

Network analysis is a method of problem solving that is based on analysing systematically and logically the relationships and time factors involved in carrying out a particular project. An appropriate project is any activity that can be considered as having a definable beginning and end, and this includes:

1 developing and launching a new product, which involves coordinating many complex and interrelated factors along with the need to be able to assess quickly

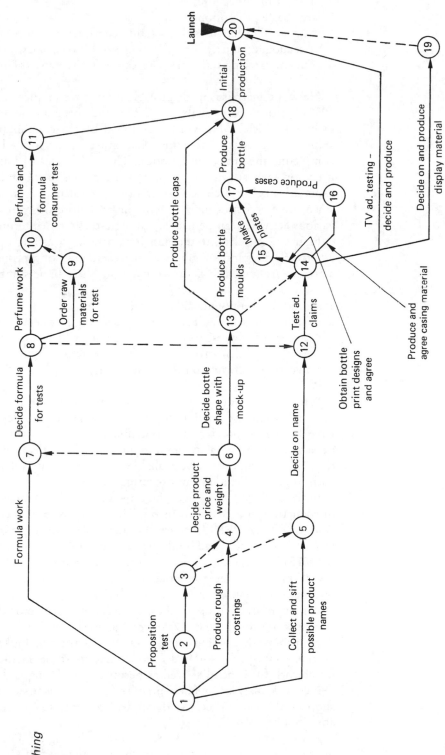

FIGURE 17.21
Network for launching a new product

the effects of changes in order to show where corrective action can best be taken;

2 product modification;

3 large-scale promotional campaigns;

4 many smaller activities that would benefit from a more rigorous approach, such as catalogue preparation; planning exhibitions, sales conferences, and training courses; carrying out market research studies; and the building of models.

Network analysis is made possible by two techniques developed during the late 1950s: critical path analysis (CPA) and programme evaluation and review technique (PERT). Networks developed by these techniques show the relationships among all the activities that must be performed in terms of time in completing the project in question. Three estimates of time are characteristically used for each activity – an optimistic, a pessimistic and a 'most likely'. The expected time for each activity can then be calculated on a probability basis, and since some activities must be completed before others can be commenced, the various activities can be laid out along a diagrammatic time-scale.

Figure 17.21 relates to the launching of a new washing-up liquid and shows that a network diagram is a graphical representation of a project, indicating how the activities are linked. It is drawn by using three basic symbols:

1 a solid line represents an *activity*;

2 a circle represents an *event* or intersection between activities;

3 a dotted line represents a *dummy* activity which is a means of showing logical relationships that are not physical activities – they may be thought of as transfers of information between events.

When the network is first drawn it is usual to omit duration times for reasons of simplicity in ascertaining the correct sequences and dependencies. After times have been incorporated it is possible to find the overall project time that is determined by those activities in sequence – the critical path. A certain amount of time ('float') will usually be available on those activities that are not on the critical path to permit flexibility in executing the project.

Basic networks only cover the time dimension, so further analysis requires the introduction of a cost dimension. This is the role of the PERT/cost technique. Both PERT and PERT/cost are designed for use in single large-scale projects, and resource allocation and multiproject scheduling (conveniently abbreviated to RAMPS) has been developed to deal with the problem of allocating resources to several projects when a number of projects are being undertaken simultaneously but there is a restriction in the availability of resources.

Although drawing up a valid network for a project is difficult, the procedure demands thorough and systematic analysis, and this discipline means that relationships that might otherwise have been overlooked are included. Furthermore, it specifies the decisions that must be made and thus provides a framework for control as well as permitting planning and scheduling.

Network analysis can fail in practice for such reasons as lack of top management support, the use of excessive detail, bad presentation, a failure to update, and the absence of feedback.

A different type of network is shown in Figure 17.22. This relates to the development of new products which was discussed in Chapter 11.

17.7 SUMMARY

Risk and uncertainty are inevitably present whenever choices need to be made among alternative claims on scarce resources. A variety of ways of accommodating

FIGURE 17.22
*New product
development network*

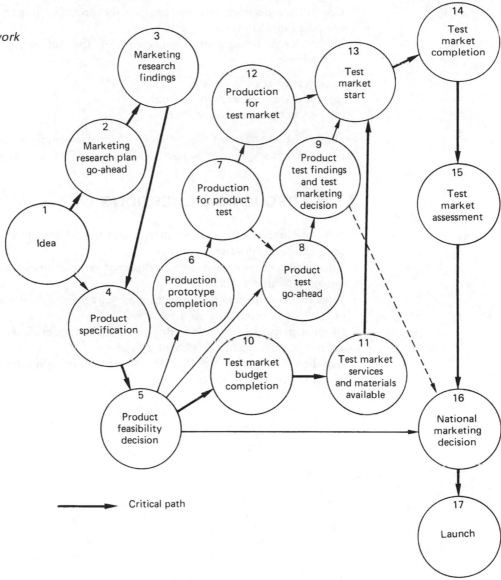

risk and uncertainty were discussed and illustrated, including probability analysis, sensitivity analysis, decision trees and, briefly, Bayesian analysis.

Some alternative matrix models were covered – the directional policy matrix, the multi-factor portfolio matrix, and the product positioning matrix – and their application to evaluating marketing plans illustrated.

Bonoma's MPA (marketing performance assessment) model warranted special attention as the most ambitious approach considered. It is still in its development phase, but holds great promise for the future. Finally, brief coverage was given to some further modelling approaches which can be used to test the robustness, feasibility and desirability of marketing plans: marketing experimentation, networking and programming.

17.8 EXERCISES

1 Illustrate with marketing examples the alternative views of the future which were mentioned on p.617.
2 List some of the *states of nature* which are relevant to a marketing project of your choice.

3 Construct a decision tree for gauging the probable impact of a promotional campaign in a competitive setting.
4 Undertake a comparative assessment of the following matrix modelling approaches:

   (a) directional policy matrix;
   (b) multi-factor portfolio matrix;
   (c) product positioning matrix.

5 Design a marketing experiment for assessing competing marketing programmes.

17.9 DISCUSSION QUESTIONS

1 Why is it necessary to allow for risk and uncertainty in evaluating marketing programme proposals?
2 What is the difference between an expected value of an event and the most likely outcome of that event?
3 What do you consider to be the main advantages and disadvantages of using one of the matrix modelling approaches?
4 In what principal ways does Bonoma's MPA model differ from other matrix approaches covered in this chapter?
5 Are there limits to the applicability of programming methods in the evaluation of marketing programmes?

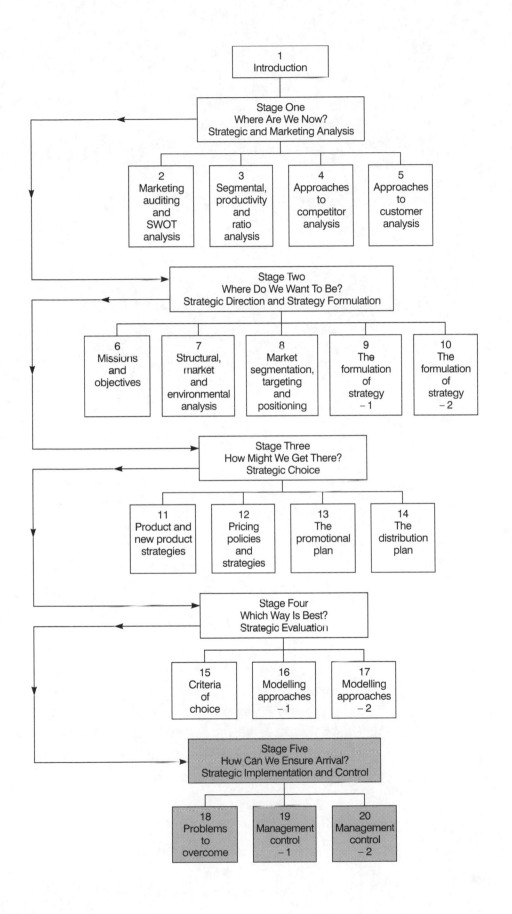

Stage Five
How Can We Ensure Arrival?
Strategic Implementation and Control

PREAMBLE

This stage of the book focuses on implementation and control. In this endeavour there are lots of problems to be overcome (e.g. relating to organizational as well as to environmental matters) which are discussed in Chapter 18.

Management controls to help in ensuring arrival are dealt with in Chapters 19 and 20. Some of these are social/behavioural in character while others are analytical.

The successful implementation of strategy is neither easy nor widely discussed in the marketing literature. If implementation is left to compete with the internal pressures of coping with crises, reacting to competitors' actions, company politics, personal career needs, and so forth, it is likely to be swamped or disrupted.

The implementation of plans poses a fundamental dilemma since to be effective it requires the reconciliation of two opposing forces: forces leading to organizational integration must be reconciled with forces leading to organizational segmentation (see Lawrence and Lorsch (1967)). In seeking to achieve this balance it is helpful if:

1 the messages contained in the plan are communicated so that there is clear recognition of what the plan says;
2 the plan must be understood so that all who need to play a role in its implementation are aware of what their roles are;
3 there is consensus about the wisdom of pursuing the plan in order to secure commitment to its accomplishment.

A flowchart showing how a strategic marketing plan might be implemented is shown in Figure 1. This suggests that a number of key elements within the organization need to be matched with the plan. These elements are:

- leadership;
- organizational culture;
- organizational structure;
- functional policies;
- resources;
- evaluation and control procedures.

There is a logical sequencing of the key elements, although some may occur simultaneously or in a different order in practice. Feedback loops are shown linking the elements in an iterative process (see McNamee (1988), pp. 323–35).

No matter how competent the analysis behind the formulation of plans and strategies it is only possible to out-perform one's competitors if those plans and strategies are executed effectively.

FIGURE 1
A flowchart showing schematically how a strategy may be implemented

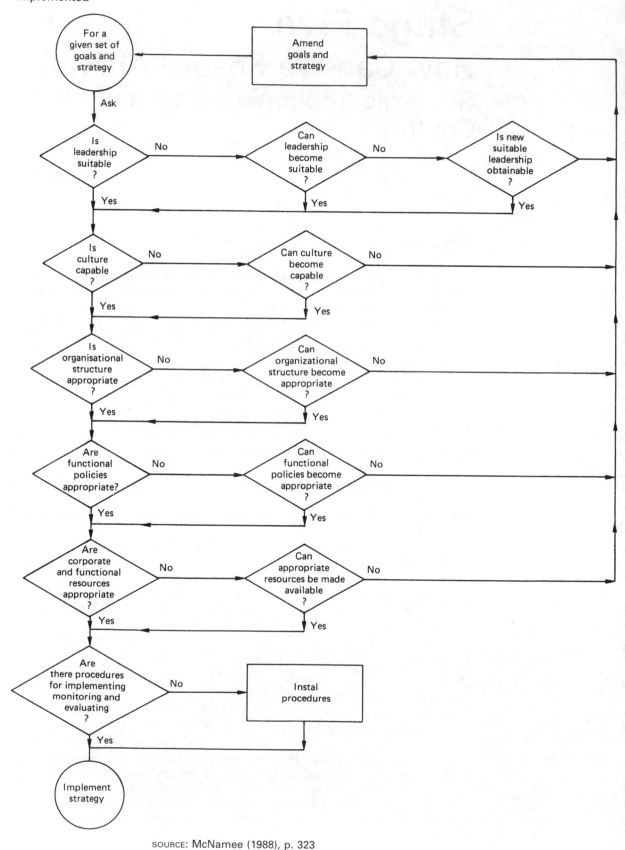

SOURCE: McNamee (1988), p. 323

FIGURE 2
*Marketing quality
assurance*

Marketing needs new sales pitch

British companies need to wake up to what the customer wants. Staying ahead when hundreds of others are going under means taking a new look at quality and service, says **Ian Griffith.**   ●

AT A TIME when the newspapers are full of stories about companies closing, there are two developments that encourage optimism.

First, there is a call from a number of chief executives for better performance in the market-place. This is a clear sign that the improvement of marketing and sales is accepted as a priority for business.

Second, quality is shaping up as one of the most important ways of staying ahead of competitors in the 1990s. Many leading companies are already on the road to total quality, where the need to identify and satisfy customer needs is given the highest priority.

The customer has not always been paramount in British business. Products have failed, not necessarily because they were poorly made but because they were not what people wanted.

The Japanese, on the other hand, have understood only too well for the past 20 years that the customer comes first. Before entering a market, they take pains to make sure they have a full understanding of customer needs and expectations. They also weigh up the competition. The Americans and the Germans have not ignored the Japanese lesson; they too are customer-conscious. If Britain is to maintain healthy businesses after 1992, it will also have to become much more market and customer focused.

The only way that this can be achieved is for companies to concentrate on improving marketing and sales effectiveness. Responsibility for this should lie with marketing departments, which not only have to represent the needs of the customer but also ensure that the company has the capability and commitment to satisfy demand with quality goods and services.

How well prepared are marketing and sales people to meet this challenge? In my experience, they are often not. Marketing is still treated by too many companies as a tactical discipline that is involved with publicity and promotion as opposed to a business philosophy that is concerned with how the whole company deals with its customers.

When competition is intensifying, this is a serious issue. Marketing must represent the customers' viewpoint as well as interests in the company boardroom.

However, reforming attitudes, ideas and quality within companies raises the questions of how people achieve such goals, how they measure that achievement and how they can maintain those standards.

The British Standard BS5750 set out the principles for product quality a decade ago, but it did not lay down how companies should identify and meet customer needs and expectations. Could those standards, which have attracted about 12,000 registrations from British companies, be applied to marketing? It was with all this in mind that the concept of Marketing Quality Assurance (MQA) was developed.

MQA, launched last October, is a third-party certification body that assesses the quality of marketing, sales and customer service in companies. It awards a certificate of excellence, and the right to use the MQA mark, if companies achieve the required standard. This is a way of signalling that the certified company is one that has independent recognition, and is a sign of marketing excellence to customers, competitors, employees and potential employees.

The specification, which is an international first and based on good practice, took five years to research and develop. An important consideration in drafting the 58 requirements in the specification was to ensure that companies were aware of the need for high-quality marketing and sales people and also understood their aspirations.

Findings showed that the most successful people are those who are able to provide a disciplined and well-planned approach based on a real understanding of the market-place and competition. They are good communicators who are able to co-ordinate the work of all parts the organisa-

tion concerned with meeting and satisfying customer needs.

Perhaps most important, they are people who can provide a creative and innovative approach, which has become vital in differentiating one organisation from another.

MQA has captured all of these needs through its specification which covers: business plans; review of market needs; marketing and sales planning; marketing and sales operations; customer assurance; purchasing of marketing and sales services; resources, personnel, training and organisation structure; quality policy, systems, control and procedures, records and audit.

MQA's specification is an associated document to the International Quality Standard ISO 9000 and therefore – as a third-party certification organisation – can grant registration to ISO 9001, EN 290012 and BS 5750 Part 1 for a company's marketing, sales and customer-assurance activities.

So the stage is set for another big step forward as the marketing enlightenment of the 1980s becomes the quality assured marketing of the 1990s.

Early indications would suggest that many chief executives acknowledge the considerable extent to which MQA registration moves their companies towards the ultimate goal of total quality, as well as providing improved marketing effectiveness.

More than 25 companies have applied for registration, with organisations such as Kodak, Sorbus, Newcastle Breweries and Southern Electric already well down the track.

There are those, however, who imagine that a formal set of standards would bring too much bureaucracy to the essentially creative business of marketing. This is not so, for marketing is more than coming up with bright ideas; it is putting those ideas into practice and making sure they work.

● *Ian Griffith is the managing director of Marketing Quality Assurance, Park House, Wick Road, Egham, Surrey TW20 0HW. Telephone: 01784 430953*

SOURCE: *The Sunday Times*, 7 July 1991, p. 4.13

This requires, inter alia, an overriding concern for quality. Japanese success in the post-war period is a clear testimony to the pursuit of quality, as reflected in the pioneering work of W. Edwards Deming. (See, for example, Mann (1989).) This success is built upon the notion of being 'right first time' which is much more than a catchy slogan: it implies providing exactly what is required by those using an organization's outputs. The *total quality management* (TQM) approach is built around this ideal.

Oakland (1989, pp. 14–15) defines TQM as '... an approach to improving the effectiveness and flexibility of businesses as a whole. It is essentially a way of organizing and involving the whole organization; every department, every activity, every single person at every level. For an organization to be truly effective, each part of it must work properly together, recognizing that every person and every activity affects, and in turn is affected by, others'.

A slightly different emphasis is offered in the definition put forward by Atkinson and Naden (1989, p. 6). They see TQM as being '... a strategy which is concerned with changing the fundamental beliefs, values and culture of an organization, harnessing the enthusiasm and participation of everyone ... towards an overall ideal of "right first time"'.

As the exhibit in Figure 2 shows, a variation on TQM can be used in a marketing context to attain BS 5750: Marketing Quality Assurance (or MQA).

In the task of implementing plans it is helpful to consider the core skills that are needed if sustainable competitive advantage is to be achieved. These core skills are the critical capabilities that the organization must possess as distinct from the skills of individuals within the organization. This is not a trivial distinction since individuals may come and go but the organization needs to have core skills (such as effective training programmes, clear performance guidelines, well-designed information systems, and incentive schemes that generate high levels of motivation) to link planning and the successful implementation of plans.

A vivid example is that of Marriott Hotels. As with many hotel chains the basic strategy is to go after business travellers with a level of service that is consistently excellent. However, the success of Marriott (as reflected in an occupancy rate that is some 10 points above the industry average) is to be found in its ability to implement the strategy in a superior way. This is achieved by institutionalizing among its 200 000 employees a fanatical eye for detail (e.g. maids follow a 66-point guide in making up bedrooms). The outcome is that Marriott Hotels is invariably at the top in customer surveys: the core organizational skill of excellent service gives a sustainable competitive advantage.

Another example can be taken from the fast food sector. In 1968 both Burger King and McDonald's had less than 1000 outlets. By 1990, despite backing from its parent company, Burger King had increased its outlets to a total of only 5500 or so, while McDonald's had emerged as the clear industry leader with over 10 000 outlets and with sales growing at 13 per cent per year. The explanation is to be found in the core skills – see Figure 3 (Irvin and Michaels, 1989, p. 7). McDonald's had the competitive edge on all counts.

FIGURE 3
Contrasting execution of core skills

Core skills	McDonald's	Burger King
Site selection	'Penchant for finding the *plum*'.	'Generally good locations'.
High-quality service	'*Unparalleled* consistency'.	'Suffers from operational sloppiness'.
Product innovation	'A *knack* for product development'.	'Spotty record with new products'.
Communications	'Surrogate man'	'Comes off as aggressive, masculine and distant'.

SOURCE: Irvin and Michaels (1989), p. 7

There are good examples to be found in the manufacturing sector as well as in the service sector, such as the VF Corporation (which makes Lee and Wrangler jeans, Jantzen swimsuits and Vanity Fair lingerie). The strong position of this company over the last 10 years is largely due to:

● high quality at competitive prices, thus offering superior value to consumers;
● accurate forecasting which means lower inventories, fewer stockouts, and less plants than most competitors;
● managing the risk that is inherent in the clothing industry by means of a focused and disciplined approach to the development of new lines.

It is important to recognize that identifying and creating core skills is far from easy. Both organizations and individuals develop particular ways of doing things and managing the process of change may require that the behaviour of thousands of people be changed in dozens of different locations. If success depends on it, then this nettle must be grasped. The approach adopted in grasping it will influence how effective the outcome is likely to be. For example, employees are more likely to show a willingness to accept change if they have a clear understanding of what is required of them, coupled with the assurance that there is some latitude for them to exercise judgement. This can be built in to the following steps *en route* to developing core skills:

1 establish a clear link between the chosen strategy and the required core skills, such as quick delivery requiring excellent distribution facilities;
2 be specific as well as selective in defining core skills so that employees will know what to do and how to do it, but in a focused way (e.g. covering no more than five core skills);
3 clarify the implications for pivotal jobs (hence recruitment and training requirements, support systems, reward schemes, etc.);
4 provide leadership from the top since the single most powerful discriminating factor between success and failure in developing core skills is the degree of top management involvement;
5 empower the organization to learn, which requires that individuals within the organization have scope for learning by doing – thereby seeing what works and what fails to work in building core skills through which strategies can be successfully implemented.

While a number of authors have written on the implementation of strategy (e.g. Lorange (1982); Bourgeois and Brodwin (1984); Nutt (1987, 1989); Reed and Buckley (1988); Reid (1989)), or more specifically on the implementation of marketing strategy (e.g. Spekman and Grønhaug (1983); McTavish (1989); Piercy and Morgan (1989a, 1989b, 1990)) as pointed out earlier there is relatively little guidance available on this important theme. Outstanding strategies are worthless if they cannot be put into effect, as Piercy and Morgan (1990), p.20 state:

> In short, the . . . reality the marketing executive faces is that implementing plans and strategies successfully is often dependent on managers and employees who are far removed from the excitement of creating new marketing strategies – people like service engineers, customer service units . . . field sales personnel, and so on.

The same authors (1989a) give examples of a museum failing to deliver a theme park strategy because employees cannot change from being 'policemen' to 'entertainers'; marketing strategies that rely on customer service failing because of employees' negative attitudes at the point of sale; and strategies based on integration and divisional cross-selling foundering because nobody recognized the human costs of change. It is not enough to develop marketing plans by focusing exclusively on customers, competitors and distributors (all *outside* the company) and ignoring those *within* the company. Almost all plans involve substantial human and organizational change: this requires 'internal marketing' which has goals such as to:

1 gain the support of key decision makers and facilitators;
2 change attitudes among those employees who deal with customers;
3 obtain employees' commitment to making the marketing plan work by involving them in the 'ownership' of the plan and by rewarding them on the plan's attainment;
4 train staff to allow them to develop new skills that will contribute to the effective implementation of plans.

Training (or management development) has been enthusiastically promoted (e.g. Hussey (1985), Brache (1986)) as a means of implementing plans. It was suggested by Hussey (1985, p. 32) that training can contribute to some of the problems of strategy implementation identified by Alexander (1985). Of the 10 most frequently encountered strategy implementation problems in US organizations, training can probably help with the top six (Figure 4).

FIGURE 4
*Implementation
problems*

Problem	Percentage of enterprises reporting problem
1 Implementation took more time than originally allocated.	76
2 Major problems surfaced during implementation that had not been identified beforehand.	74
3 Coordination of implementation activities was not effective enough.	66
4 Competing activities and crises distracted management from implementing decisions.	64
5 Capabilities of employees involved were insufficient for the task.	63
6 Training and instructions given to lower level employees were inadequate.	62

SOURCE: Adapted from Alexander (1985)

Bonoma and Crittenden (1988) have put forward a well-considered case showing that the successful implementation of marketing plans results from the interaction of structure and skills. In this context *structure* is seen to consist of:

● actions,
● programmes,
● systems,
● policies,

as portrayed in Figure 17.16 (see p. 635). Managerial *skills* embrace:

● interacting;
● allocating;
● monitoring;
● organizing.

Through a series of discussions with managers involved in implementing marketing plans Bonoma and Crittenden derived an interesting set of propositions concerning the relationship between structure and skills. These propositions are as follows:

1 There is normally a tension rather than a synergy between the enterprise's marketing structures and the skills of its managers. Whether this tension is productive or harmful depends on environmental factors.
2 The interaction between marketing structures and management skills is partially predictable using the rate of market change.
3 In low-change markets, structures and their associated systems dominate skills. Quality marketing practices result more often, and more cheaply, when strong systems and weak management skills are combined.
4 In high-change markets the reverse is true. Enterprises with weak structures and highly skilled managers get more desirable market-place results, more cheaply, than do enterprises having strong structures.
5 The complexity of tasks that marketing faces suggests whether structure or skills should dominate.
6 Routine, repetitive tasks (i.e. low complexity) are done more efficiently under strong structures with less strong execution skills.
7 Highly complex tasks require stronger execution skills and a weaker structure.

Propositions 1 to 7 can be portrayed diagrammatically (see Figure 5). If strong structures exist in circumstances characterized by rapidly changing markets and complex tasks it is likely that the enterprise's ability to adapt quickly to market needs will be constrained by rules and procedures. Conversely, if skills are dominant in a situation involving low market

FIGURE 5
*Structure/skills
dynamics*

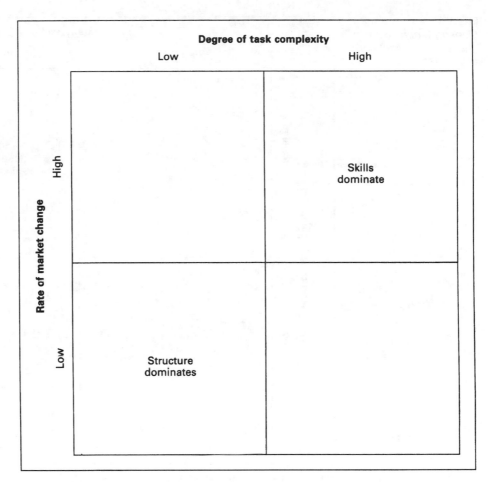

SOURCE: Adapted from Bonoma and Crittenden (1988), p. 12

change and low task complexity, the enterprise will be unable to increase its efficiency by relying on standard operating procedures.

Propositions 2 to 4 can be linked to phases of the PLC via a further proposition:

8 In the turbulent periods of the PLC (e.g. introduction, rapid growth, and, subsequently, maturity/decline) management skills will dominate execution structures in those enterprises performing better than average. In the more stable phases of the PLC structures will dominate skills.

The idea of balancing 'external' and 'internal' marketing in the implementation of marketing plans is portrayed in Figure 6.

This shows the distinction between strategy and tactics (developed with an external focus) and their implementation (via operations). However, part of the strategic thinking must be to ensure that those who will be responsible for carrying out operations are properly equipped for their tasks. If this is not the case then implementation will be poor, and failure is likely to result. Figure 7 offers the logical possibilities. Failure will follow whenever either the strategy/tactics are inappropriate or the implementation is poor.

FIGURE 6
*Strategy/tactics and
operations*

External marketing – strategy and tactics	Internal marketing – operations
External focus: setting direction	Internal focus: attaining direction
Effectiveness: doing the right thing	Efficiency: doing things right
Designing the plan	Executing the plan
Commits resources	Uses resources

SOURCE: Adapted from Kotler, et al. (1985), p. 245

FIGURE 7
Consequences of strategic and tactical implementation

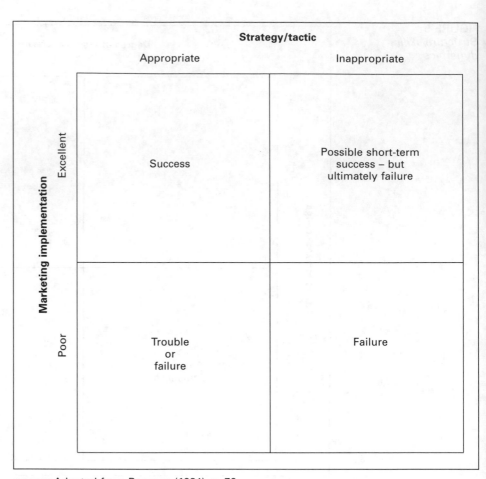

SOURCE: Adapted from Bonoma (1984), p. 72

18 | Problems to overcome

18.1 LEARNING OBJECTIVES

When you have read this chapter you should be able to:

(a) understand the importance of implementation as part of the overall process of marketing planning and control;
(b) recognize the problems that need to be addressed in implementing marketing plans and controlling marketing activities;
(c) appreciate the need for marketing orientation and a positive approach to planning if marketing objectives are to be achieved;
(d) identify the organizational design issues that are relevant to marketing planning, implementation, and control.

18.2 INTRODUCTION

Of the two major operating functions, production and marketing, the former has lent itself to rigorous analysis over many years with the result that it has been studied in great detail. Marketing, however, has not lent itself so much to critical examination until relatively recently, and for this reason it has received an unjustifiably low proportion of analytical attention. The marketing function is the most difficult area to plan and control since it is the source of sales forecasts and revenue estimates that can rarely be predicted accurately, and there is the further need to plan and control expenditure in addition to dealing with the human dimensions.

The scale of operations is determined by the sales forecast, but it may be found that the level of projected sales exceeds the short-term productive capacity of the enterprise. In such an event it may be necessary to:

1 expand the productive facilities;
2 raise prices in an attempt to ration the available output;
3 subcontract production to outside suppliers;
4 rely on inventories.

On the other hand, it may be that the projected level of sales is insufficient to produce the desired return on investment (i.e. profitability objective). Apart from increasing the overall level of sales activity it may be appropriate to reconsider the means of distribution to ensure that it is the most cost-effective, or the existing sales effort may not be properly allocated (e.g. consider exporting – see Pilcher (1989)) or individual product profit margins may be subject to adjustment by product modifications, or an analysis of credit losses may cause credit extension policies to be amended to improve profitability (see, for example, Bass (1991)).

The study, and to a lesser extent the practice, of financial management has been reduced almost to a science in parallel with the study of production. The importance of human rather than technical factors in the marketing subsystem, coupled with the complexity of the marketing interfaces with internal and external subsystems, have been the causes of the delays in rigorous marketing analysis. (See Wilson (1994).) This chapter considers some of the problems that must be overcome in controlling marketing activities along the lines suggested in Chapters 19 and 20. Problem areas that are discussed include business pressures, problems in the marketing subsystem, problems of marketing feedback and information adequacy, cost problems, problems relating to marketing orientation and problems relating to planning. Consideration is also given to the organizational problems associated with the implementation and control of marketing plans.

18.3 PRESSURES

King (1991, p. 3) has pointed out that the pressures on marketing organizations during the 1980s were formidable and it is likely that these pressures will intensify as we continue moving through the 1990s. Similar views are offered by Buckley (1991) and Hussey (1989). See also Brown (1995).

FIGURE 18.1
The influence of external factors

SOURCE: Wilson (1983), p. 209

The range of external factors impacting on organizations is shown in Figure 18.1 (Wilson, 1983, p. 209), although this is not intended to be an exhaustive portrayal. Many of these factors were discussed in Chapter 7. Pressures which are expected to have an increasing significance as we head towards the year 2000 include:

1 More confident customers due to increasing consumer awareness via consumerism, a greater willingness to experiment, more readiness to trust their own judgement, less tolerance of products that fail to contribute to their own values, higher levels of disposable income, and increased individualism.
2 New concepts of quality that reflect *real* values rather than superficial styling, plus personal added values, and a requirement for increased customer care.
3 Changing demographic and social patterns, such as fewer school leavers and a higher proportion of retired people, a shortage of skills relative to 2 above, demands for improved social conditions, and the continuing importance of 'green' issues.
4 An intensification of competition via increased global marketing, the fragmentation of markets, and the risk of excess capacity in many markets.

5 The formation of joint ventures and strategic alliances when outright acquisition is neither feasible nor desirable, or when organic expansion is not possible (see, for example, Clarke and Brennan (1988) and Devlin and Biggs (1989)) and the growing use of shared services.

6 Political changes, including deregulation, political, economic and financial integration, and change in trade policies (see, for example, Quelch, Buzzell and Salama (1990), Lynch (1992), Brown and McDonald (1994), and Bennett (1995)).

7 Technological imperatives in product and process innovations, the acceleration of technological change with an emphasis on new product development, hence shorter PLCs, and changes in the provision of service (e.g. via EFTS) – especially in retailing.

8 The harnessing of information technology in ways that build competitive advantage, which places a greater responsibility on managers both to understand the meaning of the results from the use of analytical techniques and to ensure that the quality of information in use is high.

9 Restructuring of the world economy and restructuring at a micro-economic level due to mergers, management buy-outs, leveraged buy-outs, building, unbundling, etc.

10 More market-focused organizations (i.e. increasing marketing orientation – see below), and an acceleration in the shift from a manufacturing to a service economy.

11 Short termism. On the question of short termism Heller (1990) observed that it has been argued that the spectre of the City of London has cast a shadow over British managers which makes them so uneasy that they tend to concentrate on short-term financial goals to the detriment of long-term results. However, the core of Heller's argument is that the short-term demons are, in fact, lurking within the managers themselves rather than within the City institutions (which are rarely inclined to act on a short-term basis). Managers who attach more importance to this year's results than to the organization's likely situation in the twenty-first century, or whose rewards are wholly-related to current performance, are not acting in the best interests of the organization as a whole.

The CBI set up a task force to report on the phenomenon of short termism: the resulting report (entitled *Investing for Britain's Future*) also showed short termism to be a myth insofar as it is attributable to City institutions. To the extent that it does exist it is attributable to poor management on the one hand and to underlying economic and political factors (such as high interest rates) on the other. Ferguson (1989, p. 68) has observed that share prices typically react well to announcements of strategic commitments but that 'British companies have a curious reticence about heralding their grand schemes'. The fact that there is good empirical support underlying the efficient markets hypothesis was pointed out in Chapter 15 (p. 544) (see also Puxty and Dodds (1991), pp. 69–86).

If only a few of these pressures were to occur there would be significant implications for marketing planning and control. Since most (if not all) of them are already occurring it is evident that managers must develop understanding, commitment and skills to deal proactively with new situations.

Lewis (1989) has grouped the pressures for change into four main areas, as in Figure 18.2.

The axes range from task-focused to people-focused pressures on the horizontal plane and from external to internal pressures on the vertical plane. Within the resulting cells we have:

1 market pressures, with keywords being change, variety and complexity;

2 external – people pressures involving increasing liaison with customers and developments such as the Green movement;

FIGURE 18.2
Pressures for change

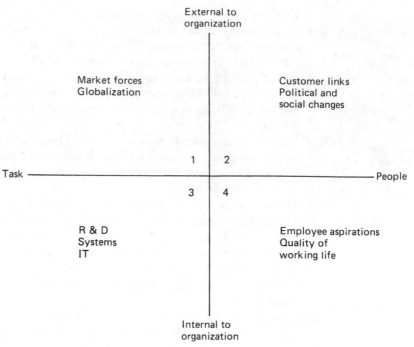

SOURCE: Lewis (1989)

3 internal – task pressures for cost reduction and systems development as well as R & D activities;

4 internal – people pressures, including increased autonomy among employees and demands for more flexibility in the way in which staff are treated in the face of reduced job security.

There are no blanket formulae for structuring organizations or motivating staff in order to cope with the problems of constant change. It is evident, however, that not all managers or their subordinates are equally amenable to change. Figure 18.3 gives one approach to assessing resistance to change (adapted from Witte (1990), p. 30).

An organization that is highly resistant to change will exhibit characteristics such as the following:

- large;
- established;
- centralized;
- hierarchic management structures;
- predictable tasks;
- manufacturing base;
- paternal orientation;
- vertical information systems;
- autocratic management style;
- unskilled workforce;
- non-professional;
- undifferentiated product lines;
- immobile workforce.

In contrast, an organization that has a low resistance to change will have characteristics as follows:

- small;
- new;
- decentralized;

FIGURE 18.3
Change resistance grid

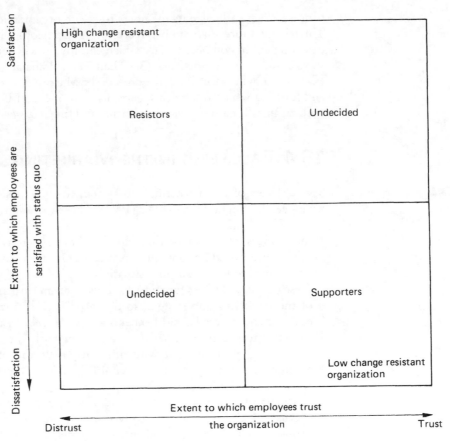

SOURCE: Adapted from Witte (1990)

- flat management structures;
- unpredictable tasks;
- service base;
- fraternal orientation;
- horizontal information systems;
- participative management style;
- skilled workforce;
- professional;
- differentiated product lines;
- mobile workforce.

The ideal environment in which to initiate change is one in which employees trust the organization but feel dissatisfied with the status quo. A classic example of this is to be found in the Virgin Group: it is a relatively young, decentralized, fast-growing service organization with diverse and innovative product lines. The workforce is skilled and mobile, the management structures are flat, and the management style is both participative and fraternal with an ethos that is virtually synonymous with change.

Innovation is clearly more likely in low-resistance organizations provided that they do not attempt too much too quickly or fail to carry through the changes that are initiated.

It has been contended (see Ulrich and Lake (1991)) that the 'traditional' means of securing competitive advantage (i.e. via financial, strategic and technological capabilities) cover only part of what managers will need to do to build sustainable competitive advantage in the 1990s. Existing capabilities must be supplemented by *organizational capability* - which can be defined as the enterprise's ability to manage people to gain competitive advantage by establishing internal structures and processes that influence its members to create organization-specific competences. This entails more than simply recruiting good people; it requires the deliberate development of competences by which employees will act to ensure the enterprise stays ahead of its competitors. (See Hamel and Prahalad (1994).) Two outstanding examples of where this is being done are the Marriott Corporation (covering hotels and food) to which reference was made on p. 654, and Borg-Warner (which deals with chemicals, automotive components and financial services).

18.4 PROBLEMS IN THE MARKETING SUB-SYSTEM

Several facets of the marketing sub-system that give rise to problems of control have been highlighted by Kotler (1972). These include the following:

1 the outputs of the marketing function have repercussions on the outputs of other corporate functions, such as credit collection having a significant bearing on the controller's cash flow situation;
2 these outputs of other functional sub-systems in turn affect subsequent outputs of the marketing sub-system, so that a poor cash flow may lead to a need to cease extending credit and hence to a lower level of sales and profit;
3 the interface of the marketing sub-system with the sub-systems formed by external agents is fraught with difficulty since the marketing manager must attempt to exercise some degree of control over advertising agents, PR consultants, wholesalers, and shipping companies;
4 the human factor that is at the heart of marketing creates problems of control because of the difficulties involved in co-ordinating the activities of sales-people, product managers, advertising agents, and marketing researchers, all of whom are essentially creative and individualistic;
5 the usual problems associated with any corporate project, such as launching a new product, entering a new territory, or executing a major promotional campaign are especially noticeable in marketing as a result of the human element and the external interfaces.

To these we can add the problem of assessing performance.

Defining marketing performance has proved to be a difficult task due to a number of problems, including (as suggested by Bonoma and Clark (1988)):

● the nature of marketing as a complex discipline having many dimensions and interfaces (e.g. internally with functions such as production, and externally with intermediaries, agencies, etc.), each of which has an impact on performance;
● the need for marketing to behave in an adaptive way in the light of environmental changes (such as competitive activities or shifts in the pattern of consumer demand) which renders performance bench-marks perishable;
● the tendency to focus on inputs rather than outputs with the presumption being that the desired outputs (such as increased market share) are 'obvious' thereby playing down the importance of both marketing performance and the implementation of marketing plans.

The marketing manager must find means of securing better co-ordination among the various functional sub-systems that are not directly under his control, including production, purchasing, and materials control. This may be achieved by improving communications and inter-organizational understandings about what is in the interest of the enterprise as a whole.

In addition, the marketing manager must strive to influence external agents as well as to motivate his internal staff to carry out their respective duties in the enterprise's best interests. This requires both flexibility in terms of tactics and adequate feedback from operations.

A co-ordinated approach requires that marketing plans are developed alongside production plans, staffing plans, financial plans, and so forth. The need for this close co-ordination is due to elements of one plan being the starting point for others: thus a sales forecast (as an element of the marketing plan) is the cornerstone of the production plan (see Chapter 15 of Fisk (1967) and Chapter 9 of Schaffir and Trentin (1973)).

Systems theory provides a conceptual framework within which management can effectively integrate the various activities of the organization, including the marketing function. (See, for example, Churchman (1968), Emery (1981), and Schoderbek, et al. (1975).) The major benefit of the systems approach lies in the facility it gives to management in recognizing the proper place and function of sub-systems within the whole, thereby focusing attention on broader issues than those contained in a single department. With particular reference to marketing, the application of systems thinking (Lazer (1962b); Wilson (1970b)) should result in at least three developments of significance to improved management:

- a more concerted emphasis on marketing planning and control;
- better systems of marketing intelligence to provide management with a clearer perspective for its marketing actions:
- following from both of the above items, a better understanding of marketing as an adjustment mechanism that is able to employ corporate resources to meet changing market conditions successfully.

With particular regard to functional co-ordination, the common flows through all departments are information, physical resources, and funds, so one or more of these can be a vehicle for integration. Let us consider some examples.

Production – Marketing Interface
A failure to control this interface effectively can lead to such problems as the sales force promising early delivery to secure an order that then causes difficulties in both production programming and delivery scheduling. Such behaviour could easily jeopardize future orders. Plant capacity and flexibility, standardization, and quality requirements must all be taken into account by planners attempting to integrate production and marketing operations.

Purchasing – Marketing Interface
Effective co-operation here should prevent material shortages from appearing and should also help to avoid the holding of excessive raw material/component stocks due to marketing management's failing to inform the purchasing department of reduced requirements. Such failure causes funds to be tied up unnecessarily in an unprofitable use, which is very inefficient. (See the discussion on supply chain management in Chapter 14.)

Personnel – Marketing Interface
Although selection procedures are imperfect this in itself is an insufficient cause to ignore the methods that are available and to rely on wholly personal judgement. Those who are to be responsible for recruiting, training, and inducting marketing personnel must have a sound knowledge of the work done in, and skill requirements of, the marketing area.

Accounting – Marketing Interface
The question of co-ordination and communication between marketing and the financial control function is of fundamental importance (e.g. Ratnatunga (1983, 1988); Ward (1989); Wilson (1970, 1975, 1981, 1998)). Our present interest is not with the keeping of books of accounts and the subsequent reporting to outside parties (e.g. via the statutory annual balance sheet and profit and loss account). This is but one decreasingly important function of the financial controller

generally referred to as the *stewardship function*. (It is so called because the controller acts as the shareholders' steward in keeping records, paying bills, collecting debts, and safeguarding the assets of the business.)

In contrast with stewardship is the controller's *service function* through which he aims to develop information flows and reporting systems to facilitate improved planning, decision making and control.

Marketing controllership is concerned with the controller's service to marketing management, and this will become increasingly important as the marketing concept is more widely adopted and as marketing becomes more dominant within the typical company.

To offer the best service to marketing involves the controller studying the company's marketing organization and its problems. One approach to this is shown in Figure 18.4 (Bancroft & Wilson (1979), p. 29).

FIGURE 18.4
A framework for improved management accounting – marketing interaction

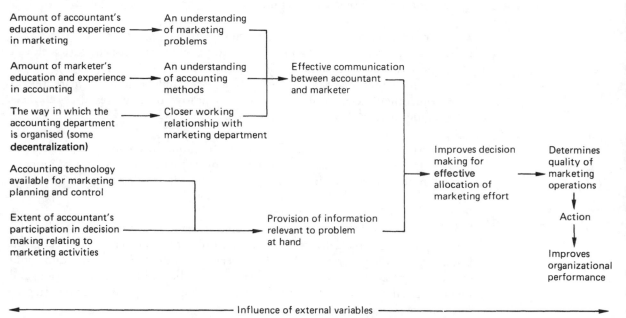

SOURCE: Bancroft and Wilson (1979), p. 29

A greater mutual understanding between marketing managers and management accountants, coupled with the greater involvement of members from both groups in the decision process, should lead to more effective outcomes. The most effective communication, and the best information flows, tend to occur where members of the controller's staff are located within the marketing function with line responsibility to the controller but with a close working relationship with the marketing staff. In their pioneering US study Schiff and Melman (1962) found this arrangement in very few companies, and in their UK study Wilson and Bancroft (1983) found a similar situation, but a deeper interest in analysing the costs of marketing seems to have developed since then, along with the spread of the marketing concept. Nevertheless, comparatively little attention has been given to marketing costs as opposed to the extensive attention given to production costs despite the very substantial scale of the former.

18.5 PROBLEMS OF MARKETING FEEDBACK

The importance of feedback is paramount since unbalanced and unstable conditions, along with an inability to exercise effective control, can develop within the marketing area if prompt, adequate, and undistorted feedback is not present.

However, the marketing manager can rarely benefit from the advantages of statistical feedback to provide an automatic corrective control over marketing activities in the same way that the production manager can use such control over much of his plant. It is necessary for the marketing manager frequently to base his decisions on experience alone, and control by relying on his ability to motivate his staff and external agents after he has personally received the feedback.

The two major reasons for the rare use of pure automatic feedback in marketing are simple to discern.

1 The fact that performance deviations can arise from a multitude of different causes. For example, a drop in sales volume may be caused by a price increase with elastic demand, as a result of competitive products or promotions, or as a result of a decline in the level of business activity over the trade cycle, and so forth.
2 The plans and standards used in the control process may be as much at fault as the apparent performance. The inability, say, of a sales representative to achieve his quota may be due to poor quota setting or unrealistic sales forecasting as well as poor performance. An investigation into such matters may result in a revision of standards or plans, but a feedback mechanism can hardly be expected to deal with mistakes in the basis of performance measurement.

All these problem areas demand that flexibility be maintained in relation to both the planning and controlling of marketing operations. Accordingly, the marketing manager must be able to redeploy his salesforce, adapt the advertising campaign, or change the various aspects of his market offer (price, packaging, product features, etc.) to meet changing conditions. This means that he is charged with the almost impossible tasks of knowing the changes to make and being able to make them.

Of the greatest importance in this setting is the suitability of the information system in enabling the marketing manager to be flexible in devising alternative plans as a matter of contingency rather than necessity. As in all such matters, the costs and benefits should be balanced in the securing of fuller control.

In considering feedback it is inevitable that delays of one kind or another will be experienced. To a large extent delay is inevitable since feedback is, by definition, *ex post*, thus only arising after the event. However, we can break delays down into their constituent categories as shown in Figure 18.5.

FIGURE 18.5
Major delays in a feedback system

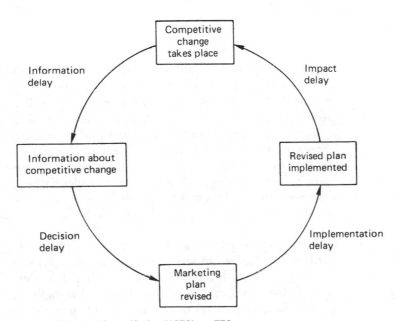

SOURCE: Adapted from Kotler (1972), p. 770

If a competitor introduces a significant change in his market offering there is a delay until this information is relayed to the marketing team. It takes time to devise a suitable response, involving revisions to marketing plans. Once the revisions are decided upon there will be a lag until they are implemented. Finally, at least for this iteration, there will be a delay following implementation before it becomes apparent what the impact of the revised course of action is on the competitive change. By the time these delays have been incurred it is quite possible that the competitor may have established a clear competitive advantage, hence feedback delays must be minimized in responding to competitive threats – or to any other relevant change. This latter situation is illustrated in Figure 18.6 (derived from Forrester (1965), pp. 357, 358 and 361) which shows positive and negative feedback loops relating to the sales growth pattern of a newly launched product.

FIGURE 18.6
Feedback effects on sales growth

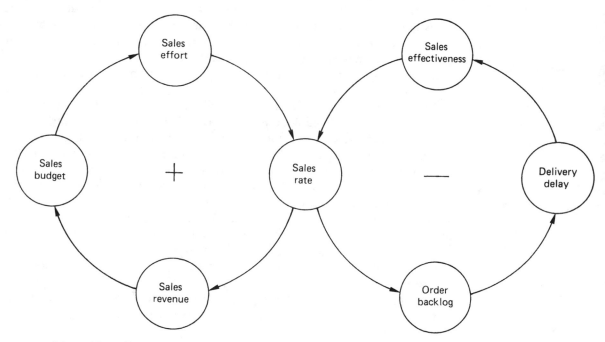

SOURCE: Adapted from Forrester (1965)

The rates of sales of the new product (i.e. the point of intersection of the positive and negative feedback loops in Figure 18.6) is a function of sales effort on the one hand and sales effectiveness on the other. If the sales rate generates a profitable level of sales revenue this is likely to lead to an increase in the sales budget, hence to further increases in the amount of sales effort. These linkages are shown in the left-hand (positive feedback) loop, and it would appear that continuous sales growth is in prospect. However, if there is insufficient productive capacity to meet the increased sales rate an order backlog will build up, along with delays in delivery. This will almost certainly cause a decrease in sales effectiveness which, in turn, will dampen the sales rate as shown in the right-hand (negative feedback) loop.

As the two loops interact it becomes clear that sales will grow when there is available productive capacity to ensure that order backlogs are avoided. Whenever the sales rate exceeds full capacity the result is that sales will then decrease due to the order backlogs, etc. This rather simplified example highlights not only the lack of synchronizing in terms of timing but also the importance of functional coordination.

18.6 INFORMATION ADEQUACY

How effective a manager is in his job will depend on how much, how relevant, and how good his information is, and how well he interprets and acts upon it.

Nevertheless, one hears frequent complaints from management that information is too late, of the wrong type, unverified, or even suppressed. It is evident, therefore, that if information is to be of value it must be clear, detailed, timely, accurate, and complete – and must not consist of vague figures thrown out by an unplanned system.

It is not enough, for example, to observe that the purpose of a particular set of procedures is to provide the information required for planning and controlling the company's marketing operation. The information requirements must be made more explicit, and the aim of a marketing analysis system defined. The aim may be to produce the internal data needed for effective planning and control of marketing activities and the requirements specified as follows:

Marketing planning

- establishing sales quotas by territory, product, industry and channel;
- developing the advertising budget, and planning the allocation of funds amongst specified media;
- evaluating the character and size of the product line;
- developing additional outlets and new channels of distribution;
- determining the need for, and location of, additional warehouses.

Measurement and control of results by:

- salesperson;
- geographic area;
- distribution channel;
- customer group;
- product.

Management must decide what needs to be done, who is to do it, ensure that it is done, and evaluate the success with which it was done. None of these functions can be performed without the necessary information. But *all* the available information may not be helpful, so the marketing manager must pay great attention to the quality, quantity, and relevance of the information that he seeks.

It is characteristic of decision making that in selecting one particular course of action the manager thereby prevents himself from moving in another direction. This constitutes a major difficulty in making decisions, and it follows that the manager's ability to make better decisions involves relying upon information that:

1 reduces the uncertainty associated with following one particular course of action;
2 improves his power to act in the right direction.

The sources of such improvement lie in the methodical selection, collection, processing, analysis, and communication of relevant information, along with the ability to formulate sound assumptions as a basis for making more accurate forecasts and decisions on the basis of that information.

However, while to manage a business is to manage information, it may be that either too much or too little information is presented. The economic wastage that results from an excess of information is *not* the incremental clerical cost of producing it, but rather the loss of executive effectiveness that it causes. This comes about in two major ways:

1 the manager may ignore the great volume of information that is presented to him, thus missing the vital as well as the irrelevant;
2 the manager may become overburdened, or even enslaved, by the excess.

On the other hand, should there be insufficient information presented for good decision making, it may be wise to postpone the decision until more information is available. A similar situation involving delay is that in which sufficient information is presented but its accuracy is in doubt and extra time must be spent if this accuracy is to be improved. In either situation the loss of control that results from delay must be weighed against the value of improved information in reducing the uncertainties implicit in the making of most decisions.

Only a limited amount of the information that flows through the typical organization is of real management significance. That which is of value, therefore, must be identified and developed in line with organizational requirements – observing the important information qualities of impartiality, validity, reliability, and internal consistency.

The organizational structure of an enterprise and its information requirements are inextricably linked. In order to translate a statement of his duties into action the manager must receive and use information. This involves using all the relevant data and intelligence – quantitative and qualitative, financial and non-financial – that is available, instead of merely relying on an existing system and the reports it produces.

As frequently happens the manager may not know precisely what information he requires or, alternatively, what information is available. Consultants can help by observing the types of decisions made, testing the adequacy of existing information, suggesting alternative information flows, and indicating the means (and costs) of collection.

The aim, then, is to provide the right information to the right people in the right quantity at the right time, and at minimum cost. The purpose of collecting, analysing, and using information is essentially the same in any size of business, whether for routine purposes or for special projects. The difference is in the relative employment of manual as opposed to computer-based systems. The increasing adoption of networked computer systems should ensure that fewer managers have cause to complain about insufficient, inaccurate or delayed information. This depends, of course, not only upon accurate information flows but also upon systematic storage in order to facilitate rapid retrieval. The need to react quickly to a changing environment demands fast and accurate retrieval as facts that take too long to find and compile are often useless when time is of the essence.

Discussions about information systems can usefully be considered against the background of the *theory of communication*. Relative to the broad subject of communication there are three major problems:

1 the accuracy with which the symbols of communication can be transmitted – the technical problem;
2 the precision with which the transmitted symbols convey the desired meaning – the semantic problem;
3 the effectiveness with which the received meaning affects behaviour in the desired manner – the effectiveness problem.

Figure 18.7 illustrates how these problems can arise in the process of selecting a message and transmitting it (i.e. in the usual decision-making process of using an information system).

FIGURE 18.7
*The communication
system*

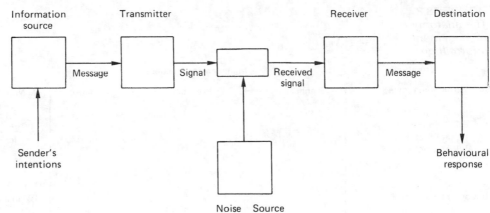

In the process of being transmitted it is unfortunately characteristic that certain things are added to (or omitted from) the signal that were not intended by the information source. Such errors, distortions, and changes are collectively termed 'noise'.

The transmitter could take a written message and use some code to encipher it into, say, a sequence of numbers (e.g. binary digits), which could then be sent over the channel as the signal. The general purpose of the transmitter thus becomes that of encoding, and the purpose of the receiver that of decoding. However, as one makes the coding more and more nearly ideal one is forced into longer and longer delays in the process of coding, and this requires the establishing of balance. But no matter how careful one is in the coding process it will always be found that, after the signal has been received, there remains some undesirable uncertainty (noise) about the precise nature of the message.

It is emphasized throughout this book that the manager needs information to assist him in decision making, to indicate performance, and to help him in making plans, setting standards and controlling outcomes. In this light the key to developing a dynamic and usable management information system is to move beyond the limits of conventional reporting and to conceive of information as it relates to the two vital elements of the management process – planning and control.

A great deal of information, while useful for planning and control, is primarily raised for some other purpose that is only tangentially related to planning and control. This covers much of the output of the accounting routine in many companies. Such information is derived from:

1 payroll procedures;
2 the order-processing cycle, beginning with the receipt of an order and ending with the collection of accounts receivable;
3 the procurement and accounts payable cycle.

The adequacy of these information flows as a basis for decision systems is highlighted by the omission of:

1 information about the future;
2 data expressed in non-financial terms, such as market share, productivity, quality levels, adequacy of customer service, etc.
3 information dealing with external conditions as they might bear on a particular enterprise's operations.

Effective business planning requires three types of information – environmental, competitive and operating. Accounting alone, therefore, is insufficient; but if the controllership function exists within a company it should ensure that

FIGURE 18.8
*The anatomy of
management
information*

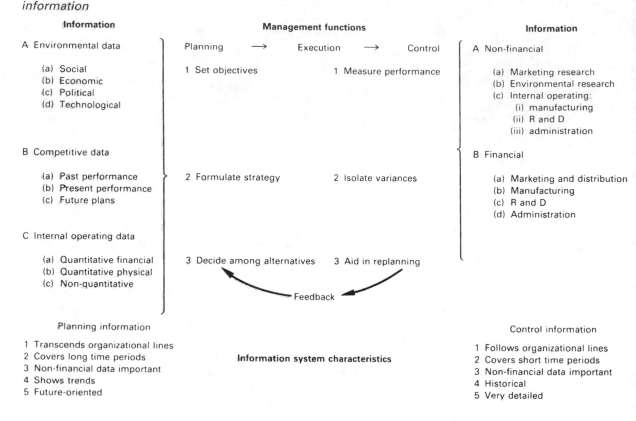

Information	Management functions	Information

A Environmental data

    (a) Social
    (b) Economic
    (c) Political
    (d) Technological

B Competitive data

    (a) Past performance
    (b) Present performance
    (c) Future plans

C Internal operating data

    (a) Quantitative financial
    (b) Quantitative physical
    (c) Non-quantitative

Management functions

Planning → Execution → Control

1 Set objectives   1 Measure performance

2 Formulate strategy   2 Isolate variances

3 Decide among alternatives   3 Aid in replanning

Feedback

Information

A Non-financial

    (a) Marketing research
    (b) Environmental research
    (c) Internal operating:
        (i) manufacturing
        (ii) R and D
        (iii) administration

B Financial

    (a) Marketing and distribution
    (b) Manufacturing
    (c) R and D
    (d) Administration

Planning information

1 Transcends organizational lines
2 Covers long time periods
3 Non-financial data important
4 Shows trends
5 Future-oriented

Information system characteristics

Control information

1 Follows organizational lines
2 Covers short time periods
3 Non-financial data important
4 Historical
5 Very detailed

economic and marketing research and forecasting are closely integrated with the systems function.

Information is the medium of control, but the flows required for planning are not necessarily the same as those required for control. Figure 18.8 outlines the general nature of information flows for planning and control. Their uses in control revolve around communication, motivation, and performance, whereas forecasting, establishing objectives, and deciding among alternatives are more important in planning.

In summary, a management information system is the means of bringing to each level of management the necessary and complete information that is accurate, timely and sufficient (but not in excessive detail), so that each manager can fulfil his responsibilities to the organization. The central purpose, then, is to aid decision making, and the system should be based on sound data, be sufficiently flexible to allow new techniques to be used, and be operated at minimum cost commensurate with the overall system results.

The three basic information flows in marketing are:

1 the inflow of environmental data;
2 internal operating data;
3 communication (usually of a persuasive nature) directed to external audiences.

The effectiveness of each flow should be continually tested by the posing of questions such as:

1 Does the procedure for developing delivery quotations to customers produce the information required to ensure that delivery promises are realistic?

2 Does the procedure for handling customers' enquiries regarding the status of their orders provide for rendering a superior form of customer service?

3 Do the sales statistical procedures produce the best internal data required to plan sales strategy, to control selling effort, and to spotlight opportunities for major improvements in the distribution programme?

4 Do the clerical-support activities provided for the sales force help to increase each sales person's productivity by maximizing the amount of time spent in direct selling work?

These representative questions point to the main uses of a marketing information system in the control effort and these fall into the following groups:

1 to spot things that are going wrong and to take corrective action before serious loss results, which constitutes the most fruitful and constructive use of control information;

2 to highlight things that have actually gone wrong and guide marketing management in either cutting the losses of failure or turning apparent failure to future advantage;

3 to determine exactly how and why failures or deviations from plan have arisen and to suggest steps that should be taken to prevent their recurrence, which is another highly constructive application since mistakes need not be repeated even if they cannot be avoided.

4 to find out who is to blame for failure which, if not done in the proper way and followed up by corrective action, is the least constructive of uses.

Careful consideration must always be applied to deciding which elements of information to include in a marketing information system if cost is not to be a prohibitive factor. The types of decisions that must be made will obviously determine the types of information that the system should provide. A few examples are given below.

Pricing (See also Chapter 12)

Before any decision on price can be made information should be available on:

1 competitive pricing policies and product prices;
2 consumer attitudes to price;
3 the relative profit contribution of the company's products at various prices;
4 distribution and production costs as a basis for 3, above;
5 volume factors (covering both market share and potential along with capacity details).

Product Management (See also Chapter 11)

This function depends completely on adequate flows of information from a variety of sources if it is to be successfully carried out. Information should be related to the PLC since this indicates when to launch new products, when to phase out declining products, and when to revitalize the marketing effort behind other products. The life cycle must be viewed in terms of total sales and market penetration on the one hand, and costs and profit outcomes on the other. Forecasts of costs and revenues will follow from forecasts of total market size and the share that is to be achieved.

Sales Operations

Up-to-date details of each live account should be an essential part of a marketing information system because this facilitates analyses that are invaluable to sales planning and control. In addition, accurate customer records mean that new sales staff can be assigned to territories or customer groups and learn a good deal about the accounts before visiting them: this avoids the situation when a poor sales-person is kept on because he is the only person knowing about his accounts in the absence of proper records, and the total sales job can be smoothly transferred to the case of promotion, transfer, or departure only if such records exist.

Analyses from sales records will give essential information to marketing management on product profitability, customer-group profitability, and regional profitability, and actual performance can be compared to the requirements of the profit plan. The extent to which variances arise from volume changes, variations in price, or adjustments in the mix of products sold can be analysed, and the usual budgetary procedures will provide information on selling expenses.

The role of the sales person as an information intermediary between the enterprise and its outlets and customers must not be overlooked since a sales person who appreciates the importance of rapid information dissemination and feedback can help his or her organization to promote new products as well as adapting quickly to environmental change.

18.7 Cost Problems

The essence of control in marketing, as in any other activity, is measurement. In relation to marketing costs, however, this measurement is not as straightforward as it may seem.

Figure 18.9 illustrates the basic elements of financial marketing performance that need to be controlled. The importance of marketing as the 'revenue generator' is made clear, but the other aspect of the financial sphere – cost incurrence – requires further consideration (see the discussion of definitions in Chapter 3, Section 3.3).

FIGURE 18.9
Key financial factors in marketing performance

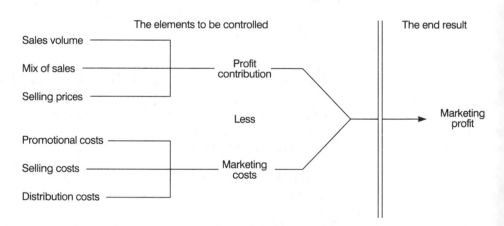

It is invariably found that the costs stemming from marketing activities are difficult to plan and control. The lowest costs are not necessarily to be preferred since these may not result in the effective attainment of the desired sales volume and profit. Most order-getting costs are 'programmed' (i.e. determined by management decision) rather than variable and tend to influence the volume of sales rather than being influenced by it.

The characteristics of marketing costs lead to problems in analysis. Such characteristics include (after Wilson (1979, 1988) but see also Kjaer-Hansen (1965) and Wilson (1992)):

1 Long-run effects (e.g. the effect of an advertising campaign lasts longer than the campaign, and is usually lagged).

2 The difficulty in measuring productivity since standards are not easily determined. (Standards can be set for sales activities, e.g. cost to create £1 of sales, average costs of each unit sold, cost to generate £1 of profit, cost per transaction, cost per customer serviced. However, in product decisions, levels of performance may be expressed in terms of the minimum required level of sales per product or the minimum profit contribution required.)

3 The non-symmetrical nature of costs. (For example, costs increase more in changing from regional to national distribution than would be saved by changing from national to regional distribution.)

4 Costs are frequently indivisible or joint costs, often intended to support a product group.

5 Some costs have discontinuities, or a stepped character shape. The special structure of marketing costs raises problems. The cost structure of every activity is related to the interaction of fixed costs (that do not vary with the level of sales activity) and variable costs (such as shipping costs that do vary with the level of activity), and is reflected in the cost per unit produced or sold at different rates of activity. However, a large number of marketing costs are semi-fixed, including, for example, sales force costs: when a sales person is appointed his or her salary is a fixed cost, but the number of sales people and the level of commission and expenses are variable, thus giving rise to a semi-fixed expenses category. In the case of marketing, which accounts for a considerable proportion of total expenditure, these stepped costs of a semi-fixed nature determine the behaviour of many other costs.

Planning in the light of these characteristics must be based to a significant extent on past experience, knowledge of competitive activities, test marketing exercises, and the estimated expenditure that desired profits at various levels of activity will permit.

Accounting data in the more conventional form provides a point of departure for marketing cost analyses, but these data must be reworked on the basis of units that are subject to management control. (The relevant control unit will depend on the purpose of the analysis, but may be a product, product line, sales territory, marketing division, customer group, etc.).

6 The costs of performing the two main tasks of marketing – order getting and order filling – have different effects and must be treated differently. The minimization principle should be applied to distribution activities whereby a given quantitative target is aimed for at the lowest possible cost. But this principle cannot be applied to promotion since the relationship between promotion and sales means that a variation in promotional expenditure will affect turnover so minimal promotion may mean minimal sales. Consequently a predictive approach must be applied and a balance struck between the desired level of sales and the level of promotional expenditure necessary to achieve that level of sales.

7 The allocation of indirect marketing costs raises questions that require solutions. Along with a general increase in the proportion of fixed costs that exists in modern businesses there has been an increasing adoption of direct costing systems (i.e. in which indirect costs are not allocated to products) which can result in indirect costs being ignored. The significance of marketing costs is so great that they must necessarily be subjected to detailed control via responsibility centre accounting (see Chapter 19, pp. 707–17) rather than be left uncontrolled as inevitable indirect outlays.

8 Further cost problems relate to the greater number of essentially different marketing conditions that have to be controlled continually and rationally. Financial control in marketing is complicated because a number of factors are influenced by the costs incurred – the product, the territory, the customer group, and the salesman's profitability, in contrast to the product alone which is the centre of attention in production accounting. The addition

of varying conditions to a series of control bases makes it difficult to know which costs are to be controlled and in relation to which base.

9 Special cost control problems arise in attempting to evaluate the results of each element of the marketing mix. It is almost impossible to isolate the role played by, say, direct selling in the marketing operation from the roles played by promotion, price, and product features. Measures of individual parameter effectiveness must be related to detailed market analyses on a before and after basis, but this requires a more comprehensive system of marketing intelligence and information than is found in the typical company.

10 The enormous range of strategic possibilities makes it impossible to include all of them in a formal analysis. Any particular marketing strategy will involve a particular combination of the elements of the marketing mix, with particular assumed environmental conditions. The number of different possible combinations is vast. This does not mean that quantitative techniques are useless, but it does mean that major measurement problems arise to complicate the issue.

11 The ever-changing environment – including the impacts of competitive activities, developments in technology, changes in consumer tastes, government action, and the other factors depicted in Figure 18.1 – makes planning difficult. As a result control is made more difficult since it is no longer clear which variances were avoidable and which unavoidable.

12 In considering the range of possible strategies the uncertainty that any one constituent factor may change at almost any time makes the question of choice even more difficult.

13 The effectiveness of costs (i.e. productivity or efficiency) is not easy to measure. The interdependent variety of elements involved and their varying long- and short-run effects are the cause of this difficulty.

14 The tendency towards 'conglomeration', with its attendant diversification of activities and sheer size, results in an increasing complexity that challenges the best efforts in securing control.

In addition there is the problem relating to the setting up and operating of decision models which strictly require a knowledge of the substitution or supplementation of the elements of the marketing mix. As with the major problem areas discussed above the latter one (i.e. understanding substitution and supplementation) is concerned with evaluating the efficiency of the marketing effort and rationalizing the pattern of expenditure. In every case it is helpful to relate marketing costs to a profit base since this is both a measure of efficiency and of goal attainment.

Essentially, costs are incurred in marketing to obtain a sufficient level of sales to give the desired profit. The necessary sales volume can be expressed as either a particular market share, or a desired depth of market penetration, in which event the interrelationships are illustrated in Figure 18.10.

The important point made by Figure 18.10 is that increasing profit is not necessarily a function of increasing market share, nor necessarily of increasing marketing expenditure. A frequently met obsession with sales managers is that of maximizing *sales volume* whereas the action that they should be recommending is the optimizing of profits. The relationship between sales and profitability should follow one of the following patterns:

1 an increase in sales with a proportionately lower increase in costs should lead to improved profitability;

2 an increase in sales with constant costs should improve profitability;

3 an increase in sales with a decrease in costs should improve profitability;

4 the maintaining of sales at a constant level with a decrease in costs should improve profitability.

FIGURE 18.10
*Marketing costs,
profits and
penetration*

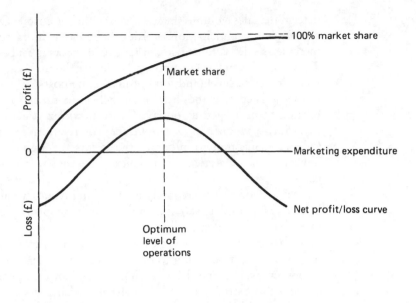

The outcome of these various matters in operational terms is that, in order to improve the effectiveness of control in marketing, the following requirements must be met:

● a frequent and accurate monitoring of the three main constituents discussed – costs, sales volume, and profit;
● a regular monitoring of the total market environment in order to detect movements and aid in evaluating the effectiveness of marketing expenditures;
● a detailed breakdown of marketing effort (expressed in financial terms) into functional/managerial responsibility centres.

In many manufacturing enterprises the costs of marketing greatly exceed the costs of production yet very little attention has been given to the analysis of marketing costs compared to the extensive attention given to production costs.

It is instructive to consider some of the reasons for this state of affairs, and these include the following:

1 While the costs of productive labour and materials can be associated with specific machines, processes, and products, the costs of the elements of the marketing mix cannot be associated so readily with outputs (such as sales and profit levels).
2 Marketing activities tend to be less routine and repetitive than is the case with many standardized production activities.
3 The dependency of marketing activities on outside agencies distinguishes them further from the more internally-regulated and predictable manufacturing activities.
4 Marketing activities tend to be performed in many locations, often distant from each other, rather than on one site.
5 Within manufacturing there is the relatively simple choice to be made between using the product or the process as the cost object. In contrast, within marketing there are many more possible cost objects – such as the product line, product range, customer, customer/industry group, sales person, sales territory, size of order, channel of distribution, etc.
6 The cost behaviour patterns of many marketing activities are the reverse of those for manufacturing activities in the sense that order getting costs tend to

determine sales volume (hence manufacturing costs). Order getting costs are committed in anticipation of sales. Whereas manufacturing costs *necessarily* increase as sales volume rises, order getting costs must be *permitted* to increase. Thus, for a given level of activity, the lower the manufacturing costs the better, while the right level (and mix) of marketing costs is a matter of judgement. It can be argued that the 'best' approach is to focus on *technical efficiency* in relation to order getting outlays (i.e. to maximize the outputs for a given level of input) and on *economic efficiency* in relation to manufacturing outlays (whereby one aims to minimize the inputs for a given level of output). This indicates the analytical complexity inherent in accounting for marketing costs.

7 Since marketing costs are rarely included in inventory valuations (being treated instead as period costs) financial accounting principles, etc., provide little incentive for detailed analysis.

8 Manufacturing activities typically have a short-run focus whereas marketing operations must pay attention to long-run considerations. This also produces a conflict over financial accounting practice in that promotional outlays in a particular period are invariably matched with the sales achieved during that period notwithstanding the fact that much promotional expenditure (and other order-getting outlays) are in the nature of capital investment intended to stimulate sales over several time periods.

9 Personnel in manufacturing roles often have a greater cost consciousness and discipline than their marketing colleagues.

10 The risk of suboptimization (whereby one particular aspect is maximized to the possible detriment of the whole) is much greater in a complex marketing context than it is in manufacturing.

11 Many marketing activities have an intangible quality that distinguishes them from the tangible characteristics of production activities. Among the intangible factors is the psychological dimension of purchase predisposition.

Although these problems are many they do not mean that no attempts should be made to plan and control marketing activities successfully. However, there is evidence to show that most accountants are not yet in tune with marketing thinking. First, accountants lack the knowledge and understanding of the information requirements necessary for the marketing function. Second, accountants in general do not accept marketing as a distinct and separate managerial function. This seemingly blind attitude was found in a survey (reported by Williamson (1979)) to be well ingrained and is an appalling indication of the failure of accountants to see the real essence of business activity (i.e. product-market interactions) and of a misplaced arrogance in looking down on a group whose purpose and function they so clearly misunderstand. Lastly, organizational design may impede adequate communications between functions. This could (and does) happen to such an extent that the accounting and marketing departments may be geographically distant from one another, although marketing *activities* are geographically dispersed in any event.

A long-established organizational design could also hinder a new pattern of resource allocation. It may be such that available resources are channelled towards the order-filling production and distribution functions rather than to the order-getting processes such as advertising, sales promotion and personal selling. Allocating to the former in preference to the latter is tantamount to saying that a firm can sell what it can make – the old sales concept – rather than the marketing concept of making what the consumers want.

The practical consequences of these inhibitions manifest themselves in the ways described below.

Schiff and Mellman as long ago as 1962, in an almost isolated empirical study, noted deficiencies of the accounting function in supplying marketing with sufficient information in certain areas, such as:

- lack of effective financial analyses of customers, channels of distribution and salespeople;
- an over-emphasis on net profit based reporting (or the full cost allocation approach);
- inadequacies in marketing cost classification (e.g. little distinction was made between fixed and variable costs or between controllable and non-controllable costs);
- return on investment was rarely used;
- there was a general lack of integration between the accounting and marketing functions.

Goodman (1970) in a later study found that accounting did not appear to have made much progress in satisfying the needs of marketing planning. These areas of failure he saw as being:

- non-use of sufficient return-on-investment criteria;
- insistence on using the traditional full-costing for decision analyses;
- inability to separate the reporting obligation of accounting from the service function;
- imperfect understanding of the marketing concept;
- lack of minimum acceptable goal criteria;
- disregard for the implications of working capital.

As various authorities have observed, there are fundamental differences between accounting and marketing. For example, accounting builds from an analysis of internal financial data, whereas marketing builds from the diagnosis of external market situations. The respective perspectives are literally poles apart (see Simmonds' *Foreword* in Wilson (1981)). Thus the marketing view that profit stems from an enterprise's position relative to its competitors (i.e. reflecting its differential advantage) and is not a function of arbitrary financial periods is not likely to meet with full-blooded approval – or even understanding – on the part of the average accountant who invariably fails to link his own profit measures either to market share or to changes in market size.

18.8 MARKETING ORIENTATION

In the absence of marketing orientation it will be difficult to implement and control marketing activities effectively since there will be no marketing plan. (The following discussion draws heavily from Wilson and Fook (1990).)

The well-documented and long-run decline in Britain's industrial competitiveness has often been attributed to a lack of adequate marketing orientation on the part of UK firms. It is widely felt that the more successful enterprises demonstrate a higher level of marketing orientation than their less successful rivals, although hard evidence to support this is rather rare. Nevertheless, despite a minority view that a preoccupation with marketing orientation is a cause of competitive decline when the former is focused on the short-run requirements of customers, there is a strong case for arguing that marketing orientation leads to improved marketing effectiveness which, in turn, leads to improved corporate effectiveness: see Figure 18.11.

FIGURE 18.11
The role of marketing orientation

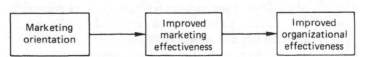

SOURCE: Wilson and Fook (1990), p. 22

If a business is to seek to improve its effectiveness in this way it needs to ask the following questions:

- What is marketing orientation?
- How can marketing orientation be recognized?
- How can marketing orientation be developed?

In this section we will address these three questions and suggest how an enterprise might develop its marketing orientation in order to improve its effectiveness.

What is Marketing Orientation?

A business can exhibit any one of a number of different orientations such as:

- production orientation;
- cost orientation;
- engineering orientation;
- sales orientation;
- marketing orientation.

The last of these is the broadest and highlights the concern the enterprise has with satisfying its customers via the adoption of the marketing concept.

Marketing orientation is concerned with implementing the marketing concept and, as such, is action oriented. However, rather than seeing it as a set of activities it is more helpful to think of marketing orientation as a process by which an enterprise seeks to maintain a continuous match betwen its products/services and its customers' needs. With a little elaboration we can build this into a formal definition:

> Marketing orientation is the process by which an enterprise's target customers' needs and wants are effectively and efficiently satisfied within the resource limitations and long-term survival requirements of that enterprise.

Doubt has been expressed by many marketing authorities on the extent to which the philosophy underlying the marketing concept has been adequately implemented – hence upon the extent to which marketing orientation really exists. Given that the practical manifestations of marketing orientation are not well known prompts our next question.

How can Marketing Orientation be Recognized?

While it should not be assumed that the following items are in order of priority, it is intended that they should be seen as constituting a reasonably comprehensive listing of the requirements that must be met if marketing orientation is to be effective.

1 Is there a good understanding within the enterprise of the needs, wants and behaviour patterns of targeted customers?
2 Is the enterprise profit-directed rather than volume-driven?
3 Does the chief executive see himself as the enterprise's senior marketing strategist or 'marketing champion'?
4 Does the enterprise have a market-driven mission (for example, a cosmetics company should see itself as being in the beauty business and the Post Office should see those in its market as users of communications)?
5 Do the enterprise's strategies reflect the realities of the market-place (including the competitive situation)?
6 Is marketing seen as being more important by managers within the enterprise than other functions and orientations?

7 Is the enterprise organized in such a way that it can be more responsive to marketing opportunities and threats than its less successful competitors?

8 Does the enterprise have a well-designed marketing information system?

9 Do managers within the enterprise make full use of marketing research inputs in their decision making?

10 Are marketing costs and revenues systematically analysed in relation to marketing activities to ensure that the latter are being carried out effectively?

11 Is there a strong link between the marketing function and the development of new products/services?

12 Does the enterprise employ staff in the marketing area who are marketing professionals (rather than, say, sales oriented in their approach)?

13 Is it understood that marketing is the responsibility of the entire organization if it is to be effective?

14 Are decisions with marketing implications made in a well-co-ordinated way and executed in an integrated manner?

These points can be linked to McKinsey & Co's 'Seven S' framework to show what is required in an effective, marketing-oriented enterprise (see Figure 18.12).

FIGURE 18.12
Requirements of marketing orientation

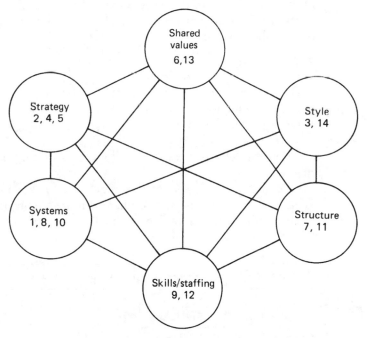

SOURCE: Adapted from Wilson and Fook (1990)

If an enterprise's responses to the points listed above contain a lot of negative answers the next question becomes important if matters are to be improved.

How can Marketing Orientation be Developed?

Developing marketing orientation is a long-term process and needs to be thought of as a form of investment. To a large extent this investment is in changing the organization's culture so that common values relating to the need to highlight service to customers, a concern for quality in all activities, and so forth are shared throughout the organization. This is not an appropriate target for the 'quick fix'.

Steps to be taken in order to enhance an enterprise's degree of marketing orientation are:

1 Secure top management support since a bottom-up approach would be doomed from the outset given the company-wide implications of marketing orientation.

2 Specify a mission relating to the development of marketing orientation. This should have a plan associated with it, and the necessary allocation of resources to enable it to be executed.

3 A task force should be set up as part of the plan to bring together managers from across the company (and consultants who can help considerably) to carry out tasks such as:

  ● identifying the current orientation of the company;
  ● carrying out a training needs analysis as a basis for a management development programme to change the company's culture in a desired way;
  ● advising on structural changes within the company to support marketing activities;
  ● ensuring commitment to change via the system of rewards (such as bonuses and promotion) that will apply to facilitate change.

4 Maintain the momentum of change by means of continuous monitoring of marketing performance to ensure that inertia does not set in. Progress towards improved marketing orientation can be measured by regularly asking questions of the following type:

  ● Are we easy to do business with?
  ● Do we keep our promises?
  ● Do we meet the standards we set?
  ● Are we responsive?
  ● Do we work together?

These elements of a process for developing marketing orientation are shown in Figure 18.13.

Developing marketing orientation requires a focus on customers, competitors, the changing environment, and company culture. Achieving it is an expensive and time-consuming endeavour. However, those companies which really make the

FIGURE 18.13
Steps in developing marketing orientation

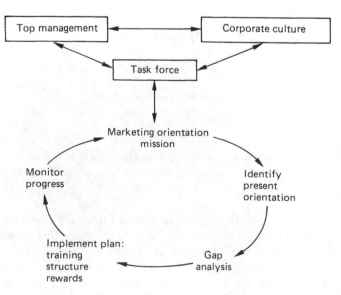

SOURCE: Wilson and Fook (1990), p. 23

effort are likely to have a higher level of marketing effectiveness and greater organizational effectiveness than their competitors.

Developing an Internal Marketing Programme

We suggested at an earlier stage in the text that the marketing concept is based upon three principal lines of thought:

1 A market focus;
2 A customer orientation;
3 Co-ordinated marketing.

However, in the case of the third of these – co-ordinated marketing – a problem that is experienced all too frequently is that not all employees are trained or motivated to work together sufficiently closely. The net effect of this is that the organization then works less than optimally. The implications of this are, in turn, exacerbated as markets become more competitive and the difficulties of achieving – and sustaining – a meaningful competitive advantage become ever greater. A programme of internal marketing in which there is a heightened emphasis upon staff training, motivation, empowerment and working in teams is therefore a potentially powerful contributor to organizational performance and, in particular, to the achievement of customer satisfaction. An effective internal marketing programme is therefore likely to be characterized by:

● a fundamental acceptance of its strategic significance by senior management;
● a willingness on the part of senior management to change the structure of the organization so that the importance of front-line staff is recognized and reflected in the structure of the organization; it is this which was referred to earlier in our discussion of the right-side-up organization (see p. 26);
● the development and communication of clear values;
● the empowerment of front-line staff so that they are given greater freedom to make decisions which will solve customers' problems;
● a commitment to staff development and training;
● a system which recognizes staff excellence and rewards it accordingly;
● the development of strong teams;
● the identification of what Jan Carlzon of Scandinavian Airlines referred to as 'moments of truth' (these are the points of contact between the customer and a member of staff where the customer can be won or lost by the quality of service and personal contact that he or she receives) and the conscious thinking through of the ways in which these can best be capitalized upon by staff training and behaviour;
● the setting of particular standards, a fundamental commitment to their achievement and a total lack of willingness to compromise in doing this; and
● the development of effective feedback systems so that the effectiveness of the internal marketing programme can be monitored. See Illustration 18.1.

Illustration 18.1: The AA and Unisys and Their Use of Internal Marketing

Customer care and satisfaction are fundamental and long-standing elements of the Automobile Association's marketing strategy. However, having positioned itself in the 1990s as 'the country's fourth emergency service' and recognising that customers generally have ever higher levels of expectation of the organisations they deal with, the AA recognised that there was a need within the organisation to re-evaluate how they might best deliver this. The answer, they felt, lay in a greater emphasis upon staff motivation and that the recognition of the achievements of its workforce could often be as effective as financial rewards. This led to the development of a number of reward schemes, with staff being nominated by their supervisors when it was felt they have 'gone the extra mile' to improve customer care and quality.

Although the AA has traditionally been characterised by a family-type atmosphere, something which in many ways made internal marketing a relatively straightforward exercise, Unisys, in common with many large multinationals, was forced to reinvent itself in the 1980s in order to focus upon customers rather than being product-driven. It chose to do this by putting customer service and quality ahead of price, but in the process was forced to make major cultural changes. Staff were retrained and taught to develop completely new mindsets. An important part of this involved a greater degree of staff empowerment which, for Unisys, meant explaining to staff what they **cannot** do and then letting them decide how they do want to run the business. At the same time, they developed a rewards system designed to recognise staff initiatives to improve quality and customer care.

Underpinning all of this is the belief that in order to understand customer service means first thinking like a customer. Unisys therefore encourages staff to imagine life on the other side of the desk and, where necessary, to take the unprompted action that can make or break customer satisfaction. However, doing this involves creating the appropriate culture rather than simply emphasising training.

Source: The Sunday Times, *11 June 1995, p. 13*

It follows from this that internal marketing should precede external marketing. This can be illustrated by the way in which, although it is relatively easy for an organization to commit itself to high levels of service, these are unlikely to be achieved until and unless the staff understand the real importance of service excellence and have been trained to deliver this. It is because of this that an increasing number of organizations, such as the AA and Unisys, are restructuring so that the typical organizational chart is inverted and a right-side-up organization created (the right-side-up and wrong-side-up organizations were discussed in Chapter 1). In this way, the pivotal importance of front-line staff to the delivery of customer satisfaction is highlighted. See Figure 18.14 and Illustration 18.2.

Illustration 18.2: The Rise and Rise of Internal Marketing

A survey of delegates at the 1996 Marketing Forum revealed that 78% of their organisations were 'fairly' or 'very seriously' committed to internal marketing. This was reflected by the way in which budgets for internal marketing are being raised, sometimes dramatically, to ensure that the corporate message is being effectively communicated to employees and the corporate identity is being maintained at all levels.

Source: Marketing, *12 December 1996, p. 4*

FIGURE 18.14
The role of internal marketing

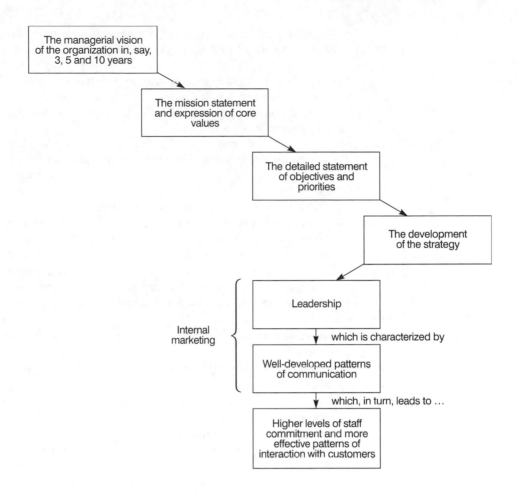

18.9 PLANNING ORIENTATION

What benefits does planning offer? Among the most important are the following:

1 Planning requires effective communication which improves the functional co-ordination of efforts throughout the organization (see below). In part this will be due to the clearer definition of objectives and policies that planning presupposes (see Porter and Roberts (1977)).
2 Planning motivates by showing what is expected of each member of the organization, and if plans have been agreed between superiors and subordinates in an appropriate way there should be a high degree of commitment to their attainment.
3 Planning should lead to the making of better decisions by requiring an explicit statement of assumptions underlying choices as well as the enumerating of alternative courses of action and relevant states of nature. In other words, systematic thought needs to be given to the future, thereby ensuring that effort is not wholly absorbed in the present.
4 Planning encourages a favourable attitude towards change, which is due in part to a better state of preparation for sudden variations (anticipated and otherwise) so that they can be turned to the organization's advantage, but which is also due to constantly striving to create a desired future. As pointed out by Charles St Thomas (1965, p. 9):

> ... the manager who successfully undertakes his planning work must begin by recognising that the primary key to his effectiveness lies in his capability to adapt.

5 Planning enables standards of performance to be established, and these in turn allow the control process to be effective.

Despite the obvious appeal of planning there are those who believe that any attempt to lay out specific and rational plans is either foolish, dangerous, or downright evil. Churchman (1968, p. 14 and pp. 215–26) refers to these individuals as anti-planners:

> ... there are all kinds of anti-planners, but the most numerous are those who believe that experience and cleverness are the hallmarks of good management.

It is easy to see what a contrast there is between the 'practical' approach based on intuition and experience and the more analytical approach being recommended in this book. Particular arguments against the adoption of planning in any given organization might include the fear that it will take power away from the chief executive, or make excessive demands on line managers, or consume time and other resources for results that cannot be guaranteed, or be a waste of effort because market forecasts are never wholly correct, and so on (see Hussey (1981), pp. 9–10).

Failings in strategic marketing planning may arise as a result of:

1 A chief executive who is not committed to planning, or who makes every decision of significance alone.
2 A planner who is too narrow in his view, or too restricted in his ability, to consider all the essential aspects of marketing planning and their impacts throughout the organization.
3 Small-scale operations which are unable adequately to support a planning function.
4 A state of corporate decline that is progressing too rapidly for planning to arrest it (see Stonich (1975)).
5 Too much emphasis being placed on *where* to compete and not enough on *how* to compete given that the latter rather than the former secures sustainable competitive advantage (see Simmonds (1985)).
6 Too little focus on uniqueness and adaptability with a tendency in many industries (e.g. security dealing, semi-conductors, biotechnology, retailing) towards a herd instinct that encourages sameness on the one hand and a limited adaptive capability on the other.
7 Inadequate emphasis on *when* to compete – such as being first into new markets or first with new products as opposed to being fast followers.
8 Too much attention being paid to competing organizations rather than focusing on individuals as competitors (e.g. chief executives' pronouncements in annual reports, etc., effectively lock their organizations into specified courses of action which highlight opportunities for others).
9 Using the wrong measures of success – especially when these favour short-term results to the detriment of long-term performance.
   Assessing marketing performance is difficult due to problems of both definition and measurement. The traditional approach has been to attempt to measure outputs relative to inputs (e.g. marketing productivity analysis – see Chapter 3). While this is feasible in broad terms, e.g. for an entire organization, it becomes more problematic as one looks in more detail at specific activities or marketing programmes. Much in marketing is unquantifiable and it follows that inputs and outputs cannot be adequately measured and manipulated if some are qualitative. Moreover, the typical result of relating inputs and outputs is the assessment of efficiency whereas effectiveness is of much greater significance. (See Bleeke (1988) for a fuller discussion of 5–9.)
10 Planning becoming a mindless ritual rather than an opportunity for sound strategic thinking.

11 Senior staff get involved in 'us versus them' battles with lower level colleagues.

12 Information that is held in one part of the organization is withheld, or only begrudgingly provided, to those who need it elsewhere in the organization.

13 Key information on which plans are based (such as sales estimates) are biased to justify a particular position rather than providing a sound basis for comparing alternatives (see Lowe and Shaw (1968)).

14 The results of the planning process are ignored when actual decisions with strategic consequences for marketing are made (such as acquisitions).

(Further coverage of points 10–14 will be found in Chapter 9 of Abell and Hammond (1979).)

18.10 ORGANIZATIONAL ISSUES

Introduction

Suggestions have been made, for example by Hayhurst and Wills (1972), that changing organizational needs may lead to the disintegration of a corporate marketing organization. This could be achieved by the separation of operational activities on the one hand and planning activities on the other. Selling and distribution might fall into the former category.

It is clear (e.g. Hooley, et al. (1984)) that the increasingly competitive environment in which marketing is undertaken has created a recognition that organizational flexibility is a necessary element of marketing orientation.

To a large extent the successful implementation of marketing strategies relies upon an appropriate structure. As Hughes (1980) has pointed out:

> Many marketing plans fail because the planner did not consider the fact that the organization was not capable of implementing the plan. Short-range plans will require adaptation to the existing organization, whereas long-range plans may require redesigning the organization.

There is thus an interdependence between strategy and structure, and this warrants our considering the issue of organizational structures in marketing. For example, organizing marketing around products or markets – rather than around functional tasks – can give an important source of competitive advantage (see Levitt (1980)). Moreover, many writers have argued that organizational structure is a key determinant of marketing effectiveness, marketing failures, and the successful implementation of the marketing concept. (See, for example, Tookey (1974), Hakansson, et al. (1979), Cascino (1967).)

Organizational Design

Apart from serving as a means of linking the organization to its environment, thereby ensuring that the outputs and activities are compatible with the external milieu in which the organization is operating, planning also serves as a means of integrating the goal-striving activities of the organization into a coordinated whole. This latter role is facilitated by effective organizational design, as Nathanson, et al. (1982, p. 93) point out:

> Organization design is conceived to be a decision process to bring about a coherence between the goals or purposes for which the organization exists, the pattern of division of labor and interunit coordination and the people who will do the work.

Organization design has similarly been defined by Pfeffer (1978) as:

> ... the process of grouping activities, roles or positions in the organization to co-ordinate effectively the interdependencies that exist ... the implicit goal of the structuring process is achieving a more rationalized and co-ordinated system of activity.

In considering a framework for organizational design (OD) we can be guided by Child's 1977 classification of the major issues within the domain of OD:

- allocating task responsibilities to individuals;
- designating formal relationships leading to hierarchical levels and spans of control;
- grouping individuals into departments, departments into divisions, etc;
- designing systems for integration and communication;
- delegating authority and evaluation;
- providing systems for appraisal and reward.

Galbraith has developed a conceptual framework in which a number of organizational variables over which choices must be made by managers in creating an organization design are identified. These are task, structure, information and decision processes, reward systems and people. In choosing how to balance these elements top management has considerable scope for varying and influencing all five. However, the organization design that emerges should be one that fits the product-market strategy of the enterprise. If a consciously developed strategy is to be effectively implemented this needs to be done via a properly designed organization: the process of organization design is the link between strategy formulation and implementation.

Nathanson, et al. (1982, p. 110) have proposed a series of 'fit' relationships which indicate the best 'fit' between particular strategies and structures. The main choices consist of:

1 single business with a functional structure;
2 a business having related products (which implies common technology and possibly common manufacturing facilities) with a multidivisional structure;
3 a business having unrelated products (hence no technological commonalities) with a holding company structure.

An enterprise's chosen strategy is a key determinant of its relationship with the environment, which in turn places particular information-processing requirements on the management of the enterprise. Different strategies help in defining different environmental settings, thus giving rise to different information processing requirements. (As an example consider the different circumstances of an enterprise choosing a strategy taking it into a high-technology sector and another enterprise adopting a strategy that focuses on a traditional, labour-intensive sector.) A good fit is found when the structure – which includes information processing among its elements – matches the strategy and produces the desired outcomes.

Figure 18.15 illustrates the best combinations of strategy and structure. ('Product relatedness' refers to common technology and 'market relatedness' refers to common customers.)

Piercy (1985) has put forward a very powerful case for viewing the marketing organization as an information-processing structure. His basic model is shown in Figure 18.16.

In developing this model Piercy reviewed major approaches to organization theory. His most significant point of departure from the traditional approach lies in his examination of information-processing models of structure and the implications of such models for organizational power and political behaviour.

Such an approach focuses on the processes required to cope with task and environmental uncertainty:

> ... in the sense both that uncertainty imposes an information-processing burden that a given structure may or may not be able to cope with, and that coping with these uncertainties critical to the organisation provides a source of power and political strength to certain sub-units or individuals.

(Piercy (1985), p. 38)

FIGURE 18.15
Fit relationships

Strategic situation Product-market strategy	Operating organization Structure	Planning process
1. High product relatedness with high market relatedness	Functional structure: necessary because of product market and geographic relatedness. No need to divisionalize.	Business-level planning focus on: competition, competitive advantage, distinctive competences, product-market segmentation, stage of product-market evolution. Synergy-integration of different functional areas. Market share, production efficiencies, technological innovation.
2. High product relatedness with low market relatedness	Functional structure: necessary because of product relatedness.	SBUs to deal with the market or geographic diversity, to focus attention on each market and allocate the functional resources to markets in most efficient manner, and to keep abreast of each market's opportunities and threats.
3. Low product relatedness with high market relatedness	Divisionalized structure: necessary because of different technologies and manufacturing processes inherent in the product.	SBUs to provide strategic approach to the market and eliminate counterproductive competition within the market- place.
4. Low product relatedness with low market relatedness	Multidivisional or holding company structure: the high degree of diversity calls for much decentralization.	SBUs, because of the large size of most of the firms in this category, the focus is primarily on goal formulation and setting on a financial basis, to place emphasis on the 'stars' that are small and might otherwise be overlooked, to serve as a span of control reducer, and to overlap any interdependencies (relatedness) that might exist.

SOURCE: Nathanson, et al. (1982)

FIGURE 18.16
*The organizational
dimensions of
marketing*

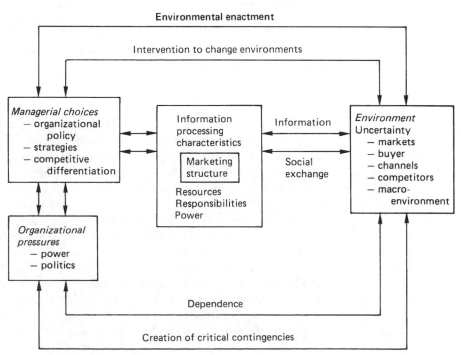

SOURCE: Piercy (1985), p. 17

The link between marketing structures and the environment, and hence to marketing decision making, is provided by the idea of information processing. The question follows as to which organizational structure is best suited to processing the information required by marketing tasks, but this question has been largely ignored by marketing experts.

One approach to dealing with some aspects of the question is provided by Weitz and Anderson (1981). They suggest that the environment may be analysed in terms of:

- *complexity* - which refers to the number of elements relevant to the organization (such as the number of product markets served);
- *interconnectedness* - which is concerned with the interdependence of key elements within the environment;
- *predictability* - which relates to the degree to which the environment is stable or unstable, hence to the degree of uncertainty.

See Figure 18.17 which relates these aspects of the environment to marketing organizations.

FIGURE 18.17
Environmental dimensions and marketing organization

Environmental unpredictability and interconnectedness

	Low	High
High (Environmental complexity)	1 Decentralized organization e.g. product divisions High differentiation i.e. marketing is organized around different products Conventional integration methods e.g. hierarchical reporting, planning systems	2 Matrix organization e.g. organized into product groups drawing on functional resources High differentiation i.e. marketing is organized around different projects Unconventional integration methods e.g. programming managers
Low (Environmental complexity)	3 Functional organization e.g. sales, advertising, marketing research, etc. Low differentiation i.e. marketing is general for all products and markets Conventional integration methods e.g. hierarchical reporting, planning systems	4 Brand management e.g. product managers plus functional specialists Low differentiation i.e. marketing is general for all brands Unconventional integration methods e.g. brand and market managers

SOURCE: Adapted from Weitz and Anderson (1981)

The tendency towards increasingly unpredictable and discontinuous change implies that organizational forms need to be considered as being short term and subject to adjustment in response to frequent changes in the contingencies that underpin them. Doyle (1979) points to such factors as an increased focus on integration, a change from volume to productivity orientation, and a move towards portfolio management as indicating that a traditional functional structure is becoming less and less appropriate. A more complex and ambiguous set of alternatives is to be found in divisional and matrix forms of organization, but these too may be transitory.

An extreme view has been put forward by Haller (1980a, 1980b) and Wills (1980a, 1980b) to suggest that marketing – as a unified function – will disappear either as a result of its being subsumed within strategic management (see Figure 18.18), or as a result of marketing planning being taken under the wing of a corporate planning department and a sales director on the one hand and a distribution director on the other emerging to take over the operational activities, with no marketing director.

FIGURE 18.18
*A strategic
management
organizational
structure*

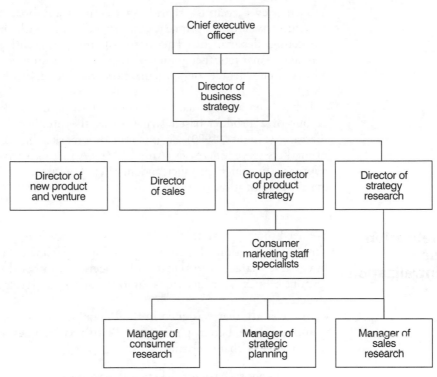

FIGURE 18.19
*Comparison of
marketing structures*

SOURCE: Adapted by Piercy (1985) from Haller (1980)

Form	Advantages	Disadvantages	Situational indicators
Functional	Specialization in task activities to develop skills. Marketing tasks and responsibilities clearly defined.	Excess levels of hierarchy may reduce unity of control. Direct lines of communication may be ignored. Conflicts may emerge. Integration problem for CME*.	Simple marketing operations. Single primary product/market.
Product/ brand	Specialization in products/brands. More management attention to marketing requirements of different products/ brands. Fast reaction to product-related change.	Dual reporting. Too much product emphasis. More management levels and cost. Conflict.	Wide product lines sold to homogeneous groups of customers, but sharing production/marketing systems, i.e. proliferation of brands and diversified products requiring different skills/ activities.
Market/ customer/ geographical	Specialization in a market entity – focus on customer needs. Fast reaction to market-related changes.	Duplication of functions. Coordination problems. More management levels.	Limited, standardized homogeneous product line sold to customers in different industries, i.e. proliferation of markets each meriting separate efforts.
Product/ market overlay	Advantages of functional product and market specialization and integration.	Allocation of responsibilities is difficult. Duplication inefficiencies.	Multiple products and multiple markets.

* Chief Marketing Executive
SOURCE: Piercy (1985)

Such views contrast sharply with the traditional approach to marketing structures where the primary concern has been with differentiation within the marketing department. The basis of this differentiation may be products, functions, markets, geographical regions or customer groups, each of which allows some degree of specialization via the division of labour. See Figure 18.19.

It has been argued that the functional structure is likely to be abandoned in favour of a product-based structure as the number of products in the range increases (Hughes, 1980), or in favour of a market-based structure as the number of markets served increases (Ames, 1971). A further variation is to adopt a hybrid approach in which product and market structures are combined in a form of matrix organization.

Centralization Versus Decentralization

We need to recognize that in the context of large, complex organizations it is not simply the creation of a single marketing department (along with its status and integrative characteristics) that is of concern but rather the allocation of marketing responsibilities and activities among different levels in the organizational structure.

In the study that was cited in the Preamble to Stage Four, Lynch, et al. (1988) found that the better performing British companies exhibited the following organizational characteristics:

- more likely to have a marketing department;
- more likely to have marketing represented directly at board level;
- more likely to adopt a market-based organizational structure;
- work more closely with other functional areas.

The study of large organizations has consistently emphasized the process of divisionalization beyond the point at which a traditional organizational structure (i.e. of a functional form) becomes incapable of effectively coping with such issues as geographic expansion, volume growth, vertical integration and product diversification (e.g. Chandler, 1962).

Buell (1966) suggested a fourfold categorization of divisionalized marketing organization:

- *Divisionalized companies with self-sufficient divisions.* At the corporate level of marketing (if it exists) policy guidelines and advice are provided, and the marketing performance of divisions is evaluated, but no marketing services are provided.
- *Divisionalized companies with corporate marketing services.* Divisions are responsible for production and selling but central marketing services deal with advertising, marketing research, etc.
- *Geographically divisionalized companies.* Divisions provide some marketing activities for their areas but central marketing services are also provided, along with national/international coordination.
- *Centralized manufacturing/decentralized marketing.* All manufacturing is centralized and marketing is undertaken through divisions.

There are benefits from both centralization and decentralization. For example, Heskett (1976) has identified the following.

Centralized Control
- Facilitates the coordination of marketing.
- Makes up for low management expertise in some areas.
- Can lead to better control.
- Ensures the transfer of ideas among marketing groups.
- Avoids duplication of effort.

Decentralization
- Encourages more effective local performance.
- Improves management development opportunities.
- Favours the development of marketing programmes that are more sensitive to local needs.

Deciding whether centralization is to be preferred to decentralization will depend on the specific circumstances of a given enterprise. For example, an enterprise having a complex and dynamic environment on the one hand and a variety of product groups on the other might be better suited to a decentralized structure. As Nonaka and Nicosia (1979) put it:

> A simple centralized organization of a marketing department is sufficient to process environmental information that is homogeneous and certain. But a complex, decentralized organization for a marketing department is required to process environmental information that is heterogeneous and uncertain ... only organisms with high internal variety can cope with and survive high variety in the environment.

See Figure 18.20.

FIGURE 18.20
Environmental variety and marketing centralization

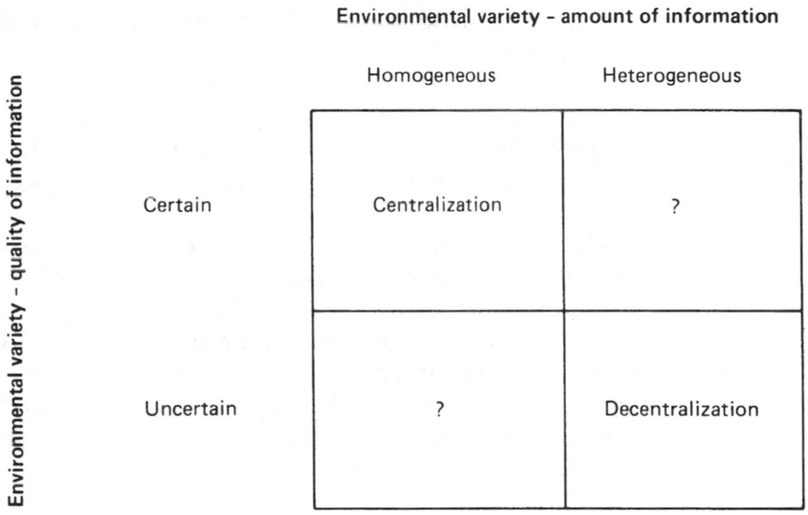

Environmental variety - amount of information

	Homogeneous	Heterogeneous
Certain	Centralization	?
Uncertain	?	Decentralization

Environmental variety - quality of information

SOURCE: Adapted from Nonaka and Nicosia (1979)

Whether or not the marketing organization should be centralized is likely to be a function of uncertainty which, in turn, reflects environmental turbulence. A centralized structure is able to cope with a relatively stable – hence predictable – environment whereas a decentralized structure is more appropriate when the environment is unstable – hence more uncertain.

18.11 SUMMARY

In this chapter we have reviewed an array of problems that need to be addressed if marketing plans are to be properly developed, adequately implemented, and the outcomes effectively controlled. The origins of problems include:

- pressures from a variety of sources (embracing consumer behaviour, economic conditions, technology, societal expectations, politics) all of which are associated with change and the imperative for enterprises to adapt to change if they are to be successful;

- the marketing subsystem with its interdependencies;
- the nature of marketing feedback;
- the adequacy of information;
- cost issues and the analysis of marketing costs as a means of establishing the effectiveness – in financial terms – and efficiency of marketing activities;
- the degree of marketing orientation that exists within the enterprise;
- the resistance to planning that is still to be found.

Successful implementation and control will be facilitated by:

- a balance between short-run programme-related measures and longer-term performance criteria;
- the attainment of synergy among the various elements of the marketing mix;
- the use of appropriate criteria for assessing performance within segments;
- the use of appropriate criteria for allocating resources to segments, coupled with flexibility in adaptive reallocations;
- executing product-market decisions in the broader context of business-level considerations relating to strategic marketing.

The need to balance strategy with a suitable structure was discussed in some detail. An emphasis was given to the principles of organizational design and the view (put forward most strongly by Piercy) of the marketing organization as an information-processing structure within an uncertain environment.

The control structure of an organization embraces the organization structure, responsibility centres, performance measures and the system of rewards. This structure needs to be properly designed if resources are to be allocated effectively in decentralized decision making.

There is a clear need for the control structure to be co-ordinated with the organization's planning system if desired behaviour is to be achieved. In assessing the adequacy of results it would be too limiting to rely solely on traditional measures such as costs, profits and profitability (e.g. return on investment) since these are partial on the one hand and on the other emphasize a relatively short-term orientation. It is better to relate short-term measures to strategic performance measures, including changes in market share, changes in growth and changes in competitive position.

18.12 EXERCISES

1 Identify the major pressures currently impacting on the marketing activities of an enterprise with which you are familiar.
2 Using the grid system shown in Figure 18.3, locate your chosen enterprise from Exercise 1 above in the change resistance grid. What does its location mean for future actions?
3 Suggest ways in which marketing and financial specialists might work together in greater harmony.
4 Outline (and justify) a suitable organizational structure for the effective implementation of marketing programmes in:

   (a) a construction company;
   (b) a professional services firm;
   (c) a non-profit enterprise.

5 Using the matrix in Figure 18.20, locate the organizations specified in Exercise 4 above, making whatever (explicit) assumptions you consider necessary.

18.13 DISCUSSION QUESTIONS

1 How might you seek to persuade those who are sceptical about the benefits of marketing planning to take a different view?
2 Is marketing orientation necessary for success? What steps might be taken to improve an enterprise's level of marketing orientation?
3 Outline the activities necessary for implementing a marketing strategy. How might these activities vary among enterprises operating in different sectors?
4 What factors are likely to influence the choice of a particular organizational design for marketing activities?
5 Are problems of marketing feedback delays getting more or less severe?

18.14 CASE STUDY

Eastman Kodak Co.

Armed with a machete, Eastman Kodak Co. Chairman Colby H. Chandler marched into a meeting with his top 75 managers last month and began whacking away at a wooden crate.

His subordinates were dumbfounded. Usually, the diminutive Mr. Chandler emphasizes a point with intricate graphs, and he rarely raises his voice. But after Kodak's second-quarter profit plunged 85% – and shocked Wall Street – only a tantrum, a vivid demonstration of how he wanted to cut costs, would suffice. 'There's no working the middle course in wartime,' Mr. Chandler asserted, borrowing a line from Winston Churchill.

The 64-year-old executive, embarking on his fourth restructuring of the company in six years, knows that it is his last chance to prove his leadership before he retires next May. Already, Kodak watchers are shaking their heads, wondering why he needs four tries to accomplish essentially one job: cut costs. Is he simply the leader of a gang that can't shoot straight? they ask.

'He's a considerate and sincere person, but he doesn't have the creativity and adaptability needed in today's markets,' says Karen Paul, a business professor at the Rochester Institute of Technology.

Even Mr. Chandler's chief lieutenants say that past restructurings, while yielding significant improvements, didn't go far enough. 'We're getting criticized by people who say, 'We've heard this all before,' and ask, 'Why haven't we delivered?' There's some justification for that,' says President Kay R. Whitmore. Indeed, a decision last month to tie annual bonuses to profits rather than to dividends on common stock was last proposed in 1986.

Vice Chairman J. Phillip Samper says, 'We have to be tougher. Our costs are still too high.' Although the company's cost structure has improved, sales per employee last year totaled only $140,000, far below the $380,000 at Kodak's chief competitor, Fuji Photo Film Co., analysts say.

But does Kodak still have enough time to rein in expenses? The plan announced last month includes elimination of 4,500 jobs and disposal or restructuring of 20 businesses with $1.25 billion in annual sales; it is designed to generate $1 billion in operating savings in 1990. But it hasn't dispelled persistent takeover rumors. Some analysts and investors consider Kodak's stock to be greatly undervalued, given the total value of its assets. Analysts say the company would fetch at least $75 a share in a takeover, compared with the $47.75-a-share closing price on the New York Stock Exchange yesterday.

Wall Street is buzzing with talk of possible raiders, including Carl Icahn – although a source close to him says 'he hasn't owned Kodak in years.' In any event, Kodak, with 324.2 million shares outstanding and a market capitalization of about $16.2 billion, would be a huge chunk to swallow. 'But it has great break-up value and a stellar name,' says a Shearson Lehman Hutton money manager.

The takeover talk is likely to intensify after a federal judge determines, in coming months, the size of the settlement in Polaroid Corp.'s successful instant-camera patent suit against Kodak. Kodak could get a multibillion-dollar bill for damages – a fact that has acted as a poison pill, discouraging takeover attempts.

For Mr. Chandler, the job of making elephant-like Kodak dance has been painful and frustrating. It has required ripping apart a 100-year-old culture that guaranteed lifetime employment but fostered complacency. Kodak had monopolized photography for so many decades that many managers didn't worry about competition – or mistakes.

After becoming chief executive six years ago, Mr. Chandler didn't dally. The methodical engineer set up more than a dozen business units, forced middle managers to make decisions, demanded shorter product-development cycles and even trimmed cafeteria hours. Some results were gratifying: a color copier went from design to manufacturing in 22 months. And a color film introduced this spring is widely considered the best in the world.

Last year, when Kodak posted a record profit of $1.4 billion, its managers believed that tough times were over. They were mistaken; in the 1989 first half, net slid 60% as operating earnings declined in most of the company's businesses.

Critics blame Mr. Chandler for not shrinking Kodak's size in one radical restructuring. Although the entire company was reorganized in 1984 into smaller divisions to make them more efficient, that wasn't enough to avoid a 10% work-force reduction and a 5% budget cut in 1986. Similarly, Kodak said earlier this year that it would slash costs for support services by 15% by 1990, only to embark on the fourth restructuring last month.

The repeated rounds of cutbacks, some observers say, have demoralized employees and still not done the trick. In spite of the cuts, Kodak's employment, at 145,300, is still at a peak because of a spate of acquisitions. And bloating of Kodak's payroll sometimes seems apparent: at a recent meeting about a small legislative matter involving Kodak's Sterling Drug unit, for example, Sterling's two managers were out-numbered by 22 Kodak staffers.

Disgruntled employees recently called for Mr. Chandler's resignation in letters to the editor of Rochester's daily newspapers. 'Perhaps it is time for you to move on and let someone else straighten up the mess,' wrote James Powless, an employee at Kodak's Elmgrove plant.

Others recommend the Jack Welch approach at General Electric Co. Asserts Bernard Ouellette, a former Sterling Drug executive: 'Divisions should have to defend why they should be kept. If you want to make motors, you have to show how you can deliver a 13% profit increase. If you can't, we'll get rid of you. It's pretty hard stuff, but a big company like Kodak has to go through it.'

But Mr. Chandler, who fondly calls his employees members of the 'Kodak family,' consciously avoided wholesale cuts. 'How big a change can you make without destroying everything in the process?' he asks. The executive, who grew up on a Maine dairy farm, is especially protective of both the company employees and the city of Rochester. 'There is not a family in Rochester that isn't touched by Kodak in some way,' he says.

Unlike a Manhattan executive who never has to face laid-off employees, Mr. Chandler is often greeted by managers on Rochester's streets with a wave and a 'Hi, Colby.' 'I agonize about every single dismissal from the company,' he declares.

Meanwhile, Kodak's diversification binge culminated in its $5.1 billion takeover of Sterling Drug last year. The camera and film company now also makes such unlikely products as artificial snow, floppy disks and aspirin. But top executives admit that they need to cull their lines of business and narrow their focus. 'We have an accumulation that we shouldn't have built up,' Mr. Chandler says.

At the same time, Kodak has been reluctant to shed products with little growth potential. For example, the carousel slide projector, a Kodak innovation that is experiencing slow growth, doesn't generate big profits, but Mr. Chandler is reluctant to part with it. 'I have a soft spot in my heart for it,' he explains.

And how could Kodak lightly abandon motion-picture film, even though the product's long-term growth is threatened by videotape and high-definition television? Years ago, movie makers sought Kodak's help in improving film; Kodak responded, and shelves lined with Emmy and Oscar awards hail its achievement. 'There's only one Kodak in the U.S.,' says John Larish, a former employee. 'People expect them to continue doing certain things.'

Certainly, Kodak faces a dilemma hamstringing many American conglomerates: it must hold down prices or risk losing market share to foreign competitors. But, at the same time, investors are demanding hefty returns *now*.

Kodak, which once set prices at will on everything from film to flash-cubes, has been forfeiting increases to stave off Fuji and others. Competition has been especially fierce in Kodak's key color print film and photographic-paper businesses. That partly explains why earnings couldn't keep pace with the healthy 9% growth in volume this year.

'Nothing in this world is simple anymore,' Mr. Chandler says, adding: 'You pay a terrible price to buy market share back.'

Yet, at times, top Kodak executives have ignored competitors' strengths. When a manager began tracking Fuji, he discovered that the Japanese company had been quietly licensing Kodak technology from Kodak's patent attorneys, who didn't inform senior executives. Fuji also had a more efficient inventory systems in the U.S. While Kodak warehouses stocked almost all its products, Fuji relied on overnight air shipments, which increased freight expenses but sharply reduced inventory costs and delivery times.

After he presented his findings about Fuji to senior management, however, the manager, who has since left the company, says he was told never to talk about it again. 'The message was, "We don't want to hear that story,"' says the departed manager, who doesn't want to be identified because his wife still works at Kodak. The company declines to comment on the incident.

Nor did Kodak always listen to its employees in Japan, who urged the company to assimilate Japanese ways. Instead, Kodak insisted on imposing its U.S. work policies and refused to offer standard Japanese benefits, such as housing assistance, according to a former Japanese manager. And until 1985, the print on its familiar yellow film boxes was in English. The result: although Kodak has gained 13% share of the Japanese color print film market, employee turnover is high, and Japanese consumers' acceptance of Kodak products is slow.

Kodak acknowledges that it has broken 'with some Japanese traditions in terms of office layout and uniforms' and says its housing assistance isn't

Exhibit 1
*Eastman Kodak's
recent troubles*

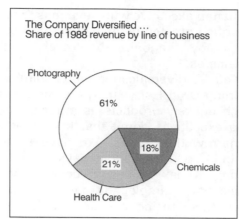

The Company Diversified ...
Share of 1988 revenue by line of business

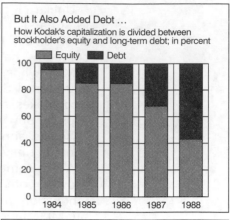

But It Also Added Debt ...
How Kodak's capitalization is divided between
stockholder's equity and long-term debt; in percent

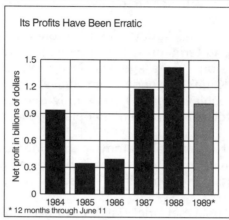

Its Profits Have Been Erratic

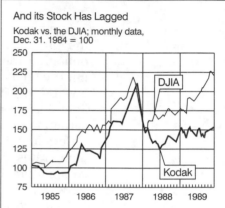

And its Stock Has Lagged
Kodak vs. the DJIA; monthly data,
Dec. 31. 1984 = 100

as high as other employers' or even offered in all cases. However, it believes that its salaries are generally higher and that it offers an attractive benefit package.

President Whitmore says the battle in Japan was 'lost by not being there earlier.' Until five years ago, Kodak executives rejected as too costly opening offices in the world's second-largest photographic market. 'The best we can do now is fight it out,' he says. 'We want to make them fight for every share point they got.'

While Kodak missed the mark in Japan, the jury is still out on Mr. Chandler's biggest, boldest move – the Sterling Drug acquisition. That shocked investors who liked blue-chip Kodak for studiously shunning high debt – and all the more because Sterling promises slight short-term returns.

The drug company does provide an entry into the fast-growing pharmaceutical business, although Kodak stock has yet to rebound to pre-Sterling highs. 'We won't know for sure if we did it right [buying Sterling] for another five years,' Mr. Whitmore says, noting that it takes at least that long to get new drugs on the market.

Absorbing Sterling hasn't been easy. Kodak wanted Sterling's top managers for their marketing savvy and knowledge of drugs, but within a year most of them left. Among them was the highly regarded former chairman, John M. Pietruski. Colleagues say Mr. Pietruski, who declines comment, felt slighted by Kodak's refusal to give him a board seat.

'Pietruski would have been a big help to Colby. He's the kind of guy who sees things as they are and not as they want them to be,' a Sterling manager says.

Kodak executives say they expected management resignations but weren't prepared for problems with Sterling's flagship product, Bayer aspirin. Kodak assumed that Bayer would take off on reports that aspirin helps heart patients. 'We didn't understand the business,' Mr. Whitmore says. 'The big part is, "I've got a headache," and that's very competitive.'

To Kodak, even Bayer is a minor headache compared with the migraine that hit when Mr. Chandler realized how badly things were going this year. Kodak's first half ended just a month after the company's annual meeting in May where – right before giving shareholders free lunch and cholesterol checks – Mr. Colby optimistically predicted a record 1989.

Although he says he was 'surprised' by the pervasiveness of problems, red flags were flying since the beginning of the year. But subordinates assured top executives that they could 'turn it around,' Vice Chairman Samper says. Such was the case in information systems, where operating profits plunged 93%, after new high-tech products stalled and over-supplied customers cut orders.

Now, Kodak is telling its employees: be productive, or you are out. But how seriously the company means that isn't clear. Rather than making hard-nosed decisions about who will go in the 4,500-employee cut-back, the company is seeking voluntary resignations with generous severance packages. 'I don't sense a lot of fear, even after the latest announcement,' says a former Kodak manager and now a consultant.

In addition, securities analysts are already saying they don't expect Kodak's profit to improve this year. They are lowering their second-half estimates in anticipation of declines in operating profits in all of Kodak's major business segments. Prudential-Bache Securities' Alex Henderson reduced his 1989 forecast to $3.60 a share from $3.70 a share, and says that may still be too high. In 1988, Kodak earned $1.4 billion, or $4.31 a share, on sales of $17.03 billion.

Mr. Chandler has only nine months before his retirement to turn things around, a time pressure that could explain his resort to machete dramatics at meetings. Mr. Whitmore explains: 'We're saying to managers, "Watch me throw a tantrum,"' in hopes that 'they'll finally understand we're serious.'

Source: Clare Ansberry and Carol Hymowitz, 'Last Chance: Kodak Chief Tries for the Fourth Time to Cut Costs,' *The Wall Street Journal*, September 19, 1989, pp. 1, A8.

Discussion Questions
1 Identify and discuss several key issues Kodak must consider in developing a marketing strategy.
2 Describe the competitive situation Kodak faces and the firm's competitive advantages.
3 Does Kodak have a market target strategy? What should Kodak's market target strategy be?
4 Discuss the actual and potential impact of restructuring on Kodak's marketing strategy and implementation.
5 Identify the important issues in designing a marketing organization that is appropriate for Kodak's business environment.

19.1 Learning Objectives

When you have read this chapter you should be able to:

(a) understand the nature of control and the control process;
(b) appreciate some different approaches to control;
(c) appreciate the importance of the behavioural aspects of control;
(d) design basic control systems.

19.2 Introduction to Control

Since control is a process whereby management ensures that the organization is achieving desired ends, it can be defined as a set of organized (adaptive) actions directed towards achieving specified goals in the face of constraints.

To bring about particular future events it is necessary to influence the factors that lie behind those events. It is the ability to bring about a desired future outcome at will that is the essence of control. In this sense it can be seen that control itself is a *process* and not an event. Moreover, the idea of control can be seen to be synonymous with such notions as adaptation, influence, manipulation and regulation. But control is *not* synonymous with coercion in the sense in which the term is used in this book. Nor does it have as its central feature (as so often seems to be thought) the detailed study of past mistakes, but rather the focusing of attention on current and, more particularly, on future activities to ensure that they are carried through in a way that leads to desired ends.

The existence of a control process enables management to know from time to time where the organization stands in relation to a predetermined future position. This requires that progress can be observed, measured, and redirected if there are discrepancies between the actual and the desired positions.

Control and planning are complementary, so each should logically presuppose the existence of the other. Planning presupposes objectives (ends), and objectives are of very limited value in the absence of a facilitating plan (means) for their attainment. In the planning process management must determine the organization's future courses of action by reconciling corporate resources with specified corporate objectives in the face of actual, and anticipated, environmental conditions. This will usually involve a consideration of various alternative courses of action and the selection of the one that is seen to be the best in the light of the objectives.

In seeking to exercise control it is important to recognize that the process is inevitably value laden: the preferred future state that one is seeking to realize is unlikely to be the same for individual A as for individual B, and that which applies to individuals also, within limits, applies to organizations.

In seeking to exercise control the major hindrances are uncertainty (since the relevant time horizon for control is the future, which cannot be totally known in advance) and the inherent complexity of socio-economic and socio-technical systems (such as business organizations). If one had an adequate understanding of the ways in which complex organizations function, and if this facilitated reliable predictions, then the information stemming from this predictive understanding would enable one to control the organization's behaviour. In this sense it can be seen that information and control have an equivalence.

Behind the presumption, therefore, that we can control anything there is an implied assertion that we know enough about the situation in question (e.g. what is being sought, how well things are going, what is going wrong, how matters might be put right, etc.).

19.3 CONTROL DEFINED

There are as many different definitions of control, and of management control, as there are authors.

Maciariello (1984, p. 5), for example, offers the following definitions of management control (MC) and management control system (MCS):

> Management control is the process of ensuring that the human, physical, and technological resources are allocated so as to achieve the overall purposes of an organization. An MCS attempts to bring unity of purpose to the diverse efforts of a multitude of organizational subunits so as to steer the overall organization and its managers toward its objectives and goals. An MCS consists of a structure and a process.

A control system's structure has relative permanence and focuses on what the system is (i.e. the designated responsibility centres, delegated authority, performance measures, etc.). Its process focuses on the way in which decisions are made to establish goals, allocate resources, evaluate performance, revise strategies, etc., in a purposive manner.

Itami (1977) emphasized the fact that management control is control within an organizational context, which implies that it is of a multi-person nature. This is also evident in Tannenbaum's (1964, p. 299) definition of control as being:

> ... any process in which a person (or a group of persons or organization of persons) determines or intentionally affects what another person or group or organization will do.

However, the idea of interpersonal influence was broadened by Hofstede (1968, p. 11) to embrace impersonal control also:

> Control within an organizational system is the process by which one element (person, group, machine, institution or norm) intentionally affects the action of another element.

The interpersonal nature of control within organizations needs to be recognized in order to relate to motivation, goal congruence and the reward system. Within Figure 19.1 there is no explicit recognition of this requirement, whereas Figure 19.2 allows for it via 'nesting'.

Within the nested model the superior exercises control by influencing the subordinate's behaviour – largely through the assessing of the subordinate's performance against agreed plans.

The behavioural aspect is highlighted by Merchant (1985, p. 4) who also refers to the strategic aspects of control:

> *Control* is seen as having one basic function: to help ensure the proper behavior of the people in the organization. These behaviors should be consistent with the organization's strategy ...

FIGURE 19.1
The control process

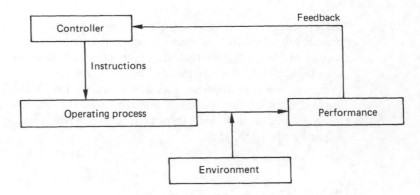

FIGURE 19.2
*A nested model of
control systems*

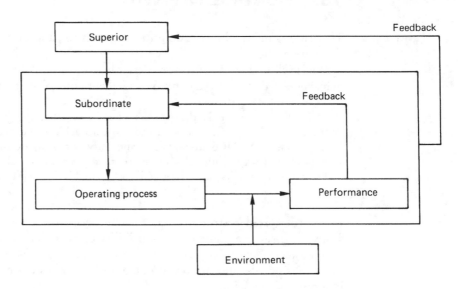

The need for control arises because individuals within the organization are not always willing to act in the organization's best interests.

Whilst strategy may be seen as being related to control it is usually separable. Thus it is possible for an enterprise having good strategies to fail because it has a poor control system, and vice versa. In general, however, the better the formulation of a strategy the greater will be the number of feasible control alternatives and the easier their implementation is likely to be.

Anthony (1988, pp. 7 and 10) also refers both to the links between control and strategic implementation on the one hand, and the interaction among individuals on the other:

> *Control* is used in the sense of assuring implementation of strategies. The management control function includes making the plans that are necessary to assure that strategies are implemented.
>
> Management control is the process by which managers influence other members of the organization to implement the organization's strategies.

Merchant (1985, p. 1) has pointed out a number of problems that have inhibited a greater understanding of control:

1 the lack of a comprehensive and generally-accepted control framework with supporting terminology;
2 control problems and solutions are discussed at different levels of analysis;
3 the solutions that are proposed also differ in accordance with the orientation of their proposers:
4 some authors argue that control should deal with (historical) facts whereas others argue that control should be future-oriented.

19.4 BASIC CONTROL CONCEPTS

In this section, which draws on Wilson and Chua (1993), we will distinguish between:

- open-loop control; and
- closed-loop control.

We shall also distinguish between two main forms of closed-loop control:

- feedforward control; and
- feedback control.

Open-loop Control

This form of control exists when an attempt is made by a system (for example, an organization) to achieve some desired goal, but when no adjustments are made to its actions once the sequence of intended acts is under way. A very simple example is that of a golfer hitting a golf ball: his aim is to get the ball into the hole, and with this in mind he will take into account the distance, the hazards, and so forth, prior to hitting the ball. Once the ball is in the air there is nothing that the golfer can do but hope that he did things right.

Two possible refinements to the basic open-loop model are:

1 To introduce a monitoring device for the continual scanning of both the environment and the transformation process of the system (that is, the process by which the organization converts inputs into outputs). This will provide a basis for modifying either initial plans or the transformation process itself if it appears that circumstances are likely to change before the plan has run its course and the goal realized. This is *feedforward control* and is illustrated in Figure 19.3.

FIGURE 19.3
A feedforward control system

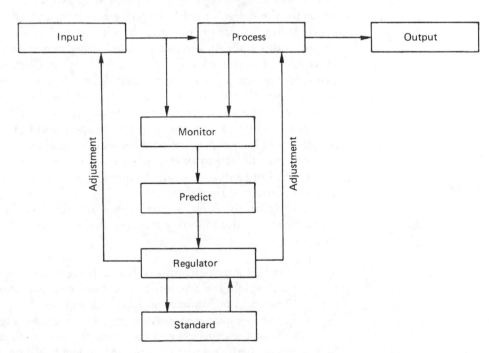

2 To monitor the outputs achieved against desired outputs from time to time, and take whatever corrective action is necessary if a deviation exists. This is *feedback control* and is illustrated in Figure 19.4.

FIGURE 19.4
A feedback control system

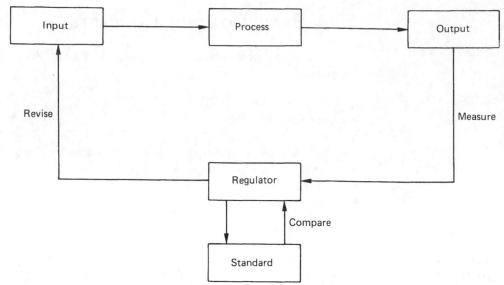

Both feedback and feedforward control entail linking outputs with other elements within the system, and this explains why they are termed *closed-loop* control systems.

Closed-loop Control

In an open-loop system errors cannot be corrected as it goes along, whereas likely errors can be anticipated and steps taken to avoid them in a feedforward control system, and actual errors along the way can be identified and subsequent behaviour modified to achieve desired ends in a feedback control system.

The inadequacy of open-loop systems as a basis for organizational control (and hence for the design of MCS) largely stems from our limited knowledge of how organizational systems operate, which in turn reflects the complexity of organizations and their environments, plus the uncertainty that clouds the likely outcome of future events. If we possessed a full understanding of organizational processes and had a perfect ability to predict the future then we would be able to rely on open-loop systems to achieve the ends we desire since we would be able to plan with the secure knowledge that our plans would be attained due to our perfect awareness of what was going to happen, and how, and when (i.e. control action would be independent of the system's output).

In our current state of awareness we must rely on closed-loop systems, whether feedforward or feedback, in which control action is dependent upon the actual or anticipated state of the system.

It is helpful to think of four types of outcome in connection with the application of closed-loop systems to the problem of organizational control. These are:

S_0 = Initial *ex ante* performance (e.g. a budget based on a set of expectations which might include: inflation at 5 per cent per annum; market growth of 10 per cent per annum; no labour disputes).

S_1 = Revised *ex ante* performance (e.g. an updated budget that has taken into account the experience of operating the system to date).

S_2 = *Ex post* performance (e.g. a revised budget based on what should have been achieved in the circumstances that prevailed during the period in question, say: inflation at 7 per cent per annum; market growth of 12 per cent per annum, and a strike lasting three weeks).

A_0 = Observed performance (i.e. that which actually occurred).

An organization's forecasting ability is shown by $A_0 - S_0$ (under feedback control) and, more precisely, by $A_0 - S_1$ (under feedforward control). The extent to which the organization is not using its resources to maximum advantage (its opportunity cost of operating) is given by $A_0 - S_2$.

A feedforward control system will function in a way that keeps revising S_0 as events are proceedings with a view to producing an eventual outcome in which $A_0 = S_1$. On the other hand, a feedback control system will, from time to time, compare $A_0 - S_0$ and S_0 will only be revised if a discrepancy has been experienced.

It is apparent that feedforward control tends to be:

- ex ante,
- proactive,
- continuous;

and seeks to predict the outcomes of proposed courses of action, while feedback control tends to be:

- ex post,
- reactive,
- episodic.

Let us look at each a litle more closely.

Feedforward Control

A feedforward system can be defined as:

> A measurement and prediction system which assesses the system and predicts the output of the system at some future date.
>
> (Bhaskar and Housden (1985), p. 199)

This differs from a feedback system in that it seeks to anticipate, and thereby to avoid, deviations between actual and desired outcomes. According to Cushing (1982, p. 83), its components are:

1 an operating process (which converts inputs into outputs);
2 a characteristic of the process (which is the subject of control);
3 a measurement system (which assesses the state of the process and its inputs, and attempts to predict its outputs);
4 a set of standards or criteria (by which the predicted state of the process can be evaluated);
5 a regulator (which compares the predictions of process outputs to the standards, and which takes corrective action where there is likely to be a deviation).

For a feedforward control system to be effective it must be based on a reasonably predictable relationship between inputs and outputs (i.e. there must be an adequate degree of understanding of the way in which the organization functions).

Guidelines for developing feedforward control systems are as follows:

1 thorough planning and analysis are required (reflecting as much understanding as possible about the links amongst inputs, process, and outputs);
2 careful discrimination must be applied in selecting those variables that are deemed to have a significant impact on output;
3 the feedforward system must be kept dynamic to allow for the inclusion of new influences on outputs;
4 a model of the system to be controlled should be developed and the most significant variables (along with their effects on process and outputs) defined within it;

5 data on significant variables must be regularly gathered and evaluated in order to assess their likely influence on future outcomes;

6 feedforward control requires action focused on the future (rather than on the correction of past errors).

Feedback Control

Feedback control should ensure self-regulation in the face of changing circumstances once the control system has been designed and installed. The essence of feedback control is to be found in the idea of *homeostasis* which defines the process whereby key variables are maintained in a state of equilibrium even when there are environmental disturbances.

As a hypothetical illustration let us consider a company planning to sell 100 000 cassette players during the next 12 months. By the end of the third month it finds that the pattern of demand has fallen to an estimated 80 000 units due to the launch by another company of a competing product. After a further three months the competitor puts up the price of its product while the original company holds its own price steady, and this suggests that the level of demand may increase to 150 000 units. Feedback signals would ensure that the company is made aware, e.g. by monthly reports, of the actual versus planned outcomes (in terms of sales levels). The launch of the competitive cassette player would be identified as the reason why sales levels were below expectations in the early months, and the competitor's price increase would be identified as the reason why sales levels subsequently increased. In response to deviations between actual and desired results (i.e. feedback) an explanation needs to be found and actions taken to correct matters. Amending production plans to manufacture fewer (or more) cassette players, allowing inventory levels to fall (or rise) to meet the new pattern of demand, modifying promotional plans to counter competitive activities and so forth, could all stem from a feedback control system.

If deviations (or *variances* to give them their usual accounting name) are minor it is probable that the process could absorb them without any modifications, and inventory control systems, for example, are normally designed to accommodate minor variations between expected and actual levels of demand with buffer stocks being held for this purpose. But in the case of extreme variations – such as the pattern of demand shifting from 100 000 units to 80 000 and then to 150 000 – it will be necessary to amend the inputs in a very deliberate way once the causes of the variations have been established. Inevitably there are costs associated with variances, and these will tend to be proportional to the length of time it takes to identify and correct them.

Some principles for the proper functioning of a feedback control system can be suggested (e.g. Cushing (1982), p. 80), and might include:

1 The benefits from the system should be at least as great as the costs of developing, installing, and operating it. This is the problem of 'the cost of control'. It is often difficult to specify precisely either the benefits (other than in broad terms – e.g. 'better customer service', 'increased efficiency') or the costs relating to different system designs, but it should be possible to make approximate assessments of both.

2 Variances, once measured, should be reported quickly to facilitate prompt control action. (This is analogous to the feedback – known as *knowledge of results* - in psychological learning theory: if one has been tested on what one has learnt it is important to be told quickly whether one is right – to reinforce the learning – or wrong – to facilitate remedial learning.)

3 Feedback reports should be simple, easy to understand, and highlight the significant factors requiring managerial attention.

4 Feedback control systems should be integrated with the organizational structure of which they are a part. The boundaries of each process subject to control should be within a given manager's span of control.

Feedforward Versus Feedback Control

The most significant features of feedforward and feedback control are shown in Figure 19.5.

Feedback systems are typically cheaper and easier to implement than are feedforward systems, and they are more effective in restoring a system that has gone out of control. Their main disadvantage, however, is that they can allow variations to persist for as long as it takes to detect and correct them. Feedforward control systems, as we have seen, depend critically for their effectiveness on the forecasting ability of those who must predict future process outputs. Both feedforward and feedback systems lend themselves to self-regulation.

FIGURE 19.5
Relative strengths

Characteristic	Feedforward	Feedback
Low cost		✓
Ease of implementation		✓
Effectiveness		✓
Minimal time delays	✓	
Self-regulation	✓	✓

The most effective approach to control comes from using the two approaches as complements since few (if any) processes could be expected to operate effectively and efficiently for any length of time if only one type of control was in use. (For example, in controlling inventory, feedback data can be used in connection with stock outs, rates of usage, etc., while feedforward data needs to be generated in gauging the raw material requirements for predicted levels of demand and the ability of suppliers to deliver on time.)

Both types of control are fundamentally intertwined with the design of MCS. In a feedback control system the functions that the system will carry out are:

- standard setting;
- performance measurement;
- reporting of results.

Within a feedforward control system the role of the MCS will encompass:

- standard setting;
- monitoring process inputs;
- monitoring operations;
- predicting process outputs.

The degree of overlap is modest relative to the degree of complementarity.

19.5 RESPONSIBILITY ACCOUNTING

In analysing organizations with a view to securing control over them there are five key variables to which one must pay attention. A change in any one of these will have consequences for one or more of the others. These variables are:

1 the task of the organization (i.e. the purpose to be served by the outputs from the organization);
2 the technology of the organization (i.e. the means whereby the inputs are converted into outputs);
3 the structure of the organization (i.e. the roles, rules, etc.);
4 the people of the organization (including their expectations, career development, etc.);

5 the environment of the organization (i.e. those factors beyond the organization's boundary).

In this section we will be concerned with aspects of 3 – the structure, as reflected through individuals' assigned responsibilities.

If an enterprise is organized in such a way that lines of authority are clearly defined, with the result that each manager knows exactly what his or her responsibilities are and precisely what is expected of him or her, then it is possible to plan and control costs, revenues, profits, etc., in order that the performance of each individual may be evaluated and, one hopes, improved. In addition, a meaningful basis can be given to the design of the reporting system if it is geared to areas of responsibility.

That is the essence of responsibility accounting which is a system of accounting that is tailored to an organization so that costs, revenues, profits, etc., can be planned, accumulated, reported, and controlled by levels of responsibility within that organization. Responsibility accounting requires that costs, revenues and profits – as appropriate – be classified by:

- responsibility centre;
- their degree of controllability within their responsibility centre (on the premise that each responsible individual in an organization should only be held accountable for those costs, revenues and profits for which he or she is responsible and over which he or she has control);
- their nature.

This approach to classification will facilitate:

- self-appraisal by lower and middle management;
- subordinate appraisal by top management;
- activity appraisal (by which top management might evaluate the performance of the overall range of corporate activities).

See Figure 19.6.

However, it is essential to the success of any control system that an individual is only held responsible for results when the following conditions prevail:

1 that he knows what he is expected to achieve;
2 that he knows what he is actually achieving;
3 that it is within his power to influence what is happening (i.e. that he can bring 1 and 2 together).

When all these conditions do not occur simultaneously it may be unjust and ineffective to hold an individual responsible, and it will be impossible to achieve the desired level of organizational performance.

From the above comments it will be apparent that targets or results should be compiled in a way that reflects one individual's 'uncontaminated' performance. Thus Manager A's budget should contain a clear set of items which are deemed to be controllable at his level of authority and a further set of items that are either fixed by company policy or are otherwise beyond Manager A's influence. These latter items are uncontrollable from A's viewpoint, and his performance should not be assessed in relation to costs, etc., over which he has no control.

Costs (as well as revenues, profits, and so forth) can only be controlled if they are related to the organizational framework: in other words, costs should be controlled in accordance with the concept of responsibility – a cost should be controlled at whatever level it is originated and initially approved by the individual who did the initiating and approving. In this way it will be clear that certain costs are the

FIGURE 19.6
*Appraisal of
performance*

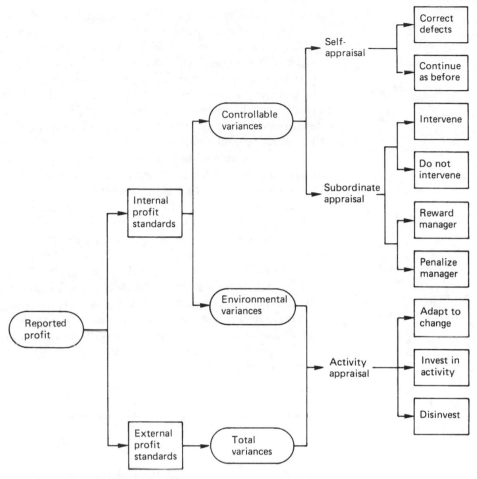

SOURCE: Shillinglaw (1964), p. 158

responsibility of, and can only be controlled by, the chief executive of a company (such as corporate public relations expenditure) whereas others are controllable by responsible individuals at lower levels of the organizational hierarchy (e.g. a departmental manager will be responsible for the salary expense of those who work within his department). It is important to distinguish between costs that are controllable at a given level of managerial authority within a given period of time and those that are not. This distinction is not the same as the one between variable costs and fixed costs. For example, rates are a fixed cost that are uncontrollable, for a given time period, by any managerial level, whereas the annual road licence fee for a particular vehicle is a fixed cost that is controllable by the fleet manager who has the power to dispense with the vehicle. In the same way the insurance premium payable on inventories is a variable cost (fluctuating with the value of the inventory from month to month) that is not controllable at the storekeeper level, but it is controllable at the level of the executive who determines inventory policy (subject, of course, to the environmental vagaries of such factors as consumer demand which can never be removed).

Controllability is affected by both managerial authority and the element of time – a short-run fixed cost will be a long-run variable cost. (Thus the managing director's salary is fixed for 12 months but variable thereafter.) All costs are controllable to some extent over the longer term even if this involves a change in the scale of operations or a relocation of the company.

The problem of distinguishing between controllable and uncontrollable costs is more difficult in relation to indirect as opposed to direct costs. It is vitally important that costs be regulated at source, and this means that for many indirect items the beneficiary of cost incurrence is very often not the person to be charged with the cost. Obvious examples are central services – maintenance, the personnel department, post room/switchboard facilities – from which all members of the company derive benefits but for which cost responsibility is accorded to the respective supervisors and managers of these service functions.

To sum up so far, the approach to control that is based on the concept of responsibility accounting involves designing the control system to match the organizational structure in order that it reflects realistically the responsibilities of departmental managers, supervisors, etc. (This method of tackling control permits the collecting and reporting of data in such a way that the performance of organizational sub-units can be evaluated.) In devising a control system for securing control that accords with the organizational structure it will usually be found necessary to define more closely the duties of responsible individuals, and various responsibilities will have to be reassigned in order to give a logical structure to an organization that may have grown in a haphazard manner. All subsequent organizational changes that lead to changes in individual responsibilities should be accompanied by suitable modifications to the control system.

Organizational charts are useful if properly detailed. Apart from showing the chain of command (i.e. who reports to whom) such a chart should also include a schedule defining the duties of those individuals and any limitations to their authority. In this way responsibilities can be unambiguously assigned, and this knowledge clearly communicated to all concerned. Figure 19.7 represents a possible marketing organization structure, giving details of duties within each functional area.

FIGURE 19.7
Marketing organization structure

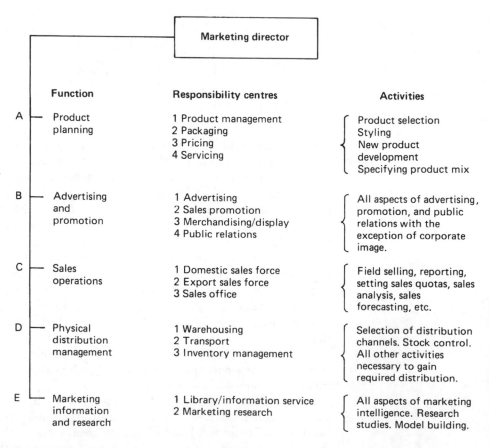

The implications of fixing responsibility and of implementing control via responsibility centres are:

- the organizational structure must be clearly defined and responsibility delegated so that each person knows his or her role;

- the extent and limits of functional control must be determined;
- the responsible individuals should be fully involved in preparing plans if they are to be held responsible for results;
- responsible individuals must be serviced with regular performance reports;
- means must be established to enable plans to be revised in line with actual performance in such a way that responsible individuals are involved;
- every item should be the responsibility of some individual within the organization.

The ability to delegate is one sign of a good manager and responsibility accounting facilitates this. The act of passing responsibility down the line to the lowest levels of supervision gives these advantages:

- it helps to create an atmosphere of cost consciousness throughout the organization;
- it tends to get control action quickly without delays resulting from the need for a senior executive to receive a monthly report before decisions can be made;
- it helps to give all levels of management a sense of team spirit with a common purpose.

A central notion in considering control is the evaluation of performance – whether *ex ante* (as in feedforward control) or *ex post* (as in feedback control). This can be undertaken at several levels: at the societal level, at the level of the enterprise as a whole, at the level of a division or other segment – such as activities, or at the levels of the group or individual. In essence what is required is a comparison of desired outcomes with expected or actual outcomes, an assessment of any divergences, and proposals for future courses of action. Putting this another way, three questions need to be posed:

1 What has happened?
2 Why has it happened?
3 What is to be done about it?

The need to view performance evaluation within a control context is highlighted by our posing all three questions, rather than just the first two.

The concept of performance measurement is a simple one to comprehend but it can only be put into practice if plans are carefully prepared before decisions are made. In the absence of a plan (expressed in terms of standards and budgeted levels of performance) there is no bench-mark for evaluating the performance of segments of an enterprise, individuals in responsible positions, or the organization as a whole, and attempting to improve upon it. The existence of standards of performance eliminates many of the opportunities and excuses for poor performance, and provides a reference point for improvements.

Measuring the performance of the various types of responsibility centre (i.e. cost, profit and investment) will usually focus on financial aspects of an organization's activity. This will not always be appropriate, although it tends to be the general case that managers are held accountable in terms of quantifiable performance rather than performance that is qualitative (such as employee morale or public relations). It is necessary to know from time to time how actual performance compares with desired performance, and this chapter focuses on this issue.

This comparison answers the question about *what* is happening, and responsibility accounting ensures that managers know *who* is to be accountable. Establishing *why* divergences occur is problematic, as is the question of deciding *how* to apply corrective action in order that control may be effective.

Individuals learn through assessing their experience and organizations learn through their members. However, the extent to which individuals – and thus organizations – can learn is constrained by the rules of the organization (governing decision making, delegation, membership and other restrictions). Dery (1982) has pursued this question by focusing on the links between erring (e.g. when variances arise) and learning. His argument is as follows:

1 the recognition of errors is a function of interpretation rather than simply an observation of events – it requires that desired and actual outcome be compared and interpreted before one can assert that an error exists;
2 the interpretation of events is influenced by organizational rules, etc., which also serve to constrain the extent to which learning can take place;
3 it is insufficient to assume that better learning at the organizational level can stem from the learning ability of individual members since the latter is constrained by the rules of the former, hence an additional factor is required that will change the organization's rules.

The level of performance of a responsibility centre from a control viewpoint can be evaluated by obtaining answers to three pairs of questions;

Quantity
● How much was accomplished?
● How much should have been accomplished?

Quality
● How good was that which was accomplished?
● How good should it have been?

Cost
● How much did the accomplishment cost?
● How much should it have cost?

Performance measurement presupposes a standard of comparison. An obvious example comes from the comparison of actual results with budgeted results – the latter being the predetermined standard of performance. Standards can be compiled for almost every business activity, such as:

● number of customer complaints;
● production costs;
● unit costs of handling and transporting products;
● market share;
● employee turnover;
● downtime;
● unfilled orders;
● return on investment;
● percentage of late deliveries of orders;
● a variety of cost/revenue/profit ratios.

Any standard can only be an effective aid to control if it is seen to be equitable: those who are being judged (i.e. the responsible individuals whose performance is being measured) must be consulted in the setting of standards otherwise no attempt may be made to reach them if they are considered to be either too high or too low. This ruins any attempt to control.

Luck and Ferrell (1979) have portrayed the links among marketing strategy, plans and standards as shown in Figure 19.8.

Control reports should be suited to the various areas of individual responsibility and as one moves further up the managerial hierarchy more items will be contained, albeit in summary form, in reports prepared for each level since more items are controllable as the scope of managerial responsibility enlarges. Top management will therefore receive a summary of all items of income and expenditure.

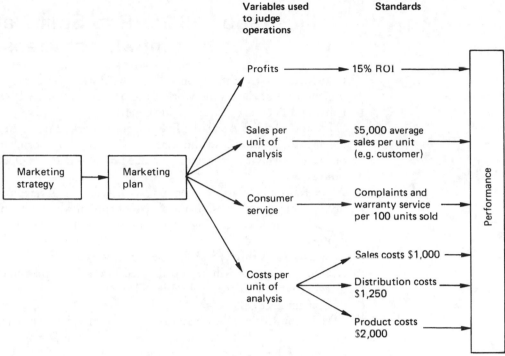

FIGURE 19.8
*Standards in the
marketing control
process*

SOURCE: Adapted from Luck and Ferrell (1979), p. 421

Such summary reports can do little to rectify past mistakes but by indicating exceptions to plans they can ensure that causes are investigated and appropriate corrective actions are taken to help in preventing future mistakes. The appropriate orientation should clearly be to the future rather than to the past.

A *responsibility centre* is made up of the various cost and revenue and investment items as appropriate for which a given individual is responsible. It is consequently a personalized concept that may be made up of one or more of the following.

- a cost centre;
- a profit centre; or
- an investment centre.

Let us look at each of these in turn.

A Cost (or Expense) Centre
This is the smallest segment of activity, or area of responsibility, for which costs are accumulated. In some cases the cost centre may correspond with a department, but in others a department may contain several cost centres.

A cost centre may be created for cost control purposes whenever management feels that the usefuless of accumulating costs for the activity in question justifies the necessary effort.

Only input costs are measured for this organizational unit: even though there is some output this is not measured in revenue terms. Thus a distribution team may deliver X units at a given total (or unit) cost, with the output being expressed either as a quantity or in terms of input costs.

A Profit Centre
This is a segment, department or division of an enterprise that is responsible for both revenue and expenditure. This is the major organizational device employed to facilitate decentralization (the essence of which is the freedom to make decisions). See Illustration 19.1.

Illustration 19.1: BR to Split National Network into Local Areas

British Rail is to embark on one of the most far-reaching changes in the organisation of the rail network since nationalisation in 1948, John Welsby, British Rail's chief executive, said yesterday.

From the end of April, the five regions, inherited from the days of private ownership, London Midland, Eastern, Western, Southern, and Scottish, will be progressively abolished and replaced by about 20 smaller units, or profit centres.

The Railways Board will retain responsibility for strategic matters, such as investment programmes, financial targets and railway safety, but most aspects of the day-to-day running of the railway will be devolved to the profit centres.

British Rail's three passenger sectors, InterCity, Network SouthEast, and Regional Railways, will be sub-divided into several profit centres, run by a director, who will effectively own all the rolling stock, track and signalling equipment needed.

Malcolm Rifkind, the transport secretary, has pledged to introduce a bill to privatise British Rail after the next general election. Transport officials are still examining the options, which include privatisation of BR as a single unit, the creation of a track authority and its break-up into regional companies.

Under the reorganization, Network SouthEast, which provides rail services in London and the South East region, will be divided into nine semi-autonomous divisions. Some of these divisions will be substantial businesses. South West, for example, which embraces all services from Waterloo, has an income of £252 million a year, employs about 8,000 staff and covers 500 route-miles. Others, such as the London, Tilbury and Southend division, with an income of £65 million, employs about 1,500 and covers 70 route-miles, will be considerably smaller.

InterCity will be divided into five route divisions. Regional Railways, which provides commuter, passenger and cross-country services, will also be split into five sub-divisions.

In an effort to make each profit centre more cost conscious, charges will be levied on trains from one profit centre using the tracks of another. Directors will know exactly what they are responsible for and accountability for shortcomings will be instant. "There will be no more alibis," Mr Welsby said.

The division of the national rail network into what is effectively 20 semi-autonomous railways, is the final phase of the radical reorganisation of the rail network introduced in the early 1980s by Sir Robert Reid, the former British Rail chairman.

By reorganising British Rail's passenger sectors around the markets rather than the regions they serve, Mr Welsby is determined to bring about a substantial improvement in the quality of services. "I'm not changing the organisation for the fun of it," he said. "The changes are vital to improve the quality of service to passengers."

The move is being watched closely by continental rail organisations, particularly those in France and Germany, which are already following the example set by British Rail with the introduction of the five sectors in the 1980s.

The reorganisation is expected to take about a year to complete, and is likely to cost in the region of £50 million. Mr Welsby said that British Rail was not trying to facilitate or impede government plans to privatise the railways.

Source: The Times, *11 April, 1991, p. 24*

Among the arguments favouring decentralized profit responsibility are:

1 a divisional manager is only in a position to make satisfactory trade-offs between revenues and costs when he has responsibility for the profit outcome of his decisions (failing which it is necessary for many day-to-day decisions to be centrally regulated);
2 a manager's performance can be evaluated more precisely if he has complete operating responsibility;
3 managers' motivation will be higher if they have greater autonomy;
4 the contribution of each division to corporate profit can be seen via divisional profit reports.

The advantages of profit centres are that they resemble miniature businesses and are a good training ground for potential general managers.

When it comes to defining profit measures several alternatives are available. An example built up from the data in Figure 19.9 will help to illustrate some of them.

FIGURE 19.9
Division A's operating data for July

Sales revenue generated by Division A	£100,000
Direct costs of Division A:	
Variable operating costs	£45,000
Fixed operating costs under control of manager of Division A	£25,000
Fixed costs not under the control of manager of Division A	£10,000
Indirect costs of Division A:	
Apportioned central costs	£15,000

This data can be analysed in ways such as those suggested in Figure 19.10. One can identify strengths and weaknesses relating to each alternative measure of profit. The *contribution margin* is useful for short-run decision making since it is not clouded by the inclusion of costs that do not respond to short-run volume changes. From a performance evaluation point of view, however, it is unsatisfactory in that it excludes all non-variable costs.

Controllable profit is a much better measure of the divisional manager's performance because it includes all the costs – whether fixed or variable – that are within his control. When non-controllable fixed costs are taken into account we

FIGURE 19.10
Analysis of Division A's operating data

	Division A contribution margin £	Division A controllable profit £	Division A direct profit £	Division A net profit £
Sales revenue	100,000	100,000	100,000	100,000
Direct costs:				
Variable	45,000	45,000	45,000	45,000
Contribution margin	£55,000			
Fixed controllable		25,000	25,000	25,000
Controllable profit		£30,000		
Fixed non-controllable			10,000	10,000
Direct profit			£20,000	
Indirect costs				15,000
Net profit				£5,000

have the *direct profit* of the division. This is more a measure of the division's performance than it is of the divisional manager's performance, so one needs to consider what it is that one is seeking to assess before one chooses a measure.

Finally, *net profit* (as pointed out in Chapter 3) helps us in assessing a division's performance in full cost terms, but this is not a relevant means of gauging the divisional manager's performance on account of the categories of cost that he is unable to influence either directly or indirectly. It could be argued that divisional managers benefit from seeing the full cost of their division's operations, but if the controllable elements are dwarfed by the uncontrollable (at the divisional level) it may not be highly motivational!

From the above we can reasonably conclude that controllable profit is the best of the specified measures for assessing a divisional manager's performance – at least in principle. In practice it may be found that the manager of a division acts in ways that improve his short-run profit position at the expense of both the division's long-run profit potential and the best interests of the organization as a whole. Examples might include:

1 eliminating training and management development activities;
2 cutting back on advertising, routine maintenance or R & D.

Countering these ways of 'playing the system' must be devised by top management in the form of policy guidelines, etc. But any measure of profit is inevitably sub-optimal as an index of divisional performance for at least one of the following reasons:

1 it typically includes items (such as interest and taxation) that are not under the control of divisional managers;
2 it only tells part of the story – something needs to be said about the investment that is needed to generate profit. The next sub-section picks up this point.

An Investment Centre

This is a segment, department or division of an enterprise under an accountable manager who is not only responsible for profit (i.e. for revenue and expenditure) but that also has his success measured by the relationship of profit to the capital invested within the division (i.e. profitability). This is most commonly measured by means of the rate of return on investment (ROI).

The logic behind this concept is that assets are used to generate profits, and the decentralizing of profit responsibility usually requires the decentralization of control over many of an enterprise's assets. The ultimate test, therefore, is the relationship of profit to invested capital within a division. Much of its appeal lies in the apparent ease with which one can compare a division's ROI with earnings opportunities elsewhere – inside or outside the company. However, ROI is an imperfect measure and needs to be used with some scepticism and in conjunction with other performance measurements.

The value of the controllable/uncontrollable cost split is primarily found in fixing responsibility and measuring efficiency. Time is an important ingredient in this context since all costs are controllable at some organizational level if a sufficiently long time-span is taken. Controllable costs are those that can be directly regulated by a given individual within a given time period.

The division of costs into controllable and uncontrollable categories is important in order that performance levels may be evaluated and also for securing the cooperation of managers at all levels. The manager who is involved in planning his performance level in the knowledge that those controllable costs for which he is responsible will be monitored, accumulated, and reported, is likely to be motivated towards attaining his predetermined level of performance. In this way it can be seen that the collecting of controllable costs by responsibility centres serves as a motivating force as well as an appraisal mechanism.

While the ideal procedure is for each responsibility centre to be assigned those costs over which its manager has sole control and for which he or she is therefore responsible, in practical terms this cannot usually be achieved. It is rare for an individual to have complete control over *all* the factors that influence a given cost element.

Apart from those costs over which a responsible individual actually has control, his responsibility centre may be charged with costs that are beyond his direct control and influence but about which management wishes him to be concerned. A good example is the cost of a company's personnel department: an operating manager may be charged with a proportion of the personnel department's costs on the grounds that either:

- he will be careful about making unnecessary requests for the services of the personnel department if he is made to feel somewhat responsible for its level of costs; or
- he may try to influence the personnel manager to exercise firm control over his department's costs.

Allocating general overheads to responsibility centres is done by many companies that practise responsibility accounting (and that therefore recognize that such costs are beyond the control of those to whom they are allocated) on the grounds that each responsible individual will be able to see the magnitude of the indirect costs incurred to support this unit. There is a major disadvantage that should be seriously considered: the manager of a small responsibility centre incurring directly controllable costs at his level in a given time period of, say, £10,000 may be allocated £45,000 of general overhead costs. In relation to the overall level of overhead costs the manager may feel that those costs for which he is responsible are so insignificant that he may give up trying to control them. The point to note is that each cost must be made the responsibility of whoever can best influence its behaviour, and allocating costs beyond this achieves at best very little from a control viewpoint and may be distinctly harmful to the cost control effort. (Since a specific example of uncontrollable costs has not been given so far the general overheads of £45,000 referred to above can be used as a suitable example. For control purposes the costs that are being considered are the costs that can be directly influenced at a given level for a specified time-span.)

While the head of a responsibility centre may not have sole responsibility for a particular cost item this item may reasonably be considered to be controllable at his level if he has a significant influence on the amount of cost incurred, and in this case his responsibility centre can properly be charged with the cost. This is one aspect of the wider problem that arises because few (if any) cost items are the sole responsibility of just one person. Guidelines that have been established for deciding which costs can appropriately be charged to a responsibility centre are, in summary:

- If an individual has authority over both the acquisition and the use of a cost incurring activity, then his responsibility centre should bear the cost of that activity.
- If an individual does not have sole responsibility for a given cost item but is able to influence to a significant extent the amount of cost incurred through his own actions, then he may reasonably be charged with the cost.
- Even if an individual cannot significantly influence the amount of cost through his own direct action, he may be charged with a portion of those elements of cost with which management wishes him to be concerned in order that he may help influence those who are more directly responsible.

That which applies to costs also, in essence, applies to revenues and assets.

19.6 Approaches to Control

Anthony's Approach to Control

The views of Robert Anthony of Harvard on management control have been very influential. They are stated in Anthony 1965 and 1988.

When Anthony published his 1965 *Framework*, the management control function was not generally recognized as a discrete activity. This has changed.

Management control is one of three types of planning and control activities that occur within organizations; the other categories are strategic planning and task control. Anthony's definition of management control, given earlier (p. 702) presumes that goals and strategies exist, but that these do not arise automatically, hence (1988, p. 10):

> Strategic planning is the process of deciding on the goals of the organization and the strategies for attaining these goals.

Authors often distinguish between

- planning (i.e. deciding what to do); and
- control (i.e. ensuring that desired results are obtained).

Anthony argues that both planning and control are undertaken at different organizational levels, hence it is more helpful to look at the mix, as shown in Figure 19.11:

FIGURE 19.11
The planning and control mix

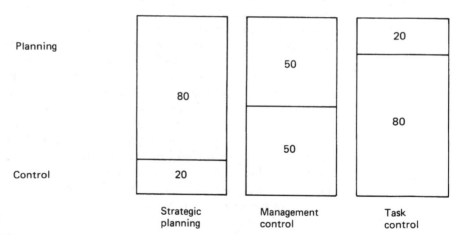

SOURCE: Adapted from Anthony (1988)

> Strategies are the courses of action that an organization has adopted as a means of attaining its goals. They include the assignment of overall responsibility for implementation . . .
>
> Strategies are big plans, important plans. They state in a general way the *direction* in which the organization is supposed to be headed. They do not have a time dimension: that is, they exist until they are changed.
>
> (1988, p. 31)

> The purpose of the MC process is to carry out the strategies arrived at in the SP process and thereby to attain the organization's goals.
>
> (1988, p. 34)

The 1988 approach links MC to the implementation of strategies in a direct way rather than to the attainment of objectives which is an indirect purpose of MC.

The key difference between MC and SP is that the latter is unsystematic: the need for strategic decisions can arise at any time – whether in response to a threat or an opportunity.

Another difference is that SP is undertaken by top management and it involves a great deal of judgement. In contrast, MC is systematic, done at all levels, and involves considerable personal interaction but less judgement than SP. SP sets the boundaries within which MC takes place.

The third element in Anthony's approach is task control:

> Task control is the process of ensuring that specific tasks are carried out effectively and efficiently.
>
> (1988, p. 12)

Anthony's framework is shown in Figure 19.12 (1988, p. 19). While dealing with SP and TC, Anthony's 1988 book focuses primarily on MC which can be described in terms of a process and the environment within which it takes place. The environment is partly external and partly internal, with the latter comprising:

- the organization's structure;
- a set of rules, procedures, etc.;
- a culture.

FIGURE 19.12
Anthony's framework

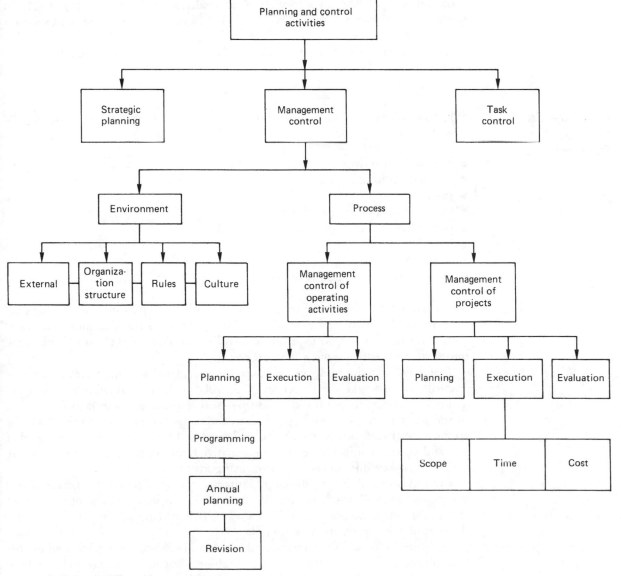

SOURCE: Anthony (1988), p. 19

The external environment contains influences that affect the level of uncertainty faced by the organization. At a highly uncertain extreme are:

- newly developed products;
- differentiated products;
- aggressive competition;
- uncertain sources of inputs;
- uncertain political circumstances.

At a less uncertain extreme are:

- mature products;
- commodity products;
- price competition;
- secure sourcing of inputs;
- political stability.

Within a highly uncertain setting an organization is likely to pay great attention to programming; to make broad budget estimates; to revise budgets frequently; to set limits to discretionary costs; to permit a good deal of management latitude; to insist on a rapid flow of information; to evaluate performance subjectively in terms of results rather than process; and to have a high proportion of bonus within the reward package.

The opposite characteristics are likely to apply in a relatively certain environment.

Merchant's Approach to Control

An organization's control system is comprised of a variety of mechanisms, including:

- personal supervision;
- job descriptions;
- rules;
- standard operating procedures;
- performance appraisal;
- budgets;
- standard costing;
- incentive compensation schemes.

However, it would be wrong to think of 'controls' – such as the above – as being the plural of 'control', and it would also be wrong to assume that more 'controls' would automatically give us more 'control' since this would assume that they meant the same thing, which they do not.

'Controls' has the same meaning as measurement, or information, whereas 'control' is more akin to direction. 'Controls' is concerned with means while 'control' is concerned with ends, and they deal respectively with facts (i.e. events of the past) and expectations (i.e. desires about the future). From this it will be appreciated that 'controls' tend to be analytical and operational (concerning what was and is) and 'control' tends to be normative (concerning what ought to be). A summary of key differences is shown in Figure 19.13.

The increasing ability to develop 'controls' has not necessarily increased our ability to 'control' organizations. If controls are to lead to control they must encourage human actors to behave in a way that facilitates adaptive behaviour on the part of the organization as a whole.

The complexity and uncertainty of the control problem are apparent when, for example, controls reveal that 'profits are falling'. But this does not indicate how one might (or should) respond – indeed, it would not be possible even to identify

FIGURE 19.13
The different focus of control and controls

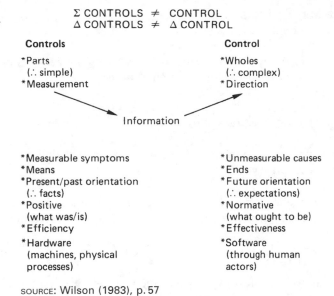

Σ CONTROLS ≠ CONTROL
Δ CONTROLS ≠ Δ CONTROL

Controls

*Parts
 (∴ simple)
*Measurement

Information

Control

*Wholes
 (∴ complex)
*Direction

*Measurable symptoms
*Means
*Present/past orientation
 (∴ facts)
*Positive
 (what was/is)
*Efficiency
*Hardware
 (machines, physical
 processes)

*Unmeasurable causes
*Ends
*Future orientation
 (∴ expectations)
*Normative
 (what ought to be)
*Effectiveness
*Software
 (through human
 actors)

SOURCE: Wilson (1983), p. 57

the whole array of potential responses. What is needed, therefore, if control is to be effective, is a basis for forming expectations about the future as well as understanding about the past that will enable us to combine these in order that we might behave in an adaptive way by either anticipating external changes and preparing to meet them, or by creating changes.

From this arises the basic question – how do we control? In large part this is resolved by the answer to another question – what do we measure in order to control? Care must be taken in measuring the key elements in any situation rather than those elements that lend themselves to easy measurement. ('Controls' are only helpful in 'control' if they are designed in the context of the overall control problem.)

Merchant (1985) offers some valuable advice on a range of controls but with a control perspective. He classifies these controls under the headings given below:

Results Controls

Reward systems – in which an individual's pay, promotion prospects, etc., depend on his performance – are a good example of results control. It is not unusual for desired results to be expressed in quantitative terms – whether financial (e.g. ROI, EPS) or not (e.g. growth rate, market share) – which gives a bench-mark for exercising results control. At senior management levels this form of control predominates since it is compatible with decentralized organizational structures. At middle-management levels, where financial goals may be less dominant, results control can be exercised through MbO (management by objectives) systems.

The effectiveness of results controls derives from the ability of this approach to address some key control problems. In particular motivational problems are eased since individuals are influenced to produce the results which will enhance both the organization's performance and their own rewards. By focusing on future expectations the results approach to control can be useful in informing managers as to what is expected of them. This emphasizes a feedforward orientation.

Three conditions need to be fulfilled before results control can be employed:

1 it is known what results are desirable;
2 the desired results can be controlled to some extent by those whose actions are being influenced;
3 the controllable results can be measured.

Action Controls

Action controls are used:

> ... to ensure that individuals perform (or do not perform) certain actions that are known to be beneficial (or harmful) to the organization.
>
> (Merchant (1985), p. 29)

Categories of action controls are:

- behavioural constraints (whether physical or administrative);
- preaction reviews;
- action accountability;
- redundancy (in which more resources are allocated to a task than is strictly necessary which increases the likelihood of its accomplishment).

Two conditions need to be fulfilled if action controls are to be effective:

1 knowledge must exist as to which actions are desirable (or undesirable);
2 the ability must be present to ensure that the desirable actions occur (or that the undesirable ones do not).

Personnel Controls

There are two categories of personnel control that can be usefully harnessed as part of the management control endeavour:

1 individual self-control which, as a naturally present force, motivates most people to want to do a good job;
2 social control which is exerted by other members of a group on those individuals who deviate from group norms and values.

If these two categories are insufficient they can be augmented by:

- selection and placement;
- training;
- cultural control.

There are several advantages that personnel controls have over results controls and action controls:

- feasibility is not a serious constraint;
- there are fewer harmful side-effects;
- their cost is typically lower.

Financial Controls

Financial controls are a form of results control which constitute the single most important type of control used in organizations of any size. The reasons favouring financial controls are fairly obvious:

- financial objectives are very important in commercial life;
- financial performance indicators are easy to derive;
- since financial results can be achieved via various routes, the use of financial controls allows for some managerial discretion;
- using financial measures is relatively inexpensive since accounting systems exist within all enterprises.

Inevitably there are negative effects which can outweigh the advantages of using financial controls. The most serious are:

- behavioural displacement – especially when the control system encourages managers to be overly concerned with short-term profits rather than longer-term strategic ends, or when it causes excessive risk aversion;
- gamesmanship.

It has been argued that there is a tendency for financial measures to drive out non-financial measures (see, for example, Munro & Cooper, 1989) within MCS design which, given the partiality of financial measures (i.e. they measure those things that can be measured in financial terms), is unfortunate.

The Approach of Johnson and Scholes

Strategic marketing involves strategic change. Johnson and Scholes (1994) have argued that there are two ways in which an organization can cope with strategic change:

1 make use of control and regulatory systems to ensure that the tasks of implementation are clear, that their execution is monitored, that individuals and groups have the capabilities to implement change, and that they are rewarded for so doing;
2 ensure that those charged with implementing change understand and work within the social, political and cultural systems that regulate organizational behaviour, and which can give rise to a resistance to strategic change.

FIGURE 19.14
The influence of organization systems on strategy implementation

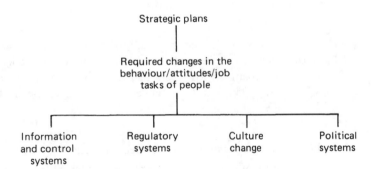

SOURCE: Adapted from Johnson and Scholes (1988), p. 292

Their approach to dealing with these issues is reflected in Figure 19.14. If we take the information and control systems first, it is widely recognized that quantitative measures are needed to see if desired results are being achieved. Such measures will typically include:

- financial analysis;
- market analysis;
- sales and distribution analysis;
- physical resource analysis;
- human resource analysis.

A set of guidelines for ensuring the effective design and operation of control systems would deal with such aspects as:

1 distinguishing between various levels of control (as proposed by Anthony (1965 and 1988)), since different levels will require different information;

2 creating responsibility centres as a means of delegation and motivation, ensuring information is provided in a suitable form for each responsible manager;
3 identifying the critical success factors and supplying information relating to these in a way that highlights their interrelationships;
4 avoiding misleading measurements by accepting that quantitative indicators of performance are not available for every activity and it is not helpful to use a measurable index as a surrogate for an unmeasurable characteristic;
5 being wary of negative monitoring in which only poor performance is reported since this can lead to risk averse behaviour or a tendency to 'pass the buck'.

The next means for ensuring the implementation of strategic change is via regulatory systems. These might range from training to the management style of an organization:

- training and development to ensure staff are capable of implementing change, which involves both new skills and attitudes;
- incentive and reward systems to encourage compliance with required change, whether in the form of pay increases or non-monetary rewards (such as promotion);
- organizational routines by which tasks are carried out may exhibit inertia so deliberate steps need to be taken to redesign them in order to facilitate change;
- management style, which embodies the organization's culture, its circumstances, and the characteristics of its managers, needs to be appropriate to the task of strategic implementation.

Moving on from regulatory systems brings us to culture change. At its most basic this focuses on the need for change to be recognized within the organization in a way that ensures those responsible for bringing change about believe in what they are doing. This can be achieved in two stages, both of which are concerned with cognitive change:

1 the beliefs and assumptions underlying the way in which the organization's members make sense of their organizational world need breaking down;
2 a reformulated set of beliefs needs to be put in their place to reorientate the culture from the past to the future. For cultural change to be meaningful it must impact upon the day-to-day experiences of individuals within the organization.

Finally there is the political system to consider. The overlaps among control systems, regulatory systems, culture and political systems is largely self-apparent, but it is important to emphasize that planning and control are inherently political rather than neutral. This will be illustrated later when we discuss the notion of entrapment.

The Approach of Luck and Ferrell

Once the plan/strategy has been determined and steps taken (e.g. via a suitable organization) to put this into effect, the control process exists to ensure that the plan will be achieved (in so far as this is feasible).

Control can operate at different levels. For example, Figure 19.15 shows *tactical* control which focuses on the implementation of plans on the right, and *strategic*

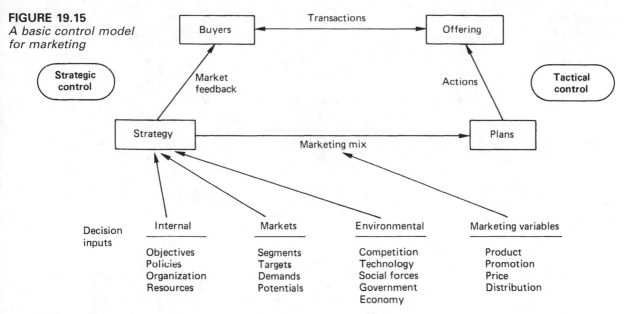

FIGURE 19.15
A basic control model for marketing

SOURCE: Adapted from Luck and Ferrell (1979), p. 15

control which focuses on the possible revision of strategy on the left. This is developed further in Figure 19.16.

Tactical control typically relates to adjustments in the execution of an established marketing plan – such as fine tuning on pricing or advertising schedules.

Strategic control deals with the reformulation of the plans themselves. For example, actual buyer behaviour patterns may indicate that a plan has been based on false premises. Strategic rethinking will thus be necessary in developing a new marketing plan (as shown in the lower half of Figure 19.16).

The role of the information system needed to facilitate tactical and strategic control is indicated in Figure 19.17.

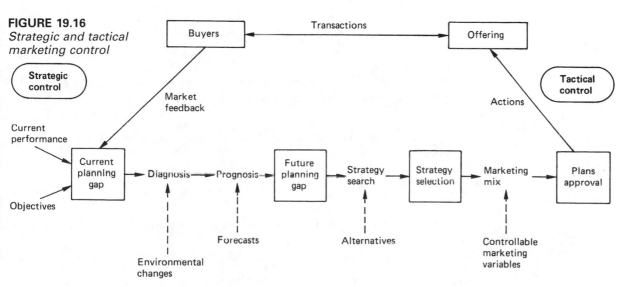

FIGURE 19.16
Strategic and tactical marketing control

SOURCE: Adapted from Luck and Ferrell (1979), p. 416

FIGURE 19.17
*The role of
information in
marketing control*

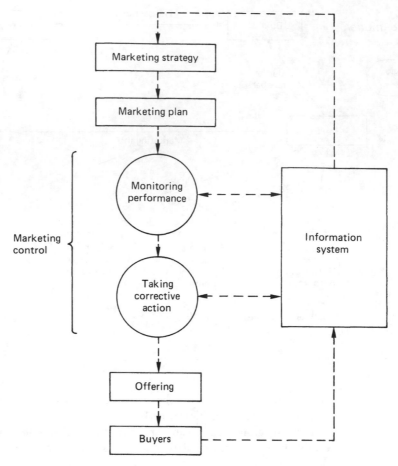

SOURCE: Luck and Ferrell (1979), p. 418

19.7 SOME BEHAVIOURAL FACTORS

Management control (MC) is based on interactions between an organization's members, hence the control process must reflect how individuals behave, as well as their knowledge, skills and personality traits.

In participating in organizations, individuals are seeking to satisfy various needs, some of which are extrinsic (i.e. satisfied by the actions of others) while others are intrinsic (i.e. satisfied by the feelings individuals have about themselves and their achievements).

The extent to which a given individual might be motivated to engage in organizational activities has been argued to be a function of:

1 beliefs regarding the outcomes that are likely to result from this individual's actions;
2 how attractive these outcomes are in relation to satisfying the individual's needs.

In designing and operating control systems, therefore, it is necessary to consider:

1 the actions that individuals are motivated to take in their perceived self-interest;

2 the best interests of the organization.

> MC is a blend of rational and behavioral considerations, and neglecting either type leads to erroneous generalizations.
>
> (Anthony (1988), p. 22)

It can also lead to harmful side effects.

Some side effects stemming from the design and implementation of control systems are inevitable and an inherent characteristic of certain types of control. On the other hand, some harmful side effects are avoidable – such as those stemming from poor design, the implementation of the wrong type of control system for a given situation, or both.

The major side effects of a negative nature are as follows.

1 Behavioural Displacement

This arises when the behaviours encouraged by the control system are inconsistent with the strategy the organization seeks to pursue. In the case of results controls, displacement can occur when there is a poor understanding of desired results or an excessive reliance on easily quantified results. In the case of action controls there is the risk of displacement due to means – ends inversion when individuals are (wrongly) encouraged by the control system to pay more attention to what they are doing (the means) rather than to what they should be accomplishing (the ends). Displacement in the context of action controls can also arise when rules and standard operating procedures are followed in a rigid, non-adaptive manner.

There is also the risk of behavioural displacement when social controls (such as group norms) induce a degree of routinized conformity that stifles any form of creative adaptation.

2 Gamesmanship

This refers to the tendency among managers to 'play the system' by means of actions intended to improve their measures of performance without producing any positive economic effects. It is particularly prevalent when either results or action controls are in use. In both, it is possible for data to be manipulated, thus rendering the control system ineffective.

3 Negative Attitudes

Such negative effects as job tension, frustration, conflict and resistance can arise even when control systems are well designed. This is most likely to be the case with poor performers since their limitations become more apparent the better the control system. However, negative attitudes can also arise in the case of potentially good performers if the control system is poorly designed.

Potential consequences of negative attitudes include gamesmanship, sabotage, or turnover, all of which can impede the achievement of strategic ends.

4 Short-Termism

> ... if long term growth of profits is the aim then rewards based on short term achievement of sales targets are not likely to be helpful.
>
> (Johnson and Scholes (1988), p. 298)

An organization's reward system is supposed to encourage goal congruence. However, control systems tend to focus on short-term results even though managers are expected to achieve both short- and long-run objectives. The reason for this is simple: the control system tends to report what has happened (e.g. over the past month) and is less capable of specifying what might happen in the long-term future.

> Our lack of knowledge about how best to measure a manager's performance is probably the most serious weakness in MCS.
>
> (Anthony (1988), p. 74)

For example, performance in a given period may not reflect the manager's real performance. Reasons for this may be that:

- outcomes (hence performance) in that period will be influenced by the actions taken in earlier periods as well as by actions of managers in other responsibility centres;
- current actions will have a lagged impact on future outcomes and it is virtually impossible to eliminate these effects from the measurement of current performance.

Dent (1990, p. 3) has commented on the way in which accounting practices have been drawn into the argument over short-termism:

> The extensive use of short-run financial calculations to appraise managerial performance is deemed to have diverted managerial attention away from fundamental value-creating activities, motivating instead opportunistic behaviours with less permanent benefits . . .

5 Entrapment and Escalation

Anthony's framework (see Figure 19.12, p. 719 above) distinguishes between MC of operating activities and MC of projects. Our focus so far has been on the former, but there are some aspects of the latter which warrant our attention.

A project can be defined as a set of activities intended to accomplish a specified end result of sufficient importance to be of interest to management.

> In a project, the focus of control is on the project itself, rather than on activities in a given time period in individual responsibility centers, as is the case with the management control of ongoing operations.
>
> (Anthony (1988), p. 16)

There are three aspects of particular interest within a project:

- its scope (i.e. the specifications for the end product);
- its schedule (i.e. the time required);
- its cost.

Trade-offs among scope, schedule and cost are usually possible in projects. For example, costs might be reduced by decreasing the project's scope, or the schedule might be reduced by increasing the cost. This is not always easy to plan since performance standards are likely to be less reliable for a one-off project than for on-going activities. Moreover, projects tend to be influenced to a greater extent by the external environment than is the case with continuing operations.

The prospect of being assessed as part of the control endeavour – whether in relation to projects or ongoing activities – typically affects the behaviour of individuals, often with dysfunctional consequences. Control activities are far from neutral in their impact, as can be shown by means of a phenomenon of recent interest: entrapment. This occurs when a responsible individual increases his commitment to an ineffective course of action in order to justify the previous allocation of resources to that task. Entrapment is seen as being one example of a broader psychological process that focuses on commitment. The commitment of an individual to a particular course of action is likely to depend on, *inter alia* (see Brockner, et al. (1986), p. 110):

1 responsibility for the action;
2 responsibility for the consequences of the action;
3 the salience of the action;
4 the consequences of the action.

While entrapment is not easily explained in terms of economic rationality, there are various plausible explanations reflecting psychological rationality. For example:

- there is a need for the decision maker to assert himself and reaffirm the wisdom of his initial decision;
- the initial commitment was made as a result of the decision maker's belief in the goodness of the course of action, hence self-justification, justification to others, and the norms of consistency are served by continuing;
- continuing avoids the waste of the investment already made (which is known as the sunk-cost fallacy);
- further investment gives further opportunities for the project to come good;
- negative feedback is treated as a learning experience (i.e. a cue to revise the inputs rather than cancel the project);
- negative feedback, alternatively, may be seen as a chance variation;
- a state of inertia has been created by which a project's financial past cannot be divorced from its future – prior investment then motivates the decision to continue;
- decisions are not made in a social vacuum, hence social costs and benefits must be considered relating to self-image, organizational image, reputation and face saving – continue so long as the social and psychological benefits are greater than the economic costs;
- information processing has behavioural underpinnings, such as selective perception in which we see what we want to see;
- an organization's reward system may work to encourage the decision maker to overlook short-term setbacks and continue with the original project through bad times.

Prospect theory (Kahneman and Tversky, 1984) has been used to explain the phenomenon of entrapment, and Figure 19.18 illustrates this. A value function (i.e. the curve in Figure 19.18) shows the relationship between objectively defined gains and losses and the subjective value placed on these by the decision maker.

At the outset the decision maker is at point A, but if the decision is unsuccessful he will find himself at point B where further losses do not result in large decreases in value. On the other hand, any gains will result in large increases in value, thus, at point B, the decision maker will risk further losses in the hope of making gains. Despite the sunk costs, risky behaviour is much more likely at point B than it was at point A.

A variation on the theme of entrapment is that of escalation (e.g. see Staw and Ross, 1987a, 1987b). These two phenomena are often related but are analytically separable: entrapment may exist in the absence of escalation. Vivid examples of escalation have been experienced in many major projects when the cost out-turns prove to be much greater than anticipated: the Sydney Opera House, Chicago's sewage system, Concorde, the Channel Tunnel.

FIGURE 19.18
The value function

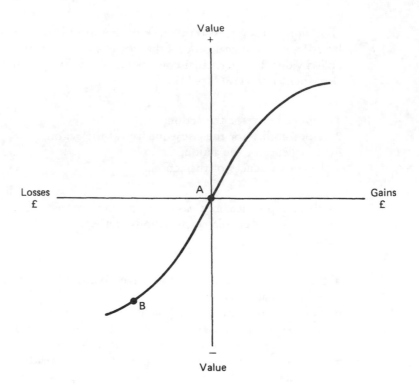

19.8 SUMMARY

Many commentators (e.g. Lamb and Shrivastava (1986)) have observed that the study of strategy implementation and control has received far less attention than its importance warrants. No matter how brilliant the formulation of strategy, it is quite useless if it cannot be effectively implemented and the subsequent performance of the organization controlled.

An array of approaches to control that focus in part on social/behavioural issues and in part on analytical techniques has been considered. Feedforward and feedback control, formal and informal controls and the approaches of authorities such as Anthony, Merchant and others were discussed. Some relevant techniques, including ratio analysis, marketing audits, and networking, have been dealt with in earlier chapters. The importance of social and behavioural issues is that analytical control techniques function only in an organizational context: social and analytical controls are complements rather than substitutes.

It can be argued (e.g. Maciariello (1984), p. 54) that the hierarchical structure of an organization is a response to the limited information-processing ability of decision makers. At each level within the hierarchy it is desirable from the viewpoint of co-ordination and control to identify the responsibilities that need to be undertaken if successful outcomes are to be achieved. One approach to this task is to define the *key success factors* over which each organizational unit has control and to assign responsibilities in accordance with these factors. The basic idea behind this approach is a simple one: if a manager's cognitive limitations constrain the amount of information that can be processed at any time it makes sense to be deliberately selective by focusing on the information that is most important in terms of fulfilling the manager's designated responsibilities.

Selecting key success factors that adequately reflect these responsibilities gives a basis for:

- establishing appropriate performance measures;
- determining resource allocation procedures;
- specifying reward systems.

The identification of key success factors gives focus to the control process. In essence the following question is being posed: to which factors are desired outcomes most sensitive? The greater the degree of sensitivity (or responsiveness) between a factor and an outcome, the more critical is that factor in controlling the organizational unit in order to bring about the desired outcome.

It is inevitable that some critical factors (such as macroeconomic variables, government actions, competitive behaviour, and suppliers' behaviour) cannot easily be influenced by a given organization, while other critical factors (which might include product design, quality, price, and level of customer service) are more readily influenced by the organization's managers. However, in control terms the point to note is that the outcome that is desired (e.g. sustained competitive advantage) can be achieved if the manager understands how the key variables behave (i.e. how they change over time and why those changes occur), since this gives the manager the ability to make future predictions. Through the ability to make accurate predictions of each key variable's future value, the manager is in a position to control the outcome of events. In part this will require the manipulation of those variables that can be directly influenced, and in part it will require an awareness of the anticipated future values of variables that the manager is unable directly to influence. Control is achieved when desired outcomes are realized, hence it is possible to be in control even though one is unable to manipulate the values of all variables. It is worth repeating the major elements underlying the above discussion:

- an understanding of the behaviour of key variables gives a basis for making predictions about their likely future values;
- on the basis of good predictions it is possible to bring about desired outcomes by manipulating the variables over which one has influence in the knowledge of the expected behaviour of those variables over which one has no direct influence.

In seeking to control marketing activities the requirements of effective control systems are:

- they must provide timely information;
- they must measure the essential nature of the activity being assessed;
- they should provide information on trends;
- they must facilitate action;
- they must be economical;
- they must be meaningful.

Two developing fields which are likely to increase in importance are those of expert systems (see McDonald and Wilson (1990)) and strategic control (see Wilson (1997)).

19.9 EXERCISES

1 Identify three examples of enterprises which have failed to adapt their marketing strategies in the light of changing circumstances, with the result that they have either withdrawn from the market or continue as laggards.
2 Identify three examples of enterprises which have managed to adapt their marketing strategies to changing circumstances and performed well as a result.

3 Develop a design for a marketing control system to suit an enterprise of your choice. Outline how it might be implemented and operated.
4 Carry out a comparative assessment of the approaches to control put forward by:

(a) Anthony;
(b) Merchant;
(b) Johnson and Scholes;
(b) Luck and Ferrell.

Which do you consider to be most useful?

5 Illustrate the application of both feedforward and feedback approaches to marketing control in situations with which you are familiar.

19.10 DISCUSSION QUESTIONS

1 Explain your understanding of *control* and why it is of value in a marketing context.
2 What purposes does a marketing control system serve?
3 How frequently should marketing activities be evaluated?
4 Is it possible for good implementation to overcome a strategy's basic limitations?
5 Is feedback control more useful in a marketing context than feedforward control? Justify your answer.

19.11 CASE STUDIES

Playboy Enterprises, Inc.

In early 1986, Christie Hefner, President and Chief Operating Officer, Playboy Enterprises, Inc., had been reviewing the company's strategies to face the changing world. Once considered a trend setter for urban sophisticates, the adult-leisure company in recent years has increasingly found its offerings out of step with the times.

As a writer on social issues put it, 'The image of the playboy in a smoking jacket is obsolete. People today are more interested in their cars and their careers than they are in sex.' While that may be open to dispute, Playboy has reason be be alarmed. The circulation of its flagship magazine has dwindled to just over four million a month from more than seven million in 1972. The number of Playboy Club key holders has fallen steadily. The cabletelevision Playboy Channel, once seen as crucial to the future, loses money and has yet to prove it can survive in its highly competitive field.

Between 1983 and 1985, Playboy's revenue fell by nearly 50%. It earned a profit on operations in only one of four years between 1982 and 1985, when it was forced by old legal problems to give up its lucrative casinos. The company was in the black (by $6.7 million) in its 1985 fiscal year only because of returns on its $60 million in investments. And its auditors have qualified their opinion on the financial statement for that year because of uncertainty over whether Playboy can collect all it is owed on one casino sale.

Company History

Initially, the Playboy Enterprises, Inc. was established as HMH Publishing Company in 1953 to publish the Playboy magazine. The present name was adopted in 1971.

Today the company's businesses, in addition to the Playboy and Games magazines, include the development and production of programming principally for pay television, and video cassettes; and products for direct sale and licensing that feature the Playboy name and trademarks for Worldwide distribution. In addition, the company owns and franchises Playboy Clubs. In the 1970s the company entered the resort hotel and casino business in different places including London, United Kingdom; Miami, Florida; Bahamas; and Atlantic City. However, in 1982 the company discontinued its resort hotel and casino operations.

Environmental Changes

Playboy is a victim of the social changes it helped promote. Attitudes toward sex have evolved rapidly since the days when the magazine could shock millions by publishing two photographs of an undraped Marilyn Monroe. Today, Playboy has to compete, not only with countless far more lurid 'skin books,' but also against the popular media; rock songs may have X-rated lyrics and an episode of 'Dynasty' on TV may be nearly as titillating as a centerfold.

As Miss Hefner puts it, 'We no longer can contrast ourselves to a gray-flannel Eisenhower society. It's now a lot more difficult for us to offer something unique.'

Yet Playboy also finds itself considerably vexed these days by those who consider its business immoral or sexist or both. Although its cable-television fare isn't hardcore, for instance, it has repeatedly been challenged in court (so far unsuccessfully) by communities that want it banned.

After ABC recently broadcast a film based on Gloria Steinem's critical account of her 1963 stint as a Bunny, Playboy President Christie Hefner fired off a memo asking her staff to 'ponder what it is Playboy and all of its resources can and should be doing to counter the . . . misimpression out there that we are not good guys.'

Perhaps a tougher problem for Miss Hefner, though, is finding a clear mission for Playboy in the 1990s, one as potent as her father's former vision for the company. In an era of aggressive careerism – by both sexes – the company no longer gets much mileage out of the so-called Playboy Philosophy, Mr. Hefner's concept of the life style of a man of leisure.

The Real Problem

Some company officials believe that one of Playboy's biggest handicaps may be its association with the public image of its founder, now 59 years old. As a Playboy executive put it, 'Pajamas just aren't as fashionable as they used to be.'

Though still the best-selling magazine for men, Playboy has fallen far behind archrival Penthouse in lucrative newsstand sales. According to Penthouse publisher Bob Guccione, 'Playboy's market is older and its readers are passing into oblivion.' But Playboy says the readership age difference is minimal. However, there are other worrisome signs. A Chicago newsstand operator who has sold a lot of copies of Playboy speaks of the typical buyer as 'a guy who thinks he's up to date but isn't.' One woman who posed for a pictorial was surprised when she saw the letters the feature generated, to find that 'a whole bunch of them were from guys in prison.' A former public-relations executive for Playboy contends that the company 'doesn't want to face reality – that time has passed them by.'

New Strategy

Against the above background, Playboy Enterprises is undertaking what Miss Hefner calls a 'repositioning.' The strategy, she says, is to go after a more upscale audience by being more in tune with current tastes and values. 'I think we should be on the cutting edge of how people who have changed their behavior to reflect a more liberal life style are going to live.'

The October 1985 issue of Playboy, marked 'Collector's Edition,' began what the company calls the magazine's next generation. This included greater coverage of such 'life-style' subjects as personal finance and home electronics. An ad in that issue asked, 'What sort of man reads Playboy?' and offers as an example race-car driver Danny Sullivan. Posing in a black silk evening jacket, he explains that he 'grew with the magazine,' learning, for instance, to care about clothes. Curiously, elsewhere in the issue was a piece satirizing the consumer society.

Sensitive to criticism that it portrays women as sex objects, Playboy intends to feature some who are more mature or more accomplished. The lead feature in the November 1985 issue was a nod in this direction, but it hardly seemed likely to defuse the moral issue. Picturing members of Mensa, the club people can join only if they have high IQs, the feature was entitled 'America's Smartest Girls Pose Nude.'

Nevertheless, Miss Hefner says Playboy's effort to move upscale is working. As evidence, she notes that the October 1985 issue carried advertising for Campbell Soup's Le Menu frozen dinners.

Covers of the new-generation Playboy are to have a glitzier look. They are planned in long meetings by a committee of fashion and art experts who try to base their designs as much on the latest fashions as on erotic content.

The graphics also are slicker and a different printing process binds pages with glue instead of staples, giving a more finished look. According to Playboy's art director, 'The magazine is supposed to look a lot more like the kind of thing you'd put on a coffee table.' That goal may be a bit optimistic, however; newsstands say that half of the buyers of Playboy still ask for a paper bag to carry it home in.

The new magazine retains many of the standard features, like the Playboy Advisor, which gives advice about sex, with answers to questions about stereos or turbochargers. Some editors complain about the uneven quality and occasionally questionable taste of color cartoons. Mr. Hefner himself is said to have rejected an editor's plea to eliminate the Party Jokes feature, which in the October 1985 issue, regales readers with one-lines like, 'What's boffo box office among milkmaids? "Pail Rider."'

The 'repositioning' also applies to the Playboy Clubs, which haven't had a major updating since they were started a quarter-century ago. Even with a recent redecorating, the club in Chicago with its plush red carpeting and black leather bar stools, looks a little like a museum for the jazz age. A gift shop up front peddling Playboy T-shirts, cigarette lighters and golf putters lends a touristy atmosphere to the place.

Rather than confront the deteriorating image of its big-city clubs, Playboy several years ago headed for the hinterlands, franchising clubs in places like Lansing, Michigan, and Des Moines, Iowa, where they might still have novelty value. But without a strong big-city base, the whole chain lost its urban gleam. The Lansing club began resorting to such decidedly unglamorous promotions as lip-sync contests and valet parking for farm tractors.

The New York Experiment

In the fall of 1985, the company reopened its newly done New York club. It was a bold experiment. The cotton-tailed bunnies were replaced by hostesses greeting guests wearing long, glittering Jean Harlow-style gowns. Some of the waiters were men. Absent were the traditional pool table, party balloons and Leroy Neiman paintings. Instead, video effects, stage acts and music by a ten-piece house orchestra were offered.

The New York club's new look was sculpted by Richard Melman who is noted for elaborate concept restaurants that are as much show-biz productions as eateries. He selected Bunnies with talent as body-builders, astrologists and jugglers. Costumes ranged from a sequined one called the Michael Jackson outfit, to sweater-dresses, to a takeoff of the current cottontail suit. The idea of male waiters (called rabbits) was to help women feel more comfortable in the club.

It remains to be seen if the company will convert the other clubs in the New York style. The company has twelve other Playboy Clubs, ten of which are franchised rather than company-owned. A section of the club called 'Cafe Playboy' may be tested as prototype for a chain of franchised bars open to the public. (A Playboy key still is needed for admittance to the clubs, though temporary memberships are readily available.)

Strategy for Other Businesses

Playboy's products division, too, is working to bolster the company image, or at least stop endangering it. The division has sold countless key chains, air fresheners and the like, even though doing so risked cheapening the company's trademark. Now Playboy is moving away from novelty items and into things like fashion apparel and branded consumer products. One success is Playboy's men's underwear, the second-best-selling brand.

Playboy still has some hard thinking to do about its video operation. The division, which launched the first sex-oriented cable channel for a mass audience five years ago, had identity problems from the start. Unable to decide how racy to be, the channel wound up alienating viewers at both ends of the spectrum.

Earlier in 1985, for instance, the channel stopped offering erotic programming during prime time, switching to mainstream movies and quasi-journalistic specials like one entitled 'Omar Sharif Hosts the Prostitutes of Paris.' Viewership dropped and Playboy soon reverted to prime-time prurience.

Partly because of its turnabouts, the Playboy Channel has had the highest disconnect rate in the industry, 13% of viewers each month. Its current level of about 762,000 subscribers isn't enough to pay for the quality programming that might attract a larger audience. At $20 million, the channel's yearly budget is less than a network might spend during a season on a single series.

As a result, Playboy is deemphasizing the channel as its main outlet for programming and will focus more on cassette sales and a recently launched pay-per-view service. It also is weighing a return to producing a late-night variety show or hour-long specials, either of which it would try to sell to one of the networks.

Still, Playboy's video operations, like the rest of its empire, is continuing to grope for the right formula for today's audience. As Miss Hefner sums up, 'We have to reflect a modern, sophisticated image.'

Required

What approaches to control do you consider appropriate for Playboy enterprises?

Hanover-Bates Chemical Corporation

James Sprague, newly appointed northeast district sales manager for the Hanover-Bates Chemical Corporation, leaned back in his chair as the door to his office slammed shut. 'Great beginning,' he thought. 'Three days in my new job and the district's most experienced sales representative is threatening to quit.'

On the previous night, Sprague, Hank Carver (the district's most experienced sales representative), and John Follet, another senior member of the district sales staff, had met for dinner at Sprague's suggestion. During dinner he had mentioned that one of his top priorities would be to conduct a sales and profit analysis of the district's business in order to identify opportunities to improve the district's profit performance. He had stated that he was confident that the analysis would indicate opportunities to reallocate district sales efforts in a manner that would increase profits. As Sprague had indicated during the conversation, 'My experience in analyzing district sales performance data for the national sales manager has convinced me that any district's allocation of sales effort to products and customer categories can be improved.' Both Carver and Follet had nodded as Sprague discussed his plans.

Carver was waiting when Sprague arrived at the district sales office this morning. It soon became apparent that Carver was very upset by what he perceived as Sprague's criticism of how he and the other district sales representatives were doing their jobs – and, more particularly, of how they were allocating their time in terms of customers and products. As he concluded his heated comments, Carver said:

> This company has made it darned clear that 34 years of experience don't count for anything . . . and now someone with not much more than two years of selling experience and two years of pushing paper for the national sales manager at corporate headquarters tells me I'm not doing my job . . . Maybe it's time for me to look for a new job . . . and since Trumbull Chemical [Hanover-Bates's major competitor] is hiring, maybe that's where I should start looking . . . and I'm not the only one who feels this way.

As Sprague reflected on the scene that had just occurred, he wondered what he should do. It had been made clear to him when he had been promoted to manager of the northeast sales district that one of his top priorities should be improvement of the district's profit performance. As the national sales manager had said, 'The northeast sales district may rank third in dollar sales, but it's our worst district in terms of profit performance.'

Prior to assuming his new position, Sprague had assembled the data presented in Exhibits 1 through 6 to assist him in analyzing the district sales and profits. The data had been compiled from records maintained in the national sales manager's office. Although he believed the data would provide a sound basis for a preliminary analysis of district sales and profit performance, Sprague had recognized that additional data would probably have to be collected when he arrived in the northeast district (District 3).

In response to the national sales manager's comment about the northeast district's poor performance, Sprague had been particularly interested in how the district had performed on its gross profit quota. He knew that district gross profit quotas were assigned in a manner that took into account variation in price competition. Thus, he felt that poor performance in the gross profit quota area reflected misallocated sales efforts either in terms of customers or in terms of the mix of product line items sold. To provide himself with a frame of reference, he had also requested data on the north-central sales district (District 7). This district is

Exhibit 1

Hanover-Bates Chemical Corporation: Summary Income Statements, 1986–1990					
	1986	**1987**	**1988**	**1989**	**1990**
Sales	$19,890,000	$21,710,000	$19,060,000	$21,980,000	$23,890,000
Production expenses	11,934,000	13,497,000	12,198,000	13,612,000	14,563,000
Gross profit	7,956,000	8,213,000	6,862,000	8,368,000	9,327,000
Administrative expenses	2,606,000	2,887,000	2,792,000	2,925,000	3,106,000
Selling expenses	2,024,000	2,241,000	2,134,000	2,274,000	2,399,000
Pretax profit	3,326,000	3,085,000	1,936,000	3,169,000	3,822,000
Taxes	1,512,000	1,388,000	790,000	1,426,000	1,718,000
Net profit	$1,814,000	$1,697,000	$1,146,000	$1,743,000	$2,104,000

generally considered to be one of the best, if not the best, in the company. Furthermore, the north-central district sales manager, who is only three years older than Sprague, is highly regarded by the national sales manager.

The Company and the Industry

The Hanover-Bates Chemical Corporation is a leading producer of processing chemicals for the chemical plating industry. The company's products are produced in four plants, located in Los Angeles, Houston, Chicago, and Newark, New Jersey. The company's production process is, in essence, a mixing operation. Chemicals purchased from a broad range of suppliers are mixed according to a variety of user-based formulas. Company sales in 1990 had reached a new high of $23.89 million, up from $21.98 million in 1989. Net pretax profit in 1990 had been $3.822 million, up from $3.169 million in 1989. Hanover-Bates has a strong balance sheet, and the company enjoys a favorable price-earnings ratio on its stock, which trades on the OTC market.

Although Hanover-Bates does not produce commodity-type chemicals (such as sulphuric acid), industry customers tend to perceive minimal quality differences among the products produced by Hanover-Bates and its competitors. Given the customers' perception of a lack of variation in product quality and the industrywide practice of limiting advertising expenditures, field sales efforts are of major importance in the marketing programs of all firms in the industry.

Exhibit 2

District Sales Quota and Gross Profit Quota Performance, 1990					
District	Number of Sales Reps	Sales Quota	Sales–Actual	Gross Profit Quota[a]	Gross Profit–Actual
1	7	$3,880,000	$3,906,000	$1,552,000	$1,589,000
2	6	3,750,000	3,740,000	1,500,000	1,529,000
3	6	3,650,000	3,406,000	1,460,000	1,239,000
4	6	3,370,000	3,318,000	1,348,000	1,295,000
5	5	3,300,000	3,210,000	1,320,000	1,186,000
6	5	3,130,000	3,205,000	1,252,000	1,179,000
7	5	2,720,000	3,105,000	1,088,000	1,310,000
		$23,800,000	$23,890,000	$9,520,000	$9,327,000

[a] District gross profit quotas were developed by the national sales manager in consultation with the district managers and took into account price competition in the respective districts.

Exhibit 3

	District Selling Expenses, 1990							
District	Sales Rep Salaries[a]	Sales Commission	Sales Rep Expenses	District Office	District Manager Salary	District Manager Expenses	Sales Support	Total Selling Expenses
1	$177,100	$19,426	$56,280	$21,150	$33,500	$11,460	$69,500	$388,416
2	143,220	18,700	50,760	21,312	34,000	12,034	71,320	351,346
3	157,380	17,030	54,436	22,123	35,000[b]	12,382	70,010	368,529
4	150,480	16,590	49,104	22,004	32,500	11,005	66,470	348,153
5	125,950	16,050	42,720	21,115	33,000	11,123	76,600	326,558
6	124,850	16,265	41,520	20,992	33,500	11,428	67,100	315,655
7	114,850	17,530	44,700	22,485	31,500	11,643	58,750	300,258
								$2,398,915

[a] Includes cost of fringe benefit program, which was 10 percent of base salary.
[b] Salary of James Sprague's predecessor.

Hanover-Bates's market consists of several thousand job-shop and captive (in-house) plating operations. Chemical platers process a wide variety of materials including industrial fasteners (for example, screws, rivets, bolts, and washers), industrial components (for example, clamps, casings, and couplings), and miscellaneous items (for example, umbrella frames, eyelets, and decorative items). The chemical plating process involves the electrolytic application of metallic coatings such as zinc, cadmium, nickel, and brass. The degree of plating precision required varies substantially, with some work being primarily decorative, some involving relatively loose standards (for example, 0.0002 zinc, which means that anything over two ten-thousandths of an inch of plate is acceptable), and some involving relatively precise standards (for example, 0.0003–0.0004 zinc).

Regardless of the degree of plating precision involved, quality control is of critical concern to all chemical platers. Extensive variation in the condition of materials received for plating requires a high level of service from the firms supplying chemicals to platers. This service is normally provided by the sales representatives of the firm(s) supplying the plater with processing chemicals.

Hanover-Bates and the majority of the firms in its industry produce the same line of basic processing chemicals for the chemical plating industry. The line consists of a trisodium phosphate cleaner (SPX); anesic aldahyde brightening agents for zinc plating (ZBX), cadmium plating (CBX), and nickel plating (NBX); a protective post-plating chromate dip (CHX); and a

Exhibit 4

	District Contribution to Corporate Administrative Expense and Profit, 1990			
District	Sales	Gross Profit	Selling Expenses	Contribution to Administrative Expense and Profit
1	$3,906,000	$1,589,000	$388,416	$1,200,544
2	3,740,000	1,529,000	351,346	1,177,654
3	3,406,000	1,239,000	368,529	870,471
4	3,318,000	1,295,000	348,153	946,847
5	3,210,000	1,186,000	326,558	859,442
6	3,205,000	1,179,000	315,376	863,624
7	3,105,000	1,310,000	300,258	1,009,742
	$23,890,000	$9,327,000	$2,398,636	$6,928,324

Exhibit 5

Northeast (#3) and North-Central (#7) District Sales and Gross Profit Performance by Account Category, 1990				
District	(A)	(B)	(C)	Total
Sales by Account Category				
Northeast	$915,000	$1,681,000	$810,000	$3,406,000
North-central	751,000	1,702,000	652,000	3,105,000
Gross Profit by Account Category				
Northeast	$356,000	$623,000	$260,000	$1,239,000
North-central	330,000	725,000	255,000	1,310,000

protective burnishing compound (BUX). The company's product line is detailed as follows:

Product	Container Size	List Price	Gross Margin
SPX	400-lb. drum	$80	$28
ZBX	50-lb. drum	76	34
CBX	50-lb. drum	76	34
NBX	50-lb. drum	80	35
CHX	100-lb. drum	220	90
BUX	400-lb. drum	120	44

Company Sales Organization

Hanover-Bates' sales organization consists of 40 sales representatives operating in seven sales districts. Most sales representatives had formerly worked for a Hanover-Bates customer, and none were college-educated. Sales representatives' salaries range from $22,000 to $30,000, with fringe-benefit costs amounting to an additional 10 percent of salary. In addition to their salaries, Hanover-Bates' sales representatives receive commissions of 0.5 percent of their dollar sales volume on all sales up to their sales quotas. The commission on sales in excess of quota is 1 percent. District sales manager salaries range from $31,500 to $35,000. Sales managers are also eligible for a bonus based on district sales performance.

In 1988 the national sales manager of Hanover-Bates had developed a sales program based on selling the full line of Hanover-Bates products. He believed that if the sales representatives could successfully carry out his program, the following benefits would accrue to Hanover-Bates and its customers:

1 Sales volume per account would be greater, and selling costs as a percentage of sales would decrease.

Exhibit 6

Potential Accounts, Active Accounts, and Account Call Coverage: Northeast and North-Central Districts, 1990									
	Potential Accounts			Active Accounts			Account Coverage (Total Calls)		
District	(A)	(B)	(C)	(A)	(B)	(C)	(A)	(B)	(C)
Northeast	90	381	635	53	210	313	1,297	3,051	2,118
North-central	60	286	499	42	182	218	1,030	2,618	1,299

2 A Hanover-Bates sales representative could justify spending more time with an account, thus becoming more knowledgeable about the account's business and becoming better able to provide technical assistance and identify selling opportunities.

3 Full-line sales would strengthen Hanover-Bates's competitive position by reducing the likelihood of account loss to other plating-chemical suppliers (a problem that existed in multiple-supplier situations).

The national sales manager's 1988 sales program had also included the following account call-frequency guidelines:

A accounts (major accounts generating $12,000 or more in yearly sales) – two calls per month

B accounts (medium-sized accounts generating $6,000–$11,999 in yearly sales) – one call per month

C accounts (small accounts generating less than $6,000 yearly in sales) – one call every two months

The account call-frequency guidelines were developed by the national sales manager after discussions with the district managers. The national sales manager had been concerned about the optimal allocation of sales effort to accounts and felt that the guidelines would increase the efficiency of the company's sales force, although not all of the district sales managers agreed with this conclusion.

It was common knowledge in Hanover-Bates' corporate sales office that Sprague's predecessor as northeast district sales manager had not been one of the company's better district sales managers. His attitude toward the sales plans and programs of the national sales manager had been one of reluctant compliance rather than acceptance and support. However, when the national sales manager succeeded in persuading Sprague's predecessor to take early retirement, no replacement was readily available.

Carver, who most of the sales representatives had assumed would get the district manager job, had been passed over in part because he would be 65 in three years. The national sales manager had not wanted to face the same replacement problem again in three years and also had wanted someone in the position who would be more likely to be responsive to the company's sales plans and policies. The appointment of Sprague as district manager had caused considerable talk, not only in the district but also at corporate headquarters. In fact, the national sales manager had warned Sprague that 'a lot of people are expecting you to fall on your face . . . they don't think you have the experience to handle the job, in particular, and to manage and motivate a group of sales representatives, most of whom are considerably older and more experienced than you.' The general sales manager had concluded by saying, 'I think you can handle the job, Jim . . . I think you can manage those sales reps and improve the district's profit performance . . . and I'm depending on you to do both.'

Source: This case was prepared by Professor Robert E. Witt, The University of Texas, Austin, as a basis for class discussion and is not designed to illustrate effective or ineffective handling of an administrative situation.

Required

What specific control procedures are applicable in Hanover-Bates?

20.1 LEARNING OBJECTIVES

When you have read this chapter you should be able to:

(a) understand the nature of controls;
(b) design and operate marketing budgeting systems;
(c) carry out variance analyses in a marketing context;
(d) recognize how to use competitive and environmental intelligence in devising corrective responses.

20.2 INTRODUCTION

Having considered in Chapter 19 the nature of control and control systems, along with a range of approaches to control, this chapter looks in more detail at the operation of some of the more widely used control systems (such as marketing audits, budgeting and variance analysis). It then goes on to consider how corrective action might be taken if outcomes are not in accordance with plans.

20.3 CONTROLS

Forms of Control

In large organizations there are a number of insidious and unobtrusive controls to be found. These are all the more dangerous and powerful because they are so deceptive. Their deceptiveness is shown in their *not* causing participants to feel their presence – there is no feeling of being oppressed by a despot. Instead there is perhaps just the experience of conforming to the logic of a situation, or of performing in accordance with some internalized standard.

Beyond this source of 'control' there are other sources. To the extent that the behaviour of members of organizations is controlled (i.e. appears to be regular and predictable) such regularity may derive from the norms and definitions of subcultural groups within the organization rather than from official rules and prescriptions. The idea that organizational rules constitute the blueprint for all behaviour within organizations is not a tenable one.

Nevertheless, the most significant form of power within organizations is the power to limit, guide and restrict the decision making of organizational personnel such that even when they are allowed (or obliged) to use their own judgement they do not deviate from official expectations. In part this is due to the organization's structure, which can be seen as a series of limitations and controls over members' decision making, and which results from powerful, senior organizational personnel choosing what the structure should be (and hence determining who is allowed to do what).

It is something of a paradox that the modern individual is freer from coercion through the power of command of superiors than most people have ever been, yet individuals in positions of power today probably exercise more control than any tyrant ever did. This is largely due to contemporary forms of power exercised within organizations and by organizations in society. There is a distinct trend that places less reliance on control through a fixed chain of command while placing more reliance on indirect forms of control. Let us pursue this in greater detail.

Forms of control have changed with the passage of time, and these forms have had impacts not only within organizations but also through them, on contemporary society.

Organizations have taken advantage of a variety of control mechanisms from time to time, ranging from ones that are obviously bureaucratic in nature (e.g. command authority and discipline) to ones that are quite unbureaucratic (such as the controlling power that is rooted in expert knowledge).

We can consider the following range of control mechanisms:

1 The prototype (bureaucratic control) is the authority exercised through a *chain of command* in which superiors give subordinates instructions which must be obeyed. This coercive form of control has strong military overtones, and an essential element is rigorous discipline that must be enforced through coercive sanctions. Such discipline is not usually a characteristic of contemporary industrial life.

2 The establishing of explicit regulations and procedures to govern decisions and operations gives a programmed form of control. Discipline is involved in this mechanism also, and close links can be seen between the idea of a set of rules that must be followed and the idea of following orders via a chain of command. However, explicit rules do restrict the arbitrary exercise of power by superiors because they apply to rulers as well as to the ruled.

  In specifying rules on how to behave in particular circumstances it is unlikely that all possible situations will be catered for. It follows that rules should ideally be related to the principles underlying decisions rather than to particular decisions – thus specifying *criteria* for decision making will be less restrictive than the stipulating of *how* specific decisions should be made.

3 Incentive systems constitute a further control mechanism. Salaries and career advancement clearly make individuals dependent to a large extent on the organization that employs them, thereby constraining them to submit to the authority exercised within that organization.

  Incentives are often tied directly to performance, with piece-work rates and sales commissions being the most obvious examples. However, performance measures can be developed for most organizational roles, and adjustments in salary levels and promotion decisions will depend at least to some extent on measured achievements.

4 Technology provides a control mechanism in two forms:

  - production technology constrains employees' performance, thereby enabling managers to control operations (e.g. the speed of an assembly line can be used to regulate productivity);
  - the technical knowledge possessed by an organization's 'technocrats' gives them the ability to understand and perform complex tasks and thereby maintain control of a situation. Management is thus able to control operations, albeit indirectly, by hiring staff with appropriate professional/technical skills to carry out the required responsibilities.

  This reduces the need to use alternative mechanisms, such as detailed rules or close supervision through a chain of command.

5 Expert knowledge is a vital requirement in managing organizations. (It could even be argued that successful management comes about through the exercising

of control over the basic knowledge.) It follows that recruiting suitable technocrats is a key mechanism for controlling the organization. If technically-qualified individuals are selectively recruited and if they have the professional ability to perform assigned tasks on their own, then if the organization gives such individuals the appropriate discretion to do what needs to be done within the broad framework of basic policies and administrative guidelines, it should be possible for control to be effective.

6 The allocation of resources (including personnel) is the ultimate mechanism of organizational control since this facilitates certain actions and inhibits others.

Within most organizations one will find several of these mechanisms of control in operation, yet there seems to be a trend towards a decreasing reliance on control through a chain of command and an increasing reliance on indirect forms of control, e.g. via recruitment policies. Incentive systems and machine technologies are perhaps the most prevalent mechanisms of contemporary organizational control; control via recruitment and resource allocation is indicative of the likely future pattern.

Controls may be informal as well as formal. The former are unwritten mechanisms that can influence either individual or group behaviour patterns within organizations in profound ways. A distinction can be made among different types of informal control by means of the level of aggregation (i.e. from individual through small groups to large groups) chosen. (See, for example, Jaworski (1988).) Three categories are:

1 Self-control in which individuals establish their own personal objectives and attempt to achieve those objectives by monitoring their own performance and adapting their behaviour whenever this is necessary. This can lead to high levels of job satisfaction but it may fail to achieve the outcomes sought by top management (i.e. those relating to the organization rather than specific individuals). In order to motivate individuals to act in accordance with top management's wishes a system of incentives will be needed.

2 Social control is applied within small group settings by members of the group. It is typically found that groups (e.g. marketing teams) set their own informal standards of behaviour and performance with which group members are expected to conform. These standards represent values and mutual commitments towards some common goal. Whenever a member of the group behaves in a deviant way by violating a group norm the other members of the group will attempt to use subtle pressures – such as humour or hints – to correct the deviance. If this fails and violations are repeated the group's reaction is likely to be to ostracize the deviant individual. In a marketing context there may be group norms for, say, expenses and sales volumes within a sales team.

3 Cultural control applies at a corporate (or divisional) level and stems from the accumulation of rituals, legends and norms of social interaction within the organization. Once an individual has internalized the cultural norms he/she can be expected to behave in accordance with those norms. This gives reason to see cultural control as being the dominant control mechanism for senior management positions involving non-routine decision making: the judgemental factor will reflect the manager's cultural conditioning.

In contrast to informal controls there are formal controls – written management-initiated mechanisms that influence the probability that individuals, or groups, will act in a manner that is supportive of marketing objectives. Three categories of formal controls can be identified, with timing being the distinguishing factor (i.e. these controls echo the sequence of managerial processes):

1 Input controls consist of measurable actions that are taken prior to the implementation of plans, such as specifying selection criteria for recruiting staff, establishing recruitment and training programmes, and various forms of resource allocation. The mix of these inputs can be manipulated in an attempt to secure control.
2 Process control relates to management's attempts to influence the means of achieving desired ends, with the emphasis being on behaviour and/or activities rather than on the end results – such as requiring individuals to follow establishing procedures. There is no clear agreement in the literature as to whether the organization's structure represents a control mechanism or not. Since it can be seen to influence and shape individual and group behaviour it is not unreasonable to think of structure as being part of process control.
3 Output controls apply when results are compared with performance standards, as in feedback control.

In considering control in marketing one might emphasize the control of marketing activities in a relatively detached and impersonal way, as is done by strategy formulation (feedforward control) and variance analysis (feedback control). Alternatively, one might emphasize the control of marketing personnel which involves finding ways to influence the behaviour of those engaging in marketing activities in order that desired ends might be achieved. Since it seems likely that marketing activities can only be controlled through marketing personnel the best way forward would seem to be a balanced combination of both approaches: in other words, feedforward and feedback need to be combined with marketing activities by those who devise and execute marketing activities.

The ultimate test of any control system is the extent to which it brings about organizational effectiveness and it is fair to say that there is little rigorously formulated evidence to demonstrate clear linkages between any approach to control and organizational effectiveness.

Audits

One approach towards assessing marketing effectiveness is the marketing audit (dealt with in detail in Chapter 2 above).

The marketing audit exists to help correct difficulties and to improve conditions that may already be good. While these aims may be achieved by a piecemeal examination of individual activities it is better achieved by a total programme of evaluation studies. The former approach is termed a 'vertical audit' as it is only concerned with one element of the marketing mix at any one time. In contrast, the latter approach, the 'horizontal audit', is concerned with optimizing the use of resources, thereby maximizing the total effectiveness of marketing efforts and outlays. As such, it is by far the more difficult of the two, and hence rarely attempted.

No matter which form of marketing audit is selected, top management (via its audit staff) should ensure that no area of marketing activity goes unevaluated and that every aspect is evaluated in accordance with standards that are compatible with the total success of the marketing organization and of the firm as a whole. This, of course, requires that all activities be related to the established hierarchy of objectives.

The Distribution Audit

In the planning and control of costs and effectiveness in distribution activities the management audit can be of considerable value. Not surprisingly, however, it entails a complex set of procedures right across the function if it is to be carried out thoroughly. The major components are the channel audit, the PDM audit, the competitive audit, and the customer service audit. Each of these will be considered briefly in turn.

1 *The channel audit*

Channels are made up of the intermediaries (such as wholesalers, factors, retailers) through which goods pass on their route from manufacture to consumption. The key channel decisions include:

- choosing intermediaries;
- determining the implications (from a PD point of view) of alternative channel structures;
- assessing the available margins.

It follows from the nature of these decisions that the main focus of a channel audit will be on structural factors on the one hand and on cost/margin factors on the other.

2 *The PDM audit*

There are three primary elements within this audit: that of company profile (which includes the handling cost characteristics of the product range and the service level that is needed in the light of market conditions); PDM developments (both of a technological and contextual nature); and the current system's capability.

Cost aspects exist in each of these elements, but operating costs loom largest in the last since it is predominantly concerned with costs and capacity. For example, some of the items that will be subjected to audit will include those shown in Figure 20.1.

3 *The competitive audit*

Through this phase it should be possible to ascertain the quality of competitors' distribution policies, etc., and especially the level of service that competitors are able to offer (and maintain). Within the competitive audit regard should also be had to channel structures, pricing and discount policies and market shares.

4 *The customer service audit*

Given that the level of service is at the centre of physical distribution management it is essential to monitor regularly its cost and quality characteristics.

A very thorough approach to the distribution audit is that developed at the Cranfield School of Management by Christopher and his colleagues (see Christopher, et al. (1977)).

Kotler (1984) has offered the view that auditing is the ultimate control measure, although it can be seen as a means of linking the notions of efficiency and effectiveness. It achieves this latter purpose by not only evaluating performance in terms of inputs used and outputs generated but also by evaluating the assumptions underlying marketing strategies. The fact that audits are expensive and time consuming – especially when undertaken in a comprehensive, horizontal manner – may appear to contradict the striving for efficiency. However, by focusing on doing the right thing they should help in ensuring effectiveness which is of greater importance.

Selecting the right person to carry out the audit has been addressed by Kling (1985). He observed that a balance of experience and objectivity is needed which tends to favour outside auditors who have a broader range of experience than insiders and who can stand back in a reasonably impartial way from policies and procedures that they were not involved in either formulating or implementing. The range of possible auditors includes:

1 self-audit;
2 audit from across (i.e. by a colleague in another function but at the same level as the manager whose activities are being audited);
3 audit from above (i.e. by the manager's superior);
4 company auditing office;

FIGURE 20.1
Distribution audit

Capacity utilization	• Warehouse • Transportation • Flexibility and expansion scope
Warehouse facilities	• Total costs • Age and maintenance costs • Flexibility throughput/period • Total throughput/period • Returns handled – number – recovery time • Picking accuracy • Service levels/back orders • Cube utilization • Cost of cube bought out

Inventory	• Total inventory holding costs
	• Product group costs
	• Service levels – total
	               – plant
	               – field
	• Field inventory holding costs
	• Transfers – number
	            – volume
	• Stock out effects – loss of business
	                    – rectification costs

Transportation	• Total costs • Production to field units • Field units to customers • Vehicle utilization • Vehicle cube utilization • Total volumes shipped • Cost per mile – volumes shipped – cases/pallets shipped • Costs of service bought out • Costs by mode/comparisons

Communications	• Total costs
	• Order communication times – method
	                         – cost
	• Time and costs per line item per order method for:
	  – order processing and registration
	  – credit investigation
	  – invoice and delivery note preparation
	  – statement preparation
	• Number and cost of customer queries
	• Salesmen's – calls/day
	          – calls/territory/day
	          – calls/product group/day
	          – calls/customer group/day
	• Salesmen's use of time – selling
	                    – inventory checking
	                    – merchandising
	                    – order processing

Unitization	• Total costs
	• Volumes shipped
	• Unitization method/proportions of
	  – pallets
	  – roll pallets
	  – containers
	• Costs of assembly and handling by load type

Service achieved (by market segment)	• Total costs • Service levels operated/costs • Delivery times • Delivery reliability • Order processing and progressing • Order picking efficiency • Claims procedure/time/cost

Volume throughput	• Total throughput – volume
	                  – weight
	                  – units
	• Total costs
	• Throughput/field locations – volume
	                          – weight
	                          – units
	• Throughput fluctuations
	• Flexibility (capacity availability/time)

5 company task-force audit (i.e. a team set up specifically to conduct the audit);

6 outside auditors.

It may be better to have a combination of 6 with one of 2–5, thereby bringing together an external view with the perspective of insiders in a joint endeavour. There is little evidence of support for 1, although it exists as a possibility in the absence of any alternative.

In carrying out a marketing audit it will be evident that the enterprise needs to exhibit adaptive behaviour if it is to remain goal striving in a dynamic environment. Effectiveness is concerned with this ability to achieve goals in an ever-changing context.

Budgeting

Budgeting (or profit planning) is perhaps the widest-ranging control technique in that it covers the entire organization rather than merely sections of it. (See Wilson (1995).)

A budget is a quantitative plan of action that aids in the co-ordination and control of the acquisition, allocation and utilization of resources over a given period of time. The building of the budget may be looked upon as the integration of the varied interests that constitute the organization into a programme that all have agreed is workable in attempting to attain objectives.

Budgetary planning and control work through the formal organization viewing it as a series of responsibility centres and attempting to isolate the performance measurement of one module from the effects of the performance of others.

Budgeting involves more than just forecasting since it involves the planned manipulation of all the variables that determine the company's performance in an effort to arrive at some preferred position in the future. The agreed plan must be developed in a co-ordinated manner if the requirements of each sub-system are to be balanced in line with company objectives. Each manager must consider the relationship of his responsibility centre (or department, or sub-system) to all others and to the company as a whole in the budgetary planning phase. This tends to reduce departmental bias and empire building, as well as isolating weaknesses in the organizational structure and highlighting problems of communication. Furthermore, it encourages the delegation of authority by a reliance on the principle of management by exception.

Having determined the plan, this provides the frame of reference for judging subsequent performance. There can be no doubt that *budgeted* performance is a better bench-mark than past performance on account of the inefficiencies that are usually hidden in the latter and the effect of constantly changing conditions.

There are essentially two types of budget – the long-term and the short-term. Time obviously distinguishes one from the other, and this raises the point that users of budgets should not be unduly influenced by conventional accounting periods: the budget period that is most meaningful to the company should be adopted. For example, the life cycle of a product from its development right through to its deletion is in many ways a more natural budgetary period than calendar units because it links marketing, production, and financial planning on a unified basis. The actual choice of a budget period will tend to depend very much on the company's ability to forecast accurately.

Typically, however, budgets tend to be compiled on an annual basis, with this time-span being broken down into lesser time intervals for reporting, scheduling and control reasons (i.e. half years, quarters, months, and even weeks in the case of production and sales activities).

Within this framework of one year the *operating budget* is prepared. This is composed of two parts, with each part looking at the same things in a slightly different way, but both arriving at the same net profit and return on investment. These two parts are:

1 The programme (or activity) budget that specifies the operations that will be performed during the forthcoming period. The most logical way to present this budget is to show, for each product, the expected revenues and their associated costs. The result is an impersonal portrayal of the expected future that is useful in ensuring that a balance exists amongst the various activities, profit margins, and volumes – in other words, this is the plan.
2 The responsibility budget that specifies the annual plan in terms of individual responsibilities. This is primarily a control device that indicates the target level of performance, but the personalized costs and revenues in this budget must be controllable at the level at which they are planned and reported.

The significance of these two ways of dealing with the operating budgets is of importance as the programme budget is the outcome of the planning phase whereas the responsibility budget is the starting point for the control phase. The former need not correspond to the organizational structure but the latter must. Consequently, the plan must be translated into the control prior to the time of execution and communicated to those involved in order that no one will be in any doubt as to precisely what is expected of him (or her).

Given these two complementary aspects of the operating budget there are two basic ways in which the budget may be prepared:

1 Periodic budgeting in which a plan is prepared for the next financial year with a minimum of revision as the year goes by. Generally the total expected annual expenditure will be spread over the year on a monthly basis on the strength of the behaviour of the elemental costs. Thus 'salaries' will be spread over the months simply as one-twelfth of the expected annual cost per month, but seasonal variations in sales will require a little more attention to be paid to marketing and production costs and their behaviour over time.
2 Continuous (or rolling) budgeting in which a tentative annual plan is prepared with, say, the first quarter by month in great detail, the second and third quarters in lesser detail, and the fourth quarter in outline only. Every month (or perhaps every quarter) the budget can then be revised by adding the required detail to the next month (or quarter), filling in some of the vagueness in the other remaining months (or quarters), and adding on a new month (or quarter) in such a way that the plan still extends one year ahead. Such a budgeting procedure attempts to accommodate changing conditions and uncertainty, and is highly desirable in that it forces management constantly to think in concrete terms about the forthcoming *year* regardless of where one happens to be in the present *financial* year.

Periodic budgeting will often be satisfactory for companies in stable industries that are able to make relatively accurate forecasts covering the planning period. Conversely, rolling budgeting is of greater value in the more usual cases of somewhat irregular cyclical activity amid the uncertainties of consumer demand.

Whether the concern is with long-term or short-term budgeting, or with continuous or period budgeting, there are certain fundamental requirements that must be met if budgeting is to be of maximum value. Briefly, these requirements are:

1 established objectives;
2 top management sponsorship and support;
3 a knowledge of cost behaviour;
4 flexibility;
5 a specified time period;
6 adequate systems support;
7 an effective organizational structure;
8 a sufficient level of education in budgetary practice.

If these prerequisites exist, then budgeting should enable the company to improve its effectiveness by planning for the future and controlling the execution of the plan by comparing actual results with the desired level of performance.

Deviations between actual and budgeted results will be of managerial concern for such reasons as the following:

1 to highlight errors in budgeting procedures;
2 to indicate the need for budget revision;
3 to pinpoint those activities requiring remedial attention.

The principles of management by exception should be applied to this process of comparison with the focusing of attention on *significant* variations. However, if the budgeted level of activity differs from the actual level of activity it will be apparent that variances of an artificial nature arise – such variances are based purely on volume rather than efficiency. This emphasizes the need for flexibility within the budgeting system: it should be able to allow for varying circumstances by recognizing and adapting to significant changes in the fundamental operating conditions of the firm. Such adaptability can be achieved by a *flexible budget*.

In a flexible budgeting system the budgeted cost is adjusted in accordance with the level of activity experienced in the budget period. For example, a budget that is based on sales of 10 000 units during a particular period is of little value for control purposes if 12 000 units (or 8000 units) are actually sold. The sales manager will be necessarily held responsible for the volume variance, but the level of commission, order processing/invoicing, freight, and similar cost-incurring activities will tend to depend on the actual level of activity which requires that the budget be adjusted in order to show the efficient budgeted level of expenditure for the achieved level of activity.

A simple way of building a flexible budget is to start with a budget for the most likely level of activity and then to derive budgets for 5 per cent, 10 per cent, 15 per cent above and below this level.

The major advantage of the flexible budget is its ability to specify the budgeted level of costs, revenues and profits *without revision* when sales and production programmes are changed. It achieves this by distinguishing between those costs that vary with changes in the level of activity and those that do not. In other words, it is based on a thorough knowledge of cost behaviour patterns.

A static budget (i.e. a fixed budget that relates to a single level of activity) can result in misleading actions. An example should make this clear. Figure 20.2

FIGURE 20.2
Fixed budget analysis

		Budget	Actual	Variance
Sales (units)		10,000	11,000	+1,000
Sales revenue		£15,000	£16,500	+£1,500
Expenditure:	Direct	10,000	11,000	+1,000
	Indirect	4,000	4,200	+200
	Profit	£1,000	£1,300	+£300

shows the comparison of a budgeted level of 10 000 units with an actual sales level of 11 000 units. It appears that profit has improved by £300 *but* not all costs vary in the same way, so a flexible budget analysis is called for. This is shown in Figure 20.3 and indicates clearly that the comparison should be between the actual level of activity and the budgeted costs, revenue, and profit for that level. While profit was higher than the budgeted figure, the difference was only £20 rather than £300.

FIGURE 20.3
*Flexible budget
analysis*

		Fixed budget	Flexible Actual	Actual	Variance
Sales (units)		10,000	11,000	11,000	–
Sales revenue		£15,000	16,500	16,500	–
Expenditure:	Direct	10,000	11,000	11,000	–
	Fixed indirect	1,500	1,500	1,450	–50
	Variable indirect	2,000	2,200	2,240	+40
	Mixed indirect	500	520	510	–10
	Profit	£1,000	£1,280	£1,300	+20

The need to distinguish fixed costs (which remain constant in total during a period) from variable costs (which remain constant per unit of output) is of paramount importance, and any costs that are neither one nor the other (i.e. semi-fixed or semi-variable expenses) can usefully be classified as mixed costs. Apart from showing the cost breakdown in some detail, Figure 20.3 shows the target level of activity (i.e. the fixed budget) as well as the efficiency with which the actual level of activity was attained. This information is vital to effective control.

It is important to appreciate that budgeting cannot take the place of management but rather forms a vital aid to management. Indeed, budgets are based on estimates, and judgement must be applied to determine how valid the estimates are and, consequently, how significant deviations are from those estimates. The adequacy of planning and controlling operations hinges critically upon the adequacy of managerial judgement.

In the light of the need for judgement it is clear that budgeting should not introduce unnecessary rigidity into the management process. A budget should be a flexible framework that is capable of accommodating changing circumstances, but care must be exercised lest the budgetary targets come to supersede the objectives of the company. The budget is a means to an end, not an end in itself.

In its traditional application budgeting has a major weakness in planning and another in control: in the planning phase there is usually consideration of too few alternative courses of action from which the best is to be selected, and in the control phase it is difficult to adjust operating budgets to reflect rapidly changing conditions – they are at best flexible with respect to changing sales or production levels.

Nevertheless, these weaknesses should not outweigh the general role of budgeting in drawing attention to problem areas, encouraging forward thinking, and developing company-wide cooperation.

Other Approaches to Budgeting: ZBB and PPBS

In order to accommodate the particular needs of non-profit organizations (such as government agencies) as well as providing a focus for more rigorous thinking in relation to *programmed* or *discretionary* costs (i.e. those which are determined purely by managerial discretion – such as R & D, training, and many marketing outlays), a number of recent developments in budgeting techniques are worthy of mention. In particular, zero-base budgeting (ZBB) and output budgeting (which is also known as a planning-programming-budgeting system, hence the initials PPBS) have generated considerable interest, so we will take note of them at this point.

- *Zero-base budgeting* (ZBB)
  Among other failings it is generally agreed that traditional budgeting (or *incremental budgeting* as it is often known due to the tendency to add on a bit

more – an increment – to last year's budget level in order to arrive at a figure for next year) is number-oriented, fails to identify priorities, and starts with the existing level of activity or expenditure as an established base, whereas it might be more useful to managers to have a technique that was decision-oriented, helped in determining priorities, and sought to reassess the current level of expenditure.

It will be appreciated from this last point that in taking as given the current level of expenditure, and the activities that this represents, the traditional approach to budgeting, by looking only at desired increases or, occasionally, decreases, is ignoring the majority of the organization's expenditure. This is rather myopic.

The zero-base budgeting alternative is to evaluate *simultaneously* existing and new ways of achieving specified ends in order to establish priorities among them which could mean that there are trade-offs between existing and new activities. For example, a new Project A that is considered to be more desirable than an existing Project B may be resourced by terminating Project B. In essence the approach is carried out in two stages:

(a) Decision packages are identified within each decision unit. These decision units are essentially discrete activities that can be described in a way that separates them from other activities of the organization. The decision packages cover both existing and projected incremental activities, and the organizational units responsible for carrying them out are much akin to the responsibility centres that were discussed earlier in the chapter. The object is to define for each decision unit the basic requirements that are needed if it is to perform the function for which it was established. Any costs in excess of this basic level are deemed increment. (It will be seen, therefore, that the title 'zero base' is something of a misnomer since the base is certainly greater than zero!) In considering what is needed in order to fulfil a particular purpose, over and above the base level, it is probable that alternative ways of achieving the same end will be identified, and these should be described and evaluated as they arise: these are the decision packages.

(b) Once the manager of a decision unit has submitted his statement of evaluated decision packages to his superior it is the latter's job to assign priorities to the various submissions from all his subordinates, and to select the highest-ranking decision packages that come within his available budget limit. There are a number of ways in which priorities can be determined, all of which presuppose some explicit criterion of effectiveness in order that competing packages may be ranked.

This approach is logical and has much to commend it in relation to discretionary outlays.

- *Output budgeting*

In the traditional approach to budgeting there tends to be an overall emphasis on the functional areas of an organization. Thus one has the budget for the marketing function, and that for the data processing department. However, no organization was ever established in order that it might have these functions as a definition of what it exists to achieve, so it is helpful to look at the situation from another angle.

In a typical business organization there will be functions such as those shown in Figure 20.4, but the organization really exists in order to achieve various purposes which have been simplified in the 'missions' of Figure 20.5. In developing a business plan the major concern is with the 'missions', subject to the resource limitations within the functions, etc., whereas the development of

FIGURE 20.4
Functional activities

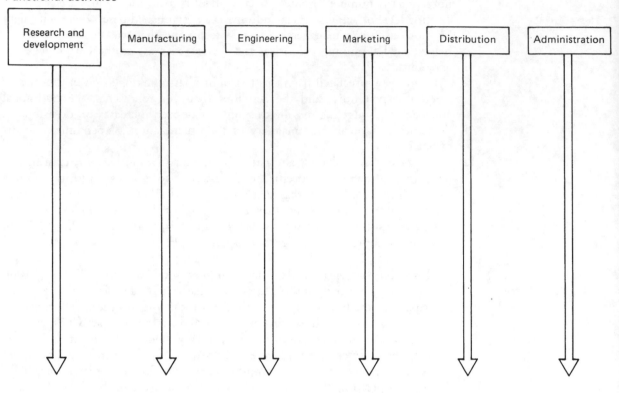

controls will usually be via the responsibility centres that are contained within the functions.

If we now superimpose the (horizontal) missions over the (vertical) functions we have the crux of the output budgeting approach. What this does is to focus attention on the purposes to be served by the organization, as shown by the missions, and the contribution that each function must make to each mission if the missions are to be successful. Figure 20.6 suggests this in the most simplified manner.

FIGURE 20.5
Missions

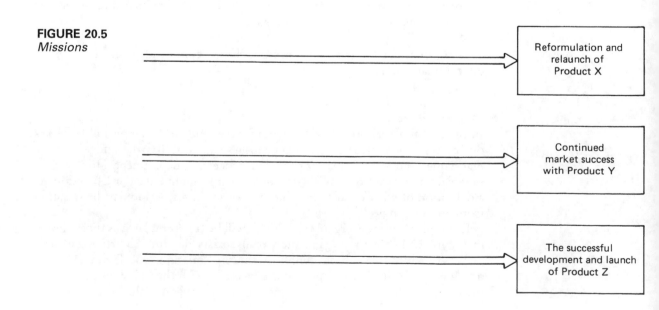

FIGURE 20.6
*A simplified output
budgeting format*

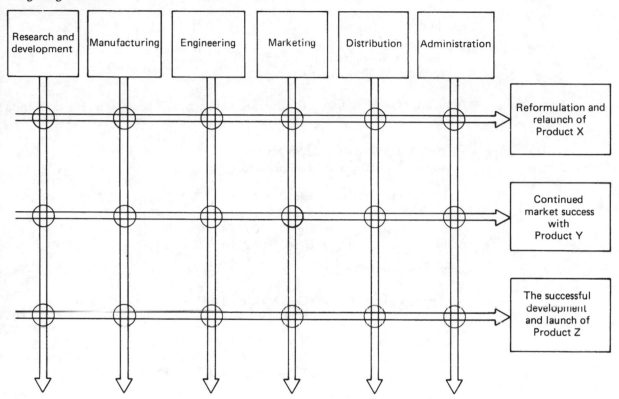

Variance
Analysis

When actual selling prices differ from standard selling prices a *sales price variance* can be computed. Standard selling prices will be used in compiling budgets, but it may be necessary to adapt to changing market conditions by raising or lowering prices, so it becomes desirable to segregate variances due to price changes from variances due to changes in quantity and product mix.

Quantity and mix are the two components of *sales volume variances*, and variations in profit can be explained to some extent by analysing sales quantity and sales mix.

The formulae for computing sales variances are:

- sales price variance = actual units sold × (actual price – standard price);
- sales volume variance = sales quantity variance + sales mix variance;
- sales quantity variance = budgeted profit on budgeted sales – expected profit on actual sales;
- sales mix variance = expected profit on actual sales – standard profit on actual sales.

'Expected profit on actual sales' is calculated as though profit increases or decreases proportionately with changes in the level of sales. 'Standard profit on actual sales' is the sum of the standard profit for all units sold. (For a single product enterprise, or in one where the profit per unit of sales is constant over the product range, the standard profit on actual sales is equal to the expected profit on actual sales, and the sales mix variance will necessarily be nil.)

Let us clarify the approach with an example. Assume budgeted sales of a company's two products for a forthcoming period were as follows:

Product A 500 units at £2.00 per unit
Product B 700 units at £1.50 per unit

and budgeted costs were:

Product A £1.75 per unit
Product B £1.30 per unit

Actual costs were in line with the budgeted costs, and actual sales for the period were:

Product A 560 units at £1.95 per unit
Product B 710 units at £1.40 per unit

Budgeted sales revenue = £[(500 × 2.00) + (700 × 1.50)] = £2,050
Actual sales revenue = £[(560 × 1.95) + (710 × 1.40)] = £2,086
Budgeted profit = £[(500 × 0.25) + (700 × 0.20)] = £265
Actual profit = £[(560 × 0.20) + (710 × 0.10)] = £183

Total sales variance   −£82

Sales price variance = £[560 × (1.95−2.00)] +
                       [710 × (1.40−1.50)]   =   −£99

Sales volume variance:
  Quantity variance = £265 − [2,086/2,050 × 265]   =   +£4
  Mix variance = £269 − [(560 × 0.25) + (710 × 0.20)] =   +£13

Sales volume variance   +£17

Total sales variance   −£82

Standards can be developed for repetitive activites, and it is possible to determine standards in a marketing context for the following illustrative activities:

1 cost per unit of sales;
2 cost per sales transaction;
3 cost per order received;
4 cost per customer account;
5 cost per mile travelled;
6 cost per sales call made.

The degree of detail can be varied to suit the particular requirements. Thus 'cost per unit of sales' may be 'advertising cost per £ of sales revenue for product X' and so on.

It is clearly more difficult to establish precise standards for most marketing activities than is the case in the manufacturing or distribution functions. Physical and mechanical factors are less influential; psychological factors are more prominent; objective measurement is less conspicuous; tolerance limits must be broader; and the range of segments for which marketing standards can be developed is much greater. But the discipline of seeking to establish standards can generate insights into relationships between effort and results that are likely to outweigh any lack of precision.

It is possible for an organization to develop marketing standards by participating in an interfirm comparison scheme (such as the one run by the Centre for Interfirm Comparison). As Westwick (1987) has shown, integrated sets of ratios and standards can be devised to allow for detailed monitoring of performance. (See Sections 3.10–3.12, pp. 98–104, in Chapter 3.)

When budget levels and standards are being developed it is vitally important to note the assumptions on which they have been based since it is inevitable that circumstances will change and a variety of unanticipated events will occur once the budget is implemented. Bearing this in mind let us work through an example. Figure 20.7 illustrates an extract from a marketing plan for Product X (column 2), with actual results (column 3) and variances (column 4) being shown for a particular operating period.

FIGURE 20.7
Operating results for Product X

Item (1)	Plan (2)	Actual (3)	Variance (4)
Revenues:			
Sales (units)	10,000,000	11,000,000	1,000,000
Price per unit (£)	1.00	0.95	0.05
Total revenue (£)	10,000,000	10,450,000	450,000
Market:			
Total market size (units)	25,000,000	30,000,000	5,000,000
Share of market (%)	40.0	36.7	(3.3)
Costs:			
Variable cost per unit (£)	0.60	0.60	–
Contribution:			
Per unit (£)	0.40	0.35	0.05
Total contribution (£)	4,000,000	3,850,000	(150,000)

The unfavourable contribution variance of £150,000 shown at the foot of column 4 is due to two principal causes:

1 a variance relating to contribution per unit; and
2 a variance relating to sales volume.

In turn, a variance relating to sales volume can be attributed to differences between:

3 actual and anticipated total market size; and
4 actual and anticipated market share.

Therefore a variation between planned and actual contribution may be due to variations in price per unit, variable cost per unit, total market size and market penetration.

In the case of Product X we have:

1 Profit variance:
$$(C_a - C_p) \times Q_a = £(0.35-0.40) \times 11,000,000$$
$$= (£550,000)$$

2 Volume variance:
$$(Q_a - Q_p) \times C_p = (11,000,000-10,000,000) \times £0.40$$
$$= £400,000$$

3 Net variance:

	£
Profit variance	(550,000)
Volume variance	400,000
	£(150,000)

where: C_a = actual contribution per unit;
$\quad\quad\quad$ C_p = planned contribution per unit;
$\quad\quad\quad$ Q_a = actual quantity sold in units;
$\quad\quad\quad$ Q_p = planned quantity of sales in units.

Figure 20.8 illustrates the relations.

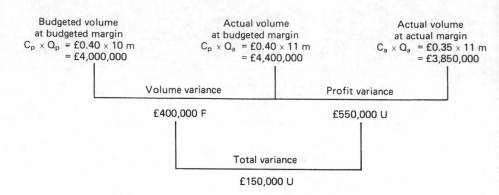

FIGURE 20.8
Marketing variances,
1

However, 2 can be analysed further to take into account the impact of market size and penetration variations.

4 Market size variance:
$$(M_a - M_p) \times S_p \times C_p = (30,000,000-25,000,000) \times 0.4 \times 0.4$$
$$= £800,000$$

5 Market share variance:
$$(S_a - S_p) \times M_a \times C_p = (0.367-0.40) \times 30,000,000 \times 0.4$$
$$= £(400,000)$$

6 Volume variance:
	£
Market size variance	800,000
Market share variance	(400,000)
	£400,000

where: M_a = actual total market in units;
$\quad\quad\quad$ M_p = planned total market in units;
$\quad\quad\quad$ S_a = actual market share;
$\quad\quad\quad$ S_p = planned market share.

See Figure 20.9 which illustrates these relationships.

In summary, the position now appears thus:

	£	£
Planned profit contribution		4,000,000
Volume variance:		
$\quad$ Market size variance	800,000	
$\quad$ Market share variance	(400,000)	400,000
Profit variance		(550,000)
Actual profit contribution		£3,850,000

FIGURE 20.9
Marketing variances, 2

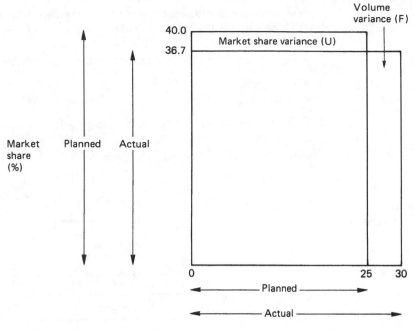

Total market (millions of units)

But this is not the end of the analysis! Variances arise because of unsatisfactory performance and unsatisfactory plans. It is desirable, therefore, to distinguish variances due to the poor *execution* of plans from those due to the poor *establishing* of plans. In the latter category are likely to be found forecasting errors reflecting faulty assumptions, and the estimates of total market size may constitute poor bench-marks for gauging subsequent managerial performance.

It is difficult to determine categorically whether market share variances are primarily the responsibility of forecasters or of those who execute the plans based on forecasts. On the face of it the primary responsibility is likely to be attached to the latter group.

In interpreting the variances for Product X it can be seen that the favourable volume variance of £400,000 resulted from two variances relating to market size and market share. Both of these are undesirable since they led to a lower contribution than intended. Had the forecasting group correctly anticipated the larger total market it should have been possible to devise a better plan to achieve the desired share and profit contribution. The actual outcome suggests that competitive position has been lost due to a loss of market share in a rapidly growing market. This is a serious pointer.

Lower prices resulted in a lower level of contribution per unit, and hence a lower overall profit contribution. The reasons for this need to be established and future plans modified as necessary.

As an approach to improved learning about the links between effort and results – especially in the face of active competitive behaviour – it is helpful to take the above analysis further and to evaluate performance by considering what *should have happened* in the circumstances (which is akin to flexible budgeting as discussed on pp. 749–50 above)..

At the end of the operating period to which Figure 20.7 refers it may become known that a large company with substantial resources made an aggressive entry into the market-place using lots of promotions and low prices. Furthermore, an unforeseen export demand for Product X may have arisen due to a prolonged strike in the USA's main manufacturer. On the basis of these details it becomes possible to carry out an *ex-post* performance analysis in which the original plans are revised to take account of what has since become known.

A clearer distinction can be made via *ex-post* performance analysis along these lines since a distinction can be made between:

1 planning variances due to environmental events that were:

- foreseeable,
- unforeseeable;

2 performance variances that are due to problems in executing the plans.

The situation is summarized in Figure 20.10.

FIGURE 20.10
Ex-post performance analysis

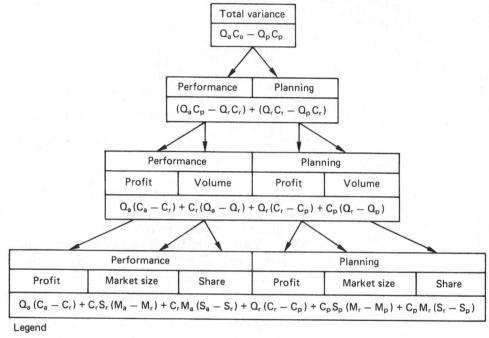

Legend

Subscripts
a = actual
p = planned
r = revised

Variables
Q = Quantity
C = Contribution margin
S = Share
M = Market

SOURCE: Adapted from Hulbert and Toy (1977)

This example has focused on a single product line (Product X), but multiproduct companies will typically have product lines with differing cost structures, prices and hence profit characteristics. It will be apparent, therefore, that the *mix* of products sold will have an impact on the overall profit outcome. For example, an enterprise may offer three product lines with budgeted characteristics relating to the next operating period as given in Figure 20.11.

FIGURE 20.11
Budgeted operating results by product line

	Product A	Product B	Product C	Total
Budget sales (units)	100,000	200,000	50,000	
Budgeted unit selling price	£12.00	£10.00	£20.00	
Budgeted unit variable cost	£6.00	£4.50	£8.00	
Budgeted unit contribution	£6.00	£5.50	£12.00	
Budgeted contribution	50%	55%	60%	
Budgeted contribution	£600,000	£1,100,000	£600,000	£2,300,000

Each product line has a different contribution per unit, so the total contribution from all lines is dependent upon the particular mix of sales across all product lines. If the actual outcomes for the period in question were as shown in Figure 20.12 we can explain the total variance of £275,000 U (i.e. actual profit contribution £2,025,000 minus budgeted profit contribution £2,300,000) as in Figure 20.13.

FIGURE 20.12
Actual operating results by product line

	Product A	Product B	Product C	Total
Actual sales (units)	90,000	220,000	45,000	
Actual unit selling price	£12.00	£9.00	£20.00	
Actual unit variable cost	£6.00	£4.50	£9.00	
Actual unit contribution	£6.00	£4.50	£11.00	
Actual contribution	50%	50%	55%	
Actual contribution	£540,000	£990,000	£495,000	£2,050,000

In summary we have:

	£
Volume variance	32,863 F
Mix variance	42,863 U
Profit variance	265,000 U
Total variance	£275,000 U

In other words the total variance was partly due to overall volume being higher than budgeted (355 000 units rather than 350 000, as budgeted), which gives a favourable variance of £32,863 made up of favourable volume variances for each individual product line; the actual mix of sales differed from budget in a way that produced an unfavourable variance of £42,863 made up of unfavourable variances for Products A and C which were partly offset by a favourable variance for product line B; and the actual margins were less than budgeted for product lines B and C, giving an unfavourable profit variance of £265,000.

The volume variance can be analysed further along the lines suggested in the previous example, but the main point to note from this example is the impact that variations in the mix of products sold can have on the profit outcome. If all product lines had the same percentage margin there would be no mix variance, but this situation is not normal, so we need to be aware of the impact of mix changes.

Variance Analysis for Distribution Cost Control

As with production costing the analysis of cost variances in distribution costing is the first step towards the goal of identifying the factors that caused the difference between the standard and actual costs so that any inefficiencies can be eliminated. To do this each enterprise will have to decide what specific variance analyses it may want to use. Often companies only compute a net variance for their distribution costs and do not attempt to break the variance down into causal factors. This practice is not to be encouraged, however, since it tends to hide inefficiencies. If the analysis is to be meaningful the variance must be further explained in terms of price and efficiency components. Such price and quantity or efficiency variances can be computed for distribution activities. The price variance is given by:

(standard price – actual price) × actual work units;

and the quantity (or efficiency) variance is given by:

(budgeted work units – actual work units) × standard price.

FIGURE 20.13
Marketing variances, 3

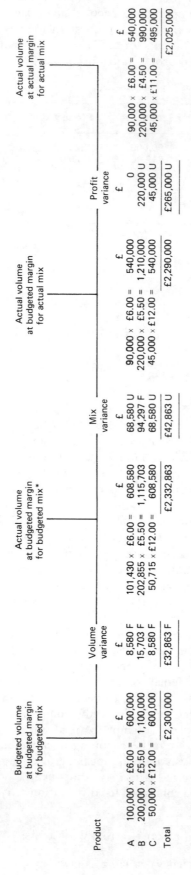

Product

		Budgeted volume at budgeted margin for budgeted mix	Volume variance	Actual volume at budgeted margin for budgeted mix*	Mix variance	Actual volume at budgeted margin for actual mix	Profit variance	Actual volume at actual margin for actual mix
		£	£	£	£	£	£	£
A	100,000 × £6.00 =	600,000	8,580 F	101,430 × £6.00 = 608,580	68,580 U	90,000 × £6.00 = 540,000	0	90,000 × £6.00 = 540,000
B	200,000 × £5.50 =	1,100,000	15,703 F	202,855 × £5.50 = 1,115,703	94,297 F	220,000 × £5.50 = 1,210,000	220,000 U	220,000 × £4.50 = 990,000
C	50,000 × £12.00 =	600,000	8,580 F	50,715 × £12.00 = 608,580	68,580 U	45,000 × £12.00 = 540,000	45,000 U	45,000 × £11.00 = 495,000
Total		£2,300,000	£32,863 F	£2,332,863	£42,863 U	£2,290,000	£265,000 U	£2,025,000

*The budgeted mix was 100,000/(100,000 + 200,000 + 50,000) = 100,000/350,000 = 28.57% for product A, and so on.
Applying this proportion to actual sales units gives 0.2857 (90,000 + 220,000 + 45,000) = 101,430 for product A,
and so on for B and C.

A Variance Reporting Example

The distribution costs of the Hill Company are analysed by territories: data for the southern territory are shown in Figure 20.14. The warehousing and handling function's standards are:

	Total standard for direct and indirect costs (£)
Variable costs:	
Receiving	21 per shipment
Pricing, tagging and marking	6 per unit handled
Sorting	5 per order
Handling returns	10 per return
Taking physical inventory	0.50 per unit warehouse unit
Clerical handling of shipping orders	2 per item
Fixed costs:	
Rent	600 per month per territory
Depreciation	450 per month per territory

The following units of variability were budgeted and recorded for the month of January, 1998:

	Budgeted	Actual
Shipments	400	420
Units handled	200	223
Orders	110	108
Returns	70	71
Warehouse unit	1,600	1,630
Item	750	780

Southern territory's actual direct costs for the month of January, 1998, were as follows:

Receiving	£6,400
Pricing, tagging and marking	1,115
Sorting	565
Handling returns	680
Taking physical inventory	880
Clerical handling of shipping orders	500
Rent	650
Depreciation	445

The company allocates the following actual indirect costs to its southern and northern territories:

Receiving (allocated on actual shipments: southern 420, northern 80)	£2,500
Clerical handling of shipping orders (allocated on actual items: southern 780, northern 120)	1,223

- *Efficiency variance*

  Shipments received is the unit of variability chosen for the receiving function. There were a total of 420 shipments made, while only 400 shipments were budgeted. This results in an unfavourable efficiency variance because actual shipments exceeded those budgeted. (It should be noted here that care must be used in analysing distribution cost variances because it is easy to misinterpret the

FIGURE 20.14
Distribution cost variances

HILL COMPANY – SOUTHERN TERRITORY
Expense variance report – warehousing and handling
January 1998

Detailed function:	Units of variability	(1) Actual cost (actual @ actual price)	(2) Actual units @ standard price	(3) Budgeted costs (budgeted units @ standard price)	(2 – 1) Price variance	(3 – 2) Efficiency variance	(3 – 1) Net variance
Receiving:							
direct costs	Shipment	£ 6,400					
indirect costs	$(\frac{420}{500}) \times £2,500$	2,100					
Total		£ 8,500	£8,820 (420 × £21)	£ 8,400 (400 × £21)	£320 F	£420 U	£100 U
Pricing, tagging and marking:							
direct costs	Unit handled	1,115	1,338 (223 × £6)	1,200 (200 × £6)	223 F	138 U	85 F
Sorting: direct costs	Order	565	540 (108 × £5)	550 (110 × £5)	25 U	10 F	15 U
Handling returns:							
direct costs	Return	680	710 (71 × £10)	700 (70 × £10)	30 F	10 U	20 F
Taking physical inventory	Warehouse unit	880	815 (1,630 × £0.50)	800 (1,600 × £0.50)	65 U	15 U	80 U
Clerical handling of shipping orders:							
direct costs	Item	£ 500					
indirect costs	$(\frac{780}{900}) \times £1,223$	1,060					
Total		£ 1,560	1,560 (780 × £2)	1,500 (750 × £2)	0	60 U	60 U
Total variable expense		£13,300		£13,150	£483 F	£633 U	£150 U
Fixed expense:							
rent		650		600			50 U
depreciation		445		450			5 F
Total warehousing and handling		£14,395		£14,200			£195 U

F = favourable; U = unfavourable

results associated with such costs. Each cost variance is considered favourable or unfavourable as far as that individual detailed function is concerned, not for its effect on the overall company.) The efficiency variance in this case is unfavourable because 20 more shipments were made than planned. Hence, orders of larger quantities should be encouraged to save costs in receiving.

- *Price variance*
  The actual cost of £20.238 (i.e. £8,500 total actual cost of receiving as shown in Figure 20.14 ÷ 420 actual units) for each shipment received is less than the standard price of £21.00 which results in a favourable price variance. This difference in price is multiplied by the actual shipments to give a total favourable price variance of £320. It is not necessary to compute the actual cost per unit using the format illustrated in Figure 20.14 since the price variance can be determined by comparing total actual cost to the actual units at standard price shown in Column 2.

Efficiency and price variance are computed for variable costs only. Only a net variance is computed for the two fixed expenses shown in Figure 20.14. This measures the difference between budgeted costs (budgeted units at standard price) and actual costs (actual units at actual price).

Other Models

A useful model for assessing product line performance has been proposed (and tested) by Diamantopoulos and Mathews (1990). The model is based on the need to evaluate product performance in a multiproduct setting using readily-available product information and widely-used performance indicators in a systematic way. Not least of all it was deemed essential that the model be clearly understood by its intended users (product managers) otherwise, from an implementation point of view, it would not have been worthwhile. Figure 20.15 shows the model.

Gross profit is used as the primary performance indicator since this measure is easily provided without additional analysis. If the gross profit being generated is below par this may be due to:

FIGURE 20.15
A model for product performance analysis

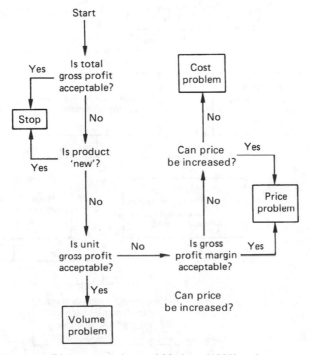

SOURCE: Diamantopoulos and Mathew (1990), p. 9

- insufficient sales volume;
- high unit cost;
- prices that are too low.

Investigation should reveal which of these possible causes applies. If the *unit* gross profit is satisfactory, for example, but the product line's *overall* gross profit is unsatisfactory, the remedy may be to increase volume by revising the marketing mix in a suitable way. There may be products having unsatisfactory gross margins that are not amenable to corrective action. In this case their continued role in the range needs to be questioned.

Areas in which the model is particularly useful are:

1 pricing (especially the effectiveness of existing pricing policies in terms of profit and volume results);
2 new product introductions (by using previous introductions to set realistic bench-mark expectations for new products);
3 product deletions (using warning signals as the stimulus to further investigations).

Despite the need to specify target values for each element of the model (i.e. total gross profit, unit gross profit, newness of product, gross profit margin, and price) this does not take away the importance of managerial judgement in arriving at an overall assessment of each product's performance. Indeed, judgement is needed in specifying the quantified target values themselves as well as in interpreting any given product's standing relative to those targets. When a particular product's performance is considered satisfactory it is not self-evident that it should be ignored: in order to ensure *sustained* satisfactory performance it may be necessary to take action in anticipation of future environmental changes (i.e. feedforward control).

FIGURE 20.16
*Analysing sales
deviations*

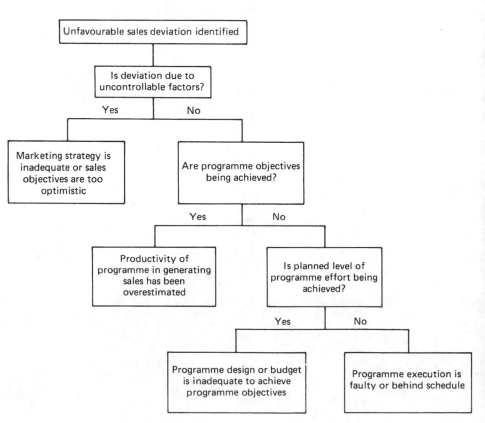

SOURCE: Guiltinan and Paul (1988), p. 399

A variation on the product line model that deals with sales deviations from plan is shown in Figure 20.16.

This protocol follows a series of logical steps. Having identified a variance that is deemed to be significant (i.e. is unlikely to have arisen by chance) the question is raised as to whether this may be due to controllable or uncontrollable factors. ('Uncontrollable' is used here in the sense of being beyond the influence of managers in the given enterprise, or beyond the forecasting ability of relevant personnel, which might cover changing market conditions leading to a decline in industry sales, or unanticipated competitive actions.)

If the explanation for the variance is not found at this first stage the next stage raises the question of the performance of marketing programmes. This can be addressed at two levels:

1 the degree to which programme objectives are being achieved;
2 the degree to which planned programme effort is being achieved.

If the degree of effort (as represented by actual sales levels, or advertising coverage) is not as planned it is unlikely that either programme objectives or sales objectives are being achieved. On the other hand, if the planned input of effort is being achieved but programme objectives (such as brand awareness levels or the number of new accounts) are not, it is probable that either the budget is inadequate or the design of the programme (e.g. sales appeal, pricing level, advertising copy) is ineffective.

It may be found that the sales variance is not attributable to faulty programmes or lack of effort but is due to the sales productivity of the programme being overstimulated, or the implementation of the programme being behind schedule.

Insofar as sales variances reflect revenue generation there is a corresponding need to examine the variances among the costs incurred and budget figures to secure control over the profit consequences of sales activities.

The Variance Investigation Decision

A major inhibiting factor in seeking to control via feedforward systems is our limited ability to make reliable estimates of the outcomes of future events. (This reflects our modest understanding of causal relationships both within the sub-systems of the enterprise and between the enterprise and its environment.) All planning is based on estimates (e.g. of prices, costs, volumes) and actual outcomes will rarely be precisely in line with these estimates: some variation is inevitable. Should we expect a manager to investigate every variance that might be reported when we know that some deviation between actual outcomes and budgeted outcomes is bound to occur? On the other hand, if no variances are investigated the control potential of this form of managerial control system is being ignored. An appropriate course of action lies somewhere between these two extremes.

Causes of variances (or 'deviations') can be categorized in the following broad way (after Demski (1980)) with particular variances often being due to one or more deviations:

1 Implementation deviation results from a human or mechanical failure to achieve an attainable outcome, e.g. if the mileage rate payable to employees using their own vehicles for business trips is 35p per mile, but due to clerical error this is being paid at only 25p per mile, the required corrective action is easy to specify. The cost of correction will be exceeded by the benefits.
2 Prediction deviation results from errors in specifying the parameter values in a decision model, e.g. in determining overhead absorption rates *ex ante* predictions must be made of, *inter alia*, the future level of activity. If the predictions are wrong then the overhead absorption rate will be wrong and variances will result.

3 Measurement deviation arises as a result of error in measuring the actual outcome – such as incorrectly adding up the number of calls made in Region X, or the number of units sold of Product P.

4 Model deviation arises as a result of an erroneous formulation in a decision model. For example, in formulating a linear programme the constraints relating to the availability of input factors may be incorrectly specified.

5 Random deviations due to chance fluctuations of a parameter for which no cause can be assigned. These deviations do not call for corrective action, but in order to identify the causes of variances it is helpful to separate random deviations from deviations 1–4 above, in order that the significance of the latter might be established.

While these five categories of deviation appear to be mutually exclusive their interdependencies should not be underestimated. The traditional view is to assume that variances are due to implementation deviations but this is patently simplistic. It is also potentially inequitable since it may deem individual managers to be responsible for variances that arise from reasons beyond their control (such as 3 and 5 above).

In setting up bench-marks (e.g. budget targets or standard costs) it is important to recognize that a range of possible outcomes in the vicinity of the bench-mark will usually be acceptable. In other words, random variations around the bench-mark are to be expected, and searching for causes of variances within the acceptable range of outcomes will incur costs without generating benefits. Only when variances fall outside the acceptable range will further investigation be desirable.

This prompts the operational question of how one actually determines whether a variance should be investigated. As Figure 20.17 suggests, if it was known in advance that a variance arose on a random basis it would not be necessary to investigate it since there will be no assignable cause. On the other hand, if a variance is of a non-random nature it would not pay to ignore it if it was significant.

FIGURE 20.17
The variance investigation decision

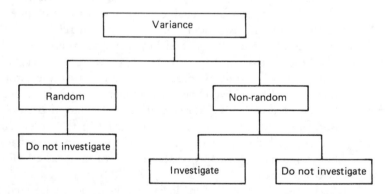

How can significance be determined? This boils down to a statistical question, and the technique that is of proven help is that developed for use in quality control situations to which we will turn very shortly.

A more conventional approach to evaluating the significance of variances is either to:

1 look at the absolute size of the variance (i.e. actual – standard) such that all variances greater than, say, £1,000 are investigated; or

2 compute the proportionate size of the variance (i.e. variance/standard) and investigate all those exceeding, say, 10 per cent.

Both 1 and 2 must depend upon the manager's intuition or some arbitrary decision rule when it comes to deciding whether or not to investigate a given variance.

The advantages of 1 and 2 are their simplicity and ease of implementation, but both fail to deal adequately with the issues of significance (in statistical terms) and balancing the costs and benefits of investigation. We can resolve these issues with the help of the approach adopted in *statistical quality control*.

Statistical quality control (SQC) is based upon the established fact that the observed quality of an item is always subject to chance variability. Some variability in the observed quality of an item will be due to assignable causes which exist beyond the boundaries due to chance cause. (Assignable causes are, by definition, identifiable and steps can be taken to remove them.) The major task of SQC is to distinguish between assignable and chance causes of error in order that the assignable causes may be identified, their causes discovered and eliminated, and acceptable quality standards maintained.

These basic principles of SQC can be applied in areas other than production. An example is given of a control chart for monitoring advertising expenditure as a percentage of sales in Figure 20.18.

FIGURE 20.18
Advertising control chart

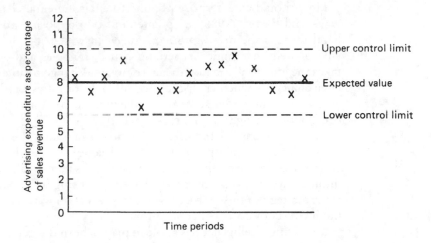

The standard of performance that is expected is that advertising expense will be 8 per cent of sales revenue, but random causes (i.e. chance) can make this figure vary from 6 per cent to 10 per cent of sales revenue. If the range of 6–10 per cent represents three standard deviations on either side of a mean of 8 per cent (i.e. $\bar{x}$ = 8 with confidence limits of $\pm 3\ \theta$), then observations would be expected to fall within this range in 998 out of 1000 cases.

However, when an observation falls outside these limits two opposing hypotheses can be put forward to explain the situation:

1 The observation is the freak one out of 1000 that exceeds the control limits by pure chance, and the company still has the situation under control.
2 The company has lost control over the situation due to some assignable cause such as a new competitor entering the market.

If hypothesis 1 is accepted it is unnecessary to investigate – with the risk that something has actually happened to cause the situation to fall out of control. On the other hand, if hypothesis 2 is accepted and investigations are begun into assignable causes there is always the risk – albeit very small – of the first hypothesis being correct and hence investigation being unecessary.

Investigations to identify the causes of variances – even when the latter are deemed to be significant – involve costs, so we must again reflect on the cost-benefit issue: if the likely penalty from *not* identifying and correcting the cause of the variance is less than the likely cost of the investigation it hardly seems worth the trouble.

Consider a hypothetical case in which the cost of investigating a reported variance is estimated at £200 while the penalty for not identifying a correctable cause is likely to be £600 (which could be the value of cost savings – or extra profit – that will arise once the cause of the variance is removed). If an investigation is undertaken and no cause is discovered, the enterprise will be £200 worse off, whereas it will be £400 better off (i.e. £600 – £200) if a cause is ascertained and corrected.

20.4 TAKING CORRECTIVE ACTION

Having implemented plans, monitored performance, and analysed significant variances, the next step is to decide on the corrective action that is needed. In this section we will concentrate on responding to environmental changes – especially those of a competitive nature.

How should an enterprise respond to environmental changes? There are many ways, and Barrett (1986) has pointed out two opposing possibilities. On the one hand there is the *deterministic approach* in which it is felt that the enterprise's environment determines its actions, hence strategies and even its structure. This takes the idea of adaptation to environmental change to an extreme: changes in the environment – whether in the form of opportunities or threats – will result in changes in competitive strategy and the implementation of these changes may well bring about changes in organizational structure.

In contrast there is the *strategic approach* in which the environment is seen as constraining the enterprise's freedom of action rather than determining it. This concentrates more on the enterprise's strengths (and weaknesses) and its ability to influence its environment rather than simply being influenced by it. One example is the strategy of raising barriers to entry which modifies the environment against the interests of potential competitors.

Marketing intelligence has a role to play in both these approaches by identifying environmental change as a basis for reactive or proactive responses. The response process is reflected in the model portrayed in Figure 20.19.

Various response stages are highlighted, with any given one being triggered when the intelligence signals pass thresholds. Thus, for example, a strong signal indicating a significant change in the environment will cross a number of thresholds and activate an appropriate high-level response. Weaker signals will cross fewer thresholds and hence prompt lower-level responses. Barrett sets his model within a framework of power relationships – especially those involved in the allocation of resources via the budgeting process. This leads to the building in of 'slack' (i.e. a greater amount of resource than is strictly needed to carry out a given task) in certain parts of the enterprise in accordance with the distribution of power. Figure 20.20 indicates in some detail the links between stages in the response process and thresholds. The sequence of stages presumes that each subsequent stage consumes more slack resources than prior stages, thereby reducing the power given from the existence of slack resources.

How should an enterprise respond to environmental changes that manifest themselves either through the gathering of environmental data (e.g. by means of a competitor intelligence system – see Cvitkovic (1989), or environmental scanning – see Sanderson and Luffman (1988)) or via variance analysis? Help is available from the technique of *competitor profiling*. The steps in this technique, developed by SRI International, are:

1 Identify the industry's four key competitive strengths. Figure 20.21 shows one set of possibilities applicable to a manufacturing situation. It is implicitly

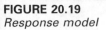

FIGURE 20.19
Response model

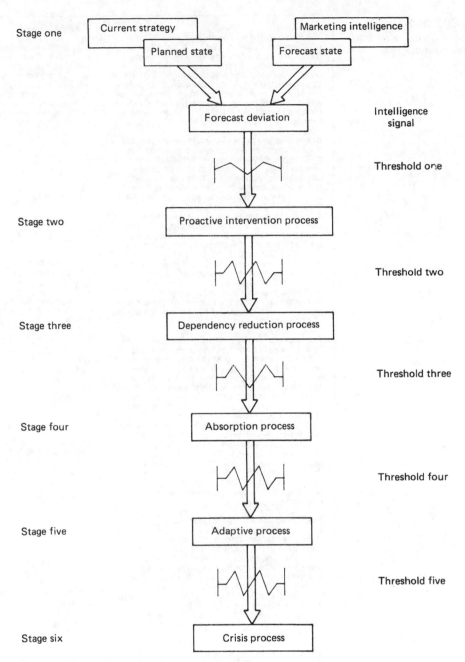

SOURCE: Barrett (1986), p. 37

assumed that both current and future success in the industry is a function of a competitor's ability to:

- meet customers' needs and communicate products' attributes;
- understand and control relevant technology;
- make superior products in a cost effective way;
- manage the co-ordination of human, financial, and technological resources.

2 Select a single specific measure of success for each of the four key competitive strengths identified in step 1 above. See Figure 20.22 for some proposals: sales level, investment in R & D, capacity utilization, and ROI are suggested for marketing, technology, manufacturing and management respectively.

3 Define linkages between adjacent pairs of competitive strengths to demonstrate their interdependence. In Figure 20.23 price has been used to link marketing and

FIGURE 20.20
Signal thresholds and response stages

Stage one
The first stage of the model suggests that the organizational plan, or budget, is based on a forecasted state of the market environment. Market intelligence provides a constantly updated forecast of the environment in which the organization operates. Differences between the original planned state of the environment on which the organization is acting, and the revised forecasted state provided by the intelligence function, gives a 'forecast deviation'.

Stage two: the proactive intervention process
If the market intelligence report indicates that the budget allowance will be exceeded, the second stage of the model is entered. In this stage the market executives may be motivated to act to prevent the forecast deviation. This proactive intervention is an attempt to engineer the market into an acceptable state. In its simplest form it may merely necessitate a minor market push. This proactive intervention in the market will, however, consume at least some of the slack resources available to the marketing executive. Successful proactive intervention may, however, require resources in excess of the slack available. In this case the intelligence report will be used to support a plea for additional marketing resources, e.g. to undertake an unabridged campaign to protect a product's position against the anticipated attack of a competitor.

Stage three: the dependency reduction process
This process is an attempt by the organization to reduce its dependency on the market in question and so reduces the significance to the organization of the perceived market adversity. This decoupling may be achieved in a number of ways – diversification, the switching of resources, adapting plant previously devoted to the market to service other markets, and so on. Dependency reduction may, however, require a long lead time and for this reason organizations are likely to engage in diversification as a policy rather than awaiting detailed intelligence reports. However, market signals which cross threshold two are likely to spur this activity. The dependency reduction process, e.g. diversification, requires the use of slack resources.

Stage four: the absorption process
This process is an attempt by the organization to sit out the market change, or at least that proportion of the change which has not been dampened by proactive intervention or dependency reduction processes. Such an absorption process consumes the stock of slack resources available to the organization. 'Belt tightening' and 'shedding' indicate the extent of the rundown of slack. All members of the organizational coalition are likely to be affected if the absorption process continues for any extended period.

Stage five: the adaptive process
In the adaptive process the organization seeks to realign its strategy and/or structure to the perceived changed environment in which it operates. It engages the organization in a 'change mode' and requires the ability by the organizational executives to adapt or react to the forecast market change. Their ability to do so is dependent on the slack resources available and the ease with which such resources can be marshalled to implement strategy/structure changes.

Stage six: the crisis process
In this, the final process, the organization is dependent on a market which is changing. It has insufficient slack to absorb the change, and both proactive intervention and adaptive response are perceived to be ineffective. Such organizations now face the possibility of being 'selected out' by the market change. The perception that such is the case is likely to induce organizational crisis leading to trauma and the termination of the organization at least in the form in which it existed prior to the onset of the market change.

Threshold one
In setting market budgets, marketing executives may build in slack, most of which will usually be cut back in the budget setting process. It is possible that not all the slack will be removed and the marketing revenue budget will be artificially high. Unless market intelligence indicates that this budget allowance is likely to be exceeded no action will be taken on the basis of the market intelligence report. The market signal will not then cross the first threshold.

Threshold two
Should the power elite within the organization be unwilling or unable to make available sufficient resources to allow successfully proactive intervention, the second threshold is crossed and the third stage of the model is entered.

Threshold three
If the organization cannot, or chooses not to, utilize its slack resources in proactive market intervention, or in dependency reduction, the market signal indicating market change will pass over the third information threshold and the fourth stage of the model is entered.

Threshold four
For organizations which do not have sufficient slack to endure the forecast market change, the intelligence signal traverses the fourth threshold and stage five of the model is entered.

Threshold five
Should the organization be unable or unwilling to adapt to the change signalled by the market intelligence report and if the lower order processes cannot effectively be engaged, the intelligence signal will cross the fifth threshold and the sixth stage is entered.

SOURCE: Barrett (1986), p. 38

FIGURE 20.21
Key competitive strengths

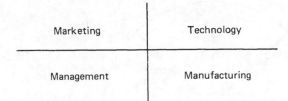

SOURCE: Cvitkovic (1989), p. 28

FIGURE 20.22
Measures of success

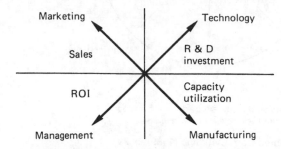

SOURCE: Adapted from Cvitkovic (1989), p. 28

FIGURE 20.23
Linkages between competitive strengths

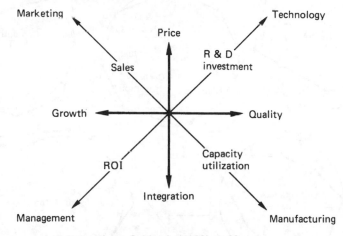

SOURCE: Adapted from Cvitkovic (1989), p. 29

technology; quality to link technology and manufacturing; integration to link manufacturing and management; and growth to link management and marketing.

4 Determine average performance scores for the measures specified in step 2 and the linkages defined in step 3. This has the effect of setting up an 'average competitor' to use as a yardstick in assessing competitors' relative positions. In Figure 20.24 average performance for the industry is shown as a circle. Above-average performance for any competitor would be plotted outside the circle and below average performance on any aspect would be plotted inside the circle. Scoring can be done by using a scale of 1 (= excellent) to 5 (= inadequate) to assess a competitor's standing on each dimension shown in Figure 20.23 and then plotting these scores and joining them up (as shown in Figure 20.25).

5 Generate competitors' profiles in order to identify relative strengths and weaknesses as a basis for taking action. The strengths and weaknesses are shown (as in Figure 20.25) relative to the 'average competitor'.

In monitoring competitors' activities the categories of activity most relevant in relation to the strategic needs of the user must be determined. Once the categories

FIGURE 20.24
Average competitor

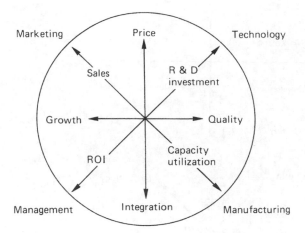

Conventions:
  outside the circle = better than average
  inside the circle = below average

source: Adapted from Cvitkovic (1989), p. 29

FIGURE 20.25
Competitive profiles

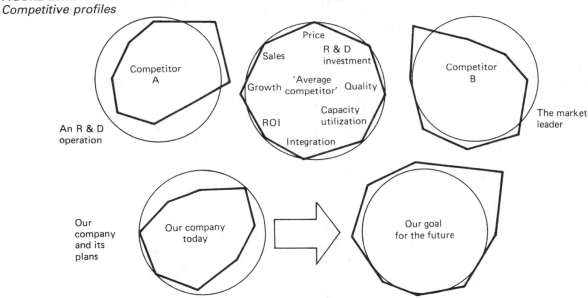

A 'second tier' competitor with some technological strengths.

Leveraging available technological strengths to improve the overall competitive position.

source: Adapted from Cvitkovic (1989), p. 30

are established, frequency of monitoring must be set. Prescott and Smith (1989) reported on a study they undertook in the USA to identify categories and frequencies. Details are given in Figure 20.26.

FIGURE 20.26
Competitive information categories and their frequency of monitoring

Continuous	Periodic	Ad hoc
● General industry trends	● Organizational goals and assumptions	● Public and international affairs
● Marketing and sales	● Customers	● Human resources
	● Acquisition/divestment programmes	● General administrative structure
● Financial	● Services provided	
● Technological development	● Operations	● Supplier and procurement practices
	● Channels of distribution	

source: Adapted from Prescott and Smith (1989), p. 10

A further aspect of the study was the extent to which different categories of information were subjected to analysis (see Figure 20.27). Three levels of analysis were used in the questionnaire sent out by Prescott and Smith – extensive, basic, and little/no analysis – with the extent to which implications were drawn from the analysis being limited to the first two levels.

FIGURE 20.27
Extent of analysis of categories of information

Extensive analysis undertaken and implications derived	Basic analysis with some implications	Little or no analysis and no implications
• General industry trends	• Technological developments	• Distribution channels
• Potential competitors	• Acquisition/divestment programmes	• Human resources
• Marketing and sales	• Customers	• General administrative structure
• Financial	• Services provided	• Public and international affairs
• Organizational goals and assumptions		• Supplier practices

SOURCE: Adapted from Prescott and Smith (1989), p. 11

Competitor cost analysis methods have been proposed by a number of authors (e.g. Beerel (1986), Brock (1984), Jones (1988), Pyne (1985) and most notably Porter (1980, 1985)). Brock (1984, p. 226) has related his discussion to the *strategic triangle* (Ohmae (1983)), see Figure 20.28.

FIGURE 20.28
The strategic triangle

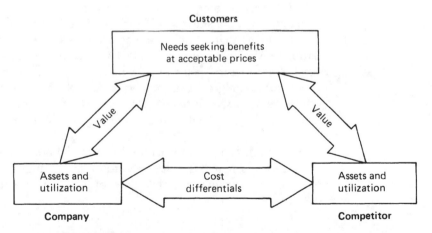

SOURCE: Brock (1984), p. 226

The focal points of the triangle were initially customers, competitors, and the company in question, but Brock has emphasized the cost differences between one's own company and competitors as a potential source of competitive advantage. Cost differentials stem from the asset bases of competing companies coupled with the way in which assets are utilized. The importance of being cost effective is evident when one considers the need to deliver value to customers at prices that are competitive while generating an adequate rate of reward to shareholders. As an example let us take a comparison between an integrated steelmaker (Maxi) and a small competitor (Mini) with the latter using scrap steel and electric furnace technology. A detailed examination of annual reports, public statements of Mini's chief executive (who was a promoter of the mini-mill within

FIGURE 20.29
Cost advantages and disadvantages

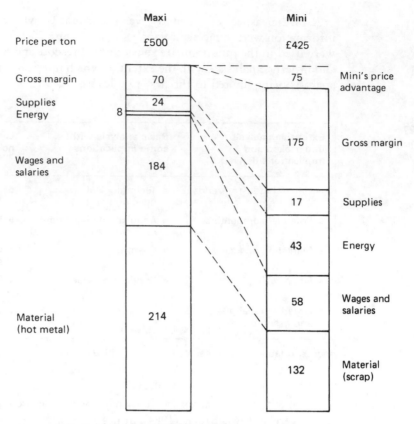

SOURCE: Adapted from Brock (1984), p. 228

the industry), and general trade literature gave sufficient information to allow the comparative profile shown in Figure 20.29 to be compiled.

It is evident that Mini's manufacturing costs are only 59 per cent of those relating to Maxi per ton of hot rolled steel ready for finishing. With a price set at £425 (as opposed to Maxi's £500) Mini not only has a clear price advantage of £75 per ton but also a gross margin advantage of £175 versus £70 which will allow for even more aggressive pricing. Maxi can see from this type of analysis that its position is being eroded, and appropriate decisions need to be made to avoid a forced decline.

Without this type of information Maxi would not be able to see how the strong strategic position it has held hitherto is being undermined by Mini. Detailed guidance on carrying out this type of cost analysis can be found in Jones (1988).

Bench-marking

This is an analytical process through which an enterprise's performance can be compared with that of its competitors. It is used by organizations such as Xerox and Ford in order to:

● identify key performance measures for each business function;
● measure one's own performance as well as that of competitors;
● identify areas of competitive advantage (and disadvantage) by comparing performance levels;
● design and implement plans to improve one's own performance on key issues relative to competitors.

Furey (1987) offers a number of US case studies showing bench-marking in use. One of these concerns a company (Company Y) that is a major vendor of

FIGURE 20.30
Sales force bench-marking

	Company Y	Direct competitor	Best-in-class competitor
Cost bench-marks			
Average total sales rep. compensation	$38,000	$44,000	$55,000
% compensation earned from commission	10%	15%	30%
Revenue per sales rep.	$835,000	$900,000	$1,200,000
Compensation as % of revenue	4.6%	4.9%	4.6%
Performance bench-marks			
Average number of calls per week per rep.	16–18	13–16	20+
Revenue quotas	Yes	Yes	No
New account quotas	Informal	No	Yes

SOURCE: Adapted from Furey (1987)

telecommunications equipment in which the senior management was curious about the cost and productivity of its sales force. The comparisons shown in Figure 20.30 were developed through a bench-marking exercise using the largest direct competitor and the best-in-class vendor of data processing equipment.

The cost of sales representatives (as a percentage of revenues) was found to be very competitive in Company Y (at 4.6 per cent), but the low commission paid by the company relative to that paid by its main competitors was matched by low productivity (in terms of revenue generated). Moreover, the direct competitor's sales force was generating more revenue with fewer calls in the absence of new account quotas than was the case in Company Y. The best-in-class competitor was paying a high rate of commission to its sales force and aggressively pursuing new customers via numerous sales calls and quotas for new accounts.

Company Y's response to this situation was to restructure the sales team's compensation and split the team into two. By raising the rate of commission substantially, and by having one part of the sales force dealing with existing accounts and the other part dealing with new accounts, Company Y's relative market share improved within six months.

Bench-marking is applicable in other functional areas and has the potential, when properly communicated throughout the enterprise, to help change the corporate culture. In the case of bench-marking products or services offered by customers but not by itself, an enterprise's senior managers can gain insights to guide its decisions: by keeping abreast of new developments in this way it will be easier to assess how to respond (see, for example, Schmid (1987) and Fifer (1989)).

In considering how to take corrective action it is important to make some assessment of the probable response of competitors to any action that might be taken. This is a vital aspect of strategic behaviour. It is assumed that the identities of the enterprise's competitors – both actual and potential – are known, although this should not be taken for granted. Once the competitors' identities are known they can be profiled (see Chapter 4) and possible responses can be explored, taking into account conjectures regarding the beliefs that competitors have of one's own enterprise (including its resources, capabilities, and strategies).

Let us look further at this, drawing on the approach of Amit, et al. (1988). In a simple situation involving an Enterprise X and its sole competitor, Y, there are four possible price policies available. In Figure 20.31 these possibilities for X are shown as the headings for the rows; the column headings show competitor Y's likely reactions. The figures in the cells represent the changes in X's profits that are expected to result from the various interactive outcomes contained in the matrix. Thus if X reduces its price by 10 per cent and Y responds by reducing its price by 20 per cent, then X's profits will fall by 25 per cent. If the data in the figure is valid, the optimal course of action for X will depend on the likelihood of Y responding in a particular way. For example, if it is felt to be most likely that Y will react to

FIGURE 20.31
Reaction function

Enterprise X's price policy (% change in price)	Competitor Y's reaction (% change in price)			
	0%	−5%	−10%	−20%
0%	0	−10	−15	−20
−5%	+7	−5	−12	−22
−10%	+30	+15	−8	−25
−20%	+12	+8	+5	−30

SOURCE: Adapted from Amit, et al. (1988), p. 432

a price reduction on the part of X by reducing price by half as much as X, then the optimal choice for X is to reduce its price by 10 per cent, giving an increase in profits of 15 per cent. It will be apparent that additional information is needed on Y's likely reaction. This can be provided via *conjectural variations*, which are beliefs about competitors' views of one's own enterprise and of their likely reactions to actions taken by one's own enterprise.

In order to gauge a competitor's likely reactions it is necessary to have information on:

- the structural characteristics of the industry and the technical ability plus desire of competitors to respond;
- competitors' conjecture about one's own behaviour.

Figure 20.32 illustrates a hypothetical situation involving different conjectural possibilities relating to a price reduction of 10 per cent. The derivation of conjectural variations is explored in detail elsewhere (see Amit, et al. (1988)) but we need to note here that it ranges from zero (when the competitor believes that the enterprise in question will not respond to changes in the competitor's strategy) to unity (when the competitor expects the enterprise in question to match any changes in strategy on the part of the competitor).

FIGURE 20.32
Conjectures and a price reduction policy

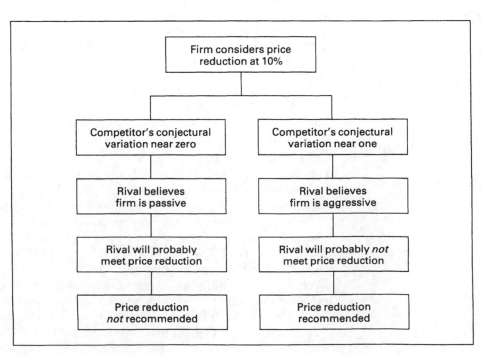

SOURCE: Amit, et al. (1988), p. 433

From Figure 20.32 it can be seen that when the competitor's conjectural variation is near to unity it believes the enterprise in question will respond aggressively to a shift in pricing policy. The obvious consequence of this will be a price war if the competitor were to match a reduction in price. As a result of this belief the competitor is unlikely to match the price reduction for fear of the consequences. The opposing situation (i.e. when the conjectural variation is near zero) is likely to have the opposite result.

20.5 MANAGEMENT REPORTS

An effective management reporting system is one that uses the available information flows to control the company's activities in accordance with objectives and plans. The process of controlling business operations depends in no small part on the devising, compiling and constant revising of an adequate and up-to-date system of reports. This should result in better decision making, faster action, greater management flexibility, and vastly improved co-ordination.

The controller must be aware of the types of decisions made at each managerial level, and the related information needs, if the best reports are to be compiled at the appropriate frequencies. In developing reports the controller must assess their ultimate utility to their recipients, which requires that they be designed specifically for the individuals who are to receive them, with due consideration being given to the conditions that govern the business and the way in which it is managed. Reports should supply information that is considered important, and this should be arranged and analysed in such a way that it is most convenient and immediately useful to those who must make decisions on the basis of it. To achieve the aim of successfully communicating the essential facts about the business to those who manage it, the controller must have a clear idea of the purposes, possibilities and limitations of the many different types of statement and report. He must, therefore, understand the problems and viewpoints of those who receive his reports and ensure that these people understand the true meaning and limitations of the information contained in those reports.

Reports should be designed to emphasize those factors that are especially important in determining success: the critical success factors.

Such factors have the following characteristics:

1 they are important in explaining success or failure;
2 they are volatile (i.e. they can change quickly);
3 prompt action is needed when a significant change occurs;
4 change is not easy to predict;
5 they can be measured.

In specifying what is to be reported at each level of management, especially at lower levels, the controller must pose two questions:

1 What are the necessary and controllable factors relevant to the level of authority in question?
2 In what form are these factors best presented to aid in decision making at this level?

The level of management in question will determine whether reports are to relate results to long-range objectives expressed in aggregate terms, or whether they should relate results to standard costs in great detail. The principles of control are the same for these extremes of top management and supervisory management, but the form of report is different.

The adoption of a structured approach to reporting, with results being reported by areas of responsibility, will enable top management to view the results and efficiencies of individual departments in the light of their contribution to overall performance and objectives. It may be, however, that the need for control action on the part of top management indicates a failure to achieve control at a more appropriate but lower level.

Similarly, a long delay between actual events and the reporting of these events via the top management control system may create the need for corrective action that is more drastic, more complex, and involves more people than if such action had been initiated at a lower level of control more closely associated with the actual events.

Within the control framework the characteristics of good reports are that they should:

1 be oriented towards the user, taking into account both his level and his function;
2 give as much information as possible in quantitative terms, and flow both ways in the organization (i.e. up and down);
3 be based on a flexible system that allows quick changes to meet new conditions;
4 be oriented towards action rather than towards curiosity.

On a tangible plane succinctness is a great virtue in reporting, while on an intangible plane a major contribution made by an adequate reporting system is that the recipient of a report is made to pause and think over the contents of that report and its implications for the enterprise.

20.6 SUMMARY

In this chapter we have built on the basic ideas of control and control systems which were introduced in Chapter 19 and looked in some detail at control methods which can be employed to advantage in a marketing context.

Audits are one such control method which was discussed in detail in Chapter 2. This highlights the fact that there is not a watertight distinction between the use of marketing audits for *taking stock* (i.e. in addressing the question 'Where are we now?') and dealing with the *flow* issue of 'How might we ensure arrival?'

Budgeting, as the most widely used form of management control, with variants such as zero based budgeting and output budgeting, was discussed, as was variance analysis, which is a diagnostic device to help explain why discrepancies between desired outcomes and actual outcomes have emerged. It was pointed out that the existence of a variance should not be taken as *prima facie* evidence that the budget level (or standard) is correct and the actual outcome is incorrect; it is often the case that the existence of a variance points to a poorly set budget target.

One straightforward refinement to a basic variance analysis approach enables a distinction to be made between *planning* variances on the one hand and *operating* variances on the other. The former are the primary responsibility of those engaged in making forecasts and setting targets, whereas the latter are the responsibility of those charged with implementing marketing plans. No matter how detailed the diagnosis of what went wrong and why, the crucial point is for this to be a prelude to action: diagnosis should be followed by prognosis. The chapter covered the importance of *responding* in a way which realigns strategic actions as a step towards achieving corporate missions.

20.7 EXERCISES

1 How would you determine whether a marketing process under your control is experiencing normal variations or is out of control? Link your answer to a specific operational context.

2 You (as Director of Marketing) are requested by your MD to set up an evaluation system for on-going marketing activities. Outline the measures, etc. which you would use and locate these within a suitable systems framework.

3 Halfway through the implementation of the current year's marketing plan you (as Marketing Manager) noted that the downward trend in market share for one of your key product lines was accelerating. What actions would you consider taking?

4 Construct an output budget for your organization's marketing activities. What problems did you need to overcome in doing this, and how successful were you in overcoming them?

5 Evaluate Barrett's response model (as portrayed in Figures 20.19 and 20.20) in terms of its applicability in a marketing situation with which you are familiar.

20.8 DISCUSSION QUESTIONS

1 Discuss alternative forms of control and their potential application in a marketing context.

2 Why is flexible budgeting more appropriate in marketing than fixed budgeting?

3 Variances presuppose some form of standard. Give examples of standards in marketing which are subject to control via variance analysis.

4 Does uncertainty over competitors' plans render control endeavours pointless? Discuss.

5 In what ways is benchmarking helpful in the control process?

20.9 CASE STUDIES

Engels & Ferrell Industries

In 1968, the Military Space (MS) Department of Engels & Ferrell Industries (EFI) first applied its extensive knowledge of space batteries to commercial uses. Until that point, the company had never attempted to market its pioneering products, mainly because they had been developed by its engineers more as their own toys/inventions than as a business venture. However, even today, any visitor who enters their well-guarded plant in Johnstown, Indiana, will be surprised to see that 12 years ago MS had developed an electric golf cart with a town range of more than 250 miles and that this vehicle is still functional. About the same time, MS had developed an electric car that achieved better than 140 miles per hour in an official time trial run in Utah, which is a recognized international record for electric car speed. Also, there are equally impressive products within the Military Space Department of EFI that have little commercial interest to the corporation.

Company History

Engels & Ferrell Industries, Inc. was established in 1894 as a railroad car manufacturing company in western Pennsylvania. The company grew steadily over the years and now has 19 operating divisions in eight states, Canada, Germany, and New Zealand. Engels & Ferrell is engaged in the industrial manufacture of several thousand different products in more than 50 plants and has a total corporate sales volume of approximately $526 million (1985). The company strategy is based on several loosely-controlled autonomous divisions and relatively small plants, most of which are located in small to middle-size communities. EFI stresses product quality and is known for its excellence in engineering and research.

The Military Space (MS) Department, the largest plant of the Electronics Division, is located in Johnstown, Indiana. The plant began operations in 1950 as a research facility for vacuum power tubes. A few years later, MS received an army contract to design and develop a battery to launch and guide a classified U.S. Army weapon. Over the next few years, MS won several more military and then space contracts. Since 1966, almost all of MS's sales have been related to military and space batteries and battery components. Today, MS employs more than 600 persons and is recognized around the free world by the military and space battery industry as the leader in terms of dollar sales volume, product diversification, and technical expertise.

Through the years, MS participated in an extensive number of projects, and this involvement resulted in the development of a large number of battery related products, most of which disappeared in the files of their creators immediately after the expiration of the contracts that generated them. The whole department had a totally engineering-oriented philosophy. MS products, usually the most precise in the industry, never enjoyed any commercial application after the expiration of their contractual restrictions. In actuality, no marketing efforts were ever made except through standard announcements in the industry literature, some product description flyers, and some participation in exhibitions and conferences. However, and in spite of the lack of any visible marketing attempts, MS sales continued growing at a satisfactory pace, with an average pretax return on sales of about 8 percent (see Exhibit 1).

Exhibit 1
Sales Volume (in $000)

Customer (end-user)	1972	1974	1976	1978	1980
U.S. Army	2721	2685	2340	2046	3048
U.S. Navy	860	704	660	2960	3641
U.S. Air Force	2142	2899	3509	3214	4684
Dept. of Energy*	820	1490	2631	3140	3966
NASA	1421	1656	2124	2291	1744
U.S. Marine Corps	160	179	130	64	0
Commercial	0	0	0	416	0
Foreign	0	36	424	622	941
Unknown/Other	0	1	71	83	20
Total	8124	9650	11889	14836	18044

*Formerly the Atomic Energy Commission and then the Energy Research Development Agency.

MS Organization in April 1981

At the end of the 1960s, MS spent significant amounts of capital to expand existing facilities, remodel the old ones, and update its equipment. This resulted in two things: first, it moved the department to the twentieth century technology and, second, it started an era of overdependence on long-term loans.

This capital expansion was necessary for MS if it was going to continue to compete successfully for military and space projects. But it was catastrophic for Wes Cooper, the department's controller, who had initiated the whole change. Cooper resigned in 1973, failing to justify the overreliance on loans and the subsequent high interest payments. Then, EFI provided some funds and a new controller, David Levine. Levine quickly proved to be extremely competent. He simplified processes, increased control, and pioneered a planning system. Subsequently, he gained for himself the title of senior vice president for EFI with planning responsibilities and designated his aggressive head accountant. Andy Parker, as the new MS controller.

Andy had joined EFI in 1977 and almost immediately started a new friendship with Bruce Jacobs, MS's newly recruited contract manager. Bruce, who had received a Ph.D. in marketing from Northwestern, had extensive experience with military sales. This was an additional communication point between the two men, since Parker had worked for 18 years as financial planner for Singer (especially associated with the B-52 mission). Therefore, both men were very glad when Andy was promoted in January 1979 to controller for MS. At that point the organizational chart for the department was as shown in Exhibit 2.

xhibit 2
)rganizational Chart –
1981

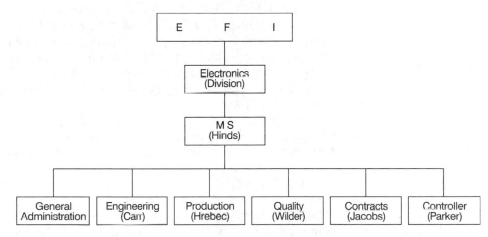

In terms of work force breakdowns, one third of the MS workers were classified as white-collar employees, almost 80 percent having an engineering orientation. In actuality, only 40 persons in MS were in administration, purchasing, accounting, controlling, personnel, and security of the facilities, leaving the main part of MS totally engineering/ production oriented (see Exhibit 3 for top executive profiles).

A Marketing Project

In May 1980, a land developing outfit in Arizona contacted MS in order to seek information and subsequently ordered 660 lithium battery systems at a price of $1,205.50 per unit (delivery 1981). Fun-Sun City, Inc., the

Exhibit 3
Top Executive Profiles
– April 1981

Name	Title	Age	Yrs. with EFI	Education
Joe Hinds	Gen. Manager	54	21	B.S.E.E.
Jim Carr	Engr. Manager	51	16	B.S.M.E.
Herb Gailey	Asst. Engr. Mgr.	46	16	B.S. (Physics)
Ed Duff	Asst. Engr. Mgr.	42	16	B.S.C.E.
Jeff Wilson	Asst. Engr. Mgr.	49	27	B.S.C.E.
Bruce Jacobs	Contract Manager	38	3	Ph.D. (Mkt.)
Dennis Hrebec	Production Mgr.	62	11	B.S. (Tech.)
Ronald Wilder	Quality Cont. Mgr.	57	4	B.A. (History)
George Hill	Purchasing Mgr.	64	47	High School
Andy Parker	Controller	43	3	M.B.A., CPA

ordering firm, was in the land developing business for retirement communities and recently had extended operations into the production of goods that potentially would be sold exclusively through their own captive markets. Fun-Sun City was operating five retirement communities with a permanent population of more than 6,000 residents and was producing an extensive line of products, ranging from T-shirts to paddle boats.

The latest addition was going to be the development of an electric golf cart, oversized and with roadworthy specifications, which was planned to be marketed even outside of the borders of their markets. This cart, which was designed to be used as a second family car, was fast (up to 39 miles per hour) and able to travel 75 miles on a single charge. The only reliable power unit that Fun-Sun City was able to find was the Li24N (lithium battery) system, patented and produced by MS exclusively.

Bruce Jacobs handled the sale with extreme care. He realized the potential of commercial sales[1] from the very beginning, but he also realized that 'rocking the boat is dangerous.' 'The life of a marketer in an engineering firm is pitiful,' he said during the last days of January 1981 to Parker. 'First of all, you do not understand their [engineers'] language; then, they want to produce whatever toys fancy their minds; and finally, they want *you* to sell it. Now, I must say that they have ideas . . . This Li24N, for example, was a very good one . . . but it applies basically to military and space programs. It is much more than what they need in a golf cart.'

'But this is what Fun-Sun City asked for, and they pay good money, too,' interrupted Parker.

'Well, that's the point,' continued Bruce. 'Golf carts do not need a space battery. They need a less demanding and a cheaper one. We must see the marketplace. The suppliers must see the real needs of the marketplace – if the buyers cannot see them. Otherwise, somebody from the competition will give Fun-Sun City a cheaper battery next year. Then, this nice door to commercial sales will close for us.'

General Manager Hinds walked in and heard the last part of the conversation. He did not say a word, but he deeply registered in his mind one further thought – to expand Jacobs' job description from contracts to a marketing direction.

Hinds felt confident about his department. He had excellent engineers, high level technology, good production facilities, competent product assurance and control workers, and an impressive backlog of military orders (see Exhibit 4).

However, in spite of all the extensive orders, Hinds also realized that profit margins were declining and that the only reason he could afford to

Exhibit 4
Current Backlog (in $000)

As of 1 April 1981:			
Thermal	$4451	U.S. Army	$2281
Ordnance (fuse)	182	U.S. Navy	127
Silver zinc	2417	U.S. Air Force	3821
Nickel cadmium (sealed)	64	Dept. of Energy	1458
Nickel hydrogen	675	NASA	1041
Lithium	1943	Foreign	696
		Commercial	308
Total	9732	Total	9732

Note: 1 April 1980 backlog was $7266.

[1] MS considers all non-government as end-user sales to be commercial. Therefore, commercial sales would include what would normally be categorized as industrial ones.

pay interest payments was that Wes Cooper, the department's previous controller, had achieved all this modernization and capital expansion when interest rates were much lower than those of 1981. The competition was already bidding lower. What if this trend were to continue? New ways to benefit from the existing innovations and new markets had to be found. Old products had to be reexamined. Marginal use of resources had to be considered. Hinds knew that costs were increasing rapidly.

A Memo

The whole MS department was truly thrilled with the new application of the Li24N. Further, one of those golf carts was given as a present to Jacobs (who, violating all existing practices, had accepted it and was using it for his transportation within the plant). When not being used, the cart was parked at the front entrance, and, since it was 'dressed up' with a blue jean outfit, it was carrying the name 'NeDim' (new dimension versus 'denim' for blue jeans). Jacobs had done an excellent job with the internal promotion of the new marketing dimensions (commercial products), and he had also instituted the 'tiny' prize, which was 1 percent of the assured sales (over $5,000) arranged by any of the company's employees using existing batteries and new customers with commercial orientation.

However, in Hinds' mind there were some doubts about the whole approach of the 'marketers.' The 'contracts' people were overperforming their roles. Everything around was like a continuous 'fair' with flags, prizes, and gimmicks. Additionally, Parker had signed a $3,600 allowance for these 'non-productive causes.' Given the ultra-conservative character of the outfit, the 'marketing directives' that Jacobs had introduced were a direct insult to the firm's practices. Hinds had to accept that sales were better than ever and that corporate pressing obligations were reduced. But he was also determined to discuss this 'monkey business' in full session of the executive team at the next meeting and to impose tighter behavioral policies.

It was then that his secretary through the intercom announced that Jacobs was there waiting to see him. Jacobs said, 'Again violating the established guidelines, I assigned to Tony Tolbs the rather ambitious task of collecting potential leads for future commercial customers. Tony has worked on this project since November 1980 and has a thorough knowledge of most of our batteries with commercial application potential. I spent two days with him summarizing the information.'

Hinds replied, 'Bruce, I admire you. I like you. But you never follow my instructions. For your own sake, I expect that you better make sense. The whole MS is upset. Workers are trying to sell batteries. People on the road wear funny T-shirts from Fun-Sun City, bought with *our* money. Good customers are complaining. I fear that some of your people do not give enough attention to our good old customers. For example, Jerry Day [Boeing/Seattle, Program Manager on the Air Launched Cruise Missile] was upset last month when he and his crew were here and you were in Colorado trying to drum up some windmill battery possibility. I am discouraged, although I am persuaded that you are right.'

Transition Period (1981–1985)

The next few weeks were hectic for the contracts department. Jacobs and his staff were extremely busy with contractual negotiations and in meetings with customers on various matters (such as schedule slippages, technical problems, and the like). As a result of this, and perhaps for other reasons, Jacobs gradually slowed down his activities regarding commercial applications. Under a directive from Hinds, in April 1981, MS did start limited production on two batteries for commercial applications. A few nickel cadmium batteries were produced and finally sold at a good profit for use in emergency lights. Some lithium batteries were produced on a speculative basis for use in fire alarms; about half were sold for an acceptable profit, and the others were eventually scrapped out for parts. Jacobs was interested in two or three other minor projects but chose not to push Hinds, and the batteries were never produced.

In late 1981, the purchasing manager, George Hill, retired and was replaced by his long-time assistant, Ralph Arnold. This management transition went very smoothly for MS.

The following year saw several changes in the key management personnel at MS. Early in the year, one of the assistant engineering managers resigned to accept an engineering position in an unrelated industry in a nearby city. He was immediately replaced internally and another project engineer was promoted to a newly established assistant engineering manager position a few weeks later. In mid-June of 1982, after a few weeks of rumors, Bruce Jacobs submitted his resignation effective the end of July. Jacobs went into college teaching the following month. While it was rumored that one of the contract administrators would move up to contract manager, this was not the case. Ronald Wilder, the quality control manager, was immediately moved to fill the position as contract manager. There were no other staffing changes in the contract department. One of the four production supervisors became the new quality control manager. Also, there was quite a bit of shifting between and among the foremen in the production and quality control departments. In August 1982, Andy Parker, controller, resigned to accept a similar position with a larger company in another state. He was replaced by an outsider in November.

1983 was a fairly uneventful year for MS. Business increased a little, with no significant product, market, or personnel changes. Wilder was now fully ingrained as contract manager and was successfully using the skills that had won him the job (negotiation tactfulness and customer contacts).

Sales increased sharply in 1984. Dennis Hrebec retired as production manager and was replaced by one of his assistants. By now most of what Jacobs had done in his five years as marketing head was largely forgotten. While there were still some commercial sales and quite a few inquiries, no formal records (logs) were kept of them. Also, the number of direct energy-related inquiries (such as for solar energy storage, windmills, and electric cars) apparently had declined.

Under the second Reagan administration, significantly more military orders were registered. Finally, 1985 was another good year for MS (see Exhibit 5). In spite of that, Hinds was concerned about the future. The unpredictability of foreign military sales (FMS) was worrying Hinds. Regions such as the Middle East appeared to be able to find cheaper, and maybe equally good, suppliers from the Far East and the People's Republic of China. It was only a matter of time to have to face foreign competitors in most other markets, too. Moreover, with the movement toward more competitive, less government regulated sales for communications and other satellites, there was an increased uncertainty about even the EFI-MS's U.S. sales. It was clear that MS had lost numerous sales of batteries for satellites because of price. Hinds realized that the whole industry was changing toward less rigorous quality requirements

Exhibit 5
Sales Volume (in $000)

Customer (end-user)	1981	1982	1983	1984	1985
U.S. Army	$ 4560	$ 6494	$ 7129	$ 9460	$11145
U.S. Navy	127	398	542	1751	600
U.S. Air Force	7314	6421	7115	6399	10754
Dept. of Energy	1880	2016	2110	1150	411
NASA	2159	2331	2560	3514	3090
U.S. Marine Corps	0	86	4	124	0
Commercial	506	411	72	0	0
Foreign	2455	1749	2889	4456	2250
Unknown/other	0	2251	1459	214	34
Total	19001	22156	23881	27065	28419

and specifications and toward more emphasis on price and delivery terms.

Moving into 1986

In January of 1986, Hinds asked Carr to concentrate on new product development and to seek out more commercial applications. In February, Carr assigned this task to John Ely, assistant engineering manager. As of mid-April, there was no evidence that Ely had taken any tangible actions concerning this assignment. Exhibits 6, 7, and 8 show the organizational chart, top executive profiles, and current backlog (all as of 1 April 1986).

Exhibit 6
Organizational Chart – 1986

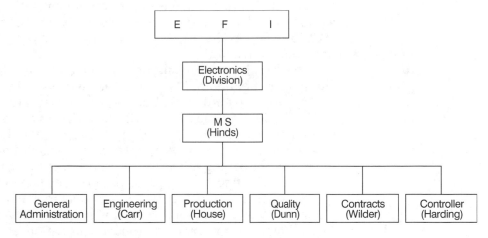

Exhibit 7
Top Executive Profiles – 1986

Name	Title	Age	Yrs with EFI	Education
Joe Hinds	Gen. Manager	59	26	B.S.E.E.
Jim Carr	Engr. Manager	56	21	B.S.M.E.
Herb Gailey	Asst. Engr. Mgr.	51	21	B.S. (Physics)
Ed Duff	Asst. Engr. Mgr.	47	21	B.S.C.E.
Bill Vernon	Asst. Engr. Mgr.	40	6	B.S.E.E.
John Ely	Asst. Engr. Mgr.	45	20	B.S.C.E.
Ronald Wilder	Contract Manager	60	7	B.A. (History)
Charles House	Production Mgr.	50	18	A.S. (Mech.)
David Dunn	Qual. Ctrl. Mgr.	39	11	B.S. (Math)
Ralph Arnold	Purchasing Mgr.	49	23	High School
Leon Harding	Controller	38	3	B.S.B.A., CPA

Exhibit 8
Current Backlog (in $000)

As of 1 April 1986:			
Thermal	$ 8570	U.S. Army	$ 6410
Ordnance (fuse)	249	U.S. Navy	1254
Silver Zinc	3866	U.S. Air Force	5210
Nickel Cadmium (sealed)	0	Dept. of Energy	0
Nickel Hydrogen	1235	NASA	2459
Lithium	2960	Foreign	1545
		Commercial	0
Total	16,880	Total	16,880

Note: 1 April 1985 backlog was $14,804.

Source: This case was prepared by Dr. John Thanopoulos, Director, International Business, and Associate Professor, Marketing at the University of Akron, and Dr. Joseph W. Leonard, Associate Professor, Department of Management at Miami University, as a basis for class discussion. All names and places have been disguised. Copyright 1987 by the authors. Reprinted with permission.

Required
Assess Engels & Ferrell from a marketing control perspective.

XYZ Corp.

The XYZ Corp. is a large electronics manufacturer located in the eastern United States. Manufacturing a very wide range of industrial and consumer electrical and electronic components, it is also a major Defense contractor. With sales of over $2 billion a year and employing more than 120,000 people, the XYZ Corp. is one of the largest electronics manufacturers in the world.

The defense manufacturing facilities are located at an industrial complex in Baltimore, Maryland. The Defense Center is divided into four main divisions: Aerospace, Surface, Underseas, and Systems Operations. Each division is headed by a vice president who reports to the Defense Center president, Mr. E. W. Briggs. Each major department within the divisions has its own marketing staff, consisting of numerous representatives who have engineering backgrounds. It has been the policy of the various marketing managers to assign specific contracts (i.e., ones the Defense Center is bidding on) to individual marketing representatives for their complete attention. It is the responsibility of these marketing representatives to obtain as much information about the contracts as possible, by whatever means they deem necessary.

The Defense Center maintains a separate sales office in Washington, D.C., under the direction of the Middle Atlantic regional manager, Mr. Clive Peters. Similar offices are located in other major cities in close proximity to other major defense installations. The purpose of these offices is to conduct as much customer contact as possible, officially and unofficially. Each of the regional salesmen is assigned particular defense agencies as clients. Salesmen are encouraged to make as many contacts with their assigned customers as possible, whether it be on the golf course, in restaurants, or, at the customer's office. Very liberal expense accounts are assigned to the salesmen.

The Defense Center solicited all branches of the armed services and other agencies such as NASA and FAA but had been most successful in the past with the Navy. In view of this, more salesmen were assigned to cover naval offices than any of the other 'targets.'

Despite the complete coverage of the market by the Defense Center sales force, sales declined sharply between 1992 and 1994. During this same period, the U.S. government's expenditure on defense increased greatly. Although XYZ's products were at least as good as competitors', actual sales were far below capacity, and many workers were laid off.

XYZ competed with numerous other electronics firms for a share of the $50 billion defense budget but often bid on contracts for which other firms generally had much more experience and competence. This bidding approach was followed because it was felt it would provide a 'foot in the door' to many agencies. In 1994, the XYZ Corp. stood only 44th on the list of total contract awards from the Defense Department, last among the major electronics manufacturers. Nevertheless, its reputation was good among its previous customers.

Mr. Briggs was worried about the poor performance of the Defense Center's representatives and regional salesmen. After an audit of sales efforts, several interesting things were brought to Mr. Briggs's attention. It was a common occurrence for numerous personnel to call directly on the same potential customers, because several products or contracts could be offered by the same contractor at the same time. Embarrassment was often the result, as two, and on occasion three, representatives were in the same waiting room awaiting the same purchasing agent. Salesmen in the decentralized sales offices were hired and trained by those offices and therefore did not have much experience with the rest of the Defense Center's operations. All sales personnel operated on a straight salary compensation plan with very little opportunity for bonuses, except for management personnel. There appeared to be little direction of the salesmen after an account was assigned. Many of the representatives complained of having very little to do.

During the 1992–94 period of declining sales, XYZ reduced its national advertising efforts considerably in an attempt to reduce overhead costs. Institutional advertising on television was completely eliminated because of its high costs with no apparent impact on sales. Sales promotion material was also eliminated in the cost saving program. These efforts were of little concern to the Defense Center personnel, since the advertising department was located at XYZ's corporate headquarters. The only active advertising carried on at the Defense Center was precise description of the Center's production facilities included with each bid proposal submitted to a government agency or Defense Department office.

Prices on contracts were very systematically computed by the accounting department through use of sophisticated computer systems. Each department planning to contribute any man-hours or material in support of the proposal submitted its input to the accounting department for compilation. A final price would be arrived at by applying standard labor and overhead rates in addition to the material costs. Once the price was computed by the accounting department, it was rarely questioned. XYZ Corp. was consistently underbid by its major competitors, sometimes by as much as 30 percent. It was generally felt by most marketing personnel that their prices were too high because the standard rates applied for direct labor and overhead costs were too high, but the accounting department explained that this was necessary to ensure sufficient profit on the contracts.

After reviewing all of the above facts, Mr. Briggs was not sure what should be done. Perhaps more advertising would make government purchasing agents more receptive to XYZ's representatives. And perhaps the sales forces should be reorganized to avoid duplication of effort. More supervision might be desirable. Or maybe the salesmen need more incentives to encourage greater effort, for example, bonuses or commissions. He was even thinking of hiring new marketing managers with successful backgrounds in consumer goods markets where competition is as tough as that faced by the Defense Center.

Required
Evaluate the Defense Center's approach to marketing. What should be done?

Appendix

Present value of £1 received each year for *n* years

Years (n)	1%	2%	3%	4%	5%	6%	7%	8%	10%	12%	14%	15%	16%	18%	20%	22%	25%	28%	30%	35%	40%	50%
1	0.990	0.980	0.971	0.962	0.952	0.943	0.935	0.926	0.909	0.893	0.877	0.870	0.862	0.847	0.833	0.820	0.800	0.781	0.769	0.741	0.714	0.667
2	1.970	1.942	1.914	1.886	1.859	1.833	1.808	1.783	1.736	1.690	1.647	1.626	1.605	1.566	1.528	1.492	1.440	1.392	1.361	1.289	1.224	1.111
3	2.941	2.884	2.829	2.775	2.723	2.673	2.624	2.577	2.487	2.402	2.322	2.283	2.246	2.174	2.106	2.043	1.952	1.868	1.816	1.696	1.589	1.407
4	3.902	3.808	3.717	3.630	3.546	3.465	3.387	3.312	3.170	3.037	2.914	2.855	2.798	2.690	2.589	2.494	2.362	2.241	2.166	1.997	1.849	1.605
5	4.853	4.713	4.580	4.452	4.329	4.212	4.100	3.993	3.791	3.605	3.433	3.352	3.274	3.127	2.991	2.864	2.689	2.532	2.436	2.220	2.035	1.737
6	5.795	5.601	5.417	5.242	5.076	4.917	4.767	4.623	4.355	4.111	3.889	3.784	3.685	3.498	3.326	3.167	2.951	2.759	2.643	2.385	2.168	1.824
7	6.728	6.472	6.230	6.002	5.786	5.582	5.389	5.206	4.868	4.564	4.288	4.160	4.039	3.812	3.605	3.416	3.161	2.937	2.802	2.508	2.263	1.883
8	7.652	7.325	7.020	6.733	6.463	6.210	5.971	5.747	5.335	4.968	4.639	4.487	4.344	4.078	3.837	3.619	3.329	3.076	2.925	2.598	2.331	1.922
9	8.566	8.162	7.786	7.435	7.108	6.802	6.515	6.247	5.759	5.328	4.946	4.772	4.607	4.303	4.031	3.786	3.463	3.184	3.019	2.665	2.379	1.948
10	9.471	8.983	8.530	8.111	7.722	7.360	7.023	6.710	6.145	5.650	5.216	5.019	4.833	4.494	4.192	3.923	3.571	3.269	3.092	2.715	2.414	1.965
11	10.368	9.787	9.253	8.760	8.306	7.887	7.499	7.139	6.495	5.938	5.453	5.234	5.029	4.656	4.327	4.035	3.656	3.335	3.147	2.757	2.438	1.977
12	11.255	10.575	9.954	9.385	8.863	8.384	7.943	7.536	6.814	6.194	5.660	5.421	5.197	4.793	4.439	4.127	3.725	3.387	3.190	2.779	2.456	1.985
13	12.134	11.348	10.635	9.986	9.393	8.853	8.358	7.904	7.103	6.424	5.842	5.583	5.342	4.910	4.533	4.203	3.780	3.427	3.223	2.799	2.469	1.990
14	13.004	12.106	11.296	10.563	9.899	9.295	8.745	8.244	7.367	6.628	6.002	5.724	5.468	5.008	4.611	4.265	3.824	3.459	3.249	2.814	2.478	1.993
15	13.865	12.849	11.938	11.118	10.380	9.712	9.108	8.559	7.606	6.811	6.142	5.847	5.575	5.092	4.675	4.315	3.859	3.483	3.268	2.825	2.484	1.995
16	14.718	13.578	12.561	11.652	10.838	10.106	9.446	8.851	7.824	6.974	6.265	5.954	5.669	5.162	4.730	4.357	3.887	3.503	3.283	2.834	2.489	1.997
17	15.562	14.292	13.166	12.166	11.274	10.477	9.763	9.122	8.022	7.120	6.373	6.047	5.749	5.222	4.775	4.391	3.910	3.518	3.295	2.840	2.492	1.998
18	16.398	14.992	13.754	12.659	11.689	10.828	10.059	9.372	8.201	7.250	6.467	6.128	5.818	5.273	4.812	4.419	3.928	3.529	3.304	2.844	2.494	1.999
19	17.226	15.678	14.324	13.134	12.085	11.158	10.335	9.604	8.365	7.366	6.550	6.198	5.877	5.316	4.843	4.442	3.942	3.539	3.311	2.848	2.496	1.999
20	18.046	16.351	14.878	13.590	12.462	11.470	10.594	9.818	8.514	7.469	6.623	6.259	5.929	5.353	4.870	4.460	3.954	3.546	3.316	2.850	2.497	1.999
21	18.857	17.011	15.415	14.029	12.821	11.764	10.835	10.017	8.649	7.562	6.687	6.312	5.973	5.384	4.891	4.476	3.963	3.551	3.320	2.852	2.498	2.000
22	19.660	17.658	15.937	14.451	13.163	12.042	11.061	10.201	8.772	7.645	6.743	6.359	6.011	5.410	4.909	4.488	3.970	3.556	3.323	2.853	2.498	2.000
23	20.456	18.292	16.444	14.857	13.488	12.303	11.272	10.371	8.883	7.718	6.792	6.399	6.044	5.432	4.925	4.499	3.976	3.559	3.325	2.854	2.499	2.000
24	21.243	18.914	16.936	15.247	13.798	12.550	11.469	10.529	8.985	7.784	6.835	6.434	6.073	5.451	4.937	4.507	3.981	3.562	3.327	2.855	2.499	2.000
25	22.023	19.523	17.413	15.622	14.094	12.783	11.653	10.675	9.077	7.843	6.873	6.464	6.097	5.467	4.948	4.514	3.985	3.564	3.329	2.856	2.499	2.000
26	22.795	20.121	17.877	15.983	14.375	13.003	11.825	10.810	9.161	7.896	6.906	6.491	6.118	5.480	4.956	4.520	3.988	3.566	3.330	2.856	2.500	2.000
27	23.560	20.707	18.327	16.330	14.643	13.211	11.986	10.935	9.237	7.943	6.935	6.514	6.136	5.492	4.964	4.524	3.990	3.567	3.331	2.856	2.500	2.000
28	24.316	21.281	18.764	16.663	14.898	13.406	12.137	11.051	9.307	7.984	6.961	6.534	6.152	5.502	4.970	4.528	3.992	3.568	3.331	2.857	2.500	2.000
29	25.066	21.844	19.188	16.984	15.141	13.591	12.277	11.158	9.370	8.022	6.983	6.551	6.166	5.510	4.975	4.531	3.994	3.569	3.332	2.857	2.500	2.000
30	25.808	22.396	19.600	17.292	15.372	13.765	12.409	11.258	9.427	8.055	7.003	6.566	6.177	5.517	4.979	4.534	3.995	3.569	3.332	2.857	2.500	2.000
40	32.835	27.355	23.115	19.793	17.159	15.046	13.331	11.925	9.779	8.244	7.105	6.642	6.233	5.548	4.997	4.544	3.999	3.571	3.333	2.857	2.500	2.000
50	39.196	31.424	25.730	21.482	18.256	15.762	13.800	12.233	9.915	8.304	7.133	6.661	6.246	5.554	4.999	4.545	4.000	3.571	3.333	2.857	2.500	2.000

Present value of £1 received n years hence, at a discount rate of x% per year

Years (n)	1%	2%	3%	4%	5%	6%	7%	8%	10%	12%	14%	15%	16%	18%	20%	22%	25%	28%	30%	35%	40%	50%
1	0.990	0.980	0.971	0.962	0.952	0.943	0.935	0.926	0.909	0.893	0.877	0.870	0.862	0.847	0.833	0.820	0.800	0.781	0.769	0.741	0.714	0.667
2	0.980	0.961	0.943	0.925	0.907	0.890	0.873	0.857	0.826	0.797	0.769	0.756	0.743	0.718	0.694	0.672	0.640	0.610	0.592	0.549	0.510	0.444
3	0.971	0.942	0.915	0.889	0.864	0.840	0.816	0.794	0.751	0.712	0.675	0.658	0.641	0.609	0.579	0.551	0.512	0.477	0.455	0.406	0.364	0.296
4	0.961	0.924	0.888	0.855	0.823	0.792	0.763	0.735	0.683	0.636	0.592	0.572	0.552	0.516	0.482	0.451	0.410	0.373	0.350	0.301	0.260	0.198
5	0.951	0.906	0.863	0.822	0.784	0.747	0.713	0.681	0.621	0.567	0.519	0.497	0.476	0.437	0.402	0.370	0.328	0.291	0.269	0.223	0.186	0.132
6	0.942	0.888	0.837	0.790	0.746	0.705	0.666	0.630	0.564	0.507	0.456	0.432	0.410	0.370	0.335	0.303	0.262	0.227	0.207	0.165	0.133	0.088
7	0.933	0.871	0.813	0.760	0.711	0.665	0.623	0.583	0.513	0.452	0.400	0.376	0.354	0.314	0.279	0.249	0.210	0.178	0.159	0.122	0.095	0.059
8	0.923	0.853	0.789	0.731	0.677	0.627	0.582	0.540	0.467	0.404	0.351	0.327	0.305	0.266	0.233	0.204	0.168	0.139	0.123	0.091	0.068	0.039
9	0.914	0.837	0.766	0.703	0.645	0.592	0.544	0.500	0.424	0.361	0.308	0.284	0.263	0.225	0.194	0.167	0.134	0.108	0.094	0.067	0.048	0.026
10	0.905	0.820	0.744	0.676	0.614	0.558	0.508	0.463	0.386	0.322	0.270	0.247	0.227	0.191	0.162	0.137	0.107	0.085	0.073	0.050	0.035	0.017
11	0.896	0.804	0.722	0.650	0.585	0.527	0.475	0.429	0.350	0.287	0.237	0.215	0.195	0.162	0.135	0.112	0.086	0.066	0.056	0.037	0.025	0.012
12	0.887	0.788	0.701	0.625	0.577	0.497	0.444	0.397	0.319	0.257	0.208	0.187	0.168	0.137	0.112	0.092	0.069	0.052	0.043	0.027	0.018	0.008
13	0.879	0.773	0.681	0.601	0.530	0.469	0.415	0.368	0.290	0.229	0.182	0.163	0.145	0.116	0.093	0.075	0.055	0.040	0.033	0.020	0.013	0.005
14	0.870	0.758	0.661	0.577	0.505	0.442	0.388	0.340	0.263	0.205	0.160	0.141	0.125	0.099	0.078	0.062	0.044	0.032	0.025	0.015	0.009	0.003
15	0.861	0.743	0.642	0.555	0.481	0.417	0.362	0.315	0.239	0.183	0.140	0.123	0.108	0.084	0.065	0.051	0.035	0.025	0.020	0.011	0.006	0.002
16	0.853	0.728	0.623	0.534	0.458	0.394	0.339	0.292	0.218	0.163	0.123	0.107	0.093	0.071	0.054	0.042	0.028	0.019	0.015	0.008	0.005	0.002
17	0.844	0.714	0.605	0.513	0.436	0.371	0.317	0.270	0.198	0.146	0.108	0.093	0.080	0.060	0.045	0.034	0.023	0.015	0.012	0.006	0.003	0.001
18	0.836	0.700	0.587	0.494	0.416	0.350	0.296	0.250	0.180	0.130	0.095	0.081	0.069	0.051	0.038	0.028	0.018	0.012	0.009	0.005	0.002	0.001
19	0.828	0.686	0.570	0.475	0.396	0.331	0.277	0.232	0.164	0.116	0.083	0.070	0.060	0.043	0.031	0.023	0.014	0.009	0.007	0.003	0.002	
20	0.820	0.673	0.554	0.456	0.377	0.312	0.258	0.215	0.149	0.104	0.073	0.061	0.051	0.037	0.026	0.019	0.012	0.007	0.005	0.002	0.001	
21	0.811	0.660	0.538	0.439	0.359	0.294	0.242	0.199	0.135	0.093	0.064	0.053	0.044	0.031	0.022	0.015	0.009	0.006	0.004	0.002	0.001	
22	0.803	0.647	0.522	0.422	0.342	0.278	0.226	0.184	0.123	0.083	0.056	0.046	0.038	0.026	0.018	0.013	0.007	0.004	0.003	0.001	0.001	
23	0.795	0.634	0.507	0.406	0.326	0.262	0.211	0.170	0.112	0.074	0.049	0.040	0.033	0.022	0.015	0.010	0.006	0.003	0.002	0.001		
24	0.788	0.622	0.492	0.390	0.310	0.247	0.197	0.158	0.102	0.066	0.043	0.035	0.028	0.019	0.013	0.008	0.005	0.003	0.002	0.001		
25	0.780	0.610	0.478	0.375	0.295	0.233	0.184	0.146	0.092	0.059	0.038	0.030	0.024	0.016	0.010	0.007	0.004	0.002	0.001	0.001		
26	0.772	0.598	0.464	0.361	0.281	0.220	0.172	0.135	0.084	0.053	0.033	0.026	0.021	0.014	0.009	0.006	0.003	0.002	0.001			
27	0.764	0.586	0.450	0.347	0.268	0.207	0.161	0.125	0.076	0.047	0.029	0.023	0.018	0.011	0.007	0.005	0.002	0.001	0.001			
28	0.757	0.574	0.437	0.333	0.255	0.196	0.150	0.116	0.069	0.042	0.026	0.020	0.016	0.010	0.006	0.004	0.002	0.001	0.001			
29	0.749	0.563	0.424	0.321	0.243	0.185	0.141	0.107	0.063	0.037	0.022	0.017	0.014	0.008	0.005	0.003	0.002	0.001	0.001			
30	0.742	0.552	0.412	0.308	0.231	0.174	0.131	0.099	0.057	0.033	0.020	0.015	0.012	0.007	0.004	0.003	0.001	0.001				
40	0.672	0.453	0.307	0.208	0.142	0.097	0.067	0.046	0.022	0.011	0.005	0.004	0.003	0.001	0.001							
50	0.608	0.372	0.228	0.141	0.087	0.054	0.034	0.021	0.009	0.003	0.001	0.001	0.001									

Bibliography

Aaker, D. A. and Day, G. S. (1972), 'Corporate Response to Consumerism Pressures', *Harvard Business Review*, Vol. 50, No. 6, November – December, pp. 114–24.

Aaker, D. A. and Day, G. S. (eds) (1974), *Consumerism*, New York: Free Press, 2nd edition.

Abbott, L. (1955), *Quality and Competition*, New York: Columbia University Press.

Abell, D. F. (1980), *Defining the Business: The Starting Point of Strategic Planning*, Englewood Cliffs, NJ: Prentice-Hall.

Abell, D. F. and Hammond, J. S. (1979), *Strategic Market Planning: Problems and Analytical Approaches*, Englewood Cliffs, NJ: Prentice-Hall.

Abratt, R. (1986), 'Industrial Buying in High-Tech Markets', *Industrial Marketing Management*, Vol. 15, pp. 293–8.

Ackoff, R. L. (1970), *A Concept of Corporate Planning*, New York: Wiley.

Adler, L. (1960), 'Phasing Research into the Marketing Plan', *Harvard Business Review*, Vol. 38, No. 3, May–June, pp. 118–21.

Adler, L. (1967), 'Systems Approach to Marketing', *Harvard Business Review*, Vol. 45, No. 3, May–June, pp. 105–18.

Aguilar, F. (1967), *Scanning the Business Environment*, New York: Macmillan.

Albrecht, K. (1979), *Stress and the Manager*, Englewood Cliffs, NJ: Prentice-Hall.

Alexander, L. (1985), 'Successfully Implementing Strategic Decisions', *Long Range Planning*, Vol. 18, No. 3, pp. 91–7.

Alexander, R. S., Cross, J. S. and Cunningham, R. M. (1961), *Industrial Marketing*, Homewood, Illinois: Irwin.

Allen, P. (1989), *Selling: Management and Practice*, London: M & E Handbooks.

Ambler, P. J. (1996) 'Brand Performance and the Product Life Cycle', MBA dissertation. Sheffield Hallam University.

American Accounting Association (1972), 'Report of Committee on Cost and Profitability Analyses for Marketing', Supplement to *The Accounting Review*, Vol. 47, pp. 575–615.

American Management Association (1959), 'The Marketing Audit: Its Nature, Purposes and Problems', in *Analyzing and Improving Marketing Performance*, AMA Management Report No. 32, New York: AMA.

American Marketing Association (1957), 'The Values and Uses of Distribution Cost Analysis', *Journal of Marketing*, Vol. 21, No. 2, April, pp. 395–400.

Ames, B. C. (1968), 'Marketing Planning for Industrial Products', *Harvard Business Review*, Vol. 46, No. 5, September–October, pp. 100–11.

Ames, B. C. (1971), 'Dilemma of Product/Market Management', *Harvard Business Review*, Vol. 49, No. 2, March–April, pp. 66–74

Ames, B. C. (1989) 'How to Devise a Winning Business Plan', *Journal of Business Strategy*, Vol. 10, No. 3, May–June, pp. 26–30.

Amit, R. (1986), 'Cost Leadership Strategy and Experience Curves', *Strategic Management Journal*, Vol. 7, No. 3, May–June, pp. 281–92.

Amit, R., Domowitz, I. and Fershtman, C. (1988), 'Thinking One Step Ahead: The Use of Conjectures in Competitor Analysis', *Strategic Management Journal*, Vol. 9, pp. 431–42.

Anandarajan, A. and Christopher, M. G. (1987), 'A Mission Approach to Customer Profitability Analysis', *International Journal of Physical Distribution and Materials Management*, Vol. 17, No. 7, pp. 55–68.

Andreason, A. R. and Belk, R. W. (1980), 'Predictors of Attendance at the Performance Arts', *Journal of Consumer Research*, Vol. 7, No. 2, September, pp. 112–20.

Ansoff, H. I. (1957), 'Strategies for Diversification', *Harvard Business Review*, Vol. 25, No. 5, September–October, pp. 113–24.

Ansoff, H. I. (1968), *Corporate Strategy*, Harmondsworth: Penguin Books.

Ansoff, H. I. (1984) *Implementing Strategic Management*, Englewood Cliffs, NJ: Prentice Hall.

Anthony, R. N. (1965), *Planning and Control Systems: A Framework for Analysis*, Cambridge, Mass: Harvard University Press.

Anthony, R. N. (1988) *The Management Control Function*, Boston, Mass: Harvard Business School Press.

Armitage, H. M. (1987), 'The Use of Management Accounting Techniques to Improve Productivity Analysis in Distribution Operations', *International Journal of Physical Distribution and Materials Management*, Vol. 17, No. 2, pp. 40–50.

Armstrong, J. S. (1982), 'The Value of Formal Planning for Strategic Decisions: Review of Empirical Research', *Strategic Management Journal*, Vol. 3, pp. 197–211.

Arthur Andersen (1997), *Differences and Similarities Between Western and Eastern Managers*, London: Arthur Andersen.

Ashton, D. J., Hopper, T. M. and Scapens, R. W. (eds) (1995) *Issues in Management Accounting*, London: Prentice Hall, 2nd edition.

Aspinal, L. (1962), 'The Characteristics of Goods Theory' in *Managerial Marketing*, edited by Lazer, W. and Kelley, E., Homewood, Illinois: Irwin.

Assael, H. (1987), *Consumer Behavior and Marketing Action*, Boston, Mass.: Kent Publishing.

Atkin, B. and Skinner, R. N. (1975), *How British Industry Prices*, London: Industrial Market Research Association.

Atkinson, P. E. and Naden, J. (1989), 'Total Quality Management: Eight Lessons to Learn from Japan', *Management Services*, Vol. 33, No. 3, pp. 6–10.

Baker, K. (1982), quoted in Clark, E., 'Acorn Finds New Friends', *Marketing*, 16 December, p. 13.

Baker, M. J. (1985), *Marketing Strategy and Management*, London: Macmillan.

Baker, M. J. (1987) 'One more time – what is marketing?' in Baker, M. J. (ed.) *The Marketing Book*, London: Heinemann, pp. 3–9.

Bancroft, A. L. and Wilson, R. M. S. (1979), 'Management Accounting in Marketing', *Management Accounting*, (CIMA), Vol. 57, No. 11, December, pp. 25–30.

Banks, S. (1964), *Experimentation in Marketing*, New York: McGraw-Hill.

Barclay, I. and Benson, M. (1990), 'Success in New Product Development: Lessons from the Past', *Leadership and Organisation Development Journal*, Vol. 11, No. 6, pp. 4–12.

Barksdale, H. C. and Harris, C. E. (1982), 'Portfolio analysis and the PLC' *Long Range Planning*, Vol. 15, No. 6, pp. 74–83.

Barnard, C. I. (1956), *The Functions of the Executive*, Cambridge, Mass: Harvard University Press.

Barrett, T. F. (1980), 'Modular Data Base System', *International Journal of Physical Distribution and Materials Management*, Vol. 10, No. 4, pp. 135–46.

Barrett, T. F. (1986), 'When the Market Says "Beware!" . . .' *Management Decision*, Vol. 24, No. 6, pp. 36–40.

Barrett, T. F. (1987), 'A Surrogate Case Flow Model of Marketing Strategy', *Irish Marketing Review*, Vol. 2, pp. 117–25.

Bartels, R. (ed.) (1963), *Ethics in Business*, Columbia, Ohio: Bureau of Business Research, Ohio State University.

Bass, R. M. V. (1991), *Credit Management*, Cheltenham: Thornes (3rd edition).

Bastable, C. W. and Bao, D. H. (1988), 'The Fiction of Sales-Mix and Sales-Quantity Variances', *Accounting Horizons*, Vol. 2, No. 2, June, pp. 10–17.

Baumol, W. J. and Sevin, C. H. (1957), 'Marketing Costs and Mathematical Programming', *Harvard Business Review*, Vol. 35, No. 5, September–October, pp. 52–60.

Beer, S. (1967), *Decision and Control*, New York: Wiley.

Beerel, A. (1986), 'Strategic Financial Control Can Provide Light and Guidance', *Accountancy*, Vol. 97, No. 1114, June, pp. 70–4.

Beishon, J. and Peters, G. (eds) (1972), *Systems Behaviour*, London: Harper & Row.

Bellis-Jones, R. (1989), 'Customer Profitability Analysis', *Management Accounting*, (CIMA) Vol. 57, No. 2, pp. 26–8.

Bennett, R. (1995), *International Marketing: Strategy, Planning, Market Entry and Implementation*, London: Kogan Page.

Bennett, R. C. and Cooper, R. G. (1982), 'The Misuse of Marketing: an American Tragedy', *McKinsey Quarterly*, Autumn, pp. 52–69.

Bernard, K. N. (1996), 'Just-in-Time as a Competitive Weapon: The Significance of Functional Integration', *Journal of Marketing Management*, Vol. 12, No. 6, August, pp. 581–597.

Bernstein, D. (1984), *Company Image and Reality*, Eastbourne: Holt, Rinehart & Winston.

Bhaskar, K. N. and Housden, R. J. W. (1985), *Accounting Information Systems and Data Processing*, Oxford: Heinemann.

Biggadike, R. (1977), *Entering New Markets: Strategies and Performance*, Cambridge, Mass: Marketing Science Institute.

Blecke, C. J. (1957), 'The Small-Order Problem in Distribution Cost Control', *NACA Bulletin*, Vol. 38, No. 10, June, pp. 1279–1284.

Bleeke, J. A. (1988), 'Peak Strategies', *Across the Board*, Vol. 25, No. 2, February, pp. 45–50.

Blenel, W. H. and Bender, H. E. (1980), *Product Service Planning*, New York: Amacom.

Bliss, M. (1980), 'Market Segmentation and Environmental Analysis', unpublished MSc thesis, University of Strathclyde.

Boag, D. A. (1987), 'Marketing Control and Performance in Early-Growth Companies', *Journal of Business Venturing*, Vol. 2, No. 4, pp. 365–9.

Bonini, C. P., Jaedicke, R. K. and Wagner, H. M. (eds) (1964), *Management Controls: New Directions in Basic Research*, New York: McGraw-Hill.

Bonoma, T. V. (1984), 'Making Your Marketing Strategy Work', *Harvard Business Review*, Vol. 62, No. 2, March–April, pp. 68–76.

Bonoma, T. V. (1985), *The Marketing Edge: Making Strategies Work*, London: Collier Macmillan.

Bonoma, T. V. and Clarke, B. H. (1988), *Marketing Performance Assessment*, Boston, Mass: Harvard Business School Press.

Bonoma, T. V. and Crittenden, V.L. (1988), 'Managing Marketing Implementation', *Sloan Management Review*, Vol. 29, No. 2, Winter, pp. 7–14.

Bonoma, T. V. and Shapiro, B. P. (1983), *Segmenting the Industrial Market*, Lexington, Mass: Lexington Books.

Bonoma, T. V. and Shapiro, B. P. (1984), 'Evaluating Market Segmentation Approaches', *Industrial Marketing Management*, Vol. 13, pp. 257–68.

Booth, J. (1986), 'If You're Not Sure Then Ask', *Accountancy*, Vol. 98, No. 1119, November, pp. 94–5.

Booz, Allen and Hamilton, (1982), *New Product Management for the 1980s*, New York: Booz, Allen & Hamilton.

Boston, Consulting Group (1971), *Perspectives on Experience*, Boston, Mass: Boston Consulting Group.

Boston Consulting Group (1982), Annual Report.

Bourantas, D. and Mandes, Y. (1987), 'Does Market Share Lead to Profitability?', *Long Range Planning*, Vol. 20, No. 5, pp. 102–8.

Bourgeois, L. J. and Brodwin, D. A. (1984), 'Strategic Implementation: Five Approaches to an Elusive Phenomenon', *Strategic Management Journal*, Vol. 5, No. 3, pp. 241–64.

Bowersox, D. J. and Closs, D. J., 'Logistics and Physical Distribution', Chapter 33, pp. 571–587, in Baker, M. J. (ed.) (1995), *Companion Encyclopaedia of Marketing*, London: Routledge.

Boyd, S. H. and Britt, J. S. (1965), 'Making Marketing Research More Effective by Using the Administrative Process', *Journal of Marketing Research*, Vol. 2, No. 1, February, pp. 13–19.

Brache, A. (1986), 'Strategy and the Middle Manager', *Training*, Vol. 23, No. 4, April, pp. 30–4.

Brighton, M. (1977), 'Pinning Down the Angels', *Market Research Society Newsletter*, No. 133, April, pp. 8–10.

Brion, J. (1967), *Corporate Marketing Planning*, New York: Wiley.

Broadbent, S. (1979), *Spending Advertising Money*, London: Business Books, 3rd edition.

Brock, J. J. (1984), 'Competitor Analysis: Some Practical Approaches', *Industrial Marketing Management*, Vol. 13, pp. 225–31.

Brockner, J., et al. (1986), 'Escalation of Commitment to an Ineffective Course of Action', *Administrative Science Quarterly*, Vol. 31, No. 1, March, pp. 109–26.

Brown, B. and McDonald, M. (1994), *Competitive Marketing Strategy for Europe*, London: Macmillan.

Brown, S. (1995), *Post-Modern Marketing*, London: Routledge.

Brownlie, D. T. (1983), 'Analytical Frameworks for Strategic Market Planning', in Baker, M. J. (ed.) (1983), *Marketing: Theory and Practice*, London: Macmillan.

Brownlie, D. T. (1987), 'Environmental Analysis', in Baker, M. J. (ed.) (1987), *The Marketing Book*, London: Heinemann.

Brownlie, D. T. and Saren, M. A. (1983), 'A Review of Technological Forecasting Techniques and Their Application', *Management Bibliographies and Reviews*, Vol. 9, No. 4.

Brownlie, D. T. and Saren, M. A. (1992), The Four Ps of the Marketing Concept: prescriptive, polemical, permanent and problematic, *European Journal of Marketing*, Vol. 26, No. 4, pp. 34–47.

Buckley, P. J. (1991), 'Developments in International Business Theory in the 1990s', *Journal of Marketing Management*, Vol. 7, No. 1, January, pp. 15–24.

Bucklin, L. P. (1978), *Productivity in Marketing*, Chicago: American Marketing Association.

Buckner, H. (1967), *How British Industry Buys*, London: Hutchinson.

Buell, V. P. (1966), *Marketing Management in Action*, New York: McGraw-Hill.

Bureau, J. R. (1981), *Brand Management*, London: Macmillan.

Burnett, L. (1961), *Communications of an Advertising Man*, New York: Leo Burnett.

Burns, T. and Stalker, G. M. (1961), *The Management of Innovation*, London: Tavistock (3rd edition, 1994, OUP).

Burton, P. W. and Miller, J. R. (1990), *Advertising Fundamentals*, Scranton, Pa: International Textbook Company.

Business Week (1977), 'The Market Mishandles a Blue Chip', *Business Week*, 20 June, p. 17

Buzzell, R. D. and Chussil, M. J. (1985), 'Managing for Tomorrow', *Sloan Management Review*, Vol. 26, No. 4, Summer, pp. 3–13.

Buzzell, R. D., Cox, D. F. and Brown, R. V. (1969), *Marketing Research and Information Systems*, New York: McGraw-Hill.

Buzzell, R. D. and Gale, B. T. (1987), *The PIMS Principles: Linking Strategy to Performance*, New York: Free Press.

Buzzell, R. D., Gale, B. T. and Sullivan, R. G. M. (1975), 'Market Share: a Key to Profitability', *Harvard Business Review*, Vol. 53, No. 1, January–February, pp. 97–106.

Buzzell, R. D. and Nourse, R. M. (1967), *Product Innovation in Food Processing*, Boston, Mass:

Division of Research, Harvard Business School.

Buzzell, R. D. and Wiersema, F. D. (1981), 'Successful Share Building Strategies', *Harvard Business Review*, Vol. 59, No. 1, January–February, pp. 135–44.

Byars, L. L. (1984), *Strategic Management*, New York: Harper & Row.

Calingo, L. M. R. (1989), 'Achieving Excellence in Strategic Planning Systems', *SAM Advanced Management Journal*, Vol. 54, No. 2, Spring, pp. 21–3.

Campbell, A., Divine, M. and Young, D. (1990), *A Sense of Mission*, London: Pitman/Financial Times.

Cannon, J. T. (1968), *Business Strategy and Policy*, New York: Harcourt, Brace & World.

Cardozo, R. N. (1980), 'Situational Segmentation of Industrial Markets', *European Journal of Marketing*, Vol. 14, No. 5/6, pp. 264–76.

Cardozo, R. N. and Smith, D. K. (1983), 'Applying Financial Portfolio Theory to Product Portfolio Decisions: An Empirical Study', *Journal of Marketing*, Vol. 47, Spring, pp. 110–19.

Carlzon, J. (1987) *Moments of Truth*, New York: Ballinger.

Carson, and Rickards (1979), 'Structured Creativity and Integrated Modelling for Industry, Technology and Research (SCIMITAR)', cited in Barclay, I. and Benson, M. (1990).

Carson, R. (1963), *Silent Spring*, Boston, Mass: Houghton Mifflin.

Carter, C. F. and Williams, B. R. (1958), *Investment in Innovation*, London: OUP.

Cascino, A. E. (1967), 'Organizational Implications of the Marketing Concept' in Kelley, E. J. and Lazer, W. (eds) (1967), *Managerial Marketing: Perspectives and Viewpoints*, Homewood, Illinois: Irwin.

Cespeds, F. V. and Piercy, N. F. (1996), 'Implementing Marketing Strategy', *Journal of Marketing Management*, Vol. 12, pp. 135–160.

Chakravarthy, B. S. (1986), 'Measuring Strategic Performance', *Strategic Management Journal*, Vol. 7, pp. 437–58.

Challagalla, G. N. and Shervani, T. A. (1996), 'Dimensions and Types of Supervisory Control: Effects on Salesperson Performance and Satisfaction', *Journal of Marketing*, Vol. 60, January, pp. 89–105.

Chandler, A. D. (1962), *Strategy and Structure*, Cambridge, Mass: MIT Press.

Channon, D. (1987), 'Through the Eyes of Customers', *Banking World*, November, pp. 26–9.

Chebat, J-C., Filiatrault, P., Katz, A., Tal, S. M. (1994), 'Strategic Auditing of Human and Financial Resource Allocation in Marketing', *Journal of Business Research*, Vol. 31, pp. 197–208.

Chevalier, M. and Charty, B. (1974), 'Don't Misuse Your Market Share Goal', *European Business*, Spring, pp. 43–51.

Child, J. (1977), *Organization*, London: Harper & Row. 1st edition.

Child, J. (1984), *Organization*, London: Harper & Row. 2nd edition.

Chisnall, P. M. (1989), *Strategic Industrial Marketing*, London Prentice Hall, 2nd edition.

Christopher, M. G. (1986), *The Strategy of Distribution Management*, London: Heinemann.

Christopher, M. G. and Walters, D. W., with Gattorna, J. L. (1977), *Distribution Planning and Control*, Farnborough: Gower.

Christopher, M. G., Majaro, S. and McDonald, M. H. B. (1987), *Strategy Search*, Aldershot: Gower.

Christopher, M. G., Payne, A. and Ballantyne, D. (1991), *Relationship Marketing*, Oxford: Heinemann.

Christopher, M. G., Schary, P. and Skjott-Larsen, T. (1979), *Customer Service and Distribution Strategy*, London: Associated Business Press.

Christopher, M. G., Jeffries, J., Kirkland, J. and Wilson, R. M. S. (1968), 'Status Report on Marketing Theory', *British Journal of Marketing*, Vol. 2, No. 3, Autumn, pp. 230–42.

Christopher, W. F. (1977), 'Marketing Achievement Reporting: A Profitability Approach', *Industrial Marketing Management*, Vol. 6, pp. 149–62.

Chua, W. F., Lowe, E. A. and Puxty, A. G. (eds) (1989), *Critical Perspectives in Management Control*, Basingstoke: Macmillan.

Churchman, C. W. (1968), *The Systems Approach*, New York: Delacorte Press.

Clarke, C. and Brennan, K. (1988), 'Allied Forces', *Management Today*, November, pp. 128–31.

Clarke, C. and Pratt, S. (1985), 'Leadership's Four Part Progress', *Management Today*, March, pp. 84–6.

Clifford, D. K. and Cavanagh, R. E. (1985), *The Winning Performance: How America's High and Mid-Size Growth Companies Succeed*, New York: Bantam Books.

Clutterbuck, D. and Dearlove, D. (1993), 'The Basic Lessons of Change', *Managing Service Quality*, Vol. 3, No. 1, March, pp. 97–101.

Coates, D., Finlay, P. and Wilson, J. (1991), 'Validation in Marketing Models', *Journal of the Market Research Society*, Vol. 33, No. 2, April, pp. 83–90.

Cochran, E. and Thompson, G. (1964), 'What New Products Fail', *The National Industrial Conference Board Review*, October, pp. 11–18.

Cohen, W. A. (1988), *The Practice of Marketing Management: Analysis Planning and Implementation*, New York: Macmillan.

Cohn, C. (1990), 'Agents of Argent', *Management Today*, March, pp. 97–8, 101.

Coleman, R. P. (1961), 'The Significance of Social Stratification in Selling', in Bell, M. (ed.) (1961) *Marketing*, New York: American Marketing Association.

Cook, R. (1992) 'Aspects of Customer Service', *ITC Magazine*, March–April, pp. 10–12.

Cook, V. J. Jr. (1985), 'The Net Present Value of Market Share', *Journal of Marketing*, Vol. 49, Summer, pp. 49–63.

Cooper, R. G. (1979), 'The Dimensions of New Product Success and Failure', *Journal of Marketing*, Vol. 43, No. 2, Summer, pp. 93 -104.

Cooper, R. G. (1980), 'Factors in New Product Success', *European Journal of Marketing*, Vol. 14, Nos. 5/6, pp. 277–92.

Coulson-Thomas, C. J. (1983), *Marketing Communications*, London: Heinemann.

Cowley, P. R. (1985), 'The Experience Curve and History of the Cellophane Business', *Long Range Planning*, Vol. 18, No. 6, pp. 84–90.

Cox, K. K. and Enis, B. M. (1969), *Experimentation for Marketing Decisions*, Scranton, Pa: Intertext.

Cox, R., Alderson, W. and Shapiro, S. J. (eds) (1964), *Theory in Marketing*, Homewood, Illinois: Irwin.

Cox, R. and Brittain, P. (1988), *Retail Management*, London: M & E Handbooks.

Cox, W. E. (1967), 'Product Life Cycles as Marketing Models', *Journal of Business*, Vol. 40, No. 4, October, pp. 375–84.

Crainer, S. (1990), 'A Niche for High Performance', *Marketing Business*, Issue 13, October, pp. 14–15.

Cravens, D. W. (1981), 'How to Match Marketing Strategies with Overall Corporate Planning', *Management Review*, Vol. 70, No. 12, December, pp. 12–19.

Cravens, D. W. (1986), 'Strategic Forces Affecting Marketing Strategy', *Business Horizons*, Vol. 29, No. 5, September–October.

Cravens, D. W. (1988), 'Gaining Strategic Marketing Advantage', *Business Horizons*, Vol. 31, No. 5, pp. 44–54.

Cravens, D. W. (1990), *Strategic Marketing*, Homewood, Illinois: Irwin. (3rd edition).

Cravens, D. W. and Lamb, C. W. (1986), *Strategic Marketing Cases and Applications*, Homewood, Illinois: Irwin. 2nd edition.

Crawford, C. M. (1979). 'New Product Failure Rates–Facts and Fallacies', *Research Management*, September, pp. 9–13.

Crissy, W. J. E., Fischer, P. M. and Mossman, F. H. (1973), 'Segmental Analysis: Key to Marketing Profitability', *MSU Business Topics*, Vol. 21, No. 2, Spring, pp. 42–9.

Crissy, W. J. E. and Kaplan, R. M. (1963), 'Matrix Models for Marketing Planning', *MSU Business Topics*, Vol. 11, No. 3, Summer, pp. 48–66.

Cross, R. H. (1987), 'Strategic Planning: What it Can and Can't Do', *SAM Advanced Management Journal*, Vol. 52, No. 1, Winter, pp. 13–16.

Culliton, J. W. (1948), *The Management of Marketing Costs*, Boston, Mass: Division of Research Harvard Business School.

Cunningham, M. I. and Roberts, D. A. (1974), 'The Role of Customer Service in Industrial Marketing', *European Journal of Marketing*, Vol. 8, No. 1, Spring, pp. 15–19.

Cushing, B. E. (1982), *Accounting Information Systems and Business Organizations*, Reading, Mass: Addison-Wesley.

Cvitkovic, E. (1989), 'Profiling Your Competitors', *Planning Review*, Vol. 17, No. 3, May–June, pp. 28–30.

Cvitkovic, E. (1993), *Competition: Forms, Facts and Fiction*, London: Macmillan.

Cyert, R. M. and March, J. G. (1963), *A Behavioral Theory of the Firm*, Englewood Cliffs, NJ: Prentice-Hall.

Dace, R. W. (1990), 'Exporting to Japan–Key Factors for Success', *Quarterly Review of Marketing*, Vol. 16, No. 1, October, pp. 1–7.

Dale, E. and Michelon, L. C. (1969), *Modern Management Methods*, Harmondsworth: Penguin.

Daniell, M. (1990) 'Webs We Weave', *Management Today*, February, pp. 81–4.

D'Aveni, R. A. and MacMillan, I. C. (1991), 'Crisis and the Content of Managerial Communications: a Study of the Focus of Attention of Top Managers in Surviving and Failing Firms', *Administrative Science Quarterly*, Vol. 35, No. 4, December, pp. 634–57.

Davidson, J. H. (1987a), *Offensive Marketing or How to Make Your Competitors Followers*, Harmondsworth: Penguin. 2nd edition.

Davidson, J. H. (1987b), 'Going on the Offensive', *Marketing*, 16 April, pp. 24–9.

Davies, G. (1988), Marks & Spencer UK Case Study. Manchester Polytechnic.

Davies, H. L. (1970), 'Dimensions of Marital Roles in Consumer Decision Making', *Journal of Marketing Research*, Vol. 7, No. 2, May, pp. 168–77.

Davis, J. (1970), *Experimental Marketing*, London: Nelson.

Day, G. S. (1983) 'Gaining Insights through Strategy Analysis', *Journal of Business Strategy*, Vol. 4, No. 1, pp. 51–8.

Day, G. S. (1984), *Strategic Market Planning: the Pursuit of Competitive Advantage*, St Paul, Minnesota: West Publishing.

Day, G. S. (1986), *Analysis for Strategic Marketing Decisions*, St Paul, Minnesota: West Publishing.

Day, G. S. (1990), *Market Driven Strategy*, New York: Free Press.

Day, G. S. (1996) 'Keeping Ahead in the Competitive Game' *Financial Times, Mastering Management*, Part 18, pp. 2–4.

Day, G. S. (1996) 'How to Learn about Markets', *Financial Times, Mastering Management*, Part 12, p. 12.

Day, G. S. and Fahey, L. (1988), 'Valuing Market Strategies', *Journal of Marketing*, Vol. 52, No. 3, July, pp. 45–57.

Day, G. S., Weitz, B. and Wensley, J. R. C. (eds) (1990), *The Interface of Marketing and Strategy*, Greenwich, Conn: JAI Press.

Day, G. S. and Wensley, J. R. C. (1988), 'Assessing Advantage: A Framework for Diagnosing Competitive Superiority', *Journal of Marketing*, Vol. 52, No. 2, April, pp. 1–20.

Dean, J. (1951), *Managerial Economics*, Englewood Cliffs, NJ: Prentice-Hall.

de Chernatony, L., Daniels, K. and Johnson, G. (1993), 'A Cognitive Perspective on Managers' Perceptions of Competition', *Journal of Marketing Management*, Vol. 9, No. 4, October, pp. 373–381.

De Jouvenal, B. (1967), *The Art of Conjecture*, New York: Basic Books.

De Kluyver, C. A. and Pessemier, E. A. (1986), 'Benefits of a Marketing Budgeting Model: Two Case Studies', *Sloan Management Review*, Vol. 28, No. 1, Fall, pp. 27–38.

Dempsey, W. A. (1978), 'Vendor Selection and the Buying Process', *Industrial Marketing Management*, Vol. 7, pp. 257–67.

Demski, J. S. (1980), *Information Analysis*, Reading, Mass.: Addison-Wesley, 2nd edition.

Deng, S. and Dart, J. (1994), 'Measuring Market Orientation: A Multi-Factor, A Multi-Item Approach', *Journal of Marketing Management*, Vol. 10, No. 8, November, pp. 725–742.

Dent, J. F. (1990), 'Strategy, Organization and Control: Some Possibilities for Accounting Research', *Accounting, Organizations and Society*, Vol. 15, No. 1/2, pp. 3–26.

Deran, E. (1987), *Low-Cost Marketing Strategies*, New York: Praeger.

Dery, D. (1982), 'Erring and Learning: An Organizational Analysis', *Accounting, Organizations and Society*, Vol. 7, No. 3, pp. 217–23.

Dev, S. F. D. (1980), 'Linear Programming and Production Planning', Chapter 7 (pp. 121–47) in Arnold, J. A., Carsberg, B. V. and Scapens, R. W. (eds) (1980), *Topics in Management Accounting*, Deddington: Philip Allen.

De Vasconcellos, J. A. S. and Hambrick, D. C. (1989), 'Key Success Factors: Test of a General Theory in the Mature Industrial-Product Sector', *Strategic Management Journal*, Vol. 10, No. 4, pp. 367–82.

Devlin, G. and Biggs, I. (1989), 'Partners in the Strategic Quickstep', *Accountancy*, Vol. 104, No. 1155, November, pp. 144–6.

Dhalla, N. K. and Yuspeh, S. (1976), 'Forget the Product Life Cycle Concept', *Harvard Business Review*, Vol. 54, No. 1, January–February, pp. 102–12.

Diamantopoulos, A. and Mathews, B. P. (1990), 'A Model for Analysing Product Performance', *Quarterly Review of Marketing*, Vol. 15, No. 3, April, pp. 7–13.

Dickinson, R. A. (1967), *Buyer Decision Making*, Berkeley, California: Institute of Business and Economic Research.

Dibb, S., Simkin, L., Pride, W. M. and Ferrell, O. C. (1991), *Marketing: concepts and strategies*, Boston: Houghton Mifflin.

Diffenbach, J. (1983), 'Corporate Environmental Analysis in Large US Corporations', *Long Range Planning*, Vol. 16, No. 3, pp. 107–16.

Dolan, R. J. (1981), 'Models of Competition: a Review of Theory and Empirical Evidence', in Enis, B. M. and Roering, K. J. (eds), *Review of Marketing*, Chicago: American Marketing Association.

Dominguez, L. V. and Page, A. (1984), 'Formulating a Strategic Portfolio of Profitable Retail Segments for Commercial Banks', *Journal of Economics and Business*, Vol. 36, No. 3, pp. 43–57.

Doyle, D. (1985), 'Marketing and ZBB', *Management*, (Eire), December, pp. 33–4.

Doyle, P. (1979), 'Management Structures and Marketing Strategies in UK Industry', *European Journal of Marketing*, Vol. 13, No. 5, pp. 319–31.

Doyle, P. (1987), 'Marketing and the British Chief Executive', *Journal of Marketing Management*, Vol. 3, No. 2, Winter, pp. 121–32.

Doyle, P. (1992), 'What are the Excellent Companies?', *Journal of Marketing Management*, Vol. 8, pp. 101–116.

Doyle, P. (1994), *Marketing Management and Strategy*, London: Prentice Hall.

Doyle, P. and Newbould, G. D. (1974), 'Advertising Management for Building Societies', *Advertising Quarterly*, Nos. 42 (1986), Marketing the True Profitability of Sales Promotions', *Journal of the Operational Research Society*, Vol. 37, No. 10, October, pp. 955–66.

Doyle, P., Saunders, J. and Wong, V. (1986), 'Japanese Marketing Strategies in the UK: A Comparative Study', *Journal of International Business Studies*, Vol. 17, No. 1, pp. 27–46.

Doyle, P., Saunders, J. and Wright, L. (1988), 'A Comparative Study of British, US, and Japanese Marketing Strategies in the British Market', *International Journal of Research in Marketing*, Vol. 5, No. 3, pp. 171–84.

Driver, J. C. (1990), 'Marketing Planning in Style', *Quarterly Review of Marketing*, Vol. 15, No. 4, July, pp. 16–21.

Drucker, P. F. (1955), *The Practice of Management*, London: Heinemann.

Drucker, P. F. (1959), 'Long Range Planning: Challenge to Management Science', *Management Science*, Vol. 5, No. 3, April, pp. 238–49.

Drucker, P. F. (1963), 'Managing for Business Effectiveness', *Harvard Business Review*, Vol. 41, No. 3, May–June, pp. 53–60.

Drucker, P. F. (1969), *The Age of Discontinuity*, New York: Harper & Row.

Drucker, P. F. (1973), *Management: Tasks, Responsibilities and Practices*, New York: Harper & Row.

Duffy, M. F. (1989), 'ZBB, MBO, PPB, and Their Effectiveness within the Planning/Marketing Process', *Strategic Management Journal*, Vol. 10, No. 2, pp. 163–73.

Düro, R. (1989), *Winning the Marketing War*, New York: Wiley.

Dutton, J. E. and Duncan, R. B. (1987), 'The Influence of the Strategic Planning Process on Strategic Change', *Strategic Management Journal*, Vol. 8, pp. 103–16.

Eells, R. and Nehemkis, P. (1984), *Corporate Intelligence and Espionage: A Blueprint for Executive Decision-Making*, New York: Macmillan.

Ehrenberg, A. S. C. (1965), 'News and Notes: American Marketing Association–50th Anniversary Speech', *Operational Research Quarterly*, Vol. 16, No. 3, September, pp. 406–12.

Emery, F. (ed.) (1981), *Systems Thinking*, Harmondsworth: Penguin. Two vols.

Engel, J. F., Kollat, D. T. and Blackwell, R. D. (1968), *Consumer Behavior*, New York: Holt, Rinehart and Winston.

Evans, F. B. (1959), 'Psychological and Objective Factors in the Prediction of Brand Choice: Ford versus Chevrolet', *Journal of Business*, Vol. 32, No. 4, October, pp. 340–69.

Fahey, L., King, W. R. and Narayanan, V. K. (1981), 'Environmental Scanning and Forecasting in Strategic Planning–the State of the Art', *Long Range Planning*, Vol. 14, No. 1, February, pp. 32–9.

Farris, P. W. and Reibstein, D. J. (1979), 'How Prices, Expenditure and Profit are Linked', *Harvard Business Review*, Vol. 57, No. 6, November–December, pp. 173–84.

Feder, R. A. (1965), 'How to Measure Marketing Performance', *Harvard Business Review*, Vol. 43, No. 3, May–June, pp. 132–42.

Feldman, W. and Cardozo, R. N. (1968), 'The Industrial Revolution and Models of Buyer Behavior', *Journal of Purchasing*, Vol. 4, November.

Feldwick, P. (ed.) (1990), *Advertising Works-5*, London: Cassell.

Ferguson, A. (1989), 'Hostage to the Short Term', *Management Today*, March, pp. 68, 70–72.

Fern, R. H. and Tipgos, M. A. (1988), 'Controllers as Business Strategists: A Progress Report', *Management Accounting*, (NAA), Vol. 69, No. 9, March, pp. 25–9.

Festinger, L. (1957), *A Theory of Cognitive Dissonance*, Stanford, California: Stanford University Press.

Fifer, R. M. (1989), 'Cost Benchmarking Functions in the Value Chain', *Planning Review*, Vol. 17, No. 3, May–June, pp. 18–23, 26–7.

Fifield, P. and Gilligan, C. T. (1996), *Strategic Marketing Management: planning and control, analysis and decision*, Oxford: Butterworth-Heinemann, second edition.

Filiatrault, P. and Chebat, J–C. (1987), 'Marketing Budgeting Practices: An Empirical Study', *Developments in Marketing Science*, Vol. 10, pp. 278–82.

Filiatrault, P. and Chebat, J–C. (1990), 'How Service Firms Set their Marketing Budgets', *Industrial Marketing Management*, Vol. 19, pp. 63–7.

Fill, C (1995), *Marketing Communications: Frameworks, theories and applications*, Hemel Hempstead: Prentice Hall.

Fisher, L. (1966), *Industrial Marketing*, London: Business Books.

Fisk, G. (1967), *Marketing Systems*, New York: Harper & Row.

Fisk, G. and Dixon, D. F. (eds) (1967), *Theories for Marketing Systems Analysis*, New York: Harper & Row.

Flamholtz, E. G. and Das, T. K. (1985), 'Toward an Integrative Framework of Organizational Control', *Accounting, Organizations and Society*, Vol. 10, No. 1, pp. 35–50.

Foreman, S. K. and Money, A. H. (1995), 'Internal Marketing: Concepts, Measurement and Application', *Journal of Marketing Management*, Vol. 11, No. 8, November, pp. 755–768.

Forrester, J. W. (1961), *Industrial Dynamics*, New York: Wiley.

Forrester, J. W. (1965), 'Modeling of Market and Company Interactions', pp. 353–64, in Bennett, P. D. (ed.) (1965), *Marketing and Economic Development*, Chicago: American Marketing Association.

Fox, H. W. (1986), 'Financial ABCs of Test Marketing', *Business Horizons*, Vol. 29, No. 5, September–October, pp. 63–70.

Foxall, G. R. (1984) 'Marketing's Domain', *European Journal of Marketing*, Vol. 18, No. 1, pp. 25–40.

Foxall, G. (1987), 'Consumer Behaviour' in Baker, M. J. (ed.) (1987), *The Marketing Book*, London: Heinemann.

Freeman, C. (1965), 'Research and Development in Electronic Capital Goods', *National Institute Economic Review*, No. 34, November, pp. 40–91.

Freund, Y. P. (1988), 'Critical Success Factors', *Planning Review*, Vol. 16, No. 4, July–August, pp. 20–3.

Frey, A. W. and Halterman, J. C. (1970), *Advertising*, New York: The Ronald Press. 4th edition.

Frey, J. B. (1982), 'Pricing Over the Competitive Life Cycle', speech presented at the 1982 Marketing Conference, New York.

Frey, J. B. (1987), *Pricing Over the Competitive Life Cycle*, The Conference Board, New York.

Fruhan, W. E. (1972), 'Pyrrhic Victories in Fights for Market Share', *Harvard Business Review*, Vol. 50, No. 5, September–October, pp. 100–7.

Fuld, L. M. (1985), *Competitor Intelligence*, New York: Wiley.

Fuld, L. M. (1988): *Monitoring the Competition: Finding Out What's Really Going on Out There*, New York: Wiley.

Fuld, L. M. (1995), *The New Competitor Intelligence*, New York: Wiley.

Furey, T. R. (1987), 'Benchmarking: The Key to Developing Competitive Advantage in Mature Markets', *Planning Review*, Vol. 15, No. 5, September–October, pp. 30–2.

Gabb, A. (1991), 'How the Discovery Took Off', *Management Today*, October, pp. 64–8.

Gable, M., Fairhurst, A., Dickinson, R. (1993), 'The Use of Benchmarking to Enhance Marketing Decision Making', *Journal of Consumer Marketing*, Vol. 10, No. 1, pp. 52–60.

Gaedeke, R. M. and Etcheson, W. W. (1972), *Consumerism*, New York: Harper & Row.

Galbraith, J. K. (1958), *The Affluent Society*, Harmondsworth: Penguin Books.

Galbraith, J. K. (1977), *The Age of Uncertainty*, London: BBC/André Deutsch.

Gale, B. T. (1994), *Managing Customer Value: Creating Quality and Service that Customers Can See*, New York: The Free Press.

Gale, B. T. and Swire, D. J. (1988), 'Business Strategies that Create Wealth', *Planning Review*, Vol. 16, No. 2, March–April, pp. 6–13, 47.

Gallagher Report (1973), cited in Barclay and Benson (1990).

Garsombke, D. J. (1989), 'International Competitor Analysis', *Planning Review*, Vol. 17, No. 3, May–June, pp. 42–7.

Geroski, P. (1996) 'Keeping out the Competition', *Financial Times, Mastering Management*, Part 16, pp. 11–12.

Gerson, R. (1992), 'Dealing with the Customers who Complain', *The Straits Times*, 27 April, p. 18.

Ghemewat, P. (1986), 'Sustainable Advantage', *Harvard Business Review*, Vol. 64, No. 5, September–October, pp. 53–8.

Gilligan, C. T. and Crowther, G. (1976), *Advertising Management*, Deddington: Philip Allen.

Gilligan, C. T. and Hird, M. (1986), *International Marketing: Strategy and Management*, London: Routledge.

Gluck, F. (1985), 'Big Bang Management', *Journal of Business Strategy*, Vol. 6, No. 1, Summer, pp. 59–64.

Gofton, K. (1984) 'The Fed Loses its Reserve', *Marketing*, 2 August, p. 15.

Goldsmith, W. and Clutterbuck, D. (1988), *The Winning Streak*, London, Weidenfeld & Nicholson.

Goodman, S. R. (1970), *Techniques of Profitability Analysis*, New York: Wiley.

Goold, M. C. and Campbell, A. E. C. (1987a), *Strategies and Styles*, Oxford: Basil Blackwell.

Goold, M. C. and Campbell, A. E. C. (1987b), 'Many Best Ways to Make Strategy', *Harvard Business Review*, Vol. 65, No. 6, November–December, pp. 70–6.

Goold, M. C. and Quinn, J. J. (1990), *Strategic Control: Milestones for Long-term Performance*, London: Hutchinson.

Govindarajan, V. and Shank, J. K. (1989), 'Profit Variance Analysis: A Strategic Focus', *Issues in Accounting Education*, Vol. 4, No. 2, Fall, pp. 396–410.

Graf, F. (1967), A speech by the A. C. Nielsen Vice-President to a grocery manufacturers' executive conference, cited by G. T. Gerlach and C. A. Wainwright (1968), *Successful Management of New Products*, New York: Hastings House, pp. 125–6.

Grashof, J. F. (1975), 'Conducting and Using a Marketing Audit' in McCarthy, E. J., Grashof, J. F. and Brogowicz, A. A. (eds) (1975), *Readings in Basic Marketing*, Homewood, Illinois: Irwin.

Green, P., Faris, P. and Wind, Y. (1968), 'The Determinants of Vendor Selection: the Evaluation Function Approach', *Journal of Purchasing*, Vol. 4, August.

Greenley, G. E. (1986a), *The Strategic and Operational Planning of Marketing*, London: McGraw-Hill.

Greenley, G. E. (1986b), 'The Interface of Strategic and Marketing Plans', *Journal of General Management*, Vol. 12, No. 1, pp. 54–62.

Greenwood, R. G. (1974), *Managerial Decentralization: A Study of the General Electric Philosophy*, Lexington, Mass: D.C. Heath.

Griffith, I. (1986) 'Cost-Cutting Doesn't Move Merchandise', *Financial Decisions*, October, pp. 77, 78, 80, 82.

Griffith, I. (1991), 'Marketing Needs New Sales Pitch', *The Sunday Times*, 7 July, p. 4.13.

Groönroos, C. (1983), *Strategic Management and Marketing in the Service Sector*, Bromley: Chartwell-Bratt.

Grundy, A. (1986), 'Why Accountants and Marketing Men Should Be Friends', *Certified Accountant*, November, pp. 12–15.

Guiltinan, J. P. and Paul G. W. (1988), *Marketing Management: Strategies and Programs*, New York: McGraw-Hill. 3rd edition.

Gummeson, E. (1987), The New Marketing – Developing Long-Term Interactive Relationships, *Long Range Planning*, Vol. 20, No. 4, pp. 10–20.

Hakansson, H. (ed.) (1981), *International Marketing and Purchasing of Industrial Goods: an Interaction Approach*, Chichester: John Wiley.

Hakansson, H., et al. (1979), 'Industrial Marketing as an Organizational Problem', *European Journal of Marketing*, Vol. 13, No. 3, pp. 81–93.

Haley, R. J. (1963), 'Benefit Segmentation: a Decision Orientated Research Tool', *Journal of Marketing*, Vol. 27, No. 3, July.

Haller, T. (1980a), 'An Organization Structure to Help You in the 1980s', *Advertising Age*, Vol. 51, No. 36, pp. 45–6.

Haller, T. (1980b), Strategic Planning: Key to Corporate Power for Marketers', *Marketing Times*, Vol. 27, No. 3, pp. 18–24.

Hambrick, D. G. and Cannella, A. A. (1989), 'Strategy Implementation as Substance and Selling', *The Academy of Management Executive*, Vol. 3, No. 4, November, pp. 278–85.

Hamel, G. and Prahalad, C. K. (1994), *Competing For The Future: breakthrough strategies for seizing control of your industry and creating the markets of tomorrow*, Boston, Mass.: Harvard Business School Press.

Hammer, M. and Champy, J. (1993), *Re-engineering the Corporation*, New York: Harper Collins.

Hamermesh, R. G., Anderson, M. J. and Harris, J. E. (1978), 'Strategies for Low Market Share Businesses', *Harvard Business Review*, Vol. 65, No. 3, May–June, pp. 95–102.

Handy, C. (1991) *The Age of Unreason*, London: Random House.

Handy, C. (1994), *The Empty Raincoat: Making Sense of the Future*, London: Random House.

Harding, M. (1966), 'Who Really Makes the Purchasing Decision?', *Industrial Marketing*, September, p. 76.

Harris, D. (1990) 'British Shoe Exports Shine', *The Times*, 5 March, 1990, p. 41.

Hart, N. A. (1978), *Industrial Advertising and Publicity*, London: Associated Business Programmes. 2nd edition.

Hartley, R. F. (1995), *Marketing Mistakes*, New York: Wiley, (6th edition).

Hartman, B. P. (1983), 'The Management Accountant's Role in Deleting a Product Line', *Management Accounting*, (NAA), Vol. 65, No. 2, August, pp. 63–6.

Harvey-Jones, Sir J. (1988), *Making it Happen*, London: Collins.

Haspelagh, P. (1982), 'Portfolio Planning: Its Uses and Limits', *Harvard Business Review*, Vol. 60, No. 1, January–February, pp. 58–73.

Hay Management Consultants (1989), *Headlines 2 000: The World as We See It*, London: Hay.

Hayhurst, R. and Wills, G. S. C. (1972), *Organizational Design for Marketing Futures*, London: Allen & Unwin,

Head, V. (1981), *Sponsorship: The Newest Marketing Skill*, Woodhead-Faulkner in association with the Institute of Marketing.

Hedley, B. (1977), 'Strategy and the Business Portfolio', *Long Range Planning*, Vol. 10, No. 1, pp. 9–15.

Heller, R. (1990), 'Pinstripe Devils', *Management Today*, September, p. 36.

Henderson, B. D. (1981), 'Understanding the Forces of Strategic and Natural Competition', *Journal of Business Strategy*, Vol. 2, Winter, pp. 11–15.

Henderson, B. D. (1982), *Henderson on Corporate Strategy*, New York: Mentor.

Henderson, B. D. (1984), *The Logic of Business Strategy*, Cambridge, Mass.: Ballinger.

Hendon, D. W. (1979), 'A New Empirical Look at the Influences of Reference Groups on Generic Product Strategy and Brand Choice: Evidence from Two Nations', in Proceedings of the Academy of International Business, *Asia Pacific Dimensions of International Business*, Honolulu: College of Business, University of Hawaii, December, pp. 752–61.

Henley, D. S. (1976), 'Evaluating Product Line Performance: A Conceptual Approach', pp. II–10 and II–11 in *Multinational Product Management*, Cambridge, Mass: Marketing Science Institute.

Hersey, P. (1988), *Selling: A Behavioral Science Approach*, Englewood Cliffs, NJ: Prentice-Hall.

Hershey, R. (1980), 'Commercial Intelligence on a Shoe-String', *Harvard Business Review*, Vol. 58, No. 5, September–October, pp. 22–4, 28, 30.

Herzberg, F. (1966), *Work and the Nature of Man*, London: Collins.

Heskett, J. L. (1976), *Marketing*, New York: Macmillan.

Hill, R. W. (1972), 'The Nature of Industrial Buying Decisions', *Industrial Marketing Management*, Vol. 2, October, pp. 45–55.

Hirsch, R. (1990), 'Getting the Ratios Right', *Management Today*, April, pp. 107–8, 110.

Hise, R. T. and Strawser, R. H. (1970), 'Application of Capital Budgeting Techniques to Marketing Operations', *MSU Business Topics*, Vol. 18, No. 3, Summer, pp. 69–75.

Hitt, M. A. and Ireland, R. D. (1985), 'Corporate Distinctive Competence, Strategy, Industry and Performance', *Strategic Management Journal*, Vol. 6, pp. 273–93.

Hlavacek, J. D. (1974), 'Towards More Successful Venture Management', *Journal of Marketing*, Vol. 38, No. 4, pp. 56–60.

Hofer, C. W. and Schendel, D. E. (1978), *Strategy Formulation: Analytical Concepts*, New York: West.

Hofstede, G. H. (1968), *The Game of Budget Control*, London: Tavistock.

Holmes, G. and Smith, N. (1987), *Salesforce Incentives*, London: Heinemann.

Hood, P. (1983), 'Sales Promotion and Merchandising' in Hart, N. A. and O'Connor, J. (eds) (1983), *The Practice of Advertising*, London: Heinemann, 2nd edition.

Hooley, G. J. (1993), 'Market-Led Quality Management', *Journal of Marketing Management*, Vol. 9, No. 3, pp. 315–335.

Hooley, G. J. and Lynch, J. E. (1985) 'Marketing Lessons From the UK's High-Flying Companies', *Journal of Marketing Management*, Vol. 1, No. 1, pp. 65–74.

Hooley, G. J. and Saunders, J. A. (1993), *Competitive Position: The Key to Market Success*, London: Prentice Hall International.

Hooley, G. J., West, C. J. and Lynch, J. E. (1983), *Marketing Management Today*, Cookham, Berks: Chartered Institute of Marketing.

Hooley, G. J., West, C. J. and Lynch, J. E. (1984), *Marketing In the UK–A Survey of Current Practice and Performance*, Cookham, Berks: Chartered Institute of Marketing.

Hopkins, D. S. and Bailey, E. L. (1971), 'New Product Pressures', *The Conference Board Record*, June, pp. 16–24.

Howard, J. (1983), 'Marketing Theory of the Firm', *Journal of Marketing*, Vol. 47, No. 4, Fall. pp. 90–100.

Howard, K. (1972), 'Network Analysis and Marketing Decisions', *European Journal of Marketing*, Vol. 6, No. 4, Winter, pp. 270–80.

Howell, S. (1994), *Analysing your Competitor's Financial Strengths*, London: Pitman Publishing/Financial Times.

Huegy, H. W. (ed.) (1963), *The Conceptual Framework for a Science of Marketing*, Urbana, Illinois: University of Illinois.

Hughes, G. D. (1980), *Marketing Management: A Planning Approach*, Reading, Mass: Addison-Wesley.

Hulbert, J. M. and Toy, N. E. (1977), 'A Strategic Framework for Marketing Control', *Journal of Marketing*, Vol. 41, No. 2, April, pp. 12–20.

Hurst, E. G. Jr. (1982), 'Controlling Strategic Plans', Ch. 7, pp. 114–23, in Lorange (ed.) (1982).

Hussey, D. E. (1971), *Introducing Coporate Planning*, Oxford, Pergamon (4th edition 1991).

Hussey, D. E. (1985), 'Implementing Corporate Strategy: Using Management Education and Training', *Long Range Planning*, Vol. 18, No. 5, pp. 28–37.

Hussey, D. E. (1989), 'Management in the 1990s', *Management Training Update*, September.

Irvin, R. A. and Michaels, E. G. (1989), 'Core Skills: Doing the Right Thing Right', *The McKinsey Quarterly*, Summer, pp. 4–19.

Itami, H. (1977), *Adaptive Behavior: Management Control and Information Analysis*, Sarasota, Florida: American Accounting Association (Studies in Accounting Research, No. 15).

Jackson, K. F. (1975), *The Art of Solving Problems*, London: Heinemann.

Jacobson, R. and Aaker, D. A. (1985), 'Is Market Share All That It is Cracked Up To Be?', *Journal of Marketing*, Vol. 49, No. 4, Fall, pp. 11–22.

Jain, S. C. (1990), *Marketing Planning and Strategy*, Cincinnati, Ohio: South-Western Publishing Company.

James, B. G. (1966), 'Emotional Buying in Industrial Markets', *Scientific Business*, Vol. 3, No. 12, Spring, pp. 326–30.

James, B. G. (1985), *Business Wargames*, Harmondsworth: Penguin.

Jaworski, B. J. (1988), 'Toward a Theory of Marketing Control: Environmental Context, Control Types, and Consequences', *Journal of Marketing*, Vol. 52, No. 3, July, pp. 23–39.

Jaworski, B. J. and MacInnis, D. J. (1989), 'Marketing Jobs and Management Controls: Toward a Framework', *Journal of Marketing Research*, Vol. 26, No. 4, pp. 406–19.

Jefkins, F. (1986), *Planned Press and Public Relations*, Glasgow: Blackie, 2nd edition.

Jefkins, F. (1990), *Modern Marketing Communications*, Glasgow: Blackie.

Jenster, P. V. (1987), 'Using Critical Success Factors in Planning', *Long Range Planning*, Vol. 20, No. 4, pp. 102–9.

Johnson, G. and Scholes, K. (1988), *Exploring Corporate Strategy*, London: Prentice-Hall. 2nd edition.

Johnson, H. G. (1967), 'Key Item Control', *Management Services*, Vol. 4, No. 1, January–February, pp. 21–6.

Johnson, H. G. and Flodhammer, A. (1980), 'Industrial Customer Segmentation', *Industrial Marketing Management*, Vol. 9, July, pp. 201–5.

Johnson, R. A., Kast, F. E. and Rosenzweig, J. E. (1973), *The Theory and Management of Systems*, New York: McGraw-Hill. 3rd edition.

Jones, C. M. (1986), 'GTE's Strategic Tracking System', *Planning Review*, Vol. 14, No. 5, September–October, pp. 27–30.

Jones, G. R. and Butler, J. E. (1988), 'Costs, Revenue and Business-Level Strategy', *Academy of Management Review*, Vol. 13, No. 2, April, pp. 202–13.

Jones, L. (1988), 'Competitor Cost Analysis at Caterpillar', *Management Accounting*, (NAA), Vol. 70, No. 4, October, pp. 32–8.

Joseph, L. and Yorke, D. (1989), 'Know Your Game Plan', *Quarterly Review of Marketing*, Vol. 15, No. 1, Autumn, pp. 8–13.

Kahaner, L. (1996), *Competitive Intelligence*, New York: Simon and Schuster.

Kahneman, D. and Tversky, A. (1984), 'Choices, Values and Frames', *American Psychologist*, Vol. 39, pp. 341–50.

Kaplan, R. S. and Norton, D. P. (1992), 'The Balanced Scorecard – Measures that Drive Performance', *Harvard Business Review*, Vol. 70, No. 1, January–February, pp. 71–9.

Kaplan, R. S. and Norton, D. P. (1993), 'Putting the Balanced Scorecard to Work', *Harvard Business Review*, Vol. 71, No. 5, September–October.

Kaplan, R. S. and Norton, D. P. (1996), *The Balanced Scorecard*, Boston, Mass.: Harvard Business School Press.

Kashani, K. (1996), 'A New Future for Brands' *Financial Times, Mastering Management*', Part 3, pp. 7–8.

Kay, J. (1993), *Foundations of Corporate Success: How Business Strategies Add Value*, Oxford: OUP.

Keiser, B. E. (1987), 'Practical Competitor Intelligence', *Planning Review*, Vol. 15, No. 5, September–October, pp. 14–18.

Kelley, W. J. (1972), *Marketing Planning and Competitive Strategy*, Englewood Cliffs, NJ: Prentice-Hall.

Kelly, J. M. (1987), *How to Check Out your Competition*, New York: Wiley.

Kerin, R. A. and Peterson, R. A. (1993), *Strategic Marketing Problems: Cases and Comments*, Boston, Mass.: Allyn and Bacon (6th edition).

Kerin, R. A., Mahajan, V. and Varadarajan, P. R. (1990), *Contemporary Perspectives on Strategic Market Planning*, Englewood Cliffs. N.J: Prentice Hall.

Kettlewood, K. (1973), 'Source Loyalty in the Freight Transport Market', Unpublished MSc Dissertation, UMIST.

Kight, L. K. (1989), 'The Search for Intelligence on Divisions and Subsidiaries', *Planning Review*, Vol. 17, No. 3, May–June, pp. 40–1.

King, S. (1991), 'Brand-building in the 1990s', *Journal of Marketing Management*, Vol. 7, No. 1, January, pp. 3–13.

King, W. (1968), 'A Conceptual Framework For Advertising Agency Compensation', *Journal of Marketing Research*, Vol. 5, No. 2, May, pp. 177–80.

Kjaer-Hanson, M. (ed.) (1965), *Cost Problems in Modern Marketing*, Amsterdam: North-Holland.

Klein, H. E. and Linneman, R. E. (1984), 'Environmental Assessment: An International Study of Corporate Practice', *Journal of Business Strategy*, Vol. 5, Summer, pp. 66–75.

Kling, N. D. (1985), 'The Marketing Audit: An Extension of the Marketing Control Process', *Managerial Finance*, Vol. 11, No. 1, pp. 23–6.

Klir, G. J. and Valach, M. (1967), *Cybernetic Modelling*, London: Iliffe.

Kohli, A. K. and Jaworski, B. J. (1990) 'Market Orientation: the construct, research propositions and managerial implications', *Journal of Marketing*, Vol. 54, April, pp. 1–18.

Kortge, G. D. (1984), 'Inverted Break-even Analysis for Profitable Marketing Decisions', *Industrial Marketing Management*, Vol. 13, pp. 219–24.

Kotler, P. (1971), *Marketing Decision-Making: A Model-Building Approach*, New York: Holt, Rinehart & Winston.

Kotler, P. (1972), *Marketing Management: Analysis, Planning and Control*, Engelwood Cliffs, NJ: Prentice-Hall, 2nd edition.

Kotler, P. (1972), 'What Consumerism Means for Marketers', *Harvard Business Review*, Vol. 50, No. 3, May–June, pp. 48–57.

Kotler, P. (1977), 'From Sales Obsession to Marketing Effectiveness', *Harvard Business Reveiw*, Vol. 55, No. 6, November–December, pp. 67–75.

Kotler, P. (1980), *Marketing Management: Analysis, Planning and Control*, Engelwood Cliffs, NJ: Prentice-Hall, 4th edition.

Kotler, P. (ed.) (1984), *Marketing Management and Strategy: A Reader*, Engelwood Cliffs, NJ: Prentice-Hall, 5th edition.

Kotler, P. (1987), *Marketing: An Introduction*, Englewood Cliffs, NJ: Prentice-Hall.

Kotler, P. (1988), *Marketing Management: Analysis, Planning, Implementation and Control*, Engelwood Cliffs, NJ: Prentice-Hall, 6th edition.

Kotler, P. (1991), ,*Marketing Management: Analysis, Planning, Implementation and Control*, Englewood Cliffs, N. J., Prentice Hall, 7th edition.

Kotler, P. (1997), *Marketing Management: Analysis, Planning, Implementation and Control*, Upper Saddle River, N. J.: Prentice Hall, 9th edition.

Kotler, P., Fahey, L. and Jatusripitak, S. (1985), *The New Competition*, Engelwood Cliffs, NJ: Prentice-Hall.

Kotler, P., Gregor, W. T. and Rodgers, W. H. (1977), 'The Marketing Audit Comes of Age', *Sloan Management Review*, Vol. 18, No. 2, Winter, pp. 25–43.

Kotler, P., Gregor, W. T. and Rodgers, W. H. (1989), 'The Marketing Audit Comes of Age', *Sloan Management Review*, Vol. 30, No. 2, Winter, pp. 49–62.

Kuehn, A. A. (1961), 'A Model For Budgeting Advertising', in Bass, F. M., et al. (eds) (1961), *Models and Methods in Marketing*, Homewood, Illinois: Irwin.

Lalonde, B. J. and Zinszer, P. H. (1976), *Customer Service: Meaning and Measurement*, Chicago: NCPDM.

Lamb, R. and Shrivastava, P. (eds) (1986), *Advances in Strategic Management*, Greenwich, Conn: JAI Press. Volume 4.

Lambert, D. M. and Sterling, J. U. (1987), 'What Types of Profitability Reports Do Marketing Managers Receive?', *Industrial Marketing Management*, Vol. 16, pp. 295–303.

Lancaster, G. and Jobber, M. D. (1985) *Sales: Technique and Management*, London: MacDonald & Evans.

Lancaster, G. and Massingham, L. (1988), *Essential of Marketing: Text and Cases*, London: McGraw-Hill.

Langrish, J., Gibbons, M., Evans, W. G. and Jevon, F. R. (1972), *Wealth from Knowledge–Studies of Innovation in Industry*, London: Macmillan.

Lawrence, P. R. and Lorsch, J. (1967), *Organization and Environment*, Boston, Mass: Harvard University Press.

Lazer, W. (1962a), 'The Role of Models in Marketing', *Journal of Marketing*, Vol. 26, No. 2, April, pp. 9–14.

Lazer, W. (1962b), 'The Systems Concept in the Evolution of Marketing Management Thought' in *Marketing Precision and Executive Action*–Proceedings of 49th Annual Conference of the American Marketing Association.

Lehmann, D. R. and O'Shaughnessy, J. (1974), 'Differences in Attribute Importance for Different Industrial Products', *Journal of Marketing*, Vol. 38, No. 2, April, pp. 36–42.

Lehmann, D. R. and Winer, R. S. (1990), *Analysis for Marketing Planning*. Homewood Illinois: Irwin, 2nd edition.

Leidecker, J. K. and Bruno, A. V. (1984), 'Identifying and Using Critical Success Factors', *Long Range Planning*, Vol. 17, February, pp. 23–32.

Leppard, J. and McDonald, M. H. B. (1987), 'A Re-Appraisal of the Role of Marketing Planning', *Journal of Marketing Management*, Vol. 3, No. 2, pp. 159–71.

Levitt, T. (1960), 'Marketing Myopia', *Harvard Business Review*, Vol. 38, No. 4, July–August, pp. 45–56.

Levitt, T. (1966), 'Innovative Imitation', *Harvard Business Review*, Vol. 44, No. 5, September–October, p. 63.

Levitt, T. (1976), 'The Augmented Product Concept' in Ruthberg, R. R. (ed.) (1976), *Corporate Strategy and Product Innovation*, New York: Free Press.

Levitt, T. (1980), 'Marketing Success Through Differentiation–of Anything', *Harvard Business Review*, Vol. 58, No. 1, January–February, pp. 83–91.

Lewis, R. (1989), 'The Shape of Organisations to Come', *Management Training Update*, December.

Lewis, R. W. (1955), 'Measuring, Reporting and Appraising Results of Operations with Reference to Goals, Plans and Budgets' in *Planning, Managing and Measuring: A Case Study of Management Planning and Control at General Electric Company*, New York: The Controllership Foundation.

Lieberman, M. B. (1987), 'The Learning Curve, Diffusion, and Competitive Strategy', *Strategic Management Journal*, Vol. 8, pp. 441–52.

Little, Arthur D. (1974), see Patel, P. and Younger, M. (1978), 'A Frame of Reference for Strategy Development', *Long Range Planning*, Vol. 11, No. 2, April, pp. 6–12.

Little, J. D. C. (1966), 'A Model of Adaptive Control of Promotional Spending', *Operations Research*, Vol. 14, No. 6, pp. 1075–97.

Littler, D. and Wilson, D. (eds) (1995), *Marketing Strategy*, Oxford: Butterworth-Heinemann.

Litwin, G., Bray, J. and Brooke, K. L. (1996), *Mobilizing the Organization: Bringing Strategy to Life*, London: Prentice Hall.

Lorange, P. (ed.) (1982), *Implementation of Strategic Planning*, Engelwood Cliffs, NJ: Prentice-Hall.

Lowe, E. A. (1971), 'On the Definition of "Systems" in Systems Engineering', *Journal of Systems Engineering*, Vol. 2, No. 1, Summer, pp. 95–8.

Lowe, E. A. and Machin, J. L. J. (eds) (1983), *New Perspectives in Mangement Control*, London: Macmillan.

Lowe, E. A. and Shaw, R. W. (1968), 'An Analysis of Managerial Biasing: Evidence from a Company's Budgeting Process', *Journal of Management Studies*, Vol. 5, No. 3, October, pp. 304–15.

Luck, D. J. and Ferrell, O. C. (1979), *Marketing Strategy and Plans*, Engelwood Cliffs, NJ: Prentice-Hall.

Luck, D. J., Ferrell, O. C. and Lucas, G. S. (1989), *Marketing Strategy and Plans*, Engelwood Cliffs, NJ: Prentice-Hall. 3rd edition.

Lunn, A., Blamires, C. and Browne, P. (1996), 'The Revitalisation of Mothercare' proceedings of The Market Research Society Annual Conference.

Lyles, M. A. (1987), 'Defining Strategic Problems: Subjective Criteria of Excellence', *Organization Studies*, Vol. 8, No. 3, pp. 263–80.

Lynch, R. (1992), *European Marketing: A Guide to the New Opportunities*, London: Kogan Page.

Lynch, J. E., Hooley, G. J. and Shepherd, J. (1988), *The Effectiveness of British Marketing*, University of Bradford Management Centre.

McCammon, B. C. Jr. (1970). 'Perspectives for Distribution Programming', in L. P. Bucklin (ed.) (1970), Glenview, Illinois: Scott, Foresman.

McCarry, C. (1972), *Citizen Nader*, London: Jonathan Cape.

McCarthy, M. J. and Perreault, W. D. Jr. (1990), *Essentials of Marketing: A Global-Managerial Approach*, Homewood, Ill.: Irwin.

McClelland, D. C. (1961), *The Achieving Society*, New York: Free Press.

McColl-Kennedy, J. R., Yau, O. H. and Kiel, G. C. (1990), 'Marketing Planning Practices in Australia: A Comparision Across Company Types', *Marketing Intelligence and Planning*, Vol. 8, No. 4, pp. 21–9.

McDonald, M. H. B. (1984), *Marketing Plans: How to Prepare Them, How to Use Them*, London: Heinemann.

McDonald, M. H. B. (1989), 'Ten Barriers to Marketing Planning', *Journal of Marketing Management*, Vol. 5, No. 1, pp. 1–18.

McDonald, M. H. B. (1990), 'SMEs – twelve factors for success in the 1990's', *Business Growth and Profitability*, Vol. 1, No. 1, pp. 11–19.

McDonald, M. H. B. (1995), *Marketing Plans: How to Prepare Them, How to Use Them*, Oxford: Butterworth-Heinemann, third edition.

McDonald, M. H. B. and Wilson, H. N. (1990), 'State-of-the-Art Developments in Expert Systems and Strategic Marketing Planning', *British Journal of Management*, Vol. 1, No. 3, September, pp. 159–70.

McGonagale, J. J. and Vella, C. M. (1993), *Outsmarting the Competition*, London: McGraw-Hill.

McGraw-Hill (1963), *Special Report on the Buying and Selling Techniques in the British Engineering Industry*, London: McGraw-Hill.

McGraw-Hill (1963), *How Advertising Affects the Cost of Selling*, London: McGraw-Hill.

McGuire, J., Schneeweis, T. and Hill, J. (1986), 'An Analysis of Alternative Measures of Strategic Performance', pp. 127–54 in Lamb and Shrivastava (eds) (1986).

McKay, E. S. (1972), *The Marketing Mystique*, New York: American Management Association.

McKenna, R. (1991), *Relationship Marketing*, Reading, Mass.: Addison Wesley.

MacLuhan, M. (1964), *Understanding Media: the Extension of Man*, London: Routledge.

MacLuhan, M. (1968), *The Medium is the Message*, New York: Random House.

McNamee, P. (1988), *Management Accounting: Strategic Planning and Marketing*, Oxford: Heinemann.

MacNeill, D. J. (1994), *Customer Service Excellence*, New York: American Media Inc.

McTavish, R. (1989), 'Implementing Marketing Strategy', *Management Decision*, Vol. 26, No. 5, pp. 9–12.

Machin, J. L. J. (1983), 'Management Control Systems: Whence & Whither?' Ch. 2, pp. 22–42, in Lowe and Machin (eds) (1983).

Maciariello, J. A. (1984), *Management Control Systems*, Englewood Cliffs, NJ: Prentice-Hall.

Madrick, J. G. (1995), *The End of Affluence: The Causes and Consequences of America's Economic Decline*, New York: Random House.

Magrath, A. J. (1988) 'People Productivity: Marketing's Most Valuable Asset', *Journal of Business Strategy*, Vol. 9, No. 4, pp. 12–14.

Magrath, A. J. and Hardy, K. G. (1986), 'Cost Containment in Marketing', *Journal of Business Strategy*, Vol. 7, No. 2, pp. 14–21.

Majaro, S. (1972), 'A Market Strategy for Europe', in Blake, J. E. (ed.) (1972), *Design For European Markets: A Management Guide*, London: Design Council.

Majaro, S. (1978), *International Marketing*, London: George Allen and Unwin.

Makens, J. C. (1989), *The 12-Day Marketing Plan*, Wellingborough: Thorsons.

Mann, N. R. (1989), *The Keys to Excellence: The Deming Philosophy*, London: Mercury.

Mansfield, E. and Wagner, S. (1975) 'Organizational and Strategic Factors Associated with Possibilities of Success in Industrial R&D', *Journal of Business*, April, pp. 179–98.

March, J. G. and Simon, H. A. (1958), *Organizations*, New York: Wiley (2nd edition 1993, Cambridge, Mass.: Blackwell).

Market Research Society (1990), *Occupational Groupings: A Job Dictionary*, London: MRS.

Markovitz, Z. N. (1987), 'Hidden Sector Competitor Analysis', *Planning Review*, Vol. 15, No. 5, pp. 20–4, 46.

Martilla, J. C. (1971), ' "Word of Mouth" Communication in the Industrial Adoption Process', *Journal of Marketing Research*, Vol. 3, No. 2, pp. 173–8.

Maslow, A. E. (1954), *Motivation and Personality*, New York: Harper & Row.

Mathur, S. S. (1986), 'Strategy: Framing Business Intentions', *Journal of General Management*, Vol. 12, No. 1, pp. 77–97.

Mehotra, S. (1984), 'How to Measure Marketing Productivity', *Journal of Advertising Research*, Vol. 24, No. 3, pp. 9–15.

Meldrum, M. J., Ward, K. and Srikanthan, S. (1987), 'Needs, Issues and Directions in the Marketing Accountancy Divide', *Quarterly Review of Marketing*, Vol. 12, Nos. 3–4, pp. 5–12.

Meldrum, M. J., Ward, K. and Srikanthan, S. (1986), 'Can You Really Account for Marketing?', *Marketing Intelligence & Planning*, Vol. 4, No. 4, pp. 39–45.

Merchant, K. A. (1985), *Control in Business*, Boston: Pitman.

Merchant, K. A. (1988), 'Progressing Toward a Theory of Marketing Control: A Comment', *Journal of Marketing*, Vol. 52, No. 3, pp. 40–4.

Miles, R. E. (1980), *Macro Organisational Behavior*, Glenview, Illinois: Scott, Foresman.

Miles, R. E. and Snow, C. C. (1978), *Organizational Strategy, Structure & Process*, New York: McGraw-Hill.

Milton, F. and Reiss, T. (1985), 'Competitive Strategy', *Accountancy Ireland*, Vol. 17, No. 5, pp. 13–17.

Milton, F. and Reiss, T. (1985), 'Developing a Competitive Strategy', *Accountancy Ireland*, Vol. 17, No. 5, pp. 19–23, 28.

Mintel Report (1988), 'Retailing: The Non-Store Alternatives–1987', London: Mintel.

Mintzberg, H. (1987), 'Crafting Strategy', *Harvard Business Review*, Vol. 65, No. 4, pp. 66–75.

Mintzberg, H. (1994), *The Rise and Fall of Strategic Planning: Reconceiving Roles for Planning, Plans, Planners*, New York: The Free Press.

Mitchell, A. (1995), 'Missing Measures', *Management Today*, November, pp. 76–8, 80.

Montgomery, D. B. and Urban, G. L. (1969), *Management Science in Marketing*, Englewood Cliffs, NJ: Prentice Hall.

Montgomery, D. B. and Urban, G. L. (eds) (1969), *Applications of Management Science in Marketing*, Englewood Cliffs, NJ: Prentice Hall.

Morgan, N. A. and Piercy, N. F. (1996), 'Competitive Advantage, Quality Strategy and the Role of Marketing', *British Journal of Management*, Vol. 7, pp. 231–245.

Morrison, A. and Wensley, J. R. C. (1991), 'Boxing Up or Boxed In?: A Short History of the Boston Consulting Group Share/Growth Matrix', *Journal of Marketing Management*, Vol. 7, No. 2, pp. 105–29.

Mossman, F. H., Fischer, P. M. and Crissy, W. J. E. (1974), 'New Approaches to Analyzing Marketing Profitability', *Journal of Marketing*, Vol. 38, No. 2, pp. 43–8.

Mossman, F. H. and Worrell, M. L. (1966), 'Analytical Methods of Measuring Marketing Profitability: A Matrix Approach', *MSU Business Topics*, Vol. 14, No. 4, pp. 35–45.

Mowen, J. C. and Gaeth, G. J. (1992), 'The Evaluation Stage in Marketing Decision Making', *Journal of the Academy of Marketing Science*, Vol. 20, No. 2, pp. 178–188.

Mulvaney, J. (1969), *The Use of Network Analysis in Marketing*, Cookham: Chartered Institute of Marketing.

Munro, R. J. B. and Cooper, P. (1989), 'The Impact of Changes in Strategic Thinking on Management Control Systems: the Selection of Non-Financial Measure in a Functional Structure'. Paper given at the Annual Conference of the British Accounting Association, University of Bath, March.

Murray, J. A. and O'Driscoll, A. (1996), *Strategy and Process in Marketing*, London: Prentice Hall.

Myers, J. H. and Samli, A. C. (1969), 'Management Control of Marketing Research', *Journal of Marketing Research*, Vol. 6, No. 3, pp. 267–77.

Myers, S. and Marquis, D. G. (1969), *Successful Industrial Innovations: a Study of Factors Underlying Innovations in Selected Firms*, New York: National Science Foundation.

Nagle, T. T. (1987), *The Strategies and Tactics of Pricing*, Englewood Cliffs, NJ: Prentice-Hall.

Naisbitt, J. and Aburdene, P. (1982), *Megatrends: Ten New Directions Transforming Our Lives*, New York: Warner Books.

Naisbitt, J. and Aburdene, P. (1990), *Megatrends 2000*, London: Sidgwick & Jackson.

Narver, J. C. and Savit, R. (1971), *The Marketing Economy*, New York: Holt, Rinehart & Winston.

Narver, J. C. and Slater, S. F. (1990) 'The Effect of a Market Orientation on Business Profitability', *Journal of Marketing*, Vol. 54, October, pp. 20–35.

Nathanson, D. A., Kazanjian, R. K. and Galbraith, J. R. (1982), 'Effective Strategic Planning and the Role of Organization Design', Chapter 6 (pp. 91–113) in Lorange, P. (ed.).

Naumann, E. (1995), 'Creating Customer Value: the path to sustainable competitive advantage', *National Productivity Review*, Vol. 14, No. 1, pp. 16–17.

Nicosia, F. M. (1966), *Consumer Decision Processes*, Englewood Cliffs, NJ: Prentice Hall.

Nilson, T. H. (1995), *Chaos Marketing: how to win in a turbulent world*, Maidenhead: McGraw-Hill.

Nonaka, I. and Nicosia, F. M. (1979), 'Marketing Management, its Environment and Information Processing: A Problem of Organization Design', *Journal of Business Research*, Vol. 7, No. 4, pp. 277–301.

Nutt, P. C. (1987), 'Identifying and Appraising How Managers Install Strategy', *Strategic Management Journal*, Vol. 8, pp. 1–14.

Nutt, P. C. (1989), 'Selecting Tactics to Implement Strategic Plans', *Strategic Management Journal*, Vol. 10, pp. 145–61.

Oakland, J. S. (1989), *Total Quality Management*, Oxford: Butterworth-Heinemann.

O'Brien, S. and Ford, R. (1988), 'Can We at Last Say Goodbye to Social Class?', *Journal of the Market Research Society*, Vol. 30, No. 3, pp. 289–332.

Ogilvy, D. (1964), *Confessions of an Advertising Man*, London: Longmans Green.

Ohmae, K. (1983), *The Mind of the Strategist*, London: Penguin.

Olins, W. (1989), *Corporate Personality – an Enquiry into the Nature of Corporate Identity*, London: Wolff Olins.

Olins, W. (1989), *Corporate Identity*, London: Thames & Hudson.

Openshaw, S. (1989), 'Making Geodemographics More Sophisticated' *Journal of the Market Research Society*, Vol. 31, No. 1, pp. 111–31.

O'Shaughnessy, J. (1995), *Competitive Marketing: A Strategic Approach*, London: Routledge (3rd edition).

Otley, D. T. and Berry, A. J. (1980), 'Control, Organization and Accounting', *Accounting, Organizations and Society*, Vol. 5, No. 2, pp. 231–46.

Ouchi, W. (1983), *Theory Z*, Reading, Mass: Addison-Wesley.

Oxenfeldt, A. R. (1973), 'A Decision Making Structure for Price Decisions', *Journal of Marketing*, Vol. 37, No. 1, January, pp. 48–54.

Packard, V. (1957), *The Hidden Persuaders*, Harmondsworth: Penguin Books.

Palin, R. (1985), 'Operational PR' in Howards, W. (ed.) (1985), *The Practice of Public Relations*, London: Heinemann.

Parkinson, S. (1995), *Manufacturing – The Marketing Solution*, Cookham: The Chartered Institute of Marketing.

Pascale, R. T. (1990), *Managing on the Edge: how successful companies use conflict to stay ahead*. New York: Simon and Schuster.

Pearson, G. J. (1979), 'Setting Corporate Objectives as a Basis for Action', *Long Range Planning*, Vol. 12, August, pp. 13–19.

Pearson, G. J. (1993), 'Business Orientation: Cliché or Substance?', *Journal of Marketing Management*, Vol. 9, No. 3, July, pp. 233–243.

Peattie, K. J. and Notley, D. S. (1989), 'The Marketing and Strategic Planning Interface', *Journal of Marketing Management*, Vol. 4, No. 3, pp. 330–49.

Peters, T. J. (1992) *Liberation Management*, New York: Knopf.

Peters, T. J. and Waterman, R. H. (1982), *In Search of Excellence: Lessons from America's Best Run Companies*, New York: Harper & Row.

Pettigrew, A. M. (1975), 'The Industrial Purchasing Decision as a Political Process', *European Journal of Marketing*, Vol. 9, No. 1, pp. 4–19.

Pfeffer, J. (1978), *Organizational Design*, Arlington Heights, Illinois: AHM.

Piercy, N. F. (1985), *Marketing Organisation: An Analysis of Information Processing, Power and Politics*, London: Allen & Unwin.

Piercy, N. F. (1986), *Marketing Budgeting*, London: Croom Helm.

Piercy, N. F. (1987), 'Servicing the Needs of Marketing Management', *Management Accounting*, (CIMA), Vol. 65, No. 3, March, pp. 42–3.

Piercy, N. F. (1987), 'The Marketing Budgeting Process: Marketing Management Implications', *Journal of Marketing*, Vol. 51, No. 4, October, pp. 45–9.

Piercy, N. F. (1991), *Market-led Strategic Change*, London: Thorsons.

Piercy, N. F. and Morgan, N. (1989a), 'Good Plans Need Internal Marketing', *The Sunday Times*, 10 September, p. E1.

Piercy, N. F. and Morgan, N. (198b), 'Learning to Love the Marketing Task', *The Sunday Times*, 12 November, p. E14.

Piercy, N. F. and Morgan, N. (1990), 'Making Marketing Strategies Happen in the Real World', *Marketing Business*, Issue 9, February, pp. 20–1.

Piercy, N. F. and Morgan, N. A. (1994), 'The Marketing Planning Process: Behavioral Problems Compared to Analytical Techniques and Explaining Marketing Plan Credibility', *Journal of Business Research*, Vol. 29, pp. 167–178.

Pilcher, R. (1989), 'Managing Exports Effectively', *Accountancy*, Vol. 103, No. 1148, April, pp. 75–8.

Pilditch, J. (1987), 'Winning Companies Concentrate on Their People and Products', *The Times*, 25 June, p. 29.

Planning Review: Competitve Intelligence Issues: Vol. 15, No. 5, September–October 1987; Vol. 17, No. 3, May–June 1989.

Platchta, J. (1990), 'Does Sweet Talk Pay?', *Management Today*, March, pp. 91–2, 94.

Ploos Van Austel, M. J. (1987), 'Physical Distribution Cost Control', *International Journal of Physical Distribution and Materials Management*, Vol. 17, No. 2, pp. 67–78.

Poczter, A. and Siegel, J. G. (1986), 'How to Finance Your Marketing Strategy', *FE*, Vol. 2, No. 2, February, pp. 41–4.

Polli, R. and Cook, V. (1969), 'The Validity of the Product Life Cycle', *Journal of Business*, Vol. 42, No. 4, October, pp. 385–400.

Porter, L. M. and Roberts, K. H. (eds) (1977), *Communication in Organizations*, Harmondsworth: Penguin.

Porter, M. E. (1979), 'How Competitive Forces Shape Strategy', *Harvard Business Review*, Vol. 57, No. 2, March–April, pp. 137–45.

Porter, M. E. (1980), *Competitive Strategy*, New York: Free Press.

Porter, M. E. (1985), 'How to Attack the Industry Leader', *Fortune*, Vol. 111, 29 April, pp. 97–9, 102, 104.

Porter, M. E. (1985), *Competitive Advantage: Creating and Sustaining Superior Performance*, New York: Free Press.

Porter, M. E. (1990), *The Competitive Advantage of Nations*, New York: Free Press.

Posner, M. (1986), 'Sales and Finance Staff Should Harmonise', *Accountancy*, Vol. 98, No. 1116, August, pp. 113–14.

Powers, T. L. (1987), 'Breakeven Analysis with Semifixed Costs', *Industrial Marketing Management*, Vol. 16, No. 1, February, pp. 35–42.

Prescott, J. E. (ed.) (1989), *Advances in Competitor Intelligence*, Vienna, Virginia: Society of Competitor Intelligence Professionals.

Prescott, J. E., Kohli, A. K. and Venkatraman, N. (1986), 'The Market Share–Profitability Relationship: An Empirical Assessment of Major Assertions and Contradictions', *Strategic Management Journal*, Vol. 7, No. 4, July–August, pp. 377–94.

Prescott, J. E. and Smith, D. C. (1989), 'The Largest Survey of 'Leading Edge' Competitor Intelligence Managers', *Planning Review*, Vol. 17, No. 3, May–June, pp. 6–13.

Project SAPPHO (n.d.) *A Study of Success and Failure in Innovation*, Science Policy Research Unit, University of Sussex.

Puxty, A. G. and Dodds, J. C. (1991), *Financial Management: Method and Meaning*, London: Chapman & Hall. 2nd edition.

Pyne, F. G. (1984), 'Better, Operating Statements for the Marketing Director', *Accountancy*, Vol. 95, No. 1086, February, pp. 87–90.

Pyne, F. G. (1985), 'Accountancy that Helps to Meet and Beat Competition', *Accountancy*, Vol. 96, No. 1104, August, pp. 104 -7.

Quelch, J. A., Buzzell, R. D. and Salama, E. R. (1990), *The Marketing Challenge of 1992*, Reading, Mass: Addison-Wesley.

Rabino, S. and Wright, A. (1984), 'Applying Financial Portfolio and Multiple Criteria Approaches to Product Line Decisions', *Industrial Marketing Management*, Vol. 13, pp. 233–40.

Rafiq, M. and Ahmed, P. K. (1993), 'The Scope of Internal Marketing: Defining the Boundary Between Marketing and Human Resource Management', *Journal of Marketing Management*, Vol. 9, No. 3, pp. 219–232.

Rapp, S. and Collins, T. L. (1987), *Maxi Marketing*, New York: McGraw-Hill.

Rapp, S. and Collins, T. L. (1990), *The Great Marketing Turnaround: The Age of the Individual and How to Profit From It*, Englewood Cliffs, N.J.: Prentice Hall.

Rappaport, A. (1967), 'Sensitivity Analysis in Decision-Making', *The Accounting Review*, Vol. 42, No. 3, July, pp. 441–56.

Rappaport, A. (1986), *Creating Shareholder Value: The New Standard for Business Performance*, New York: Free Press.

Ratnatunga, J. T. D. (1983), *Financial Controls in Marketing: The Accounting-Marketing Interface*, Canberra: Canberra College of Advanced Education.

Ratnatunga, J. T. D. (1988), *Accounting for Competitive Marketing*, London: CIMA (Occasional Paper Series).

Reading, B. (1988), 'Why it's Time for Us to Save', *The Sunday Times*, 11 December.

Reed, R. and Buckley, M. R. (1988), 'Strategy in Action–Techniques for Implementing Strategy', *Long Range Planning*, Vol. 21, No. 3, pp. 67–74.

Reeves, R. (1961), *Reality in Advertising*, New York: Knopf.

Reid, D. M. (1989), 'Operationalizing Strategic Planning', *Strategic Management Journal*, Vol. 10, pp. 553–67.

Reid, D. M. and Hinckley, L. C. (1989), 'Strategic Planning: The Cultural Impact', *Marketing Intelligence and Planning*, Vol. 7, No. 11/12, pp. 4 -11.

Reimann, B. C. (1989), *Managing for Value*, Oxford: Basil Blackwell.

Resnik, A. J., Turney, P. B. B. and Mason, J. B. (1979), 'Marketers Turn to Countersegmentation', *Harvard Business Review*, Vol. 57, No. 5, September–October, pp. 100–6.

Rhyne, L. C. (1986), 'The Relationship of Strategic Planning to Financial Performance', *Strategic Management Journal*, Vol. 7, pp. 423–36.

Richards, M. (1978), *Organizational Goal Structures*, St Paul, Minnesota: West Publishing Company.

Richardson, P. R. (1988), *Cost Containment: The Ultimate Advantage*, New York: Free Press.

Richardson, W. and Richardson, R. (1989), *Business Planning: a Strategic Approach to World Markets*, London: Pitman.

Ries, A. and Trout, J. (1982), *Positioning: the Battle for Your Mind*, New York: Warner Books.

Ries, A. and Trout, J. (1986), *Marketing Warfare*, New York: McGraw Hill.

Riesman, D., Glazer, N. and Dinny, R. (1950), *The Lonely Crowd*, Newhaven, Conn: Yale University Press.

Rivkin, J. (1995), *The End of Work: The Decline of the Global Labor Force and the Dawn of the Post-Market Era*, G. P. Putnam's Sons: New York.

Roach, J. D. C. (1981), 'From Strategic Planning to Strategic Performance: Closing the Achievement Gap', *Outlook*, Spring, New York: Booz, Allen & Hamilton.

Robert, M. M. (1990), 'Managing Your Competitor's Strategy', *Journal of Business Strategy*, Vol. 11, No. 2, pp. 24–8.

Robertson, R. S. (1967), 'The Process of Innovation and the Diffusion of Innovation', *Journal of Marketing*, Vol. 3, No. 1, January, pp. 14–19.

Robinson, P. J., Faris, C. W. and Wind, Y. (1967), *Industrial Buying and Creative Marketing*, Boston, Mass: Allyn & Bacon.

Robinson, S. J. Q., Hichens, R. E. and Wade, D. P. (1978), 'The Directional Policy Matrix–Tool for Strategic Planning', *Long Range Planning*, Vol. 11, No. 3, June, pp. 8–15.

Robinson, W. T. and Fornell, C. (1985), 'Market Pioneering and Sustainable Market Share Advantages', *PIMSletter*, 39, Cambridge, Mass: Strategic Planning Institute.

Robinson, W. T. and Fornell, C. (1985), 'Sources of Market Pioneer Advantages in Consumer Goods Industries', *Journal of Marketing Research*, Vol. 22, No. 3, August, pp. 305–17.

Rockart, J. F. (1979), 'Chief Executives Define Their Own Data Needs', *Harvard Business Review*, Vol. 57, No. 2, March–April, pp. 81–93.

Rodger, L. W. (1965), *Marketing in a Competitive Economy*, London: Hutchinson.

Rogers, E. M. (1962), *Diffusion of Innovations*, New York: Free Press.

Rosenbloom, B. (1995), 'Channel Management', Chapter 32, pp. 551–570, in M. J. Baker (ed.) (1995), *Companion Encyclopaedia of Marketing*, London: Routledge.

Rothman, L. J. (1989), 'Different Measures of Social Grade', *Journal of The Market Research Society*, Vol. 31, No. 1, pp. 139–40.

Rothschild, W. E. (1984), *How to Gain (and Maintain) the Competitive Advantage*, New York: McGraw-Hill.

Rothwell, R. (1972), Project SAPPHO: An Interim Report, Working Paper, Science Policy Unit, University of Sussex.

Rothwell, R. (1974), SAPPHO Updated–Project SAPPHO Phase II, *Research Policy*, Vol. 3, pp. 258–91.

Rothwell, R. (1977), 'The Characteristics of Successful Innovators and Technically Progressive Firms', *R & D Management*, Vol. 7, No. 3, pp. 191–206.

Ruekert, R. W., Walker, O. C. and Roering, K. J. (1985), 'The Organization of Marketing Activities: A Contingency Theory of Structure and Performance', *Journal of Marketing*, Vol. 49, pp. 13–25.

St. Thomas, C. E. (1965), *Practical Business Planning*, New York: AMA.

Salancik, G. R. and Upah, G. D. (1978), Directions for Interorganisational Marketing, Unpublished paper, University of Illinois, August.

Sanderson, S. M. and Luffman, G. A. (1988), 'Strategic Planning and Environmental Analysis', *European Journal of Marketing*, Vol. 22, No. 2, pp. 14–27.

Saunders, J. A. (1987), 'Marketing and Competitive Success' in Baker, M. J. (ed.) (1987), *The Marketing Book*, London: Macmillan.

Saunders, J. A. (1987), 'Attitudes, Structure and Behaviour in a Successful Company', *Journal of Marketing Management*, Vol. 3, No. 2, pp. 173–183.

Saunders, J. A., Saker, J. M., Smith, I. G. (eds.) (1996), 'Exploring Marketing Planning', Special Issue of *Journal of Marketing Management*, Vol. 12, Nos. 1–3.

Schaffir, K. H. and Trentin, H. G. (1973), *Marketing Information Systems*, New York: Amacom.

Scherer, F. M. (1980), *Industrial Market Structure and Economic Performance*, Chicago: Rand McNally. 2nd edition.

Schiff, M. and Mellman, M. (1962), *The Financial Management of the Marketing Function*, New York: FERF.

Schiffman, L. G. and Kanuk, L. L. (1983), *Consumer Behavior*, Englewood Cliffs, NJ: Prentice-Hall. 2nd edition.

Schmid, R. D. (1987), 'Reverse Engineering a Service Product', *Planning Review*, Vol. 15, No. 5, September–October, pp. 33–5.

Schoderbeck, P. P. (ed.) (1971), *Management Systems: A Book of Readings*, New York: Wiley. 2nd edition.

Schoderbek, P. P., Kefalas, A. G. and Schoderbek, C. G. (1975), *Management Systems: Conceptual Considerations*, Dallas: Business Publications.

Schoeffler, S. (1977), 'Market Position: Build, Hold or Harvest?', *The PIMSletter on Business Strategy*, No. 3, Cambridge, Mass: Strategic Planning Institute.

Schwartz, D. (1973), *Marketing Today*, New York: Harcourt, Brace, Jovanovich.

Schwartz, G. (ed.) (1965), *Science in Marketing*, New York: Wiley.

Sevin, C. H. (1965), *Marketing Productivity Analysis*, New York: McGraw-Hill.

Shapiro, B. P., et al. (1987), 'Manage Customers for Profits (Not Just Sales)', *Harvard Business Review*, Vol. 65, No. 5, September–October, pp. 101–8.

Shapiro, S. J. and Kirpalani, V. H. (eds) (1984), *Marketing Effectiveness*, Boston: Allyn & Bacon.

Shell Chemical Company (1975), *The Directional Policy Matrix: a New Aid to Corporate Planning*, London: Shell.

Sheth, J. N. (1969), *The Theory of Buyer Behavior*, New York: Wiley.

Sheth, J. N. (1973), 'Industrial Buyer Behavior', *Journal of Marketing*, Vol. 37, No. 4, October, pp. 50–6.

Shillinglaw, G. (1964), 'Divisional Performance Review: An Extension of Budgetary Control', in Bonini, C. P., Jaedicke, R. K. and Wagner, H. M. (eds) (1964).

Shuchman, A. (1950), 'The Marketing Audit: its Nature, Purposes and Problems', in Oxenfeldt, A. R., & Crisp, R. D. (eds) *Analysing and Improving Marketing Performance*, New York: American Management Association Report No. 32.

Simkin, L. (1996), 'People and Processes in Marketing Planning: The Benefits of Controlling Implementation', *Journal of Marketing Management*, Vol. 12, No. 5, July, pp. 375–390.

Simmonds, K. (1980), '*Strategic Mangement Accounting*', Paper presented to ICMA Technical Symposium, Oxford.

Simmonds, K. (1981), 'Strategic Management Accounting', *Management Accounting*, Vol. 59, No. 4, April, pp. 26–9. Reprinted in Cowe, R. (ed.) (1988), *Handbook of Management Accounting*, Aldershot: Gower (2nd edition) pp. 14–36.

Simmonds, K. (1982), 'Strategic Management Accounting for Pricing: A Case Example', *Accounting and Business Research*, Vol. 12, No. 47, Summer, pp. 206–14.

Simmonds, K. (1985), 'How to Compete', *Management Today*, August, pp. 39–43, 84.

Simmonds, K. (1986), 'The Accounting Assessment of Competitive Position', *European Journal of Marketing*, Vol. 20, No. 1, pp. 16–31.

Simmonds, K. (1989), 'Strategic Management Accounting: The Emerging Paradigm', Plenary lecture given at 12th Annual Conference of the European Accounting Association, University of Stuttgart, April.

Simmons, W. W. (1972), 'Practical Planning', *Long Range Planning*, Vol. 5, No. 2, June pp. 32–9.

Simms, J. (1995), 'Market or Die', *Marketing Business*, June, pp. 12–13.

Simon, H. A. (1960), *The New Science of Management Decision*, New York: Harper & Row.

Simons, R. (1987), 'Accounting Control Systems and Business Strategy: An Empirical Analysis', *Accounting, Organizations and Society*, Vol. 12, No. 4, pp. 357–74.

Simons, R. (1990), 'The Role of Management Control Systems in Creating Competitive Advantage: New Perspectives', *Accounting, Organizations and Society*, Vol. 15, Nos. 1/2, pp. 127–43.

Slevin, D. P. and Pinto, J. K. (1987), 'Balancing Strategy and Tactics in Project Implementation', *Sloan Management Review*, Vol. 29, No. 1, Fall, pp. 33–41.

Smith, D. C. and Prescott, J. E. (1987), 'Demystifying Competitive Analysis', *Planning Review*, Vol. 15, No. 5, September–October, pp. 8–13.

Sofer, C. (1972), *Organizations in Theory and Practice*, London: Heinemann.

Spekman, R. E. and Grønhaug, K. (1983), 'Insights on Implementation: A Conceptual Framework for Better Understanding the Strategic Marketing Planning Process', AMA Conference Proceedings, 1983, Chicago: American Marketing Association.

Srikanthan, S., Ward, K. and Meldrum, M. J. (1986), 'Reducing the Costs of the Marketing Game', *Management Accounting*, (CIMA), Vol. 64, No. 10, November, pp. 48–51.

Srikanthan, S., Ward, K. and Meldrum, M. J. (1987), 'Segment Profitability: A Positive Contribution', *Management Accounting*, (CIMA) Vol. 65, No. 4, April, pp. 27–30.

Srikanthan, S., Ward, K. and Meldrum, M. J. (1987), 'Marketing: The Unrecognised Asset', *Management Accounting*, (CIMA), Vol. 65, No. 5, May, pp. 38–42.

Stacey, R. (1991), *The Chaos Frontier: Creative Strategic Control for Business*, Oxford: Butterworth-Heinemann.

Stacey, R. D.(1994), 'Order from Chaos', *Management Today*, November, pp. 62–65.

Stacey, R. D. (1996). *Strategic Management and Organisational Dynamics*, London: Pitman (2nd edition).

Stapleton, C. (1991), 'Strategic Alliances', *Management Consultancy*, April, pp. 40, 43.

Starr, M. K. (1971), *Management: A Modern Approach*, New York: Harcourt, Brace, Jovanovich.

Stasch, S. F. (1972), *Systems Analysis for Marketing Planning and Control*, Glenview, Ill: Scott, Foresman.

Staw, B. M. and Ross, J. (1987a), 'Knowing When to Pull the Plug', *Harvard Business Review*, Vol. 65, No. 2, March–April, pp. 68–74.

Staw, B. M. and Ross, J. (1987b), 'Behavior in Escalation Situations: Antecedents, Prototypes and Solutions', *Research in Organizational Behavior*, Vol. 9, pp. 39–78.

Steiner, G. (1969), *Strategic Factors in Business Success*, New York: FERF.

Stern, M. E. (1966), *Marketing Planning: A Systems Approach*, New York: McGraw-Hill.

Stone, M. and Young, L. D. (1992), *Competitive Customer Care: a guide to keeping customers*, London: Croner.

Stonich, P. L. (1975), 'Formal Planning Pitfalls and How to Avoid Them', *Management Review*, No. 64, July.

Strauss, G. (1962), 'Tactics of Lateral Relationships: The Purchasing Agent', *Administrative Science Quarterly*, Vol. 7, No. 3, September, pp. 161–86.

Strebel, P. (1996), 'Breakpoint: how to stay in the game', *Financial Times, Mastering Management*, Part 17, pp. 13–14.

Sturges, J. (1991), 'Top Marketers', *Marketing Week*, 22 March, pp. 26–33.

Sutton, H. (1988), *Competitive Intelligence* (Research Report No. 913), New York: The Conference Board.

Swan, J. E. and Rink, D. R. (1982), 'Variations on the Product Life Cycle', *Business Horizons*, Vol. 25, No. 1, January–February, pp. 72–6.

Tannenbaum, A. S. (1964), 'Control in Organizations: Individual Adjustment and Organizational Performance', in Bonini, Jaedicke and Wagner (eds) (1964).

Taylor, J. W. (1992), 'Competitive Intelligence: A Status Report on US Business Practices', *Journal of Marketing Management*, Vol. 8, No. 2, April, pp. 117–125.

Test, D. L., Hawley, J. D. and Cortright, M. F. (1987), 'Determining Strategic Value', *Management Accounting*, (CIMA), Vol. 68, No. 12, June, pp. 39–42.

Thomas, M. J. (1984), 'The Meaning of Marketing Productivity Analysis', *Marketing Intelligence and Planning*, Vol. 2, No. 2, pp. 13–28.

Thomas, M. J. (1986), 'Marketing Productivity Analysis: A Research Report', *Marketing Intelligence and Planning*, Vol. 4, No. 2,

Thomas, M. J. (1987a), 'Does Your Marketing Pay?', *Management Decision*, Vol. 25, No. 4, pp. 41–5.

Thomas, M. J. (1987b), in Baker, M. J. (ed.) (1987), *The Marketing Book*, London: Heinemann.

Thomas, M. J. (1993), 'Marketing – In Chaos or Transition?' in Brownlie, D. (ed.) *Rethinking Marketing*, Coventry: Warwick Business School Research Bureau, pp. 114–23.

Thomas, P. S. (1980), 'Environmental Scanning–the State of the Art', *Long Range Planning*, Vol. 13, No. 1, pp. 20–8.

Tilles, S. (1963), 'How To Evaluate Corporate Strategy', *Harvard Business Review*, Vol. 41, No. 4, July–August, pp. 111–21.

Tocher, K. (1970), 'Control', *Operational Research Quarterly*, Vol. 21, No. 2, June, pp. 159–80.

Tocher, K. (1976), 'Notes for Discussion on "Control"', *Operational Research Quarterly*, Vol. 27, No. 2, June, pp. 231–39.

Toffler, A. (1970), *Future Shock*, New York: Bantam Books.

Toffler, A. (1980), *The Third Wave*, New York: Bantam Books.

Tomkins, C. R. (1991), *Corporate Resource Allocation: Financial, Strategic and Organizational Perspectives*, Oxford: Blackwell.

Tookey, D. A. (1974), 'The Marketing Function in its Organisational Context', in *Marketing as a Non-American Activity*, Proceedings, MEG Conference, July.

Treacy, M. and Wiersema, F. (1995), *The Discipline of Market Leaders*, Reading, Mass: Addison Wesley.

Tschohl, J. (1991) 'Courtesy, Friendliness and Speed: customer service importance', *Supervision*, Vol. 52, No. 2, February, pp. 9–11.

Turnbull, P. W. (1987), 'Organisational Buying Behaviour', in Baker, M. J. (ed.) (1987), *The Marketing Book*, London: Heinemann.

Turnbull, P. W. and Cunningham, M. T. (1981), *International Marketing and Purchasing*, London: Macmillan.

Tushman, M. L. and Nadler, P. A. (1978), 'Information Processing as an Integrating Concept in Organizational Design', *Academy of Management Review*, Vol. 3, No. 3, pp. 613–24.

Udell, J. G. (1964), 'How Important is Pricing in Competitive Strategy?', *Journal of Marketing*, Vol. 28, No. 1, pp. 44–8.

Ule, M. (1957), 'A Media Plan for Sputnik Cigarettes', *How to Plan Media Strategy*, American Association of Advertising Agencies.

Ulrich, D. and Lake, D. (1991), 'Organizational Capability: Creating Competitive Advantage', *The Executive*, Vol. 5, No. 1, February, pp. 77–92.

Vangermeersch, R. and Brosnan, W. T. (1985), 'Enhancing Revenues Via Distribution Cost Control', *Management Accounting*) (NAA), Vol. 67, No. 2, August, 56–60.

Veblen, T. (1899), *The Theory of the Leisure Class*, London: Macmillan.

Vella, C. M. and McGonagle, J. J. (1987), 'Shadowing Markets: A New Competitive Intelligence Technique', *Planning Review*, Vol. 15, No. 5, September–October, pp. 36–8.

Venkatesan, M. and Holloway, R. J. (1971), *An Introduction to Marketing Experimentation: Methods, Applications and Problems*, New York: Free Press.

Verhage, B. J. and Waarts, E. (1988), 'Marketing Planning for Improved Performance: A Comparative Analysis', *International Marketing Review*, Vol. 8, No. 5, Summer, pp. 20–30.

Vickers, Sir G. (1965), *The Art of Judgement*, London: Chapman & Hall.

Vickers, Sir G. (1968), *Value Systems and Social Process*, London: Tavistock.

Vickers, Sir G. (1972), *Freedom in a Rocking Boat: Changing Values in an Unstable Society*, London: Penguin.

Vidale, M. L. and Wolfe, H. B. (1957), 'An Operations Research Study of Sales Responses to Advertising', *Operations Research*, Vol. 5, No. 3, June, pp. 370–81.

Walden, G. and Lawler, E. O. (1993), *Marketing Masters: Secrets of America's Best Companies*, New York: HarperCollins.

Walker, O. C. and Ruekert, R. W. (1987), 'Marketing's Role in the Implementation of Business Strategies: A Critical Review and Conceptual Framework', *Journal of Marketing*, Vol. 51, No. 3, July, pp. 15–33.

Wall, S. L. (1974), 'What the Competition is Doing: You Need to Know', *Harvard Business Review*, Vol. 52, No. 6, November–December, pp. 22–4, 28, 30, 32, 34, 36, 38, 162–6, 168, 170.

Walleck, A. S., O'Halloran, J. D. and Leader, C. A. (1991), 'Benchmarking World Class Performance', *The McKinsey Quarterly*, No. 1, pp. 3–24.

Walters, C. G. and Paul, G. W. (1970), *Consumer Behavior: An Integrated Framework*, Homewood, Illinois: Irwin.

Ward, A. J. (1968), *Measuring, Directing and Controlling New Product Development*, London: In Com Tec.

Ward, K. (1989), *Financial Aspects of Marketing*, Oxford: Heinemann.

Webster, F. E. (1970), 'Informal Communications in Industrial Markets', *Journal of Marketing Research*, Vol. 7, No. 2, May, pp. 186–9

Webster, F. E. (1988) 'The Rediscovery of the Marketing Concept', *Business Horizons*, Vol. 31, No. 3, pp. 29–39.

Webster, F. E. and Wind, Y. (1972), *Organisational Buying Behavior*, Englewood Cliffs, NJ: Prentice-Hall.

Weigand, R. (1966), 'Identifying Industrial Buying Responsibilities', *Journal of Marketing Research*, Vol. 3, No. 1, February, pp. 81–4.

Weigand, R. (1968), 'Why Studying the Purchasing Agent is Not Enough', *Journal of Marketing*, Vol. 32, No. 1, January, pp. 41–5.

Weihrich, H. (1982), 'The TOWS Matrix: a tool for situational analysis', *Long Range Planning*, Vol. 15, No. 2, p. 60.

Weinberg, R. (1969), Paper presented at a seminar on Developing Marketing Strategies for Short-Term Profits and Long-Term Growth, sponsored by Advanced Management Research, Inc. Regency Hotel, New York, 29 September.

Weinshall, T. D. (ed.) (1977), *Culture and Management*, Harmondsworth: Penguin.

Weitz, B. A. and Anderson, L. (1981), 'Organizing the Marketing Function', in *AMA Review of Marketing 1981*, Chicago: American Marketing Association.

Wells, W. D. and Gubar, G. (1966), 'Life Cycle Concepts in Marketing Research', *Journal of Marketing Research*, Vol. 3, No. 4, November, pp. 355–63.

Wenner, D. L. and LeBer, R. W. (1989), 'Managing Shareholder Value–From Top to Bottom', *Harvard Business Review*, Vol. 67, No. 6, November–December, pp. 1–8.

Wensley, J. R. C. (1981), 'Strategic Marketing: Betas, Boxes or Basics', *Journal of Marketing*, Vol. 45, No. 3, Summer, pp. 173–83.

Wensley, J. R. C. (1987), 'Marketing Strategy', in Baker, M. J. (ed.) (1987), *The Marketing Book*, London: Heinemann.

Wernerfelt, B. (1986), 'The Relation Between Market Share and Profitability', *Journal of Business Strategy*, Vol. 6, No. 4, Spring, pp. 67–74.

West, A. (1967), *Modern Sales Management*, London: Macmillan Education.

Westfall, R. (1962), 'Psychological Factors in Predicting Product Choice', *Journal of Marketing*, Vol. 36, April, pp. 34–40.

Westwick, C. A. (1987), *How to Use Management Ratios*, Aldershot: Gower, 2nd edition.

White, J. (1969), 'Some Aspects of The Marketing of Machine Tools in Great Britain', unpublished PhD thesis, UMIST.

Williamson, R. J. (1979), *Marketing for Accountants and Managers*, London: Heinemann.

Wills, G. S. C. (1980a), 'Sweeping Marketing Overboard', *European Journal of Marketing*, Vol. 14, No. 4, p. 1.

Wills, G. S. C. (1980b), 'Commercial Phoenix', *European Journal of Marketing*, Vol. 14, No. 6, p. 1.

Wills, G. S. C., Christopher, M. G. and Walters, D. W. (1972), *Output Budgeting in Marketing*, Bradford: MCB.

Wills, G. S. C., Wilson, R. M. S., Hildebrandt, R. and Manning, N. (1972), *Technological Forecasting*, London: Penguin Books.

Wilson, A. (1982), *Marketing Audit Check Lists*, London: McGraw-Hill.

Wilson, I. (ed.) (1994), *Marketing Interfaces: Exploring the Marketing and Business Relationship*, London: Pitman.

Wilson, R. M. S. (1970), 'Accounting Approaches to Marketing Control', *Management Accounting*, (CIMA), Vol. 48, No. 2, February, pp. 51–8.

Wilson, R. M. S. (1970), 'The Development and Application of a Systems Approach', *Marketing Forum*, July–August, pp. 5–28.

Wilson, R. M. S. (1971), 'The Role of the Accountant in Marketing', *Marketing Forum*, May–June, pp. 21–33.

Wilson, R. M. S. (1971), 'Implications of Technological Forecasting for Industrial Marketing', Ch. 21 (pp. 326–46) in Wills, G. S. C. (ed.) *Exploration in Marketing Thought*, London: Crosby Lockwood/ Bradford University Press.

Wilson, R. M. S. (1971), 'The Role of Marketing in Conglomerates', *European Journal of Marketing*, Vol. 5, No. 3, Autumn, pp. 116–22.

Wilson, R. M. S. (1972), 'Financial Control of Physical Distribution Management: Some Basic Considerations', *International Journal of Physical Distribution*, Vol. 3, No. 1, Autumn, pp. 7–20.

Wilson, R. M. S. (1973), *Management Controls in Marketing*, London: Heinemann.

Wilson, R. M. S. (1974), *Financial Control: A Systems Approach*, London: McGraw-Hill.

Wilson, R. M. S. (1975), 'Marketing Control: A Financial Perspective', *The Business Graduate*, Vol. 5, No. 2, Summer, pp. 15–20.

Wilson, R. M. S. (1979), *Management Controls and Marketing Planning*, London: Heinemann.

Wilson, R. M. S. (ed.) (1980), *The Marketing of Financial Services*, Bradford: MCB.

Wilson, R. M. S. (compiler) (1981), *Financial Dimensions of Marketing*. London: Macmillan. Two volumes.

Wilson, R. M. S. (1983), *Cost Control Handbook*, Aldershot: Gower. 2nd edition.

Wilson, R. M. S. (1984), 'Financial Control of the Marketing Function', Ch. 12 (pp. 130–53) in Hart, N. A. (ed.), *The Marketing of Industrial Products*, London: McGraw-Hill. 2nd edition.

Wilson, R. M. S. (1986), 'Accounting for Marketing Assets', *European Journal of Marketing*, Vol. 20, No. 1, pp. 51–74.

Wilson, R. M. S. (1988), 'Cost Analysis', Ch. 11 (pp. 150–88) in Lock, D. and Farrow, N. A. E. (eds), *The Gower Handbook of Management*, Aldershot: Gower. 2nd edition.

Wilson, R. M. S. (1988), 'Marketing and the Management Accountant', Ch. 13 (pp. 255–95) in Cowe, R. (ed.) (1988), *Handbook of Management Accounting*, Aldershot: Gower. 2nd edition.

Wilson, R. M. S. (1990), 'Strategic Cost Analysis', *Management Accounting*, Vol. 68, No. 9, October, pp. 42–3.

Wilson, R. M. S. (1995), 'Strategic Management Accounting', Ch. 8 (pp. 159–190) in Ashton, D. J., Hopper, T. M. and Scapens, R. W. (eds) *Issues in Management Accounting*, London: Prentice Hall (2nd edition).

Wilson, R. M. S. (1991), 'Corporate Strategy and Management Control', Ch. 4, (pp. 115–65) in Hussey, D. E. (ed.), *International Review of Strategic Management*, Chichester: Wiley.

Wilson, R. M. S. (1995), 'Marketing Budgeting and Resource Allocation', pp. 277–300, in Baker, M. J. (ed) (1995), *Companion Encyclopaedia of Marketing*, London: Routledge.

Wilson, R. M. S. (1997), 'The Case for Strategic Control', pp. 152–181, in I. Lapsley and R. M. S. Wilson (eds) (1997), *Explorations in Financial Control*, London: International Thomson Business Press.

Wilson, R. M. S. (Forthcoming), *Accounting for Marketing*, London: Academic Press.

Wilson, R. M. S. and Bancroft, A. L. (1983), 'Management Accounting for Marketing–Some Industry Practices', *Management Accounting*, (CIMA), Vol. 61, No. 2, February, pp. 26–8.

Wilson, R. M. S. and Bancroft, A. L. (1983), *The Application of Management Accounting Techniques to the Planning and Control of Marketing*, London: CIMA.

Wilson, R. M. S. and Chua, W. F. (1993), *Managerial Accounting: Method and Meaning*, London: Chapman & Hall. 2nd edition (1st edition, 1988).

Wilson, R. M. S. and Fook, N. Y. M. (1990), 'Improving Marketing Orientation', *Marketing Business*, Issue 11, June, pp. 22–3.

Wilson, R. M. S. and McHugh, G. J. P. (1987), *Financial Analysis*, London: Cassell.

Wind, Y. (1978), 'Issues and Advances in Segmentation Research', *Journal of Marketing Research*, Vol. 15, No. 3, August, pp. 317–37.

Wind, J. (1996) 'Big Questions for the 21st Century', *Financial Times, Mastering Management*, Part 15, pp. 6–7.

Wind, Y. and Claycamp, H. J. (1976), 'Planning Product Line Strategy: A Matrix Approach', *Journal of Marketing*, Vol. 40, No. 1, January, pp. 2–9.

Winer, L. (1966), 'A Profit-Oriented Decision System', *Journal of Marketing*, Vol. 30, No. 2, April, pp. 38–44.

Witcher, B. J. (1990), 'Total Marketing: Total Quality and the Marketing Concept', *The Quarterly Review of Marketing*, Vol. 15, No. 2, Winter, pp. 1–6.

Witte, M. (1990), 'Organising to Make the Most of Change', *Management Consultancy*, March, pp. 29–30, 32–3.

Wong, V. and Saunders, J. A. (1993), 'Business orientations and corporate success', *Journal of Strategic Marketing*, Vol. 1, No. 1, pp. 20–40.

Wong, V., Saunders, J. A. and Doyle, P. (1988), 'The Quality of British Marketing: A Comparison with US and Japanese Multinationals in the UK Market', *Journal of Marketing Management*, Vol. 4, No. 2, pp. 107–30.

Woo, C. Y. and Cooper, A. C. (1982), 'The Surprising Case for Low Market Share', *Harvard Business Review*, Vol. 60, No. 6, November–December, pp. 106–13.

Wright, R. V. L. (1974), *A System for Managing Diversity*, Cambridge, Mass: Arthur D. Little.

Yale, J. P. (1964), *Modern Textiles Magazine*, February, p. 33.

Yankelovich, D. (1964), 'New Criteria for Market Segmentation', *Harvard Business Review*, Vol. 42, No. 2, March–April, pp. 83–90.

Author index

Subject index